CRIMINAL LITIGATION
PRACTICE AND PROCEDURE

CRIMINAL LITIGATION PRACTICE AND PROCEDURE

Gary Atkinson

With acknowledgements to Frederick Price (Chapter 5, 'Police Complaints')

Published by

College of Law Publishing,
Braboeuf Manor, Portsmouth Road, St Catherines, Guildford GU3 1HA

British Library Cataloguing-in-Publication Data

A catalogue record for this book is available from the British Library.

ISBN 10: 1 905391 16 1

ISBN 13: 978 1 905391 16 5

Typeset by Style Photosetting Ltd, Mayfield, East Sussex

Printed in Great Britain by Ashford Colour Press Ltd, Gosport, Hants.

Preface

This book has been written principally for students studying criminal litigation as part of the Legal Practice Course (LPC). The book is designed so that it may be used both by students studying the basics of criminal litigation on the compulsory part of the LPC, and also students studying advanced criminal litigation as an elective subject. Although intended primarily as a student text, it is hoped that the level of detail in the book will also make it of use to trainee and newly qualified solicitors.

The book concentrates on the practice and procedure of criminal litigation, from the initial investigations carried out by the police through to appeals following conviction. Matters of substantive criminal law only arise where necessary to illustrate a point of practice or procedure, or in the context of the law of evidence.

The book employs a case study which has been integrated into the text to illustrate the most common documents that are created during the course of criminal proceedings, and how such documents should be drafted. In addition, worked examples are used to explain complex points of procedure and evidence. Flowcharts are provided, where appropriate, to demonstrate procedures. Each chapter concludes with a checklist, summarising the key points the chapter has covered. The appendix includes extracts from the Criminal Procedure Rules 2005 and the Codes of Practice which supplement the provisions of the Police and Criminal Evidence Act 1984. It also contains extracts from the Magistrates' Court Sentencing Guidelines.

Criminal litigation, like so many other areas of legal practice, has been subject to significant change in recent years. Whether such changes will improve the criminal justice system remains to be seen. The most momentous changes were made by the Criminal Justice Act 2003, which has had an impact on virtually all areas of criminal practice and procedure. Although most parts of the Act have now been brought into force, certain parts of the Act (for example, the new rules on allocation, the increased sentencing powers given to the magistrates' court and the new types of custodial sentence for offenders sent to prison for a period of less than 12 months) have yet to be implemented. At the time of writing, the clear indication from the Government is that these outstanding parts of the Act will be brought into force in Autumn 2006. For this reason, the book has been written on the premise that the entirety of the Criminal Justice Act 2003 is in force.

Subject to the above, I have endeavoured to state the law as at 30 June 2006.

In the interests of brevity, the masculine pronoun has been used throughout to include the feminine.

GARY ATKINSON
York

Acknowledgements

Writing a new textbook on the practice and procedure of criminal litigation has proved to be a Herculean task. That task has, however, been made considerably easier by the assistance I have received from my colleagues at the College of Law, and in particular Frederick Price (who is largely responsible for the contents of Chapter 5) and Sean Hutton. I also owe a huge debt of gratitude to Carolyn Thompson for the excellent secretarial assistance she has provided, and to David Stott for his editorial support and guidance. Alistair MacQueen at CLP has been unstinting in his support of this project. More generally, I would like to thank all those colleagues who have taken an interest in the writing of the book and have provided a boost to my morale when required.

Finally, I would like to give special thanks to my colleague, John Holtam. Although this is a new book, I am indebted to John for the work he has done over a number of years in writing the textbook, *Criminal Litigation*, previously published by CLP. John's book was an inspiration for this text and I have used a number of examples and diagrams from John's book where appropriate.

To my family. Thank you for everything.

Contents

Table of Cases

S

Table of Statutes

Table of Statutory Instruments

Table of Abbreviations

CJA	Criminal Justice Act [date]
CJPOA 1994	Criminal Justice and Public Order Act 1994
CPIA 1996	Criminal Procedure and Investigations Act 1996
CPO	community punishment order
CPS	Crown Prosecution Service
CrimPR	Criminal Procedure Rules 2005
EAH	early administrative hearing
IPCC	Independent Police Complaints Commission
EFH	early first hearing
MCA 1980	Magistrates' Courts Act 1980
PACE 1984	Police and Criminal Evidence Act 1984
PCC(S)A 2000	Powers of Criminal Courts (Sentencing) Act 2000
PCMA	plea and case management hearing
PH	preparatory hearing
PTR	pre-trial review
RDCO	recovery of defence costs order
SOCA	Serious Organised Crime Agency
SOCPA 2005	Serious Organised Crime and Police Act 2005
TIC	(offences) taken into consideration
YJCEA 1999	Youth Justice and Criminal Evidence Act 1999

Part 1
INTRODUCTION

Chapter 1

Introduction to Criminal Procedure

1.1 Introduction

If a member of the general public was asked to explain what he thought the job of a solicitor entailed, there is a very good chance that in his reply he would say that solicitors spend much of their time in court representing those who are accused of having committed criminal offences. Whilst it is not the case that every solicitor in practice spends his time representing clients charged with having committed a criminal offence, all solicitors need to have a thorough understanding of the criminal litigation process. At some stage in his professional life, a solicitor will be asked to advise a client (whether an individual or a limited company) on a matter of criminal law or procedure.

The purpose of this book is to provide an introduction to criminal procedure and evidence. Whilst the book is intended primarily for use by students studying the Legal Practice Course (LPC), it is hoped that it will also be of use to trainee and newly-qualified solicitors.

This introductory chapter (**Part 1**) covers a number of preliminary matters which are necessary for an understanding of how the criminal litigation process works. The chapter will begin by defining the role played by various persons or bodies within the criminal justice system. It will then go on to explain how criminal offences are classified and how this classification determines which type of court may deal with a particular offence. The chapter will also cover matters of professional conduct and human rights, together with an introduction to the Criminal Procedure Rules 2005.

Subsequent chapters will examine the functions and powers of the police in the criminal litigation process, and the role played by a solicitor who represents a client at the police station (**Part 2**). This will be followed by an explanation of the procedures that take place in both the magistrates' court and the Crown Court between a defendant being charged with an offence and his trial taking place (**Part 3**). The rules governing sentencing and the making of an appeal against conviction and/or sentence will then be examined (**Part 4**). Specific chapters are devoted to proceedings in the youth court and to the prosecution of road traffic offences (**Part 5**). The book will conclude with an introduction to the law of evidence and an explanation of the key evidential issues which commonly arise in the course of criminal proceedings (**Part 6**).

1.2 Key personnel

1.2.1 Defence solicitors

Although there is nothing to prevent a defendant in criminal proceedings from representing himself at court, most defendants will be represented by a solicitor. The defence solicitor will often become involved in a criminal case by providing advice and assistance to a suspect in the police station, before the suspect is charged. If the suspect is charged, the defence solicitor will then represent that person in proceedings before the magistrates' court and, if necessary, the Crown Court. If the case reaches the Crown Court, it is likely that the defence solicitor will instruct a barrister to be the client's advocate in court (although the solicitor will still have a significant role to play – see **Chapter 10**).

The majority of defence solicitors are solicitors in private practice, although in certain parts of the country a government-funded public defender service exists.

1.2.2 The police

The police are responsible for the investigation of suspected criminal offences and the apprehension of persons alleged to have committed those offences. The police possess a wide range of powers which they may exercise in the investigation of suspected criminal offences. These include powers to stop and search suspected offenders, powers to search premises and the power to arrest suspects. Following an arrest, the police have additional powers which they may exercise whilst a suspect is detained at the police station. The extent of the powers which the police may exercise in the investigation of a criminal offence is examined in **Chapters 2 and 3**. The role played by the solicitor who is representing a suspect in the police station will be explained in **Chapter 4**. **Chapter 5** will examine the various options open to an individual in the event that the police exercise their powers improperly or are otherwise guilty of misconduct.

Although the police will investigate the overwhelming majority of alleged criminal offences, other agencies exist to investigate particular types of crime (for example, HM Revenue & Customs). The Serious Organised Crime and Police Act 2005 created a new body, the Serious Organised Crime Agency (SOCA). The rationale behind its creation was the establishment of a national agency able to combat criminal enterprises specialising in drugs and violence, together with tax evasion and serious fraud. Although the powers of agencies such as SOCA are beyond the scope of this book, it should be appreciated that they have extensive investigative powers which sometime exceed those which the police may exercise.

1.2.3 The Crown Prosecution Service

The Crown Prosecution Service (CPS) is responsible for prosecuting individuals (and companies) charged with having committed a criminal offence. The head of the CPS is the Director of Public Prosecutions (DPP).

Historically the police were responsible for deciding what charge a suspect should face. Once the police had charged the suspect, they would then pass the file to the CPS who would take over responsibility for the prosecution of the case before the criminal courts.

As a result of changes brought about by the Criminal Justice Act 2003, the CPS now plays a much fuller role at an earlier stage in the criminal process. For all but the most minor offences, responsibility for deciding the charge the suspect faces now rests with the CPS rather than the police. Representatives from the CPS are based in police stations, and once the police have completed their investigations, they will pass the file to the relevant CPS representative who will then decide if the suspect should be charged and, if so, what charge the suspect should face.

After a suspect has been charged, the CPS retains responsibility for the prosecution of the case. Solicitors from the CPS are responsible for collating the evidence on which the prosecution seek to rely and presenting this evidence to the court.

Although the CPS works closely with the police, it is an independent organisation. In deciding whether a prosecution should be brought, the CPS must apply the test set out in the Code for Crown Prosecutors. This provides that a prosecution should be brought only if there is enough evidence to provide a realistic prospect of conviction *and* it is in the public interest for a prosecution to be brought. Full details of the Code can be found on the CPS website (www.cps.gov.uk).

1.2.4   The magistrates' court

After a suspect has been charged with an offence, he will make his first appearance in court before the magistrates' court (unless he is aged 17 or under, in which case he will be normally be dealt with in the Youth Court – see **Chapter 14**). Depending on the type of offence with which the suspect has been charged, the case may either remain in the magistrates' court or be sent to the Crown Court for trial (see **1.3** below).

Approximately 95% of all criminal cases are dealt with by the magistrates' court. The functions of the magistrates' court include:

(a)   issuing search and arrest warrants (see **Chapter 2**);

(b)   issuing warrants for further detention under the Police and Criminal Evidence Act 1984 (see **Chapter 3**);

(c)   trying summary offences and some either way offences (see **1.3** below);

(d)   sending indictable only offences and some either way offences to the Crown Court for trial (see **1.3** below);

(e)   dealing with applications for a representation order (see **Chapter 6**); and

(f)   dealing with applications for bail (see **Chapter 6**).

Most magistrates are not legally qualified (although they do receive some training). They are members of the local community who have volunteered their services. It is usual for three magistrates to sit in court at any one time. The magistrates will be advised on matters of law, practice and procedure by a legal adviser (commonly referred to as the clerk to the justices). The legal adviser is responsible for the efficient running of the magistrates' court, and plays a significant role in proceedings. The legal adviser should not advise magistrates on questions of fact, only on matters of law.

In some magistrates' courts (particularly in large cities), a legally qualified magistrate known as a District Judge (Magistrates' Court) will sit alone to hear cases. This judge will be either a qualified solicitor, or a barrister.

1.2.5   The Crown Court

The Crown Court is the venue which deals with offenders charged with the most serious types of criminal offence. The main functions of the Crown Court are:

(a)   to conduct the trial of and, following conviction, to sentence offenders convicted of all indictable only and some either way offences (see **1.3** below);

(b)   to determine questions of bail and representation, particularly appeals by a defendant against the refusal of bail by the magistrates' court (see **Chapter 6**); and

(c)   to hear appeals against conviction and/or sentence from the magistrates' court (see **Chapter 11**).

Proceedings in the Crown Court are before a judge and, if the case goes to trial, before a judge and jury. Judges of varying levels of seniority sit in the Crown Court. Most cases will be dealt with by a Circuit Judge. More serious cases (typically cases where the defendant is charged with murder, manslaughter or rape), and cases which are particularly high profile, will be heard before a High Court Judge. If the defendant pleads not guilty and the case goes to trial, the judge will decide matters of law and the jury matters of fact. If the Crown Court is hearing an appeal against sentence and/or conviction from the magistrates' court, no jury will be present but the judge will sit with between two and four magistrates.

Most advocacy in the Crown Court is performed by barristers (collectively referred to as counsel). Both the CPS and the solicitor representing the defendant will usually instruct a barrister to conduct their case in the Crown Court. Solicitors have very limited rights of audience in the Crown Court (see **Chapter 10**), although it is possible for solicitors achieve full rights of audience by passing a written and practical test.

1.2.6   The Probation Service

A representative from the Probation Service will always be present in court (whether the magistrates' court or the Crown Court) when a case is being heard. The Probation Service is responsible for compiling reports on defendants who have been convicted, should the court require a report before sentencing the defendant. Such reports are known as pre-sentence reports and focus on the defendant's background, previous convictions and likelihood of re-offending (see **Chapter 12**).

The Probation Service is also responsible for the administration of various types of community order which the court may impose as part of the sentence a defendant receives (see **Chapter 11**).

1.2.7   The Criminal Defence Service

The Criminal Defence Service (CDS) was created by the Access to Justice Act 1999. The purpose of the CDS is to provide funding for legal services for those suspected of having committed a criminal offence or facing criminal proceedings.

The CDS is funded by the Legal Services Commission. The CDS provides funding for defendants either by entering into a 'general criminal contract' with solicitors in private practice, or by providing salaried public defenders in certain parts of the country. All solicitors in private practice who wish to secure public funding for their clients must enter into a 'general criminal contract'.

Details of how a solicitor obtains public funding for a client charged with having committed a criminal offence are given in **Chapter 6**.

1.3   Classification of offences

1.3.1   Introduction

All criminal offences fall into one of three categories of offence: indictable only, either way or summary offences. It is necessary to know into which category a particular offence falls because the procedure at court for dealing with each type of offence is different.

1.3.2   Indictable-only offences

Indictable-only offences are the most serious form of criminal offence and must be dealt with by the Crown Court. Although a defendant charged with an indictable-only offence will make his first appearance before the magistrates' court, the magistrates will immediately send the case to the Crown Court for trial (see **Chapter 10**).

Examples of indictable-only offences include:

- murder;
- manslaughter;
- rape;
- robbery;
- wounding/causing gbh with intent (s 18 of the Offences Against the Person Act 1861);
- causing death by dangerous driving; and
- burglary involving the commission of, or intent to commit, an offence triable only on indictment.

1.3.3   Either way offences

Either way offences can be dealt with either by the magistrates' court, or by the Crown Court. A defendant charged with an either way offence will make his first appearance before the magistrates' court, and the magistrates will then decide whether to keep the case before them or to send the case to the Crown Court for trial because it is too serious for them to deal with. This is known as the allocation procedure. If the magistrates do decide to keep the case before them, the defendant has the right to elect trial by a judge and jury in the Crown Court (see **Chapter 6**).

Examples of either way offences include:

- theft;
- wounding/inflicting gbh with intent (s 20 of the Offences Against the Person Act 1861);
- assault occasioning actual bodily harm (s 47 of the Offences Against the Person Act 1861);
- obtaining property by deception;
- handling stolen goods;
- burglaries (other than those covered in **1.3.2** above);
- criminal damage (where the value of the damage exceeds £5,000); and
- affray.

Some of the powers which the police are granted by the Police and Criminal Evidence Act (PACE) 1984 may only be exercised in respect of offences which are termed 'indictable'. An indictable offence will be an indictable only offence *or* an either way offence.

1.3.4 Summary offences

Summary offences are the least serious form of criminal offence and may be dealt with only by the magistrates' court (see **Chapter 6**).

Examples of summary offences include:

- common assault;
- taking a conveyance without consent (TWOC);
- criminal damage (where the value of the damage caused is less than £5,000); and
- various road traffic offences, such as driving whilst over the prescribed alcohol limit, speeding and careless driving.

Flowcharts giving an overview of the procedure for each type of offence are provided at **1.11** below.

1.4 The Criminal Procedure Rules 2005

1.4.1 Introduction

Prior to April 2005, the rules of procedure for both the magistrates' court and the Crown Court were to be found in a number of different statutes, statutory instruments and practice directions. The Criminal Procedure Rules (CrimPR), which came into effect in April 2005, placed these rules for the first time in one specific document. These rules are supplemented by the Consolidated Criminal Practice Direction. The Rules and Practice Direction can be found at www.dca.gov.uk.

The format of the CrimPR is very similar to that of the Civil Procedure Rules, which have been use in civil litigation cases for several years. Like the Civil Procedure Rules, the CrimPR provide the courts with an 'overriding objective' and impose a number of duties on participants in a criminal case. The Rules also provide criminal courts with specific case management powers. Set out below is an overview of Parts 1 and 3 of the Rules, which deal with the 'overriding objective', the duty of participants in criminal case and the case management powers which the court may exercise.

1.4.2 The overriding objective (CrimPR, Part 1)

Rule 1.1(1) of the CrimPR states that the overriding objective of the Rules is 'that criminal cases be dealt with justly'. Under r 1.1(2), dealing with a criminal case 'justly' includes doing the following:

(a)   acquitting the innocent and convicting the guilty;

(b)   dealing with the prosecution and the defence fairly;

(c)   recognising the rights of a defendant (particularly the right to a fair trial under Article 6 of the European Convention on Human Rights);

(d)   respecting the interests of witnesses, victims and jurors, and keeping them informed of the progress of the case;

(e)   dealing with the case efficiently and expeditiously;

(f) ensuring that appropriate information is available to the court when bail and sentence are considered;

(g) dealing with the case in ways that take into account the gravity of the offence alleged, the complexity of what is in issue, the severity of the consequences for the defendant and others affected, and the needs of other cases.

1.4.3 The duty of participants in a criminal case (CrimPR, Part 1)

Rule 1.2(2) of the CrimPR defines a participant as being 'anyone involved in any way with a criminal case'. This includes solicitors who are either prosecuting a case or representing the defendant. Each participant in a criminal case must prepare and conduct the case in accordance with the overriding objective and comply with the CrimPR. In particular, a participant must at once inform the court and all parties to the case of any significant failure to take any step required by the Rules (CrimPR, r 1.2(1)(c)).

1.4.4 The court's case management powers (CrimPR, Part 3)

Rule 1.3 of the CrimPR provides that the court must further the overriding objective. Under r 3.2(1), the court must do this by 'actively managing the case'. Active case management includes the following:

(a) the early identification of the real issues;

(b) the early identification of the needs of witnesses;

(c) achieving certainty as to what must be done, by whom, and when, in particular by the early setting of a timetable for the progress of the case;

(d) monitoring the progress of the case and compliance with directions;

(e) ensuring that evidence, whether disputed or not, is presented in the shortest and clearest way;

(f) discouraging delay, dealing with as many aspects of the case as possible on the same occasion, and avoiding unnecessary hearings (if the case is adjourned, the court must identify a good reason for an adjournment being necessary);

(g) encouraging the participants to cooperate in the progression of the case;

(h) making use of technology.

Rule 3.3 provides that the parties in the case must assist the court in its duty actively to manage the case.

Under r 3.4(1), at the beginning of a case each party (ie, the CPS and the solicitor representing the defendant) must nominate an individual responsible for the progress of the case, and must tell the other parties and the court who that individual is and how he may be contacted. Similarly, the court itself will nominate a court officer who is responsible for the progress of case (the 'case progression officer'). The case progression officer will ensure that the parties comply with any directions given by the court and keep the court informed about events which might affect the progress of the case.

Rule 3.5(1) provides the court with substantial case management powers to enable it actively to manage the case. The court is given the power to make any direction or take any step actively to manage a case, unless such a direction or step would contravene legislation. In particular the court may:

(a) nominate a judge, magistrate, justices' clerk or assistant to a justices' clerk to manage the case;

(b)   give a direction on its own initiative or on application by a party;

(c)   ask or allow a party to propose a direction;

(d)   for the purpose of giving directions, receive applications and representations by letter, by telephone or by any other means of electronic communication, and conduct a hearing by such means;

(e)   give a direction without a hearing;

(f)   fix, postpone, bring forward, extend or cancel a hearing;

(g)   shorten or extend a time limit fixed by a direction;

(h)   require that issues in the case should be determined separately, and decide in what order they should be determined; and

(i)   specify the consequences of failing to comply with a direction.

Integral to the court's active management of the case is r 3.8(1), which provides that whenever a case comes before the court, if the case cannot be concluded at that hearing, the court must give directions so that it can be concluded either at the next hearing or as soon as possible after that. Under r 3.8(2), at every hearing the court must, where relevant:

(a)   if the defendant is absent – because he has failed to answer his bail – decide whether to proceed nonetheless (in *R v O'Hare* [2006] EWCA Crim 471, the Court of Appeal held that a trial could proceed in the absence of the defendant if he chose not to appear);

(b)   ask the defendant to enter his plea of guilty or not guilty (unless he has already done so at an earlier hearing). If no plea can be taken, the court should ask what the defendant's plea is likely to be;

(c)   set, follow or revise a timetable for the progress of the case;

(d)   where a direction has not been complied with, find out why, identify who was responsible, and take appropriate action.

In a number of instances the Court of Appeal has endorsed the view that courts should take a robust view towards the progression of cases before them, and that judges should be less concerned with purely technical matters and more concerned with the overall interests of justice (see, for example, *R v Ashton* [2006] EWCA Crim 794).

Extracts from the key parts of the CrimPR are contained in **Appendix 3**.

1.5   The Criminal Justice Act 2003

In addition to the changes made to the management and organisation of the criminal litigation process by the CrimPR, huge changes to the substantive law of criminal procedure, evidence and sentencing have been made by the Criminal Justice Act 2003. The White Paper, *Justice for All* (2002), which preceded the Act, stated that the central purpose of the Act was to rebalance the criminal justice system in favour of victims and the community as a whole, whilst ensuring that suspects and offenders received fair treatment. Whether the Act has achieved this objective is perhaps too early to say. What can be said, however, is that the Act has made significant changes to most parts of the criminal litigation process, from the initial investigations carried out by the police through to the sentencing of offenders by the courts. Key sections of the Act will be analysed in subsequent chapters, although it should be recognised that many of the changes made by this statute are so fundamental that its true impact may not be appreciated for several years.

1.6 Professional conduct

1.6.1 Introduction

A solicitor involved in criminal litigation is likely to face issues of professional conduct on a regular basis. The areas where such issues frequently arise are highlighted where appropriate in subsequent chapters. Set out below is a summary of the duties imposed on solicitors in criminal proceedings, and an overview of key areas of professional conduct of which a solicitor practising in this area should be aware.

1.6.2 Duty not to mislead the court

All solicitors involved in criminal proceedings (whether they are prosecuting or defending a case) owe an overriding duty not to mislead or deceive the court in any way (*The Law Society's Code of Conduct* (2004), Rule 11.01). This has particular significance for a solicitor representing a defendant in criminal proceedings. Although that solicitor owes a duty to his client to act in that client's best interests, this duty does not extend to the solicitor misleading or deceiving the court in any way. Rule 1.03 of *The Law Society's Code of Conduct* (2004) provides that the solicitor must treat the interests of clients as paramount, provided they do not conflict with the solicitor's professional conduct obligations.

1.6.3 The prosecution

Prosecuting advocates are under a duty to ensure that all material evidence supporting the prosecution case is put before the court in a dispassionate and fair manner. In particular:

(a)   all relevant facts known to the prosecution should be placed before the court, including (after conviction) facts relevant to mitigation;

(b)   if a prosecution witness gives evidence in court which is inconsistent with any earlier statement made by that witness, the prosecuting solicitor should disclose this fact to the defence; and

(c)   when arguing a point of law, all relevant legal authorities should be cited, including those authorities which are against the prosecution and in favour of the defence.

1.6.4 The defence

1.6.4.1 Accepting instructions from a third party

It is often the case that a solicitor will be asked by a relative or friend of a person who has been arrested to attend the police station to advise that person. Although there is nothing improper in this, the first step the solicitor should take in such circumstances is to telephone the police station and ask to speak to the arrested person, to determine if he wants the solicitor to attend the police station to act on his behalf. The solicitor should tell the arrested person that he is entitled to free legal advice from a solicitor of his choice, and he is not obliged to use him just because he has been contacted by his family or friends. Only if the arrested person decides to instruct the solicitor should that solicitor then attend the police station to represent the client.

1.6.4.2 The client who admits his guilt

A client may admit his guilt to his solicitor during the course of the legal proceedings. Although it is still the client's decision as to what plea he should enter, the solicitor should advise the client that he would receive credit from the court when it comes to sentencing were he to enter an early guilty plea (see **Chapter 11**). If the client wishes to plead not guilty and insists on giving evidence in the witness box denying his guilt, the solicitor should decline to act. To act in such circumstances would involve misleading or deceiving the court (see **1.6.2** above). The solicitor may, however, properly continue to act on a not guilty plea if the defendant merely intends to put the prosecution to proof of its case without any evidence being given either by him or by any witnesses called on his behalf. Putting the prosecution to proof of its case means asking questions of prosecution witnesses in order to undermine or discredit their evidence. Such questioning should not, however, suggest facts to the court which the defence solicitor knows to be false. This important area of professional conduct is examined more fully in **Chapter 6**.

If a client admits his guilt to his solicitor at the end of a trial at which the client has been acquitted, the solicitor should not take any steps in response to this. As the court proceedings have concluded, there is no danger of the solicitor misleading the court. The solicitor does, however, owe a continuing duty of confidentiality to his client (see **1.6.4.5** below) which lasts beyond the end of the case, and so the solicitor should not disclose this admission to anyone else.

1.6.4.3   The client with a defence who wants to plead guilty

Occasionally a client will wish to plead guilty despite the fact that his instructions indicate that he has a defence to the charge he faces. Typically this arises with clients who are apprehensive at the thought of having to take part in a trial. Such a client should be advised on the defence available to him. If he insists on pleading guilty, the solicitor may continue to act on his behalf. The client should be advised, however, that when delivering a plea of mitigation on the client's behalf, the solicitor will not be able to rely on the facts that may constitute a defence.

The solicitor should attempt to dissuade a client from pleading guilty to an offence the client denies having committed if the client wants to plead guilty as a matter of convenience or to get the case out of the way without the need for a trial to take place.

1.6.4.4   The client who gives inconsistent instructions

Defence solicitors regularly encounter clients who change their instructions. Typically a client will say one thing in the initial statement which he gives to his solicitor and will then change his story when he sees the evidence which the CPS seeks to rely upon. The mere fact that a client gives inconsistent instructions to his solicitor does not make it improper for the solicitor to continue to act on the client's behalf. If, however, it becomes clear to the solicitor that the client is changing his instructions with a view to putting forward false evidence to the court, the solicitor should refuse to act.

1.6.4.5   Disclosure of the defence case

A solicitor owes a duty of confidentiality to his client (*The Law Society's Code of Conduct* (2004), Rules 1.04 and 4.01). A solicitor should not, therefore, without the express consent of his client, disclose details of his client's case to any other party. A typical example of when a request for disclosure may arise is when the client is jointly charged with another person, and the solicitors representing the co-defendant ask for disclosure of the client's case. Such a request should be treated with caution and the client's instructions taken. Only rarely will it be in the client's interests for his defence to be disclosed. If the solicitor does consider it to be in the client's interests to disclose information, the solicitor will need to explain to the client why he considers this to be the case.

Ideally, the solicitor should obtain his client's written consent before disclosing details of the client's defence.

1.6.4.6 Arguing a point of law

When a point of law is in issue, the defendant's solicitor (like the prosecuting advocate) is under a positive duty to assist the court and to supply the court with all relevant authorities, including those which are unfavourable. This is in contrast to the position where there is a dispute over a matter of fact. In such a situation the only duty imposed on the defence solicitor is a negative one, namely, not to mislead the court.

1.6.4.7 The client who gives a false name to the court

A solicitor should not act for a client who, to the knowledge of the solicitor, provides the court with a false name, address or date of birth. If faced with this problem, the solicitor should try to persuade the client to change his mind. If the client refuses to do so, the solicitor should cease to act on the client's behalf.

1.6.4.8 Knowledge of previous convictions

On occasions, and particularly before the defendant is sentenced, the prosecution will provide to the court a list of the defendant's previous convictions. Sometimes this list may be inaccurate or incomplete because not all the defendant's convictions have been recorded. If asked to confirm the accuracy of the list, the defence solicitor should decline to comment. To confirm the list as accurate would amount to a positive deception of the court. On the other hand, disclosing previous convictions without the client's express consent would be a breach of the duty of confidentiality owed to the client. To avoid such difficulties, the solicitor should always attempt to obtain from the CPS a list of his client's previous convictions prior to going to court so that the solicitor may discuss any problems with his client. The client should be warned of the dangers of misleading the court. If the client indicates that, if asked, he will pretend the list is accurate, the solicitor must cease to act.

1.6.4.9 Conflicts of interest

A solicitor may not continue to act for two or more defendants where a conflict of interest arises, or may potentially arise, between them (*The Law Society's Code of Conduct* (2004), Rules 1.05 and 3.01). The most obvious example of where a conflict can arise is where two defendants are jointly charged with having committed an offence and each defendant blames his co-defendant for the commission of the offence. Even if a solicitor is representing two defendants who both decide to plead guilty, a conflict of interest may still arise. For example, one defendant may wish to say in mitigation that he played a very small role in the offence and the larger role was played by his co-defendant. If a conflict of interest arises whilst a solicitor is acting for both defendants, the solicitor should consider withdrawing from the case entirely. This would be appropriate where the solicitor has information in his possession about one defendant which could be used to assist the other defendant in the case.

The Law Society has provided specific advice to defence solicitors who may be asked to represent more than one defendant in criminal proceedings. This advice forms part of the guidance notes to Rule 3 (conflicts of interest) in *The Law Society's Code of Conduct* (2004).

Further details about how a solicitor should deal with potential or actual conflicts of interest between clients are provided in **Chapter 4**.

1.6.4.10   Interviewing prosecution witnesses

Although there is a general rule that there is 'no property in a witness', defence solicitors should always proceed with caution if they intend to interview a prosecution witness. The usual course of action would be to notify the prosecution of the fact that a witness is to be interviewed and to invite a representative from the CPS to attend the interview as an observer. Such a step will avoid suspicion that the solicitor is attempting to pervert the course of justice. It should also prevent a later allegation that a witness has been pressured in some way to change his evidence.

1.6.4.11   Withdrawing from the case

If circumstances arise which require a solicitor to withdraw from a case, the reason for withdrawal should not normally be given to the court. To do so would breach the duty of confidentiality owed to the client (see **1.6.4.5** above). The solicitor should simply explain that a matter has arisen which makes it impossible for him to continue to act in the case. A common euphemism that solicitors often employ is to tell the court that they must withdraw from the case 'for professional reasons'.

1.7   Legal professional privilege

Communications between a client and his solicitor are privileged if the purpose of the communication is the giving or receiving of legal advice. This will include all letters, records of telephone calls, witness statements and other documents prepared by the defence solicitor. The defence cannot be compelled to reveal the contents of such communications to any other party, and the defendant cannot be asked about their contents when being cross-examined.

This privilege extends to communications between the defendant or his solicitor and a third party, provided such communications are made in contemplation of pending or anticipated proceedings and the purpose, or dominant purpose, was to prepare for the litigation. Common examples of such communications include statements taken from witnesses who will give evidence on the defendant's behalf and letters of instruction to experts. The defence cannot be compelled to reveal the contents of such communications to any other party.

When giving evidence at trial, a defendant may (often inadvertently) waive privilege. For example, a defendant may say that he remained silent when interviewed at the police station after receiving advice from his solicitor that he was not in a fit state to be interviewed. Such a defendant has waived privilege and may then be cross-examined about the detailed legal advice which he received at the police station, including any other reasons for him remaining silent in interview (such as not having any plausible explanation for his conduct which would stand up to police scrutiny). This area is examined more fully in **Chapter 4**.

1.8   Human rights

1.8.1   Introduction

Human rights issues sometimes arise during the course of criminal proceedings and, where appropriate, have been highlighted in subsequent chapters. This chapter will provide a general introduction to the subject of human rights by discussing the key sections of the Human Rights Act 1998 and the significant parts of the European Convention for the Protection of Human Rights and Fundamental Freedoms 1950.

1.8.2   The Human Rights Act 1998

The Human Rights Act (HRA) 1998 came into force on 2 October 2000. The Act gives effect in domestic law to the rights and freedoms guaranteed by the European Convention for the Protection of Human Rights and Fundamental Freedoms 1950 (ECHR), to which the UK is a signatory.

Section 3 of the HRA 1998 provides that courts must, so far as it is possible to do so, interpret and give effect to legislation in a way which is compatible with the ECHR. If it is not possible to interpret legislation so as to be compatible with the ECHR, courts do not have the power to 'strike down' that legislation. However s 4 of the HRA 1998 enables the High Court, the Court of Appeal and the House of Lords to declare such legislation to be incompatible with the ECHR ('a declaration of incompatibility'). Such a declaration operates as a clear signal to Parliament and the Government that an incompatibility has been found. Section 10 of the 1998 Act allows Government Ministers to make a remedial order to amend the relevant legislation to make it compatible with the ECHR.

Section 6 of the HRA 1998 provides that it is 'unlawful for a public authority to act in a way which is incompatible with a convention right'. The term 'public authority' is widely defined and will include a criminal court. An individual who claims that a public authority has contravened s 6 may rely on the rights granted to him by the ECHR as a defence in civil and criminal proceedings, or as the basis of an appeal. Alternatively, an individual may seek judicial review of a decision or action taken by a public authority, or bring civil proceedings for damages against that authority.

Section 8(1) of the HRA 1998 provides that

> in relation to any act (or proposed act) of a public authority which the court finds is (or would be) unlawful, it may grant such relief or remedy, or make such order, within its powers as it considers just and appropriate.

This means that criminal courts will have the power to stay proceedings as an abuse of process (ie, stop a case where the police or the prosecution have abused their powers – see **Chapter 21**), quash a charge which a defendant faces, make a ruling that evidence is inadmissible or quash a conviction. A considerable body of case law has built up concerning human rights issues within the criminal litigation process, and a defence solicitor should always be alert to such issues arising when he is representing a client in the police station or at court.

1.8.3   The European Convention for the Protection of Human Rights and Fundamental Freedoms 1950

Since the HRA 1998 came into force, defence solicitors have been able to rely on the ECHR in criminal proceedings. Defence solicitors are now able to test domestic law and practice for compliance with the ECHR, and in particular the following articles:

(a)   Article 3 – the prohibition of torture;

(b)   Article 5 – the right to liberty and security;

(c)   Article 6 – the right to a fair trial;

(d)   Article 7 – no punishment without law;

(e)   Article 8 – the right to respect for private and family life.

Extracts from each article are set out below.

Article 3

Prohibition of torture

No one shall be subjected to torture or to inhuman or degrading treatment or punishment.

Article 5

Right to liberty and security

1.   Everyone has the right to liberty and security of person. No one shall be deprived of his liberty save in the following cases and in accordance with a procedure prescribed by law:

   (a)   the lawful detention of a person after conviction by a competent court;

   (b)   the lawful arrest or detention of a person for non-compliance with the lawful order of a court or in order to secure the fulfilment of any obligation prescribed by law;

   (c)   the lawful arrest or detention of a person effected for the purpose of bringing him before the competent legal authority on reasonable suspicion of having committed an offence or when it is reasonably considered necessary to prevent his committing an offence or fleeing after having done so;

   (d)   the detention of a minor by lawful order for the purpose of educational supervision or his lawful detention for the purpose of bringing him before the competent legal authority;

   (e)   the lawful detention of persons for the prevention of the spreading of infectious diseases, of persons of unsound mind, alcoholics or drug addicts or vagrants;

   (f)   the lawful arrest or detention of a person to prevent his effecting an unauthorised entry into the country or of a person against whom action is being taken with a view to deportation or extradition.

2.   Everyone who is arrested shall be informed promptly, in a language which he understands, of the reasons for his arrest and of any charge against him.

3.   Everyone arrested or detained in accordance with the provisions of paragraph 1(c) of this article shall be brought promptly before a judge or other officer authorised by law to exercise judicial power and shall be entitled to trial within a reasonable time or to release pending trial. Release may be conditioned by guarantees to appear for trial.

4.   Everyone who is deprived of his liberty by arrest or detention shall be entitled to take proceedings by which the lawfulness of his detention shall be decided speedily by a court and his release ordered if the detention is not lawful.

5.   Everyone who has been the victim of arrest or detention in contravention of the provisions of this article shall have an enforceable right to compensation.

Article 6

Right to a fair trial

1.   In the determination of his civil rights and obligations or of any criminal charge against him, everyone is entitled to a fair and public hearing within a reasonable time by an independent and impartial tribunal established by law.

Judgment shall be pronounced publicly but the press and public may be excluded from all or part of the trial in the interest of morals, public order or national security in a democratic society, where the interests of juveniles or the protection of the private life of the parties so require, or to the extent strictly necessary in the opinion of the court in special circumstances where publicity would prejudice the interests of justice.

2.   Everyone charged with a criminal offence shall be presumed innocent until proved guilty according to law.

3.   Everyone charged with a criminal offence has the following minimum rights:

(a)   to be informed promptly, in a language which he understands and in detail, of the nature and cause of the accusation against him;

(b)   to have adequate time and facilities for the preparation of his defence;

(c)   to defend himself in person or through legal assistance of his own choosing or, if he has not sufficient means to pay for legal assistance, to be given it free when the interests of justice so require;

(d)   to examine or have examined witnesses against him and to obtain the attendance and examination of witnesses on his behalf under the same conditions as witnesses against him;

(e)   to have the free assistance of an interpreter if he cannot understand or speak the language used in court

Article 7

No punishment without law

1.   No one shall be held guilty of any criminal offence on account of any act or omission which did not constitute a criminal offence under national or international law at the time when it was committed. Nor shall a heavier penalty be imposed than the one that was applicable at the time the criminal offence was committed.

2.   This article shall not prejudice the trial and punishment of any person for any act or omission which, at the time when it was committed, was criminal according to the general principles of law recognised by civilised nations.

Article 8

Right to respect for private and family life

1.   Everyone has the right to respect for his private and family life, his home and his correspondence.

2.   There shall be no interference by a public authority with the exercise of this right except such as is in accordance with the law and is necessary in a democratic society in the interests of national security, public safety or the economic well-being of the country, for the prevention of disorder or crime, for the protection of health or morals, or for the protection of the rights and freedoms of others.

1.9 Gary Dickson case study

1.9.1 Introduction

Criminal litigation is a 'hands-on' area of law which requires a solicitor to develop skills in case analysis, drafting and advocacy. The Gary Dickson case study provides a practical illustration of some of the most significant points which arise in subsequent chapters. In particular, the case study is designed to enable readers to see how the most important documents in a criminal case should be drafted, and to illustrate how the different types of advocacy that may be required during the course of a criminal case should be performed. The documents making up the case study have been integrated into the text at appropriate places to provide a practical illustration of the key skill or document under discussion.

1.9.2 Overview of the Gary Dickson case study

Gary Dickson is arrested by the police on Monday, 18 December 2006, on suspicion of having committed an assault during the early hours of that morning in Chester city centre. He is taken to Chester police station where his detention for questioning is authorised (**Key Document: Custody Record – Chapter 3**). He is subsequently interviewed on tape (without having a solicitor present), and then takes part in a video identification procedure. He is picked out by an eye-witness to the assault. Dickson is charged with assault occasioning actual bodily harm under s 47 of the Offences Against the Person Act 1861 (**Key Document: Charge Sheet – Chapter 3**), and is remanded in police custody to appear before Chester magistrates' court the following day.

Dickson asks a solicitor who has represented him in previous criminal matters to act on his behalf. Dickson's solicitor takes a detailed statement from him (**Key Skill: Drafting the Client's Statement – Chapter 6**), and prepares an application for a legal representation order on his behalf (**Key Skill: Completing an Application for a Legal Representation Order – Chapter 6**). This application is successful (**Key Document: Representation Order – Chapter 6**). Dickson indicates to his solicitor that he will plead not guilty to the charge, on the basis that at the time of the alleged assault he was at home in bed asleep. At the early administrative hearing before the magistrates' court, the magistrates adjourn the case to enable the CPS to provide advance disclosure of its case to Dickson's solicitor. The solicitor makes an application for bail on Dickson's behalf (**Key Skill: Making an Application for Bail – Chapter 7**). This application is unsuccessful, and after a further bail application to the magistrates made one week later also fails, a successful appeal against the refusal of bail is made to a Crown Court judge in chambers (**Key Skill: Drafting a Bail Appeal Notice – Chapter 7**).

The CPS serves advance disclosure on Dickson's solicitor and the solicitor obtains Dickson's comments on this (**Key Document: Advance Disclosure – Chapter 6**). Dickson's solicitor obtains a statement from Jill Summers, who will give evidence at trial confirming Dickson's alibi defence.

At the next hearing (the plea before venue hearing) Dickson enters a not guilty plea to the charge. The magistrates accept jurisdiction, but Dickson elects trial before the Crown Court. The magistrates send the case to Crown Court for trial and give directions to be complied with prior to the plea and case management hearing taking place at the Crown Court. As part of these directions, the CPS serves on Dickson's solicitor a schedule listing the unused material in its possession (**Key document: Police Schedule of Non-sensitive Unused Material – Chapter 8**), and Dickson's solicitor serves a defence statement on the CPS confirming Dickson's alibi defence (**Key Skill: Drafting a Defence Statement – Chapter 10**).

Dickson's solicitor instructs counsel to represent Dickson in the Crown Court (**Key Skill: Preparing a Brief to Counsel – Chapter 10**). At the plea and case management hearing, Dickson enters a not guilty plea to the count on the indictment (**Key Document: Indictment – Chapter 10**) and the case is listed for trial. On the day of the trial Dickson changes his plea from not guilty to guilty. The judge adjourns the case so that the Probation Service can prepare a pre-sentence report on Dickson (**Key Document: Pre-sentence report – Chapter 12**).

At the sentencing hearing, the prosecution outline the facts of the case and Dickson's counsel gives a plea in mitigation on his behalf (**Key Skill: Delivering a**

Plea in Mitigation – Chapter 12). Dickson receives a generic community order. Under the terms of the order, he is required to complete 300 hours' unpaid work and to take part in an anger management programme. He is also ordered to pay £750 in compensation to his victim and £250 towards the prosecution costs. No defence costs recovery order is made.

1.10 Additional sources of information

1.10.1 Practitioner texts

This book is designed to provide an introduction to criminal procedure and the law of evidence. There are several practitioner texts which can be consulted to check more detailed points of practice or procedure:

Blackstone's Criminal Practice (2006) – this is an authoritative guide to practice and procedure in both the magistrates' court and the Crown Court. It also has very full sections dealing with substantive criminal offences, the investigative powers of the police and the law of evidence. (See also the companion website at www.oup.co.uk.)

Archbold: Criminal Pleading, Evidence and Practice (2006) – this is very similar in its scope and format to the *Blackstone's* text, and is used mainly by practitioners in the Crown Court.

Archbold: Magistrates' Courts Criminal Practice (2006) – this book is intended for the solicitor in the magistrates' court. It contains a section dealing with the substantive law, with other helpful sections dealing with procedural and evidential matters.

Stone's Justices' Manual (2006) – a comprehensive guide to all matters of practice and procedure in the magistrates' court.

Anthony and Berryman's Magistrates' Courts Guide (2006) – this provides useful information about all the offences that are likely to arise in the magistrates' court, including a particularly helpful section on road traffic offences.

Wilkinson's Road Traffic Offences (22nd edn, 2005) – this is the standard reference work on all matters of law, practice and procedure concerning road traffic offences.

Ed Cape with Jawaid Luqmani, *Defending Suspects at Police Stations* (4th edn, 2003) – this is an excellent guide to how a solicitor should represent a client at the police station. It contains numerous hints and tips for newly-qualified solicitors in what is a difficult area of practice.

In addition to the above there are several other textbooks which provide detailed guidance on various matters of criminal procedure, particularly in relation to applications for bail and sentencing. Similarly, there are several books which outline the immense changes made to the criminal justice system by the provisions of the Criminal Justice Act 2003.

1.10.2 Websites

There are a number of websites that are useful sources of information for the busy criminal litigation solicitor:

www.dca.gov.uk – the website of the Department for Constitutional Affairs. This gives access to the Criminal Procedure Rules 2005 and amendments that have been made to the Rules.

www.courtservice.gov.uk – the website of the Court Service. This gives access to various court forms and also key judgments.

www.sentencing-guidelines.gov.uk – the website of the Sentencing Guidelines Council, which contains sentencing guidelines issued by the Council (see **Chapter 11**).

www.cps.gov.uk – the website of the CPS, which contains the Code for Crown Prosecutors and a useful summary of various evidential matters.

www.homeoffice.gov.uk – the website of the Home Office. This gives access to the Codes of Practice for police conduct issued under PACE 1984, and also details of proposed further reforms to the criminal justice system.

www.lawsociety.org.uk/home.law – the website of the Law Society. The Criminal Law Committee of the Law Society produce a quarterly newsletter called the 'Criminal Practitioners newsletter', which contains useful information about recent developments in matters of criminal practice.

www.jsboard.co.uk – the website of the Judicial Studies Board (JSB). The JSB is responsible for training members of the judiciary. The website contains specimen directions for judges to give in criminal cases, and is particularly useful for specimen directions about evidential matters. It also provides access to the Magistrates' Court Sentencing Guidelines (see **Chapter 11**).

www.clsa.co.uk – the website of the Criminal Law Solicitors' Association. This provides regular updates on matters of law, procedure and evidence for solicitors specialising in criminal litigation work.

www.legalservices.gov.uk – the website of the Legal Services Commission, which contains details of the various forms of public funding available in criminal litigation matters, together with the payment rates solicitors may claim and the forms which must be completed in order to obtain payment.

1.11 Procedural flowcharts

1.11.1 Introduction

In **1.3** above, the classification of offences into the categories of indictable only, either way or summary offences was explained. One of the hardest tasks facing a student of criminal litigation is to understand the different procedures that are followed in respect of each type of offence from the arrest of the suspect through to the conclusion of the case at court. To assist with this, set out below are three flowcharts which provide a general overview of the procedural steps that are followed for each type of offence. The details of each stage in the process will be explained in subsequent chapters.

1.11.2   Indictable only offences

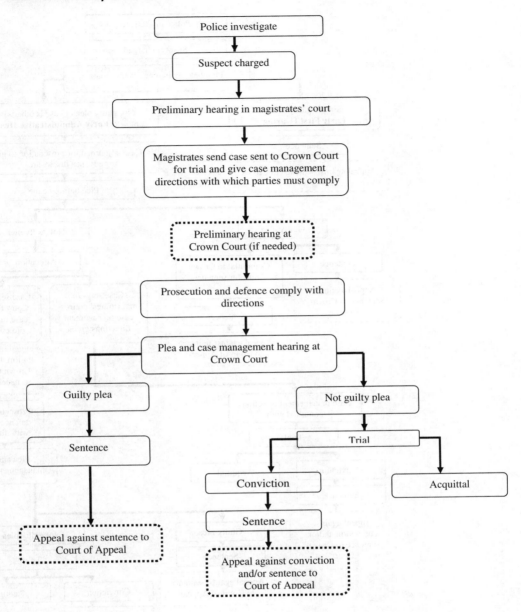

1.11.3 Either way offences

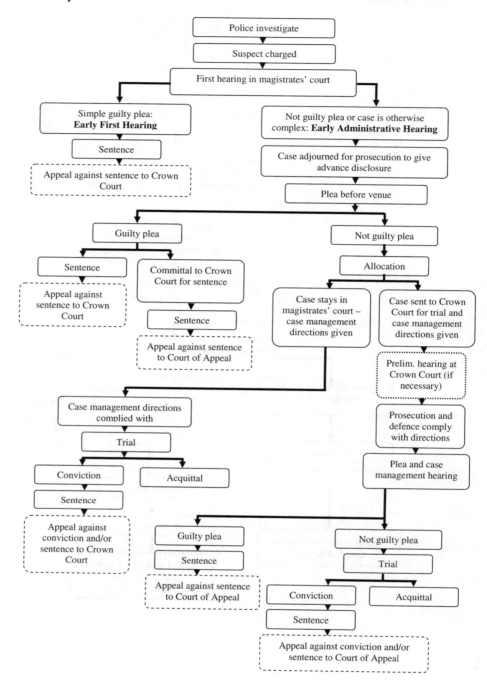

1.11.4 Summary offences

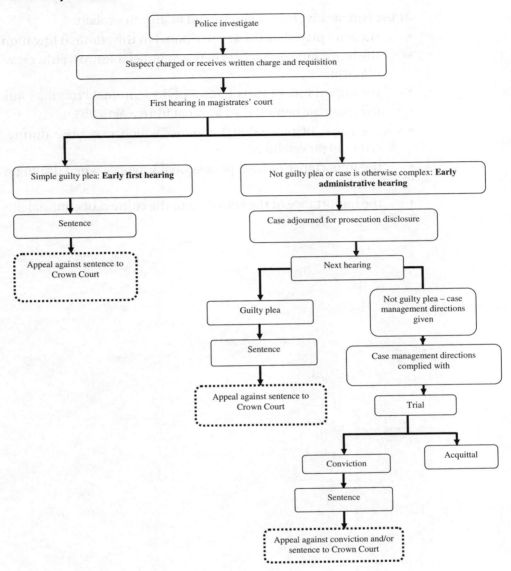

1.12 Checklist

At the end of this chapter you should be able to explain:

- the roles played by the key personnel in the criminal litigation process;
- the procedural differences between indictable only, either way and summary offences;
- the importance of Parts 1 and 3 of the Criminal Procedure Rules 2005;
- the rationale behind the Criminal Justice Act 2003;
- the issues of professional conduct which may arise during the course of criminal proceedings;
- the importance of legal professional privilege when dealing with a criminal case;
- the importance of the HRA1998 in the context of criminal litigation.

Part 2
THE CLIENT AND THE POLICE

Chapter 2

The Investigative Powers of the Police (1) – Outside the Police Station

2.1 Introduction

The criminal litigation process begins before a solicitor is asked to represent a suspect in the police station or a defendant at court. The first stage in the process involves the police carrying out investigations after a criminal offence has been committed. Only when the police have investigated an offence and arrested a suspect is a solicitor likely to become involved.

This chapter will look at the powers the police exercise *outside* the police station when investigating an offence. The powers that will be described are:

(a) the power to stop and search persons and vehicles;

(b) the power of arrest; and

(c) the power to enter and search premises (and to seize and retain items found on premises).

Most powers exercised by the police are granted to them by the Police and Criminal Evidence Act (PACE) 1984. The Act is supplemented by seven Codes of Practice (A to G) which provide police officers with detailed guidance as to how to exercise these powers. References to section numbers in this chapter are, unless otherwise stated, to PACE 1984. References to Code A are to the Code of Practice on the Exercise by Police Officers of Statutory Powers of Stop and Search. References to Code B are to the Code of Practice for Searches of Property and the Seizure of Property. References to Code C are to the Code of Practice for the Detention, Treatment and Questioning of Persons by Police Officers. References to Code G are to the Code of Practice for the Statutory Power of Arrest by Police Officers. In July 2006 a new Code H will be added (detention, treatment and questioning by police officers of persons under the Terrorism Act 2000).

2.2 Powers of stop and search

2.2.1 What can the police search for?

This section will examine the powers of stop and search the police may exercise under PACE 1984. Brief details of the main additional powers of stop and search which the police may exercise are set out at **2.2.7** below.

Under s 1(2), a police officer is given the power to search any person or vehicle (or anything which is in or on a vehicle) for stolen or prohibited articles, or any articles to which s 1(8A) applies. The officer can detain a person or vehicle for the purpose of carrying out such a search. Section 1(2) also allows the police to search a person or vehicle for prohibited fireworks.

Stolen articles have their ordinary meaning. Prohibited articles are articles which are offensive weapons (see below), or which are either:

(a)   made or adapted for use in the course of or in connection with the offences set out in s 1(8); or

(b)   intended by the person having that article for such use by him or by some other person.

The offences listed in s 1(8) are:

(a)   burglary;

(b)   theft;

(c)   taking a motor vehicle or other conveyance without authority;

(d)   obtaining property by deception;

(e)   destroying or damaging property (Criminal Damage Act 1971, s 1).

Examples of articles which could fall into this category are a crowbar, wrench or jemmy.

Offensive weapons are defined in s 1(9) as being any article which is either:

(a)   made or adapted for use for causing injury to persons (such as a cosh or a gun); or

(b)   intended by the person having it with him for such use by him or by some other person (such as a baseball bat which is not manufactured for use as an offensive weapon.

Articles to which s 1(8A) applies are any articles which would contravene the offence of having an article with a blade or a point in a public place contrary to s 139(1) of the Criminal Justice Act 1988. This covers most types of knife, except a folding pocket knife.

A police officer may seize any article discovered during a search if he has reasonable grounds for suspecting the article to be a stolen or prohibited article, or an article to which s 1(8A) applies (s 1(6)).

2.2.2   Where can the power to stop and search be exercised?

The basic rule is that this power can be exercised only in a public place. Section 1(1)(a) allows a police officer to carry out a stop and search:

(a)   in any place to which at the time of the search the public, or any part of the public, have access, whether by payment or otherwise, and whether the access is as of right or by virtue of express or implied permission; or

(b)   in any other place (other than a dwelling) to which people have ready access at the time the officer intends to carry out the search.

Examples of locations which would fall into the first category above are shopping centres, public houses, parks and bus stations, as well as the public highway. The second category could include the garden or yard attached to a house (but not the house itself), as these are places to which the public have ready access.

2.2.3   When can the power of stop and search be exercised?

Before exercising the power of stop and search conferred by s 1(2), a police officer must have 'reasonable grounds for suspecting that he will find stolen or prohibited articles or any article to which [s 1(8A)] applies' (s 1(3)). Paragraph 2.2 of Code A provides that:

> Reasonable grounds for suspicion depend on the circumstances in each case. There must be an objective basis for that suspicion based on facts, information, and/or intelligence which are relevant to finding an article of a certain kind ...

The police cannot use a person's age, appearance or race, or the knowledge that a person has a previous conviction as valid grounds for searching that person. Reasonable suspicion should be based on accurate and current intelligence or information. This could, for example, be information about an article a person is carrying, about a suspected offender, or about a person seen carrying a type of item that is known to have been stolen recently from local premises. The police do not have the power to stop or detain a person in order to find grounds for a search (Code A, para 2.11).

Paragraph 1.4 of Code A stresses that the main function of stop and search powers is 'to enable officers to allay or confirm suspicions about individuals without exercising their power of arrest'. If an officer who has reasonable grounds for suspicion detains a person in order to carry out a search, the officer may ask questions about the person's behaviour or presence in circumstances which gave rise to the suspicion. Any response to such questions might confirm the reasonable grounds for suspicion required to detain the person, or might remove those grounds (if, for example, the detained person gives a satisfactory explanation).

If the person is in the garden or yard of a dwelling, a police officer can exercise his power of stop and search only if he has reasonable grounds for believing that the person does not live in the dwelling and does not have the express or implied permission of the owner of the dwelling to be there (s 1(4)).

Similarly, if a vehicle is in the garden or yard of a dwelling, a police officer can exercise his power of stop and search only if he has reasonable grounds for believing that the person in charge of the vehicle does not live in the dwelling and the vehicle is not in the garden or yard with the express or implied permission of the owner of the dwelling.

2.2.4   What steps need to be taken prior to search?

If a police officer intends to search a person or a vehicle which is attended by a person, the officer must first take reasonable steps, if he is not in uniform, to bring to the attention of the person to be searched or in charge of the vehicle documentary evidence that he is a police officer (by producing his warrant card).

The officer, whether or not he is in uniform, must then take reasonable steps to bring to the attention of that person the following information:

(a)   the fact that the person is being detained for the purposes of a search;

(b)   the officer's name and the name of the police station to which he is attached;

(c)   the object of the proposed search (ie, details of the article(s) for which there is a power to search); and

(d)   the officer's grounds for proposing to carry out the search (s 2(2)).

2.2.5   How should the search be conducted?

Paragraph 3.1 of Code A provides that all stops and searches 'must be carried out with courtesy, consideration and respect for the person concerned'.

Under s 117, a police officer is allowed to use 'reasonable force' in the exercise of any other powers contained within PACE 1984. Force may be used for a stop and search only if the person is unwilling to cooperate or resists. The exercise of reasonable force is a 'last resort' (Code A, para 3.2).

The period of time during which a person or vehicle is detained must be kept to a minimum, and the thoroughness and extent of the search depends on what is suspected of being carried, and by whom (Code A, para 3.3). The search must be carried out 'at or near the place where the person or vehicle was first detained' (Code A, para 3.4).

The only items of clothing a detained person can be required to remove in public are an outer coat, jacket and gloves (Code A, para 3.5). A search in public of a detained person's clothing which has not been removed can be only a 'superficial examination of outer garments' (Code A, para 3.5). If a police officer has reasonable grounds for considering it necessary that a more thorough search be conducted (for example, by requiring a detained person to remove a shirt), this must be done out of public view, such as in a police van (Code A, para 3.6).

2.2.6   What must be done after the search?

The police officer who carried out the search must make a record of it at the time, unless there are exceptional circumstances making this wholly impracticable (such as in a public disorder situation, or if the officer's presence is urgently required elsewhere). If a record is not made at the time, it must be made as soon as practicable afterwards (Code A, para 4.1).

A copy of a record made at the time must be given immediately to the person who has been searched (Code A, para 4.2).

2.2.7   What other powers of stop and search may the police exercise?

Annex A to Code A summarises the main stop and search powers enjoyed by the police. The other significant powers of stop and search the police may exercise in addition to those powers granted by PACE 1984 are:

(a)   powers to search persons and vehicles for controlled drugs (and to seize and detain anything found which appears to be evidence of an offence) under s 23(2) of the Misuse of Drugs Act 1971;

(b)   powers to search persons and vehicles for offensive weapons or dangerous instruments to prevent incidents of serious violence, or to deal with the carrying of such items under s 60 of the Criminal Justice and Public Order Act 1994; and

(c)   powers of search of persons and vehicles under anti-terrorist legislation (particularly ss 44–47 of the Terrorism Act 2000).

Changes proposed in the Police and Justice Bill which is currently before Parliament would also give the police the power to search any person, vehicle or aircraft in an aerodrome (or anything which is in or on such a vehicle or aircraft) for stolen or prohibited articles.

Unless they are exercising the specific statutory powers of stop and search noted above, the police have no general statutory or common law right to detain a person for the purpose of making enquiries, or to require a person to give his name and address (*Rice v Connolly* [1966] 2 All ER 649). There are, however, some exceptions to this. For example, provisions in the Road Traffic Act 1988 permit the police to stop a motorist and require him to undergo a breath alcohol test if the police suspect the motorist of driving whilst over the prescribed alcohol limit (see **Chapter 15**).

2.3 Arrest

2.3.1 Introduction

A police officer's decision to arrest a suspect is a pivotal stage in the criminal process. In *Christie v Leachinsky* [1974] AC 573, Lord Simonds characterised arrest as being the beginning of imprisonment. Arrest will be the first occasion when a suspect has been deprived of his liberty, and must therefore have both a clear legal justification and be necessary. Arresting or detaining someone who it is reasonably suspected has committed a criminal offence is one of the exceptions to an individual's right to liberty and security under Article 5 of the ECHR (see **Chapter 1**). However, such action is justified only if the arrest is 'lawful'.

Paragraphs 1.2 and 1.3 of Code G state:

> 1.2 The right to liberty is a key principle of the Human Rights Act 1998. The exercise of the power of arrest represents an obvious and significant interference with that right.
>
> 1.3 The use of the power must be fully justified and officers exercising the power should consider if the necessary objectives can be met by other, less intrusive means.

Paragraph 1.4 of Code G provides that failure by the police to observe PACE 1984 and the Codes of Practice when exercising the statutory power of arrest may prejudice both the legality of the arrest and the conduct of any subsequent investigation into the offence.

This section will look at what constitutes a lawful arrest, the sources of the police powers of arrest and how the police should exercise those powers. It will also examine the safeguards that exist and the rules with which the police must comply should they wish to question a person about his suspected involvement in a criminal offence prior to him being arrested.

2.3.2 What is an arrest?

An arrest is a restraint on the liberty of the person under due process of law. There are two requirements for an arrest to be valid:

(a) there must be a *power* of arrest (see **2.3.4** below); and

(b) the arrest must be carried out in the proper *manner* (see **2.3.5** below).

If either of these requirements is not fulfilled, an arrest will be invalid and the detention of any person following such an arrest will be unlawful and in breach of his right to liberty under Article 5 of the ECHR. The person wrongfully detained would be entitled to claim damages in such circumstances (see **Chapter 5**).

2.3.3 Interviews prior to arrest – the 'anti-verballing' rules

2.3.3.1 Introduction

Most interviews which the police carry out with suspects will take place at the police station after the suspect has been arrested. Such interviews will be audio-recorded, and the recording can be played at any subsequent trial if there is a dispute as to what was said during the interview. It will, however, often be the case that, outside of the police station and prior to that person's arrest, the police will want to ask questions of a person whom they suspect of having committed an offence to ascertain if their suspicions are justified and to enable them to establish the necessary grounds for then arresting that person.

Prior to arresting a suspect, the police are permitted to question that person about his suspected involvement in a criminal offence, although the suspect is under no legal obligation to answer such questions. The police may not detain a suspect to ask such questions prior to arrest (*Kenlin v Gardiner* [1967] 2 QB 510). The only exception to this is if the police are exercising their powers of stop and search under s 1 (see **2.2** above).

If the police do interview a suspect prior to arrest and the suspect makes an admission or a confession, detailed requirements are set out in Code C to ensure both that any such comment is properly recorded and that the suspect is given the opportunity to comment on any remarks that he is alleged to have made. These provisions are commonly referred to as the 'anti-verballing rules' and are designed as safeguards to prevent the police from later misrepresenting (whether deliberately or otherwise) what the suspect has said. Prior to interviews at the police station being recorded, it was common for defendants to argue at trial that admissions or confessions which the police claimed had been made were in fact fabricated by the police (colloquially called being 'done up in the verbals'). This led to several well-publicised miscarriages of justice. The recording of interviews at the police station and the requirements of Code C below in respect of interviews which take place outside the police station are designed to prevent such miscarriages of justice occurring again.

2.3.3.2   What constitutes an interview?

Paragraph 11.1A of Code C states that:

> An interview is the questioning of a person regarding their involvement or suspected involvement in a criminal offence or offences which, under paragraph 10.1, must be carried out under caution. . . .

This means that if the police question a suspect in the street *before* that suspect has actually been arrested, this may count as an interview. Questioning a suspect prior to arrest will count as an interview only if the police have 'some reasonable, objective grounds for suspicion, based on known facts or information which are relevant to the likelihood the offence has been committed and the person to be questioned committed it' (Code C, Notes for Guidance, para 10A).

The significance of such questioning being an interview is contained in para 10.1 of Code C, which provides that:

> A person whom there are grounds to suspect of an offence, see *Note 10A*, must be cautioned before any questions about an offence, or further questions if the answers provide the grounds for suspicion, are put to them if either the suspect's answers or silence, (ie failure or refusal to answer or answer satisfactorily) may be given in evidence to a court in a prosecution. . . .

In other words, a police officer must caution a suspect before carrying out an interview as defined by para 11.1A above. The wording of the caution is as follows:

> You do not have to say anything. But it may harm your defence if you do not mention when questioned something which you later rely on in court. Anything you do say may be given in evidence. (Code C, para 10.5)

Example

PC Singh is called to a public house where one of the customers has been assaulted. The customer did not recognise his assailant but is able to provide PC Singh with an accurate description of this person. PC Singh leaves the public house and sees Oliver nearby. Oliver closely matches the description of the assailant given by the customer. PC Singh asks Oliver where he has just come from. Oliver tells him that he has come from the same public house where the assault occurred. This gives PC Singh reasonable grounds to suspect that Oliver may have committed the assault. PC Singh should therefore caution Oliver before asking him any further questions about the assault.

Should a police officer fail to caution a suspect before conducting an interview in these circumstances, this may result in any subsequent admission or confession made by the suspect being ruled inadmissible at trial under s 78 of PACE 1984, on the basis that it would be unfair to permit the prosecution to rely on such evidence (see **Chapters 20** and **21**).

2.3.3.3 Recording interviews outside the police station

Paragraph 11.7(a) of Code C states that 'an accurate record must be made of each interview, whether or not the interview takes place at a police station'. If the record is not made at the time of the interview, it must be made as soon as practicable after the completion of the interview (Code C, para 11.7(c)). Paragraph 11.11 of Code C provides that a person who has been interviewed shall, unless it is impracticable, be given the opportunity to read the interview record and sign it as correct, or to indicate how they consider it inaccurate. To comply with these paragraphs, if the interview takes place outside the police station, the police officer will usually make a note of the interview in his pocket book, and then invite the suspect to read the note and sign this as being correct.

The police must also make a written record of any comments made by a suspect (including any unsolicited comments) which are outside the context of an interview but which might be relevant to the offence (Code C, para 11.13). As with the record of an interview, if practicable the suspect should be given the opportunity to read the record and either to sign it as correct, or to indicate how he considers it inaccurate.

Once a suspect has been arrested, any further interview(s) with that suspect should generally take place only at the police station, where they can be audio-recorded (see **2.3.7** below). At the start of such an interview at the police station, the police will put to the suspect any significant statement made by the suspect either prior to his arrest, or after his arrest but prior to the start of the interview (Code C, para 11.4; see **Chapter 3**).

2.3.4 The sources of the police powers of arrest

2.3.4.1 Introduction

Arrests that are made by the police will be carried out either after a warrant for the arrest of the relevant person has been issued, or without a warrant.

Arrests under a warrant are rare and usually arise when a defendant fails to attend court and the court issues a warrant for the defendant's arrest.

Example

Malcolm is charged with theft and is bailed to appear before the magistrates' court. Malcolm fails to attend court at the required time so the magistrates issue a warrant for Malcolm's arrest. The warrant gives the police the power to arrest Malcolm, whom they will then bring before the court as soon as possible after his arrest.

Of much greater importance are arrests carried out without a warrant. The powers of the police to arrest without a warrant derive from two sources:

(a)   powers of arrest in PACE 1984;

(b)   the common law power to arrest for a breach of the peace.

Each of these powers will be examined in turn.

2.3.4.2   Powers of arrest in PACE 1984

Powers of arrest granted only to the police

The statutory powers of arrest which the police may exercise are contained in s 24 of PACE 1984. Section 24 gives police officers a power of arrest in respect of any criminal offence (no matter how minor that offence may be), provided that certain conditions are satisfied. These conditions are explained in Code G, which states that a lawful arrest made under s 24 requires two elements:

(a)   a person's involvement, or suspected involvement or attempted involvement in the commission of a criminal offence; *and*

(b)   reasonable grounds for believing that the arrest is necessary (Code G, para 2.1).

The wording of s 24 is as follows:

> **24   Arrest without warrant: constables**
>
> (1)   A constable may arrest without a warrant—
>
> > (a)   anyone who is about to commit an offence;
> >
> > (b)   anyone who is in the act of committing an offence;
> >
> > (c)   anyone whom he has reasonable grounds for suspecting to be about to commit an offence;
> >
> > (d)   anyone whom he has reasonable grounds for suspecting to be committing an offence.
>
> (2)   If a constable has reasonable grounds for suspecting that an offence has been committed, he may arrest without a warrant anyone whom he has reasonable grounds to suspect of being guilty of it.
>
> (3)   If an offence has been committed, a constable may arrest without a warrant—
>
> > (a)   anyone who is guilty of the offence;
> >
> > (b)   anyone whom he has reasonable grounds for suspecting to be guilty of it.
>
> (4)   But the power of summary arrest conferred by subsection (1), (2) or (3) is exercisable only if the constable has reasonable grounds for believing that for any of the reasons mentioned in subsection (5) it is necessary to arrest the person in question.
>
> (5)   The reasons are—
>
> > (a)   to enable the name of the person in question to be ascertained (in the case where the constable does not know, and cannot readily ascertain, the person's name, or has reasonable grounds for doubting whether a name given by the person as his name is his real name);
> >
> > (b)   correspondingly as regards the person's address;
> >
> > (c)   to prevent the person in question—
> >
> > > (i)   causing physical injury to himself or any other person,

            (ii)   suffering physical injury,

            (iii)   causing loss of or damage to property,

            (iv)   committing an offence against public decency (subject to subsection (6)), or

            (v)   causing an unlawful obstruction of the highway;

    (d)   to protect a child or other vulnerable person from the person in question;

    (e)   to allow the prompt and effective investigation of the offence or of the conduct of the person in question;

    (f)   to prevent any prosecution for the offence from being hindered by the disappearance of the person in question.

  (6)   Subsection (5)(c)(iv) applies only where members of the public going about their normal business cannot reasonably be expected to avoid the person in question.

Section 24 therefore enables a police officer to arrest anyone who is, or whom he reasonably suspects is:

(a)   about to commit an offence; or

(b)   in the act of committing an offence; or

(c)   guilty of having committed an offence,

provided that the officer has reasonable grounds for believing that it is necessary to arrest the suspect for one or more of the reasons set out in s 24(5).

Example 1

PC Smith sees Tony break a window to gain access to a house. PC Smith arrests Tony on suspicion of burglary. It transpires that the house belongs to Tony and he broke the window to get in because he had lost his key. PC Smith had valid grounds for arresting Tony under s 24(1)(d) if he reasonably suspected that Tony was committing a burglary and one or more of the conditions in s 24(5) was satisfied.

Example 2

Abdul is the victim of an assault which results in his sustaining a broken nose. Abdul gives a detailed description of his assailant to PC Smith. Shortly after the assault, PC Smith sees Brian near the scene of the assault. Brian matches the description of the assailant given by Abdul and Brian's shirt is covered in blood. PC Smith arrests Brian on suspicion of assault occasioning actual bodily harm. It later transpires that Brian was not the assailant. Brian merely resembled the assailant and his shirt was covered in blood following a nosebleed. PC Smith had valid grounds for the arrest under s 24(3)(b) if he reasonably suspected that Brian was guilty of the assault and one or more of the conditions in s 24(5) was satisfied.

Example 3

From a distance PC Smith sees Martin punch Patrick in the face, causing Patrick's nose to break. PC Smith runs after Martin and arrests him on suspicion of assault occasioning actual bodily harm. At his trial, Martin is acquitted on the basis that (unknown to PC Smith) Patrick had attacked him first and Martin was acting in reasonable self-defence. Even though Martin had therefore not committed an offence, PC Smith had valid grounds for the arrest under s 24(2) if he reasonably suspected an offence had been committed by Martin and one or more of the conditions in s 24(5) was satisfied.

Example 4

There has been a spate of robberies in a particular park. Rachel knows that her friend Alison will be walking through the park late one evening. She decides to play a trick on Alison by hiding in some bushes and jumping out in front of her as she walks by. PC Smith sees Rachel hiding in the bushes. Thinking that she may be about to commit a robbery, PC Smith arrests Rachel as she is waiting for Alison to walk past. PC Smith had valid grounds for the arrest under s 24(1)(c) if he reasonably believed that Rachel was about to commit a robbery, as long as one or more of the conditions in s 24(5) was satisfied.

The conditions in s 24(5) (referred to in Code G as the 'necessity criteria') are deliberately drawn widely, and a police officer should have little difficulty in persuading a court that one or more of these conditions was satisfied at the time he decided to make the arrest. Most of these conditions are self-explanatory and require no further discussion. Even if none of the other conditions in s 24(5) is satisfied, a police officer will normally be able to justify an arrest under s 24(5)(e) on the basis that he has reasonable grounds for believing that the arrest was necessary for the 'prompt and effective investigation of the offence or of the conduct of the person in question'. This wording is sufficiently wide to cover most situations. Paragraph 2.9 of Code G gives several examples of when the condition in s 24(5)(e) will be satisfied:

(a)   where there are grounds to believe that:
    (i)   the person has made false statements,
    (ii)   the person has made statements which cannot be readily verified,
    (iii) the person has presented false evidence,
    (iv)   the person may steal or destroy evidence,
    (v)   the person may make contact with co-suspects or conspirators,
    (vi)   the person may intimidate, or threaten or make contact with witnesses,
    (vii) it is necessary to obtain evidence by questioning; or
(b)   when the offence is indictable, there is a need to:
    (i)   enter and search any premises occupied or controlled by a person,
    (ii)   search the person,
    (iii) prevent contact with others,
    (iv)   take fingerprints, footwear impressions, samples or photographs of the suspect.

When applying the necessary criteria, the officer must 'take into account the situation of the victim, the nature of the offence, the circumstances of the suspect and the needs of the investigation process' (Code G, para 2.8).

Powers of arrest granted to other persons

In addition to the powers of arrest given to the police under s 24, persons other than police officers (ie, members of the public) are given a more limited power of arrest under s 24A of PACE 1984:

> **24A Arrest without warrant: other persons**
> (1)   A person other than a constable may arrest without a warrant—
>   (a)   anyone who is in the act of committing an indictable offence;
>   (b)   anyone whom he has reasonable grounds for suspecting to be committing an indictable offence.
> (2)   Where an indictable offence has been committed, a person other than a constable may arrest without a warrant—
>   (a)   anyone who is guilty of the offence;

> (b)   anyone whom he has reasonable grounds for suspecting to be guilty of it.
>
> (3)   But the power of summary arrest conferred by subsection (1) or (2) is exercisable only if—
>
> (a)   the person making the arrest has reasonable grounds for believing that for any of the reasons mentioned in subsection (4) it is necessary to arrest the person in question; and
>
> (b)   it appears to the person making the arrest that it is not reasonably practicable for a constable to make it instead.
>
> (4)   The reasons are to prevent the person in question—
>
> (a)   causing physical injury to himself or any other person;
>
> (b)   suffering physical injury;
>
> (c)   causing loss of or damage to property; or
>
> (d)   making off before a constable can assume responsibility for him.

2.3.4.3 Arrest to prevent a breach of the peace

The only remaining power of arrest at common law is the power to arrest to prevent a breach of the peace. The Court of Appeal defined what is meant by the term 'breach of the peace' in *R v Howell* [1982] QB 416, where it was held that a police officer was entitled to arrest a defendant who had been swearing in the street at 4 am. The Court said that:

> ... there is a breach of the peace whenever harm is actually done or is likely to be done to a person or in his presence to his property or a person is in fear of being so harmed through an assault, an affray, a riot or other disturbance.

Any person (not just a police officer) may arrest for a breach of the peace:

(a)   committed in his presence;

(b)   when he has reasonable cause to believe that a breach of the peace will be committed by a person in the immediate future; or

(c)   when a breach of the peace has been committed and he has reasonable grounds to believe that it will be renewed if the person is not arrested.

2.3.5 How should the police conduct an arrest?

2.3.5.1 Use of force

An arrested person must understand that he is under physical restraint. Words alone can suffice to make a suspect understand that he is no longer a 'free agent', but if the suspect does not submit to words alone the police officer may be required to use a form of physical restraint (such as handcuffs).

The police are permitted to use force in carrying out an arrest. Section 117 permits the police to use 'reasonable force' in exercising any other power conferred by PACE 1984. In addition, s 3 of the Criminal Law Act 1967 provides that any person may use such force as is reasonable in the circumstances for effecting or assisting in the lawful arrest of offenders or suspected offenders.

2.3.5.2 Information to be given to the suspect

A police officer making an arrest must tell the suspect:

(a)   that he is under arrest, even if the fact of the arrest is obvious. If it is not possible to give this information immediately (for example, because the suspect has passed out drunk), the suspect must be told that he is under arrest as soon as practicable after his arrest (s 28(1)); and

(b)   the ground(s) for the arrest, even if the ground(s) are obvious. If it is not possible to give this information immediately (for example, because the suspect is acting violently), the suspect must be told of the ground(s) for his arrest as soon as is practicable after the arrest (s 28(3)).

Paragraph 2.2 of Code G confirms this by providing that an arresting officer must inform the suspect that:

(a)   he is being arrested (even if this is obvious);

(b)   he is being arrested as a result of his involvement, or suspected involvement or attempted involvement in the commission of a criminal offence; and

(c)   there are reasonable grounds for believing that his arrest is necessary.

The arresting officer must also inform the custody officer of this information when the suspect arrives at the police station and is brought before the custody officer in order for the suspect's ongoing detention at the police station to be authorised (Code C, para 2.2) – see **Chapter 3**.

A suspect must also be cautioned on being arrested (Code C, para 10.5). The wording of the caution is set out at **2.3.3.2** above. The giving of the caution may be delayed if it is impracticable to caution the suspect immediately because of the suspect's condition or behaviour (Code G, para 3.4 (a)).

Under para 4.1 of Code G, a police officer carrying out an arrest must record the following information (normally in his pocket book):

(a)   the nature and circumstances of the offence leading to the arrest;

(b)   the reason or reasons why the arrest was necessary;

(c)   the giving of the caution; and

(d)   anything said by the person at the time of the arrest.

Such information should be recorded at the time of the arrest unless it is impracticable to do so, in which case the record should be made as soon as possible thereafter (Code G, para 4.2). This information must also be recorded in the custody record when the suspect arrives at the police station (Code G, para 4.3; see **3.2.2.2**).

2.3.6   Searches following arrest

Section 32(1) permits a police officer to search a person who is arrested anywhere other than at a police station, if the officer has reasonable grounds for believing that the person may present a danger to himself or to others.

Under s 32(2)(a), a police officer may also search an arrested person for anything which he might use to assist him to escape from custody, or which might be evidence relating to an offence. A search for items under s 32(2)(a) may be carried out only if the police officer has reasonable grounds to believe that the person to be searched may have concealed on his person anything for which a search is permitted under that subsection (s 32(5)).

Under s 32(2)(b), a police officer is permitted to enter and search any premises in which the arrested person was when he was arrested or immediately before he was arrested, for evidence relating to the offence for which he has been arrested. This power of search applies only to offences which can be tried on indictment. Offences which are triable on indictment are indictable only offences (ie, offences which can be tried only in the Crown Court) *and* offences that are triable either way (ie, offences which can be tried in either the Crown Court or the magistrates' court).

A police officer may search premises under s 32(2)(b) only if he has reasonable grounds for believing that there is evidence for which a search is permitted on the premises (s 32(6)).

Example

Basil uses a pistol to commit an armed robbery (an indictable offence). PC Morgan chases Basil and follows him into a warehouse. As Basil attempts to leave the warehouse he is arrested by PC Jones. When arrested Basil does not have the pistol on his person. PCs Morgan and Jones may search the warehouse to see if Basil has deposited the pistol there, because Basil was in the warehouse immediately before he was arrested and there are reasonable grounds for believing the pistol may be there.

The power of search in s 32(2) is only a power to search to the extent that is reasonably required for the purpose of discovering any such item or evidence (s 32(3)).

The powers of search in s 32 do not permit a police officer to require a person to remove any item of clothing in public other than an outer coat, a jacket or gloves. The powers do, however, authorise a search of a person's mouth (s 32(4)).

2.3.7 Interviews after arrest

When a police officer has made a decision to arrest a suspect, that suspect should not be interviewed about the relevant offence except at a police station or other authorised place of detention. The only exceptions to this are if the delay caused by having to take the suspect to the police station to be interviewed would be likely to:

(a)   lead to interference with, or harm to, evidence connected with an offence; or

(b)   lead to interference with, or physical harm to, other people; or

(c)   lead to serious loss of, or damage to, property; or

(d)   lead to alerting other people suspected of committing an offence but not yet arrested for it; or

(e)   hinder the recovery of property obtained in consequence of the commission of an offence (Code C, para 11.1).

The rules concerning the conduct of interviews at the police station are described in **Chapter 3**.

2.3.8 What happens after arrest?

A person arrested at any place other than a police station must be taken to a police station 'as soon as practicable after the arrest' (s 30(1A)). There is an exception to this in s 30A, which permits a police officer to release an arrested person on bail at any time before he arrives at the police station. This exception was created by s 4 of the Criminal Justice Act 2003 and has attracted the label 'street bail'. The rationale behind this is that, at the time of the arrest, the police officer may still be investigating the offence and, rather than wanting to interview the arrested person at the police station immediately, may prefer to delay interviewing the arrested person until the investigations are complete. If the police officer does grant the suspect 'street bail', he must give the arrested person a notice informing him when he should attend for interview and at which police station. The police have the power to arrest without warrant a suspect who fails to answer street bail.

Under changes proposed in the Police and Justice Bill currently before Parliament, s 30A will be amended to allow a police officer to impose conditions on street bail if such conditions are necessary:

(a) to secure that the person surrenders to custody;

(b) to secure that the person does not commit an offence while on bail;

(c) to secure that the person does not interfere with witnesses or otherwise obstruct the course of justice, whether in relation to himself or any other person; or

(d) for the person's own protection, or, if aged under 17, for the person's own welfare or in the person's own interests.

A police officer will be able to impose any conditions other than requiring the arrested person to provide a security or surety, or to reside in a bail hostel (see **Chapter 7**). The arrested person will be able to ask the police or the magistrates' court to vary the conditions imposed on street bail. The police will have the power to arrest without warrant a suspect who breaches conditions attached to street bail.

2.4 Entry, search and seizure

2.4.1 Introduction

This chapter has already looked at the following powers of search granted to the police:

(a) the power to carry out a stop and search of persons and vehicles under s 1 of PACE 1984 (see **2.2** above); and

(b) the power to search an arrested person, or the premises where that person was arrested or where that person was immediately prior to arrest, under s 32 of PACE 1984 (see **2.3** above).

The rest of the chapter will look at the other powers to enter and search premises conferred on police officers by the 1984 Act.

When exercising any powers of search, entry and seizure, police officers must comply with the requirements of Code B. Paragraph 1.3 of Code B states:

> The right to privacy and respect for personal property are key principles of the Human Rights Act 1998. Powers of entry, search and seizure should be fully and clearly justified before use because they may significantly interfere with the occupier's privacy. Officers should consider if the necessary objectives can be met by less intrusive means.

A search which is carried out illegally will contravene a suspect's right to respect for his private life under Article 8 of the ECHR, and may entitle the suspect to claim damages for trespass in civil proceedings.

Paragraph 1.4 of Code B provides that any powers of search should be exercised courteously and with respect, and that any force used in carrying out a search should be both reasonable and necessary and proportionate in the circumstances.

2.4.2   Section 8

2.4.2.1   When may a search warrant be issued under s 8?

Section 8(1) permits a police officer to apply to a magistrate for a warrant to enter and search premises. A magistrate may issue such a warrant if he is satisfied that there are reasonable grounds for believing:

(a)   that an indictable offence has been committed;

(b)   that there is material on the premises specified in the application which is likely to be of substantial value (whether by itself or together with other material) to the investigation of the offence;

(c)   that the material is likely to be relevant evidence;

(d)   that it does not consist of or include items subject to legal privilege, excluded material or special procedure material (such as health records or journalistic material); and

(e)   that *any* of the conditions specified in s 8(3) apply.

The conditions in s 8(3) are:

(a)   that it is not practicable to communicate with any person entitled to grant entry to the premises;

(b)   that it is practicable to communicate with a person entitled to grant entry to the premises but it is not practicable to communicate with any person entitled to grant access to the evidence;

(c)   that entry to the premises will not be granted unless a warrant is produced; or

(d)   that the purpose of a search may be frustrated or seriously prejudiced unless a police officer arriving at the premises can secure immediate entry to them.

Under s 8(2), a police officer may seize and retain anything for which a search has been authorised by the magistrate.

In the light of the very wide powers of search granted by other sections of PACE 1984 (and particularly s 18, which is explained at **2.4.4** below), search warrants are usually confined to premises other than those controlled by an arrested person.

Example

Sanjay is arrested on suspicion of smuggling stolen paintings into the country for onward sale. The police believe that documents confirming the sale of these paintings are located in an office controlled by Richard, Sanjay's business partner. The police can apply to a magistrate under s 8 to obtain a warrant to search Richard's office if the requirements of s 8(1) are satisfied.

2.4.2.2   Procedural safeguards

The appellate courts have on several occasions stated that the issuing of a search warrant is a very severe interference with the liberty of an individual and is a step which should be taken only after a thorough examination of the facts.

A number of safeguards are provided by ss 15 and 16, and any entry on or search of premises by a police officer under a warrant is unlawful unless these safeguards are complied with.

Under s 15(2), a police officer applying for a warrant must:

(a)   state the ground on which he makes the application and the statute under which the warrant would be issued;

(b)   specify the premises which the officer wants to enter and search (there may be more than one set of premises specified but, if so, the details of each set of premises must be set out);

(c)   identify, so far as is practicable, the articles or persons to be sought.

Paragraph 3.1 of Code B states that the officer must take reasonable steps to check that the information on which an application for a search warrant is based is 'accurate, recent and not provided maliciously or irresponsibly'.

An application for a warrant under s 8 will be made in writing to a magistrate, but without notice of the application being given to the owner or occupier of the premises which are the subject matter of the warrant. The police officer making the application is required to answer on oath any question that the magistrate may put to him about the application. The application must be supported by a signed written authority from an officer of at least the rank of inspector (Code B, para 3.4(a)).

If the police are unable to specify all the premises which a person occupies or controls, they may ask the court to issue an 'all premises warrant', as opposed to the usual warrant to search a specific set or sets of premises (s 8(1A)(a) and (b)). Such a warrant will enable the police to search both the specific premises noted in the warrant and, in addition, any further premises which are occupied or controlled by the person, even though the details of such premises are currently unknown (and will become known only when the police have carried out further investigations). All premises warrants are likely to be issued in cases of high-level fraud or organised crime.

2.4.2.3   Contents of the warrant

Any warrant that is issued will normally authorise entry on one occasion only (s 15(5)) and the warrant itself will specify:

(a)   the name of the person who applied for it;

(b)   the date on which it was issued;

(c)   the statute under which it was issued; and

(d)   the premises to be searched.

Additionally the warrant must identify, as far as practicable, the articles or persons to be sought (s 15(6)).

Section 15(5) does permits the court to issue a search warrant authorising entry and search of premises on more than one occasion, but *only* if it is necessary to carry out multiple searches to achieve the objective of the search.

2.4.2.4   Execution of the warrant

The warrant to enter and search premises must be executed within three months from the date of its issue (s 16(3)). The warrant must be executed at a reasonable hour, unless the police officer executing the warrant believes that the purpose of the search may be frustrated by entry at a reasonable hour (s 16(4)).

If the occupier of the premises to be entered and searched is present when the police officer executes the warrant, the officer must:

(a)   identify himself to the occupier (and show him his warrant card to prove he is a police officer if he is not in uniform);

(b)   show the warrant to the occupier; and

(c)   supply the occupier with a copy of the warrant.

If the occupier of the premises is not present when the police officer executes the warrant, but some other person is present who appears to be in charge of the premises, the above steps must be taken in relation to that person. If nobody is present who appears to be in charge of the premises when the police officer executes the warrant, a copy of the warrant must be left in a prominent place on the premises.

Section 16(8) provides that any search under a warrant 'may only be a search to the extent required for the purpose for which the warrant was issued'.

2.4.3 Section 17

Section 17 allows a police officer to enter and search any premises for the purpose of:

(a) executing a warrant of arrest;

(b) arresting a person for an indictable offence;

(c) arresting a person for any one of a specified list of non-indictable offences, including an offence under s 4 of the Public Order Act 1986 (fear or provocation of violence) and the offence of driving whilst under the influence of drink or drugs (Road Traffic Act 1988, s 4);

(d) recapturing any person who is unlawfully at large and whom he is pursuing; or

(e) saving life or limb, or preventing serious damage to property.

The powers of entry and search for all but the last of the above purposes may be exercised only if the police officer has reasonable grounds for believing that the person he is seeking is on the premises (s 17(2)(b)).

Example

Mark commits a burglary of shop premises (an indictable offence) and his image is captured on a CCTV camera. The police investigate and are informed by Mark's parents that Mark is hiding in a flat belonging to Carol, his girlfriend. The police may enter and search Carol's flat to arrest Mark for the offence of burglary, as they will have reasonable grounds for believing that he is there.

The power of search in s 17 is only a power to search to the extent that is reasonably required for the purpose for which the power of entry is exercised (s 17(4)).

Section 17(6) expressly preserves the common law power the police have to enter premises to deal with or prevent a breach of the peace.

2.4.4 Section 18

Section 18(1) allows a constable to enter and search any premises *occupied or controlled* by a person who has been arrested for an indictable offence. This section allows the police to search a suspect's home address (since these will be premises occupied by the suspect) and also other premises over which the suspect has some form of control (eg business premises). In order to carry out such a search and entry, the police officer must have reasonable grounds for suspecting that there is on the premises evidence (other than items subject to legal privilege) that relates:

(a) to that offence; or

(b) to some other indictable offence which is connected with or similar to that offence.

Example

Frank, a bank manager, is arrested on suspicion of obtaining a pecuniary advantage by deception (an indictable offence). The police are informed by one of Frank's colleagues that documents relating to the offence are located in Frank's office at the branch of the bank where he works. The police will be able to search Frank's office under s 18 because these are premises controlled by Frank and the police have reasonable grounds for suspecting that evidence relating to the offence is on the premises.

Under s 18(2), a police officer may seize and retain any items for which he is permitted to search under s 18(1). The power to search in s 18(1) is only a power to search to the extent that is reasonably required for the purpose of discovering such evidence (s 18(3)).

The power of search under s 18 may be exercised only if it has been authorised in writing by an officer with the rank of inspector or above (s 18(4)). The only exception to this is s 18(5), which permits an officer to search premises before obtaining such authorisation (and before taking the arrested person to the police station or releasing him on 'street bail') if the police officer considers that the presence of the arrested person at the premises is necessary for the effective investigation of the offence. This situation is likely to arise only when there is evidence at the premises which is about to be destroyed and taking the person to the police station would facilitate its destruction.

2.4.5 Powers of seizure

Section 19 provides the police with a general power to seize items when an officer is 'lawfully on any premises'. A police officer will be lawfully on any premises if he is there:

(a)   with the consent of the occupier (since there is nothing to prevent a police officer asking an occupier if he may enter and search premises when he has no other authority to enter);

(b)   to execute a search warrant under s 8; or

(c)   pursuant to any of the powers granted by ss 17, 18 or 32.

Under s 19(2), a police officer may seize *anything* which is on the premises if he has reasonable grounds for believing that:

(a)   it has been obtained in consequence of the commission of an offence (not necessarily the offence he is currently investigating); and

(b)   it is necessary to seize it in order to prevent it being concealed, lost, damaged, altered or destroyed.

Example

Julian is arrested on suspicion of handling stolen bank notes following the robbery of a local bank. PC Briggs enters Julian's house to carry out a search under s 18 for evidence relating to that offence. Whilst carrying out the search, PC Briggs finds a suitcase full of items of jewellery, recently reported as stolen following a burglary at a local hotel. PC Briggs will be able to seize the jewellery if he considers that it has been obtained by Julian as a result of the commission of an offence and it is necessary to seize the jewellery to prevent it being concealed, lost, damaged, altered or destroyed.

Under s 19(3), a police officer may seize *anything* which is on the premises if he has reasonable grounds for believing that:

(a)   it is evidence in relation to an offence which he is investigating or any other offence; and

(b)   it is necessary to seize it in order to prevent the evidence being concealed, lost, altered or destroyed.

Example

Reginald is arrested on suspicion of having taken part in a robbery at a local bank. PC Briggs enters Reginald's house to carry out a search under s 18 for the missing bank notes. Whilst carrying out the search, PC Briggs finds a set of scales, a quantity of plastic bags and some weights. PC Briggs suspects that these items are evidence that Julian is concerned in the cultivation and/or supply of controlled drugs. PC Briggs will be able to seize these items if he considers that such items are evidence in relation to an offence and it is necessary to seize the items to prevent them from being concealed, lost, altered or destroyed.

The power of seizure in s 19 is wider than the power of seizure granted by s 18, because under s 19 a police officer may seize any item found on the premises. Under s 18 a police officer can seize only items relating to the specific offence he is investigating, or some other indictable offence which is connected with or similar to that offence.

The only limitation on the power of seizure in s 19 is that a police officer cannot seize any item that he has reasonable grounds for believing is subject to legal privilege.

2.4.6   Powers of retention

Under s 22, anything which a police officer has seized by virtue of s 19 may be retained by the police 'so long as is necessary in all the circumstances' (s 22(1)).

Section 22(2) provides that anything seized for the purposes of a criminal investigation may be retained:

(a)   for use as evidence at a criminal trial; or

(b)   for forensic examination, or for investigation in connection with an offence.

If a person is no longer in police detention or custody, or has been released on bail by a court, nothing seized from him on one of a number of specified grounds may be retained (s 22(3)). These grounds are that the item was seized so that it could not be used:

(a)   to cause physical injury to any person;

(b)   to damage property;

(c)   to interfere with evidence; or

(d)   to assist in escape from police detention or lawful custody.

2.4.7   Other powers of search, seizure and retention

In addition to the powers contained in PACE 1984, the police enjoy additional powers of search, seizure and retention in respect of certain specific offences. The most common example of such a power is s 23(3) of the Misuse of Drugs Act 1971. This enables the police to enter any premises (by force if necessary) to search both the premises and anyone found on the premises either for controlled drugs, or for documents related to the production of such drugs. The police may seize and retain any drugs or documents found. Before exercising this power the police must obtain a warrant from a magistrate authorising them to enter the premises.

2.5 Checklist

At the end of this chapter you should be able to explain:

- the powers which the police may exercise to stop and search persons and vehicles (PACE 1984, s 1);
- the safeguards which are in place should the police wish to interview a person prior to arrest and to record any comments made during that interview (the 'anti-verballing rules');
- the powers of arrest which the police may exercise (PACE 1984, s 24);
- how an arrest should lawfully be carried out by the police (PACE 1984, s 28);
- the powers which the police may exercise to search a person following arrest (PACE 1984, s 32);
- the powers which the police may exercise to enter and search premises (PACE 1984, ss 8, 17 and 18);
- the powers which the police may exercise to seize and retain items found during a search (PACE 1984, ss 19 and 22).
- the importance of the police complying with the requirements of the Codes of Practice when exercising their investigative powers outside the police station.

Chapter 3

The Investigative Powers of the Police (2) – Inside the Police Station

3.1 Introduction

This chapter examines the powers the police may exercise when a suspect has been arrested and is detained at the police station. What occurs at the police station can be of great significance when a case gets to trial, particularly if the defendant's solicitor attempts to argue that prosecution evidence obtained whilst his client was detained at the police station is inadmissible because the police breached the provisions of PACE 1984 or the Codes of Practice issued under that Act.

References to section numbers in this chapter are, unless otherwise stated, to PACE 1984. References to Code C are to the Code of Practice for the Detention, Treatment and Questioning of Persons by Police Officers. References to Code D are to the Code of Practice for the Identification of Persons by Police Officers. References to Code E are to the Code of Practice on Audio Recording Interviews with Suspects, and references to Code F are to the Code of Practice on Visual Recording with Sound of Interviews with Suspects.

3.2 Procedure on arrival at the police station

3.2.1 Introduction

A suspect who has been arrested other than at a police station must be taken to the police station 'as soon as is practicable after the arrest' (s 30(1A)), unless the arresting officer decides to grant 'street bail' (see **Chapter 2**).

Occasionally a suspect may be arrested at the police station. If the police do not have sufficient evidence to arrest a suspect, they may ask that person to attend voluntarily at the police station to answer questions. There is no obligation to do this and a 'volunteer' who attends a police station is free to leave at any time. He can be prevented from leaving only if the police decide to place him under arrest before he leaves the police station (s 29). The police will often arrest a 'volunteer' if, when interviewed, the volunteer makes admissions which then give the police sufficient evidence to arrest him.

Paragraph 1.1 of Code C provides that 'all persons in custody must be dealt with expeditiously, and be released as soon as the need for detention no longer arises'.

3.2.2 The custody officer

3.2.2.1 Who will the custody officer be?

A suspect who has been arrested must be brought before a custody officer in the custody suite on his arrival at the police station (or after his arrest if he was arrested at the police station). The custody officer is responsible for authorising the detention of the suspect and supervising his welfare whilst in police custody. The custody officer will normally be a police officer holding at least the rank of sergeant, who should not be involved in the investigation of the offence for which the suspect has been arrested. Changes introduced by the Serious Organised Crime and Police Act 2005 now permit civilian custody officers to work alongside the police in custody suites and to perform the role of custody officer. Such persons will be known as 'designated staff custody officers'.

Paragraph 2.1A of Code C confirms that a suspect who has been arrested (or who is attending the police station to answer bail) should be brought before the custody officer as 'soon as practicable'.

When the arresting officer brings the suspect before the custody officer, he must tell the custody officer:

(a)   that the suspect was arrested as a result of his involvement, or suspected involvement or attempted involvement in the commission of a criminal offence; and

(b)   why he considered it was necessary to arrest the suspect (Code G, para 2.2).

3.2.2.2 What initial steps must the custody officer take?

The custody officer is responsible for opening and then maintaining a custody record for each suspect who has been arrested and brought to the police station. This is a written document which records certain key information:

(a)   the suspect's name, address, telephone number, date of birth and occupation;

(b)   the offence for which the suspect has been arrested and why the arresting officer considered it necessary to arrest the suspect;

(c)   the time of the suspect's arrest and the time of his arrival at the police station;

(d)   the reason why the suspect's ongoing detention at the police station has been authorised by the custody officer (see **3.3.2** below);

(e)   the time such detention was authorised;

(f)   confirmation that the suspect has been given details of the rights he may exercise whilst detained at the police station (see below), and whether he has requested legal advice from a solicitor; and

(g)   details of the items of property the suspect has on his person, and details of any medical condition he suffers from.

The custody record will also have attached to it a detention log. This is a record of all the significant events that occur whilst the suspect is in police custody.

The custody officer must also inform the suspect about his ongoing rights which may be exercised at any time whilst the suspect is in custody. These rights are:

(a)   the right to have someone informed of the suspect's arrest (s 56);

(b)   the right for the suspect to consult privately with a solicitor (the suspect must be told that free independent legal advice is available; s 58); and

(c)   the right to consult the Codes of Practice.

3.2.2.3 Search of the detained person

The custody officer must also find out what items of property a suspect has on his person, and he may make a record of these items (s 54(1) and (2)). The custody officer may either search the suspect himself, or may authorise a search of the suspect, to the extent he considers necessary to ascertain what items the suspect has on his person. Detailed rules are set out in Annex A to Code C if the custody officer wants to search intimate parts of the suspect's body, or if the custody officer requires a suspect to remove more than his outer clothing during the conduct of the search.

Section 54(3) permits the custody officer to seize and retain any items the suspect has on his person. Items of clothing and personal effects may be seized only if the custody officer has reasonable grounds for believing that they may be evidence (for example, a blood-soaked shirt), or if the custody officer believes that the suspect may use them:

(a)   to cause physical injury to himself or others;

(b)   to cause damage to property;

(c)   to interfere with evidence; or

(d)   to assist him to escape.

Examples of such items may include a penknife, a key, a sharpened comb or a razor blade.

Key Document – The Custody Record

CHESHIRE POLICE

CUSTODY RECORD

Station: Chester	EM No:		Custody No:	CH		000687	06

1. Reasons for Arrest: Suspicion of assault contrary s 47 of the Offences Against the Person Act 1861 2. Comment made by person if present when facts of arrest explained Yes ☐ No ☒ If 'yes' record on Detention Log Place of Arrest: …17 Marsh Street, Chester, CH3 7LW	8. PERSONAL Details Surname: ..Dickson.. Forename(s) ..Gary Paul… Address: 17 Marsh Street, Chester, CH3 7LW Telephone No: 431809 (Chester) Occupation: Unemployed ….. Age: 27….. Date of Birth: ..28/10/79 Height: 1m 80cm..Sex: Male/~~Female~~ Ethnic Origin: British………. Place of Birth: …York………

3.	Time	Date 18/12/06
Arrested at:	11.40	18/12/06
Arrived at Station:	12.00	18/12/06
Relevant Time:	12.00	18/12/06

Condition on Arrival: **Nil of Note…….**
Relevant time not applicable: ☐
If appropriate

9. Arresting officer: G Chambers
Rank: PC No 911. Station: Chester

10. Officer in the case: G Chambers
Rank: PC 911 Station: Chester

4. DETENTION DECISION
*Delete as appropriate
A. Detention authorised*.
B. ~~Detention not authorised*.~~
Signature: …S. Dunn
Name: ..Steven Dunn
Time: 12.30 Date: 18/12/06
REASON FOR DETENTION:
     (i) To Charge …………… ☐
    &/or (ii) Other authority (state) ……..☐
    &/or (iii) Other secure or preserve evidence ………… ☐
    &/or (iv) To obtain evidence by questioning ………..☒
Record grounds for detention – MUST complete for (iii) And (iv)
Arrested on suspicion of assault. Detention necessary to obtain evidence by questioning …………
Person present when grounds recorded: Yes ☒ No ☐
Person informed of grounds: Yes ☒ No ☐
If no case, record reasons(s) in Log of Events

11. DETAINED PERSON'S RIGHTS
An extract from a notice setting out my rights has been read to me and I have been given a copy. I have also been provided with a written notice setting out my entitlements while in custody.
Signature: G. Dickson
Time: 12.30 Date 18/12/06

LEGAL ADVICE REQUESTED
I want to speak to a solicitor as soon as practicable:
Signature: ………………….
Time: ………. Date: ………………..

LEGAL ADVICE DECLINED

I have been informed that I may speak to a solicitor IN PERSON or ON THE TELEPHONE:
Signature: ..G Dickson …..
Time: …12.30…. Date: ….18/12/06
I DO NOT WANT TO SPEAK TO A SOLICITOR at this time:
Signature: G Dickson
Time: ..12.30 …. Date:..18/12/06
Reasons, if given, for not wanting legal advice:
……NOT GIVEN…………………………………..

5. Comment made by person when informed of detention   Yes ☐   No ☒   if yes record on Log of Events

Notification of named person: Requested Yes ☐ No ☐
Nominated person: ………………………..
Detainee's signature …………………………..

6. Drugs Referral Information leaflet issued: Time: ………… Date: ………………..

APPROPRIATE ADULT		INTERPRETER	
Yes ☐ No ☐		Yes ☐ No ☐	

Notices served, rights and grounds for detention explained in presence of Appropriate Adult/Interpreter
Signature of A/Adult …………..
Time: ……… Date: ………………..
Signature of interpreter: ……………
Time: ………..Date:……………….

OFFICER OPENING CUSTODY RECORD
Signature: S. Dunn
Name: Steven Dunn
Rank No: SGT 568
Time: 12.30 …. Date: 18/12/06……

FOREIGN NATIONALS
Embassy/Consulate informed: Yes ☐ No ☐ N/A ☐
Record details in Log of Events
Force Immigration Dept informed: Yes ☐ : Record on 7k

RECORD OF RIGHTS

Surname: Dickson   Custody Record No.   CH | 000687 | 06

Interpreter present   Yes ☐   No ☒   Detained person informed of rights   Yes ☒   No ☐
(if no, record reason on detention log)

"You have the right to have someone informed that you have been detained. You have the right to consult privately with an independent solicitor either in person, in writing or on the telephone. Independent legal advice is available from the duty solicitor free of charge. You also have the right to consult a copy of the Codes of Practice covering police powers and procedures. You may do any of these things now, but if you do not you may still do so at any time whilst detained at the police station".

Solicitor requested: Yes ☐   No ☒
(If no, remind the person of the right to speak to a solicitor, in person, or on the telephone.)

Solicitor requested: Yes ☐   No ☒
(If no, ask for and if applicable, record reason.)

Name of solicitor requested: _____

Reason, if given, for not
wanting legal advice: _____

Notification of named person requested   Yes ☐   No ☒

Details of nominated person (if appropriate)

Name

Address

Telephone Number

Details of appropriate adult (if appropriate)

Name

Address

Telephone Number

An extract from a notice setting out a detained person's rights has been read to me and I have been given a copy. I have been provided with a written notice setting out a detained person's entitlements while in custody.

I ~~do~~/do not..........want a person informed.

I understand that my right to speak to a solicitor includes the right to speak on the telephone.

I ~~do~~/do not want to speak to a solicitor at this time.

Signature: G. Dickson   Time: 12.30   Date: 18/1/2006

CHESHIRE POLICE
DETENTION LOG

| Surname: | ..Dickson…….. | | Forename(s): ..Gary Paul………… |
| Custody Ref: | CH/000687/06……… | | Cell No: ….4……. |

Date	Time	Full details of any action/occurrence involving detained person (include full particulars of all visitors/officers) Individual entries need not be restricted to one line All entries to be signed by the writer (include rank and number)
18/12/06	12.25	COMMENTS
		Dp brought to desk. Arrested at his home address on suspicion of assault following information received (PACE, s 24(2)). Arrest necessary to prevent person causing physical injury to others (s 24(5)(c)(i)) & to allow prompt and efficient investigation of offence (s 24(5)(e)).
		Dp understands
	12.30	CHAMBERS PC 911
		CUSTODY RECORD CREATED
		Detention authorised by PS 568 DUNN. Grounds for detention are to obtain evidence by questioning
		DUNN PS 568
	12.30	RIGHTS GIVEN
		DUNN PS 568
	12.35	POST-DETENTION SEARCH RECORDED
		Searched by ANDREWS PC 210 and contents of pockets retained
		DUNN PS 568
	12.40	DOCTOR NOT CONTACTED
		Dp states he is fit well and uninjured. Does not suffer any ailments, epilepsy, asthma, diabetes, heart condition. Does not self harm. Doctor not requested or required.
		DUNN PS 568
	13.00	CELL ALLOCATED
		Placed in cell 4 by DUNN PS 568
		DUNN PS 568
	14.00	Visited dp – awake. Provided with cup of tea
		DUNN PS 568
	15.00	Visited dp – awake. Refused cup of tea
		DUNN PS 568
	16.00	Dp visited awake
		DUNN PS 568
	17.00	Dp visited awake. Meal refused
		DUNN PS 568

CHESHIRE POLICE
DETENTION LOG

Surname: ..Dickson……..	Forename(s): ..Gary Paul…………
Custody Ref: CH/000687/06………	Cell No: ….4…….

Date	Time	Full details of any action/occurrence involving detained person (include full particulars of all visitors/officers) Individual entries need not be restricted to one line All entries to be signed by the writer (include rank and number)
	17.45	Dp visited – awake
		DUNN PS 568
	18.00	Detention reviewed.
		HUDSON Insp. 420
		PC 911 CHAMBERS
	18.20	Dp transferred to custody of PC 911 CHAMBERS. Taken to interview room. Interviewed by PC 911 CHAMBERS
		DUNN PS 568
	18.45	Dp returned to custody of PC 568 DUNN
		DUNN PS 568
	19.00	Dp charged with assault occasioning actual bodily harm. No reply made on charge
		DUNN PS 568
	19.05	Dp refused bail.
		Reasonable grounds to believe dp will fail to appear in court and will cause injury to others if bail granted.
		DUNN PS 568

3.3   Detention at the police station

3.3.1   Is there sufficient evidence to charge the suspect?

After opening the custody record and informing the suspect of his rights, the custody officer's next responsibility is to determine whether there is already 'sufficient evidence' to charge the suspect with the offence for which he has been arrested (s 37(1)). To do this, the custody officer will ask the investigating officer – usually in the presence of the suspect – for details of the evidence that already exists against the suspect and what steps the officer proposes to take if the further detention of the suspect is authorised (this will normally be some form of investigative procedure such as an audio-recorded interview with the suspect or the holding of an identification procedure – see **3.5** below). The custody officer should note in the custody record any comments made by the suspect in relation to the account given by the arresting officer of the reasons for the arrest (Code C, para 3.4). The custody officer should not himself put any questions to the arrested person about his involvement in any offence (Code C, para 3.4).

The custody officer may detain the suspect at the police station for as long as it is necessary for him to determine if sufficient evidence exists to charge the suspect. If there is such evidence, the suspect should be charged straight away, and either released on bail to appear before the magistrates' court or remanded in police custody until he can be brought before the magistrates.

3.3.2   Grounds for detention

If there is not sufficient evidence to charge a suspect immediately, the suspect should be released either on bail or without bail, unless:

(a)   the custody officer has reasonable grounds for believing that detaining the suspect without charge is necessary to *secure* or *preserve* evidence relating to an offence for which he is under arrest; or

(b)   it is necessary to obtain such evidence by *questioning* (s 37(2)).

If either of these grounds is satisfied, the custody officer may authorise the suspect to be kept in police detention (s 37(3)).

The usual ground upon which a custody officer will authorise detention is to enable the officer investigating the offence to obtain evidence by questioning the suspect about his involvement in the offence under investigation. Many suspects who are interviewed by the police make admissions during interview which assist the case against them, and the investigating officer will want to carry out an audio recorded interview with the suspect in almost every case.

The first ground above may be useful in situations where the police want to carry out a search of the suspect's premises under s 18 (see **Chapter 2**), or where they are still looking for evidence of the offence. In such cases the police may want to detain the suspect in the police station so that he has no opportunity to hide or destroy the evidence before it can be found. This ground can also be used where the police want to obtain some form of identification evidence and can do so only whilst the suspect is in the police station. The police may, for example, want the suspect to take part in an identification procedure, or to obtain the suspect's fingerprints.

Example 1

Jackie is arrested on suspicion of theft of a necklace from a jewellery shop. The police believe that Jackie has hidden the necklace somewhere in her flat and want to carry out a search of the flat under s 18. The custody officer may authorise Jackie's detention at the police station if he has reasonable grounds for believing that, if released, Jackie may remove or destroy the necklace before the officer conducting the search is able to find it.

Example 2

Anthony is arrested on suspicion of the burglary of a factory. The police have found fingerprints on the frame of the window which was smashed by the burglar to gain entry to the property. The custody officer may authorise Anthony's detention at the police station if he has reasonable grounds for believing that Anthony's detention will be necessary in order for Anthony's fingerprints to be taken to see if they match those found at the factory.

If the custody officer becomes aware at any time that the grounds on which a suspect's detention was authorised have ceased to apply (and that no other grounds to justify his continued detention exist), the suspect must be released immediately (s 39).

3.3.3 Conditions of detention

Code C specifies the conditions in which a suspect should be held whilst in police detention.

The cell in which a suspect is held must be adequately heated, cleaned and ventilated, and also adequately lit (Code C, para 8.2). Any bedding supplied to a suspect must be of a reasonable standard and in a clean and sanitary condition (Code C, para 8.3). A suspect must be provided with access to toilet and washing facilities (Code C, para 8.4).

A suspect must be offered at least two light meals and one main meal in any 24-hour period, and drinks should be provided at meal times and upon reasonable request between meals (Code C, para 8.6). A suspect should be offered brief outdoor exercise daily if this is practicable (Code C, para 8.7).

Suspects should be visited in their cells at least every hour (Code C, para 9.3).

If the custody officer considers that a suspect is injured, appears to be suffering from physical illness or mental disorder, or appears to need clinical attention, the custody officer must make arrangements to ensure that the suspect receives appropriate clinical attention as soon as reasonably practicable (Code C, para 9.5). Normally in such cases the custody officer will arrange for the suspect to be seen by the police surgeon.

3.3.4 Periods of detention

3.3.4.1 Introduction

Invariably, the first question a suspect will ask his solicitor following the solicitor's arrival at the police station is how long the police can detain him there. Many suspects do not appreciate that the police are able to detain them only for a specified period of time. A volunteer who attends the police station is free to leave at any time unless the police arrest him (see **3.2.1**).

3.3.4.2 The initial maximum period

Section 41 provides that a person 'shall not be kept in police detention for more than 24 hours without being charged'. This 24-hour period begins from the 'relevant time'. The relevant time is determined as follows:

(a)   in the case of a person attending voluntarily at the police station who is then arrested at the police station, *the time of his arrest* (s 41(2)(c));

(b)   in the case of a person who attends a police station to answer 'street bail' granted under s 30A, *the time when he arrives at the police station* (s 41(2)(ca));

(c)   in any other case, the relevant time is *the time when the suspect arrested arrives at the first police station to which he is taken after his arrest* (s 41(1)(d)).

Example 1

Stuart is attending the police station as a volunteer to answer questions about his suspected involvement in an assault. Stuart arrives at the police station at 11 am. His interview begins at 11.15 am and ends at 12.00 pm. Stuart is arrested at 12.10 pm. The 'detention clock' will start running from 12.10 pm, the time of Stuart's arrest. The police will be able to detain Stuart for a maximum period of 24 hours from this time.

Example 2

Eric is arrested by PC Long on suspicion of theft. There are witnesses to the theft from whom PC Long wants to take statements before interviewing Eric. He therefore grants Eric street bail, requiring him to attend at the police station at 1 pm the following day. Eric complies with the terms of his street bail, and attends the police station at 1 pm the following day. The 'detention clock' will start running from this time. The police will be able to detain Eric for a maximum period of 24 hours from this time.

Example 3

Hussein is arrested at home at 3.30 pm on suspicion of theft. He is taken to the police station and arrives there at 3.45 pm. His detention is authorised by the custody officer at 4.00 pm. The 'detention clock' will start running from 3.45 pm, the time of Hussein's arrival at the police station. The police will be able to detain Hussein for a maximum period of 24 hours from this time.

3.3.4.3   Can the police extend the maximum period of detention?

Under s 42, the police have the power to extend the period of a suspect's detention in the police station up to a period of 36 hours from the 'relevant time' if certain conditions are met.

Such an authorisation must be given by an officer of the rank of superintendent or above, and may only be given if the superintendent has reasonable grounds for believing that:

(a)   the detention of the suspect without charge is necessary to secure or preserve evidence relating to an offence for which the suspect is under arrest, or to obtain such evidence by questioning him;

(b)   the offence is an indictable offence (ie, an either way or an indictable only offence); and

(c)   the investigation is being carried out diligently and expeditiously.

Example

Victor is arrested on suspicion of the murder of Margaret. He arrives at the police station at 9.00 am and is questioned about the offence. Victor refuses to answer any questions, but at 8.00 am the following day, during the course of searching Victor's house, the police find a bloodstained knife that they believe Victor used as the murder weapon. The investigating officer wants to question Victor about this new piece of evidence, and asks the superintendent to authorise Victor's continued detention to enable him to do this.

The superintendent is likely to authorise the extension of the initial detention period. Murder is an indictable offence and the investigating officer wants to question Victor to find out what Victor has to say about the knife which has only just been found. As long as the superintendent believes that the investigating officer is carrying out the investigation diligently and expeditiously, the officer's request will be granted. If the request is granted, Victor may be detained at the police station until 9 pm that day.

3.3.4.4   Are any further extensions possible?

The police are able to obtain a warrant of further detention from a magistrates' court if the conditions set out below are satisfied (s 43). If the magistrates are persuaded to grant a warrant of further detention, this can be for such period of time as the magistrates think fit, but up to a maximum period of 36 hours. This is on top of the police superintendent's power to extend the basic detention period up to a maximum of 36 hours from the 'relevant time'. Therefore, if the magistrates grant a warrant of further detention, this may result in the suspect being detained in the police station for a total of 72 hours (ie, three days).

The police may apply for a warrant of further detention only if the offence under investigation is an indictable offence (s 43(4)(b)). The application to the magistrates' court must be made on oath by a police officer and must be supported by a written application (called an 'information'). A copy of the information must be supplied to the suspect, and the suspect must be brought to court for the hearing. The suspect is entitled to legal representation at the hearing.

The magistrates will grant a warrant of further detention only if they consider that there are 'reasonable grounds for believing that the further detention of the person to whom the application relates is justified' (s 43(1)). Such detention can be justified only if:

(a)   the suspect's detention without charge is necessary to secure or preserve evidence relating to an offence for which he is under arrest, or to obtain such evidence by questioning him; and

(b)   the investigation is being conducted diligently and expeditiously (s 43(4)).

Example

Clare is arrested at 4 pm on 15 March on suspicion of robbery and is taken to the police station, arriving there at 4.30 pm. This is the relevant time for detention purposes. Clare can be detained initially for a maximum period of 24 hours, and so must be released or charged no later than 4.30 pm on 16 March. If, before 4.30 pm on 16 March, a superintendent authorises Clare's continued detention under s 42, Clare can be detained until 4.30 am on 17 March, at which point she must be released or charged. But if, before this time, the police apply to the magistrates' court for a warrant of further detention and a warrant is granted for a 36-hour period, the police will be able to detain Clare until 4.30 pm on 18 March, at which point she must be released or charged.

In exceptional cases, the police can make an additional application to a magistrates' court under s 44 for an extension of the warrant of further detention granted under s 43. The same procedural requirements as are required for an application under s 43 must be complied with, and the magistrates will grant an extension only if the grounds under s 43 above are satisfied and there are reasonable grounds for believing that the further detention is justified (s 44(1)).

An extension granted under s 44 'shall be for any period as the court thinks fit' but cannot:

(a)   be longer than 36 hours; or

(b)   end later than 96 hours after the 'relevant time'.

This means that the police can detain a suspect in police custody for a maximum period of *four days* before that suspect must be either released or charged (the only exception to this is the powers of detention in respect of certain terrorist offences, which are beyond the scope of this book).

Example

Continuing with the example of Clare above, the police may apply for an extension of the warrant of further detention at any time before the warrant granted under s 43 expires. This extension can be for a maximum of 36 hours but cannot end later than 96 hours after the 'relevant time'. The relevant time in this case is 4.30 pm on 15 March. Therefore the extension cannot go beyond 4.30 pm on 19 March. At this point Clare must be released or charged with an offence.

3.3.4.5   Detention reviews

In addition to the time limits for detention set out in **3.3.4.4** above, the police are obliged to carry out periodic reviews of the suspect's detention to ensure that the grounds on which the detention was initially authorised by the custody officer are still applicable (s 40). This is a mandatory requirement and, if such reviews are not carried out, any detention after this time will be unlawful and will amount to the tort of false imprisonment (*Roberts v Chief Constable of the Cheshire Constabulary* [1999] 1 WLR 662).

Reviews of detention that take place before a suspect is charged are carried out by an officer of at least the rank of inspector who is not directly involved in the investigation (s 40(2)(b)). This officer is usually referred to as the 'review officer'.

The first review must take place no later than six hours after the custody officer first authorised the detention of the suspect (*not* six hours after the suspect first arrived at the police station). The second review must take place no later than nine hours after the first review. Subsequent reviews must take place at intervals of not more than nine hours.

Example

Simeon is arrested at 10 am. He arrives at the police station at 10.15 am (the 'relevant time' for the purpose of calculating the maximum period of detention). The custody officer authorises his detention at 10.30 am. The first custody review must be carried out no later than 4.30 pm. If that review takes place at, for example, 4.15 pm, the next review would need to take place no later than 1.15 am the following day (ie, no more than nine hours after the first review). Further reviews after that would then need to take place at intervals of no more than nine hours.

Under s 40A, a review of detention may be carried out by means of a telephone discussion rather than the 'review officer' having to be physically present in the police station.

3.4   Rights of the suspect

3.4.1   Right to have someone informed of the arrest

Section 56(1) states:

Where a person has been arrested and is being held in custody in a police station or other premises, he shall be entitled, if he so requests, to have one friend or relative or other person who is known to him or who is likely to take an interest in his welfare told, as soon as practicable ... that he has been arrested and is being detained there.

In certain situations the police may delay (but not deny) the exercise of this right. Any delay must be authorised by an officer of at least the rank of inspector and can only be authorised when the suspect has been detained for an indictable offence (s 56(2)(a) and (b)). The length of any delay can be for a maximum of 36 hours from the 'relevant time' (s 56(3)). Authorisation may be given orally but, if it is, must be confirmed in writing as soon as is practicable (s 56(4)).

The police officer who authorises the delay may do so only if he has reasonable grounds for believing that telling the named person of the arrest *will*:

(a)   lead to interference with or harm to evidence connected with an indictable offence, or interference with or physical injury to other persons;

(b)   lead to the alerting of other persons suspected of having committed such an offence but not yet arrested for it; or

(c)   hinder the recovery of any property obtained as a result of such an offence (s 56(5)).

The right not to be held incommunicado in the police station is a fundamental right, and the police cannot delay the exercise of this right if they have merely have reasonable grounds for believing that telling the named person of the arrest *might* lead to any of the above consequences. The police need to have reasonable grounds for believing that telling the named person *will* lead to any one or more of these consequences.

Example

Fred is a member of a notorious criminal gang whose members all have previous convictions for armed robbery. Fred is arrested on suspicion of having taken part in an armed robbery at a bank, after an image of his face was captured on the bank's CCTV system. A number of other people took part in the robbery, but they have not yet been identified. Several thousand pounds were stolen in the robbery.

Fred wants to notify Vince, his brother, that he has been arrested. Vince is known to be a member of the gang. The police believe that, if notified that Fred has been arrested, Vince will alert the other gang members who participated in the robbery and these people will then take steps to dispose of the money that was stolen. The police will be able to take advantage of the provisions in s 56 to delay Vince being notified of Fred's arrest for up to 36 hours. Armed robbery is an indictable offence, and the police appear to have reasonable grounds for believing that notifying Vince of Fred's arrest will lead to the alerting of other suspects and will hinder the recovery of property obtained as a result of the offence.

3.4.2   Right to legal advice

3.4.2.1   The basic right to legal advice

The most important right that a suspect who has been arrested and detained at the police station has is the right to receive free and independent legal advice from a solicitor (or an accredited police station representative).

Section 58(1) states: 'A person arrested and held in custody in a police station or other premises shall be entitled, if he so requests, to consult a solicitor privately at any time.' If a suspect makes such a request, he must be permitted to consult a solicitor 'as soon as practicable' (s 58(4)).

Paragraph 6.1 of Code C reinforces this by providing that:

... all detainees must be informed that they may at any time consult and communicate privately with a solicitor, whether in person, in writing or by telephone, and that free independent legal advice is available from the duty solicitor.

If a solicitor attends the police station to see a particular suspect, that suspect must be informed of the solicitor's arrival at the police station (whether or not he is being interviewed at the time of the solicitor's arrival). The suspect must then be asked if he would like to see the solicitor, even if he has previously declined legal advice (Code C, para 6.15). The solicitor's attendance and the suspect's decision must be noted in the custody record.

Code C also states that at no time should a police officer do or say anything with the intention of dissuading a person from obtaining legal advice (Code C, para 6.4).

3.4.2.2 When can the right to legal advice be delayed?

The police have a very limited right to *delay* (but not deny) the exercise of this right. Any delay must be authorised by an officer with at least the rank of superintendent, and can be authorised only when a suspect has been arrested for an indictable offence (s 58(6)). The length of any delay can be for a maximum of 36 hours from the relevant time (s 58(5)). Authorisation for delaying a suspect's access to legal advice can be given orally but, if it is, must be confirmed in writing as soon as is practicable (s 58(7)).

A police officer may authorise a delay in the suspect receiving access to legal advice only if he has reasonable grounds for believing that the exercise of this right, at the time when the suspect wishes to exercise it, *will*:

(a)   lead to interference with or harm to evidence connected with an indictable offence, or interference with or physical injury to other persons;

(b)   lead to the alerting of other persons suspected of having committed such an offence but not yet arrested for it; or

(c)   hinder the recovery of any property obtained as a result of such an offence (s 58(8)).

These are the same grounds as are set out in s 56 (see **3.4.1** above), and again the key word is *will*. Access to legal advice is a fundamental right, and the police cannot delay the exercise of this right if they think merely that allowing the suspect to exercise his right to obtain legal advice *might* lead to one or more of the above consequences. The police must reasonably believe that allowing the suspect to exercise this right *will* lead to one or more of these consequences. This is a very difficult test for the police to satisfy. Guidelines which the police must follow when determining whether to delay a suspect's access to legal advice are contained in Annex B to Code C (see **Appendix 1**).

Occasionally the police will attempt to use their powers under s 58 if they consider that the particular solicitor a suspect has asked to consult may himself be involved or implicated in criminal activity. It will of course be very rare for a police officer to believe that a solicitor would knowingly pass on information in breach of s 58, and any grounds put forward by the police to justify delaying the right would need to be specific to the solicitor concerned.

If the police have reasonable grounds for such a belief in respect of the particular solicitor a suspect has asked to consult, the suspect should still be offered the opportunity to consult the duty solicitor. The duty solicitor will be a solicitor chosen from a list of local solicitors who have agree to be members of the 'Duty

Solicitor Scheme' for the relevant police station, and who are available to attend the police station on a rota basis to represent those suspects who do not have a solicitor of their own (or whose solicitor is unavailable). The identity of the particular duty solicitor who attends the police station will depend on which solicitor on the rota is 'on call' at the time the suspect requests access to legal advice. This means that the duty solicitor could be any one of a number of individuals, and in these circumstances it will be very difficult for the police to establish the necessary grounds for delaying access to legal advice.

Alternatively, the police may think that a solicitor will be an unwitting dupe and may inadvertently pass on information to other suspects still at liberty. This point was considered in *R v Samuel* [1988] QB 115. The Court of Appeal held that the police officer must have a reasonable belief that one of the statutory grounds for exclusion applies and that the consequence will very probably happen. The Court went on to say that it would be a rare occurrence for a solicitor to be an unwitting dupe, and any suspicion that a suspect will try to use the solicitor in this role would have to be specific to the suspect, such as where the suspect is known or suspected to be a member of a criminal gang.

Although ss 56 and 58 enable the police to keep a suspect incommunicado and to deny the suspect access to legal advice for up to 36 hours, the exercise of this power by the police can be for a period of less than 36 hours, and a suspect must be told as soon as the grounds on which delay was authorised no longer apply.

Example

George is arrested on suspicion of murder. It is alleged that George committed the murder together with Jeremy. At the time of George's arrest Jeremy has not been apprehended, and the police delay the exercise of George's rights under s 56 and s 58 on the basis that exercising these rights will lead to the alerting of Jeremy. Ten hours after George arrives at the police station, the police arrest Jeremy. The only ground on which the exercise of George's rights under s 56 and s 58 was delayed has now been removed. The police should now inform George of his right to have someone informed of his arrest and his right to obtain free and independent legal advice.

3.4.3 Right to consult the Codes of Practice

A suspect who has been arrested is also entitled to ask to consult the Codes of Practice (A–G) which supplement the provisions of PACE 1984.

3.5 Interviews and identification evidence

3.5.1 Introduction

Once the custody officer has authorised the detention of a suspect at the police station, the officer investigating the offence will then take steps to further his investigation. The steps that an investigating officer can take to secure, preserve or obtain evidence whilst the suspect is detained at the police station will involve one or more of the following:

(a)   carrying out an audio-recorded interview with the suspect about the suspect's alleged involvement in the offence(s);

(b)   carrying out a form of identification procedure (such as an identification parade or video identification) to see if a witness to, or a victim of, the offence is able to recognise the suspect;

(c)   taking fingerprints from the suspect to see if these match fingerprints found at the scene of the crime, or on any relevant objects or articles which the police have recovered;

(d)   taking samples from the suspect to see if these match any samples obtained during the course of the police investigation; and

(e)   taking photographs of the suspect.

These investigative powers will be examined further below.

3.5.2   Interviews with the suspect

3.5.2.1   Introduction

Interviews that take place in the police station must comply with the requirements of Codes C and E. Such interviews are recorded (usually on a tape) and are referred to in the Codes of Practice as 'audio recorded' interviews. Code E provides detailed guidance as to the procedure that need to be followed in such interviews.

(If the police decide to record an interview with a suspect visually, guidance on how and when this should be done is contained in Code F. The visual recording of police station interviews is rare, and will usually be carried out only in the case of very serious offences or when a suspect has a disability which requires him to use sign language to communicate.)

Paragraph 2.1 of Code E states: 'Recording of interviews shall be carried out openly to instil confidence in its reliability as an impartial and accurate record of the interview.'

The interview will normally be recorded on two tapes. One of the tapes, the master tape, is sealed in the presence of the suspect at the end of the interview. This seal will be broken and the tape opened at trial only if there is any dispute about what was said. The other tape is called the working copy and will be used by the police to prepare a written summary or transcript of the interview if the suspect is subsequently charged with an offence. Some police forces will use three tapes, with the third tape being given to the suspect if he is subsequently charged so that he may pass this on to his solicitor for the solicitor to listen to (see **Chapter 6**).

3.5.2.2   Should the suspect be interviewed at all?

Paragraph 11.18 of Code C provides that suspects who, at the time of the interview, appear unable to:

(a)   appreciate the significance of questions or their answers; or

(b)   understand what is happening because of the effects of drink, drugs, or any illness, ailment or condition,

should not generally be interviewed (although there are some limited exceptions to this in cases where an interview needs to be held as a matter of urgency).

Paragraph 2(b) of Annex G to Code C states that a suspect might be 'at risk' in an interview if '... anything the [suspect] says in the interview ... *might* be considered unreliable in subsequent court proceedings because of their physical or mental state'.

If a suspect is deemed to be at risk, the custody officer will normally ask a health care professional to see the suspect, and then ask that professional to advise on whether the suspect is fit to be interviewed

3.5.2.3 Start of the interview

The caution

At the start of the interview, the police officer conducting the interview will caution the suspect. The wording of the caution is as follows:

> You do not have to say anything. However it may harm your defence if you do not mention when questioned something which you later rely on in court. Anything you do say may be given in evidence. (Code C, para 10.5)

The caution is worded in this way because, although the suspect has a right to remain silent and cannot be compelled to answer questions in the interview, if the suspect exercises this right but then at his trial raises facts as part of his defence which he could have mentioned during the interview, the court may draw an 'adverse inference' from his silence under s 34 of the Criminal Justice and Public Order Act 1994 (see **Chapter 18**). The court may, for example, infer that the defendant said nothing at the police station because he did not have any answer to the questions put by the police, and fabricated his defence only when he had left the police station and had the time to concoct a story.

If, however, the interviewing officer wants the suspect to account for an object, substance or mark found on his person, in or on his clothing or footwear, otherwise in his possession or in the place where he was arrested, a 'special caution' must be given. Such a caution will also be required if the suspect was arrested at the place where the offence was committed at or about the time of the offence, and the officer wants the suspect to account for his presence. If the special caution is given and the suspect then fails to answer the question (or to answer the question satisfactorily), the court at trial will be able to draw an adverse inference from this pursuant to ss 36–37 of the Criminal Justice and Public Order Act 1994 (see **Chapter 18**). If the officer fails to administer the special caution, no such inference may be drawn at trial.

The special caution requires the suspect to be informed of the following matters (in ordinary language):

(a)   what offence is being investigated;

(b)   what fact the suspect is being asked to account for;

(c)   this fact may be due to the suspect taking part in the commission of the offence;

(d)   a court may draw a proper inference if the suspect fails or refuses to account for this fact; and

(e)   a record is being made of the interview and it may be given in evidence if the suspect is brought to trial (Code C, para 10.11).

After cautioning the suspect, the officer must also remind the suspect that he is entitled to free and independent legal advice, even if the suspect has his solicitor present at the interview (Code C, para 11.2). The caution and the reminder that the suspect is entitled to free and independent advice must be given at the start of every interview the police have with the suspect (so, if a suspect is interviewed more than once, the same information must be given at the start of each interview).

Significant statements and silences

After complying with the above formalities, the interviewing officer must then put to the suspect 'any significant statement or silence which occurred in the presence and hearing of a police officer ... before the start of the interview' (Code C, para 11.4). The interviewing officer must ask the suspect whether he confirms or denies that earlier statement or silence, and if he wants to add anything to it. The terms 'significant statement' and 'significant silence' are defined in Code C, para 11.4A. A 'significant statement' is a statement which appears capable of being used in evidence against the suspect at trial, in particular a direct admission of guilt. A 'significant silence' is a failure or refusal to answer a question, or which might allow the court to draw adverse inferences from that silence at trial (see **Chapter 18**).

Example 1

(This is a continuation of the example involving Oliver and PC Singh at **2.3.3.2** above.)

If, on being asked where he had come from when being questioned in the street by PC Singh, Oliver told PC Singh 'I came from the pub but it wasn't me that hit him', this would be a significant statement. Oliver has not been told by PC Singh that an assault took place at the pub, and the only explanation for Oliver's comments is that he was at the pub and knows something about the assault. This is an admission by Oliver, and should be put to him at the start of the interview.

Example 2

PC Rogers is called to a jewellery shop in connection with the suspected theft of a gold bracelet by Alex. Following PC Roger's arrival at the shop, and in his hearing, the owner of the shop says to Alex: 'I saw you pick the bracelet up and put it in your pocket when you thought I wasn't looking. Why did you try to steal it?' Alex doesn't reply to this. This is a significant silence. Although Alex has not admitted his guilt, had he not done what the owner of the shop accused him if doing, it would have been reasonable to expect him to have denied the shop owner's version of events. The significant silence should be put to Alex at the start of his interview at the police station.

Should the police officer fail to put to a suspect at the start of the interview a significant statement or silence made outside the police station, this may result in the contents of that statement or the nature of that silence being ruled inadmissible at trial under s 78 of PACE 1984 (see **Chapter 21**).

3.5.2.4 Conduct of the interview

The way in which the interviewing officer may conduct the interview is subject to limitations imposed by Code C. Paragraph 11.5 provides: 'No interviewer may try to obtain answers or elicit a statement by the use of oppression.'

'Oppression' might occur if the interviewing officer:

(a)   raises his voice or shouts at the suspect;

(b)   makes threatening gestures towards the suspect;

(c)   leans towards the suspect so that he is 'in the suspect's face';

(d)   stands over or behind the suspect; or

(e)   threatens to detain the suspect indefinitely unless he makes a confession.

Paragraph 11.5 also states that: '... no interviewer shall indicate, except to answer a direct question, what action will be taken by the police if the person being questioned answers questions, makes a statement or refuses to do either.' This means that an interviewing officer should not offer any inducements to a suspect to admit his guilt. This may occur if the interviewing officer indicates to the suspect that he will be released from police detention much more quickly if he admits to having committed the offence under investigation.

The interview must cease when

> the officer in charge of the investigation is satisfied all the questions they consider relevant to obtaining accurate and reliable information about the offence have been put to the suspect, this includes allowing the suspect an opportunity to give an innocent explanation and asking questions to test if the explanation is accurate and reliable, eg to clear up ambiguities or clarify what the suspect said. (Code C, para 11.6)

If interviews with a suspect take place over more than one day, in any period of 24 hours the suspect must be given a continuous period of at least eight hours for rest. This period will usually be at night and must be free from questioning or any other interruption in connection with the offence (Code C, para 12.2).

Similarly, breaks from interviews should take place at recognised meal times, and short refreshment breaks should be taken at approximately two-hour intervals (Code C, para 12.8).

If the conduct of an interview breaches any of the above provisions of Code C, at any subsequent trial the court may rule inadmissible any admission or confession made by the defendant in that interview (see **Chapter 20**).

3.5.2.5   Can a suspect be interviewed before receiving legal advice?

The general position

In general, a suspect who requires legal advice should not be interviewed (or continue to be interviewed) until such advice has been received (Code C, para 6.6). This means that the police should not seek to interview a suspect who has indicated that he requires legal advice. Similarly, where a suspect has indicated that he does not require legal advice, is then interviewed and indicates at some point during the interview that he has changed his mind and now requires legal advice, the police should stop the interview to allow the suspect to obtain such advice.

Exceptions to the general position

The police may interview a suspect before that suspect has obtained independent legal advice in the following situations:

(a)   As noted at **3.4.2.2** above, s 58 allows the police to delay a suspect receiving any legal advice for up to 36 hours. If the police exercise their powers under s 58 to delay a suspect's access to legal advice, the police may (and usually will) want to interview the suspect prior to allowing him access to legal advice.

(b)   Even if the police do not exercise their powers under s 58 to delay the suspect having access to legal advice, they are still permitted to interview a suspect before that suspect has received legal advice if an officer of at least the rank of superintendent reasonably believes that the delay which would be caused by the time taken to obtain such advice might:

(i)   lead to interference with, or harm to, evidence connected with an offence;

(ii)   lead to interference with, or physical harm to, other people;

(iii) lead to serious loss of, or damage to, property;

(iv)   lead to alerting other people suspected of having committed an offence but not yet arrested for it; or

(v)   hinder the recovery of property obtained in consequence of the commission of an offence (Code C, para 6.6(b)(i)).

(c)   The police are also permitted to interview a suspect before that suspect has received legal advice if the relevant solicitor has agreed to attend the police station, but awaiting his arrival would 'cause unreasonable delay to the process of investigation' (Code C, para 6.6(b)(ii)).

(d)   The police may interview a suspect before the suspect has received legal advice if the solicitor the suspect has asked to speak to either cannot be contacted or has declined to attend the police station, and the suspect has then declined the opportunity to consult the duty solicitor (Code C, para 6.6(c)).

(e)   If a suspect asks for legal advice but then changes his mind about this, the police may interview the suspect provided the suspect agrees to this (either in writing or during the interview) and an officer with at least the rank of inspector has given authority for the interview to proceed (Code C, para 6.6(d)).

In the situations at (a), (b) and (c) above, the caution given to the suspect at the start of the interview will be as follows: 'You do not have to say anything, but anything you do say may be given in evidence.' The reason for this wording is that no adverse inferences may be drawn at trial from the suspect's silence in interview if the suspect had not at the time of the interview been allowed access to legal advice (Youth Justice and Criminal Evidence Act 1999, s 58). This will not apply to the situations at (d) and (e) above, because in these cases the suspect is allowed to speak to the duty solicitor (situation (d)) or a solicitor of his own choice (situation (e)). The caution in these cases will be the normal caution given at the start of the interview (see 3.5.2.3 above).

3.5.3   Identification procedures

3.5.3.1   Introduction

In addition to wanting to interview an arrested person about his suspected involvement in a criminal offence, the other main reason for the police to arrest a suspect is to enable them to obtain additional evidence which points to that suspect's guilt. The most common method which the police use to obtain such evidence is to see if the victim of and/or witnesses to the offence are able visually to identify the suspect.

The procedures which the police need to follow when obtaining identification evidence are contained in Code D. Paragraph 1.2 of Code D provides:

> Identification by witnesses arises, eg if the offender is seen committing the crime and a witness is given an opportunity to identify the suspect in a video identification, identification parade or similar procedure. The procedures are designed to:
> *   test the witness' ability to identify the person they saw on a previous occasion
> *   provide safeguards against mistaken identification.

If the police do not know the identity of the suspect, they are permitted to take a witness to a particular neighbourhood or place to see if that witness is able to identify the person he saw.

If the identity of the suspect is known to the police and the suspect has been arrested, the police may then use a form of identification procedure to see if the witness can identify the suspect. There are four different types of identification procedure:

(a)   video identification;

(b)   an identification parade;

(c)   a group identification; and

(d)   confrontation by a witness.

The police must keep a record of the suspect's description as *first* given to them by a potential witness (Code D, para 3.1). Before any form of identification procedure takes place, a copy of this record should be given to the suspect or his solicitor. This may prove useful at trial if there are discrepancies between this description and the appearance of the suspect.

3.5.3.2   Video identification (Code D, Annex A)

A video identification occurs when the witness is shown moving images of a known suspect, together with similar images of others who resemble the suspect.

The images must include the suspect and 'at least eight other people who, so far as possible, resemble the suspect in age, height, general appearance and position in life' (Code D, Annex A, para 2). The images that are shown to the witness show the suspect and the other people in the same positions, or carrying out the same sequence of movements (Code D, Annex A, para 3).

The suspect or his solicitor must be given a reasonable opportunity to see the full set of images (normally referred to as 'foils') before they are shown to any witness. If there is a 'reasonable objection' to the images or to any of the other participants (such as one of the other participants not resembling the suspect), the police must take steps, if practicable, to remove the grounds for objection (Code D, Annex A, para 7). Such steps may include not using the image of a participant who does not resemble the suspect, and instead replacing this with an image of someone who does resemble the suspect.

If a suspect has any unusual features (such as a facial scar, a tattoo, or distinctive hair style or colour) which do not appear on the images of the other people, the police may take steps to conceal those features on the video or to replicate those features on the images of the other people (Code D, Annex A, para 2A). Such concealment or replication may be done electronically. If a witness, having seen video images where concealment or replication has been used, wants to see an image without the concealment or replication of the unusual feature, the witness may be allowed to do so (Code D, Annex A, para 2C).

A suspect will not be present at the video identification, although the suspect will have attended the police station on an earlier date to be video-taped for the purpose of the video identification. The suspect's solicitor should be given reasonable notice of the time and place of the video identification so that he may attend to ensure that it is carried out properly (Code D, Annex A, para 9).

Only one witness may see the video at a time. The playback of the video may be frozen and there is no limit on the number of times the suspect may see the video (Code D, Annex A, para 11). Before they see the set of images, witnesses must not be able to:

(a)   communicate with each other about the case;

(b)   see any of the images which are to be shown;

(c)   see, or be reminded of, any photograph or description of the suspect, or be given any other indication as to the suspect's identity; or

(d)   overhear a witness who has already seen the material (Code D, Annex A, para 10).

The police must not discuss with the witness the composition of the set of images, and a witness must not be told whether a previous witness has made an identification.

If a suspect refuses to consent to take part in a video identification, the police are permitted to proceed with a covert video identification.

3.5.3.3   Identification parades (Code D, Annex B)

An identification parade occurs when a witness sees the suspect in a line of other persons who resemble the suspect.

The identification parade will consist of at least eight people (in addition to the suspect) who, so far as possible, resemble the suspect in age, height, general appearance and position in life (Code D, Annex B, para 9).

If a suspect has any unusual features (such as a facial scar, tattoo or distinctive hair style or colour) which it is not possible to replicate on the other participants in the parade, the police may take steps to conceal those features. For example, a plaster may be used to hide a facial scar, or a hat may be used to hide distinctive hair colour (Code D, Annex B, para 10).

Paragraph 14 of Code D, Annex B provides that the police must make appropriate arrangements to ensure that, before attending the parade, witnesses are not able to:

(a)   communicate with each other about the case, or overhear a witness who has already seen the identification parade;

(b)   see any member of the identification parade;

(c)   see, or be reminded of, any photograph or description of the suspect, or be given any other indication as to the suspect's identity; or

(d)   see the suspect before or after the identification parade.

The suspect is allowed to choose his own position in the line (and may change positions between witnesses if more than one witness is to attend the parade), but cannot otherwise alter the order of people forming the line. Paragraph 16 of Code D, Annex B states:

> Witnesses shall be brought in one at a time. Immediately before the witness inspects the identification parade, they shall be told the person they saw on a specified earlier occasion may, or may not, be present and if they cannot make a positive identification, they should say so. The witness must also be told they should not make any decision about whether the person they saw is on the identification parade until they have looked at each member twice.

Sometimes a witness will ask to have a parade member speak, move or adopt a particular posture. If a witness makes such a request, he should first be asked whether he can identify any person on the parade on the basis of appearance only. A witness who asks a parade member to speak must be reminded that the participants in the parade have been chosen on the basis of physical appearance only. Only when the police have done that may a member of the parade then be asked to comply with the request to hear him speak, move or adopt a particular posture. (If a suspect is picked out after he has been asked to speak, whilst this evidence will be admissible at trial, the judge will give a very strong warning to the jury to treat such evidence with the utmost caution.)

A colour photograph or video recording of the identification parade should always be taken (Code D, Annex B, para 23).

The police cannot compel a suspect to take part in an identification parade should the suspect refuse to consent to taking part.

3.5.3.4 Group identification (Code D, Annex C)

A group identification occurs when the witness sees the suspect in an informal group of people.

Group identifications may take place either with the consent and cooperation of the suspect, or covertly if the suspect does not consent (Code D, Annex C, para 2).

The place where a group identification should be held is a place where other people are passing by or waiting around informally (such as on an escalator, or in a shopping centre or bus station). The suspect should be able to join these people and be capable of being seen by the witness at the same time as others in the group (Code D, Annex C, para 4).

In selecting the location for the holding of a group identification, the police must reasonably expect that the witness will see some people whose appearance is broadly similar to that of the suspect (Code D, Annex C, para 6). Beyond that, however, there is no requirement that the other persons whom the witness sees in addition to the suspect have any particular likeness to the suspect.

If a suspect refuses to consent to a group identification and such an identification is held covertly, the police will be required to take the witness to a place where the suspect is likely to be at a given time. If, for example, the suspect is in employment, the group identification could take place outside the suspect's place of work at the time when the suspect is known to start or finish work, since it is likely that the suspect would then be in a group of fellow workers arriving or leaving work at the same time.

3.5.3.5 Confrontation (Code D, Annex D)

A confrontation occurs when a witness is brought face to face with a suspect in the police station. Confrontations are extremely rare.

Prior to a confrontation taking place, the witness must be told that the person he saw may, or may not, be the person he is to confront and that if he is not that person, the witness should say so (Code D, Annex D, para 1).

Confrontations will usually take place in the presence of the suspect's solicitor.

3.5.3.6 Who arranges the identification procedure?

The identification officer

Identification procedures are the responsibility of an officer not below the rank of inspector who is not involved with the investigation. This officer is known as the 'identification officer' (Code D, para 3.11). The identification officer will be in charge of the identification procedure and must ensure that it complies with the requirements of Code D. The identification officer will be present throughout the procedure and must be in uniform. When an identification procedure needs to be held, para 3.11 of Code D provides that 'it must be held as soon as practicable'. If the police decide to hold an identification procedure, the suspect will normally be released on police bail (see **3.7.3** below) with a requirement to re-attend the police station at a later date when the identification procedure will take place. This will then enable the police to arrange for witnesses to attend the police station (in the case of an identification parade) or to obtain the necessary images (in the case of a video identification).

The investigating officer will have no involvement in the conduct of the identification procedure. Paragraph 3.11 of Code D states: 'No officer ... involved with the investigation of the case against the suspect ... may take part in [identification] procedures or act as the identification officer.' This ensures that there is no risk of the investigating officer seeking to influence in any way the witnesses who are to take part in the identification procedure.

Steps to be taken by the identification officer

Before a video identification, identification parade or group identification is arranged, the identification officer must explain the following matters to the suspect:

(a)   the purpose of the identification procedure to be used;

(b)   the suspect's entitlement to free legal advice;

(c)   the procedure to be followed, including the suspect's right to have a solicitor or friend present;

(d)   that if the suspect refuses to consent to the identification procedure taking place, such refusal may be given in evidence at trial, or the police may proceed covertly without the suspect's consent (ie, by holding a covert video or group identification), or make other arrangements to test whether a witness can identify the suspect (ie, by arranging a confrontation);

(e)   that if the suspect has significantly altered his appearance between being offered an identification procedure and the time of the procedure, this may be given in evidence at trial and the identification officer may consider other forms of identification;

(f)   whether, before the suspect's identity became known, the witness was shown photographs, or a computerised or artist's composite likeness or image by the police; and

(g)   that the suspect or his solicitor will be provided with details of the description of the suspect as first given by any witnesses who are to attend the identification procedure *before* the procedure takes place (Code D, para 3.17).

3.5.3.7   When must an identification procedure be held?

If:

(a)   a witness has identified or purported to have identified a suspect; or

(b)   a witness thinks he can identify the suspect, or there is a reasonable chance that the witness can identify the suspect,

and the suspect disputes being the person the witness claims to have seen, para 3.12 of Code D states that an identification procedure *shall* be held unless it is not practicable or would serve no purpose in proving or disproving whether the suspect was involved in committing the offence. Code D goes on to give an example of when it would not be necessary to hold an identification procedure, namely when it is not disputed that the suspect is already *well known* to the witness. In such a case, an identification procedure would serve no purpose because the witness would inevitably pick out the suspect.

An identification procedure should be held if a witness to a crime has purported to identify the suspect in the street some time after the crime was committed, since the purpose of an identification procedure is to test the reliability of the eye-witness's identification.

Example 1

Tom is arrested on suspicion of assault. A witness, Barbara, saw the assault. She does not know Tom, but thinks she can identify the person she saw commit the assault. Tom disputes being the person Barbara claims to have seen. An identification procedure should be held to see if Barbara can pick out Tom as the person she saw committing the assault.

Example 2

Tom is arrested on suspicion of assault. A witness, Barbara, saw the assault. She recognised Tom as the person who committed the assault because he was at school with her some years previously. Tom disputes being the person Barbara claims to have seen. He also says that he vaguely recalls Barbara from school, but didn't know her very well. He also comments that it is several years since he left school and Barbara was two years ahead of him. An identification procedure should be held to see if Barbara can pick out Tom, since Tom is disputing the fact that he is well known to Barbara.

Example 3

Tom is arrested on suspicion of assault. A witness, Barbara, saw the assault. She identifies Tom as the person who committed the assault. Tom disputes being the person Barbara claims to have seen. Barbara has known Tom for several years as they are both members of the same gym. Tom does not dispute that he is *well known* to Barbara. There would be no useful purpose in holding an identification procedure since Barbara would clearly pick out Tom were a procedure to be held.

Example 4

An assault takes place outside a pub and is witnessed by Barbara. The assailant runs away before he can be apprehended. Barbara does not know the identity of the person who carried out the assault, but thinks she will be able to identify this person if she sees him again. PC Smith later takes Barbara to the area where the assault occurred. Barbara sees Tom and recognises him as the person who committed the assault. An identification procedure should be held to test the reliability of Barbara's street identification of Tom.

An identification procedure may also be held if the officer in charge of the investigation considers it would be useful (Code D, para 3.13).

3.5.3.8 Which type of identification procedure should be used?

Paragraph 3.14 of Code D provides that a suspect should initially be offered a video identification unless:

(a) a video identification is not practicable;

(b) an identification parade is both practicable and more suitable than a video identification; or

(c) the officer in charge of the investigation considers that a group identification is more suitable than a video identification or identification parade, and the identification officer considers it practicable to arrange a group identification.

The decision on which type of procedure is offered to the suspect will be made by the investigating officer in conjunction with the identification officer. A video identification is now by far the most common form of identification procedure used by the police. Identification parades are held only very rarely. A video identification is normally preferred to an identification parade, if it can be arranged and completed sooner than an identification parade. Paragraph 3.14 states:

> An identification parade may not be practicable because of factors relating to the witnesses, such as their number, state of health, availability and travelling requirements. A video identification would normally be more suitable if it could be arranged and completed sooner than an identification parade.

A group identification may be offered if the officer in charge of the investigation considers it to be more suitable than a video identification or identification parade, and the identification officer considers it practicable to arrange (Code D, para 3.16).

Confrontations are very much a last resort.

3.5.3.9   Can an identification procedure be used if a witness has recognised a suspect from a photograph?

The police will keep photographs of individuals with previous convictions, and may show these photographs to a witness when they are trying to identify the person responsible for a crime (see **3.5.7** below).

Before a witness is shown any photographs, that witness's first description of the suspect must have been recorded (Code D, Annex E, para 2).

The witness must be shown at least 12 photographs at a time (Code D, Annex E, para 4). As soon as a witness makes a positive identification from photographs, no other witnesses should be shown the photographs. The witness who made the identification and any other witnesses should then be asked to take part in one of the identification procedures outlined above (Code D, Annex E, para 6).

The suspect or his solicitor must be notified if a witness attending an identification procedure has previously been shown photographs, or a computerised or artist's composite (Code D, Annex E, para 9).

If the case subsequently comes to trial, when giving evidence the witness will not be permitted to say that he originally identified the suspect from photographs shown to him by the police.

3.5.4   Fingerprints and impressions of footwear

3.5.4.1   Fingerprints

Fingerprints are another form of identification evidence. The police may want to take a suspect's fingerprints to see if they match fingerprints found at the scene of a crime, or fingerprints found on an object or article which the police have recovered during their investigation (such as a weapon, or an item which it is alleged the suspect has stolen).

A suspect's fingerprints may be taken either with or without his consent under s 61 (Code D, para 4.2). Consent must be given in writing if the suspect is at the police station. Section 61 allows the police to take fingerprints from a person who has been detained at the police station for a recordable offence, or charged with or convicted of such an offence. Fingerprints may also be taken from a person who had been given a caution, reprimand or warning for a recordable offence. The term 'recordable offence' relates to those offences for which convictions, cautions, reprimands and warnings may be recorded in national police records. At present, a recordable offence is any offence which carries a possible sentence of imprisonment upon conviction.

The police may also take a person's fingerprints away from the police station if the officer reasonably suspects that the person is committing or attempting to commit an offence, or has committed or attempted to commit an offence, and either the name of the person is unknown or cannot reasonably be ascertained by the officer, or the officer has reasonable grounds for doubting whether the name given by the person is his real name (s 61). These provisions will enable 'street bail' (see **Chapter 2**) to work effectively.

The police may use reasonable force if necessary to take a person's fingerprints without his consent (Code D, para 4.6).

Before fingerprints are taken, the suspect must be informed:

(a)   why the fingerprints are being taken;

(b)   of the grounds relied on if the fingerprints are not taken with consent; and

(c)   that the fingerprints may be retained and made the subject of a speculative search (Code D, para 4.7).

3.5.4.2   Impressions of footwear

Section 61A of PACE 1984 allows the police to take impressions of a suspect's footwear. A suspect can either give written consent to having such an impression taken, or the police may take an impression without consent. An impression can be taken without consent if:

(a)   the suspect is arrested, charged or told that he will be reported for a recordable offence (see **3.5.4.1** above); and

(b)   he has not already had such an impression taken in the course of the investigation (s 61A(3)).

Reasonable force may be used to take an impression of footwear (Code D, para 4.18).

Before an impression of footwear is taken, the suspect must be informed:

(a)   of the reason for the taking of the impression;

(b)   that the impression may be retained and made the subject of a speculative search (s 61A(5) and (6)).

3.5.5   Samples

3.5.5.1   Types of sample

Samples are another form of identification evidence which the police may use to link a suspect to a crime or crime scene. For example:

(a)   in a burglary investigation, the police may use paint samples from underneath a suspect's fingernails to match with paint on the window frame of the property that was burgled;

(b)   in a case of assault by biting, the police may use a dental impression from a suspect to match with the bite mark left on the victim;

(c)   in a rape investigation, the police may use a sample of semen from a suspect to match with semen recovered from the victim.

Samples are divided into two types, intimate and non-intimate (s 65).

An *intimate sample* is:

(a)   a dental impression;

(b)   a sample of blood, semen or any other tissue fluid;

(c)   a sample of urine;

(d)   a sample of pubic hair;

(e)   a swab taken from a person's body orifice other than the mouth; or

(f)   a swab taken from any part of a person's genitals (including pubic hair).

A *non-intimate* sample is:

(a)   a sample of hair other than pubic hair;

(b)   a sample taken from a nail or from under a nail;

(c)   any swab taken from a person's body, unless the swab would satisfy the definition of an intimate sample;

(d)   saliva; or

(e)   a skin impression other than a fingerprint.

3.5.5.2   When can intimate samples be taken?

Under s 62, intimate samples may be taken only on the authority of a police officer with at least the rank of inspector *and* with the 'appropriate consent' (this means the consent in writing of the suspect if over 17, the suspect's parent or guardian if he is under 14, or the consent of both the suspect and his parent or guardian if he is aged between 14 and 17 inclusive).

The officer who authorises the taking of the sample must have reasonable grounds for suspecting the suspect's involvement in a recordable offence (see **3.5.4.1** above). He must also believe that the sample will tend to confirm or disprove the suspect's involvement in that offence.

Example

Trevor is arrested on suspicion of murdering his girlfriend, Carol. Carol was struck on the head with a hammer. The police have recovered the hammer which was covered in blood. Forensic examination has revealed that there are two distinct blood types on the hammer. One of the blood types is Carol's blood. The police believe the other blood type to be Trevor's. The police would be able to take a sample of Trevor's blood to confirm or disprove this if the necessary authority is obtained from an officer with at least the rank of inspector and the appropriate consent is obtained from Trevor.

3.5.5.3   Why should a suspect consent to an intimate sample being taken?

A court is entitled to 'draw such inferences as appear proper' if a suspect refuses, without good cause, to consent to the taking of an intimate sample (s 62(10)). If, for example, a suspect charged with rape refused to provide a sample of semen to the police, the court may draw from this refusal an inference that the suspect does not want to give such a sample because the sample would match semen recovered from the victim of the alleged rape.

Paragraph 6.3 of Code D states: 'Before a suspect is asked to provide an intimate sample, they must be warned that if they refuse without good cause, their refusal may harm their case if it comes to trial ...'

3.5.5.4 When may non-intimate samples be taken?

A non-intimate sample may be taken with the written consent of the suspect. In addition, s 63 allows for non-intimate samples to be taken from persons in police custody without their consent in the following circumstances:

(a) if the person is in police detention following his arrest for a recordable offence (see **3.5.4.1**) and he has not had a non-intimate sample of the same type and from the same part of his body taken in the course of the investigation, or such a sample has been taken but it has proved to be insufficient (s 63(2A)–(2C));

(b) if the person is being held in custody by the police on the authority of the court and an officer of at least the rank of inspector authorises such a sample to be taken (s 63(3)); or

(c) if a person has been charged with a recordable offence or told that he will be reported for such an offence, and either that person has not had a non-intimate sample taken from him during the course of the investigation or, if such a sample has been taken, it has proved to be unsuitable or insufficient (s 63(3A));

(d) if the person has been convicted of a recordable offence (s 63(3B)).

The police are permitted to use reasonable force to take a non-intimate sample from a person without that person's consent (Code D, para 6.7).

3.5.5.5 Conclusion

Intimate and non-intimate samples may be used for speculative searches (see **3.5.6** below).

Before the police take from a suspect any intimate sample with consent or a non-intimate sample with or without consent, the person from whom the sample is to be taken must be told:

(a) the reason for taking the sample;

(b) the grounds on which the relevant authority has been given; and

(c) that the sample may be retained and be made the subject of a speculative search (Code D, para 6.8).

3.5.6 Speculative searches

Fingerprints, impressions of footwear or DNA samples taken by the police may be the subject of a 'speculative search'. This means that the fingerprints, impressions of footwear or DNA sample may be checked against other records held by the police to see if the suspect may be linked to other crimes which the police are investigating (s 63A).

3.5.7 Taking photographs of the suspect

Section 64A permits a police officer to photograph a person detained at a police station either with his consent, or without his consent if it is withheld or it is not possible to obtain it. Section 64A also permits the police to take photographs of a suspect with or without his consent when that suspect is away from the police station if the suspect falls within one of the categories set out in s 64(1B). The most important category is suspects who have been arrested. Other categories include suspects who have received various forms of fixed penalty notice.

Section 64A also permits the police to retain and use or disclose any photographs of the suspect which they have taken for the following purposes:

(a)   the prevention or detection of offences;

(b)   the investigation of offences; or

(c)   the conduct of prosecutions.

Example

Sam is arrested on suspicion of theft. His photograph is taken whilst he is at the police station. Sam is subsequently charged and convicted of theft. The police may retain the photograph. When a further theft takes place and a witness sees (but does not recognise) the thief, the police may show the witness Sam's photograph, together with at least 11 others, to see if the witness recognises Sam or one of the other people as the thief (see **3.5.3.9** above). This would be using the photograph for the purpose of investigating an offence.

If a suspect refuses to consent to having his photograph taken, the police may use reasonable force to take the photograph if the photograph cannot be taken covertly (Code D, para 5.14).

When the police take a photograph of a suspect, the suspect must be told the purposes for which the photograph may be used, disclosed or retained (Code D, para 5.16).

3.6   Special categories of suspect

3.6.1   Introduction

A solicitor will often be called to the police station to represent an individual who falls within one of several special categories of suspect, and to whom specific rules apply. These categories are:

(a)   juveniles – suspects who are aged between 10 and 16 inclusive (although para 1.5 of Code C provides that the police should treat anyone who *appears* to be under 17 as a juvenile in the absence of clear evidence to the contrary);

(b)   suspects who suffer from a mental disability or otherwise appear to be mentally vulnerable;

(c)   suspects who are deaf, dumb or blind; and

(d)   suspects who cannot speak or understand English.

3.6.2   Initial steps the custody officer must take

3.6.2.1   The need for an interpreter

Under para 3.12 of Code C, if a detainee appears to be deaf or there is any doubt about his hearing or speaking ability, or his ability to understand English, and the custody officer is unable to communicate effectively with him, the custody officer should, as soon as practicable, call an interpreter for assistance so that the custody officer can properly explain to the suspect the reason for his detention and the rights he may exercise whilst in police custody. Interpreters should normally be drawn from the National Register of Public Service Interpreters (NRPSI).

3.6.2.2   Juveniles

A juvenile who has been arrested and detained at the police station has the right to have a person informed of his arrest under s 56 (see **3.4.1** above) and the right to receive free and independent legal advice from a solicitor under s 58 (see **3.4.2** above), in just the same way as an adult suspect.

In addition, however, if a juvenile has been arrested, the custody officer must, if practicable, find out the person responsible for his welfare (Code C, para 3.13). That person may be:

(a)   the juvenile's parent or guardian;

(b)   if the juvenile is in local authority or voluntary organisation care, the person appointed by that authority or organisation to have responsibility for the juvenile's welfare (Children and Young Persons Act 1933, s 34(8)); or

(c)   any other person who has, for the time being, assumed responsibility for the juvenile's welfare.

That person must be informed as soon as practicable that the juvenile has been arrested, why he has been arrested and where he is being detained. This right is in addition to the juvenile's right under s 56 to have a person informed of his arrest (see **3.4.1** above).

If a juvenile is known to be the subject of a court order under which a person or organisation is given any statutory responsibility to supervise or monitor him (for example, a supervision order), reasonable steps must also be taken to notify that person or organisation. The person notified is known as the 'responsible officer' and will usually be a member of a Youth Offending Team (Code C, para 3.14).

3.6.2.3   Informing the appropriate adult

Under para 3.15 of Code C, in the case of a juvenile, or a mentally disordered or otherwise mentally vulnerable person, the custody officer must, as soon as practicable:

(a)   inform the 'appropriate adult' (who, in the case of a juvenile, is likely to be the same person who is responsible for his welfare) of the grounds of his detention and his whereabouts; and

(b)   request that the adult comes to the police station to see the detainee.

The appropriate adult and his role are discussed in more detail in **3.6.3** below.

3.6.3   The appropriate adult

3.6.3.1   Who may be an appropriate adult?

The 'appropriate adult' is a person who attends the police station to provide support and assistance to the suspect. In the case of a juvenile, the appropriate adult will come from one of three potential categories of person. There is a hierarchical order the police should follow when contacting an appropriate adult for a juvenile, as follows:

(a)   The police should initially attempt to contact the juvenile's parent or guardian (or a representative from the local authority where the juvenile is in local authority care) to act as an appropriate adult.

(b)   If no one in (a) is available, the police should then ask a social worker from the local authority to act as an appropriate adult.

(c)   If a social worker is not available, the police should finally contact another responsible adult who is aged 18 or over and not connected to the police (Code C, para 1.7). This may, for example, be an aunt or uncle, or a grandparent. Although the adult must be aged 18 or over, the police may consider that an adult who is only just 18 or over may not be sufficiently responsible to fulfil the role.

In the case of a mentally disordered or otherwise mentally vulnerable suspect, the appropriate adult is likely to be a representative from the local authority's social services department, such as a social worker.

A solicitor should never be an appropriate adult, because support and assistance from an appropriate adult is in addition to any legal advice a suspect receives from his solicitor at the police station. Other persons who should not fulfil the role of appropriate adult include:

(a)   police officers or persons employed by the police;

(b)   an interested party such as the victim of the offence, another suspect, a potential witness or anyone else involved in the investigation (this would, for example, prevent a juvenile's mother acting as appropriate adult if the juvenile has been arrested on suspicion of assaulting her, as she would be the victim);

(c)   a person, such as a parent or social worker, to whom the juvenile has made admissions *prior* to that person being asked to attend the police station to fulfil the role of an appropriate adult; and

(d)   an estranged parent (but only when the juvenile expressly and specifically objects to the presence of such a person).

3.6.3.2   What is the role of the appropriate adult?

Although Code C does not specify exactly what role the appropriate adult should play at the police station, the Home Office has produced a document entitled 'Guidance for Appropriate Adults' that will be issued to an appropriate adult upon his arrival at the police station. The guidance can be found on the Home Office website (www.homeoffice.gov.uk).

The guidance provides that the appropriate adult has 'a positive and important role', and that the appropriate adult is not at the police station simply to act as an observer but rather to ensure that the suspect 'understands what is happening to them and why'. The key roles and responsibilities of an appropriate adult are:

(a)   to support, advise and assist the suspect, particularly when the suspect is being questioned;

(b)   to ensure that the suspect understands his rights whilst at the police station, and the role played by the appropriate adult in protecting those rights;

(c)   to observe whether the police are acting properly, fairly and with respect for the rights of the suspect; and

(d)   to assist with communication between the suspect and the police.

The guidance makes it clear that it is not the role of the appropriate adult to provide the suspect with legal advice, and any conversations the appropriate adult has with the suspect are not covered by legal privilege (see **Chapter 4**).

The defendant's solicitor needs to ensure that the appropriate adult is aware of his role, and must ensure that the appropriate adult understands that it is not his role to help the police. The solicitor should also make it clear to the appropriate adult that, whilst he is there to help the suspect understand what the police are doing, he should not answer questions on behalf of the suspect, particularly in an interview situation. The appropriate adult should, however, intervene in an interview if he considers that the juvenile has not understood a question which has been asked and that clarification of the question is necessary.

The custody officer should explain his rights whilst at the police station to a suspect in the presence of the appropriate adult, or repeat those rights in the presence of the appropriate adult if he had already explained these rights to the suspect before the appropriate adult arrived at the police station (Code C, para 3.17). The custody officer should also advise the suspect that:

(a)   the duties of the appropriate adult include giving advice and assistance; and

(b)   the suspect may consult privately with the appropriate adult at any time (Code C, para 3.18).

If a suspect is blind, seriously visually impaired or unable to read, the custody officer must ensure that his solicitor, relative, appropriate adult or some other person likely to take an interest in him and not involved in the investigation is available to help check any documentation (Code C, para 3.20). Paragraph 3.20 also provides that if a suspect needs to sign a document or give written consent to any step being taken, such a person may be asked to sign on his behalf.

3.6.4   Interviews

3.6.4.1   Suspects who require an appropriate adult

Paragraph 10.12 of Code C provides that if a juvenile or a person who is mentally impaired or otherwise mentally vulnerable is cautioned in the absence of the appropriate adult, this caution must be repeated in the appropriate adult's presence.

Similarly, such a suspect must not normally be interviewed, or asked to provide or sign a written statement under caution or record of interview, in the absence of the appropriate adult (Code C, para 11.15).

When an appropriate adult is present in an interview, he must be informed by the police that he is not there simply to act as an observer, and that the purpose of his presence in the interview is to:

(a)   advise the person being interviewed;

(b)   observe whether the interview is being conducted properly and fairly; and

(c)   facilitate communication with the person being interviewed (Code C, para 11.17).

The appropriate adult's presence at the police station (and particularly during the interview) is necessary to help the suspect cope with the demands of custody and questioning, and to appreciate the seriousness of the situation. The appropriate adult should help the suspect gain a degree of understanding of what is taking place so that the suspect can make a sensible decision as to the course of action he should take. The appropriate adult should not, however, attempt to answer questions on behalf of the suspect during the interview.

The 'Notes for guidance' to Code C clarify the role an appropriate adult should play in an interview. Paragraph 11C states that:

> Although juveniles or people who are mentally disordered or otherwise mentally vulnerable are often capable of providing reliable evidence, they may, without knowing or wishing to do so, be particularly prone in certain circumstances to provide information that may be unreliable, misleading or self-incriminating. Special care should always be taken when questioning such a person, and the

appropriate adult should be involved if there is any doubt about a person's age, mental state or capacity. Because of the risk of unreliable evidence it is also important to obtain corroboration of any facts admitted whenever possible.

There are very limited situations when a suspect can be interviewed in the absence of the appropriate adult. These are detailed in para 11.18 of Code C.

3.6.4.2 Suspects who are unable to speak or understand English

In the case of a suspect who speaks only a foreign language, para 13.2 of Code C provides that such a person must not normally be interviewed in the absence of an interpreter if:

(a)   the suspect has difficulty understanding English;

(b)   the interviewer cannot speak the suspect's own language; or

(c)   the suspect wants an interpreter present.

The interviewer must ensure that the interpreter makes a note of the interview at the time in the person's language (for use in the event of the interpreter being called to give evidence) and also certify the accuracy of the note (Code C, para 13.3). The suspect should be allowed to read this record or have it read to him, and sign it as correct or indicate the respects in which he considers it to be inaccurate.

If a suspect makes a written statement to the police that is other than in English:

(a)   the interpreter must record the statement in the language in which it is made;

(b)   the suspect shall be invited to sign it; and

(c)   an official English translation shall be made in due course (Code C, para 13.4).

In the case of suspects who are deaf, or where there is doubt about their hearing or speaking ability, they must not normally be interviewed in the absence of an interpreter unless they agree in writing to being interviewed without one (Code C, para 13.5).

An interpreter should also normally be called if a juvenile is being interviewed and the parent or guardian present as the appropriate adult appears to be deaf, or if there is doubt as to that adult's hearing or speaking ability, unless the adult agrees in writing to the interview proceeding without one (Code C, para 13.6).

There are very limited situations when a suspect who has difficulty understanding English or has a hearing disability may be interviewed without an interpreter being present. These situations are detailed in para 11.18 of Code C.

3.6.5   Suspects who require an interpreter – additional provisions

The police must make all reasonable attempts to ensure that a detainee understands that any interpreter will be provided at the public expense (Code C, para 13.8).

An interpreter must be called if a detainee cannot communicate with a solicitor because of language, hearing or speech difficulties (Code C, para 13.9). Such an interpreter must not be a police officer when interpretation is required for the purposes of obtaining legal advice.

If a custody officer is unable to establish 'effective communication' with a person charged with an offence who appears to be deaf, or where there is doubt about his ability to hear, speak or to understand English, arrangements must be made as soon as practicable for an interpreter to explain the offence and any other information given by the custody officer (Code C, para 13.10).

3.6.6 Identification procedures

In addition to the requirements imposed by Code C, if the police require a suspect who falls into a special category to take part in an identification procedure, to provide a sample, or to give his fingerprints or an impression of his footwear, they must comply with additional provisions in Code D.

Paragraph 2.12 of Code D provides that where any procedure in Code D requires a person's consent (for example, if a suspect is asked to consent to taking part in an identification parade or video identification), the following conditions apply:

(a)   if the suspect is mentally disordered or otherwise mentally vulnerable, his consent is valid only if given in the presence of the appropriate adult;

(b)   if the suspect is a juvenile aged 14 or over, consent must be obtained both from the juvenile *and* from the juvenile's parent or guardian;

(c)   if the suspect is a juvenile aged under 14, consent must be obtained from the juvenile's parent or guardian (rather than from the juvenile).

If the suspect is blind, seriously visually impaired or unable to read, the custody officer must ensure that his solicitor, relative, appropriate adult or some other person likely to take an interest in him and not involved in the investigation is available to help check any documentation (Code D, para 2.13).

If any procedure in Code D requires information to be given to or sought from a suspect (for example, the suspect being given details of the first description of the suspect by a witness who is to attend an identification procedure), such information must be given or sought in the presence of the appropriate adult if the suspect is mentally disordered, otherwise mentally vulnerable or a juvenile (Code D, para 2.14). Similarly, any procedure in Code D involving the participation of a suspect who is mentally disordered, otherwise mentally vulnerable or a juvenile must take place in the presence of the appropriate adult (Code D, para 2.15). This means that the appropriate adult will be present when an identification procedure takes place.

3.7 Charging the suspect

3.7.1 Introduction

Once the police have exercised their investigative powers whilst the suspect is detained in the police station, they will then need to determine what step to take next in the case. The investigating officer will tell the custody officer what he wishes to do, but the actual decision on what to do next will be made by the custody officer. The custody officer has four possible options:

(a)   release the suspect without charge and without bail;

(b)   release the suspect without charge but on bail whilst the police make further enquiries;

(c)   release the suspect without charge but on bail for the purpose of enabling the CPS to decide whether there is sufficient evidence to charge the suspect and, if so, whether the suspect should be charged or the matter dealt with other than by way of charge; or

(d)   charge the suspect.

Each of these options will be examined in turn.

3.7.2   Release without charge and without bail

If, having investigated the offence, the police determine that the suspect did not in fact commit the crime under investigation (or there is insufficient evidence against the suspect and it is unlikely that any further evidence will be obtained), the custody officer should release the suspect without charge and without any requirement that the suspect return to the police station at a later date. This means that, from the suspect's point of view, the matter is closed, although there is nothing to prevent the police from re-arresting the suspect at a later date should any further evidence come to light which implicates the suspect.

Example

Aftab is arrested on suspicion of assault. Aftab is interviewed and denies the assault. The only witness to the assault is the victim, Louise. A video identification is arranged but Louise fails to pick out Aftab as the person who assaulted her. The police have no additional evidence against Aftab. He should be released without charge and should not be required to return to the police station at a later date.

If there is sufficient evidence to charge the suspect but the offence is a minor one, the police may decide to release the suspect without charge but to give him an informal warning (see **3.9.1.2** below).

3.7.3   Release on bail whilst the police make further enquiries

It is often the case that, after exercising their investigative powers in the police station, the police will need to make further enquiries before deciding whether to charge a suspect or to pass their file to the CPS to determine if there is sufficient evidence to charge the suspect. In such circumstances the police will release the suspect on bail under s 47(3)(b).

Example

Richard is arrested on suspicion of assaulting Wayne in a nightclub. Wayne has given a statement saying that this was an unprovoked attack. In an audio-recorded interview at the police station, Richard states that he was initially attacked by Wayne, and that any violence he used was only in self-defence. Richard also gives the interviewing officer the names of two of his friends who witnessed the incident and who will confirm his version of events. The police did not take statements from these people when carrying out their initial investigations. The police will need to speak to these witnesses to see if they back up Richard's version of events, and also speak to Wayne again to put to him what Richard has said. The police should therefore release Richard without charge but on bail, with a requirement that Richard attend the police station again at a future date when the police have determined what course of action they are going to take after carrying out their further investigations.

Details of the time and date when the suspect needs to re-attend the police station will be contained in a written notice which will be given to him by the police. The police are not permitted to add conditions to bail granted to a suspect in these circumstances (so, continuing with the above example, the police would not be able to impose a condition on Richard's bail that he does not attempt to make contact with Wayne).

When the suspect answers his bail, the police may:

(a)   release him without charge (if, after making further enquiries, the police have insufficient evidence to charge);

(b)   exercise further investigative powers (such as re-interviewing the suspect);

(c)   release the suspect again on bail if their further enquiries are incomplete or, having completed their enquiries, they wish to pass their file to the CPS for advice (see **3.7.4** below);or

(d)   charge the suspect (if, after making further enquiries, the police have sufficient evidence to charge).

If the suspect fails to answer his bail at the police station, he may be arrested without warrant (s 46A).

Under changes proposed in the Police and Justice Bill which is currently before Parliament, the police will be permitted to impose conditions on bail granted to a suspect whilst the police make further enquiries into the alleged offence (for example, a condition of residence or a condition not to enter a particular area). If the suspect breaches any conditions that are imposed, the police will have the power to arrest him without warrant.

3.7.4   Release on bail whilst the file is passed to the CPS

The Criminal Justice Act 2003 has made significant changes to the procedure for deciding when a suspect should be charged and what offence that suspect should be charged with. Schedule 2 to the Act sets out new arrangements for the charging of suspects. The significance of these changes is that the CPS (rather than the police) will normally determine what charge (if any) should be brought. The Act creates a new s 37B of PACE 1984, which provides that it is for the CPS to determine whether the suspect should be charged and, if so, with what offence. The rationale behind this is that, as the CPS is the body responsible for conducting the case at court, it should be the CPS who decides what the most appropriate charge is. More generally, the CPS and the police now work together in local 'Criminal Justice Units', rather than being separate entities.

It will therefore usually be the case that once the police believe there is sufficient evidence to charge a suspect, the police will need to send the case papers to the CPS for it to determine the exact charge. Lawyers from the CPS are often present at the police station to advise on charging and so, in a straightforward case, a decision on the appropriate charge can be made there and then. However, in many cases (and particularly where the case is serious or complex) the standard practice will be for the police to send their file to the CPS for it to review the case and make a decision as to the appropriate charge.

The CPS will apply a two-part test to determine whether or not the suspect should be charged:

(a)   the CPS will need to determine if there is sufficient evidence to charge the suspect; and

(a)   if there is sufficient evidence, the CPS will then need to determine if it is in the public interest to charge the suspect, or whether the matter should be dealt with other than by way of charge (see **3.9** below).

It will often take a number of weeks for the CPS to review a file, and the police will therefore need to release the suspect on bail under s 47(3)(b) whilst this is done. As with releasing the suspect on bail whilst the police make further enquiries, the suspect will be required to re-attend the police station at a future time and date, and will be given a notice to this effect. When the suspect answers his bail, the police may:

(a)   charge the suspect (if the CPS found there was sufficient evidence to charge and a charge was in the public interest);

(b)   exercise further investigative powers if the CPS considered that further evidence was needed (eg, re-interviewing the suspect);

(c)   release the suspect without charge (if the CPS found there was insufficient evidence to charge); or

(d)   deal with the matter other than by way of a charge if the CPS found there was sufficient evidence to charge the suspect but a charge was not in the public interest (see **3.9** below).

Under the new s 47(1A) which has been inserted into PACE 1984 by the Criminal Justice Act 2003, the police may impose conditions on a suspect who is released on bail pending consultations with the CPS. For example, conditions might be imposed requiring a suspect to reside at a particular address, not to enter a specified area or not to contact specified persons.

Example

Francis is arrested on suspicion of assaulting his wife, Laura. The police refer the file to the CPS to determine what charge Francis should face. Francis is released on bail whilst the CPS reviews the papers. Francis tells the police that he will be staying at his brother's house rather than returning to the matrimonial home. The police impose conditions on the bail granted to Francis, requiring him to live at his brother's address and not to speak to, or try to communicate with, Laura.

If the suspect fails to answer his bail at the police station, or the police reasonably suspect that the suspect has broken any conditions attached to his bail, he may be arrested without warrant (s 46A).

3.7.5 Charging the suspect

3.7.5.1 Procedure

If the police consider that they have sufficient evidence to charge the suspect, they will either charge him themselves or pass the case papers to the CPS for it to determine what the appropriate charge should be.

As stated at **3.6.4** above, the usual practice will be for the police to refer the case to the CPS for it to determine the appropriate charge. However, the police will still decide on the appropriate charge themselves in minor cases, particularly if the offence is summary only and it is expected that the suspect will enter a guilty plea.

When a decision has been made (either by the police, or by the CPS) to charge a suspect, the suspect will be formally charged at the police station. In accordance with para 16.2 of Code C, the suspect must be cautioned on charge and anything the suspect says in response to the charge should be written down. The wording of the caution is the same as that used at both the time of the suspect's arrest the start of the interview in the police station (see **3.5.2**).

The suspect should also be given a written notice (the 'charge sheet') which gives the particulars of the offence. Paragraph 16.3 of Code C states: ' ... As far as possible the particulars of the charge shall be stated in simple terms, but they shall also show the precise offence in law with which the detainee is charged ...'

If the suspect is a juvenile, mentally disordered or otherwise mentally vulnerable, the written notice should be given to the appropriate adult (Code C, para 16.3).

3.7.5.2 Further interviews after charge

A suspect who has been charged cannot be interviewed further by the police about the offence for which he has been charged, unless the interview is necessary:

(a) to prevent or minimise harm or loss to some other persons, or the public;

(b) to clear up an ambiguity in a previous answer or statement; or

(c) in the interests of justice for the suspect to have put to him, and to have an opportunity to comment on, information concerning the offence which has come to light since he was charged (Code C, para 16.5).

If the police do interview a suspect after he has been charged, the suspect must be cautioned before any interview takes place. The wording of the caution is the 'old' caution which was used prior to the court being given the power under the Criminal Justice and Public Order Act 1994 to draw an adverse inference from a suspect's silence at the police station. The wording of the caution will be: 'You do not have to say anything, but anything you do say may be given in evidence.' This means that the suspect may remain silent in the interview and not have any adverse inference drawn from that silence at his trial.

Key Document – Charge Sheet

CHESHIRE POLICE   Form MG4
CHARGE (S)

Collaws Solicitors

Surname:	DICKSON		Custody No.	CH	000687	06
Forename:	GARY PAUL		Arrest Date:	18	DEC	06
Address:	17 MARSH STREET	YO☐ PYO☐	Station	CHESTER		
	CHESTER	M ☒ F ☐	Date of Birth	28	10	1979
		PO☐ Ethnicity: 1		Self Class: W1		
	Post Code: CH3 7LW	Name of interpreter				

You are charged with the offence(s) shown below. You do not have to say anything. But it may harm your defence if you do not mention now something which you may later rely on in court. Anything you do say may be given in evidence.

Consec. No.	Charge(s)
	That you on Monday 18th December 2006 assaulted Vincent Lamb causing him actual bodily harm CONTRARY TO SECTION 47 OF THE OFFENCES AGAINST THE PERSON ACT 1861.

Continuation charges: Yes   No X

Reply (if any): ....

Signed (person charged): ...*Gary Paul Dickson*.. Signed (appropriate adult):
....

Officer charging   Surname: DUNN   Rank: ...SGT... No. ...568......... Station: ...CHESTER

Officer in case   Surname: CHAMBERS Rank: ......PC....... No. ...911............Station: ...CHESTER

Charge accepted   Surname: .... Rank: .... No. ....Time: ....Date.............

BAIL WITHOUT CONDITIONS (FOR BAIL WITH CONDITIONS – USE FORM MG4A)

I understand that I am granted bail and must surrender to the custody of   Court at

(full address)

on   time

I have been informed that if I fail to do so I may commit an offence and be fined, imprisoned or both.

Signed (person bailed) .... Signed (appropriate adult) ....

Officer Granting Surname: ....Rank: .... No: .... Time: .... Date ....

File copy ☐   Court copy ☐   Custody record ☒   Person charged ☐

3.8 Bail after charge

3.8.1 When may the police deny bail to a suspect?

When a suspect is charged at the police station, the custody officer must then decide:

(a)   whether to keep him in police custody until he can be brought before a magistrates' court, or to release him; and

(b)   if the latter, whether to release him on bail with conditions or without conditions (s 38(1)).

Section 38(1)(a) provides that bail can be denied to a suspect who has been charged only in certain circumstances. These circumstances are that:

(a)   the suspect refuses to provide his name and address (or the police have doubts as to the accuracy of the name and address that the person has given); or

(b)   the custody officer has *reasonable grounds* to believe that:

   (i)   the suspect will fail to appear in court;

   (ii)   continued detention of the suspect is necessary to prevent the suspect from committing a further offence (only if the offence for which the suspect was arrested is imprisonable);

   (iii) where the police are permitted to take a sample from the suspect under s 63B (see **3.5.5.4** above), detention of the suspect is necessary for the sample to be taken.

   (iv)   continued detention of the suspect is necessary to prevent him from causing physical injury to any other person or from causing damage to property (only if the offence for which the suspect was arrested is non-imprisonable);

   (v)   detention of the suspect is necessary to prevent the suspect from interfering with the administration of justice or with police investigations; or

   (vi)   continued detention of the suspect is necessary for his own protection.

Example 1

Rashid is charged with burglary. He has several previous convictions for failing to attend court to answer bail. The custody officer may refuse bail as he would have reasonable grounds for believing that Rashid would fail to appear in court if he was granted bail.

Example 2

Melanie is charged with theft. She has numerous previous convictions for theft and related offences, including several offences that were committed whilst she was on bail in the course of previous proceedings. The custody officer may refuse bail as he would have reasonable grounds for believing that Melanie would commit further offences whilst on bail.

Example 3

Charles is a member of a notorious criminal gang and has been charged with assault. The name and address of the victim of the assault are known to Charles, and he has a previous conviction for intimidating a witness. The custody officer may refuse bail as he would have reasonable grounds for believing that, if granted bail, Charles might attempt to intimidate the victim and so interfere with the police investigation or the administration of justice.

If the suspect is a juvenile, the custody officer may also deny the suspect bail if he has reasonable grounds for believing that it is in the suspect's 'own interests' to be detained (s 38(1)(b)). This will include situations where the custody officer has concerns about the suspect's home environment.

3.8.2   Conditional bail

If the custody officer decides to grant bail to a suspect who has been charged, he must then decide whether it is necessary to impose conditions on that bail. Conditions may be imposed only if they are necessary:

(a)   to prevent the suspect from failing to surrender to custody;

(b)   to prevent the suspect from committing an offence whilst on bail;

(c)   to prevent the suspect from interfering with witnesses or otherwise obstructing the course of justice (whether in relation to himself or another person); or

(d)   for the suspect's own protection or, if the suspect is a child or young person (ie 17 or under), for his own welfare or in his own interests (Bail Act 1976, s 3A(5)).

The custody officer may impose most of the same types of condition which a magistrates' court could impose on bail granted to a defendant (see **Chapter 7**), although he cannot impose a condition that a suspect reside at a bail hostel, undergo medical examination or see his legal adviser. The custody officer may, for example, impose conditions requiring the suspect:

(a)   to reside at a particular address;

(b)   not to speak to or contact any witnesses;

(c)   not to enter a particular area or set of premises; or

(d)   to observe a curfew at night between specified hours.

A suspect who wishes to vary conditions imposed on bail which the police have granted may either:

(a)   ask the custody officer who imposed the conditions (or another custody officer at the same police station) to vary the conditions (Bail Act 1976, s 3A(4)); or

(b)   make an application to the magistrates' court for the conditions to be varied (Magistrates' Courts Act 1980, s 43(B)(1) and CrimPR, r 19.1).

3.8.3   When will the suspect make his first appearance at court?

3.8.3.1   Suspects granted bail by the police

If a suspect is granted bail by the police after being charged, the date of his first appearance in the magistrates' court will be the first sitting of the court after he is charged with the offence (s 47(3A)), unless his appearance cannot be accommodated by the court until a later date. In practice, this means that a suspect is likely to make his first appearance in court within at most one to two weeks of being charged.

3.8.3.2   Suspects denied bail by the police

If the police refuse to grant bail to a suspect after he has been charged, the suspect will be kept in police custody (unless he is a juvenile – see **3.8.3.3** below) and must be brought before the magistrates' court as soon as is practicable, and in any event not later than the first sitting of the court after he is charged with the offence (s 46(2)). In practice this means that the suspect will normally appear before the court within 24 hours of being charged.

3.8.3.3   Juveniles refused bail after charge

If the custody officer denies bail after charge to a juvenile, the suspect will normally be kept in local authority accommodation rather than at the police station pending his first appearance before the Youth Court. The only two situations when a juvenile may be kept in police custody after charge are:

(a)   if it is impracticable to move the suspect to local authority accommodation; or

(b) if the juvenile is aged at least 12, there is no *secure* local authority accommodation available and keeping him in other local authority accommodation would not be adequate to protect the public from serious harm from him (s 38(6)). 'Secure accommodation' is accommodation provided for the purpose of restricting liberty (Children Act 1989, s 25(1)).

If either of these criteria is satisfied and the juvenile is detained at the police station, para 8.8 of Code C provides that the juvenile must be kept separate from adult suspects and must not be detained in a cell unless it is not practicable to supervise the juvenile other than in a cell. The suspect will normally be kept in a juvenile detention room.

The guidance notes to Code C provide that, unless one of the conditions in s 38(6) is satisfied, neither a juvenile's behaviour nor the nature of the offence provides grounds for the custody officer to decide that it is impracticable to arrange the juvenile's transfer to local authority care (Code C, Notes for Guidance, para 16D). This paragraph also states that the lack of secure local authority accommodation does not make it impracticable to transfer the juvenile unless the juvenile is aged 12 or over *and* the local authority accommodation would not be adequate to protect the public from serious harm by the juvenile. In *R (M) v Gateshead Borough Council* [2006] EWCA Civ 221, the Court of Appeal held that any local authority receiving a request from the police under s 38(6) to provide secure accommodation for a juvenile had to comply with such a request, regardless of the area the juvenile came from.

3.8.4 Breaching police bail

If a suspect has been bailed to attend court following charge, s 7(3) of the Bail Act 1976 gives a police officer the power to arrest that person where he reasonably believes either that the person is unlikely to surrender to custody, or that the person has breached, or is likely to breach, his bail conditions. A person who is arrested under s 7 must be brought before a magistrates' court within 24 hours. The magistrates will determine if there has been a breach of bail conditions (usually by hearing evidence from the arresting officer and the defendant) and, if so, whether they should grant bail to the defendant or remand him in custody. Breach of bail conditions is *not* in itself a criminal offence, although a defendant who has breached police bail may experience difficulties in persuading the magistrates to grant him bail subsequently.

3.9 Alternatives to charging

3.9.1 Adult offenders

3.9.1.1 Introduction

It is not inevitable that a suspect against whom there is sufficient evidence to bring a charge will always be charged with an offence. Where the suspect is aged over 17, rather than charging him, it may be possible to deal with the matter in one of the following ways:

(a) an informal warning;

(b) a formal caution;

(c) a conditional caution.

Each of these is examined further below.

3.9.1.2   Informal warnings

In minor cases the police have always had discretion to release a suspect without charge but to give him an informal warning about his future conduct. Such informal warnings are often given to individuals arrested for minor public order offences. An informal warning will not appear on a defendant's list of previous convictions if he is later charged with another offence.

3.9.1.3   Formal cautions

Instead of giving an informal warning, the police may instead decide to issue a formal caution (although, with the changes brought about by the Criminal Justice Act 2003, it is likely that such a decision will now be made by the CPS rather than the police). The giving of formal cautions was originally developed for cases involving juveniles, but can now be used only for adult offenders.

Although records are kept of cautions that are given, a formal caution is not the same as a conviction. If a defendant who has received a caution is later convicted of a separate offence, the caution may be mentioned to the court when the court is considering what sentence to pass. In reality this rarely happens, although a caution given for the same kind of offence as the offence to be sentenced will normally be cited.

Cautions are usually given in the police station by a police officer with at least the rank of inspector. The offender must sign a form acknowledging that he agrees to the caution and that he admits the offence for which the caution is being given. Before a caution is given, three conditions must be satisfied:

(a)   sufficient evidence must have been collected to have justified a prosecution;

(b)   the offender must admit that he is guilty of the offence; and

(c)   the offender must agree to being cautioned, having been made aware that the caution might be raised in court were he to be convicted of a later offence.

The types of offender who are most likely to receive cautions are:

(a)   the elderly;

(b)   the infirm;

(c)   those suffering from severe physical illness;

(d)   those suffering from some form of mental illness or impairment, particularly if the strain of the proceedings would cause this to worsen; and

(e)   those showing signs of severe emotional distress.

Offenders are unlikely to receive more than one caution. Usually an offender with a caution on his record will be charged if he commits a further offence.

A solicitor should only ever advise a client to accept a caution if the client admits his guilt and the solicitor considers that the evidence against the client would be sufficient to result in a conviction if the client were prosecuted. A client should not accept a caution as a matter of convenience.

3.9.1.4   Conditional cautions

One of the principal goals of the Criminal Justice Act 2003 is to achieve 'restorative justice'. This is best described as bringing offenders and their victims into some form of contact, with a view to an agreement being reached as to what the offender should do to make reparation for the crime he has committed. The intention is to make an offender appreciate the effect his crime has had upon his victim, and to improve victim satisfaction with the criminal justice process. Conditional cautions must be seen against this backdrop.

Conditional cautions do not replace the system of police cautioning detailed at **3.9.1.3** above. However, in contrast to formal cautions, they have a statutory basis and may be given only with the approval of the CPS.

Under s 22 of the Criminal Justice Act 2003, a conditional caution can be given to a person aged 18 or over, provided that the five requirements set out in s 22(3) of the Act (see below) are satisfied. The conditions that are imposed must have as their objective either or both of the following:

(a)   facilitating the rehabilitation of the offender;

(b)   ensuring that the offender makes reparation for the offence.

In the Police and Justice Bill currently before Parliament, an additional objective is proposed, namely, the punishment of the offender.

The five requirements that must be satisfied before a conditional caution may be given are:

(a)   there must be evidence that the offender has committed an offence;

(b)   the relevant prosecutor (usually the CPS) must decide that there is sufficient evidence to charge the offender with the offence, and that a conditional caution should be given to the offender in respect of that offence;

(c)   the offender must admit that he committed the offence;

(d)   the effect of the conditional caution must be explained to the offender, and he must be warned that any failure to comply with any of the conditions attached to the caution may result in his being prosecuted for the offence itself; and

(e)   the offender must sign a document containing the details of the offence, an admission that he committed the offence, his consent to a conditional caution and the conditions attached to the caution (Criminal Justice Act 2003, s 22(3)).

Section 25 of the Criminal Justice Act 2003 provides that if an offender fails 'without reasonable excuse' to comply with any conditions attached to the caution, he may be arrested and prosecuted for the original offence and the document he has signed may be used in evidence against him (ie, as evidence that he has admits having committed the offence).

The conditions that are likely to be attached to cautions will be geared either towards *rehabilitating* the offender, or towards the offender making *reparation* to his victim. The former may include, for example, a condition that the offender takes part in an anger management course, receives treatment for drug or alcohol dependency (such as joining Alcoholics Anonymous), or attends driver rectification classes. The latter may include paying financial compensation to the victim, restoring to the victim stolen goods, or making good damage caused to property (such as cleaning off graffiti). Changes proposed by the Police and Justice Bill would also permit the police to impose a condition that the offender pay a financial penalty, or that the offender attend at a specified place at specified times. Any financial penalty would be either one-quarter of the maximum fine the magistrates could impose for the offence or £500, whichever is lower.

Conditional cautions are effectively a form of sentencing without the involvement of the court, and are very similar to the generic community order which a court may impose on a defendant following conviction (see **Chapter 11**).

As with formal cautions, a solicitor should only ever advise a client to accept a conditional caution if the client admits his guilt and the solicitor considers that the evidence against the client would be sufficient to result in a conviction if the client were prosecuted. A client should not accept a conditional caution as a matter of convenience.

3.9.2 Suspects aged 17 and under

3.9.2.1 Reprimands and final warnings

Before a defendant aged 17 or under ever comes before a Youth Court (see **Chapter 14**), it is likely that he will have been through the formal system of reprimands and warnings created by ss 65 and 66 of the Crime and Disorder Act 1998. Reprimands and final warnings are the equivalent of police cautions for adult offenders (see **3.9.1.3** above). They may be given both to juveniles (ie, offenders aged 16 and under) and to offenders aged 17.

Reprimands and final warnings are not court orders and can be given only by the police. They can, however, be referred to in court when the court is being given details of a defendant's antecedents.

An offender is likely to receive a reprimand or final warning from the police when the following conditions are satisfied:

(a)   there is sufficient evidence against the offender to provide a realistic prospect of conviction;

(b)   the offender admits to having committed the offence;

(c)   the offender has no previous convictions; and

(d)   it would not be in the public interest to prosecute the offender.

The police must also take into account the seriousness of the offence when deciding whether to administer a reprimand or final warning, or whether to charge the offender. In determining the seriousness of the offence, the police will use a guidance document prepared by the Association of Chief Police Officers (ACPO), entitled 'Final Warning Scheme: Guidance for the Police and Youth Offending Teams'. The guidance operates by giving each criminal offence a 'gravity score' and then suggesting what the most appropriate course of action is for the police depending on the score for the offence(s) the offender has committed. The gravity score may be raised or lowered depending on the presence of any aggravating or mitigating factors. The guidance can be found on the Home Office website (www.homeoffice.gov.uk).

If an offence is suitable for a reprimand or final warning, the police will start by administering a reprimand to the offender. A reprimand may be given only if the offender has not previously been reprimanded or given a final warning. If an offender has received a reprimand and then offends again, he may be likely to receive a final warning instead of being charged with the offence. An offender who has received a final warning cannot receive another final warning in respect of any further offence unless more than two years have elapsed since the previous warning *and* the further offence is not sufficiently serious as to require a charge to be brought. Such an offender must be charged with the offence.

Reprimands and final warnings can be given by the police only when an offender admits his guilt. A Youth Court may take them into account when deciding whether to grant bail to a defendant, or when sentencing a defendant (see **Chapter 14**). A defendant who is convicted of a further offence within two years of receiving a final warning cannot be given a conditional discharge by the Youth Court unless exceptional circumstances exist.

3.9.2.2 What is the effect of a final warning or reprimand?

A solicitor advising a client at the police station needs to identify the circumstances when the client may be eligible to receive a reprimand or final warning, and to be able to advise the client on the consequences of accepting a reprimand or a final warning. The solicitor must also ensure that he does not persuade the client to agree to a reprimand or a final warning when the client is adamant that he did not commit the offence. A client should not be permitted to admit to something he has not done simply because this may appear to be the easiest short-term option.

The advantages of a client accepting a reprimand or final warning are that:

(a)   this avoids the client being charged with the offence and having to appear before the Youth Court; and

(b)   a reprimand or final warning is not a criminal conviction (which may be important when the client is completing a future job application).

There are, however, consequences of accepting a reprimand or final warning which must be pointed out to the client:

(a)   A record of the reprimand or final warning will be retained until the offender is 18 or for a period of five years, whichever is the longer (this includes fingerprints, photographs and any DNA samples taken).

(b)   If a final warning is given, the police must refer the client to the Youth Offending Team, who will then assess him and probably require him to take part in some form of programme (this is very similar to a 'referral order' – see **Chapter 14**).

(c)   Although a reprimand or final warning will not generally need to be disclosed when making a future job application, it may need to be disclosed if the juvenile wishes to enter a profession (eg, law, teaching or medicine).

(d)   A juvenile who accepts a reprimand or final warning will lose the option of having a further offence dealt with in this way should he reoffend (unless he does not reoffend for at least two years *and* the further offence is not sufficiently serious as to require a charge to be brought – see **3.9.2.1** above).

3.10 Commencing a case other than by charge

For some summary only offences (particularly relatively minor road traffic offences such as careless driving), a suspect may not have been arrested by the police and may not even have needed to attend the police station. An alternative method of commencing criminal proceedings exists for such offences.

Prior to the enactment of the Criminal Justice Act 2003, in such cases the police would 'lay an information' (ie, supply written details of the case) before the magistrates' court, and the court would then issue a summons requiring the defendant to attend court at a particular time on a particular day. The 2003 Act has put in place new arrangements for commencing prosecutions in this type of case. Under these arrangements, a prosecutor (ie, the police or the CPS) will send to the person a document called a 'written charge', which charges that person with the offence (Criminal Justice Act 2003, s 29(1)). The prosecutor must also send the person charged a document called a 'requisition', requiring that person to appear before a magistrates' court at a given time and place to answer the charge (Criminal Justice Act 2003, s 29(2)).

3.11 Flowchart – procedure at the police station

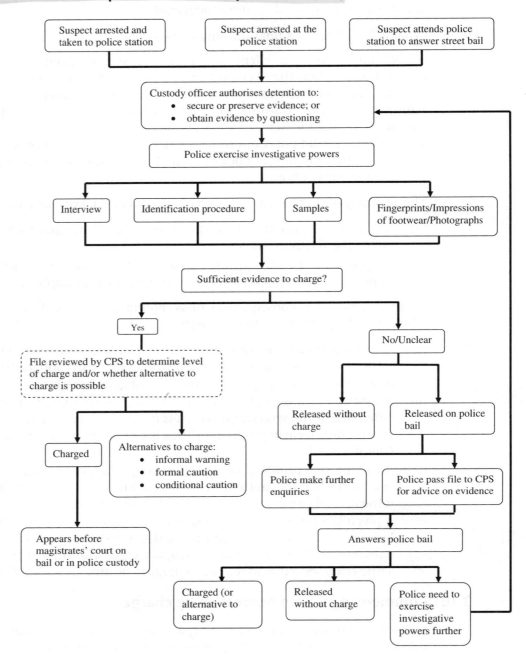

3.12 Checklist

At the end of this chapter you should be able to explain:

- the procedure which takes place when a suspect who has been arrested arrives at the police station, and the role played by the custody officer at this stage (PACE 1984, s 37);
- the powers of detention which the police may exercise (PACE 1984, ss 41–44);
- the rights of a suspect who has been arrested and detained at the police station, and the power the police have to delay the exercise of those rights (PACE 1984, ss 56 and 58);
- the conditions in which a suspect should be held whilst detained at the police station (PACE 1984, Code C);
- the investigative powers which the police may exercise in respect of a suspect who has been arrested and detained at the police station:
  — interviewing the suspect,
  — requiring the suspect to take part in an identification procedure,
  — taking fingerprints or impressions of footwear from the suspect,
  — taking intimate or non-intimate samples from the suspect,
  — taking photographs of the suspect.
- the manner in which the police should conduct an interview with the suspect (PACE 1984, Code C);
- when an identification procedure should be held, and the different types of identification procedure which the police may use (PACE 1984, Code D);
- the additional matters which must be taken into account by the police when a suspect who falls into a special category has been arrested and detained at the police station;
- the procedure for charging a suspect with having committed a criminal offence (including the role played by the CPS), and the alternatives to charging the suspect;
- the power of the police to refuse to grant bail to a suspect who has been charged with a criminal offence (PACE 1984, s 38) and the conditions which may be attached to any bail that is granted (Bail Act, s 3A);
- the importance of the police complying with the requirements of the Codes of Practice when exercising their investigative powers inside the police station.

Chapter 4

The Role of the Solicitor at the Police Station

4.1 Introduction

A suspect who has been arrested and detained at the police station is entitled to free legal advice and to be represented by a solicitor (PACE 1984, s 58). Representing a client at the police station is highly pressurised work. The client will often be in an agitated or emotional state, and the solicitor will be required to give advice (often on the basis of limited information) which may have significant evidential consequences when the client's case comes to trial.

The role which a solicitor plays at the police station is clearly set out in para 6D of the Notes for Guidance to Code C (the Code of Practice for the Detention, Treatment and Questioning of Persons by Police Officers). This states:

> The solicitor's *only* role in the police station is to *protect and advance* the legal rights of their client. On occasions this may require the solicitor to give advice which has the effect of the client avoiding giving evidence which strengthens the prosecution case. . . . (emphasis added)

Protecting and advancing the legal rights of clients may bring a solicitor into conflict with the police, who are likely to view the solicitor's attendance at the police station as at best a nuisance which gets in the way of their investigation.

This chapter *must* be read in conjunction with **Chapter 18**, which deals with the evidential implications of a client exercising his right to remain silent when interviewed at the police station.

4.2 Preparation for attending the police station

4.2.1 The initial telephone contact

4.2.1.1 To whom will the solicitor speak?

A solicitor may be required to attend the police station at any time of the day or night (particularly if the solicitor is a member of the duty solicitor scheme – see **Chapter 3**). The solicitor will usually be telephoned by the custody officer at the police station to say that a suspect who has been arrested wants the solicitor to attend the police station to represent him. The custody officer is unlikely to provide any details of the case against the client at this stage, other than to confirm the client's name and the offence he is alleged to have committed.

After speaking to the custody officer, the solicitor should speak to the client. The solicitor will need to identify himself (if he has not represented the client on a previous occasion), ask the client to confirm that he wants the solicitor to come to the police station to represent him, and remind the client that any advice given will be free. The solicitor will also need to give some brief initial advice to the client. Although the telephone conversation should be private, the solicitor should not assume that the conversation will be completely confidential, and the client should therefore be advised to confine himself to 'Yes/No' answers in response to any questions from the solicitor. The solicitor should not allow the client to give his detailed version of events in case the client can be overheard by the police. The solicitor will need to tell client:

(a)   when he will attend the police station and what he will do when he does attend;

(b)   not to talk to anyone about the case; and

(c)   in the solicitor's absence, not to agree to be interviewed, not to sign anything, not to give any samples and not to take part in an identification procedure.

4.2.1.2   The attendance kit

Solicitors who attend the police station on a regular basis will have a standard 'kit' of materials which they take with them whenever required to attend the police station. This kit will normally include a pro forma on which to record the client's instructions, together with an up-to-date copy of PACE 1984 and the Codes of Practice. What happens at the police station can have major repercussions later in the case, and it is therefore vital that the solicitor records everything of significance that happens whilst he is at police station. An example of a standard police station attendance pro forma is set out at **4.11** below.

4.2.2   When must the solicitor attend the police station?

A solicitor is not obliged to attend the police station immediately after the initial telephone contact, even if the client has insisted that the solicitor attends straight away. If, for example, the client is drunk and the custody officer tells the solicitor that the investigating officer is not proposing to take any further steps until the client has sobered up and is ready for interview, the solicitor need not usually attend until the police notify him that they are ready to interview the client. The solicitor must attend the police station straight away, however, in the following situations:

(a)   the offence is a serious one;

(b)   the police intend to carry out an interview or other investigative procedure (such as taking samples or conducting an identification procedure) straight away;

(c)   the client is vulnerable (eg, a juvenile or a client with mental problems);

(d)   the client complains that he has been mistreated by the police;

(e)   the solicitor needs to make representations about the client's detention and he cannot do this effectively over the telephone; or

(f)   the client needs to speak to the solicitor in confidence.

In deciding whether it is necessary to attend the police station straight away, the solicitor should *not* take into account the fact that:

(a)   the client insists the solicitor attends (unless any of the above factors is present);

(b)   this may be inconvenient for the solicitor;

(c)   the client has experience of police detention or questioning, or the client reassures the solicitor that he can cope on his own.

4.2.3   Other steps the solicitor needs to take

If the solicitor does not need to attend the police station immediately, there are two other steps which he may usefully take in preparation for his later attendance, as noted below.

4.2.3.1   Check the law

The solicitor will know the offence(s) which the client has been arrested on suspicion of having committed from his conversation with the custody officer. The solicitor should check the legal elements of each offence so that he is aware of what will need to be proved to secure a conviction against the client. This may be relevant when the solicitor is assessing the strength of the police case and advising the client on his strategy in interview.

4.2.3.2   Check old files

If the solicitor (or his firm) has represented the client in previous criminal proceedings, the solicitor should check the outcome of such proceedings to see if the client has any previous convictions and, if so, whether these are for the same type of offence that the police are currently investigating. This may be relevant if the police choose to question the client about such convictions. The old files may also reveal whether the client is under any form of disability or mental impairment which makes him 'vulnerable' and which may in turn affect the advice the solicitor will give as to whether the client should answer questions in interview.

4.3   Information gathering on arrival at the police station

4.3.1   The custody officer

On arrival at the police station the first person the solicitor is likely to speak to is the custody officer. Although the custody officer is not involved in the investigation of the offence, he will be able to supply the solicitor with much basic information about the circumstances of the client's detention in police custody. In particular, the custody officer should allow the solicitor to view the custody record and detention log (Code C, para 2.4) in which the custody officer will have recorded all the significant events which have occurred since the client arrived at the police station (see **Chapter 3**). The solicitor should use the custody record to obtain (or confirm) his client's basic details (name, address, date of birth, etc), unless he already has this information. The solicitor then needs to obtain (or confirm) the following additional details from the custody officer and/or the custody record:

(a)   the alleged offence(s) for which the client has been arrested;

(b)   the time at which the custody officer authorised the client's detention and the reason such authorisation was given (ie, was detention authorised to obtain or preserve evidence, or to obtain such evidence by questioning?);

(c)   any significant comments made by the client whilst at the police station (for example, an admission of guilt);

(d) any samples, fingerprints or impressions of footwear which may already have been taken from the client (see **3.5.4** and **3.5.5**);

(e) any identification procedure which may already have taken place (see **3.5.3**);

(f) any interview which may already have taken place at the police station (if, for example, the client has decided to obtain legal advice only after already having been interviewed by the police);

(g) whether the client is under any form of physical or mental disability, or requires the attendance of an appropriate adult (see **3.6**);

(h) any illness which the client may be suffering from, or any indication that the client is in any way vulnerable or requires medical treatment (or details of any medical treatment which the client has already received whilst at the police station). Similarly, the solicitor should find out if the client is suffering from the effects of drink and/or drugs;

(i) any significant items found as a result of a search either of the client's person, or of any premises owned, used or occupied by the client or premises where the client was arrested (for example, items it is alleged the client has stolen or used in the commission of the offence); and

(j) if the client has already been at the police station for six hours or more, details of any detention reviews which have been carried out and the reason why the client's continued detention has been authorised (see **3.3.4.5**).

4.3.2 The investigating officer

Once the solicitor has obtained some basic details about the circumstances of the client's detention, he will then need to speak to the officer who is dealing with the case. The purpose of speaking to the investigating officer is to obtain the following information:

(a) the facts of the offence;

(b) disclosure;

(c) significant statements; and

(d) the next steps the investigation officer proposes to take.

4.3.2.1 The facts of the offence

The solicitor needs to know what his client is alleged to have done which constitutes a criminal offence.

4.3.2.2 Disclosure

Although the police are not obliged to provide the solicitor with any details of the case against the client, they will normally provide the solicitor with some (if not all) of the evidence they have. The investigating officer will summarise orally the contents of the witness statements which he has obtained, allow the solicitor to view copies of such statements or supply the solicitor with a typed disclosure statement summarising the evidence which the police have. The last form of disclosure is the more common method now used by the police. The solicitor should push the investigating officer to disclose as much information as possible about the case against his client. He should try to find out if the police have any other evidence in addition to statements from witnesses. The police may, for example, have obtained samples or fingerprints, the suspect may have been caught committing the offence on CCTV, or there may be an item of documentary or real evidence (such as a weapon it is alleged the suspect used, or drugs found on the suspect's person). If the investigating officer refuses to make any disclosure, or discloses only a very limited amount of information, the solicitor should point out to him that in those circumstances the solicitor cannot properly advise his client as to the nature of the case against him and will only be able to advise his client to give a 'no comment' interview (see **4.4.3** below). In such a situation the solicitor could usefully employ the 'DEAL' technique to persuade the officer to give proper disclosure by:

(a)   Describing the offending behaviour – telling the officer that he is making insufficient disclosure of the case against the client;

(b)   Explaining why it offends – insufficient disclosure means that the solicitor will be unable properly to advise his client;

(c)   Asking the officer to refrain from the offending behaviour – asking the officer to make proper disclosure;

(d)   Letting the officer know what will happen if he refuses to refrain from such behaviour – the solicitor will advise the client to give a 'no comment' interview, state the reason for this during the interview and request that the officer's refusal to disclose details of the case against the client be noted in the custody record. The solicitor will also tell the officer that he will make a record of the officer's refusal to give disclosure of the case against his client in the solicitor's police station attendance log.

Example

Vincent is arrested on suspicion of burglary and is detained at the police station for questioning. Vincent's solicitor attends the police station and seeks disclosure of the police case from PC Thomas, the investigating officer. PC Thomas refuses to disclose any details of the police case, telling the solicitor that the police case will be put in full to Vincent in interview. The solicitor would respond as follows:

'Officer, whilst I appreciate that you are under no legal obligation to disclose to me the evidence you have obtained against my client, if I am to advise my client properly I need to know what the case against my client is. I would ask you to reconsider your decision. If you are unwilling to provide me with such details, I will have no alternative other than to advise my client to give a "no comment" interview and not to answer any questions you might put to him. I will also state during the interview the reasons I have given this advice, and insist that your refusal to provide me with any details of the case against my client is recorded in the custody record. I will also make a written record of your refusal to supply these details.'

4.3.2.3   Significant statements

The solicitor needs to find out if, prior to his arrival at the police station, the client has made any significant statement (or if there has been a significant silence) that is likely to be put to the client in interview (see **3.5.2.3**). The client may, for example, have made an admission on arrest which the police will wish to put to him at the start of the interview.

4.3.2.4   The next steps which the investigating officer proposes to take

The solicitor needs to find out from the investigating officer what his intentions are. For example, is the client going to be interviewed straight away, or will the police require the client to take part in an identification procedure, or to provide fingerprints or samples?

4.3.3   The client

The solicitor should speak to his client only once he has obtained as much information as he can about the case from the custody officer and the investigating officer. The solicitor needs to discuss the following matters with his client:

(a)   *The solicitor's identity and role.* Unless the solicitor has represented the client previously, this is likely to be the first meeting between the solicitor and the client. Although the solicitor may have already spoken to the client on the telephone (see **4.2.1** above), this is likely to have been several hours earlier and the client is unlikely to recall much of what the solicitor said. Furthermore, the client may be in a vulnerable emotional state and may not fully understand who the solicitor is and what his role is at the police station. The solicitor needs to make it clear to the client that he is there to provide the client with free independent legal advice and that he has no connection with the police. The solicitor should point out to the client that his only role at the police station will be to protect and advance the client's legal rights. The solicitor must also tell the client that anything he is told by the client will remain confidential (even after the solicitor has stopped acting for him), although the solicitor is bound by certain rules of professional conduct which in certain circumstances may limit what he is able to do or say on the client's behalf (see **4.3.4** below).

(b)   *Details of the alleged offence.* The solicitor should give the client details of what he has been told by the investigating officer about the offence the client is alleged to have committed. The level of information the solicitor can give to the client will depend upon the level of disclosure given by the police (see **4.3.2.2** above), but it is important that the client has a clear picture of what the solicitor has been told. As part of telling the client about the police case, the solicitor should also advise the client about the relevant substantive law. In particular, the solicitor should advise the client as to what the police will need to prove in order to obtain a conviction for the offence for which the client has been arrested.

(c)   *The client's instructions.* Once the client knows what the police case against him is, the solicitor should then get the client's version of events. Given the pressures of time that exist at the police station, it may not be possible for the solicitor to obtain a full proof of evidence from the client. The solicitor should, however, try to take detailed instructions from the client. Any advice which the solicitor subsequently gives to the client will be based on this information, and it is therefore important that the solicitor takes as full instructions as time permits.

(d)   *The next step in the police investigation.* The client may already have been detained at the police station for several hours and be anxious to know what the police intend to do. The solicitor needs to advise the client as to what the next step in the police investigation will be. In the majority of cases, the next step will be for the police to require the client to take part in an audio recorded interview.

(e)   *Prepare the client for interview.* This involves:

  (i)   advising the client on whether or not to answer questions put to him in the interview (ie, advising the client what is the 'safest option' in the interview – see **4.4.6** below);

  (ii)   preparing a written statement on the client's behalf if the client is to give a 'no comment' interview, but hand the statement to the police so that his defence is put 'on record' (see **4.4.5** below);

  (iii) advising the client how the interview will be conducted by the police (see **4.5** below); and

  (iv)   advising the client what role the solicitor will play in the interview (see **4.5** below).

4.3.4 Conduct issues

4.3.4.1 The client who admits his guilt

A solicitor may take instructions from a client who confirms that he has in fact committed the offence for which he has been arrested, but who wants to deny the offence when interviewed by the police. If the client admits his guilt to his solicitor, the solicitor must advise the client that he cannot then attend an interview to represent the client if the client intends to deny having committed the offence. The solicitor cannot be a party to the client giving information to the police which the solicitor knows to be false since this would amount to a breach of the solicitor's duty not to mislead the court (see **1.6.2**). The solicitor could attend an interview where the client intends to give a 'no comment' response to police questions, since this would not involve the giving of false information.

If the client insists on giving false information in interview, the solicitor should decline to act any further on the client's behalf. As the solicitor owes an ongoing duty of confidentiality to the client, the police should not be told why the solicitor is no longer acting on the client's behalf. It is usual in such a case for a solicitor to say that he is withdrawing from the case for 'professional reasons'.

A solicitor representing a client who intends to lie to the police in interview should attempt to dissuade the client from doing so. It is appropriate for the solicitor to advise the client that, if he admits his guilt in the interview, he will receive credit from the court for cooperating with the police when he is later sentenced (see **Chapter 11**).

4.3.4.2 Conflicts of interest

When may a conflict arise?

A solicitor will often be asked to advise two (or more) individuals at the police station who are jointly suspected of having committed an offence. Although a solicitor is permitted to act for two or more suspects where there is no conflict of interest, the difficulty faced by a solicitor at the police station is spotting when a potential conflict of interest may arise. On arrival at the police station the solicitor will know little more than the names of the clients and the offence for which they have been arrested. Until the solicitor knows what the police version of events is (and what version of events his potential clients are giving), he is not going to know whether there is an actual or potential conflict of interest. It is the responsibility of the solicitor to determine whether a conflict of interest exists. If the custody officer suggests to the solicitor that there is a conflict, the solicitor should ask the officer to clarify why he considers this to be the case, but stress to the officer that ultimately it is the decision of the solicitor alone as to whether a conflict exists and not that of the police (Code C, Notes for Guidance, para 6G).

Steps the solicitor should take

Once he has spoken to the investigating officer, the solicitor should speak to one of the suspects (usually the first suspect to have requested the solicitor's attendance at the police station). If that suspect's account suggests a clear conflict of interest (if, for example, the suspect denies guilt and accuses the other suspect of having committed the offence), the solicitor should decline to act for the second suspect and inform the police that he should receive separate legal advice. Even if there is no obvious conflict of interest, the solicitor should be alert to a potential conflict of interest arising later in the case. This could occur, for example, if both suspects admit the offence but, when the case comes to court, the mitigation for one of the suspects is going to be that he played only a minor role in the commission of the offence and that the larger role was played by the other suspect.

If, after speaking to the first suspect, the solicitor considers there is any risk of a conflict of interest developing, he should decline to see the second suspect and tell the police that this suspect must get legal advice elsewhere. If a conflict of interest emerges only after the solicitor has seen both suspects, the appropriate course of action is for the solicitor to withdraw from the case completely. To continue acting for both suspects would be a clear conflict of interest, and it would be inappropriate to continue to act for only one of the suspects because the solicitor would be in possession of confidential information about the other suspect. Only if the solicitor could act for one suspect without breaching his duty of confidentiality to the other suspect could he continue to act for that suspect. This is unlikely ever to be the case.

Detailed advice for solicitors asked to represent more than one client at the police station is contained in *The Law Society's Code of Conduct* (2004) in the guidance notes to Rule 3 (conflicts of interest).

Should a solicitor disclose to one client information he has been given by another client?

If a solicitor decides that there is no conflict of interest and he is able to represent both suspects, he must still not disclose to one client anything he has been told by the other (in order to comply with his duty of confidentiality), unless:

(a)   he has obtained the other client's consent (preferably in writing) to disclose this information;

(b)   both clients are putting forward the same defence; and

(c)   he considers it in his client's best interests for the information to be disclosed.

If the client is a juvenile, the client would need to provide written authority for the solicitor to disclose any information, and such authority must be given in the presence of the appropriate adult.

Even if the above considerations are satisfied, the solicitor must also have regard to his overriding duty not to mislead the court. Co-accused who are represented by the same solicitor may attempt to use that solicitor to pass information between each other so that they can jointly fabricate a defence and give the police a consistent 'story'. To guard against this, the solicitor should ensure that before telling the second client what he has been told by the first client, he obtains an account of the second client's version of events. If this is consistent with the account given by the first client, the solicitor will be able to pass on the relevant information. If, however, the stories are inconsistent, the solicitor will need to withdraw from the case. It would be inappropriate for the solicitor to continue to act for just one of the clients because he would be in possession of confidential information about the other.

4.3.4.3   Disclosing the client's case to a third party

A solicitor representing a client at the police station may be asked for details of his client's defence by another solicitor representing a co-accused who has been arrested in connection with the same matter. Such a request should be treated with caution. The solicitor owes a duty of confidentiality to his client and should therefore not respond to such a request by releasing any such information. The only exception to this is if the solicitor considers it is in the client's best interests for such information to be disclosed. This will only very rarely be the case. If the solicitor does consider that it would be in the client's interests to disclose this information, the solicitor should explain his reasoning to the client and obtain the client's express instructions (ideally in writing) to disclose the information.

4.3.4.4   The appropriate adult

If an appropriate adult is required, the solicitor must ensure that the appropriate adult understands what his role is, that he is not present simply as an observer and that he is *not* at the police station to assist the police.

Issues of professional conduct may arise when an appropriate adult attends the police station to assist a juvenile or a mentally disordered suspect. Some common issues which may arise are as follows.

A conflict in instructions between the appropriate adult and the detained person

It will often be the case that a detainee wishes to pursue one course of action whilst the appropriate adult wants him to do something else.

Example

Jacob is aged 15 and has been arrested on suspicion of theft. He asks for legal advice from a solicitor and his father is also called to the police station as the appropriate adult. Jacob admits to his solicitor that he committed the theft, but the solicitor considers that the police have insufficient evidence to prove the allegation. The solicitor therefore advises Jacob to remain silent in interview. Jacob's father is unhappy about this and instructs the solicitor that Jacob must tell the truth.

In this situation the solicitor's client is the person under arrest, not the appropriate adult. The solicitor's duty is to act in the client's best interests. The solicitor would attempt to explain to the appropriate adult why it would be in the best interests of the person under arrest to follow his advice.

The duty of confidentiality

Appropriate adults do not owe the suspect a duty of confidentiality. In the example given above, Jacob's father could therefore tell the police what Jacob had said. He would also be able to give evidence for the prosecution at Jacob's trial, repeating what Jacob had said. The solicitor could ask the appropriate adult, prior to the solicitor giving advice, if the appropriate adult is willing to be bound by confidentiality during the consultation (and to confirm this in writing). If the appropriate adult agrees to this, there is nothing to prevent the appropriate adult changing his mind and disclosing such information to the police. If the appropriate adult refuses to be bound by confidentiality, the solicitor should tell the police that he objects to that person continuing to act as the appropriate adult.

Legal professional privilege

Even if the appropriate adult agrees to treat the consultation as being confidential, since legal professional privilege does not apply to appropriate adults, there is nothing to prevent the prosecution from calling the appropriate adult to give evidence at trial as to what was said during the consultation.

To circumvent these potential problems, para 1E of the Notes for Guidance to Code C provides that a suspect should always be given the opportunity to consult privately with a solicitor in the absence of the appropriate adult (if the appropriate adult is a social worker, it is standard practice for social workers not to sit in on the consultation, so such problems do not arise). A solicitor attending the police station will usually ask the suspect whether he wants the appropriate adult to attend any consultation prior to the consultation starting. If the suspect indicates that he does want the appropriate adult to be present, the solicitor will then ask the appropriate adult if he is prepared to treat the consultation as confidential. If the appropriate adult is not prepared to agree to this, the solicitor should suggest to the suspect that he reconsider his decision to have the appropriate adult present at the consultation. If the appropriate adult is prepared to treat the consultation as confidential, the solicitor should ask him to sign something to this effect. Ultimately, it is the decision of the suspect as to whether he wants the appropriate adult to attend the consultation with his solicitor.

4.3.4.5 Withdrawing from acting

If, for reasons of professional conduct, a solicitor is unable to continue acting for a client (or clients) at the police station, the solicitor needs to do the following:

(a)   explain to the client why he is no longer able to represent him;

(b)   tell the client that he is entitled to free legal advice from another solicitor of his choice or the duty solicitor;

(c)   tell the client that, although he is no longer able to represent him, the solicitor owes to the client an ongoing duty of confidentiality and will not therefore tell the police why he is unable to act; and

(d)   tell the custody officer that he is no longer able to act, but not disclose the reason why.

4.4 Should the suspect answer questions in interview?

4.4.1 Introduction

The usual ground upon which the custody officer will authorise the detention of a suspect at the police station under s 37 of PACE 1984 is to enable the investigating officer to obtain evidence by questioning the suspect in an audio recorded interview. The reason for the police wanting to interview a suspect is their hope that the suspect will 'crack' and say something incriminating when put under the pressure of an interview situation. Most suspects who are interviewed by the police end up either making an admission of guilt or contradicting themselves, so that their account of the case is shown to lack credibility when the interview is either played or read out to the court at trial (see **Chapter 9**). The most important role the solicitor has at the police station is to advise his client whether or not to answer questions in police interview. A client whom the police wish to interview has four options:

(a)   to answer all the questions put to him;

(b)   to give a 'no comment interview';

(c)   to give a 'mixed interview', where he answers some questions but not others;

(d)   to give a 'no comment interview', but either during the interview or before being charged hand a written statement to the police setting out facts he will rely upon in his defence at trial.

Each of these options will be examined in turn below. Whilst the final decision as to which option to take is that of the client, the client is likely to follow the advice received from his solicitor. It is therefore vital that the solicitor makes an accurate note of the advice given to the client, and the reasons for giving such advice.

In certain serious fraud investigations, provisions in the Serious Organised Crime and Police Act 2005 effectively enable the police to compel potential suspects to answer questions, since refusal to answer will in itself be a criminal offence. The details of this are beyond the scope of this book.

4.4.2 Answer all questions

4.4.2.1 Advantages

The advantage of a client answering all questions in interview is that this allows the client to put his version of events on record straight away. This can be particularly important if the client is raising a specific defence which imposes an evidential burden on him, such as self-defence or the defence of alibi (see **Chapter 16**). If the client's defence is particularly strong and the client comes across well when interviewed, answering questions in full may even result in the police deciding not to pursue the case any further if they accept the truth of the client's version of events. Even if the client is subsequently charged by the police, the credibility of his evidence at trial will be boosted if he can show that he placed his defence on record at the earliest opportunity, and has told a consistent 'story' throughout.

Answering all the questions put by the police is also likely to ensure that at trial the court or jury will not be permitted to draw adverse inferences against the client under ss 34, 36 or 37 of the Criminal Justice and Public Order Act (CJPOA) 1994 (see **Chapter 18** and **4.4.3** below).

If the client is admitting his guilt, it may also be sensible to answer questions in interview to confirm this. This will enable the client's solicitor to say in mitigation, when the client later comes to be sentenced at court, that his client cooperated with police from the first opportunity and that, by making a prompt admission of guilt at the police station, the client saved the police from having to spend additional time and resources investigating the offence.

4.4.2.2 Disadvantages

The disadvantage in answering questions put by the police in interview is that many suspects will either say something incriminating or make comments which undermine their credibility. Police officers are particularly adept at 'tripping up' suspects in interview, and it is very easy for a suspect to become flustered, confused or angry, particularly if he is in an emotional condition. Suspects in such a state may be led into admitting their involvement in the offence, or into asserting facts which are contradictory or which the police can show to be untrue.

If the suspect is subsequently charged with the offence and pleads not guilty, a transcript of the interview record will be read out at court (or the recording of the interview may be played). A suspect who comes across as being confused or angry, who makes admissions, or who gives a contradictory or implausible account of events is likely to have his credibility severely damaged in the eyes of the jury or magistrates. In reality, suspects who answer questions in police interview normally give the police that missing piece of evidence they are looking for.

Even clients who are able to give their solicitor a clear version of events may be vulnerable to confusion in an interview situation. This is particularly the case with young or immature clients, clients who have not previously been in trouble with the police or clients who the solicitor believes may be emotionally vulnerable.

The solicitor also needs to consider whether the police have provided sufficient disclosure of the evidence which they have obtained in the course of their investigations in order to enable the client to answer all the questions which the police put. A common tactic employed by the police is to hold back from the suspect's solicitor a particular piece of information which is then put to the suspect in interview, hoping to catch him off-guard. If the solicitor does not consider that the police have made a full disclosure of their case, it is a hazardous step for the solicitor then to advise the client to answer questions in police interview. The client is likely to be caught out when the police raise a matter which was not disclosed to his solicitor.

An additional potential problem in the client answering questions is that the line of questioning pursued by the police may lead the client to make an attack on the character of another person. If, for example, the client is alleged to have committed an assault, the police may ask him why the alleged victim of the assault would have made a complaint unless it was true. If, in reply, the client alleges that the victim has fabricated his story because of a pre-existing grudge, this will constitute an attack on the character of the victim. If the client is subsequently prosecuted for the offence, such an attack will enable the CPS to raise in evidence at trial any previous convictions the client may have, either to show that the client has a propensity to commit that particular type of offence or to show that he has a propensity to be untruthful (see **Chapter 22** and **4.5.3.3** below).

4.4.3   Give a 'no comment' interview

4.4.3.1   Advantages

The advantage of a client declining to answer questions in interview (other than to say 'no comment' in reply to each question) is that there is no danger of the client incriminating himself by making any admissions, or inadvertently giving the police a piece of evidence which they would not otherwise have had. If the case against the client is weak and the police are hoping to bolster it by getting the client to say something damaging in interview, giving a 'no comment' interview may mean that the police will not then have sufficient evidence to enable them to charge the client with the offence, and the client is likely to be released without charge.

4.4.3.2   Disadvantages

The disadvantage of a client giving a 'no comment' interview is that, if the client is subsequently charged and pleads not guilty, the magistrates or jury may in certain circumstances draw an adverse inference under ss 34, 36 or 37 of the CJPOA 1994 from the client's silence in interview. The circumstances in which an adverse inference may be drawn are examined fully in **Chapter 18**. In summary, however, if the client fails to answer questions in police interview and then at trial raises a defence the details of which could have been given to the police in interview, the court or jury are entitled to conclude that the defence is a sham and was fabricated by the defendant after he had left the police station, when he had the opportunity to 'get his story straight'.

4.4.3.3   When is a solicitor likely to advise the client to give a 'no comment' interview?

A solicitor is permitted to advise a client who admits his guilt to the solicitor to give a 'no comment' interview. This will be important if the solicitor considers that the case against the client is weak and the police do not currently have sufficient evidence to prove the allegation. A client who answers questions in such a situation may make a damaging admission which will give the police sufficient evidence to charge him. This course of action would not involve the solicitor being a party to the client lying to or misleading the police, and the police may decide not to pursue the case if they are unable to obtain any admissions from the client in interview.

The other occasions on which a solicitor may advise his client to give a 'no comment' interview are if:

(a) he considers that the police have not provided him with full disclosure of the evidence they have obtained against his client (so that the solicitor is unable properly to advise his client on the strength police case against him). Lack of full disclosure from the police creates a real risk that the client may implicate himself if he answers questions in interview. This is a particularly important consideration if a co-accused has also been arrested and interviewed by the police, especially if the police are not prepared to disclose what they consider the role of the co-accused to have been, or if the police are not prepared to disclose what the co-accused has said in interview;

(b) linked to (a), the solicitor considers that the police may attempt to 'ambush' the client during the interview by revealing a piece of evidence which they had not disclosed to the solicitor in advance of the interview (in the hope that, when confronted with this evidence, the client will say something incriminating or be lost for words);

(c) the client denies involvement in the offence and the police do not currently have sufficient evidence to charge the client (since if the client agrees to answer questions in interview he runs the risk of giving the police the additional evidence they need to enable them to charge him);

(d) the client is physically or mentally unfit to be interviewed (if, for example, the client is suffering from the effects of drink or drugs), or the solicitor considers that the client would fail to give a good account of his case in interview because the client is distressed, emotional or fatigued. This is likely to be the case if the interview is to take place late at night, the client has been at the police station for a number of hours before the interview takes place, or the client has been involved in an upsetting incident (often in connection with the alleged offence);

(e) the client is likely to perform badly in interview due to his:

(i) age,

(ii) lack of maturity,

(iii) psychological vulnerability, or

(iv) previous inexperience of police detention and questioning.

If the client is particularly young, he may lack the maturity to answer questions properly or may become aggressive during the interview. Older clients often become easily confused or 'lost' during interviews at the police station. If the client appears particularly agitated or ill at ease, the solicitor may consider that the client is psychologically vulnerable to the questioning techniques the police may employ during the interview. Similar considerations will apply if this is the first time the client has been arrested and he has no previous experience of custody or questioning by the police. A solicitor may also have suspicions that the client could be suffering from some form of mental impairment if the client is behaving strangely, or if the client is unable to give the solicitor coherent instructions;

(f)   the facts of the case are so complex, or relate to matters occurring so long ago, that the client cannot reasonably be expected to provide an immediate response to the allegations made against him, or that any immediate response he is able to give will not be accurate. This may be a particular consideration in a fraud case in which the police want to ask the client about complex financial matters, or in a case involving allegations of physical or sexual abuse carried out many years previously;

(g)   although the client says he did not commit the offence, the client does not have a viable case or defence. If the solicitor considers that the client has no case that will, at that time, stand up to police questioning, the best course of action may be to give a 'no comment' interview, since the client will only come across badly in interview if he attempts to answer questions to which he has no real response; or

(h)   the client has any other good personal reasons for staying silent. A common situation when a client may have a good personal reason for staying silent is if the client would suffer extreme embarrassment if he were to tell the police what actually happened.

Example

Gerry is arrested on suspicion of the burglary of a shop in the early hours of the morning. Gerry instructs his solicitor that he did not commit the burglary and has an alibi. The alibi is that, at the time the burglary is alleged to have occurred, Gerry was at the home of Anthea, with whom he is having an affair. Gerry is married and doesn't want his wife to find out about the affair. If, when interviewed, Gerry tells the police details of his alibi, the police will check it and it is likely that Gerry's wife will find out about the affair. Gerry will have a good personal reason for wanting to remain silent. (In this situation the solicitor would advise Gerry that he would need to balance the risk that his wife might find out about the affair against the greater likelihood of his being convicted if he fails to put forward a defence to the allegation made against him.)

If a client decides to give a 'no comment' interview on the basis of the legal advice he has received, the solicitor must explain to the client that this will not necessarily prevent a court from drawing adverse inferences from this silence at any subsequent trial (see **Chapter 18**). If the solicitor has advised a client to remain silent, he should ensure that he makes a full written note of the reasons for his advising this. Such a record may have important evidential value at trial (see **Chapter 18**).

4.4.4   Give a 'mixed interview'

A solicitor should *not* advise a client to answer some of the questions put by the police but not others. Doing this comes across very badly at trial when the interview transcript is read out or the recording of the interview is played to the court. By answering some questions but not others, it will appear to the magistrates or the jury that the defendant has something to hide and is refusing to reply to those difficult questions for which he has no satisfactory answer.

4.4.5   Hand in a written statement

4.4.5.1   When might a written statement be used?

Handing in a written statement to the police is a useful strategy to employ if the solicitor considers that his client needs to place his version of events on record to avoid an adverse inference being drawn at trial (if, for example, the client has a positive defence such as self-defence or alibi), but the solicitor is concerned that the client may perform badly if he answers questions in interview. This is likely to be the case if the client is young, emotional, or has never previously been arrested and detained at the police station. If the client is to hand in a written statement to the police, the solicitor will advise him to answer 'no comment' to questions put by the police in interview. The written statement will be handed to the police either during the interview, or after the interview but prior to the client being charged.

4.4.5.2 What should the statement contain?

A written statement will be drafted by the solicitor and will allow the client to set out his defence in a clear and logical way. As long as the written statement sets out all the facts which the client later relies upon in his defence at trial, handing in a written statement should avoid the risk of any inferences being drawn at trial under s 34 of the CJPOA 1994 (see **4.4.3.2**), even if the client answers 'no comment' to the questions put to him by the police in interview. In drafting the statement, the solicitor should also take care to cover those matters about which the police might ask the client in interview and which may at trial be the subject of an adverse inference under s 36 or s 37 of the CJPOA 1994 (see **Chapter 18**).

4.4.5.3 When should the statement be handed in to the police?

The written statement can be handed in to the police either during the interview, or just prior to charge. It is normal practice for the statement to be handed in at the start of the interview and for the suspect then to answer 'no comment' to questions put by the police during the interview. If, however, the defence solicitor feels that the police case is particularly weak, it may be better to hold back the handing in of the defence statement until the police have actually decided to charge the client (but before the client is formally charged). Handing in the statement earlier may give the police some additional information, which might lead them to decide to charge the client when otherwise they might not have done so. For example, in the statement the client may make a partial admission which gives the police sufficient evidence to enable them to charge him with the offence.

Example

Julia is arrested on suspicion of burglary of shop premises and is to be interviewed at the police station. Before the interview takes place, Julia's solicitor obtains disclosure of the case against Julia from the investigating officer. The solicitor considers that the police case against Julia is weak and that Julia is unlikely to be charged if she gives a 'no comment' interview. In particular, the police do not have any direct evidence placing Julia at the shop premises at the time of the burglary.

When the solicitor takes instructions from Julia, she tells him that she did not commit the burglary but was outside the shop premises when the burglary took place. Julia's solicitor advises her that if she discloses this fact to the police, this will strengthen the case against her and make it more likely that she will be charged. Julia accepts her solicitor's advice and gives a 'no comment' interview. However, Julia's solicitor also prepares a written statement in Julia's name setting out her defence. The solicitor will not hand this statement in to the police during the interview. If the police do decide to charge Julia, however, the solicitor will hand in the statement before Julia is charged. If the statement contains the facts Julia will later raise in her defence at trial, this will prevent any adverse inferences being drawn.

Very occasionally a solicitor will take a written statement from his client but, rather than hand the statement to the police whilst the client is at the police station, retain the statement on the client's file. This may occur when the solicitor has doubts as to the accuracy of the instructions he has received from his client and is reluctant to disclose the client's defence to the police because he suspects that the facts put forward by the client either will not stand up to scrutiny, or may 'change' later in the case. In such circumstances, the solicitor will retain the statement on his file and produce it at a later stage in the case, if necessary, to prevent the court drawing an inference that the client's defence was fabricated after he had left the police station. Adopting such a tactic will not, however, prevent other adverse inferences being drawn by the court at trial. These could include an inference that the defendant made up his defence prior to interview but was not sufficiently confident to expose it to police questioning, or that he had not thought up all the details of the defence at the time of the police interview.

Example

Paul is arrested on suspicion of assault and is to be interviewed at the police station. Paul tells his solicitor that it is a case of mistaken identity and that he was elsewhere at the time of the assault (although he cannot recall exactly where he was). The identification evidence against Paul is extremely strong and Paul's solicitor doubts that Paul's account will stand up to police scrutiny. The solicitor takes a written statement from Paul who then gives a 'no comment' interview. The solicitor does not hand a copy of the statement to the police but retains the statement on his file.

Scenario 1 – Paul is subsequently charged with assault. Paul's defence at trial is the same as the account he gave to his solicitor at the police station. Paul's solicitor can produce the statement to the court to prevent the court drawing an inference of recent fabrication (that Paul thought up his defence only after he had left the police station). The court will, however, be able to draw the adverse inference that Paul was not sufficiently confident in his defence to expose it to police questioning at the police station.

Scenario 2 – Paul is subsequently charged with assault. Paul changes his version of events and now tells his solicitor that he was present at the time of the assault but claims to have been acting only in self-defence. The solicitor will not use Paul's statement obtained at the police station because the basis of Paul's defence has changed. The court will be able to draw an inference of recent fabrication. However, by not handing in Paul's statement when Paul was originally detained at the police station, Paul's solicitor has avoided the far more damaging situation of Paul saying one thing at the police station and then saying something totally different when his case comes to trial.

4.4.6 Conclusion

Giving the correct advice to a client on whether or not to answer questions in an interview at the police station is one of the hardest tasks a defence solicitor will face, because there are a number of considerations that need to be taken into account. To help solicitors who advise clients at the police station to give the correct advice, The Law Society has produced a 'Safest defence: decision-making template' for solicitors to use at the police station when deciding what advice to give to their clients. A copy of the template is reproduced below. It lists a number of factors which the solicitor should take into account when advising a client on whether to answer questions, and the matters the solicitor should consider when assessing the importance of each factor. The factors are:

(a)   the degree of disclosure given by the police;

(b)   the strength of the prosecution case;

(c)   the age and maturity of the client;

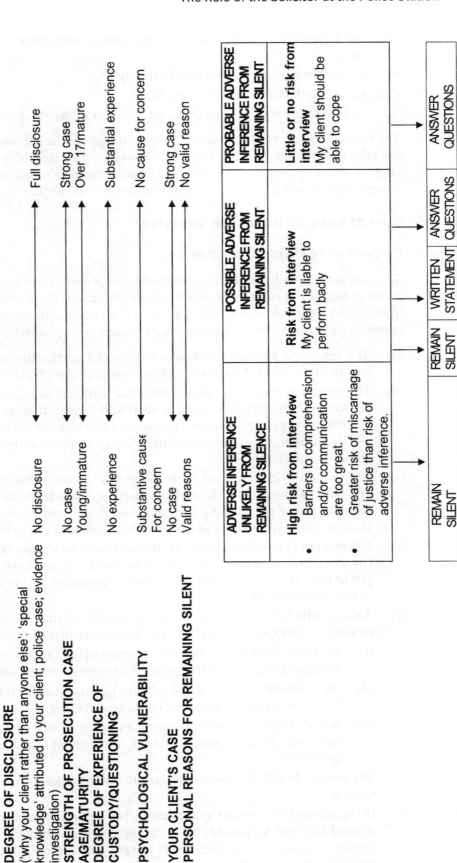

DEGREE OF DISCLOSURE
('why your client rather than anyone else': 'special knowledge' attributed to your client; police case; evidence investigation)

No disclosure → Full disclosure

STRENGTH OF PROSECUTION CASE

No case → Strong case

AGE/MATURITY

Young/immature → Over 17/mature

DEGREE OF EXPERIENCE OF CUSTODY/QUESTIONING

No experience → Substantial experience

PSYCHOLOGICAL VULNERABILITY

Substantive cause
For concern → No cause for concern

YOUR CLIENT'S CASE

No case → Strong case

PERSONAL REASONS FOR REMAINING SILENT

Valid reasons → No valid reason

ADVERSE INFERENCE UNLIKELY FROM REMAINING SILENCE	POSSIBLE ADVERSE INFERENCE FROM REMAINING SILENT		PROBABLE ADVERSE INFERENCE FROM REMAINING SILENT
High risk from interview • Barriers to comprehension and/or communication are too great. • Greater risk of miscarriage of justice than risk of adverse inference.	**Risk from interview** My client is liable to perform badly		**Little or no risk from interview** My client should be able to cope
REMAIN SILENT	REMAIN SILENT	WRITTEN STATEMENT	ANSWER QUESTIONS	ANSWER QUESTIONS

Safest defence: decision-making template

(d)   the degree of experience of police questioning and custody which the client has;

(e)   the psychological vulnerability of the client;

(f)   the strength of the client's case; and

(g)   whether the client has any personal reasons for staying silent.

The template also sets out the most appropriate advice the solicitor should give to his client, dependent on the solicitor's assessment of the risks involved in the client answering questions. A solicitor attending the police station should include a copy of the template as part of his standard attendance kit.

4.5   Role of the solicitor in the interview

4.5.1   Preparing the client for interview

The solicitor needs to explain to his client the procedure to be followed in the audio recorded interview, and to warn the client about the tactics the police are likely to adopt in an attempt to get him to answer questions if he gives a 'no comment' interview. The following points need to be explained to the client:

(a)   The interview will be audio-recorded and all parties (including the client and the solicitor) will be asked to identify themselves on the recording.

(b)   The interview can be stopped at any time if the client requires further legal advice from the solicitor. The client should be told that he can ask for the interview to be stopped for this purpose, or the solicitor may intervene of his own volition to suggest that the interview be stopped so he can give further advice to the client.

(c)   The solicitor will be present in the interview to protect the client's interests, and will intervene in the interview when necessary if the solicitor considers that the police questioning is in any way inappropriate, or if he considers that the client would benefit from further legal advice in private.

(d)   If the client is to remain silent in the interview, he should be advised to use the stock phrase of 'no comment' in answer to all the questions which are put to him. It is easier for clients to answer questions in this way rather than to remain totally silent.

(e)   A client who is to remain silent should be advised that the police will often employ certain tactics to get him to talk. In particular the police may:

(i)   try to get him to talk by asking apparently innocuous questions that have nothing to do with the offence under investigation;

(ii)   try to alienate him from the solicitor by suggesting that the legal advice he has received from his solicitor is incorrect; or

(iii)   warn him that certain consequences may arise (for example, he may be detained at the police station indefinitely) unless he answers questions.

The client should be advised to ignore such tactics and to maintain his silence.

(f)   If the client is to answer questions in the interview, the solicitor should remind him not to 'lose his cool' during the interview, and not to become hostile or abusive in his comments towards the interviewing officer. If the recording of the interview is subsequently played out at his trial, the client is likely to lose credibility in the eyes of the jury or magistrates if he acts in this way. The client should also be warned against making personal attacks on others during the interview. An attack on the character of another person made during the course of an interview may enable to prosecution to adduce evidence of the suspect's previous convictions at his trial.

4.5.2 The interview

4.5.2.1 Seating arrangements

The solicitor should ensure that he is permitted to sit beside his client during the interview and must never allow the police to prevent him from being able to make eye contact with his client. The police will occasionally try to 'distance' the client from his solicitor by asking the solicitor to sit behind him, so that he is unable to make proper eye contact with the client, thereby isolating the client and making him feel more alone and vulnerable in the interview. The client and the solicitor need to be able to make eye contact, both to give the client the psychological support of being reminded that the solicitor is present in the interview and so that the solicitor can detect from the client's facial expressions or gestures if he is becoming fatigued, emotional, confused or frustrated.

4.5.2.2 The solicitor's role

The solicitor will not play a passive role in the interview. It may be necessary for the solicitor to intervene to object to improper questioning, or to give the client further advice (which may entail the interview being stopped if such advice needs to be given in private).

Paragraph 6D of the Notes for Guidance to Code C states:

> ... the solicitor may intervene [in interview] in order to seek clarification, challenge an improper question to their client or the manner in which it is put, advise their client not to reply to particular questions, or if they wish to give their client further legal advice.

A solicitor attending an interview must be particularly vigilant when representing a juvenile or a person under a disability. The solicitor needs to ensure that the officer conducting the interview does not employ questioning techniques which take advantage of the suspect's age or disability.

Paragraph 6D provides that a solicitor may be excluded from the interview only in very limited circumstances when he is deemed to be engaging in 'unacceptable conduct', such as answering questions on behalf of his client or writing down answers for the client to read out (see **4.5.5** below).

4.5.2.3 Opening statement by the solicitor

It is standard practice at the start of the interview for the solicitor to make an opening statement explaining the role which he will play in the interview. This will put the police officer(s) conducting the interview on notice that the solicitor intends to play an active role in the interview, and will also provide an opportunity for the solicitor to state the advice given to the client and the reasons for that advice. A suggested form of wording for the statement is as follows:

> I am [name], a solicitor/accredited or probationary representative with [firm name]. I am now required to explain my role. My role is to advance and protect my client's rights. I shall continue to advise my client throughout the interview and if necessary I shall ask that the interview be stopped in order to allow me to advise my client in private.
> I shall intervene in the interview if:
> — my client asks for, or needs, legal advice;
> — your questioning or behaviour is inappropriate;

— information or evidence is referred to that has not been disclosed to me before this interview;

— clarification of any matter is required; or

— a break is required.

After receiving legal advice my client has decided:

[either]

— to exercise his right to silence [if appropriate, give a reason for this advice] because [reason]. Please respect that decision. [My client is however prepared to hand to you a written statement about this matter.]

[or]

— to answer questions which you may raise which are relevant to my client's arrest/voluntary attendance.

It is important that a solicitor makes an opening statement, both to make it clear to the police that the solicitor knows his role (and if the solicitor does need to intervene, to justify such intervention in advance) and to give the client confidence in the solicitor's ability, which in turn will give the client important psychological support.

4.5.3   When should a solicitor intervene during the interview?

4.5.3.1   Examples of when a solicitor should intervene

A solicitor should intervene during the course of the interview if he considers that:

(a)   the questioning techniques employed by the police are inappropriate or improper;

(b)   the police are behaving in an inappropriate manner; or

(c)   his client would benefit from further (private) legal advice.

Set out below is a non-exhaustive list of the types of situation which may occur during an interview when it would be appropriate for the solicitor to intervene.

The solicitor is unhappy about the seating arrangements for the interview

Even before the interview has commenced, the solicitor should intervene if the police have arranged the seats so that he cannot properly advise his client (for example, by seating the solicitor behind the client so that the solicitor cannot make eye contact with the client), or if the solicitor considers the seating to be oppressive (if, for example, the interviewing officer places his chair right next to the client's chair). See **4.5.2.1** above.

The police are acting in an oppressive manner

This would encompass situations in which, for example, the interviewing officer raises his voice or shouts at the client, uses threatening gestures towards the client, or if he leans towards or stands over the client. The interviewing officer will also be acting oppressively if he insists that the client makes eye contact with him (there is no requirement for the client to do this), or insists that the client answer questions. Oppressive behaviour further includes long silences during the interview when the police hope the client will 'crack' and start to answer questions. Continued repetitive questioning of a suspect in the face of a suspect's sustained denial of guilt may also amount to oppressive conduct.

Multiple/unclear questions

This covers the situation where the interviewing officer asks the client several questions at once without giving the client a proper opportunity to reply, or if the officer interrupts a reply the client is making. The solicitor will also intervene if the questions being asked are unclear and require clarification by the officer, or if the questions are too wide or so lengthy that the client is unable to understand what he is actually being asked about (or to know which question to answer).

Irrelevant questions

The solicitor should intervene if the interviewing officer asks questions that have nothing to do with the allegations against the client or the reasons for the client's arrest (if, for example, the officer asks the client about his involvement in another offence for which the client has not been arrested, or if the officer asks the client personal questions that are not related to the offence under investigation). A common police tactic is to ask such questions in the hope of 'wearing down' the suspect.

Making a statement/asserting facts

This refers to the situation where the interviewing officer makes a statement to the client as opposed to putting a question to him, particularly if that statement is an allegation of guilt that is not supported by any evidence (if, for example, the officer states to the client: 'I think you are guilty of this offence. You're just making up a story as you go along').

Misrepresenting the law

If the interviewing officer gives an incorrect explanation of the law concerning the offence(s) the client has been arrested for, the solicitor should intervene, particularly if this is done to suggest to the client that the police case is stronger than it actually is.

Misrepresenting the strength of the case against the client

Again, the solicitor should intervene if the interviewing officer suggests that the case against the client is stronger than it actually is (this is sometimes done by the police in the hope that the client will think there is no point in denying his involvement in the offence).

'Upgrading' a response from the client/putting words in the client's mouth/making assumptions

The interviewing officer will sometimes ask a question based on an earlier reply from the client which the officer has upgraded. For example, if a client says that he is unable to remember being in a particular pub, it would be an upgrading of this response for the officer then to say: 'So you admit being in the pub ...' The solicitor should also intervene if, when asking further questions, the interviewing officer makes false or inaccurate assumptions based on answers given by the client, or if the officer asks leading questions which assume the existence of a fact which has not yet been established. If the officer asks such a question, the solicitor should ask the officer to disclose any additional evidence which the officer has to justify his assertion that a particular fact exists.

Threats/consequences of silence

The solicitor should intervene if, for example, the interviewing officer threatens to keep the client at the police station indefinitely, or until the client answers questions or makes an admission. Alternatively, the interviewing officer may tell the client that he will come across badly at court if he doesn't answer questions, or that he will get a heavier sentence if he doesn't admit his guilt. The solicitor should intervene immediately if the interviewing officer questions the client's decision to exercise his right of silence. He should also intervene if the police attempt to undermine the advice he has given to his client by, for example, telling the client that advice he has received to stay silent is bad advice or will get him into trouble at court.

Inducements

If, for example, the interviewing officer tells the client that he will get a lighter sentence if he admits his guilt, or that he will be able to leave the police station immediately if he confesses, the solicitor should intervene at once. A common tactic adopted by the police is to tell a suspect that he will get bail only if he answers questions and admits his guilt.

Previous convictions

The purpose of the interview is to enable the police to obtain evidence about the current offence, not to discuss a suspect's previous convictions. Although a defendant's previous convictions may be admissible in evidence at trial (see below and also **Chapter 22**), such convictions should not need to be discussed in the interview about the offence the police are currently investigating, and the solicitor should object if these convictions are raised by the officer conducting the interview (but see **4.5.3.2** below).

New information

The solicitor should intervene if the interviewing officer asks questions based on evidence which has not previously been disclosed to the solicitor and which the police have kept back. The solicitor should ask the officer to disclose this evidence to him so that he can then take his client's instructions upon it before the interview proceeds any further.

Hypothetical/speculative questions

An interviewing officer may sometimes say to a suspect: 'How do you think this would look to somebody else? If you were in my place, wouldn't you think that this evidence is pretty strong?' The client is not in the interview to answer hypothetical questions but rather to answer factual questions about the alleged offence. The officer should be asked to refrain from asking such questions. Similarly, the police should not ask questions requiring the client to give his opinion or to give a speculative answer. The solicitor should be particularly on his guard to prevent the client being asked to give his opinion about the character of another person. Any critical comments made by the client could lead to his own bad character or previous convictions being used in evidence against him at trial (see further below).

'This is your chance to tell your story'

Interviewing officers will sometimes suggest to a client that the purpose of the interview is for the client to put his account on record. This is not the case; the purpose is for the police to obtain evidence, not for the police to invite the client to give his story. The solicitor should intervene in such a situation.

The officer asks the client if he would be prepared to take part in further investigative procedures

The interviewing officer may, during the course of the interview, ask the client if he is prepared to take part in an identification procedure, or to provide fingerprints or samples. Such matters should not be raised in interview because the client is entitled to receive legal advice from his solicitor in private before agreeing to take part in any such procedure.

The solicitor is concerned about the client's behaviour or conduct

The solicitor should intervene to suggest to the client that further confidential advice is required if the client:

(a) shows signs of stress, confusion or emotion;

(b) begins to tell lies, or starts to answer questions having agreed that he would give a 'no comment' interview; or

(c) becomes abusive or hostile towards the interviewing officer.

The client is making comments that may have adverse consequences later in the case

If the client makes derogatory or critical comments about any other person (such as a prosecution witness or a co-accused), this may result in any previous convictions the client has becoming admissible at his later trial (see **Chapter 22**). The solicitor should intervene immediately if he considers that the client is in danger of putting his own bad character in issue by attacking the character of another person. The solicitor should also intervene if the client makes comments that might cause the police to refuse the client bail if he is charged or if he would otherwise be released on bail pending further enquiries or consultations with the CPS (if, for example, the client makes a threat of physical violence against a potential prosecution witness).

Inaccurate summary

If, at the end of the interview, the officer summarises the interview in an inaccurate way (by suggesting that the client has admitted more than he has actually said) and then asks the client to confirm that the summary is accurate, the solicitor should intervene.

Sufficient evidence to charge

The solicitor should intervene at any point during the interview if the police say anything to suggest that they think there is sufficient evidence to charge the client (if, for example, the police say to the client: 'The judge is going to come down heavily on you when you're sentenced'). The interview should not be prolonged if the client has given any explanation he wishes to give and the police consider there is sufficient evidence to charge (Code C, para 11.6 – see **3.3.1**).

4.5.3.2 Previous convictions

There is currently an ongoing debate as to whether, in the light of changes made by the Criminal Justice Act 2003 to the admissibility of bad character evidence at trial (see **Chapter 22**), the police are now permitted to question a suspect about his previous convictions on the basis that such convictions will have some evidential value as they might show that the suspect either has a propensity to commit offences of the same kind as the offence about which he is being questioned, or a propensity to be untruthful. However, even if the police are permitted to ask such questions, it should be accepted practice for them to ask them in a separate interview, rather than in the interview when the suspect is being questioned about the alleged offence for which he has been arrested. This will ensure that if such previous convictions are ruled at trial to be inadmissible, the record of the interview will not need to be edited but rather the separate interview will simply not be used as part of the prosecution case.

If the police do carry out a separate interview to ask the defendant about his previous convictions, the advice to be given to a suspect will depend on whether the interviewing officer is making general enquiries about the suspect's previous convictions, or is asking more detailed questions in an attempt to show that there are factual similarities between the suspect's previous convictions and the offence currently under investigation.

In the former case, the suspect should be advised to give a 'no comment' interview. If the interviewing officer is simply going through the list of the suspect's previous convictions without making reference to the actual facts of those convictions, there is no possibility of the court drawing an adverse inference from the suspect's silence, and if the suspect answers questions he runs the risk of giving the police evidence about the facts of the previous offences which they might otherwise have had difficulty proving.

If, however, the interviewing officer has made enquiries before the interview about the facts of the defendant's previous convictions, he may put these facts to the suspect in interview to establish similarities with the facts of the current offence. If the suspect fails to answer such questions but then seeks to argue at trial that the facts of his previous convictions are different from the facts of the current offence, the court may draw an adverse inference from his silence at the police station under s 34 of the CJPOA 1994 (see **4.4.3** above). In such a situation the best advice to give is again for the suspect to give a 'no comment' interview (so that there is no chance that the suspect might give the police details about the facts of his previous convictions which they would not otherwise have obtained), but at the same time for the suspect's solicitor to take a statement from the suspect detailing the facts of the suspect's previous convictions. The statement should be retained on the solicitor's file (rather than being handed in to the police) so that it may be used if necessary later in the case to rebut any suggestion that the facts of the previous convictions have been recently fabricated by the suspect.

4.5.4 How to intervene

A solicitor who intervenes in police interview needs to ensure that his intervention follows a proper structure, so that the police can understand why he has intervened and what he is asking the police to do. A useful structure for interventions is the 'DEAL' technique described at **4.3.2.2** above.

Key skill – intervening in the police interview

Set out below is a transcript of the record of the audio-recorded interview carried out by the police in the Gary Dickson case study. Mr Dickson did not have a solicitor present in the interview. Had a solicitor been present, he should have intervened on several occasions.

CHESHIRE POLICE

RECORD OF AUDIO-RECORDED INTERVIEW

INTERVIEW OF: Gary Dickson   **DATE OF BIRTH:** 28.10.79

ADDRESS: 17 Marsh Street, Chester   **DATE:** 18.12.2006

INTERVIEW AT: Chester Police Station

TIME COMENCED: 6.30 pm   **TIME CONCLUDED:** 6.40 pm

DURATION OF INTERVIEW: 10 mins   **TAPE REFERENCE NO:** SG01/4351

INTERVIEWING OFFICER: PC G Chambers   **OTHER PERSONS PRESENT** None

Signature of officer preparing record: *Gareth Chambers* PC911

Tape times	PARTICULARS OF INTERVIEW
0.00	Introductions.
	Caution. Reminded of right to free legal advice.
0.50	PC911: Right Mr Dickson, I think you know why you're here, don't you? You have been arrested for assaulting a man near to Connolley's Nightclub.
1.12	GD: I've been here most of the day and I haven't had much sleep, so do you think you could let me go now or what?
	PC911: Just answer the question Mr Dickson and we can both go home.
	GD: Look, just because I work at the club that doesn't mean you can pin any kind of trouble on me. I'm saying nothing.
2.42	PC911: Mr Dickson, why don't we just get this over with? Look I'm going off duty soon and if we don't deal with this interview now I won't be back on duty until tomorrow afternoon. You don't want to have to wait until then, do you?
	GD: No I don't. My girlfriend will be worried about me – she will think that I'm in some sort of trouble. Could I at least telephone her?
3.20	PC911: Don't worry, this will be over sooner than you think. Let's make a start then. Where were you at 3.15 am this morning?
3.56	GD: I would have finished work by then so I'd be at home.
	PC911: Are you sure about that, because I have reason to believe you were still near to the club and you assaulted a man there?
	GD: No. That's not true. I had been at the club earlier but I left much earlier than 3.15 am.
	PC911 Oh come on Mr Dickson, don't play the innocent with me or we'll be here all night.
4.20	GD: Look I don't know where you are getting the idea in your head that I've been assaulting someone. It's just rubbish.

Tape times	PARTICULARS OF INTERVIEW
4.50	PC911: Come on Mr Dickson, let's be serious, shall we? You chased him in your car didn't you? And you got out of the car and then you beat him?
	GD: No, I did not.
	PC911: You were seen Mr Dickson. Driving your own car at the time wasn't very clever was it?
	GD: No, you are seriously barking up the wrong tree here. The person who saw me is obviously confused. I was at the club and I did drive it to work and home again. But I didn't stop to beat anyone up and I wasn't on the road at 3.15 am. I would have got home much earlier than that.
5.20	PC911: That's rubbish isn't it? We have a witness who says that he saw you go over to the victim, hit him in the face several times and then drive away back in the direction towards Marsh Street.
	GD: He's making it up.
6.40	PC911: Why would the witness lie? You must realise this is a very serious charge, Mr Dickson. We're not going to get anywhere if you're going to play these stupid games with me. Perhaps you'd like to stop being clever or I'll take you back to the cells. Don't you want to get out of here tonight? What's it to be?
	GD: I've told you already what happened.
	PC911: Oh come on.
	GD: You lot have really got it in for me haven't you?
7.20	PC911: We both know you've been in trouble before – so it's likely you did exactly what our witness says.
	GD: Why don't you get off my back and go and find the person that really did it.
7.50	PC911: Come on, Dickson that isn't very helpful is it? We both know it was you so it seems futile to deny it.
	GD: Well if it makes you happy, so what if it was me? You should know that I always get even with people who get on the wrong side of me.
8.20	PC911: I think you're getting carried away again. Why don't we just finish this interview and then you can go and get some sleep? I think we both know that it's going to be better for you if you just tell me what really happened. The courts tend to come down heavy on repeat offenders you know. All I need is for you to accept that you assaulted Vince Lamb. Do you admit you did that?
	GD: Yes, I suppose so.
	PC911: You don't mean you suppose so, do you? You mean you did it.

Tape times	PARTICULARS OF INTERVIEW
9.10	GD: Yes.
	PC911: Do you have anything further you wish to say before I terminate this interview?
	GD: No.
9.50	INTERVIEW TERMINATED AT 6.40 PM
10.00	

Some examples of when a solicitor might have intervened in this interview using the DEAL technique follow:

Example 1

At 2.42 on the interview tape PC Chambers states:

'Look I am going off duty soon and if we don't deal with this interview now I won't be back on duty until tomorrow afternoon. You don't want to have to wait until then, do you?'

The solicitor's intervention would have been as follows:

'Officer I object to this line of questioning. You are threatening to keep my client in the police station unless my client makes an admission of guilt. You are not permitted to make such threats to my client. I would ask you to refrain from making such threats. If you continue to make such threats I will ask you to terminate the interview so that I may make representations to your superior officers. I will record the reason for the termination of the interview in my attendance record, and also ask that a note of the reason for the termination of the interview be made in the custody record.'

Example 2

At 4.50 on the interview tape PC Chambers states:

'Come on Mr Dickson, let's be serious, shall we? You chased him in your car didn't you? And you got out of the car and then you beat him?'

The solicitor's intervention would have been as follows:

'Officer you are asking my client multiple questions. You have asked my client three questions without giving my client a proper opportunity to reply. I would ask you to refrain from this behaviour. Please ask my client one question at a time and allow my client to reply fully before asking a further question. If you continue to ask my client multiple questions I will advise my client not to answer such questions.'

Example 3

At 6.40 on the interview tape PC Chambers states:

'Why would the witness lie? You must realise this is a very serious charge, Mr Dickson. We're not going to get anywhere if you're going to play these stupid games with me. Perhaps you'd like to stop being clever or I'll take you back to the cells. Don't you want to get out of here tonight? What's it to be?'

The solicitor's intervention would have been as follows:

'Officer my client has not been charged with an offence. If you consider that you already have sufficient evidence to charge my client, please terminate the interview immediately. If you do not have sufficient evidence to charge my client, I would remind you that the purpose of the interview is to ask my client factual questions, not for you to make threats against my client. You are putting pressure on my client to admit his guilt by threatening to keep him here indefinitely. I also consider that the language you have used is oppressive. I would ask you to refrain from using such language and stop threatening my client. If you are not prepared to do this, I ask that you end the interview so that I may make representations to your senior officer. I shall make a note of the reason for the termination of the interview in my attendance record, and I will ask the custody officer to record the reason for the termination of the interview in the custody record.'

Example 4

At 8.20 on the interview tape PC Chambers states:

'I think we both know it is going to be better for you if you just tell me what really happened. The courts tend to come down heavy on repeat offenders you know. All I need is for you to accept that you assaulted Vince Lamb. Do you admit you did that?'

The solicitor's intervention would have been as follows:

'Officer you are offering an inducement to my client in the hope that he will make an admission. You are also making reference to previous convictions which my client has. My client's previous convictions are not relevant to your enquiry and you should not attempt to persuade my client to admit his guilt in the hope that he will receive a lesser sentence. I would ask you to refrain from doing this. If you make any further reference to my client's previous convictions, or offer any further inducements to my client to admit guilt, I will ask you to stop the interview. I will record the reason for the termination of the interview in my attendance record, and also ask that a note of the reason for the termination of the interview be made in the custody record.'

There are several other occasions when a solicitor would have intervened during the course of this interview had he been present.

4.5.5 Can a solicitor be removed from the interview?

Paragraph 6.9 of Code C states that a solicitor may be required to leave the interview only 'if their conduct is such that the interviewer is unable properly to put questions to the suspect'. Paragraph 6D of the Notes for Guidance to Code C provides that para 6.9 will apply only if the solicitor's approach or conduct prevents or unreasonably obstructs proper questions being put to the suspect, or the suspect's response being recorded. Examples of such unacceptable conduct would include answering questions on a suspect's behalf, or providing written replies for the suspect to quote. A solicitor should not be removed from the interview simply because he tells his client not to answer questions, or because he intervenes when he considers that the police are asking questions in an inappropriate manner.

If the officer conducting the interview considers that the conduct of the solicitor is preventing him from properly putting questions to the suspect, the interviewer must stop the interview and consult an officer of at least the rank of superintendent (Code C, para 6.10). This officer must then speak to the solicitor and decide if the interview should continue in the presence of the solicitor or not. If it is decided that the solicitor should be excluded from the interview, the suspect must be given the opportunity to consult another solicitor before the interview continues, and that other solicitor must be given an opportunity to be present at the interview.

4.6   Identification procedures

4.6.1   Initial advice to the client

If the police do not want to interview a suspect immediately, it is likely that they will require the suspect to take part in an identification procedure (probably a video identification or possibly an identification parade). In such circumstances, there are several matters which the solicitor will need to explain to his client, and various checks which the solicitor will need to carry out prior to the identification procedure taking place. On the assumption that the police will want to hold a video identification or identification parade, the solicitor should advise the client to agree to such a procedure being carried out. In the event that the client does not agree, the solicitor should warn the client that the police may hold a less satisfactory form of identification procedure, such as group identification or even a confrontation (see **Chapter 3**). These procedures are less satisfactory than a video identification or an identification parade because it is more likely that the suspect will be identified by the witness, as the suspect will not be seen in a group of people who resemble him in appearance. The police may also choose to video the suspect covertly for a video identification.

Even if the police do not decide to organise a form of identification procedure that does not require the consent of the suspect, refusal to take part in an identification procedure is admissible at trial, and the court may therefore draw an adverse inference from the refusal of a suspect to take part in a video identification or an identification procedure. The adverse inference will be that the suspect refused to take part in the procedure because he thought he would be recognised by the witness(es) who would have attended the procedure.

Occasionally the police will decide not to organise an identification procedure, even if the suspect disputes the identification made by the witness and is not well known to the witness. For the police not to hold an identification procedure in such circumstances is a breach of Code C, para 3.12 (see **3.5.3.7**). If the solicitor considers that the police should carry out an identification procedure in order to comply with Code C, he should make representations to this effect to the investigating officer. If the solicitor fails to make such representations, it is unlikely that at trial the court would look favourably on an application by the defendant to exclude the identification evidence under s 78 of PACE 1984 (see **Chapter 21**). Although the failure to hold an identification procedure would be a clear breach of the Codes of Practice, the court is likely to conclude that it would not be unfair to admit the identification evidence from the witness because the defendant's solicitor had the opportunity to make representations about the need for an identification procedure to be held when he was at the police station.

4.6.2   Identification parades

Before the parade takes place, the solicitor should ensure that the police provide him with details of the first description of the suspect given by the potential witness (Code D, para 3.1). The solicitor should explain to the client what will happen at the parade (see **3.5.3.3**). The solicitor should tell the client that he may choose where to stand on the parade and that whilst the parade is taking place he should not speak or do anything to draw attention to himself.

The solicitor needs to check that the other participants in the parade resemble the client in age, height, general appearance and position in life. If they do not, the solicitor should make representations to the identification officer and ask either for the parade to be postponed, or for some form of disguise to be used to overcome any disparity in the appearance of the other participants. If, for example, the other participants in the parade are taller than the suspect, the solicitor may ask that all the people taking part in the parade be seated. Alternatively, if the suspect has a distinctive style or colour of hair, the solicitor could ask that all participants in the parade wear hats.

The solicitor should check that the witnesses are properly segregated before the parade and that there is no opportunity for the witnesses to see either the client or the other participants in the parade before the parade takes place. This may involve the solicitor checking the route which the witnesses will take to get to the parade and ensuring that the witnesses who are waiting to take part in the procedure are kept in separate rooms. The solicitor should ensure that there is no opportunity for a witness who has already attended the parade to speak to another witness before that witness has attended the parade. The solicitor should ensure that the investigating officer is to play no part in the identification parade.

If the solicitor considers that the parade has been contaminated in any way, he should ask the witness if he has discussed the description of the offender with anyone, either before attending or whilst at the police station. He should also ask that a note of his concerns be made by the identification officer in the written record of the parade.

4.6.3 Video identification

If the police intend to hold a video identification, the solicitor will be entitled to attend this procedure (see **3.5.3.2**). The solicitor needs to obtain from the police details of the first description of the suspect given by the potential witness (Code D, para 3.1). The solicitor needs to check in advance that the images which are to be used (referred to as the 'foils') resemble the suspect in age, height, general appearance and position in life. Again, the solicitor will need to object if the images do not comply with this requirement, and ensure that the police obtain further images. If the suspect has a distinctive feature (such as a prominent tattoo) the solicitor should ensure that this is covered up both on the image of the client and on the other foils.

The solicitor should attend the video identification to ensure that the witnesses attending the procedure are segregated from each other and that no unauthorised persons (such as the investigating officer) are present. The solicitor should check the number of witnesses who are to attend, where the witnesses will be kept before and after the procedure (making sure that a witness who has attended the procedure has no opportunity to speak to a witness who has not yet taken part), and the route the witnesses will take both to view and then to leave the procedure.

If the solicitor considers that the video identification has been contaminated in any way, he should ask the witness if he has discussed the description of the offender with anyone, either before attending or whilst at the police station. He should also ask that a note of his concerns be made by the identification officer in the written record of the video identification procedure.

4.6.4 Written records

Whichever form of identification procedure is used, the solicitor needs to keep a detailed record of what happens. The solicitor must ensure that the identification officer complies with the procedural requirements of Code D, Annex A (in the case of a video identification), or Code D, Annex B (in the case of an identification parade) when conducting the procedure. The solicitor should also make sure that

that any objections he makes to the conduct of the procedure (if, for example, the solicitor considers that the witnesses have not been properly segregated before an identification parade takes place) are recorded in full by the identification officer. Any comments made during the procedure (whether by the witness, the identification officer or anyone else) should also be recorded.

4.7 Fingerprints and samples

The solicitor should advise his client to cooperate in the giving of fingerprints, impressions of footwear or non-intimate samples. If the client refuses to consent to such samples being taken, the police are entitled to obtain such samples using reasonable force (see **3.5.4.1**).

Although a client is not obliged to provide the police with an intimate sample, the solicitor should warn his client that if he refuses to provide such a sample, an adverse inference may be drawn from this by the magistrates or jury at trial under s 62(10) of PACE 1984 (see **3.5.5.3**). The inference that will be drawn by the court is that the client has something to hide. Such a refusal is also capable of amounting to corroboration of other evidence that may exist against the client.

Example

Norman is being questioned about a rape. He denies having intercourse with the victim but refuses to give a sample of semen. This refusal is capable of corroborating evidence from the victim that non-consensual sexual intercourse between her and Norman took place.

4.8 Charge and bail after charge

When the police have completed their investigations, the solicitor may consider that the evidence the police have compiled indicates either that his client is not guilty, or that there is insufficient evidence to justify his client being charged. The solicitor should draw this to the attention of both the investigating and the custody officer, and make appropriate representations to persuade the custody officer to release the client without charge.

If the police decide that there is sufficient evidence to charge the client, the solicitor should (in cases where the client admits his guilt and the evidence against him is strong) consider making representations to the police that the client should be dealt with other than by way of charge. For an adult offender this would mean persuading the police to deal with the offender by way of an informal warning, a formal caution or a conditional caution. For an offender aged 17 or under, this would mean persuading the police to consider a reprimand or final warning. (See **3.9** above for further details of these alternatives to charging the client.) A solicitor should only ever advise a client to accept such a disposal if the client admits his guilt and the solicitor considers that the evidence against the client is such that the client would be convicted were he to be charged. A client who denies his guilt should not be advised to accept a caution, reprimand or final warning merely to get the matter out of the way. The client also needs to be advised about the potential consequences of accepting one of these options (see **Chapter 3**).

If the police decide to charge a suspect, the custody officer will then need to consider if the suspect should be granted bail pending his first appearance before the magistrates' court, or whether he should instead be remanded in police custody. If the custody officer indicates that he is minded to refuse bail, the suspect's solicitor should consider making representations in support of bail being granted. This will often involve the solicitor suggesting that the custody officer should consider granting bail with appropriate conditions, rather than the suspect being denied bail altogether (see **3.8** above).

Example

Trevor is interviewed at the police station about his suspected involvement in several night-time burglaries of commercial premises on a particular industrial estate. Trevor is subsequently charged with these burglaries. The custody officer informs Trevor's solicitor that he is reluctant to grant bail to Trevor as he believes that, if released on bail, Trevor will commit further offences. Trevor's solicitor should suggest to the custody officer that he consider imposing bail with conditions (to prevent Trevor committing further offences), rather than refusing bail. Such conditions might involve the imposition of a curfew, or a restriction on Trevor entering the area where the industrial estate is located.

4.9   The Police Station Representative Accreditation Scheme

A suspect who is detained at the police station may receive legal advice from a solicitor or an accredited police station representative. An accredited police station representative will be an individual who is accredited by the Legal Services Commission (LSC) to provide advice to suspects in the police station. The aim of the Police Station Representative Accreditation Scheme is to certify non-solicitors to advise and assist suspects being held at a police station, and to allow them to claim payment from the LSC for having provided such assistance.

If a trainee solicitor wishes to represent suspects at the police station, he must become an accredited representative. In order to do this, the trainee solicitor must first register as a probationary police station representative with the LSC. This will enable him to claim payment from the LSC for any police station work he does before he gains full accreditation. In order to gain full accreditation, the trainee then has one year from registering as a probationary representative to complete two forms of assessment:

(a)   The trainee will be required to attend the police station on a specified number of occasions to represent suspects. The trainee will be expected to produce a 'portfolio' of these attendances, detailing what each case involved, the issues that arose, how the trainee responded to these issues and how the trainee feels he could have performed more effectively.

(b)   The trainee will be required to take a 'critical incidents' test. This simulates police station situations on audio cassette and tests the trainee's proficiency in such situations by recording his response or the advice he gives.

Those other than trainee solicitors who wish to gain accreditation (such as ex-police officers employed by a firm of solicitors) must also pass a written test on matters of criminal law, evidence and procedure. Those who have successfully completed the Legal Practice Course are exempt from this requirement.

4.10   Checklist

At the end of this chapter you should be able to explain:

*   the role played by a solicitor when representing a client at the police station;
*   the steps the solicitor should take prior to attending the police station to represent a client;
*   the steps the solicitor should take, and the information he should seek to obtain, upon arrival at the police station;

- the advantages and disadvantages of the solicitor advising the suspect to adopt the following courses of action in a police interview:
    — answer all the questions put by the police,
    — give a 'no comment interview',
    — give a 'no comment' interview but also hand in to the police a written statement;
- the relationship between the advice a solicitor may give to a suspect at the police station and the ability of the court under ss 34, 36 and 37 of the CJPOA 1994 to draw adverse inferences at trial from the defendant's refusal to answer questions in a police station interview;
- the role played by the solicitor in an audio-recorded interview at the police station, including when a solicitor should intervene during the course of an interview and how an intervention should be made;
- the role played by the solicitor, and the advice that should be given to the suspect, should the police decide to hold an identification procedure;
- the advice the solicitor should give to a suspect from whom the police wish to obtain fingerprints, impressions of footwear or samples (intimate and non-intimate);
- the representations the solicitor should make to the police (in an appropriate case) to deal with the matter other than by charging the suspect;
- the representations the solicitor should make to the custody officer to obtain police bail for the suspect in the event that the suspect is charged with an offence.

4.11   Police station attendance record

INFORMATION FROM POLICE	
Inspected custody record: Yes/No	

Search of client: Yes/No Tick if intimate	Client's consent given: Yes/No
Legal authority & reason:	
Evidence obtained:	

Search of premises: Yes/No	Address
Legal authority & reason s.32/s.18	
Evidence obtained	

Samples taken: Yes/No	Client's consent given: Yes/No
Type: Intimate/non-intimate	Refusal implications explained: Yes/No
Legal authority & reason:	

Previous questioning/interview: Yes/No	
Details:	
Previous attendance at police station: Yes/No	Was legal advice received: Yes/No Was it sought: Yes/No

Client fit for interview: Yes/No	Police Surgeon called/attended: Yes/No

Co-accused: Yes/No

Name	Solicitor	Known to client?	In custody?	Conflict?

Significant statement or silence: Yes/No	Advised client to comment on this in interview: Yes/No

Consultation with officer	Name:

NAME:						
UFN:						
TELEPHONE CALLS						
Date	Time	R/A	Person spoken to	F/E	Instructions /Advice / Action	Duration

IDENTIFICATION PROCEDURES		
Obtained original description provided by each witness: Yes/No		
Advised client on methods of identification & procedure: Yes/No		
Advised client of right of refusal & implications thereof: Yes/No		
Advised client to consent to:		
Client consented to:	Representation made:	
Date of ID procedure:	Place: Type:	
Result:		
Witness	Identified?	Witness remarks
1.	Yes/No	
2.	Yes/No	
3.	Yes/No	
4.	Yes/No	

Make full note separately of procedure used and checks made

ATTENDANCE DETAILS		
Date of attendance	Outcome (enter bail to return/place: date: time)	Fee earner attending
1.		
2.		
3.		
4.		

OUTCOME	
No further action: Yes/No	
Caution/warning/reprimand: Yes/No	Advised client of implications: Yes/No
Charge: Yes/No	
Advised client on implications of reply to charge & inference from silence: Yes/No	
Advise to client: reply to charge/remain silent	
Reasons:	
Time of charge:	Reply:
Advised client on prints, photos & DNA: Yes/No	
Bail refused: Yes/No Procedure for future application explained: Yes/No	Representations Made: Yes/No Prospects of success: low/medium/high
Bail granted: Yes/No Conditions:	Explained consequences of FTA: Yes/No Explained consequences of breach: Yes/No
Charge (including date):	
Court:	Venue:	Date:	Time:
File allocated to		
Costs form completed: Yes/No	

CONSULTATION WITH CLIENT	
Previous convictions/cautions: Yes/No	
Details	
Outstanding criminal cases/on bail: Yes/No	
Details	
Health problems: Yes/No	
Details (including nature & effect of illness, & medication taken):	
Police Surgeon called: Yes/No	Note in custody record: Yes/No
Other vulnerabilities (e.g. language): Yes/No	
Details:	
Injuries: Yes/No	
Details (including description & cause):	
Witness to injuries: Yes/No	Name:
Police Surgeon called: Yes/No	Affects fitness for IV: Yes/No
Note on custody record: Yes/No	Photographs required: Yes/No
Searches made/samples taken: Yes/No	Consent given: Yes/No
Witness(es): Yes/No	
Name & Address:	
Alibi: Yes/No	
Where & When:	
Name & Address of alibi witness:	
Advised client on implications from silence under s34: Yes/No ss36&37: Yes/No	
Advised client to answer questions/remain silent/issued prepared statement	
Reasons:	
In interview, client answered questions/remained silent/issued statement/mixed	
Complaint against police: Yes/No	Advised client on procedure for
Make complaint prior to release: Yes/No	Complaint: Yes/No

Note: attach client's instructions on substance of allegations and issues in dispute.
Include instructions on role of co-suspects; and anything said by them.
Keep full note of any interview

CASE NARRATIVE

Date & Time	Person spoken to	Relevant details / instructions / advice / representations

Chapter 5

Police Complaints

5.1 Introduction

This chapter will examine the options open to an individual who believes that he has suffered as a result of misconduct by the police. The term 'misconduct' is broad, ranging from a police officer being unnecessarily rude to a member of the public to a police officer assaulting a suspect who has been detained in police custody. The chapter will begin by examining the role of the Independent Police Complaints Commission (IPCC). It will then examine the taking of civil or criminal proceedings against the police, before providing a summary of when a public enquiry into police conduct may take place. It will end with a reference to inquests.

5.2 The Independent Police Complaints Commission (IPCC)

5.2.1 Why was the IPCC created?

The IPCC is the public body that took over responsibility for handling complaints against the police from 1 April 2004 onwards. The IPCC replaced the Police Complaints Authority (PCA) and was part of a series of reforms brought into force under the terms of the Police Reform Act 2002.

The introduction of an independent body to oversee and investigate complaints against the police had been under consideration for a number of years, and had been called for by several pressure groups, such as 'Liberty', the human rights organisation. These calls were given added impetus following the publication of the Macpherson Report into the death of Stephen Lawrence and the subsequent police investigation.

Dissatisfaction with the PCA centred on the fact that the Authority was perceived to be biased in favour of the police and was not sufficiently independent.

5.2.2 How does the IPCC differ from the PCA?

The IPCC is run by 18 commissioners, none of whom must previously have worked for the police. The IPCC is completely separate from any government department and any decisions it makes can be overruled only by the courts. Acting under the commissioners are a number of investigation teams who can investigate incidents of alleged police misconduct independently of the police. These investigators have full police powers whilst carrying out their investigations and must, on request, be given full access to police records and premises.

More generally the IPCC has overall 'guardianship' of the complaints system, which means it can produce statutory guidance on complaints handling for police forces and report and make recommendations to the Home Secretary on police practice.

5.2.3   Making a complaint

Any individual can make a complaint alleging police misconduct. Although it is possible to make complaints orally at a police station, the IPCC encourages complaints to be made in writing. Complaints should in the first instance be made directly to the police force concerned. Any complaints made directly to the IPCC will be passed to the relevant police force.

Complaints must be made within one year of the incident complained of, and must be about a particular officer or officers, rather than about general police practice or policy. Complaints made outside this one-year period will not be considered if good reason for the delay cannot be shown or unless injustice would be caused by the delay.

Complaints may be made against any of the following categories of person:

(a)   any member of a police force;

(b)   anyone employed by a police authority and under the direction and control of the Chief Constable; or

(c)   any special constables or staff designated as detention and escort officers.

Any unsuccessful complaint previously dealt with by the PCA cannot be reopened.

5.2.4   Local resolution

This procedure is used to resolve approximately one-third of complaints against the police and is appropriate for less serious types of complaint, such as an allegation that a police officer has spoken to a member of the public in a rude, aggressive or otherwise unprofessional manner.

In such a case the police will ask the individual making the complaint if he is willing to have his complaint resolved through dialogue rather than a formal investigation. The dialogue is likely to involve a member of the police service meeting with the complainant to find out what his concerns are, and then a further meeting between the member of the police service and the officer complained about. An attempt is then made to address the complainant's concerns either through an explanation, or by an apology.

A complainant may not want his complaint to go through local resolution. He can instead ask for the IPCC to progress instead directly to an investigation. Such requests are dealt with by the IPCC's Professional Standards Department who will decide whether such a step is merited.

If, however, a complainant agrees to local resolution, he cannot appeal against the outcome (for example, if he is dissatisfied with the explanation). A complainant only has a right of appeal to the IPCC following local resolution (see **5.2.6.3** below) if the police fail to follow the correct procedure when local resolution is used.

5.2.5   Complaints resolved through investigation

Certain complaints that are made against the police must be referred to the IPCC by the police. These categories of complaint are:

(a)   allegations of assault;

(b)   allegations of 'hate crime';

(c)   allegations of corruption;

(d)   allegations of serious offences;

(e)   cases that involve deaths in police custody; and

(f)   when the police have used firearms.

The death of the Brazilian Jean Charles de Menezes serves to illustrate the IPCC approach to the use of firearms, although the case is an exceptional and untypical one. In July 2005, in the aftermath of several terrorist bombings in London, Mr Menezes was shot and killed by police officers at Stockwell underground station. At the time he was mistaken for a suspected suicide bomber.

With any incident involving firearms, investigators would expect to be at the scene within hours to secure the area, gather forensic evidence, and take statements. In line with the usual practices, an IPCC investigation into Mr Menezes' death was carried out. At the time of writing the IPCC's report is with the Crown Prosecution Service (CPS).

In cases not covered by the above categories, the police have the option of referring the complaint to the IPCC. If the police refer a case to the IPCC, the Commission can deal with it in one of three ways:

(a)   In the most serious cases the IPCC will carry out an independent investigation that will not have any police involvement.

(b)   In less serious cases the IPCC will arrange for the police themselves to carry out an investigation which the IPCC will manage. This is referred to as a 'managed' investigation.

(c)   In most cases the police will deal with the complaint and the IPCC will either have a supervisory role (a 'supervised' investigation), or have no formal role at all (a 'local' investigation). A 'local' investigation should not be confused with the 'local resolution' procedure described at **5.2.4** above.

5.2.6   Appeals to the IPCC

5.2.6.1   Introduction

In addition to its investigative powers, the IPCC can consider three types of appeal from aggrieved complainants:

(a)   appeals against the refusal by the police to record a complaint;

(b)   appeals against the local resolution process; and

(c)   appeals against the outcome of a 'supervised' or 'local' investigation.

5.2.6.2   Appeals against the refusal by the police to record a complaint

As stated at **5.2.3** above, all complaints must initially be made to the relevant local police force. Under the Police Reform Act 2002, each police force must either record an individual's complaint, or give that individual an explanation of why it has been decided not to record that complaint.

If the police refuse to record a complaint (for example, if the police believe the complaint is groundless), the individual making the complaint can appeal to the IPCC to overturn the police decision not to record the complaint. Such an appeal must be made within 28 days of the individual being notified by the police that his complaint has not been recorded.

5.2.6.3   Appeals against the local resolution process

An individual has no right of appeal against the outcome of the local resolution process, but there is a right of appeal to the IPCC if an individual considers that the procedures he agreed to for the local resolution of his complaint were not followed. This right of appeal must be exercised within 28 days of the date on which the individual believes the procedures were followed incorrectly.

5.2.6.4   Appeals against the outcome of a 'supervised' or 'local' investigation

A 'supervised' or 'local' investigation will be carried out by the police with the IPCC playing a very minor role. An individual may be dissatisfied with the outcome of such an investigation in two circumstances:

(a)   if the individual disagrees with the findings of the investigation (for example, because the police did not interview all the relevant witnesses); or

(b)   if the individual disagrees with the action the police propose to take as a result of the investigation.

In such circumstances the individual has a right of appeal to the IPCC to have the decision made by the police overturned. The appeal must be made within 28 days of the individual being notified of the outcome of the investigation.

There is no right of appeal if the investigation was 'managed' by the IPCC, or to investigations which the IPCC undertakes completely independently of the police. The only way in which such investigations can be challenged is through judicial review.

5.2.7   Powers of the IPCC

If an individual has appealed to the IPCC as in **5.2.6** above, the IPCC can overturn a decision made by the police and give instructions to the relevant Chief Constable as to the future handling of the complaint.

If an investigation has been carried out (either by the IPCC, or by the police under the management or supervision of the IPCC), a report will be prepared. If the complaint is serious and an individual's complaint is upheld, this can result in disciplinary proceedings being taken against the relevant police officer(s) and, in appropriate cases, criminal proceedings.

Since April 2006, the IPCC has also had an agreement with the Serious Organised Crime Agency (SOCA) to handle complaints against SOCA. The agreement means that the IPCC can investigate matters involving those employed by or on secondment to SOCA, whether they are police personnel or personnel from Customs and Excise, the Immigration and Nationality Directorate, or other government agencies.

5.2.8   Disciplinary charges against individual officers

As noted at **5.2.7** above, complaints by the public or investigations by the IPCC could in some circumstances lead to disciplinary action against police officers. Although such disciplinary initiatives are similar to those available to any employer, there is the added element that there will often be public interest in the outcome. It is not possible for a member of the public to compel a police force to commence disciplinary proceedings, but this process is often sparked by concerns of the public.

In *French and Others v Chief Constable of Sussex* [2006] EWCA Civ 312, a number of police officers brought a claim for negligence against their police force following disciplinary proceedings against them. An IPCC enquiry was initiated against police officers following a fatal shooting. None of the officers had witnessed the shooting. Disciplinary proceedings were brought against some of them by the Chief Constable, but these were then discontinued.

The officers then brought civil claims for damages for stress-related illnesses caused by the disciplinary process. Their claims failed. It was held by the Court of Appeal that there was no prospect of the officers establishing foreseeability of psychiatric injury, even if there were alleged failings in the procedures followed by their police force.

The Court of Appeal decision indicates that the judiciary will be reluctant to compromise the need to hold officers to account through internal processes such as disciplinary proceedings.

For more information on employment procedures and related matters, see *Employment Law.*

5.2.9 Police reports to the IPCC even if no complaint

Under the original provisions of the Police Reform Act 2002, certain deaths or serious injuries involving the police had to be reported to the IPCC only if prompted by a complaint, or if there was a suggestion that there had been a disciplinary or criminal offence by a person serving with the police. In practice, the police are quick to inform the IPCC of any death where there is police involvement, but it was decided that more legislative uniformity should be introduced. This was achieved by s 160 of the Serious Organised Crime and Police Act 2005 and the Police (Complaints and Misconduct) (Amendment) Regulations 2006 (SI 2006/1406).

As a result of these provisions, there is now a further category of case, known as a 'death or serious injury (DSI) matter', which must be reported to the IPCC. Any DSI occurring during or following police contact must be reported, even if there has been no complaint against the police, and regardless of whether there has been questionable conduct by arresting or investigating officers or other police personnel.

The 2006 Regulations also changed the timescale regarding when the police are required to report matters to the IPCC. For all qualifying matters (issues where the police are required by statute to draw matters to the attention of the IPCC), a report must be filed by the end of the day following the incident, rather than by the end of the next working day. This provision removes the possibility of there being a delay in notifying the IPCC over a weekend or bank holiday.

5.3 Criminal proceedings

The IPCC has the power to refer cases to the CPS with a view to criminal proceedings being taken against police officers whose conduct amounts to a criminal offence. An example of when such a referral might occur is if the IPCC considers that a police officer has assaulted a suspect whilst that suspect was in police custody. The CPS will determine whether charges should be brought against the officer concerned.

If the CPS decides not to bring a prosecution, it is possible for an individual to bring a private prosecution against the relevant police officer. Such prosecutions are extremely rare. Public funding will not be available to finance such a prosecution, and the cost of funding such proceedings privately is prohibitively expensive. In addition, if the CPS has determined that there is insufficient evidence to charge the officer, such a prosecution has little chance of resulting in a conviction.

If a police officer is prosecuted and convicted (whether by the CPS or through a private prosecution), the court when passing sentence has the power to order the defendant to pay compensation to the victim of the crime.

5.4 Civil proceedings

5.4.1 Introduction

A victim of police misconduct may want to do more than initiate a complaint or follow the progress of criminal proceedings. In many instances there may be an entitlement to compensation, which will involve the need to contemplate and prepare for action in the civil courts. Many successful claims for compensation have followed a failed complaint, so a legal adviser should be alert to the possibilities of civil action even if the complaints process has proved fruitless.

5.4.2 Type of claim

Most claims against the police will lie in tort. There are various types of claim that can be made:

(a)   Battery – if the police have used an excessive amount of force in carrying out an arrest or during a suspect's detention.

(b)   Trespass – if the police enter and search property without the necessary authority to do so.

(c)   False imprisonment – if the police detain a suspect without justification, or if a suspect is held in police detention beyond detention time limits or without proper reviews of detention being carried out.

(d)   Malicious prosecution – if the police bring a prosecution from malicious motives and without reasonable or probable cause.

(e)   Claims for unlawful killing or personal injury – where there is an allegation of death or injury at the hands of the police, either when in custody or in other circumstances.

(f)   Damage to goods – for example, impounding a vehicle and damaging it, or damaging items of property during a search.

(g)   Claims for race discrimination under the Race Relations (Amendment) Act 2000 and related legislation.

Any civil claim against the police will be made against the Chief Constable of the relevant force, as he is deemed to be vicariously liable for any torts committed by his officers. Public funding from the Community Legal Service is available for civil claims against the police, depending on the merits of the case and the individual's financial means. It is likely the Legal Services Commission will require an attempt to have been made to settle a grievance by way of the complaints process as a condition of providing funding.

5.4.3 Pre-action matters

A number of pre-action steps will take place. Disclosure will need to take place, a medical report commissioned where a claimant has suffered injury (whether physical or psychiatric), and the possibility of settlement explored. It is usual for the parties' legal advisers to agree at the outset that the timescale for the Personal

Injury Protocol be followed, with the letter of claim to be acknowledged within 21 days, and a full response provided by the defendant within three months of acknowledgement. For more details on the Personal Injury Protocol, see *Personal Injury and Clinical Negligence Litigation*.

5.4.4 Commencing the claim and progressing to trial

The usual rules relating to commencing proceedings will apply to claims against the police. The claim form will be issued in the county court or, for higher-value or more complex matters, the Queen's Bench Division of the High Court. Trials for false imprisonment and malicious prosecution take place before a judge and jury. In the county court there are eight jurors and in the High Court 12. Otherwise, trials are heard before a judge alone.

5.4.5 Disclosure

Disclosure of documents will be guided by the usual civil litigation principles. Typical documents that a claimant's solicitor would expect to receive would include custody records, property, charge and bail sheets, records of premises searches, interview transcripts, CCTV footage (edited and unedited), officer personnel files, details of disciplinary hearings, and records of previous complaints. This is not an exhaustive list but gives a flavour of the sort of documentation which exists and which should be provided, depending on the facts of each scenario.

Exactly what should be provided by way of disclosure varies from case to case, and is subject to CPR, Part 31 and its interpretation. In *Scott v Chief Constable of South Yorkshire* [2006] Lawtel, 28 March, the Court of Appeal held that there was no duty on the defendant police force to disclose documents relating to certain complaints against a police officer. The officer in question arrested the claimant outside a club, prompting litigation against the Chief Constable alleging false imprisonment, assault and battery. At first instance the case was dismissed, and the claimant appealed. The appeal was also dismissed, the Court saying that there was no requirement for the defendant to disclose papers relating to another complaint against the same officer in respect of an allegedly unlawful arrest.

5.4.6 Damages

Guidance on the level of damages that the courts should award in claims against the police was given by the Court of Appeal in *Thompson v The Commissioner of Police for the Metropolis* [1997] 2 All ER 762.

Such damages usually fall into one or more of three categories:

(a) Basic damages – based on the usual premise that a claimant should be awarded a sum of money to compensate him for injuries or damage caused. The aim of such damages is to put the claimant back to the position he was in had the tort never occurred.

(b) Aggravated damages – reflecting humiliating circumstances at the time of the arrest, or alternatively high-handed, insulting, malicious or oppressive behaviour in relation to arrest, imprisonment or the conduct of the prosecution.

(c) Exemplary damages – where the action of the police is deemed oppressive, arbitrary or unconstitutional, and the aim is to 'punish' the police for their actions. Juries have traditionally struggled with the distinction between aggravated and exemplary damages. Awards combining the two are often appealed by defendants on the basis that an award including both is likely to overcompensate the claimant.

In *Thompson*, the Court provided the following guidelines on what type of damages should be awarded and the quantum of such damages:

(a)   In false imprisonment cases, the Court said that a figure of £500 should be awarded for the first hour of detention, reaching £3,000 for 24 hours.

(b)   For cases involving malicious prosecution, the Court suggested that damages of between £2,000 and £10,000 would be appropriate.

(c)   For aggravated damages, the amount would be unlikely to be less than £1,000. It would, however, be rare for the sum to be more than twice the basic damages (except where those damages were modest).

(d)   For exemplary damages, a minimum figure of £5,000 and an absolute maximum figure of £50,000 would be appropriate.

5.4.7   Compensation for wrongful conviction

Where a person has been wrongfully convicted or charged, a compensation scheme for miscarriages of justice operates by virtue of s 133 of the Criminal Justice Act 1988. Applications should be made in writing to the Home Secretary and sent to the Compensation Section of the Home Office.

This is not a measure directed specifically at the police, but misconduct would be caught by the provisions of s 133. Decisions on compensation are made by an assessor appointed by the Home Secretary, and factors the assessor will have regard to include the seriousness of the offence for which the person was convicted, the severity of the punishment, the conduct of the investigation and prosecution of the offence, and any other convictions of the person and any punishment resulting from them.

In April 2006 the Government introduced reforms to this statutory scheme. It was announced that time limits would be introduced for applications, and that legal fees would be assessed by reference to public funding rates rather than on any other basis. In addition, an applicant's criminal record will have a wider impact on the amount awarded, and greater scrutiny will be given to conduct at the time of the miscarriage of justice. It was also stated that the maximum sum awardable under the scheme would be capped at £500,000.

As part of the same initiative, a discretionary scheme, whereby the Home Secretary had the power to make an ex gratia payment in certain exceptional cases which did not fall within s 133, was abolished. Individuals wishing to claim compensation following serious default on the part of the authorities must now satisfy the provisions of the amended s 133 procedure, or alternatively bring a civil claim.

5.4.8   Damages under the Human Rights Act 1998

The Human Rights Act 1998 incorporates the European Convention on Human Rights (ECHR) and provides an individual with another potential civil cause of action against the police. Under Article 5(5) of the ECHR, the victim of an arrest or detention that breaches the other clauses of Article 5 has 'an enforceable right to compensation'. This would provide an individual who is unlawfully arrested by the police or unlawfully detained at the police station with a right to damages.

5.4.9   Negligence and the police

Many claims for negligence against the police are unsuccessful because the courts are reluctant to find that a relevant duty of care exists. So while it is not uncommon for a claim to succeed where a police vehicle in a chase has crashed and injured another road user, it is unlikely that a victim of crime would succeed in an allegation that the police had failed to protect him, or alternatively had not progressed a criminal investigation with the necessary expedition or efficiency. In *Brooks v Commissioner of Police for the Metropolis* [2005] UKHL 24, it was held that the police owed no duty of care to assess whether the claimant was a victim of crime, nor was there a duty to give him protection and support. It was also held that there was no duty to give reasonable weight to the account the claimant gave as an eye-witness and to act on that account. *Brooks* is one of several cases and actions stemming from the Stephen Lawrence case mentioned at **5.5** below.

5.5 Public enquiries

The Home Secretary has the power to arrange for an independent enquiry to take place to investigate any matter concerning the police in England and Wales. The scope of such an enquiry can encompass alleged misconduct by particular police officers, but can also cover more general policing policies and practices. An example of a high-profile public enquiry into police practices was the Macpherson Enquiry of 1999 into the death of Stephen Lawrence and the police investigation that followed. The Report concluded that the investigation was inadequate and suggested that the Metropolitan Police were 'institutionally racist'.

Another example of a public enquiry (although not directed at the police) was that into the death of Zahid Mubarek announced in 2004. Mr Mubarek was killed by an allegedly racist cellmate whilst detained in a young offenders institution in West London. One of the terms of reference for the enquiry was to make recommendations as to the prevention of such attacks in the future.

5.6 Inquests

Where someone has died in police custody or as a result of police actions, an inquest will take place before a coroner and a jury. For details about inquests, see ***Personal Injury and Clinical Negligence Litigation***. As with any inquest, the procedure is not designed to establish liability or apportion blame, but evidence gathered at an inquest will be helpful in framing and supporting any subsequent civil claim. The inquest should comply with the requirements of Article 2 of the ECHR, and in particular the House of Lords case of *R v Coroner for Western Somerset, ex p Middleton* [2004] UKHL 10. It was held in *Middleton* that where a death occurred at the hands of a State authority, the scope of an inquest could be broadened so that the question of how the deceased came by his death should be interpreted to mean by what means and in what circumstances, rather than having a more limited interpretation.

5.7 Checklist

By the end of this chapter you should be able to explain:

- the role played by the IPCC and the powers which the IPCC may exercise;
- when criminal proceedings might be commenced against a police officer;
- the types of civil claim which may be made against the police, and the principles governing compensation in such cases;
- the role of public enquiries in maintaining police accountability;
- the significance of inquests where a death has allegedly occurred in police custody or otherwise at the hands of the police.

5.8   Flowchart – remedies for police misconduct

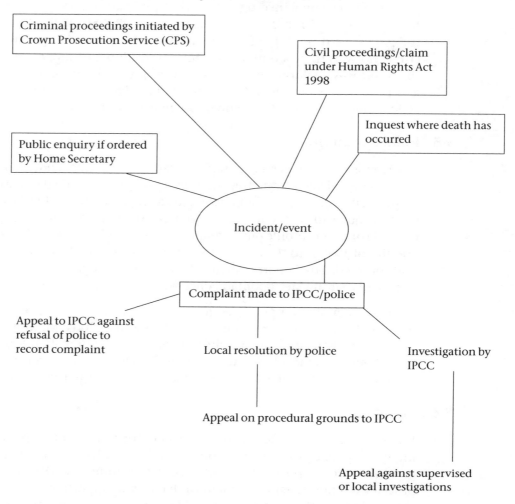

Part 3

PROCEDURE FROM CHARGE TO TRIAL

Chapter 6

Initial Hearings in the Magistrates' Court

6.1 Introduction

All defendants aged 18 or over who are charged with a criminal offence will make their first appearance at court before the magistrates' court. If the defendant is charged with an indictable only offence, the magistrates will immediately send the case to the Crown Court for trial under s 51 of the Crime and Disorder Act 1998. The procedure for doing this is described in **Chapter 10**. Defendants aged 17 and under will usually be dealt with in the Youth Court (see **Chapter 14**).

This chapter will concentrate on adult defendants who are charged with an either way offence or a summary offence. It will describe what happens when the defendant makes his initial appearance at court and the role played by the defence solicitor at this stage in obtaining funding for the case, finding out details of the prosecution case against his client and advising the client as to his plea. It will also examine the procedure which takes place to determine whether an either way offence will ultimately be dealt with by the magistrates' court or by the Crown Court.

6.2 The first hearing

6.2.1 Defendants on bail

If the defendant was charged by the police he will either:

(a) come to court in custody if the police refused to grant him bail; or

(b) attend court to 'answer' his bail if he was granted bail by the police.

A defendant who has received a written charge and requisition (see **3.10**) will come to court on the date and at the time specified in the requisition.

If the defendant is attending court having been granted bail by the police, the first hearing will be either an Early First Hearing (EFH) or an Early Administrative Hearing (EAH). Which type of hearing takes place will depend on the complexity of the case and the plea which the defendant is expected to enter.

6.2.2 Early First Hearing

6.2.2.1 Introduction

If a defendant is going to enter a 'simple guilty plea' to the offence, his first appearance before the court will be an EFH. A 'simple guilty plea' is when the defendant admits all the elements of the offence and there are no complex issues involved.

6.2.2.2 Summary offences

If the offence is a summary matter which can be dealt with only by the magistrates, the defendant will appear before a full bench of three magistrates. The charge will be read out to the defendant and he will enter a guilty plea. A representative from the CPS will then tell the magistrates the facts of the case and the defendant's solicitor will give a plea in mitigation on the defendant's behalf. The magistrates will then either sentence the defendant straight away, or adjourn the case to a later date if they want to obtain any reports (such as a report from the Probation Service) before sentencing the defendant. If the case is adjourned, the magistrates will consider whether the defendant should be granted bail or remanded in custody prior to the next hearing (see **Chapter 7**).

> **Example**
>
> Bhupinder is charged with careless driving (a summary only offence) after he drove his car into the rear of another vehicle at a set of traffic lights. Bhupinder intends to plead guilty to the offence. At the EFH, Bhupinder enters a guilty plea. The CPS representative outlines the facts of the case to the magistrates, and Bhupinder's solicitor then gives a plea in mitigation on Bhupinder's behalf. The magistrates decide that they do not require a pre-sentence report from the Probation Service before deciding on their sentence. Bhupinder is sentenced straight away.

6.2.2.3 Either way offences

If the offence is an either way matter, the defendant will again appear before a full bench of magistrates. The charge will be put to him and he will enter a guilty plea. After the defendant enters his guilty plea, the magistrates will then need to determine whether they should sentence the defendant, or whether the defendant should be committed to the Crown Court for sentence because, given the seriousness of the case, their sentencing powers will be insufficient (see **6.9** below).

As with summary offences, if the case is adjourned the magistrates will go on to consider whether the defendant should be granted bail or remanded in custody prior to the next hearing (see **Chapter 7**). The case may need to be adjourned either for the magistrates to obtain a pre-sentence report from the Probation Service before sentencing the defendant, or, if the magistrates have decided to commit the defendant to Crown Court to be sentenced, for the sentencing hearing at the Crown Court to take place.

> **Example**
>
> Carol is charged with the theft (an either way offence) of an iPod from an electrical shop. Carol intends to plead guilty to the offence. At the EFH, Carol enters a guilty plea. The CPS representative outlines the facts of the case to the magistrates, and Carol's solicitor gives a plea in mitigation on Carol's behalf. The magistrates decide that they will sentence Carol (rather than her being committed to the Crown Court for sentence). However, the magistrates decide that, before sentencing Carol, they require a pre-sentence report from the Probation Service. Carol's case is adjourned for

three weeks to enable the report to be prepared. The magistrates grant bail to Carol prior to the sentencing hearing.

6.2.3   Early Administrative Hearing

An EAH is essentially an organisational or administrative hearing, and will follow the same format whether the defendant is charged with a summary only or an either way offence. The magistrates will check if the defendant has legal representation, and the case may be adjourned to enable the defendant to see a solicitor and to obtain public funding for his case (see **6.4** below). Even if the defendant has already secured legal representation, the case is likely to be adjourned so that the solicitor instructed by the defendant may advise the defendant on the strength of the prosecution case and the plea he should enter. In order to do this, the solicitor will need to obtain disclosure of the prosecution case (see **6.6** below). The solicitor may have received some details of the prosecution case (such as copy witness statements) at court, but will need time to read these fully and to take his client's instructions on their contents. The solicitor will also need to listen to the tape(s) of his client's interview in the police station, and to view any CCTV recordings which may form part of the prosecution case.

When the case is adjourned the magistrates will consider whether the defendant should be granted bail or remanded in custody prior to the next hearing (see **Chapter 7**). The case will typically be adjourned for two to three weeks. When the defendant appears before the court again, the magistrates will expect him to be in a position to enter his plea (see **6.8** below). There are several steps the defendant's solicitor needs to take prior to this next hearing. These are outlined at **6.3** below.

As an EAH normally deals with purely administrative matters, it can be conducted by the magistrate's clerk/legal adviser rather than before a bench of magistrates. However, if there is any prosecution objection to the defendant being granted bail, the hearing should take place before a bench of magistrates so that an application for bail can be made by the defendant's solicitor.

Example

Vikram is charged with affray following a fight outside a nightclub. He intends to enter a not guilty plea. At the EAH, the magistrates check that Vikram has obtained legal representation. Vikram has instructed a solicitor to represent him. Vikram's solicitor has been handed a bundle of witness statements from the CPS, but has not yet had the opportunity to read these or to obtain Vikram's instructions on their contents. He has also received a tape showing CCTV footage of the alleged affray, which he will need to view. At the EAH, Vikram's solicitor explains to the magistrates that Vikram will not be in a position to enter a plea until the solicitor has taken the above steps. The magistrates therefore adjourn the case for three weeks to enable the solicitor to take these steps. The magistrates grant bail to Vikram prior to the next hearing.

6.2.4   Defendants refused police bail

If the police refused to grant the defendant bail after he was charged, the defendant will be kept in police custody until he can be brought before a magistrates' court. This will normally be either later on the day on which the defendant was charged, or on the following day.

Defendants who make their first appearance before the court in custody appear at what are termed 'remand hearings'. What happens at a remand hearing will be similar to either an EFH or an EAH, depending on whether the defendant is pleading guilty or not. Unless the defendant is pleading guilty to the charge and can be sentenced there and then, the most significant part of the remand hearing will be when the court considers whether to grant the defendant bail prior to the next hearing. If the police refused bail it is likely that the CPS will oppose bail being granted to the defendant, and a full bail hearing will be necessary to determine whether the defendant should be granted bail or remanded in custody prior to the next hearing (see **Chapter 7**).

6.3 Role of the defence solicitor

Unless the case involves a straightforward summary only offence, few defendants will enter their plea (whether guilty or not guilty) at their first appearance before the magistrates' court. Usually their cases will be adjourned for them to take advice from their solicitors.

The solicitor's role at this stage involves taking the following steps:

(a)   obtaining funding from the LSC to pay for the work he will do on his client's behalf (unless the client is paying his solicitor privately);

(b)   taking a statement from the client;

(c)   obtaining details of the prosecution case from the CPS;

(d)   advising the client on the strength of the prosecution evidence and the plea the client should enter; and

(e)   in the case of an either way offence, informing the client that his case may be dealt with either by the magistrates' court or by the Crown Court, and advising the client about the advantages and disadvantages of each court.

Each of these matters is considered in greater detail below.

6.4 Funding the case

6.4.1 Introduction

Most defendants in criminal proceedings do not pay their solicitors on a private basis for the legal work done on their behalf. Rather, defence solicitors will normally make applications on behalf of their clients for the clients' cases to receive public funding from the LSC. The public funding of a defendant's legal representation in a criminal case is specifically provided for by Article 6(3) of the ECHR (see **1.8.3**), which states that defendants who do not have sufficient means to pay for legal assistance should receive this free from charge when this is in the interests of justice.

The public funding of criminal defence work is administered by the Criminal Defence Service, which is itself part of the LSC. Full details of the different types of public funding that are available in criminal litigation matters can be found on the LSC website (www.legalservices.gov.uk), together with details of the rates of payment that solicitors receive and the various forms which must be completed to obtain payment. In order to obtain public funding for their clients, a firm of solicitors must have a contract with the LSC to represent defendants in criminal proceedings. This is known as a 'general criminal contract'. To be eligible for such a contract, a firm must first pass a preliminary audit to obtain a 'Specialist Quality Mark' (formerly known as a franchise). Firms awarded a contract will be subject to an annual audit by the LSC to ensure that their files are being run properly and that the firm's case management systems are working correctly. A firm which fails to pass the audit may have its contract removed, in which case it will no longer be able to obtain public funding for its clients.

6.4.2 Work done before the client is charged

6.4.2.1 Work done at the police station

The first advice solicitors normally provide to their clients will be at the police station. All persons attending at the police station (whether under arrest, or attending voluntarily – see **3.2.1**) are entitled to free legal advice, regardless of their means. Work done by a solicitor at the police station will be claimed under the Police Station Advice and Assistance Scheme. The work done by the solicitor (ie, travelling to and from the police station, waiting at the police station, and providing advice and assistance to the client) may be claimed for under fixed hourly rates. The solicitor is also entitled to claim a fixed sum for any initial advice given to the client over the telephone. Non-solicitors (such as trainees) can attend the police station and charge for this work as long as they are either accredited or probationary police station representatives (see **4.9** above).

Some solicitors are members of duty solicitor schemes for a given police station. These solicitors have their names entered on a rota, and they may be called out to attend the police station if they are 'on duty' and the person who has been arrested does not have his own solicitor. The duty solicitor scheme has separate arrangements for payment.

6.4.2.2 Work done outside the police station

If a client is of limited means (ie, in receipt of income support or income-based jobseeker's allowance), the solicitor will be able to fund any preliminary work he carries out on the client's behalf outside the police station under the Advice and Assistance Scheme. This scheme covers work done before the client is charged. It may, for example, cover taking initial instructions from a client who has been released on police bail and is due to return to the police station at a later date. The scheme does not cover any work done for a client after the client has been charged. In such cases it will be necessary for the client to apply for a representation order (see **6.4.3.2** below). Any work done under the Advice and Assistance Scheme can be claimed for by the solicitor under fixed hourly rates.

6.4.3 Work done after the client is charged

6.4.3.1 The duty solicitor scheme

The duty solicitor scheme operates in the magistrates' court in a similar way to at the police station (see **6.4.2.1** above). Solicitors who are members of a court duty scheme will again have their names on a rota. On the day when it is his turn to attend court as the duty solicitor, the particular solicitor will be available to advise any defendants who do not have their own solicitors but who require legal representation. The duty solicitor will claim his costs in attending court from the LSC under the Advocacy Assistance (Court Duty Solicitor) Scheme.

In recent years the duty solicitor scheme has been extended to allow solicitors who are members of the scheme to represent defendants at preliminary hearings in their capacity as duty solicitors, even though they are not on the rota to attend court as the duty solicitor that day. A solicitor who is on a particular court's duty solicitor panel may represent a client as that client's 'duty solicitor of choice' at an EFH or EAH, and at one further hearing. The solicitor will claim his costs in attending court from the LSC under the Advocacy Assistance Scheme.

Example

Roger is charged with theft. He has admitted his guilt in police interview and is bailed to appear at the magistrates' court. Roger asks his solicitor, Charles, to represent him before the magistrates. Charles is a member of the duty solicitor scheme but is not on the rota to attend court that day as the duty solicitor. Charles can attend court to represent Roger as Roger's 'duty solicitor of choice'.

As Roger is pleading guilty, his first appearance is an EFH. After Roger enters his guilty plea the magistrates decide to adjourn sentencing because they want to obtain a pre-sentence report on Roger from the Probation Service. Charles will be able to represent Roger at this further hearing as Roger's 'duty solicitor of choice'.

The 'duty solicitor of choice' scheme will cover straightforward cases where a defendant pleads guilty and is sentenced either immediately or after one further hearing. For any other type of case (and particularly cases where the defendant is pleading not guilty) it will be necessary for the defendant to apply for a representation order, discussed below.

6.4.3.2   Applying for a representation order

A defendant who wants to apply for a representation order must fill in an application form and send this to the magistrates' court where his case is being heard. The grant of a representation order is subject to a 'merits' test, but not currently to a means test (this will change when the provisions contained in the Criminal Defence Service Act 2006 are brought into effect – see **6.4.5** below).

A representation order will be granted by the magistrates' court only if it is in the interests of justice for the defendant to have his legal costs paid from public funds. This ensures compliance with Article 6(3)(a) of the ECHR, which provides that a defendant who does not have sufficient means to pay for legal assistance should receive this free 'when the interests of justice so require' (see **1.8.3** above).

The factors that are taken into account in deciding whether a defendant can satisfy the interests of justice test are set out in Sch 3, para 5(2) to the Access to Justice Act 1999:

> In deciding what the interests of justice consist of in relation to any individual, the following factors must be taken into account—
>
> (a)   whether the individual would, if any matter arising in the proceedings is decided against him, be likely to lose his liberty or livelihood or suffer serious damage to his reputation,
>
> (b)   whether the determination of any matter arising in the proceedings may involve consideration of a substantial question of law,
>
> (c)   whether the individual may be unable to understand the proceedings or to state his own case,
>
> (d)   whether the proceedings may involve the tracing, interviewing or expert cross-examination of witnesses on behalf of the individual, and
>
> (e)   whether it is in the interests of another person that the individual be represented.

These factors are replicated in Part 5 of the application form for a representation order (Form A – see pages 157–62 below). A solicitor filling in an application for a representation order must discuss each factor with the client and, if that factor is relevant, provide further details in the appropriate box. Further guidance on what might go in each box is set out below:

'5a. It is likely that I will lose my liberty'

This box should be completed if the defendant is facing a serious charge which is likely to result in a prison sentence. A solicitor can find out the likely sentence for a particular offence by consulting the Magistrates' Court Sentencing Guidelines, or, for cases which are likely to be tried in the Crown Court, guidelines set by the Court of Appeal or the Sentencing Guidelines Council (see **Chapter 11**). In completing this box, the solicitor will effectively be presenting the prosecution case against his client 'taken at its most serious' in order to justify why his client should receive public funding for his case.

Magistrates' court

Extracts from the Magistrates' Court Sentencing Guidelines are set out in **Appendix 2**. For each offence that may be dealt with by the magistrates' court, the guidelines set out the maximum penalty for the offence and then a guideline sentence. The guideline sentence is the usual sentence the magistrates would pass on a first-time offender who has entered a guilty plea but been convicted following a trial. By way of example, the guideline sentence for assault occasioning actual bodily harm is a custodial sentence. Even if the sentencing guidelines do not indicate that the magistrates would normally impose a custodial sentence for that offence, the solicitor should consider whether there are any aggravating factors which make the offence more serious than it otherwise would be, and which may in turn lead the magistrates to impose a custodial sentence. The sentencing guidelines set out a list of potentially aggravating factors for each offence. For example, the guideline sentence for theft is a community penalty, but if aggravating factors are present the magistrates might consider custody. Aggravating factors in a theft case will include that the theft was of an item of high value, that it was planned (as opposed to being opportunistic) or that the victim of the theft was vulnerable (such as an elderly person). Aggravating factors in an assault case would include the use of a weapon, premeditation, kicking or biting, or if the victim was vulnerable or serving the public (such as a nurse or bus driver).

Similarly, even if the offence is not particularly serious in itself and would not usually warrant a custodial sentence, if the client has numerous previous convictions for the same type of offence this could result in the client receiving a prison sentence, because the court will treat such convictions as aggravating factors which make the offence more serious.

Crown Court

If the client is charged with an indictable only offence, there should be no difficulty in completing box 5a. Defendants convicted of such offences will almost inevitably receive a custodial sentence. Similarly, if the client is charged with an either way offence which the solicitor considers will be dealt with by the Crown Court (because the specific facts of the offence mean that the magistrates are likely to decide that it is too serious for them to deal with – see **6.10.2.1** below), completing this box should be straightforward. To find out the sentence his client is likely to receive if sentenced in the Crown Court, the solicitor will need to access the case compendium which can be found on the Sentencing Guidelines Council website (www.sentencing-guidelines.gov.uk). The compendium contains details of significant cases in which the Court of Appeal has set out sentencing guidelines for the types of case likely to come before the Crown Court. The Sentencing Guidelines Council has also provided its own definitive sentencing guidelines for certain offences.

'5b. I am currently subject to a sentence that is suspended or non-custodial that if breached may allow the court to deal with me for the original offence'

This box will be relevant if the defendant is subject to a suspended prison sentence (see **Chapter 11**) and commits a further offence during the period of the suspension. There is a statutory presumption that a defendant who is convicted of a further offence during the period of suspension will have his sentence activated and so will go to prison (Criminal Justice Act 2003, Sch 8, para 12).

This box will also be relevant if the defendant is currently the subject of a generic community order (see **Chapter 11**) imposed on a previous occasion when the defendant was before the court for another offence. If the defendant is convicted of the current offence, the court can revoke the order and re-sentence him. The likely 'new' sentence will be a term of imprisonment.

'5c. It is likely that I will lose my livelihood'

This box needs to be completed if the defendant is in employment and a conviction is likely to lead to the loss of that employment. This will apply to any defendant in employment who is likely to face a prison sentence if convicted, but may also be relevant for other defendants who are not likely to receive a prison sentence but who have particular types of job. For example, the defendant may be a bus driver charged with a road traffic offence which will result in his disqualification from driving if he is convicted. Alternatively, the defendant may be a teacher charged with common assault (since a conviction for an offence of violence will preclude a defendant from working with children in the future). This box is also useful for a defendant who is in a position of trust at work and who may lose his job if convicted of an offence involving dishonesty (such as a bank manager accused of a minor theft).

'5d. It is likely that I will suffer serious damage to my reputation'

This box will apply only to defendants with no previous convictions, or with convictions for very minor offences (usually minor road traffic offence such as speeding). If the defendant has no previous convictions and has a position of standing or respect in the community (such as a vicar or a local councillor), a conviction for any criminal offence, even if the offence is relatively minor, may cause serious damage to his reputation. This box is useful for defendants with no previous convictions who are accused of minor offences which would not otherwise receive public funding.

'5e. A substantial question of law is involved'

This box will usually be relevant when a piece of prosecution evidence is in dispute and it will be necessary to challenge the admissibility or credibility of this evidence at trial. Examples of when this may arise are:

(a)   if there is disputed identification evidence and the court needs to apply the *Turnbull* guidelines to assess the credibility of such evidence (see **Chapter 17**);

(b)   if there is a possibility that the court may draw adverse inferences from the defendant's refusal to answer questions at the police station (see **Chapter 18**);

(c)   if either the prosecution or the defence are seeking to persuade the court to admit hearsay evidence (see **Chapter 19**);

(d)   if the defence are seeking to exclude a confession made by the defendant under s 76 or s 78 of PACE 1984 (see **Chapters 20 and 21**);

(e)   if the defence are seeking to exclude any prosecution evidence which has been unfairly obtained under s 78 of PACE 1984 (see **Chapter 2**);

(f)   if the prosecution want to raise the defendant's previous convictions in evidence at trial, or either party is seeking to raise the previous convictions of any other person (see **Chapter 22**).

'5f. I shall be unable to understand the court proceedings or state my own case ...'

Box 5f enables the applicant to apply for representation for the following reason:

> I shall be unable to understand the court proceedings or state my own case because:
>
> (i)   My understanding of English is inadequate ...
>
> (ii)   I suffer from a disability ...

This box should be completed if the defendant is from overseas and does not have a full understanding of spoken or written English, or if the defendant has a disability. A disability can be either some form of mental problem or illness, or a physical disability (such as a defendant who is deaf, blind or unable to speak).

'5g. Witnesses have to be traced and/or interviewed on my behalf'

This box will often be relevant if the defendant is accused of an assault or public order offence in a public place and the defendant believes that there are people who saw the incident who will back up his version of events. For example, a defendant may deny a charge that he assaulted somebody in a nightclub by arguing that he was acting in self-defence. It may be necessary to trace other people who were present in the nightclub at the time who can support what the defendant says.

'5h. The case involves expert cross-examination of a prosecution witness'

This box is likely to be relevant if a witness needs to be cross-examined to determine a question of law, or to decide on the admissibility of a particular piece of evidence. For example, if a defence solicitor is attempting to persuade the court to exclude a confession his client is alleged to have made on the basis that the police have acted improperly, it may be necessary to cross-examine a police officer who is giving evidence for the prosecution to establish that the Codes of Practice issued under PACE 1984 were breached. Only a person with legal expertise could properly conduct such a cross-examination. Similarly, only someone with a detailed knowledge of the law concerning disputed identification evidence could properly conduct a cross-examination of a prosecution witness who claims to have identified the defendant when the defendant disputes this. Box 5h will also be relevant if the prosecution seek to rely on any expert evidence, such as a report from a forensic scientist. If the contents of the report from the forensic scientist are disputed, this will require expert cross-examination to cast doubt upon the expert's conclusions.

'5i. It is in someone else's interests that I am represented'

This box should be completed when it would be inappropriate for a defendant to represent himself and so need to cross-examine prosecution witnesses in person. It would, for example, be inappropriate for a defendant to cross-examine a child witness in person (particularly if the defendant was charged with having abused the child), or for a husband to cross-examine his wife in a domestic abuse case. In certain circumstances, a defendant will not be permitted to cross-examine in person a prosecution witness (see **9.8.3.1**).

'5j. Any other reasons'

This is a 'catch all' box designed to cover any matters not falling under the other headings. Unless there is something specific to the particular case that needs to go in this box, if the defendant is pleading not guilty it is common practice to state here that the defendant intends to enter a not guilty plea.

6.4.3.3   The scope of a representation order

If a defendant is able to satisfy the interests of justice test, the magistrates' court will grant a criminal defence representation order (CDRO) and the order will be sent to the defendant's solicitor. At the conclusion of the case the defendant's solicitor will claim back any costs incurred under the representation order from the LSC (see **6.4.4** below). A magistrates' court has no power to order at the end of the case that a defendant who has received a representation order and who has been convicted should make any payment towards the cost of his publicly funded legal representation. A defendant who is convicted before the Crown Court may be ordered to make such a contribution (see **6.11.3** below).

The representation order granted to a defendant in respect of an either way or summary only matter will cover all the work done by the solicitor in connection with those proceedings in the magistrates' court, and may be extended to cover an appeal to the Crown Court against conviction and/or sentence (see **Chapter 13**). If, for an either way matter, the magistrates decline jurisdiction or the defendant elects trial in the Crown Court (see **6.10** below), the defendant's solicitor will need to ask the magistrates to extend the representation order to cover the proceedings in the Crown Court (see **10.4.2.1**). A representation order granted in respect of an indictable only offence will automatically cover proceedings in both the magistrates' court and the Crown Court, and is referred to as a 'through order' (see **10.4.1.2**).

An example of a completed application for a representation order is set out below, together with an example of the representation order itself.

Key skill – applying for a representation order

APPLICATION FOR THE RIGHT TO REPRESENTATION IN CRIMINAL PROCEEDINGS	FORM A

I apply for the right to representation for the purposes of criminal proceedings in accordance with the Access to Justice Act 1999 and the Criminal Defence Service (General) (No 2) Regulations 2001

1. Personal details

1a. Surname

DICKSON

1b. Forenames

GARY PAUL

1c. Title (Mr, Mrs, Ms, Miss or another)

MR

1d. Date of birth

29.10.79

1e. Home address

17 MARSH STREET
CHESTER
CH3 7LW

1f. Present address (if different from above)

2. Case details

2a. What charges have been brought against you? Describe briefly what it is that you are accused of doing; e.g. theft of £10 worth of CDs or assault on a neighbour

ASSAULT OCCASIONING ACTUAL BODILY HARM (ABH) CONTRARY TO SECTION 47 OF THE OFFENCES AGAINST THE PERSON ACT 1861.

2b. Are there any co-defendants in this matter

No

2c. Give reasons why you and your co-defendants cannot be represented by the same solicitors

3. The Court Proceedings

3a. I am due to appear before

CHESTER MAGISTRATES	court
Date 19th DECEMBER 2006	at 10 am

or

3b. I appeared before

The
Date

And (tick whichever applies)	My case has been sent to the Crown Court for trial under Section 51 of the Crime and Disorder Act 1998	
	My case has been transferred to the Crown Court for trial	
	I was committed for trial to the Crown Court	
	I was convicted and/or* sentenced and I wish to appeal against the conviction/sentence* to the Crown Court/Court of Appeal/ House of Lords*(*Delete as appropriate)	
	I was convicted and committed for sentence to the Crown Court	
	A retrial has been ordered under Section 7 of the Criminal Appeal Act 1968	
	Other (please specify nature of hearing)	

4. Outstanding matters

If there are any other *outstanding* criminal charges or cases against you give details including the court where you are due to appear.

N/A

5. Reasons for wanting representation

To avoid the possibility of your application being delayed, or publicly funded representation being refused because the court does not have enough information about the case, you must complete the rest of this form. When deciding whether to grant publicly funded representation the court will need to know why it is in the interests of justice for you to be represented. If you need help in completing the form you should speak to a solicitor.

	Details	Reasons for grant or refusal (for Details court use only)
5a It is likely that I will lose my liberty (*you should consider seeing a solicitor before answering this question*)	I am accused of committing an unprovoked assault involving multiple blows to the head. The guideline sentence for this offence in the magistrates' court sentencing guidelines is custody. I have one previous conviction for the same offence and two previous convictions for other offences of violence.	
5b. I am currently subject to a sentence that is suspended or non-custodial that if breached may allow the court to deal with me for the original offence. (*Please give details*)		
5c. It is likely that I will lose my livelihood	I work as both a scaffolder/steeplejack and as a nightclub doorman. I will lose both jobs if I am sent to prison. A prison sentence will also preclude me from working as a doorman in the future.	
5d. It is likely that I will suffer serious damage to my reputation		
5e. A substantial question of law is involved. (*You will need the help of a solicitor to answer this question*)	(Please give authorities to be quoted with law reports references.) (i) I will dispute the credibility of identification evidence to be given by a prosecution witness – *R v Turnbull* (1977).	

	(ii) I wish to challenge the admissibility of a confession I made at the police station under ss 76 and 78 of PACE 1984. (iii) The prosecution may seek leave to adduce in evidence under s 101(d) of the Criminal Justice Act 2003 previous convictions I have for offences of violence. I will oppose such an application on the basis that these previous convictions do not demonstrate a propensity to act violently, and that the admission of such convictions at trial would be more prejudicial than probative – *R v Hanson and Others* (2005).	
5f. I shall be unable to understand the court proceedings or state my own case because: i) My understanding of English is inadequate* ii) I suffer from a disability* (* *Delete as appropriate*)		
5g. Witnesses have to be traced and/or interviewed on my behalf (State circumstances)	My girlfriend will provide me with an alibi. She needs to be interviewed by my solicitor so a statement may be taken from her.	

5h. The case involves expert cross examination of a prosecution witness (*give brief details*)	(i) The *Turnbull* witness requires expert cross-examination to undermine the credibility of the identification evidence he will give. (ii) The police officer who interviewed me at the police station requires expert cross-examination to establish that he breached PACE 1984 and the Codes of Practice.	
5i. It is in someone else's interests that I am represented		
5j. Any other reasons (*Give full particulars*)	I am pleading not guilty and the case is likely to be tried in the Crown Court	

6. Legal Representation

a)   If you do not give the name of a solicitor, the court will select a solicitor for you.

b)   You must tell the solicitor that you have named him.

c)   If you have been charged together with another person or persons, the court may assign a solicitor other than the solicitor of your choice.

The solicitor I wish to act for me is:
MR MATTHEW SIMPSON

Give the firm's name and address (if known)
COLLAWS SOLICITORS, 129 WESTGATE, CHESTER

Declaration to be completed by the legal representative
[The legal representative may wish to confirm with the Legal Services Commission the status of the above named solicitor should he/she not be sure of the above named solicitor's authorisation to provide publicly funded representation] I,..., representing the above named applicant, certify that the named solicitor above is authorised to provide representation under a crime franchise contract, or a general criminal contract, or an individual case contract.

I understand that only firms with a general criminal contract or individual case contract may provide representation in the magistrates' court.

or

I,.., representing the above named applicant, certify that the named solicitor above is employed by the Legal Services Commission in a Public Defender Office and is authorised to provide representation.

Signed..Date...

7. Declaration

If you knowingly make a statement which is false, or knowingly withhold information, you may be prosecuted.

If convicted, you may be sent to prison for up to three months or be fined or both (section 21 Access to Justice Act 1999)

I apply for representation for the proceedings set out in Section 3 of this form.

I understand that should my case proceed to the Crown Court or any higher court, the court may order that I pay for some or all of the costs of representation incurred in the proceedings by way of a Recovery of Defence Costs Order. I understand that should my case proceed to the Crown Court or any higher court, I will have to furnish details of my means to the court and/or the Legal Services Commission.

Signed   *Gary Paul Dickson*   dated *19th December 2006*

FOR COURT USE ONLY

Any additional factors considered when determining the application, including any information given orally.

Decision on Interests of Justice Test

I have considered all available details of all the charges and it/is not in the interests of justice that representation be granted for the following reasons:

Signed...Appropriate Officer

Date...

To be completed where right to representation extends to Crown Court

Statement of means Form B given to defendant on..........................(date)

Indicate type of case: Sent case under s 51 Crime and Disorder Act 1998 Transferred for trial Committal for trial/sentence*Appeal against conviction/sentence*Retrial under s 7 of the Criminal Appeal Act 1968 Other (specify)....................................(* Delete as appropriate)

First date of hearing at Crown Court..

Key Document – Representation Order

Royal
coat of
arms

Chester Magistrates' Court
The Square
Chester
CH1 1PF

BOARD COPY

Mr Gary Paul Dickson
17 Marsh Street
Chester
CH3 7LW

Date: 19.12.2006
Order Number: LO 45756567   Board Number: LA/474575/05/06
Date of Grant: 19.12.2006

Date of Hearing:19.12.2006

In accordance with the provisions of Section 12(2) of the Access to Justice Act 1999 the court now grants representation to Gary Paul Dickson for proceedings before a Magistrates' Court in connection with:-

Assault occasioning actual bodily harm, contrary to Section 47 of the Offences Against the Person Act 1861.

The representation granted shall consist of the following:-

Solicitor
including advice on the preparation of the case for the proceedings.

The solicitor assigned is:-

Mr M. Simpson
Collaws
129 Westgate
Chester

Clerk to the Justices

White Copy – Legal Aid Board *Pink Copy* – Solicitor *Blue Copy* – Court *Green Copy* – Defendant *Yellow* - C.P.S.

6.4.3.4   Rates of payment under a representation order

In most cases where the client has the benefit of a representation order, the solicitor will claim a 'standard fee' for the work done on the client's behalf. This is a fixed payment, the level of which is determined by the way in which the case was dealt with. For example, a case where the client pleads not guilty and the matter goes to trial attracts a higher standard fee than a case in which the client enters an immediate plea, because of the extra work involved in representing a client on a not guilty plea. In addition to the standard fee, the solicitor may also claim for travelling and waiting time. If the amount of work done by the solicitor is in excess of the level of the standard fee, the solicitor may claim payment for the work done on the basis of set hourly charging rates prescribed by the LSC.

6.4.4   Claiming payment

When a solicitor has attended the police station to represent a client, he will complete a Claim Costs Summary Sheet (Form CDS 11) which details the work he has done for the client, the times involved and the fees claimed. If the client is charged and the solicitor then obtains a representation order in respect of the court proceedings, a separate CDS 11 will be completed to record the work done by the solicitor at court. A copy of Form CDS 11 is set out at **6.14** below. Any CDS 11 forms that are completed will be retained on the client's file and not sent to the LSC. At the end of each month, the solicitor's firm will send a Contract Work Report Form (Form CDS 6) to the LSC to claim payment for all the police station attendances and court work the firm has carried out during that month. This form will contain a summary of all the individual CDS 11 forms which the firm has completed for that month. When the LSC carries out its annual audit of the firm, the LSC will check a sample of the CDS 11 forms retained on the solicitor's files to ensure that these have been completed correctly.

6.4.5   The Criminal Defence Service Act 2006

The Criminal Defence Service Act 2006 received Royal Assent on 30 March 2006. The Act makes significant changes to the public funding of criminal cases. The principal changes are as follows:

(a)   Responsibility for the granting of representation orders will be transferred from the court to the LSC, although court staff will still carry out the day-to-day processing of criminal legal aid applications.

(b)   In addition to applicants for a representation order needing to demonstrate that it is in the interests of justice that public funding be granted, there will also be a means test. Applicants will only be granted a representation order in the magistrates' court if they satisfy financial eligibility criteria. In the Crown Court an applicant who falls outside the financial eligibility criteria may still be granted public funding, although a system of means testing for cases in the Crown Court is likely to be introduced in 2007.

(c)   Applications for a representation order will need to be supported by financial documentation (such as payslips and bank statements) to confirm that the applicant satisfies the means test.

Although the Act means that large numbers of defendants will either be ineligible for public funding, this is unlikely to lead to arguments that the Act is incompatible with the provisions of the ECHR. Article 6(3) provides that the State is required to provide free legal assistance to a person charged with an offence only if he does not have sufficient means to pay for legal assistance himself (and if the interests of justice so require). Introducing a means test for public funding should not breach this requirement.

Although the Act has received Royal Assent, its provisions will only come into force when the Lord Chancellor introduces the necessary regulations by way of statutory instrument. Notes on the Department of Constitutional Affairs (DCA) website (www.dca.gov.uk) indicate that the new funding arrangements will be brought into force in October 2006. Four draft sets of regulations have been published by the DCA and are currently the subject of consultation with various bodies (including The Law Society):

(a) *The Criminal Defence Service (General) (No 2) (Amendment) Regulations 2006.* These regulations introduce the new test of financial eligibility for publicly-funded representation in criminal proceedings in the magistrates' court, and transfer the responsibility for granting representation orders from the court to the LSC. In practice, however, the LSC will delegate to the court the power to grant representation orders to applicants who satisfy both the interests of justice and the financial eligibility tests.

(b) *The Criminal Defence Service (Financial Eligibility) Regulations 2006.* These regulations set out the criteria relating to financial eligibility which must be satisfied before individuals involved in criminal proceedings may receive publicly-funded representation in the magistrates' court.

Individuals in receipt of certain benefits (such as income support) are automatically eligible, as are those under 16 or under 18 and in full-time education. If an individual has a partner, the partner's resources are to be treated as those of the individual, unless the individual has a contrary interest in the proceedings (for example, a husband charged with assaulting his wife would not have his wife's resources taken into account).

An individual will be financially eligible for a representation order if his *gross income*, adjusted to take account of any partner or children living with him, is £11,590 or less, and ineligible if his *gross income* is £20,740 or more. Where his gross income falls between these amounts, the LSC (or the court under powers delegated to it by the LSC) will calculate the individual's *annual disposable income*, making deductions in respect of any income tax, national insurance, council tax, housing expenses, child care costs, maintenance and living expenses. The individual will be eligible for a representation order if his *annual disposable income* does not exceed £3,156.

(c) *The Criminal Defence Service (Representation Orders and Consequential Amendments) Regulations 2006.* These regulations empower the LSC, instead of the court, to grant a right to publicly-funded representation in criminal proceedings in the magistrates' court. The regulations set out the procedure to be followed by applicants for representation orders. The LSC (or more probably the court acting under powers delegated to it by the LSC) will grant a representation order if an individual is financially eligible and the interests of justice require that an order be granted. Where a representation order is granted, the order extends to the Crown Court if the proceedings continue there.

(d) *The Criminal Defence Service (Representation Orders: Appeals etc) Regulations 2006.* These regulations provide for appeals or renewed applications where an individual has been refused publicly-funded representation on the grounds that the interests of justice do not require him to be granted a representation order. In the case of proceedings in the magistrates' court, the individual may appeal to the court. In the case of proceedings in other courts (most commonly the Crown Court), the individual may make a renewed application to the person who, or court which, refused the application.

An individual will have no automatic right of appeal if his application is refused because he fails to satisfy the financial eligibility criteria. An individual who is unable to pay for his defence costs because of particularly high outgoings, or because the case is likely to be unusually expensive, will be able to apply to the LSC for special consideration under hardship criteria.

6.4.6   The Carter Report

In addition to the changes made by the Criminal Defence Service Act 2006, the Government has recently undertaken a comprehensive review of the way in which criminal litigation work is funded, prompted by concerns regarding the increasing amount of public money being spent in this area. Lord Carter (the chairman of the review panel) published his report on 9 February 2006. The report is entitled *Procurement of Criminal Defence Services* and recommends a number of market-based reforms. These include a system of 'fixed pricing' for all types of work and solicitors doing police station work as part of a 'block contract'. The aim of these recommendations is to concentrate criminal defence work in a small number of large firms to achieve economies of scale and therefore save costs.

6.5   Taking a statement from the client

A defence solicitor will usually meet his client for the first time either at the police station, or when the client makes his first appearance at court. On neither occasion is the solicitor likely to have sufficient time to take a detailed statement from the client. Given the pressures on a solicitor's time in the police station or at court, the best the solicitor is likely to be able to do is take some personal information from his client and brief details about the facts of the case.

A full and accurate statement needs to be taken from the client as soon as possible. Some solicitors will delay taking a statement until they have received details of the prosecution case and can take their client's instructions on this at the same time. Other solicitors prefer to obtain their client's version of events first and then consider the prosecution witness statements when these are received.

There is no set formula for taking a statement from a client, but any statement, whatever its format, needs to be full, accurate and user-friendly. The statement will not be disclosed to the court or the prosecution and can be written using the type of language which the client would normally use. It is good practice to get the statement checked and signed by the client so that there are no misunderstandings as to what the client's 'story' is later in the case. The matters that should be included in a statement are as follows:

(a)   the client's personal details – name, address date of birth, contact telephone number, National Insurance number, etc;

(b)   details of the charge and the court where the client's case is being heard;

(c)   the client's education and employment history;

(d)   details of the client's family circumstances;

(e)   any health problems the client may have;

(f)   any previous convictions the client has;

(g)   what the client has to say about the current offence;

(h)   any factors that might be relevant to mitigation (particularly if the client intends to plead guilty);

(i)   any factors that might be relevant to a bail application, such as a potential surety (see **7.5.1**);

(j)   the client's comments on the prosecution evidence – these can be added to the statement when details of the prosecution case are received.

An example of a completed client's statement is set out below. The prosecution witness statements referred to in the latter half of the client's statement are included in the advance disclosure package set out at **Key Document – Advance Disclosure** at p 172 below.

Key skill – drafting the client's statement

STATEMENT OF GARY PAUL DICKSON

Statement of Gary Paul Dickson will say as follows:

Personal Details

My full name is Gary Paul Dickson and I reside at 17 Marsh Street, Chester CH3 7LW with my girlfriend Jill Summers. The property is owned by Jill's parents and we share a flat on the top floor.

I am 27 years old, having been born on 28th October 1979. I have two jobs. My main occupation is as a scaffolder/steeplejack. I am self-employed and do contract work throughout the country. Basically I go wherever there is work. I also do some part-time work as a doorman/bouncer on a weekend and the odd night during the week at Connolley's Nightclub in Chester.

My contact telephone numbers are:

HOME – Chester 431809

MOBILE – 05573 372537

Charge

I am charged with a s 47 assault on Vincent Lamb in the early hours of the morning of 18th December 2006. I know nothing about any assault on Mr Lamb and it is my intention to enter a not guilty plea to this charge.

Education and Employment History

I was born and brought up in York. I attended Burnholme Community College until I was 16. I left school with GCSEs in English Language, Maths, History and Art.

After leaving school I joined the army. I served as a private and latterly as a corporal with the Green Howards regiment. I left the army in 2001 and moved to Chester to live with some former school friends.

I started doing some scaffolding work for a firm based in Chester on a part-time basis and found that I liked the work. I was never an employee of the firm, but just did contract work as and when it became available. I started doing similar work for a couple of other firms and was soon doing this work all the time. I can earn good money doing the scaffolding. The work takes me to all parts of the country and occasionally I go abroad to work.

I've been doing the work as a doorman for about three years. I'm quite a big lad and when I was having a drink in Connolley's one day, the manager asked if I'd like to do some door work. I jumped at the chance because I thought it was a way to earn some easy money.

Family Circumstances

I've been with my girlfriend Jill Summers for about 18 months. Our relationship is serious and we hope to get married at some point in the future. We are saving up money to get our own place together. Sharing a flat is fine for the moment but we'd like to start a family and need the extra space.

Health

As far as I am aware I don't have any health problems. The army gets you fairly fit and I need to stay in good physical shape to do the work as a doorman.

Previous Convictions

I have 2 convictions for threatening behaviour and one conviction for assault occasioning actual bodily harm. I also have a conviction for failing to answer bail in a previous case.

The violence convictions are all as a result of customers at the nightclub getting aggressive or drunk and needing to be ejected from the premises. Sometimes customers get a bit lippy or even try to punch you when they are being thrown out. I was only ever doing my job, but the customers occasionally complain to the police that they have been assaulted. The police don't like professional doormen and so always press charges if they can. I pleaded guilty to these offences because it was my word against the customers and a lot of their mates.

Current Offence

At about 11.00 am on Monday 18th December 2006 I was asleep in bed with Jill at 17 Marsh Street. I had been working at the nightclub until the early hours and Jill had been out the previous evening as well. As far as I was concerned it had been a normal evening at the nightclub. I had to deal with a couple of drunks but nothing other than that.

A policeman woke me up by banging on the door. I answered the door and he asked me if I was the owner of a dark blue VW Golf registration number L251 CVM. I told him I was, but as it was parked outside the house I thought this was obvious. He then asked me to confirm my whereabouts at 3.15 am that morning. I told him I was in bed with Jill. I asked him what was going on, and he told me that there had been a complaint of an assault by a man driving a car which matched the description and registration number of my car. I told him I didn't know what he was talking about.

He asked me if I would accompany him to the police station to answer some questions. I refused to go so he arrested me. When we got to the police station I was put in a cell for several hours. I hadn't had anything to eat or drink since the previous night, but the police wouldn't give me a drink or a meal. They didn't tell me why I had been stuck in a cell.

At about 6.00 pm I was told that I was going to be interviewed. I asked to speak to a solicitor before I was taken to the interview room. They said that I had to be interviewed there and then, or wait until the following morning. I didn't want to stay there any longer than necessary and so agreed to be interviewed without a solicitor. By the time the interview started I was totally pissed off with the way I had been treated. I said some stupid things which weren't true and which I now regret. They kept asking me the same questions over and over again, and it was clear that they weren't going to believe a word I said when I told them that I knew nothing about the assault. I eventually said it was me just to get out of there.

Mitigation

I have nothing to say in mitigation because I am not guilty of this offence and I will be pleading not guilty when the charge is put to me at court. I know nothing about the attack on Mr Lamb. At the time of the attack I was asleep at home.

Matters Relevant to Bail

I intend to continue working at Connolley's because the money is good. I suppose there is always the chance of more trouble with the public, but this is an occupational hazard. All the other doormen have previous convictions. We are an east target for the police because there is no shortage of lads who want to try it on with us and then go squealing to the police when they get a smack.

The conviction I have for failing to answer my bail was just a mix up over court dates I thought my trial was going to be dealt with in the afternoon, and didn't appreciate that I needed to be at court for 10.00 am regardless. I did turn up at court in the afternoon, but a warrant for my arrest had already been issued. I was arrested at court. This was a genuine oversight on my part but the magistrates convicted me anyway.

I am due to go away to Kerry in the Republic of Ireland in two months' time to do some scaffolding work. The job pays very well and will last for five weeks.

I understand that any bail the court grants me may be subject to conditions. Until I am due to go away with work I would be able to abide by a condition that I report to the police station daily or that I live at 17 Marsh Street.

I could afford to pay a security if required.

Signed: *Gary Dickson*

Dated: 19th December 2006

Comments on Prosecution Witness Statements

PC Gareth Chambers

This is pretty much correct. I have been arrested by PC Chambers before and he obviously has it in for me. He knows about my previous convictions. He obviously wasn't going to let me out of the interview until I said I was guilty, even though I didn't do it.

John Barnard

He must be mistaken. If he had been drinking all night as he claims, his recollection can't be reliable. He says I have short hair and a white tight-fitting T-shirt. This is actually the uniform worn by all the staff at Connolley's so that description could apply to any of the door staff or many of the customers as well.

He isn't very sure of the car registration number. He has either not remembered it properly or the police have told him the number. He did pick me out at the video identification, but he got that wrong as well. Perhaps the police told him who to pick.

Vincent Lamb

I don't know and have never heard of Vincent Lamb. He may have been the guest disc jockey that night. I don't really know what is going on inside the nightclub unless there is any trouble. I spend all my time at the entrance and on the street outside. I am adamant that I have never met Vincent Lamb. I'm sorry if he got his face smashed in, but I had nothing to do with it.

Peter Hansen

There is nothing I can say about this. There must be loads of dark VW Golfs on the road.

Record of audio recorded interview

This seems to be right in terms of what was said, but the confession I made is just not true. I only said I assaulted Vincent Lamb because this was the only way I could think of to get out of the police station. Even though PC Chambers said I would be allowed to leave the police station on bail if I admitted my guilt, after I was charged the custody officer wouldn't let me have bail and I was kept in the cells overnight until court the next day.

Record of previous convictions

This is correct. As I said in my statement, you get plenty of grief on the door of the club. I sometimes gave the odd customer a smack if I thought they deserved it.

6.6 Obtaining disclosure from the prosecution

6.6.1 Introduction

If the solicitor has represented the client at the police station, he may have some knowledge as to what the prosecution case against his client is and what evidence the CPS has to support this case. He is unlikely, however, to have seen copies of the witness statements which the police have obtained. It is vital for the defendant's solicitor to see all the prosecution evidence as soon as possible after the defendant has been charged so he may advise the defendant as to the strength of the case against him and take his instructions on what the prosecution witnesses are saying.

What the CPS must disclose to the defendant's solicitor varies depending on whether the offence the defendant has been charged with is a summary offence or an either way offence.

6.6.2 Summary offences

If the offence is summary only, there is no statutory obligation on the CPS to disclose details of the prosecution case to the defendant's solicitor. As a matter of good practice, however, the CPS will provide the defendant's solicitor with at least a summary of the case against his client, and more usually with copies of the statements of the witnesses upon whose evidence the prosecution are going to rely at trial. The Attorney-General has issued guidelines to prosecutors to this effect, stating that the CPS should disclose to the defence all the evidence upon which the prosecution will seek to rely at trial (*Attorney-General's Guidelines on Disclosure of Information in Criminal Proceedings 2000*).

6.6.3 Either way offences

A defendant charged with an either way offence in entitled to receive 'advance disclosure' of the prosecution case (CrimPR, r 21.3). The CPS will serve on the defendant's solicitor an advance disclosure package containing:

(a)   copies of the written statements given by prosecution witnesses;

(b)   a transcript of any audibly recorded interviews with the defendant in the police station (together with a copy of the interview tape, unless the suspect was given a copy of the tape on charge – see **3.5.2.1**); and

(c)   details of any previous convictions which the defendant may have.

Should the CPS fail to disclose to the defence details of the evidence on which the prosecution will seek to rely at trial, this would constitute a breach of the 'equality of arms' principle enshrined in Article 6(3) of the ECHR (see **1.8.3**).

Key Document – Advance Disclosure

Set out below is the advance disclosure package provided to the solicitor representing Gary Dickson.

CHESHIRE POLICE

WITNESS STATEMENT

(CJ Act 1967, s 9; MC Act 1980, ss 5A(3)(a) and 5B; MC Rules 1981, r 70)

Station or Section: Chester   Division: G

Statement of (name of witness): VINCENT LAMB   Date: 20 December 2006
(in full – Block letters)

Date and place of birth: Over 18 England

Occupation: Entertainer

This statement (consisting of 1 page signed by me) is true to the best of my knowledge and belief and I make it knowing that if it is tendered in evidence I shall be liable to prosecution if I have wilfully stated in it anything which I know to be false or do not believe to be true.

Dated: 20th December 2006   Signed: *Vincent Lamb*

I am employed as a freelance disc jockey.

At about 3.15 am on 18th December 2006, I was walking away from Connolley's Nightclub intending to go to the nearby multi-storey car park to get my van and then return to the club to pack away all my equipment. I was in a really good mood as I had finished an evening as the guest disc jockey at the club and I thought it had gone extremely well.

It was very dark as I walked along. I heard a car approach from behind me at speed. I turned and was dazzled by the headlights so I couldn't see very much at all. The car screeched to a halt and the driver's side door opened. Someone got out and I was aware of the shadow of a large man silhouetted against the headlights of the car. I could not see what the man looked like or what he was wearing. He walked straight up to me and struck me in the face with his fist. I was struck several times in the face and was knocked to the ground. I must have lost consciousness because the next thing I remember was coming around on the pavement after my attacker had gone.

A passer-by called an ambulance and I was taken to Chester Hospital where I received treatment. As a result of the attack I have a broken nose and a deep cut above my left eyebrow. A splint was put on my nose and some stitches were put in my eyebrow. I have to go back to hospital next week to have the stitches removed.

I can't think why anyone would want to attack me. Nothing untoward had occurred during the evening and I had got on well with all the customers at the nightclub. My wallet was still in my pocket and nothing was missing.

Signed: *Vincent Lamb*   Signature witnessed by: *PC Chambers*

CHESHIRE POLICE

WITNESS STATEMENT

(CJ Act 1967, s 9; MC Act 1980, ss 5A(3)(a) and 5B; MC Rules 1981, r 70)

Station or Section: Chester   Division: G

Statement of (name of witness): JOHN BARNARD   Date: 20th December 2006

(in full – Block letters)

Date and place of birth: Over 18 England

Occupation: Engineer

This statement (consisting of 1 page signed by me) is true to the best of my knowledge and belief and I make it knowing that if it is tendered in evidence I shall be liable to prosecution if I have wilfully stated in it anything which I know to be false or do not believe to be true.

Dated: 20th December 2006   Signed: *John Barnard*

I am a mechanical engineer employed by Imperial Chemicals at Bootle Merseyside and live at 10 Tower Court, Belleview Road, Liverpool.

On 17th December 2006 I had been out for the evening in Chester. I had been to a club called Toffs and had quite a bit to drink; about seven pints over the course of the evening.

At approximately 3.15 am on Monday 18th December I was walking back to a friend's house where I had agreed to stay the night. I noticed a dark coloured VW Golf zoom past me at speed and pull up sharply next to a young man who was walking about 50 metres in front of me. A well-built man got out of the driver's seat and proceeded to hit the other man in the face several times. There didn't seem to be any provocation for the attack. The man who was hit didn't put up any real resistance, as he was quite a lot smaller than the well-built man. The big man then got back in his car and sped back the way he had just come, so that he passed me again. He must have been travelling at about 40 mph by the time he passed me so I only managed to glimpse him as he passed. He was white, clean shaven with short dark hair and a tight-fitting white T-shirt. As the car disappeared I tried to remember the registration. I used to be in the army and I have done checkpoint duty in Northern Ireland so I have had some training in vehicle recognition. I made a mental note at the time and told a police officer later that evening that I thought the registration number was either C251 CVM or L251 CVM. It was a dark blue Golf. It did not appear to have any body damage on the side I saw. I am not sure of the numbers as I had quite a bit to drink that night but I'm quite certain it was 'CVM' at the end.

I was subsequently asked to see if I could pick out the man in the car at a video identification. I picked out foil number four in the video identification.

[Gary Dickson was foil number four]

Signed: *John Barnard*

Taken by: PC244 Hansen

CHESHIRE POLICE

WITNESS STATEMENT

(CJ Act 1967, s 9; MC Act 1980, ss 5A(3)(a) and 5B; MC Rules 1981, r 70)

Station or Section: Chester   Division: G

Statement of (name of witness): GARETH CHAMBERS   Date: 18 December 2006
(in full – Block letters)

Date and place of birth: Over 18 England

Occupation: Policeman

This statement (consisting of 1 page signed by me) is true to the best of my knowledge and belief and I make it knowing that if it is tendered in evidence I shall be liable to prosecution if I have wilfully stated in it anything which I know to be false or do not believe to be true.

Dated: 18th December 2006   Signed: *Gareth Chambers*

I am Police Constable 911 of Cheshire Police based at Chester.

On Monday 18th December 2006 I was on mobile patrol in Chester town centre. Acting on information received I attended at 17 Marsh Street at 11.10 am. I knocked on the door of 17 Marsh Street and a man known to me as Gary Dickson answered. I asked Mr Dickson if he was the owner of a dark blue VW Golf registration number L251 CVM. He said that he was. I then asked Mr Dickson to confirm his whereabouts in the early hours of 18th December at approximately 3.15 am. I explained that if he would accompany me to the station then I could take a statement and it may be that he would be eliminated from our enquiries.

Mr Dickson refused to accompany me so I returned to my vehicle and called for back up. Once further police officers attended following my request I again asked Mr Dickson to accompany me to the station. He refused so I arrested him on suspicion of having committed an assault on Vince Lamb the previous evening. He made no reply.

I conveyed Gary Dickson and myself to Chester Police Station. At the police station the custody officer authorised the detention of Gary Dickson for questioning. I later interviewed Mr Dickson in Interview Room 2 at Chester Police Station in accordance with the Codes of Practice. Two tapes were used and the sealed master tape is available as exhibit 'GC1'.

At 18.30 hours the interview was commenced and it was concluded at 18.40 hours.

I have prepared a copy of the salient points of the interview, which I produce as exhibit 'GC1'.

At 19.45 hours, after Mr Dickson had taken part in a video identification, I took Mr Dickson before the custody officer who charged him with assault occasioning actual bodily harm. He made no reply.

Signed: *Gareth Chambers*

Taken by: PC 244 Hansen

CHESHIRE POLICE

WITNESS STATEMENT

(CJ Act 1967, s 9; MC Act 1980, ss 5A(3)(a) and 5B; MC Rules 1981, r 70)

Station or Section: Chester   Division: G

Statement of (name of witness): PETER HANSEN   Date: 29th December 2006
(in full – Block letters)

Date and place of birth: Over 18 England

Occupation: Police Constable

This statement (consisting of 1 page signed by me) is true to the best of my knowledge and belief and I make it knowing that if it is tendered in evidence I shall be liable to prosecution if I have wilfully stated in it anything which I know to be false or do not believe to be true.

Dated: 19th December 2006   Signed: *Peter Hansen*

I am Police Constable 244 of Cheshire Police based at Chester.

On 18th December 2006 I made a request to the Vehicle Licensing Authority at Swansea for confirmation of the details of the registered keeper and registered address of the vehicles with the registration number C251 CVM and L251 CVM. C251 CVM is a silver BMW and L251 CVM is a dark blue VW Golf. The registered keeper of the latter vehicle is Gary Paul Dickson.

Signed: *P Hansen*

Taken by: PC244 Hansen

CHESHIRE POLICE

WITNESS STATEMENT

(CJ Act 1967, s 9; MC Act 1980, ss 5A(3)(a) and 5B; MC Rules 1981, r 70)

Station or Section: Chester   Division: G

Statement of (name of witness): HARBHAJAN SINGH   Date: 29th December 2006
(in full – Block letters)

Date and place of birth: Over 18 England

Occupation: Doctor

This statement (consisting of 1 page signed by me) is true to the best of my knowledge and belief and I make it knowing that if it is tendered in evidence I shall be liable to prosecution if I have wilfully stated in it anything which I know to be false or do not believe to be true.

Dated: 29th December 2006   Signed: *Harbhajan Singh*

I am a Senior House Officer employed by Chester Hospital in the Accident and Emergency Department.

This statement is taken from the notes which I made at the time of my examination of Vincent Lamb.

Mr Lamb was seen in the Accident and Emergency Department on 18th December 2006 at about 3.45 am. Mr Lamb alleged that he had been assaulted and had sustained facial injuries. He had lost consciousness following the assault, but had not vomited or suffered any visual disturbance.

When examined Mr Lamb was slightly groggy and had a laceration over his left eyebrow and swelling over the bridge of his nose. An X-ray of his facial bones was organised and this showed a fracture in the bone over the bridge of the nose.

Four stitches were put into the laceration over the left eyebrow and a splint was provided for the broken nose. Mr Lamb was advised about possible problems following a head injury, and was allowed home.

Mr Lamb was seen again 7 days later when the stitches and the splint were removed.

Signed: *Harbhajan Singh*

Taken by: PC244 Hansen

CHESHIRE POLICE

RECORD OF AUDIO-RECORDED INTERVIEW

INTERVIEW OF: Gary Dickson   **DATE OF BIRTH:** 28.10.79

ADDRESS: 17 Marsh Street, Chester   **DATE:** 18.12.2006

INTERVIEW AT: Chester Police Station

TIME COMENCED: 6.30 pm   **TIME CONCLUDED:** 6.40 pm

DURATION OF INTERVIEW: 10 mins   **TAPE REFERENCE NO:** SG01/4351

INTERVIEWING OFFICER: PC G Chambers   **OTHER PERSONS PRESENT** None

Signature of officer preparing record: *Gareth Chambers* PC911

Tape times	PARTICULARS OF INTERVIEW
0.00	Introductions.
	Caution. Reminded of right to free legal advice.
0.50	PC911: Right Mr Dickson, I think you know why you're here, don't you? You have been arrested for assaulting a man near to Connolley's Nightclub.
1.12	GD: I've been here most of the day and I haven't had much sleep, so do you think you could let me go now or what?
	PC911: Just answer the question Mr Dickson and we can both go home.
	GD: Look, just because I work at the club that doesn't mean you can pin any kind of trouble on me. I'm saying nothing.
2.42	PC911: Mr Dickson, why don't we just get this over with? Look I'm going off duty soon and if we don't deal with this interview now I won't be back on duty until tomorrow afternoon. You don't want to have to wait until then, do you?
	GD: No I don't. My girlfriend will be worried about me – she will think that I'm in some sort of trouble. Could I at least telephone her?
3.20	PC911: Don't worry, this will be over sooner than you think. Let's make a start then. Where were you at 3.15 am this morning?
3.56	GD: I would have finished work by then so I'd be at home.
	PC911: Are you sure about that, because I have reason to believe you were still near to the club and you assaulted a man there?
	GD: No. That's not true. I had been at the club earlier but I left much earlier than 3.15 am.
	PC911 Oh come on Mr Dickson, don't play the innocent with me or we'll be here all night.
4.20	GD: Look I don't know where you are getting the idea in your head that I've been assaulting someone. It's just rubbish.

Tape times	PARTICULARS OF INTERVIEW
4.50	PC911: Come on Mr Dickson, let's be serious, shall we? You chased him in your car didn't you? And you got out of the car and then you beat him?
	GD: No, I did not.
	PC911: You were seen Mr Dickson. Driving your own car at the time wasn't very clever was it?
	GD: No, you are seriously barking up the wrong tree here. The person who saw me is obviously confused. I was at the club and I did drive it to work and home again. But I didn't stop to beat anyone up and I wasn't on the road at 3.15 am. I would have got home much earlier than that.
5.20	PC911: That's rubbish isn't it? We have a witness who says that he saw you go over to the victim, hit him in the face several times and then drive away back in the direction towards Marsh Street.
	GD: He's making it up.
6.40	PC911: Why would the witness lie? You must realise this is a very serious charge, Mr Dickson. We're not going to get anywhere if you're going to play these stupid games with me. Perhaps you'd like to stop being clever or I'll take you back to the cells. Don't you want to get out of here tonight? What's it to be?
	GD: I've told you already what happened.
	PC911: Oh come on.
	GD: You lot have really got it in for me haven't you?
7.20	PC911: We both know you've been in trouble before – so it's likely you did exactly what our witness says.
	GD: Why don't you get off my back and go and find the person that really did it.
7.50	PC911: Come on, Dickson that isn't very helpful is it? We both know it was you so it seems futile to deny it.
	GD: Well if it makes you happy, so what if it was me? You should know that I always get even with people who get on the wrong side of me.
8.20	PC911: I think you're getting carried away again. Why don't we just finish this interview and then you can go and get some sleep? I think we both know that it's going to be better for you if you just tell me what really happened. The courts tend to come down heavy on repeat offenders you know. All I need is for you to accept that you assaulted Vince Lamb. Do you admit you did that?
	GD: Yes, I suppose so.
	PC911: You don't mean you suppose so, do you? You mean you did it.

Tape times	PARTICULARS OF INTERVIEW
9.10	GD: Yes.
	PC911: Do you have anything further you wish to say before I terminate this interview?
	GD: No.
9.50	INTERVIEW TERMINATED AT 6.40 PM
10.00	

CHESHIRE POLICE

RECORD OF PREVIOUS CONVICTIONS

THIS PRINTOUT IS PRODUCED FOR THE USE OF THE COURT, DEFENCE
AND PROBATION SERVICE ONLY AND MUST NOT BE DISCLOSED TO ANY
OTHER PARTY

DATA PROTECTION LEGISLATION

THESE PERSONAL DATA ARE PROVIDED TO YOU FOR THE AGREED
SPECIFICATION PURPOSE(S).   KEEP THE DATA SECURE AND PROTECT
THEM AGAINST LOSS OR UNAUTHORISED ACCESS

COURT/DEFENCE/PROBATION PRINT

PRINT OF PNC RECORD

PRINT FOR: DEFENDANT PRINT

TOTAL NUMBER OF PAGES ATTACHED   3

PLEASE NOTE THAT IN THE ABSENCE OF FINGERPRINTS, IDENTITY
CANNOT BE POSITIVELY CONFIRMED WITH THE SUBJECT OF YOUR
ENQUIRY AND YOU SHOULD CONFIRM THE INFORMATION WITH THE PERSON

YOUR ATTENTION IS DRAWN TO THE PROVISIONS OF THE
REHABILITATION OF OFFENDERS ACT 1974

THIS PRINTOUT IS PRODUCED FOR THE USE OF THE COURT, DEFENCE AND PROBATION SERVICE ONLY AND MUST NOT BE DISCLOSED TO ANY OTHER PARTY

YOUR ATTENTION IS DRAWN TO THE PROVISIONS OF THE REHABILITATION OF OFFENDERS ACT 1974

DATA PROTECTION LEGISLATION

THESE PERSONAL DATA ARE PROVIDED TO YOU FOR THE AGREED SPECIFICATION PURPOSE(S). KEEP THE DATA SECURE AND PROTECT THEM AGAINST LOSS OR UNAUTHORISED ACCESS

```
SURNAME        :    DICKSON
FORENAME(S)    :    GARY PAUL
BORN           :    28/10/79
ADDRESS        :    17 MARSH STREET
                    CHESTER
                    CH3 7LW
```

SUMMARY OF CONVICTIONS AND REPRIMANDS/WARNINGS/CAUTIONS

CONVICTION(S)   :   OFFENCE(S): 4

DATE FIRST CONVICTED: 10/09/04 DATE LAST CONVICTED: 13/12/05

1 OFFENCE AGAINST THE PERSON   (2005)

2 PUBLIC ORDER ACT OFFENCES   (2004-2005)

1 MISCELLANEOUS OFFENCE   (2005)

            SUMMARY OF REPRIMANDS/WARNINGS/CAUTIONS

                        NONE

END OF SUMMARY OF CONVICTIONS AND REPRIMANDS/WARNINGS/CAUTIONS

CONVICTIONS
----

1. 10/09/04 CHESTER MAGISTRATES COURT

    1. THREATENING BEHAVIOUR   FINE £150
        PUBLIC ORDER ACT 1986 s 4   COSTS £25
----

2. 17/03/05 CHESTER MAGISTRATES COURT

    1. THREATENING BEHAVIOUR   FINE £250
        PUBLIC ORDER ACT 1986 s 4   COSTS £25

----

3. 13/12/05 CHESTER MAGISTRATES COURT

    1. ABH   GENERIC COMMUNITY ORDER-
        OFFENCES AGAINST THE PERSON 200 HOURS UNPAID WORK
        ACT 1861 s 47   COMPENSATION £100
                                    COSTS   £50

    2. FAILURE TO SURRENDER   FINE   £300

END OF CONVICTION REPORTS

6.7 Advising the client on plea

6.7.1 Matters to discuss with the client

After he has obtained details of the prosecution case, the defendant's solicitor will then need to take further instructions from his client. The following matters will have to be discussed:

(a) the client's response to the prosecution case – each prosecution witness statement needs to be discussed with the client and an accurate note taken of any points of dispute. This note should then be added to the client's statement. The solicitor should also listen to the interview tape to check that the transcript with which he has been provided is accurate. If the client made any admissions when interviewed, the solicitor needs to take instructions from his client – are the admissions correct, or did the client make admissions because of the manner in which the interview was conducted or just to get out of the police station as quickly as possible? Does the client come across well on tape (in which case, should the solicitor ask for the interview to be played out at trial rather than the transcript being read out)? Are there grounds on which an application may be made to the court to exclude the interview record from being used in evidence at trial? (See **Chapters 20** and **21**.);

(b) the strength of the prosecution case – whilst it is the client's decision as to the plea he will enter, if the prosecution case is overwhelming the solicitor should inform the client of this, and remind the client that he will be given credit for entering an early guilty plea when he is subsequently sentenced (see **Chapter 11**);

(c) whether it is necessary to obtain any further evidence in support of the defendant's case – for example, in the light of the prosecution evidence which has been disclosed, the client may recall the identity of other witnesses who could give evidence on his behalf;

(d) if the defendant has been charged with an either way offence and is pleading not guilty, whether he should elect to be tried in the magistrates' court, or before a judge and jury in the Crown Court (see **6.11** below).

The ultimate decision the client will need to take once the CPS has disclosed details of its case is what plea to enter. This is the client's decision, not the solicitor's. As mentioned in (b) above, as part of his duty to act in the best interests of his client, the solicitor should give the client his view of the strength of the evidence against him. It is also appropriate for the solicitor to advise the client that, when it comes to sentencing, the client will receive a reduced sentence for entering an early guilty plea. But if a client steadfastly maintains his innocence, the solicitor should not attempt to browbeat the client into pleading guilty, even if the solicitor considers that the evidence against him is overwhelming.

6.7.2 Professional conduct

Occasionally a client will tell his solicitor that he is guilty of the offence but nevertheless intends to enter a not guilty plea at court. This will raise issues of professional conduct for the solicitor who, whilst under a duty to act in his client's best interests, is under an overriding duty not to mislead the court. In such circumstances the client has two options – to plead guilty, or to plead not guilty. To comply with his duty to act in his client's best interests, the solicitor will need to advise the client of the benefits were the client to enter a guilty plea, and of the limitations on the solicitor's ability to continue representing the client were he to enter a plea of not guilty.

6.7.2.1 Benefits of pleading guilty

The solicitor should advise the client that, were he to plead guilty, the client would receive credit from the court for entering an early guilty plea when the court was deciding what sentence to impose (see **Chapter 11**). Similarly, if the client enters a guilty plea, the solicitor will be able to give a plea in mitigation on the client's behalf before the client is sentenced (see **Chapter 12**).

6.7.2.2 Limitations if the client pleads not guilty

If the client insists on maintaining a not guilty plea, he must be advised that the solicitor may still represent him at his trial but that the solicitor is limited in what he can do on the client's behalf because of his overriding duty not to mislead the court. At trial, the solicitor would be able to cross-examine prosecution witnesses and put the prosecution to proof of their case, since this would not involve misleading the court (although, in cross-examining the prosecution witnesses, the solicitor would need to be careful not to assert any positive defence that he knew to be false). Similarly, the solicitor would be able to make a submission of no case to answer at the end of the prosecution case and to ask the magistrates to dismiss the case, as again this would not involve misleading the court. Such a submission could be made if the prosecution failed to discharge their evidential burden to show that the defendant had a case to answer (see **9.5**).

The defendant's solicitor would, however, be unable to continue acting for the defendant if the submission of no case to answer was unsuccessful and the defendant then insisted on entering the witness box to give evidence which the solicitor knew to be false. In this situation, the defendant's solicitor could not be a party to misleading the court and would need to withdraw from the case. The solicitor would nevertheless still owe a duty of confidentiality to his client and so could not indicate to the court the reason for his withdrawal from the case. A common euphemism that defence solicitors use in such situations is to tell the court that they are withdrawing from the case 'for professional reasons'.

Example

Shane is charged with theft from a shop. The evidence against him consists only of identification evidence from the owner of the shop. Shane admits his guilt to his solicitor but enters a not guilty plea, believing that he may be acquitted if the evidence given by the shop owner at court is unconvincing. Shane's solicitor is entitled to cross-examine the owner of the shop at trial to cast doubt on the credibility of the evidence he gives. For example, the shop owner may have caught only a fleeting glimpse of Shane from a long distance away, and may admit under cross-examination that he cannot be certain of the identification he has made. If the evidence given by the shop owner is unconvincing, Shane's solicitor will then be able to make a submission of no case to answer at the conclusion of the prosecution case and ask the magistrates to dismiss the case. If, however, the magistrates decline to dismiss the case and Shane then insisted on giving evidence in his own defence, his solicitor would need to withdraw from the case so as not to be a party to the court being misled. The solicitor would tell the court that he could not continue to act in the case for 'professional reasons' so as not to breach his duty of confidentiality to Shane.

6.8   The next hearing – entering a plea

6.8.1   Introduction

Once the defendant's solicitor has had the opportunity to obtain details of the prosecution case and to discuss these with his client, the court will expect the defendant to be in a position to enter his plea at the next hearing following the EAH.

6.8.2   Summary offences

If the offence is a summary one, the defendant will enter a plea of guilty or not guilty. If the defendant pleads guilty, the magistrates will then either sentence the defendant immediately, or adjourn the case for the preparation of reports (usually from the Probation Service) before sentencing the defendant. The magistrates may also need to adjourn the case if the defendant pleads guilty but disputes the specific factual allegations made by the CPS. In such a situation a separate hearing (called a 'Newton hearing' – see **12.4**) will be necessary to determine the factual basis upon which the defendant will be sentenced. The sentencing procedure in the magistrates' court is described in **Chapter 12**.

If the defendant is pleading not guilty, the court will fix a date for the defendant's trial to take place and issue case management directions which both prosecution and defence must comply with before trial. Details of the directions the court will make are given in **Chapter 8**.

Whether the defendant is pleading guilty or not guilty, if the case is adjourned the magistrates will need to determine whether the defendant should be released on bail or remanded in custody prior to the next hearing (see **Chapter 7**).

6.8.3   Either way offences

If the offence is an either way matter, the defendant may still enter his plea as for a summary only offence. However, before going any further, the magistrates must then determine whether the defendant is to be sentenced (if he is pleading guilty) or tried (if he is pleading not guilty) in the magistrates' court, or in the Crown Court. This is known as the plea before venue and allocation procedure, discussed in further detail at **6.9** and **6.10** below.

6.9   Plea before venue

The procedure that will take place when the defendant appears before the magistrates is as follows:

(a)   The charge will be read out to the defendant by the court clerk/legal adviser, who will also check that the defendant's solicitor has received advance disclosure of the prosecution case.

(b)   The clerk will then tell the defendant that he may indicate to the court how he would plead if the matter were to proceed to trial (the defendant is under no obligation to indicate his plea). The clerk will also tell the defendant that, if he indicates a guilty plea, he will then be treated as having pleaded guilty before the magistrates, who may then either sentence him or commit him to the Crown Court to be sentenced if they consider their own sentencing powers to be inadequate.

(c)   The clerk will then ask the defendant to give his plea.

(d)   If the defendant indicates a guilty plea, the CPS representative will then outline the facts of the case to the magistrates and tell the magistrates about any previous convictions the defendant may have. The defendant's solicitor will then give a plea in mitigation on the defendant's behalf. At this point the magistrates will need to determine if their sentencing powers are sufficient to deal with the case, or if the defendant should be sentenced by a Crown Court judge who has greater sentencing powers. The maximum sentence a magistrates' court may pass is 12 months' imprisonment for a defendant who is convicted of one either way offence, rising to a maximum of 65 weeks where a defendant is convicted of two or more either way offences. The magistrates will determine whether their sentencing powers are sufficient by assessing the overall seriousness of the offence, looking at the guideline sentence in the Magistrates' Court Sentencing Guidelines (see **11.4.3.2** and **Appendix 2**) and considering whether there are any aggravating or mitigating factors present which make the offence either more or less serious.

(e)   If the magistrates decide that their sentencing powers are sufficient, they will then either sentence the defendant straight away, or adjourn the case for reports before sentencing the defendant (the magistrates will also need to adjourn the case if they consider that a '*Newton* hearing' is necessary – see **6.8.2** above). If the case is adjourned for sentence, the defendant will be released on bail or remanded in custody prior to the sentencing hearing.

Example

Hamish is charged with theft of a necklace. At the plea before venue hearing he enters a guilty plea. The CPS representative then outlines the facts of the case to the magistrates. The magistrates hear that the necklace was worth £100 and that Hamish has returned the necklace to the police. They also hear that Hamish has no previous convictions for any kind of offence. The magistrates decide that their sentencing powers are sufficient. They will either sentence Hamish immediately, or adjourn the case for reports before sentencing Hamish.

(f)   If the magistrates decide that their sentencing powers are insufficient, they will commit the defendant to Crown Court for sentence pursuant to the Powers of Criminal Courts (Sentencing) Act 2000, s 3. This section allows the magistrates to commit the defendant to Crown Court for sentence if they consider that the offence (or, if there is more than one offence, the combination of the offences) is so serious that the Crown Court should have the power to deal with the defendant as if he had been convicted at a Crown Court trial. The procedural rules which must be complied with when a defendant is committed to the Crown Court for sentence are set out in Part 43 of the Criminal Procedure Rules 2005.

Example

Danny is charged with theft of a necklace. At the plea before venue hearing he enters a guilty plea. The CPS representative then outline the facts of the case to the magistrates. The magistrates hear that the necklace was worth £10,000 and has not been recovered. They are also told that Danny has numerous previous convictions for theft. In the light of this information the magistrates decide that their sentencing powers are insufficient, and they to commit Danny to the Crown Court for sentence.

If the defendant is committed to the Crown Court for sentence, he will be remanded either in custody, or on bail. In most cases where a defendant pleads guilty at the plea before venue hearing and is committed to Crown Court for sentence, the magistrates will not alter the position as regards bail or custody. Thus when a defendant who has been on bail enters a guilty plea, the magistrates are likely to grant him bail, even if they anticipate that the defendant will receive a custodial sentence at the Crown Court. If a defendant who has been in custody enters a guilty plea at the plea before venue hearing, he is likely to remain in custody prior to the sentencing hearing at the Crown Court (*R v Rafferty* [1999] 1 Cr App R 235).

(g) If the defendant either refuses to enter a plea (as he is entitled to do) or enters a not guilty plea, a procedure called 'allocation' will then occur. This will conclude with the case either staying in the magistrates' court for trial, or being sent to the Crown Court for trial.

6.10 Allocation

6.10.1 Introduction

The allocation process has two stages. At the first stage, the magistrates will determine in which type of court it is more appropriate for the defendant to be tried. If the magistrates decide that the case is more suitable for a summary trial before them, the second stage will then take place. At this stage, the defendant has the option either of agreeing to his trial taking place in the magistrates' court, or of electing trial before a judge and jury at the Crown Court.

6.10.2 The first stage

6.10.2.1 Procedure

The first stage in the allocation process is for the *magistrates* to decide whether the offence is more suitable for summary trial in the magistrates' court, or trial on indictment in the Crown Court. Under s 19(2) of the Magistrates' Courts Act 1980, before the court makes this decision it must:

(a) give the prosecution an opportunity to tell the court about any previous convictions the defendant has; and

(b) give the prosecution and the defence the opportunity to make representations as to whether summary trial or trial on indictment is more suitable.

In practice, the CPS representative will outline the facts of the case to the magistrates, tell the magistrates about any previous convictions the defendant has and suggest in which court (magistrates' court or Crown Court) he thinks the trial ought to be held. The defendant's solicitor will then tell the magistrates in which court he thinks the trial ought to be held.

Once the magistrates have heard from the prosecution and the defence, they will then decide whether the case is more suitable for trial in the magistrates' court or in the Crown Court. In making this decision the magistrates must take into account the following considerations:

(a) whether their sentencing powers (see **6.9** above) would be adequate in the event that the defendant was found guilty of the offence;

(b) any representations that have been made by the prosecution or the defence; and

(c) any allocation guidelines issued by the Sentencing Guidelines Council under s 170 of the Criminal Justice Act 2003 (the Council have issued a draft set of guidelines entitled National Allocation Guidelines (2006) – see **6.10.2.2** below) (Magistrates' Courts Act 1980, s 19(3)).

6.10.2.2   The National Allocation Guidelines (2006)

The National Allocation Guidelines are published by the Sentencing Guidelines Council (SGC) for use by the magistrates' court when deciding whether an either way offence should remain in the magistrates' court for trial, or should be sent to the Crown Court for trial. The purpose behind the Guidelines is to ensure there is consistency between magistrates' courts throughout the country as to the types of case which are sent to the Crown Court for trial. The court must have regard to these Guidelines when deciding whether a case should be sent for trial. The Guidelines are currently in draft form and are likely to be finalised in the latter part of 2006.

The draft Guidelines set out the following general principles which the magistrates should apply when making their decision as to trial venue:

(a)   The court should begin with the presumption that the case will be suitable for trial in the magistrates' court.

(b)   The primary test as to whether the magistrates should retain jurisdiction or send the case to the Crown Court for trial is the adequacy of their sentencing powers were the defendant to be convicted.

(c)   The magistrates should decide whether their sentencing powers will be sufficient according to the seriousness of the alleged offence.

(d)   To determine the seriousness of the alleged offence, the magistrates should look at the case at its worst from the point of view of the defendant (ie, their decision should be based on the prosecution case taken at its highest and they should assume that all the factual allegations made against the defendant are correct).

(e)   How seriously the magistrates view the case will be based on representations made by the prosecution and defence as to the nature and circumstances of the offence (including the presence of any aggravating or mitigating factors). The court must also have regard to any definitive sentencing guidelines issued by the SGC, and to any relevant guideline judgments from the Court of Appeal. As the magistrates must assume that the prosecution version of events is correct, any representations by the defence should be limited to identifying any inaccuracies in the factual outline of the case, assessing the adequacy of the court's sentencing powers and determining the relevance of the defendant's previous convictions.

(f)   In assessing the seriousness of the offence, the magistrates must consider the existence and relevance of any previous convictions, taking into consideration the nature of the offences to which the previous convictions relate, the relevance of these convictions to the current offence, and the time that has elapsed since the convictions.

(g)   It will be rare for the magistrates to decline jurisdiction for reasons that are not connected with the adequacy of its sentencing powers, although there may be a few exceptional cases where it is important to have the separation between judge and jury that is possible in the Crown Court (the Guidelines cite as an example a case where there are complex issues of disclosure that need to be resolved by a judge).

(h)   If the magistrates are uncertain as to whether their sentencing powers will be adequate if the defendant is convicted, they should send the matter to Crown Court for trial.

(i)   If there is more than one defendant, the presumption is that a single trial will be in the interests of justice (ie, the magistrates should either send all the defendants to the Crown Court for trial or retain jurisdiction in respect of each defendant).

It is anticipated that, in time the SGC will provide more detailed guidelines for specific offences. The full set of draft Guidelines can be found on the SGC website (www.sentencing-guidelines.gov.uk).

6.10.2.3   The magistrates' decision

If the magistrates decide that the case is more suitable for trial in the Crown Court, they will 'send' the defendant to the Crown Court for trial under s 51(1) of the Crime and Disorder Act 1998. The procedure for sending a case to the Crown Court is described in **Chapter 10**. The magistrates will either grant the defendant bail, or remand the defendant in custody pending his first appearance at the Crown Court.

Example

Veronica is charged with assault occasioning actual bodily harm. At the plea before venue hearing she indicates a not guilty plea. The CPS representative and Veronica's solicitor then address the magistrates as to the most appropriate venue for trial. The magistrates hear from the CPS representative that the alleged assault was premeditated and involved the use of a weapon. They are also told that Veronica has several previous convictions for offences involving violence. The magistrates decide that the case is too serious for them to deal with because, in the event that Veronica is convicted, their sentencing powers will be insufficient. The magistrates will send Veronica's case to the Crown Court for trial.

If the magistrates decide that the case is suitable for summary trial, the second stage will take place.

6.10.3   The second stage

If the magistrates decide that the case is suitable for summary trial before them, they must then explain to the defendant that he may either consent to summary trial in the magistrates' court, or may elect to be tried on indictment in the Crown Court. The magistrates will also warn the defendant that if he consents to summary trial, if convicted he may still be committed to the Crown Court for sentence under s 3A of the Powers of Criminal Courts (Sentencing) Act 2000 if the magistrates consider that he is a 'dangerous offender' (see below and **Chapter 11**).

Before he makes this choice, the defendant may ask the magistrates to give an 'indication of sentence'. In other words, he may ask the magistrates whether a custodial sentence or some other form of sentence would be more likely to be imposed were he to plead guilty there and then before the magistrates. The magistrates may choose whether or not to give such an indication. If the magistrates do give an indication of sentence, they will then ask the defendant if he wants to reconsider his plea (ie, allow him to enter a guilty plea).

The rationale behind this is that often a defendant who has hitherto pleaded not guilty will enter a guilty plea on the day of his trial, causing unnecessary inconvenience and anxiety to the witnesses who have had to prepare themselves to attend court to give evidence, and also wasting the time which the court has set aside for the trial to take place. By allowing the magistrates to give an indication of sentence at an earlier stage in the proceedings, it is hoped that more defendants will be encouraged to enter guilty pleas at an earlier stage. This is most likely to occur in cases where the magistrates indicate that the sentence they would impose would be a non-custodial sentence (such as a community sentence or a fine). The draft National Allocation Guidelines (2006) prepared by the Sentencing Guidelines Council (see **6.10.2.2** above) suggest that, when indicating a sentence, the magistrates should make a reduction of a maximum of one-quarter from the sentence they would have imposed had the defendant been convicted following a trial.

If the defendant does decide to change his plea to guilty (which he may very well do if the magistrates have indicated that a non-custodial sentence is more likely), he will then be convicted of the offence and the magistrates will proceed to sentence him. The magistrates may either sentence the defendant immediately, or adjourn the case for reports before sentencing. If the latter, the magistrates will either grant the defendant bail, or remand him in custody prior to the sentencing hearing. The defendant may be sent to prison only if, when asked to give an indication of sentence, the magistrates indicated that a prison sentence was likely to be imposed.

If the defendant does not ask for an indication of sentence, if the magistrates refuse to give an indication of sentence or if, following an indication of sentence, the defendant does not wish to reconsider his plea, the defendant will then be asked if he consents to summary trial in the magistrates' court or if he wishes to elect trial before a judge and jury in the Crown Court.

If the defendant consents to summary trial, the magistrates will then fix a date for the trial to take place and issue case management directions with which the prosecution and defence must comply before trial (see **Chapter 8**). If the defendant elects trial in the Crown Court, the magistrates will send the case to the Crown Court for trial under s 51(1) of the Crime and Disorder Act 1998, and fix a date for the plea and case management hearing to take place at the Crown Court (see **Chapter 10**). In either case the magistrates will grant the defendant bail, or remand the defendant in custody, pending the next hearing.

Example 1

Shona is charged with theft. At the plea before venue hearing she indicates a not guilty plea. After hearing representations from the CPS representative and Shona's solicitor as to the most appropriate venue for trial, the magistrates decide that the facts of the case mean that it is more suitable for the trial to take place in the magistrates' court. In particular they are told that the alleged theft appears to have been opportunistic, the item stolen was of low value and Shona has no previous convictions for offences involving theft. The magistrates then explain to Shona that she may consent to summary trial, or elect trial before the Crown Court. Before making her decision, Shona asks the magistrates to give an indication of the likely sentence were she to plead guilty immediately. The magistrates indicate that, in view of the facts of the case, the likely sentence would be a community penalty. Shona then reconsiders her plea and enters a guilty plea to the charge. The magistrates will either sentence Shona immediately, or adjourn the case for pre-sentence reports before sentencing her.

Example 2

Trudy is charged with assault occasioning actual bodily harm. At the plea before venue hearing she indicates a not guilty plea. After hearing representations from the CPS representative and Trudy's solicitor as to the most appropriate venue for trial, the magistrates decide that the facts of the case mean that it is more suitable for the trial to take place in the magistrates' court. In particular they are told that the assault is not alleged to have been premeditated, there was no use of a weapon and Trudy has no previous convictions for offences involving violence. The magistrates then explain to Trudy that she may consent to summary trial before them, or may elect trial at the Crown Court. Trudy decides not to ask the magistrates for an indication of sentence and tells the magistrates that she wishes to elect trial at the Crown Court. The magistrates will then send Trudy's case to the Crown Court for trial. Had Trudy consented to a summary trial, the magistrates would then have fixed a date for the trial to take place and issued case management directions.

If the defendant enters a not guilty plea, the magistrates accept jurisdiction and the defendant does not elect trial at the Crown Court, the magistrates will *not* have the power to send the defendant to the Crown Court to be sentenced if, at the end of the trial before them, the defendant is convicted and the magistrates consider that a custodial sentence should be imposed which exceeds their maximum sentencing powers. The only exception to this is if the magistrates consider that the defendant satisfies the definition of a 'dangerous offender' (see **11.5.3.2**). Following a trial before them, the magistrates will commit such an offender to Crown Court for sentence so that he may be given either a custodial sentence for public protection, or an extended custodial sentence under Pt 12 of the Criminal Justice Act 2003.

This may be contrasted with the position of a defendant who enters a *guilty* plea at the plea before venue hearing (see **6.9** above). Such a defendant may be committed to the Crown Court for sentence if the magistrates consider their sentencing powers to be inadequate, even if the defendant does not satisfy the definition of a 'dangerous offender'.

A flowchart summarising the plea before venue and allocation procedure is set out at **6.12** below.

6.10.4 Different pleas at the plea before venue hearing

Occasionally a defendant who is charged with more than one either way offence will indicate different pleas at the plea before venue hearing. He may indicate a plea of guilty to one offence, but a plea of not guilty to the other. In such circumstances the magistrates will proceed with the allocation hearing in respect of the offence to which the defendant has indicated a not guilty plea.

If, at the allocation hearing, the magistrates accept jurisdiction (and the defendant does not elect trial at the Crown Court), the magistrates will either sentence the defendant immediately for the offence to which he has pleaded guilty, or adjourn sentence until the end of the trial of the offence to which he has entered a not guilty plea.

If, at the allocation hearing, the magistrates decline jurisdiction (or the defendant elects trial at the Crown Court), the magistrates will then send the offence to which the defendant has entered a not guilty plea to the Crown Court for trial, pursuant to s 51(1) of the Crime and Disorder Act 1998 (see **6.10.2.3** above). In this situation, the magistrates will then have a choice as to what to do with the offence to which the defendant has pleaded guilty. The magistrates may either sentence the defendant themselves, or the defendant may be committed to the Crown Court for sentence.

The defendant may be committed to the Crown Court for sentence in one of two situations:

(a) if the magistrates consider that their sentencing powers in respect of the offence to which the defendant has pleaded guilty are inadequate, they will commit the defendant to Crown Court for sentence under s 3 of the Powers of Criminal Courts (Sentencing) Act 2000 (see **6.9** above);

(b)　if the magistrates consider their sentencing powers in respect of the offence to which the defendant has pleaded guilty to be adequate, the magistrates may still commit the defendant to the Crown Court for sentence if the offence is 'related' to the offence for which the defendant has been sent for trial (Powers of Criminal Courts (Sentencing) Act 2000, s 4). 'Related' offences are offences which can be tried on the same indictment (see **10.5.5**). It is common practice for the magistrates to commit 'related' offences to the Crown Court for sentence, so that all the offences the defendant is convicted of can be dealt with at the same time.

Example

Jackie is charged with theft and assault occasioning actual bodily harm. She is alleged to have stolen a watch from a market stall and then assaulted the stallholder when he attempted to chase after her. At the plea before venue hearing, Jackie pleads guilty to the theft but not guilty to the assault. The magistrates accept jurisdiction in respect of the assault charge, but Jackie elects trial at the Crown Court. The magistrates may:

* sentence Jackie themselves for the theft; or
* commit Jackie to the Crown Court to be sentenced for the theft if they consider their sentencing powers to be inadequate; or
* if they consider their sentencing powers in respect of the theft charge to be adequate, commit Jackie to the Crown Court to be sentenced for the theft because this is 'related' to the assault (as both offences arose out of the same set of factual circumstances).

The Crown Court will sentence a defendant committed for sentence under s 4 only at the end of the trial for the offence to which the defendant pleaded not guilty (ie, the assault in the above example). The sentencing powers of the Crown Court in such circumstances depend on whether the defendant is subsequently convicted of the offence to which he pleaded not guilty. If he is convicted of this offence, the Crown Court will have the power to impose any sentence which it would have had the power to impose had the defendant been convicted following a Crown Court trial. If the defendant is acquitted of the offence to which he pleaded not guilty, the Crown Court's sentencing powers are limited to those of the magistrates' court.

In the above example, if at trial Jackie is convicted of the assault, she could receive a sentence of up to seven years' imprisonment for the theft (being the maximum sentence this offence carries in the Crown Court). If she is acquitted of the assault, though, the maximum sentence she could receive for the theft would be 12 months' imprisonment.

6.11　Advising the client on trial venue

6.11.1　Introduction

If the magistrates consider that an either way case is suitable for summary trial, the defendant will then have a choice as to whether he wants his trial to take place in the magistrates' court or the Crown Court. The defendant's solicitor must advise him about the factors in favour of each venue.

6.11.2　Factors in favour of the Crown Court

6.11.2.1　Greater chance of acquittal

Statistically, more defendants are acquitted following a jury trial in the Crown Court than are acquitted following a trial before a bench of magistrates or a district judges in the magistrates' court. Juries are perceived to be more sympathetic to defendants than 'case-hardened' magistrates. In particular, if the prosecution case includes evidence from police officers who often give evidence before the same magistrates' court, it is felt that a defendant will get a fairer hearing in the Crown Court where the jurors are hearing from each of the witnesses for the first time. Magistrates may be pre-disposed to favour the evidence of police officers from whom they may have heard evidence in previous cases, whereas jurors are perhaps more likely to question the testimony of police officers whose evidence is disputed by the defendant. Similarly, if the defendant has several previous convictions before the same magistrates' court, the magistrates before whom he is tried may be aware of such convictions and may be prejudiced against him.

6.11.2.2 Better procedure for challenging admissibility of prosecution evidence

The procedure for deciding the admissibility of disputed prosecution evidence is better for the defendant in the Crown Court than in the magistrates' court.

In the Crown Court, when a dispute over the admissibility of a piece of prosecution evidence (such as a confession) arises, the jury will be asked to leave the courtroom and the judge will conduct a mini-trial to decide whether or not the evidence should be admitted. This mini-hearing is known as a voire dire (or a 'trial within a trial'). Only if the judge decides that the evidence is admissible will the jury ever hear about it. If the judge rules the evidence to be inadmissible, the evidence will not be placed before the jury.

Were such a situation to arise in the magistrates' court, because the magistrates are responsible for determining both matters of law and matters of fact, the magistrates themselves would need to determine whether the evidence was admissible. If the magistrates decided that a piece of prosecution evidence was inadmissible, when considering their verdict the magistrates would need to set to one side their knowledge of the existence of that piece of evidence. There is a risk that such knowledge would remain in the back of their minds and affect their decision as to the defendant's guilt or innocence.

(Although the Crown Court remains the better venue for determining the admissibility of disputed items of prosecution evidence, most magistrates' courts do now attempt to determine issues of admissibility of evidence at pre-trial hearings rather than at the hearing itself. Such hearings will take place before a different bench of magistrates from the bench who hear the trial, so there is no risk that the defendant will be prejudiced at trial by the magistrates being aware of any item of prosecution evidence which has been found to be inadmissible. Such hearings regularly take place in relation to applications to adduce bad character or hearsay evidence (see **Chapters 19 and 22**), although in *R (Robinson) v Sutton Coldfield Magistrates' Court* [2006] EWHC (Admin) 307, the High Court said that the inadmissibility of a defendant's previous convictions could be determined by the magistrates at trial and that, if the magistrates decided that such convictions were admissible, this would not prevent them from conducting the trial. Some magistrates' courts have extended these pre-trial hearings to cover the admissibility of disputed confession evidence under ss 76 and 78 of PACE 1984 (see **Chapter 20**), or other evidence which the defendant's solicitor argues should be excluded under s 78 (for example, identification evidence where it is alleged that the police have failed to comply with Code D of the Codes of Practice, or the record of the defendant's interview at the police station where it is alleged the police employed inappropriate questioning techniques) – see **Chapter 21**.)

6.11.3   Factors in favour of magistrates' court

6.11.3.1   Limited sentencing powers

The biggest advantage in a defendant choosing to have his trial before the magistrates' court is the limited sentencing powers the magistrates possess. The maximum sentence a defendant may receive in the magistrates' court is 12 months' imprisonment for one either way offence (rising to 65 weeks for two or more either way offences), together with a fine not exceeding £5,000. The sentencing powers available to a judge in the Crown Court are considerably wider. For example, a defendant convicted of theft in the Crown Court may receive a sentence of up to seven years' imprisonment and an unlimited fine.

In very limited circumstances the magistrates do have the power to commit the defendant to Crown Court for sentence even if they had previously accepted jurisdiction and the trial took place in the magistrates' court. Such a power may be exercised only if the magistrates consider the defendant to be a 'dangerous offender' (see **6.10.3** above and **Chapter 11**).

6.11.3.2   Speed and stress

A trial in the magistrates' court takes place much sooner than a trial in the Crown Court. Cases in the magistrates' court generally get to trial within a matter of weeks, whilst in the Crown Court it can often take several months for a case to come to trial. This may be significant for a defendant who needs his case to be concluded relatively quickly, such as a defendant who has been offered employment in another part of the country or overseas. This will also be a very important consideration for a defendant who has been denied bail and is remanded in custody prior to trial.

Cases in the magistrates' court are also less stressful for defendants. The procedure in the magistrates' court is less formal than and not as intimidating as the Crown Court (for example, the judge and the barristers in the Crown Court wear wigs and gowns, whereas the magistrates and the advocates in the magistrates' court do not). This may be significant for a defendant who has never previously been charged with an offence, and who is likely to be intimidated by the greater formality of the Crown Court. This is, however, unlikely to be a significant consideration for a defendant with numerous previous convictions who is no stranger to the criminal courts.

6.11.3.3   Prosecution costs

If a defendant is convicted in either the magistrates' court or the Crown Court, he is likely to be ordered to make a contribution towards the costs incurred by the CPS in bringing the case against him. Such costs are likely to be higher in the Crown Court because of the greater amount of work that goes into preparing a case for trial in the Crown Court (such as the need to instruct counsel).

6.11.3.4   Defence costs

A defendant who is convicted in the Crown Court may be ordered to pay a contribution towards his solicitor's costs if his case was funded by way of a representation order. Representation orders are currently non-means tested and are granted solely if it is in the interests of justice for the defendant's case to be publicly funded (see **6.4.3.2** above). However, a defendant whose case is sent to the Crown Court for trial will need to complete a statement of means for the Crown Court. At the end of the case, if the defendant is convicted, the trial judge has the power to order that the defendant make a contribution towards those costs which the defendant's solicitor will claim from the Legal Services Commission for acting on the defendant's behalf (CrimPR, Part 77). This is called a recovery of defence costs order (RDCO). The court will have regard to the defendant's statement of means when deciding whether or not to make such an order. This is a significant consideration to be borne in mind by a solicitor representing a defendant with substantial financial means and assets. A magistrates' court cannot make such an order in respect of a defendant who has been convicted following a trial before them.

When the changes made by the Criminal Defence Service Act 2006 (see **6.4.5** above) take effect, a defendant who is of significant financial means will not satisfy the financial criteria for obtaining a representation order in proceedings before the magistrates' court. If the defendant's case is sent to the Crown Court for trial, the defendant may become eligible for a representation order. The changes made by the Act will not, however, affect the ability of the judge at the Crown Court to make an RDCO, although the amount of the RDCO cannot exceed the total value of the legal work carried out on the defendant's behalf.

Until the financial eligibility test for the granting of a representation order introduced by the 2006 Act is extended to Crown Court proceedings (this is likely to happen some time during 2007), it will arguably cheaper for a defendant charged with an either way offence who does not satisfy the financial eligibility criteria that apply in the magistrates' court to elect trial in the Crown Court rather than agree to a summary trial.

If the defendant funds his case privately, proceedings in the magistrates' court will be significantly cheaper than the Crown Court. His case will come to trial much more quickly, and it will not be necessary for his solicitor to brief counsel to represent him at trial (see **Chapter 10**).

6.11.3.5   No obligation to serve defence statement

A defendant pleading not guilty in the Crown Court is effectively obliged to serve on both the Crown Court and the prosecution a defence statement under ss 5, 6 and 6A of the Criminal Procedure and Investigations Act 1996 (see **10.8.2**). Such a statement must set out the nature of the defence, indicate any factual matters on which the defendant takes issue with the prosecution, and indicate any points of law the defendant will rely on at trial. The giving of a defence statement will put the prosecution on notice about the defence which the defendant is going to raise well in advance of the trial, and will allow the CPS time to prepare to rebut such a defence. The defendant will therefore lose any element of surprise at trial.

In the magistrates' court there is no obligation on the defendant to provide a defence statement either to the court or to the CPS. The giving of such a statement in the magistrates' court is entirely optional, and in practice is very rarely done.

6.12 Flowchart – plea before venue and allocation

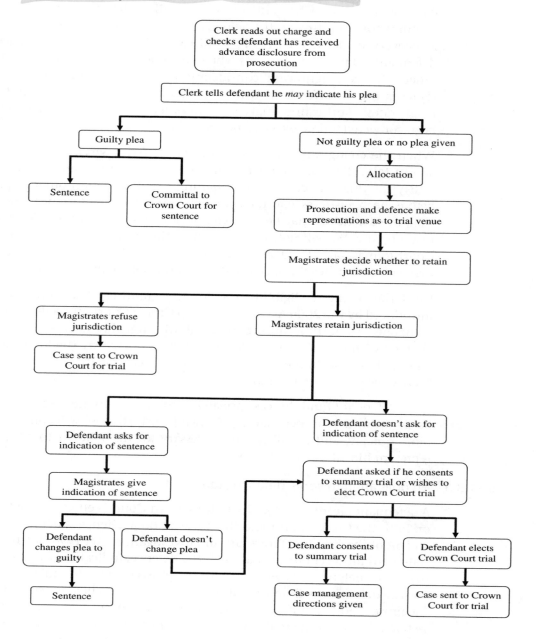

6.13 Checklist

At the end of this chapter you should be able to explain:

- the matters which will be dealt with at an EFH, an EAH and a remand hearing;

- the role played by the defendant's solicitor at the above hearings;

- the forms of public funding available to a defendant in a criminal case;

- how to complete an application for a representation order;

- how to take a statement from a client;

- the obligations on the CPS to make disclosure to the defendant's solicitor of the details of the case against a defendant charged with a summary or either way offence;

- the matters to be taken into account when the defendant's solicitor advises his client on the plea to be entered;

- the procedure which is followed at the plea before venue and allocation hearings;

- the matters to be taken into account by the defendant's solicitor when advising his client whether to elect trial in the Crown Court.

6.14 Form CDS 11

Claim Cost Summary Sheet   CDS11

Class (delete where appropriate) - Criminal Investigations / Criminal Proceedings / Appeals and Reviews / Prison Law / Associated CLS

a **One form should be completed for each claim you make**
a **Where this claim relates to a Lower Standard Fee, do not complete Profit / Core Cost information**
a **Where this claim relates to the Associated CLS Class of Work, only Legal Help claims should be recorded on this form. Where Investigative Help and Legal Representation are being claimed the appropriate CLS claim form should be used.**

Client surname and initial: _____   UFN: _____

Our reference: _____

Profit Costs

Description	Rate £	Hours / Mins	Net Total £	VAT £	Gross Total
		Total			

Disbursements

Description	Rate £	Total	VAT	Gross Total
Mileage	@ p			

Travel

Description	Rate (£)	Hours / Mins	Total £	VAT £	Gross Total
		Total			

Waiting

Description	Rate (£)	Hours / Mins	Total £	VAT £	Gross Total
		Total			

Where the claim is in the Proceedings Class and a Representation Order has been granted, where applicable indicate level of standard fee claimed i.e. lower or higher standard fee category.

Pre-order work? ☐   Standard Fee [   ]

Date order granted____/____/____   Total Core Costs £[   ]

CDS11   Page 1   Version 4 October 2003   (c) Criminal Defence Service

Chapter 7

Bail

7.1 Introduction

It is rare for a criminal case to be completed on the first occasion on which the defendant appears before the magistrates' court. This is likely to happen only in the case of a straightforward summary offence where the defendant pleads guilty at the early first hearing and the magistrates sentence him immediately (see **6.2.2.2**). In any other type of case there will need to be one or more adjournments before the case is concluded. Common reasons for cases needing to be adjourned are:

(a) for the CPS to provide the defendant's solicitor with details of the case against the defendant prior to the defendant entering his plea (see **Chapter 6**);

(b) for the CPS and the defendant's solicitor to comply with case management directions given by the court after the defendant has entered a not guilty plea and prior to the defendant's trial taking place (see **Chapter 8**);

(c) for a hearing date to take place at the Crown Court if the magistrates have declined jurisdiction in an either way matter, or have sent an indictable only case to the Crown Court for trial (see **Chapter 10**); and

(d) for the court to obtain reports on the defendant before passing sentence (see **Chapter 12**).

This chapter will look at the ways in which a magistrates' court may adjourn a case and the time limits that apply when a case is adjourned. It will then go on to examine a defendant's right to be granted bail when his case is adjourned and the grounds on which the court may refuse bail. The chapter will explain the types of condition which the magistrates may impose on a bail which has been granted to a defendant, and will consider the options open to a defendant who is refused bail by the magistrates. It will also examine the consequences for a defendant who either breaches conditions imposed on his bail, or fails to attend court to answer bail.

7.2 Remand periods

7.2.1 What is a remand?

When a case is adjourned by the magistrates (or by a judge in the Crown Court) the defendant will be remanded. A 'remand' is an adjournment where the court attempts to ensure the defendant will attend the next hearing. A defendant may be remanded in one of three ways:

(a)   a remand in custody;

(b)   a remand on bail with conditions attached to that bail; or

(c)   a remand on unconditional bail.

7.2.2 Remands prior to conviction

7.2.2.1 Remands in custody

The basic rule

The basic rule is that a defendant may not be remanded in custody for more than eight clear days at a time. However, where there are successive remands in custody, the defendant need be brought before the court only on every fourth remand, provided he has consented to this and has legal representation. In addition, the court may remand a defendant in custody for up to 28 days if:

(a)   it has previously remanded him in custody for the same offence; and

(b)   he is before the court; and

(c)   it can set a date to remand him to on which it expects the next stage of the proceedings to take place.

Example

Abdul is charged with theft. He is refused bail by the police and appears before the magistrates' court in custody on 2 April. Abdul's solicitor makes an application for bail which is refused. Abdul is remanded in custody by the magistrates for seven days and so appears before the court again on 9 April. At the hearing on 9 April the prosecution confirm that they will shortly be in a position to serve advance disclosure on Abdul's solicitor. The magistrates refuse bail again and remand Abdul in custody for 28 days until 7 May when the plea before venue hearing will take place. The magistrates are able to do this because Abdul is before the court, he has previously been remanded in custody, and the next stage of proceedings (plea before venue) can take place at the next hearing. (In practice, the hearing on 9 April will usually be conducted by live video link with the prison or remand centre where Abdul is being held, rather than Abdul being brought to court.)

Custody time limits

Time limits exist to ensure that defendants who are remanded in custody have their cases brought promptly to trial. The overall maximum period of remand in custody (normally referred to as the custody time limit) in the magistrates' court is 70 days before summary trial for an either way offence and 56 days before trial for a summary only offence. However, if the case involves an either way offence and the decision to hold a summary trial (ie, the allocation hearing) is taken within 56 days, the custody time limit for the either way offence is reduced to 56 days.

The prosecution may apply to the court to extend the custody time limit, although for an application to be successful the prosecution will need to show on the balance of probabilities that there is good and sufficient cause to do this and that it has acted with due diligence and expedition. Unless the prosecution make a successful application to extend the custody time limit, once the time limit has expired the defendant must be released on bail until his trial. If the magistrates grant a prosecution application to extend the custody time limit, the defendant has a right of appeal to the Crown Court. Similarly, the prosecution may appeal to the Crown Court against the magistrates' refusal to extend the custody time limit. The relevant procedural rules that must be complied with when an appeal is made are contained in Part 20 of the Criminal Procedure Rules 2005. The custody time limits which apply to cases in the Crown Court are detailed in **Chapter 10**.

Where will the defendant be kept whilst in custody?

Defendants who are remanded in custody will normally be kept at a prison or remand centre. However, s 128(7) of the Magistrates' Courts Act 1980 allows a magistrates' court to remand a defendant to police custody for up to three days if this is necessary for the purposes of making enquiries in relation to offences other than the offence for which the defendant had been charged. The CPS is likely to apply for such a remand when a defendant has been arrested and charged for one offence but the police suspect his involvement in other matters about which they wish to interview him. A defendant made subject to such a remand must be brought back before the magistrates as soon as the need to make enquiries has ceased. Whilst he is at the police station, the defendant is entitled to the same rights as if he had been arrested and detained prior to charge (for example, the right to free legal advice; see **3.4** above).

7.2.2.2   Remands on bail

A defendant who is on bail can be remanded prior to conviction for any period of time, subject to his consent.

7.2.3   Remands after conviction

Following conviction a defendant may be remanded in custody prior to sentence (usually for the preparation of pre-sentence reports) for successive periods of not more than three weeks. If the defendant is remanded on bail this may be for successive periods of not more than four weeks.

7.2.4   Remands after case committed or sent to Crown Court

A defendant who is committed to the Crown Court for sentence (see **6.9**), or whose case is sent to the Crown Court for trial (see **Chapter 10**), may be remanded in custody or on bail until the case comes before the Crown Court.

7.3   The right to bail

Whenever a case is adjourned the magistrates (or judge) must then consider whether to remand the defendant in custody, or to remand the defendant on bail (with or without conditions).

The substantive law concerning the grant or refusal of bail is contained predominantly in the Bail Act 1976. The procedural rules which are relevant to the issue of bail are found in Parts 18 to 21 of the Criminal Procedure Rules 2005.

Under s 4 of the Bail Act 1976, there is a presumption that bail will be granted to the following types of defendants (unless one or more exceptions apply):

(a)   all defendants prior to conviction;

(b)   defendants who have been convicted if their case has been adjourned for the court to obtain reports before sentencing (see **Chapter 12**); and

(c)   defendants who are appearing before the court for breach of a community sentence (see **Chapter 11**).

The presumption in favour of bail does not apply to defendants:

(a)   who have been committed to the Crown Court for sentence by the magistrates (see **6.10** above); or

(b)   who are appealing against conviction or sentence (see **Chapter 13**).

The only other limitation on the presumption that bail will be granted is in respect of defendants charged with the most serious types of offence. Under s 25 of the Criminal Justice and Public Order Act 1994, if the defendant is charged with one of a number of specified offences and has previously been convicted of any of these offences (not necessarily the same offence as he is currently charged with), a court can grant bail to that defendant only if exceptional circumstances exist (and the court must state what those circumstances are and the reason bail has been granted). The specified offences are:

(a)   murder;

(b)   attempted murder;

(c)   manslaughter;

(d)   rape;

(e)   attempted rape.

7.4   Exceptions to the right to bail

7.4.1   Imprisonable offences

The exceptions to the presumption in favour of bail for defendants who are charged with imprisonable offences are set out in paras 2 to 7 of Sch 1, Pt 1 to the Bail Act 1976:

2.— (1)   The defendant need not be granted bail if the court is satisfied that there are substantial grounds for believing that the defendant, if released on bail (whether subject to conditions or not) would—

(a)   fail to surrender to custody, or

(b)   commit an offence while on bail, or

(c)   interfere with witnesses or otherwise obstruct the course of justice, whether in relation to himself or any other person.

2A.—(1)   If the defendant falls within this paragraph he may not be granted bail unless the court is satisfied that there is no significant risk of his committing an offence while on bail (whether subject to conditions or not).

(2)   The defendant falls within this paragraph if—

(a)   he is aged 18 or over, and

(b)   it appears to the court that he was on bail in criminal proceedings on the date of the offence.

3.   The defendant need not be granted bail if the court is satisfied that the defendant should be kept in custody for his own protection or, if he is a child or young person, for his own welfare.

4.   The defendant need not be granted bail if he is in custody in pursuance of the sentence of a court or of any authority acting under any of the Service Acts.

5. The defendant need not be granted bail where the court is satisfied that it has not been practicable to obtain sufficient information for the purpose of taking the decisions required by this Part of the Schedule for want of time since the institution of proceedings against him.

6.— (1) If the defendant falls within this paragraph, he may not be granted bail unless the court is satisfied that there is no significant risk that, if released on bail (whether subject to conditions or not), he would fail to surrender to custody.

(2) Subject to sub-paragraph (3) below, the defendant falls within this paragraph if—

(a) he is aged 18 or over, and

(b) it appears to the court that, having been released on bail or in connection with the proceedings for the offence, he failed to surrender to custody.

(3) Where it appears to the court that the defendant has reasonable cause for his failure to surrender to custody, he does not fall within this paragraph unless it also appears to the court that he failed to surrender to custody at the appointed place as soon as reasonably practicable after the appointed time.

(4) For the purpose of sub-paragraph (3) above, a failure to give to the defendant a copy of the record of the decision to grant him bail shall not constitute a reasonable cause for his failure to surrender to custody.

7. Where his case is adjourned for inquiries or a report, the defendant need not be granted bail if it appears to the court that it would be impracticable to complete the inquiries or make the report without keeping the defendant in custody.

The most significant grounds on which bail is normally refused are those set out in paras 2, 2A and 6 above. In deciding whether any of these *grounds* is made out the court must take into account the following *factors*:

(a) the nature and seriousness of the offence (and the probable sentence the defendant will receive for it);

(b) the character, antecedents, associations and community ties of the defendant;

(c) the defendant's record in respect of previous grants of bail in criminal proceedings; and

(d) the strength of the evidence against the defendant. (Bail Act 1976, Sch 1, Pt 1, para 9).

Each of these factors will be examined in turn.

7.4.1.1 The nature and seriousness of the offence and the probable method of dealing with the defendant for it

This factor is most likely to be relevant to a prosecution argument that there are substantial grounds for believing that the defendant would fail to surrender to custody if he were to be granted bail. If the defendant has been charged with a serious offence that is likely to result in a prison sentence if he is convicted, the CPS may argue that the defendant will fail to surrender to custody (usually referred to as absconding – see 7.9 below) to avoid such a fate.

Example

Neil pleads not guilty to a charge of wounding with intent. The prosecution allege that Neil attacked his victim with a hammer in an unprovoked assault, causing the victim to suffer head injuries from which he will never fully recover. This is a serious offence and, if convicted, Neil will receive a lengthy prison sentence. The prosecution will argue that Neil should be denied bail as there are substantial grounds for believing that, if granted bail, Neil will fail to surrender to custody. The factor they will rely on to support this is that if Neil is convicted, the court will deal with the matter by way of a custodial sentence, and Neil will abscond to avoid being sent to prison.

This can be a difficult argument for the defence to counter. If the defendant's solicitor considers that the offence is not as serious as the prosecution suggest (and so will not inevitably result in a custodial sentence were the defendant to be convicted), this should be pointed out to the court. To assess whether the defendant is likely to receive a custodial sentence if convicted, the defendant's solicitor will need to check the guideline sentence in the Magistrates' Court Sentencing Guidelines (see **11.4.2.2**) or, for more serious offences, either any definitive sentencing guidelines issued by the Sentencing Guidelines Council (SGC) or the case compendium of guideline sentences given by the Court of Appeal, both of which may be found at www.sentencing-guidelines.gov.uk. He will also need to consider whether the guideline sentence is likely to be affected by the presence of any aggravating or mitigating factors.

Example

Nicola is charged with theft of a bracelet (worth £50) from a shop. The allegation is that, after paying for some other goods which she had purchased, as she was leaving the shop Nicola grabbed the bracelet and ran. Nicola denies the charge. She has several previous convictions for shoplifting offences. The prosecution oppose bail on the ground that there are substantial grounds for believing that Nicola will abscond if granted bail. The prosecution argue that, because of her previous convictions, Nicola is likely to receive a custodial sentence if convicted and so will abscond to avoid this possibility. Nicola's solicitor will argue that the offence will not merit a custodial sentence. The item stolen was not of high value, the offence does not appear to have been planned and is not in any way sophisticated, and the alleged victim is not 'vulnerable'.

Often, however, the best response to an argument concerning the seriousness of the offence is to acknowledge that the offence is serious but to go on to say that the defendant is pleading not guilty and is anxious to attend court to ensure that he is acquitted and his name cleared. The defendant's solicitor may also say that the very seriousness of the offence will make it more likely that his client will answer his bail, because the defendant will not want to make matters any worse for himself by not turning up at court.

A defendant who has been convicted but whose case is adjourned for reports has a prima facie right to bail (see **7.3** above). A defendant who is convicted of a serious offence and whose case is adjourned for reports is likely to be refused bail, however, if the court considers that there are substantial grounds to believe that the defendant will abscond to avoid an inevitable custodial sentence.

7.4.1.2 The defendant's character, antecedents, associations and community ties

Character and antecedents

The reference to a defendant's character and antecedents is a reference to the defendant's previous convictions. A defendant's criminal record may be raised by the CPS when bail is being considered, to suggest that there are substantial grounds for believing that the defendant will commit further offences if he is released on bail. This is likely to be relevant if a defendant has a history of committing the same type of offence as that with which he has been charged in the current proceedings, particularly if the reason for the previous offending is ongoing (such as a serial shoplifter who steals to fund a drug habit) or if the previous offences were committed on bail. Even if a defendant has several previous convictions for the same type of offence, unless the last of these convictions was relatively recent, the defendant's solicitor may suggest that there are not 'substantial grounds' for believing that the defendant will commit further offences. Similarly, if the CPS suggests that the defendant offends for a particular reason, his solicitor may suggest that there is no longer any need for such offending if the defendant's circumstances have changed (if, for example, the defendant stole previously to fund a drug addiction, but that addiction has now been successfully treated).

The CPS will certainly raise this factor to support an argument that the defendant will commit offences if granted bail should the defendant's previous convictions reveal a history of committing offences whilst on bail for other matters. If the defendant was already on bail for another offence at the time he is alleged to have committed the current offence, the exception to granting bail contained in para 2A in **7.4.1** above is likely to be relied on by the prosecution. Such a defendant is unlikely to be granted bail for the current offence.

The prosecution may also rely on this factor to support an allegation that there are substantial grounds for believing that the defendant will fail to surrender to custody if released on bail, particularly if the evidence against the defendant is strong. If the defendant is convicted of the offence with which he is currently charged, when he comes to be sentenced the court will treat any previous convictions he has as aggravating factors (particularly if they are for the same type of offence). Such aggravating factors are likely to result in the defendant receiving a harsher sentence than would normally be the case. This may be particularly significant if the defendant's previous convictions might lead a court to consider imposing a custodial sentence when otherwise it would not have done so. The CPS will argue that in such a case the defendant may abscond rather than run the risk of imprisonment. This will also be a strong argument if the defendant is currently subject to a suspended sentence of imprisonment which is likely to be 'activated' if the defendant is convicted of the current offence (see **11.5.6.4**).

Example 1

Dawn pleads not guilty to a charge of shoplifting. Dawn has 10 previous convictions for the same type of offence within the preceding three years. Dawn's previous offences were committed to obtain money to support her heroin addiction (which is ongoing). The CPS will argue that Dawn should be denied bail as there are substantial grounds for believing that, if granted bail, Dawn will commit further offences. The factor it will rely to support this is that Dawn's character and antecedents indicate that she commits this type of offence on a regular basis to support her ongoing drug addiction.

Example 2

Adam pleads not guilty to a charge of theft. Adam's list of previous convictions reveals that he has twice been convicted of other property-related offences which were committed whilst he was on bail for other matters. The CPS will argue that Adam should be denied bail as there are substantial grounds for believing that, if released on bail, Adam will commit further offences. The factor it will rely on to support this is that Adam's previous convictions show a history of offending whilst on bail.

Example 3

Morgan pleads not guilty to a charge of assault occasioning actual bodily harm. Six months previously, Morgan was convicted of unlawful wounding and received a sentence of 12 months' imprisonment, suspended for two years. The evidence against Morgan in respect of the current charge is strong, consisting of good quality identification evidence and a confession Morgan is alleged to have made when first arrested. The CPS will argue that Morgan should be denied bail as there are substantial grounds for believing that, if released on bail, Morgan would fail to surrender to custody. The factor it will rely on to support this is that Morgan's antecedents show he is subject to a suspended sentence of imprisonment which is likely to be activated if Morgan is convicted of the current offence. Morgan is likely to be convicted because of the strength of the evidence against him.

Associations

The reference to the defendant's associations may be relevant to a prosecution argument that, if released on bail, there are substantial grounds for believing that the defendant will commit further offences, abscond or interfere with witnesses.

If a defendant is known to associate with other criminals, or is alleged to be a member of a criminal gang, the CPS may use this to suggest there are 'substantial grounds' to believe that he may commit further offences if released on bail. Similarly, if the defendant has criminal connections in other countries, the CPS may suggest that the defendant will use these connections to enable him to leave the country and so fail to surrender to bail.

The CPS may also suggest that a defendant's associations are relevant if a witness is known to the defendant and there is a fear that the defendant may attempt to interfere with the witness. This often arises in the case of domestic assaults when the victim is a relative of the defendant and there is a fear that the defendant may put pressure on the victim to 'change his story'. To counter this argument, the defence will normally suggest that appropriate conditions be imposed on any bail granted to the defendant to prevent the defendant from contacting the witness or victim (see 7.5 below).

Example 1

James pleads not guilty to a charge of armed robbery of a bank. The CPS alleges that James is a member of criminal gang responsible for several similar armed robberies. None of the other members of the gang has as yet been identified or arrested by the police, and none of the proceeds from the bank robberies have been recovered. The CPS will argue that James should be denied bail as there are substantial grounds for believing that, if released on bail, James would commit further offences. The factor it will rely on is that James's associations include membership of a gang responsible for a series of armed robberies, the other members of which are still at large.

Example 2

Nigel pleads not guilty to a charge of indecent assault. The CPS alleges that Nigel indecently assaulted his 11-year-old daughter (who lives at the same address as Nigel). In her statement to the police, Nigel's daughter has said that Nigel has threatened to 'shut her up' unless she changes her story. The CPS will argue that Nigel should be denied bail on the basis that there are substantial grounds for believing that, if granted bail, Nigel will attempt to interfere with a witness. The factor it will rely on to support this is that Nigel is closely associated with his alleged victim. Nigel and his victim share the same home, and the victim has already indicated that he has attempted to persuade her to change her story.

Community ties

The strength or otherwise of a defendant's community ties will be relevant to an argument that there are substantial grounds for believing that the defendant will fail to surrender to custody if released on bail. If, for example, the defendant is unemployed, has no relatives in the local area, has lived in area only for a short time or is of no fixed abode, the CPS may argue that there is nothing to keep him in the area and nothing to prevent him from absconding. From the opposite point of view, if the defendant is in employment (or at least has a written offer of employment), has family in the area, has lived in the area for a long time or owns a property in the locality, the defendant's solicitor may argue that the defendant has every reason to stay in the area and so will not abscond.

Example

Naveed pleads not guilty to a charge of possession of Class A drugs. Naveed is unemployed and lives alone in bedsit accommodation. Naveed has no family or known friends in the local area, and most of his relatives are known to live some 200 miles away. Naveed moved to the area only some three months ago. The CPS will argue that Naveed should be denied bail as there are substantial grounds for believing that, if granted bail, Naveed will fail to surrender to custody. The factor it will rely on to support this is Naveed's lack of community ties, because Naveed appears to have nothing to tie him to the local area.

7.4.1.3 The defendant's record in relation to previous grants of bail

If a defendant has previous convictions, it is almost certain that at some stage he will have been granted bail by the court whilst being dealt with for these previous offences. If his criminal record discloses that he has a conviction for the offence of absconding (ie, failing to answer his bail – see **7.9** below), the CPS is likely to raise this to suggest there are substantial grounds for believing that the defendant will fail to surrender if he is granted bail in the current proceedings. If such an argument is raised by the CPS, the circumstances of the absconding need to be investigated further by the defendant's solicitor to see if there is some explanation for the absconding: Did the defendant purposely fail to attend court, or was there simply a mix up over the date of the hearing? Was the defendant arrested for breaching his bail, or did he voluntarily surrender himself to custody? If the defendant has been convicted of absconding, the way in which the court sentenced him for this offence may be relevant. If, for example, the court imposed no separate penalty for the offence, or if the defendant received a further grant of bail in the substantive proceedings, this would suggest that the court did not view the absconding as being particularly serious.

A defendant with an extensive criminal record who has no convictions for absconding is in a strong position to argue that he is unlikely to fail to answer his bail. Such a defendant will have been granted bail many times previously, and the absence of any convictions for absconding will show that the defendant has always answered his bail in the past. This is a particularly strong argument for a defendant who has previously answered bail for an offence for which he was mistakenly imprisoned.

If the defendant has been granted bail in the current proceedings at an earlier hearing, but then fails without reasonable cause to answer his bail, is arrested for breaching his bail and then applies for bail again, the exception to granting bail contained in para 6 in **7.4.1** above will be relied on by the prosecution. Such a defendant is unlikely to be granted bail again (see **7.9.1** below).

Example 1

Jack pleads not guilty to a charge of affray. Jack has three previous convictions for failing to answer bail in relation to other public order offences with which he was charged. The CPS will argue that Jack should be denied bail as there are substantial grounds for believing that, if granted bail, Jack will fail to surrender to custody. The factor it will rely to support this is that Jack's record in relation to previous grants of bail shows that he has a history of failing to answer his bail.

Example 2

Janine pleads not guilty to a charge of theft. Janine has numerous previous convictions for theft and other property-related offences. Janine has no previous convictions for absconding. The CPS is unlikely to be able to establish that there are substantial grounds for believing that, if granted bail, Janine would fail to surrender to custody. The fact that Janine has appeared before the courts (and presumably been granted bail) on a regular basis, but has no previous convictions for absconding, shows that Janine always answers her bail.

7.4.1.4   The strength of the evidence

If the CPS considers the evidence against the defendant to be strong (for example, good quality identification evidence from an eye-witness, or a confession made by the defendant when interviewed by the police), it may use this to argue that if released on bail there are substantial grounds for believing that the defendant would fail to surrender to custody. Such an argument is often combined with an argument that the offence is serious and will result in a custodial sentence if the defendant is convicted.

Example

Vivian pleads not guilty to a charge of unlawful wounding. The CPS alleges that he struck his victim in the face with a broken bottle, causing the victim to suffer a severe laceration needing 15 stitches. There were numerous witnesses to the incident who will say that Vivian launched an unprovoked attack, and when interviewed at the police station, Vivian made several admissions. The CPS will argue that Vivian should be denied bail as there are substantial grounds for believing that, if granted bail, Vivian will fail to surrender to custody. The factors it will rely to support this are that the seriousness of the offence means that Vivian will receive a prison sentence if convicted and, given the strength of the evidence against Vivian, a conviction is likely.

The defendant's solicitor will often try to counter this by arguing that the evidence is not as strong as the prosecution have suggested. He may, for example, argue that identification evidence on which the prosecution are relying is disputed (and that the quality of such evidence is poor), or that there will be a challenge to the admissibility of the confession evidence on which the CPS seeks to rely. The defendant's solicitor may also say that the defendant has an innocent explanation for a piece of evidence on which the CPS seeks to rely (such as the defendant's fingerprints being found on an item of stolen property).

Example

Sharon is charged with theft of items of clothing from a shop. She denies the charge, claiming that she was elsewhere at the time of the theft. Sharon has extensive previous convictions and the CPS opposes bail, arguing that there are substantial grounds for believing that Sharon will abscond because, if convicted, she is likely to face a custodial sentence as a result of her previous record. The CPS argues that Sharon is likely to be convicted because the evidence against her is strong. The evidence against Sharon consists of identification evidence from a store detective, who claims to recognise Sharon as the person he saw running from the shop after committing the theft. Sharon's solicitor will challenge the alleged strength of such evidence by suggesting that it is weak and unlikely to result in a conviction. He will argue that that the store detective got only a brief glimpse of the thief, that the store detective did not see the thief's face, and that his description of the thief does not match Sharon's appearance. He will argue that Sharon is unlikely to be convicted on the basis of such evidence.

7.4.2 Non-imprisonable offences

It is extremely rare for a defendant charged with a non-imprisonable offence not to be granted bail, as there are only very limited circumstances in which the CPS would ever oppose the grant of bail to such a defendant. Under Sch 1, Pt 2 to the Bail Act 1976, the court may refuse bail to a defendant charged with a non-imprisonable offence only if:

(a) the defendant was granted bail in previous criminal proceedings but failed to answer this bail and the court believes that, if granted bail in the current proceedings, the defendant would again fail to surrender to custody;

(b) the defendant needs to be kept in custody for his own protection or, in the case of a defendant under 18 years of age, for his own welfare;

(c) the defendant is currently serving a custodial sentence in respect of a separate offence; or

(d) the defendant was granted bail at an earlier hearing in the same proceedings, but has been arrested either for failing to answer his bail or for breaking any conditions of his bail, and the court is satisfied that there are substantial grounds for believing that, if released on bail, the defendant would fail to surrender to custody, commit an offence or interfere with witnesses or otherwise obstruct the course of justice

7.5 Conditional bail

A court has the power to grant bail to a defendant subject to the defendant complying with one or more conditions that the court attaches to that bail. The conditions must be necessary to:

(a) prevent the defendant from absconding;

(b) prevent the defendant committing a further offence whilst on bail;

(c) prevent the defendant interfering with witnesses or obstructing the course of justice;

(d) ensure that the defendant makes himself available for the purpose of obtaining medical or other reports;

(e) ensure that the defendant keeps an appointment with his solicitor (Bail Act 1976, s 3); or

(f) ensure the defendant's own protection or, in the case of a defendant aged under 18, for his own welfare or in his own interests.

When he is making an application for bail on behalf of his client, the defendant's solicitor will normally invite the magistrates to consider granting conditional bail to his client if the magistrates are not minded to grant bail on an unconditional basis. The most common conditions that the court may impose are described at **7.5.1 to 7.5.8** below.

7.5.1   Sureties

A surety may be used to ensure that a defendant answers his bail. A surety is a person who enters into what is termed a 'recognisance' of money and is under an obligation to use every reasonable effort to ensure that the defendant attends court. The surety will be required to appear before the court at the bail hearing to confirm his willingness to be a surety, although he will not be required to pay over any money at this stage.

If the defendant fails to answer his bail at the next hearing, the court must declare the immediate and automatic forfeiture of the recognisance. The court will order the surety to appear before the court to explain why he should not pay over the sum. The court will then determine whether some or all of the surety should be paid.

Before accepting a proposed surety, the court will want to ensure that the person who is proposed as the surety is suitable. The surety will be required to give evidence to the court about his financial resources, his character and any previous convictions he has, and his relationship to the defendant. As the surety is meant to ensure that the defendant attends the next hearing, the court will also want to find out how close the surety lives to the defendant and how regularly the surety sees the defendant.

A court is unlikely to accept as a surety a person who has a criminal record, who lives a long distance from the defendant or who has no financial means. As a matter of professional conduct, a solicitor should never stand surety for a defendant.

7.5.2   Security

A security may be required by the court to ensure that the defendant answers his bail. If the court orders a security, the defendant will be required to deposit a sum of money (or goods) with the court. If the defendant fails to attend court to answer his bail, he will forfeit the security he has given. For obvious reasons a security can be used only for defendants of substantial financial means.

7.5.3   Reporting to a police station

This is another condition which may be used to ensure that the defendant will not abscond. The court may order the defendant to report to his local police station on a regular basis (often once each day at a specified time) so that the police may ensure that the defendant remains in the local area.

7.5.4   Residence

This is a common condition which the courts use to ensure that defendants will not fail to surrender to custody. If such a condition is imposed, the court will require the defendant to reside at a specified address. The police will often check that such a condition is being complied with by visiting the address late at night or early in the morning to check that the defendant is there.

If a defendant does not have a permanent address, the court may impose a condition of residence in a bail hostel run by the Probation Service (if a place is available). This can also be useful if the circumstances of the case mean that a defendant cannot reside at his normal home address. The most common example of this is when there is an allegation of a domestic assault where the defendant and his alleged victim reside in the same property.

To support a condition of residence, the court may order that the defendant be electronically monitored (commonly referred to as 'tagging').

7.5.5 Curfew

This condition may be used to prevent a defendant committing further offences whilst on bail. The court can require a defendant to remain at his place of residence between certain specified hours (for example, between 8 pm and 7 am). As with a condition of residence, the police may visit the residence during these hours to check that the defendant is there. A curfew is often used for a defendant with a history of night-time offending. To support a curfew, the court may order that the defendant be electronically monitored.

7.5.6 Non-communication with prosecution witnesses

This condition may be used to prevent a defendant interfering with prosecution witnesses if the court is concerned that the defendant may try to intimidate a witness. The condition can cover not only face-to-face contact with the witnesses, but also contacting the witnesses by telephone or in writing. If a witness resides in the same property as the defendant, the defendant will need to secure alternative accommodation (see 7.5.4 above).

7.5.7 Restriction on entering specified areas

This condition can be use either to prevent the defendant interfering with prosecution witnesses, or to prevent the defendant committing further offences whilst on bail. A condition may be imposed preventing the defendant from entering the geographical area or town where a prosecution witness resides. Such a condition may also be used where the defendant habitually commits offences in the same place or type of place. For example, a defendant with a history of committing thefts at a certain shopping centre may be prohibited from entering that shopping centre or a defendant with a history of committing serious assaults in a city centre may be prohibited from entering that city centre.

7.5.8 Attending appointments with his solicitor or the Probation Service

A common condition which magistrates impose is to require a defendant to keep in regular touch with his solicitor and to attend meetings with his solicitor as and when required. The purpose behind such a condition is to ensure that the case is not delayed because the defendant has failed to provide his solicitor with prompt instructions.

Similarly, if following conviction the magistrates want to obtain a pre-sentence report from the Probation Service or a medical report on the defendant before passing sentence, a condition will be imposed requiring the defendant to attend such meetings or appointments as are necessary for the preparation of such reports. This is designed to ensure that cases are not delayed because a defendant has failed to keep an appointment.

7.6 Procedure for applying for bail

If the CPS objects to bail being granted, the following procedure will take place at court:

(a)   The CPS representative will apply to the magistrates for the defendant to be remanded in custody. He will give the magistrates a list of the defendant's previous convictions and then outline the *grounds* on which the prosecution object to bail being granted. He will support these grounds by citing the relevant details of the case and applying the *factors* referred to at **7.4.1** above.

(b)   The defendant's solicitor will then make an application for bail on his client's behalf. He will take each of the prosecution *grounds* for objecting to bail in turn and respond to these, applying, where appropriate, the same *factors*. The defendant's solicitor should ask the magistrates to grant his client unconditional bail, but should also suggest appropriate conditions, which the magistrates may impose if they are not prepared to grant unconditional bail.

(c)   The magistrates may hear evidence from other persons in support of the defendant's application for bail, such as a prospective employer if the defendant has recently been offered employment, or a person who is prepared to provide the defendant with accommodation if the defendant is currently of no fixed abode.

(d)   The magistrates will then decide whether to remand the defendant in custody or on bail. If the magistrates grant bail to the defendant, they will specify any conditions on that bail which they consider necessary. If bail is granted subject to a surety, the court will hear evidence on oath from the surety to ensure that he is suitable to act in that capacity.

A record of the magistrates' decision will be made and a copy of this given to the defendant. If the magistrates refuse bail or grants bail subject to conditions, reasons for the refusal or reasons for the conditions which have been imposed must also be recorded and a copy given to the defendant. If the CPS opposed bail but bail is granted by the magistrates, a record must be made of the reasons for granting bail and a copy given to the CPS upon request.

A court which has granted conditional bail to a defendant may, at a later hearing, vary these conditions on the application either of the CPS, or of the defendant's solicitor. A common situation that arises regularly in the magistrates' court is for the defendant to ask the magistrates to vary a condition that he does not enter a specified area, because he has just gained employment and his place of work is in that area. In such a case, the magistrates will vary the condition to permit the defendant to enter the specified area solely for the purposes of employment.

If the magistrates grant unconditional bail to the defendant, they may subsequently impose conditions on such bail if they consider that conditions have become necessary for one or more of the reasons specified at **7.5** above.

Key skill – making an application for bail

PROSECUTION SUBMISSION

Sir, the prosecution wish to raise objections to bail being granted to the defendant under Schedule 1, Part 1 of the Bail Act 1976. In particular the prosecution consider that, if released on bail, there are substantial grounds for believing that the defendant either will fail to surrender to custody, or will commit further offences whilst on bail. I will deal with each of these grounds in turn.

Starting with the risk that the defendant will fail to surrender to custody, the evidence against the defendant is such that a conviction is very likely. The defendant was picked out by an eye-witness to the assault at a video identification and, when questioned by the police, the defendant confessed to having committed the assault. The defendant is accused of having committed a prolonged and unprovoked attack on his victim, punching the victim in the face several times and causing the victim to suffer a fractured nose and split eyebrow. If convicted, the defendant is likely to receive a custodial sentence, particularly given the fact that the defendant has a previous conviction for the same offence. In these circumstances, the defendant may very well fail to surrender to custody so as to avoid this significant risk of imprisonment.

Another factor which may lead the defendant to fail to surrender to custody is the defendant's lack of community ties. The prosecution understand that the defendant has no close friends or family in the Chester area and does not own his own property in the area. The prosecution also understand that the defendant works as a scaffolder and regularly works away from the Chester area, including some work that is done out of the country.

As can be seen from the defendant's list of previous convictions, the defendant already has one recent previous conviction for failing to surrender to bail. This was also in respect of an assault charge which the defendant faced. When seen in the context of the current offence, this must raise substantial doubts that the defendant will surrender to custody.

The second objection to bail being granted is that the defendant may commit further offences if released on bail. Sir, this is a defendant with a history of violent offending. The defendant has been convicted of three offences involving violence within the last three years. One of these convictions was for the same offence with which the defendant is currently charged. Furthermore, all these offences appear to be connected to the defendant's employment as a nightclub bouncer. Given that the defendant is likely to continue in this employment, the prosecution would say that it is only a matter of time before the defendant offends again.

Sir, for the reasons I have outlined, I oppose bail being granted to the defendant and ask that the defendant be remanded in custody until this matter next comes before the court.

DEFENCE SUBMISSION

Sir, I wish to apply for unconditional bail on behalf of Mr Dickson. I will take the prosecution objections to bail being granted in turn, but before doing so I would like to remind you that under section 4 of the Bail Act 1976 there is a presumption that bail will be granted to Mr Dickson. Bail can be refused only if you consider that there are substantial grounds for believing that Mr Dickson would either fail to surrender to custody, or would commit further offences were he to be released on bail. This is a very high test for the prosecution to satisfy and, in my submission, the prosecution have failed to do this.

I will deal first with the allegation that Mr Dickson will fail to surrender to custody if released on bail. Whilst I concede that the charge Mr Dickson faces is a serious one, this makes it all the more likely that Mr Dickson will in fact attend the next hearing. Mr Dickson will be pleading not guilty in this matter. He is anxious to clear his name and does not wish to worsen the situation by failing to answer his bail.

The prosecution suggest that Mr Dickson is unlikely to come to court of his own volition because the evidence against him is strong. I would dispute the supposed strength of the prosecution evidence. Mr Dickson has a good defence to this charge and wants nothing more than to come to court to clear his name. A challenge to the admissibility of Mr Dickson's confession will be made at trial under sections 76 and 78 of PACE 1984. In addition, the identification evidence of the eye-witness will be challenged as being inaccurate. At trial, Mr Dickson intends calling an alibi witness to confirm that he was not the person who committed the assault.

The prosecution also seek to place reliance upon Mr Dickson's previous conviction for failing to surrender to bail. This must be placed in context. Mr Dickson did not actively abscond. Rather, there was a misunderstanding over the time Mr Dickson's case was due to start. Mr Dickson thought his case was due to start in the afternoon, and did not appreciate that he needed to be at court at 10.00 am. Mr Dickson did turn up at court in the afternoon at the time he thought he was supposed to attend. This is not the same thing as purposely seeking to avoid coming to court and I would urge you to give little significance to the prosecution's arguments on this point.

The prosecution suggest that Mr Dickson's lack of community ties mean that he is likely to abscond. Mr Dickson does in fact have strong ties to his local community. He is living with his partner in a property owned by his partner's parents, and has employment in the area from the evening and weekend work he does as a bouncer.

The second ground raised by the prosecution is that Mr Dickson will commit further offences if released on bail. I would submit that this is not the case. First I would reiterate that Mr Dickson will be pleading not guilty to this offence. In addition, Mr Dickson does not have a lengthy list of previous convictions and he has not previously offended whilst on bail. Whilst he has three previous convictions for relevant offences, these convictions are spread over more than two years and do not create substantial grounds for believing that Mr Dickson will offend again.

Furthermore, all of Mr Dickson's previous convictions relate to incidents when he was working as a nightclub bouncer. The allegation in this case is that the assault occurred away from the nightclub where Mr Dickson was working, and there is no suggestion that the assault had anything to do with the circumstances of Mr Dickson's employment as a bouncer, save that the victim of the assault had been working at the nightclub as a disc jockey.

Sir, for the reasons I have set out I would ask that you grant unconditional bail to Mr Dickson. Should you feel unable to grant bail on an unconditional basis, there are a number of conditions which I would invite you to consider imposing to remove any concerns you might have as to Mr Dickson's willingness to attend court on the next occasion. If you deem conditions to be appropriate, you might wish to consider imposing a condition that Mr Dickson report to his local police station on a daily basis, or a condition that he resides at 17 Marsh Street. Mr Dickson would also be able to provide a security to the court should one be required. I would submit that the imposition of such conditions would remove any substantial grounds for believing that Mr Dickson would fail to come to court on the next occasion.

Sir, unless I can be of any further assistance, those are my submissions.

7.7 Further applications for bail

If bail is refused, the magistrates are under a duty to consider the question of bail at any subsequent hearing if the defendant is still in custody and the presumption in favour of bail (see 7.3 above) still applies. However, this does not mean that the defendant's solicitor is permitted to make a full bail application at each subsequent hearing.

At the first hearing after the hearing at which the court refused to grant bail, the defendant's solicitor is permitted to make a full application for bail using *any* argument as to fact or law, even if he used the same arguments in his first unsuccessful application. At any subsequent hearing, the court need not hear arguments as to fact or law which it has heard previously (Bail Act 1976, Sch 1, Pt IIA).

Thus, a defendant who is refused bail is entitled to have his solicitor make one further full bail application, but if this is refused his solicitor may make a further bail application only if he is able to raise a *new* legal or factual argument as to why bail should be granted.

Example

Amir makes his first appearance before the magistrates on 14 May. His solicitor makes a full application for bail, but this is refused and Amir is remanded in custody for seven days. When Amir appears before the court again on 21 May, his solicitor may make a further full application for bail using any argument as to fact or law, whether or not this argument was used in the bail application made on 14 May. If the magistrates refuse bail on 21 May, Amir's solicitor can make a further application for bail only if he can raise a new argument that he has not used previously. For example, a potential surety might have become available (who can ensure Amir's attendance at subsequent hearings), or Amir might have been offered employment (in which case he will be less likely to abscond).

In applying the above rule, the magistrates will ignore a hearing at which bail was refused on the basis that it had not been practicable to obtain sufficient information about the defendant to determine whether bail should be granted (see 7.4.1 above).

If the magistrates' court remands a defendant in custody after hearing a fully argued bail application, it must issue a certificate confirming that it has heard such an application. This is known as a 'full argument certificate' and will be handed to the defendant's solicitor.

7.8 Appeals against decisions on bail

7.8.1 Appeals by the defendant (CrimPR, r 19.18)

A defendant who is refused bail by the magistrates' court may appeal against this decision to the Crown Court provided the magistrates have issued the 'full argument certificate' referred to in **7.7** above. Although a defendant may make an appeal to the Crown Court after the magistrates have made an initial refusal of bail, for tactical reasons most defence solicitors will delay making an appeal to the Crown Court until they have made two full applications for bail before the magistrates' court. Delaying an appeal until after the second full application before the magistrates maximises the number of potentially successful applications for bail which the defendant will be able to make.

To appeal to the Crown Court against a refusal of bail by the magistrates, the defendant's solicitor must complete a notice of application, which needs to be sent to the Crown Court and served on the CPS (at least 24 hours before the hearing). The notice of application will contain details of the defendant's previous applications for bail, details of the stage the case has reached before the magistrates, the nature and grounds of the defendant's appeal, and details of any proposed sureties.

The appeal will be heard before a Crown Court judge in chambers and will normally take place within a matter of days of the notice of application being sent to the Crown Court (it is normal practice to obtain a date for the hearing from the Crown Court at the same time as completing the application). The judge will need to have the following documents before him when considering the application:

(a)   the notice of application;

(b)   the 'full argument certificate'; and

(c)   a record of the defendant's previous convictions.

The defendant's solicitor should ensure that he sends the 'full argument certificate' and details of the defendant's previous convictions to the court prior to the appeal being heard. Failure to do so may mean that the judge refuses to consider the appeal.

At the hearing in chambers, the judge will hear representations from the CPS and the defendant's solicitor. The judge may refuse the defendant's application or grant bail to the defendant, with or without conditions. If the judge grants bail, a copy of the judge's order will need to be sent to the prison or remand centre where the defendant is being held so that the defendant may be released from custody.

Although the hearing of an appeal will usually take place in chambers, if the defendant applies for the hearing to be held in public in open court, such an application should be granted unless there are good reasons for excluding the public (*Malik v (1) Central Criminal Court (2) Crown Prosecution Service* [2006] EWHC (Admin) 1539).

Key skill – drafting a bail appeal notice

NOTICE OF APPLICATION RELATING TO BAIL TO BE MADE TO THE CROWN COURT

AT CHESTER   **CROWN COURT**

NAME AND LOCATION OF MAGISTRATES COURT CHESTER

Note: The appropriate office of the Crown Court should be consulted about the time and place of
hearing before this notice is sent to the other party to the application.
A copy of this notice should be sent to the Crown Court.
In the case of an application for bail in the course of proceedings being held before
Magistrates the certificate prescribed by Section 5 (6)A of the Bail Act 1976 (as amended)
should accompany this notice when it is lodged at the Court office.

**TAKE NOTICE that an application relating to bail will be made to the
Crown Court**

at   Chester

on   3rd January 2007

at   10.00 am

On behalf of the defendant/appellant/prosecutor/respondent

1.   **Defendant/appellant (block letters please)**

Surname: DICKSON   **Date of Birth:** 29.10.79

Forename: GARY PAUL

Home Address: 17 Marsh Street
Chester
CH3 7LW

2.   **If defendant/appellant is in custody state:**

Place of Detention: Chester Remand Centre

Prison number (if applicable): CRC100213

Length of time in custody since: 8 days since 19.12.06

Date of last remand: 26.12.06

3.   **Solicitors for the appellant**

Name: Collaws

4.   **State the particulars of proceedings during which the defendant/appellant was committed to custody or bailed (un)conditionally including:**

(a) **the stage reached in the proceedings at the date of the application:**

Remand hearing on 19/12/06 and further remand hearing on 26/12/06. Case adjourned for prosecution to give advance disclosure. Plea before venue to take place on 8/01/07.

(b) **The offences alleged:**

Assault occasioning actual bodily harm, contrary to s 47 of the Offences Against the Person Act 1861.

(c) **(if the application relates to a case pending before Magistrates) Give details of the next appearance:**

Place: Chester Magistrates Court

Date: 8/01/07   **Time:** 10.00 am

5.   **Give details of any relevant previous applications for bail or variation of conditions of bail**

19/12/06 – first full application for bail

26/12/06 – second full bail application

6.   **Nature and grounds of application:**

(a) **State fully the grounds relied on and list previous conditions (if any):**

SEE ATTACHED

(b) **Give details of any proposed sureties and answer any objections raised previously:**

N/A

NATURE AND GROUNDS:

The following arguments will be raised to counter the prosecution objections to bail:

<u>**Fail to surrender to custody**</u>

Mr Dickson has one previous conviction for failure to surrender to custody. This failure was due to a genuine misunderstanding as to the time that Mr Dickson's case was due to start. Mr Dickson did attend court of his own volition later in the day.

Mr Dickson is pleading not guilty to the one charge he faces and will come to court to clear his name. Mr Dickson has a strong defence to this charge and the evidence against him will be challenged. It will be alleged that the eye witness who purports to identify Mr Dickson as the assailant is mistaken. The admissibility of the confession evidence obtained by the police will be challenged under ss 76 & 78 of PACE 1984. An alibi witness will be called on Mr Dickson's behalf.

Mr Dickson has strong community ties. Mr Dickson resides in the Chester area with his partner. He and his partner reside in a property owned by his partner's parents. Mr Dickson has some part-time employment in the Chester area from his employment as a nightclub doorman.

<u>**Commit offences on bail**</u>

Mr Dickson is pleading not guilty to the current charge. He has never previously committed an offence whilst on bail, and he does not have a lengthy list of previously convictions. Mr Dickson's last conviction was over one year ago. All of Mr Dickson's previous convictions relate to incidents when Mr Dickson was working as a nightclub doorman and was dealing with customers. The current charge relates to an alleged incident which occurred after Mr Dickson left his place of employment. There is no reason to believe that Mr Dickson will offend again whilst on bail.

<u>**Bail Conditions**</u>

The following bail conditions will be put forward:

i) residence at 17 Marsh Street, Chester
ii) reporting to Chester Police Station on regular basis
iii) security

7.8.2 Appeals by the prosecution (CrimPR, rr 19.16 and 19.17)

If the magistrates grant bail to a defendant who has been charged with an imprisonable offence, s 1 of the Bail (Amendment) Act 1993 gives the CPS the right to appeal against this decision to a Crown Court judge in chambers. The CPS must have initially objected to the grant of bail before the magistrates' court, and oral notice of the appeal must be given by the CPS representative at the conclusion of the hearing in the magistrates court at which bail was granted *before* the defendant is released from custody. This oral notice must be confirmed in writing and served on the defendant within two hours of the hearing in the magistrates' court concluding. The appeal must be heard at the Crown Court within 48 hours of the magistrates' decision to grant bail. The defendant will be remanded in custody by the magistrates until the appeal is heard.

The CPS will not appeal against the grant of bail to a defendant in every case where it initially opposed the grant of bail. The Code for Crown Prosecutors provides that appeals should be made only in cases of 'grave concern', and should not be made merely because the Crown prosecutor disagrees with the magistrates' decision. Prosecution appeals to the Crown Court are likely to be made only where the prosecution have grave concerns that a defendant released on bail might cause injury to another, or might abscond by leaving the country.

7.9 Failing to surrender (absconding)

7.9.1 What steps will the court take if the defendant fails to surrender?

A defendant who is granted bail (either by the police after he has been charged, or by the court following a hearing) is under a duty to surrender to the court at the time and place appointed for the next hearing. If the defendant fails to attend court to answer his bail at the appointed time and date, the magistrates will issue a warrant for his arrest (Bail Act 1976, s 7(1)). The warrant will either be backed with bail (which means that the police, having arrested the defendant, will then release him again pending his next court appearance), or, as is much more common, not backed with bail. If the warrant is not backed with bail, the police will arrest the defendant and then keep him in police custody until he can be brought before the court. The defendant will be brought before the magistrates' court at the next hearing (which will usually be on the day following his arrest).

7.9.2 Will the defendant be charged with failing to surrender?

What happens when the defendant is brought before the court will depend on whether the defendant has breached bail which has been granted by the police or bail granted by the court.

A defendant who has been charged by the police and bailed to appear before the magistrates' court will be in breach of *police* bail if he fails to attend court at the appointed date and time. When that defendant is arrested and brought before the court, whether he is charged with failing to surrender to custody under s 6(1) or (2) of the Bail Act 1976 (see **7.9.3** below) is a matter for the CPS. If the defendant's solicitor can persuade the CPS representative that there is a reasonable explanation for the defendant failing to attend court (if, for example, the defendant made a genuine mistake as to the date of his first appearance at court), the CPS representative may decide not to take proceedings against the client for failing to surrender.

If, however, the defendant has already made an appearance before the court, was been granted bail by the court and then failed to surrender at the next hearing, the decision to commence proceedings against him for failing to surrender will be made by the court rather than the CPS because the defendant will be in breach of *court* bail.

7.9.3 What offence(s) might the defendant be charged with?

The Bail Act 1976 creates two offences with which a defendant who fails to surrender to custody at the appointed time and date may be charged:

(a) if the defendant fails without reasonable cause to surrender to custody, he will be guilty of the offence of absconding under s 6(1);

(b) if the defendant did have a reasonable cause for failing to surrender, he will still be guilty of an offence under s 6(2) unless he surrendered to custody as soon as it was reasonably practicable for him to do so. For example, a defendant who is unable to answer his bail because he is injured in a road traffic accident and has to go to hospital will still be guilty of an offence under s 6(2) unless he answers his bail as soon as reasonably practicable after his release from hospital.

Since absconding is a separate criminal offence, a solicitor who represents a defendant charged under s 6(1) or (2) above will be able to claim payment for representing the defendant in connection with the absconding charge only if he asks the court to extend his client's representation order (see **6.4.3.2**) to cover not only the substantive offence with which the client has been charged but also the absconding offence.

7.9.4 Procedure at court

If the defendant has failed to answer *police* bail (see **7.9.2** above) and the CPS wishes to pursue the matter, the CPS representative will ask that a charge under either s 6(1) or s 6(2) be put to the defendant. The defendant may then plead either guilty or not guilty to the charge.

If the defendant has failed to answer *court* bail, when the defendant is brought before the court he will be asked informally by the court clerk the reason for his failure to surrender. If the defendant puts forward a reasonable excuse, it is unlikely that the court will take the matter any further. If the defendant is unable to put forward a reasonable excuse, however, the charge of absconding will then be put to him and he will plead guilty or not guilty.

If the defendant pleads guilty to a charge of absconding (whether in respect of police bail or court bail), the court may either sentence him immediately or adjourn sentence until the conclusion of the substantive proceedings. If the defendant pleads not guilty, the court will deal with the matter straight away, with the defendant giving evidence and being cross-examined on the reasons for his failing to attend. The burden of proof will be on the defendant to show, on a balance of probabilities, that he had reasonable cause for his failure to surrender.

7.9.5 The sentence

The maximum sentence for a defendant convicted of absconding is a prison sentence and/or a fine. The Magistrates' Courts Sentencing Guidelines (see **Chapter 11**) recommend a community penalty as the 'guideline' sentence for a defendant convicted of absconding after pleading not guilty to such a charge. Even if the magistrates decide not to impose a separate penalty for the absconding offence, they may decide to refuse the defendant bail in the substantive proceedings, or grant bail but with a much more stringent package of conditions.

A defendant convicted of absconding may be sentenced immediately or at the end of the trial in respect of the substantive offence. How the court sentences a defendant who is convicted of absconding will depend on the factual circumstances of the offence, with the court considering any aggravating or mitigating factors. Aggravating factors will include:

(a)   wilful absconding by the defendant;

(b)   absconding over a long period of time;

(c)   previous convictions for absconding;

(d)   a defendant who left the jurisdiction; and

(e)   absconding which causes a trial date to be postponed (although the court does have the power to conduct a trial in the absence of a defendant who has absconded).

Mitigating factors will include:

(a)   a genuine misunderstanding (for example, a defendant who made a genuine mistake as to the time he was due to appear at court);

(b)   a defendant who, having realised his mistake, attends court later that day; and

(c)   a defendant who wilfully absconded but then surrendered voluntarily to custody.

7.9.6 Will the defendant receive a further grant of bail in the substantive proceedings?

Although a defendant who has absconded may still receive a further grant of bail in the substantive proceedings, much will depend on the actual circumstances of the failure to surrender. The CPS is likely to object to a further grant of bail being made on the basis that there are substantial grounds to believe that, if released on bail, the defendant will fail to surrender. Paragraph 6 of Sch 1, Pt 1 to the Bail Act 1976 provides that a defendant who has failed to surrender in the current proceedings shall not be granted bail again unless the court is satisfied that there is no 'significant risk' of him failing to surrender again (see **7.4.1** above).

The court may be persuaded to make a further grant of bail to the defendant if his failure to surrender was the result of a genuine misunderstanding, or if the defendant voluntarily surrendered. In such a case, the court may grant bail on the same conditions as previously, or bail subject to more stringent conditions. The defendant is unlikely to be granted bail again, however, if he wilfully failed to surrender and had to be arrested by the police. In such a case, the court is likely to apply para 6 of Sch 1, Pt 1 to the Bail Act 1976 (see above) and deny him bail.

> ### Example 1
>
> Donald is charged with assault occasioning actual bodily harm. He makes his first appearance before the magistrates' court on unconditional bail, and his case is adjourned so that the CPS can make advance disclosure of its case to his solicitor. Donald is granted bail by the magistrates. Donald fails to attend the next hearing and a warrant for his arrest is issued. Donald is eventually arrested by the police some 200 miles away four weeks later. Donald has two previous convictions for absconding. When Donald is brought before the magistrates following his arrest, the magistrates refuse him bail on the basis that there are substantial grounds for believing that he will fail to surrender to custody if a further grant of bail is made, and that there is a

significant risk that he will abscond if granted bail again. Donald will be remanded in custody until the next hearing.

Example 2

Michaela is charged with theft and makes her first appearance before the magistrates' court on unconditional bail. Her case is adjourned so that the CPS can make advance disclosure of its case to her solicitor. Michaela fails to attend the next hearing and a warrant for her arrest is issued. Michaela then arrives at court the day after the hearing was due to take place. She explains that her failure to attend was a genuine oversight on her part after she got the dates mixed up. When Michaela is brought before the magistrates, the magistrates accept that she made a mistake and they also take into account the fact that she surrendered voluntarily. The magistrates make a further grant of bail to Michaela, although this is now subject to a condition of residence and a condition that she report daily to the police station.

If a defendant absconds prior to his trial, the court may proceed with the trial in his absence (*R v O'Hare* [2006] EWCA Crim 471).

7.10 Breaches of bail

A defendant who breaches any bail conditions other than a condition to attend the next court hearing (for example, a defendant who fails to comply with a curfew, a condition of residence or a condition not to contact a prosecution witness) does *not* commit a criminal offence by breaching such conditions. However, a defendant who breaches his bail conditions is likely to have his bail reviewed by the magistrates, who may decide that his failure to comply with the conditions necessitates a remand in custody. As breach of a bail condition is not a separate criminal offence, any work carried out by the defendant's solicitor in connection with the breach proceedings will be covered under the representation order granted to the defendant for the substantive offence with which he has been charged.

Section 7(3) of the Bail Act 1976 empowers a police officer to arrest a person who has been bailed to attend court (either by the police following charge, or by the court at a previous hearing) if the officer reasonably believes that the person:

(a)   is not likely to surrender to bail; or

(b)   has broken, or is likely to break, his bail conditions.

A defendant who is arrested will be detained in police custody and must then be brought before the magistrates' court within 24 hours. The magistrates will then decide whether to remand the defendant in custody, or whether to grant bail with or without conditions pending the next substantive hearing in the case. The magistrates will adopt a two-stage approach:

(a)   The magistrates will determine if there has been a breach of the bail conditions previously imposed. Unless the defendant admits to breaching his bail conditions, the magistrates are likely to hear oral evidence from both the police officer who arrested the defendant and the defendant himself to determine whether a breach has occurred.

(b)   If the magistrates determine that there has been a breach of bail conditions, they will decide whether the defendant should be remanded in custody or on bail pending the next hearing (unless the case can be disposed of at that hearing). The magistrates will assess the seriousness of the breach and the reasons for the breach. The magistrates will hear representations from the CPS (the CPS is likely to be opposing the further grant of bail) and the defendant's solicitor before coming to a decision. A defendant who has breached his bail conditions without good reason is likely to be remanded in custody, although the magistrates may be persuaded to make a further grant of bail but with more stringent conditions attached to it.

Example 1

The police charge Qasim with theft and release him on conditional bail pending his first appearance before the magistrates' court one week later. The condition is that Qasim does not contact any prosecution witnesses. Two days after being charged, Qasim is arrested for breaching this condition. Manaz, an eye-witness to the theft, alleges that Qasim approached her and asked her to change her story. The police arrest Qasim and bring him before the magistrates' court within 24 hours of his arrest. Qasim denies contacting Manaz but, after a hearing at which both Qasim and the police officer who arrested him for breaching his bail condition give evidence, the magistrates decide that Qasim did breach his bail conditions. Qasim's solicitor makes an application for Qasim to be granted bail prior to the next hearing. This is opposed by the CPS, and the magistrates refuse bail on the basis that there are substantial grounds for believing that, if released on bail, Qasim will interfere with witnesses. Qasim is remanded in custody until the next hearing.

Example 2

The police charge Nick with affray following an incident at a city centre pub, and release him on conditional bail pending his first appearance before the magistrates' court one week later. The condition is that Nick does not enter a defined area in the city centre. The following day Nick attends the birthday party of a friend at another pub. This pub is within the area Nick is not supposed to enter, although Nick genuinely thought that it was outside this area. Nick is arrested for breaching his bail condition and is brought before the magistrates' court within 24 hours. Nick accepts that he breached his bail condition, but explains that he made an honest mistake. Nick makes a further application for bail and this is opposed by the CPS. The magistrates nevertheless decide to make a further grant of bail to Nick, although this is made subject to more onerous conditions. In addition to keeping out of the city centre, the magistrates impose an additional condition that Nick is not to enter any public house.

7.11   Bail and the Human Rights Act 1998

In June 2001, the Law Commission published *Bail and the Human Rights Act*, which examined the compatibility of the provisions of the Bail Act 1976 with Article 5(3) of the ECHR, which provides that those charged with a criminal offence 'shall be entitled to trial within a reasonable time or to release pending trial'. The Commission also published *Law Commission Guidance for Bail Decision-makers and their Advisers*, giving advice to magistrates and their clerks on the human rights considerations which had to be taken into account when a decision whether to grant bail was being made. This guidance is reproduced at **7.14** below.

7.12 Flowchart – contested bail application

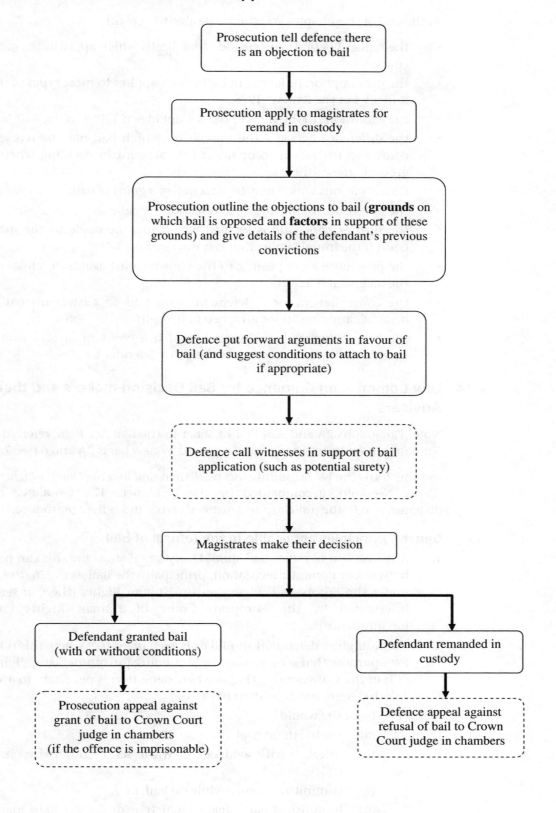

Prosecution tell defence there is an objection to bail

Prosecution apply to magistrates for remand in custody

Prosecution outline the objections to bail (**grounds** on which bail is opposed and **factors** in support of these grounds) and give details of the defendant's previous convictions

Defence put forward arguments in favour of bail (and suggest conditions to attach to bail if appropriate)

Defence call witnesses in support of bail application (such as potential surety)

Magistrates make their decision

Defendant granted bail (with or without conditions)

Defendant remanded in custody

Prosecution appeal against grant of bail to Crown Court judge in chambers (if the offence is imprisonable)

Defence appeal against refusal of bail to Crown Court judge in chambers

7.13 Checklist

At the end of this chapter you should be able to explain:

- the remand periods and custody time limits which apply in the magistrates' court;

- the presumption in favour of bail which applies to most types of defendant under s 4 of the Bail Act 1976;

- the exceptions to the right to bail set out in Sch 1, Pt 1 to the Bail Act 1976;

- the difference between the *grounds* on which bail may be refused by the court and the *factors* to be taken into account in deciding whether those grounds are satisfied;

- the conditions which may be attached to a grant of bail;

- the procedure for making an application for bail;

- the further applications for bail which may be made to the magistrates' court if the initial application is unsuccessful;

- the procedure for appealing to the Crown Court against a refusal of bail by the magistrates' court;

- the consequences for a defendant who fails to answer his bail, or who breaches any conditions attached to his bail;

- the human rights considerations which a court must take into account when deciding whether to grant bail to a defendant.

7.14 Law Commission Guidance for Bail Decision-makers and their Advisers

Note: Paragraphs 2A and 6 of Pt 1 of Sch 1 to the Bail Act 1976, referred to in the Guidance, have been repealed and replaced by new paras 2A and 6 (see **7.4.1**).

In June 2001, the Law Commission published *Bail and the Human Rights Act 1998* (Paper No 269), accompanied by the Guidance. The Guidance has been disseminated to the judiciary and justices' clerks and is here reproduced in full.

General principles applicable to the refusal of bail

1. Any decision to refuse bail should only be taken where this can be justified both under domestic legislation, principally the Bail Act 1976 (the Act), and under the European Convention on Human Rights (the Convention), as interpreted by the European Court of Human Rights (Strasbourg jurisprudence).

2. Accordingly, a defendant should only be refused bail where this is necessary for a purpose that is recognised by Strasbourg jurisprudence applying Article 5(3) of the Convention. That is where detention is necessary to avoid a real risk that, were the defendant released,

   (1) he or she would

      (a) fail to attend trial; or

      (b) interfere with evidence or witnesses, or otherwise obstruct the course of justice; or

      (c) commit an offence while on bail; or

      (d) be at risk of harm against which he or she would be inadequately protected; or

   (2) a disturbance to public order would result.

3. Detention will only be necessary if the risk could not be adequately addressed by the imposition of appropriate bail conditions that would make detention unnecessary.

4. Any court refusing bail should give reasons that explain why detention is necessary. Those reasons should be closely related to the individual circumstances of the defendant.

The exceptions to the right to bail in English law

5. Some of the exceptions to the right to bail found in the Act correlate so closely with the above purposes recognised by the Strasbourg jurisprudence that there is no need to consider separately how they should be applied in a way that complies with the Convention. These are the exceptions in paragraph 2(a) (fail to surrender to custody) and (c) (interfere with witnesses or otherwise obstruct the course of justice) and paragraph 7 (impracticable to complete inquiries or report without keeping defendant in custody) of Part I, and paragraph 2 of Part II (also based on failure to surrender to custody), of Schedule 1 to the Act.

6. In respect of the remaining exceptions to the right to bail we offer the following guidance as an aid to compliance with the Convention.

The risk of offending on bail

7. The decision-taker must consider whether it may properly be inferred from any previous convictions and other circumstances relating to the defendant that there is a real risk that the defendant will commit an offence if granted bail, and that the defendant therefore falls within paragraph 2(b) of Part I of Schedule 1 to the Act. Provided that a decision to withhold bail is a necessary and proportionate response to a *real risk* that, if released, the defendant would commit an offence while on bail, such a decision will comply with the Convention.

Defendant on bail at the time of the alleged offence

8. The factor in paragraph 2A of Part I of Schedule 1 to the Act (a defendant who commits an indictable offence whilst on bail) does not, in itself, establish any Article 5(3) purpose.

9. Consequently, a court should not base a decision to withhold bail solely on paragraph 2A. To do so would infringe Article 5 and would be unlawful under sections 3 and 6 of the Human Rights Act 1998 (HRA)

10. That factor may, however, be relevant to a decision whether to withhold bail on the basis of another relevant exception, for example the risk that the defendant will commit an offence while on bail.

Detention for the defendant's own protection

11. A decision to refuse bail to a defendant under the exception in paragraph 3 of Part I of Schedule 1 to the Act, that is for the defendant's own protection (from self-harm or harm from others) would comply with the Convention, where

    (1) detention is *necessary* to address a *real risk* that, if granted bail, the defendant would suffer harm, against which detention could provide protection; and

    (2) there are exceptional circumstances in the nature of the alleged offence and/or the conditions or context in which it is alleged to have been committed.

12.   A decision of a court to order detention because of a risk of *self*-harm may be compatible with the ECHR even where the circumstances giving rise to the risk are unconnected with the alleged offence, provided that the court is satisfied that there is a real risk of self-harm, and that a proper medical examination will take place rapidly so that the court may then consider exercising its powers of detention under the Mental Health Act 1983.

Detention because of a lack of information

13.   The refusal of bail under paragraph 5 of Part I of Schedule 1 to the Act, where it has not been practicable to obtain sufficient information for the taking of a full bail decision for want of time since the institution of proceedings against the defendant, would be compatible with Article 5 provided that

(1)   detention is for a short period, which is no longer than necessary to enable the required information to be obtained, and

(2)   the lack of information is not due to a failure of the prosecution, the police, the court or another state body to act with 'special diligence'.

14.   There is no need in such a case for the court to be satisfied of any of the recognised purposes set out in paragraph 2 above.

15.   After the initial short period of time has passed, a lack of information that is not due to a failure of a state body to act with 'special diligence' may be taken into account as a factor militating in favour of detention on *another* Convention compliant ground for detention.

Detention following arrest under section 7

Paragraph 6 of Part I and paragraph 5 of Part II of Schedule 1

16.   The broad provisions in paragraph 6 of Part I and paragraph 5 of Part II of Schedule 1 to the Act, that a defendant arrested pursuant to section 7 need not be granted bail, should be read subject to the narrower provisions governing bail following a section 7(3) arrest, set out in section 7(5) of the Act. That provision requires that bail should again be granted unless the justice is of the opinion that the defendant is not likely to surrender to custody, or has broken or is likely to break any condition of bail. Detention on one of these grounds will comply with the Convention only where this is necessary for one or more of the recognised purposes set out above in paragraph 2.

Section 7(5) hearings

17.   At the hearing of section 7(5) proceedings there is no requirement that oral evidence should be heard in every case, but account should be taken of the quality of material presented. This may range from mere assertion to documentary proof. If the material includes oral evidence, the defendant must be given an opportunity to cross-examine. Likewise, a defendant should be permitted to give relevant oral evidence if he or she wishes to do so.

Section 25 of the Criminal Justice and Public Order Act 1994

18.   The expression 'exceptional circumstances' in section 25 of the Criminal Justice and Public Order Act 1994 should be construed so that it encompasses a defendant who, if released on bail, would not pose a real risk of committing a serious offence. This construction achieves the purpose of Parliament to ensure that, when making bail decisions about defendants to

whom section 25 applies, decision-takers focus on the risk the defendant may pose to the public by re-offending.

19. It is possible that's some other circumstance might constitute 'exceptional circumstances'. Even if 'exceptional circumstances' do exist, bail may, nonetheless, be withheld on a Convention-compatible ground if this is deemed to be necessary in the individual case.

Conditional bail

Conditional bail as an alternative to custody

20. A defendant must be released, if need be subject to conditions, unless:

(1) that would create a risk of the kind which can, in principle, justify pretrial detention (set out above in paragraph 2), and

(2) that risk cannot, by imposing suitable bail conditions, be averted, or reduced to a level at which it would not justify detention.

Conditional bail as an alternative to unconditional bail

21. A court should only impose bail conditions for one of the purposes which Strasbourg jurisprudence recognises as capable of justifying detention (set out above in paragraph 2).

22. A bail condition should only be imposed where, if the defendant were to break that condition or be reasonably thought likely to do so, it may be necessary to arrest the defendant in order to pursue the purpose for which the condition was imposed.

Reasons for imposing conditions

23. Decision-takers should state their reasons for imposing bail conditions and specify the purposes for which any conditions are imposed.

24. Decision-takers should also be alert to ensure that any bail conditions they impose do not violate the defendants other Convention rights, such as those protected by Articles 8–11 of the Convention (the right to respect for family life, freedom of thought, conscience and religion, freedom of expression and freedom of assembly and association).

Giving reasons for bail decisions

25. It is of particular importance that decision-takers or their clerks make, and retain for the file, a note of the gist of the arguments for and against the grant of bail, and the oral reasons given by the tribunal for their decision.

26. Standard forms should be completed accurately to show that a decision has been taken in a way that complies with the Convention.

Participation of the defendant

27. Strasbourg jurisprudence recognises it as sufficient participation of the defendant in bail proceedings if, where necessary, he or she participates through a legal representative. Nevertheless, a domestic court should not hear a bail application to a conclusion in the absence of a defendant where the defendant's presence is essential to fair proceedings.

Form of evidence

28. It is not necessary to hear sworn evidence in the great majority of cases. Courts should, in particular cases, consider whether fairness requires the calling of evidence on oath for the determination of the application, as a

failure to call such evidence may cause a particular decision to fall foul of Article 5(4).

29. A court hearing bail proceedings should take account of the quality of the material presented. It may range from mere assertion to documentary proof. If the material includes sworn oral evidence, the defendant must be given an opportunity to cross-examine. Likewise, the defendant should be permitted to give relevant oral evidence if he or she wishes to do so.

Disclosure

30. *Ex parte Lee* recognises an ongoing duty of disclosure from the time of arrest. The Court of Appeal emphasised that at the stage before committal, there are continuing obligations on the prosecutor to make such disclosure as justice and fairness may require in the particular circumstances of the case, that is, where it could reasonably be expected to assist the defence when applying for bail. This will ensure that the defendant enjoys 'equality of arms' with the prosecution.

31. Compliance with this requirement, together with those imposed by the Attorney-General's guidelines to prosecutors, should ensure compliance with the Convention. This will apply equally to hearings pursuant to section 7(5) (see above).

32. The duty of disclosure does not require that the whole of the prosecution file be disclosed to the defence prior to the hearing. It is sufficient if disclosure is provided of the material the defendant needs in order to enjoy 'equality of arms' with the prosecution in relation to the matter to be decided by the court.

Public hearing

33. Where normally the hearing would be in chambers, if the defendant requests that the bail hearing be held in public, it should be held in public unless there is a good reason not to do so.

The right to challenge pre-trial detention

34. The Convention gives a detained person the right to make further court challenges to the legality of his or her detention despite having already made one or more such challenges, where for example, with the passage of time, the circumstances which once were considered by a court to justify detention may have changed.

35. To ensure compliance with the Convention, Part 11A of Schedule I to the Act should be applied on the basis that courts should be willing, at intervals of 28 days, to consider arguments that the passage of time constitutes, in the particular case, a change in circumstances relevant to the need to detain the defendant, so as to require the hearing of all the arguments on the question of bail. It may be, for example, that the time served on remand may have reduced the risk of the defendant absconding.

36. If the court finds that the passage of time does amount to a relevant change of circumstances then a full bail application should follow in which all the arguments, old and new, could be put forward and taken into account.

Chapter 8
Preparation for Trial in the Magistrates' Court

8.1 Introduction

After a defendant has entered a not guilty plea to a summary offence, or has pleaded not guilty to an either way offence and has consented to a trial in the magistrates' court (see **Chapter 6**), the magistrates will fix the date when the defendant's trial is take place. The magistrates will also give a series of directions that the CPS and the defendant's solicitor must comply with prior to the trial. This chapter will describe the directions that the magistrates will give and will also look at the steps which the defendant's solicitor needs to take in order to prepare his client's case for trial. These steps include obtaining evidence from witnesses other than the defendant and obtaining details of any 'unused' material the CPS has which may assist the defence case.

8.2 Directions

8.2.1 Introduction

Prior to the Criminal Procedure Rules 2005 coming into effect, there were no standard case management directions that the magistrates' court would give in order to ensure that the CPS and the defendant's solicitor were properly prepared for trial. Once a defendant had entered his not guilty plea, the court would either fix a trial date immediately (if the case was straightforward) or would arrange for a hearing called a pre-trial review to take place. The purpose of the pre-trial review was to make arrangements for the trial in a more complex case and to ensure that the parties were ready for trial. The Criminal Procedure Rules 2005 have replaced this system with a formal set of case management directions with which the parties must comply.

8.2.2 Case management hearing

The court will give case management directions either at the same hearing at which the defendant enters his plea of not guilty (and, in the case of an either way matter, after the plea before venue/allocation hearing has taken place and the defendant has consented to trial before the magistrates), or at a subsequent hearing. The hearing at which case management directions are given is referred to in the Criminal Procedure Rules as a case management hearing, although many magistrates' courts continue to refer to this as a pre-trial review.

The case management directions are intended to be standard directions which can be used for any case, although they may be varied by the court in a particular case if necessary. The directions allow the parties eight weeks to prepare the case for trial (or 14 weeks when expert evidence is to be called at trial).

Before the court gives case management directions, the court will expect both the CPS and the defendant's solicitor to nominate case progression officers in accordance with CrimPR, r 3.4 (see **1.4.4**). The case progression officer is responsible for ensuring that the directions given by the court are complied with and must notify the court immediately if there is any difficulty in complying with them.

After the defendant has given his not guilty plea, the court will ask the defendant's solicitor to answer the following questions:

(a)   Has the defendant been advised about credit for pleading guilty? YES/NO

(b)   Has the defendant been warned that if he is on bail and fails to attend, the proceedings may continue in his absence? YES/NO

The defendant's solicitor must ensure that he discusses these questions with his client prior to the case management hearing. He must in addition obtain express authority from his client to answer these questions since the questions ask about advice given to the client that would normally be legally privileged information.

8.2.3   Content of the directions

After asking the questions referred to in **8.2.2** above, the magistrates will then give the case a trial date (with an estimated duration of the trial) before giving the parties the directions listed at (a) to (k) below. (All the time limits shown in square brackets below may be varied by the court if it deems it appropriate to do so. Where the directions refer to a document being 'served', this means that it must be sent to the other parties in the case (in other words, the defence or prosecution, as the case may be, and also any co-accused) and filed with the court.)

(a)   *Prosecution case and disclosure.* Unless it has already done so, the CPS must serve copies of the documents containing the evidence on which the charge or charges are based, including witness statements and any documentary exhibits, tapes of interviews, video tapes and CCTV tapes within *[28] days*. Unless it has already done so, the CPS must also comply with its initial duty to disclose to the defendant any unused material it has within *[28] days* (see **8.4.6** below).

(b)   *The defence statement.* If the defendant intends to provide a defence statement (see **8.4.7** below), this must be served this within *14 days* of the CPS complying with its initial duty of disclosure of any unused material it has. If, following receipt of the defence statement, the CPS needs to make further disclosure of any unused material it has, this must be done at least *[14] days* before the trial date.

(c)   *Witness statements.* If the defendant wants a prosecution witness to give evidence in person at trial, his solicitor must notify the prosecution within *7 days* of receiving details of the prosecution case under (a) above. The defendant must serve any statements of defence witnesses who the defence propose not to give evidence in person at trial within *[14] days* of receiving the prosecution case under (a) above. If either the CPS or any co-accused requires such a witness to give evidence in person at trial, they must notify the defendant within *7 days* of being served with the statement(s) (see **8.4.5** below).

(d)   *Hearsay evidence.* If the CPS wishes to rely on any hearsay evidence at trial (see **Chapter 19**), it must serve a notice of intention to introduce hearsay evidence at the same time as it complies with its initial duty to disclose to the defendant's solicitor any unused material it has. If the defendant wishes to oppose this, he must serve a notice opposing the prosecution's notice within *14 days* of receiving this notice.

If the defendant wishes to rely on any hearsay evidence at trial, he must serve a notice of intention to introduce hearsay evidence within *14 days* of the date on which the CPS complies with its initial duty to disclose to the defence any unused material it has. If the CPS wishes to oppose this, it must serve a notice opposing the defendant's notice within *14 days* of receiving this.

(e) *Bad character evidence.* If the defendant wishes to introduce the previous convictions of a prosecution witness at trial (see **Chapter 22**), he must serve an application for permission to do this within *14 days* of the date on which the CPS discloses the existence of such convictions. The CPS should disclose the existence of such convictions as part of its obligation to disclose to the defence any material capable of undermining the prosecution case (see **8.4.6.2** below). If the CPS wishes to oppose the defendant's application, it must serve a notice doing so within *14 days* of receiving the application.

If the CPS wishes to introduce the defendant's bad character at trial, it must serve a notice of intention to do this at the same time as it complies with its initial duty to disclose any unused material it has. The defendant must serve any application he wishes to make to exclude evidence of his bad character at trial within *14 days* of receiving the prosecution notice. The court has the discretion to make any further orders it wishes in relation to the use of bad character evidence at trial.

(f) *Written admissions.* If either the CPS or the defendant wishes to make a written admission under s 10 of the Criminal Justice Act 1967, such an admission must be made within *[56] days*.

(g) *Points of law.* If either the CPS or the defendant wishes to argue a point of law at trial (for example, the admissibility of a confession allegedly made by the defendant), if the party raising the point considers that a skeleton argument would be helpful, such an argument must be served together with any supporting authorities at least *[21] days* prior to the trial. The other party must serve a skeleton argument in reply together with authorities at least *[7] days* prior to the trial. (A skeleton argument is a brief form of written submission setting out the basic arguments to be raised and any legal authorities to be relied on.)

(h) *Special measures.* If the CPS requires a special measures direction to enable prosecution witnesses to give their evidence (see **16.5.4**), it must serve an application for such measures within *14 days*. If the defendant opposes this application, any response must be served within *14 days* of service of the prosecution application.

(i) *Expert evidence.* If either the CPS or the defendant seeks to rely on evidence from an expert at trial, a copy of that expert's report must be served within *[28] days*. The party served with the expert's report must indicate whether the expert is required to attend at the trial, and either serve their own expert evidence in response or indicate that they are not intending to rely on expert evidence within *[28] days* of receipt of the other party's expert evidence.

A meeting of experts to agree non-contentious matters and identify issues, if appropriate and the parties agree, must take place within *[28] days* of service of both parties' expert evidence.

The parties must notify the court within *[14] days* of an experts' meeting whether the length of the trial is affected by the outcome of the meeting.

(j)   *Trial readiness.* The CPS and the defendant must certify readiness for trial by filing a certificate of readiness for trial (if appropriate) at least *[7] days* before trial.

(k)   *Further case management.* Where the case is complex, the court may arrange a further case management hearing. If it chooses to do so, the court will specify in the directions when that hearing is to take place.

A copy of the case progression form used by the magistrates' court to give case management directions is set out at **8.6** below.

8.3   Case analysis

To provide his client with a properly argued defence at trial, the defendant's solicitor must carry out an analysis of the case against his client to determine what the issues in the case are and what evidence can be placed before the court to ensure that those issues are resolved in the defendant's favour and that the defendant is ultimately acquitted.

Set out below is a six-point template which should be followed by the defendant's solicitor when analysing the prosecution case against his client:

(a)   *What are the legal elements of the offence charged?* The first step in analysing a case is to determine what it is that the CPS will need to prove in order to secure a conviction. To do this the defendant's solicitor must find out what the *actus reus* and *mens rea* are for the offence with which his client is charged.

(b)   *What is the prosecution account of the case?* What story does the CPS want the court to believe? To discover this the defendant's solicitor should prepare a brief narrative account of the prosecution case. If the prosecutor could tell the magistrates what it is alleged the defendant did when the offence was committed, what would he say?

(c)   *What is the defendant's account of the case?* This is the same procedure as in (b) above, but from the defendant's point of view. If the defendant was telling the court his 'story', what would he say?

(d)   *What are the facts in issue?* If steps (b) and (c) have been properly completed, the defendant's solicitor should now have two accounts or versions of what the court is going to be asked to believe happened. Wherever the accounts diverge there is a fact in issue. The defendant's solicitor needs to make a list detailing each fact in issue in the case.

(e)   *How is each party going to prove its version of the facts in issue?* Once the defendant's solicitor has a list of the factual issues that the court needs to resolve, he must then analyse the evidence which exists. For each fact in issue he needs to determine what evidence the CPS has to support its version of events and what evidence his client has to rebut this.

(f)   *Is any further evidence required?* The final stage in the case analysis model is for the defendant's solicitor to assess the adequacy of the evidence that currently exists to support the defendant's case. Will this evidence be sufficient to result in an acquittal, or is further evidence necessary? If there are weaknesses in the defendant's case, where is the further evidence going to come from to strengthen this case?

8.4   Obtaining additional evidence

8.4.1   Introduction

If the case analysis described in **8.3** above shows that additional evidence in support of the defendant's case is necessary, the defendant's solicitor should consider with his client where such evidence may be obtained. Additional evidence may come from witnesses as to fact, from expert witnesses, or it may be in the form of documentary evidence. Such documentary evidence is likely to be 'unused material' which the CPS has compiled but does not wish to rely on as part of its case against the defendant. The defendant's solicitor must ensure that he obtains from the CPS any 'unused material' which may assist the defence case (see **8.4.6** below).

8.4.2   Witnesses as to fact

8.4.2.1   Introduction

The defendant's solicitor needs to find out from his client if he is aware of any witnesses who might be prepared to give evidence on his behalf. For example, a defendant charged with assault who is pleading not guilty on the basis that he acted in self-defence, may have been with a friend at the time of the assault who will support the defendant's account of what happened.

Any witnesses who are located need to be interviewed and a signed statement taken from them. The defendant's solicitor needs to take a view on how helpful a particular witness will be to his client's case, and how credible that witness will be if he gives evidence at court. Very careful consideration needs to be given before calling a defence witness who has previous convictions, since the CPS may attempt to raise such convictions when the witness is being cross-examined in order to undermine the credibility of his evidence (see **Chapter 22**).

8.4.2.2   Securing the attendance of the witness at trial

Witnesses who are prepared to give a written statement are often reluctant to attend court to give oral evidence at trial, and a prudent solicitor will secure their attendance by obtaining a witness summons from the magistrates' court. The procedural rules which apply when an application for a witness summons is necessary are contained in Part 28 of the Criminal Procedure Rules 2005.

The court will issue a witness summons if it is satisfied that the witness can give material evidence in the proceedings and it is in the interests of justice for a summons to be issued (Magistrates' Courts Act 1980, s 97). The defendant's solicitor will usually ask a potential defence witness to confirm in writing that he will attend court. If a negative response is received, or if, as is much more likely, no response is received, the solicitor should then write to the court requesting that it issue a witness summons. The court will issue a witness summons requiring the witness to attend the trial. The court has the power to summons a witness to give evidence (whether for the prosecution or defence) even if that witness has not provided a written statement. The court may also summons a witness who may be able to give material evidence in a case to attend court and give a deposition (ie, a statement).

Since the Criminal Procedure Rules 2005 came into effect, the courts have been increasingly unwilling to adjourn trials, even when crucial witnesses have failed to attend to give evidence. In view of this, the safest course of action for a defence solicitor may now be to ask the court for a witness summons in respect of any witness whose evidence is vital for the defence case, even if that witness has said that he is willing and able to attend court.

8.4.2.3   Disclosure obligations

Under s 6C of the Criminal Procedure and Investigations Act (CPIA) 1996, a defendant must serve on the CPS a notice setting out the names, addresses and dates of birth of any witnesses he intends to call to give evidence. This rule was introduced to enable the CPS to check whether any defence witnesses have previous convictions, although there is nothing to stop the CPS, via the police, interviewing these witnesses (since there is no property in a witness). Should the police wish to interview a defence witness, a code of practice exists which governs the conduct of the interview (CPIA 1996, s 21A).

Unlike civil proceedings, there is no requirement for a defendant in a criminal case to serve on the CPS copies of the statements taken from the witnesses whom he intends to call to give evidence at trial. The only exception to this are reports from any expert witnesses whom the defendant wishes to call to give evidence at trial. These must be served on the CPS (see **8.4.3** below). A defendant may, however, serve a more general defence statement on the prosecution (see **8.4.7** below).

8.4.3   Expert witnesses

8.4.3.1   When may an expert be required?

Expert evidence may be required at trial in respect of any technical matter which is outside the competence of the magistrates. Evidence may, for example, be required from a forensic scientist or a medical expert, particularly if the CPS has already obtained expert evidence which the defendant disputes. Expert evidence should be obtained as soon as possible, although if the defendant's case is funded by way of a representation order, the defendant's solicitor should obtain prior authority from the Legal Services Commission (LSC) to instruct the expert. If authority is not obtained, the cost of the report may not be paid for by the LSC at the end of the case.

8.4.3.2   Disclosure obligations

If the defendant's solicitor wishes to call an expert to give evidence at trial, he must serve a copy of the expert's report on the CPS in advance of trial (there is no obligation to serve the statements of any other defence witnesses on the CPS – see **8.4.2.3** above). An expert witness is unlikely to require a witness summons, although the defendant's solicitor must check the expert's availability to attend trial so that the trial can be fixed on a date when the expert is available to attend court.

Under s 6D of the CPIA 1996, the defendant is obliged to serve on the CPS a notice giving the name and address of any expert witness who has been *consulted* (in addition to serving a copy of the report from an expert who will actually give evidence at trial). This means that if the defendant's solicitor has obtained a report from an expert but does not intend to call that expert to give evidence at trial (because the expert's opinion does not assist the defendant's case), it will be open to the CPS to approach that expert and possibly call him to give evidence *against* the defendant (since there is no property in a witness).

Example

Eric is charged with the burglary of a domestic property. The CPS case is that paint found under Eric's fingernails is the same paint as on the frame of the window through which it is alleged Eric gained access to the property. Eric denies the offence and claims that the paint under his fingernails is from some decorating he was doing at home, and is a different type of paint from that on the window frame at the property. Eric's solicitor instructs a forensic expert to confirm that the paint found under Eric's fingernails is different from that at the property. In his report, the expert states that in his opinion the paint under Eric's fingernails is in fact exactly the same paint as was found at the property. This report will not be used as part of Eric's defence and a copy will not be served on the CPS. Eric's solicitor must, however, notify the CPS of the name and address of the expert. The CPS may then approach the same expert to give evidence against Eric.

8.4.4   Do all witnesses need to attend the trial?

Some witnesses may give evidence that is not in dispute. For example, in an assault case the CPS may obtain a statement from a doctor who treated the victim for his injuries. If the defendant accepts that he caused these injuries but claims that he was acting in self-defence, there is little point in the CPS having to call the doctor to give evidence if the nature of the injuries is accepted and the doctor's evidence will go unchallenged by the defendant.

Section 9 of the Criminal Justice Act 1967 provides that a written statement from a witness will be admissible at trial (as opposed to the witness having to come to court to give evidence) provided that:

(a)   it is signed and dated;

(b)   it contains the following declaration:

This statement (consisting of [1] page signed by me) is true to the best of my knowledge and belief and I make it knowing that if it is tendered in evidence I shall be liable to prosecution if I have wilfully stated in it anything which I know to be false or do not believe to be true.

(c)   a copy has been served before the hearing on the other parties in the case; and

(d)   none of the other parties has objected within seven days.

The statement may only contain matters which would have been admissible if the witness had given oral evidence at court.

'Section 9' witness statements should be used only for evidence which is not in dispute (although the CPS routinely serves the statements of all prosecution witnesses in the form of a s 9 statement). If the party receiving a statement which is served in this form wishes to challenge the admissibility of anything said in the statement, or to cross-examine the maker of the statement, it should object in writing within seven days.

Example

Nosheen is charged with theft of a bracelet from a shop. Nosheen denies the theft on the basis of mistaken identity and will state that she was elsewhere at the time of the theft. The CPS serves on Nosheen's solicitor statements it has obtained from the owner of the shop and a customer who claims to identify Nosheen as the person who took the bracelet. Both statements are served under s 9 of the Criminal Justice Act 1967. The statement from the shop owner merely confirms that the bracelet is missing and the value of the bracelet. The shop owner states that he did not witness the theft because he was elsewhere at the time. Nosheen's solicitor will write to the CPS within seven days of receiving the statements, confirming that he objects to the customer's statement being used at trial without the customer being called to give oral evidence. The customer will need to be cross-examined at trial as the identification evidence he gives is disputed. Nosheen's solicitor will not object to the statement from the shop owner being used at trial without the shop owner needing to attend court. The shop owner did not see the alleged theft and says nothing that Nosheen will dispute. He merely confirms the fact of the theft, which Nosheen is not disputing.

8.4.5 Documentary evidence

Documentary evidence which may be used at trial will often take the form of plans or photographs of the place where the alleged crime occurred (the court is likely to find such items particularly helpful). Any plans or photographs should be verified by a witness statement from the person who prepared the plan or took the photographs. Photographs may be helpful in supporting the defendant's case or undermining prosecution evidence. They can be particularly useful in undermining the credibility of a prosecution witness who claims to have had an unobstructed view of an incident.

Example

Linda is charged with common assault. The CPS alleges that she punched a fellow customer at a pub when that customer accidentally knocked over Linda's drink. Another customer who was sitting close by will give evidence for the prosecution stating that, from where he was sitting, he had a clear view of the incident. Linda's solicitor obtains photographs which show that the other customer could not in fact have seen the incident as he described it because, given his position, there was a pillar blocking his view. This evidence may be put to the other customer in cross-examination to undermine the credibility of his evidence.

8.4.6 Obtaining unused material from the CPS

8.4.6.1 Introduction

When the police investigate an alleged offence they will compile a large amount of documentary evidence (for example, witness statements, business records, CCTV footage, etc). In the case of an either way offence, any evidence obtained which will subsequently be relied upon as part of the prosecution case at trial will be supplied to the defendant's solicitor as part of the 'advance disclosure' package (see **6.6.3** above). In a summary only matter, the CPS has no such duty of disclosure but will, in accordance with guidelines given by the Attorney-General (see **6.6.2**), supply the defence with details of the evidence the prosecution seek to rely on.

The remaining material which the CPS has in its possession but which it does not propose to rely upon at trial is referred to as 'unused material'. A common example of unused material is statements taken from witnesses who the police initially think may help the prosecution case, but who in fact do not say anything which assists the case against the defendant.

8.4.6.2 The prosecution's duty to disclose unused material

The CPS is under an obligation to retain any unused material which it receives from the police. If the defendant subsequently enters a not guilty plea, the CPS is obliged to disclose this material to the defendant's solicitor if certain conditions are satisfied. Those conditions are set out in s 3 of the CPIA 1996, which provides that the CPS must disclose:

... any prosecution material which has not previously been disclosed to the accused and which might reasonably be considered capable of *undermining the case for the prosecution against the accused*, or of *assisting the case for the accused*. (emphasis added)

The types of unused material which may need to be disclosed by the CPS under the above test include:

(a)   records of the first description of a suspect given to the police by a potential eye-witness if that description differs from that of the defendant;

(b)   any information provided by the defendant which indicates an innocent explanation for the offence for which he has been charged;

(c)   any material casting doubt on the reliability of a witness, such as any previous convictions the witness may have;

(d)   any material casting doubt on the reliability of a confession;

(e)   any statement taken from a witness which appears to support the defendant's version of events.

Example 1

Adam is charged with theft from a shop. Adam denies the offence on the basis of mistaken identity. As part of its advance disclosure obligations, the CPS serves on Adam's solicitors statements from two witnesses who saw the theft and who give a description of the thief which matches Adam's description. Adam is 5 feet 8 inches tall, of slim build and with short brown hair. The CPS has also obtained a statement from another witness to the theft, who describes the thief as being 6 feet tall, of medium build and with long brown hair. The CPS does not intend to call this witness to give evidence at trial, but it is under an obligation to serve a copy of the statement on Adam's solicitors. The statement undermines the prosecution case that Adam was the thief and supports Adam's defence of mistaken identity.

Example 2

Gregory is charged with assaulting Trevor. Gregory denies the offence and claims that Trevor threw the first punch, and that he was acting only in self-defence. The CPS serves on Gregory's solicitor several statements from eye-witnesses who state that Gregory threw the first punch. The CPS also has a statement from another witness who says that Trevor threw the first punch. The CPS does not intend to rely on evidence from this witness at trial, but it is under an obligation to serve a copy of the statement on Gregory's solicitor. The statement undermines the prosecution case that Gregory threw the first punch and assists Gregory's case that he was acting in self-defence after being attacked.

Example 3

Paul is charged with assaulting Sunil. Paul's defence is that Sunil attacked him first and that he was acting in self-defence. Sunil has several previous convictions for offence of violence. The CPS is under a duty to disclose this information to Paul's solicitor. This information casts doubt on the reliability of Sunil's evidence (that Paul attacked him) and so will undermine the prosecution case (the CPS Disclosure Manual provides that all previous convictions of prosecution witnesses be disclosed to the defence, regardless of their likely relevance to the case).

This duty of disclosure is a continuing duty and so the CPS must keep under review the question of whether there is any material that meets the above test (CPIA 1996, s 7A).

If the CPS does disclose any unused material to the defendant's solicitor, the solicitor must consider how best to make use of such material. He should, for example, seek to interview a witness who appears to assist the defendant's case, and ask that witness if he would be prepared to give evidence at trial on behalf of the defendant. Alternatively, if the CPS discloses the fact that a prosecution witness has previous convictions, the defendant's solicitor should consider making an application for permission to raise such convictions at trial when cross-examining that witness (see **Chapter 22**).

8.4.6.3   Procedure for disclosure of unused material

When the CPS makes disclosure of any unused material in its possession, the defendant's solicitor will be sent a standard disclosure letter by the CPS which will have attached to it a document headed 'Police Schedule of Non-sensitive Unused Material'. This is a list which records all the non-sensitive items of unused material the CPS has. It will also record whether such documents are to be supplied to the defence (because they satisfy the test set out at **8.4.6.2** above), or whether such documents should not be supplied to the defence because they do not appear either to undermine the case for the prosecution or to assist the case for the defence. Any documents which are to be supplied to the defence will normally be provided at the same time as the list is sent to the defendant's solicitor.

When he receives this list from the CPS, the defendant's solicitor may ask for clarification of any items on the list (if, for example, the items are described in such a vague manner that the defendant's solicitor is unable to determine what they actually are). He may also ask the CPS to supply a copy of an item from the list (which the CPS has not already supplied) if he considers that the item may satisfy the test at **8.4.6.2** above. If the list does not include items which the defendant's solicitor suspects the CPS may have, he may challenge the contents of the list, and ask the CPS to confirm that the list is a full schedule of all the unused material it has.

Example 1

Scott is charged with handling stolen DVDs which the police seized following a search of his flat. When Scott's solicitor receives the list of unused material from the CPS, one of the items listed reads: 'Various receipts found at the accused's flat.'

These documents are not supplied to Scott's solicitor because the CPS states that they do not satisfy the test for disclosure under s 3. Scott's defence is that he bought the DVDs from a market stall and that one of the documents the police removed from his flat (which is not being relied upon as part of the prosecution case) is a receipt for these items. Scott's solicitor will ask the CPS to clarify the contents of the list by giving a proper description for each receipt. If the receipt for the DVDs is found to be among these receipts, Scott's solicitor will then ask the CPS to supply a copy of this document since it would satisfy the test under s 3.

Example 2

Guy is charged with assault following an altercation outside a nightclub. Guy's defence is that he was attacked first and was acting only in self-defence. Guy tells his solicitor that he recalls several witnesses to the incident giving statements to the police at the time of the incident. The only eye-witness evidence the CPS seeks to rely on at Guy's trial is from the alleged victim. When the CPS serves the list of unused material, there in no reference to statements being obtained from any other witnesses. Guy's solicitor suspects that such statements were obtained by the police and that these may support Guy's defence. Guy's solicitor will write to the CPS to challenge the extent of the disclosure of unused material that has been made.

An example of a schedule of non-sensitive unused material is set out at **Key Document – Police Schedule of Non-sensitive Unused Material**, below.

8.4.6.4   Can the prosecution withhold disclosure of any unused material?

In addition to having items of unused material which are non-sensitive, the CPS may also have in its possession 'sensitive' items, the existence of which the CPS is not obliged to disclose to the defence because these items are protected by 'public interest immunity'. The CPS will normally make an application to the court for a ruling that it is not in the public interest to disclose such documents as part of the list of unused material because these items are 'sensitive' material. Examples of such material include:

(a)   material relating to matters of national security or intelligence;

(b)   material relating to the identity of police informants or under-cover police officers;

(c)   material revealing techniques and methods relied upon by the police in the course of their investigations (such as covert surveillance techniques in use); and

(d)   material relating to a child witness (such as material generated by a local authority social services department).

It is normal practice when drafting a defence statement (see **10.8.3**) for the CPS to be asked if a schedule of sensitive materials has been prepared and, if so, whether the CPS has made an application to court for an order that it is not obliged to disclose the existence of such material.

Key Document – Disclosure Letter and Police Schedule of Non-sensitive Unused Material

(Although the Gary Dickson case is dealt with in the Crown Court, the schedule prepared by the police will be in the same format as it would be were the case being heard in the magistrates' court.)

CPS

Chester Office
East Chambers
Saville Street
Chester
CH1 4NJ

Switchboard:
Facsimile: 01245 123423
DX No: 61616 Chester

Direct Line: 01245 423123

Our Ref:
Your Ref:
Date: 10th January 2007

Collaws Solicitor
Chester

Dear Sirs

DISCLOSURE OF PROSECUTION MATERIAL UNDER SECTION 3 CRIMINAL PROCEDURE AND INVESTIGATIONS ACT 1996

R v   Gary Paul Dickson

URN   CH/000/687/06

COURT   CHESTER CROWN COURT

I am required by section 3 Criminal Procedure and Investigations Act 1996 (CPIA) to disclose to you any prosecution material which has not previously been disclosed, and which in my opinion might undermine the case for the prosecution against your client or which might reasonably be expected to assist the case for your client.

Attached to this letter is a copy of a schedule of non-sensitive unused material prepared by the police in compliance with their duty under Part II CPIA and the provisions of the Code of Practice. The schedule has been prepared by the police Disclosure Officer, who in this case is PC 911 Chambers.

Unless the word 'evidence' appears alongside any item, all the items listed on the schedule are not intended to be used as part of the prosecution case. You will receive a written notice should the position change.

At this stage, it is my opinion that there is no prosecution material which requires disclosure to you, other than item 2 on the schedule. A copy of this item is enclosed with this letter.

If you supply a written defence statement to me and to the court within 14 days, the material will be further reviewed in the light of that statement.

A defence statement is required by section 5 CPIA in Crown Court cases. In magistrates' court cases, section 6 CPIA makes a defence statement optional. Please bear in mind that we will rely upon the information you provide in the statement to identify any remaining material which has not already been disclosed but which might reasonably assist the defence case as you have described it. The statement will also be relied on by the court if you later make an application under section 8 CPIA.

If you do not make a defence statement where one is required, or provide one late, the court may permit comment and/or draw an adverse inference.

If you have a query in connection with this letter, please contact the writer.

Yours faithfully

CPS

Crown Prosecution Service.

CHESHIRE POLICE

POLICE SCHEDULE OF NON-SENSITIVE UNUSED MATERIAL

Page No ....1...of....2......

R v ..Gary Paul Dickson.......

URN:

CH	000	687	06

Is there any material in this case which has not been examined by either the investigating or disclosure officer? Yes   No

If 'yes' please attach MG11 (refer to para. 7.9.11 of the Manual of Guidance)

The Disclosure Officer believes that the following material which does not form part of the prosecution case is NOT SENSITIVE

Item No.	DESCRIPTION AND RELEVANCE (Give sufficient details for CPS to decide if material should be disclosed or requires more detailed examination)	LOCATION	FOR CPS USE: *Enter D = Disclosure to Defence 1 = Defence may inspect COMMENT
			*
1.	Computer entry of general incident 10067579		Does not appear to undermine case / assist defence do not disclose
2.	Full copy file of Gary Paul Dickson including all MG forms, CPS and memos, previous convictions of Dickson		Disclosure – Common Law
3.	Pocket note book entries for PC Chambers		Does not appear to undermine case / assist defence do not disclose
4.	Computer printout held on Cheshire Police computer		Does not appear to undermine case / assist defence do not disclose
5.	Rough notes of Gary Paul Dickson interview		Does not appear to undermine case / assist defence do not disclose
6.	input documents – description of Gary Paul Dickson held on PNC		Does not appear to undermine case / assist defence do not disclose

Signature: *G Chambers*   Name : G Chambers PC 911

Date: 27.01.2006

Reviewing lawyer signature: *P Jones*

Print name: P JONES

Date: 12.02.2006

CHESHIRE POLICE

POLICE SCHEDULE OF NON-SENSITIVE UNUSED MATERIAL

URN: | CH | 000 | 687 | 06

Page No ...2....of....2........

R v ..Gary Paul Dickson........

Is there any material in this case which has not been examined by either the investigating or
disclosure officer? Yes No   If 'yes' please attach MG11 (refer to para. 7.9.11 of the Manual of Guidance)

The Disclosure Officer believes that the following material which does not form part of the prosecution case is NOT
SENSITIVE

Item No.	DESCRIPTION AND RELEVANCE (Give sufficient details for CPS to decide if material should be disclosed or requires more detailed examination)	LOCATION
7.	Pocket note book entry for PC Chambers (details present during interview)	Officer's possession
8.	Charge set of fingerprints of Gary Paul Dickson	Force Records
9.	Video identification record of Inspector Greene	Officer's possession Secure Store

Signature: G Chambers

Name : G Chambers PC 911

Date: 27.01.2006

FOR CPS USE: *Enter D = Disclosure to Defence

1 = Defence may inspect

*	COMMENT
	Does not appear to undermine case / assist defence do not disclose
	Does not appear to undermine case / assist defence do not disclose
	Does not appear to undermine case / assist defence do not disclose

Reviewing lawyer signature: P Jones

Print name: P JONES

Date: 12.02.2006

8.4.7   Serving a defence statement on the prosecution

A defendant in the magistrates' court may serve on the CPS a defence statement under ss 5, 5A and 6 of the CPIA 1996. Defence statements are dealt with only very briefly in this chapter because it is unusual for a defence statement to be given in the magistrates' court (for reasons which are set out below). The giving of a defence statement is examined in much more detail in **Chapter 10**, which describes procedures in the Crown Court where defence statements are much more common.

The defence statement is a document which sets out the nature of the defence, the factual issues in the case where the defendant takes issue with the prosecution version of events, and any points of law the defendant will seek to rely on in the case. The giving of such a statement is discretionary in the magistrates' court.

For a case in the magistrates' court, the defendant's solicitor should consider serving a defence statement on the CPS only if he thinks that the CPS will, in the light of the information disclosed in the statement, be in a position to disclose to him additional unused material that may assist the defence case. Such a situation is likely to arise only if the defence statement contains additional details about the defence of which the CPS was previously unaware. An example of when such a situation may arise is provided at **10.8.7**.

In reality it is extremely rare for a defence statement to be served on the prosecution in the magistrates' court. The possible advantage of gaining additional disclosure from the CPS is heavily outweighed by the disadvantage of giving away details of the defence case to the CPS prior to the trial when there is no obligation to do so. The giving of a defence statement is normally confined to the Crown Court, where the service of such a statement on the CPS is effectively obligatory (see **10.8.2**).

8.5   Checklist

At the end of this chapter you should be able to explain:

*   the case management directions with which the CPS and the defendant's solicitor must comply prior to a trial in the magistrates' court, and the time limits for compliance with these directions;
*   how to carry out an effective case analysis and to identify any additional evidence that needs to be obtained in support of the defendant's case;
*   the forms of additional evidence which may assist the defendant's case and how such additional evidence should be obtained;
*   the disclosure obligations imposed on the CPS in respect of any unused material in its possession;
*   when the defendant's solicitor may challenge the extent of the disclosure of unused material given by the CPS, and how this should be done;
*   the circumstances in which a defence statement may be given in the magistrates' court and the reason why such statements are given only rarely.

8.6   Magistrates' court case progression form

MAGISTRATES' COURT
CASE PROGRESSION

CASE TO BE TRIED IN THE MAGISTRATES' COURT

Date of hearing: /   /

The court will fix the trial date at (or shortly after) the hearing at which the defendant pleads not guilty. The directions below apply from that hearing unless they are modified or deleted by the court.

<u>DEFENDANT</u>

Name of defendant_____Age___Date of Birth_____
Address_____
_____
In custody /on bail Contact telephone number (if defendant agrees)_____

<u>CASE</u>

No. of case in Magistrates' Court: [   ]   URN: [   ]
Charges:_____
_____
_____
_____

<u>LEGAL REPRESENTATION</u>

Prosecution Reviewing Lawyer: _____Address:_____
_____
Tel.: _____   Fax: _____
Email: _____   DX _____

Defence Solicitor: _____Solicitors Firm & Address:_____
_____
Tel.: _____   Fax: _____
Email: _____   DX _____

<u>CASE PROGRESSION OFFICERS</u>

<u>Magistrates' Court</u>	<u>Prosecution</u>	<u>Defence</u>
Name:	Name:	Name:
Address:	Address:	Address:
Tel:	Tel:	Tel:
Fax:	Fax:	Fax:
Email:	Email:	Email:
DX:	DX:	DX:

Has the defendant been advised about credit for pleading guilty? YES/NO

Has the defendant been warned that if he is on bail and fails to attend, the proceedings may continue in his absence? YES/NO

TRIAL DATE *The trial will take place on:*   *and is expected to last for:*

DIRECTIONS

Special measures

a.   The prosecution to serve any application for special measures within **14 days**.

b.   The defence to serve any response to the application for special measures within **14 days** of service of the prosecution application.

Prosecution case and disclosure

c.   To the extent it has not done so, the prosecution must serve copies of the documents containing the evidence on which the charge or charges are based, including witness statements and any documentary exhibits, tapes of interview, video tapes and CCTV tapes within **[28] days**.

d.   To the extent it has not done so, the prosecution must comply with its initial duty of disclosure within **[28] days**.

Hearsay evidence

e.   The prosecution to serve any notice of intention to introduce hearsay evidence at the same time as it complies, or purports to comply with its initial duty of disclosure.

f.   The defence to serve any notice opposing the prosecution's notice under e., within **14 days** of receipt of the notice.

g.   The defence to serve any notice of intention to introduce hearsay evidence within **14 days** of the date on which the prosecution complied, or purported to comply, with its initial duty of disclosure.

h.   The prosecution to serve any notice opposing the defence's notice under g. within **14 days** of receipt of the application.

Bad character evidence

i.   The defence to serve any application to introduce the bad character of a prosecution witness within **14 days** of the date on which the prosecution complied, or purported to comply, with its initial duty of disclosure.

j.   The prosecution to serve any notice opposing the defence application to introduce the bad character of a prosecution witness under i. within **14 days** of receipt of the application.

k.   The prosecution to serve any notice to introduce the defendant's bad character at the same time as it complies, or purports to comply with its initial duty of disclosure.

l.   The defence to serve any application to exclude evidence of the defendant's bad character within **7 days** of receipt of the prosecution application under k.

m.   *Any further orders relating to bad character:*

Defence statement

n. If a defence statement is to be given, the defence must serve it within **14 days** of the prosecution complying or purporting to comply with its initial duty of disclosure.

Witness statements

o. If the defence wish a prosecution witness to give evidence in person at the trial, the defence shall so notify the prosecution within **7** days of receiving the prosecution case under c.

p. The defence must serve any statements of defence witnesses who the defence propose not to give evidence in person at the trial within **[14] days** of receiving the prosecution case under c.

q. If a party requires a witness whose statement has been served under p. to give evidence in person at the trial, the party shall so notify the prosecution within **7** days of service of the statement.

Further disclosure

r. The prosecution to complete any further disclosure at least **[14]** days before the trial.

Written admissions

s. The parties must file any written admissions made under section 10 of the Criminal Justice Act 1967 within **[56] days**.

Expert evidence

t. If either party intends to rely on expert evidence, the directions below apply.

Point of law

u. If any point of law is to be taken by a party and a skeleton argument would be helpful, it must be served together with authorities at least **[21] days** prior to the trial.

v. The other party must serve a skeleton argument in reply together with authorities at least **[7] days** prior to the trial.

Trial readiness

w. The parties must certify readiness for trial, by filing a certificate of readiness if appropriate, at least **[7] days** prior to the trial.

x. *Any other orders:*

Further case management

y. *A further case management hearing will take place on:*

EXPERT EVIDENCE

a. A party seeking to rely on expert evidence must serve the expert's report within **[28] days**.

b. A party served with expert evidence must indicate whether the expert is required to attend at the trial, and either serve their own expert evidence in response or indicate that they are not intending to rely on expert evidence within **[28] days** of receipt of the other party's expert evidence.

c. A meeting of experts to agree non-contentious matters and identify issues, if appropriate and if the parties agree, must take place within **[28] days** of service of both parties' expert evidence.

d. The parties must notify the court within **[14] days** of an experts' meeting whether the length of the trial is affected by the outcome of the meeting.

MAGISTRATES' COURT
CASE PROGRESSION

CASE TO BE TRIED IN THE MAGISTRATES' COURT

GUIDANCE NOTES

General notes

These notes accompany the standard directions form for cases to be tried in the Magistrates' Court. The directions in this form will apply when a defendant pleads not guilty to a summary offence, or a defendant pleads not guilty to an offence triable either way and it is determined that the case will be tried in the magistrates' court. The timetable begins on the date of the not guilty plea.

The directions in this form allow parties 8 weeks in which to prepare for trial, or 14 weeks where there is to be expert evidence. Not all those directions will be needed in every case. If the court fixes a trial date less than 8 weeks after the date of the not guilty plea then directions relevant to the case will need to be modified.

If the defendant intends to plead guilty but there is a dispute over the facts of the offence, and a Newton Hearing is to be held, the relevant directions will apply and any reference to the trial should be read as a reference to the Newton Hearing. The timetable begins on the date of the guilty plea

The directions are default directions, which will apply where the defendant pleads not guilty unless the justices, a District Judge (Magistrates' Court), a justices' clerk or an assistant to a justices' clerk, as the case may be, direct otherwise. Except where they appear in square brackets, the time limits are mandatory except to the extent that there is power to vary them. .

Parties must come to the hearing prepared to provide the information set out on page 1 of the form (to the extent that this has not already been done) and to answer the questions in bold. Local practice will determine whether the parties will be required to complete the form and make it available to the District Judge or magistrate at or before the start of the hearing.

If the defendant decides later to plead guilty the defence should inform the prosecution and the court immediately and the court should made an appropriate order so that the defendant can be sentenced as soon as possible.

Except where otherwise required, a direction in the form to "serve" material, means serve on the other party(ies) and file with the Magistrates' Court.

If there is more than one defendant use a second form only to record the details on page 1 and the answers to the questions in bold and record the directions on one form only.

Notes relevant to specific sections

a. See Rule 29.1(4) of the Criminal Procedure Rules 2005.

b. See Rule 29.1(6) of the Criminal Procedure Rules 2005.

c. This is a suggested time limit only: the prosecution must provide copies of written statements and a summary of the prosecution case to the defence "as soon as practicable" after a request for advance information by the defence – see rule 21.3 of the Criminal Procedure Rules 2005.

d. This is a suggested time limit only: the prosecution must comply with their initial duty of disclosure "as soon as reasonably practicable"– see section 13 of the Criminal Procedure and Investigations Act 1996.

e. See Rule 34.3 of the Criminal Procedure Rules 2005.

f. See Rule 34.5 of the Criminal Procedure Rules 2005. The court may vary the period, see Rule 34.7.

g. See Rule 34.4 of the Criminal Procedure Rules 2005. The court may vary the period, see Rule 34.7.

h. See Rule 34.5 of the Criminal Procedure Rules 2005. The court may vary the period, see Rule 34.7.

i. See Rule 35 .2 of the Criminal Procedure Rules 2005. The court may vary the period, see Rule 35.8.

j. See Rule 35.3 of the Criminal Procedure Rules 2005. The court may vary the period, see Rule 35.8.

k. See Rule 35.4 of the Criminal Procedure Rules 2005. The court may vary the period, see Rule 35.8.

l. See Rule 35.6 of the Criminal Procedure Rules 2005. The court may vary the period, see Rule 35.8.

m. Any further orders not covered by the bad character provisions in i-l should be set out here.

n. See sections 6 and 12, Criminal Procedure and Investigations Act 1996 and Regulation 3 of the Criminal Procedure and Investigations Act 1996 (Defence Disclosure Time Limits) Regulations 1997. By virtue of Regulation 4, the period may be extended only if the application is made before its expiry.

o. A written statement of a witness served under section 9 Criminal Justice Act 1967 is "admissible as evidence to the like extent as oral evidence" if, amongst other things, "none of the other parties or their solicitors, within **seven** days from the service of the copy of the statement, serves a notice ... objecting to the statement being tendered in evidence under this section" (see section 9(2)(d)). The court may require the witness to give evidence orally notwithstanding a failure to comply with this requirement, see section 9(4).

p. See section 9 Criminal Justice Act 1967. This is a suggested period only and is subject to the discretion of the court.

q. See note o.

r. This is a suggested time limit only: the prosecution must comply with this duty as soon as reasonably practicable - see section 9, Criminal Procedure and Investigation Act 1996.

s. This is a suggested period only and is subject to the discretion of the court.

w. A formal certificate of readiness may not be necessary. The form and timing of confirmation of trial readiness is subject to the discretion of the court.

y. As part of the court's duty to actively manage cases, any unnecessary hearings should be avoided - see Rule 3.2 (2) (f) of the Criminal Procedure Rules 2005.

EXPERT EVIDENCE

a-d. See Rule 24.1 of the Criminal Procedure Rules 2005. These are suggested periods only and subject to the discretion of the court. Expert evidence not disclosed before trial may not be introduced without the court's permission - see Rule 24.3.

Chapter 9
Summary Trial and Advocacy Techniques

9.1 Introduction

For a defendant who has entered a plea of not guilty, the trial represents the culmination of his case, when the magistrates will decide whether or not he is guilty of the offence he is charged with having committed. This chapter will begin by giving an outline of the sequence of events at a summary trial in the magistrates' court. It will then examine particular aspects of the trial process in more depth, before concluding with an introduction to some basic advocacy skills. Although the chapter will focus on a trial in the magistrates' court, the advocacy techniques described will be just as applicable to a trial in the Crown Court. The trial process in the Crown Court is described in **Chapter 10**.

9.2 Order of events at trial (CrimPR, Part 37)

The normal order of events at a trial in the magistrates' court is as follows:

(a) Opening speech by the solicitor from the CPS.

(b) The prosecution witnesses will then be called in turn to give evidence. Each witness will be examined in chief by the prosecuting solicitor and then cross-examined by the defendant's solicitor. The prosecuting solicitor may then choose to re-examine the witness.

(c) (Possible submission of no case to answer by defendant's solicitor.)

(d) The defence witnesses will then be called in turn to give evidence (with the defendant being called first). Each witness will be examined in chief by the defendant's solicitor and will then be cross-examined by the prosecuting solicitor. The defendant's solicitor may then choose to re-examine the witness.

(e) Closing speech by the defendant's solicitor (the prosecuting solicitor is not entitled to make a closing speech).

(f) The magistrates retire to consider their verdict.

(g) The magistrates deliver their verdict.

(h) If the defendant is found guilty, the magistrates will then either sentence the defendant immediately, or adjourn sentence until a later date if they wish to obtain pre-sentence reports on the defendant. If the defendant is acquitted, he will be formally discharged by the magistrates and told that he is free to go.

A flowchart summarising the above procedure is provided at **9.9.1** below.

9.3 Professional conduct

9.3.1 Duties of the defendant's solicitor

A solicitor representing a defendant in a trial before the magistrates is under a duty to say on behalf of his client what that client would properly say for himself were he to have the necessary skills and knowledge to do this. In other words, it is the duty of the defence solicitor to act in his client's best interests and to ensure that the CPS discharges the onus placed upon it to prove the client's guilt. Therefore, even if a client has admitted his guilt, it would still be appropriate for the defence solicitor to put the prosecution to proof of its case (see **Chapter 6**).

The defendant's solicitor nevertheless remains under an overriding duty not to mislead the court (*The Law Society's Code of Conduct* (2004), Rule 11.01). He cannot therefore say anything in his client's defence which he knows to be untrue. Although the defendant's solicitor is not under a duty to inform the CPS or the court of any facts which may have been overlooked, he is under a duty to tell the court what the relevant law is, even if this proves detrimental to the client's case.

The defendant's solicitor also owes a duty of confidentiality to his client. This means that if the defendant's solicitor has to cease to act for his client (if, for example, the client insists on the solicitor putting false or misleading information before the court), the defence solicitor should not tell the court why he is ceasing to act for his client. A defence solicitor who withdraws from acting in such circumstances will tell the court that he is no longer able to act for his client for 'professional reasons'.

The professional duties imposed on a solicitor when acting as the advocate for the prosecution are summarised at **1.6.3**.

The detailed rules of professional conduct with which a solicitor must comply when acting as an advocate (whether for the prosecution or the defence) are contained in Rule 11 ('Litigation and Advocacy') of *The Law Society's Code of Conduct* (2004).

9.3.2 Preparing the defendant to give evidence

Prior to the trial, the defendant's solicitor must tell his client what is likely to happen at the trial. If the client is to give evidence in his own defence, it is a sensible step to supply the client with a copy of his witness statement, so that he can read it before the trial commences. The client will not be able to refer to his witness statement when giving evidence, but it is useful for him to be able to refresh his memory as to what he first told his solicitor about the offence.

The defendant's solicitor should be careful, however, not to 'coach' his client (or indeed any other defence witness). Advocates in the magistrates' court (whether representing the prosecution or the defence) should not rehearse or coach witnesses in relation to their evidence, or in the way in which that evidence should be given.

9.3.3 Modes of address

A trial in the magistrates' court will normally be conducted before a bench of three magistrates. Traditionally magistrates were addressed collectively as 'Your Worships', although it is now more common for remarks to be addressed to the chairperson of the bench of magistrates, using 'Sir' or 'Madam' as appropriate. If the trial takes place before a District Judge, 'Sir' or 'Madam' should be used as appropriate.

9.4 The prosecution case

9.4.1 Opening speech

A trial in the magistrates' court will begin with the solicitor from the CPS giving an opening speech. This does not form part of the evidence on which the magistrates will decide the case and is more a matter of 'setting the scene'. The opening speech will normally begin with the prosecuting solicitor telling the magistrates the factual details about the charge which the defendant faces. He will then explain to the magistrates the relevant substantive law and will tell them what the prosecution will need to prove in order to secure a conviction. The prosecuting solicitor should remind the magistrates that the prosecution have the burden of proving beyond a reasonable doubt that the defendant is guilty, and that the defendant is entitled to an acquittal unless the magistrates are sure that he is guilty (see **16.2**). The prosecuting solicitor will outline what the prosecution case consists of, tell the court which witnesses he intends to call to give evidence for the prosecution, and summarise briefly the evidence that is to be given by these witnesses. He may also refer the magistrates to any points of law which he anticipates may arise during the trial (for example, the *Turnbull* guidelines if the case consists of disputed identification evidence (see **17.2**), or ss 76 or 78 of PACE 1984 if there is disputed confession evidence (see **20.4** and **20.5**).

9.4.2 Prosecution evidence

After completing his opening speech, the prosecuting solicitor will call his first witness to give evidence. It is customary for the first prosecution witness to be the 'victim' of the alleged crime. For example, in an assault case the first prosecution witness is likely to be the person who was injured in the assault. In a theft case the first prosecution witness is likely to be the person whose property has been stolen. After the victim has given evidence, other prosecution witnesses (including any expert witnesses) will be called to give evidence.

Each prosecution witness who is called to give evidence will initially be asked questions by the prosecuting solicitor. This is called examination in chief and is designed to allow the witness to place his account before the court (see **9.8.1** below). The defendant's solicitor will then have the opportunity to cross-examine the witness (see **9.8.2** below). At the end of the cross-examination, the prosecuting solicitor may, if he chooses, briefly re-examine the witness (see **9.8.3** below).

Any prosecution witnesses who are not being called to give evidence (for example, witnesses who have given a statement under s 9 of the Criminal Justice Act 1967 to which the defence have not objected – see **8.4.4** – or witnesses whose statements are to be read out as hearsay evidence – see **Chapter 19**), will have their statements read out to the court by the prosecuting solicitor.

If the defendant was interviewed at the police station, either a summary or the full transcript of the interview will be read out to the court, unless the defendant's solicitor objects to this. If the defence solicitor does object (if, for example, the summary does not include points made by the defendant in support of his defence, or if the solicitor considers that the defendant came across well in the interview), the audio recording of the interview will be played to the court.

9.4.3 Arguments on points of law

During the presentation of his case, the prosecuting solicitor may seek to place evidence before the court which the defendant's solicitor considers to be inadmissible. A common example of this is when the prosecution seek to adduce evidence that the defendant made a confession, and the defendant's solicitor seeks to challenge the admissibility of this confession under s 76 of PACE 1984 on the basis that the confession was obtained in circumstances rendering it unreliable (see **20.4.3**). Another example is if the prosecution seek to adduce evidence that the defendant was visually identified by a witness following an identification procedure, and the defendant's solicitor seeks to challenge the admissibility of this evidence under s 78 of PACE 1984 on the basis that the identification procedure was not carried out in accordance with the requirements of Code D (see **3.5.3** and **17.5**).

If such a situation arises, the magistrates will normally hold a hearing called a voire dire to determine the admissibility of the particular piece of evidence in dispute. Such hearings are also often referred to as 'a trial within a trial'.

A voire dire will involve witnesses giving evidence on matters relevant to the admissibility of the evidence (for example, in the case of a disputed confession made in the context of an interview at the police station, both the police officer who conducted the interview and the defendant are likely to give evidence). After the witnesses have given evidence, the prosecuting solicitor and the defendant's solicitor will make legal submissions as to the admissibility of the disputed evidence.

If the magistrates decide that the evidence is inadmissible, the prosecuting solicitor will not be permitted to make any further reference to such evidence during the course of the trial. If the evidence is ruled to be admissible, it may then be produced by the prosecuting solicitor as part of the prosecution case (although the defendant's solicitor will still be entitled to attempt to undermine the reliability or cogency of such evidence during the trial).

Example 1

Robert is charged with theft. In an audio-recorded interview at the police station he confessed to the theft, and the CPS wishes to adduce evidence of this at Robert's trial. Robert's solicitor challenges the admissibility of the confession, arguing that it was obtained in circumstances which make it unreliable. The basis of this argument is that Robert claims that he confessed only after being told by the interviewing officer that he was going to be kept at the police station until he made a confession. At the voire dire the magistrates are likely to hear evidence from Robert and the interviewing officer, and they will also read a transcript of the interview or have the recording of the interview played out. Submissions will also be made by the prosecuting solicitor and Robert's solicitor. At the conclusion of the voire dire, the magistrates decide that the confession is inadmissible. This means that the prosecuting solicitor cannot use the confession as part of his case against Robert.

Example 2

Fiona is charged with common assault. In an audio-recorded interview at the police station, Fiona confessed to having committed the assault. Fiona's solicitor argues that the magistrates should rule the confession to be inadmissible because in the police interview the interviewing officer told Fiona that if she confessed to the offence she would receive a lighter sentence. Fiona's solicitor argues that this renders the confession unreliable. At the voire dire the magistrates will hear evidence from both the interviewing officer and Fiona, and will also either read a transcript of the interview or have the recording of the interview played out. The magistrates will also hear legal submissions from the prosecuting solicitor and from Fiona's solicitor. At the conclusion of the voire dire, the magistrates decide that the confession is admissible. The prosecuting solicitor will therefore be able to place evidence of the confession before the magistrates as part of his case against Fiona. Fiona's solicitor will still be permitted to attempt to undermine the reliability or cogency of this evidence during the trial (both when cross-examining the interviewing officer and when Fiona is giving evidence in chief), and will be able to make reference to this in his closing speech.

The difficulty faced by the defendant's solicitor when conducting a voire dire in the magistrates' court is that the magistrates decide matters of both law and fact. This means that even if the magistrates decide that a piece of prosecution evidence is inadmissible, the magistrates will still be aware of the existence of that item of evidence. Thus, when deciding their verdict, the magistrates will need to perform 'mental gymnastics' so as to set aside their knowledge of the inadmissible evidence. This situation will not arise in a Crown Court trial where the judge will conduct a voire dire in the absence of the jury, who will therefore never hear about any prosecution evidence which the judge rules to be inadmissible. The absence of a satisfactory procedure for dealing with the question of the admissibility of disputed prosecution evidence in a magistrates' court trial is one of the reasons why a defendant may elect trial in the Crown Court when charged with an either way matter (see **6.11.2.2**).

As an alternative to holding a separate 'trial within a trial', the magistrates may sometimes hear the disputed evidence as part of the trial itself, and then consider the question of the admissibility of such evidence either when the defendant's solicitor makes a submission of no case to answer at the conclusion of the prosecution case (see **9.5** below), or when he makes his closing submissions at the end of the trial.

To overcome problems at trial with magistrates being aware of the existence of an item of prosecution evidence even if they have decided that such evidence is admissible, many magistrates' courts now hold pre-trial hearings to determine the admissibility of disputed items of evidence. Such hearings are particularly common in respect of applications to adduce hearsay evidence, or evidence of the defendant's bad character. Pre-trial hearings will be held before a different bench of magistrates to the bench which ultimately conducts the trial, thus ensuring that the magistrates who actually decide the case need never be aware of items of evidence which are inadmissible.

9.5 Submission of no case to answer

When presenting his case to the magistrates, the prosecuting solicitor bears an evidential burden. This burden is to present sufficient evidence to the court to justify a finding of guilt (see **16.2.2.1**). If the prosecuting solicitor fails to satisfy this burden, the defendant's solicitor should make a submission of no case to answer at the conclusion of the prosecution case, asking the magistrates to dismiss the case.

A submission of no case to answer will be made by the defendant's solicitor if either:

(a) the prosecution have failed to put forward evidence to prove an essential element of the alleged offence; or

(b)   the evidence produced by the prosecution has been so discredited as a result of cross-examination, or is so manifestly unreliable, that no reasonable tribunal could safely convict on it.

Example 1

Harvinder is charged with the theft of a bicycle. In presenting his case, the prosecuting solicitor fails to produce evidence that the bicycle belonged to another person. Proving that the item stolen belonged to another person is an essential element in the offence of theft. Harvinder's solicitor should therefore make a submission of no case to answer and request that the magistrates dismiss the case.

Example 2

Matthew is charged with assault occasioning actual bodily harm following an incident outside a night club. The victim of the alleged assault was attacked from behind and never saw his attacker. The prosecution case is based solely on evidence from a passer-by who witnessed the assault. This witness has identified Matthew, but in cross-examination by Matthews's solicitor this evidence is shown to be unreliable. The witness confirms in cross-examination that it was dark at the time of the assault, he was standing some distance away, he got only a fleeting glimpse of the assault and he didn't see the attacker's face. At the conclusion of the prosecution case, Matthew's solicitor will make a submission of no case to answer on the basis that the prosecution evidence is so manifestly unreliable that the court cannot safely convict on it.

If the magistrates accept a submission of no case to answer, the charge against the defendant will be dismissed. If the magistrates reject the submission of no case to answer, the defendant may then present his case and call witnesses. The fact that the prosecution have satisfied the evidential burden does not mean that the prosecution are entitled to a conviction at that stage. This is because the court will not yet have heard either from the defendant, or from any witnesses the defendant wishes to call in support of his defence.

Although a defendant who has made an unsuccessful submission of no case to answer may still be acquitted at the end of his trial even if he fails to produce any evidence in support of his defence (*DPP v Uddin* 2006 WL 1518702), the overwhelming majority of defendants will need to place evidence before the court in order to secure an acquittal.

9.6   The defence case

9.6.1   Should the defendant give evidence?

9.6.1.1   Competence and compellability of the defendant

A defendant is a competent witness for the defence but is not compellable. This means that a defendant can give evidence on his own behalf but he is not obliged to do so (Criminal Evidence Act 1898, s 1(1)). Prior to the trial taking place the defendant's solicitor should always discuss with the defendant whether or not he should give evidence in his own defence. A defendant may be reluctant to give evidence, particularly if he is young or nervous, or if he fears that his 'story' will not stand up to cross-examination by the prosecuting solicitor.

In the normal course of events it will be necessary for the defendant to give evidence (assuming there has not been a successful submission of no case to answer by his solicitor). For example, a defendant who is raising a defence such as self-defence or alibi has the evidential burden of placing some evidence of this defence before the court (see **16.2.2.2**). The simplest way to discharge this burden is for the defendant himself to give evidence. Similarly, if the prosecution have adduced evidence of a confession made by the defendant, and the defendant disputes the truth of this confession, the defendant will need to give evidence to explain why he made a false confession.

A defendant who answered questions (or provided a written statement) at the police station will have the credibility of this evidence enhanced if he goes into the witness box at trial and repeats what he said at the police station. A defendant who does this will enable his solicitor, when giving his closing speech, to say that the defendant has put forward a consistent defence since first being arrested and questioned.

9.6.1.2   Criminal Justice and Public Order Act 1994, s 35

In addition to the above, as a result of s 35 of the CJPOA 1994, a defendant who fails to give evidence on his own behalf at trial is likely to find that the court will draw an adverse inference from such failure. Section 35(2) provides that:

> ... the court shall, at the conclusion of the evidence for the prosecution, satisfy itself ... that the accused is aware that the stage has been reached at which evidence can be given for the defence and that he can, if he wishes, give evidence and that, if he chooses not to give evidence, or having been sworn, without good cause refuses to answer any question, it will be permissible for the court or jury to draw such inferences as appear proper from his failure to give evidence or his refusal, without good cause, to answer any question.

The effect of s 35 is that, if the prosecution have raised issues which call for an explanation from the defendant, should the defendant then fail to give evidence the court will be entitled to infer from that failure that the defendant has either no explanation, or no explanation that will stand up to cross-examination.

Example

Marcus is charged with common assault. Marcus pleads not guilty on the basis that he was acting in self-defence. At the end of the prosecution case, Marcus declines to enter the witness box to give evidence on his own behalf. The court is entitled to infer from this that Marcus has no defence to the charge, or no defence that will stand up to cross-examination (in other words, an inference that Marcus is guilty of the offence).

In the cases of *R v Cowan; R v Gayle; R v Ricciardy* [1995] 4 All ER 939, the Court of Appeal stated that the court had to take into account the following matters when considering the application of s 35:

(a)   the burden of proof remains on the prosecution throughout;

(b)   the defendant is entitled to remain silent;

(c)   before drawing an adverse inference from the defendant's silence, the court had to be satisfied that there was a case to answer on the prosecution evidence;

(d)   an adverse inference from the defendant's failure to give evidence cannot on its own prove guilt; and

(e)   no adverse inference could be drawn unless the only sensible explanation for the defendant's silence was that he had no answer to the case against him, or none that could have stood up to cross-examination.

In *R v Whitehead* [2006] EWCA Crim 1486, the Court of Appeal stated that the jury or magistrates should start by considering the prosecution evidence rather than the defendant's silence. They had to conclude that this evidence was sufficiently cogent to call for an explanation before considering the implications of the defendant's silence. Once that threshold had been crossed, the jury or magistrates were then entitled to consider the defendant's silence as a further evidential factor and in the context of the evidence as a whole.

9.6.1.3   Advice to the defendant

In light of s 35, it will be very rare for a defendant's solicitor to advise his client not to give evidence. The only potential advantage to not giving evidence is that this will prevent a defendant either incriminating himself, or coming across as lacking credibility in the witness box; but this is heavily outweighed by the risk that an adverse inference will be drawn from such silence. A defendant who is raising a specific defence (such as alibi or self-defence) will need to enter the witness box to discharge his evidential burden and to substantiate that defence. Similarly, there may be a need for the defendant to give evidence if it is necessary to 'explain' away a piece of evidence on which the CPS seeks to rely. For example, a defendant may have an explanation for having made an admission or confession upon which the CPS seeks to rely, or there may be a need to explain why an adverse inference should not be drawn under s 36 or s 37 of the CJPOA 1994 if, when interviewed by the police, the defendant failed to account for the presence of a mark, object or substance, or he failed to account for his presence at a particular location.

In *Ebanks v The Queen* [2006] UKPC 16, the Privy Council stated that where a defendant decided not to give evidence, his legal representative should made a written record of this, together with a brief summary of the reasons for the decision. Wherever possible this record should be endorsed by the defendant. The Privy Council also held that it is the duty of the defendant's legal representative to put the defendant's case, whether or not he intends to call evidence to support that case. Similarly, if it is alleged that a prosecution witness has lied, a defendant's legal representative may properly cross-examine that witness to expose such lies, even if the defendant does not subsequently enter the witness box to give positive evidence about those lies.

A flowchart summarising whether the defendant will be required to give evidence and the consequences of a defendant not giving evidence is set out at **9.9.2** below.

9.6.2   Order of defence witnesses

If a defendant is to give evidence on his own behalf, he must be called prior to any other witnesses for the defence unless the court 'otherwise directs' (PACE 1984, s 79). The rationale behind this is that the defendant will be in court throughout the proceedings. Therefore, if other defence witnesses were to give evidence before the defendant, the defendant would have the opportunity to hear what they said and could then tailor his own testimony to take account of the comments made by the other defence witnesses.

Defence witnesses will give evidence in the same way as prosecution witnesses. Each defence witness will be examined in chief by the defendant's solicitor and will then be cross-examined by the prosecuting solicitor. The defendant's solicitor will then have the opportunity to re-examine the witness.

9.6.3   The closing speech

The defendant's solicitor has a choice in the magistrates' court as to whether to make an opening or a closing speech. In practice, solicitors representing the defendant will nearly always choose to make a closing speech, given the tactical importance of having the last word after all the evidence has been presented to the court. Like the prosecution opening speech (see **9.4.1** above), the defence closing speech is not itself evidence. It does, however, allow the defendant's solicitor to sum up the case from the defence point of view, to point out all the weaknesses in the prosecution case and to remind the court of all the points in favour of the defendant.

Although there is no set format for making a closing speech, the following points should be borne in mind:

(a)   The closing speech should be kept short and to the point. Closing speeches that are too long often have little impact on the magistrates.

(b)   The defendant's solicitor must always remind the magistrates that the CPS bears the burden of proving beyond a reasonable doubt that the defendant is guilty of the offence with which he is charged. The magistrates should be told that the defendant is entitled to an acquittal unless they are sure that the defendant is guilty (see **16.2.1**). The defendant does not need to prove that he is innocent. All he need do to secure an acquittal is to demonstrate that the CPS has failed to prove its case beyond a reasonable doubt.

(c)   The defendant's solicitor should refer back to the opening speech made by the prosecuting solicitor, in which the prosecuting solicitor set out what he was going to prove. The defendant's solicitor should point out each and every area where the prosecution case has 'come up short'. The defendant's solicitor should place particular emphasis on the factual weaknesses or discrepancies in the prosecution case.

(d)   The defendant's solicitor may also need to cover evidential issues during the closing speech. If, for example, the prosecution have relied upon disputed identification evidence, the defendant's solicitor will need to give a *Turnbull* warning (see **17.4**) to the magistrates. Alternatively, if the CPS has have been permitted to rely on disputed confession evidence, the defendant's solicitor should seek to undermine the credibility of such evidence. If the evidence of the defendant's bad character has emerged at trial (see **Chapter 22**), the defendant's solicitor will need to downplay the significance of such evidence. If, on the other hand, the defendant is of good character, it should be pointed out to the magistrates that this is of relevance both to the defendant's propensity to commit the offence with which he has been charged, and also as to his credibility as a witness (see **22.8**).

(e)   The closing speech is all about persuasion. In other words, the defendant's solicitor should 'show' the magistrates how to find the defendant not guilty. It is often a sensible tactic to conclude the closing speech by listing all the weaknesses of the prosecution case (and the strengths of the defence case), and then invite the magistrates to conclude that the only possible verdict is one of not guilty.

9.7   The verdict

The magistrates will normally retire to consider their verdict. Most trials in the magistrates' court will be before a bench of three magistrates. The magistrates may make their decision by majority. There does not need to be unanimous agreement on the verdict. When the magistrates return to court after deciding upon the verdict, the defendant will be asked to stand and will be told by the chairperson of the bench that he has been found either not guilty or guilty.

If the defendant is found guilty, the magistrates will move on to consider the sentence to be imposed. The magistrates will either sentence the defendant immediately, or adjourn the case for a number of weeks if they wish to obtain medical or other reports before passing sentence. If the defendant is sentenced immediately, his solicitor will deliver a plea in mitigation to the magistrates prior to sentence (see **12.7**). If the magistrates adjourn the case before passing sentence, they will need to consider whether the defendant should be granted bail or remanded in custody prior to the sentencing hearing (see **7.3**). A defendant who has been found guilty following a trial in the magistrates' court has the right to appeal against his conviction and/or sentence to the Crown Court. The procedure for doing this is described in **Chapter 13**.

If the defendant is acquitted by the magistrates, he will be formally discharged and told that he is free to go. In such a case, if the defendant's case was not funded by way of a representation order, the magistrates will usually direct that his legal costs be paid for from central funds (ie, by the State).

9.8　Advocacy techniques

9.8.1　Introduction

Although this chapter is principally concerned with the procedure at a summary trial in the magistrates' court, the advocacy techniques suggested below are equally applicable to a trial in the Crown Court.

The evidence which a bench of magistrates (or a jury in the Crown Court) will consider when deciding the defendant's guilt or innocence will be the oral evidence they have heard from witnesses at the trial, together with any statements which have been read out at trial and any documentary or real evidence (such as the audio-recording of the defendant's interview at the police station, any CCTV footage that exists, or any items produced as exhibits such as a weapon used in an assault or allegedly stolen goods). The evidence which the court hears from each witness who is called to give evidence at trial falls into three parts:

(a)　examination-in-chief;

(b)　cross-examination;

(c)　re-examination.

9.8.2　Examination in chief

9.8.2.1　Purpose

The purpose of examination-in-chief is to allow a witness to 'tell his story'. The advocate conducting the examination-in-chief should ask questions which enable the witness to repeat the version of events which that witness has provided in his witness statement.

The difficulty in conducting an examination-in-chief is that the advocate is not allowed to ask leading questions. Leading questions are questions which are suggestive of the answer.

> #### Example
>
> Murray is called as a prosecution witness. He is to testify to the fact that at 2 pm on 5 June he saw Grant steal a tin of baked beans from Sainsbury's.
>
> The prosecuting solicitor cannot say to Murray: 'Did you see Grant steal a tin of baked beans from Sainsbury's at 2 pm on 5 June?' This is a leading question.

9.8.2.2 Techniques

Instead of asking leading questions, an advocate conducting an examination-in-chief should use 'open' questions to elicit the information from the witness.

Example

Continuing with the example at **9.8.2.1** above, the prosecutor could elicit the information from Murray in the following way:

Q   Where were you on 5 June at about 2 pm?

A   In Sainsbury's.

Q   Did anything unusual happen whilst you were in Sainsbury's?

A   Yes, I saw Grant pick up a tin of baked beans and put this in his pocket.

Q   What happened next?

A   I saw Grant walk out of the shop without paying for the tin of baked beans.

Inexperienced advocates sometimes find that their conduct of an examination-in-chief involves repeating the same question to the witness ('And what happened next?') time after time. This can become tedious for the court. A far better technique to adopt is 'piggy-backing', where each question builds on the answer to the last question.

Example

Q   Are you in employment, Mr Brown?

A   Yes, I am the manager at Barclays Bank in Bishopthorpe.

Q   Were you at work at the bank on 15 November?

A   Yes.

Q   What time did you get to work?

A   About 8.30 am.

Q   What did you after you got to work?

A   I opened up the bank and made myself a cup of coffee. Whilst I was waiting for other members of staff to arrive, I opened that morning's post.

Q   What did you do after you had opened the post?

A   I went to open the front door of the bank to let in the other members of staff.

Q   Did anything unusual happen as you went to open the front door?

A   Yes, I was confronted by a man wearing a balaclava and brandishing a sawn-off shotgun.

9.8.2.3 Witnesses who don't 'come up to proof'

A witness who is called to give evidence for either the prosecution or the defence will usually have provided a written statement (sometimes referred to as a 'proof of evidence') to the party for whom he is going to give evidence. The questions asked in examination-in-chief will be designed to allow the witness to state orally for the court what he has already said on paper in his witness statement.

A witness who is called to give evidence may not give the evidence expected of him. This is known colloquially as a witness 'not coming up to proof'. If the failure to 'come up to proof' is not deliberate (and occurs only because the witness is nervous, forgetful or ignorant), the party calling the witness is not allowed to contradict or to try to discredit the witness. If, however, the witness appears to be unwilling (rather than unable) to tell the truth on behalf of the party calling him, that party may then apply to the magistrates (or the judge in the Crown Court) to declare the witness to be 'hostile'. If the witness is declared hostile, he may:

(a)   be cross-examined by the party calling him (this will allow that party to put leading questions to the witness to show that he is being untruthful); and

(b)   have any previous inconsistent statement put to him by the party calling him (see **9.8.3.2** below).

In practice, witnesses are commonly shown to be hostile by proving that they have made an earlier out-of-court statement from which they appear to be deliberately and dishonestly departing.

Example

Michael is a member of a criminal gang. A fellow gang member, Robby, is on trial for theft, and Michael is due to give evidence for the prosecution confirming that Robby committed the theft. Michael has given a written statement to the police confirming this. However at Robby's trial, Michael denies that Robby had anything to do with the theft. The prosecution can apply to the court to declare Michael to be 'hostile'. If Michael is declared hostile, he can be asked leading questions by the prosecution to show that he is being untruthful, and his previous inconsistent statement (in which he said that Robby committed the theft) may be put to him.

9.8.2.4   May a witness refresh his memory in the witness box?

A witness who attends court to give oral evidence is not allowed to have a copy of his statement in front of him when giving evidence. However, the party calling that witness may apply to the court for the witness to refresh his memory in the witness box from a document which was made or verified by him at an earlier time. Section 139(1) of the Criminal Justice Act 2003 allows a witness to do this if the witness confirms to the court that the document records his recollection of the matters at that earlier time, and his recollection of the matters is likely to have been significantly better at the earlier time than it is at the time of his giving evidence.

Example 1

Roderick is charged with theft from a shop. On leaving the shop he was apprehended by PC White, who will say that Roderick immediately confessed to having committed the theft as soon as he had been stopped. PC White then made a note of the exact words used by Roderick. When giving evidence in the witness box, PC White will be permitted to refer to his note book to refresh his memory as to exactly what Roderick said, as long as the court is satisfied that PC White made the entry in his note book contemporaneously and whilst the comments made by Roderick were still fresh in his mind.

Example 2

Joanne witnesses a burglary taking place at factory premises. She sees the burglars drive off in a vehicle and makes a note of the vehicle registration number in her pocket diary. When giving evidence for the prosecution in the witness box, Joanne will be permitted to refer to her pocket diary to refresh her memory as to the details of the registration number, as long as the court is satisfied that Joanne made the record in her pocket diary contemporaneously and whilst details of the registration number of the vehicle were still fresh in her mind.

If a witness is permitted to use a document to refresh his memory whilst in the witness box and is cross-examined on the contents of the document, the document will itself become an item of evidence in the proceedings, and will be admissible as evidence of any matter of which oral evidence by the witness would have been admissible (Criminal Justice Act 2003, s 120(3)). Thus, in Example 2 above, Joanne's entry in her pocket diary will be admissible as evidence to show that the burglars drove away in a vehicle with the relevant registration number.

9.8.2.5 Previous consistent statements

The common law position

Prior to the Criminal Justice Act 2003 coming into force, there was a common law rule against previous consistent or self-serving statements, which prevented a witness from being asked about a previous oral or written statement made by him and consistent with his evidence. For example, in *R v Roberts* [1942] 1 All ER 187, the defendant was convicted of murdering his girlfriend by shooting her. The Court of Appeal held that the trial judge had correctly excluded evidence from the defendant that, two days after the shooting, he had told his father that the gun had gone off accidentally. The Court held that this type of evidence had no evidential value, because the fact that a defendant said something to another person on a previous occasion did not confirm his evidence at court.

This common law rule was subject to an exception in cases involving a sexual offence. If the victim of an alleged sexual offence made a voluntary complaint shortly after the offence had been committed, the prosecution were permitted to call to give evidence the person to whom the complaint was made. Evidence from this person was not admissible to prove that the offence had actually taken place, but was admissible to show that the victim had acted in a consistent way and was therefore a credible witness.

Criminal Justice Act 2003

Section 120(4) of the Criminal Justice Act 2003 has extended the above common law exception to all types of offence, by providing that a previous statement made by a witness is admissible as evidence of any matter stated of which oral evidence by the witness would be admissible, provided one or more of certain conditions is satisfied.

Section 120(4) states:

> (4)   A previous statement by the witness is admissible as evidence of any matter stated of which oral evidence by him would be admissible if—
>
> (a)   any of the following three conditions is satisfied, and
>
> (b)   while giving evidence the witness indicates that to the best of his belief he made the statement, and that to the best of his belief it states the truth.

The first condition is that the statement identifies or describes a person, place or object (s 120(5)).

The second condition is that the statement was made by the witness when the matters stated were fresh in his memory, but he does not remember them, and cannot reasonably be expected to remember them, well enough to give oral evidence of them in the proceedings (s 120(6)).

The third condition is set out in s 120(7), which provides:

(a)   the witness claims to be a person against whom an offence has been committed;

(b)   the offence is one to which the current criminal proceedings relate;

(c)   the statement consists of a complaint made by a witness about conduct which would, if proved, constitute the offence;

(d)   the complaint was made as soon as could reasonably be expected after the alleged conduct;

(e)   the complaint was not made as a result of a threat or promise; and

(f)   before the statement is adduced, the witness gives oral evidence in connection with its subject matter.

A statement which is repeated in evidence at trial under s 120(4) will be admissible both to prove the truth of the matters contained in the statement and also to show the credibility of the complainant by demonstrating that the complainant has given a consistent version of events throughout. Such a statement will constitute hearsay evidence, but will be admissible by virtue of s 114(1)(a) of the Criminal Justice Act 2003. Both 'first hand' and 'multiple' hearsay are admissible under s 120 (see **Chapter 19**).

Example

Derrick, a student, is charged with raping Samantha at an end-of-term party held at Derrick's house. Derrick denies the charge, claiming that Samantha consented to sexual intercourse. The rape is alleged to have occurred at approximately 11.00 pm. Samantha left the house 15 minutes after the alleged rape occurred, in the company of a friend, Rachel. On their way home, Samantha broke down in tears and told Rachel what had happened. A few days later Samantha made a complaint to the police, claiming that she had been raped by Derrick. Rachel also gave a statement to the police, detailing what she had been told by Samantha on their way home from Derrick's house. At Derrick's trial, Samantha will give evidence as to what she told Rachel, and Rachel will be permitted to give evidence confirming what she was told by Samantha, provided the above conditions in s 120(4) and (7) are satisfied. The evidence will be admissible both to show that the rape occurred and also that Samantha has acted consistently (ie, by making an immediate allegation of rape to Rachel and subsequently reporting this to the police).

Rebutting a suggestion of recent fabrication

Subject to s 120(4) of the Criminal Justice Act 2003 (see above), the common law rule against the admissibility of previous self-serving statements remains. However, if in cross-examination it is put to the witness that his evidence has recently been fabricated, in re-examination the witness may be asked about evidence of a previous consistent statement to negative the suggestion of recent fabrication and to confirm his credibility.

Example 1

Fergus is on trial for theft and raises an alibi defence. When interviewed about the theft at the police station following his arrest, Fergus gave a 'no comment' interview. Whilst at the police station Fergus did give a statement to his solicitor setting out his defence of alibi, but the solicitor did not hand the statement to the police. In cross-examination at trial, it is put to Fergus that his alibi defence was made up after he left the police station. In re-examination, Fergus will be permitted to give evidence that he gave a statement to his solicitor at the police station setting out his defence. This evidence will be used to refute the suggestion of recent fabrication.

Example 2

In *R v Oyesiku* (1971) 56 Cr App R 240, the defendant was convicted of assaulting a police officer. His wife gave evidence that the police officer had been the aggressor. It was put to her in cross-examination that she had fabricated this account. The Court of Appeal held that the trial judge had properly allowed it to be put to her in re-examination that she had in fact made a prior statement to her husband's solicitor confirming the police officer as being the aggressor. This statement had been made just after her husband's arrest but before she had been able to speak to him. The Court of Appeal held that the trial judge should also have permitted the jury to inspect the statement itself to enable them to judge the extent to which the statement refuted the suggestion that the wife's evidence had been fabricated.

If a previous statement made by a witness is admitted as evidence to rebut a suggestion that the evidence given by the witness has been fabricated, the statement is admissible not only to show the consistency of the witness, but also as to the truth of its contents (Criminal Justice Act 2003, s 120(2)).

9.8.2.6 Anticipating cross-examination

In addition to letting the witness tell his story, an advocate conducting an examination-in-chief should also anticipate any matters which are likely to arise in cross-examination. If the advocate considers that there are any damaging matters which are likely to come out in cross-examination, he may minimise such damage by raising these matters in examination-in-chief. This is particularly relevant for a defendant's solicitor who is carrying out an examination-in-chief of a client who has a number of previous convictions which are likely to be raised in cross-examination by the prosecuting solicitor (see **Chapter 22**). If the defendant's solicitor knows that evidence of his client's previous convictions is going to emerge in cross-examination, it is better for him to raise such convictions himself in examination-in-chief. Doing this will take the 'sting' out of a prosecution attack on the defendant's character and enable the defendant to give a proper explanation for his previous conduct.

9.8.2.7 Example of an examination in chief

Set out below is an extract from the examination-in-chief of John Barnard, which would have been carried out by the prosecuting solicitor had Gary Dickson's case been tried in the magistrates' court:

Q   Mr Barnard, do you recall 17 December 2006?

A   Yes, I was at work during the day and then I went out that evening.

Q   When you went out for the evening, where did you go?

A   I went out to a club called Toffs in Chester city centre at about 10.30 pm.

Q   How long were you in Toffs?

A   Four or five hours. I left at approximately 3 am the following morning.

Q   What did you do when you left the club?

A   I set off to walk to a friend's house where I was going to spend the night.

Q   Did anything happen as you walked to your friend's house?

A   About 15 minutes after I set off I saw a dark coloured VW Golf zoom past me then stop sharply next to a young man who was walking ahead of me.

Q   Did anything happen after the car stopped?

A   The driver of the car got out.

Q   Did the driver of the car do anything after he got out of the car?

A   Yes, he hit the other man in the face several times.

Q   Did the other man do anything to provoke the attack?

A   No.

Q   What happened after the attack had finished?

A   The man got back in his car and drove away, passing me again.

Q   Can you describe the man who carried out the attack?

A   Yes, he was a well-built man with short dark hair and a tight-fitting white t-shirt. He was white and clean shaven.

Q   Do you recall any further details about the car?

A   It was a dark blue Golf. The registration number was either C251 CVM or L251 CVM.

Q   How can you be sure of this?

A   I used to be in the army and have had training in vehicle recognition. I made a mental note of the registration number at the time and told a police officer later on in the evening.

Q   Mr Barnard did you subsequently attend at a video identification at Chester police station?

A   Yes.

Q   At the video identification were you able to pick out the person you had seen on 18 December?

A   Yes.

Q   Do you see that person in court today?

A   Yes, it's Mr Dickson, the defendant.

9.8.3 Cross-examination

9.8.3.1 Purpose

The cross-examination of a witness called by the other party in the case has two purposes:

(a)   to enable the party conducting the cross-examination to put his case to the witness; and

(b)   to undermine the credibility of the evidence which that witness has just given in examination-in-chief.

In some circumstances, a defendant is not permitted to cross-examine in person certain categories of prosecution witness (Youth Justice and Criminal Evidence Act 1999, ss 34–36). The detailed provisions of this are beyond the scope of this book, but in summary a defendant may not cross-examine in person a complainant in a case involving an alleged sexual offence (YJCEA 1999, s 34). For some offences, restrictions also exist on a defendant being able to cross-examine in person a complainant who is a child, or any other child witness (YJCEA 1999, s 35). Where the witness is neither a child nor the victim of alleged sexual offence, the court may make an order preventing the defendant from personally cross-examining that witness if:

(a)   the quality of evidence given by the witness on cross-examination:
  (i)   is likely to be diminished if the cross-examination is conducted by the defendant in person, and
  (ii)   the quality of such evidence would be likely to be improved if the witness were not cross-examined by the defendant in person; and

(b)   it would not be contrary to the interests of justice to prevent the defendant from cross-examining the witness in person (YJCEA 1999, s 36).

9.8.3.2 'Putting your case'

'Putting your case' means suggesting to a witness that the version of events which that witness has just put forward in examination-in-chief is incorrect, and suggesting an alternative version of events. It is always necessary for an advocate to put his client's version of events to a witness in cross-examination. For example, in an assault case where the defendant is claiming he acted only in self-defence, the defendant's solicitor must, when cross-examining the alleged victim of the assault, put to the victim that he (the victim) attacked the defendant first and that the defendant was acting only in self-defence. If the defendant's solicitor fails to put to the witness that the defendant was acting in self-defence, the defendant will then not be entitled to enter the witness box and say that he was acting in self-defence.

Putting your case often means asking a witness a series of questions which elicit a negative response. This is something which can be disconcerting for inexperienced advocates but is still something which needs to be done.

Example

Q   Mr Green, you have told the court that my client attacked you without provocation?

A   Yes.

Q   That's not correct is it Mr Green?

A   Yes it is correct.

Q   Mr Green, isn't it the case that you attacked my client first?

A   No.

Q   Mr Green, I put it to you that you punched my client in the face and my client was only defending himself?

A   No.

Q   Mr Green, my client was only acting in self-defence wasn't he?

A   No.

9.8.3.3 Discrediting the witness

Discrediting the testimony the witness has just given in examination in chief is all about undermining the credibility of the witness and exposing any weaknesses in his evidence. For example, if the court gives leave, the witness should be cross-examined about any previous convictions he has for offences involving untruthfulness (such as perjury or obtaining property by deception) to suggest that his testimony should not be relied upon. Alternatively, if the defendant is charged with assault and raises the defence of self-defence, the victim of the alleged assault should be cross-examined about any previous convictions he has for offences involving violence. (See **Chapter 22.**) If the witness is unsure or uncertain about any point, this should be exploited to suggest that the witness's recollection of events is incomplete and unreliable. If possible, advocates should avoid suggesting to a witness that his evidence has been intentionally fabricated, or that the witness is intentionally lying. Most witnesses in criminal cases do attempt to tell the truth, and witnesses are far more liable to give contradictory evidence as a result of being confused or unsure, rather than from any malicious motive. An allegation made in cross-examination that a prosecution witness has deliberately fabricated or made up evidence is likely to lead to the court allowing the prosecuting solicitor to adduce evidence of any previous convictions the defendant might have (see **Chapter 22**).

9.8.3.4 Restrictions on questions to undermine the credibility of the witness

There are no general restrictions on the type of questions that may be asked of a witness to undermine the credibility of the evidence given by him. However, in cases where the defendant has been charged with a sexual offence, s 41 of the Youth Justice and Criminal Evidence Act 1999 imposes restrictions on the defendant adducing evidence about the complainant's previous sexual behaviour, or the complainant being cross-examined about such behaviour. A defendant is not permitted to adduce evidence or ask questions in cross-examination about the previous sexual conduct of the complainant unless leave of the court is obtained. In the leading case of *R v A (Complainant's Sexual History)* [2001] 3 All ER 1, the

House of Lords considered when leave should be given in the context of a case where the defendant raised the defence of consent and wanted to adduce evidence of his previous sexual relationship with the complainant. Their Lordships held that leave should be given in such a case when the evidence and the questioning in relation to it was so relevant to the issue of consent that to exclude it would endanger the fairness of the trial under Article 6 of the ECHR (see **1.8.3**). The procedural steps which must be followed by a defendant seeking leave to adduce evidence at trial of a complainant's previous sexual history are contained in Part 36 of the Criminal Procedure Rules.

There is a general rule that the answer given by a witness to a question designed to undermine the credibility of that witness shall be final and no further questions may be put to the witness on the same point. This rule is subject to a number of exceptions which permit further questions if the witness responds negatively to such a question. These exceptions are:

(a)   a question asked to prove that the witness is *biased* (if the witness responds by denying that he is biased, further questions may be asked of the witness to establish that bias exists);

(b)   a question asked to prove that the witness has made a *previous inconsistent statement* (see **9.8.3.5** below); and

(c)   a question asked to prove that the witness has a relevant *previous conviction* (if the witness denies having such a conviction, further questions may be asked to establish this and a memorandum of conviction may be placed before the court – see **22.7.6**).

9.8.3.5   Previous inconsistent statements

A previous inconsistent statement may be put to a witness in cross-examination (or to a witness during examination-in-chief if the court has declared the witness to be 'hostile') in order to undermine the credibility of the oral evidence given by the witness. In addition, s 119(1) of the Criminal Justice Act 2003 provides that if a person giving oral evidence at trial admits that he made a previous inconsistent statement, or it is proved that such a statement was made, that previous statement will itself be admissible in evidence to show that the contents of this statement are in fact correct. The previous inconsistent statement will be hearsay evidence, but will be admissible by virtue of s 114(1)(a) of the Criminal Justice Act 2003. Both 'first hand' and 'multiple' hearsay evidence is admissible under s 119 (see **Chapter 19**).

Example

Graham is charged with theft and raises the defence of alibi, claiming that he was at home with his wife Gillian at the time of the theft. While Graham is being questioned at the police station, the police take a statement from Gillian. Gillian states that, at the time the theft is alleged to have taken place, Graham was not with her but had gone out shopping. Gillian subsequently refuses to give evidence for the prosecution at Graham's trial (as Graham's spouse she cannot be compelled to give evidence for the prosecution – see **Chapter 16**). Gillian is then called as a defence witness at Graham's trial. She gives evidence that, at the time Graham is alleged to have committed the theft, Graham was at home with her. In cross-examination the prosecuting solicitor will be able to put to Gillian the previous inconsistent statement to the police, in order to undermine the credibility of the evidence Gillian has given in support of Graham's alibi. Gillian's statement to the police will itself also be admissible in evidence to show that the contents of the statement are correct, and that Graham was not in fact at home with her at the time of the theft.

9.8.3.6   Techniques of cross-examination

Carrying out an effective cross-examination requires an advocate to 'control' the answers which the witness gives. This is done by asking 'closed' questions. 'Closed' questions are questions which require a Yes/No answer. 'Open' questions, which allow the witness to expand upon the evidence he has given when examined in chief, should never be asked in cross-examination.

Example

Q   Mr Green, you had been out drinking on the night in question hadn't you?

A   Yes.

Q   You'd been in the pub for several hours hadn't you?

A   Yes.

Q   And you drank six pints of lager and a couple of whisky chasers?

A   Yes.

Q   So you would agree with me that you had a lot to drink?

A   Yes.

Q   Having a lot to drink will impair your judgement, won't it Mr Green?

A   Not necessarily.

Q   Would you drink six pints of lager and a couple of whisky chasers before driving your car?

A   No.

Q   Because it would impair your judgement wouldn't it?

A   Yes.

9.8.3.7   Example of a cross-examination

Set out below is an extract from the cross-examination of John Barnard, which would have been carried out by Gary Dickson's solicitor had his case been tried in the magistrates' court:

Q   Mr Barnard, you told the court that you spent the evening of 17 December at a club?

A   That's correct.

Q   You had quite a bit to drink, didn't you Mr Barnard?

A   I wouldn't say I had that much.

Q   Well according to your statement you had seven pints to drink. Is that correct?

A   Yes.

Q   That's quite a lot isn't it Mr Barnard?

A   I suppose so.

Q   You have said that as you were walking to your friend's house a car zoomed past you and pulled up 50 metres away?

A   Yes.

Q   50 metres is just a guess?

A   Yes.

Q   It could have been further couldn't it?

A   Yes.

Q   And this was at 3.15 am in the middle of December wasn't it?

A   Yes.

Q   So it must have been very dark?

A   Yes.

Q   You say that a well-built man got out of the car and attacked a pedestrian?

A   Yes.

Q   That's not a very full description is it?

A   I suppose not, but I saw the man again when he drove past me after he had done the assault.

Q   When the man drove past you after committing the assault you have said he was travelling at about 40 mph?

A   Yes, but I got a fair look at him.

Q   That's not what you said in your statement Mr Barnard. In your statement you said you only managed to glimpse him. That's correct isn't it?

A   Yes.

Q   Mr Barnard, are you familiar with Connelley's nightclub?

A   Yes

Q   Mr Barnard do the staff at Connelley's wear a uniform?

A   Yes.

Q   What is that uniform?

A   They all wear tight-fitting white t-shirts.

Q   And the driver of the car was wearing a tight-fitting white t-shirt wasn't he Mr Barnard?

A   Yes.

Q   So you saw an incident from a long distance away, it was dark at the time, you'd had a lot to drink and the only description you can give could apply to numerous other people. That's correct isn't it?

A   Yes.

9.8.4 Re-examination

Following cross-examination, the advocate who originally called the witness to give evidence in chief may carry out a brief re-examination of the witness. Re-examinations are rare and should be carried out only where a case has been damaged in cross-examination *and* the advocate considers that some of that damage can be repaired by way of re-examination. An advocate should seek to avoid carrying out a re-examination if at all possible, because this is a clear indication to the court that the advocate's case has been damaged. Re-examination can only ever cover matters which have been raised in cross-examination. An advocate who has forgotten to raise a matter with witness in examination-in-chief cannot raise that matter in re-examination, unless the matter has been brought up in cross-examination by the opposing advocate.

9.9 Procedural flowcharts

9.9.1 Trial procedure in the magistrates' court

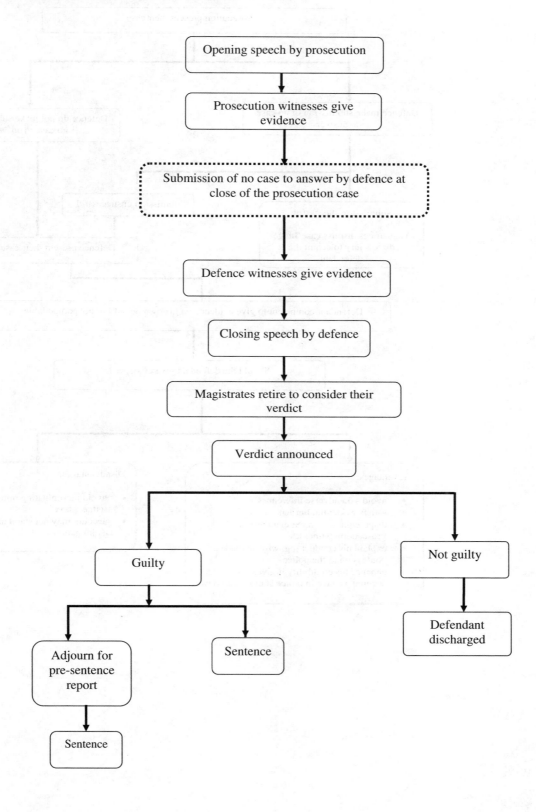

9.9.2   Will the defendant need to give evidence?

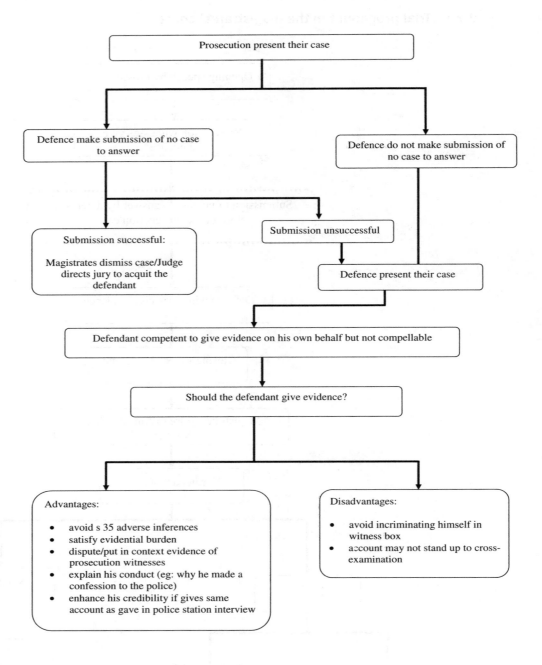

9.10 Checklist

At the end of this chapter you should be able to explain:

- the order in which events take place at a trial in the magistrates' court;
- matters of professional conduct which may arise at or prior to a trial in the magistrates' court;
- how the CPS will present its case at a trial in the magistrates' court;
- how and when to make a submission of no case to answer at a trial in the magistrates' court;
- how the defendant's solicitor will present his client's case at a trial in the magistrates' court;
- whether a defendant should give evidence in support of his defence at trial;
- the purpose of an examination-in-chief of a witness, and how this should be carried out;
- the purpose of the cross-examination of a witness and how this should be carried out;
- the purpose of the re-examination of a witness.

Chapter 10

The Crown Court

10.1 Introduction

This chapter will begin by describing the types of case which may be dealt with by the Crown Court and will then go on to examine the procedure by which an indictable-only offence or an either way offence (where the magistrates have declined jurisdiction or the defendant has elected Crown Court trial) is sent to the Crown Court for trial. The standard case management directions which apply in Crown Court cases will be explained, as will the significance of the plea and case management hearing. The chapter will describe the role played by the defendant's solicitor in a Crown Court case, with particular emphasis placed on how to 'brief' counsel and the drafting of the defence statement. The chapter will conclude with a description of the procedure which takes place at a trial in the Crown Court.

10.2 Cases dealt with in the Crown Court

The Crown Court has jurisdiction to deal with the following types of case:

(a) *Indictable-only offences* – these offences must be dealt with before the Crown Court. The procedure by which these cases reach the Crown Court is described at **10.4** below.

(b) *Either way offences where the defendant pleads not guilty* – these offences will be sent to the Crown Court for trial by the magistrates if either the magistrates refuse jurisdiction, or if the magistrates accept jurisdiction but the defendant elects Crown Court trial (see **6.10** above).

(c) *Either way offences where the defendant pleads guilty* – if the magistrates consider their sentencing powers to be inadequate, a defendant who has appeared before them and entered a guilty plea to an either way offence at the plea before venue hearing will be committed to the Crown Court for sentence (see **6.9** above).

(d) *Appeals from the magistrates' court* – a defendant who wishes to appeal against his conviction and/or sentence imposed by the magistrates' court for an either way or summary only offence has a right of appeal to the Crown Court (see **13.2.1**).

Defence appeals against the refusal of bail by the magistrates' court, or appeals by the CPS against a decision by the magistrates to grant bail to a defendant, will also be heard before the Crown Court. Such appeals will take place before a Crown Court judge in chambers (see **7.8**).

This chapter will focus on the procedure to be followed in respect of:

(a)   indictable-only offences; and

(b)   either way offences where the defendant pleads not guilty and the magistrates decline jurisdiction or the defendant elects Crown Court trial.

10.3   Trial by judge and jury

In the magistrates' court, the magistrates decide matters of both fact and law (the latter with the assistance of their clerk/legal adviser). In a Crown Court trial these functions are split between the judge and the jury. The jury (which is made up of 12 members of the public) will decide any matters of fact which are in dispute, and will ultimately decide upon the defendant's guilt or innocence. The judge will resolve any disputes that arise over points of law during the course of a trial, and will direct the jury as to the relevant law which they must apply to the facts of the case when they retire to consider their verdict. Although the judge will also sum up for the jury the evidence which they have heard before the jury retire to consider their verdict, the jury are solely responsible for deciding what the true facts of the case are. The judge will also be responsible for sentencing the defendant in the event that he is found guilty.

There are some limited situations in which trials may take place without a jury being present, so-called 'judge-alone' trials. The detailed rules as to when such a trial can take place are outside the scope of this book, but in summary, judge-only trials can take place in the following circumstances:

(a)   the CPS may apply for a judge-only trial if it anticipates that there may be an attempt to tamper with the jury (CJA 2003, s 44). The CPS may anticipate an attempt to tamper with a jury if there has been an attempt to intimidate a prosecution witness, or if a previous trial has collapsed due to jury tampering;

(b)   if a trial has collapsed due to jury tampering (such as an attempt to bribe or intimidate a juror), the trial judge has a discretion to carry on with the trial in the absence of the jury (CJA 2003, s 46);

(c)   in a serious or complex fraud case, the CPS may to apply to a Crown Court judge for the case to be tried without a jury if the complexity of the trial or the length of the trial (or both) is likely to make the trial so burdensome to the members of a jury hearing the trial that the interests of justice require that serious consideration should be given to the question of whether the trial should be conducted without a jury. This power is not yet in force because the further approval of Parliament is required before it is implemented. The Government has indicated that currently it has no plans to seek such approval.

In any judge-only trial, the judge will be the sole arbiter of both the facts and the law.

10.4 Sending for trial (CrimPR, Part 12)

10.4.1 Indictable-only offences

10.4.1.1 Which offences qualify?

Where an adult appears before a magistrates' court charged with an indictable-only offence, the court must send him to the Crown Court for trial pursuant to s 51(1) of the Crime and Disorder Act 1998:

(a) for that offence; and

(b) for any either way offence or summary offence with which he is charged which fulfils the 'requisite conditions'.

The 'requisite conditions' are that:

(a) the either way or summary offence appears to the court to be related to the indictable-only offence; and

(b) in the case of a summary only offence, it is punishable with imprisonment, or involves obligatory or discretionary disqualification from driving (Crime and Disorder Act 1998, s 51(11)).

Example

Tony is charged with robbery and assault occasioning actual bodily harm. The CPS alleges that Tony attacked his victim to steal the victim's mobile phone and in the process struck the victim in the face, causing the victim to sustain a fractured nose. Robbery is an indictable-only offence and so must be sent to the Crown Court for trial. Assault occasioning actual bodily harm is an either way offence. It fulfils the 'requisite conditions' because it is related to the indictable-only offence.

If Tony had been charged with common assault (a summary only offence) instead of assault occasioning actual bodily harm, the 'requisite conditions' would still be satisfied. The common assault charge is related to the indictable-only offence, and common assault is punishable by imprisonment.

10.4.1.2 The preliminary hearing in the magistrates' court

An adult defendant charged with an indictable-only offence will be sent straight to the Crown Court for trial following a preliminary hearing in the magistrates' court, pursuant to s 51(1) of the Crime and Disorder Act 1998. This preliminary hearing will usually take place at the first available court sitting after the defendant has been charged by the police. The purpose of the preliminary hearing is to determine whether an indictable-only offence is charged and whether there are related offences which should also be sent to the Crown Court (see **10.4.1.1** above). The magistrates will set a date for the plea and case management hearing at the Crown Court (see **10.6** below), and also a date for a preliminary hearing in the Crown Court if such a hearing is necessary (see **10.5.2** below), and will remand the defendant either on bail or in custody to appear at the Crown Court. The magistrates will also give a set of standard case management directions for the CPS and the defendant's solicitor to comply with (see **10.5.1** below).

The magistrates have the power at the preliminary hearing to make a representation order (see **6.4.3.2**) to cover the defendant's legal representation in both the magistrates' court and the Crown Court. This is often referred to as a 'through order'. Although a representation order is currently granted solely on the 'interests of justice' test and is not subject to the defendant's means, at the conclusion of the case in the Crown Court the judge has the power to order a defendant who has been convicted to pay some or all of the costs of his defence (see **Chapter 11**). If the magistrates grant the defendant a representation order to cover his legal representation in the Crown Court, the magistrates' clerk will ask him to complete a statement of means (Form B) which he will then need to return to the Crown Court. This will be used by the Crown Court judge at the end of the defendant's trial if the judge is considering making an order that the defendant pay some or all of his defence costs. A copy of Form B is included at **10.13.1** below.

When the changes made by the Criminal Defence Service Act 2006 are brought into effect, making financial eligibility a requirement for the grant of a representation order (see **6.4.5** above), the defendant will complete a statement of means when he first applies for a representation order, rather than completing a statement of means only after his case has been sent to the Crown Court for trial.

10.4.2 Either way offences

10.4.2.1 Procedure

A defendant charged with an either way offence who enters a not guilty plea (or who declines to enter a plea) at the plea before venue hearing will have his case sent to Crown Court either if the magistrates decline jurisdiction, or if the defendant himself elects to be tried before a judge and jury. The plea before venue and allocation procedure is described in **6.9**.

If the magistrates decline jurisdiction or the defendant elects Crown Court trial, the magistrates will immediately send the case to the Crown Court for trial using the procedure set out under s 51(1) of the Crime and Disorder Act 1998, as described at **10.4.1.2** above. The magistrates will set a date for the plea and directions hearing at the Crown Court (see **10.6** below), and a date for a preliminary hearing at the Crown Court if such a hearing is necessary (see **10.5.2** below), and will remand the defendant on bail or in custody to appear before the Crown Court. As with indictable-only offences, the magistrates will also give a set of standard case management directions for the CPS and the defendant's solicitor to comply with (**see 10.5.1** below). The magistrates will also extend the defendant's representation order to cover the Crown Court proceedings, and ask the defendant to complete a statement of means to be sent to the Crown Court for the use of the judge if he judge orders the defendant to pay some or all of his defence costs at the end of the case (see **10.4.1.2** above).

10.4.2.2 Linked summary offences

Just as with indictable-only offences, a defendant who is sent for trial in respect of an either way offence may also be charged with another offence that is summary only.

If the summary only offence is common assault, taking a conveyance without consent, driving whilst disqualified or criminal damage, the defendant may be tried for these offences at the Crown Court if the offence is founded on the same facts as the either way offence, or is part of a series of offences of the same or a similar character (CJA 1988, s 40(1)).

Example

Jarvis is charged with theft of goods from a motor vehicle and taking a conveyance without consent. The CPS alleges that Jarvis took a vehicle without the owner's consent and stole some CDs from the vehicle whilst it was in his possession. Jarvis is sent to the Crown Court for trial on the theft charge after he enters a not guilty plea at the plea before venue hearing and elects Crown Court trial. The summary only offence of taking a conveyance without consent can also be tried in the Crown Court as it is founded on the same facts as the either way offence.

In addition to the above, if the magistrates send a defendant for trial for one or more either way offences, they may also send him for trial of any summary only offence with which he is also charged if the summary only offence:

(a)   is punishable with imprisonment or disqualification from driving; and

(b)   arises out of circumstances which are the same as or connected to the circumstances of the either way offence (CJA1988, s 41(1)).

If the defendant, on conviction for the either way offence, pleads guilty to the summary only offence, the Crown Court can sentence for the summary offence, although its sentencing powers are limited to those of the magistrates. If the defendant is acquitted of the either way offence, or pleads not guilty to the summary only offence, this offence must be remitted back to the magistrates' court for trial.

Example

Len is sent for trial to the Crown Court on a charge of assault occasioning actual bodily harm. He also faces a charge for the summary only public order offence of using threatening behaviour. Both charges arise out of the same incident. If Len is convicted of the assault charge at the Crown Court, he can also be sentenced for the public order offence if he pleads guilty to it. If Len is acquitted of the assault charge or pleads not guilty to the public order offence, however, the Crown Court must remit the public order offence back to the magistrates' court for trial.

10.5 Standard case management directions and other preliminary matters

10.5.1 Standard case management directions

After the magistrates have made an order under s 51(1) of the Crime and Disorder Act 1998 sending the defendant to the Crown Court for trial, the magistrates' clerk will send a notice to the Crown Court specifying the charge(s) upon which the defendant has been sent for trial.

Prior to the Criminal Procedure Rules 2005 coming into effect, the defendant would then make his first appearance before the Crown Court at a preliminary hearing, which took place between eight and 28 days after the hearing at which the defendant was sent for trial. The Criminal Procedure Rules altered this system by creating a set of standard case management directions that will be issued by the magistrates when they send the case for trial (see **10.4.1** and **10.4.2** above). The directions are intended to replicate the type of directions a judge would previously have made at a preliminary hearing and so remove the need for such a hearing to take place. The directions that the magistrates will give for the parties to comply with are as set out at **10.5.1.1 to 10.5.1.6** below.

10.5.1.1 Prosecution case and disclosure

The CPS will be required to serve on the defendant (or his solicitor) the evidence on which it seeks to rely within *50 days* if the defendant is remanded in custody and within *70 days* if the defendant is on bail. This will include a draft indictment (the Crown Court version of the charges the defendant faces, in which each allegation against the defendant is set out in the form of a count – see **10.5.5** below), witness statements, documentary exhibits, tapes of interview, video tapes and CCTV tapes. The same time limits apply for the CPS to make initial disclosure of any unused material it has to the defendant (see **10.8** below). The final version of the indictment must be sent to the Crown Court within *28 days* of the service of the prosecution evidence.

10.5.1.2   Obligations on the defence

If the defendant requires a prosecution witness to give evidence in person at trial, he must give notice of this to the CPS within *7 days* of receiving the prosecution evidence. Following receipt of this notice, the police will then be required to notify the CPS and the Crown Court of the dates when any prosecution witness is unavailable to give evidence, and the reasons for this.

The defendant will also have *14 days* from the date on which the CPS complies with its initial duty of disclosure in respect of unused material to serve a defence statement (see **10.8** below), and to make an application to dismiss the charges (see **10.5.3** below).

10.5.1.3   Hearsay evidence

The CPS must serve any notice of intention to introduce hearsay evidence within *14 days* of the service of the prosecution papers. The defendant must serve any notice opposing the prosecution notice within *14 days* of receiving it.

The defendant must serve any notice of intention to introduce hearsay evidence within *14 days* of the date on which the CPS complies with its initial duty of disclosure of unused material. The CPS must serve any notice opposing the defence notice within *14 days* of receiving it.

10.5.1.4   Bad character evidence

The defendant must serve any application to introduce the previous convictions of a prosecution witness at trial within *14 days* of the date on which the CPS discloses the existence of any such convictions. The CPS should disclose the existence of such convictions as part of its obligation to disclose to the defendant any material capable of undermining the prosecution case (see **10.8.1** below). The CPS must serve any notice opposing the defendant's application within *14 days* of receiving the application.

The CPS must serve any notice of intention to introduce the defendant's bad character at trial within *14 days* of serving on the defendant the papers containing details of the prosecution case. The defendant must serve any application to exclude evidence of his bad character at trial within *14 days* of receiving the prosecution notice.

The court has the discretion to make any further orders it wishes in relation to the use of bad character evidence at trial.

10.5.1.5   Special measures

The CPS must serve any application for permission to use special measures (see **Chapter 16**) at trial within *28 days* of the service of the papers containing details of the prosecution case. The defendant must serve any response to the application made by the CPS within *14 days* of service of this application.

10.5.1.6   Case progression

Within *14 days* the parties must give to the Crown Court case progression officer responsible for the case all relevant information to enable the Crown Court Case Details Form to be completed.

A copy of the form used by the magistrates when giving directions (which sets out the full set of standard directions that the prosecution and defence will be required to comply with) is at **10.13.2** below. It will be the responsibility of the case progression officers from both the CPS and the defendant's firm of solicitors (see **Chapter 1**) to ensure that the directions are complied with within the relevant time limits.

At the same time as giving case management directions, the magistrates will fix a date for the plea and case management hearing in the Crown Court (see **10.6** below) and, if necessary, the preliminary hearing (see **10.5.2** below). The plea and case management hearing must take place within 14 weeks of the case being sent for trial when the defendant is remanded in custody, and 17 weeks when the defendant is on bail.

10.5.2 Preliminary hearings in the Crown Court

Although the objective behind the introduction of standard case management directions was to prevent there being the need for a preliminary hearing in the Crown Court, such a hearing may still take place. A preliminary hearing will take place either if the resident (ie, senior) judge at the relevant Crown Court has given a direction that all cases sent to the Crown Court should be given a preliminary hearing, or if the magistrates who send the case to the Crown Court deem a preliminary hearing to be necessary because:

(a)   there are case management issues the Crown Court needs to resolve;

(b)   the trial is likely to last more than four weeks;

(c)   it is desirable to set an early trial date;

(d)   the defendant is a child or young person (ie, under 18 years of age); or

(e)   there is likely to be a guilty plea and the defendant could be sentenced at the preliminary hearing (this will be rare in practice because the preliminary hearing is likely to take place before the defendant has received the details of the prosecution case, and so his solicitor will not be in a position to advise him on the strength of the prosecution case and what his plea should be).

Either the prosecution or defence may also make an application that a case sent to the Crown Court be listed for a preliminary hearing.

If, when sending the case for trial, the magistrates make an order for a preliminary hearing to take place at the Crown Court, this hearing will take place within 14 days of the date on which the magistrates send the case to the Crown Court. A copy of the case progression form which the advocates for both the prosecution and defence must complete prior to a preliminary hearing taking place is set out at **10.13.2** below.

If a preliminary hearing takes place at the Crown Court in a case where the defendant indicates that he is likely to plead not guilty at the subsequent plea and case management hearing (see **10.6** below), the judge will give any further directions which he considers necessary (beyond those standard case management directions already given by the magistrates) for the parties to prepare the case prior to the plea and case management hearing. The defendant will either be released on bail, or remanded in custody pending the plea and case management hearing. If the defendant pleads guilty at the preliminary hearing, the judge will sentence him immediately, or adjourn the case to obtain pre-sentence reports. If the judge adjourns sentence, the defendant will either be remanded in custody or released on bail.

10.5.3 Challenging a case sent for trial under s 51 (CrimPR, Part 13)

A defendant whose case is sent to the Crown Court for trial may apply to a Crown Court judge for the charge(s) against him to be dismissed prior to his trial taking place if the evidence against him is particularly weak. Section 6(1) of the CJA 1987 provides that a judge 'shall dismiss a charge ... if it appears to him that the evidence against the [defendant] would not be sufficient for a jury to properly convict him'.

The procedure which must be followed when a defendant seeks to challenge a case sent for trial is set out in Part 13 of the Criminal Procedure Rules. To make an application to challenge a case sent for trial, the defendant must give written notice both to the CPS and the court within 14 days of the CPS disclosing its case to the defendant (see **10.5.2** above). This notice may include an application for leave to call witnesses to give oral evidence at the hearing. The CPS then has seven days to file a reply to the application. The court will list the matter for a hearing, at which the judge will either dismiss the charge against the defendant or refuse the application to dismiss the charge.

10.5.4 Custody time limits

Just as in the magistrates' court, limits exist for the maximum period of time a defendant may be remanded in custody prior to the start of his trial at the Crown Court. The maximum period a defendant may be remanded in custody is 182 days from the date on which the magistrates sent the case for trial to the start of the trial, less any period of time during which the defendant was in the custody of the magistrates' court after making his first appearance before the magistrates.

Example

Kim is charged with robbery on 1 February and makes her first appearance in the magistrates' court on the same day. The magistrates send her case to Crown Court for trial and remand Kim in custody to appear before the Crown Court. The trial must begin within 182 days of the date on which the magistrates sent the case the Crown Court for trial.

The CPS may apply to the Crown Court to extend the custody time limit at any time before its expiry. The application may be made orally, although a written notice of intention must be served on the defendant within two days. In order to obtain an extension, the CPS will need to persuade the court that (on the balance of probabilities):

(a)   there is good and sufficient cause for extending the custody time limit; and

(b)   the CPS has acted with due diligence and expedition throughout.

Reasons that do *not* come within (a) or (b) above include the seriousness of the charge the defendant faces, the fact that a refusal of the court to extend the custody time limit would lead to an automatic right to bail, and police delays in obtaining evidence due to understaffing or sickness.

If the initial custody time limit has expired and the Crown Court has not extended this period, the defendant must be released on bail until the start of his trial.

10.5.5 The indictment (CrimPR, Part 14)

The indictment is the formal document that sets out the charge(s) upon which the defendant is to be tried in the Crown Court. The indictment is drafted by the

CPS and is referred to initially as the 'bill of indictment'. The CPS will send the final version of the draft indictment to the Crown Court, where it will be signed and dated by an officer of the court and so become the indictment. This must be done within 28 days of the CPS serving the case papers on the defence (CrimPR, r 14.2) – see **10.5.2** above.

The charge(s) a defendant faces are set out in the indictment in the form of counts. There can be more than one count on an indictment.

Detailed rules for the drafting of the indictment in the Crown Court are contained in the Indictment Rules 1971 (SI 1971/1253). These rules are beyond the scope of this book, but an explanation of the rules can be found either in *Blackstone's Criminal Practice*, or in *Archbold: Criminal Pleading, Evidence and Practice* (see **1.10.1**).

An example of an indictment is set out below.

Key Document – Indictment

No CH 060248

INDICTMENT

IN THE CROWN COURT AT CHESTER

THE QUEEN – v – GARY PAUL DICKSON

GARY PAUL DICKSON is charged as follows:

STATEMENT OF OFFENCE

Assault occasioning actual bodily harm, contrary to section 47 of the Offences Against the Person Act 1861

PARTICULARS OF OFFENCE

Gary Paul Dickson on or about the 18th day of December 2006 assaulted Vincent Lamb causing him actual bodily harm

Michael Richards
Officer of the court

10.6 Plea and case management hearing

10.6.1 Introduction

If the defendant has been charged with an indictable-only offence, the plea and case management hearing (PCMH) will be the first occasion at which the defendant makes an appearance before the court after having seen details of the prosecution case. If the defendant has been charged with an either way offence, the defendant will already have seen some details of the prosecution case in the advance disclosure package supplied to his solicitor prior to the plea before venue and allocation hearing (see **6.6.3**). In such a case, the PCMH will, however, still be the first occasion on which the defendant makes an appearance before the court knowing the full extent of the evidence the CPS will seek to rely on at trial.

The purpose of the PCMH is to enable the defendant to enter his plea and, if the defendant is pleading not guilty, to enable the judge to give further case management directions for the CPS and the defendant's solicitor to comply with prior to trial.

The PCMH will take place within 14 weeks of the case being sent for trial when the defendant is remanded in custody, and 17 weeks when the defendant is on bail.

10.6.2 The arraignment

At the start of the PCMH the defendant will be arraigned. This means that the count(s) on the indictment will be put to the defendant and he will either plead guilty or not guilty. If the defendant pleads guilty to some counts but not guilty to others, the jury at the defendant's trial in respect of the counts to which he pleaded not guilty will not be told about the counts to which he has pleaded guilty (so they are not in any way prejudiced against the defendant).

It will sometimes be the case that a defendant charged with several counts will agree with the CPS that he will plead guilty to certain counts if the CPS does not proceed with other counts. If this happens, at the arraignment the CPS will offer no evidence in respect of these other counts and the judge will order that a verdict of not guilty be entered. The CPS will also offer no evidence at the arraignment if, since the case was sent for trial, further evidence has become available which leads it to conclude that there is no longer a reasonable prospect of securing a conviction. In this case, the judge will again order that a not guilty verdict be entered and the defendant will be formally discharged.

As an alternative to offering no evidence, the CPS may ask that a count 'lie on the court file'. This may happen when there are several counts on the indictment and the CPS evidence in respect of each count is strong. If the defendant is prepared to plead guilty to the more serious counts, the CPS may agree to lesser counts being left on the file. In such a case a not guilty verdict will not be entered and (in theory) with the leave of the court the CPS may be permitted to re-open the case at a later date.

10.6.3 Guilty pleas

If the defendant pleads guilty at the PCMH, the judge will either sentence him immediately or, if necessary, adjourn sentence for the preparation of pre-sentence reports, such as medical reports or reports from the Probation Service (see **12.2**). The judge may also need to adjourn the case if the defendant pleads guilty but disputes the specific factual allegations made against him by the prosecution witnesses. In such a situation a separate hearing (called a '*Newton* hearing' – see

12.4) will be necessary to determine the factual basis on which the defendant will be sentenced. If the case is adjourned, the defendant will either be released on bail or remanded in custody pending either the sentencing hearing or the 'Newton hearing'.

10.6.4   Indication of sentence

Following the judgment of the Court of Appeal in *R v Goodyear* [2005] EWCA Crim 888, a judge is now permitted at the PCMH to give a defendant an advance indication of the likely sentence he would receive were he to enter a guilty plea at that stage. The defendant must specifically ask for such an indication. If the judge gives an indication and the defendant then enters a guilty plea, the indication given by the judge will be binding (this is very similar to the defendant's ability to ask for an indication of sentence at the allocation hearing in the magistrates' court – see **6.10.3**). It is likely that a defendant will ask for an indication of plea in case where he would be prepared to enter a guilty plea if the judge indicated that he would deal with the case other than by way of a custodial sentence.

10.6.5   Not guilty pleas

If the defendant pleads not guilty at the PCMH, the judge will then consider if any further directions are necessary to prepare the case for trial. To determine whether further directions may be necessary, the judge will require the prosecution and defence advocates present at the PCMH to be in a position to supply him with the following information:

(a)   a summary of the issues in the case;

(b)   details of the number of witnesses who will be giving oral evidence at trial and the estimated length of the trial;

(c)   whether the transcript(s) of the defendant's police station interview(s) require(s) editing;

(d)   whether a defence statement has been served and, if so, whether there is there any issue as to the adequacy of the statement;

(e)   whether the prosecution will be serving any additional evidence;

(f)   whether there is any dispute as to the adequacy of disclosure of unused material by the prosecution;

(g)   whether any expert evidence is to be called and, if so, whether any additional directions are needed in respect of this;

(h)   whether any further directions are necessary concerning hearsay or bad character evidence;

(i)   whether special measures are required for any witnesses;

(j)   any facts which can be formally admitted;

(k)   any points of law or issues concerning the admissibility of evidence which are likely to arise at trial;

(l)   dates of availability to attend trial of the witnesses and the advocates.

A copy of the prescribed form that the advocates must complete prior to the PCMH taking place is set out at **10.13.4** below.

10.6.6   Listing the case for trial

At the PCMH, the judge will give any further case management directions that are necessary in the light of the information disclosed by the parties (see **10.6.5** above), and then either fix a date for the defendant's trial or place the case in the 'warned list'. The warned list is a list of cases awaiting trial that have not been given a fixed date for the trial to start. If a case is placed in the warned list, the Crown Court will contact the defendant's solicitor to let him know that the case has been listed for trial shortly before the date when the trial is due to start.

At the conclusion of the PCMH, the defendant will either be released on bail, or remanded in custody pending his trial.

10.6.7 Change of plea

A defendant who initially enters a not guilty plea may, at the discretion of the judge, change this to a guilty plea at any time before the jury return their verdict. This is likely to happen if a defendant admitted his guilt but pleaded not guilty in the hope that a successful submission of no case to answer could be made at the end of the prosecution case but before the defendant needed to give evidence. If the submission is unsuccessful, the defendant will change his plea to guilty. A defendant may also change his plea to guilty during the trial if the judge makes a ruling on a point of law or the admissibility of a piece of evidence which deprives the defendant of a defence he wanted to rely on.

10.7 Role of the defence solicitor

10.7.1 Rights of audience

Most advocacy in the Crown Court is carried out by barristers (collectively referred to as counsel), whom the solicitor will 'brief' to represent the defendant in the Crown Court proceedings. Similarly the CPS will brief counsel to conduct the prosecution case in the Crown Court.

Solicitors generally have rights of audience in the Crown Court which are limited to:

(a)   appeals against the refusal of bail by the magistrates (see **7.8**);

(b)   appeals against conviction and/or sentence from a magistrates' court, provided a member of the solicitor's firm conducted the hearing in the magistrates' court (see **13.2.1**);

(c)   representing a defendant who has been committed by the magistrates' court to the Crown Court for sentence following a guilty plea at the plea before venue hearing in the magistrates' court, provided a member of the solicitor's firm conducted the hearing in the magistrates' court (see **6.9**); and

(d)   preliminary hearings in the Crown Court where the defendant has been sent for trial (see **10.5.2** above).

A solicitor is therefore unable to represent his client at a trial in the Crown Court, unless the solicitor has obtained an additional qualification (which is available from The Law Society) giving him rights of audience in the higher courts (which includes the Crown Court).

Although some solicitors have obtained such qualifications, most criminal defence solicitors still prefer to brief counsel to conduct a Crown Court trial.

10.7.2 Briefing counsel

If counsel is to be instructed in the Crown Court, a brief to counsel should be prepared and sent to counsel's clerk as soon as the case has been sent for trial by the magistrates' court. The brief should be as full as possible and should be broken down into sections, as follows:

(a)   *Enclosures* – this will list all the documents that are being sent to the barrister along with the brief (such as prosecution witness statements, correspondence with the prosecution, the draft indictment, police station interview transcripts, a copy of the representation order, the defendant's witness statement, copies of any hearsay or bad character notices given or received, etc).

(b)   *Introduction* – this deals with basic personal information about the defendant, the charge, the history of the case, bail arrangements and the prosecution witnesses who are to attend trial.

(c)   *Prosecution case* – this contains a summary of the evidence to be given by each prosecution witness (and may also contain an analysis of the strengths and weaknesses of the prosecution case).

(d)   *Defence case* – this contains a summary of the defence evidence, including details of the defendant's version of events and any supporting evidence, such as a witness who supports the defendant's alibi (the solicitor may also attempt to assess the strengths and weaknesses of the defendant's case).

(e)   *Evidence and related procedural issues* – any significant points of evidence likely to arise at trial should be highlighted for the benefit of counsel. This may include, for example, issues relating to the admissibility of a confession, hearsay evidence or bad character evidence, whether adverse inferences may be drawn from the defendant's silence at the police station, or whether the case involves evidence from a '*Turnbull* witness'. Any related procedural issues should be covered as well, such as the preparation of the defence statement, and the giving or receiving of notices or applications under Parts 34 and 35 of the Criminal Procedure Rules in relation to hearsay evidence or bad character evidence (see **Chapters 19** and **22**).

(f)   *Mitigation* – any facts relevant to mitigation in the event of the defendant being convicted should be mentioned. If the defendant has any previous convictions, these should (if possible) be distinguished from the facts of the current offence. In the case of a defendant who is pleading not guilty, this section of the brief will focus on 'offender' rather than 'offence' mitigation, since the defendant is denying having committed the offence (see **12.7.4**).

(g)   *Conclusion* – counsel will normally be asked in the conclusion to advise the defendant in conference, to attend the PCMH, to represent the defendant at trial and, if necessary, to make a plea in mitigation on the defendant's behalf following conviction. If the defendant is convicted, counsel should also be asked to provide written advice on whether there is any merit in an appeal against conviction and/or sentence being made.

An example of a completed brief to counsel is set out below.

Key skill – preparing a brief to counsel

BRIEF TO COUNSEL

IN THE CROWN COURT   Case No CH 060248

AT CHESTER

R

—v—

GARY PAUL DICKSON

BRIEF TO COUNSEL ON BEHALF OF THE DEFENDANT TO APPEAR AT THE PLEA
AND CASE MANAGEMENT HEARING ON THURSDAY 5TH APRIL 2007 AT
10.30AM AND AT THE TRIAL ON A DATE TO BE FIXED

Counsel has copies of the following documents:

1. Representation order
2. Custody record
3. Charge sheet
4. Draft indictment
5. Prosecution case papers comprising:
    statement of PC Gareth Chambers
    statement of John Barnard
    statement of Vince Lamb
    statement of Peter Hansen
    statement of Dr Harbhajan Singh
    record of audio-recorded interview at police station
6. List of Dickson's previous convictions
7. Statement of Gary Paul Dickson
8. Dickson's comments on the prosecution witness statements
9. Statement of Jill Summers
10. Directions given by magistrates (for case sent to Crown Court under s 51)
11. Prosecution schedule of non-sensitive unused material
12. Defence statement
13. Initial description of assailant given by John Barnard
14. Video identification record
15. Prosecution notice of intention to adduce evidence of the defendant's bad character at trial
16. Defence application to exclude evidence of the defendant's bad character at trial.
17. Correspondence received from the CPS.

INTRODUCTION

Counsel is instructed on behalf of Gary Paul Dickson of 17 Marsh Street, Chester
CH3 7LW. The defendant is on conditional bail, the condition being that he reside
at this address and report to his local police station every second day. The
defendant is charged with assaulting one Vincent Lamb on 18th December 2006,
causing Mr Lamb actual bodily harm, contrary to s 47 of the Offences Against the
Person Act 1861. The defendant will plead not guilty. At a plea before venue before
Chester Magistrates' Court on 8th January 2007, the magistrates declined

jurisdiction and the case was sent to the Crown Court for trial pursuant to s 51 of the Crime and Disorder Act 1998. No preliminary hearing at the Crown Court was deemed necessary, and the magistrates gave directions for the parties to prepare for the plea and case management hearing on 5th April 2007.

In accordance with these directions, the prosecution have served the evidence on which they seek to rely at trial. The defence have confirmed that all prosecution witnesses will be required to attend the trial to give oral evidence, with the exception of PC Peter Hansen and Dr Singh. The prosecution have confirmed in writing that they do not have any unused material which might reasonably undermine the case for the prosecution or assist the case for the defence, and a schedule of non-sensitive unused material has been supplied. A defence statement has been served. The prosecution have reviewed their position in respect of the disclosure of unused material following the service of the defence statement, and have served a copy of the first description of the individual who committed the assault on Vincent Lamb given to the police by the prosecution witness, John Barnard, together with the video identification record referred to at item 9 in the schedule of non-sensitive unused prosecution material. The prosecution have served notice that they intend to introduce evidence of the defendant's bad character at trial. An application to exclude evidence of the defendant's bad character at trial has been made.

THE PROSECUTION CASE

The prosecution case is that on the evening of Monday 18th December 2006 the defendant was working as a bouncer at Connolley's nightclub in Chester. The defendant left work at just prior to 3.15 am the following morning, driving a dark blue VW Golf registration number L251 CVM. On his way home, the defendant stopped his car, got out and assaulted Vince Lamb, who had been a guest disc jockey at Connolley's nightclub that evening. The defendant then got back in his car and drove away. At the time of the assault, Mr Lamb was walking back to the multi-storey car park where his own car was parked. The allegation is that the defendant punched Mr Lamb several times in the face. The assault was witnessed by John Barnard, who later picked out the defendant in a video identification at Chester police station. Mr Lamb sustained a fractured nose and a split left eyebrow. When interviewed about the assault at the police station, the defendant confessed to having committed the offence.

THE DEFENCE CASE

The defendant accepts that he was working as a bouncer at Connolley's that evening and that he does own a VW Golf registration number L251 CVM. The defendant does not know Vince Lamb. Whilst Mr Lamb may have been a guest disc jockey at Connolley's that evening, the defendant was not aware of this because he was standing at the entrance to the nightclub rather than inside the nightclub premises. The defendant left work at 1.30 am and drove straight home to 17 Marsh Street, Chester. At the time of the alleged assault on Mr Lamb, the defendant was asleep in bed with his partner, Ms Jill Summers. John Barnard has made a mistake in identifying the defendant as the person who committed the assault. The defendant accepts that he made a confession at the police station, but says he made the confession only as a result of the conduct of the police both before and during the interview. The defendant will say that the confession is untrue.

EVIDENCE

Counsel's attention is particularly drawn to the following points of evidence:

(i) The identification evidence given by John Barnard – Mr Barnard is not known to the defendant and there is no suggestion that Mr Barnard's evidence has been intentionally fabricated. The defendant will say that Mr Barnard is simply mistaken. There do not appear to be any grounds on which the admissibility of the identification evidence given by John Barnard may be challenged under s 78 of PACE 1984. The record of the video identification suggests that the video identification procedure was carried out in accordance with the requirements of Code D. The credibility of the evidence given by Mr Barnard will need to be challenged at trial under the *Turnbull* guidelines, in particular that Mr Barnard saw the assault from a distance of some 50 metres away, at a time when it was dark and after he had consumed a substantial amount of alcohol. Further, the initial description of the attacker which Mr Barnard gave to the police differs in several respects from the actual appearance of Mr Dickson.

(ii) The confession – the admissibility of the defendant's confession will need to be challenged at trial under s 76 and s 78 of the Police and Criminal Evidence Act 1984. The police appear to have actively dissuaded the defendant from obtaining legal advice prior to being interviewed, and the conduct of the interview could be said to be oppressive or, at the very least, such as to render the defendant's confession unreliable. The interviewing officer gives a clear impression to the defendant that he will be detained at the police station until he makes a confession. There are several breaches of Code C.

(iii) The defendant's previous convictions – the defendant has one previous conviction for s 47 assault in December 2005, and two convictions for threatening behaviour in September 2004 and March 2005. The prosecution have given notice that they intend to adduce evidence of these convictions at trial under s 101(1)(d) of the Criminal Justice Act 2003 in order to demonstrate that the defendant has a propensity to commit offences of this kind. This application has been opposed because there is no factual similarity between these offences and the current offence, and these convictions do not demonstrate a propensity to commit offences of the kind charged (*R v Hanson & Others* [2005] Crim LR 787). The previous offences were all committed in the course of the defendant's employment as a bouncer, whereas the current offence is alleged to have occurred outside the course of the defendant's employment. The admissibility of these convictions is also challenged under s 101(3) of the Criminal Justice Act 2003, on the basis that to raise such convictions would be unfair to the defendant as, in the eyes of the jury, such convictions would be more prejudicial than probative of the defendant's guilt.

(iv) The alibi defence – this defence has been confirmed in the defence statement which has been served on the prosecution. Ms Summers has provided a statement confirming details of the alibi, and has confirmed that she will attend trial to give evidence on the defendant's behalf.

MITIGATION

Instructing solicitors have considered the question of a plea in mitigation if the defendant is convicted. The defendant is aged 27 and resides with Ms Summers in a property owned by Ms Summer's parents. In addition to working on a part-time basis as a bouncer, the defendant works on a contract basis as a scaffolder and steeplejack. The defendant left school at 16 and joined the army. The defendant left the army in 2001 when he moved to the Chester area.

CONFERENCE

Counsel is requested to advise in conference, to attend the plea and case management hearing, to represent the defendant at trial on a plea of not guilty and, if necessary, to make a plea in mitigation on behalf of the defendant. In the event of the defendant being convicted, counsel is asked to advise in writing on the prospects of a successful appeal being made to the Court of Appeal against conviction and/or sentence.

Dated this 1st day of March 2007

Collaws Solicitors

10.7.3 Conference with counsel

Counsel will usually be instructed immediately after the hearing at which the magistrates send the case to Crown Court for trial. Unless a preliminary hearing is necessary, any conference with counsel is likely to take place prior to the PCMH. Although a conference will not take place in every case, it is sensible for a conference to be arranged, if for no other reason than to introduce counsel to the client before the PCMH. It can be an unnerving experience for a client to meet counsel who is to represent him for the first time on the morning of the PCMH.

A conference with counsel should always be held when:

(a)   the defendant is to enter a not guilty plea (counsel will need to make an assessment as to how the defendant will perform as a witness and to 'test' the defendant on the strength of his case);

(b)   the defendant requires advice from counsel as to the plea he should enter;

(c)   there are any particular complications in the case, or if the case may involve serious consequences (such as a custodial sentence being likely in the event that the defendant is convicted); or

(d)   there is a need to consider with the defendant any tactical or evidential matters (for example, whether the defendant should give evidence at trial, or whether the defendant's previous convictions are likely to emerge in evidence at trial).

10.7.4 Preparation for trial

Although the barrister will present the defendant's case at trial, the defendant's solicitor still has an important role to play in preparing the case for trial. For example, at the conference with counsel, counsel may indicate that he requires a statement to be obtained from a particular witness, or that the CPS should be asked to divulge some additional information or document. It will be the solicitor's job to contact the relevant witness, or to write to the CPS in such circumstances.

Similarly, the defendant's solicitor will need ensure that a representative from his office attends the trial to assist counsel and, in particular, to take a detailed note of what each witness says when giving evidence. Such a note will often be used by counsel when preparing his closing argument for the jury (see **10.10** below). A note of the evidence and the judge's summing up may also be helpful when drafting grounds of appeal against sentence and/or conviction (see **Chapter 13**).

10.8 Disclosure

10.8.1 Introduction

The disclosure obligations with which both the CPS and the defendant must comply in a case before the Crown Court are, just as in a case before the magistrates' court, contained in the Criminal Procedure and Investigations Act (CPIA) 1996. In addition, however, the parties in a Crown Court case must comply with a Disclosure Protocol published in February 2006, 'Disclosure: A Protocol for the Control and Management of Unused Material in the Crown Court'. The Protocol provides that, when a party is obliged to provide disclosure, such disclosure should be given promptly. When checking and recording the existence of any unused material (see **10.8.2** below), the police must act 'thoroughly, scrupulously and fairly'. The CPS must then make full and prompt disclosure of unused material to the defendant's solicitor to ensure that 'justice is not delayed, denied or frustrated'. Defence statements (see **10.8.3** below) must be sufficiently detailed to comply with the requirements of the CPIA 1996 and must be served by the due date. In *R v K* [2006] EWCA Crim 724, the Court of Appeal held that the Protocol must be applied by trial judges, and prosecuting and defence counsel.

10.8.2 Prosecution duty of disclosure

Just as in the magistrates' court, the CPS is obliged to serve on the defendant all the evidence on which it wishes to rely at trial to prove the defendant's guilt. The directions referred to at **10.5.1** above provide for the prosecution to serve their evidence on the defence within specified time limits.

In addition to this evidence, the prosecution will also have a quantity of 'unused material', such as statements from witnesses whom the CPS does not intend to call to give evidence at trial. The CPS is obliged to retain this material; and in the event of the defendant entering a not guilty plea, the CPS must disclose any such material to the defendant if the material satisfies the test set out in s 3 of the CPIA 1996. Section 3 provides that such material must be disclosed if it 'might reasonably be considered capable of undermining the case for the prosecution ... or of assisting the case for the accused'. This is the same test as is applied in the magistrates' court, and examples of the types of material that may need to be disclosed by the CPS are given in **8.4.6.2**. The case management directions referred to at **10.5.1** above provide that the CPS must make initial disclosure of any unused material in its possession which satisfies the above test at the same time as disclosing the evidence on which it wishes to rely at court. In practice the CPS will send to the defendant's solicitor a schedule of all the unused material in its possession, together with copies of any items on the schedule which the CPS considers satisfy the above test for disclosure.

The duty of disclosure on the CPS is ongoing, and so the CPS must apply this test to any further material it receives after making initial disclosure (CPIA 1996, s 7A). The CPS must also consider the need to make further disclosure in the light of any information received from the defence about the nature of the defence case (see **10.8.3** below).

If the defendant's solicitor considers that the disclosure made by the CPS is incomplete, he will request disclosure of any 'missing' items when drafting the defence statement (see **10.8.4** below). The disclosure given by the CPS may be incomplete if:

(a)   the CPS has failed to supply a copy of a document listed on the schedule of unused material because it erroneously considers that document does not satisfy the above disclosure test; or

(b)   the CPS has failed to include on the list a document which the defendant's solicitor believes it may have in its possession (for example, a statement from a witness whose evidence may assist the defendant's case).

10.8.3   Defence disclosure

Once the CPS has made its initial disclosure of unused material, the onus switches to the defendant's solicitor. If the defendant is to enter a not guilty plea, within 14 days of the CPS making initial disclosure of any unused material it has, the defendant should serve a defence statement (sometimes referred to as a 'Defence Case Statement' or DCS) on the CPS and send a copy of the statement to the Crown Court. This is a part of the standard case management directions that the magistrates will give when the case is sent to Crown Court for trial (see **10.5.1** above). This time limit applies even if the initial disclosure made by the CPS is incomplete or otherwise defective (*DPP v Wood; DPP v McGillicuddy* [2006] EWHC (Admin) 32). If the case is particularly complex and 14 days will be insufficient, the defendant may apply to the court for a longer period within which to serve the defence statement. In a case involving two or more co-accused, s 5A of the CPIA 1996 permits the court to make an order that a copy of the defence statement made by each defendant is to be served on the other defendants in the case. The requirements for the contents of a defence statement are set out at **10.8.4** below.

Although the giving of a defence statement is not strictly a mandatory requirement, in practice a defence statement will always be given in the Crown Court if the defendant is to plead not guilty. This is because the court is permitted to draw an adverse inference against the defendant if a defence statement is not provided (see **10.8.6** below). This represents a significant difference between the magistrates' court and the Crown Court. In the magistrates' court, defence statements are very rarely given because the court is not permitted to draw an adverse inference from the absence of such a statement, and solicitors representing defendants are unwilling to provide the CPS with details of their clients' defence in advance of trial.

10.8.4   Contents of the defence statement

The contents of the defence statement are prescribed by s 6A of the CPIA 1996. The defence statement must be a written statement which:

(a)   sets out the nature of the defence, including any particular defences on which the defendant intends to rely (for example, alibi or self-defence);

(b)   indicates the matters of fact on which the defendant takes issue with the prosecution and why he takes such issue;

(c)   indicates any points of law (including any point as to the admissibility of evidence) that the defendant wishes to take at trial, and any legal authority on which the defendant intends to rely for this purpose; and

(d)   in the case of an alibi defence, provides the name, address and date of birth of any alibi witness, or as many of these details as are known to the defendant.

It is normal practice when drafting a defence statement also to include a paragraph asking if a schedule of sensitive material has been prepared and, if so, if the prosecution have made an application to court for an order that they are not obliged to disclose any such material. The types of document that might fall under this heading are described at **8.4.6.4**.

The Disclosure Protocol referred to at **10.8.1** above states:

> [The defence statement] must identify the matters of fact upon which the accused takes issue with the prosecution, and the reason why, in relation to each disputed matter of fact. It must further identify any point of law (including points as to the admissibility of evidence, or abuse of process) which the accused proposes to take, and identify authorities relied on in relation to each point of law. Where an alibi defence is relied on, the particulars must [be given]. Judges will expect to see defence statements that contain a clear and detailed exposition of the issues of fact and law in the case.

The defence are under a continuing duty to update the defence statement if the details to be given under any of the above points should change before trial (if, for example, a witness comes forward who is able to support an alibi given by the defendant and whose existence was unknown at the time the initial defence statement was prepared) (CPIA 1996, s 6B(3)).

An example of a completed defence statement is set out below.

Key skill – drafting the defence statement

DEFENCE STATEMENT

(Criminal Procedure and Investigations Act 1996, sections 5 & 6)

<u>Crown Court Case No CH 060248</u>

To the prosecutor: Crown Prosecution Service (Cheshire)

To the Court: Chester Crown Court

Name of accused: Gary Paul Dickson

Charge: Assault Occasioning Actual Bodily Harm (Offences Against the Person Act 1861, section 47)

Name and address of solicitors for the accused: Collaws Solicitors, 129 Westgate, Chester CH1 5RJ

Date:

If called upon to establish a defence at trial, the following statement is served in accordance with the provisions of the Criminal Procedure and Investigations Act 1996.

1.   **The nature of the accused's defence is:** alibi.

2.   **The accused takes issue with the prosecution in relation to the following matters of fact:**
   (i)   the allegation that the accused was in the vicinity of Connelley's nightclub in Chester city centre at or about 3.15 am on 18th December 2006;
   (ii)   the allegation that the accused's vehicle registration number L251 CVM was in the vicinity of Connelley's nightclub in Chester city centre at or about 3.15 am on 18th December 2006;
   (iii) the allegation that the accused assaulted the complainant Vincent Lamb causing him actual bodily harm.
   (iv)   the truthfulness of the confession made by the accused when questioned by the police about the assault at Chester Police Station on 18th December 2006.

3.   **The accused takes issue with the prosecution in relation to the matters of fact noted above for the following reasons:**
   (i)   the prosecution witness John Barnard is mistaken both in his identification of accused as the individual who committed the assault, and in his identification of the accused's vehicle as the vehicle driven by the individual who committed the assault;

   (ii)   the confession is untrue and was made by the accused only as a result of the police interviewing the accused at the police station in an improper manner.

4.   **The accused will give the following evidence of alibi:** that at 3.15 am on 18th December 2006 the accused was at his home address of 17 Marsh Street, Chester CH3 7LW. The accused will call a witness in support of this alibi. The name of the witness is Jill Summers (date of birth: 16/03/80). The address of the witness is 17 Marsh Street, Chester CH3 7LW.

5.   **The accused will raise the following points of law at trial:**

   (i)   the reliability of the identification evidence given by the prosecution witness John Barnard will be challenged under the principles set out in *R v Turnbull* [1977] QB 224;

   (ii) the admissibility of the confession made by the accused will be challenged under sections 76 and 78 of the Police and Criminal Evidence Act 1984, on the basis that the conduct of the interview contravened Code C of the Codes of Practice;

   (iii) the prosecution has served notice that, pursuant to s 101(d) of the Criminal Justice Act 2003, it will at trial introduce evidence of the accused's convictions for the following offences in order to demonstrate that the accused has a propensity to commit offences of the kind charged: (a) assault occasioning actual bodily harm – 13 December 2005; (b) threatening behaviour – 17 March 2005; and (c) threatening behaviour – 10 September 2004.

   This application will be opposed because these convictions do not demonstrate a propensity for the accused to commit offences of the kind with which he is charged (*R v Hanson, Gilmore & Pickstone* [2005] Crim LR 787). Should the court determine that these convictions do establish such a propensity, an application will be made to exclude such convictions under s 101(3) of the Criminal Justice Act 2003 on the basis that the admission of these convictions would have such an adverse effect on the fairness of the proceedings that the court ought not to admit them.

6.   **The accused requests the following disclosure of material which might undermine the prosecution case or which might assist the defence disclosed by this statement:**

   The first description given to the police by the prosecution witness John Barnard of the individual who committed the assault on Vincent Lamb on 18th December 2006.

   The video identification record referred to at item 9 in the schedule of non-sensitive unused prosecution material.

   [*The statement would list here any material the prosecution have not disclosed which the defence suspect the prosecution may have, any items mentioned on the schedule of non-sensitive unused material which have not actually been supplied to the defence, or any items mentioned in the schedule which should in fact have been disclosed as part of the prosecution case In each case, such items would be mentioned only if the defence solicitor considered that they would satisfy the test for disclosure.*]

7.   **Sensitive materials**

   (i)   Has a sensitive materials schedule been prepared?

   (ii) Has the prosecutor been informed separately of the existence of material deemed to be too sensitive to be included in the schedule?

   (iii) Has the prosecutor been informed separately of information about any prosecution witnesses' previous convictions (including spent convictions) or disciplinary issues involving police officers relating to this matter?

   (iv) If the answer to (i), (ii) or (iii) above is yes, has the prosecutor decided that he is not under a duty to disclose:

      (a)   any material in (i) above?

(b)   any material in (ii) above?

(c)   any material in (iii) above?

(v)   If the answer to (i), (ii) or (iii) above is yes, has an application been made to the court to order non-disclosure of any such material?

The defence reserves the right to amend the above statement on the receipt of further evidence.

Signed: *Gary Paul Dickson*

Dated: *19th February 2007*

10.8.5   Obtaining the defendant's approval of the defence statement

Prior to the enactment of the CJA 2003, there was some confusion as to what a trial judge should do when a defendant claimed that his solicitor had not shown him a copy of his defence statement and the defence he raised at trial was different to the defence disclosed in that statement. It was unclear whether or not a judge was permitted invite a jury to draw adverse inferences in such circumstances.

Any doubts have been removed by provisions in Pt 5 of the CJA 2003, which inserts a new s 6E into the CPIA 1996. This stipulates that defence statements will be deemed to be given with the authority of the defendant unless the contrary is proved. A defendant's solicitor should therefore ensure that the defendant sees and approves a copy of the defence statement before this is served. As the defence statement will be drafted either by the defendant's solicitor or, if time permits, by counsel, the usual practice will be for the defendant's solicitor (or counsel) to sign the original statement which is served, and for the defendant to sign a copy of the statement which will be kept on the solicitor's file.

10.8.6   When may the court draw an adverse inference?

The reason why defence statements are effectively obligatory for defendants pleading not guilty in the Crown Court is that if there are any 'faults' in disclosure given by the defence, the court may draw an adverse inference from this when determining the defendant's guilt (CPIA 1996, s 11). These faults include:

(a)   failing to provide a defence statement at all;

(b)   late service of the defence statement;

(c)   serving a defence statement that is incomplete;

(d)   serving a defence statement which is not consistent with the defence put forward at trial; and

(e)   failing to update a defence statement.

If any of these faults occurs the court or, with leave, any other party (such as the prosecution or any co-accused) may make such comments as appear appropriate, and the court or jury may draw such inferences as appear proper when deciding whether the defendant is guilty.

Example 1

Philippa is charged with theft. Her case is case is sent for trial at the Crown Court. She enters a not guilty plea at the PCMH. Philippa fails to serve a defence statement on the CPS. At her trial Philippa raises the defence of alibi, and claims that the prosecution witnesses who identified her as the person who committed the theft are mistaken. As Philippa failed to serve a defence statement setting out this defence, the trial judge or, with leave, the prosecution may comment on this and the jury may draw such inferences as appear proper.

Example 2

Javed is charged with unlawful wounding. His case is sent for trial at Crown Court. At the PCMH he enters a not guilty plea. In his defence statement, Javed claims that he was not present at the time of the alleged incident and raises the defence of alibi. At his trial, Javed accepts that he was present at the time of the incident and instead raises the defence of self-defence. As there is a disparity between what was said in his defence statement and the defence he is raising at trial, the judge or, with leave, the prosecution may comment on this and the jury may draw such inferences as appear proper.

Example 3

Veronica is charged with theft. She enters a not guilty plea and the magistrates send her case to Crown Court for trial. In her defence statement, Veronica raises the defence of alibi and names Gregory as an alibi witness. At her trial Veronica calls three witnesses (Gregory, Richard and Megan) to support her alibi. As no reference was made to Richard or Megan in her defence statement, the judge or, with leave, the prosecution may comment on this and the jury may draw such inferences as appear proper.

In addition to the above, the trial judge has the power to order that a copy of the defence statement be disclosed to the jury to assist them in understanding the issues in the case (CPIA 1996, s 6E).

The judge may also order that a copy of the defence statement be supplied to any co-accused in a case where there are two or more defendants.

10.8.7 Other defence disclosure obligations

As in the magistrates' court, the defendant is not required to provide notice in advance that he will or will not be giving evidence on his own behalf at trial. However, under s 6C of the CPIA 1996, the defendant must serve a notice on the CPS and the court giving the names, addresses and dates of birth of any witnesses that he intends to call to give evidence on his behalf. Under s 6D of the CPIA 1996, the defendant must also serve details of the name and address of any expert witness he has consulted, even if that expert is not to be called to give evidence (see 8.4.2.3).

10.8.8 Further disclosure obligations on the prosecution

The only 'reward' for a defendant who provides a defence statement is that the CPS must review its initial disclosure of unused material and determine if there is any further unused material in its possession which, in light of the matters contained in the defence statement, might now be deemed capable of undermining the case for the prosecution or of assisting the case for the defendant.

Example

Gavin is jointly charged with Philip with the production of cannabis at premises owned by Philip. Gavin's defence is that he knows nothing about the production of cannabis at the premises and was employed by Philip at the premises solely to clean and valet cars. The CPS is not aware that this is the basis of Gavin's defence because he refused to answer any questions when interviewed at the police station. As part of their investigations, the police recover from the premises a number of documents, including receipts for various items of car-cleaning equipment. The CPS does not intend to use these receipts in evidence and is not under a duty to disclose such documents to Gavin's solicitor, because the documents neither undermine the prosecution case nor assist the case for the defence (because there has been no indication as to what the defence case is).

Gavin's solicitor subsequently serves a defence statement on the CPS stating that Gavin knew nothing about the premises being used for the production of cannabis and confirming that Gavin was employed at the premises solely to valet cars. The CPS is under a continuing duty of disclosure and so, in the light of the defence statement, it must now disclose the receipts to Gavin's solicitor, as the receipts assist Gavin's defence that he had an innocent explanation for being at the premises.

Section 8 of the CPIA 1996 enables a defendant who has provided a defence statement to make application to the court if the CPS has failed to comply with its continuing duty of disclosure in light of the matters contained in the defence statement. The defendant may ask the court for an order that the CPS disclose material provided the defendant has reasonable cause to believe that there is prosecution material which should have been, but has not been, disclosed. The defendant will only be permitted to make such an application if he has set out in detail in his defence statement the material which he considers the CPS has in its possession which it has not subsequently disclosed.

A flowchart summarising the disclosure obligations imposed on both the CPS and the defendant in respect of summary, either way or indictable-only offences is provided at **10.11** below.

10.9   Pre-trial hearings, preparatory hearings and further evidence

10.9.1   Pre-trial hearings

Section 40 of the CPIA 1996 allows a judge, prior to the trial starting, to rule on the admissibility of evidence and on any question of law relating to the case. The rulings can be made on the application of the prosecution or defence, or on the judge's own motion. During the course of a pre-trial hearing, a judge may use his case management powers to deal with issues (such as the admissibility of disputed points of evidence) by reference to written submissions rather than hearing oral argument (*R v K & Others* – see **10.8.1** above).

10.9.2   Preparatory hearings (CrimPR, Part 15)

Part 3 of the CPIA 1996 creates a statutory scheme for preparatory hearings in long or complex Crown Court cases. A judge, acting either on his own motion or on the application of the prosecution or defence, can order such a hearing to take place if it is likely to bring substantial benefits because of the complexity or likely length of the case. The hearing can be use for any of the following purposes:

(a)   to identify important issues for the jury;

(b)   to help the jury's understanding of the issues;

(c)   to speed up proceedings before the jury;

(d)   to help the judge's management of the trial.

The judge conducting a preparatory hearing has the power to make rulings as to the admissibility of evidence, or on any point of law. Both the CPS and the defendant have the right to appeal to the Court of Appeal against any ruling made by the judge at a preparatory hearing (CrimPR, Part 65).

In addition, the CPS must ask for a preparatory hearing to take place in order to enable an application to be made for the trial to take place without a jury under s 44 of the CJA 2003 (see **10.3** above). A preparatory hearing must also take place if the defendant is charged with a terrorist offence or an offence which has terrorist connections.

10.9.3 Notices of further evidence

A witness may be called to give evidence for the prosecution in the Crown Court even though his witness statement was not served on the defendant in accordance with the standard case management directions given by the magistrates when the case was sent to the Crown Court for trial. It may be, for example, that the witness came forward only after the PCMH had taken place. If the CPS wishes to call additional evidence from a 'new' witness at trial, a notice of intention to do so will be served on the defendant and the Crown Court. The notice will be accompanied by a copy of the relevant statement.

10.10 Trial procedure

10.10.1 Order of events

The procedure at a trial in the Crown Court is very similar to that in the magistrates' court (see **Chapter 9**). The order of events is as follows:

(a) The jury will be sworn in (commonly referred to as being 'empanelled'). The jury will comprise a randomly selected panel of 12 members of the public between the ages of 18 and 70, whose names are on the electoral roll for the local area and who have resided in the UK for at least five years. Certain persons are ineligible for jury service (for example, anyone suffering from a mental disorder), and certain classes of people are disqualified from being jurors (for example, anyone currently on bail in criminal proceedings).

(b) Prosecuting counsel will then give an opening speech to the jury, explaining what the case is about and what evidence he intends to call. The opening speech will usually contain the following elements:

    (i)   the legal elements of the offence(s) on the indictment;

    (ii) an outline of the evidence the prosecutor intends to call;

    (iii) an explanation of the operation of the burden and standard of proof in a criminal case (see **Chapter 16**);

Depending on the facts of the case, prosecuting counsel may highlight to the jury any points of law that he anticipates may arise during the case and possible defences open to the defendant.

(c) Each prosecution witness will then be called in turn to give evidence, starting with the 'victim' of the alleged crime. Each witness will be examined in chief by prosecuting counsel, cross-examined by defence counsel, and then (if necessary) re-examined by prosecuting counsel. Prosecuting counsel will read out the statements of any witness whose evidence has been accepted by the defendant under the s 9 procedure (see **8.4.4**) without the witness who gave the statement being required to attend court in person. He will also read out the statement of an witness whose evidence is to be admitted as hearsay evidence (see **Chapter 19**).

(d) If any disputes as to points of law or arguments as to the admissibility of evidence arise, a hearing known as a 'voire dire' (or a 'trial within a trial') will take place in the absence of the jury. Such hearings normally arise in the context of disputes as to the admissibility of a piece of evidence upon which the prosecution seek to rely (for example, a disputed confession). It is normal practice for defence counsel to notify prosecuting counsel prior to the trial of any items of prosecution evidence of which he will seek to challenge the admissibility at trial. Prosecuting counsel will not mention these items of evidence during his opening speech.

When the relevant point is reached during the presentation of the prosecution case, the judge will ask the jury to retire and he will then conduct the voire dire. The judge will hear evidence from witnesses, and then legal submissions from both prosecuting and defence counsel about the item of evidence in dispute. The judge will then make his ruling. If the judge rules that a particular piece of evidence is inadmissible, the jury will never hear about that piece of evidence. If the judge rules that the evidence is admissible, the party wishing to rely on that evidence (usually the prosecution) may then raise it during the trial. It will still be open to the other party (usually the defence) to attempt to undermine the reliability or cogency of that evidence either when cross-examining the witness giving the evidence, or when examining their own witnesses in chief.

(e)   At the conclusion of the prosecution case, defence counsel may make a submission that there is no case for the defendant to answer. This submission will be made to the judge in the absence of the jury. The test which the judge will apply in deciding whether there is a case to answer is known as the 'Galbraith test', following the case of R v Galbraith [1981] 2 All ER 1060 in which it was first set out. The judge will ask himself if the prosecution evidence, taken at its highest, is such that a jury properly directed could not properly convict on it. For the submission to succeed, defence counsel will need to show that the prosecution have failed to adduce evidence in support of an essential element of the offence, or that, even taking the best possible view of the prosecution evidence, the case against the defendant is so unreliable that a jury could not convict on it. If the judge rejects a submission of no case to answer, he should give brief reasons for deciding that there is sufficient evidence to go before the jury (R v Powell [2006] All ER (D) 146 (Jan)).

(f)   If the submission of no case to answer is successful, the jury will be asked to return and the judge will instruct them to return a verdict of not guilty. If the submission of no case to answer is unsuccessful, the judge may permit a defendant to change his plea from not guilty to guilty at this stage. A defendant may wish to do this if, for example, he has admitted his guilt to his solicitor but put the prosecution to proof of their case. A defendant may also wish to change his plea to guilty at the end of the prosecution case if the trial judge has made a ruling on a point of law, or on the admissibility of a piece of evidence, which deprives the defendant of a defence he had hoped to rely upon.

(g)   If the submission of no case to answer is unsuccessful (and the defendant does not seek to change his plea), defence counsel will then present the defendant's case. If the defence intend calling a witness or witnesses in addition to the defendant, defence counsel is entitled to make an opening speech to the jury. He is not entitled to do this if only the defendant is to give evidence. If there is more than one defendant, each defendant will present his case in turn. The order in which this is done will follow the order in which the defendants' names appear on the indictment.

(h)   Witnesses for the defence will then be called to give evidence. The defendant will be called first (assuming he is to give evidence). Should the defendant fail to give evidence, the judge will direct the jury that they may draw an adverse inference from such silence under s 35 of the CJPOA 1994 (see **9.6.1.2**). Each defence witness will be examined in chief by defence counsel, cross-examined by the prosecuting counsel and then (if necessary) re-examined by defence counsel.

(i)   At the conclusion of the defence case, both prosecuting and defence counsel will deliver a closing speech to the jury. Prosecuting counsel will give his closing speech first, followed by defence counsel.

(j)   Before the jury retire to consider their verdict, the judge will then give his 'summing up' to the jury. The summing up has two parts, namely directions on the law and a summary of the evidence.

When the judge directs the jury on the law he will cover three areas:

(i)   the burden and standard of proof (see **Chapter 16**);

(ii)   the legal requirements of the offence; and

(iii) any other issues of law and evidence that have arisen during the trial (for example, a *Turnbull* warning in the case of disputed identification evidence, or a direction as to the drawing of adverse inferences under ss 34 to 37 of the CJPOA 2004).

A very common ground of appeal raised by defendants following conviction at a trial in the Crown Court is that the judge has misdirected the jury on a point of law or evidence. To prevent judges misdirecting the jury, the Judicial Studies Board (JSB) has produced a set of specimen directions for judges to use. These directions cover most issues of law and evidence that are likely to arise during a trial. These directions may be found on the JSB website (www.jsboard.co.uk).

When the judge gives the jury a summary of the evidence, he will provide the following:

(i)   a succinct summary of the issues of fact that the jury has to decide;

(ii)   an accurate and concise summary of the evidence and arguments raised by both prosecution and defence; and

(iii) a correct statement of the inferences the jury are entitled to draw from their conclusions about the facts.

At the end of his summing up, the judge will tell the jury member to appoint a foreman, and will instruct them to retire to consider their verdict and to reach a unanimous conclusion.

(k)   The jury will then retire to consider their verdict. The deliberations of the jury are in private and must remain completely secret. The jurors are permitted to consider only the evidence they have heard at trial when deciding their verdict, and are not permitted to discuss the case with anyone other than their fellow jurors. The jury must decide their verdict unanimously, although a majority verdict of 11:1 or 10:2 will be accepted if, after at least 2 hours and 10 minutes, unanimity is not possible (Juries Act 1974, s 17). If the case was lengthy or in any way complex, the judge is likely to wait much longer than this minimum period before telling the jury that he is prepared to accept a majority verdict.

(l)   If the jury cannot reach a majority verdict within a reasonable time, the judge will discharge the jury. The CPS may then request a re-trial before a new jury.

(m) If the jury find the defendant not guilty, the defendant will be discharged by the judge and told that he is free to go. If the defendant's case was not funded by way of a representation order, the judge will usually order that his legal costs be paid from central funds (ie, by the State).

(n)   If the jury find the defendant guilty, the judge will then proceed to sentence the defendant. The judge will either sentence the defendant immediately, or, if necessary, adjourn sentence so that pre-sentence reports can be obtained (see **Chapter 12**). If the judge adjourns sentence, he will remand the defendant either on bail or in custody. Although there is a presumption in favour of bail for a defendant who has been convicted but not yet sentenced, if the sentencing hearing has been adjourned so that pre-sentence reports may be prepared (see **Chapter 7**), a defendant who has been convicted of a serious offence is very unlikely to be granted bail before sentence. The judge is likely to refuse him bail on the grounds either that the defendant will fail to surrender to custody, or that it would be impractical to prepare the report unless the defendant is in custody. The procedure for sentencing a defendant is described in **Chapter 12**.

A flowchart summarising the above is set out at **10.11.2** below.

10.10.2   Role of the solicitor at trial

If counsel is representing the defendant at trial, it is rare for the solicitor who has been dealing with the matter in the magistrates' court to attend the whole trial. In a complex or lengthy case, the solicitor may attend the first day of the trial, but more commonly a paralegal or trainee solicitor will be sent to 'sit behind counsel'. The representative from the solicitor's firm who attends court will be present at any conference that take place between defence counsel and the defendant at court, and will assist counsel during the trial by taking notes of the evidence given by witnesses, and by making a note of any directions or evidential rulings made by the judge. Such notes will be important because counsel may wish to rely on them either when cross-examining a witness, or when giving his closing speech to the jury. Similarly, notes of comments made by the judge may be useful when a notice of appeal is being drafted based on a misdirection given by the judge (see **Chapter 13**).

The other important function played by the representative from the solicitor's firm who attends the trial is to meet any defence witnesses who are to attend court, and to ensure that such witnesses are ready to give evidence when called. As with witnesses called to give evidence on behalf of a defendant in the magistrates' court, a witness summons should have been obtained for any defence witness required to give evidence. The Crown Court will issue a summons for a witness to attend trial if that witness is likely to give evidence material to the case and it is in the interests of justice for a summons to be issued (Criminal Procedure (Attendance of Witnesses) Act 1965, s 2). The procedural requirements for obtaining a witness summons from the Crown Court are set out in Part 28 of the Criminal Procedure Rules.

At the end of the case, if the defendant has been convicted, counsel will have a further conference with the defendant to advise on the prospects of an appeal against conviction and/or sentence. Such a conference is likely to take place in the cells at the Crown Court. The representative from the solicitor's firm will attend this conference and again take a note of any advice given by counsel.

10.11   Procedural flowcharts

10.11.1   Disclosure (both magistrates' court and Crown Court)

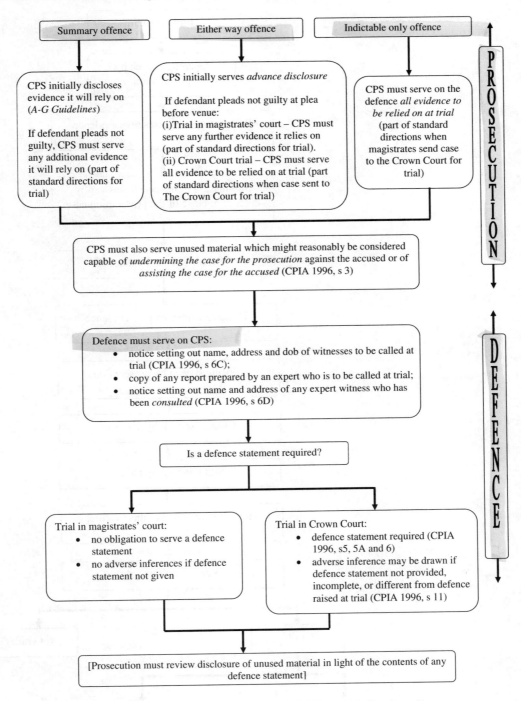

Summary offence

Either way offence

Indictable only offence

CPS initially discloses evidence it will rely on (*A-G Guidelines*)

If defendant pleads not guilty, CPS must serve any additional evidence it will rely on (part of standard directions for trial)

CPS initially serves *advance disclosure*

If defendant pleads not guilty at plea before venue:
(i) Trial in magistrates' court – CPS must serve any further evidence it relies on (part of standard directions for trial).
(ii) Crown Court trial – CPS must serve all evidence to be relied on at trial (part of standard directions when case sent to The Crown Court for trial)

CPS must serve on the defence *all evidence to be relied on at trial* (part of standard directions when magistrates send case to the Crown Court for trial)

CPS must also serve unused material which might reasonably be considered capable of *undermining the case for the prosecution* against the accused or of *assisting the case for the accused* (CPIA 1996, s 3)

Defence must serve on CPS:
- notice setting out name, address and dob of witnesses to be called at trial (CPIA 1996, s 6C);
- copy of any report prepared by an expert who is to be called at trial;
- notice setting out name and address of any expert witness who has been *consulted* (CPIA 1996, s 6D)

Is a defence statement required?

Trial in magistrates' court:
- no obligation to serve a defence statement
- no adverse inferences if defence statement not given

Trial in Crown Court:
- defence statement required (CPIA 1996, s5, 5A and 6)
- adverse inference may be drawn if defence statement not provided, incomplete, or different from defence raised at trial (CPIA 1996, s 11)

[Prosecution must review disclosure of unused material in light of the contents of any defence statement]

PROSECUTION

DEFENCE

10.11.2   Trial procedure in the Crown Court

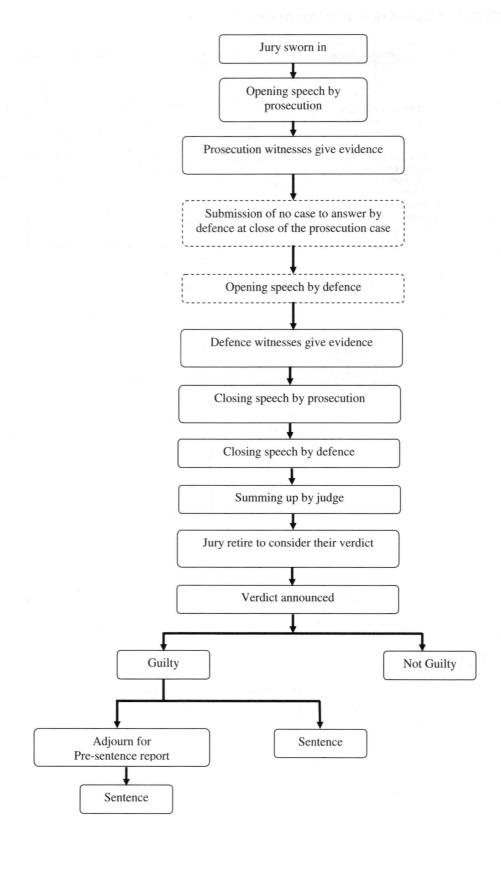

10.12 Checklist

At the end of this chapter you should be able to explain:

- the types of case which are dealt with in the Crown Court;
- the role played by the judge and the jury at a trial in the Crown Court;
- the procedure by which an indictable-only or either way offence is sent for trial in the Crown Court;
- how a defendant may challenge a case that has been sent for trial to the Crown Court;
- the case management directions with which the CPS and the defendant's solicitor will need to comply in a case sent to the Crown Court for trial;
- the purpose of the preliminary hearing and the plea and case management hearing in the Crown Court;
- how to brief counsel to represent the defendant at Crown Court;
- how the defence statement should be drafted;
- the potential consequence in the Crown Court for a defendant who fails to provide a defence statement, or who provides a defence statement which is inaccurate or incomplete;
- the order of events at a trial in the Crown Court.
- the role played by the defence solicitor at a Crown Court trial.

10.13   Key forms

10.13.1   Form B

Statement of Means for Right to Representation in Criminal Proceedings in the Crown Court

Form B

Reference

Now that you have been granted publicly funded representation in the Crown Court you must complete this form and return it to the court at least **4 days** before your first hearing at the Crown Court. If you do not comply, the judge may make a Court Order against you requiring you to pay for all costs incurred in your defence.

If you or your partner are receiving one of the following benefits, you are only required to complete Parts 1 and 2A of this form:

> Income-based Job Seeker's Allowance
>
> Income Support
>
> Pension Credit (Guarantee element)

If you indicate one of the above, and no further enquiries are made of you or your partner, only this information will go before the judge to consider whether to make a Recovery of Defence Costs Order.

A partner is a person with whom the applicant lives as a couple and includes a person with whom the person concerned is not currently living but from whom he or she is not living separate and apart.

You should inform the Court if your circumstances change once you have completed this form and returned it to the Crown Court.

See the Declaration at the end of this form for enquiries that can be made about the information you provide.

Part 1 - Personal details

1a	Surname	
1b	Surname at birth *If different*	
1c	Title *Mr/Mrs/Miss/Ms/other*	1d Date of birth
1e	Forename(s)	
1f	Home address *Including postcode*	
1g	Address where we can contact you *If different from above*	

1h   Marital status
Tick as appropriate

Single ☐   Cohabiting ☐   Widowed ☐

Married ☐   Married but separated ☐   Divorced ☐

Part 2 - Financial position
Part A - Benefits

If you or your partner receive Income-based Job Seeker's Allowance, Income Support or the Guarantee Pension Credit, please provide the following details:

(i)   The address of the Social Security Office, Jobcentre or Pension Credit Office that is/was dealing with you or your partner's claim.

(ii) National Insurance number of the person claiming benefit.
      This is required so that we can verify your, or your partner's, claim with the Benefits Agency, Inland Revenue or Department of Work and Pensions.

(iii) Name of Benefit

(iv) Name of recipient of Benefit

(v)   Date of birth of recipient of Benefit

Please go to the end of the form and sign the Declarations if you have completed this section.

Part B - Income from work

In this section you are asked to give details of the money you receive.
You should answer these questions with annual amounts. Where you are paid monthly, multiply the amount by 12 or where you are paid weekly, multiply the amount by 52.

		You	**Your partner**	**Additional details**	**Court use**
1	Provide details of gross earnings, including bonuses, overtime or commission.				
	Do you or your partner receive benefits from work that are not money? *For example: luncheon vouchers, company car, free health insurance etc. Please specify.*	Yes ☐ No ☐	Yes ☐ No ☐		
	Employer's name and address				
2	Are you or your partner, self-employed/in partnership?	Yes ☐ No ☐	Yes ☐ No ☐	(i) Turnover	
	Indicate nature of work for you and/or your partner.			(ii) Business expenses (not taken out for personal use)	
	Indicate you and/or your partner's role in company.			(iii) Net profit (Turnover minus business expenses) (iv) Period of trading	

Part B - Income (continued)

		You		Your partner		Additional details	Court use
3	Part-time work: gross earnings including bonuses, commission and overtime.						
	Employer's name and address						
4	Are you or your partner a shareholder in a private limited company, or are you or your partner a company director?	Yes ☐	No ☐	Yes ☐	No ☐	Provide details for you and/or your partner.	
5	Is anybody else, including a company or other body, supporting either you or your partner financially or making resources available to either of you?	Yes ☐	No ☐	Yes ☐	No ☐	Examples of, non-financial support may include the following: Do you live in someone else's house or drive someone else's car? Indicate the nature of the support and what period this support covered. Provide details of connection to individual or company, and name the individual or company.	
6	Do you receive any other income not mentioned in any of the above questions?	Yes ☐	No ☐	Yes ☐	No ☐	Indicate the nature of this income. For example, an allowance or income from trust. Indicate how often this income is received.	
7	Do you receive any income from state benefits or tax credits? *Give details of benefit received, how much and how often.*	Yes ☐	No ☐	Yes ☐	No ☐	If you are in receipt of more than one tax credit, provide details of each credit and any elements that are now included in the award.	

Part C - Capital and Savings

Please provide details of all your capital and savings.

		You		Your partner		Additional details	Court use
I	**Main dwelling** Do you and/or your partner own the house/property that you treat as your main dwelling?	Yes ☐	No ☐	Yes ☐	No ☐	If **Yes**, please provide the following details: i) What is the out-standing mortgage on your property? ii) What is its current market value? iii) What share do you own in this property and if not shared with your partner, who do you own this property with? iv) What type of property is this? *For example, flat.* v) How many bedrooms does this property have?	
2	**Other property** Do you and/or your partner own any other property?	Yes ☐	No ☐	Yes ☐	No ☐	If **Yes**, provide the following details: i) What is the out-standing mortgage on this property? ii) What is its current market value? iii) What share do you own in this property and if not with your partner, who do you own this property with? iv) What type of property is this? *For example, flat.* v) How many bedrooms does this property have?	

Part C - Capital and Savings (continued)

		You	Your partner	Additional details	Court use
3	Savings *Please provide details, of savings, including money in the bank, building society, or at home or in current accounts, National Savings Certificates, ISAs.*			If you have savings certificates, provide details of the issue and how many units you have.	
4	Do you and/or your partner own any stocks or shares? *Include Unit Trusts, PEPs or ISAs.*	Yes ☐ No ☐	Yes ☐ No ☐	If **Yes**, please provide details of the company and name of the fund if appropriate. Also provide the present value and the amount of the yearly dividend.	
5	Do you and/or your partner have any rights under a trust fund?	Yes ☐ No ☐	Yes ☐ No ☐	If **Yes**, what are the details of the fund and what rights do you have?	
6	Articles of value *Please provide details of any articles of value that you and/or your partner own, and their approximate value.*			Include antiques jewellery, art etc.	
7	Do you or your partner have any other capital assets that you have not indicated above?	Yes ☐ No ☐	Yes ☐ No ☐	If **Yes**, please provide details of the same.	

Part D - Financial commitments

		You		Your partner		Additional details	Court use
I	Do you have any dependants who live with you?	Yes ☐	No ☐	Yes ☐	No ☐	If **Yes**, please provide details of how many, their relationship and their ages.	
2	Do you and/or your partner have any financial orders that this court should know about?	Yes ☐	No ☐	Yes ☐	No ☐	If **Yes**, please indicate the nature of the order(s) and the amount(s).	
3	How much do you and/or your partner pay in housing costs?					Provide details of rent or mortgage on your main dwelling. Indicate the period that this amount covers.	

Part E - Further information

		You		Your partner		Additional details	Court use
I	Has any other person been paying towards your legal costs and expenses in these or any other proceedings prior to your grant of representation?	Yes ☐	No ☐			If **Yes**, please provide details of the amount and from whom this support came. Indicate their relationship.	
2	Are any of your and/ or your partner's assets subject to a mareva injunction or freezing order?	Yes ☐	No ☐	Yes ☐	No ☐	If **Yes**, please provide details of the nature of the assets, the value of the order and whose order or injunction it is.	

Part E - Further information (continued)

	You		Your partner		Additional details	Court use
3 Do you and/or your partner have interests in any business abroad?	Yes ☐	No ☐	Yes ☐	No ☐	If **Yes**, please provide details of the nature of the business, its name and address and your and/or your partner's interest in it.	
4 Are you and/or your partner currently bankrupt or subject to bankruptcy proceedings or subject to an Individual Voluntary Arrangement?	Yes ☐	No ☐	Yes ☐	No ☐	If **Yes**, please provide full details.	

Is there any other information that you feel is relevant to the Court or the Legal Services Commission which should be taken into account when considering your means?
Please provide details where relevant.

Declaration

1. I declare that to the best of my knowledge and belief, I have given a complete and correct statement of my income and/or savings and/or capital and those of my partner.

2. I understand I may be required to provide evidence to support the information I have supplied on this form.

3. I authorise such enquiries as are considered necessary to enable the Court or the Legal Services Commission to ascertain mine and/or my partner's income, outgoings, savings, business interests.

4. I consent to the disclosure of any information by other parties that may assist in their enquiries.

5. I authorise the Court or the Legal Services Commission to make such enquiries to other parties as they feel necessary and I consent to the disclosure of information to confirm that I am in receipt of such benefits or tax credit or guarantee pension credit as I have stated.

6. I understand that the Court and the Legal Services Commission can provide a report on my financial position to the trial judge and my representative, with a view to a Recovery of Defence Costs Order being made for up to the full amount of the costs incurred in defending me in the proceedings, in this and any other court.

7. I understand that if I knowingly make a statement which is false or knowingly withhold information I may be prosecuted. If convicted of such an offence I may be sent to prison for up to three months or fined or both (section 21 Access to Justice Act 1999).

8. I understand that I must co-operate fully and immediately with any enquiry into my financial circumstances by the Court or Legal Services Commission, and that if the information I have provided is not correct or complete, then an Order may be made against me requiring me to pay all costs incurred in defending me in the proceedings, in this and any other court.

Signature

Date

Full name
in BLOCK CAPITALS

Declaration and authority by person receiving the benefit

This additional declaration should be signed by the person receiving the benefit if they are not the person applying for publicly funded representation.

I consent to the Court or Legal Services Commission disclosing information about me to any parties and making such enquiries as may be necessary to check the information provided in this application. Other parties may carry out such processing as is necessary to check this information remains correct and may inform the Court or the Legal Services Commission of any relevant changes.

Signature

Date

10.13.2   Magistrates' court case progression form – case sent to Crown Court under s 51 of the Crime and Disorder Act 1998

**MAGISTRATES' COURT
CASE PROGRESSION**

**CASE SENT TO THE CROWN COURT UNDER SECTION 51 OF THE
CRIME AND DISORDER ACT 1998**

Sent to Crown Court at _____ on __ / __ / __

Prosecution advocate:

D1	[bail][custody] represented by:
D2	[bail][custody] represented by:
D3	[bail][custody] represented by:
D4	[bail][custody] represented by:
D5	[bail][custody] represented by:

No. of case in Magistrates' Court: _____ URN: _____

	D1	D2	D3	D4	D5
Has the defendant been advised about credit for pleading guilty?					
Is the defendant likely to plead guilty?					
Has the defendant been warned that if he is on bail and fails to attend, the proceedings may continue in his absence?					

1. PRELIMINARY HEARING & PLEA AND CASE MANAGEMENT HEARING

   a. *If this is a case for which a preliminary hearing in the Crown Court is necessary the preliminary hearing will take place on:*   __ / __
   b. *The plea and case management hearing will take place on:*   __ / __
   c. *If a defendant is likely to plead guilty, and a pre-sentence report would be appropriate, the court orders:*

   d. **If a defendant is likely to plead guilty, are there any other matters which should be dealt with at the same time as these proceedings (other offences/TICs)?**   D1   D2   D3   D4   D5
   e. **If yes, give brief details:**

   f. *If there are other matters, the court orders:*

   g. *Further orders (e.g. orders re medical or psychiatric reports):*

2. FURTHER DIRECTIONS

   a. The prosecution to serve copies of the documents containing the evidence on which the charge or charges are based ("the prosecution case papers") together with a draft indictment within 50 days where the defendant is in custody and within 70 days in other cases.
   b. The indictment to be preferred within 28 days of the service of the prosecution case papers.

c. Any notice of application by the defence to dismiss the charges shall be made within 14 days of the service of the prosecution case papers.

d. If the defence wish a prosecution witness to be called to give evidence in person at the trial, the defence shall so notify the prosecution and the Crown Court within 7 days of receiving the prosecution case papers.

e. Following receipt of the notification referred to in d., the police to notify the prosecution and the Crown Court of the dates when the witness is unavailable to give evidence and the reasons therefor so that the information is available for the plea and case management hearing.

f. The prosecution to comply with its initial duty of disclosure at the same time as service of the prosecution case papers.

g. The defence to serve the defence statement, including alibi details if appropriate, within 14 days of the date on which the prosecution complied, or purported to comply, with its initial duty of disclosure.

h. The prosecution to serve any application for special measures within 28 days of the service of the prosecution case papers.

i. The defence to serve any response to the application for special measures within 14 days of service of the application.

j. The prosecution to serve any notice of intention to introduce hearsay evidence within 14 days of the service of the prosecution case papers.

k. The defence to serve any notice opposing the prosecution notice under j. within 14 days of receipt of that notice.

l. The defence to serve any notice of intention to introduce hearsay evidence within 14 days of the date on which the prosecution complied, or purported to comply, with its initial duty of disclosure.

m. The prosecution to serve any notice opposing the defence notice under l. within 14 days of receipt of that notice.

n. The defence to serve any application to introduce the bad character of a prosecution witness within 14 days of the date on which the prosecution complied, or purported to comply, with its initial duty of disclosure.

o. The prosecution to serve any notice opposing the defence application under n. to introduce the bad character of a prosecution witness within 14 days of receipt of the application.

p. The prosecution to serve any notice to introduce the defendant's bad character within 14 days of the service of the prosecution case papers.

q. The defence to serve any application to exclude evidence of the defendant's bad character within 7 days of receipt of the prosecution notice under p.

r. *Any further orders relating to bad character:*

s. The parties shall, within 14 days, give to the Crown Court case progression officer responsible for this case all the relevant information to enable the Crown Court Case Details form to be completed.

t. *Further orders:*

....
....
....

MAGISTRATES' COURT
CASE PROGRESSION

CASE SENT TO THE CROWN COURT UNDER SECTION 51 OF THE CRIME AND DISORDER ACT 1998

<u>GUIDANCE NOTES</u>

General notes

These notes accompany the standard directions form for cases sent to the Crown Court.

The Consolidated Criminal Practice Direction states:

> V.56.4 A preliminary hearing ('PH') is not required in every case sent for trial under section 51 of the Crime and Disorder Act 1998: see rule 12.2 (which altered the Crown Court rule from which it derived). A PH should be ordered only where such a hearing is considered necessary. The PH should be held about 14 days after sending.

> V.56.5 Whether or not a magistrates' court orders a PH, a plea and case management hearing ('PCMH') should be ordered in every case sent or committed to the Crown Court for trial. The PCMH should be held ... within about 14 weeks after sending for trial where a defendant is in custody and within about 17 weeks after sending for trial where a defendant is on bail.

Parties must come to the hearing prepared to provide the information set out on page 1 of the form (to the extent that this has not already been done) and to answer the questions in bold. Local practice will determine whether the parties will be required to complete the form and make it available to the District Judge or Magistrate at or before the start of the hearing.

If the defendant intends to plead guilty the court should make appropriate orders so that the defendant can be sentenced at the preliminary hearing if possible.

The directions set out in section 2 are default directions, which will apply unless a contrary order is made. Most of these directions are laid down by the Criminal Procedure Rules 2005. The purpose of the directions is to enable the PCMH to be an effective hearing.

The proposed italicised orders should be filled in, if relevant.

Except where otherwise required, a direction in the form to "serve" material means serve on the other party(ies) and file with the Crown Court.

If there are more than 5 defendants use a second form only to record the details on page 1 and the answers to the questions in bold and record the direction on one form only.

Notes relevant to specific sections

1. PRELIMINARY HEARING & PLEA AND CASE MANAGEMENT HEARING

Where a preliminary hearing is fixed, the date of the plea and case management hearing should be fixed at the same time. Both dates should be obtained from the Crown Court.

Subject to any direction of the Resident Judge, a preliminary hearing should normally only be ordered where:

> i) there are case management issues which call for such a hearing;

> ii) the case is likely to last for more than 4 weeks;

> iii) it would be desirable to set an early trial date;

1

iv) the defendant is a child or young person;

v) there is likely to be a guilty plea and the defendant could be sentenced at the preliminary hearing; or

vi) it seems to the court that it is a case suitable for a preparatory hearing in the Crown Court (see sections 7 and 9 of the Criminal Justice Act 1987 and sections 29-32 of the Criminal Procedure and Investigations Act 1996, as amended by sections 43-45 of the Criminal Justice Act 2003).

A preliminary hearing should be fixed for a date about 14 days after sending. The plea and case management hearing should be fixed for a date within about 14 weeks of sending where the defendant is in custody and within about 17 weeks of sending where the defendant is on bail.

No preliminary hearing should be fixed where a case is sent for trial to the Central Criminal Court. If necessary, one will be fixed by that Court.

1e. If the defendant is facing charges in other courts give brief details of offence, court and court number.

2. DIRECTIONS

2a. For a case sent to the Crown Court under section 51 of the Crime and Disorder Act 1998, the Crime and Disorder Act 1998 (Service of Prosecution Evidence) Regulations 2000 (as amended) provide that the prosecution case papers must be served within 50 days of sending where the defendant is in custody and within 70 days of sending in other cases. The Magistrates' Court has no power to enlarge this period: see paragraph 1 of Schedule 3 to the Crime and Disorder Act 1998 ("the 1998 Act"). Only a Crown Court judge can extend the period.

2b. See Rule 14.2(1)(d) of the Criminal Procedure Rules 2005.

2c. See Rule 13.2(2)(c) and Rule 13.3(4)(c) of the Criminal Procedure Rules 2005.

2d. By virtue of section 9(1) of the Criminal Justice Act 1967 a written statement of a witness is "admissible as evidence to the like extent as oral evidence" if, amongst other things, "none of the other parties or their solicitors, within **seven** days from the service of the copy of the statement, serves a notice ... objecting to the statement being tendered in evidence under this section" (s. 9(2)(d)). The period includes weekends and bank holidays. By virtue of s. 9 (4) and (5), a judge in the Crown Court may require that person to attend before the court and give evidence even though the notice was not given in time.

2g. See regulation 2 of the Criminal Procedure and Investigations Act 1996 (Defence Disclosure Time Limits) Regulations 1997, S.I. 1997 No. 684. If the prescribed period would expire on a weekend, Christmas Day, Good Friday or a bank holiday, the period is treated as expiring on the next working day. By virtue of regulation 3(1): "The period referred to in regulation 2 shall, if the [Crown] court so orders, be extended by so many days as the court specifies". By virtue of Regulation 3(2): "The court may only make such an order if an application which complies with paragraph (3) below is made by the accused before the expiration of the period referred to in regulation 2."

2h. See Rule 29.1(4) of the Criminal Procedure Rules 2005. The Crown Court may extend the time: see Rule 29.2; and there is provision for late applications: see Rule 29.3.

2i. See Rule 29.1(6) of the Criminal Procedure Rules 2005. (The Crown Court has no explicit power to extend the time for opposition under 29.1(6): see 29.2(1).)

2j. See Rule 34 3 of the Criminal Procedure Rules 2005. The Crown Court may vary the period, see Rule 34.7.

2k. See Rule 34.5 of the Criminal Procedure Rules 2005. The Crown Court may vary the period, see Rule 34.7.

2

2l. See Rule 34.4 of the Criminal Procedure Rules 2005. The Crown Court may vary the period, see Rule 34.7.

2m. See Rule 34 .5 of the Criminal Procedure Rules 2005. The Crown Court may vary the period, see Rule 34.7.

2n. See Rule 35.2 of the Criminal Procedure Rules 2005. The Crown Court may vary the period, see Rule 35.8.

2o. See Rule 35.3 of the Criminal Procedure Rules 2005. The Crown Court may vary the period, see Rule 35.8.

2p. See Rule 35.4 of the Criminal Procedure Rules 2005. The Crown Court may vary the period, see Rule 35.8.

2q. See Rule 35.6 of the Criminal Procedure Rules 2005. The Crown Court may vary the period, see Rule 35.8.

2r. Any orders not covered by the bad character provisions in 2n. to 2q should be noted here.

2t. Where a case is sent for trial to the Central Criminal Court the prosecution should be required to serve, 7 days before the plea and case management hearing, an extended case summary prepared or approved by the advocate who will attend that hearing.

10.13.3   Crown Court case progression form – preliminary hearing

CROWN COURT

CASE PROGRESSION

PRELIMINARY HEARING

Date of hearing: /   /   Judge:

Prosecution advocate:		
D1	[bail][custody] represented by:	
D2	[bail][custody] represented by:	
D3	[bail][custody] represented by:	
D4	[bail][custody] represented by:	
D5	[bail][custody] represented by:	

No. of case in Crown Court: [   ]   URN: [   ]

Has the defendant been advised about credit for pleading guilty?

D1	D2	D3	D4	D5

Has the defendant been warned that if he is on bail and fails to attend, the proceedings may continue in his absence?

1) TRIAL JUDGE

Should the future management of the case be under the supervision of the trial judge or a nominated judge?   YES/NO

2) PLEA

a.   **Is it likely that the case can be concluded by the defendant pleading guilty?**

D1	D2	D3	D4	D5

b.   If yes and if the defendant cannot be sentenced at the preliminary hearing, go to 3) and/or 4) as appropriate

3) LIKELY GUILTY PLEA

a.   *The defendant will be sentenced on: /   /   or at the plea and case management hearing*

b.   *The directions made by the magistrates' court when the case was sent shall apply subject to the following amendments:*

c.   *The pre-sentence report (if required) to be received by the Crown Court and made available to the defence and the prosecution by:*

d.   *The defence to serve any material which it wishes the court to consider when sentencing by:*

e.   **Does the defence intend to make "derogatory assertions" against a person's character in the course of mitigation?**

D1	D2	D3	D4	D5

f.   *If yes, the court orders:*

g. **Are there any other matters against a defendant which should be dealt with at the same time as the proceedings in this case (other offences/TIC's)?**

D1	D2	D3	D4	D5

h. **If yes, give brief details:**

i. *If there are other matters, the court orders:*

j. *Further orders (e.g. orders re medical, psychiatric reports, confiscation proceedings or Newton hearings):*

4) DIRECTIONS FOR PLEA AND CASE MANAGEMENT HEARING

a. *The directions made by the Magistrates' Court when the case was sent shall apply subject to the following amendments:*

b. *Further orders:*

5) EXPERT EVIDENCE

a. **Is this a case in which the parties will rely on expert evidence?**

P	D1	D2	D3	D4	D5

b. *If yes, the court orders:*

6) TRIAL

a. **Can the date of the trial or the period during which the trial will take place be fixed now?**
                                                                    YES/NO

b. *If yes, the trial will take place on:*
or within the period of :
and it is estimated that it will last:

CROWN COURT

CASE PROGRESSION

PRELIMINARY HEARING

<u>GUIDANCE NOTES</u>

General notes

These notes accompany the preliminary hearing form.

The parties must ensure that the Court has a copy of the "CASE SENT TO THE CROWN COURT UNDER SECTION 51 OF THE CRIME AND DISORDER ACT 1998" form completed in the Magistrates' Court.

The answers to the questions in bold must be filled in before the hearing. The proposed italicised orders should be filled in before the hearing, if possible (if there are more than five defendants, a further form should be filled in only so far as necessary).

Except where otherwise required, a direction in the form to "serve" material means serve on the other party(ies) and file with the Crown Court.

Notes relevant to specific sections

1) TRIAL JUDGE OR NOMINATED JUDGE

If the case is due to last for more than 4 weeks or if it seems likely that a preparatory hearing will be ordered, the future case management should normally be under the supervision of the trial judge or a nominated judge. It may also be desirable for the future case management to be under the supervision of the trial judge or a nominated judge in other cases where, for example there are difficult issues of law to be considered or where the prosecution intends to make a public interest immunity application.

If the case fits into this category, the court should normally make the necessary directions for the plea and case management hearing and then direct that the case be considered by the Resident Judge.

2) PLEA

If it is likely that the case can be concluded by all the defendants pleading guilty then 3) should be completed and there should be no need to make any orders under 4). Otherwise any appropriate orders under 3) should be made in respect of those defendants likely to plead guilty and 4) should be completed.

3) LIKELY GUILTY PLEA

3b. The Crown Court has a greater power to vary the time limits than the magistrates' court.

3c. A pre-sentence report will not be required in every case.

3e. Advance notice of the fact that such an assertion is going to be made should be given to the prosecution to enable it to decide whether to challenge the assertion and to enable the sentencing court to consider whether to make an order restricting the publication of the assertion under sections 58-61 of the Criminal Procedure and Investigations Act 1996 ("CPIA").

3i. If the defendant is facing charges in other courts give brief details of offence, court and court number.

4) DIRECTIONS FOR PLEA AND CASE MANAGEMENT HEARING

4a. The Crown Court has a greater power to vary the time limits than the Magistrates' Court.

5) EXPERT EVIDENCE

The court should identify any issues in relation to which it is appropriate to call expert evidence and set a timetable for obtaining, serving, and (if possible) agreeing such evidence or identifying the issues in dispute. See also paragraph 15 of the guidance notes to the PCMH form.

The parties should consider whether orders being considered by the court will involve costs being incurred which may not be met by the Legal Services Commission.

7) TRIAL

The court should consider whether it is possible and desirable to set the trial date or period because, for example, of the health, vulnerability or availability of a witness or the defendant or because the defendant falls within the definition of a persistent young offender, or because experts and/or leading counsel may have to be instructed and, before any such instructions can be expected, it is necessary to know the date.

10.13.4 Plea and case management hearing in the Crown Court form

PLEA AND CASE MANAGEMENT HEARING IN THE CROWN COURT

Date of hearing: Judge:

P			represented by:		☐
D1		in custody/on bail	represented by:		☐
D2		in custody/on bail	represented by:		☐
D3		in custody/on bail	represented by:		☐
D4		in custody/on bail	represented by:		☐
D5		in custody/on bail	represented by:		☐

Tick right hand column if the advocate is instructed for trial

No. of case in Crown Court: URN:

	D1	D2	D3	D4	D5
Has the defendant been advised about credit for pleading guilty?	☐	☐	☐	☐	☐
Has the defendant been warned that if he is on bail and fails to attend, the proceedings may continue in his absence?	☐	☐	☐	☐	☐
Is the Crown Court Case Details form up-to-date? (P ☐)	☐	☐	☐	☐	☐

Matters likely to be applicable to all trials

1) **TRIAL JUDGE**
Should the future management of the case be under the supervision of the trial or a nominated judge?   **YES/NO**

2) **RESOLVING THE CASE WITHOUT A TRIAL**   **Not applicable ☐**

	D1	D2	D3	D4	D5
a. **Might the case against a defendant be resolved by a plea of guilty to some counts on the indictment or to a lesser offence?**	☐	☐	☐	☐	☐
b. **If so, how?**					
c. **Is the prosecution prepared to resolve the case in this way?**	☐	☐	☐	☐	☐
d. **If no, does the court take the provisional view that the case should be resolved in this way?**	☐	☐	☐	☐	☐

   e. *If yes, the court orders:*

3) **GUILTY PLEA**   **Not applicable ☐**

	D1	D2	D3	D4	D5
a. **Is there a written basis of plea?**	☐	☐	☐	☐	☐
b. **Is the basis of plea acceptable to the prosecution?**	☐	☐	☐	☐	☐
a. Is the basis of plea acceptable to the court?	☐	☐	☐	☐	☐

   b. If not acceptable, section 25 (Newton Hearing) will also apply.
   c. *The defendant(s) will be sentenced on:*
   d. *The prosecution to serve any further material relevant to sentence by:*
   e. *The pre-sentence report, if required, to be received by the Crown Court and made available to the defence and the prosecution by:*
   f. *The defence to serve any material which it wishes the court to consider when sentencing the defendant by:*

1

g. **Will "derogatory assertions" be made in mitigation?**   ☐ ☐ ☐ ☐ ☐

h. *If yes, the court orders:*

i. **Are there any other matters which should be dealt with at the same**   ☐ ☐ ☐ ☐ ☐
   time as these proceedings (other offences/TICs)?
j. **If yes, give brief details:**

k. *If there are other matters, the court orders:*

l. *Further orders (e.g. orders re medical or psychiatric reports or confiscation proceedings):*

4) NOT GUILTY - TRIAL DATE   Not applicable ☐
  a.   **If the defendant is in custody and if the provisions regarding custody time limits apply, when**
    does the custody time limit (or any extension thereof) expire?
    D1:   ; **D2:**   ; **D3:**   ; **D4:**   ; **D5:**   .
  b.   **Set out other reasons why the trial should take place earlier or later than it might otherwise?**

  c.   *If the defendant is in custody and the date of the trial is outside the custody time limit period, the*
    court makes the following orders:

  d.   **What is the estimated length of the prosecution, defence cases?**
    Prosecution   **Defence**
  e.   *The trial will take place on:*   *and the length of it will be:*

5) READINESS FOR TRIAL
*The parties' case progression officers to inform the Crown Court case progression officer in writing
that the case is ready for trial, that it will proceed as a trial on the date in 4e and will take no more/less
time than the period in 4e, by:*

6) EVIDENCE - WITNESSES
  a.   **Have the parties completed Annex A?**   **YES/NO**
  b.   If yes, does the court approve Annex A?   YES/NO
  c.   *If the list of witnesses to be called orally is not agreed or approved, agreement (which is subject to
    the court's approval) must be reached and notified to the court by:*
  d.   *Absent agreement, the prosecution shall seek further directions by:*

7) EVIDENCE - DEFENDANTS' INTERVIEWS   Not applicable ☐
  a.   **Should the interviews be edited before the trial?**   P   D1 D2 D3 D4 D5
                                      ☐   ☐   ☐   ☐   ☐   ☐

  b.   *Proposals for the editing of interviews shall be drafted by:*   *and served by:*
  c.   *The other parties shall respond by:*
  d.   *The agreed interviews shall be filed with the Court by:*
  e.   *Absent agreement, the party(ies) named in b) shall seek further directions by:*

8) DEFENCE STATEMENT
  a.   **Has a defence statement been served?**   D1 D2 D3 D4 D5
                                       ☐   ☐   ☐   ☐   ☐

  b.   **Is there an issue as to its adequacy?**   ☐   ☐   ☐   ☐   ☐
  c.   *The court gives a warning to:*   ☐   ☐   ☐   ☐   ☐
  d.   *The court orders:*

9) PROSECUTION ADDITIONAL EVIDENCE   Not applicable ☐
   a.   *Any additional evidence to be served by*:

   b.   **Which topic/issue will the additional evidence relate to?**

10) FURTHER PROSECUTION DISCLOSURE   Not applicable ☐
   a.   *The prosecution to complete any further disclosure by*:
   b.   **Is the defence alleging that the prosecution has not complied with its**   D1 D2 D3 D4 D5
        obligation to disclose material?   ☐   ☐   ☐   ☐   ☐
   c.   *If yes, the court orders*:

11) EVIDENCE - ADMISSIONS/SCHEDULES
   a.   **Have the parties considered which admissions/schedules can be agreed:**   **YES/NO**
   b.   *If yes and if the court agrees that the proposed admissions/schedules are sufficient, they shall be drafted by*:
   c.   *and sent to the other parties by*:
   d.   *The other parties shall respond by*:
   e.   *The agreed admissions/schedules shall be filed with the court by*:
   f.   *Absent agreement, the named party in b) shall seek further directions by*:
   g.   *If the answer to question a. is no or if the court does not approve the proposed admissions/schedules, the court orders*:

Matters which may apply to any trial

12) EVIDENCE - EXHIBITS
   a.   **Have the parties completed and agreed Annex B?**   **YES/NO**
   b.   *If Annex B is not agreed, agreement must be reached and notified to the court by*:
   c.   *In the absence of agreement, the prosecution shall seek further directions by*:
   d.   *If, in the view of the court, any exhibits should be presented in a particular way in order to be more easily understood by the jury, the court orders*:

   e.   *Further orders*:

13) EVIDENCE - VIDEO EVIDENCE   Not applicable ☐
                                                       D1 D2 D3 D4 D5
   a.   **Has the prosecution delivered to the defence the transcript of video**   ☐   ☐   ☐   ☐   ☐
        witness evidence upon which it proposes to rely?
   b.   *If no, the prosecution to do so by*:
   c.   *The defence shall submit any editing proposals by*:
   d.   *The prosecution shall respond by*:
   e.   *The agreed transcripts and edited video shall be filed with the court by*:
   f.   *Absent agreement, the prosecution shall seek further directions by*:

14) EVIDENCE - CCTV EVIDENCE   Not applicable ☐
                                                       P   D1 D2 D3 D4 D5
   a.   **Has any unedited CCTV evidence been made available in full to**   ☐   ☐   ☐   ☐   ☐   ☐
        the other parties?
   b.   *If yes, copy of proposed composite/edited film/stills to be served by*:
   c.   *The other parties to respond by*:
   d.   *Absent agreement, the party seeking to rely on the evidence shall seek directions by*:

15) EVIDENCE - EXPERT EVIDENCE   Not applicable ☐
                                                       P   D1 D2 D3 D4 D5
   a.   **Expert evidence is likely to be called by:**   ☐   ☐   ☐   ☐   ☐   ☐

3

b. **To prove/disprove:** P:
D1/2/3/4/5:

c. Does the court approve of the need for the identified expert evidence?   ☐ ☐ ☐ ☐ ☐ ☐
d. If no, why?

e. *In any event the evidence to be served by:*

f. **Should the expert evidence be presented in a particular way in order to be more easily understood by the jury?**   ☐ ☐ ☐ ☐ ☐ ☐
g. *If yes, the court orders:*

h. **Would it be helpful if the experts consulted together and if possible agreed a written note of points of agreement or disagreement with a summary of reasons?**   ☐ ☐ ☐ ☐ ☐ ☐
i. *If yes, and if the parties agree, the court orders:*

16) ELECTRONIC EQUIPMENT – COMPATIBILITY   Not applicable ☐

P	D1	D2	D3	D4	D5
☐	☐	☐	☐	☐	☐

a. **Does the trial courtroom have the appropriate equipment to allow the presentation of electronic evidence (CCTV, live link, audio recordings, DVD etc)?**
b. *If no, the court orders:*

17) EVIDENCE - SPECIAL MEASURES AND LIVE LINK   Not applicable ☐

D1	D2	D3	D4	D5
☐	☐	☐	☐	☐

a. **Any outstanding issues about special measures or live links?**
b. If yes, the court orders:

18) MISCELLANEOUS ORDERS RE. WITNESSES AND DEFENDANT   Not applicable ☐

P	D1	D2	D3	D4	D5
☐	☐	☐	☐	☐	☐

a. **Does any witness or defendant need an interpreter or have special needs for which arrangements should be made?**
b. *If yes, the court orders:*

c. **Are any special arrangements needed for a child defendant?**   ☐ ☐ ☐ ☐ ☐ ☐
d. *If yes, the court orders:*

e. **Will a defendant be unrepresented at trial?**   ☐ ☐ ☐ ☐ ☐ ☐
f. *If yes, the court orders:*

19) HEARSAY / BAD CHARACTER EVIDENCE   Not applicable ☐

P	D1	D2	D3	D4	D5
☐	☐	☐	☐	☐	☐

a. **Further applications regarding hearsay evidence or bad character evidence are to be made by:**
b. *The court orders:*

20) PRODUCTION OF MATERIAL FROM THIRD PARTIES   Not applicable ☐

P	D1	D2	D3	D4	D5
☐	☐	☐	☐	☐	☐

a. **Applications for production of material (e.g. social services, hospital, banking records) from third parties to be made by:**
b. *The court orders:*

21) PRE-TRIAL RESOLUTION OF ISSUES   Not applicable ☐

4

a. **What are the legal or factual issues which should be resolved before the trial:**

b. *If the issues are not capable of being resolved at the plea and case management hearing, the necessary hearing will take place on   and will last:*

c. **Do the parties wish to call witnesses to give evidence orally to enable the court to resolve the issues?**

P	D1	D2	D3	D4	D5
☐	☐	☐	☐	☐	☐

d. *If yes, and if the court approves, the court makes the following orders:*

e. *Skeleton arguments to be submitted by:* P by: D1/2/3/4/5 by:

22) PUBLIC INTEREST IMMUNITY: ON NOTICE APPLICATIONS   Not applicable ☐

a. **What is the nature of the prosecution's application on notice for public interest immunity?**

b. *The court orders:*

23) FURTHER ORDERS CONCERNING THE CONDUCT OF THE TRIAL

a. *Prosecution case summary/opening, if necessary, to be served by:*

b. *To ensure that the trial does not take more time than the period in 4e., the court orders:*

24) ANY FURTHER MISCELLANEOUS ORDERS - INCLUDING ORDERS RE. LITIGATION SUPPORT

25) NEWTON HEARING   Not applicable ☐

a. *The Newton hearing will take place on:*   *and the length of it will be:*

b. *The issues to be resolved are:*

c. *The prosecution to serve any further material by:*   *and the defence by:*

d. *The following witnesses will be called to give evidence orally:*

e. *Further orders (including any orders re. hearsay/bad character):*

Judge's signature:

ANNEX A
Witnesses upon whom the prosecution intends to rely and who will give evidence orally

Name of witness	Page No	Type of witness	Required by:						Order of calling
			P ☐	D1 ☐	D2 ☐	D3 ☐	D4 ☐	D5 ☐	
			P ☐	D1 ☐	D2 ☐	D3 ☐	D4 ☐	D5 ☐	
			P ☐	D1 ☐	D2 ☐	D3 ☐	D4 ☐	D5 ☐	
			P ☐	D1 ☐	D2 ☐	D3 ☐	D4 ☐	D5 ☐	
			P ☐	D1 ☐	D2 ☐	D3 ☐	D4 ☐	D5 ☐	
			P ☐	D1 ☐	D2 ☐	D3 ☐	D4 ☐	D5 ☐	
			P ☐	D1 ☐	D2 ☐	D3 ☐	D4 ☐	D5 ☐	
			P ☐	D1 ☐	D2 ☐	D3 ☐	D4 ☐	D5 ☐	
			P ☐	D1 ☐	D2 ☐	D3 ☐	D4 ☐	D5 ☐	
			P ☐	D1 ☐	D2 ☐	D3 ☐	D4 ☐	D5 ☐	
			P ☐	D1 ☐	D2 ☐	D3 ☐	D4 ☐	D5 ☐	
			P ☐	D1 ☐	D2 ☐	D3 ☐	D4 ☐	D5 ☐	
			P ☐	D1 ☐	D2 ☐	D3 ☐	D4 ☐	D5 ☐	
			P ☐	D1 ☐	D2 ☐	D3 ☐	D4 ☐	D5 ☐	
			P ☐	D1 ☐	D2 ☐	D3 ☐	D4 ☐	D5 ☐	
			P ☐	D1 ☐	D2 ☐	D3 ☐	D4 ☐	D5 ☐	
			P ☐	D1 ☐	D2 ☐	D3 ☐	D4 ☐	D5 ☐	
			P ☐	D1 ☐	D2 ☐	D3 ☐	D4 ☐	D5 ☐	
			P ☐	D1 ☐	D2 ☐	D3 ☐	D4 ☐	D5 ☐	

ANNEX B
Exhibits which the prosecution intends to make available to the jury at the start of the trial

Exhibit reference	Page No	Exhibit reference	Page No.	Exhibit reference	Page No.

Use continuation sheets as necessary

6

PLEA AND CASE MANAGEMENT HEARING IN THE CROWN COURT
GUIDANCE NOTES

General notes

These notes accompany the plea and case management hearing ('PCMH') form. The Consolidated Criminal Practice Direction provides:

IV.41.8   Active case management at the PCMH should reduce the number of ineffective and cracked trials and delays during the trial to resolve legal issues. The effectiveness of a PCMH hearing in a contested case depends in large measure upon preparation by all concerned and upon the presence of the trial advocate or an advocate who is able to make decisions and give the court the assistance which the trial advocate could be expected to give. Resident Judges in setting the listing policy should ensure that list officers fix cases as far as possible to enable the trial advocate to conduct the PCMH and the trial.

IV.41.9   In Class 1 and Class 2 cases, and in all cases involving a serious sexual offence against a child, the PCMH must be conducted by a High Court judge; by a circuit judge or by a recorder to whom the case has been assigned in accordance with paragraph IV.33 (allocation of business within the Crown Court); or by a judge authorised by the Presiding Judges to conduct such hearings. In the event of a guilty plea before such an authorised judge, the case will be adjourned for sentencing by a High Court judge or by a circuit judge or recorder to whom the case has been assigned.

Use of the PCMH form: pilot schemes

IV.41.10   The pilot courts will be the Central Criminal Court, Preston Crown Court and Nottingham Crown Court. In pilot courts the PCMH form as set out in annex E will be used in accordance with the guidance notes.

Use of the PCMH form: general

IV.41.11   In other courts the Resident Judge should exercise discretion as to the manner in which the form is used taking account of the views of the local criminal justice agencies and of practitioners. In the event of the Resident Judge deciding to use the form in a manner that is not agreed to by either the local criminal justice agencies or the practitioners, the Resident Judge should consult the Presiding Judge of his circuit before doing so.

Further pre-trial hearings after the PCMH

IV. 41.12   Additional pre-trial hearings should be held only if needed for some compelling reason. Where necessary the power to give, vary or revoke a direction without a hearing should be used. Paragraph 5 of the PCMH form enables the Court to require the parties' case progression officers to inform the Crown Court case progression officer that the case is ready for trial, that it will proceed as a trial on the date fixed and will take no more or less time than that previously ordered.

The parties must complete only one copy of the form and make it available to the judge at or before the hearing (if there are more than five defendants, a further form should be filled in only so far as necessary). The answers to the questions in bold must be filled in before the hearing. The proposed italicised orders should be filled in before the hearing, if possible. Tick the "Not applicable" box if no part of the section is relevant. Local practice will determine how the form should be completed and by whom and whether electronically or not. The directions must be easily understood by, and made available to, the case

1

progression officers. Time limits should normally be expressed by reference to a particular date rather than by the number of days allowed, to make the task of the case progression officers easier.

The court may make rulings which have binding effect (subject to being discharged or varied) under section 40 of the Criminal Procedure and Investigations Act 1996 as to:

> "(a) any question as to the admissibility of evidence;
> (b) any other question of law relating to the case concerned."

The extent to which courts exercise the power to make these rulings at this hearing is a matter for the court, after considering representations.

Except where otherwise required, a direction to "serve" material means serve on the other party(ies) and file with the Crown Court.

Where a direction requires a party to respond to a proposal (e.g. a proposed edited interview) the party responding will be expected to suggest a counter-proposal.

Notes relevant to specific sections

1) TRIAL OR NOMINATED JUDGE

If the case is due to last for more than 4 weeks or if there are issues of law to be considered or if the prosecution intends to make a public interest immunity application, then the future management of the case should normally be under the supervision of the trial judge or a nominated judge.

Where it is deemed appropriate for the management of the case to be under the supervision of the trial judge or a nominated judge the court should normally continue with the plea and case management hearing and then direct that the case be considered by the Resident Judge.

2) RESOLVING THE CASE WITHOUT A TRIAL

2e. The court should normally grant the prosecution a very short adjournment to resolve the issue.

3) GUILTY PLEA

If there is an issue about whether the defendant is fit to plead the court should be informed for the court to make appropriate orders.

3i. Where the defence intend to make a "derogatory assertion" against a person's character in the course of mitigation advance notice of that intention enables the prosecution to decide whether to challenge the assertion and enables the sentencing court to consider whether to make an order restricting the publication of the assertion under sections 58-61 of the Criminal Procedure and Investigations Act 1996 ("CPIA1996").

3l. If the defendant is facing charges in other courts give brief details of offence, court and court number.

4) NOT GUILTY – TRIAL DATE

4b. These reasons could include the health, vulnerability or availability of a witness or of the defendant or the fact that the defendant falls within the definition of a persistent young offender.

4c. The court should, if possible, deal with the extension of a custody time limit at this stage rather than adjourn any application to a subsequent date. Regulation 7 of the Prosecution of Offences (Custody Time Limits) Regulations 1987 permits the defendant to waive the requirements of notice and gives the court authority to waive them.

4e. It will often not be possible to fill in these answers until the balance of the form has been considered.

2

6) EVIDENCE - WITNESSES

The parties shall before the hearing agree or try to agree which witnesses are properly required to give oral evidence, on which day of the trial and in which order the witnesses will be called.

The parties must use their best endeavours to reduce the amount of oral evidence to a minimum, in particular by reducing the number of witnesses who give similar evidence, or by the deletion of challenged passages the omission of which will not materially affect the case for the party calling that witness, or by the use of admissions which make the calling of the witness in person unnecessary.

The parties will be expected to be able to justify to the court what they have agreed.

7) EVIDENCE – DEFENDANTS' INTERVIEWS

In order to assist editing of defendants' interviews it will be helpful if the prosecution can supply interviews to the defence in an electronic form.

In the absence of agreement before the trial, the party responsible for the editing shall have available at the trial the interviews in electronic form so that the necessary editing can be done during the trial.

See also the provisions of paragraph IV 43 of the Consolidated Criminal Practice Direction in relation to interviews.

8) DEFENCE STATEMENT

The defence is required to serve a defence statement by section 5 of the CPIA 1996. The defence statement will have to comply with new section 6A as inserted by section 33 of the Criminal Justice Act 2003. If the defendant has not provided a defence statement, the court should be told what are the issues in his case.

8b. See s. 11 of the CPIA 1996 as substituted by section 39 of the Criminal Justice Act 2003.

8c. The judge will have to consider whether to give a warning under section 6E of the CPIA 1996, as substituted by section 36 of the Criminal Justice Act 2003.

9) PROSECUTION ADDITIONAL EVIDENCE

The court may wish to order that any evidence served after the due date may not be introduced without the court's permission. If so, insert that in the box.

10) FURTHER PROSECUTION DISCLOSURE

10b. Section 8 of the CPIA 1996 provides for an application to be made by the defence for an order obliging the prosecution to disclose material where the accused has reasonable cause to believe that the prosecution has not complied with its obligation to disclose.

11) EVIDENCE – ADMISSIONS / SCHEDULES

11a. See section 10 of the Criminal Justice Act 1967.

12) EVIDENCE - EXHIBITS

Exhibits should be presented so that they can be easily understood by the jury, for example by the jury being given edited or summarized versions of documents, by the use of schedules, electronic presentation of material, or by the use of graphics.

13) EVIDENCE - VIDEO EVIDENCE

Transcripts are costly and time consuming to obtain. It is the video which is the evidence, not the transcript. Therefore a transcript should normally only be obtained when there is to be a trial and a need for a transcript is identified.

3

14) EVIDENCE - CCTV EVIDENCE

14b. Consideration should be given to requiring the videos to be copied on to a DVD.

15) EVIDENCE - EXPERT EVIDENCE

15c. If the court does approve the need for the instruction of an expert on behalf of a publicly funded defendant, the court may wish to explain why, so that the Legal Services Commission can be informed accordingly. If the court does not approve the need for the expert evidence, the court may wish to note the reasons. If the court does give reasons, those reasons must be notified to the Legal Services Commission if an application is being made for public funding of the expert's fees.

15f. In order that expert evidence can be easily understood by the jury the court may order, for example, that the jury be given a copy of the report, or an edited or summarized version thereof, or may direct the use of schedules or graphics.

15i. The words "if the parties agree" have been included because such an order, in the absence of agreement, may raise issues of costs and of privilege, which the Criminal Procedure Rule Committee has not yet addressed.

It must be borne in mind that the costs of an expert may not be met by the Legal Services Commission.

18) MISCELLANEOUS ORDERS RE. WITNESSES AND DEFENDANT

18a. In the event of an interpreter being required, set out the relevant language and, where applicable, the dialect. The Court should establish in each case who is responsible for providing the interpreter.

18c. If the defendant is a child the parties and the court should consider what provisions are required so that, in accordance with Part IV.39 of the Consolidated Criminal Practice Direction, the defendant is not exposed to avoidable intimidation, humiliation or distress.

18e. If the defendant will not be represented at trial there are orders which may have to be made prohibiting him from cross-examining certain witnesses (see Youth Justice and Criminal Evidence Act 1999, Chapter II).

20) PRODUCTION OF MATERIAL FROM THIRD PARTIES

Note the Attorney General's 2005 Guidelines on disclosure of information in criminal proceedings.

21) PRE-TRIAL RESOLUTION OF ISSUES

The parties shall, before the hearing, agree or try to agree what legal issues are likely to be raised (joinder, severance, admissibility of evidence, abuse of process, issues of substantive law etc) and at what stage they should properly be resolved and will be expected to be able to justify to the court what they have agreed. Although paragraph IV 36.1 of the Consolidated Criminal Practice Direction provides that written notice of an application to stay an indictment on the grounds of abuse of process must be given not later than 14 days before the date fixed or warned for trial, this issue should be considered at the PCMH.

22) PUBLIC INTEREST IMMUNITY: ON NOTICE APPLICATIONS

If the prosecution does not make an application for public interest immunity until later, the court and the defence must be informed as soon thereafter as practicable.

24) ANY FURTHER MISCELLANEOUS ORDERS – INCLUDING ORDERS RE. LITIGATION SUPPORT

Note the Guide to the Award of Costs in Criminal Proceedings on www.jsboard.co.uk.

4

25) NEWTON HEARING

The parties must agree or try to agree which witnesses are properly required to give oral evidence, in which order the witnesses will be called and what special arrangements need to be made to facilitate the giving of evidence. The parties must use their best endeavours to reduce the amount of oral evidence to a minimum, in particular by reducing the number of witnesses who give similar evidence, or by the deletion of challenged passages the omission of which will not materially affect the case for the party calling that witness, or by the use of admissions which makes the calling of the witness in person unnecessary. The court will decide which witnesses should be called to give oral evidence.

Part 4

SENTENCING AND APPEALS

Chapter 11

Sentencing – The Law

11.1 Introduction

The majority of defendants charged with having committed a criminal offence will either plead guilty, or be convicted after a trial in either the magistrates' court or the Crown Court. The final stage in the criminal litigation process (subject to any appeal the defendant may make – see **Chapter 13**) is for the defendant to be sentenced.

This chapter will examine the statutory provisions which are relevant to the sentencing of offenders. It will begin by explaining the purpose of sentencing, the types of sentence which the court may impose upon a defendant, and the factors which must be considered by the court when determining the type of sentence a defendant is to receive. The chapter will conclude by looking in more detail at the particular types of sentence which the court may impose.

11.2 Purpose of sentencing

Section 142(1) of the Criminal Justice Act (CJA) 2003 states that a court sentencing an offender aged 18 or over must have regard to the following five purposes of sentencing:

(a)   the punishment of offenders;

(b)   the reduction of crime (including its reduction by deterrence);

(c)   the reform and rehabilitation of offenders;

(d)   the protection of the public; and

(e)   the making of reparation by offenders to persons affected by their offence.

The court need not have such regard if the sentence is fixed by law or subject to a statutory minimum (see **11.5.1**) or if the defendant is classed as a dangerous offender (see **11.5.3.2**).

Section 174 of the CJA 2003 imposes a duty on the court to give reasons for the particular sentence which is imposed on a defendant. When a defendant is being sentenced, the court must 'state in open court, in ordinary language and in general terms, its reasons for deciding on the sentence passed ...' (s 174(1)).

11.3 Types of sentence

11.3.1 The basic sentence

There are four basic types of sentence which a court may impose on an adult defendant (the types of sentence that may be imposed on a juvenile appearing before the Youth Court are detailed in **Chapter 14**). In descending order of severity, these sentences are as follows:

(a) *Custodial sentence* – this involves the defendant being deprived of his liberty by being detained in custody for a specified period of time (see **11.5** below). Defendants aged 21 and over will serve a custodial sentence in prison. Defendants aged 18 to 20 (inclusive) will serve a custodial sentence in a young offenders institution.

(b) *Community sentence* – this involves the defendant being required to take part in one or more activities within the community whilst still retaining his liberty (see **11.6** below).

(c) *Fine* – this involves the defendant having to pay a financial penalty for his offending (see **11.7** below).

(d) *Discharge* – no immediate penalty is imposed on the defendant who receives a discharge, but if the discharge is conditional, the defendant may be sentenced for the original offence if he commits another offence within a period of time specified by the court (see **11.8** below).

The above list is sometimes referred to as the 'sentencing ladder', with the particular rung of the ladder upon which a defendant finds himself being determined by the seriousness of the offence. A flowchart depicting the sentencing ladder is to be found at **11.9** below.

11.3.2 Additional orders

11.3.2.1 Introduction

In addition to the basic sentence which he receives, the court may also impose additional orders on a defendant convicted of a criminal offence. The most common types of additional order are set out below.

11.3.2.2 Compensation

A defendant may be ordered to pay compensation to the victim of an offence for any injury or other loss suffered by the victim. An order to pay compensation is particularly common in cases of assault where the victim has suffered physical injury, but it can also be used in other cases (for example, a theft case where goods stolen by the defendant are destroyed or damaged). Magistrates may order a defendant to pay compensation up to a maximum figure of £5,000 per offence. There is no financial limit on the amount of compensation which may be ordered in the Crown Court, although the judge must have regard to the defendant's means when making an order.

11.3.2.3 Prosecution costs

A defendant convicted of a criminal offence may be ordered by the court sentencing him to pay some or all of the costs incurred by the CPS in bringing the case against him. Such costs must be just and reasonable. The court must specify the exact amount to be paid by the defendant.

11.3.2.4 Defence costs

A defendant whose case is being funded by way of a representation order will not be required to make any contribution towards the costs of his case whilst the case is ongoing. However, in the Crown Court, following conviction the judge has the power to order a defendant who has the benefit of a representation order to pay some or all of the costs of his defence. This is referred to as a 'recovery of defence costs order' (RDCO).

The judge will consider whether to make an RDCO *after* he has taken into account any other financial orders and penalties that may be made. An RDCO should be made against every defendant who is convicted and has the financial means to pay towards the cost of his legal representation.

An RDCO may *not* be made against a defendant who:

(a) only appears in the magistrates' court;

(b) has been committed for sentence to the Crown Court having entered a guilty plea at the plea and directions hearing in the magistrates' court; or

(c) is appealing to the Crown Court against a sentence imposed by the magistrates' court.

11.3.2.5 Forfeiture orders

A court may order the forfeiture of any property which was in the defendant's possession or control at the time he was apprehended, if the property was:

(a) used for committing or facilitating any offence;

(b) intended to be used for committing or facilitating any offence; or

(c) unlawfully in his possession (Powers of Criminal Courts (Sentencing) Act 2000).

In addition, there are a number of specific statutory powers which provide for the forfeiture of drugs, firearms and offensive weapons.

Examples of items which may be the subject of a forfeiture order include:

(a) implements used in the production and/or distribution of drugs (for example, a set of scales);

(b) offensive weapons (such as guns, knives or a baseball bat);

(c) items used to gain unlawful access to premises (such as a jemmy or crowbar).

The court will normally order that any property subject to a forfeiture order should be destroyed (a 'destruction order').

An order for the forfeiture and destruction of a controlled drug will be made by the court under s 27 of the Misuse of Drugs Act 1971.

11.3.2.6 Confiscation and restitution orders

A defendant appearing in the Crown Court may be made the subject of a confiscation order in respect of the proceeds of his criminal activity (for example, a defendant who has made substantial profits from the supply of controlled drugs). Such orders were created by the Proceeds of Crime Act 2002. The detailed provisions of confiscation orders are beyond the scope of this book.

Section 28 of the Theft Act 1968 enables the court to make a restitution order. A restitution order is designed to restore to a person entitled to them goods which have been stolen or otherwise unlawfully removed from him, or to restore to him a sum of money representing the proceeds of the sale of the goods from money found in the defendant's possession.

11.3.2.7 Anti-social behaviour orders

A criminal court may make an anti-social behaviour order (ASBO) pursuant to s 1C of the Crime and Disorder Act 1998. This section applies where a defendant is convicted of an offence and the court considers that the defendant has acted in an anti-social manner (ie, a manner that caused, or was likely to cause, harassment, alarm or distress to one or more persons not of the same household as the defendant). If the court considers that an order under s 1C is *necessary* to protect any person from further anti-social acts by him, the court may make an order prohibiting the defendant from doing anything described in that order (*R v Boness & Others* [2005] EWCA Crim 2395). The most common types of order are those prohibiting defendants from entering particular places or areas, or from contacting specified individuals.

An ASBO can be made only in addition to a sentence imposed for an offence, or in addition to a conditional discharge (see **11.8** below). The order will have effect for a period (which must not be less than two years) specified in the order. A defendant who, without reasonable excuse, breaches the terms of an ASBO may receive a custodial sentence and/or a fine.

> #### Example
>
> Danny (aged 18) is a member of a gang which has been using a local housing estate as a place to race their cars in the early hours of the morning. Following an altercation with a local resident, Danny is charged with affray and subsequently convicted. In addition to the sentence for the affray, the court also makes an ASBO on the basis that Danny's behaviour (racing cars late at night) is anti-social, and an order is necessary to stop Danny committing further anti-social acts. The order prohibits Danny from entering the housing estate and is expressed to last for two years.

A court which makes an ASBO must ensure that the terms of the order are proportionate and commensurate with the risk to be guarded against. If not, the order may infringe the defendant's rights under the ECHR (*R v Boness & Others* – above).

In the case of *R v W* [2006] EWCA Crim 686, the Court of Appeal issued the following points of guidance for a court considering the imposition of an ASBO following conviction:

(a)   the court must be satisfied to the criminal standard (ie, beyond a reasonable doubt) that the defendant has acted in the anti-social manner alleged;

(b)   the ASBO must be 'necessary', but this does not require proof beyond a reasonable doubt that the order is necessary;

(c)   the terms of the ASBO must be precise and capable of being understood by the offender;

(d)   the conditions in the ASBO must be enforceable, so that they should allow a breach to be readily identified and proved (ie, the order should not be general, but should rather prohibit the particular type of anti-social behaviour that gives rise to the necessity for an ASBO – see *CPS v T* [2006] EWHC (Admin) 782);

(e)   each prohibition must be necessary to protect persons from anti-social behaviour by the offender;

(f)   not all conditions in an ASBO have to run for the full term of the order itself (the test is what is necessary and proportionate);

(g)   the court should not impose an ASBO which prohibits an offender from committing specified criminal offences if the sentence which could be passed following conviction for the offence should be a sufficient deterrent;

(h)   it is unlawful to make an ASBO as if it were a further sentence or punishment – an ASBO must not be used merely to increase the sentence the offender is liable to receive; and

(i)   as proceedings under s 1C of the Crime and Disorder Act 1998 are civil in nature, hearsay evidence in support of the application for the ASBO is admissible.

11.3.2.8   Binding over

A magistrates' court may make an order that anyone appearing before it be bound over to keep the peace. A bind over is not a sentence as such, and is often used by magistrates in cases involving minor disturbances, typically disputes between neighbours which have resulted in proceedings for offences under ss 4, 4A and 5 of the Public Order Act 1996, or for common assault. Magistrates have the power to bind over anyone before the court. This may include the victim of the alleged criminal behaviour, a witness, and even a defendant who has been acquitted of the offence with which he was charged.

Magistrates should make a bind over order only when a person is before the court and his behaviour in connection with the current offence leads the magistrates to believe that a breach of the peace may arise from his behaviour in future. The magistrates may make an order that the person be bound over to keep the peace for a specified period of time and for a given sum of money (usually referred to as a 'recognisance'). If the person fails to keep the peace within the specified period of time, he will be obliged to pay the recognisance. A person before the court may be bound over to keep the peace only with his consent (although consent is normally given because refusal to give consent amounts to a contempt of court for which the person may be imprisoned).

Example

Toyah and Leanne start a fight with each other at the pub after Toyah accuses Leanne of sleeping with her boyfriend. Toyah scratches Leanne's face and is subsequently charged with common assault. At her trial, Toyah is acquitted by the magistrates. The magistrates are concerned, however, that as Toyah and Leanne live near to each other and frequent the same pub, there is a risk that their future behaviour might cause a breach of the peace to occur. The magistrates therefore make an order that both Toyah and Leanne are to be bound over to keep the peace for 12 months in the sum of £50. If either of them breaches the peace within the following 12-month period, she will be ordered to forfeit the sum of £50.

11.4   Principles of sentencing

11.4.1   The traditional approach to sentencing

Prior to the CJA 2003 coming into force, guidelines existed to ensure that a degree of consistency was achieved when courts were sentencing offenders for particular types of offence. For cases in the Crown Court, the Court of Appeal provided guidance in 'guideline' cases as to what the 'starting point' sentence should be for any given offence. In the magistrates' court, the Magistrates' Association published a set of guidelines (the Magistrates' Court Sentencing Guidelines) indicating what the 'starting point' was for any given offence. The starting point sentence was based on a first-time offender who pleaded not guilty and was convicted following trial.

Once the judge or bench of magistrates had found the appropriate starting point, it would then be necessary to determine whether the facts of the specific offence being dealt with made the offence more or less serious than a 'standard' offence of that type. To determine this, the judge or magistrates would consider the existence of any aggravating or mitigating factors, and also whether the defendant had previous convictions for the same or for similar offences. Aggravating factors are factors which make an offence more serious than would otherwise be the case. Examples of aggravating factors included an offence being premeditated, the victim of the offence being chosen for his vulnerability (such as an elderly person) or, in the case of a violent offence, the use of a weapon. Mitigating factors are factors which make an offence less serious than would otherwise be the case. Examples of mitigating factors include a defendant committing an offence on impulse or out of desperation, the victim suffering only minor injuries (in the case of an assault) or an item stolen being of low value (in a theft case).

Finally the judge or magistrates would take into account whether the defendant had entered a guilty plea and, if he had, at what stage in the case the plea had been entered. The defendant would be entitled to a discount on his sentence for pleading guilty, although the size of this reduction would depend upon at which stage in the proceedings the plea had been entered. A defendant who entered a guilty plea at the first opportunity (ie, at his first court appearance) would be entitled to a discount of a maximum of one-third of the sentence he would have received had he pleaded not guilty and been convicted following a trial.

11.4.2   The Criminal Justice Act 2003

11.4.2.1   Introduction

Although the system described in **11.4.1** above has not been completely removed, the CJA 2003 has made a number of significant changes to the way in which defendants are sentenced. In particular, the relative informality of the pre-CJA procedure has been replaced with procedures that are clearly set out in statute and are designed to ensure a uniformity of approach to sentencing in both the Crown Court and the magistrates' courts.

11.4.2.2   The Sentencing Guidelines Council

One of the most important changes made by the CJA 2003 is the creation (by s 167) of the Sentencing Guidelines Council (SGC). The SGC is made up of the Lord Chief Justice (the senior criminal judge), seven judicial members and four non-judicial members. Its purpose is to encourage consistency in sentencing by producing definitive sentencing guidelines to which all courts (ie, the magistrates' court, the Crown Court, the Court of Appeal and the House of Lords) must have regard. In producing these guidelines, the SGC is assisted by a separate Sentencing Advisory Panel (SAP), which will produce reports and research papers for the SGC to consider.

In time, the guidelines produced by the SGC will replace the guidance given by the Court of Appeal in guideline cases and the Magistrates' Court Sentencing Guidelines. So far the SGC has produced sentencing guidelines only for a limited range of offences. It has not as yet issued guidance for most types of offence and, until it does, the previous guidelines – either from the Court of Appeal (for Crown

Court cases) or contained in the Magistrates' Court Sentencing Guidelines (for cases in the magistrates' court) – will continue to be used by the courts. Indeed the SGC has produced a case compendium which comprises summaries of key current sentencing guideline cases from the Court of Appeal. This compendium can be found on the SGC website (www.sentencing-guidelines.gov.uk). Extracts from the Magistrates' Court Sentencing Guidelines, dealing with the most common cases dealt with in the magistrates' court, are set out in **Appendix 2**. The full set of Guidelines can be found on the Judicial Studies Board website (www.jsboard.co.uk).

The current edition of the Magistrates' Court Sentencing Guidelines was prepared before s 154 of the CJA 2003 came into effect. Section 154 increases the maximum sentencing powers of the magistrates' court (see **11.5.4** below).

The importance of the sentencing guidelines issued by the SGC is highlighted by s 172 of the CJA 2003, which provides that a court, when sentencing a defendant, must have regard to any guidelines which are relevant to the defendant's case. If the sentencing court chooses to depart from the guideline sentence, it must give reasons for so doing (CJA 2003, s 174(2)). The appellate courts have stressed, though, that guidelines are distinct from strict rules, and that magistrates or judges passing sentence always need to have regard to the particular facts of the case before them (*R v Martin* [2006] EWCA Crim 1035).

The SGC has produced three more general sets of guidelines dealing with the following matters:

(a)   the new sentences created by the CJA 2003 (see **11.5 and 11.6** below);

(b)   reductions in sentence for a guilty plea (see **11.4.2.5** below);

(c)   the principle of 'seriousness' (see **11.4.2.3** below).

The full text of these guidelines can be found on the SGC website (see above).

11.4.2.3   The principle of seriousness

Prior to the CJA 2003 coming into force, the seriousness of an offence would determine the 'starting point' for the sentence the court would impose. The sentencing court would then take into account the presence of any aggravating or mitigating factors to arrive at its sentence.

The CJA 2003 does not change this. It does, however, list those matters which the sentencing court must consider when determining how serious an offence is. Section 143(1) of the Act provides that:

> In considering the seriousness of any offence, the court must consider the offender's *culpability* in committing the offence and any *harm* which the offence caused, was intended to cause or might foreseeably have caused. (emphasis added)

Culpability

The SGC has published a guideline, 'Overarching Principles: Seriousness'. In this guideline, the SGC identifies four levels of criminal culpability for sentencing purposes. In descending order of seriousness, the four levels are where the offender:

(a)   has the *intention* to cause harm, with the highest culpability being when an offence is planned. The worse the harm intended, the greater the seriousness;

(b)   is *reckless* as to whether harm is caused. This covers situations when the defendant appreciates that some harm would be caused but goes ahead, giving no thought to the consequences even though the extent of the risk would be obvious to most people;

(c) has *knowledge* of the specific risks entailed by his actions, even though he does not intend to cause the harm that results;

(d) is guilty of *negligence*.

The SGC guideline provides that the culpability of the defendant in the particular circumstances of the case should be the initial factor in determining the seriousness of an offence.

Harm

The SGC guideline on 'Seriousness' confirms that 'harm' not only includes harm which is actually caused, but also where there is a risk of harm even though no harm actually results.

Harm may be caused either to individuals, or to the community at large. The types of harm that may be caused include:

(a) physical injury;

(b) sexual violation;

(c) financial loss;

(d) damage to health; and

(e) psychological distress.

Prevalence

Although courts throughout the country should pass the same sentence for the same type of offence, in exceptional circumstances a court in a particular area may treat an offence more seriously than elsewhere. This may occur if the particular type of offence is prevalent in the area and the court has before it evidence that these offences are causing harm to the community at large. Common examples of offences which may be prevalent in a particular area are drugs-related offences and street robberies. In *R v Oosthuizen* [2005] Crim LR 979, the Court of Appeal endorsed the principle that a court, when sentencing a defendant, may treat an offence more seriously than it would be treated elsewhere on the basis of prevalence.

11.4.2.4   Aggravating and mitigating factors

Statutory aggravating factors

The concept of aggravating and mitigating factors has not been changed by the CJA 2003. There are, however, now four situations when the 2003 Act obliges the sentencing court to treat an offence as being more serious than it would otherwise have done (and so to impose a greater penalty):

(a) *Previous convictions* – under s 143(2), the court must treat any previous convictions as an aggravating factor if, having regard to the nature of the previous conviction and the time that has elapsed since the conviction, the court considers it reasonable to do so. In practice this means that previous convictions are likely to be regarded as aggravating factors if the offences have been committed recently and/or are for similar types of offence. For example, if a defendant convicted of a theft from a supermarket has several previous convictions for the same type of offence, these previous convictions will be seen by the sentencing court as an aggravating factor.

(b) *Offences committed whilst on bail* – under s 143(3), if the offender was on bail in respect of another offence at the time of the current offence, the court must treat this as an aggravating factor.

(c) *Racial or religious aggravation* – under s 145, any racial or religious motive for committing the offence must be treated as an aggravating factor.

(d) *Hostility based on sexual orientation or disability* – under s 146, any hostility towards the victim of an offence based on that victim's sexual orientation or any physical or mental disability, must be treated as an aggravating factor.

Other aggravating and mitigating factors

The SGC guideline on 'Seriousness' lists other factors which a sentencing court may consider to be aggravating or mitigating factors.

The list of *aggravating* factors includes:

(a) offences that are planned or premeditated;

(b) offenders operating in groups or gangs;

(c) the deliberate targeting of vulnerable groups (such as the elderly or disabled victims);

(d) offences committed whilst under the influence of drink or drugs;

(e) the use of a weapon;

(f) deliberate and gratuitous violence or damage to property, beyond that required to carry out the offence;

(g) offences involving the abuse of a position of trust;

(h) offences committed against those working in the public sector or providing a service to the public;

(i) in property offences, the high value (including sentimental value) of property to the victim.

The list of *mitigating* factors includes:

(a) offences where the defendant has acted on impulse;

(b) when the defendant has experienced a greater degree of provocation than normally expected;

(c) defendants who are suffering from mental illness or physical disability;

(d) if the defendant is particularly young or old (particularly in the case of young offenders who are immature and have been led astray by others);

(e) the fact that the defendant played only a minor role in the offending;

(f) defendants who were motivated by genuine fear;

(g) defendants who have made attempts to make reparation to their victim.

11.4.2.5 Reduction in sentence for a guilty plea

Why is a reduction made?

The sentencing guidelines provided by the SGC (for the Crown Court) and contained in the Magistrates' Court Sentencing Guidelines (for the magistrates' court) are based on a defendant who is convicted following a trial. Often, however, the court will be required to sentence a defendant who has pleaded guilty to the offence with which he has been charged.

Section 144 of the CJA 2003 provides that when sentencing a defendant who has entered a guilty plea, the court must 'take into account' the stage in the proceedings at which the defendant gave his indication of a guilty plea and the circumstances in which the indication was given. The rationale behind a reduction in sentence for defendants who pleads guilty is that a guilty plea avoids the need for a trial (and therefore enables other cases to be dealt with more quickly), saves money and, if made early in the case, saves victims and witnesses from stress and anxiety about having to attend court to give oral evidence.

The SGC guideline 'Reduction in Sentence for a Guilty Plea' confirms that the sentencing court should treat reductions in sentence for a guilty plea as being a separate issue from the presence of aggravating and mitigating factors. The court should first address the issue of the defendant's remorse, together with any mitigating features, when deciding the appropriate length of sentence, *before* calculating the reduction to be made for the guilty plea.

The SGC has also confirmed that where an offence crosses the threshold for the imposition of a community or custodial sentence (see **11.5** and **11.6** below), a sufficiently early guilty plea may allow the court to impose a fine or a discharge rather than a community sentence, or an alternative to an immediate custodial sentence.

What level of reduction will be made?

The level of the reduction in sentence will depend upon the stage in the proceedings at which the guilty plea was entered. For all offences other than murder, the SGC has stated that the level of the reduction should be on a sliding scale, ranging from a maximum of *one-third* (where the guilty plea was entered at the first reasonable opportunity), reducing to a maximum of *one-quarter* (where the guilty plea is entered after a date for trial has been set), and to a maximum of *one-tenth* (for a guilty plea 'at the door of the court' or after the trial has begun). Set out below is a diagram reproduced from the SGC guideline which depicts this sliding scale.

For the offence of murder, the defendant will receive a mandatory sentence of life imprisonment (see **11.5.1** below). The sentencing judge will then specify the tariff for the offence (ie, the actual length of the custodial sentence to be served by the defendant). A defendant who pleads guilty at the first reasonable opportunity will be entitled to a maximum reduction of his tariff of one sixth or five years, whichever is less.

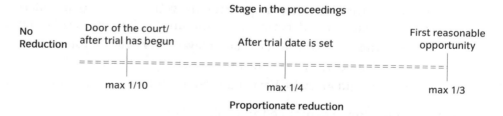

In *R v Oosthuizen* [2005] Crim LR 979, the Court of Appeal held that a defendant who pleads guilty at the first opportunity should receive a full discount, even if the defendant was caught red-handed and had no choice other than to plead guilty because of the strength of the evidence against him. This was confirmed in *R v Bowering* [2005] EWCA Crim 3215.

In *Attorney-General's Reference (Nos 14 & 15 of 2006)* [2006] EWCA Crim 1335, the defendant was convicted of various sexual offences, the most serious being the rape of a 12-week-old baby. The defendant pleaded guilty at the first opportunity, and he received a one-third discount on his sentence (because the defendant received a discretionary life sentence, the 'discount' represented a reduction of the minimum period of time the defendant would need to serve in custody before being eligible to apply to the Parole Board for release on licence – see **11.5.3.2**). The Attorney-General argued on appeal that this discount was excessive because the defendant had effectively been caught 'red-handed' (there were photographs of him committing the rape) and therefore had no alternative other than to plead guilty. The Court of Appeal rejected this submission. Applying the *Oosthuizen* case, the Court said that credit for a guilty plea should not be withheld or reduced where the defendant was caught 'red-handed', and the strength of the prosecution case should not, in itself, be regarded as a reason for reducing the discount otherwise appropriate for a prompt guilty plea. The Court did, however, go on to say that there was significant judicial concern about the guidelines issued by the SGC in relation to defendants who had no option other than to plead guilty, and the Court recommended that the guidelines be reviewed as a matter of urgency. The SGC is now conducting a review of the above guidelines, and has launched a consultation with various bodies (including The Law Society) to determine if the guidelines ought to be amended.

11.4.2.6   The totality principle

Introduction

When an offender is being sentenced, the court will take into account both the offence he is being sentenced for and any associated offences. An associated offence is an offence for which the defendant has been convicted in the same proceedings or for which he is to be sentenced at the same time, *or* an offence which the defendant has asked the court to take into consideration when passing sentence.

Offences for which the defendant is convicted in the same proceedings or is to be sentenced at the same time

It will often be the case that a defendant will be convicted of more than one offence in the same set of proceedings, or that a defendant who has been convicted of offences in different sets of proceedings will be sentenced for all of the offences at the same hearing. Whenever a court is sentencing a defendant who has been convicted of more than one offence, it must, when deciding on the appropriate sentence, look at the totality of the offending rather than considering each offence in isolation.

Example

Ruth is convicted of three separate offences of theft in the same proceedings. When Ruth is being sentenced, the court will not look at each offence separately, but will rather assess the total extent of Ruth's offending in determining the sentence that Ruth will be given. Only if the totality of Ruth's offending passes the appropriate thresholds (see **11.5** and **11.6** below) may a custodial or community sentence be imposed by the court.

Offences taken into consideration

Defendants who are being sentenced for a particular offence may ask the court to take other offences into consideration (TIC) when considering the sentence to be imposed. This is particularly common with offenders convicted of property-related offences. In addition to the offence for which he was charged and convicted, a defendant may have committed several similar types of offence for which he has not yet been prosecuted but for which he may subsequently face prosecution. It is likely to be in the defendant's interests that all matters outstanding (or potentially outstanding) against him should be dealt with at the same time.

The usual practice is for the police to present the defendant with a list of additional offences for which he is under investigation and may subsequently be charged. The defendant may ask the court to take these other offences into consideration when deciding the sentence he is to receive for the offence(s) for which he is currently before the court. The offences to be taken into consideration should be of a similar nature to, or less serious than, the offence(s) for which the defendant has been convicted.

When sentencing the defendant, the court is entitled to take these additional offences into account. It may take other offences into consideration, however, only if the defendant expressly agrees to this (*R v Miles* [2006] EWCA Crim 256). The manner in which the court deals with offences taken into consideration depends on the context of such offences. Although in theory these additional offences should increase the severity of the sentence the defendant receives; in practice they might add nothing, or very little, to the sentence the court would otherwise have imposed. They are, however, capable of leading to a substantial increase in the sentence the defendant receives if the offences demonstrate a pattern of criminal activity which suggests careful planning, or if the offences were committed on bail after an earlier arrest.

The advantage to the defendant of having offences taken into consideration is that this 'wipes the slate clean', because he will not subsequently be prosecuted for such offences. The advantage to the police is that a large number of TICs improves their clear-up rates without the need to commence a fresh prosecution against the defendant.

Example

Sarfraz is convicted of one charge of burglary of commercial premises. Sarfraz asks the court to take into consideration three other burglaries of commercial premises which he admits to having carried out and which the police are currently investigating. If the court agrees to take these offences into consideration when deciding the sentence to be imposed on Sarfraz, he cannot subsequently be prosecuted for these offences. Sarfraz is, however, likely to receive a more severe sentence than if he had just been sentenced for the offence with which he was initially charged.

The procedure which takes place when a defendant asks that other offences be taken into consideration is that the defendant will be given a form by the police giving details of the other offences which the police suspect the defendant may have committed. The defendant may then sign the form and will be asked to admit before the court that he wishes the other offences to be taken into consideration on sentence.

11.5 Custodial sentences

11.5.1 Mandatory custodial sentences

Most criminal offences which carry custody as a possible sentence allow the sentencing court some discretion, firstly as to whether a custodial sentence should be imposed and, secondly, as to the length of the sentence. There are some exceptions to this for offences which carry either a fixed custodial sentence or a custodial sentence which is subject to a statutory minimum period:

(a)   *Murder* – a defendant convicted of murder will receive a mandatory sentence of life imprisonment (although the sentencing judge will determine the minimum number of years which the defendant must actually serve in prison before becoming eligible for release on licence upon the recommendation of the Parole Board).

(b) *Burglary of domestic premises* – a defendant who receives a third conviction for burglary of domestic premises will receive a minimum sentence of three years' imprisonment, unless the court is of the opinion that there are particular circumstances relating either to the offender or to any of the offences which would make the imposition of the minimum sentence unjust.

(c) *Trafficking in Class A drugs* – a defendant who receives a third conviction for trafficking in Class A drugs will receive a minimum sentence of seven years' imprisonment, unless the court is of the opinion that there are particular circumstances which relate to any of the offences or to the offender which would make it unjust to impose such a sentence.

(d) *Firearms offences* – under s 51A of the Firearms Act 1968, a defendant who commits any one of a defined list of offences involving the possession of a firearm will receive a minimum sentence of five years' imprisonment if over 18 (or three years if aged between 16 and 18), unless there are exceptional circumstances relating to the offence or the offender.

11.5.2 Discretionary custodial sentences

Where the court has discretion as to whether to pass a custodial sentence, it must apply the test set out in s 152(2) of the CJA 2003:

> The court must not pass a custodial sentence unless it is of the opinion that the offence, or the combination of the offence and one or more offences associated with it, was so serious that neither a fine alone nor a community sentence can be justified for the offence.

This test is known as the custody threshold. Only if this threshold is passed may the court impose a custodial sentence. The only circumstance in which this test will not be relevant is if the court considers that the defendant satisfies the definition of a 'dangerous offender' in ss 224–236 of the CJA 2003 (see **11.5.3** below). In such circumstances the court is obliged to impose a custodial sentence and so need not consider whether the custody threshold is satisfied.

If the custody threshold is passed, the court must then consider the length of the custodial sentence. To determine the length of the sentence, the court must apply s 153(2) of the CJA 2003. This provides that a custodial sentence

> ... must be for the shortest term (not exceeding the permitted maximum) that in the opinion of the court is commensurate with the seriousness of the offence, or the combination of the offence and one or more other offences associated with it.

Separate sentences of imprisonment imposed on defendants convicted of two or more offences may be expressed by the sentencing court to be either concurrent or consecutive. A *concurrent* sentence means that the custodial terms are deemed to be served at the same time. A *consecutive* sentence means that one custodial sentence will start after the other one has finished.

Example

Alison is convicted in the Crown Court of unlawful wounding and theft. She is sentenced to three years' imprisonment for the unlawful wounding offence and one year's imprisonment for the theft. The judge tells Alison that the sentences are to run concurrently. This means that Alison has effectively received a total sentence of three years' imprisonment because the sentence for the theft will run at the same time as the first year of the sentence for the unlawful wounding.

Had the judge expressed the custodial terms to be consecutive, Alison's total sentence would amount to four years. The one-year sentence for the theft would take effect after Alison had served the three-year sentence for the unlawful wounding.

Consecutive sentences should not generally be imposed where matters of fact arise out of the same incident (*R v Lawrence* (1989) 11 Cr App R (S) 580).

11.5.3 Discretionary custodial sentences in the Crown Court

11.5.3.1 The 'normal' approach to sentencing

Judges in the Crown Court have the power to sentence a defendant to a term of imprisonment up to the maximum permitted for that offence. Examples of the maximum prison sentences that may be imposed for some of the most common crimes dealt with in the Crown Court are:

(a)   robbery – life imprisonment;

(b)   wounding/causing gbh with intent (Offences Against the Person Act 1861, s 18) – life imprisonment;

(c)   wounding/inflicting gbh (Offences Against the Person Act 1861, s 20) – five years;

(d)   assault occasioning actual bodily harm (Offences Against the Person Act 1861, s 47) – five years;

(e)   theft – seven years;

(f)   burglary of domestic premises – 14 years;

(g)   burglary of other premises – 10 years.

In practice, very few defendants receive the maximum sentence which the offence carries. In determining the length of the sentence, the judge will have regard to the guideline cases previously considered by the Court of Appeal. The SGC has put these cases together in a document entitled 'Guideline Judgments Case Compendium', which may be accessed from the SGC website (see **11.4.2.2** above).

11.5.3.2 Dangerous offenders

Introduction

When the judge imposes a discretionary custodial sentence, he will normally impose such a sentence only if the test set out in s 152(2) of the CJA 2003 (see **11.5.2** above) is satisfied. Similarly, he will determine the actual length of the sentence by applying the test set out in s 153(2) above. These tests are modified, however, in the case of 'dangerous offenders', against whom it is considered the public require greater protection. Such offenders will receive longer sentences than they would were the court to apply the tests in ss 152(2) and 153(2).

If a defendant is classified as 'dangerous', the court will impose one of the following types of custodial sentence:

(a)   life imprisonment;

(b)   a sentence required for public protection; or

(c)   an extended sentence.

Each type of sentence will be examined below, after the new terminology employed by the CJA 2003 has been explained.

Terminology

The CJA 2003 has introduced the following terms:

(a) *Specified offence* – s 224(1) divides specified offences into:

    (i)   specified violent offences – these offences include manslaughter, kidnapping, riot, affray, robbery, actual and grievous bodily harm and aggravated burglary; and

    (ii)   specified sexual offences – these offences include rape, indecent assault, unlawful sexual intercourse and a range of offences known generically as 'paedophile offences'.

(b) *Serious offences* – s 224(2) defines a serious offence as being a specified offence (as described above) which is punishable by a maximum sentence of either life imprisonment, or a prison sentence of at least 10 years.

(c) *Serious harm* – this is defined in s 224(3) as meaning 'death or serious personal injury, whether physical or psychological'.

Life sentences and sentences for public protection

If a defendant is convicted of a serious offence *and* the court considers that there is a significant risk to members of the public of serious harm as a result of the defendant committing further specified offences, s 225 provides that the court must pass one of the following sentences:

(a) a discretionary life sentence (if the offence itself carries such a sentence as a maximum penalty and the seriousness of the offence justifies such a sentence). The judge will determine the minimum period the defendant must serve in custody before he becomes eligible for release on licence upon the recommendation of the Parole Board; or

(b) if a discretionary life sentence is not possible, a sentence of imprisonment for public protection. This will be a sentence of detention for an indeterminate period. The judge will set the minimum period of time that is to be served in custody for the purposes of punishment and deterrence, following which the defendant will become eligible for release on licence upon the recommendation of the Parole Board.

Extended sentences

A defendant will receive an extended sentence if he has been convicted of a specified violent or sexual offence (but which is not a serious offence) *and* the court considers that there is a significant risk of serious harm occasioned by him committing further offences (CJA 2003, s 227(1)).

An extended sentence is made up of two parts:

(a) the appropriate custodial sentence (ie, the 'normal' sentence the court would impose, subject to a minimum sentence of 12 months); plus

(b) an additional period (referred to as the 'extension period') during which the defendant will be released on licence. The extension period will begin at the end of the full custodial term imposed by the judge (whether or not the defendant has already been released early on licence) and will be for as long as the court considers necessary for the purposes of protecting the public from serious harm caused by the defendant committing further offences. The extension period must not exceed five years in the case of a specified violent offence, or eight years in the case of a specified sexual offence. The overall term of the extended sentence must not exceed the maximum term permitted for the offence.

11.5.4 Discretionary custodial sentences in the magistrates' court

The CJA 2003 has made significant changes to the maximum sentencing powers available to a magistrates' court. Prior to the Act coming into force, the maximum custodial sentence which a magistrates' court was permitted to impose on a defendant was six months for one offence, rising to a maximum of 12 months where a defendant was convicted of two or more either way offences.

Section 154 of the CJA 2003 increases the upper sentencing limit for an individual offence in the magistrates' court to 12 months. This is subject to the statute which created the offence imposing a lower maximum sentence. If the magistrates are sentencing a defendant on the same occasion in respect two or more offences which carry a potential custodial sentence, s 155 of the Act permits the magistrates to impose consecutive custodial sentences up to a maximum of 65 weeks (ie, 15 months). The same section now permits the magistrates to sentence a defendant convicted of two or more either way offences to receive a maximum sentence of 65 weeks.

Example

George is convicted in the magistrates' court of the offences of theft and assault occasioning actual bodily harm. The magistrates decide to impose consecutive prison sentences for each offence. George is sentenced to nine months' imprisonment for the theft and a further four months' imprisonment for the assault. The magistrates are permitted to pass such a sentence because the total sentence imposed on George will not exceed 65 weeks.

The rationale behind the increase in the sentencing powers available to the magistrates is that this should result in more either way cases being dealt with by the magistrates' court rather than by the Crown Court (where the cost of cases is far more expensive). The changes should result in the magistrates being prepared to accept jurisdiction in far more either way cases at the plea before venue hearing than is presently the case (see **Chapter 6**).

11.5.5 How long will a defendant actually spend in prison?

The first question a solicitor is usually asked by a client who is sentenced to a term of imprisonment is how much time the client will actually spend in prison.

For defendants who receive a prison sentence of 12 months or more, unless the defendant is convicted of murder (see **11.5.1**) or is classified as a 'dangerous offender' (see **11.5.3.2**), he will be entitled to release from custody after completing half of his sentence. During the second half of the sentence the defendant will be released on licence and will be required to comply with licence requirements imposed either by the sentencing court, or by the Probation Service (such as observing a curfew, attending appointments with the Probation Service or undergoing periodic drug tests). If the defendant breaches the term of his licence, he can be returned to prison to serve the remainder of his sentence.

The position in respect of a defendant who receives a prison sentence of less than 12 months is set out in **11.5.6** below.

Any time which a defendant has spent in custody on remand before the custodial sentence is passed will count as time served as part of the sentence, unless the court is of the opinion that it is just in all the circumstances for this time not to be counted towards the sentence (CJA 2003, s 240(3) and (4)). If the court is of this opinion, reasons must be given (CJA 2003, s 240(5) and *R v Barber* [2006] EWCA Crim 162).

11.5.6 Custodial sentences of less than 12 months

11.5.6.1 Introduction

As a result of changes introduced by the CJA 2003, all custodial sentences of less than 12 months (whether imposed by the Crown Court or the magistrates' court) must be one of the new-style shorter sentences:

(a)   custody plus (see **11.5.6.2** below); or

(b)   intermittent custody (see **11.5.6.3** below); or

(c)   a suspended sentence, sometimes referred to as 'custody minus' (see **11.5.6.4** below).

11.5.6.2 Custody plus

This new form of sentence was created by s 181 of the CJA 2003.

A defendant who is sentenced to an immediate term of imprisonment of less than 12 months will have his sentence divided into two parts:

(a)   a short custodial period of between two and 13 weeks; and

(b)   a longer licence period, which must be at least 26 weeks in length.

The combined totals of the custodial and the licence periods must be for a minimum of 28 weeks and a maximum of 51 weeks. This means that the shortest prison sentence a court may now in effect pass is one of 28 weeks (two weeks in custody and 26 weeks on licence). To allow for such a sentence to be given in the magistrates' court, the Act has increased the maximum custodial sentence permitted in the magistrates' court for summary only offences which carry a possible sentence of imprisonment following conviction, from six months to 51 weeks (CJA 2003, ss 280 and 281).

Example 1

Brian is convicted of criminal damage by the magistrates' court, and the magistrates decide to impose a custodial sentence of less than 12 months. The magistrates decide that the custodial period should be four weeks. The magistrates may set the licence period anywhere between 26 and 47 weeks.

Example 2

Marcia is convicted of common assault by the magistrates' court, and the magistrates decide to impose a custodial sentence of less than 12 months. The magistrates decide that the custodial period should be 12 weeks. The magistrates may set the licence period anywhere between 26 and 39 weeks.

During the licence period, the defendant will be obliged to comply with licence requirements set by the court when he is sentenced. Should he fail to comply with these requirements, he may be returned to prison for the remainder of the licence period. The menu of requirements from which the court may choose is similar to that from which a court may choose when imposing a generic community order (see **11.6** below):

(a)   an unpaid work requirement;

(b)   an activity requirement;

(c)   a programme requirement;

(d)   a prohibited activity requirement;

(e)   a curfew requirement (enforced by electronic monitoring);

(f)   an exclusion requirement (enforced by electronic monitoring);

(g)   a supervision requirement;

(h)   an attendance centre requirement (for defendants under 25 years of age only).

Details of what each requirement entails are set out at **11.6** below.

When a court imposes a sentence of 'custody plus', it will follow the following procedure:

(a)   the court will set the overall term of imprisonment;

(b)   then it will specify what part of that term is the 'custodial period';

(c)   then it will state that the remaining part of the term is the licence period; and

(d)   lastly, it will set the requirements with which the defendant must comply during the licence period.

The Sentencing Guidelines Council (SGC) published a draft guideline for consultation on the new 'custody plus' sentence on 30 March 2006. (Definitive guidelines are expected in the second half of 2006.)

11.5.6.3   Intermittent custody

Intermittent custody is a concept borrowed from other European jurisdictions and is a variant of custody plus. It was created by s 183 of the CJA 2003. A sentence of intermittent custody allows a defendant to serve his custodial sentence at weekends or at other times fixed by the court, as opposed to having to serve the 'custodial period' of his sentence in one continuous term of imprisonment. Such a sentence may be appropriate for defendants for whom the court has decided that a short custodial sentence is required, but who might lose their employment if a custody plus sentence were to be imposed, or who might lose other community or family ties which they might have.

As with custody plus, if the court decides to impose a sentence of intermittent custody, it must first set an overall prison term of between 28 and 51 weeks. The court will then specify the number of 'custodial days' which the defendant must serve in prison before being released on licence for the remainder of the term. The number of 'custodial days' must be between 14 and 90. The court will then specify the periods when the defendant is to be released temporarily from prison on licence before he has served the full number of 'custodial days'. Lastly, the court will impose conditions with which the defendant must comply during the licence period. The licence period will comprise both the days when the defendant is released temporarily from custody and any weeks remaining as part of the overall prison term after the defendant has served his 'custodial days'. The conditions which the court may impose are essentially the same type of conditions which the court may impose under custody plus (see **11.5.6.2** above).

Example

Oscar is convicted of handling stolen goods by the magistrates' court. The magistrates decide to impose a custodial sentence of less than 12 months. In his plea in mitigation, Oscar's solicitor informs the magistrates that Oscar works on a production line in a local factory between Monday and Friday, and Oscar will lose this job if he receives an immediate custodial sentence (ie, a sentence of custody plus). The magistrates therefore decide to impose a sentence of intermittent custody.

Oscar is given an overall prison term of 36 weeks and is told that he must serve 24 custodial days. The court specifies that Oscar is to be released temporarily from prison on licence between Monday and Friday (so that in effect he serves his custodial days at the weekend). Oscar will serve his 24 custodial days over the following 12 weekends. During the period of time when he is released intermittently from custody (ie, the weekdays during the first 12 weeks of his sentence), and also during the remaining period of his overall sentence after he has completed his custodial days, the magistrates may impose conditions with which Oscar must comply.

11.5.6.4 Suspended sentence orders ('custody minus')

The 'new-style' suspended sentence

Prior to the CJA 2003 coming into force, both the magistrates' court and the Crown Court had the power to sentence a defendant to a term of imprisonment, but to suspend that term of imprisonment so that the defendant would not be sent to prison immediately and would be required to serve a prison sentence only if he committed further offences during the period for which the sentence was suspended. The court could impose a suspended sentence only if there were 'exceptional circumstances' which justified the suspension of the custodial term. 'Exceptional circumstances' normally related to the particular family circumstances of the defendant (for example, a defendant who was the sole carer for an elderly parent, or a defendant who was a single parent looking after a disabled child). Whilst the CJA 2003 preserves suspended sentences as a form of sentence which the court may impose, it makes significant changes to the way in which such sentences will operate in future. The 'new-style' suspended sentences are created by s 189 of the Act.

Under s 189, when a court passes a sentence of imprisonment of at least 28 weeks but not more than 51 weeks (ie, custody plus), the court has a discretion to make an order that:

(a) for a period of time specified in the order, the offender must comply with one or more requirements; and

(b) the sentence of imprisonment imposed is not to take effect unless, during the period of suspension, the offender either fails to comply with the requirements specified in (a) or commits a further offence and, in either case, the court orders that the original sentence is to take effect.

The period of suspension and the period of time during which the offender must comply with the requirements must be between six months and two years.

The requirements which the court can attach to a suspended sentence order are the same type of activities that a court can impose as part of a generic community order (see **11.6** below).

The court may suspend a sentence of imprisonment either in respect of a prison sentence (for offenders aged 21 and over), or in respect of detention in a young offenders institution (for offenders aged 18 to 20 inclusive).

There is no longer a requirement that the court must find 'exceptional circumstances' to justify the suspension of the custodial sentence. It is likely, however, that suspended sentences will continue to be used in the same way as prior to the CJA 2003 coming into effect, ie where the court decides that the custody threshold has been passed but finds that there are particular circumstances relating to the defendant which justify not sending him to prison immediately.

As a suspended sentence order is a variant of custody plus, the magistrates will need to set an overall term of imprisonment, a 'custodial period' (of between two and 13 weeks) and a 'licence period' (of at least 26 weeks).

Example

Ellen is convicted of common assault by the magistrates' court. The magistrates decide to impose a custodial sentence of less than 12 months and impose an overall term of imprisonment of 40 weeks. The custodial period is set at 10 weeks and the licence period is set at 30 weeks. The magistrates exercise their discretion to suspend the sentence for 12 months, but impose requirements that during those 12 months Ellen must undertake 100 hours' unpaid work within the community. If Ellen fails to comply with this requirement, or commits another offence during the 12-month period, the court may order that the original sentence take effect (see 'Breach of a suspended sentence', below).

Breach of a suspended sentence

A defendant who has received a suspended sentence can breach such a sentence in one of two ways:

(a)   by failing without reasonable excuse to comply with a requirement imposed as part of the sentence; or

(b)   by committing a further offence in the period during which the sentence is suspended (even if the further offence is itself non-imprisonable).

Paragraph 8 of Sch 12 to the CJA 2003 creates a presumption that, in either case, the court will order that the suspended sentence take effect (often referred to as 'activating' the sentence), unless the court considers that it would be unjust to do this, in which case the court must give reasons for its decision not to activate the sentence. Case law on suspended sentences prior to the CJA 2003 coming into effect suggests that the court may consider it unjust to activate a suspended sentence if a defendant commits a further offence towards the end of the suspension period, or if a defendant commits an offence of a completely different type from that for which the suspended sentence was originally given.

Example 1

Kate is convicted of theft by the magistrates' court. The magistrates impose a sentence of custody plus (with a custodial period of six weeks), but exercise their discretion to suspend this for a period of 18 months. The magistrates also impose a requirement that Kate does 200 hours of unpaid work in the community.

Kate fails to attend at the times when she is supposed to do this work and the Probation Service (which organises the work) brings this to the attention of the court. When Kate appears before the court there is a presumption that the original sentence will be activated. Unless Kate has a reasonable excuse for not attending to carry out her unpaid work, the magistrates will order that the original sentence will take effect. Kate will therefore immediately be sent to prison to complete the 'custodial period' of her original sentence.

Example 2

Jim is convicted of obtaining property by deception in the magistrates' court. The magistrates impose a sentence of custody plus (with a custodial period of four weeks), but exercise their discretion to suspend this for two years. The magistrates also impose a requirement that Jim performs 150 hours of unpaid work in the community. Two weeks before the end of the suspension period (and after having completed the 150 hours of unpaid work), Jim is convicted of theft. There is a presumption that the suspended sentence will be activated, but in such a case the magistrates are likely to decide that it would be unjust to do this because the suspension period has almost expired and Jim has completed his unpaid work. To activate the suspended sentence (and so send Jim to prison to complete the custodial period of his sentence) would be unjust.

11.5.7 Deferred sentence

Section 278 of the CJA 2003 permits a court to defer sentencing a defendant for up to six months to enable the court to observe both the defendant's conduct during the deferment period and any changes in the defendant's circumstances during this period. Deferment of sentence may be used when a court is considering imposing an immediate custodial sentence, but a change (for the better) in the defendant's circumstances is imminent and the court wants to assess the effect of such change on the defendant before passing sentence. Typical examples of when a deferred sentence may be appropriate are when a defendant is just about to start a new job, or when a defendant has been given the opportunity to move away from the area where he committed his offences so that he may 'make a fresh start'.

The CJA 2003 permits a court, when deferring sentence, both to specify activities which the defendant should undertake during the deferment period and to assess the defendant's compliance with these activities when the case comes back before the court for sentence. Such activities will usually involve some form of reparation to the victim of the offence (for example, the court may require an offender convicted of causing criminal damage by covering premises with graffiti, to remove the graffiti). A defendant must consent to his sentence being deferred and must also undertake to comply with the requirements imposed by the court.

11.6 Community sentences

11.6.1 Threshold

The CJA 2003 has swept away various community-based penalties which a sentencing court previously had the power to impose on an defendant, and has replaced this with one type of community sentence – the generic community order.

Section 148 of the Act sets out the threshold which must be reached before a court can impose such an order:

(1) A court must not pass a community sentence on an offender unless it is of the opinion that the offence, or the combination of the offence and one or more offences associated with it, was serious enough to warrant such a sentence.

(2) Where a court passes a community sentence which consists of or includes a community order—

(a) a particular requirement or requirements forming part of the community order must be such as, in the opinion of the court, is, or taken together are, the most suitable for the offender, and

(b) the restrictions on liberty imposed by the order must be such as in the opinion of the court are commensurate with the seriousness of the offence, or the combination of the offence and one or more offences associated with it.

In addition to the threshold set out in s 148, s 151 of the CJA 2003 permits a court to impose a community sentence on persistent offenders who do not satisfy the s 148 test. 'Persistent offenders' are offenders who have three or more previous convictions, each of which was dealt with by the court by way of a fine only.

11.6.2 Contents of the generic community order

In making a generic community order the court may choose from a 'menu' of options and select those which are most appropriate for the defendant. Any limitations which the sentence imposes on the defendant must be proportionate to the seriousness of the offence and must reflect the principal aim of preventing the defendant from re-offending.

The order can last for up to three years, although certain requirements are subject to shorter time limits. For example, a requirement for the offender to carry out unpaid work within the community must be completed within 12 months of the order being made.

The options from which the court may choose are as follows:

(a) *Unpaid work requirement* – this requires the defendant to perform unpaid work in the community for between 40 and 300 hours. This work must be completed within a 12-month period.

(b) *Activity requirement* – this requires the defendant to take part in specified activities which may be designed to help the defendant overcome a particular problem (such as finding work), or which may be activities to make reparation to the victim (such as repairing damage caused).

(c) *Programme requirement* – this requires the defendant to take part in one or more courses to address the defendant's offending behaviour, such as courses in anger management, sex offending or substance misuse.

(d) *Prohibited activity requirement* – this requires the defendant to refrain from taking part in specified activities. This type of order is unlikely to be made in the case of adult defendants and is more appropriate for defendants in the Youth Court (see **Chapter 14**).

(e) *Curfew requirement* – this requires the defendant to remain at a particular location (normally the defendant's place of residence) specified by the court between specified times. The order can last for up to six months and the defendant will be electronically monitored.

(f) *Exclusion requirement* – this prohibits the defendant from entering a place or places (such as a city centre, or a particular type of establishment like a shop or a pub) for a period not exceeding two years. Again the defendant will be electronically monitored.

(g) *Residence requirement* – this requires the defendant to live at a particular place as specified in the court order.

(h) *Mental health treatment requirement* – this requires the defendant to submit to treatment from a mental health practitioner for a specified period of time.

(i) *Drug rehabilitation requirement* – this requires the defendant to submit to treatment to reduce or eliminate his dependency on drugs, and to submit to providing samples to determine whether he has drugs in his body. This will be for a period of time specified by the court, but it must be for at least six months.

(j) *Alcohol treatment requirement* – this requires the defendant to submit, during a period of time specified by the court, to treatment to reduce or eliminate his dependency on alcohol. The period must last for at least six months.

(k) *Supervision requirement* – this requires the defendant to attend appointments with a member of the Probation Service. The purpose of such meetings is to promote the defendant's rehabilitation, and the meetings will involve confronting the defendant's offending behaviour, discussing how the defendant might 'manage' his life and generally monitoring the defendant's progress. A supervision requirement may be imposed for up to three years.

(l) *Attendance centre requirement* – this requires the defendant to attend an attendance centre for a total of between 12 and 36 hours. Such an order can only be imposed on defendants who are under 25 years of age. Further details of the requirements of this type of order are provided in **Chapter 14**.

The sentencing court will choose one or more of these options to make up the overall community sentence to be imposed on the defendant.

The court may order that electronic monitoring be used to check the defendant's compliance with any of the specific requirements imposed under a generic community order (in the case of a curfew or exclusion requirement, such monitoring is mandatory).

11.6.3 Guidance from the SGC

Given the extremely wide scope of the potential requirements a court may impose as part of a generic community order, the SGC has provided guidelines as to how the court should approach the making of such an order.

In its guideline 'New Sentences: Criminal Justice Act 2003', the SGC stipulates that the court should initially decide (in consultation with the Probation Service if necessary) whether a community sentence is justified, and then, if it is justified, the court must decide which requirements should be included in the order. When deciding which requirements to include, the court must be satisfied as to three matters:

(a) that the restriction on liberty is commensurate with the seriousness of the offence;

(b) that the requirements are most suitable for the defendant; and

(c) that where two or more requirements are included, they are compatible with each other.

The guiding principles behind the making of a generic community order are said by the SGC to be 'proportionality and suitability'. The court should impose an order which has the maximum chance of successful completion. The SGC has identified three sentencing ranges (low, medium, and high) within the community sentence band, and a court considering the imposition of such a sentence must decide into which band the particular offence(s) with which it is dealing falls:

(a) *The low range* – this is for defendants whose offence was relatively minor and will include persistent petty offenders and those who have failed to respond to the previous imposition of fines. The types of offence this may cover are some public order offences, some thefts from shops and interference with a motor vehicle. Suitable requirements for defendants in the low range may include:

(i) 40 to 80 hours of unpaid work; or

(ii) a curfew requirement of up to 12 hours per day for a few weeks; or

(iii) an exclusion requirement lasting a few months; or

(iv) a prohibited activity requirement; or

(v) an attendance centre requirement (where available).

(b) *The medium range* – this range is for offences which obviously fall within the community sentence band. The SGC guidelines suggest that the types of offence falling within this band will include handling stolen goods worth less than £1,000 acquired for resale, or somewhat more valuable goods acquired for the handler's own use, some cases of burglary in commercial premises, some cases of taking a motor vehicle without consent and some cases of obtaining property by deception. Suitable requirements for defendants in the medium range may include:

    (i) between 80 and 150 hours of unpaid work; or

    (ii) an activity requirement in the middle range (20 to 30 days); or

    (iii) a curfew requirement of up to 12 hours for two to three months; or

    (iv) an exclusion requirement lasting approximately six months; or

    (v) a prohibited activity requirement.

(c) *The high range* – this range is for offences that only just fall below the custody threshold, or where the custody threshold has been crossed but the court considers that a community sentences is appropriate in all the circumstances. The SGC suggests that an example of the latter type of offence might be a standard domestic burglary committed by a first-time offender. Suitable requirements for defendants in the high range may include two or more of the following requirements:

    (i) between 150 and 300 hours of unpaid work;

    (ii) an activity requirement up to the maximum 60 days;

    (iii) an exclusion order lasting approximately 12 months;

    (iv) a curfew requirement of up to 12 hours for four to six months.

In *Attorney-General's Reference* (No 11 of 2006) [2006] EWCA Crim 856, the Court of Appeal held that where a defendant was on the brink of receiving a custodial sentence, a judge was entitled to take into account the extent to which prisons were overcrowded in determining the sentence to be imposed. The Court held that prison overcrowding hindered the work of rehabilitating offenders that a prison should normally provide, and this was therefore a matter which the judge could properly take into account in deciding that a community sentence was more appropriate. The Court stressed that the reform and rehabilitation of offenders was an important function of sentencing to which the court must always have regard (see **11.2** above).

11.6.4 Breach of a community sentence

The consequences for an offender who breaches the terms of a generic community order are dealt with by s 179 of the CJA 2003, which invokes Sch 8 to the Act.

The first thing that will happen when a defendant, without reasonable excuse, breaches a community order, is that defendant will receive a warning from a 'responsible officer'. This person is likely to be the member of the Probation Service who is supervising the defendant's compliance with his generic community order. The warning must:

(a) describe the circumstances of the failure;

(b) state that the failure is unacceptable; and

(c) inform the defendant that if, within the next 12 months, he again fails to comply with any of the requirements of the order, he will be liable to be brought before a court.

If, within the following 12 months, the defendant again fails without reasonable excuse to comply with the requirements of the order, the responsible officer will report this matter to the court which imposed the order in the first place and the defendant will be required to appear before that court.

If the court is satisfied that that the defendant has, without reasonable excuse, failed to comply with the requirements of the order, the court *must*:

(a)   amend the order so as to impose requirements on the defendant which are more onerous (for example, by increasing the amount of unpaid work the defendant is required to complete); or

(b)   revoke the order completely and re-sentence the defendant for the offence, but without taking into account the usual custody threshold (see **11.5.2** above); or

(c)   where the defendant has wilfully and persistently failed to comply with the order, the court may revoke the order and impose a custodial sentence of up to 51 weeks (ie, custody plus). This can be done even if the original offence was not punishable by way of a custodial sentence.

Example

Gavin is convicted of assault occasioning actual bodily harm by the magistrates' court. He receives a generic community order which includes a requirement to complete 250 hours of unpaid work.

Gavin fails to attend his first unpaid work session. The probation officer supervising Gavin's sentence gives Gavin a warning. Gavin then fails to attend his second unpaid work session and is brought back before the magistrates' court. The magistrates must, if they are satisfied that Gavin had no reasonable excuse for failing to attend the unpaid work sessions, either amend the generic community order to add more onerous requirements or revoke the order and re-sentence Gavin. If the magistrates choose the latter course, the inevitable sentence will be custodial.

The options open to the court in the event that the defendant breaches his community sentence are incremental. Thus, in the above example, Gavin is likely to have his original order amended to impose more onerous requirements. Should Gavin fail to comply with these further requirements, the magistrates will then consider revoking the original order and re-sentencing Gavin.

11.6.5   Further offences committed during the currency of the generic community order

It will often be the case that a defendant who has received a generic community sentence is convicted of a further offence during the period when the generic community order is still in force. In such a situation, the magistrates may either allow the original generic community order to continue, or, if it is in the interests of justice having regard to the circumstances that have arisen since the original order was made, they may:

(a)   revoke the order (this will be done if the magistrates are imposing a custodial sentence for the 'new' offence, since an offender in prison cannot comply with a community sentence); or

(b)   revoke the order and re-sentence the defendant for the original offence as if he had just been convicted of it. If this is done, the court must have regard to the extent to which the defendant has complied with the original order.

It is likely that, in practice, the magistrates will take one of the steps in (a) or (b) above only if they are intending to impose a custodial sentence for the 'new' offence, or if they consider that it is appropriate to re-sentence the defendant for the original offence (perhaps because the defendant has re-offended only a short time after the original generic community order was imposed).

Example 1

Barry is convicted of common assault by the magistrates' court and receives a two-year generic community order with a supervision requirement, under which he must meet a probation officer once a fortnight. Barry complies with this requirement. Two months before the order is to come to an end, Barry is convicted of a minor public order offence. The magistrates are very unlikely to revoke the original order. Barry will not receive a custodial sentence for the public order offence and it would not be in the interests of justice to revoke the original order and re-sentence Barry, given that the order is almost at an end and Barry has complied with the terms of the order throughout its duration. The magistrates will allow the generic community order to continue, and sentence Barry separately for the public order offence.

Example 2

Miranda is convicted of assault occasioning actual bodily harm by the magistrates' court and receives a two-year generic community order. One year into the order Miranda is convicted of two charges of unlawful wounding. It is likely that the court will want to impose a sentence of imprisonment for these offences. If so, the court will revoke the generic community order and impose a custodial sentence for the offences of unlawful wounding.

Example 3

Tarquin is convicted by the magistrates' court of the possession of a Class A drug and receives an 18-month generic community order, which includes a requirement that Tarquin complies with a drug rehabilitation requirement. Three months after the order is made, Tarquin is convicted of possession of a Class B drug. Whilst this offence would not in itself be likely to lead to a custodial sentence, the magistrates are likely to take the view that the generic community order has been unsuccessful because Tarquin is still taking drugs. The magistrates may therefore decide to revoke the generic community order and re-sentence Tarquin to a term of imprisonment for the original offence of possessing Class A drugs.

11.7 Fines

11.7.1 Introduction

Fines are the most common penalty imposed on those convicted of criminal offences. Approximately 70% of all offenders are dealt with by way of a fine.

11.7.2 Fines in the magistrates' court

In the magistrates' court, the maximum level of fine which the magistrates can impose is set by the statute which creates the offence for which the offender has been convicted. The statute will usually stipulate the maximum fine to be one of five standard levels:

(a)   Level 1 – £200;

(b)   Level 2 – £500;

(c)   Level 3 – £1,000;

(d)   Level 4 – £2,500;

(e)   Level 5 – £5,000.

By way of example, the maximum fine a magistrates' court may impose for the offence of theft is a level 5 fine (£5,000).

The actual size of fine a defendant receives will be determined by the totality principle (if the defendant has been convicted of more than one offence), proportionality and the defendant's personal financial circumstances. Most magistrates' courts that are considering imposing a fine (or other financial penalty) on a defendant will require the defendant to complete a statement of means for this purpose.

To ensure consistency between different magistrates' courts, the Magistrates' Court Sentencing Guidelines suggest that, where a fine is to be imposed, the fine should be in a particular band depending on the seriousness of the offence. The Guidelines give three bands – A, B and C. These bands represent 50%, 100% and 150% of the defendant's weekly take-home pay or benefit.

11.7.3 Fines in the Crown Court

For most offences, the Crown Court has the power to impose a fine instead of, or in addition to, any other sentence it imposes on the defendant (CJA 2003, s 163). There is no maximum limit to the size of fines in the Crown Court. However, as in the magistrates' court, the court will enquire into the financial circumstances of the defendant and take such circumstances into account when deciding on the level of the fine.

Both the Crown Court and the magistrates' court have the power to order a defendant to disclose details of his financial circumstances so that the court may determine the appropriate level of fine to impose (CJA 2003, s 162).

11.8 Conditional and absolute discharges

11.8.1 Conditional discharges

If the court decides to impose a conditional discharge on a defendant, the effect of this is that the defendant will not receive any immediate penalty for the offence he has committed. If, however, the defendant commits a further offence during a period of time specified by the court, the court may sentence him for the original offence. This period of time for which a person can be discharged conditionally is up to three years.

The court will impose a conditional discharge if it is satisfied that, having regard to the circumstances, the nature of the offence and the character of the defendant, any punishment would be inexpedient. For example, a conditional discharge may be imposed where a person of previous good character commits a petty theft. The court may feel that a court appearance and the attendant publicity is punishment enough.

Example

Emily is 50 years of age. She is convicted of the theft of a tin of baked beans from her local supermarket. Emily is of previous good character and the court hears in mitigation that at the time of the offence Emily was taking anti-depressant medication, which had been prescribed by her GP after Emily's husband had confessed to having an extra-marital affair. The magistrates decide that the loss of her good name and the publicity surrounding the case is sufficient punishment for Emily. The magistrates impose a conditional discharge on Emily for a period of two years. The effect of this is that no immediate penalty will be imposed on Emily; but were she to commit a further offence within the specified two-year period, she would be liable to be re-sentenced for her original offence.

11.8.2 Absolute discharges

Absolute discharges are rare. A defendant who receives an absolute discharge will not be subject to any immediate penalty and cannot be subsequently sentenced for the offence if he later commits further offences. An absolute discharge is often imposed where the court feels that the defendant, although technically guilty of an offence, is morally blameless.

11.9 Flowchart – the sentencing ladder

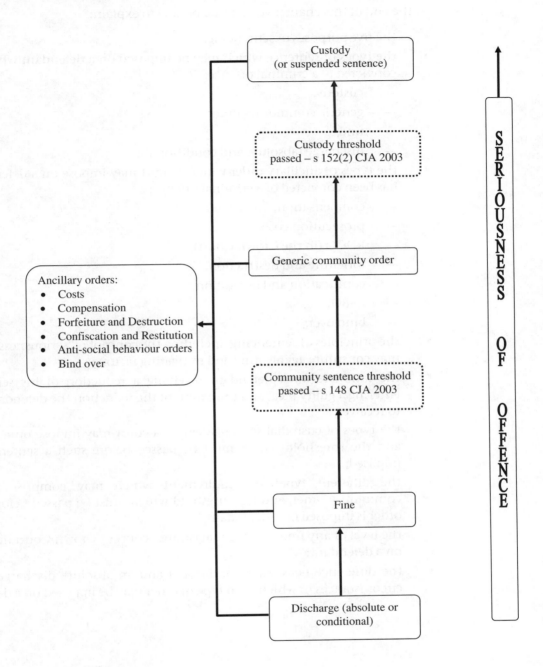

11.10   Checklist

At the end of this chapter you should be able to explain:

- the five purposes of sentencing;
- the types of sentence which may be imposed on a defendant who has been convicted of a criminal offence:
  — custody,
  — generic community order,
  — fine,
  — discharge (absolute and conditional);
- the types of ancillary order which a court may impose on a defendant who has been convicted of a criminal offence:
  — compensation,
  — prosecution costs,
  — RDCO (in the Crown Court),
  — forfeiture and destruction,
  — confiscation and restitution,
  — ASBO,
  — bind over;
- the principles of sentencing, including the concept of 'seriousness' and what may constitute aggravating and mitigating factors;
- the rationale for a defendant receiving a reduction of his sentence for entering a guilty plea, and the extent of the reduction the defendant is likely to receive;
- the types of custodial sentence which a court may impose on a defendant and the threshold which must be passed before such a sentence can be imposed;
- the different types of requirement which may comprise a generic community order, and the threshold which must be passed before such an order is imposed on a defendant;
- the level of any fine which a magistrates' court or Crown Court may impose on a defendant;
- the difference between a conditional and an absolute discharge, and the circumstances in which each type of order may be imposed on a defendant.

Chapter 12

Sentencing in Practice

12.1 Introduction

A defendant will be sentenced by the court either after entering a plea of guilty, or, if he pleaded not guilty, following his conviction at trial. In both situations the court may sentence the defendant immediately, or, if the court thinks it necessary, sentencing may be adjourned until the court has obtained one or more pre-sentence reports dealing with such matters as the defendant's personal history, his current family circumstances, his employment position and his attitude towards the offence for which he has been convicted.

This chapter will examine the practical aspects of sentencing. It will begin by looking at the types of pre-sentence reports that may be required by the court, and will then go on to examine the role played by the defendant's solicitor in the sentencing process. The procedure that is followed when a defendant is sentenced will be explained, and the chapter will conclude with some practical guidance on how the defendant's solicitor should deliver a plea in mitigation on his client's behalf.

12.2 Pre-sentence reports

12.2.1 Pre-sentence reports from the Probation Service

12.2.1.1 Contents

The most common type of pre-sentence report which the court may require before sentencing a defendant is a pre-sentence report from the Probation Service. Such a report is prepared 'with a view to assisting the court in determining the most suitable method of dealing with an offender' (CJA 2003, s 158(1)). If the judge or magistrates require a report from the Probation Service, the sentencing of the defendant will be adjourned (usually for three weeks if the defendant is remanded in custody, or four weeks if the defendant is remanded on bail) to enable an officer from the Probation Service to meet the defendant and to prepare the report. Pre-sentence reports from the Probation Service follow a standard format and contain the following information:

(a) details of the offence and the defendant's attitude towards it – whether he now admit his guilt (if he had pleaded not guilty), or if he feels any genuine remorse for his crimes;

(b)   information about the defendant's personal history and family situation, and any medical problems the defendant may have;

(c)   the Probation Service officer's assessment of the risk of harm to the public from the defendant re-offending; and

(d)   a conclusion incorporating the sentence which the officer preparing the report considers most appropriate for the defendant (and in particular a proposal in relation to what requirements could most appropriately be included in a generic community order).

12.2.1.2   When will the court require a report?

Section 156(1) of the CJA 2003 provides that before deciding on whether a particular type of sentence is appropriate, the court must 'take into account all such information as is available to it about the circumstances of the offence or ... of the offence and the offence or offences associated with it, including any aggravating or mitigating factors'. Section 156(3) stipulates that the court must 'obtain and consider' a pre-sentence report before deciding the following:

(a)   whether the custody threshold has been passed and, if it has, how long the custodial sentence should be (see **11.5.2**); and

(b)   whether the threshold for imposing a community sentence has been passed and, if it has, the requirements that should be imposed on the defendant under a generic community order and the suitability of those requirements for that particular defendant (see **11.6.1**).

The court does not need to obtain such a report if it is of the opinion that a report is 'unnecessary' (s 154(1)). Such a situation is most likely to arise in the Crown Court where a defendant has been convicted of a serious offence and a lengthy custodial sentence is inevitable.

If the judge or magistrates adjourn sentence for the preparation of a pre-sentence report, the defendant will either be released on bail, or remanded in custody (see **7.3**). If the defendant is remanded in custody pending the preparation of a report, he may be remanded for a maximum period of three weeks at any one hearing. Remands on bail may be for a maximum period of four weeks at any one time.

An example of a pre-sentence report in the Gary Dickson case study is set out below.

Key Document – Pre-sentence Report

PRE-SENTENCE REPORT ON GARY DICKSON

INTRODUCTION

1.   This report is based upon two interviews with Mr Dickson, both of which were carried out at 17 Marsh Street, Chester. Mr Dickson has pleaded guilty to one charge of assault occasioning actual bodily harm. I have read the prosecution papers and have seen the record of Mr Dickson's previous convictions.

OFFENCE ANALYSIS

2.   I have discussed the circumstances of the offence with Mr Dickson. Mr Dickson pleaded not guilty initially but changed his plea to guilty on the morning of the trial. Mr Dickson now accepts that he assaulted his victim in an unprovoked attack, punching Mr Lamb several times in the face. Mr Dickson's only explanation for his actions is that Mr Lamb had spent most of

the evening taunting Mr Dickson because he was 'only' a bouncer and Mr Lamb had at one point during the evening tried to proposition Mr Dickson's girlfriend.

3.   Mr Dickson has two previous convictions for offences of threatening behaviour and one previous conviction for the offence of assault occasioning actual bodily harm. Mr Dickson informs me that all three offences occurred whilst he was working as a bouncer, when he was attempting to eject customers from nightclub premises.

INFORMATION ABOUT THE OFFENDER

4.   Mr Dickson is 27 years old and was born and brought up in York. He lives with his girlfriend and her parents in Chester.

5.   Mr Dickson left school at 16 with 4 GCSEs. He joined the army, and remained in the army until 2001.

6.   Mr Dickson works full time as a scaffolder and steeplejack. He is self-employed and does contract work throughout the country. Mr Dickson has also had an evening and weekend job working as a bouncer at a nightclub in Chester. Mr Dickson informs me that he has recently been dismissed from this job as a result of the current proceedings. Mr Dickson has indicated that, as a result of being offered a well-paid, long-term contract to do some scaffolding work at a new building site in Chester, he will not be seeking to get another job as a bouncer.

7.   Mr Dickson's partner has just found out that she is expecting his child. Mr Dickson is very excited at the prospect of becoming a father. He is anxious to fulfil his obligations as a father to his child, and is fearful of losing both his partner and his child should he receive a custodial sentence.

RISK TO THE PUBLIC OF RE-OFFENDING

8.   Mr Dickson's history of offending appears to be tied closely to his employment as a bouncer. Mr Dickson tells me that when he was in the army he obeyed orders from senior officers without question. This made it hard for Mr Dickson to tolerate being abused by members of the public to whom he had given orders when he was working as a bouncer. All too often he would lose his temper and commit acts of violence.

9.   If Mr Dickson were to return to work as a bouncer, I think Mr Dickson would present a significant risk to the public of re-offending. However, Mr Dickson has lost his job as a bouncer and will not be seeking another job in this area. As long as Mr Dickson stays away from this type of work, I would assess the risk of Mr Dickson re-offending as low. Mr Dickson does have anger management issues that he needs to address.

CONCLUSION

10.   Mr Dickson's personal circumstances will change shortly with the birth of his child. He wants to do the best for his family and has the opportunity to take up a well-paid and long-term scaffolding contract.

11.   Mr Dickson has pleaded guilty to a serious and unprovoked assault. I am aware that the court will be considering an immediate custodial sentence. However, I believe that Mr Dickson has learned from his past mistakes and will not be returning to work as a bouncer.

12.   To take account of the seriousness of the offence, the court may wish to impose a generic community order with significant limitations on Mr

Dickson's free time. Mr Dickson would be suitable for such an order with the imposition of an unpaid work requirement and also a programme requirement under which he would have to attend an anger management course run by the Probation Service.

Signed: *Lucinda Smythe*

Probation Officer

12.2.1.3   Specific sentence reports

If the court is minded to impose a generic community order (see **11.6** above) and wants to ensure that the defendant is suitable for such a sentence, rather than asking the Probation Service to prepare a full pre-sentence report the court may ask for a specific sentence report . This report will be shorter than a full pre-sentence report and will concentrate on the defendant's suitability for the terms of the order which the court is considering. The advantage of requesting such a report is that there will normally be a probation officer present in court who can see the defendant and prepare a report straight away, thus enabling the court to sentence the defendant immediately rather than having to adjourn the case for several weeks. These reports are often referred to as 'stand down' reports, since the case will be 'stood down' by the court whilst the report is being prepared.

12.2.1.4   Who sees the pre-sentence report?

Section 159 of the CJA 2003 provides that the court must supply a copy of the report to:

(a)   the defendant or his legal representative; and

(b)   the prosecutor.

The prosecutor has the right to make representations to the court if there is any information in the report about the offence which may be incorrect or misleading. The contents of the pre-sentence report are otherwise confidential, and the defendant's solicitor should not therefore disclose the contents of the report to anyone other than the defendant.

12.2.2   Medical reports

Under s 157 of the CJA 2003, the court is obliged to obtain and consider a medical report before it imposes a custodial sentence (other than a sentence fixed by law) if the defendant 'is or appears to be mentally disordered'.

Even if the defendant is not mentally disordered, the defendant's solicitor will often ask the court to adjourn sentence so that he (rather than the court) may obtain a medical report to assist in the plea in mitigation he is to give on his client's behalf. Such a report may be useful if the defendant is suffering from some ongoing illness or injury, or if the defendant's medical condition at the time of his offending may go some way towards explaining the reason for his offending.

Example

Jenny has pleaded guilty in the magistrates' court to the offence of stealing from her employers. Jenny is 50 years of age and has no previous convictions. At the time she committed the offence, Jenny was in the middle of an acrimonious divorce and had been prescribed anti-depressant medication by her doctor. Jenny's solicitor will need to obtain a report from Jenny's doctor confirming this, to use in mitigation on Jenny's behalf.

12.3 Role of the defendant's solicitor

12.3.1 Introduction

The role of the solicitor whose client has either pleaded guilty or has been convicted following a trial, is to present to the court a plea in mitigation on the client's behalf before the client is sentenced. The purpose of the plea in mitigation is to reduce the severity of the sentence to be passed, and to seek to persuade the court to impose the most lenient penalty which might reasonably be given for the offence(s) the defendant has committed. Guidance on how to structure a plea in mitigation is provided at **12.7** below.

12.3.2 Preparation for the sentencing hearing

There are several steps which the defendant's solicitor needs to take prior to the sentencing hearing if he is going to be able to deliver an effective plea in mitigation on his client's behalf. These are examined in **12.3.2.1** to **12.3.2.3** below.

12.3.2.1 Research the likely sentence

Magistrates' court

The first step is to carry out some research into the likely range of penalties to be imposed for the offence. In the magistrates' court the solicitor will need to consult the Magistrates' Court Sentencing Guidelines (or, in future, any guidelines issued by the SGC – see **Chapter 11**). The starting point for any plea in mitigation is to attempt to make a realistic assessment of the likely range of sentences that will be in the mind of the court. There is little point in the defendant's solicitor seeking to persuade the magistrates that a fine is appropriate when the offence clearly warrants either custody or a community sentence. Similarly, the defendant's solicitor should not be seeking to persuade the court not to impose a prison sentence if the offence clearly has not passed the custody threshold.

For each offence which may be dealt with by the magistrates, the Magistrates' Court Sentencing Guidelines contain a chart which the magistrates must work through to arrive at their sentence. The chart begins by specifying both the maximum sentence for the offence and a 'guideline' sentence for a first-time offender who pleads not guilty and is then convicted following a trial. The chart then provides a list of potential aggravating and mitigating factors in respect of the offence, together with possible points of 'offender' mitigation which may be present (ie, factors personal to the defendant which may be relevant to mitigation). The chart also reminds the magistrates that the defendant is entitled to credit if he has entered a guilty plea and so removed the need for a trial to take place. Only when the magistrates have worked thought the chart should they decide upon the appropriate sentence.

Extracts from the Guidelines can be found in **Appendix 2**.

Crown Court

In the Crown Court the plea in mitigation will be delivered by counsel rather than by the defendant's solicitor. The defence solicitor should still nevertheless find out the likely range of penalties to be imposed for the offence by checking either the guideline sentences given by the Court of Appeal and set out in the sentencing compendium prepared by the SGC (see **Chapter 11**), or any definitive guidelines the SGC has given for the relevant offence.

12.3.2.2   See the client

The defendant's solicitor needs to take further instructions from his client before the sentencing hearing, covering the following matters:

(a)   *The likely sentence* – the client will want to know 'what he is likely to get' for the offence.

(b)   *The client's previous convictions* – if the client has previous convictions, the court may view these as an aggravating feature which will increase the severity of the sentence (see **11.4.2.4**). The defendant's solicitor needs to take full instructions on his client's previous convictions so that he may 'explain' to the court the circumstances behind such convictions and, if possible, attempt to distinguish them from the current offence. This is particularly important if the previous convictions are for the same type of offence as the offence for which the client is to be sentenced.

Example

George is to be sentenced for the offence of common assault following a drunken brawl in a pub. George has a previous conviction for common assault, which the magistrates may treat as an aggravating factor. George instructs his solicitor that the previous conviction occurred following a petty disagreement with a neighbour (which got out of hand) concerning the moving of a garden fence. George's solicitor will need to explain this in his plea in mitigation in order to distinguish this offence from the offence for which George is to be sentenced.

(c)   *The client's financial circumstances* – it is likely that the defendant may be ordered to make some form of financial payment by the court. This may be a fine, an order to pay compensation to the victim, an order to pay prosecution costs, or, in the Crown Court, an order to pay or to contribute towards the defence costs. If the court makes such an order, it will expect the defendant's solicitor to put forward the defendant's proposals for payment. The defendant will normally instruct his solicitor that he can make payment within a specified number of days, or that he can make weekly payments of a certain amount until the amount due has been discharged. The court will expect the defendant's solicitor to have this information to hand when he is asked what the defendant's proposals for payment are.

(d)   *Character references* – if the defendant is of previous good character (see **22.8**), the defendant's solicitor should discuss with his client whether there is anyone who occupies a position of respect or trust within the community (such as a teacher) who may be prepared to provide a character reference for the client, or to attend court to give such a reference in person at the sentencing hearing. If the client is in employment, it is particularly useful mitigation to obtain such a reference from the client's employer.

(d)   *Medical reports* – as explained in **12.2.2** above, the defendant's solicitor may need to obtain a medical report from his client's doctor for use when delivering the plea in mitigation on the client's behalf. To obtain such a report, the defendant's solicitor will need to get a signed form of authority from his client to send to the doctor, authorising the doctor to release information about the client's medical situation.

12.3.2.3   Obtain a copy of the pre-sentence report prepared by the Probation Service

As the pre-sentence report is prepared at the court's request, the Probation Service officer who prepared it is unlikely to disclose a copy of his report to the defendant's solicitor until the day of the sentencing hearing. The report may often be very detailed, and the solicitor needs to get to court sufficiently early to read the report and discuss its contents with the defendant. The solicitor needs to ensure that there is nothing in the report which is factually incorrect. He must also discuss with the defendant the sentencing recommendation set out in the report. The court will place great emphasis on the report's recommendations when deciding on the sentence to be imposed, and the solicitor needs to explain to the client exactly what the suggested sentence entails. This is particularly important when the report recommends that the defendant should comply with specific requirements as part of a generic community order (see **11.6**).

12.4 *Newton* hearings

Occasionally a defendant may plead guilty to the charge against him but dispute the specific factual version of events put forward by the CPS. If the dispute concerning the correct version of events is substantial (ie, if it may have a bearing on the type of sentence the court imposes), the court must either accept the defendant's version of events or allow both the CPS and the defendant to call evidence so that the court can determine the true factual circumstances of the offence on which the defendant's sentence will be based. If evidence is to be called, a hearing must be arranged so that witnesses can attend court to give evidence. This is referred to as a *Newton* hearing, following the case of *R v Newton* (1983) 77 Cr App R 13.

Example 1

Stephen pleads guilty to a charge of assault occasioning actual bodily harm. The CPS alleges that Stephen launched an unprovoked attack on his victim, punching him in the head several times. Stephen accepts that he is guilty of the offence, but says that he attacked the victim only after being subjected to racial abuse by him. Stephen also says that he punched his victim only once. The difference between the prosecution and the defence version of events is significant, and is likely to affect the type of sentence the court will impose. The court must therefore either hold a *Newton* hearing to determine the facts on which Stephen will be sentenced, or alternatively accept Stephen's account as being the correct version of events.

Example 2

Stanley pleads guilty to a charge of burglary of a dwelling. The CPS alleges that Stanley broke into the dwelling by smashing a window, ransacked several rooms in the property, soiled the carpets and took several items of high value. Stanley says that he got into the property through an open window (causing no damage to the window), denies ransacking the property or soiling the carpets, and says that he removed only a small transistor radio. The difference between the prosecution and the defence version of events is significant, and is likely to affect the type of sentence the court will impose. The court must therefore either hold a *Newton* hearing, or alternatively accept Stanley's account as being the correct version of events.

12.5 Sentencing procedure

12.5.1 Magistrates' court

The procedure that is followed at a sentencing hearing in the magistrates' court is as follows:

(a) The defendant will either enter a guilty plea, or will be convicted following a trial.

(b) If the defendant has entered a guilty plea, the court will be supplied with details of any offences which the defendant wishes to have taken into consideration (see **11.4.2.6**) and the prosecuting solicitor will outline the facts of the case to the magistrates (there will be no need to do this if the defendant is convicted following a trial because the magistrates will have heard the facts of the case during the course of the trial). The prosecutor may, as part of his submission, read out to the court a statement from the victim of the crime detailing the effect the crime has had on his or her life. This is known as a 'victim personal statement'. The court should take the statement into account prior to passing sentence (although the opinion of the victim as to what the sentence should be is not relevant).

(c)   The prosecuting solicitor will then supply the court with a list of the defendant's previous convictions (if any). The court will check to make sure that a copy of this list has been supplied to the defendant's solicitor.

(d)   The prosecuting solicitor will conclude his remarks by asking for any ancillary orders he wishes the magistrates to make (such as an application for the defendant to pay the prosecution costs).

(e)   The defendant's solicitor will then address the magistrates. He may ask the magistrates to adjourn the case at his request (should he wish to obtain medical or other reports for use in mitigation), or he may ask the magistrates if they wish to adjourn the case so that a pre-sentence report may be obtained from the Probation Service.

(f)   If the case is not adjourned, the defendant's solicitor will then give a plea in mitigation on his client's behalf. He may also call character witnesses to give evidence on the defendant's behalf.

(g)   The magistrates will then sentence the defendant.

(h)   If the magistrates decide to adjourn the case so that reports can be prepared, the case is likely to be adjourned for three or four weeks. During this period, the defendant will either be released on bail, or be remanded in custody (see **12.2.1.2** above). There is a presumption that a defendant whose case is adjourned for the preparation of reports will be granted bail (see **7.3**), although if the magistrates are considering a custodial sentence they may decide to refuse bail on the ground that the defendant may fail to surrender to custody.

(i)   When the case comes back before the court for sentence, it is likely to be dealt with by a different bench of magistrates. The prosecuting solicitor will therefore need to repeat the facts of the case to the court (whether or not the defendant pleaded guilty), to check that the magistrates have before them details of the defendant's previous convictions, and to make an application for any ancillary orders he may require.

(j)   The defendant's solicitor will then give a plea in mitigation on his client's behalf.

(k)   The magistrates will then sentence the defendant. The court must explain to the defendant both the reasons for, and the effect of, the sentence which is imposed (CJA 2003, s 174(1)).

A flowchart summarising the above is set out at **12.8** below

12.5.2   Crown Court

The procedure which takes place when a judge sentences a defendant in the Crown Court is essentially the same as in the magistrates' court.

Unless the defendant has been convicted following a trial, prosecuting counsel will tell the judge what the facts of the case are. He will also provide the judge with details of the defendant's previous convictions and request any ancillary orders (such as an order for the payment of compensation or prosecution costs). If the judge considers that a pre-sentence report is necessary, he will adjourn sentencing for the preparation of reports and remand the defendant either on bail or in custody. When a judge who has presided over the defendant's trial adjourns sentencing for the preparation of pre-sentence reports, the judge will normally 'reserve' the case to himself to ensure that he will ultimately sentence the defendant once the necessary reports have been prepared. Although there is a presumption that a defendant whose case has been adjourned for the preparation of reports will be granted bail (see **7.3**), if the defendant has been convicted of a serious offence the judge is likely to refuse bail on the grounds either that the defendant will fail to surrender to custody, or that it would be impractical to prepare the report without keeping him in custody. Before the judge sentences the defendant, defence counsel will deliver a plea in mitigation on the defendant's behalf.

As in the magistrates' court, prosecuting counsel may read out to the judge a victim personal statement from the victim of the offence. In cases of murder or manslaughter, the Government is currently piloting a 'Victims' Advocate Scheme', which gives the families of victims of these offences the opportunity to make a statement to the court (whether verbally in writing) about the effect the crime has had on them. The judge must take the contents of the statement into account when passing sentence.

12.5.3   Reasons for and effect of sentence

When the judge or the magistrates sentence the defendant, the defendant must be told both the reasons for the sentence and the effect of the sentence (CJA 2003, s 174(1)). If guidelines (such as sentencing guidelines issued by the SGC – see **11.4.2.2**) indicate that a sentence of a particular kind, or in a particular range, would normally be appropriate for the offence, if the judge or magistrates impose a sentence of a different kind, or outside the particular range, the defendant must be told the reasons for this (CJA 2003, s 174(2)). Section 172 of the CJA 2003 requires the court to have regard to any guidelines that exist when sentencing an offender.

12.6   Professional conduct

Issues of professional conduct may arise for the defendant's solicitor when the list of his client's previous convictions (which the CPS produces to the court) is either inaccurate or incomplete. The defendant's solicitor should never be asked by the court clerk/legal adviser to confirm the accuracy of the list. If the solicitor is asked to do this, he should decline to comment. To confirm the list as being accurate would be a positive deception of the court, breaching the solicitor's duty not to mislead the court. However, the solicitor also owes a duty of confidentiality to his client, and disclosing to the court details of a client's previous convictions without the client's consent is a breach of this duty.

To prevent such problems occurring, the defendant's solicitor should obtain details of his client's previous convictions from the CPS in advance of the sentencing hearing. The solicitor should then discuss the accuracy of this list with his client. The client must be warned about the dangers of misleading the court. If the client insists that, if asked, he will pretend the list is accurate, or if the client asks the solicitor to pretend the list is accurate, the solicitor must cease to act for the client and withdraw from the case.

12.7 Plea in mitigation

12.7.1 Purpose and structure

The purpose of the plea in mitigation is to persuade the sentencing court to impose upon the defendant the most lenient sentence which the court could reasonably be expected to give for that offence. The structure of a plea in mitigation may be divided into four parts:

(a) *The 'starting point' sentence* – the defendant's solicitor should begin by identifying the 'starting point' sentence. This is the sentence which the court is likely to impose for a 'standard' offence of the type the defendant has committed, with no significant aggravating or mitigating features.

(b) *The offence* – the defendant's solicitor should then address the circumstances of the offence, minimising the impact of any aggravating factors and stressing the importance of any mitigating factors that are present.

(c) *The offender* – after dealing with the offence, the defendant's solicitor should then emphasise any personal mitigation which the defendant may have.

(d) *The suggested sentence* – the plea in mitigation should conclude with the defendant's solicitor suggesting to the court the type of sentence which he considers it would be most appropriate for the court to impose.

Each of these four parts will now be looked at in more detail. Although what is set out below concentrates on the delivery of a plea in mitigation in the magistrates' court, the same principles will apply when a plea in mitigation is being delivered in the Crown Court.

12.7.2 The 'starting point' sentence

If the defendant's solicitor has properly researched the likely range of sentences which will be in the mind of the court, he should be able to identify what the 'starting point' sentence is likely to be (see **12.3.2** above). The 'starting point' sentence is the sentence the magistrates are going to have at the back of their minds before they have heard any mitigation put forward on behalf of the defendant. The objective of the plea in mitigation is to persuade the magistrates to impose a sentence which is less severe than the 'starting point' sentence. The Magistrates' Court Sentencing Guidelines helpfully provide for each offence covered a guideline sentence for a first-time offender who has pleaded not guilty. The defendant's solicitor should identify to the magistrates what he considers the starting point sentence to be and then tell the magistrates that he hopes to persuade then to impose a lesser sentence.

In the Crown Court, the 'starting point' sentence may be found in the compendium of Court of Appeal sentencing guideline cases found on the SGC website (www.sentencing-guidelines.gov.uk) or in any definitive guidelines the SGC has issued for the relevant offence.

12.7.3 The offence

After identifying the 'starting point' sentence, the plea in mitigation should then focus on the offence itself. This requires the defendant's solicitor to:

- minimise the impact of any aggravating factors surrounding the offence; and

- emphasise the importance of any mitigating factors.

For each offence covered by the Magistrates' Courts Sentencing Guidelines, there is a list of possible aggravating and mitigating factors. For example, aggravating factors in a case involving the use of violence against another may include:

(a)   the use of a weapon;

(b)   extensive injuries to the victim;

(c)   premeditation;

(d)   a group action;

(e)   the use of kicking;

(f)   a victim who is particularly vulnerable (such as an elderly or disabled person, or a child).

Possible mitigating factors in such a case may include:

(a)   minor injuries to the victim;

(b)   an element of provocation;

(c)   the use of a single blow;

(d)   no weapon used;

(e)   no element of premeditation.

Aggravating factors for a property-related offence such as the burglary of a dwelling house may include:

(a)   the threat or use of force;

(b)   stealing items of a high financial or sentimental value;

(c)   an element of planning;

(d)   significant damage to the property (eg, a house being ransacked, or significant damage caused when gaining entry);

(e)   the presence of the victim at the time of the burglary (particularly if the burglary is at night).

Mitigating factors in such a case may include:

(a)   no use of force or violence;

(b)   only items of low value being stolen;

(c)   an offence committed on impulse or an opportunistic crime;

(d)   no damage caused to the property;

(e)   the burglary being carried out when the property was vacant.

The defendant's solicitor should identify any aggravating factors which would normally lead the court to impose a sentence in excess of the 'starting point' sentence, and attempt (if possible) to disassociate the defendant's case from those factors. Similarly, the defendant's solicitor should emphasise to the court the presence of any mitigating factors.

12.7.4   The offender

After dealing with the facts of the offence, the plea in mitigation should move on to consider any personal mitigation the defendant may have. Factors which may be relevant here are set out below.

12.7.4.1   The age of the defendant

The younger the defendant is, the more likely it will be that the court will want to pass a sentence designed to 'help' the defendant rather than to punish him. This is particularly the case if the court thinks that a young defendant who is immature and impressionable has been led astray by older co-defendants. The courts are also generally more likely to give sympathetic treatment to a defendant of advanced years, particularly if this is his first offence.

12.7.4.2   The health of the defendant

It is unwise to suggest to the court in mitigation that the defendant committed an offence only because he was under the influence of drink or drugs at the time. The court is likely to regard this as an aggravating feature of the offence. If, however, there is evidence that the defendant is a drug addict or an alcoholic, this may be used to suggest to the court that a sentence designed to help the defendant overcome this addiction (for example, a generic community order that incorporates a drug rehabilitation requirement or an alcohol treatment requirement) may be more appropriate than a custodial sentence. Similarly, a defendant who is suffering from a long-term illness or injury is likely to receive some sympathy from the court, as is a defendant who may have been suffering from some form of mental illness (such as depression) at the time the offence was committed.

12.7.4.3   Cooperation with the police/early guilty plea

The court will give the defendant credit for entering an early guilty plea to the offence (since the sentencing guidelines are based on the appropriate sentence for a defendant who is convicted following a trial). The amount of credit the defendant will receive depends upon the stage in the proceedings at which the defendant entered his guilty plea (see **11.4.2.5**). Such credit may amount to a maximum reduction of one-third of the sentence the defendant would have received had he pleaded not guilty (if the defendant has pleaded guilty at the first opportunity). The defendant's solicitor should (if appropriate) always remind the court of this. It would also be appropriate to tell the court if the defendant has positively assisted the police in their enquiries, for example by naming others involved in the crime or by revealing the whereabouts of stolen property. The fact that the defendant made a prompt confession when questioned by the police is also useful mitigation, showing that the defendant did not waste police time during the investigation process.

12.7.4.4   Voluntary compensation

A defendant who voluntarily makes good the damage which he has caused, or who makes a voluntary payment of compensation to his victim, is likely to receive credit for this. This is particularly the case if the defendant is of limited means.

12.7.4.5   Remorse

Evidence of *true* remorse is effective mitigation. A mere apology made by the defendant's solicitor to the court on behalf of his client is unlikely to have much effect, but the court will take into account any positive steps which the defendant has made to tackle the problems which led him to commit the offence. For example, the court is likely to give credit to a defendant who is to be sentenced for several public order offences committed whilst in a drunken state, if that defendant has begun to attend classes organised by Alcoholics Anonymous to combat his addiction. Similarly, the court will give credit to a defendant who has committed thefts to fund a drug habit, but who has voluntarily sought treatment for this.

12.7.4.6 Character

As noted in **Chapter 11** and in **12.3.2** above, if the defendant has previous convictions which the court may view as aggravating factors, his solicitor should attempt to distinguish such convictions from the facts of the current offence and 'explain' the circumstances of the defendant's previous offending. For example, a defendant convicted of theft may have several previous convictions for thefts which were committed in order to fund a drug habit. If the defendant is no longer taking drugs and the reason for the defendant having committed the current offence is different from his motive for committing the previous offences, his solicitor should explain this to the court.

Just as having previous convictions may be seen as an aggravating factor, so a defendant with no previous convictions (and so of previous good character) is entitled to have this taken into account. This is particularly important when there is a specific reason or explanation for a defendant of previous good character having committed an offence.

Example

Violet is 50 years of age and is of previous good character. She works on the check-out at her local supermarket and has been charged with stealing £500 in cash from her employers. The reason for Violet having committed the offence is that her husband has recently left her, taking all her savings and leaving her with insufficient funds to pay the rent on her house. Violet's solicitor can ask the court to take Violet's previous good character into account and suggest that there is a specific 'one-off' explanation for her committing a criminal offence.

The defendant's solicitor may call character witnesses (see **12.3.2.2**) to give evidence as to the defendant's previous good character.

It is also appropriate to say in mitigation that, aside from any sentence imposed by the court, a defendant of hitherto good character will have lost his good name as a result of being convicted, and will suffer shame as a result. This will certainly be the case if the defendant has a respected position within the community (eg, is a doctor or a teacher).

12.7.4.7 Family circumstances

If the court has requested a pre-sentence report from the Probation Service, this will look in depth at the defendant's personal background and family circumstances. The defendant's solicitor should also refer to the defendant's personal circumstances in the plea in mitigation, particularly if the defendant has a regular home and job, and has family who will be supportive in his attempts to stay out of trouble in the future. Although there is little to be gained from saying that the defendant's family will be caused upset or inconvenience if a custodial sentence is imposed, if exceptional circumstances exist, explaining to the magistrates the effect the defendant's imprisonment will have on his immediate family can be effective mitigation. For example, the defendant may have a partner who is dangerously ill or who is expecting a child, or the defendant may have a handicapped child. The defendant's solicitor should also tell the court if a custodial sentence will result in the defendant losing his job. This may persuade the court to impose a community penalty instead of imprisonment. It is often the case that defendants who are due to be sentenced may have received a recent offer of employment. This should be raised in mitigation, although the magistrates are likely to give this credence only if the defendant is able to produce a letter or other document confirming the offer.

If the defendant has had a troubled family background, it would also be appropriate to refer to this in mitigation, particularly if the defendant is still young. For example, a defendant may have come from a broken home, or have been physically or sexually abused as a child. Similarly, young defendants will often have become addicted to drugs or involved in prostitution at an early age. This will be particularly effective mitigation if the defendant's solicitor is able to say that the client has made a genuine attempt to overcome such a background.

12.7.4.8   Other consequences of conviction

It is also appropriate to point out to the court any other adverse consequence suffered by the defendant as a result of the conviction. For example, a defendant convicted of a minor theft may have lost his job following his conviction if he worked in a professional capacity or in a position of trust. A defendant may also have had to relinquish other positions of responsibility following his conviction (for example, a defendant who was a member of a local council or a school governor).

12.7.4.9   Low risk of re-offending

The pre-sentence report from the Probation Service will address the risk of the defendant committing further offences. If this risk is assessed as being low, the defendant's solicitor should mention this in the plea in mitigation to support an argument that the defendant's offending was a one-off aberration for which the defendant has shown remorse and a willingness to change.

12.7.5   The suggested sentence

The plea in mitigation should conclude with the defendant's solicitor suggesting to the court the sentence which he thinks the court should impose upon his client. This should be lower than the 'starting point' sentence, and should reflect the all the mitigating factors which the defendant's solicitor has placed before the court. The sentence which the defendant's solicitor suggests to the court must be realistic, and so should be at the lower end of the range of possible sentences which will be in the mind of the court. If the sentence which the defendant's solicitor suggests as being appropriate is the same sentence as is recommended in the pre-sentence report, the solicitor should emphasise this point (given that the pre-sentence report is requested by the court to assist it in determining sentence).

An example of a plea in mitigation to be delivered to the court is set out below.

Key Skill – Delivering a Plea in Mitigation

(Although this is a plea in mitigation delivered in the Crown Court, the same comments would be made were it in the magistrates' court. The only difference is in the modes of address used.)

PLEA IN MITIGATION

Your Honour, before you pass sentence on Mr Dickson, it falls to me to give a plea in mitigation on his behalf. Has your Honour had the opportunity to read the pre-sentence report prepared by the Probation Service?

[The judge indicates that he has read the report.]

Clearly, your Honour, this is a serious matter, and your Honour may be minded to consider imposing an immediate custodial sentence on Mr Dickson. I hope to persuade your Honour that a more suitable method of disposing of this case would be for your Honour to impose a community sentence as recommended in the pre-sentence report. I will begin by addressing the circumstances of the offence. I will then provide your Honour with details of Mr Dickson's personal circumstances, before concluding by addressing the format of the generic community order which I hope to persuade you Honour to impose.

Your Honour, Mr Dickson accepts the prosecution version of events as outlined to you by my learned friend [the prosecution barrister who will have outlined the facts of the case to the judge], save that there was an element of provocation in this matter. Whilst it is true to say that Mr Dickson assaulted Mr Lamb after Mr Lamb had left Connolley's nightclub, this incident must be placed in the context of events which occurred earlier in the evening. Mr Lamb had been working at Connolley's that evening as a disc jockey, with Mr Dickson working there as a bouncer. Throughout the evening Mr Lamb had taunted Mr Dickson about his status as a bouncer and, at one stage, had attempted to proposition Mr Dickson's partner. Whilst such conduct on the part of Mr Lamb should in no way condone Mr Dickson's later actions, it does help to explain why Mr Dickson acted in the way he did.

I would also ask your Honour to note that Mr Dickson did to a certain extent act on impulse. As he was driving home from the nightclub, Mr Dickson noticed Mr Lamb also leaving the nightclub. Mr Dickson saw his opportunity to get back at Mr Lamb for Mr Lamb's conduct earlier in the evening. Your Honour, this was not a planned or premeditated attack, nor was any weapon used by Mr Dickson in carrying out the attack. It was the impulsive act of a man who had been subjected to taunts throughout the evening.

Whilst it is correct that Mr Dickson initially entered a plea of not guilty to this offence, I would ask your Honour to give such credit as your Honour feels able for the fact that Mr Dickson did ultimately changed his plea to one of guilty.

Your Honour, Mr Dickson is 27 years of age. He has lived in the Chester area since 2001. Prior to moving to Chester, Mr Dickson served in the army for five years. Mr Dickson has been in full-time employment since leaving the army. In addition to working as a bouncer on a weekend and some weekday evenings, Mr Dickson also does contract work as a scaffolder and steeplejack.

Mr Dickson does have previous convictions, of which your Honour will be aware from the list of Mr Dickson's antecedents. These previous convictions arose from Mr Dickson's work as a bouncer at Connolley's, and followed altercations which Mr Dickson had with abusive customers at the nightclub. Mr Dickson would say that these convictions resulted from incidents where he had been provoked by such customers to the point at which he felt compelled to react in a violent manner.

Your Honour, Mr Dickson's personal circumstances have recently changed. Mr Dickson has been living with his partner for 18 months. His partner has just been informed that she is expecting their first child, and Mr Dickson is acutely aware of the responsibilities impending fatherhood will impose on him. Mr Dickson has also recently been offered a long-term contract to do some scaffolding work in Chester. The financial value of this work is such that Mr Dickson will no longer need to continue with his part-time work as a bouncer. As your Honour has read in the pre-sentence report, Mr Dickson has been dismissed from his job at Connolley's, but has no intention of seeking further work as a bouncer.

Your Honour, there is a theme running through Mr Dickson's offending. That theme is that Mr Dickson has difficulty in controlling his temper in situations where he is open to verbal provocation from others. As Mr Dickson will not be seeking further employment as a nightclub bouncer, Mr Dickson is effectively removing himself from the possibility of becoming involved in such situations. Indeed the pre-sentence report suggests that as long as Mr Dickson does not return to work as a bouncer, the risk of his re-offending is low.

Your Honour will be aware that Mr Dickson has previously received a community sentence involving an unpaid work requirement. However, in my respectful submission, whilst that sentence served to punish Mr Dickson for his offending, the sentence failed to address the underlying reason for that offending.

As your Honour will be aware, one of the five purposes of sentencing set out in section 142(1) of the Criminal Justice Act 2003 is the reform and rehabilitation of offenders. The sentence suggested by Ms Smythe in the pre-sentence report is a generic community order comprising an unpaid work requirement and, significantly, a programme requirement under which Mr Dickson would need to attend an anger management course. Your Honour may think that such a sentence is appropriate as it would satisfy the need to punish Mr Dickson, but also the need to prevent him from offending again in the future. I would submit that the imposition of an immediate custodial sentence, whilst achieving the goal of punishing Mr Dickson, would not address this latter point. Your Honour will be aware that many offenders who receive prison sentences offend again shortly after leaving prison.

Your Honour will also be aware that another purpose of sentencing is the making of reparation by offenders to those affected by their offences. I would submit that such a purpose could be satisfied in this case by the making of an order that Mr Dickson pay compensation to Mr Lamb. Should your Honour order compensation to be paid, or should your Honour order that Mr Dickson pay the costs of the prosecution or a contribution towards his defence costs, I am instructed that such payment can be made by Mr Dickson within 14 days.

Unless your Honour has any questions, that concludes my submissions on behalf of Mr Dickson.

12.8   Flowchart – sentencing procedure

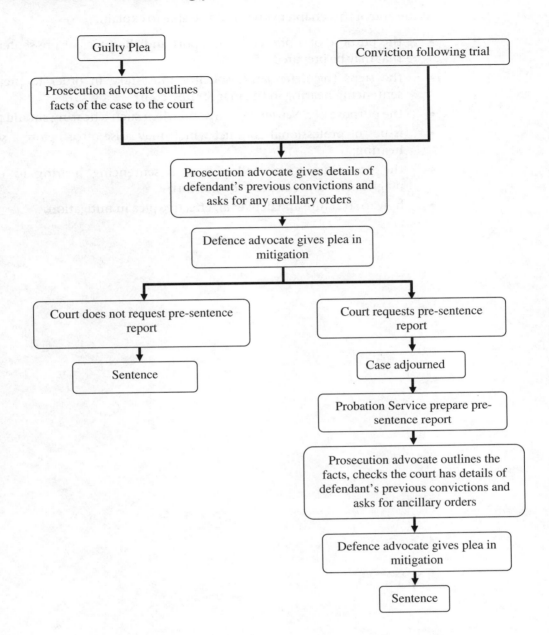

12.9 Checklist

At the end of this chapter you should be able to explain:

- the purpose of a pre-sentence report and the types of pre-sentence report that may be prepared;
- the steps the defendant's solicitor must take in order to prepare for a sentencing hearing in the magistrates' court.
- the purpose of a *Newton* hearing and when such a hearing should take place;
- issues of professional conduct which may arise at or before a sentencing hearing;
- the procedure to be followed at a sentencing hearing in either the magistrates' court or the Crown Court;
- how to structure and deliver an effective plea in mitigation.

Chapter 13

Appeals

13.1 Introduction

Most criminal cases will end either following the acquittal of the defendant at trial, or, if the defendant is convicted or pleads guilty, following sentence. This chapter will consider the options open to the defendant to appeal against his conviction or the sentence he has received. It will also examine the more limited rights of appeal that may be exercised by the CPS following the acquittal of the defendant or the imposition of a sentence which the CPS considers to be insufficient.

The rules which govern the procedure for the making of an appeal (either by the defendant, or by the CPS) are in Parts 63–74 of the Criminal Procedure Rules 2005.

13.2 Appeals from the magistrates' court (including the Youth Court)

13.2.1 Appeals to the Crown Court (CrimPR, Part 63)

13.2.1.1 Who may appeal?

Section 108(1) of the Magistrates' Courts Act 1980 provides that a defendant convicted in the magistrates' court may appeal to the Crown Court in the following circumstances:

(a) if he pleaded guilty before the magistrates, he may appeal against the sentence he has received;

(b) if he pleaded not guilty before the magistrates, he may appeal against the conviction and/or sentence he has received.

Appeals by juveniles against conviction and/or sentence in the Youth Court (see **Chapter 14**) are also covered by these provisions (since Youth Courts are deemed to be a particular type of magistrates' court).

The prosecution do not have the right to appeal to the Crown Court against either the acquittal of a defendant by the magistrates, or the sentence imposed on a defendant by the magistrates.

13.2.1.2 Who hears the appeal?

The appeal (whether against conviction and/or sentence) will be heard by a circuit judge or recorder, who will sit with an even number of magistrates. This will normally be two magistrates, although up to four magistrates may sit on an appeal.

13.2.1.3   Appeals against conviction

A defendant convicted following a trial in the magistrates' court may appeal against his conviction to the Crown Court on the basis that the magistrates made errors of fact and/or law.

The Crown Court will not consider an appeal against conviction from a defendant who pleaded guilty in the magistrates' court if the defendant subsequently regrets pleading guilty and thinks he has an arguable defence (*R v Marylebone Justices, ex p Westminster City Council* [1971] 1 WLR 567). The Crown Court will only consider an appeal against conviction from a defendant who pleaded guilty before the magistrates if either the defendant made an 'equivocal plea', or his plea of guilty was made under duress. An equivocal plea will occur when the defendant pleads guilty but subsequently makes a comment (often in mitigation) which suggests that his plea was a misunderstanding of the correct legal position.

Example

Anil is accused of the theft of a lawnmower from his neighbour Geoffrey. Anil decides not to seek legal representation. He enters a plea of guilty and the magistrates adjourn the case for a pre-sentence report. When Anil comes before the court for sentence, he says in mitigation that he took the lawnmower only because he thought it belonged to him. This would make his plea equivocal, because such a belief would have provided him with a possible defence to the charge.

In such cases, the Crown Court will remit the case back to the magistrates' court for trial, with a direction that the magistrates should treat the case as if a plea of not guilty had been entered.

An appeal against conviction in the Crown Court is a full rehearing of the case (in effect another trial). Both the CPS and the defendant will need to call all those witnesses whose evidence they seek to rely on. The witnesses do not necessarily need to be the same witnesses who were called to give evidence at the original trial in the magistrates' court; new witnesses may be called, and new or different points of law may be relied on.

13.2.1.4   Appeals against sentence

A defendant may appeal to the Crown Court against a sentence imposed by the magistrates' court if he considers that the sentence imposed by the magistrates is excessive. The Crown Court should carry out a full rehearing of the issues and take an independent view, based on the evidence, of what the correct sentence should be, rather than simply reviewing the sentence passed by the magistrates' court. The Crown Court is entitled to decide the appeal on a different factual basis to that determined by the magistrates' court, and the Crown Court is not bound by any findings of fact made by the magistrates.

13.2.1.5   Procedure for appealing against conviction and/or sentence

A defendant wishing to appeal from the magistrates' court to the Crown Court must file a notice of appeal with both the magistrates' court and the CPS within 21 days of the magistrates passing sentence. The notice will not provide any detailed grounds of appeal and it is normal practice for a standard form of wording to be used. For an appeal against conviction the wording is usually: 'This appeal is based on the grounds that the magistrates erred in fact and law.' For an appeal against sentence only, the wording is usually: 'This appeal is based on the ground that the sentence imposed by the magistrates was excessive [or too harsh] in all the circumstances.'

The clerk to the magistrates' court will send the notice of appeal to the relevant Crown Court, and the Crown Court will then arrange a date for the hearing of the appeal to take place. The Crown Court does not have any discretion to turn down an appeal at the notice stage. A defendant who has filed the notice in time is entitled to have his appeal heard.

If a defendant files his notice outside the 21 days, a Crown Court judge does have the discretionary power to extend this time limit if the defendant provides reasons (in writing) for the notice not being filed in time.

An example of a notice of appeal to the Crown Court is set out at **13.8.1** below.

13.2.1.6 Will the defendant be granted bail pending the hearing of the appeal?

When the magistrates impose a custodial sentence on a defendant, the magistrates may grant bail to the defendant pending an appeal to the Crown Court. There is, however, no presumption in favour of bail, as s 4 of the Bail Act 1976 does not apply to defendants appealing against conviction or sentence (see **7.3**). If the magistrates do not grant bail, the defendant may apply to the Crown Court for bail pending the hearing of the appeal. Defendants who apply to the Crown Court for bail commonly raise the argument that, if bail is not granted, by the time their appeal is heard they are likely to have served a substantial part of their sentence.

13.2.1.7 Powers of the Crown Court

The powers which the Crown Court may exercise on hearing an appeal from the magistrates' court are set out in s 48 of the Supreme Court Act 1981. The Crown Court may:

(a) confirm, reverse or vary the decision of the magistrates;

(b) remit the case back to the magistrates' court with a direction (as in the case of an equivocal plea – see **13.2.1.3** above); or

(c) make any other orders that the court thinks are just, as long as such orders could have been made by the magistrates' court (for example, make an order for the payment of costs or compensation by the defendant).

The Crown Court has the power to impose on the defendant any sentence, as long as it is a sentence which the magistrates' court had the power to impose. This means that a defendant appealing against a sentence imposed by the magistrates may have that sentence increased if the Crown Court takes a more serious view of the case than did the magistrates. A solicitor instructed by a defendant who wishes to appeal should always point this out to the defendant before the appeal is made.

Example

Jonathan is convicted in the magistrates' court of careless driving. The magistrates disqualify Jonathan from driving for two months. Jonathan appeals against this sentence to the Crown Court. On hearing the appeal, the Crown Court takes a more serious view of the case and increases the sentence to one of four months' disqualification. The Crown Court is able to do this because this is a sentence which the magistrates' court had the power to pass.

Both the CPS and the defendant are able to appeal to the High Court by way of case stated against any decision or order made by the Crown Court following an appeal from the magistrates' court. The appeal must be based either on a point of law, or on an argument that the Crown Court has exceeded its jurisdiction (see **13.2.2** below).

13.2.2 Appeal to the High Court by way of case stated (CrimPR, Part 64)

13.2.2.1 Who may appeal?

Either the CPS or the defendant may appeal from a decision of the magistrates' court to the Queen's Bench Division of the High Court. Such a right of appeal exists when either:

(a)   the decision which has been made by the magistrates is wrong in law; or

(b)   the magistrates have acted outside their jurisdiction (Magistrates' Courts Act 1980, s 111).

Arguments often raised in an appeal by way of case stated are that:

(a)   the magistrates misread, misunderstood or misapplied the law;

(b)   the magistrates decided to hear a case when they did not have the jurisdiction to hear it;

(c)   the magistrates made errors in deciding the admissibility or otherwise of evidence;

(d)   the magistrates erred in their decision following a submission of no case to answer.

Example

Hugh is convicted by the magistrates of assault occasioning actual bodily harm. The key piece of evidence against him was a confession given in an audio-recorded interview at the police station. Hugh's solicitor argued before the magistrates that the confession should be excluded, because the interview was conducted without Hugh being allowed access to legal advice and the police conducted the interview in an oppressive manner. The magistrates refused to exclude the confession evidence and Hugh was subsequently convicted. Hugh may appeal to the High Court by way of case stated, raising the argument that the magistrates made an error in deciding that the confession was admissible in evidence.

Appeals by way of case stated should not be used to appeal against a finding of fact made by the magistrates (*Spillman v DPP* [2006] All ER (D) 78). Similarly, a defendant wanting to appeal against a sentence imposed by the magistrates which he considers to be excessive should appeal to the Crown Court (see **13.2.1** above) rather than by way of case stated.

13.2.2.2 Procedure

The party wishing to appeal by way of case stated must apply to the magistrates' court within 21 days of the relevant decision being made by the magistrates. This is normally done by writing to the clerk to the magistrates' court. The application must identify the question of law on which the aggrieved party seeks the view of the High Court. Following receipt of this letter, the magistrates must then 'state a case' for the opinion of the High Court.

To do this, the clerk to the magistrates (in conjunction with the magistrates who heard the case) will prepare a 'statement of case' that will contain the following information:

(a)   the facts which were in dispute in the case;

(b)   any findings of fact made by the magistrates;

(c)   the findings made by the magistrates on the point of law in question;

(d)   details of any legal authorities the magistrates relied on; and

(e)   the question of law the High Court is being asked to consider.

Once an initial draft of the 'statement of case' has been prepared, the clerk will send this out to the CPS and the defendant's solicitor to enable them to suggest any necessary amendments. Once a final version of the statement of case has been agreed, the clerk will send this to the party making the appeal. That party must then lodge this with the High Court in London, and give notice that this has been done to the other party.

13.2.2.3   The hearing

The appeal is heard by the Divisional Court of the Queen's Bench Division, and will normally be heard by three judges. No evidence is given by witnesses (since the appeal is not concerned with matters of fact) and the hearing will be confined to legal argument based on the agreed facts set out in the statement of case.

The Divisional Court has the power to reverse, vary or affirm the decision made by the magistrates. It may also remit the case back to the same magistrates' court with a direction to acquit or convict the defendant, or to remit the case to a different bench of magistrates (if the case needs to be reheard). The Divisional Court may make an order that the costs of either party be paid from central funds (ie, by the state).

Both the CPS and the defendant are able to appeal to the House of Lords in respect of any decision or order made by the High Court following an appeal to the High Court by way of case stated. Any such appeal must be on a point of law only, and the High Court must certify it to be a point of law of general public importance. Further, either the High Court or the House of Lords must grant leave to appeal.

13.2.3   Judicial review

An application for judicial review is not strictly a form of appeal. It does, however, represent an alternative method of challenging a decision made by the magistrates' court. An application for judicial review may be made either by the CPS or the defendant if:

(a)   the magistrates have made an order that they had no power to make (and so have acted 'ultra vires', or beyond their powers); or

(b)   the magistrates have breached the rules of natural justice (either by contravening a party's right to a fair hearing, or by appearing to be biased).

An applicant for judicial review will seek an order from the Divisional Court either quashing the decision made the magistrates, or compelling the magistrates to act (or not act) in a certain way.

13.3   Appeals from the Crown Court

13.3.1   Rights of appeal open to the defendant (CrimPR, Part 68)

A defendant who is convicted in the Crown Court has the following rights of appeal to the Criminal Division of the Court of Appeal:

(a)   *Appeal against conviction (Criminal Appeal Act 1968, s 1(1))*. The defendant may appeal against his conviction if either the Court of Appeal grants him leave to appeal, or the trial judge grants a certificate that the case is fit for appeal (Criminal Appeal Act 1968, s 1(2)). The appeal may be on a point of law or fact, or both (see **13.3.2** below).

(b)   *Appeal against sentence (Criminal Appeal Act 1968, s 9)*. The defendant may appeal against the sentence he has received if either the Court of Appeal grants him leave to appeal, or the judge who passes sentence has granted a certificate that the case is fit for appeal against sentence (Criminal Appeal Act 1968, s 11). The potential grounds of appeal against sentence are set out at **13.3.3** below.

If a Crown Court judge grants a certificate that a case is fit for appeal (whether against conviction or sentence), he may also grant bail to the defendant pending the hearing of the appeal. There is, however, no presumption in favour of bail being granted (see **7.3**). Alternatively, the defendant may ask the Court of Appeal to grant him bail pending the hearing of his appeal. This power to grant bail will be exercised by a single judge (see **13.3.2.2** below). It is rare for the Court of Appeal to grant bail pending the outcome of the appeal, unless the grounds of the appeal are very strong.

13.3.2   Appeals against conviction

13.3.2.1   When will an appeal against conviction be allowed?

If the Court of Appeal considers a conviction to be 'unsafe', it must allow the appeal (Criminal Appeal Act 1968, s 2). In all other cases, the Court of Appeal must dismiss the appeal.

This means that a conviction may be upheld if there was an error or mistake at the defendant's trial in the Crown Court, if the Court of Appeal considers that, even had the mistake not been made, the correct and only reasonable verdict would have been one of guilty.

> **Example**
>
> Trevor is convicted of the armed robbery of a bank. At his trial, the CPS relies on identification evidence from several eye-witnesses to the robbery, fingerprint evidence from the scene of the crime, bank notes found following a search of Trevor's home and an admission made by Trevor in interview. Trevor appeals against his conviction. He argues that the conviction is unsafe because the admission he made should have been ruled inadmissible by the trial judge, as the police failed to caution him at the start of his interview.
>
> The Court of Appeal agrees that the trial judge erred in allowing the admission to be used in evidence against Trevor. However, the Court turns down the appeal because, even if the trial judge had excluded the admission, there was still other, overwhelming evidence that Trevor was guilty, and the only proper and reasonable verdict was one of guilty. The Court is satisfied that Trevor's conviction is not unsafe.

Examples of the most common grounds of appeal raised by defendants to argue that their convictions are unsafe are:

(a)   *a failure by the trial judge to direct the jury correctly* as to:
  (i)   the burden and standard of proof (see **Chapter 16**),
  (ii)   the substantive law concerning the offence(s),
  (iii)   the fact that it is for the jury rather than the judge to determine what the facts of the case are (although it is the role of the judge to remind the jury of the prominent features of the evidence when summing up, it is the sole responsibility of the jury to judge the evidence and decide all the relevant facts of the case),

(iv)   the fact that the jury should try to return a unanimous verdict (and the judge will notify them when the time has arisen when he may be prepared to accept a majority verdict – see **10.10.1**);

(b)   *the trial judge wrongfully admitting or excluding evidence*, for example:

(i)   the judge wrongfully admitting in evidence a disputed confession or the defendant's previous convictions (see **Chapters 20** and **22**),

(ii)   the judge wrongfully excluding hearsay evidence which would have assisted the defendant's case (see **Chapter 19**);

(c)   *the trial judge failing to administer the correct warnings to the jury*, for example:

(i)   the judge failing to give a '*Turnbull*' warning in a case of disputed identification, or a corroboration warning where the defendant alleges that a witness has a purpose of his own to serve in giving evidence against the defendant (see **Chapter 17**),

(ii)   the judge failing to give a proper direction to the jury as to the drawing of adverse inferences (see **Chapter 18**);

(d)   *inappropriate interventions by the trial judge* – if, for example, the judge had constantly interrupted defence counsel during the cross-examination of a prosecution witness;

(e)   *a failure by the trial judge when summing up the case to the jury to*:

(i)   deal with the essential points of the defence case,

(ii)   identify any inconsistencies in the prosecution case,

(iii)   summarise the evidence on which the jury may properly rely in order to convict the defendant,

(iv)   give a '*Vye*' direction where the defendant is of good character (see **22.8**) (when summing up, the judge should not usually tell the jury to place any evidential significance on a prosecution witness being of good character; this is 'oath-helping' and is not permitted – see **22.8.2**),

(v)   tell the jury, when special measures have been used to enable a prosecution witness to give evidence, that they should not allow this to prejudice them against the defendant, nor assume that the use of special measures means the defendant has behaved improperly (see **16.5.4**),

(vi)   explain to the jury the evidential significance of any previous sexual relationship between the defendant and the complainant where the defendant is charged with rape and raises the defence of consent (see **Chapter 9**);

(f)   *new evidence* – even if the trial has been properly conducted, the defendant may argue his conviction is unsafe if fresh evidence comes to light which casts doubt upon his guilt (if, for example, a new witness comes forward to substantiate an alibi which the defendant gave at trial but which was disbelieved by the jury, or if expert evidence on which the prosecution relied at trial is subsequently shown to be flawed). The key issue for the Court of Appeal will be the effect such evidence may have had on the jury (*R v Boreman & Others* (2006) WL 1635086). The question the Court will ask is whether, had the evidence been placed before the jury, the verdict might have been different. If so, the Court will set aside the conviction as being unsafe.

At the end of the trial, defence counsel will normally prepare a written advice on the merits of an appeal against conviction in accordance with the instructions contained in his brief (see **10.7.2**).

13.3.2.2 Procedure for making the appeal (CrimPR, Part 68)

Only rarely will the defendant ask the trial judge to certify that the case is fit for appeal. In *R v Inskip* [2005] EWCA Crim 3372, the Court of Appeal said that such a certificate should be granted only in truly exceptional circumstances, and that the normal rule is that it is for the Court of Appeal to consider whether a case is suitable for the granting of leave. This rule was established in *R v Bansal* [1999] Crim LR 484.

The usual method of commencing an appeal against conviction is for the defendant to seek leave to appeal from the Court of Appeal direct.

The procedure is as follows:

(a)   Within 28 days of his *conviction* (not sentence), the defendant must send to the Registrar of Criminal Appeals a notice of application for leave to appeal together with draft grounds of appeal. The notice is on a standard form which is reproduced at **13.7.2** below. The grounds are a separate document prepared by defence counsel, setting out the detailed arguments as to why the conviction is unsafe. The Court may grant the defendant leave to appeal out of time (if, for example, the defendant is appealing against his conviction on the basis of new evidence which only comes to light a long time after his original conviction).

(b)   On receipt of these documents, the Registrar will obtain a transcript of the evidence that was given at trial and of the judge's summing up to the jury. The Registrar will then put the case papers before a single judge, who will determine whether leave to appeal ought to be granted. This is a filtering stage, designed to weed out appeals that are frivolous and have no chance of success. If leave to appeal is granted, the single judge will also grant the defendant public funding for the hearing of the appeal. The single judge may grant the bail to the defendant pending the hearing of the appeal. He also has the power to order a witness to attend for examination at the appeal.
      In appeals that are completely without merit, the single judge may, when dismissing the appeal, make a direction as to loss of time. This means that any time spent by the defendant in custody awaiting the outcome of the appeal will not count towards the total time the defendant must serve for his sentence (as would normally be the case). This provision is designed to deter defendants from pursuing frivolous appeals.

(c)   The hearing of the appeal will then take place before the full Court of Appeal, which will comprise a three-judge panel. The Court will hear oral arguments from the parties, and may also hear fresh evidence (including expert evidence) if that evidence:
      (i)   appears to be credible;
      (ii)   would have been admissible at the defendant's trial; and
      (iii) there is a reasonable explanation for the failure to adduce this evidence at the defendant's trial (Criminal Appeal Act 1968, s 23).

13.3.2.3 Powers of the Court of Appeal

Section 2 of the Criminal Appeal Act 1968 (as amended by the Criminal Appeal Act 1995) permits the Court of Appeal to do any of the following:

(a)   quash the conviction and acquit the defendant – if, for example, new evidence has come to light which the Court considers would have led to the defendant's acquittal had such evidence been available at the defendant's trial;

(b)   quash the conviction and order that a retrial take place – if, for example, the conviction is unsafe because the judge failed to direct the jury properly when summing up the case;

(c)   allow part of the appeal and dismiss other parts of the appeal (if the defendant was appealing against conviction for more than one offence). In such a case the Court will probably then re-sentence the defendant in respect of the offences for which his conviction was upheld;

(d)   find the defendant guilty of an alternative offence (in which case the Court will probably re-sentence the defendant); or

(e)   dismiss the appeal.

The Court will dismiss the appeal unless it thinks that the conviction is unsafe. If the conviction is unsafe, the Court must then decide whether to order a retrial. A retrial will normally be ordered unless holding a retrial would be unfair to the defendant or in some other way inappropriate. If a significant amount of time has elapsed since the original trial, the Court is unlikely to order a retrial since the recollection of the witnesses is likely to be poor and unreliable.

13.3.3   Appeals against sentence

13.3.3.1   Procedure (CrimPR, Part 68)

A defendant may also appeal to the Court of Appeal against the sentence imposed by the Crown Court (Criminal Appeal Act 1968, s 9). The procedure to be followed when an appeal against sentence is made to the Court of Appeal is essentially the same as for an appeal against conviction, with the defendant either requiring a certificate from the sentencing judge that the case is fit for appeal, or the defendant seeking leave from the Court of Appeal to proceed. It is rare for the sentencing judge to grant a certificate, and most defendants will seek leave of the Court of Appeal to proceed. If the defendant seeks leave from the Court of Appeal, a notice of application for leave to appeal together with draft grounds of appeal must be sent to the Registrar of Criminal Appeals within 28 days of *sentence* being passed in the Crown Court. The draft grounds of appeal will state why it is considered that the sentence passed in the Crown Court is either wrong or excessive. Assuming leave to appeal is granted by the single judge (see **13.3.2.2** above), the appeal will then be considered by a two- or three-judge panel. The appeal will usually be confined to legal submissions on what the appropriate sentence (or sentencing range) is in the particular case.

13.3.3.2   When will an appeal be successful?

An appeal against sentence will be successful only if:

(a)   the sentence passed by the trial judge is wrong in law (if, for example, the trial judge were to pass a sentence or make an order that he did not have the power to pass or make);

(b)   the sentence passed by the trial judge is wrong in principle (if, for example, the trial judge passes a custodial sentence when the offence was not serious enough to merit such a sentence);

(c)   the judge adopted the wrong approach when sentencing. Examples of a judge adopting the wrong approach when sentencing are:

(i)   if the judge increased the sentence because the defendant had pleaded not guilty (since the 'guideline' sentencing cases from the Court of

Appeal and any guidelines issued by the SGC start from the assumption that the defendant is convicted following a not guilty plea);

(ii)   if the judge failed to give the defendant an appropriate discount for entering a guilty plea (see **11.4.2.5**); or

(iii)   if the judge should have held a *Newton* hearing before determining the facts of the offence upon which the sentence was to be based (see **12.4** above);

(d)   in the case of co-defendants, there is an unjustified disparity in the sentence each defendant received (particularly where both co-defendants appear to have been equally culpable); or

(e)   the sentence passed is manifestly excessive. This is the most common ground of appeal. A Crown Court judge sentencing a defendant will impose a sentence within a range of possible sentences which may be appropriate for the offence. The Court of Appeal will interfere only if the sentencing judge has gone beyond the upper limit of this range. The Court of Appeal will not reduce a sentence simply because it would have imposed a lower sentence within the appropriate range. For most offences, the Court of Appeal will have set out guidelines for appropriate sentences in previous cases before it and, if a judge in the Crown Court imposes a sentence which is within these guidelines, the Court of Appeal is unlikely to alter the sentence. In future, definitive sentencing guidelines will be given by the SGC established under the CJA 2003 (see **11.4.2.2**). Guideline sentences for all types of offence dealt with in the Crown Court can be found in a compendium on the SGC website (www.sentencing-guidelines.gov.uk).

After the defendant has been sentenced, defence counsel will normally provide a written advice on the prospects of a successful appeal against sentence in accordance with the instructions contained in his brief (see **10.7.2**).

13.3.3.3   Powers of the Court of Appeal

The Court of Appeal may confirm a sentence passed by the Crown Court, or quash the sentence and replace it with an alternative sentence or order as it thinks appropriate. The Court of Appeal *cannot*, however, increase the sentence imposed by the judge in the Crown Court.

13.3.4   Prosecution appeals (CrimPR, Parts 66 and 70)

13.3.4.1   Termination and evidential rulings

Introduction

The CPS has no right of appeal in respect of a defendant who has been acquitted by a jury following a Crown Court trial. Sections 58–63 of the CJA 2003 do, however, give the CPS a right of appeal to the Court of Appeal in respect of rulings made by a trial judge either before or during the trial which:

(a)   either effectively terminate the trial ('termination rulings'); or

(b)   significantly weaken the prosecution case ('evidential rulings').

Termination rulings

Examples of termination rulings include:

(a)   a ruling at the end of the prosecution case that the defendant has no case to answer (and that the case should be dismissed); or

(b)   a ruling that a vital piece of prosecution evidence is inadmissible, leaving the CPS with no alternative than to offer no evidence against the defendant because it no longer has sufficient evidence to secure a conviction (for example, a ruling by the trial judge that evidence of a confession made by the defendant is inadmissible when this is the *only* evidence against the defendant).

If the CPS wishes to appeal against a termination ruling, it must inform the trial judge that it intends to appeal, or request an adjournment to consider whether to appeal. Leave to appeal must be obtained either from the trial judge, or from the Court of Appeal. Prosecuting counsel must agree with the trial judge that if leave to appeal is refused, or if the appeal is later abandoned, the defendant will be acquitted. If leave to appeal is granted, the appeal may be expedited (in which case the defendant's trial will be adjourned pending the outcome of the appeal) or non-expedited (in which case the jury will be discharged). In either case, the termination ruling and the subsequent acquittal of the defendant are placed 'on hold' until any appeal is heard or abandoned. The Court of Appeal may either uphold the trial judge's ruling and acquit the defendant, or reverse or vary the ruling and order either that the trial should continue or that a new trial should take place.

Evidential rulings

Examples of rulings which significantly weaken the prosecution case are:

(a)   a confession being ruled inadmissible by the trial judge under ss 76 or 78 of PACE 1984 (see **Chapter 20**);

(b)   identification evidence being ruled inadmissible by the trial judge under s 78 of PACE 1984 due to breaches of the Act or the Codes of Practice by the police (see **Chapter 17**); or

(c)   the trial judge ruling that the defendant's previous convictions are inadmissible (see **Chapter 22**).

The CPS has a limited right of appeal to the Court of Appeal in respect of evidential rulings made by the trial judge which *significantly* weaken the prosecution case. This right is confined to more serious offences (for example, murder, manslaughter, rape and other serious sexual offences, robbery with a weapon and certain drugs offences). As with appeals against termination rulings, leave to appeal must be obtained either from the trial judge, or from the Court of Appeal. The trial judge must decide whether the appeal should be expedited (in which case the defendant's trial will be adjourned) or non-expedited (in which case the jury will be discharged). The Court of Appeal may confirm, vary or reverse the evidential ruling and, dependent on this, will order either that the defendant be acquitted, or that the trial be resumed or that a fresh trial take place.

13.3.4.2   Powers of the Attorney-General

The CPS has a right of appeal to the Court of Appeal if it considers that the Crown Court has passed a sentence which is 'unduly lenient'. Section 36 of Criminal Justice Act 1988 allows the Attorney-General to refer such a case to the Court of Appeal, which in turn has the power to increase the sentence. The Attorney-General may only refer a case to the Court of Appeal if the offence is indictable-only or is a specified either way offence. The list of specified either way offences includes indecent assault, a number of offences under the Misuse of Drugs Act 1971 and racially motivated public order offences. This right of appeal is being used with increasing frequency by the Attorney-General, often in high-profile cases where the public and the media perceive a sentence to have been unduly lenient.

The Attorney-General must obtain leave from the Court of Appeal before proceeding with the appeal. If the appeal is successful, the Court of Appeal will quash the sentence passed in the Crown Court and pass the sentence it considers appropriate. Any sentence imposed by the Court of Appeal must be a sentence that could have been passed in the Crown Court. The Court of Appeal is not permitted to take into account new material that was not available to the sentencing judge. The task of the Court of Appeal is to decide whether the judge's sentence, in the light of the material then before the judge, could properly be characterised as unduly lenient (*Attorney-General's Reference (No 19 of 2005); R v Bowden* [2006] All ER (D) 247).

13.3.4.3   Applications for a retrial

The rule against double jeopardy

Prior to the enactment of the CJA 2003, a defendant could never be tried twice for the same offence. Legally this was known as 'autrefois acquit', although it was known more commonly as the rule against 'double jeopardy'.

The rule (traceable back to the Magna Carta) was based on the argument that a defendant was entitled to finality, and the further argument that, if the CPS was given a 'second chance', it might prepare the case less thoroughly and less fairly from the outset.

However, recent advances in technology (in particular DNA testing) mean that new evidence may now come to light that was unavailable at the time of trial, and which may conclusively prove guilt (or innocence). Such advances led to calls for the reform of the rule against double jeopardy. These calls for reform were given added impetus following the Stephen Lawrence case, in which four defendants were acquitted of an allegedly racist murder. After the case, a campaign developed for some of those accused of the murder to be retried after 'better' evidence emerged.

The result of this are the changes to the rule against double jeopardy contained in the CJA 2003.

The new provisions

Section 75 of the 2003 Act lists those offences for which a retrial is possible following the acquittal of a defendant. The list includes:

(a)   murder and attempted murder;

(b)   manslaughter;

(c)   kidnapping;

(d)   a number of sexual offences under the Sexual Offences Acts of 1956 and 2003, including rape, attempted rape and assault by penetration;

(e)   various offences in relation to Class A drugs, such as unlawful importation and production; and

(f)   arson endangering life or property;

A retrial may take place even if the defendant was acquitted before the passing of the CJA 2003. It remains to be seen whether this provision will be compatible with the right to a fair trial enshrined in Article 6 of the ECHR.

Procedure

In order to prosecute a defendant for a second time for the same offence, the CPS must initially apply to the Court of Appeal for an order that:

(a) quashes the acquittal of the defendant; and

(b) provides for the defendant to be retried for that particular offence.

The Director of Public Prosecutions (who is the head of the CPS) must consent to such an application being made to the Court of Appeal. He may give such consent only if it is in the interests of justice for such an application to be made and the evidential requirements of s 78 of the Act (see below) are met.

The Court of Appeal must either make the order applied for or dismiss the application, depending on whether the evidential test and the interests of justice test (see below) are met (s 77(1)).

The evidential test

The evidential test is set out in s 78 of the CJA 2003. This requires that there be 'new and compelling' evidence of the defendant's guilt. 'New' evidence means evidence not adduced when the defendant was acquitted. To be 'compelling', this evidence must be reliable, substantial and highly probative of the case against the defendant.

The interests of justice test

This test is set out in s 79, which provides that the Court of Appeal should have particular (but not exclusive) regard to the following factors:

(a) whether existing circumstances make a fair trial unlikely;

(b) the length of time since the offence was allegedly committed;

(c) whether it is likely that the new evidence would have been adduced in the earlier proceedings, but for the failure of the police or the prosecution to act with due diligence and expedition; and

(d) whether, since the earlier proceedings, the police or prosecutor have failed to act with due diligence or expedition.

The last two points are aimed at preventing sloppy or incomplete investigations by the police or the CPS.

Additional provisions

Section 80 of the 2003 Act gives details of the procedural steps required if the CPS wishes to make an application to the Court of Appeal for a defendant to be retried. Section 80 also amends the Criminal Appeal Act 1968, to allow for an appeal to the House of Lords against the decision of the Court of Appeal either to allow or disallow a retrial.

It is important that if a retrial may occur, reporting restrictions are put in place so as not to prejudice it. These are provided for in s 82, which allows the Court of Appeal to order that the proceedings before it must not be reported if such reporting would give rise to a substantial risk of prejudice to the fairness of a retrial. In *Re D (Acquitted Person Retrial)* (2006) *The Times*, 6 March, the Court of Appeal held that where an application was made to quash an acquittal and a new trial was ordered, publicity of the fact that the Court of Appeal had concluded that there was compelling evidence for making such an order might reasonably be regarded as prejudicial to the subsequent trial. In light of this judgment, it is likely that the Court of Appeal will make an order under s 82 in most cases when it is asked to quash a conviction and order a new trial. Orders made under s 82 may cover both the making of an application to quash a conviction and the judgment of the court if the application is successful and a new trial is ordered.

13.3.5 The Criminal Cases Review Commission

The Criminal Cases Review Commission was created under the provisions of the Criminal Appeal Act 1995. The purpose of the Commission is to investigate alleged miscarriages of justice and, where appropriate, to refer such cases to the Court of Appeal. The Commission may refer to the Court of Appeal either a conviction following a Crown Court trial, or a sentence imposed following a Crown Court trial (Criminal Appeal Act 1995, s 9). The Commission also has the power to refer to the Crown Court a conviction or sentence imposed in the magistrates' court (Criminal Appeal Act 1995, s 11).

The Commission will refer a case to the Court of Appeal (or the Crown Court) only if the test set out in s 13 of the 1995 Act is satisfied. Section 13 provides that a reference should not be made unless the Commission considers that there is a real possibility that the conviction or sentence would not be upheld were the reference to be made. The Court of Appeal may direct the Commission to carry out investigations in any particular case as the Commission sees fit (Criminal Appeal Act 1995, s 15). Other provisions of the 1995 Act empower the Commission to obtain documentary and other evidence.

13.4 Appeals to the House of Lords

Section 33 of the Criminal Appeal Act 1968 allows either the CPS or the defendant to appeal to the House of Lords from a decision made by the Court of Appeal if:

(a) the Court of Appeal certifies that the decision involves a point of law of general public importance; *and*

(b) either the Court of Appeal or the House of Lords gives leave to appeal.

The procedural requirements for appeals to the House of Lords are set out in Part 74 of the Criminal Procedure Rules 2005.

13.5 Procedural flowcharts

13.5.1 Appeals from the magistrates' court and the Youth Court

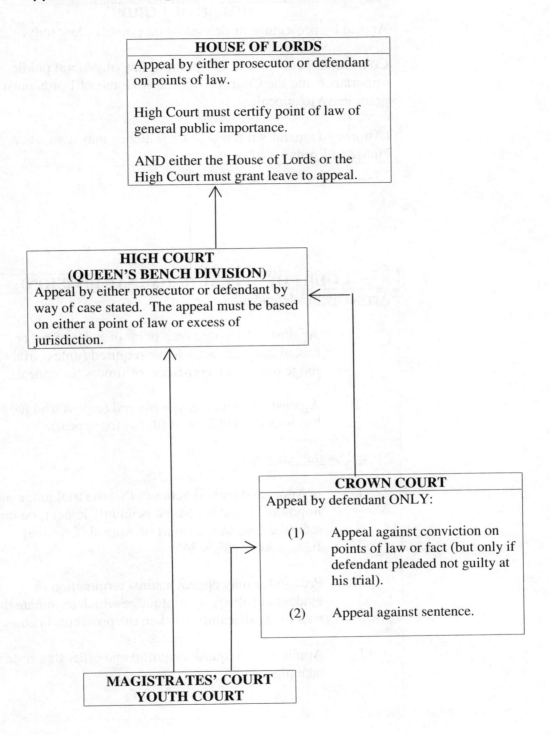

HOUSE OF LORDS

Appeal by either prosecutor or defendant on points of law.

High Court must certify point of law of general public importance.

AND either the House of Lords or the High Court must grant leave to appeal.

HIGH COURT
(QUEEN'S BENCH DIVISION)

Appeal by either prosecutor or defendant by way of case stated. The appeal must be based on either a point of law or excess of jurisdiction.

CROWN COURT

Appeal by defendant ONLY:

(1) Appeal against conviction on points of law or fact (but only if defendant pleaded not guilty at his trial).

(2) Appeal against sentence.

MAGISTRATES' COURT
YOUTH COURT

13.5.2   Appeals from the Crown Court

HOUSE OF LORDS

Appeal by prosecutor or defendant on points of law only.

Court of Appeal must certify point of law of general public importance and the Court of Appeal or House of Lords must grant leave to appeal.

(Attorney-General's references on sentence may also reach House of Lords.)

↑

COURT OF APPEAL (CRIMINAL DIVISION)

Appeal by the defendant:

(1)   Against conviction: on a point of law or fact, or mixed law and fact – leave required (unless trial judge has issued certificate of fitness for appeal).

(2)   Against sentence: leave required (unless trial judge has issued certificate of fitness for appeal).

Appeal by the prosecutor:

(1)   If Attorney-General believes that the trial judge has imposed a sentence which is unduly lenient, he may refer the case to the Court of Appeal (Criminal Justice Act 1988, s 36).

(2)   Prosecutor may appeal against termination or evidential rulings by trial judge which terminate the trial or significantly weaken the prosecution case.

(3)   Application to quash acquittal and order that re-trial take place.

↑

CROWN COURT

13.6 Checklist

At the end of this chapter you should be able to explain:

- the rights of appeal to the Crown Court the defendant may exercise following conviction or sentence in the magistrates' court;

- the right, exercisable by either the defendant or the CPS, to appeal to the High Court by way of case stated against a decision made by the magistrates' court;

- the use of judicial review proceedings as an alternative to appealing against a decision made by the magistrates' court;

- the rights of appeal to the Court of Appeal the defendant may exercise following conviction or sentence in the Crown Court;

- the rights of appeal to the Court of Appeal the CPS may exercise in respect of a Crown Court matter:

  - appeals against a termination or evidential ruling made by the trial judge,

  - the Attorney General's power to refer unduly lenient sentences to the Court of Appeal,

  - applications for a conviction to be quashed and a retrial ordered;

- the right, exercisable by either the defendant or the CPS, to appeal to the House of Lords against a ruling on a point of law made by the Court of Appeal.

13.7 Key forms

13.7.1 Notice of appeal to Crown Court against conviction, order or sentence

TO: the Justices' Clerk of the Magistrates' Court sitting at [place]

AND TO: the Branch Crown Prosecutor, Crown Prosecution Service, [address]

On the   [date]   , I   [name]

of   [address]

was convicted by the above Magistrates' Court as follows

Offence(s):   [state details of offence(s)]

for which the court on the   [date]   ordered   [sentence]

I give notice that I intend to appeal to the Crown Court at   [venue]   against conviction and/or the order or sentence.

The general grounds of appeal are as follows: [state general grounds of appeal]

[appeal against conviction – this appeal is based on the grounds that the magistrates erred in fact and law]

[appeal against sentence – this appeal is based on the grounds that the sentence imposed by the magistrates was excessive in all the circumstances]

Dated   [date]

Signed   [signature of appellant]

13.7.2   Notice and grounds of appeal or application for leave to appeal to the Court of Appeal Criminal Division

Notice and grounds of appeal or application for leave to appeal

(Criminal Procedure Rules, r 68.3(1), (2))

FOR OFFICIAL USE	CAO No. / /	Form **NG**

NOTICE and **GROUNDS** of appeal or application for leave to appeal to **THE COURT OF APPEAL CRIMINAL DIVISION**

ON COMPLETION PLEASE SEND THIS FORM TO THE CROWN COURT WHERE TRIED OR SENTENCED

Please read the notes for guidance attached. Write in **BLACK INK** and use **BLOCK CAPITALS**

The Appellant

Surname _____   Prison Index No _____

Forenames _____

Address _____   Prison _____
(if not in custody) _____   _____
_____   _____
_____

postcode _____   Date of birth _____

The Court where tried Or sentenced

The Crown Court at _____   Name of Judge _____

Date Trial started _____   Date of conviction _____

Date of sentence _____

Total period of remand in custody prior to sentence _____

The Conviction(s) and/or sentence(s)

The full Crown Court case number(s) must be given, and particulars of ALL counts, offences and sentences included

Crown Court Case number(s)	Court Or Charge No.	Offence(s)	Sentence
		Total sentence	

Applications

The appellant Is applying for:

Please tick (✓) as appropriate

☐ Extension of time in which to apply for leave to Appeal against conviction and/or sentence

☐ Leave to appeal against conviction

☐ Leave to appeal against sentence

☐ Representation Order

☐ Bail

☐ Leave to call witness

Legal Representation (please use BLOCK CAPITALS)	Name of **Counsel** _____ Address_____
	Telephone No _____
	Reference _____ Postcode _____ DX No _____
	Name of **Solicitor** _____ Address _____
	Telephone No _____
	Reference _____ Postcode _____ DX No _____

Grounds of Appeal	There is no specific format which is required for grounds of appeal but it is helpful for the grounds to be listed separately for conviction or sentence, under the appropriate heading. The grounds must be attached to this application form. Please also see the attached guidance notes, particularly note 8.
	NB. (1) Where grounds have been settled by counsel **they must be signed by counsel** with the name of counsel printed underneath. Counsel should also indicate whether s/he wishes to perfect grounds.
	(2) Any report which is relied upon and which was not retained by Crown Court must be copied and attached to this application form.
	(3) If an extension of time is needed, the detailed reasons for the delay must be attached to the grounds of appeal, preferably under a separate heading—grounds for extension of time.

| Transcripts | On an application for **leave to appeal against conviction** a transcript of the trial judge's summing up is obtained by the Registrar as a matter of course. On an application for **leave to appeal against sentence** the Registrar will obtain a transcript of the sentencing judge's remarks |
| | If ADDITIONAL transcript is sought, please specify below or, if preferred, within the grounds of appeal, giving specific dates and times of the part of the proceedings for which the transcript is requested. **Failure to give such details could result in unnecessary delay and prejudice the applicant**. |

TRANSCRIPT	DATE	TIME

Please note that transcript obtained by means other than through the Registrar may result in the cost of the transcript not being allowed upon taxation in cases subject to a Representation Order.

			* delete as appropriate

REMINDER

Have You:

a) included reasons in support of any application for extension of time? Yes/No*

b) included Form B if applying for bail? Yes/No*

c) included Form W and witness statement (conviction cases only) if seeking to call a witness Yes/No*

d) (i) attached your grounds of appeal? Yes/No*

    (ii) are the grounds of appeal signed by counsel/solicitor? Yes/No*

    (iii) does counsel wish to perfect grounds? Yes/No*

e) (i) attached your request for additional transcript? Yes/No*

    (ii) specified the dates and times of transcript requested? Yes/No*

SIGNATURE

APPELLANTS **IN CUSTODY ONLY**

I understand that if the single judge and/or the Court is of the opinion that the application for leave to appeal is plainly without merit, an order may be made that time spent in custody as an appellant shall not count towards sentence.

ALL APPELLANTS

I understand that if the court dismisses my appeal or application it may make an order for payment of costs against me, including the cost of any transcript obtained.

[This form should be signed by the appellant but may be signed by his/her legal representative provided the WARNINGS set out above have been explained to him/her. **NB** if signed by a legal representative, the appellant will be given the opportunity to request a copy of the form.]

Signature   Date

_____   _____

(of appellant or legal representative signing on *behalf* of the appellant)

NOW PLEASE SEND THIS FORM TO THE CROWN COURT WHERE TRIED OR SENTENCED

FOR PRISON USE

This notice was handed to me by appellant today.

Signed _____

Date _____   Prison Officer

Appellant's Index No   _____

EDR   _____

PED   _____

FOR CROWN COURT USE

Immediately upon receipt of Form NG the Crown Court must complete and send tear-off slips 1-3 overleaf as applicable. These tear-off slips **must** be used so that the correct notifications are sent out.

Slip 1
(Acknowledgement)

☐ sent to _____

Slip 2
(Notification / statements)

☐ Prosecutor _____

Date sent _____

Slip 3
(Monetary penalty/order)

☐   Mags. Ct   _____

Form NG received in Crown Court:

Signed _____   Date _____

Sent to the Criminal Appeal Office

Signed _____   Date _____

Name and full address / DX number of Prosecuting Authority (e.g. CPS, Customs & Excise, H & S Executive)

_____

_____

_____

Slip 3   Notification to Magistrates of appeal in cases involving monetary penalty or order
(to be sent in all cases involving monetary penalty or order)

To: Clerk to the Justices   From: Court Manager
                          Magistrates   Crown Court at

Dear Sir / Madam,   Date

R -v-   Crown Court Ref:

I write to inform you that in this case, in which you are responsible for enforcing the monetary penalty or order, the above-named has lodged notice of appeal to the Court of Appeal Criminal Division.

Yours faithfully,

Slip 2   Notification to Prosecuting Authority of receipt of Application for leave to appeal to the Court of Appeal (to be sent in all cases)

To: From: Crown Court at

                                                    Date:

Dear Sir / Madam,

R -v-   Crown Court Ref:

Please note that an application for leave to appeal has been received in the above matter. All exhibits must be retained in safe custody pending the determination of the appeal. If the matter involves a committal for sentence, please forward forthwith witness statements / statements of facts, enclosing this slip for reference purposes to:

The Registrar, Criminal Appeal Office   Telephone 020 7947 6011/6014   Yours faithfully
Royal Courts of Justice   DX: RCJ 44450 STRAND
Strand, London WC2A 2LL   FAX: 020 7947 6900

                                                                        (on behalf of the Registrar)

Slip 1   Acknowledgement of Form NG (to be sent in all cases to sender of Form NG)

                                        From: Court Manager
                                              Crown Court at
                                              Crown Court Ref:
                                              Date:

To
                                              Your Ref:

R -v-

Dear Sir / Madam,

I acknowledge receipt of form(s) NG (B* W*) which have been forwarded to the Registrar of Criminal Appeals for attention. All further communications should be addressed to:

The Registrar, Criminal Appeal Office   Yours faithfully,
Royal Courts of Justice
Strand, London WC2A 2LL
(Tel: 020 7947 6011/6014: DX: RCJ 44450 Strand: Fax: 020 7947 6900)

*Delete as appropriate

Notes for guidance on the completion of this form

1.   Everyone who is convicted or sentenced in the Crown Court in circumstances where the appeal is to the Court of Appeal Criminal Division is entitled to have advice or assistance on appeal. Provision for this is included in a trial Representation Order.

2. Solicitors and Counsel are expected to be familiar with "A Guide to Proceedings in the Court of Appeal Criminal Division" copies of which are available from any Crown Court Centre. The Guide is also available on the Court Service Internet site (**www.courtservice.gov.uk),** as are all necessary forms.

3. Separate application forms should be submitted for conviction or sentences that do not arise in the same proceedings.

4.   This notice will be treated as a notice of appeal where leave to appeal is not required.

5. In the initial stages the Court is reliant upon the information that you provide. It is in your own interests to assist by providing accurate and complete information in the form. Please indicate if you or your legal advisers have already been in correspondence with this office.

6. Please give details of the appellant's full name; if in custody give the prison index number and address where detained. If not in custody give details of address at which residing and which correspondence should be sent.

7. Applications

This form should be sent to the Crown Court within 28 days of the conviction, sentence, verdict or finding appealed against. If the appellant is in custody the form should be handed to the prison authority (or other person having custody) for forwarding to the Crown Court, and the date of handing in should be recorded on the form.

- **Extension of time** The period of 28 days cannot be extended except by leave of the Court of Appeal Criminal Division and detailed reasons for the delay must be attached to this form. Please Note: the time for applying for leave to appeal against conviction runs from the **date of conviction** even where sentence is passed on a later date.

- **Leave to appeal against conviction.**

⎫
⎬ See Note 8 below
⎭

- **Leave to appeal against sentence.**

- **Representation Order** A Representation Order made in the Crown Court does not provide for oral argument before the Court of Appeal. If a Representation Order is sought for this purpose it should be applied for.

- **Bail** Where bail is applied for Form B (CAO) must also be completed. If Form B (CAO) accompanies Form NG it should be submitted to the Crown Court but if submitted later should be sent to:- *The Registrar, Criminal Appeal Office, Royal Courts of Justice, Strand, London WC2A 2LL.*

- **Leave to call a witness (<u>conviction appellants only</u>)** Where leave is sought to call a witness in support of an application for leave to appeal against **conviction** an application should be made on **Form W (CAO).** A separate form is required for each witness. A signed statement from the witness should be appended to Form W (CAO) and, if it is said that the witness was not available at trial, an affidavit, sworn by the appellant's solicitor, should also be lodged, describing the circumstances in which the witness came forward and the circumstances in which the statement was made. If Form W (CAO) accompanies Form NG it should be sent to the Crown Court but if submitted later should be sent to:- *The Registrar* at the address given above.

8. Grounds of appeal If a positive advice on appeal is given it should always be incorporated into the same document as the grounds of appeal, as a single document. Grounds must be settled with sufficient detail to enable matters relied upon to be clearly identified. Wording such as "the conviction is unsafe" or "the sentence is in all the circumstances too severe" will be ineffective as grounds unless accompanied by detailed reasons. Ineffective applications will be rejected, thus causing delay and possibly making it necessary for an extension of time to be sought (see note 7 above). Unsigned grounds will be returned, again with resulting delay to the application.

An appeal against **conviction** is <u>not</u> another trial which looks again at the facts of the case in the way the jury did to decide if the appellant is guilty or innocent. The Court of Appeal will only be concerned with whether the conviction is unsafe and will consider issues such as: whether the trial as a whole was fair; whether the trial Judge made the correct legal rulings during the course of the trial (for example, in relation to disclosure of evidence, the admissibility of evidence or a submission of no case to answer); whether the trial Judge fairly summed up the case to the jury with the appropriate legal directions; "fresh evidence" that was not presented at trial.

An appeal against **sentence** will only succeed if the sentence was **"manifestly excessive"** (i.e. the sentence was too high given the facts of the offence or in light of any available personal mitigation) and/or **"wrong in principle"** (i.e. the sentencing Judge made some mistake when imposing the sentence. For example, there was no power to pass the particular sentence imposed or the sentence was passed on some incorrect factual or legal basis). Grounds should therefore explain <u>why</u> the sentence was "manifestly excessive" and/or "wrong in principle".

9.   Where a certificate that the case is fit for appeal is granted by the trial judge this should be stated (and see generally paragraph 17 of "A Guide to proceedings in the Court of Appeal Criminal Division").

10. Where an appellant has been **granted** leave to appeal s/he is entitled to be present on the hearing of the appeal only. If the appellant is in custody and wishes to be present at any hearing for which leave to be present is required s/he must apply for leave in writing.

[Note: Formerly forms NG 2 & 3 of the Criminal Appeal Rules 1968 (SI 1968/1262), relating to rule 2 of those Rules]

Part 5
SPECIFIC TYPES OF PROCEEDINGS

Chapter 14

The Youth Court

14.1 Introduction

14.1.1 Which defendants appear before the Youth Court?

The Youth Court is a particular form of magistrates' court. A hearing in the Youth Court will therefore take place either before a district judge or a bench of magistrates. The Youth Court deals with cases involving defendants aged between 10 and 17 inclusive. There is a conclusive presumption that children under the age of 10 cannot be guilty of committing a criminal offence (the doctrine of *doli incapax*). Children aged 10 and over are subject to the criminal law in the same way as adults.

Defendants in the Youth Court are sometimes referred to as either 'children' or 'young people'. 'Children' are defendants aged between 10 and 13 inclusive. 'Young people' are defendants aged between 14 and 17 inclusive. This distinction is relevant in terms of the sentencing powers of the court (see **14.9** below).

Collectively defendants in the Youth Court are referred to as youths or 'juveniles'. There is a difference between the term 'juveniles' when applied to defendants in the Youth Court and 'juveniles' at the police station. A 'juvenile' at the police station is a suspect who is, or appears to be, under *17* years of age (see **3.6.1**). A 'juvenile' in the Youth Court is a defendant under *18* years of age.

Some defendants appearing before the Youth Court are classified by the court and the police as 'persistent young offenders' (PYOs). The Home Office categorises a PYO as a defendant who has been sentenced on three separate occasions for one or more recordable offences (a recordable offence is any offence for which a defendant may receive a custodial sentence). A defendant who is a PYO will have his case expedited so the Youth Court may deal with him as quickly as possible.

14.1.2 Differences between the adult magistrates' court and the Youth Court

Procedures in the Youth Court are modified to take account of the age of the defendant. The layout of the courtroom is less formal than the magistrates' court, with all participants in the case sitting at the same level rather than there being a raised dock or bench. The defendant will usually sit on a chair in front of the CPS representative and his own solicitor, and in full view of the magistrates. The use of straightforward language rather than legal terminology is encouraged, and solicitors remain seated when addressing the court. Defendants (and any child witnesses) are usually spoken to and referred to by their first name. Witnesses 'promise' rather than 'swear' to tell the truth, and child witnesses under the age of 14 must give unsworn evidence (as, in fact, is the case in the adult magistrates' court). Emphasis is placed on there being as much communication as possible between the magistrates, the defendant and his parents or guardian.

Magistrates receive special training in youth justice matters before being allowed to sit in the Youth Court. If a case in the Youth Court is heard before a bench of magistrates (rather than a district judge), there must be three magistrates, one of whom must be female and one of whom must be male.

Some of the terminology in the Youth Court also differs from that in the adult magistrates' court. For example, there will be a 'finding of guilt' rather than a conviction, and the court will make an 'order upon a finding of guilt' rather than give a sentence.

Most of the procedural and evidential issues that may arise in the context of a case before the Youth Court are the same as for the case of an adult defendant before the magistrates' court. In particular, a trial in the Youth Court will follow the same procedure as a trial in the magistrates' court (see **9.2**).

14.2   Aims of the youth justice system

The principal aim of the youth justice system is to prevent offending by children and young persons (Crime and Disorder Act 1998, s 37(1)). All those involved in the youth justice system (including solicitors representing defendants) must have regard to this aim. The Youth Court must also have regard to the welfare of the defendant (Children and Young Persons Act 1933, s 44(1)).

14.3   Youth offending teams

Youth offending teams (YOTs) are responsible for co-ordinating the provision of youth justice services in their particular local area. A member of the YOT will attend each sitting of the Youth Court. This is likely to be a member of the Probation Service who has received training in dealing with youth justice matters.

The YOT will assist the Youth Court with the following matters:

(a)   investigating and confirming the personal circumstances and previous convictions of defendants;

(b)   providing support for defendants who are granted bail;

(c)   preparing pre-sentence reports; and

(d)   administering any non-custodial sentence imposed by the Youth Court.

14.4   Role of parents and guardians

A defendant appearing before the Youth Court who is aged under 16 must be accompanied by his parents or guardian during each stage of the proceedings, unless the court is satisfied that it would be unreasonable to require such attendance (Children and Young Persons Act 1933, s 34A). For defendants aged 16 or 17, the court has a discretion as to whether to make an order requiring the attendance of the defendant's parents or guardian.

Parents or guardians who attend the Youth Court play an active role in the proceedings. The court will want to hear their views (particularly in relation to sentencing) and may direct questions to them.

14.5 Reporting restrictions

The only people who are usually allowed to attend a hearing in the Youth Court are:

(a)   the magistrates;

(b)   court staff (such as the court clerk and usher);

(c)   the defendant and his parents or guardian;

(d)   the CPS representative;

(e)   the defendant's solicitor;

(f)   a representative from the YOT;

(g)   members of the press.

The press are restricted in what they are permitted to report about a hearing before the Youth Court. They cannot report the name, address or school, or any other details which are likely to lead to the identification of the defendant or any other child or young person (such as a witness) involved in the case.

Section 49 of the Children and Young Persons Act 1933 allows the court to lift these restrictions either to avoid injustice, or, following conviction, if the court is satisfied that it is in the public interest to reveal the defendant's identity. The courts should use this ability to 'name and shame' defendants only when doing so will provide some real benefit to the community, such as making the public aware of the identity of a prolific offender. This power should not be used as an 'extra' punishment imposed on the defendant.

14.6 Legal representation

Subject to having regard to s 37(1) of the Crime and Disorder Act 1998 (see **14.2** above), the solicitor representing a defendant in the Youth Court plays the same role as he would were he representing an adult defendant in the magistrates' court (see **6.3** above). Representation orders are applied for in the same manner as in the adult court and will be determined by the court applying the same interests of justice test.

The court must, however, take into account the age of the defendant when deciding whether a representation order should be granted.

14.7 Jurisdiction

14.7.1 Age

The Youth Court may only deal with defendants aged between 10 and 17 inclusive. Problems may arise when a defendant commits an offence when aged under 18, but reaches 18 before the proceedings in the Youth Court have been concluded.

If a defendant is charged with an offence when aged 17, but turns 18 prior to his *first* appearance in the Youth Court, the court does not have jurisdiction to deal with him and the case must be dealt with in the adult magistrates' court (*R v Uxbridge Youth Court, ex p H* (1998) 162 JP 327). If convicted, the defendant will be subject to the full range of sentencing powers which the magistrates' court may exercise.

If a defendant makes his first appearance in the Youth Court before his 18th birthday, but becomes 18 whilst the case is ongoing, the Youth Court may either remit the case to the adult magistrates' court, or retain the case (Children and Young Persons Act 1963, s 29). If the Youth Court retains the case, it will have the full range of sentencing powers that the adult magistrates' court would have were it dealing with the defendant (see **Chapter 11**).

14.7.2   Gravity of the offence

14.7.2.1   Homicide

There is no plea before venue procedure in the Youth Court and defendants do not have the right to elect trial by jury.

The Youth Court has jurisdiction to deal with all offences committed by juvenile offenders other than offences of homicide, such as murder and manslaughter. These offences may be dealt with by the Crown Court only (Magistrates' Courts Act 1980, s 24(1)). The only exceptions to this are if the juvenile has been charged with a 'grave crime' (see **14.7.2.2** below), or if the juvenile is classified as a 'dangerous offender' as defined by ss 226–228 of the CJA 2003 (see **14.7.2.3** below).

14.7.2.2   Grave crimes

Under s 24(1) of the Magistrates' Courts Act 1980, the Youth Court has a discretion whether to deal with a case involving a 'grave' crime, or to send such a case to the Crown Court for trial. 'Grave' crimes are generally offences for which an adult offender may receive a custodial sentence of 14 years or more (such as robbery or rape). Section 91 of the Powers of Criminal Courts (Sentencing) Act 2000 gives the Crown Court power to sentence a defendant aged between 10 and 17 to a period of long-term detention if the defendant is convicted of a grave crime.

The Youth Court should only send a case involving a grave crime to the Crown Court for trial if there is a real prospect that, were the defendant to be convicted, a sentence of long-term detention would be imposed and that consequently the maximum sentence the Youth Court may impose (a two-year detention and training order – see **14.9** below) would be insufficient (*R (H) v South and South East Hampshire Youth Court* (28 April 2006); *R (G) v Llanelli Magistrates' Court* (6 June 2006)).

> #### Example
>
> Vicky (aged 16) is charged with robbery and appears before the Youth Court. She has a previous conviction for the same offence. When it hears the facts of the case, the Youth Court decides that its sentencing powers are insufficient because, were Vicky to be convicted, there is a real prospect that a sentence of long-term detention would be required. The Youth Court therefore decides to send Vicky's case to the Crown Court for trial.

In *R (H, A and O) v Southampton Youth Court* [2004] EWHC (Admin) 2912, the High Court said that, when considering whether a case involving young offenders should be sent to the Crown Court, the Youth Court should have regard to the following:

(a)   The general policy of the legislature was that offenders under 18 years old, and in particular those under the age of 15, should wherever possible be tried in a Youth Court. A Crown Court trial (with its greater formality) should be reserved for the most serious cases.

(b) Generally, first-time offenders aged 12–14 and younger should not be detained in custody, and should be tried in the Crown Court only in exceptional circumstances (which would be rare).

(c) In each case a court should ask itself whether there was a real prospect, having regard to the offender's age, that a two-year detention and training order would be imposed, or whether the offence had other unusual features which might make it more suitable for the Crown Court.

In *R (W, s and B) v Brent, Enfield and Richmond Youth Courts* [2006] EWHC (Admin) 95, the High Court held that when the Youth Court is considering whether to send a juvenile to the Crown Court for trial under s 91, it must have all the necessary information before it to enable it to make an informed decision. This means that the CPS must explain the facts of the case to the court as accurately as possible (and the court must assume these facts to be true when making its decision), the record of the defendant's previous convictions which is before the court must be accurate, and the court must be told of any undisputed mitigation or (in appropriate cases) if the defendant intends to enter a not guilty plea.

14.7.2.3 Dangerous offenders

The provisions set out in **11.5.3.2** concerning the sentencing of adult offenders who are classified as 'dangerous' apply equally to juveniles. Sections 226 and 228 of the CJA 2003 permit a Crown Court, in an appropriate case, to sentence a juvenile to life imprisonment, to impose a sentence of detention for public protection, or to impose an extended sentence. If the Youth Court considers that a defendant may be classed as a 'dangerous offender', the court will decline jurisdiction and send the case to the Crown Court.

14.7.3 Defendants jointly charged with adult offenders

14.7.3.1 Magistrates' court

If a youth aged 17 or under is jointly charged with an adult and the offence is either summary only or an either way offence which is to be tried in the magistrates' court, both defendants will be tried together in the adult magistrates' court. If the youth is convicted, the magistrates may sentence him or remit his case to the Youth Court for sentence. If the juvenile is convicted, the magistrates will normally remit his case to the Youth Court for sentence unless they propose to deal with the matter by way of a fine or a discharge, in which case they will sentence the defendant themselves.

14.7.3.2 Crown Court

If a youth aged 17 or under is jointly charged with an adult and the offence is either indictable-only or an either way offence which is to be tried in the Crown Court, there is a presumption that both defendants will be sent for trial at the Crown Court. However, this presumption must be balanced with the general presumption that young offenders should be dealt with in the Youth Court. To assist magistrates to determine whether to send both defendants for trial in the Crown Court or to separate the youth and the adult offender, the SGC has listed examples of factors the magistrates should take into account:

(a) the young age of the youth, particularly when there is a substantial age gap between the juvenile and the adult;

(b)   the immaturity and intellect of the youth;

(c)   the relative culpability of the youth compared with the adult, and whether or not the role played by the youth was minor;

(d)   lack of previous convictions on the part of the youth compared with the adult; and

(e)   whether the respective trials of the youth and the adult can be held separately without inconvenience to witnesses or injustice to the case as a whole (draft National Allocation Guidelines 2006).

If a juvenile jointly charged with an adult is tried in the Crown Court, following conviction the judge may exercise any of the sentencing powers that would be open to the Youth Court had the defendant been convicted before the Youth Court (see **14.9** below).

14.8   Bail

14.8.1   Powers of the Youth Court

The Youth Court has the power to remand a defendant:

(a)   on bail (with or without conditions);

(b)   into local authority accommodation; or

(c)   in the case of 17-year-olds, into custody.

The provisions of the Bail Act 1976 (see **Chapter 7**) apply to defendants in the Youth Court, although a defendant may be refused bail for his 'own welfare' rather than for his 'own protection' as is the case with adult offenders (Bail Act 1976, Sch 1, Pt 1, para 3). This power is particularly important in situations when the court has concerns about the defendant's home environment. If a parent or guardian is required to act as a surety for a defendant, the court may require that person to ensure not only that the defendant answers his bail, but also that any other conditions imposed on bail are complied with by the defendant. If the defendant fails to comply with these conditions, the recognisance will become payable (see **7.5.1**).

Paragraphs 2A and 6 of the Bail Act 1976 (whereby a court will normally refuse bail to a defendant who is either alleged to have committed his current offence whilst on bail for another matter, or who has already absconded whilst on bail for the current offence – see **7.4.1**) apply only to defendants aged 18 or over. However, when the Youth Court is considering whether a defendant aged 17 or under would commit a further offence if released on bail, the court must give 'particular weight' to the fact that the defendant was on bail for another matter at the time he was alleged to have committed the current offence (Bail Act 1976, Sch 1, Pt 1, para 9AA). Similarly, 'particular weight' must be given to the fact that the defendant had previously been granted bail and failed to surrender to custody in connection with the offence if the Youth Court is considering whether to make a further grant of bail to the defendant (Bail Act 1976, Sch 1, Pt 1, para 9AB).

In deciding whether to grant bail, the Youth Court will normally have before it a report from the YOT providing details of the defendant's antecedents and also his record in relation to previous grants of bail. In addition, the report will inform the court about the defendant's home situation and his attendance record at school, college or work. The YOT report will examine the viability of imposing conditions on any bail which is granted to the defendant and may prepare a 'bail support package' for the court to consider if bail is in issue. If the court is considering refusing bail, the report will comment on the availability of local authority accommodation into which the defendant may be remanded.

14.8.2 Refusal of bail

Defendants in the Youth Court will normally be granted bail, with or without conditions. If a defendant is granted conditional bail, electronic monitoring may be used on defendants aged between 12 and 17 inclusive to ensure that the defendant complies with such conditions. If, however, the defendant is aged under 17, electronic monitoring may be used only if:

(a)   either (i) the defendant is charged with a violent or sexual offence, or an offence carrying at least 14 years' imprisonment, or (ii) the defendant is charged with an imprisonable offence and he has a recent history of repeatedly committing imprisonable offences while remanded on bail or to local authority accommodation; *and*

(b)   a YOT has informed the court of its opinion that the imposition of electronic monitoring is suitable.

14.8.2.1 Defendant aged between 10 and 16

Defendants aged between 10 and 16 who are refused bail will be remanded to the care of the local authority. This means that the defendant should stay in local authority accommodation. Often, however, no local authority accommodation will be available, in which case the defendant will return to live at home (although this will be under the care and supervision of the local authority).

In some circumstances the court may order that the defendant is to be remanded to secure local authority accommodation. For such a remand to be made, the defendant must be aged between 12 and 16 (inclusive), and the criteria set out in s 23(5) of the Children and Young Persons Act 1969 must be met. These criteria are that either:

(a)   the defendant is charged with, or has been convicted of, a violent or sexual offence, or an offence punishable in the case of an adult offender with at least 14 years' imprisonment; or

(a)   the defendant has a recent history of absconding whilst remanded to local authority accommodation, and is charged with, or has been convicted of, an imprisonable offence alleged or found to have been committed while he was so remanded;

and, in either case, the court is of the opinion that imposing a security requirement is the only way to protect the public from serious harm from the defendant, or to stop the defendant from committing imprisonable offences.

Although defendants aged between 12 and 16 may be remanded into secure accommodation, in practice shortages in such accommodation mean that the court is only ever likely to make such an order in respect of 15- or 16-year-olds.

14.8.2.2 Male defendants aged 15 or 16

For defendants who are male and aged 15 or 16, if the court considers that the defendant satisfies the criteria set out in s 23(5) (see **14.8.2.1** above), the court will remand the defendant in custody rather than in secure local authority accommodation. The only restriction on this is that a remand in custody should not be made if there are concerns about the vulnerability of the defendant by reason of either his immaturity or his propensity to self-harm.

14.8.2.3 Defendants aged 17

Defendants aged 17 who are refused bail will be remanded in custody. Such defendants will be remanded either to a remand centre, or to prison.

If bail is refused by the Youth Court, a defendant has the same right of appeal to the Crown Court as an adult offender in the magistrates' court (see **7.8.1** above).

14.9 Sentencing

14.9.1 Background and procedure

14.9.1.1 Objective of sentencing

Before a defendant ever comes before a Youth Court, it is likely that he will have been through the formal system of reprimands and warnings created by ss 65 and 66 of the Crime and Disorder Act 1998 (see **Chapter 3**). When the Youth Court sentences a defendant, it must balance the seriousness of the offence (and the defendant's previous record) with the welfare requirements of the defendant. The court must at all times have regard to the principal aim of preventing offending.

14.9.1.2 Sentencing procedure

Sentencing in the Youth Court follows a similar procedure to that in the adult magistrates' court (see **12.5.1**). The CPS representative will give the facts of the case to the magistrates (assuming the defendant has pleaded guilty rather than having been convicted following a trial), and the defendant's solicitor will then give a plea in mitigation. The court is also likely to want to hear from the defendant's parents or guardian before deciding the appropriate penalty.

A key document in the sentencing process is the pre-sentence report prepared by the YOT. The Youth Court must obtain this report before sentencing the defendant, unless the defendant has recently been sentenced by the Youth Court for another matter and the court is able to use the pre-sentence report prepared for that earlier matter (CJA 2003, s 156). The court is likely to indicate the type of sentence it has in mind when it orders a report, and the report will address the defendant's suitability for that type of sentence. The court will place great emphasis on the contents of the report when deciding the sentence to impose. The Youth Court may either adjourn the sentencing hearing to enable the YOT to prepare the pre-sentence report, or may ask the member of the YOT who is present in court to prepare a 'stand down' report (see **12.2.1.3**) so that sentencing can take place without the need for the case to be adjourned.

14.9.2 Types of sentence available

14.9.2.1 Absolute and conditional discharges

The Youth Court has the power to order an absolute or a conditional discharge for a defendant in the same way as the magistrates' court may for an adult offender (see **11.8** above). A conditional discharge can be imposed for a maximum period of three years.

It is rare for such a sentence to be given in practice. A defendant coming before the Youth Court is likely to have been through the system of reprimands and final warnings at the police station (see **Chapter 3**), and the court is more likely impose a sentence which will actively help to prevent the defendant from re-offending than to give the defendant an absolute or conditional discharge. A conditional discharge is only likely to be given when the defendant has been convicted following a trial, the defendant has no previous convictions (and has not received any reprimands or final warnings from the police), and the court takes the view that immediate punishment of the defendant is unnecessary. A defendant who satisfies the above conditions but who pleaded guilty will receive a referral order rather than a conditional discharge (see **14.9.2.2** below).

14.9.2.2 Referral orders

Referral orders were introduced by s 16 of the Powers of Criminal Courts (Sentencing) Act 2000. Referral orders can only be made in respect of a defendant who has not previously been convicted or bound over by a court.

A referral order *must* be made for a defendant who pleads guilty to an offence (which carries a possible custodial sentence) and who has never previously been convicted or bound over by a court, unless the court is proposing either to impose a custodial sentence or to make an absolute discharge. Referral orders *cannot* be made unless the defendant pleads guilty to the offence with which he is charged, although if the defendant has entered a mixed plea (ie, guilty to one or more offences but not guilty to others), the court has the power to make a referral order but is not obliged to do so.

If the court makes a referral order, the defendant will be referred to a 'youth offender panel'. The panel will speak with the defendant and his parents or guardian to help prevent any further offending. The referral order will require the defendant to attend meetings with the youth offender panel and specify the length of the youth offender contract (see below). The referral order will be 'spent' when the defendant has successfully complied with the terms of the youth offender contract.

The youth offender panel comprises a member of the YOT and two community volunteers. At the meetings the panel will speak to the defendant and his family with a view to:

(a)   stopping any further offending;

(b)   helping the defendant right the wrong he did to his victim; and

(c)   helping the defendant with any problems he may have.

The panel will agree with the defendant a 'youth offender contract'. This is a programme of behaviour designed to prevent the defendant re-offending, and will last between three and 12 months. The terms of the contract are agreed between the defendant and the panel members, rather than by the Youth Court.

At the same time as making a referral order, the court may make an order for the payment of costs and/or compensation (see **14.9.2.3** below). A referral order may be combined with a parenting order (see **14.9.4** below).

14.9.2.3 Fines, compensation and costs

Fines

The level of any fine imposed by a Youth Court must have regard to the seriousness of the offence and the defendant's financial circumstances. The maximum level of fine a Youth Court may impose is determined by the defendant's age. For defendants aged 10 to 13 inclusive, the maximum fine is £250. For defendants aged 14 to 17 inclusive, the maximum fine is £1,000.

If the court imposes a fine on a defendant aged under 16, it must order that the fine be paid by the parents or guardian of the defendant, although if the defendant has a source of income the court will often express its wish that the fine be paid from this. In the case of defendants aged 16 or 17, the court may order that the fine be paid either by the defendant, or by his parents or guardian.

Compensation

An order to pay compensation may be made against a defendant as a penalty in itself, or in addition to any other penalty which the court imposes. Such an order may be made by the Youth Court if it considers that the defendant's victim has suffered a loss which deserves to be compensated. For defendants aged under 16, any compensation ordered by the court will be payable by the defendant's parents or guardian. For defendants aged 16 or 17, the court may order that the compensation be paid either by the defendant, or by his parents or guardian.

Costs

The court may also order a defendant to make a contribution towards costs incurred by the CPS in bringing the case. This is not subject to any maximum figure. As with fines and compensation, for defendants aged under 16 the parents or guardian of the defendant will be ordered to pay this sum; and for defendants aged 16 or 17 the court may order that such costs be paid either by the defendant, or by his parents or guardian.

14.9.2.4   Reparation orders

Reparation orders were introduced by s 73 of the Powers of Criminal Courts (Sentencing) Act 2000. These orders are based on the concept of 'restorative justice', in which the defendant is required to make reparation to his victim for the damage caused by his crime. Reparation orders are distinct from the community penalties described at **14.9.2.5** below.

Under the terms of the order, the defendant will be required to do some work to make reparation either to his victim, or to the community at large. This may, for example, include such tasks as cleaning off graffiti or tidying up damage caused to the victim's property. The order may require the defendant to do up to 24 hours' work. Before such an order is made, the court must obtain a report from the YOT confirming that the defendant is suitable to do such work, and also detailing the attitude of the victim to the making of such an order. The work required to be done under the reparation order will be supervised by the YOT and must be completed within a period of three months.

14.9.2.5   Community penalties

Introduction

The CJA 2003 has made significant changes to the types of community penalty which the Youth Court may impose. The Act differentiates between offenders who are aged 15 and under, and offenders aged 16 or 17.

Defendants aged 15 and under

If the Youth Court decides to impose a community sentence on an offender who is aged 15 or under, the sentence will be a 'youth community order' (CJA 2003, s 147). A youth community order will be made up of one or more of the following:

(a)   a curfew order;

(b)   an exclusion order;

(c)   an attendance centre order;

(d)   a supervision order;

(e)   an action plan order.

Each type of order is described below. A Youth Court should not make a youth community order unless it is of the opinion that the offence (or the combination of the offence and one or more offences associated with it) is serious enough to warrant such a sentence (CJA 2003, s 148(1)). A Youth Court making such an order must be satisfied that the component parts of the order are suitable for the defendant, and that the restrictions on the defendant's liberty imposed by the order are commensurate with the seriousness of the offending (CJA 2003, s 148(3)).

Curfew orders

The Youth Court may make such an order by virtue of ss 37 and 38 of the Powers of Criminal Courts (Sentencing) Act 2000. A curfew order may last for a maximum period of three months. The order will require the defendant to be indoors at a specified address between certain hours. The defendant may be electronically monitored to ensure that he complies with the order.

Exclusion orders

The Youth Court may make an exclusion order by virtue of s 40A(1) of the Powers of Criminal Courts (Sentencing) Act 2000. An exclusion order will prevent the defendant from entering a place or area as specified in the order. Orders may last for a maximum period of three months. Before making an order, the Youth Court must find out about the defendant's family circumstances and the likely effect of an order on those circumstances. A defendant may be electronically monitored to ensure that he complies with the order.

Attendance centre orders

A Youth Court may make such an order under s 60 of the Powers of Criminal Courts (Sentencing) Act 2000. An attendance centre order requires a defendant to attend a centre normally run either by the police, or by the YOT. This will usually take place on alternate Saturdays, when the defendant will be required to attend for up to three hours and take part in a planned series of activities.

The total number of hours a defendant can be ordered to complete is dependent on the defendant's age, although the total number of hours will usually between 12 and 24.

Supervision orders

This type of order was created by s 65 of the Powers of Criminal Courts (Sentencing) Act 2000. A supervision order enables the court to place a defendant under the supervision of the YOT for a minimum period of six months and a maximum period of three years. An officer from the YOT will 'advise, assist and befriend' the defendant, with a view to preventing him from re-offending. The court may impose conditions when making a supervision order, such as a requirement that the defendant live at a particular address, attend meetings with his supervisor, participate in certain activities, or make reparation to the victim of his offence.

Action plan orders

Action plan orders were created by s 69 of the Powers of Criminal Courts (Sentencing) Act 2000. An action plan order places a defendant under intense supervision for a fixed period of three months. The purpose of the order is to enable the YOT to 'take control' during this period, and ensure that the defendant attends regular meetings with the YOT. The court (or the officer from the YOT who provides the supervision) will also specify certain things the defendant must do during the three-month period, such as attending at an attendance centre, making reparation to the victim, attending school or some other form of training, meeting a drugs counsellor for advice or staying away from a particular location. The court will normally fix another hearing for some time during the course of the three-month period so that it can monitor the defendant's progress.

Defendants aged 16 and 17

If the Youth Court wishes to impose a community sentence on a defendant aged 16 or 17, it must make a generic community order in the same way as the magistrates' court would for an adult offender (see **11.6** above).

A Youth Court will not be able to make such an order for defendants who are 16 or over unless the court is of the opinion that the offence (or the combination of the offence and one or more offences associated with it) is serious enough to warrant such a sentence (CJA 2003, s 148(1)).

In making a generic community order, the Youth Court will be able to choose from the same 'menu' of options as can the magistrates' court for an adult defendant (see **11.6.2**), and select those options which are most appropriate for the defendant. Any limitations which the order imposes on the defendant must be proportionate to the seriousness of the offence and must be the most suitable for the defendant (CJA 2003, s 148(2)). They must reflect the principal aim of preventing the defendant from re-offending.

Instead of making a generic community order, the Youth Court may impose a supervision order or an action plan order. Such orders will operate in the same way as for offenders aged 15 and under (see above).

14.9.2.6   Detention and training orders

The making of a detention and training order is provided for in ss 100 to 103 of the Power of Criminal Courts (Sentencing) Act 2000. A detention and training order is the only type of custodial sentence that the Youth Court has the power to impose. The Youth Court should not impose a detention and training order unless it is of the opinion that the offence (or the combination of the offence and one or more offences associated with it) is so serious that neither a fine alone nor a community sentence can be justified for the offence (CJA 2003, s 152(2)).

Detention and training orders cannot be imposed on defendants aged 10 or 11. If a defendant is aged between 12 and 14 inclusive, an order may only be made if the court considers that the defendant is a 'persistent young offender' (see **14.1.2** above). For defendants aged 15 or over, there is no restriction on the making of such an order, save that the threshold set out in s 152 above must be met.

An order may be imposed for fixed periods of 4, 6, 8, 10, 12, 18 or 24 months. The length of the order must be for the shortest period of time the court considers commensurate with the seriousness of the offence, or the offence and one or more offences associated with it (CJA 2003, s 153(2)). A detention and training order may be imposed only if the court has received from the YOT a pre-sentence report that specifically addresses custody as a possible sentencing option.

When the court makes such an order, the defendant will be held in detention in a young offenders institution for one half of the period of the order. He will then be released into the community under the supervision of the YOT for the second half of the order. The degree of supervision is decided upon by the YOT (not the court), but is likely to include electronic monitoring and intensive supervision.

Example

Kevin appears before the Youth Court and is convicted of the burglary of domestic premises. The magistrates impose a detention and training order for a period of 12 months. Kevin will spend the first six months in detention at a young offenders institution. He will spend the second six months in the community under the supervision of the YOT.

Detention and training orders have become particularly common in recent years as a way of dealing with juveniles who commit street robberies to get mobile phones, or juveniles who commit other robberies against fellow school pupils.

14.9.3 Anti-social behaviour orders

A Youth Court can make an anti-social behaviour order (ASBO) where:

(a)   a defendant has committed an offence;

(b)   the court considers that the defendant has acted in a manner that was likely to cause harassment, alarm or distress to one or more people not in the same household as the defendant; and

(c)   the court considers that such an order is necessary to protect persons from further anti-social acts committed by the defendant (see **11.3.2.7**).

The order will impose prohibitions on the defendant, such as a prohibition against entering a particular area or place, or not to engage in a particular type of behaviour. The order may last for a minimum of two years and a maximum of five years. If the defendant breaches the order, this will constitute a separate offence for which the defendant may be prosecuted.

A Youth Court that makes an ASBO may also make an individual support order (ISO). The idea behind such an order is that, at the same time as imposing restrictions on the defendant, the defendant is also given support by requiring him to participate in specified activities or follow directions given by a member of the YOT.

14.9.4 Parenting orders

Under ss 8 to 10 of the Crime and Disorder Act 1998, a Youth Court may make a parenting order when a defendant has been convicted of an offence. A parenting order can be imposed on the parents or guardian of a defendant. Such an order is mandatory where the defendant is aged under 16 and the court considers that such an order is necessary to prevent the defendant from re-offending. The order is discretionary when the defendant is 16 or over.

The order will require the defendant's parents or guardian to comply with any requirements that are specified in the order and to attend counselling or guidance sessions. The objective is to make parents accept responsibility for their children's offending and to prevent further offending.

The order may be imposed for a maximum period of 12 months, although the requirement to attend counselling or guidance sessions may last for a maximum period of three months only.

The Youth Court also has power to make an order binding over the parent or guardian of a defendant who is aged below 16, if the court is satisfied that to make such an order would be desirable in the interests of preventing the defendant committing further offences. The parent or guardian may be bound over in a sum not exceeding £1,000 to take proper care of the defendant and exercise proper control over him.

14.10 Appeals

As the Youth Court is a type of magistrates' court, a defendant convicted or sentenced by the Youth Court has the same rights of appeal as a defendant who is convicted or sentenced by the adult magistrates' court (see **Chapter 13**).

14.11   Flowchart – the sentencing ladder in the Youth Court

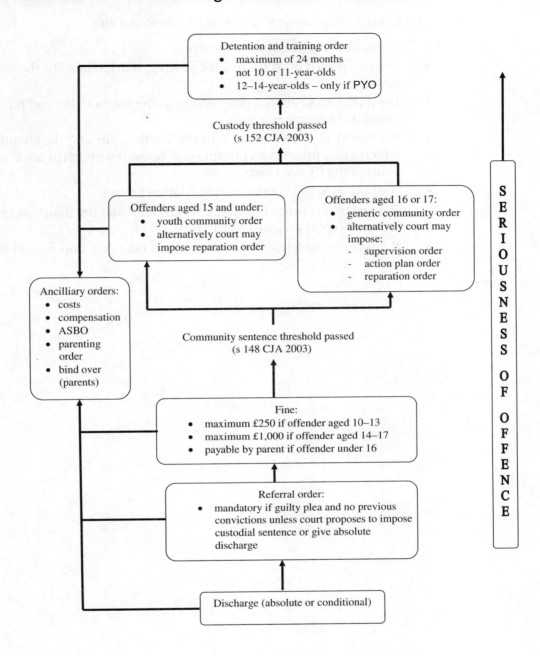

14.12 Checklist

At the end of this chapter you should be able to explain:

- the aims of the youth justice system;
- the role played by YOTs and the parents of defendants in the youth justice system;
- the differences between proceedings in the Youth Court and proceedings in the adult magistrates' court;
- the extent of the jurisdiction of the Youth Court and the circumstances in which a case involving a juvenile may be dealt with in the adult magistrates' court or the Crown Court;
- the powers of the Youth Court in relation to bail;
- the sentencing procedure in the Youth Court and the significance of the pre-sentence report prepared by the YOT;
- the types of sentence which the Youth Court may impose and the purpose behind such sentences.

Chapter 15

Road Traffic Offences

15.1 Introduction

Road traffic offences are the 'bread and butter' of the average solicitor specialising in criminal litigation. Attend any magistrates' court and the list of cases to be dealt with that day will invariably include several road traffic matters. Most newly-qualified solicitors perform their first advocacy in the magistrates' court representing clients charged with such offences.

This chapter will begin by listing the most common road traffic offences. It will then go on to consider what is meant by the 'endorsement' of a driving licence, to explain how the penalty points system works, and to look at when a defendant may be disqualified from driving. The chapter will conclude by examining the meaning of the terms 'mitigating factors', 'mitigating circumstances' and 'special reasons', and looking at the situations when these may be raised by a defendant.

For a more in-depth analysis of road traffic offences, the standard work of reference is *Wilkinson's Road Traffic Offences*. This two-volume publication is normally published every second year. It is accepted by the courts as an authoritative source of the law in road traffic matters, and should be consulted in all but the most straightforward of cases. The current, 22nd edition was published in 2005.

A number of changes both to substantive road traffic law and the practice and procedure concerning the prosecution of road traffic offences are contained in the Road Safety Bill which is currently before Parliament. It is anticipated that the Bill will receive Royal assent during the latter part of 2006. Changes proposed in the Bill are, where relevant, described in this chapter.

15.2 Specific offences

Prosecutions for road traffic offences will follow the same procedure at court as for any other type of offence. Road traffic offences may be summary only (eg, careless driving), either way (eg. dangerous driving) or indictable only (eg, causing death by dangerous driving). What sets road traffic offences apart from other offences is that, in addition to any other penalty which the offence may carry, most traffic offences will carry the following additional penalties:

(a)   details of the conviction will be endorsed on the defendant's driving licence (see **15.3** below);

(b)   the defendant may be subject to an obligatory or a discretionary disqualification from driving (see **15.5** below); and

(c)   if the defendant is not disqualified from driving for the offence itself, a number of penalty points will be endorsed on the defendant's driving licence (see **15.4** below).

The table set out below lists all 'endorsable' road traffic offences, the number of penalty points each offence carries, and whether, following conviction, disqualification for the offence is obligatory or discretionary. (Offences for which disqualification from driving is obligatory still carry penalty points. This is because, if the defendant is able to avoid obligatory disqualification by successfully arguing that 'special reasons' exist (see **15.6.3** below), the court may still impose penalty points.)

Offence	Legislative provision	Number of penalty points	Disqualification
Manslaughter (or in Scotland culpable homicide) by driver of a motor vehicle	(common law)	3–11	Obligatory
1988 Act			
Causing death by dangerous driving	s 1	3–11	Obligatory
Dangerous driving	s 2	3–11	Obligatory
Careless or inconsiderate driving	s 3	3–9	Discretionary
Causing death by careless driving when under influence of drink or drugs	s 3A	3–11	Obligatory
Driving or attempting to drive when unfit through drink or drugs	s 4(1)	3–11	Obligatory
Being in charge when unfit through drink or drugs	s 4(2)	10	Discretionary
Driving or attempting to drive with excess alcohol	s 5(1)(a)	3–11	Obligatory
In charge with excess alcohol	s 5(1)(b)	10	Discretionary
Failing or refusing to provide breath for preliminary test	s 6(4)	4	Discretionary
Failing or refusing to provide specimens for analysis when driving or attempting to drive	s 7(6)	3–11	Obligatory
Failing or refusing to provide specimens for analysis when not driving or attempting to drive	s 7(6)	10	Discretionary
Failing to allow specimen to be subjected to laboratory test when driving or attempting to drive	s 7A	3–11	Obligatory
Failing to allow specimen to be subjected to laboratory test when not driving or attempting to drive	s 7A	10	Discretionary
Motor racing or speed trials on highway	s 12	3–11	Obligatory

Offence	Legislative provision	Number of penalty points	Disqualification
Leaving motor vehicle in dangerous position	s 22	3	Discretionary
Carrying passenger on motor cycle other than astride and on a seat	s 23	3	Discretionary
Failing to comply with traffic directions or signals in respect of motor vehicle	ss 35, 36	3	Discretionary
Using vehicle in dangerous condition	s 40(A)	3	Discretionary
Breach of requirement as to brakes, steering gear or tyres	s 41A	3	Discretionary
Driving otherwise than in accordance with a licence	s 87(1)	3–6	Discretionary
Driving after making false declarations as to physical fitness	s 92(10)	3–6	Discretionary
Driving after failure to notify disability	s 94(3A)	3–6	Discretionary
Driving after refusal or revocation of licence	s 94A	3–6	Discretionary
Driving with uncorrected defective eyesight	s 96(1)	3	Discretionary
Refusing eyesight test	s 96(3)	3	Discretionary
Driving while disqualified by court order	s 103(1)(b)	6	Discretionary
Using motor vehicle whilst uninsured	s 143	6–8	Discretionary
Failing to stop after accident	s 170(4)	5–10	Discretionary
Failing to give particulars or report accident	s 170(4)	5–10	Discretionary
Failure to give information as to identity of driver	s 172	3	Discretionary
Taking, etc, a motor vehicle in Scotland without authority	s 178		Discretionary
Theft Act 1968			
Stealing or attempting to steal a motor vehicle	s 1		Discretionary
Taking or attempting to take etc, a motor vehicle without authority	s 12		Discretionary
Aggravated vehicle-taking	s 12A	3–11	Obligatory
Going equipped for stealing or for taking motor vehicles	s 25		Discretionary
RTR Act 1984			
Contravention of temporary speed restriction	s 16(1)	3–6 or 3 (fixed penalty)	Discretionary

Offence	Legislative provision	Number of penalty points	Disqualification
Motorway offences	s 17(4)	3–6 or 3 (fixed penalty) if speeding, otherwise 3	Discretionary
Pedestrian crossing offence in respect of motor vehicle	s 25	3	Discretionary
School crossing patrol offence in respect of motor vehicle	s 28	3	Discretionary
Street playground offence in respect of motor vehicle	ss 29, 30	2	Discretionary
Speeding offences	s 89	3–6 or 3 (fixed penalty)	Discretionary
RTO Act 1988			
Aiding and abetting, etc, an obligatory disqualifiable offence	s 28(1)(b)	10	Discretionary

For serious road traffic offences (such as dangerous driving), the court may impose a community penalty or custody in just the same way as for a non-road traffic offence. Similarly for minor road traffic offences (such as careless driving), the court may impose a fine. These penalties will be in addition to any order disqualifying the defendant from driving or imposing penalty points. **Appendix 2** contains extracts from the Magistrates' Court Sentencing Guidelines for the most common road traffic offences dealt with in the magistrates' court.

The Road Safety Bill proposes a number of new offences. The most significant of these offences are:

(a)   causing death by careless or inconsiderate driving – disqualification for the offence will be obligatory and the offence will carry 3–11 penalty points;

(b)   causing death by driving when the driver is unlicensed, disqualified or uninsured – disqualification for the offence will be obligatory and the offence will carry 3–11 penalty points.

15.3   Endorsement

Most road traffic offences are said to be 'endorsable'. This will result in two things if the defendant is convicted:

(a)   details of the offence will be endorsed on the defendant's driving licence and the details sent to the Driver and Vehicle Licensing Authority (DVLA) in Swansea; and

(b)   unless the defendant is disqualified from driving for the offence, a number of penalty points will also be endorsed on his licence (see **15.4** below).

Part 55 of the Criminal Procedure Rules provides that the following information must be recorded on a licence which is endorsed:

(a)   the name of the magistrates' court which dealt with the offence;

(b)   the date on which the offence was committed and details of the type of offence committed (this is recorded by means of a code; for example, CD is the code for careless driving and DR10 is the code for driving whilst over the prescribed alcohol limit);

(c)   the date of conviction and the date of sentence (if different); and

(d)   the penalty imposed, including the number of penalty points.

What happens in practice is that the defendant will surrender his licence to the court, which will then send this to the DVLA. The DVLA will enter the appropriate endorsement on the licence and then return this to the defendant. The DVLA will also retain details of the endorsement on its database, so that if in any subsequent proceedings there is a dispute about any endorsements on a licence, the court will be able to obtain a print out from the DVLA. Under changes proposed in the Road Safety Bill, the Secretary of State will in future hold a 'driving record' for all road traffic offenders. The 'driving record' will record all the endorsements an offender has received, and may be accessed by the courts and the police.

Endorsable offences may be divided into two separate categories: (i) offences where the court is obliged to disqualify the defendant (unless the defendant can establish the existence of 'special reasons – see **15.6.3** below); and (ii) offences where the court has a discretion as to whether to disqualify the defendant. Examples of the former type of offence are dangerous driving and driving whilst over the prescribed alcohol limit. Examples of the latter type of offence are careless driving and speeding.

15.4 Penalty points

15.4.1 How many points will the court impose?

The court will impose penalty points only if it does not disqualify the defendant from driving for the offence for which he has been convicted. A defendant *cannot* both be disqualified from driving and receive penalty points in respect of the same offence (see below).

The number of points to be endorsed is fixed in respect of some offences and variable in respect of others. Where the number of points is variable, the court will decide on the number of points to be imposed by reference to the seriousness of the offence. For example, a defendant convicted of careless driving may receive between 3 and 9 points. The actual number of points the court imposes will depend on the facts of the case and the view the court takes as to the seriousness of the offence.

If a defendant commits more than one endorsable offence on the same occasion, the number of penalty points he receives will usually be the number of points imposed for the offence that incurs the highest number of penalty points, although details of each offence will still be endorsed on the licence.

Example

John is convicted on the same occasion of careless driving (for which the court may impose 3 to 9 points – see above) and using a vehicle with defective tyres (which carries 3 points). The magistrates decide that 6 points are appropriate for the offence of careless driving. This is the total number of points that will be imposed (although details of *both* offences will be endorsed on John's licence).

The court does have the power to impose points for both offences if it thinks it fit to do so (Road Traffic Offenders Act 1988, s 28(4)). It is very rare for the court to exercise this power. In the above example, if there was evidence that John had been using his vehicle with defective tyres for some time, the court could in principle impose a further 3 points for this offence, making an overall total of 9 points.

If a defendant is convicted of an offence that carries penalty points, the court must endorse the defendant's licence with the appropriate number of penalty points unless either the court can find 'special reasons' for not doing so (see **15.6.3** below), or the court is proposing to disqualify the defendant for the offence itself.

If a court decides to disqualify a defendant for the offence itself, the defendant's licence will still be endorsed with the details of that offence but no penalty points will be endorsed on the licence.

Example

Michael is convicted of careless driving. The court may disqualify Michael from driving for this offence. If Michael is disqualified for this offence, his licence will be endorsed with details of the conviction but he will not receive any penalty points. If Michael is not disqualified for this offence, the court will impose between 3 and 9 penalty points on Michael's licence.

15.4.2   When will a defendant be disqualified under the points system?

A defendant will be disqualified under the penalty points system if he collects 12 or more 'relevant points' on his licence (Road Traffic Offenders Act 1988, s 35). Relevant points are any penalty points imposed for any offences that are *committed* within a period of three years. This is often referred to as the 'totting up system'. When the number of points on a defendant's licence is being calculated, the court will start with the date the current offence was committed and then work back three years, adding together the points imposed for the current offence and any other offences committed within this three-year period (see **Example 1** below).

When adding up the number of points, the court will not need to go back the full three years if the defendant has an earlier penalty points disqualification during this period. The effect of such a disqualification is to 'wipe the slate clean' of any earlier penalty points, including any points awarded for the offence following which the defendant was disqualified under the penalty points scheme (see **Example 2** below).

If, however, a defendant is disqualified other than under the penalty points system during the three-year period prior to the commission of the current offence (ie, a disqualification for an offence carrying obligatory or discretionary disqualification), any penalty points already on the defendant's licence that were imposed prior to this disqualification will *not* be cleared away as a result of the disqualification (see **Example 3** below).

Example 1

Raj has convictions for offences committed on the following dates:

14 May 2005	careless driving – licence endorsed with 7 points
23 October 2006	speeding – licence endorsed with 3 points
11 January 2007	defective tyres – licence endorsed with 3 points

After conviction for the offence committed on 11 January 2007, Raj will be liable to disqualification under the penalty points system because he will have 12 or more points on his licence in respect of offences committed within a three-year period.

Example 2

Jane has convictions for offences committed on the following dates:

20 June 2004	failing to stop – licence endorsed with 6 points
12 February 2005	careless driving – licence endorsed with 8 points (disqualified under the penalty points system for 6 months)
3 March 2006	defective brakes – licence endorsed with 3 points
31 July 2006	speeding – licence endorsed with 4 points
2 February 2007	careless driving – licence endorsed with 4 points

Following the offence committed on 12 February 2005, Jane was disqualified under the points system for having 12 points or more on her licence in respect of offences committed within a three-year period. This disqualification 'wipes the slate clean', so that the points imposed for the offences on 20 June 2004 and 12 February 2005 will not be taken into account again. Therefore, following the offence committed on 2 February 2007 Jane will have only 11 points on her licence and so will not be liable to disqualification under the penalty points system.

Example 3

Seema has convictions for offences committed on the following dates:

11 November 2004	speeding – licence endorsed with 6 points
9 April 2005	drink driving – disqualified from driving for 12 months (obligatory)
13 August 2006	careless driving – 5 points
1 March 2007	defective tyres – 3 points

Following the conviction for the offence committed on 1 March 2007, Seema will be liable to disqualification under the penalty points system because she will have 12 points or more on her licence in respect of offences committed within a three-year period. The disqualification for drink driving on 9 April 2005 does not wipe the slate clean of the 6 points imposed for the speeding offence on 11 November 2004 because this was *not* a disqualification under the penalty points system.

15.4.3   How long is the period of disqualification?

If a defendant is disqualified under the penalty points system, the minimum period of disqualification is six months, unless the court finds there to be 'mitigating circumstances' either for not imposing a disqualification under the penalty points system, or for disqualifying the defendant for less than six months (see **15.6.2** below)

This minimum period is increased to one year for a defendant who has previously been disqualified for 56 days or more during the three-year period prior to the commission of the most recent offence in respect of which penalty points have been taken into account. If a defendant has more than one disqualification for 56 days or more within this three-year period, the minimum period is increased to two years.

When the minimum period is increased because of a previous disqualification of 56 days or more, the previous disqualification does not need to be under the penalty points scheme. It also includes offences where disqualification was obligatory, or where the magistrates exercised their discretion to disqualify the defendant. Thus in Example 3 at **15.4.2** above, Seema will receive a minimum disqualification of 12 months because she has one previous disqualification of 56 days or more in the three years prior to the commission of the most recent offence for which she received penalty points.

15.4.4 Newly-qualified drivers

The penalty points system operates differently for newly-qualified drivers, who must undergo a probationary period for two years after passing the driving test. If a newly-qualified driver receives 6 or more penalty points within this two-year period, his full driving licence will be revoked automatically and he will be required to pass a further driving test. However, he will not be disqualified from driving until he passes such a test; rather, he will revert to the status of a driver who has only a provisional licence (for which he will need to apply) and so, for example, he will not be allowed to drive unaccompanied or without displaying 'L' plates.

15.4.5 Road Safety Bill

Under changes proposed in the Road Safety Bill, for certain specified offences (including speeding and careless and inconsiderate driving), where the court proposes to deal with the offence by way of penalty points rather than a disqualification, the court may offer the defendant the opportunity to take part in a driver rehabilitation course. The court may do this only if, after taking into account the number of points the court proposes to award for the current offence, the defendant will have between 7 and 11 points (inclusive) on his licence. If the defendant successfully completes the course, the court may order that 3 of the points imposed for the offence shall not be taken into account by a later court if, after 12 months have elapsed, the defendant is convicted of a further offence for which penalty points are imposed (and which may result in the defendant being disqualified from driving under the penalty points scheme).

15.5 Disqualification from driving

15.5.1 Obligatory disqualification

A court has an obligation to disqualify a defendant in the following situations:

(a) A court must disqualify a defendant for at least 12 months if the defendant is convicted of an offence carrying obligatory disqualification (such as driving whilst over the prescribed alcohol limit or dangerous driving). The only exception to this is if the court finds that there are 'special reasons' for not disqualifying the defendant (see **15.6.3** below).

(b) The minimum period of disqualification in (a) is increased to two years if:
   (i) the defendant is convicted of causing death by dangerous driving, or causing death by careless driving whilst under the influence of drink or drugs; or
   (ii) in the three years prior to the current offence, the defendant has received more than one disqualification for a fixed period of at least 56 days.

(c) The minimum period of disqualification in (a) is increased to three years if the defendant is convicted of any offence involving 'drink driving' or driving whilst unfit through drugs, and the defendant has a conviction within the 10 years preceding the current offence for any similar type of offence.

(d) A court must disqualify a defendant for at least six months under the penalty points scheme when that defendant acquires 12 or more relevant points on his licence (see **15.4.3** above). The only exception to this is if the court finds that there are 'mitigating circumstances' for not disqualifying the defendant (see **15.6.2** below). If a defendant is disqualified under the penalty points scheme, the court *may* require him to undergo an extended driving test at the end of his period of disqualification before his licence is returned.

(e) A court must disqualify a defendant until he passes an extended driving test if the defendant is convicted of motor-related manslaughter, causing death by dangerous driving, dangerous driving or causing death by careless driving when under the influence of drink or drugs. The defendant will only be able to take such a test once the period of disqualification imposed for the offence has expired. For any other offence which carries an obligatory disqualification, the court *may* require the defendant to take an extended driving test at the end of his period of disqualification before his licence is returned.

Obligatory disqualification is merely part of the overall sentence the court may impose on a defendant, and in a serious case (such as dangerous driving) the court may impose a custodial or community penalty. If the court is considering such a sentence it will normally adjourn the case so that a pre-sentence report may be prepared by the Probation Service (see **12.2** above). In such circumstances the court has the power to impose an interim period of disqualification on the defendant until sentence is passed (Road Traffic Offenders Act 1988, s 26). It is important that a solicitor advises his client if an interim disqualification is likely, so that the client does not drive to court. The client should also be advised to have his driving licence with him at court if an interim disqualification is likely, as the licence will need to be handed in to the court.

The magistrates may also impose an interim disqualification if they commit the defendant to the Crown Court to be sentenced following a guilty plea because they consider their sentencing powers to be insufficient (see **6.9**).

15.5.2 'Drink drive' cases

15.5.2.1 Drink-Drive Rehabilitation Scheme/alcohol ignition locks

A defendant convicted of an offence involving 'drink driving' can obtain a reduction in the length of his disqualification by agreeing to take part in the 'Drink-Drive Rehabilitation Scheme'. A court sentencing such a defendant will usually offer the defendant the opportunity to attend a rehabilitation course, the purpose of which is to reduce the risk of further offending. The defendant will be required to pay to attend such a course. Following satisfactory completion of the course, the reduction in the length of the period of disqualification will be at least three months but not more than one-quarter of the period originally imposed (Road Traffic Offenders Act 1988, ss 34A–34C). For example, a defendant who receives a 12-month disqualification for driving whilst over the prescribed alcohol limit, would have this reduced to nine months upon successful completion of the course.

Under changes proposed in the Road Safety Bill, an experimental programme for the use of alcohol ignition locks is proposed. This programme may be offered to a defendant who is convicted of a second drink driving offence within a period of two years and who is to be disqualified for no less than two years. Under the programme, the overall period of disqualification will be reduced if the offender complies with the conditions of the programme. The programme will last for at least at least 12 months, but must not exceed one-half of the original unreduced disqualification period. The conditions will include an element of education and counselling (in a similar way to the existing rehabilitation course), but the key feature of the programme is that, at the end of the reduced period of disqualification, the defendant agrees to drive only a vehicle fitted with an alcohol interlock device, which is designed to prevent the vehicle being driven until a specimen of breath has been given in which the proportion of alcohol does not exceed a specified amount. A driver who fails to comply with these conditions will have his full original disqualification period restored.

15.5.2.2 'High risk offenders'

The Road Safety Bill also proposes that if a driver convicted of a drink drive offence is categorised as being a 'high risk offender', he will not be able to apply for the return of his licence at the end of the period of his disqualification until he has undergone a medical examination certifying that he is medically fit to drive. High risk offenders will be:

(a)   offenders disqualified from driving whilst two and a half times (or more) over the prescribed limit;

(b)   offenders disqualified on two or more occasions within 10 years for either exceeding the legal limit of alcohol in their breath, blood, or urine, or being unfit to drive through drink; and

(c)   offenders disqualified for failure (without reasonable excuse) to provide a specimen for analysis.

15.5.3 Discretionary disqualification

A court has a discretion to disqualify a defendant in the following situations:

(a)   A defendant convicted of an endorsable offence (such as careless driving or speeding) may be disqualified for that offence itself. There is no minimum or maximum period of disqualification, although in practice such disqualifications are generally between two weeks and six months. The only exception to this is if, as a result of committing the offence, the defendant is liable to disqualification under the penalty points system (because he has accumulated 12 or more relevant points on his licence). In such a case, any disqualification imposed on the defendant will be under the points system, and will be for a minimum period of six months (see **15.4** above).

There are proposals in the Road Safety Bill to expand the existing scheme whereby drivers convicted of various alcohol-related offences may obtain a reduction in their period of disqualification if they successfully complete a driver rehabilitation course (see **15.5.2** above). The Bill proposes expanding the scheme to cover a number of specified offences which carry discretionary disqualification in the event of conviction (including speeding and careless and inconsiderate driving). If the court decides to disqualify the defendant from driving for at least 12 months following conviction for a specified offence, the court may offer the defendant a reduction in the period of disqualification if he successfully completes a driver rehabilitation course. As with the existing scheme for drivers convicted of alcohol-related offences, the length of the reduction will be at least three months but not more than one-quarter of the period originally imposed.

(b)   A defendant convicted of an endorsable offence may be disqualified until he passes a driving test.

(c)   A defendant convicted of stealing or attempting to steal a motor vehicle, TWOC, or going equipped for stealing or taking motor vehicles may be disqualified.

(d)   A defendant convicted of any form of assault may be disqualified if the assault was committed using a motor vehicle (Powers of Criminal Courts (Sentencing) Act 2000, s 147(1)).

(e)   A Crown Court may disqualify a defendant where a motor vehicle has been used in the commission of any indictable offence for which the defendant could receive a custodial sentence of two years or more (Powers of Criminal Courts (Sentencing) Act 2000, s 147(2)). The Crown Court may exercise this power either where the defendant is convicted following a trial in the Crown Court, or where the defendant is committed to the Crown Court for sentence having entered a guilty plea in the magistrates' court.

In addition to the above, s 146 of the Powers of Criminal Courts (Sentencing) Act 2000 provides courts with a general power to disqualify a defendant from driving for such period as the court thinks fit in respect of any offence (whatever the nature of the offence) either in addition to or, in certain cases, instead of dealing with the defendant via an alternative type of sentence. Although this power appears remarkably wide, it is normally interpreted by the courts as giving them an additional power to disqualify a defendant who has not committed a driving-related offence and who has not used a vehicle in the commission of an offence. A court that chooses to disqualify a defendant convicted of a driving-related offence will use the other statutory powers at its disposal to impose the disqualification rather than the power under s 146.

15.5.4   Removal of disqualification

Section 42 of the Road Traffic Offenders Act 1988 gives the court power to make an order removing a disqualification, subject to the defendant having served part of the period of disqualification originally imposed. Applications under s 42 are normally made by defendants given a lengthy period of disqualification, who wish to show the court that they have reformed. The earliest date on which a defendant is permitted to make an application under s 42 is as follows:

(a)   if the disqualification was for less than four years, *two years* after the disqualification was imposed;

(b)   if the disqualification was for less than 10 years but not less than four years, after *one-half of the period of disqualification*;

(c)   if the disqualification was for 10 years or more, *five years* after the disqualification was imposed (Road Traffic Offenders Act 1988, s 42(3)).

When the court is considering an application to remove a disqualification, it may have regard to the following factors:

(a)   the character of the person disqualified and his conduct subsequent to the order;

(b)   the nature of the offence;

(c)   any other circumstances of the case (Road Traffic Offenders Act 1988, s 42(2)).

The court may either remove the disqualification from whichever date it sees fit, or refuse the application. Even if the applicant persuades the court to remove the disqualification, the court is likely to order him to pay the costs of the application. The court is only likely to exercise its powers under s 42 if the applicant has taken steps to reform (for example, by successfully completing a rehabilitation course – see **15.5.2** above) and there is a pressing need for him to be able to drive (for example, the nature of his employment requires him to be able to drive).

15.6 Mitigation

15.6.1 Mitigating factors

15.6.1.1 Introduction

Unless the defendant is seeking to avoid either a mandatory disqualification from driving under the penalty points scheme (see **15.6.2** below), or an obligatory disqualification from driving or the obligatory endorsement of his licence with penalty points (see **15.6.3** below), the defendant's solicitor will give the normal plea in mitigation before the defendant is sentenced, just as he would for any other type of offence. In delivering such a plea, the defendant's solicitor may raise any mitigating factors which he considers relevant to his client's case.

Thus:

(a)   if a defendant is convicted of an offence for which the court has a discretion to disqualify him (such as careless driving), mitigating factors may be raised to persuade the court:

    (i)   not to disqualify him, and

    (ii)   if the court decides not to disqualify him, to impose the lowest number of points the court feels able for the offence (where the court has a discretion as to the number of points that may be imposed), or

    (iii)   if the court decides to disqualify him, to reduce the period of disqualification to the shortest period of time the court feels able to impose, and

    (iv)   whether or not the defendant is disqualified, to limit the level of any other penalty that is imposed (such as a fine or an order to pay prosecution costs);

(b)   if the defendant is convicted of an offence which carries obligatory disqualification (such as driving whilst over the prescribed alcohol limit), mitigating factors may be raised to persuade the court to limit the period of disqualification to the shortest period of time the court feels able to impose and to limit the level of any financial penalty;

(c)   for serious offences (such as dangerous driving), where the court will be considering a custodial sentence in addition to disqualifying the defendant from driving, mitigating factors may be raised to persuade the court to deal with the matter other than by way of imprisonment. For example, a community sentence or a fine may be suggested as an alternative to custody.

15.6.1.2 Examples of mitigating factors

Mitigating factors can relate to the circumstances of the offence itself, or to the personal circumstances of the defendant.

Some of the most common points that may be raised by way of 'offence mitigation' (particularly for offences such as careless driving when the defendant is seeking to avoid a discretionary disqualification, or to limit the number of penalty points to be imposed) are:

(a)   the defendant's speed was not excessive;

(b)   there was not much traffic on the road;

(c)   the defendant was guilty only of a momentary lapse in concentration;

(d)   only minor damage or injury was caused; and

(e)   the defendant entered a timely guilty plea.

Examples of points commonly raised as 'offender mitigation' include:

(a)   the defendant's age and the number of years he has been driving;

(b)   the defendant having a 'clean' driving licence;

(c)   the defendant's job requiring him to have a driving licence; and

(d)   the fact that the defendant drives a large number of miles each year.

Example 1

Imran is convicted of careless driving. This is Imran's third conviction for careless driving, and the magistrates indicate that they are considering disqualifying Imran from driving for the current offence.

Imran is employed as a fork lift truck driver and has been told by his employer that if he is disqualified from driving he will lose his job. Imran's solicitor may raise this as a mitigating factor when seeking to persuade the court not to disqualify Imran from driving.

Example 2

Crystal is convicted of careless driving. Crystal has been driving for 25 years and this is her first conviction. The offence involved a momentary lapse in concentration when Crystal pulled out at a junction into the path of another vehicle. Very minor damage was caused to the vehicle, and Crystal pleaded guilty at the first opportunity. The magistrates indicate that they are not considering imposing a disqualification. They are, however, obliged to impose between 3 and 9 penalty points. Crystal's solicitor may raise the above matters as mitigating factors when seeking to persuade the court to impose the lowest number of points it feels able for the offence.

Example 3

Walter is convicted of driving whilst over the prescribed alcohol limit. Walter's breath/alcohol reading was only just over the limit. Walter was stopped by the police in the early hours of the morning when there were few other vehicles on the road. Walter pleaded guilty at the first opportunity. The offence carries obligatory disqualification from driving. Walter's solicitor will be able to use the above matters as mitigating factors to persuade the court to disqualify Walter from driving for as short a period as possible (the minimum period of disqualification being 12 months – see **15.5.1** above).

Example 4

Diane is convicted of driving whilst over the prescribed alcohol limit. Diane was three times the legal limit when stopped by the police, and the magistrates indicate that they are considering imposing a custodial sentence (in addition to a lengthy disqualification from driving). Diane has been driving for 30 years and has had no previous convictions. Diane drove on this occasion only after storming out of her house following a blazing row with her husband who had just disclosed that he had been having an affair with his secretary. Diane's solicitor will be able to raise these matters as mitigating factors to persuade the court not to impose a custodial sentence, and to consider an alternative penalty (such as a fine or a community penalty).

15.6.1.3   Procedure

Where a defendant seeks to rely only on mitigating factors (and is not seeking to avoid a penalty points disqualification by raising mitigating circumstances, or an obligatory disqualification or endorsement by raising special reasons – see **15.6.2** and **15.6.3** below), the procedure at the sentencing hearing will be the same as for any other type of offence (see **12.7** above). The prosecutor will outline the facts of the case to the court (assuming the defendant entered a guilty plea) and the defendant's solicitor will then deliver a plea in mitigation, highlighting the mitigating factors that exist and arguing for the lowest possible penalty that the court feels able to impose. The magistrates will then retire to consider their sentence, before returning to court to announce the sentence.

15.6.2 Mitigating circumstances

15.6.2.1 What are mitigating circumstances?

If a defendant accumulates 12 or more relevant penalty points on his driving licence, he will become liable to a mandatory disqualification under the penalty points system for at least six months (see **15.4.3** above). If, however, the defendant is able to prove on the balance of probabilities that mitigating circumstances exist, the magistrates have a discretion either not to disqualify him from driving under the penalty points scheme, or to disqualify him but for less than six months.

Mitigating circumstances may relate either to the offence itself, or to the personal circumstances of the defendant. They are, however, more limited in their scope than mitigating factors (see **15.6.1.2** above), because the following circumstances will *not* be taken into account by the court:

(a)   the triviality of any of the offences for which points were imposed (since the penalty points system already takes into account differences in the seriousness of different offences, by allocating varying numbers of points to each offence depending on the seriousness of the offence);

(b)   any hardship that will be suffered as a result of a disqualification, unless that hardship is *exceptional*. This may be hardship to the defendant or, more usually, someone other than the defendant, such as a family member or an employer. The fact that a defendant will lose his employment if he is disqualified will not normally be sufficient to constitute exceptional hardship. It is the knock-on effect of that loss of employment which may constitute exceptional hardship (if, for example, the defendant will no longer be able to pay his mortgage and his family are therefore at risk of having their home repossessed). The court will normally only find hardship to be exceptional if the disqualification would cause someone other than the defendant to suffer such hardship (for example, a sick or elderly relative whom the defendant takes to hospital by car on a regular basis; or an employer who relies on the defendant to drive in the course of his employment, and whose business will suffer badly if the defendant is no longer able to drive);

(c)   any mitigating circumstances the defendant has previously raised in the three years prior to the current conviction in an attempt to avoid a disqualification under the penalty points system (this is because the defendant should not be allowed to escape disqualification by perpetually using the same argument).

In practice, a defendant seeking to avoid a disqualification under the penalty points system will normally need to persuade the court that such a disqualification would cause exceptional hardship to someone other than himself. The burden will be on the defendant to prove, on the balance of probabilities, that exceptional hardship will be caused, and the defendant will need to give evidence at court in support of this, and possibly call evidence from others (such as his employer).

Example 1

Dwayne is convicted of careless driving following an incident when his car momentarily left the road and he collided with a bollard. The incident occurred in the early hours of the morning when no other drivers were using the road, and no damage was caused (other than to Dwayne's car). The magistrates impose 3 penalty points for this offence (the minimum number of points they could impose). Dwayne already has 9 relevant points on his licence, which means that he now has 12 relevant points and is liable to a disqualification under the penalty points scheme. Dwayne will not be permitted to raise the triviality of the current offence as a reason for not disqualifying him under the penalty points scheme.

Example 2

Fred accumulates 12 relevant penalty points on his licence. He drives to work, which is 20 miles away from his home address. He claims that if he is disqualified from driving he will be unable to get to work, and so will lose his job and suffer exceptional hardship.

The magistrates will first want to be satisfied that Fred will actually lose his job – could he get to work by means of public transport, or could he get a lift to work? Would he lose his job if they imposed a period of disqualification that was under six months? Even if Fred would lose his job, how easily could he find another job? If he could find another job easily, this would not cause exceptional hardship. Even if Fred would lose his job and would find it difficult to get another job, the magistrates are unlikely to find that exceptional hardship will be caused if only Fred is affected as a result of the disqualification.

Example 3

Albert accumulates 12 relevant points on his licence. Albert works as a sales representative for a publishing company, for which he receives a large salary. Albert usually drives over 1,000 miles per week in the course of his employment. Albert is told by his employer that he will lose his job if he is disqualified from driving. Albert and his wife Sue have a large mortgage. The monthly mortgage instalments are paid out of Albert's salary. Sue is not in employment. She stays at home to look after their two infant children. Albert argues that his family will suffer exceptional hardship if he is disqualified from driving because he will no longer be able to pay the mortgage from his salary and the family home will be repossessed.

The magistrates are likely to accept that, because of the nature of his job, Albert is likely to lose his employment if he is disqualified. However, before finding that exceptional hardship will be caused if Albert is disqualified, the magistrates will want to know how easy it would be for Albert to find alternative employment in order to fund the mortgage payments. Similarly, they would want to know if Sue could find employment to contribute towards the mortgage payments.

Example 4

Alan accumulates 12 relevant points on his licence. Alan works as a delivery driver for a small bakery in a rural area. The only other person who works at the bakery is Neville, the owner of the bakery. Neville does not have a driving licence and relies on Alan to make the deliveries. If Alan is disqualified from driving, the deliveries will not be made and the bakery will suffer large financial losses. Alan therefore argues that exceptional hardship will be suffered by Neville if he is disqualified from driving.

Before finding that exceptional hardship exists, the magistrates are likely to want to hear evidence from Neville. How easily could he find another delivery driver? What losses would he actually suffer if Alan was unavailable to drive? If Alan was disqualified for less than six months, would this still cause Neville exceptional hardship?

Example 5

Shabnam accumulates 12 relevant points on her licence. Her 6-year-old daughter suffers from leukaemia and Shabnam drives her to the local hospital on a weekly basis for medical treatment. The hospital is five miles away from their home address. Shabnam claims that if she is disqualified from driving she will be unable to drive her daughter to the hospital, which will cause her daughter exceptional hardship.

The magistrates will want to be satisfied that Shabnam is the only person who could drive her daughter to the hospital – is there anybody else who could take her, or is an ambulance service available? Given the proximity of the hospital, would it be possible to make the journey by public transport?

Example 6

Roger accumulates 12 relevant points on his licence. He avoided a disqualification under the points system two years ago by persuading the magistrates that disqualification would cause him exceptional hardship, because he lives in a rural area with no public transport and he suffers from arthritis which prevents him from being able to walk very far.

Roger will not be able to raise these circumstances again at the current hearing because he has already used such arguments within the previous three years to avoid a disqualification under the penalty points scheme.

The magistrates must find that mitigating circumstances exist before exercising their discretion not to disqualify the defendant for at least six months. If the magistrates do find that mitigating circumstances exist, they may choose either not to disqualify the defendant or to disqualify the defendant but for a reduced period (ie, for less than six months).

15.6.2.2 Procedure

A defendant who is liable to be disqualified under the penalty points system and wishes to raise mitigating circumstances, either to avoid such a disqualification or to reduce the period of the disqualification, has the burden of proving (on the balance of probabilities) that mitigating circumstances exist. The hearing at which the defendant will argue the existence of mitigating circumstances is first and foremost a sentencing hearing. The procedure that will take place at the hearing is as follows:

(a) The hearing will begin with the prosecutor outlining the facts of the case to the magistrates.

(b) The defendant will then give evidence in support of his argument that mitigating circumstances exist. The defendant will be examined in chief by his solicitor, cross-examined by the prosecutor (usually to put the defendant to proof that exceptional hardship would genuinely be caused were the defendant to be disqualified) and, if necessary, re-examined.

(c) Any other evidence which the defendant wishes to call will then be adduced. For example, the defendant's employer may attend court to confirm that the defendant will lose his job if he is disqualified, or a letter from the employer to this effect may be read out to the court. If the defendant argues that, as a result of losing his job, he will have his property repossessed because he will no longer be able to afford his mortgage, the magistrates will expect him to produce evidence to show what his monthly mortgage payments are.

(d) When all the evidence has been given, the defendant's solicitor will make submissions to the court in support of his argument that mitigating circumstances exist, and will also make a general plea in mitigation in respect of any other penalty the court may impose for the substantive offence (such as a fine or an order to pay the prosecution costs). In some magistrates' courts, the practice is for the defendant's solicitor to make his submissions *prior* to the defendant giving evidence.

(e)   The prosecutor has the right to respond to the submissions made by the defendant's solicitor if there are any points of law in relation to mitigating circumstances which he wishes to bring to the attention of the court.

(f)   The magistrates will then retire to consider whether the defendant has established, on the balance of probabilities, that mitigating circumstances exist.

(g)   The magistrates will then return to court and announce whether such circumstances exist. They will then proceed to sentence the defendant. If the magistrates find that mitigating circumstances do exist, the defendant will either not be disqualified from driving under the penalty points scheme, or will be disqualified but for a period of less than six months. Whether or not the defendant is disqualified under the penalty points scheme, the court may impose other penalties (in addition to points) for the substantive offence which led to him having 12 (or more) points on his licence. This penalty is likely to be a fine together with an order to pay the prosecution costs.

If a defendant avoids a disqualification by raising mitigating circumstances, any points on his licence will remain. If he subsequently commits another offence for which he receives penalty points, the defendant will be liable once again to a disqualification under the penalty points scheme.

Example

Sadie has convictions for offences on the following dates:

12 March 2005	speeding	licence endorsed with 3 points
15 September 2006	careless driving	licence endorsed with 7 points
2 January 2007	speeding	licence endorsed with 3 points

Following the conviction for the offence on 2 January 2007, Sadie was liable to a disqualification under the penalty points scheme because she had accumulated 12 or more relevant points on her licence. However, Sadie was able to avoid a disqualification by raising as a mitigating circumstance the fact that an elderly relative whom she drove to a hospital appointment each week would suffer exceptional hardship were she to be disqualified.

On 5 April 2007 Sadie commits the offence of failing to stop after an accident, for which she receives 5 points. Sadie will now have a total of 18 points on her licence and will be liable to a disqualification under the penalty points scheme. Although Sadie may attempt to avoid such a disqualification by raising mitigating circumstances, she will not be able to raise the same argument as she did on the last occasion to avoid disqualification (see **15.6.2.1** above).

15.6.3   Special reasons

15.6.3.1   When might special reasons apply?

If a defendant is convicted of an offence that carries either an obligatory disqualification from driving, or the obligatory endorsement of his licence with penalty points, he may avoid such penalties only if he is able to persuade a court that there are 'special reasons' why such a penalty should not be imposed.

Example 1

Erica is convicted of driving whilst over the prescribed alcohol limit, an offence which carries obligatory disqualification from driving for a minimum period of 12 months. Erica will be able to avoid such a penalty only if she is able to persuade the court that special reasons exist not to disqualify.

Example 2

Robin is convicted of careless driving. The magistrates decide not to disqualify Robin from driving for the offence, but they are obliged to impose between 3 and 9 penalty points. Robin will be able to avoid this penalty only if he is able to persuade the court that special reasons exist not to impose penalty points.

Special reasons are *not* a defence to the charge, and even if the existence of special reasons is established, the defendant will still be liable to any other penalty which the court may impose (such as a fine or the payment of costs). A defendant who argues the existence of special reasons bears the burden of proving (on the balance of probabilities) that such reasons exist.

15.6.3.2 What are special reasons?

There is no statutory definition of what may amount to a special reason. The accepted definition of the term was given in the case of *R v Crossen* [1939] NI 106:

> A 'special reason' ... is one which is special to the facts of the particular case, that is special to the facts which constitute the offence. It is, in other words, a mitigating or extenuating circumstance, not amounting in law to a defence to the charge, yet directly connected with the commission of the offence and one which the court ought properly to take into consideration when imposing punishment. A circumstance peculiar to the offender as distinguished from the offence is not a 'special reason' within the exception.

In *R v Wickens* (1958) 42 Cr App R 236, the court said that four criteria had to be satisfied for a matter to amount to a special reason. The matter must:

(a)   be a mitigating or an extenuating circumstance;

(b)   not amount to a defence to the charge;

(c)   be directly connected with the commission of the offence (and not the personal circumstances of the offender); and

(d)   be a matter which the court ought properly to take into account when imposing a sentence.

As special reasons must be directly connected with the commission of the offence, factors that are relevant to the particular circumstances of an individual defendant *cannot* amount to special reasons. Thus a defendant cannot say that his previous good character is a special reason. Neither can a defendant argue that a special reason exists when he (or his family, his employers or anybody else) will suffer hardship, however severe this might be.

Example

Gordon, a doctor, is convicted of driving whilst over the prescribed alcohol limit. Gordon lives in a rural area and is the only doctor serving his community. Gordon cannot argue that there are special reasons not to disqualify him from driving because his job benefits the public and the public will suffer if he is disqualified. His particular circumstances are irrelevant, as they are not connected to the circumstances of the offence itself.

15.6.3.3   What may amount to special reasons?

Each case will turn on its own facts and it is not possible to say with certainty when a special reason will exist. It is, however, possible to identify matters which have been held capable of amounting to special reasons. Special reasons are most commonly raised by defendants convicted of 'drink drive' offences, particularly the offence of driving whilst over the prescribed limit. Defendants in such cases commonly argue that special reasons exist for one of the following reasons:

(a)   their drinks were spiked;

(b)   the distance driven was extremely short; or

(c)   the only reason for driving was in response to an emergency.

Spiked drinks

Defendants often raise the argument that drinks they had consumed were spiked so that either the defendant did not realise that he was drinking alcohol at all, or the defendant knew he was drinking alcohol but was misled as to the alcoholic content of the drink.

In *Pugsley v Hunter* [1973] RTR 284, it was held that a court could find special reasons if a defendant was able to show that:

(a)   his drink had been spiked by another person;

(b)   he wasn't aware and didn't suspect that his drink had been spiked; and

(c)   had his drink not been spiked, the level of any other alcohol in his blood would not have exceeded the prescribed limit.

In order to prove (c) above, it was held that the defendant would need to establish this by using medical or scientific evidence, unless it was obvious to a layman that the excess was explained by the added alcohol. In practice, a defendant will need to obtain expert evidence to show that, but for the spiking of his drinks, the amount of alcohol he says he consumed would not have put him above the prescribed limit.

In the *Pugsley* case, the court found that special reasons existed where the defendant was found to have an excessive amount of alcohol in his blood as a result of having taken cough medicine which he hadn't realised contained alcohol.

In *DPP v Younas* [1990] RTR 22, the defendant had been served with two pints of lager. Each pint had, without his knowledge, been spiked with a double Bacardi. The defendant drank one and three-quarter pints of the lager. The defendant was found to have an excessive amount of alcohol in his blood, and sought to persuade the court that special reasons existed. The magistrates, in the absence of any medical evidence, found that, but for drinking the Bacardi, the defendant would not have been over the limit, because it would have been obvious to the layman that one and three-quarter pints of lager would not have taken the defendant over the prescribed limit.

This case may be contrasted with *Smith v DPP* [1990] RTR 17. Here the Crown Court dismissed an appeal from the magistrates' court. The defendant had drunk one and a half pints of lager and had then consumed a fruit drink which, unknown to him, included one measure of vodka. The defendant failed to produce any medical evidence, and the court was not prepared to find that the additional alcohol in the fruit drink was the cause of his being over the prescribed limit.

In order to prove to the magistrates' court that special reasons exist, the defendant will need to place appropriate evidence before the court. Ideally, the defendant will need to find at least one witness to the spiking of the drink, and expert medical or scientific evidence should be sought to show that the defendant would not have exceeded the prescribed limit had the drink not been spiked.

Even if a defendant can persuade a court that special reasons exist, the court still has to determine whether or not to exercise its discretion not to disqualify the defendant from driving. Although the victim of a spiked drink may have an excuse for starting to drive, if the amount of alcohol in the defendant's blood is substantial, the court is likely to find that the defendant should have realised his faculties were impaired and to have then stopped driving immediately.

The courts have adopted a twofold approach in such cases. First, the court needs to determine if special reasons exist. If they do, the court should then determine whether the defendant should have realised that the amount of alcohol in his body made him unfit to drive (*R v Newton (David)* [1974] RTR 451).

In *Donahue v DPP* [1993] RTR 156, the court found that special reasons existed but nevertheless disqualified the defendant. The defendant had been served with alcoholic wine at a business function when he had asked for non-alcoholic wine. On leaving the function he crashed his car into a hedge and was found to be over the prescribed limit. A doctor told the court that the defendant might have attributed the effect of the alcohol mistakenly to tiredness, due to his having spent the previous evening looking after an ill relative. The magistrates found that the defendant was experienced enough to have realised that he had consumed alcohol which made him unfit to drive.

Shortness of distance driven

If a defendant has driven his vehicle only a very short distance (and particularly if this has been done at the request of another), this may amount to special reason as long as the distance driven was such that the defendant was unlikely to come into contact with other road users and danger would be unlikely to arise.

In *R v Agnew* [1969] Crim LR 152, special reasons were found when a passenger in a car was asked by the owner of the car to move it a distance of six feet. However, in *R v Mullarkey* [1970] Crim LR 406, special reasons were found not to exist in respect of a defendant who drove his vehicle some 400 yards in the early hours of the morning during the winter when there was very little traffic on the road.

In *Chatters v Burke* [1986] 3 All ER 168, the court considered the factors to be taken into account when a defendant convicted of driving whilst over the prescribed alcohol limit claimed special reasons existed on the basis of the shortness of the distance he had driven. The court said that the shortness of distance driven was only one of seven factors which the court needed to consider, as follows:

(a)   the distance the vehicle was driven;

(b)   the manner in which the vehicle was driven;

(c)   the state of the vehicle;

(d)   how much further (if at all) the defendant intended to drive;

(e)   the road and traffic conditions at the time of the offence;

(f)   if danger was a possibility as a result of the vehicle coming into contact with other vehicles or pedestrians; and

(g)   the reason for the vehicle being driven.

In the *Chatters* case, the defendant was a passenger in a vehicle. The driver of the vehicle lost control, causing the vehicle to leave the road and roll over into an adjacent field. The defendant drove the vehicle back onto the road, but stopped it there and didn't intend driving it any further. The court found that special reasons did exist.

In *DPP v Bristow* [1998] RTR 100, the Divisional Court held that in such a case, the key question the magistrates should ask themselves in determining whether special reasons exist is this: would a sober, reasonable and responsible friend of the defendant who was present at the time of the incident (but a non-driver and so unable to assist himself) have advised the passenger to drive the vehicle or not to drive the vehicle?

Emergency

Special reasons can arise when the only reason for the defendant having driven a vehicle was a genuine emergency. In *Brown v Dyerson* [1969] 1 QB 45, the court held that a sudden medical emergency, which was the only reason for the defendant driving, could amount to a special reason. However, a defendant seeking to raise this argument will need to prove that:

(a)   there was a genuine emergency;

(b)   there was no alternative other than for the defendant to drive; and

(c)   the defendant had looked at all reasonable possible alternatives before driving.

In *R v Baines* [1970] Crim LR 590, the court refused to find special reasons when the defendant used his car to 'rescue' his partner's sick and elderly mother who had run out of petrol at night. The defendant had failed to look at any alternatives to driving, and the emergency had therefore not made it necessary for the defendant to drive.

In cases involving non-medical emergencies the courts have adopted a similar approach. For example, in *Jacobs v Reed* [1974] RTR 81, the defendant drove home from an airport whilst over the prescribed limit, after being telephoned by his wife following their daughter's failure to arrive at school. The court refused to find special reasons as the defendant had not considered any alternative method of getting home.

In *DPP v Cox* [1996] RTR 123, the Divisional Court upheld a finding of special reasons by magistrates in the case of a club steward who drove 300 yards from his home whilst over the prescribed limit in response to notification from the alarm company that the burglar alarm at the club had gone off. The defendant did not consider using alternative means of transport, or phoning another person who had a key to the club. The court took the view, however, that the shortness of the distance driven and the steward's responsibilities as a keyholder together constituted special reasons. The court gave particular emphasis to the fact that the club premises might have been the subject of vandalism, and the steward had no way of knowing how long it would be before the police arrived in response to the alarm.

15.6.3.4   Procedure – what evidence will be placed before the court?

A defendant who argues the existence of special reasons must prove on the balance of probabilities that such reasons exist. The defendant is required to produce evidence to show the existence of special reasons. It is not enough for the defendant's solicitor simply to assert that special reasons exist. The usual procedure is for the defendant to enter a guilty plea to the offence and for the case then to be adjourned so that there can be a hearing to determine if special reasons exist before the court sentences the defendant.

As with a hearing at which the defendant seeks to argue the existence of mitigating circumstances, the hearing at which the defendant seeks to argue the existence of special reasons is still a sentencing hearing. The procedure that will take place at the hearing is as follows:

(a)   The prosecutor will outline the facts of the case to the magistrates.

(b)   The defendant will then adduce evidence in support of his argument that special reasons exist. The defendant will be required to give evidence himself. He will be examined in chief by his solicitor, cross-examined by the prosecutor (to test his version of events and put him to proof of what he says occurred) and, if necessary, re-examined.

(c)   The defendant will then adduce any other evidence he wishes to call. If the defendant alleges that his drink was spiked, expert scientific or medical evidence will usually be required to show that, but for the alleged spiking of the drink, the defendant would have been below the prescribed alcohol limit (assuming the court accepts the defendant's account of what he thought he had drunk). Such expert evidence is normally accepted by the prosecution without the expert needing to attend court to give oral evidence. The defendant may also call any other witnesses whose evidence may be relevant (for example, a witness who saw the defendant's drink being spiked).

(d)   The prosecutor may call witnesses to rebut anything the defendant has said (for example, if the defendant alleges that a particular person spiked his drink, the prosecutor may call that person to give evidence to deny having done this).

(e)   After the witnesses have given evidence, the defendant's solicitor will make a submission to the court to argue that, on the basis of the evidence given, special reasons exist, and to persuade the court not to disqualify the defendant (or not to endorse his licence). The defendant's solicitor will also give a plea in mitigation in relation to the other sentencing powers the court may exercise (such as the level of any fine or an order to pay the prosecution costs).

(f)   The prosecutor is entitled to reply to the submission made as to the existence of special reasons if there are any points of law which need to be brought to the court's attention.

(g)   The magistrates will then retire to consider whether special reasons exist. When they return to court, the magistrates will announce whether or not they find that special reasons exist, and they will then proceed to sentence the defendant. Whether or not the defendant is able to establish the existence of special reasons for him not to be disqualified (or for penalty points not to be endorsed on his licence), he is still liable to receive any other penalty which the court may impose for the offence. This is likely to be a fine together with an order that the defendant pay the prosecution costs.

15.6.3.5   What may the court do if it finds that special reasons exist?

The court's discretion

If a defendant can establish the existence of special reasons, the court has a discretion not to disqualify the defendant from driving for the minimum period, or to not endorse his licence with the appropriate number of penalty points. The court is not obliged to do this, however. Thus, in the examples at **15.6.3.1** above, even if Erica and Robin both established the existence of special reasons, the magistrates would still have the power:

(a)   in Erica's case, to disqualify her from driving for a minimum period of 12 months; and

(b)   in Robin's case, to endorse his licence with between 3 and 9 penalty points.

Special reasons not to endorse the licence with penalty points

If a court finds that special reasons exist for not endorsing the defendant's licence with the appropriate number of penalty points, the court cannot impose a lower number of points than the offence would normally carry. The court must either endorse the licence with the appropriate number of points (despite the existence of 'special reasons'), or not endorse the licence at all.

Example

Stuart pleads guilty to the offence of careless driving, but raises special reasons as to why his licence should not be endorsed with the appropriate number of penalty points. The magistrates find that special reasons exist. The magistrates must either endorse Stuart's licence with between 3 and 9 penalty points (despite the existence of special reasons), or not endorse the licence at all. The magistrates are not permitted to impose a lower number of penalty points than the offence would normally carry.

Special reasons not to disqualify

In a case where disqualification is obligatory (such as driving whilst over the prescribed limit), even if the court finds that special reasons exist not to disqualify the defendant, the court will still be obliged to endorse the defendant's licence with the appropriate number of penalty points which the offence carries. The court need not do this, however, if it considers that the facts making up the special reasons for not disqualifying are also special reasons for not endorsing the licence with penalty points.

Example

Gregg is charged with driving whilst over the prescribed alcohol limit. He pleads guilty, but claims that he was over the prescribed limit only because his drinks had been spiked. The magistrates find that special reasons exist and exercise their discretion not to disqualify Gregg from driving. The magistrates must, however, endorse Gregg's licence with the appropriate number of penalty points (between 3 and 11 points for this offence), unless they find that the facts making up the special reasons for not disqualifying are also special reasons for not endorsing the licence with penalty points.

15.7   Flowchart – avoiding penalty points or disqualification from driving

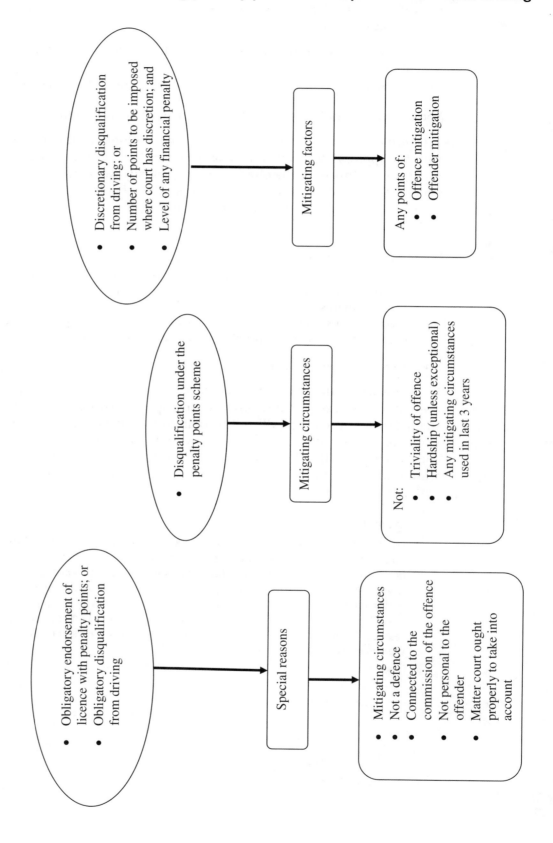

15.8 Checklist

At the end of this chapter you should be able to explain:

- what the most common road traffic offences are, how many points each offence carries, and whether a defendant convicted of a particular offence is liable to an obligatory or a discretionary disqualification;

- what is meant by a road traffic offence being 'endorsable';

- the operation of the penalty points scheme and the circumstances when a defendant may be disqualified from driving under this scheme;

- the offences which carry an obligatory disqualification from driving and the length of such disqualification;

- the circumstances in which a defendant may be subject to a discretionary disqualification from driving;

- the difference between mitigating factors, mitigating circumstances and special reasons, and the circumstances in which a defendant who has been convicted of a road traffic offence is entitled to raise these;

- the procedure which will take place when the defendant seeks to persuade the court that mitigating circumstances or special reasons exist.

Part 6
EVIDENCE

Chapter 16

Introduction to Evidence

16.1 Introduction

Whether a defendant who pleads not guilty to an offence is convicted or acquitted depends on the strengths and weaknesses of the evidence which is placed before the court by the prosecution and the defence. The next seven chapters will analyse the law concerning the admissibility of evidence in criminal proceedings. This chapter will provide a general introduction to the law of evidence, with subsequent chapters focusing on more specific areas.

This chapter will begin by examining the burdens and standards of proof which operate in a criminal case. It will then look at what is meant by 'evidence', before summarising the various types of evidence which may exist in criminal proceedings. The chapter will conclude by looking at particular rules relating to evidence from witnesses, including the use of special measures to enable a witness to give evidence and the admissibility of evidence from expert witnesses.

16.2 Burdens and standards of proof

16.2.1 The legal burden

In the overwhelming majority of criminal cases, the CPS will bear the legal burden of proving the defendant's guilt. The standard of proof that the CPS needs to satisfy in order to do this is to prove beyond a reasonable doubt that the defendant is guilty of the offence with which he has been charged. In other words, the magistrates or jury should convict the defendant only if they are *sure* of his guilt (*Woolmington v DPP* [1925] AC 462).

Occasionally the legal burden of proof will fall upon the defendant. An example of this is the defendant who pleads not guilty and raises the defence of insanity. A defendant pleading insanity is required to prove that fact. In cases where the defendant bears the legal burden of proof, the standard of proof that is required is proof on the balance of probabilities. This is a lower standard of proof than proof beyond a reasonable doubt, and simply means 'more probable than not'.

If a defendant raises a particular defence (for example, a defendant who asserts that he has an alibi, or that he was acting in self-defence), the defendant does *not* have the burden of proving that defence (see **16.2.2.2** below). The burden rests with the CPS (as part of the requirement that the prosecution prove the defendant's guilt beyond a reasonable doubt) to satisfy the magistrates or the jury that the defence is not true (see the example at **16.2.2.2** below).

16.2.2   The evidential burden

16.2.2.1   The burden on the prosecution

As was explained in **Chapter 9**, the CPS will present its case first at trial. At the conclusion of its case, the CPS must have presented sufficient evidence to the court to justify a finding of guilt and to show that the defendant has a case to answer (this is before the defendant has adduced any evidence). If the CPS fails to do this, the defendant's solicitor (or counsel) will be entitled to make a submission of no case to answer, and to ask the court to dismiss the case (see **Chapters 9** and **10**).

16.2.2.2   The burden on the defence

The defendant is not obliged to place any evidence before the court to show that he is innocent of the offence with which he has been charged. If the defendant does not adduce any evidence in his own defence, in his closing speech the defendant's solicitor or counsel may still ask the court to acquit the defendant on the basis that the evidence put forward by the CPS is not sufficient to prove the case against the defendant beyond a reasonable doubt (*DPP v Uddin* 2006 WL 1518702). However, a defendant who is raising a specific defence (such as the defence of alibi or self-defence) must place *some* evidence of that defence before the court if he wishes the magistrates or jury to consider that defence when deciding the verdict. This is the evidential burden that the defendant bears. It is relatively simple for the defendant to satisfy such a burden. All he need do is enter the witness box and give details of his defence. The onus will then fall on the CPS, as part of its legal burden (see **16.2.1**), to prove beyond a reasonable doubt that the defence which has been raised is not true.

> #### Example
>
> Alex is on trial for murder and raises the defence of alibi, claiming that at the time of the murder he was at home with his girlfriend. When presenting its case at court, the CPS must first satisfy its evidential burden by presenting sufficient evidence to the court to to show that Alex has a case to answer. Should the CPS fail to do this, Alex's counsel will make a submission of no case to answer and ask the judge to dismiss the case. If the CPS satisfies its evidential burden, Alex then bears the evidential burden of placing some evidence of his alibi defence before the court. Alex will satisfy this burden by entering the witness box and giving details of his alibi (he will probably also call his girlfriend to give evidence). In order to secure a conviction and to satisfy its legal burden, the CPS will then need to prove beyond a reasonable doubt both that Alex's alibi is untrue *and* that Alex did commit the murder.

16.3   What is evidence?

16.3.1   Introduction

In **Chapter 8** a case analysis model was described. The purpose of carrying out a case analysis is to determine the facts in issue in the case (ie, those areas where there is disagreement between the CPS and the defendant as to the facts). 'Evidence' is the information or material which the CPS and the defendant will then place before the court in order to persuade the court that their version of the facts which are in issue is in fact the correct version.

16.3.2 Requirements of evidence

There are two basic requirements which need to be satisfied if the jury or the magistrates are to take a piece of evidence into account in deciding what the facts of the case are:

(a)   Evidence must be *relevant*. Historically it was said that evidence had to be 'logically probative of a fact in issue'. If evidence is not relevant to a fact in issue, the court will not be concerned with it.

(b)   Even if the evidence is relevant, it must be *admissible*. This means that the rules which comprise the law of evidence must permit such evidence to be used in a criminal trial. Subsequent chapters will examine rules of admissibility in relation to particular types of evidence. If evidence is deemed to be admissible, the magistrates or jury will then need to determine the reliability or cogency of such evidence (ie, how much weight should be attached to that piece of evidence).

Evidence that is both relevant and admissible may be either direct evidence of a defendant's guilt, or circumstantial evidence from which a defendant's guilt may be inferred.

Example

Janice is charged with the murder of Leslie. The CPS alleges that Janice stabbed Leslie with a knife whilst Leslie was drinking in a busy pub. The CPS has an eye-witness who identifies Janice as the assailant. The CPS also has a letter sent by Janice to Leslie shortly before the stabbing, in which Janice threatened to 'get even' with Leslie following an argument between them over some money. The evidence from the eye-witness will be direct evidence of Janice's guilt. The letter will be circumstantial evidence, since it is evidence that Janice had a motive for killing Leslie.

16.3.3 Matters that do not need to be proved by evidence

In deciding whether the CPS has proved its case against the defendant beyond a reasonable doubt, the jury or magistrates may only take into account a fact which has been proved by evidence. This rule is subject to some exceptions, the most important of which are as follows:

(a)   Either the CPS or the defendant may formally admit certain facts either in advance of trial, or at trial itself (CJA 1967, s 10). There is no set procedure for doing this, although facts admitted in advance of trial will usually be admitted in writing, whereas facts admitted at trial will be admitted orally.

A common use for admissions under s 10 is when the court has ruled that the previous convictions of a defendant or other witness will be admissible in evidence at trial (see **Chapter 22**). Rather than making the party that seeks to rely on these convictions prove at trial that such convictions exist, the other party will often make an admission to this effect under s 10.

(b)   If a court takes judicial notice of a fact, evidence of that fact will not then be required. For example, a court will take judicial notice of matters of law and so there is no requirement to prove the contents of a statute. A court will also take judicial notice of matters of common knowledge. For example, in a prosecution for dangerous driving where it is alleged the defendant drove at 80 miles per hour on the wrong side of the road, the CPS would not be required to prove that in Britain motorists should drive on the left hand side of the road, or that the standard national maximum speed limit is 60 miles per hour.

16.4 Types of evidence

16.4.1 Introduction

There are three types of evidence which may be used in criminal proceedings:

(a)   oral testimony from witnesses;

(b)   documentary evidence;

(c)   real evidence.

Each of these forms of evidence will be examined in more detail below.

16.4.2 Oral testimony from witnesses

16.4.2.1 Witnesses as to fact

The most common form of evidence given at a criminal trial is oral evidence from witnesses who attend trial to be examined on their evidence. The witness will be examined in chief by the party that has called the witness to give evidence, cross-examined by the other party, and then possibly re-examined (see **Chapter 9**). Most witnesses who attend court to give evidence are 'witnesses as to fact' (for example, the victim of an assault or an eye-witness to a theft). Such witnesses are entitled to give evidence as to factual matters but, subject to a very limited number of exceptions, are not permitted to give evidence which amounts to an opinion. The rationale behind this rule is that opinion evidence from a witness will intrude on the role of the magistrates or jury to form their own opinion based on the facts that are adduced in evidence. The most common exceptions to this rule allow witnesses as to fact to give opinion evidence based on their perceptions, such as an estimate as to the speed at which a vehicle was travelling, or describing a person's demeanour or whether they considered a person to be in a drunken state.

Further rules concerning the admissibility of evidence from witnesses as to fact are examined at **16.5** below.

16.4.2.2 Expert witnesses (CrimPR, Part 24)

The other type of witness that may be called in criminal proceedings is an expert witness. Unlike witnesses as to fact, expert witnesses are permitted to express opinion evidence (but only within the expert's particular sphere of expertise). The court will need the assistance of an expert when the matter on which the expert is to comment is a technical matter which is beyond the competence of the magistrates or jury (for example, whether a sample of paint found underneath the defendant's fingernails matches a sample of paint taken from the window sill of the house that the defendant is alleged to have burgled, or whether a particular type of knife found at the defendant's home could have caused the injuries inflicted on the person the defendant is alleged to have stabbed).

Examples of the types of expert who appear regularly in criminal proceedings include:

(a)   forensic scientists (who may, for example, comment on DNA or other samples found at the scene of the crime and whether these match with samples taken from the defendant);

(b)   fingerprint, handwriting or voice analysis experts;

(c)   pathologists (to comment on the cause of death in a murder case); and

(d)   forensic accountants (particularly in fraud cases).

Further rules concerning the admissibility of evidence from expert witnesses are examined at **16.6** below.

16.4.3 Documentary evidence

Documents may be placed before the court as pieces of evidence. Examples of documentary evidence include:

(a)   the transcript of a defendant's audio-recorded interview at the police station;

(b)   entries in a business ledger;

(c)   invoices or receipts; and

(d)   photographs or plans.

A document must be authenticated by a witness if it is to be admitted in evidence. This will usually involve the witness giving oral evidence to explain what the document is and how the document came into existence. For example, the police officer who interviewed the defendant at the police station will give a statement confirming that the interview took place and will attach as an exhibit to his statement the transcript of the interview record. When he gives evidence at trial, the officer will confirm that the interview took place and the transcript will then be read out to the court (unless the defence ask for the audio recording of the interview to be played).

The contents of a document may constitute hearsay evidence. The rules governing the admissibility of 'documentary hearsay' are discussed in **Chapter 19**.

16.4.4 Real evidence

Examples of items of real evidence include:

(a)   stolen goods which have been recovered by the police;

(b)   a weapon which it is alleged was used in an assault;

(c)   drugs found by the police in a search of a suspect's premises;

(d)   CCTV footage showing a crime being committed.

As with documentary evidence, in order for real evidence to be admissible it will normally be necessary for such evidence to be authenticated by a witness, explaining the significance of the real evidence to the prosecution or defence case and how such evidence was obtained. For example, if the defendant is alleged to have assaulted his victim with a baseball bat later found at the defendant's home, the police officer who found the bat will need to give evidence confirming where, when and in what circumstances the bat was found.

16.5 Witnesses as to fact

16.5.1 Competence and compellability

16.5.1.1 Introduction

Rules exist to determine whether potential witnesses are both competent and compellable to give evidence at trial. The issue of 'competence' is concerned with whether the witness will be permitted to give evidence at all. 'Compellability' is concerned with whether a witness who is competent to give evidence may be made to attend court to give evidence (usually through the service of a witness summons).

16.5.1.2   The defendant

A defendant is competent to give evidence on his own behalf at trial (Criminal Evidence Act 1898, s 1(1)). A defendant is not competent to be a witness for the prosecution.

A defendant cannot be compelled to give evidence on his own behalf at trial, although it is normal practice for a defendant to give such evidence. A defendant who chooses not to enter the witness box to give evidence is likely to have an adverse inference drawn from his silence at trial under s 35 of the CJPOA 1994 (see **Chapters 9** and **18**).

16.5.1.3   Co-defendants

Co-defendants who are tried together are not competent to be called as prosecution witnesses to give evidence against each other. However, if two defendants are jointly charged with the same offence, the CPS may call one defendant as a witness against the other if that defendant has either pleaded guilty at an earlier hearing, or is tried separately from the other defendant.

Example 1

David and Geoff are jointly charged with the production of a controlled drug. Both are pleading not guilty on the basis that they knew nothing about the production of the controlled drug and their co-defendant is solely responsible. The CPS will not be permitted to call David to give evidence against Geoff, or to call Geoff to give evidence against David. Neither is competent to be a prosecution witness.

Example 2

Amanda and Claire are jointly charged with assault. Amanda pleads guilty to the offence but Claire pleads not guilty. Amanda is now competent to give evidence for the CPS at Claire's trial to say that she and Claire committed the assault together.

If a defendant gives evidence in his own defence at trial, and in doing so implicates a co-defendant, this will be admissible in evidence against the co-defendant.

Example 1

Nick and Chris are jointly charged with assaulting Tina in a pub. Both plead not guilty on the basis that the assault was committed by the other. At trial, Nick gives evidence in his own defence and claims the assault was carried out by Chris. Chris then gives evidence in his own defence and claims the assault was carried out by Nick. The evidence given by each defendant will be admissible against his respective co-defendant.

Example 2

Pauline and Mary are jointly charged with the theft of goods from an electrical shop. Both plead not guilty and raise the defence of alibi, claiming that they were at home at the time of the alleged theft. When Pauline gives evidence in her own defence, however, she admits that both she and Mary were in the shop at the time of the theft, although she denies that either of them had anything to do with the theft. Pauline's admission that she and Mary were in fact in the shop will be admissible in evidence against Mary.

16.5.1.4   The defendant's spouse

The spouse of a defendant is competent to give evidence for the CPS. A spouse cannot be compelled to do so, however, except in certain specified cases (the most common example being where the offence involves an assault on that spouse, and the spouse had provided the police with a statement to that effect).

Example

Stuart is charged with burglary. His defence is one of alibi. He complains that at the time of the burglary he was at home with his wife Anne. The police take a statement from Anne, who says that she was not at home at the relevant time because she was away visiting her sister. Anne is competent to give evidence for the CPS at Stuart's trial, but cannot be compelled to do so.

A defendant's spouse is always competent to give evidence on behalf of the defendant, and can be compelled (by means of a witness summons) to do so.

16.5.1.5 Other witnesses

The general rule is that all other witnesses are competent to give evidence. Only if a witness either cannot understand the questions that will be asked of him in court, or cannot answer them in a way that can be understood, will the witness not be competent to give evidence. The competence of a witness to give evidence maybe challenged by the CPS, the defendant or the court. In assessing whether a witness is competent to give evidence, the court must consider providing the witness with 'special measures' (see **16.5.6** below) to assist the witness in either understanding questions, or being able to answer questions. It is the responsibility of the party calling the witness to satisfy the court that the witness is competent to give evidence.

Before he gives evidence a witness will either swear on oath to tell the truth, or make an affirmation that he will do so. Children under the age of 14 are not permitted to swear on oath or make an affirmation. Such children are, however, permitted to give unsworn evidence. If the child is very young, questions may arise as to whether the child is too young to give evidence. In such a case the court must apply the test set out in s 53(3) of the Youth Justice and Criminal Evidence Act 1999, namely whether the child understands the questions being asked and whether the jury could understand the child's answers. The usual practice in such cases is for the child's evidence to be taken as soon as possible (usually by way of a video-recorded interview – see **16.5.4.1** below), and for the trial to be 'fast-tracked' so that the child may be cross-examined whilst he is still able to recall the relevant events (*R v Powell* [2006] EWCA Crim 3). If a defendant challenges the admissibility of such evidence under s 78 of PACE 1984 on the basis that the child was too young to give evidence and it would therefore be unfair for such evidence to be admitted (see **21.2**), the trial judge will allow such video-recorded evidence to be used only if he considers that a reasonable jury properly directed could be sure that the child had given a credible and accurate account on the video tape (*R v Hanton* [2005] EWCA Crim 2009; *R v K (Evidence: Child video interview)* [2006] EWCA Crim 472). The court should determine the competence of a very young child to give evidence as a preliminary issue to be dealt with at the start of the trial. The court will watch the videotaped interview with the child and/or ask the child questions to assess his competence (*R v MacPherson* [2005] EWCA Crim 3605).

In *R v H* [2006] EHWC Crim 853, the defendant was convicted of a series of rapes. The evidence against him came from children, including the 6-year-old victim. There were numerous inconsistencies in the evidence given and, on appeal, the defendant argued that the trial judge should have found there to be no case to answer on the basis of such inconsistencies. The Court of Appeal rejected this argument, finding that the judge was in a much better position than an appellate court to decide whether the inconsistencies were such that the trial ought to be stopped.

Children over the age of 14 are eligible to give sworn evidence only if they understand the solemnity of a criminal trial and that taking an oath places a particular responsibility on them to tell the truth. There is a presumption that, unless evidence is offered to the contrary, such witnesses will give sworn evidence.

Witnesses other than the defendant and the defendant's spouse may be compelled to attend court to give evidence by the service of a witness summons.

16.5.2 Self-made evidence

A witness is not permitted to back up the oral evidence he gives at trial by referring to a statement he made on a previous occasion. For example, a defendant who is charged with assault and claims at trial that he was acting in self-defence will not be permitted to tell the court that, when he was detained at the police station, he gave a 'no comment' interview to the police but also provided a statement to his solicitor (which was not given to the police) saying that he had acted in self-defence. Similarly, his solicitor would not be able to give evidence as to what he had been told. This is known as the rule against self-made evidence. There are, however, several exceptions to this rule:

(a) *Rebutting a suggestion of recent fabrication.* If during cross-examination it is put to a witness that he has recently concocted his evidence, evidence of a previous statement made by the witness may be admitted to rebut this allegation. In the above example, if it was put to the defendant that he had fabricated his defence of self-defence just before trial, both he and his solicitor would be permitted to give evidence confirming that he had provided the solicitor with a written statement whilst at the police station, stating that he had been acting in self-defence in order to show that the allegation of recent fabrication was incorrect. In addition, if the written statement of a witness is admitted as evidence to rebut the suggestion that his oral evidence at trial has been fabricated, that statement is admissible as evidence of any matter stated of which oral evidence by the witness would be admissible (CJA 2003, s 120(2)). Thus, in the above example, as well as being admissible to refute the allegation of recent fabrication, the written statement given by the defendant to his solicitor would be admissible in evidence to support his claim that he had been acting in self-defence.

(b) *Statements forming part of the* res gestae. The *res gestae* principle applies to a statement made so spontaneously that there is no possibility of its having been concocted (*Ratten v The Queen* [1972] AC 378). The principle permits the court to hear about a statement made at the time of an event, since the statement may help to explain the event. The *res gestae* principle is an exception to the rule excluding hearsay evidence and is explained more fully in **Chapter 19**.

(c) *Exculpatory statements made to the police.* When a defendant is questioned at the police station about his alleged involvement in an offence, he may put forward an explanation which, if later accepted by the court at trial, would lead to his acquittal. Such statements are admissible in evidence to show consistency between the account given by the defendant at the police station and the evidence he later gives at trial.

Example

Nicholas is charged with common assault. When interviewed at the police station, he claims to have been acting in self-defence. If, when giving evidence at his trial, Nicholas repeats this defence, the comments made at the police station will be admissible to show that Nicholas has given a consistent account since first being arrested.

As a matter of practice, although such statements in interview will not assist the prosecution case, when giving evidence at the defendant's trial the interviewing officer will give evidence of what was said in the interview at the police station, and the court will accept such evidence as an exception to the rule against self-made evidence.

(d)   *Documents used to refresh the memory of the witness.* A witness attending court to give oral evidence is not permitted to have a copy of his statement before him when giving evidence. The witness may, however, ask the court for leave to refresh his memory from a document which was made or verified by him at an earlier time (CJA 2003, s 139(1)). If the court permits a witness to use a document for this purpose and the witness is then cross-examined on the contents of the document, the document will become a piece of evidence and will be admissible as evidence of any matter of which oral evidence by the witness would have been admissible. Some examples of the operation of s 139 are set out at **9.8.2.4**.

(e)   *Previous consistent statements.* Section 120(4) of the CJA 2003 permits a previous consistent statement made by a witness to be admissible as evidence of any matter stated of which oral evidence by the witness would be admissible, provided certain conditions are satisfied. These conditions are explained at **9.8.2.5**.

16.5.3   Do witnesses need to attend court to give evidence?

Most witnesses will attend court to give oral evidence and be cross-examined on such evidence. If the evidence to be given by the witness is not disputed by the other party, the witness's statement will normally be read out to the court pursuant to s 9 of the CJA 1967 rather than the witness attending court to give oral evidence (see **8.4.4**). In certain circumstances, if a witness is not available to attend court, his written statement may be read out to the court as hearsay evidence under s 116 or 117 of the CJA 2003, even if that statement has not been accepted under the s 9 procedure. This will be considered more fully in **Chapter 19**.

16.5.4   Special measures (CrimPR, Part 29)

16.5.4.1   The Youth Justice and Criminal Evidence Act 1999

Sections 16 to 33 of the Youth Justice and Criminal Evidence Act 1999 introduced a number of 'special measures' which are available to assist witnesses (other than the defendant) who might otherwise have difficulty in giving evidence in criminal proceedings, or who might be reluctant to do so. The following categories of witness may apply to the court for the assistance of special measures to help them give evidence in court:

(a)   children aged under 17;

(b)   those suffering from a mental or physical disorder, or having a disability or impairment that is likely to affect their evidence;

(c)   those whose evidence is likely to be affected by their fear or distress at giving evidence in the proceedings (Youth Justice and Criminal Evidence Act 1999, ss 16 and 17).

Witnesses who are alleged to be the victims of a sexual offence will automatically be considered eligible for special measures under (c) above when giving evidence, unless the witness tells the court that he or she does not want such assistance. In all other cases, it is for the court to determine whether a witness falls into any of these categories.

Under s 116(2)(e) of the CJA 2003, a witness who is fearful about having to give evidence at trial may, with the leave of the court, have his written statement read out to the court rather than having to attend court in person to give oral evidence (see **19.5.1.2**). If leave is granted, the defendant will be deprived of the opportunity to cross-examine the witness on his account. Thus, before giving leave, the trial judge should assess whether the fears of the witness may be allayed by the employment of special measures to enable the witness to give evidence. If special measures are used, the defendant will not be deprived of the opportunity to cross-examine the witness.

The types of special measure which may be used are:

(a)   screens, to ensure that the witness does not see the defendant (YJCEA 1999, s 23);

(b)   allowing a witness to give evidence from outside the court by live television link (s 24);

(c)   clearing people from the court so evidence can be given in private (s 25);

(d)   in a Crown Court case, the judge and barristers removing their wigs and gowns (s 26);

(e)   allowing a witness to be examined in chief before the trial and a video-recording of that examination-in-chief to be shown at trial, instead of the witness being examined in chief at trial;

(f)   allowing a witness to be cross-examined (and re-examined) before the trial and a video-recording of that cross-examination (and re-examination) to be shown at trial, instead of the witness being cross-examined (or re-examined) at trial (s 28);

(g)   allowing an approved intermediary (such as an interpreter or speech therapist) to help a witness communicate when giving evidence at the court (s 29);

(h)   allowing a witness to use communication aids, such as sign language or a hearing loop (s 30).

Where a witness is eligible for assistance, the court must determine, in all the circumstances of the case, whether (and which) special measure(s) would be likely to improve (and then maximise) the quality of the witness's evidence (see YJCEA 1999, s 19(2) and (3)).

Where special measures are directed, s 32 of the 1999 Act contains an important evidential safeguard for the defendant. Section 32 obliges the trial judge to warn the jury that the fact that special measures have been used should not in any way prejudice them against the defendant, or give rise to any suggestion that the defendant has behaved in any way improperly towards the witness so as to necessitate the use of special measures.

A defendant is unlikely to succeed in raising an argument that the use of special measures for prosecution witnesses contravenes his right to fair trial under Article 6 of the ECHR. In *R v H* (see **16.5.1.5** above), a 13-year-old defendant was convicted of four counts of rape on the basis of evidence given by other children, including the victim who was 6 years old. The witnesses gave evidence in chief by way of a video-recording and their cross-examination was carried out by way of a video link. There were numerous inconsistencies in the evidence given, and the defendant argued on appeal that, inter alia, the use of special measures had prevented him from effectively participating in the trial and that he did not have a fair trial as a result. The Court of Appeal dismissed the appeal and found that, although the trial did not comply fully with the directions for the trial of children in the Crown Court, any criticisms of the trial process were not so grave as to prevent the defendant from having a fair trial.

16.5.4.2   The Criminal Justice Act 2003

Section 51

Section 51 of the CJA 2003 allows the court to make an order that *any* witness other than the defendant (ie, not just those special categories of witness listed at 16.5.4.1 above) be permitted to give evidence by live link if it is in the interests of the efficient or effective administration of justice for the person concerned to give evidence in this way. This will enable witnesses to give evidence from a part of the country other than where the trial is taking place (and even from overseas). In considering whether to use a live link, the court must consider all the circumstances of the case, and in particular:

(a)   the availability of witnesses;

(b)   the need for a witness to attend in person;

(c)   the importance to the case of the witness's evidence;

(d)   the views of the witness;

(e)   the suitability of the facilities at the place where the witness would give evidence via a live link; and

(f)   whether allowing a witness to give evidence in this way might tend to inhibit any party from effectively testing the witness's evidence in cross-examination (s 51(7)).

Section 137

Section 137 of the 2003 Act allows a video-recording of the account of an eye-witness other than the defendant, given whilst events were still fresh in the mind of the witness, to amount to the evidence-in-chief of that witness. The witness must claim to have seen events alleged by the prosecution to include conduct constituting the offence or part of the offence, or events closely connected with such events. Section 137 applies to all indictable-only offences and some prescribed either way offences. Leave of the court will be required to admit evidence under s 137. The court may grant leave only if the witness's recollection of the events in question is likely to have been significantly better when he gave the recorded account than it will be when he gives oral evidence in the proceedings, *and* it is in the interests of justice for the recording to be admitted (s 137(3)(b)). In deciding whether it is in the interests of justice, the court must consider:

(a)   the time interval between the events and the making of the video;

(b)   factors affecting the reliability of what is said in the video (for example, if made shortly after the event, the comments may be tainted by anger or grief);

(c)   the quality of the recording itself;

(d)   any view of the witness as to whether his account should be given orally or by way of video (s 137(4)).

16.5.4.3 Witness anonymity

In addition to the special measures introduced by statute, the court has always had an inherent jurisdiction at common law to control its own proceedings. This power has on occasions been used to enable a witness to give evidence anonymously, with the defendant and his legal representatives being unaware of the true identity of the witness. The court is likely to exercise this power only where the witness would genuinely be in fear of his life if the defendant became aware of his identity. In *R v Davis & Others* [2006] EWCA Crim 1155, the defendants were convicted of murder after key prosecution witnesses had given evidence anonymously. The defendants appealed against conviction, arguing that the preservation of the witnesses' anonymity had prevented them from properly cross-examining the witnesses and so had infringed their rights under Article 6(3)(d) of the ECHR 'to examine or have examined witnesses against [them]'. Rejecting the appeals, the Court considered that the concealment of the identity of witnesses was not inconsistent with the right to a fair trial, provided that the following conditions were met:

(a)   the need to preserve the anonymity of the witness was clearly established;

(b)   defence counsel was permitted to cross-examine the witness; and

(c)   ultimately, the trial was fair.

16.5.4.4 Procedure

Parts 29 and 30 of the Criminal Procedure Rules contain the procedural rules which must be followed when a party seeks a special measures directions, or when evidence is to be given by live television link.

Both the CPS and the defendant may make a pre-trial application to the court for a direction authorising the use of special measures for a particular witness who is to be called. The standard directions that will normally be given for not guilty cases in both the Crown Court (see **Chapter 10**) and the magistrates' court (see **Chapter 8**) provide time limits for the making of such an application.

An application for a special measures direction must be made in writing, using a prescribed form (CrimPR, r 29.1(1)). A party opposing the use of special measures at trial must notify both the court and the party that made the application (CrimPR, r 29.1(6)). This notification must be in writing and must set out the reasons for the objection.

In the Crown Court, a party seeking a special measures direction from the court must serve an application for such a direction within 28 days of the service of the prosecution case papers (CrimPR, r 29.1(4)(c)). Any party opposing the application then has 14 days in which to respond (CrimPR, r 29.1(6)).

In the magistrates' court, an application for a special measures direction must be made within 14 days of the defendant indicating his intention to plead not guilty (CrimPR, r 29.1(4)(a)). As in the Crown Court, any party opposing the application will then have 14 days in which to respond (CrimPR, r 29.1(6)).

16.6 Expert evidence

16.6.1 Introduction

Any witness who is designated as an expert is allowed to give opinion evidence to the court on any matter within his particular field of expertise.

Example

Laurie is charged with murdering Steve by stabbing him with a particular type of kitchen knife that was one of a set of knives found by the police in Laurie's kitchen. The CPS wishes to adduce evidence from a pathologist who has examined Steve's body and who will say that the wound on the body is consistent with the type of wound that would be caused by that particular type of knife. This is opinion evidence on the part of the pathologist, but will be permitted by the court because this matter is within the pathologist's field of expertise.

Experts who give opinion evidence in criminal proceedings are immune from later civil claims by a party to the case who disagrees with the evidence given, although a trial judge (or the Court of Appeal) may refer the expert's conduct to his relevant professional disciplinary body if satisfied that such conduct had fallen so far below what was expected of him as to merit some disciplinary action. Such a referral would not be justified unless the expert's failings were sufficiently serious for the judge to believe that he might need to be removed from practice, or at least be subjected to conditions regulating his practice such as a prohibition on him acting as an expert witness. Normally evidence given honestly and in good faith by an expert would not merit a referral (*Meadows v General Medical Council* [2006] All ER (D) 229).

16.6.2 Disclosure of experts' reports

16.6.2.1 The requirements of the Criminal Procedure Rules, Part 24

Both the CPS and the defendant may call expert evidence at trial, and it will often be the case that experts called by the prosecution and defence will differ in the opinions they put forward. Any party seeking to rely on expert evidence at trial must serve a copy of the expert's report on the other party in advance of trial. Detailed rules concerning the disclosure of expert evidence are set out in Part 24 of the Criminal Procedure Rules. Rule 24.1 provides that a party seeking to adduce evidence from an expert at trial must supply the other parties in the case with a copy of the expert's report 'as soon as practicable' after either:

(a) the defendant has entered a not guilty plea (in a case to be tried in the magistrates' court); or

(b) the case has been sent for trial under s 51 of the Crime and Disorder Act 1998 (in a case to be tried in the Crown Court).

16.6.2.2 Standard directions

Directions for the service of experts' reports will form part of the directions that the court will give prior to trial in both the magistrates' court (see **Chapter 8**) and the Crown Court (see **Chapter 10**). In addition to serving on the CPS the report of any expert on whose evidence he seeks to rely at trial, the defendant must also supply the CPS with the name and address of any expert who has been *consulted* but on whose evidence he does not seek to rely (Criminal Procedure and Investigations Act 1996, s 6D; see **8.4.3.2**).

Magistrates' court

In the magistrates' court, the standard directions to be given in a not guilty case provide that:

(a) if either the CPS or the defendant seeks to rely on evidence from an expert, they must serve a copy of that expert's report within *28 days* of the directions being given;

(b)   the party served with the expert's report must indicate whether the expert is required to attend at the trial, and either serve its own expert evidence in response or indicate that it is not intending to rely on expert evidence, within *28 days* of receipt of the other party's expert evidence;

(c)   a meeting of experts to agree non-contentious matters and identify issues, if appropriate and the parties agree, must take place within *28 days* of service of both parties' expert evidence;

(d)   the parties must notify the court within *14 days* of an experts' meeting whether the length of the trial is affected by the outcome of the meeting.

Crown Court

In the Crown Court, the list of standard directions to be given by the magistrates when the case is sent for trial does not contain any specific reference to the disclosure of expert evidence. However, the CPS will include the report of any expert on whose evidence it seeks to rely at trial in the prosecution case papers which must be served on the defendant. The judge will give further directions as to the disclosure of expert evidence at the preliminary hearing (if such a hearing is necessary), or at the plea and case management hearing (see **Chapter 10**).

16.6.3   Role of the expert witness in criminal proceedings

An expert witness in criminal proceedings owes an overriding duty to the court (see *R v Puaca* [2005] Crim 3001). In *R v Harris* [2005] EWCA Crim 1980, the Court of Appeal made the following comments about expert evidence in criminal proceedings:

(a)   Expert evidence presented to the court should be and be seen to be the independent product of the expert, uninfluenced as to form or content by the requirements of litigation.

(b)   An expert witness should provide independent assistance to the court by way of objective unbiased opinion in relation to matters within his expertise.

(c)   An expert witness should state the facts or assumptions on which his opinion is based. He should not omit to consider material facts which detract from his concluded opinions.

(d)   An expert should make it clear when a particular question or issue falls outside his expertise.

(e)   If an expert's opinion is not properly researched because he considers that insufficient data are available then this must be stated, with an indication that the opinion is no more than a provisional one.

(f)   If, after exchange of reports, an expert witness changes his view on material matters, such change of view should be communicated to the other side without delay and, when appropriate, to the court.

In *R v Bowman* [2006] EWCA Crim 417, it was held that the above duties are owed to the court and override any obligation to the party from whom the expert has received instructions or by whom the expert is paid. It was also held that an expert's report prepared for use in criminal proceedings should contain:

(a)   details of the expert's academic and professional qualifications, experience and accreditation relevant to the opinions expressed in the report, and the range and extent of his expertise and any limitations upon his expertise;

(b)   a statement setting out the substance of all the instructions received (whether written or oral), questions upon which an opinion is sought, the materials provided and considered, and the documents, statements, evidence, information or assumptions which are material to the opinions expressed or upon which those opinions are based;

(c) information relating to who has carried out measurements, examinations or tests and the methodology used, and whether or not such measurements, examinations or tests were carried out under the expert's supervision;

(d) where there is a range of opinion on the matters dealt with in the report, a summary of the range of opinion and the reasons for the opinion given. In this connection any material facts or matters which detract from the expert's opinions and any points which should fairly be made against any opinions expressed should be set out;

(e) relevant extracts of literature or any other material which might assist the court;

(f) a statement to the effect that the expert has complied with his duty to the court to provide independent assistance by way of objective unbiased opinion in relation to matters within his or her expertise, and an acknowledgement that the expert will inform all parties and, where appropriate, the court in the event that his opinion changes on any material issues.

On 14 February 2006, the Attorney-General published a guidance booklet for experts, entitled 'Disclosure: Experts' evidence and unused material – Guidance Booklet for Experts'. This guidance was felt to be necessary following a number of high-profile cases in which defendants convicted of murdering their infant children had their convictions quashed by the Court of Appeal after it emerged that there were significant defects in the expert paediatric evidence which had been adduced at their original trials (*R v Clark* [2003] EWCA Crim 1020; *R v Cannings* [2004] 1 All ER 725). The guidance reminds prosecution experts that:

(a) the expert has an overriding duty to the court;

(b) the expert's duty is to the court and not to the CPS;

(c) the expert is required to comply with the Criminal Procedure and Investigations Act 1996, and the surrounding case law on disclosure; and

(d) the expert must not give evidence beyond his area of expertise.

This guidance does not apply to experts instructed by the defendant.

16.6.4 Does the expert need to give oral evidence at trial?

Although it is normal practice for an expert witness to attend trial to give oral evidence, s 30 of the CJA 1988 enables the court to give leave for an expert's report to be admissible as an item of hearsay evidence (see **16.6.5** below) without the expert needing to attend court to give oral evidence. Before giving such leave, the court needs to consider a number of criteria, including:

(a) the contents of the report;

(b) the reasons for the non-attendance of the expert; and

(c) the risk of unfairness to the defendant, particularly if the contents of the report are controversial and the defendant will be deprived of the opportunity to cross-examine the expert on his report.

It is unlikely that a court will grant leave when the expert's evidence is of any real importance to the prosecution case and the defendant wishes to take issue with the contents of his report.

16.6.5   The contents of an expert's report and the rule excluding hearsay evidence

16.6.5.1   Criminal Justice Act 2003, s 118(1)

Hearsay evidence is an out-of-court statement that is repeated at court in order to prove the truth of the matter stated out of court. Such evidence is inadmissible in criminal proceedings unless it falls within one of four exceptions set out in s 114(1) of the CJA 2003 (see **19.4.2**). One of these exceptions comprises a list of common law rules of evidence set out in s 118 of the same Act. This list includes 'any rule of law under which in criminal proceedings an expert witness may draw on the body of expertise relevant to his field' (CJA 2003, s 118(1)).

> **Example**
>
> Terry is charged with burglary of shop premises. A forensic expert in glass analysis gives evidence for the CPS that glass found embedded in Terry's shoe is identical to glass from a window that was smashed during the burglary, and that such glass is extremely rare. To reach his opinion about the rarity of the glass, the expert had to draw on the published findings of others within his field of expertise. This is hearsay evidence, but will nevertheless be admissible by virtue of s 118(1).

16.6.5.2   Criminal Justice Act 2003, s 127

Section 127 of the CJA 2003 permits a court to admit in evidence a statement on which an expert bases his opinion, even if the maker of the statement does not attend court to give evidence (thus making the statement hearsay evidence). This provision is designed to allow an expert to give an opinion based on information gathered by anyone assisting him in the preparation of his report, without that person needing to attend court to give evidence. It may also be used in more controversial circumstances, however, as set out in the example below.

> **Example**
>
> Nancy is charged with dangerous driving following a serious road traffic accident. The CPS intends to call an accident reconstruction expert to give his opinion on the likely cause of the accident. The expert will say that the accident was caused by Nancy driving her vehicle at an excessive speed. The expert's opinion is in part based on eye-witness accounts of the accident. The eye-witnesses will not be attending court to give evidence. The prosecution will seek to have the expert's opinion evidence admitted under s 127.

The court may refuse to admit evidence under s 127 if another party to the case opposes this and the court considers that it is not in the interests of justice for the evidence to be admitted (CJA 2003, s 127(4)). In deciding whether it is in the interests of justice for the evidence to be admitted, the court must consider:

(a)   the expense of calling as a witness the person who prepared the statement;

(b)   whether relevant evidence could be given by that person which could not be given by the expert; and

(c)   whether that person can reasonably be expected to remember the matters stated well enough to give oral evidence of them (CJA 2003, s 127(5)).

16.7 Flowchart – admissibility of evidence

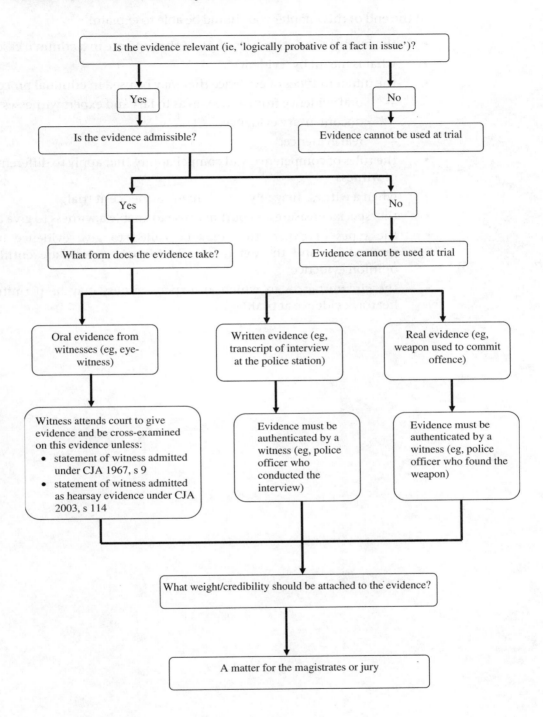

16.8 Checklist

At the end of this chapter you should be able to explain:

- the burdens and standards of proof that operate in a criminal case;
- what is meant by 'evidence';
- the different types of evidence that may be used in criminal proceedings:
  — oral evidence from witnesses as to fact and expert witnesses,
  — documentary evidence,
  — real evidence;
- the rules of competence and compellability that apply to different categories of witness;
- when a witness may rely on self-made evidence at trial;
- the 'special measures' a court may use to enable a witness to give evidence;
- the types of expert that may be called to give evidence in criminal proceedings and the extent to which such experts are entitled to give opinion evidence;
- the circumstances in which an expert witness may be permitted to give hearsay evidence at trial.

Chapter 17

Visual Identification Evidence and Corroboration

17.1 Introduction

One of the most common forms of evidence relied upon by the CPS in a criminal trial is visual identification evidence from a witness who claims to have seen the defendant committing the crime with which he has been charged. Evidence from eye-witnesses is, however, notoriously unreliable, and the defendant will often dispute the visual identification which the eye-witness claims to have made. This chapter will examine the guidelines which apply in such cases and will look at the factors the court will take into account in deciding whether disputed visual identification evidence is admissible and, if it is, how the quality of that evidence should be assessed. The chapter will also look at what is meant by the term 'corroboration' and when corroboration of evidence given by a witness is either essential or desirable.

17.2 The *Turnbull* guidelines

Special guidelines apply when a witness who gives evidence for the CPS visually identifies the defendant as the person who committed the crime, *and* the defendant disputes that identification. The guidelines were laid down in the case of *R v Turnbull* [1977] QB 224.

A witness will identify the defendant as the person who committed the offence if:

(a) the witness picks out the defendant informally (if, for example, a witness points out to a police officer in the street an individual whom the witness recognises as the person he saw committing an offence earlier that day); or

(b) the witness identifies the defendant at a formal identification procedure at the police station (ie, a video identification, identification parade, group identification or confrontation – see **Chapter 3**); or

(c) the witness claims to recognise the defendant as someone previously known to him.

Such a witness is known as a '*Turnbull* witness'. In all three cases, the *Turnbull* guidelines will apply *only* if the defendant disputes the visual identification made by the witness.

Example 1

Joe is on trial for theft. A witness called by the CPS tells the court that he saw a man committing the theft and later identified Joe as that man at a video identification held at the police station.

(a)   If Joe denies being at the scene of the theft, the *Turnbull* guidelines will apply.

(b)   If Joe admits to being at the scene of the theft but denies that he was the person who committed the theft, and suggests that it was somebody else who was present at the time who committed the theft, the *Turnbull* guidelines will apply.

(c)   If Joe admits taking the item but denies acting dishonestly because he claims to have had the right to take the item, the *Turnbull* guidelines will not apply. In this case Joe will not be disputing the identification evidence given by the witness.

Example 2

Jane is on trial for assault. A witness tells the court that he saw Jane commit the offence. He says that he knows Jane because he has occasionally seen her walking past his house.

(a)   If Jane denies being at the scene of the assault, the *Turnbull* guidelines will apply.

(b)   If Jane admits to being at the scene of the assault but denies that she was the person who committed the assault, and states that it was somebody else who was present at the time who committed the assault, the *Turnbull* guidelines will apply.

(c)   If Jane admits striking the victim but claims that she was acting only in self-defence, the *Turnbull* guidelines will not apply because Jane does not dispute the identification evidence given by the witness.

If a witness simply gives a description to the court of the person who committed the crime, but there is no direct evidence that it was the defendant (other than the fact that the defendant's physical appearance matches the description given), the *Turnbull* guidelines will not apply.

Example

Peter is on trial for burglary. A witness who saw the burglary tells the court that it was committed by a man who was 'approximately 6ft tall, with brown, spiky hair and a moustache'. Peter matches this description, but the witness failed to pick Peter out at a video identification at the police station.

The *Turnbull* guidelines will not apply in this case, because there is no direct evidence from the witness identifying Peter as the person responsible for the burglary.

17.3   The *Turnbull* guidelines in the Crown Court

17.3.1   Role of the trial judge

In the Crown Court the trial judge is responsible for assessing the quality of the identification evidence given by a witness called by the CPS. The judge must look at the circumstances of the *original* sighting of the defendant by the witness, and determine how strong this evidence is. The *original* sighting is the sighting of the defendant made by the eye-witness at the time the offence was committed.

In assessing the quality of this evidence, the trial judge will take into account a number of factors, including the following:

(a)   *The length of the observation* – did the witness see the defendant for a lengthy period of time, or did he just get a fleeting glimpse?

(b)   *Distance* – was the witness close to the defendant, or did he see the defendant only from a long distance away?

(c)   *Lighting* – did the observation happen in daylight or at night? If at night, was there any street lighting? If the observation occurred inside a building, was the building well lit or was it dark?

(d)   *Conditions* – if the sighting was outside, what were the weather conditions at the time? Was it a clear day, or was it raining or foggy? How many other people were present at the time and did they obstruct the witness's view? Did anything else obstruct the view? If the sighting was in a building such as a pub, was there a smoky atmosphere, or did any part of the building (such as a pillar) obstruct the view?

(e)   *How much of the suspect's face did the witness actually see* – did the witness see all of the suspect's face, or merely part of it? Can the witness give a clear description of the suspect's face, or is the description vague and lacking detail?

(f)   *Whether the person identified was someone who was already known to the witness (a recognition case), or someone the witness had never seen before.* Might the person identified have been seen by the witness in earlier, innocent circumstances, with the witness then mistakenly thinking he had seen that person committing the offence?

(g)   *How closely does the original description given by the witness to the police match the actual physical appearance of the defendant?* Are there any discrepancies in height, build, hair colour/length or age?

The judge will base his assessment of the strength of the identification evidence on what the witness who gives this evidence has said both in examination-in-chief and in cross-examination. It is therefore important for the defendant's solicitor or counsel to seek to undermine the credibility of the identification evidence when cross-examining the *Turnbull* witness. The mnemonic 'ADVOKATE' may be used as a reminder to ensure that the necessary issues are raised in the cross-examination of a *Turnbull* witness:

Amount of time the person was under observation.

Distance between the witness and the person observed.

Visibility.

Obstructions blocking the witness's view.

Known or seen before (ie, did the witness know the person observed, or had he seen that person before)?

Any reason to remember (ie, was there any particular reason why the witness should remember the person he saw)?

Time lapses (between the sighting of the person by the witness and the witness giving a statement describing that person to the police, or identifying that person at an identification procedure).

Errors or discrepancies between the first description of the person seen given by the witness to the police and the actual appearance of the defendant.

17.3.2 Identification poor and without support

If the judge considers the identification evidence to be of poor quality, and it is not supported by any other prosecution evidence, the judge should stop the trial at the end of the prosecution case and direct the jury to acquit the defendant. This will normally follow a submission of no case to answer being made by the defendant's counsel (see **10.10.1**).

Example

Rebecca is charged with theft. The only evidence called by the CPS is from an eye-witness who picked Rebecca out at a video identification at the police station. When cross- examined at court, the witness concedes that she got only a fleeting glimpse of the person who committed the theft, and that this was from a long distance away at a time when it was raining heavily and a lot of other people were present to obstruct her view. At the end of the prosecution case, Rebecca's counsel will make a submission of no case to answer. If the judge assesses the identification evidence which has been given to be of poor quality and unsupported, he will stop the trial and direct the jury to acquit Rebecca.

17.3.3 Identification good

If the judge considers the quality of the original sighting made by the eye-witness to be good, when he sums up the case to the jury before they retire to consider their verdict he will point out to them the dangers of relying on identification evidence, and the special need for caution when such evidence is relied on. He will tell the jury that it is very easy for an honest witness to be mistaken as to identity, and he will direct the jury to examine closely the circumstances of the original sighting and take into account the factors listed at **17.3.1** above when considering the quality of the identification evidence. This is usually referred to as a '*Turnbull* warning'.

Example

Nigel is charged with assault occasioning actual bodily harm. The CPS seeks to rely on evidence from an eye-witness to the assault who later picked out Nigel at a video identification at the police station. When giving evidence at court, the witness states that he saw the assault take place over a period of 40 seconds. He also says that he had an unobstructed view of the assault from only 5 metres away, and that the assault occurred in daylight when the weather conditions were bright and clear. The judge considers that the quality of the initial sighting by the eye-witness is good. When summing up the case at the end of the trial he will give a '*Turnbull* warning' to the jury. He will warn the jury about relying on identification evidence and will direct them to take into account the factors listed in **17.3.1** above when considering the quality of the identification evidence.

If the prosecution case is based solely on identification evidence by a single witness which the judge considers to be of good quality, the judge must exercise particular care when summing up to the jury. In particular, the judge must set out fully the strengths and weaknesses of the identification evidence given by the witness (*R v Garnett Edwards* [2006] UKPC 23).

In *R v Capron* [2006] UKPC 34, the Privy Council held that a *Turnbull* warning should be given even in a case where the witness claims to have recognised the defendant as someone already known to him (ie, a recognition case).

17.3.4 Identification poor but supported

If the judge considers the quality of the initial sighting by the eye-witness to be poor but this sighting is supported by other evidence, a '*Turnbull* warning' similar to that described at **17.3.3** above should be given. Supporting evidence means some other independent evidence which suggests that the identification made by the witness may be correct. The judge will direct the jury as to what other evidence is capable of amounting to supporting evidence, and direct them not to convict on the strength of the identification evidence alone but to look for other supporting evidence before they decide to convict. Examples of supporting evidence include:

(a)   a confession made by the defendant;

(b)   other evidence which places the defendant at the scene of the crime (such as the defendant's fingerprints being found at premises he is alleged to have broken into);

(c)   in a theft case, the defendant having been found by the police in possession of stolen property;

(d)   the defendant having previous convictions which show a propensity for him to commit the type of offence with which he is charged (see **Chapter 22**).

Example

Frank is charged with unlawful wounding. The CPS has two items of evidence: (i) Frank's fingerprints, found on a knife which it is alleged he used as a weapon; and (ii) evidence from an eye-witness to the wounding who picked Frank out in a video identification at the police station. When giving evidence at Frank's trial, the eye-witness concedes that the incident occurred at night in an alley where there was no lighting. The eye-witness also says that he observed the incident only for a moment and saw only part of the attacker's face.

At the end of the prosecution case, the judge assesses the identification evidence given by the eye-witness as being of poor quality. However, this evidence is supported by Frank's fingerprints on the knife. The judge will therefore not stop the trial. However, when summing up the case at the end of the trial, he will warn the jury about relying on identification evidence and will direct the jury to take into account the factors listed in **17.3.1** above when considering the quality of the evidence. The judge will tell the jury what other evidence is capable of amounting to supporting evidence (ie, the fingerprints on the knife), and tell the jury not to convict on the strength of the identification evidence alone.

17.4   The *Turnbull* guidelines in the magistrates' court

In the magistrates' court, the magistrates decide matters of both fact and law, and it will therefore be necessary for the defendant's solicitor to address the magistrates on the *Turnbull* guidelines during the course of the trial.

If the defendant's solicitor considers that the quality of the identification evidence given by an eye-witness is poor, and the CPS has no other supporting evidence, he should make a submission of no case to answer at the end of the prosecution case (see **9.5** above). The submission will be on the basis that the evidence called by the prosecution is manifestly unreliable. In making his submission the defence solicitor should list the relevant factors mentioned at **17.3.1** above, and point out to the magistrates why he considers the identification evidence to be of poor quality.

If the identification evidence given by the eye-witness is either good or is poor but supported by other evidence called by the CPS, the defendant's solicitor is unlikely to make a submission of no case to answer. He will instead address the *Turnbull* guidelines in his closing speech to the magistrates, and will point out that, however strong it might appear, identification evidence from an eye-witness is notoriously unreliable and the magistrates should exercise caution when considering such evidence. The defendant's solicitor will also point out any weaknesses in the identification evidence that has been given. The ADVOKATE mnemonic is useful here as a checklist for areas of potential weakness in the quality of the identification evidence (see **17.3.1** above). The defendant's solicitor may also use his closing speech to undermine the significance or credibility of any other evidence adduced by the CPS which supports the disputed identification evidence. For example, if the supporting evidence consists of the defendant's fingerprints being found on a stolen item, the defendant's solicitor may suggest an innocent explanation for this.

17.5   Disputed identification evidence and PACE, s 78

Section 78 of PACE 1984 provides the court with the discretion to exclude evidence upon which the prosecution seek to rely if 'the admission of such evidence would have such an adverse effect on the fairness of proceedings that the court ought not to admit it'. Section 78 is examined more fully in **Chapter 21**; in summary, however, it is commonly raised by the defendant's solicitor when the methods employed by the police to obtain evidence constitute a serious and substantial breach either of PACE 1984, or of the Codes of Practice (see **Chapters 2 and 3**).

In the context of disputed visual identification evidence, such a situation may occur if the police breach the rules for holding an identification procedure contained in Code D of the Codes of Practice (see **3.5** above). For example:

(a)   at a video identification the police may breach the requirement that the other images shown to the witness must resemble the suspect in age, general appearance and position in life (Code D, Annex A, para 2);

(b)   at an identification parade the police may breach the requirement that the witnesses attending the parade are segregated both from each other and from the suspect before and after the parade (Code D, Annex B, para 14);

(c)   a breach of the Codes of Practice will occur if, whilst the defendant was detained at the police station, the police failed to hold an identification procedure when such a procedure should have been held pursuant to para 3.12 of Code D (see **3.5.3.7**).

If the defendant's solicitor considers that disputed identification evidence has been obtained following serious and substantial breaches of Code D, he should first attempt to persuade the court to rule such evidence inadmissible under PACE 1984, s 78. Only if the court declines to exercise its discretion under s 78 should the defence solicitor then consider how the quality of the *original* sighting made by the witness may be undermined in cross-examination, and what representations may be made to the court in respect of the *Turnbull* guidelines.

Example

George is charged with robbery. Mildred, the victim of the robbery, gives a statement to the police describing her attacker. She comments that she got only a brief glimpse of her attacker's face, and there are several dissimilarities between the description she gives and the actual appearance of George. Mildred is nevertheless able to pick George out at an identification parade carried out at the police station. The identification parade was carried out in breach of Code D because four of the other participants in the parade did not resemble George and the officers investigating the robbery were present during the parade. George denies taking part in the robbery and claims that Mildred is mistaken.

At trial, George's solicitor will make an application to the court under PACE 1984, s 78, for the identification evidence given by Mildred to be excluded, on the basis of the breaches of Code D which occurred when the identification parade took place. Only if this application is unsuccessful will George's solicitor then need to consider how in cross-examination he may undermine the quality of Mildred's original sighting of her attacker at the time of the robbery, and what representations he should make to the court in respect of the *Turnbull* guidelines.

Where an application has been made under s 78 to exclude disputed identification evidence because the police failed to hold an identification procedure in accordance with para 3.12 of Code C (see **3.5.3.7** above), if the judge rejects the application and allows the prosecution to adduce the identification evidence at trial, the judge must nevertheless warn the jury that 'an identification procedure enables a suspect to put the reliability of an eye-witness's identification to the test, that the suspect has lost the benefit of that safeguard and that the jury should take account of that fact in its assessment of the whole case, giving it such weight as it thinks fair' (*R v Forbes* [2001] 1 AC 473, HL). Such a situation may arise when a witness makes a street identification of the person he saw committing the offence some time after the offence has occurred. Although in such circumstances the police should hold an identification procedure to test the reliability of the witness's identification evidence, the judge is unlikely to exclude the identification evidence from the witness as a result of any failure to hold an identification procedure (on the basis that there would have been little value in holding such a procedure because the suspect would in all probability have been picked out by the witness given that he was identified by the witness in the street). The judge must, however, give the above warning to the jury. A failure by the judge to give such a warning is likely to render any subsequent conviction unsafe (*R v Muhidinz* [2005] EWCA Crim 2464).

17.6 Corroboration

17.6.1 What is corroboration?

When a jury or bench of magistrates are deciding their verdict, they will assess the strength of the evidence which has been placed before them. Although the law does not say that one particular form of evidence is 'better' than another, rules do exist as to when evidence which has been given by a witness should be corroborated.

Corroboration is other, independent evidence which supports the evidence to be corroborated and which implicates the defendant in the crime with which he has been charged.

17.6.2 Examples of corroboration

The following is a non-exhaustive list of examples of evidence which may corroborate evidence given by a witness called by the CPS:

(a)   The evidence of another witness.

Example

Lisa is accused of theft. A witness called by the CPS visually identifies Lisa as the person he saw committing the theft. Lisa disputes this identification evidence. The CPS has evidence from another eye-witness who saw Lisa running away from the scene of the theft at the time the theft was alleged to have taken place. This will corroborate the account given by the eye-witness who identified Lisa as the thief.

(b)   A confession which has been made by the defendant.

Example

Daniel is accused of murder. An eye-witness has identified Daniel as the person who committed the murder. Daniel disputes this identification but confessed to the murder when interviewed at the police station. The confession corroborates the identification made by the eye-witness.

(c)   Circumstantial evidence such as possession of stolen property, or forensic evidence.

Example 1

Scott is charged with theft. An eye-witness has visually identified Scott as the person who committed the theft. Scott disputes this identification. When the police arrested Scott on suspicion of theft, his flat was searched and a number of items of property that were stolen when the theft took place were recovered. The stolen items corroborate the account given by the eye-witness.

Example 2

Marie is charged with the burglary of a house. An eye-witness has visually identified Marie as the person who committed the burglary. Marie disputes this identification evidence. The police obtain samples of paint from underneath Marie's fingernails which match paint on the frame of the window of the house through which the burglar gained access to the premises. The samples corroborate the account given by the eye-witness.

(d)   The refusal of a defendant to give an intimate body sample.

Example

Jason is charged with raping Charlotte. Charlotte has given a statement to the police stating that Jason had sexual intercourse with her without her consent. Jason denies that sexual intercourse took place. Jason refuses to produce a sample of semen. This will corroborate Charlotte's claim that sexual intercourse took place.

(e)   The refusal of a defendant to take part in an identification procedure.

Example

Fiona is charged with theft. The CPS has obtained a statement from an eye-witness who visually identifies Fiona as the person who committed the theft. Fiona denies committing the theft, and claims that she was elsewhere at the time. However, Fiona refuses to take part in an identification procedure at the police station. Her refusal corroborates the evidence given by the eye-witness.

(f)   An adverse inference from the defendant's silence when questioned at the police station.

Example

Laurie is charged with burglary. The CPS has obtained a statement from an eye-witness who visually identifies Laurie as the person who committed the burglary. At trial, Laurie disputes this identification and claims that he was elsewhere at the time of the burglary, and so has an alibi. When he was interviewed at the police station, however, Laurie refused to answer any questions about the burglary and said nothing about his alibi. The adverse inference that may be drawn at trial from Laurie's silence (see **Chapter 18**) will corroborate the account given by the eye-witness.

17.6.3   When is corroboration essential?

For a limited number of offences, the defendant cannot be convicted solely on the evidence of a single witness. For such offences some form of corroboration is required. These offences include treason, perjury and driving in excess of the speed limit (unless the evidence is from a roadside camera). If the CPS fails to produce evidence which is capable of amounting to corroboration, a submission of no case to answer made by the defendant's solicitor or counsel at the end of the prosecution case will be successful. If there is evidence which is capable of amounting to corroboration, it will then be left to the jury or the magistrates to decide whether or not to accept that evidence as corroboration.

A defendant may not be convicted of any offence if the only evidence against him is an adverse inference under ss 34, 36, or 37 of the CJPOA 1994 (see **Chapter 18**). Such an inference may, however, itself amount to corroboration of other evidence adduced by the CPS (see **17.6.2(f)** above).

17.6.4   When is corroboration desirable?

In some cases, corroboration may be desirable because the evidence given by a witness is in some way 'suspect'. Examples include:

(a)   witnesses with a purpose of their own to serve in giving false evidence; and

(b)   where the prosecution witness is a mental patient.

Category (a) above may include evidence from a co-defendant, evidence from a witness with a grudge against the defendant, or evidence from a witness whom the defendant alleges committed the offence. Corroboration is particularly important in a situation where a co-defendant has entered a guilty plea on an earlier occasion and is now giving evidence for the CPS against his fellow defendant who has pleaded not guilty.

Example 1

Nicola and Zoe are jointly charged with theft. Both enter pleas of not guilty and, when giving evidence in their respective defences at trial, place the blame for the theft on the other. It is desirable for the evidence that Nicola gives implicating Zoe, and for the evidence that Zoe gives implicating Nicola, to be corroborated.

Example 2

Steven and John are jointly charged with common assault. Steven pleads not guilty. John pleads guilty and the court adjourns sentencing in his case until the end of Steven's trial. Having pleaded guilty, John now gives evidence for the CPS at Steven's trial, stating that Steven played a more significant role in the assault than he did. John may be giving evidence against Steven in the hope of minimising his role in the offence and so getting a lighter sentence. It is therefore desirable that the evidence given by John be corroborated.

Example 3

Kevin (a pub landlord) is charged with assaulting Frederick (a customer at the pub). Kevin denies that the assault ever took place. At trial, it emerges that Frederick had a grudge against Kevin, because some months previously Kevin had banned Frederick from entering the pub after a violent altercation between Frederick and another customer. It is desirable that the evidence to be given by Frederick at Kevin's trial be corroborated.

Example 4

Joanna is charged with assault. Lucy was an eye-witness to the assault and will give evidence for the prosecution confirming that Joanna committed the assault. Joanna denies having committed the assault. Her defence is that the assault was in fact carried out by Lucy. It is desirable that the evidence to be given by Lucy is corroborated.

In the Crown Court, if the judge considers that evidence given by a witness is in any way unreliable, or that the witness has a purpose of his own to serve in giving evidence, he will direct the jury that there is a special need for caution to be exercised by them when considering this evidence, and that it would be dangerous to convict the defendant on the basis of this evidence alone (*R v Makanjuola* [1995] 1 WLR 1348).

In the magistrates' court, when making his closing speech, the defendant's solicitor should warn the magistrates about the dangers of convicting solely on the evidence of a witness who is either unreliable, or who has a purpose of his own to serve in giving evidence against the defendant.

17.7   Flowchart – visual identification evidence

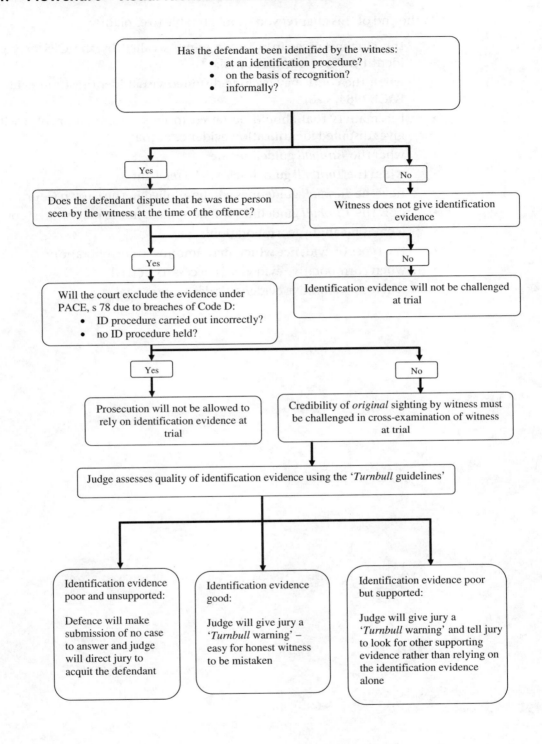

17.8 Checklist

At the end of this chapter you should be able to explain:

- the circumstances in which a witness called by the CPS may give visual identification evidence at trial;
- when the court may exclude disputed visual identification evidence under PACE 1984, s 78;
- the matters that should be raised in cross-examination of a witness who gives disputed identification evidence at trial;
- what the *Turnbull* guidelines are;
- when the *Turnbull* guidelines will be relevant;
- how the *Turnbull* guidelines will be applied in the Crown Court;
- how the *Turnbull* guidelines will be applied in the magistrates' court;
- what is meant by 'corroboration';
- the types of evidence which may amount to corroboration;
- when corroborative evidence is necessary at trial;
- when corroborative evidence is desirable at trial.

Chapter 18

Inferences from Silence

18.1 Introduction

18.1.1 The 'right to silence'

Anyone who is arrested on suspicion of having committed a criminal offence is entitled to remain silent when interviewed at the police station. The police do not have the power to force people to answer questions. However, under the provisions of the Criminal Justice and Public Order Act (CJPOA) 1994, when a defendant's case comes to trial, the court may be permitted to draw what are termed 'adverse inferences' from his earlier silence when being questioned about the offence. This chapter will examine when a court is permitted to draw such inferences, and the potential evidential consequences which may arise at trial when a solicitor advises a client not to answer questions when interviewed at the police station. This chapter must be read in conjunction with **Chapter 4**, which looks, inter alia, at the advice a solicitor may give to a suspect at the police station as to whether to answer questions in interview.

18.1.2 What is an adverse inference?

The term 'adverse inference' means that the court is permitted to draw a negative conclusion from the defendant's silence when interviewed at the police station. In other words, the court may hold a defendant's silence against him. For example, the court may draw an inference that the defendant remained silent when interviewed because he had had no adequate explanation to give for his conduct, or no adequate explanation that would stand up to subsequent investigation by the police. Another adverse inference the court may draw is one of recent fabrication, namely that the defendant kept silent at the police station because he had no satisfactory explanation for his conduct and 'thought up' his defence only after being charged by the police.

Although the court may draw an adverse inference from the defendant's silence when interviewed, silence on its own *cannot* prove guilt (CJPOA 1994, s 38(3)). The CPS will therefore need to adduce other evidence of the defendant's guilt before it may ask the court to draw an adverse inference from the defendant's silence in interview.

The court is not permitted to draw an adverse inference from a defendant's silence if that silence occurred at a time when the defendant had not been allowed the opportunity to consult a solicitor to obtain independent legal advice (Youth Justice and Criminal Evidence Act 1999, s 58). Inferences may be drawn only when a defendant has been given the opportunity to take independent legal advice. In cases where the police are allowed to delay a suspect receiving legal advice (see **Chapter 3**), no inferences may be drawn from the defendant's silence in any interview which takes place before the defendant is permitted to obtain legal advice.

18.2   Criminal Justice and Public Order Act 1994, s 34

18.2.1   Introduction

Section 34 permits the court or jury to draw an adverse inference from a defendant's silence when the defendant was being questioned or charged at the police station. Section 34 provides:

(1)   Where in any proceedings against a person for an offence, evidence is given that the accused—

(a)   at any time before he was charged with the offence, on being questioned under caution by a constable trying to discover whether or by whom the offence had been committed, failed to mention any fact relied on in his defence in those proceedings; or

(a)   on being charged with the offence or officially informed that he might be prosecuted for it, failed to mention any such fact,

being a fact which in the circumstances existing at the time the accused could reasonably have been expected to mention ... the court or jury ... may draw such inferences from the failure as appear proper.

Example 1

Derek is arrested on suspicion of assault. Derek refuses to answer any questions put to him by the police in interview at the police station. Derek is subsequently charged with the assault. At his trial, Derek claims to have been acting in self-defence. Section 34 allows the court to draw an adverse inference from Derek's failure to mention this defence when being questioned by the police.

Example 2

Erica is arrested on suspicion of theft. Erica refuses to answer questions put to her by the police when interviewed at the police station. Erica is subsequently charged with the theft. At her trial, Erica raises the defence of alibi, claiming that she was at a friend's house at the time the alleged theft took place. Section 34 allows the court to draw an adverse inference from Erica's failure to mention her alibi defence when being questioned by the police.

18.2.2   When will s 34 apply?

In *R v Argent* [1997] 2 Cr App R 27, the Court of Appeal said that certain conditions had to be satisfied before adverse inferences could be drawn from a defendant's silence in police interview:

(a)   the interview had to be an interview under caution;

(b)   the defendant had to fail to mention any fact later relied on in his defence at trial;

(c)   the failure to mention this fact had to occur *before* the defendant was charged;

(d)   the questioning of the defendant at the interview in which the defendant failed to mention the fact had to be directed to trying to discover whether or by whom the alleged offence had been committed; and

(e)   the fact which the defendant failed to mention had to be a fact which, in the circumstances existing at the time, the defendant could reasonably have been expected to mention when questioned.

Only if these conditions are satisfied may an adverse inference be drawn under s 34(1)(a). In *R v Betts and Hall* [2001] 2 Cr App R 257, the Court of Appeal stated that if a defendant remained silent during his initial interview at the police station and then answered questions during a subsequent interview, inferences from his failure to answer questions in the first interview might still be drawn at trial.

Of the five conditions set out above, the condition which normally gives rise to a dispute between the CPS and the defendant is (e), ie whether in the circumstances existing at the time the defendant could reasonably have been expected to mention the fact which he later relied on in his defence at court.

It is unlikely that, in practice, a court will seek to draw an inference under s 34(1)(b). If a defendant places his factual defence on record when interviewed by the police, a court will not draw an adverse inference if he says nothing when he is subsequently charged. If, conversely, the defendant remains silent in interview and then raises a defence at trial, the court will draw an adverse inference under s 34(1)(a). The only occasion when the court is likely to draw an adverse inference under s 34(1)(b) is if the defendant was not actually interviewed by the police (so there is no possibility of an inference under s 34(1)(a)), but was simply told that he was to be charged with an offence.

Example

In *R v Goodsir* [2006] All ER (D) 326, the defendant was stopped by a police officer in connection with a road traffic offence. He was twice cautioned by the officer, but at no time was he questioned in relation to the offence. He was told that he would be reported for summons, and was subsequently summonsed for the offence of dangerous driving. The defendant pleaded not guilty and raised the defence of duress of circumstances. The trial judge told the jury that they were entitled to draw an adverse inference from the defendant's silence on caution. The defendant was convicted and appealed on the basis that the judge was wrong to allow the jury to draw an adverse inference, since the defendant had not been asked any questions, nor been given the opportunity to explain his behaviour. The Court of Appeal held that the judge had properly left the issue of adverse inferences to the jury because, under s 34(1)(b), the defendant could reasonably be expected to have explained the manner of his driving *after* being informed that he would be reported for summons.

18.2.3 Use of a written statement

A solicitor advising a client at a police station will often suggest to a client that rather than answering questions in interview, the client should instead hand to the police a written statement, which the solicitor will prepare on the client's behalf (see **4.4.5**). The advantage of this is that it allows the client's version of events to be set out in a clear and logical way. This is particularly useful for a client whom the solicitor feels may not come across well in interview (for example, a client who is distressed, emotional or tired).

At one time it was thought that the two inferences which the court was permitted to draw from a defendant's failure to mention facts *in interview* were either that the facts had subsequently been fabricated by the defendant (ie, the defendant had made up his defence only after leaving the police station), or that the defendant did have an account to give but not an account that he wanted to subject to police questioning during the interview. However, in *R v Knight* [2003] EWCA Crim 1977, the Court of Appeal held that the purpose of s 34 was to encourage defendants to make an early disclosure of their defence to the police, not to permit the police to scrutinise and test that defence *in interview* (although of course the police would be able to investigate the facts of the defence *outside* of the interview by, for example, speaking to witnesses who the defendant said would support his case). Therefore, as long as a written statement which is handed to the police contains all the facts which a defendant later relies on in his defence at court, the court will not be able to draw an adverse inference under s 34 if, having handed in the statement, the defendant then refuses to answer questions from the police based on the contents of that written statement.

In the rare situations when a defence solicitor prepares a written statement for his client but does not hand this in to the police (see **4.4.5.3**), whilst this will prevent the court at trial from drawing the inference of recent fabrication, it will not prevent the court from drawing an inference that the defendant was not sufficiently confident about his defence to expose this to investigation by the police following the interview.

18.2.4 When may a solicitor advise a suspect to remain silent?

Much of the case law surrounding s 34 comes from cases where a defendant remained silent at the police station on the basis of legal advice from his solicitor. The courts have said that in a number of situations it may be appropriate for a solicitor to advise his client to remain silent when interviewed by the police, as follows:

(a) *Level of disclosure given by the police* – although the police are not under a general duty to disclose to the suspect's solicitor details of the evidence which they have obtained against the suspect, the courts have held that if the absence of meaningful disclosure means that a solicitor is unable properly to advise his client, this may amount to a good reason for advising the client to remain silent (*R v Argent* (see **18.2.2** above); *R v Roble* [1997] Crim LR 449).

(b) *Nature of the case* – if the material the police have is particularly complex, or relates to events which occurred a long time ago, the solicitor may advise his client to remain silent when it would not be sensible to give an immediate response to the police (*R v Roble* (see above); *R v Howell* [2003] Crim LR 405).

(c) *Personal circumstances of the suspect* – if the solicitor considers the suspect to be suffering from some form of ill health, the suspect is mentally disordered or vulnerable, is excessively tired or is otherwise confused, shocked or intoxicated, the solicitor would be justified in advising the suspect to remain silent (*R v Howell*, above).

18.2.5 Can a defendant avoid an adverse inference by claiming his refusal to answer questions was based on legal advice?

A defendant who at trial claims that the only reason for his silence when interviewed by the police was as a result of legal advice he received from his solicitor will *not* automatically prevent the court from drawing an adverse inference if he subsequently raises in his defence a fact which he failed to mention at the police station (*R v Condron* [1997] 1 Cr App R 185). The European Court of Human Rights has accepted that this does not breach a defendant's right to a fair trial under Article 6 of the ECHR (see **1.8** above), although the Court has pointed out that legal advice is a fundamental part of the right to a fair trial and, as such, the fact that a defendant was advised by his solicitor to not answer questions in the police station must be given appropriate weight at trial (*Condron v UK* [2000] Crim LR 679).

Following the *Condron* case, two conflicting lines of authority emerged concerning the position when a suspect refused to answer questions at the police station as a result of legal advice received from his solicitor. In *R v Betts and Hall* [2001] Crim LR 754, it was held that adverse inferences could not be drawn from a defendant's silence in the police station where that silence was based on legal advice the defendant had received, if the court or jury were satisfied that this was a genuine reason for the defendant's failure to mention at the police station facts which he later relied on in his defence at trial. In *R v Howell* [2003] Crim LR 405, however, it was held that even if the court or jury were satisfied that the legal advice he had received was a genuine reason for the defendant's silence, it would still be permissible for the court draw adverse inferences from that silence.

The situation was resolved by the Court of Appeal in *R v Beckles* [2004] EWCA Crim 2766. The Court held that where a defendant explained his reason for silence as being his reliance on legal advice, the ultimate question for the court or jury under s 34 was whether the facts relied on trial were facts which the defendant could *reasonably* have been expected to mention in police interview. If they were not then no adverse inference could be drawn. If the court or jury considered that the defendant *genuinely* relied on the advice he had received from his solicitor, that would not necessarily be the end of the matter because it still might not have been reasonable for him to rely on the advice, or the advice might not have been the true explanation for his silence. Lord Justice Kay commented that 'a person who is anxious not to answer questions because he has no adequate explanation to offer, gains no protection from his lawyer's advice because that advice is no more than a convenient way of disguising his true motivation for not mentioning facts'.

Following the *Beckles* case, the jury will now be directed by the trial judge that adverse inferences should not be drawn under s 34 if the jury believe that the defendant *genuinely and reasonably* relied on the legal advice to remain silent.

18.2.6 Legal privilege

Conversations between a suspect and his solicitor in the police station, and details of any advice given by the solicitor to the suspect, are ordinarily subject to legal privilege. In an interview the police are not permitted to ask a suspect what advice he has received from his solicitor (or, if the police were to ask, the solicitor would instruct his client not to answer).

If at trial a defendant states that he only remained silent in interview following advice from his solicitor, this will not in itself waive privilege. Equally, however, this is unlikely on its own to prevent an adverse inference being drawn from his silence. If an adverse inference is to be avoided, the court will want to know the reasons for the advice that was given. The risk for a defendant in providing this information to the court is that privilege is 'indivisible'. This means that if a defendant says that he remained silent on the basis of legal advice, the defendant (and conceivably his solicitor) may be cross-examined by the CPS as to the reasons behind the solicitor's decision to advise his client to remain silent. For example, the solicitor who advised a client to remain silent because the police had only made a limited disclosure only of their case might also have advised his client to remain silent because there were inconsistencies in his client's story which would be exposed in the interview.

To counter problems with privilege, some solicitors who advise suspects to remain silent in interview in the police station will now give their advice at the start of the interview itself. The solicitor will normally use the following form of words:

> I *now* advise you to remain silent because ... [the disclosure given by the police is so limited that I cannot properly advise you/I do not consider you to be in a fit state to be interviewed/the offences you are alleged to have committed occurred so long ago or are so complex that you cannot be expected to give an immediate response, etc].

This does not amount to a waiver of privilege because the advice is being given to the client there and then, and the solicitor is not merely confirming advice given to the client before the interview took place.

18.3 Criminal Justice and Public Order Act 1994, s 36

Section 36 permits the court or jury to draw an adverse inference if, when interviewed by the police, the defendant failed to account for the presence of an object, substance or mark. Section 36 provides:

(1)   Where—

    (a)   a person is arrested by a constable, and there is:

        (i)   on his person; or

        (ii)   in or on his clothing or footwear; or

        (iii)   otherwise in his possession; or

        (iv)   in any place in which he is at the time of his arrest,

    any object, substance or mark, or there is any mark on any such object; and

    (b)   that or another constable investigating the case reasonably believes that the presence of the object, substance or mark may be attributable to the participation of the person arrested in the commission of an offence specified by the constable; and

    (c)   the constable informs the person arrested that he so believes, and requests him to account for the presence of the object, substance or mark; and

    (d)   the person fails or refuses to do so,

    then ... the court or jury ... may draw such inferences from the failure or refusal as appear proper.

Example 1

Joe is arrested on suspicion of assaulting Fred. In an interview at the police station, Joe is asked to account for the fact that when he was arrested there was blood on his shirt and his knuckles were grazed. Joe does not reply to this question. Section 36 permits a court to draw an adverse inference from Joe's failure to account for his bloodstained shirt and grazed knuckles.

Example 2

Ronald is arrested on suspicion of the burglary of commercial premises. Entry to the premises was gained by the use of a crowbar to open a window. In an interview at the police station, Ronald is asked to account for the fact that when he was arrested he had in his possession a crowbar. Ronald does not reply to this question. Section 36 permits a court to draw an adverse inference from Ronald's failure to account for his possession of the crowbar.

Although there is a degree of overlap between ss 34 and 36, whilst s 34 will apply only if a defendant raises a fact, which he failed to mention at the police station, in his defence at trial, s 36 will operate irrespective of any defence put forward. It may apply even if no defence is raised at trial, because the inference arises from the defendant's failure to account for the object, substance, or mark *at the time he is interviewed.* The inference which is likely to arise in such a case is that the defendant has no explanation for the presence of the object, substance or mark, or no explanation that will stand up to police questioning.

Example

An assault occurs in the street. The police are called and they arrest Keith nearby. Keith's shirt is bloodstained. In an interview at the police station, Keith is asked to account for the fact that his shirt is bloodstained. Keith refuses to answer this question.

Were Keith to give evidence at his trial that he was walking home from a night club, tripped up and as a result injured his arm and got blood on his shirt, s 34 will apply (as Keith did not mention this fact in interview). Whether or not Keith puts forward an explanation for his bloodstained shirt, s 36 will apply because Keith failed to explain the reason for his shirt being bloodstained when he was interviewed at the police station.

Inferences may only be drawn under s 36 if the police officer requesting the explanation for the object, substance or mark has told the suspect certain specified matters before requesting the explanation (the 'special caution'). The suspect must be told:

(a)   what the offence under investigation is;

(b)   what fact the suspect is being asked to account for;

(c)   that the officer believes this fact may be due to the suspect taking part in the commission of the offence in question;

(d)   that a court may draw an adverse inference from failure to comply with the request; and

(e)   that a record is being made of the interview and that it may be given in evidence if the suspect is brought to trial (PACE Code C, para 10.11).

18.4 Criminal Justice and Public Order Act 1994, s 37

Section 37 allows the court to draw an adverse inference if, when questioned at the police station, the defendant failed to account for his presence at a particular place. Section 37 provides:

(1)   Where—

(a)   a person arrested by a constable was found by him at a place at or about the time the offence for which he was arrested is alleged to have been committed; and

(b)   that or another constable investigating the offence reasonably believes that the presence of the person at that place and at that time may be attributed to his participation in the commission of the offence; and

(c)   the constable informs the person that he so believes, and requests him to account for that presence; and

(d)   the person fails or refuses to do so,

then ... the court or jury ... may draw such inferences from the failure or refusal as appear proper.

Example

Leonard is arrested on suspicion of the burglary of a jewellery shop. Leonard is arrested by the police whilst standing outside the jewellery shop, only two minutes after the shop's burglar alarm went off. When interviewed at the police station,

Leonard is asked to account for his presence near the shop at or about the time of the burglary. Leonard does not reply to this question. Section 37 permits the court to draw an adverse inference from Leonard's failure to account for his presence near the shop at or about the time of the burglary.

There is some overlap between ss 34 and 37. Whilst s 34 will apply only if a defendant raises a fact, which he failed to mention at the police station, in his defence at trial, s 37 will operate irrespective of any defence put forward. It may apply even if no defence is raised at trial, because the inference arises from the defendant's failure to account for his presence at a particular place at or about the time of the offence *at the time he is interviewed.*

Example

Sophie is arrested whilst walking late at night along an alley behind a house which has just been burgled. Sophie is interviewed at the police station and is asked to account for her presence in the alley at or about the time of the burglary. Sophie refuses to answer this question.

If, at her trial, Sophie states that she was walking along the alley because she was taking a short cut home, s 34 will apply because Sophie did not mention this fact when interviewed at the police station. Whether or not at trial Sophie puts forward an explanation for her presence in the alley, s 37 will apply because Sophie failed to explain the reason for her presence in the alley when she was interviewed at the police station.

As with s 36, inferences may be drawn under s 37 only if a suspect has been given the 'special caution' (see **18.3** above).

18.5 Silence at trial

Unless at his trial a defendant makes a successful submission of no case to answer at the end of the prosecution case, the defendant will then have the opportunity to put his case before the court. A defendant is not obliged to give evidence on his own behalf at trial. Neither is a defendant obliged to raise any facts in his own defence. The defendant is entitled to remain silent at trial (Criminal Evidence Act 1898, s 1(1)) and rely on an argument that the CPS has failed to prove his guilt beyond a reasonable doubt. In this situation, since the defendant will not be raising any facts in his defence at trial which he did not mention in the police station, no adverse inferences may be drawn under s 34.

However, a defendant who fails to give evidence on his own behalf at trial may be subject to an adverse inference being drawn by the court or jury under s 35 of the CJPOA 1994 (see **9.6.1.2**). In particular, if the defendant raises a specific defence, such as self-defence or alibi, his failure to enter the witness box to substantiate this defence may lead the court to draw an adverse inference. The inference in such a case will be that the defendant has no plausible explanation, or that any explanation he does have is too weak to stand up to cross-examination by the prosecution. Similarly, if the CPS has adduced evidence of a confession made by the defendant, and the defendant denies that the confession is true, the defendant will need to give evidence to explain why he made a false confession. Should he fail to do so, the court will draw an adverse inference that the defendant has no satisfactory explanation for giving the confession other than the fact that the confession is in fact true.

18.6   Procedural flowcharts

18.6.1   Adverse inferences under s 34

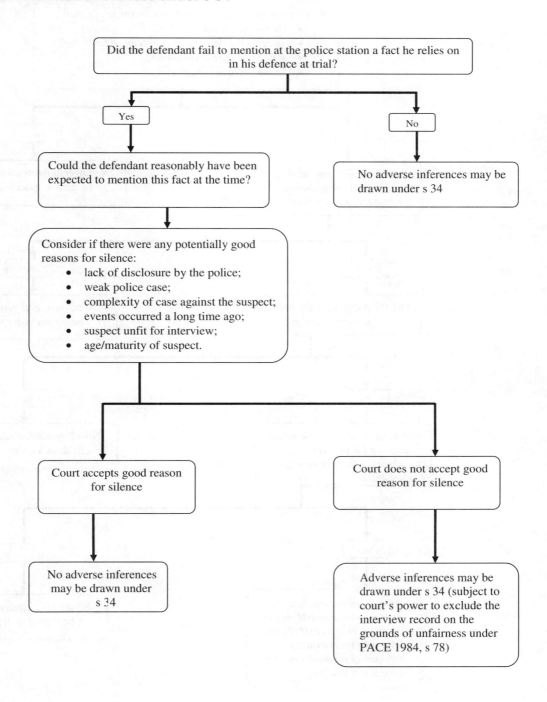

18.6.2   Adverse inferences under s 36

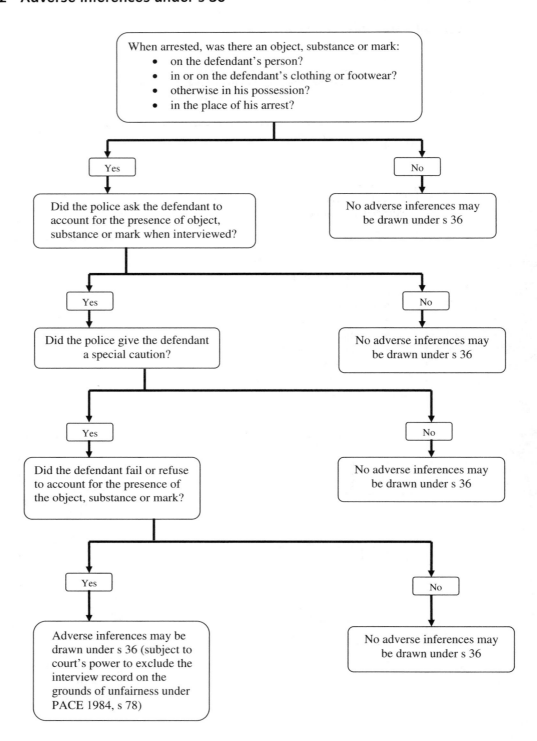

18.6.3   Adverse inferences under s 37

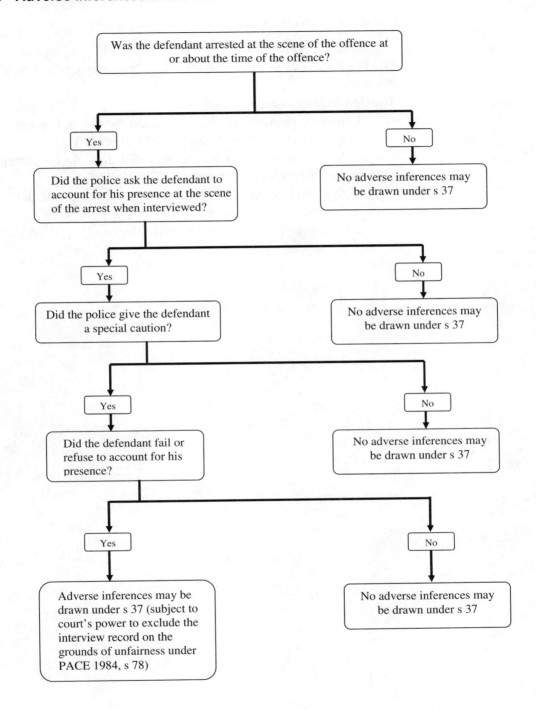

18.7 Checklist

At the end of this chapter you should be able to explain:

- the meaning of an 'adverse inference';
- the types of adverse inference which a court may draw from a defendant's silence;
- the significance of a defendant:
  — failing to mention when questioned by the police any fact he later relies on as part of his defence (CJPOA 1994, s 34),
  — failing to account for the presence of an object, substance or mark when interviewed by the police (CJPOA 1994, s 36),
  — failing to account for his presence at a particular place when interviewed by the police (CJPOA 1994, s 37),
  — failing to give evidence in his own defence at trial (CJPOA 1994, s 35).

Chapter 19
Hearsay Evidence

19.1 Introduction

This chapter will begin by explaining what has historically constituted hearsay evidence and the general common law rule that excluded such evidence from being used in criminal proceedings. It will then examine the statutory definition of hearsay evidence provided by the Criminal Justice Act (CJA) 2003, and the various forms of hearsay evidence that are made admissible in criminal proceedings by virtue of the Act. The chapter will examine how hearsay evidence made admissible under the 2003 Act may be excluded at trial, before concluding with an examination of the procedural requirements that must be complied with should either the CPS or the defendant seek to adduce hearsay evidence at trial.

19.2 What is hearsay evidence?

Historically, hearsay evidence could be broken down into four parts:

(a) an oral or written statement;

(b) made out of court;

(c) repeated in court;

(d) to prove the truth of the matter stated out of court.

Examples of such hearsay evidence include a witness repeating at court what he had been told by another person, a witness statement being read out in evidence at court rather than the witness attending court to give oral evidence, or a business document (such as an entry in a ledger or a handwritten receipt) being produced in evidence.

19.3 The rule against hearsay evidence

Prior to the CJA 2003 coming into effect, there was a general common law rule that hearsay evidence was inadmissible in criminal proceedings. The rationale behind this rule was the inherent unreliability of such evidence. Hearsay evidence was deemed to be 'second-hand' evidence because it was repeating something that had been said elsewhere, and the maker of the original statement could not therefore be directly cross-examined on its contents. This general rule was subject to a number of exceptions, contained both in the common law and in a number of statutory sources. Dissatisfaction with this variety of exceptions led to the CJA 2003 abolishing the common law rule and putting in place a new statutory framework under which hearsay evidence may be admissible only if it satisfies certain requirements.

19.4   The statutory definition of hearsay evidence

19.4.1   How is hearsay evidence defined?

19.4.1.1   The statutory definition

The CJA 2003 provides a statutory definition of hearsay evidence and stipulates that such evidence will be admissible only in four separately defined circumstances (see **19.4.2** below).

A 'hearsay statement' is defined in s 121(2) as 'a statement, not made in oral evidence, that is relied on as evidence of a matter in it'.

> ### Example 1
>
> Garth is charged with handling a stolen bike. At Garth's trial, the CPS calls Adam to give evidence. Adam tells the court: 'Garth showed me a bike. He told me he had just been given it by a mate of his who had nicked it from somewhere else.' This will be hearsay evidence because the CPS will rely on the statement made by Garth to show that he was in possession of a bike which he knew to be stolen. The statement by Garth is being relied on as evidence of a matter stated in it.
>
> ### Example 2
>
> Mark is charged with assaulting Janine. The CPS alleges that Mark went round to Janine's house and punched her in the face. Mark accepts that he went round to Janine's house, but denies punching her. When giving evidence at his trial, Mark says: 'I went round to Janine's house because my son told me that she had used abusive language towards him.'
>
> This will not be hearsay. Although the statement from Mark's son is not made in oral evidence, Mark is not seeking to rely on the statement to show that Janine did in fact use abusive language towards his son. Rather, he is using his son's statement to explain why he went round to Janine's house. The statement made by Mark's son is not being relied on as evidence of a matter stated in it.

A 'statement' is defined in s 115(2) as 'any representation of fact or opinion made by a person by whatever means; and it includes a representation made in a sketch, photofit or other pictorial form'. This definition means that a statement does not necessarily need to be in writing. An oral statement (such as that made by the store detective in the example in (a) at **19.4.1.2** below) will satisfy the definition. Similarly, a statement could be made by way of a gesture, such as someone nodding or shaking his head in answer to a question. A sketch or photofit of a person alleged to have committed an offence, which is put together by the police in conjunction with a victim or a witness, will also be a statement, as will a diagram prepared by a witness (for example, a plan of the layout of a building or shop). A piece of video or CCTV footage will not satisfy this definition, however, since neither would be a statement of fact or opinion made by a *person*. Computerised records may constitute hearsay evidence (see **19.4.1.3** below).

The purpose, or one of the purposes, of the person making the statement must appear to the court to have been to cause another person to believe that the matter, or to cause another person to act (or a machine to operate) on the basis that the matter, is as stated (CJA 2003, s 115(3)).

19.4.1.2 Examples of hearsay evidence in criminal proceedings

Examples of hearsay evidence that commonly arise in criminal proceedings are:

(a) a witness repeating at trial what he has been told by another person;

Example

PC Smith gives evidence for the CPS in a shoplifting case. He says to the court: 'When I arrived at the shop I was told by the store detective that the defendant had left the store without paying for the goods.'

This will be hearsay evidence because the statement by the store detective was not made by him in oral evidence and the statement is being relied upon to show that the defendant left the shop without paying for the goods.

(b) a statement from a witness being read out at trial instead of the witness attending court to give oral evidence;

Example

Suzanne is charged with common assault. Marie witnesses the assault and gives a statement to the police confirming what she saw. Marie is subsequently unavailable to attend Suzanne's trial to give oral evidence. If the CPS seeks to read out Marie's written statement at Suzanne's trial, this will be hearsay evidence, because the statement by Marie was not made by her in oral evidence and the statement is being relied upon to show that Suzanne committed the assault.

(c) a police officer repeating at trial a confession made to him by the defendant at or before the time of the defendant's arrest;

Example

Sean is charged with assault occasioning actual bodily harm. At Sean's trial, the arresting officer tells the court: 'When I arrested the defendant, he told me that he punched the complainant because the complainant had been rude to his girlfriend.'

This will be hearsay evidence because the statement by Sean was not made by him in oral evidence and the statement is being relied upon to show that Sean committed the assault.

(d) a transcript of the defendant's interview at the police station being read out at trial;

Example

Michael is arrested on suspicion of theft and is interviewed at the police station. During the interview, Michael admits to having carried out the theft and is charged with this offence. Michael subsequently pleads not guilty to the charge. The police prepare a written transcript of the interview to be read out at Michael's trial. The written transcript will be hearsay evidence. The statement made by Michael (ie, the admission that he carried out the theft) was not made by him in oral evidence and the statement is being relied upon to show that Michael committed the theft.

(e) a business document (such as an entry in a ledger, a receipt or an invoice) being introduced in evidence at trial.

Example

Rupert is charged with stealing £500 in cash from the safe at the bank where he works. The CPS seeks to adduce in evidence a ledger entry compiled by a clerk at the bank showing that, on the day of the alleged offence, £500 was deposited in the safe. The ledger entry will be hearsay evidence because the statement by the clerk (ie, the entry in the ledger) was not made by him in oral evidence and the statement is being relied upon to show that the £500 was deposited in the safe.

19.4.1.3   Do computer records constitute hearsay evidence?

Records produced by a computer or other machine may constitute hearsay evidence. If a computer is used to store information supplied by a person, and a party then seeks to rely on this information at trial by producing a printout from the computer, this will be hearsay evidence. If, however, a computer is used merely to perform a calculation (for example, an automated ticket machine that calculates the payment due when a driver leaves a car park), any printout which records this calculation this will not be hearsay evidence because the court is not being asked to accept the truth of a matter stated by *a person*. In such a case, a record generated by the computer will be admissible as long as it is proved that any information supplied to the computer to enable it to perform the calculation was correct (CJA 2003, s 129(1)).

Example

Leonard is charged with the theft of a quantity of metal bars from a builder's yard after the police recover a number of bars from his house. Leonard pleads not guilty, and the CPS obtains forensic evidence from tests on samples of the metal to show that the metal bars recovered from Leonard's house are of exactly the same chemical composition as other metal bars that were at the builder's yard but were not stolen. The forensic scientist who carried out the tests used a computer to carry out calculations based on the data obtained from the tests. At Leonard's trial, the CPS produces printouts from the computer to prove the results of the calculations. These printouts will not constitute hearsay evidence since the court is not being asked to accept the truth of a matter stated by a person. It will, however, be necessary for the forensic scientist who carried out the tests to give evidence of the data obtained from the tests, since the printout could not be used to prove that the information fed into the computer was correct, merely that the actual calculations performed by the computer were correct.

19.4.1.4   First-hand and multiple hearsay

Hearsay evidence may be either 'first-hand' hearsay, or 'multiple' hearsay.

Example 1

Jason is on trial for theft. The arresting officer (PC Blake) gives evidence that when he arrested Jason, Jason made the following confession: 'Okay, fair enough, it was me. I only did it for drug money.'

This is first-hand hearsay evidence, because PC Blake is repeating a statement that he heard Jason make. Details of the contents of Jason's statement did not pass through anyone else before getting to PC Blake.

Example 2

Bill sees a burglary take place and recognises Roger as the person committing the burglary. Bill tells Susan that he saw Roger commit the burglary. Susan in turn tells Anthea what she has been told by Bill. Anthea then gives a statement to the police repeating this. If Anthea gives evidence at court in accordance with the contents of her statement, her evidence will be multiple hearsay. She is repeating what she heard from Susan, who had in turn repeated to Anthea what she (Susan) had heard from Bill.

Example 3

Andrea is a bank clerk. She receives a cash deposit of £5,000 from a customer and places this in the bank's safe. She tells Brian, the senior cashier, who in turn tells Fred, the manager. Fred makes a record of the deposit in a ledger. An armed robbery subsequently takes place and the £5,000 is stolen. At the robber's trial, the CPS seeks to use the entry in the ledger to show how much money was in the safe. The entry in the ledger will be multiple hearsay. The details of the amount of money placed in the safe have passed from Andrea to Brian, then from Brian to Fred, and then from Fred into the ledger itself.

The circumstances in which multiple hearsay evidence will be admissible are more limited than for first-hand hearsay (see **19.5.5** below).

19.4.2 When will hearsay evidence be admissible?

Hearsay evidence will be admissible if it falls within one of four categories. Section 114 of the CJA 2003 states:

> (1) In criminal proceedings a statement not made in oral evidence in the proceedings is admissible as evidence of any matter stated if, but only if—
>
>   (a) any provision of this Chapter or any other statutory provision makes it admissible,
>
>   (b) any rule of law preserved by section 118 makes it admissible,
>
>   (c) all parties to the proceedings agree to it being admissible, or
>
>   (d) the court is satisfied that it is in the interests of justice for it to be admissible.

Each of the four circumstances in which hearsay evidence is admissible in criminal proceedings by virtue of s 114 is examined in detail at **19.5** below. A flowchart summarising the admissibility of hearsay evidence in criminal proceedings is provided at **19.10.1** below.

19.5 Exceptions to the rule excluding hearsay evidence

19.5.1 Hearsay admissible under a statutory provision – s 114(1)(a)

19.5.1.1 Introduction

The first category of hearsay evidence which is admissible by virtue of s 114 is hearsay made admissible by virtue of any statutory provision. Hearsay evidence is made admissible as a result of a statutory provision in the following situations:

(a) cases where a witness in unavailable – CJA 2003, s 116 (see **19.5.1.2** below);

(b) business and other documents – CJA 2003, s 117 (see **19.5.1.3** below);

(c) previous inconsistent statements of a witness – CJA 2003, s 119 (see **9.8.3.5**);

(d) previous consistent statements by a witness – CJA 2003, s 120 (see **9.8.2.5**);

(e) reports prepared by experts (if leave of the court is obtained) – CJA 1988, s 30 (see **16.6.4**);

(f) evidence of a confession made by the defendant – PACE 1984, s 76(1) (see **19.5.2.2** below and **20.3.1**);

(g) evidence raised by a defendant of a confession made by a co-accused – PACE 1984, s 76A(1) (see **20.3.3.2**);

(h) statements from a witness which are not in dispute – CJA 1967, s 9 (see **8.4.4**); and

(i) formal admissions – CJA 1967, s 10 (see **16.3.3**).

19.5.1.2 Cases where a witness is unavailable to attend court

Section 116 of the CJA 2003 provides:

> (1) In criminal proceedings a statement not made in oral evidence in the proceedings is admissible as evidence of any matter stated if—

(a)   oral evidence given in the proceedings by the person who made the statement would be admissible as evidence of that matter [ie, the statement must be 'first-hand hearsay', see **19.4.1.4** above],

(b)   the person who made the statement (the relevant person) is identified to the court's satisfaction, and

(c)   any of the five conditions mentioned in subsection (2) is satisfied.

The conditions referred to in s 116(2)(a)–(e) are that:

(a)   the relevant person is dead;

(b)   the relevant person is unfit to be a witness because of his bodily or mental condition;

(c)   the relevant person is outside the United Kingdom and it is not reasonably practicable to secure his attendance;

(d)   the relevant person cannot be found, although such steps as it is reasonably practicable to take to find him have been taken;

(e)   through fear the relevant person does not give oral evidence in the proceedings, either at all or in connection with the subject matter of the statement, *and* the court gives leave for the statement to be given in evidence.

Before s 116(2)(c) is satisfied, the court will want to know what steps have been taken by the party wishing to rely on the evidence from the witness to secure the attendance of the witness at trial, since whether it is fair to admit the statement under s 116(2)(c) depends in part on what efforts should reasonably be made to secure the attendance of the witness (*R v C and K* [2006] EWCA Crim 197).

'Fear' in s 116(2)(e) is 'to be widely construed and includes, for example, fear of the death or injury of another person or of financial loss' (CJA 2003, s 116(3)). The court will give leave under s 116(2)(e) only if it considers that the statement 'ought to be admitted in the interests of justice', having regard to:

(a)   the contents of the statement (ie, how important the statement is in the context of the case as a whole);

(b)   any risk that its admission or exclusion will result in unfairness to any party to the proceedings (and in particular to how difficult it will be to challenge the statement if the relevant person does not give oral evidence and so cannot be cross-examined on his evidence);

(c)   the court's power in appropriate cases to use special measures for the giving of evidence by fearful witnesses (such as the witness giving evidence from behind a screen, or by a live TV link away from the court – see **16.5.4.1**); and

(d)   any other relevant circumstances (s 116(4)).

If at all possible, the court should seek to use special measures to enable the prosecution witness to give evidence rather than allow the statement of the witness to be read out at court, particularly if the evidence to be given by the witness forms a significant part of the case. This will at least give the defendant an opportunity to cross-examine the witness on his account. In *R (Robinson) v Sutton Coldfield Magistrates' Court* [2006] EWHC (Admin) 307, the Divisional Court held that in such a case, it was the responsibility of the defendant's solicitor or counsel to suggest to the court that special measures be employed to enable the witness to come to court to give evidence.

Leave of the court will be required only in the case of s 116(2)(e). If any of the conditions in s 116(2)(a)–(d) is relied on, leave of the court is *not* required (as long as the relevant condition is satisfied).

Example 1

Zoë witnesses an assault and gives a signed statement to the police describing what she saw. Before the case comes to trial, Zoë is killed in a road traffic accident. Zoë's written statement will be admissible in evidence because she satisfies the condition in s 116(2)(a) and oral evidence given by her of what she saw when the assault occurred would have been admissible at trial.

Example 2

Anne witnesses an armed robbery at the bank where she works, and provides a witness statement describing what happened and identifying the robbers. Before the case comes to trial, Anne is involved in a serious road traffic accident and is placed on a life support machine. Anne's witness statement will be admissible in evidence because she satisfies the condition in s 116(2(b) and oral evidence given by her of what she saw when the robbery occurred and her identification of the robbers would have been admissible at trial.

Example 3

Arthur, a serving soldier, witnesses a theft and gives a signed statement to the police describing what he saw. Before the case comes to trial, Arthur is posted abroad. Arthur's written statement will be admissible in evidence because he satisfies the condition in s 116(2)(c) (assuming it is not reasonably practicable to secure his attendance at trial) and oral evidence given by him of what he saw when the theft occurred would have been admissible at trial.

Example 4

Iqbal lives in a shelter for the homeless. He witnesses a road traffic accident in which a young child is seriously injured. Iqbal gives a witness statement to the police, and the driver involved in the accident is subsequently charged with dangerous driving. Before the trial takes place, Iqbal leaves the shelter. Despite making extensive enquiries, the police are unable to locate Iqbal's current whereabouts. Iqbal's written statement will be admissible in evidence because the condition in s 116(2)(d) appears to be satisfied and oral evidence given by Iqbal of what he saw when the accident occurred would have been admissible at trial.

Example 5

Emily witnesses a murder. She gives a signed statement to the police describing what she saw. Before the case comes to trial, Emily receives several anonymous letters telling her that if she gives evidence at court her baby son will be killed. Emily refuses to attend court to give oral evidence of what she saw. Emily's written statement may be admissible in evidence. She appears to satisfy the condition in s 116(2)(e) and oral evidence given by her of what she saw when the murder occurred would have been admissible at trial. However, the trial judge will still need to give leave for her written statement to be admitted in evidence, having regard to the matters listed in s 116(4) above.

Example 6

Fred owns an off-licence. At the end of each day's trading, Fred makes a record in a ledger detailing how much money he has taken that day. He then places the money in a safe at the back of his shop premises. One evening, after making a record in the ledger, but before putting the money in the safe, two robbers enter Fred's shop. Fred is knocked unconscious and the robbers steal the takings. Fred is traumatised by these events and suffers a mental breakdown, which renders him incapable of attending court to give evidence. Fred's entry in the ledger may be admissible in evidence. He appears to satisfy the condition in s 116(2)(b) and oral evidence given by him as to the amount of the day's takings that were stolen in the robbery would have been admissible. (Fred's entry in the ledger will also be admissible under s 117 – see **19.5.1.3** below.)

In all of the above examples it will be necessary for the party wanting to adduce the hearsay evidence to demonstrate that the appropriate condition in s 116(2) is satisfied. By way of illustration, in **Examples 2 and 6** above the court will require medical reports to show that Anne and Fred are unable to give evidence; and in **Example 4** the court will require evidence to show what steps have been taken to attempt to locate Iqbal.

Section 116 applies only to 'first-hand' hearsay. In other words, a statement can be admissible under this section only if the person who made that statement would have been permitted to give oral evidence at trial of the matters contained in the statement. In the six examples given above, the statement of each witness who was unable to come to court to give oral evidence would constitute 'first-hand' hearsay because their evidence had not passed through any other hands and was direct evidence of what they either saw (in the cases of Zoe, Arthur, Emily and Iqbal) or did (in the case of Anne and Fred). Below is an example of 'second-hand' or multiple hearsay. Such evidence is not admissible under s 116.

Example

Lydia witnesses an assault. She tells Jenny what she saw when the assault occurred. Jenny then gives a signed statement to the police repeating what she had been told by Lydia. Before the case comes to trial, Jenny is killed in a road traffic accident. Jenny's statement will *not* be admissible under s 116. Although Jenny satisfies the condition in s 116(2)(a) above, she would not have been permitted to give oral evidence at court as to the contents of her statement because her statement merely repeated what she had been told by Lydia and was itself hearsay. Any evidence given by Jenny would be multiple hearsay and therefore not admissible under s 116 (Jenny's statement may, however, be admissible under s 114(1)(d) – see **19.5.4** below).

A flowchart summarising the operation of s 116 is set out at **19.10.1** below.

19.5.1.3 Business and other documents

Introduction

Section 117 of the CJA 2003 provides:

(1) In criminal proceedings a statement contained in a document is admissible as evidence of any matter stated if—

    (a) oral evidence given in the proceedings would be evidence of that matter,

    (b) the requirements of subsection (2) are satisfied, and

    (c) the requirements of subsection (5) are satisfied, in a case where subsection (4) requires them to be.

The requirements of s 117(2) are that:

(a) the document (or the part of it containing the statement) must have been created or received by a person in the course of a trade, business, profession or other occupation, or as the holder of a paid or unpaid office;

(b) the person who supplied the information contained in the statement (the relevant person) had, or may reasonably be supposed to have had, personal knowledge of the matters dealt with; and

(c) each person (if any) through whom the information was supplied from the relevant person to the person mentioned in paragraph (a) received the information in the course of a trade, business, profession or other occupation, or as the holder of a paid or unpaid office.

The practical effect of s 117 is to make both 'first-hand' and 'multiple' hearsay in certain documents admissible in evidence.

Business records

Section 117 will commonly be used to ensure the admissibility in evidence of business ledgers or records.

Example 1

Robin is charged with armed robbery. The CPS alleges that Robin bought the shotgun used in the robbery from a local gun shop two weeks prior to the robbery taking place. The CPS seeks to adduce in evidence a handwritten receipt given to Robin at the time the shotgun was purchased. The receipt was prepared by Neville, the owner of the gun shop.

Neville → the receipt prepared by Neville → 'first-hand hearsay'

The receipt will be first-hand hearsay evidence and will be admissible under s 117. The receipt is a statement in a document and was prepared by Neville in the course of his business from information about which he had first-hand knowledge, namely Robin's purchase of the shotgun.

Example 2

Paul deposits £500 in a safe at the bank where he works. He tells Geoffrey, a clerk at the bank, who records the deposit in a ledger.

Paul → Geoffrey → Geoffrey's entry in the ledger → 'multiple hearsay'

The ledger is multiple hearsay, but it will be admissible under s 117. The entry in the ledger is a statement in a document and was created by Geoffrey in the course of business. The person who supplied the information contained in the ledger (Paul) had personal knowledge of the making of the deposit.

Example 3

Anthony deposits £1,000 in a safe at the betting shop where he works. He tells Shona, one of his colleagues. Shona passes this information on to Gavin, the owner of the shop, who records the deposit in a ledger.

Anthony → Shona → Gavin → Gavin's entry in the ledger → 'multiple hearsay'

The entry in the ledger is multiple hearsay, but it will be admissible under s 117. The entry in the ledger is a statement in a document which was created by Gavin in the course of business. The person who supplied the information contained in the ledger (Anthony) had personal knowledge of the making of the deposit, and the person through whom the information was passed (Shona) received the information in the course of business.

Example 4

Quentin is charged with theft of £5,000 in cash after the police find this money in a suitcase at Quentin's flat. Quentin's defence is that he won the money following a successful bet on the horses which he placed two days earlier at a local bookmakers. Quentin produces a betting slip to support this. The betting slip is a statement in a document. It is therefore hearsay evidence, but will be admissible by virtue of s 117 if Quentin can show that the betting slip was created by a person at the bookmakers' shop where Quentin placed the bet. If the person who created the betting slip was not the person to whom Quentin actually spoke when the bet was made, Quentin will need to show that the information on the betting slip was supplied by the person he dealt with, and that anyone through whom this information passed before the slip was actually created also worked for the bookmakers.

Example 5

Younis is charged with the theft of a car from Shoaib. Younis claims to have bought the car from a local garage. Younis produces a sales receipt for the car to support this defence. The sales receipt is a statement in a document and is therefore hearsay evidence. It will be admissible by virtue of s 117 if Younis can show that the sales receipt was created by a person at the garage from which he purchased the car. If the person who created the sales receipt was not the same person with whom Younis actually dealt when he purchased the car, Younis will need to show that the information on the sales receipt was supplied by the person with whom he dealt, and that anyone through whom this information passed before the receipt was created also worked at the garage.

Statements prepared for use in criminal proceedings

If the statement was prepared for 'the purposes of pending or contemplated criminal proceedings, or for a criminal investigation' (s 117(4)), the requirements of s 117(5) must be satisfied. The requirements of s 117(5) will be satisfied if:

(a)   any of the five conditions mentioned in s 116(2) is satisfied (see **19.5.2** above); or

(b)   the relevant person cannot reasonably be expected to have any recollection of the matters dealt with in the statement (having regard to the length of time since he supplied the information and all other circumstances).

Example 1

Roberta witnesses an assault. She tells PC Smith what she saw. PC Smith prepares a statement for Roberta to sign, setting out what Roberta told him. Before Roberta has the opportunity to check and sign the statement, she is killed in a road traffic accident (had she been able to sign the statement before her death, it would have been admissible under s 116(2)(a) – see **19.5.1.2** above). The written statement prepared by PC Smith will be multiple hearsay, but will be admissible in evidence under s 117. The written statement is a statement in a document. PC Smith created the statement in the course of his profession as a police officer and the person who supplied the information contained in the statement (Roberta) had personal knowledge of the matters dealt with in the statement. As the statement was prepared for the purpose of criminal proceedings, the requirements of s 117(5) must be satisfied. These requirements are satisfied because Roberta is dead and so satisfies s 116(2)(a).

Example 2

A burglary occurs at a shop. The police ask Charles, the owner of the shop, to prepare a list of all the items taken in the burglary. Charles tells PC Briggs what he thinks was taken in the burglary and PC Briggs writes out a list. Two years later the police arrest Robert and charge him with the burglary. At Robert's trial, the CPS seeks to use the list to prove what was taken in the burglary. Charles is able to attend trial to give evidence but, given the time which has elapsed since the time of the burglary, he is unable to recall what he told PC Briggs should go in the list. The list of stolen items compiled by PC Briggs is multiple hearsay but should nevertheless be admissible in evidence under s 117. The list of stolen items is a statement in a document. PC Briggs created the list in the course of his job as a police officer and the person who supplied the information contained in the list (Charles) had personal knowledge of the matters dealt with in the list. As the list was complied for use in contemplated criminal proceedings, one of the requirements in s 117(5) must be satisfied. These requirements are satisfied because, although Charles can attend court to give oral evidence, due to the time which has elapsed since the list was complied, he cannot reasonably be expected to have any recollection of the matters dealt with in the statement.

Can the court refuse to admit a statement under s 117?

The court retains a discretionary power to make a direction that a statement shall not be admitted under s 117 (CJA 2003, s 117(6)). The court may make such a direction if it is satisfied that the statement's reliability as evidence for the purpose for which it is tendered is doubtful in view of:

(a) its contents;

(b) the source of the information contained in it;

(c) the way in which or the circumstances in which the information was supplied or received; or

(d) the way in which or the circumstances in which the document concerned was created or received (CJA 2003, s 117(7)).

A flowchart summarising the operation of s 117 is set out at **19.10.3** below.

19.5.1.4 Human rights considerations

Article 6(3)(d) of the ECHR provides that a defendant has the right 'to examine or have examined witnesses against him'. Sections 116 and 117 of the CJA 2003 (see **19.5.1.2** and **19.5.1.3** above) allow the CPS to adduce evidence given by witnesses who will not attend court to give oral evidence upon which they may be cross-examined. Do these sections breach Article 6(3)(d)?

In *R v Trivedi* [1997] EHRLR 521, the European Court of Human Rights held that the statutory provisions which ss 116 and 117 replaced (and which were worded in a very similar way) were compatible with Article 6. The same conclusion was reached by the Court of Appeal in *R v Xhabri* [2005] EWCA Crim 3135. The Court held that Article 6(3)(d) did not give a defendant an absolute right to examine every witness whose testimony was adduced against him. Rather, Article 6(3)(d) would be breached only if the fairness of the trial required that a witness be available for cross-examination, and this could be determined only by looking at the facts of each individual case.

In *R v Campbell* [2005] EWCA Crim 2078, the Court of Appeal found that there was no automatic breach of the defendant's right to a fair trial even when the sole substantial evidence against the defendant was hearsay evidence, provided it was in the interests of justice for such evidence to be admitted.

In *R v Al-Khawaja* [2005] EWCA Crim 2697, the defendant was convicted on two counts of indecent assault. The sole witness to one of the assaults was the victim of the assault, who had since died. The trial judge permitted her statement to be read in evidence by virtue of s 116(2)(a). The defendant argued that this breached his right to a fair trial under Article 6(3)(d). The Court of Appeal held that where a witness who was the sole witness to a crime had made a statement to be used in the prosecution of that crime and had since died, there would be a strong public interest in the admission of the statement in evidence so that the prosecution might proceed. Whilst that public interest should not be permitted to override the requirement for the defendant to have a fair trial, the provision in Article 6(3)(d) stipulating that the defendant should be able to cross-examine the witness against him was merely one part of a fair trial. If, as in this case, such a witness could not be cross-examined, it was necessary to examine whether the proceedings as a whole were fair. The Court of Appeal concluded that the proceedings as a whole were fair, and the defendant had received a fair trial, because the defendant had been given the opportunity at trial to attack the credibility of the victim's statement both through expert evidence and by exposing the inconsistencies between the victim's account and evidence given by other witnesses.

In *R (Robinson) v Sutton Coldfield Magistrates' Court* (see **19.5.1.2** above), the defendant was charged with assault occasioning actual bodily harm. The magistrates gave leave for the complainant's statement to be admitted under s 116(2)(e) (see **19.5.1.2** above) on the basis that, since the assault took place, the complainant had moved house and she was fearful that, if she attended trial to give oral evidence, the defendant might follow her home and discover her new address. Following conviction, the defendant appealed on the basis that his rights under Article 6(3)(d) had been breached because he was denied the opportunity to cross-examine the complainant. The Divisional Court rejected his appeal. The court said that there was other evidence against the defendant in addition to that given by the complainant, and the defendant had himself accepted when interviewed that the complainant was an honest witness.

There are provisions in the CJA 2003 which permit a party to challenge the credibility of evidence adduced under ss 116 and 117 (see **19.6** below), and in the Crown Court a judge has the power in certain circumstances to stop a case based largely on unconvincing hearsay evidence (see **19.7** below). A court will also have the power to exclude hearsay evidence under s 126 of the Act if the hearsay evidence is of limited importance and its admission would take up an inordinate amount of time (see **19.8** below). In addition, the court will always have a general discretion to exclude any prosecution evidence under s 78 of PACE 1984, if the admission of the evidence would have such an adverse effect on the fairness of proceedings that the court ought not to admit it (see **Chapter 21**).

19.5.2 Common law exceptions to the rule against hearsay evidence – s 114(1)(b)

19.5.2.1 Introduction

Section 118(1) of the CJA 2003 preserves several common law exceptions to the rule excluding hearsay evidence. The most important exceptions preserved by s 118(1) are:

(a)   evidence of a confession made by the defendant (see **19.5.2.2** below);

(b)   evidence admitted as part of the *res gestae* (see **19.5.2.3** below);

(c)   opinion evidence from an expert based on previously published works (see **19.5.2.4** below); and

(d)   statements made by a party to a common enterprise being admissible against another party to the enterprise (see **19.5.2.5** below).

Other common law exceptions which are preserved include matters of general public information, evidence concerning a family's reputation or tradition, and public documents.

Section 118(2) provides that, with the exception of the rules preserved by s 118(1), the common law rules governing the admissibility of hearsay evidence are abolished.

19.5.2.2 Confessions

Prior to the enactment of the CJA 2003, evidence that the defendant had made a confession was admissible at common law as an exception to the rule excluding hearsay evidence. This rule was subsequently codified by s 76(1) of PACE 1984, which provides:

(1)   In any proceedings a confession made by an accused person may be given in evidence against him insofar as it is relevant to any matter in issue in the proceedings and is not excluded by the court in pursuance of this section.

A confession which is prima facie admissible under s 76(1) may be inadmissible as a result either of s 76(2), or of the court exercising its power to exclude unlawfully obtained evidence under s 78 (see **20.4** and **20.5**).

Section 118(1) preserves the common law rule that a confession made by a defendant will be admissible in evidence against him, even if the confession is hearsay evidence.

19.5.2.3   Evidence admitted as part of the *res gestae*

The common law principle of evidence being admitted as part of the *res gestae* (sometimes referred to in other jurisdictions as the 'excited utterance rule') provided that a statement made contemporaneously with an event would be admissible as an exception to the hearsay rule because the spontaneity of the statement meant that any possibility of concoction could be disregarded.

Example

Gerry is charged with murder. The CPS alleges that Gerry shot his victim with a rifle. Gerry's defence is that the rifle went off by accident as he was examining it. Gerry wants to call a witness to give evidence on his behalf who will say that, just after the gun went off, Gerry said: 'Oh God, my hand just slipped!' This would be hearsay evidence, but would be admissible as part of the *res gestae*.

Section 118(1) of the CJA 2003 preserves the common law rule admitting evidence that forms part of the *res gestae*. Such statements will now be admissible if one of the following conditions is satisfied:

(a)   the statement was made by a person so emotionally overpowered by an event that the possibility of concoction or distortion can be disregarded;

(b)   the statement accompanied an act which can properly be evaluated as evidence only if considered in conjunction with the statement; or

(c)   the statement relates to a physical sensation or a mental state (such as intention or emotion) (CJA 2003, s 118(1)).

19.5.2.4   Expert evidence

Section 118(1) permits an expert to give opinion evidence at trial which is based on other published works within that expert's body of expertise. For example, a pathologist giving evidence in a murder case as to the cause of death may state that, in his opinion, the cause of death was due to the deceased suffocating after being exposed to excessive quantities of a particular noxious gas. The expert will be permitted to draw on the findings of research by others (which will therefore be hearsay) to explain to the court what would constitute an excessive quantity of such gas. This rule is examine more fully in **Chapter 16** (which looks more generally at the admissibility of expert evidence in criminal proceedings).

19.5.2.5   Statements made by a party to a common enterprise being admissible against another party to the enterprise

Section 118(1) of the CJA 2003 preserves the common law rule whereby a statement made by a party to a common enterprise is admissible against another party to the enterprise as evidence of any matter stated. This rule allows the actions or comments of one party to be used in evidence against the other, and usually arises in cases of alleged conspiracy.

Example

In *R v Singh* [2006] EWCA Crim 660, the defendant was convicted of conspiracy to kidnap. The CPS alleged that the defendant was at the time of the kidnapping the user of two mobile phones, which he used to make and receive a number of calls from his co-conspirators at or around the time the kidnapping took place. The Court of Appeal held that the trial judge had properly allowed the CPS to adduce in evidence against him the entries in mobile phone records belonging to other conspirators which showed the calls that been made between these phones and the phones owned by the defendant. The entries were hearsay evidence, but were admissible by virtue of s 118(1) because they constituted a statement made by a co-conspirator which implicated the defendant.

19.5.3 Hearsay admissible by agreement – s 114(1)(c)

This is largely self-explanatory. If all the parties in the case agree, any form of hearsay evidence can be admissible in evidence.

Example

Brian is charged with unlawful wounding. The CPS alleges that Brian punched someone who pushed in front of him whilst he was waiting to get off a bus. Brian accepts that he punched the other person, but says that he was only acting in self-defence after this person had attacked him. Trevor, the bus driver, is to give evidence for the prosecution. Trevor will say that, after Brain had got off the bus, one of the other passengers approached Trevor and identified Brian by name as one of the people involved in the incident. Although Trevor's evidence will be hearsay (because he will be repeating what he was told by the other passenger), Brian will not object to such evidence being adduced. Brian does not dispute being identified as one of the people involved in the incident. His defence will be that, although he was involved, he was only acting in self-defence.

19.5.4 Hearsay admissible in the interests of justice – s 114(1)(d)

The most significant change made to the admissibility of hearsay evidence by the CJA 2003 has been to introduce a 'catch-all' provision, allowing the court to admit hearsay evidence that would not otherwise be admissible if it is in the interests of justice to do so. The objective of this provision is to give the courts a very wide discretion to admit hearsay evidence which is cogent and reliable, and then to allow the magistrates or jury to determine the weight to be attached to such evidence.

In deciding whether to admit hearsay evidence under s 114(1)(d), the court must have regard to the following factors:

(a)   how much probative value the statement has (assuming it to be true) in relation to a matter in issue in the proceedings, or how valuable it is for the understanding of other evidence in the case;

(b)   what other evidence has been, or can be, given on the matter or evidence mentioned in para (a);

(c)   how important the matter or evidence mentioned in para (a) is in the context of the case as a whole;

(d)   the circumstances in which the statement was made;

(e)   how reliable the maker of the statement appears to be;

(f)   how reliable the evidence of the making of the statement appears to be;

(g)   whether oral evidence of the matter stated can be given and, if not, why not;

(h)   the amount of difficulty involved in challenging the statement; and

(i)   the extent to which that difficulty would be likely to prejudice the party facing it (CJA 2003, s 114(2)).

In assessing these factors, the court will need to have regard to the defendant's right to a fair trial enshrined in Article 6 of the ECHR (see **1.8.3**).

The Court of Appeal considered the application of s 114(1)(d) and s 114(2) in *R v Taylor* [2006] EWCA Crim 260. The defendant was charged with causing grievous bodily harm with intent, the allegation being that he (along with a number of others) attacked his victim by repeatedly kicking and punching him in the head. The defendant admitted being present but denied any involvement in the attack. Two witnesses (J and N) who were previously known to the defendant, named the defendant as having taken part in the attack, having been told this by another. N was told the name by her ex-boyfriend who knew the defendant, and N then told J. There was other eye-witness and forensic evidence against the defendant. J and N gave their evidence in chief by video-recorded interviews (see **16.5.4.1**), and the defendant applied under s 114(2) to exclude the reference in the interviews to the defendant's name on the basis that this amounted to inadmissible hearsay evidence (and multiple hearsay in the case of J).

The trial judge said he was unable to apply all the factors in s 114(2) because he knew nothing about N's ex-boyfriend and so could not form a view on his reliability. Further, the circumstances in which J and N were informed of the defendant's name were unclear, and it was not known whether N's ex-boyfriend could be identified and attend court to give evidence as to the circumstances. The trial judge held that, having regard to the factors in s 114(2), it was in the interests of justice to admit the hearsay evidence from J and N, and that admitting such evidence would not have an adverse effect on the fairness of the trial because it was open to the defendant to give evidence challenging the assertion that he had participated in the assault.

The defendant appealed on the basis that the trial judge had failed to reach a conclusion on all nine factors set out in s 114(2) and should not therefore have admitted the hearsay evidence from J and N. The Court of Appeal rejected this argument, stating that the judge was not obliged to come to a conclusion on all of the factors before admitting the hearsay evidence. The Court held that to reach a proper conclusion on whether the evidence should be admitted, the trial judge was required to exercise his judgment in the light of the factors in s 114(2), give consideration to them and to any other factors he considered relevant, and then to assess their significance and the weight that in his judgment they carried. The Court found that the trial judge had correctly followed this approach. The hearsay evidence from J and N had been properly admitted.

In *Maher v DPP* [2006] EWHC (Admin) 1271, the High Court gave further guidance on the circumstances in which s 114(1)(d) might be used to introduce hearsay evidence at trial. The appellant (M) appealed by way of case stated against her convictions for careless driving, failing to stop at the scene of an accident and failing to report an accident to the police. The DPP had alleged that, whilst reversing her car in a car park, M had struck a parked car owned by a third party (X), causing damage to that car. The DPP further alleged that M then left the scene of the accident without leaving her contact details. An individual claimed to have seen the accident as it occurred and left a note on X's car with the registration number of the car that allegedly struck X's car. X's girlfriend saw the note and immediately rang the police, who made a record of the contents of the note on their incident log. Thereafter M was traced through the registration given in the note, and she admitted in a police interview that she had driven her car in the car park on the day that the alleged accident occurred. She claimed, however, that she did not hit X's car. At the date of trial the original note was lost and the DPP sought to adduce the police log as hearsay evidence pursuant to s 117 (see **19.5.1.3** above). M challenged the admissibility of the log and contended that the requirements under s 117(2)(c) for the person supplying the information to have been acting in the course of a trade or business were not met. The magistrates' court rejected M's submission and convicted her.

The High Court held that the magistrates' court erred in admitting the log as hearsay evidence pursuant to s 117. The log was based upon the information supplied by X's girlfriend. She was not acting in the course of her business when she informed the police of the information that she received via the note. However, the court went on to say that the evidence contained in the log fell within the magistrates' court's discretion under s 114(1)(d), and it would therefore have been appropriate to admit the police log as hearsay evidence in the interests of justice.

Other examples of when the court *may* be prepared to admit hearsay evidence under s 114(1)(d) are set out below.

Example 1

Sean witnesses a bank robbery taking place and makes mental note of the registration number of the car used by the criminals to make their getaway. Sean is too frightened to go to the police station to make a statement and instead makes an anonymous telephone call to the police, giving them the car registration number. Sean's anonymous telephone call is automatically tape-recorded. Acting on this information, the police trace the car (which was itself stolen). The police obtain fingerprints from the car which belong to members of a well-known criminal gang whom the police suspect to be behind the bank robbery.

Will the transcript of the tape-recording of Sean's anonymous telephone call be admissible in evidence? The recording will not be admissible under s 116 because the person making the statement (Sean) cannot be identified. The statement will not be admissible under s 117 because, as the transcript was prepared for the purpose of criminal proceedings, the requirements of s 116 need to be satisfied (see **19.5.1.3** above). These requirements are not met because Sean cannot be identified. The court may exercise its discretion to admit the transcript in evidence under s 114(1)(d), however. In deciding whether to admit the transcript in evidence under this provision, the court will need to apply the factors listed at (a)–(i) above.

Example 2

Tony is charged with assault. Richard, who is not charged, admits to Stephen that he carried out the assault. Tony and Richard are similar in appearance. Tony's defence is one of mistaken identity. He will ask the court to exercise its discretion under s 114(1)(d) to allow Stephen to give evidence of the confession that was made to him by Richard.

19.5.5 Additional requirements for the admissibility of multiple hearsay evidence

If the hearsay evidence on which a party seeks to rely is 'multiple hearsay' (see **19.4.1.4** above), such evidence may be adduced only if:

(a)   it is admissible under s 117 – business documents (see **19.5.1.3** above);

(b)   it is admissible under s 119 – a previous inconsistent statement by a witness (see **9.8.3.5**);

(c)   it is admissible under s 120 – a previous consistent statement by a witness (see **9.8.2.5**);

(d)   all the parties agree to it being admitted (see **19.5.3** above); or

(e)   the court is satisfied that the value of the evidence in question, taking into account how reliable the evidence appears to be, is so high that the interests of justice require the later evidence to be admissible (CJA 2003, s 121).

19.6 Challenging the credibility of hearsay evidence

If hearsay evidence is admitted by the court, the maker of the statement will not be in attendance at court to give oral evidence. This will deprive the other party of the opportunity to cross-examine the maker of the statement in an attempt to undermine that person's credibility as a witness. In such a case, however, s 124 of the CJA 2003 permits the following evidence to be admissible:

(a)   any evidence which (if the witness had given oral evidence) would have been admissible as relevant to his credibility as a witness; and

(b)   with the leave of the court, any evidence which (if the witness had given oral evidence) could have been put to him in cross-examination as relevant to his credibility as a witness (for example, evidence that the witness had previous convictions for offences where he had been untruthful, such as perjury).

Example

Peter is on trial in the Crown Court for theft. Part of the prosecution case consists of a witness statement from Julia, Peter's ex-girlfriend, who claims to have witnessed Peter committing the theft. Julia's witness statement has been admitted as hearsay evidence under s 116(2)(b) because Julia had a serious accident just prior to the trial and is in a critical condition in hospital. Peter alleges that Julia fabricated her statement to get revenge on him after he broke off their relationship. Julia also has two previous convictions for offences of perjury. As Julia will not be attending trial to give oral evidence, Peter will be unable to put to her in cross-examination that she has a grudge against him and so has a reason for giving a false statement. Neither will he be able to cross-examine her about her previous convictions (assuming the judge would have given him leave to do so – see **Chapter 22**). Peter will, however, be able to place before the jury evidence of his breaking off the relationship to show that Julia might have had a grudge against him, as this is a matter relevant to Julia's credibility as a witness. Peter will also seek leave to place before the jury evidence of Julia's previous convictions, as again these are matters relevant to her credibility as a witness and are matters which could, with the leave of the court, have been put to her in cross-examination.

19.7 Stopping the case where evidence is unconvincing

In a Crown Court trial, if the judge is satisfied at any time after the close of the prosecution case that:

(a)   the case against the defendant is based wholly or partly on hearsay evidence; and

(b)   the hearsay evidence is so unconvincing that, considering its importance to the case against the defendant, his conviction of the offence would be unsafe,

the judge must direct the jury to acquit the defendant (or discharge the jury if the judge considers there ought to be a retrial) (CJA 2003, s 125).

Example

Erica is charged with unlawful wounding. The only evidence against Erica is from two witnesses who claim to have seen Erica commit the alleged assault. Both witnesses gave statements to the police but have since disappeared, despite the police having taken steps to find them. The statements are admissible as hearsay evidence under s 116(2)(d), as the makers of the statements cannot be found although such steps as it is reasonably practical to take to find them have been taken. However, the quality of the identification evidence given in the statements is weak and, at trial, Erica adduces evidence under s 124 (see **19.6** above) that both witnesses have previous convictions for offences involving deception. If the trial judge considers that the evidence provided by the statements is so unconvincing that it would render any conviction unsafe, he must direct the jury to acquit Erica.

19.8   The general discretion to exclude evidence

Section 126(1) of the CJA 2003 gives the court a general discretion to refuse to admit a statement that constitutes hearsay evidence if 'the court is satisfied that the case for excluding the statement, taking account of the danger that to admit it would result in undue waste of time, substantially outweighs the case for admitting it, taking account of the value of the evidence'.

This provision allows a court to exclude a piece of hearsay evidence if the evidence is of limited importance to the case and an inordinate amount of time would be spent in the evidence actually being given. In *R v Xhabri* (see **19.5.1.4** above), however, the Court of Appeal said that s 126 could be used more generally to exclude hearsay evidence where the court considered that the admission of such evidence would have an adverse effect on the fairness of the trial. This much wider interpretation of s 126 was upheld by the Court of Appeal in *R v C and K* (see **19.5.1.2** above). The Court interpreted s 126 as giving the court 'a general discretion to exclude evidence in criminal proceedings'.

Section 126(2) provides that nothing in the CJA 2003 concerning the admissibility of hearsay evidence prejudices the court's overriding general power to exclude evidence under s 78 of PACE 1984. The provisions of s 78 are examined in detail in **Chapter 21**, but essentially s 78 provides the court with a discretionary power to exclude evidence if the admission of such evidence would have such an adverse effect on the fairness of proceedings that it ought to be excluded.

19.9   Procedure for admitting hearsay evidence

19.9.1   Introduction

The procedural rules to be followed should a party seek to rely on hearsay evidence at trial (or to challenge the admissibility of hearsay evidence on which another party seeks to rely) are contained in Part 34 of the Criminal Procedure Rules (CrimPR). These rules do not, however, apply in all cases when a party wishes to use hearsay evidence at trial. The rules in Part 34 only apply to cases where:

(a)   it is in the interests of justice for the hearsay evidence to be admissible (s 114(1)(d));

(b)   the witness is unavailable to attend court (s 116);

(c)   the evidence is contained in a business or other document (s 117); or

(d)   the evidence is multiple hearsay (s 121) (CrimPR, r 34.1).

For hearsay evidence which is admissible on any other grounds, the procedural rules contained in Part 34 do not apply. If, for example, the defendant made a confession at the time of his arrest, the rules in Part 34 will not apply should the CPS seek to rely on the arresting officer repeating details of that confession when he gives evidence at the defendant's trial. Similarly, the rules in Part 34 will not apply if the hearsay evidence is admissible under any of the preserved common law exceptions to the rule excluding hearsay evidence. The significance of this is that, if the hearsay evidence to be adduced at trial does not fall within one or more of the four sections noted at (a) to (d) above, the party seeking to rely on that evidence will not need to serve on the other party notice of its intention to rely on such evidence (see below).

A party wishing to adduce hearsay evidence to which Part 34 applies, or to oppose another party's application to introduce such evidence, must give notice of its intention to do this both to the court and to the other parties in the case (CrimPR, r 34.2). Notice must be given using a set of prescribed forms which are set out at **19.12** below. As part of the standard directions that will be given in both the magistrates' court (see **Chapter 8**) and the Crown Court (see **Chapter 10**), the court will impose time limits for the CPS and the defendant to give notice of their intention to adduce hearsay evidence at trial. The relevant time limits are set out in r 34.3 (for the CPS) and r 34.4 (for the defendant). If a party opposes the introduction of hearsay evidence, it must serve a counter notice. The time limits for serving a counter notice are set out in r 34.5.

19.9.2   Magistrates' court

In the magistrates' court, if the CPS wishes to adduce hearsay evidence to which Part 34 applies, it must serve a notice of intention to introduce hearsay evidence at the same time as it complies with its initial duty to disclose to the defendant any unused material it has (CrimPR, r 34.3(a)). If the defendant wishes to oppose this, he must serve a notice opposing the prosecution notice within *14 days* of receiving this notice (CrimPR, r 34.5).

If the defendant seeks to rely on hearsay evidence to which Part 34 applies, he must serve a notice of intention to introduce hearsay evidence within *14 days* of the date on which the CPS complies with its initial duty to disclose to him any unused material it has (CrimPR, r 34.4). If the CPS wishes to oppose this, it must serve a notice opposing the defendant's notice within *14 days* of receiving this (CrimPR, r 34.5).

19.9.3   Crown Court

If the prosecution seek to adduce hearsay evidence to which Part 34 applies, they must serve on the defendant notice of their intention to do so within *14 days* of service of the prosecution case papers (CrimPR, r 34.3(b)). The defendant then has *14 days* from receipt of this notice to serve a notice opposing the prosecution notice (CrimPR, r 34.5).

The defendant has *14 days* from the date on which the CPS complies with its initial duty of disclosure in respect of unused material to make an application to adduce hearsay evidence at trial (CrimPr, r 34.4). The CPS will then have *14 days* from the receipt of this notice to serve a notice opposing this (CrimPR, r 34.5).

19.9.4   Must the parties comply with the above time limits?

Rule 34.7 of the Criminal Procedure Rules permits the court to dispense with the requirement to give notice of hearsay evidence, to allow notice to be given orally rather than in writing, and to shorten or extend the time limits for giving notice. In *R (Robinson) v Sutton Coldfield Magistrates' Court* [2006] EWHC (Admin) 307 (see **19.5.1.2** above), the Divisional Court upheld permission given by the magistrates to allow the CPS to adduce a witness statement from the complainant as hearsay evidence when the application was made the day before trial.

19.9.5   Determining the admissibility of hearsay evidence

When either the CPS or the defendant has made an application to adduce hearsay evidence at trial, and this application is opposed by the other party, the court will usually determine the admissibility of such evidence at a pre-trial hearing. In the magistrates' court, this is likely to be at the case management hearing/pre-trial review, or at a specific pre-trial hearing to resolve disputes about the admissibility of evidence (see **Chapter 8**). In the Crown Court, this is likely to be at the plea and case management hearing, or at a specific pre-trial hearing (see **Chapter 10**).

Completed examples of the forms used in both the magistrates' court and the Crown Court to apply to give notice of an intention to introduce hearsay evidence or to oppose the introduction of such evidence are set out at **19.12** below.

19.10 Procedural flowcharts

19.10.1 Criminal Justice Act 2003, s 114

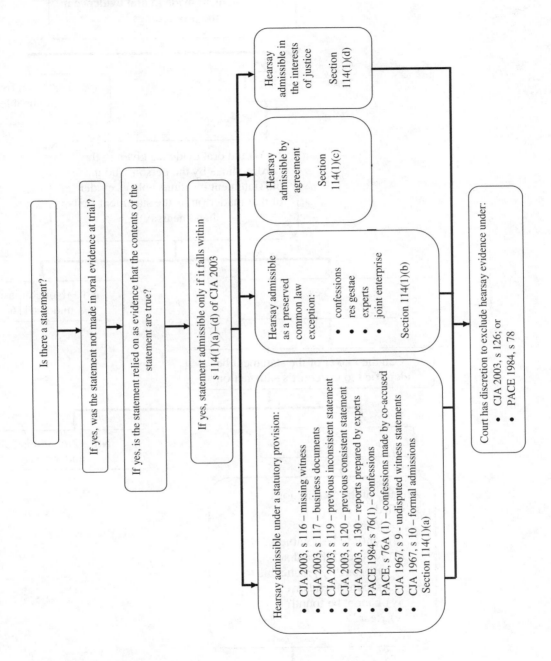

Is there a statement?

If yes, was the statement not made in oral evidence at trial?

If yes, is the statement relied on as evidence that the contents of the statement are true?

If yes, statement admissible only if it falls within s 114(1)(a)–(d) of CJA 2003

Hearsay admissible as a preserved common law exception:

- confessions
- res gestae
- experts
- joint enterprise

Section 114(1)(b)

Hearsay admissible by agreement

Section 114(1)(c)

Hearsay admissible in the interests of justice

Section 114(1)(d)

Hearsay admissible under a statutory provision:

- CJA 2003, s 116 – missing witness
- CJA 2003, s 117 – business documents
- CJA 2003, s 119 – previous inconsistent statement
- CJA 2003, s 120 – previous consistent statement
- CJA 2003, s 130 – reports prepared by experts
- PACE 1984, s 76(1) – confessions
- PACE, s 76A (1) – confessions made by co-accused
- CJA 1967, s 9 - undisputed witness statements
- CJA 1967, s 10 – formal admissions

Section 114(1)(a)

Court has discretion to exclude hearsay evidence under:

- CJA 2003, s 126; or
- PACE 1984, s 78

19.10.2 Criminal Justice Act 2003, s 116 – the 'missing witness'

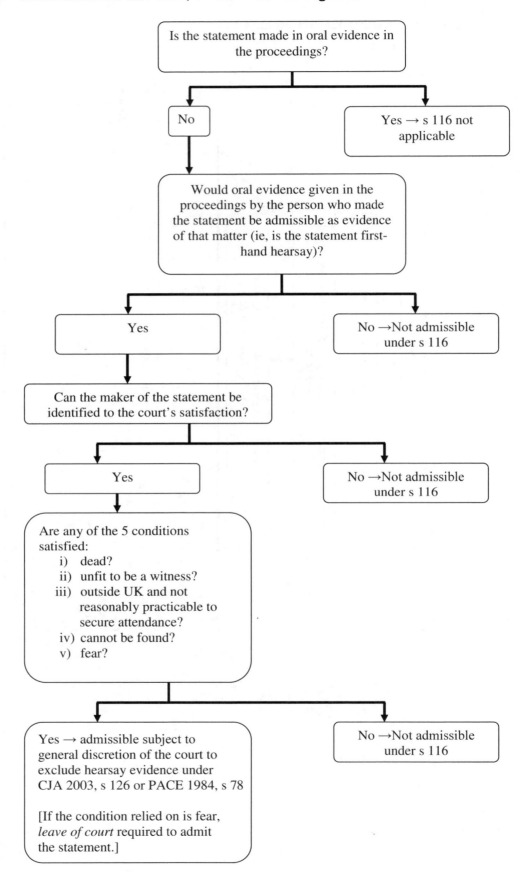

19.10.3 Criminal Justice Act 2003, s 117 – business documents and documents prepared for criminal proceedings

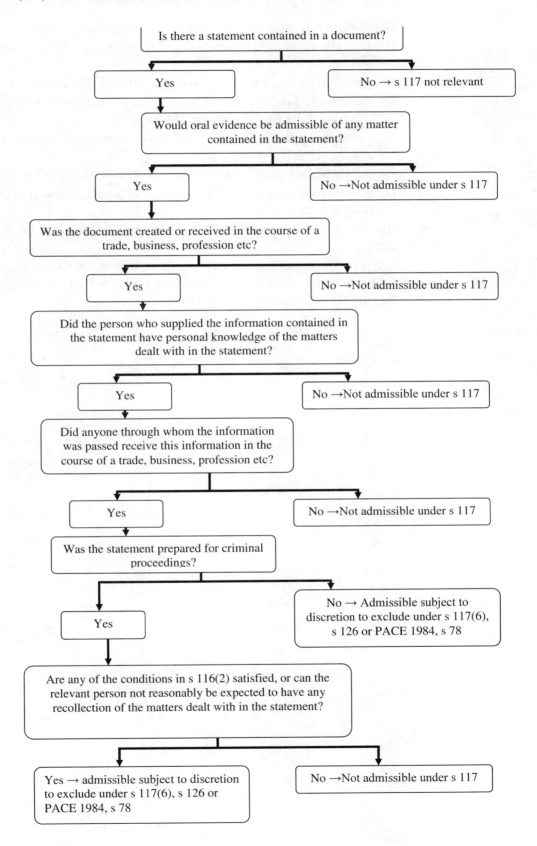

19.11 Checklist

At the end of this chapter you should be able to explain:

- the statutory definition of hearsay evidence in the CJA 2003;
- the four circumstances in which hearsay evidence is admissible in criminal proceedings:
  - evidence admissible by virtue of a statutory provision (s 114(1)(a));
  - common law exceptions to the rule excluding hearsay evidence preserved by the CJA 2003 (s 114(1)(b));
  - evidence which all the parties agree shall be admissible (s 114(1)(c)); and
  - evidence which it is in the interests of justice to admit (s 114(1)(d)).
- the power of the court to exclude hearsay evidence that would otherwise be admissible at trial;
- the way in which the credibility of hearsay evidence may be challenged at trial;
- the procedural rules to be followed if a party wishes to rely upon hearsay evidence at trial, or to challenge hearsay evidence that another party seeks to rely upon at trial (CrimPR, Part 34).

19.12 Key forms

19.12.1 Introduction

Two forms are set out below:

(a)   notice of intention to introduce hearsay evidence (see **19.12.2**); and

(b)   notice of opposition to the introduction of hearsay evidence (see **19.12.3**).

Each form has been completed to illustrate the level of detail required when these forms are being filled in.

19.12.2 Notice of intention to introduce hearsay evidence

<table>
<tr>
<td colspan="2">
Notice of intention to introduce hearsay evidence
Under s 114, Criminal Justice Act 2003

(Criminal Procedure Rules, rr 34.2, 68.20(1))
</td>
</tr>
<tr>
<td colspan="2">
This form must be used to give notice of intention to introduce hearsay evidence on one or more of the grounds set out in s 114(1)(d), s 116, s 117 and s 121, Criminal Justice Act 2003.
</td>
</tr>
<tr>
<td>
Details of party giving notice

Surname: Crown Prosecution Service

Forename(s): N/A
Address: 7 Market Street, Christlethorpe, Guildshire
</td>
<td>
State the name and address of the party giving notice of hearsay evidence. (If in custody give address where detained)
</td>
</tr>
<tr>
<td>
Case Details

The Crown Court at Christlethorpe
Case Reference Number CH/0931/07
Name of Judge: HHJ Hutton

Date the trial or proceedings is due to start/started:
7th April 2007

Name the prosecuting agency (if relevant): CPS
Name of defendant(s): Alison Davies
</td>
<td>
Enter the name of the Court and the case no.
</td>
</tr>
<tr>
<td>
Charges:
Theft of gold necklace (valued at £1,500) from Scriveners jewellery shop on 15th November 2006
</td>
<td>
Give brief details of the charges to which this notice applies.
</td>
</tr>
<tr>
<td colspan="2">
To the named recipient(s) of this notice: Alison Davies
</td>
</tr>
<tr>
<td colspan="2">
I give you notice of my intention to introduce hearsay evidence, details of which are set out below, in these proceedings.
</td>
</tr>
</table>

Grounds for introducing the hearsay evidence

On which of the following grounds do you intend to introduce the hearsay evidence?

(a) ☐	It is in the interests of justice for it to be admissible.	Tick as appropriate to show which of ss 114(1)(d), 116, 117 or 121 of the CJA 2003 you rely on to introduce the evidence.
(b) ☑	The witness is unavailable to attend.	Where box (a) is ticked you must specify below which of the factors set out in s 114(2), CJA 2003 are relevant and explain how they are relevant.
(c) ☐	It is in the interests of justice for it to be admissible.	
(d) ☐	The evidence is multiple hearsay.	

Further details of grounds:

Criminal Justice Act 2003, s 116(2)(c) – that the relevant person is outside the UK and it is not reasonably practicable to secure her attendance. The witness in question has returned to live and work in Australia, and will not be returning to the UK in the foreseeable future.

Details of hearsay evidence

The details of the hearsay evidence are as follows:	Give brief details of the evidence that you want to introduce as hearsay evidence
Written witness statement from Kylie Donovan who was a shop assistant at Scriveners jewellers and who witnessed the defendant pick up the gold necklace from a display stand, place it in her coat pocket and then leave the shop without paying.	A complete copy of that evidence must be attached to this notice, if it has not already been served on the other parties.
A copy of Miss Donovan's witness statement is attached and has been served on the defendant Alison Davies through her solicitors Messrs Johnson & Brown.	

Extension of time

Are you applying for an extension of time within which to give
This notice? ~~Yes~~/No

If yes, state your reasons:

Signed: *J Smith*

Dated: *23rd February 2007*

19.12.3 Notice of opposition to the introduction of hearsay evidence

Notice of opposition to the introduction of hearsay evidence **Under s 114, Criminal Justice Act 2003** (Criminal Procedure Rules, rr 34.3, 34.5, 68.20(1))	
This form shall be used to give notice of opposition to the introduction of hearsay evidence, as specified in a notice of hearsay evidence given under rule 34(2)	
Details of party opposing the introduction of hearsay evidence	
Surname: *Davies* Forename(s): *Alison* Address: *24 The Limes, Christlethorpe, Guildshire GU3 7TX* Date that you were given notice that hearsay evidence will be introduced in these proceedings: *23rd February 2007*	State the name and address of the party giving notice of their opposition to the introduction of hearsay evidence. (If in custody give address where detained)
Case Details The *Crown* Court at *Christlethorpe* Case Reference Number *CH/0931/07* Name of Judge: *HHJ Hutton* Date the trial or proceedings is due to start/started: *7th April 2007* Name the prosecuting agency (if relevant): *CPS* Name of defendant(s): *Alison Davies* Charges: *Theft of gold necklace (valued at £1,500) from Scriveners jewellery shop on 15th November 2006*	Enter the name of the Court and the case no. Give brief details of the charges to which this notice applies.

Details of the hearsay evidence that you want to exclude

Written witness statement from Kylie Donovan dated 15th November 2006. Objection to the entire witness statement.

Give brief description of the hearsay evidence that you want to exclude from the proceedings. Specify whether you object to all or part of that evidence.

Grounds for excluding the evidence

The evidence given by the witness is an eye-witness account of what occurred when the alleged theft took place. The defence is that this is a case of mistaken identification by the witness. If the witness statement is admitted as hearsay evidence, there will be no opportunity to cross-examine the witness as to the quality of the identification evidence she gives.

The court is asked to exercise its discretion under s 126(1) of the Criminal Justice Act 2003 and s 78 of PACE 1984 to exclude the statement on the grounds that its admission would have an adverse effect on the fairness of the trial.

Set out the grounds for excluding the hearsay evidence that you object to.

Any relevant skeleton argument or case law that might bear on the issue may be attached to this notice.

Extension of time

Are you applying for an extension of time within which to give this notice?   *Yes/No

If yes, state your reasons:

*delete as appropriate

Signed: *Johnson & Brown*

Dated: *4th March 2007*

Chapter 20

Confessions

20.1 Introduction

Although there are no rules saying what weight or credibility a court should attach to a particular piece of evidence, it is likely that a jury or a bench of magistrates will place great significance on the CPS producing evidence that a defendant who is pleading not guilty has confessed to having committed the offence with which he is charged. This chapter will examine what constitutes a confession and when confession evidence is admissible in evidence at trial. The chapter will also look at the circumstances in which confession evidence may be excluded and the procedure to be followed when the defendant challenges the admissibility of confession evidence upon which the CPS seeks to rely.

20.2 What is a confession?

20.2.1 PACE 1984, s 82(1)

A confession is 'any statement wholly or partly adverse to the person who made it, whether made to a person in authority or not and whether made in words or otherwise' (PACE 1984, s 82(1)).

Confessions will usually be made by a suspect when interviewed at the police station, although a defendant may also make a confession outside the police station, either to the police or to someone else. If, for example, a defendant admits to a friend that he committed a theft, this would be a confession. Confessions do not need to amount to a full admission of guilt. Anything said by a suspect that constitutes an admission of any element of the offence with which he is subsequently charged will satisfy the definition of a confession.

Example 1

Julian is arrested on suspicion of theft from a supermarket. When interviewed at the police station, Julian tells the police: 'Yeah, it was me who nicked the stuff. I wanted to sell it to get money for drugs.' Julian's comments satisfy the definition of a confession in s 82(1) because he has admitted to carrying out the theft.

Example 2

Claudia, a juvenile, is charged with the theft of a mobile phone. The prosecution allege that Claudia took the phone from a bag belonging to Kate, a pupil in Claudia's class at school. The prosecution have obtained a witness statement from Naomi, another pupil at the same school. Naomi claims to have overheard Claudia telling one of her friends that she (Claudia) hid the phone inside her bra when the class teacher was searching the bags of all the pupils in the class after the phone was stolen. Although Naomi did not overhear Claudia admitting to taking the phone from Kate's bag, Claudia's remark will still satisfy s 82(1). The comment made by Claudia is adverse to her case because she has admitted to being in possession of the stolen phone and to hiding the phone when a search was being conducted.

Example 3

PC Jones is called to a pub where an assault has taken place. On arriving at the pub, PC Jones obtains a description of the person alleged to have committed the assault. Shortly after leaving the pub, PC Jones sees Michael in the street. Michael matches the description of the person who committed the assault. PC Jones asks Michael if he has been at the pub that evening. Michael replies: 'I was at the pub but it wasn't me that hit him.' Although Michael has not said that he committed the assault, his comments still satisfy the definition of a confession in s 82(1) above. This is because, in the event that Michael is later charged with the assault, the comments he made will be adverse to his case. Michael admits to having being at the pub, and also admits to knowing that an assault has taken place (for which he may be a suspect).

A suspect who makes a confession to the police may make the confession either orally in answer to a question from the police, or in writing if he provides the police with a written statement. A confession may also be made through gestures or actions. For example, a suspect may nod his head or put his thumb up when asked if he committed an offence.

20.2.2   Can silence amount to a confession?

The general rule is that an accused's silence in the face of an allegation made against him that would normally call for some kind of denial or allegation from him, is not admissible as evidence to show that he admits the allegation.

Example

In *R v Christie* [1914] AC 545, the defendant was charged with indecently assaulting a young boy. Shortly after the alleged assault occurred, and in the presence of the boy's mother and a police officer, the boy confronted the defendant with the words, 'That is the man', and then went on to give details of the alleged assault. The defendant replied with the comment: 'I am innocent.' The Court of Appeal held that, had the defendant remained silent in the face of the allegation made by the boy, this could not be evidence to show that he admitted the allegation made, even though the making of such an allegation would reasonably call for some kind of explanation from the defendant. The defendant had, however, responded, and although the response was a denial of guilt, the Court held that the nature of the defendant's response was such that it was open to the jury to infer that the defendant accepted the boy's allegation (although the jury were not obliged to do so).

The situation is the same if the police put to a suspect an allegation which has been made against him by a co-accused. The suspect's silence in the face of such an allegation is not evidence that the suspect accepts the truth of the allegation. The position is different, however, if a suspect remains silent when, *in his presence*, a co-accused makes a confession in which he is implicated (see **20.3.3.1** below).

20.3 Admissibility of confession evidence

20.3.1 Confessions

A confession made by a defendant will be admissible in evidence at the defendant's trial as an exception to the rule excluding hearsay evidence. Confessions are admissible in evidence by virtue of s 76(1) of PACE 1984 (see below) and so fall within the exception to the rule excluding hearsay evidence contained in s 114(1)(a) of the CJA 2003 (which provides that hearsay evidence will be admissible at trial if it is made admissible by virtue of any statutory provision – see **19.5.1**).

Section 76(1) provides:

> In any proceedings a confession made by an accused person may be given in evidence against him insofar as it is relevant to any matter in issue in the proceedings and is not excluded by the court in pursuance of this section.

This means that a confession made by a defendant prior to his trial will be admissible at trial to prove the truth of the confession (ie, to prove the defendant's guilt).

Example 1

James is charged with theft. He admits the theft in an audio-recorded interview at the police station. A transcript of the interview is subsequently read out at James's trial. The transcript is hearsay evidence, but it will be admissible in evidence by virtue of s 76(1).

Example 2

James is arrested on suspicion of theft. As he is being arrested, James tells the arresting officer: 'Okay I did it. You know I only steal because I have no money.'

When he is later interviewed at the police station, James denies having made this confession. At James's trial, the arresting officer repeats the comment made by James at the time of his arrest. This will be hearsay evidence, but it will be admissible in evidence by virtue of s 76(1).

Example 3

James is charged with theft. He denied the theft when interviewed at the police station, but later admits to his friend Margaret that he committed the theft. Margaret has provided the CPS with a statement in which she repeats the confession which James has made. If Margaret repeats this at court when giving oral evidence, this will be hearsay evidence, but it will be admissible in evidence by virtue of s 76(1).

20.3.2 Mixed statements

A confession may sometimes also include a statement which is favourable to the defendant. These are referred to as 'mixed statements'. The whole statement will be admissible under s 76(1) as an exception to the rule excluding hearsay evidence.

Example

Cedric is charged with assault. When interviewed at the police station, he says: 'I hit the victim in the face but I only did this in self-defence.' This is a mixed statement, because Cedric makes a confession (admitting he hit the victim in the face) but he also makes a statement favourable to his defence (saying that he was acting in self-defence). The entire statement will be admissible under s 76(1).

20.3.3   Confessions and a co-accused

20.3.3.1   Is a confession made by one defendant admissible in evidence against his co-defendant?

Pre-trial confessions

Confessions made out of court are admissible in evidence only against the person making the confession (PACE 1984, s 76(1)). A confession made to the police by one defendant is therefore not admissible in evidence against a co-defendant who may be implicated in that confession (see 'Confessions made at trial', below, for the position if the confession is repeated in oral evidence at trial).

> #### Example 1
>
> Violet and Jason are jointly charged with arson. Both are pleading not guilty. When interviewed by the police, Violet made a confession, stating that she and Jason committed the offence together. Violet now claims that this confession was untrue. If, at trial, the CPS adduces evidence of Violet's confession, the confession will only be admissible in evidence against Violet as the person who made the confession. The confession will not be admissible in evidence against Jason.

> #### Example 2
>
> Sunita and Jack are jointly charged with burglary. Both are pleading not guilty. Sunita confesses to her friend Joanne that she and Jack committed the burglary, and Joanne then gives a statement to this effect to the police. If Joanne repeats details of the confession made to her by Sunita when she gives oral evidence at court, the confession will be admissible in evidence against Sunita because Sunita was the person who made the confession. The confession will not be admissible in evidence against Jack.

The only exception to this is that, at common law, a confession made by a defendant which also implicates a co-defendant may be admissible in evidence against the co-defendant if the confession was made *in the co-defendant's presence* and the co-defendant does nothing at that time to challenge what the defendant has said about his involvement in the offence (*R v Coll* [2005] All ER (D) 82).

> #### Example
>
> Gary and Eric are jointly charged with criminal damage, the allegation being that they smashed the windows on a car. They were seen doing this by an eye-witness who gave their descriptions to the police. The police found them together at a local pub and, when asked about their involvement, Gary said (in the presence and hearing of Eric): 'Okay, it was us that did it. I smashed the wing mirrors and Eric did the windscreen.'
>
> This confession will be admissible to prove Gary's guilt. It will also be admissible in evidence against Eric, if Eric says nothing at the time of Gary's comment to challenge what Gary has said about his involvement in the offence. It will then be a matter for the magistrates or jury to decide whether Eric's failure to respond to Gary's incriminating remark could amount to an admission of guilt on his part.

Confessions made at trial

Any evidence given by a co-defendant at trial which implicates the defendant (including a confession or an admission made by the co-defendant) will be admissible in evidence against the defendant. Also, if the co-defendant has pleaded guilty at an earlier hearing and is giving evidence on behalf of the prosecution at the trial of the defendant, any evidence he gives implicating the defendant in the commission of the offence will be admissible in evidence against the defendant.

Example 1

Trisha and Marlon are jointly charged with theft. Tricia is to plead guilty and Marlon will plead not guilty. Tricia enters her guilty plea on her first appearance before the court. She then gives a statement to the CPS stating that she and Marlon committed the theft together. As Tricia is no longer being tried with Marlon (because she has pleaded guilty), she will be able to give evidence as a prosecution witness at Marlon's trial. If, when giving evidence, Tricia states that she and Marlon committed the theft together, this will be admissible in evidence against Marlon.

Example 2

Barry and Colin are jointly charged with assault occasioning actual bodily harm. The allegation is that they attacked a fellow customer in a restaurant. Both plead not guilty. Barry raises the defence of alibi and claims that he was at home with his wife at the time of the assault. Colin accepts that he was at the restaurant (with Barry), but denies that either of them had anything to do with the assault. When giving evidence at trial, Colin says: 'I was having a meal with Barry when a fight started. Neither of us had anything to do with it.'

This is an admission. Although Colin is not admitting his guilt, he does accept that he was in the restaurant at the time of the assault. Colin's comments will also be admissible in evidence against Barry. They suggest that Barry was in the restaurant at the time of the assault, and that Barry's alibi may therefore be untrue (although they also suggest that Barry had nothing to do with the assault).

20.3.3.2 Can one defendant adduce evidence of a confession made by another defendant?

Although a pre-trial confession made by one defendant cannot be adduced by the prosecution in evidence against a co-defendant (see **20.3.3.1** above), s 76A(1) of PACE 1984 allows a defendant to adduce as part of his defence evidence that a co-defendant or co-accused has made a confession. Evidence of such a confession is relevant both to the guilt of the co-defendant and to the credibility of any evidence given by the co-defendant.

Example 1

Robert and Patrick are jointly charged with common assault. Both are pleading not guilty. Robert's defence is that he had nothing to do with the assault and that the assault was committed by Patrick alone. Before the case comes to trial Patrick dies, and so Robert is tried alone. When Patrick was interviewed by the police he confessed to having committed the crime. Robert is entitled to raise Patrick's confession in evidence at his trial to show that it was Patrick rather than he who committed the assault.

Example 2

Sarah and Rachel are jointly charged with theft. Both are pleading not guilty. Shortly after being charged, Sarah told Diane (a friend of Rachel), that she committed the theft alone. Rachel will be able to adduce evidence of Sarah's confession at trial (by calling Diane to give oral evidence) both to show that Sarah is guilty of the offence and to undermine the credibility of any evidence which Sarah gives at trial.

20.4 Challenging the admissibility of a confession: PACE 1984, s 76

20.4.1 Introduction

A defendant who is alleged to have made a confession may challenge the admissibility of this confession at his trial by arguing either:

(a) that he did not make the confession at all, and that the person (usually a police officer) to whom he made the alleged confession was either mistaken as to what he heard or has fabricated evidence of the confession; or

(b) that he did make the confession, but only for reasons other than the fact that he was actually guilty of having committed the offence. In this case, the defendant will say that the confession is untrue.

If the defendant accepts that he made a confession but denies that the confession is true, he will usually challenge the admissibility of the confession under s 76(2) of PACE 1984:

> If, in any proceedings where the prosecution proposes to give in evidence a confession made by an accused person, it is represented to the court that the confession was or may have been obtained—
>
> (a)   by *oppression* of the person who made it; or
>
> (b)   in consequence of anything said or done which was likely, in the circumstances existing at the time, to render *unreliable* any confession which might be made by him in consequence thereof,
>
> the court shall not allow the confession to be given in evidence against him except in so far as the prosecution proves to the court beyond reasonable doubt that the confession (notwithstanding that it may be true) was not obtained as aforesaid. (emphasis added)

This means that if a defendant argues that a confession was obtained in the manner or circumstances detailed under paras (a) or (b) above, the court must not allow that confession to be used as evidence by the prosecution, unless the prosecution prove beyond a reasonable doubt that the confession was not so obtained. Even if the court thinks that the confession is true, the court must still rule that the prosecution cannot use the confession in evidence unless the prosecution can prove that the confession was not obtained by oppression or in circumstances which render it unreliable.

Example

Jeff is charged with murder. When interviewed at the police station he confessed to having committed the murder. At his trial, Jeff argues that the confession was obtained by oppression and should be ruled inadmissible by the trial judge. The CPS must prove beyond a reasonable doubt that the confession was not obtained by oppression, even if the judge believes the confession to be true. If the prosecution fail to do this, the judge must not allow evidence of the confession to be placed before the jury.

20.4.2 Oppression

The Police and Criminal Evidence Act 1984 provides a partial definition of the term 'oppression'. Section 76(8) states that 'oppression' includes 'torture, inhuman or degrading treatment, and the use or threat of violence (whether or not amounting to torture)'. This was not intended to be a full definition of the meaning of the term, and it will be very rare for a defendant to argue that he confessed only because the police subjected him to this kind of treatment. In *R v Fulling* [1987] 2 WLR 923, the Court of Appeal said that the word 'oppression' was to be given its ordinary meaning. The Court said that oppression consisted of 'the exercise of authority or power in a burdensome, harsh or wrongful manner; unjust or cruel treatment of subjects, inferiors, etc; the imposition of unreasonable or unjust burdens'.

An argument that a confession should be excluded under s 76(2)(a) on the grounds of oppression is likely to arise only where there has been deliberate and serious misconduct on the part of the police. Examples of when the court has found oppression are:

(a) *R v Davison* [1998] Crim LR 442 – the defendant confessed after being unlawfully held at the police station, unlawfully denied access to legal advice and questioned about an offence for which he had not been arrested.

(b) *R v Paris* (1993) 97 Cr App R 1999 – in an audio-recorded interview at the police station, the defendant was bullied and hectored into making a confession. The Court of Appeal said that, other than actual physical violence, it would find it hard to think of a more hostile and intimidating approach adopted by interviewing officers.

Paragraph 11.5 of Code C of PACE 1984 (the Code of Practice for the Detention, Treatment and Questioning of Persons by Police Officers) specifically states that no police officer may try to obtain answers or elicit a statement from a suspect by the use of oppression (see **3.5.2.4**).

20.4.3 Unreliability

Findings of oppression are rare, and it is more likely that a defendant will argue that his confession should be excluded under s 76(2)(b) because it is unreliable.

For the court to exclude a confession under s 76(2)(b), something must be said or done which, in the circumstances that existed at the time, would render any confession which the defendant made unreliable. In other words, something must have been said or done which might have caused the defendant to make a confession for reasons other than the fact that he had actually committed the offence and wanted to admit his guilt. Although s 76(2)(b) does not require deliberate misconduct on the part of the police, the thing which is said or done will usually involve an alleged breach of Code C (see **20.4.2** above). Examples of the types of breach of Code C which may lead to a confession being excluded on the grounds of unreliability include:

(a) *denying a suspect refreshments or appropriate periods of rest between interviews*, so that the suspect either is not in a fit state to answer questions properly, or makes admissions in interview simply to get out of the police station as soon as possible or to obtain rest or refreshments (this may be particularly relevant if the suspect is suffering from some form of illness or ailment, even if the police are not aware of this condition);

(b) *offering a suspect an inducement to confess*, for example, telling a suspect that if he confesses he will receive a lesser sentence, suggesting to the suspect that he will be able to leave the police station much more quickly if he admits his guilt, or telling the suspect that he will only be granted police bail if he makes a confession;

(c) *misrepresenting the strength of the prosecution case*, for example by telling a suspect that the prosecution case is much stronger than it actually is and that there is no point in denying his guilt;

(d)   *questioning a suspect in an inappropriate way*, for example by repeatedly asking a suspect the same question, or badgering a suspect until he gives the answer which the officer wants;

(e)   *questioning a suspect who the police should have known was not in a fit state to be interviewed* either because the suspect had consumed drink or drugs, or because the suspect was suffering from some form of medical condition or ailment. The answers given by such a suspect in interview may be unreliable;

(f)   *threatening a suspect*, for example by telling him that he will be kept at the police station until he makes a confession, so that that the suspect thinks he has no option other than to confess if he wants to get out of the police station.

A very common example of an argument used to exclude a confession on the unreliability ground under s 76(2)(b) is for a defendant to argue that his confession is unreliable because he was denied access to legal advice at the police station in breach of Code C and s 58 of PACE 1984 (see **3.4.2**). A breach of s 58 and Code C will not, however, in itself lead to the exclusion of the confession. In order for the confession to be excluded, there must be a causal link between the breach and the unreliability of the confession that was subsequently made. The defendant will need to show that had he been allowed access to legal advice, he would not have made a confession. Therefore, if denial of access to legal advice is relied upon as an argument to exclude a confession under s 76(2)(b), a defendant will find it hard to establish a causal link if he is an experienced criminal who was fully aware of his rights when detained at the police station. In contrast, a suspect who has never previously been arrested and has no experience of police detention or knowledge of his rights when at the police station, may find it easier to have a confession excluded under s 76(2)(b) if he raises the same argument.

Example 1

In *R v Trussler* [1998] Crim LR 446, the defendant was a drug addict who was kept in custody for 18 hours. He was interviewed several times without being given any rest and was denied access to legal advice. His confession was excluded under s 76(2)(b).

Example 2

In *R v Alladice* (1998) 87 Cr App R 380, the defendant was denied access to legal advice and confessed to a robbery. When giving evidence at trial, the defendant stated that he knew of his rights and that understood the police caution. The defendant's application to exclude his confession was rejected by the trial judge. Although denying access to legal advice was a serious breach of Code C, there was nothing to suggest that this might render any confession he had made unreliable, because he was fully aware of what his rights were.

20.4.4   Challenging the admissibility of a confession adduced in evidence by a co-defendant

Section 76A(1) of PACE 1984 permits a defendant to adduce in evidence as part of his defence the fact that that a co-accused or co-defendant with whom he is jointly charged has confessed to having committed the offence (see **20.3.3.2** above).

Under s 76A(2), if the co-defendant who made the confession represents to the court that his confession was obtained as a result of oppression, or in circumstances rendering it unreliable (as described in **20.4.3** above), the court must exclude the evidence of the confession (even if the court believes the confession to be true), unless the court is satisfied that the confession was not obtained in such a way. The court need only be satisfied on the balance of probabilities that the confession was not obtained either by oppression or in circumstances rendering it unreliable in order for the confession to be admissible (in contrast to confessions adduced by the prosecution which, if challenged by the defendant, must be excluded under s 76(2) unless the court is satisfied beyond a reasonable doubt that the confession was not obtained by oppression or in circumstances making it unreliable – see **20.4.1** above).

Example

Richard and Paul are jointly charged with common assault. Both are pleading not guilty. Richard's defence is that he had nothing to do with the assault and that the assault was committed by Paul alone. When Paul was interviewed by the police he confessed to having committed the crime. Richard is entitled to raise Paul's confession in evidence at trial to show that it was Paul rather than he who committed the assault. However, Paul argues at trial that the confession he made when interviewed was obtained only as a result of threats made by the police to keep him in custody indefinitely until he confessed, and so is unreliable. If Richard attempts to adduce evidence of Paul's confession and Paul challenges this, the court must exclude the evidence of Paul's confession (even if the court believes the confession to be true) unless the court is satisfied on the balance of probabilities that the confession was not obtained in circumstances making it unreliable.

20.5 Challenging the admissibility of a confession: PACE 1984, s 78

20.5.1 Introduction

Section 76 of PACE 1984 deals exclusively with the court's power to exclude evidence of a confession made by the defendant (see **20.4** above). Under s 78, the court has a more general discretion to exclude prosecution evidence (see **Chapter 21**). This includes evidence of a confession made by a defendant. Section 78 provides the court with the *discretion* to exclude confession evidence on which the CPS seeks to rely if the court considers that the admission of the confession would have such an adverse effect on the fairness of proceedings that it ought not to be admitted. Section 78 may be relied on either when the defendant admits making a confession but claims that the confession is untrue, or when the defendant denies making the confession at all.

20.5.2 Confessions the defendant accepts having made

When a defendant alleges that the police breached the provisions of PACE 1984 and/or the Codes of Practice in obtaining a confession from him, the court is likely to exercise its discretion under s 78 to exclude such evidence only if these breaches are both significant and substantial (*R v Walsh* (1989) 91 Cr App R 161; *R v Keenan* [1990] 2 QB 54).

For example, if the police fail to caution a suspect at the start of an interview at the police station and the suspect then makes a confession during the interview, the failure to caution the suspect will be a significant and substantial breach of Code C. Paragraph 10.1 of Code C provides that a suspect must be cautioned before he is questioned about an offence (see **3.5.2.3**). If the police failed to caution the suspect, the suspect might not have appreciated that he was under no obligation to answer questions in the interview. In such circumstances, it would be unfair at trial to allow the CPS to rely on a confession made in the interview because, had he been properly cautioned, the suspect might have chosen to stay silent in interview.

There is a significant degree of overlap between the court's discretion to exclude a confession (which the defendant admits to having made) under s 78, and the duty of the court to exclude a confession under the 'unreliability' ground in s 76(2)(b). The examples of breaches of Code C at **20.4.3** above, which would lead the court to exclude a confession on the grounds of unreliability under s 76(2)(b), could also be raised to support an argument under s 78 that it would be unfair to allow the prosecution to rely on confession evidence. If, for example, the defendant made a confession only after being told by the police that he would be able to leave the police station much sooner if he admitted his guilt, an argument could be made under s 78 that it would be unfair to allow the prosecution to rely on the confession because the defendant might have confessed as a means of ensuring his prompt release from police custody, rather than because he was actually guilty of the offence.

Many of the cases in which the court has exercised its discretion to exclude evidence of a confession made by the defendant under s 78 are concerned with suspects who have been denied access to legal advice. In *R v Walsh* (1989) 91 Cr App R 161, the Court of Appeal said that in most cases where a defendant had been denied access to legal advice in breach of s 58 of PACE 1984 or the provisions of Code C, this would lead to the court exercising its discretion to exclude any confession that the defendant subsequently made, since allowing the CPS to rely on such evidence would have an adverse effect on the fairness of the proceedings.

Another example of when the court has used s 78 to exclude evidence of a confession made by the defendant is when the police have deliberately misled the defendant as to the strength of the evidence they have obtained, in order to make the defendant think that he has no option other than to confess. In *R v Mason* [1998] 1 WLR 139, a police officer told the defendant's solicitor that fingerprint evidence existed, tying the defendant in to the crime he was suspected of having committed. The defendant then made a confession. In fact there was no such fingerprint evidence, and this was a deliberate lie on the part of the police officer. The Court of Appeal held that the trial judge should have exercised his discretion under s 78 to exclude the confession.

Where s 78 differs from s 76 (and in particular the unreliability ground in s 76(2)(b)) is that a confession which the defendant accepts having made may be excluded under s 78 even when nothing has been said or done (either by the defendant, or by the police), and where there is no suggestion that the police have acted improperly or in breach of the Codes of Practice. This may occur when:

(a)   the physical condition of the defendant renders the confession unreliable. This may be the case if the defendant was tired, emotional, or suffering from the effects of illness or medication (about which he had not told the police) at the time the confession was made;

Example

Ruth is arrested on suspicion of theft. Ruth is a diabetic but fails to disclose this to the custody officer or interviewing officer. Whilst at the police station Ruth's blood sugar level falls, and as a consequence Ruth becomes light-headed and is unaware of what she is saying. In interview, Ruth admits to having committing the offence. At her subsequent trial, she denies the theft. In such circumstances the court is likely to exclude the confession under s 78 because Ruth was aware of what she was saying.

(b)   the defendant has an ulterior motive for making a confession, such as needing to get out of the police station as soon as possible for reasons unconnected to the police investigation, or wanting to protect another person.

Example 1

Emma is arrested at a supermarket on suspicion of shoplifting. She is subsequently taken to the police station. Emma has two young children whom she has left at home while shopping. Emma does not disclose this fact to the police, because she is worried that the police might inform the social services department at the local council that she has left her children at home unattended. When interviewed about the offence, even though she was not in fact shoplifting, Emma makes an immediate confession so that she can leave the police station as soon as possible and return to her children. Again, the court is likely to exclude such a confession under s 78, as the reason for the confession was not Emma's guilt but rather her concern about getting into trouble with social services.

Example 2

Peter and his wife Jenny are arrested on suspicion of assaulting a neighbour. Although Peter had nothing to do with the alleged assault, when interviewed by the police he admits his guilt. He does this because Jenny has a heart condition and he is worried about the effect if Jenny were to be prosecuted. Prior to Peter's trial, Jenny dies. It is likely that at trial a court would exclude Peter's confession under s 78 if the court believed that the reason for Peter's confession was his desire to protect Jenny rather than his actually being guilty of the assault.

20.5.3 Confessions the defendant denies having made

A defendant will often be alleged to have made a confession 'outside' the police station when first approached by the police. If the defendant subsequently denies having made such a confession, he may challenge the admissibility of this confession under s 78.

A confession allegedly made by the defendant when questioned by the police in an interview 'outside' the police station is likely to be excluded under s 78 if the police breached the provisions of Code C of PACE 1984 by:

(a) failing to caution the defendant before conducting the interview (Code C, para 10.1), as the defendant would not then appreciate the legal significance and consequences of any comments he might make;

(b) failing to make an accurate record of the defendant's comments (Code C, para 11.7(a)), as the police would not then be able to substantiate that such comments were in fact made by the defendant;

(c) failing to give the defendant an opportunity to view the record of his comments and to sign this record as being accurate, or to dispute the accuracy of the record (Code C, para 11.11), as the defendant would then be deprived of the opportunity to challenge the accuracy of the police record; or

(d) failing to put this admission or confession to the defendant at the start of his subsequent interview at the police station (Code C, para 11.4), as the whole point of putting the confession to the defendant at the start of the audio-recorded interview is to ensure that the defendant has the opportunity to confirm or deny 'on the record' what he is alleged to have said.

In *R v Canale* [1990] 2 All ER 187, the police alleged that the defendant had made certain admissions to them. The defendant denied making these admissions. The interviewing officer to whom these admissions had allegedly been made failed to make a contemporaneous note of the interviews as required by Code C (see

2.3.3.3), and the defendant was therefore denied the opportunity to comment on the accuracy of the record of these interviews. The evidence was excluded by the court under s 78 because its admission would have been unfair to the defendant.

This case may be contrasted with *Watson v DPP* [2003] EWHC 1466. The magistrates' court convicted the defendant of drink driving. The police officer who attended the road traffic accident in which the defendant had been involved spoke to the defendant, who admitted being the driver of the vehicle. The officer was unable to make a contemporaneous note of the interview, or to invite the defendant to sign such a note, because he was called away to attend another emergency. The defence raised by the defendant at his trial was that he had not been the driver of the vehicle. He argued that the police officer's breaches of the Codes of Practice meant that his alleged admission that he had been the driver should have been excluded at his trial under s 78. His appeal was dismissed. Whilst it was accepted that there had been a breach of Code C, the court had nevertheless been entitled to admit evidence of the alleged admission because the defendant had ample opportunity at the police station to deny that he had been the driver of the vehicle, and the only reason the officer had failed to make a contemporaneous note was because he had been called away in an emergency. In those circumstances, there was nothing unfair about the evidence of the admission being used at trial. This case illustrates the limitations of s 78, and in particular the fact that excluding evidence under s 78 is very much within the *discretion* of the court.

20.6 Procedure for challenging the admissibility of a confession

20.6.1 Crown Court

In the Crown Court, the admissibility of disputed confession evidence will be determined by the trial judge in the absence of the jury at a voire dire (see **10.10.1**). If the confession was made by the defendant in an interview at the police station, the interviewing officer will give evidence as to how the confession was obtained and the defendant will then give his version of events. The record of the interview will also be played. If the confession was made 'outside' the police station, the officer to who the confession was made will give evidence, as again will the defendant. Prosecuting and defence counsel will then make submissions to the judge on whether the confession should be excluded in the light of the evidence given. The judge will then make his ruling.

If the judge rules the confession to be inadmissible, the jury will hear nothing about the confession. If the judge rules the confession to be admissible, the interviewing officer will then give evidence of the confession when giving his evidence to the jury. The defendant will still be able to attack the cogency of the confession (either when giving evidence himself, or when the police officer is being questioned) in an attempt to persuade the jury to attach little or no weight to it. In his summing up to the jury, the trial judge must direct the jury that, if they consider the confession to have been obtained by oppression or other improper conduct, they should disregard it (*R v Mushtaq* [2005] 1 WLR 1513).

20.6.2 Magistrates' court

In the magistrates' court, a ruling as to the admissibility of the disputed confession will normally be sought when the interviewing officer gives evidence. If the defendant seeks to exclude evidence of the confession under s 76 of PACE 1984, the magistrates must hold a voire dire (see **9.4.3**). If the defendant raises submissions under s 76 and s 78, both arguments should be dealt with at the same voire dire. If the defendant seeks to rely only on s 78, there is no obligation to hold a voire dire. In such cases, a challenge to the admissibility of the confession may be left either to the close of the prosecution case (if the defendant's solicitor wishes to make a submission of no case to answer), or to the end of the trial when the defendant's solicitor makes his closing speech.

20.6.3 Challenging the credibility of a disputed confession not excluded by the court

If the trial judge or the magistrates rule that a confession is not to be excluded under s 76 or s 78, the defendant may still challenge the credibility or reliability of the confession during the trial. For example, the defendant may give evidence-in-chief that he made the confession for reasons other than the fact that he was guilty, or that he never actually made the confession and evidence of the confession has been fabricated. Similarly, the defendant's solicitor or counsel may cross-examine the police officers to whom the confession was made to suggest either that the confession was obtained only after breaches of PACE 1984 or the Codes of Practice had occurred, or that evidence of the confession has been fabricated. It will then be a matter for the jury or magistrates (when considering their verdict) as to what weight should be attached to the confession as an item of prosecution evidence.

20.7 Evidence obtained as the result of an inadmissible confession

The fact that the court excludes evidence of a confession made by a defendant will not affect the admissibility in evidence of any facts discovered as a result of the confession, although the CPS will not be able to tell the court that such facts were discovered as a result of a confession made by the defendant.

Example

Martin is charged with murder. As a result of a confession made by Martin, the police are able to recover both the murder weapon and the body of his victim. The trial judge rules that the confession made by Martin is inadmissible under s 76(2)(b). The CPS will be able to adduce evidence as to where and when the murder weapon and the body were discovered, but it will not be able to raise in evidence that these items were discovered as a result of a confession made by Martin.

20.8 Procedural flowchart – confession evidence

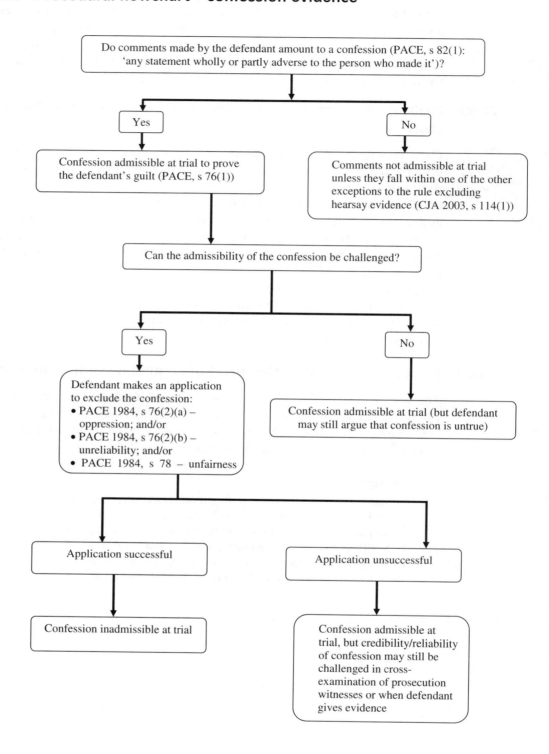

20.9 Checklist

At the end of this chapter you should be able to explain:

- the statutory definition of a confession (PACE 1984, s 82(1));
- the basic rule as to the admissibility of confession evidence at trial (PACE 1984, s 76(1));
- the circumstances in which a confession made by one defendant is admissible in evidence against a co-defendant;
- the circumstances in which one defendant may adduce evidence of a confession made by a co-defendant;
- how to challenge the admissibility of a confession using PACE 1984, s 76(2)(a) – confession obtained by *oppression*;
- how to challenge the admissibility of a confession using PACE 1984, s 76(2)(b) – *unreliability* of the confession;
- how to challenge the admissibility of a confession using PACE 1984, s 78 – *unfair* to admit the confession in evidence;
- the procedure by which a defendant may challenge the admissibility of a disputed confession in either the Crown Court, or the magistrates' court;
- the admissibility of evidence obtained as the result of a confession which the court has ruled to be inadmissible.

Chapter 21

Exclusion of Evidence

21.1 Introduction

There are occasions when the CPS may seek to rely on evidence which has been obtained by the police in an illegal or unfair manner. This chapter will examine the principles which the court will apply in deciding whether or not such evidence is admissible at trial. It will begin with an explanation of the power the court has to exclude such evidence under s 78 of PACE 1984. It will then examine how this power is exercised in relation to particular types of evidence. The chapter will conclude by examining situations when the court may stop a case entirely for 'abuse of process' by the police.

21.2 Police and Criminal Evidence Act 1984, s 78

Prior to PACE 1984 coming into force, the position at common law was that evidence which had been obtained by the police illegally or unfairly was still admissible in evidence at the defendant's trial. For example, in *Jeffrey v Black* [1978] QB 490, drugs were seized from the defendant's property following an illegal search. At his trial for the illegal possession of these drugs, the defendant argued that the court should rule this evidence to be inadmissible. The court declined to do so. The court said that the key issue in deciding the admissibility of the evidence was not whether it had been obtained unfairly, but rather whether it was *relevant* to the charge which the defendant faced. Finding the drugs at the defendant's premises was clearly relevant to a charge of illegal possession drugs, and the evidence was therefore admissible. The court said that an irregularity in obtaining evidence did not render such evidence inadmissible.

Following the enactment of PACE 1984, the courts were given a statutory power to exclude prosecution evidence by virtue of s 78(1):

> In any proceedings a court may refuse to allow evidence on which the prosecution proposes to rely to be given if it appears to the court that, having regard to all of the circumstances, including the circumstances in which the evidence was obtained, the admission of the evidence would have such an adverse effect on the fairness of the proceedings that the court ought not to admit it.

Case law on s 78 suggests that this section has been interpreted broadly in line with the pre-existing common law position. The power in s 78 is *discretionary*, and the court is likely to exercise its discretion to exclude prosecution evidence under s 78 only if there is something unreliable about the evidence which the police have obtained, which in turn means that it would be unfair to allow the CPS to rely on such evidence. If the evidence is relevant to the charge faced by the defendant, and there is nothing in the way in which it has been obtained which casts doubt on its reliability, the evidence is unlikely to be excluded under s 78, even if the police have breached the provisions of PACE 1984 and/or the Codes of Practice when obtaining it.

The courts have said repeatedly that applications by defendants to exclude prosecution evidence under s 78 on the ground that the police have breached PACE 1984 or the Codes of Practice in the obtaining of such evidence, should be granted only if the breaches are 'significant and substantial' (*R v Walsh* (1989) 91 Cr App R 161; *R v Keenan* [1990] 2 QB 54).

Even if the court has doubts as to the reliability of evidence, it is not *obliged* to exclude such evidence under s 78. The use of the word 'may' in s 78 means that this is a discretionary power which the court can choose to exercise or not. This may be contrasted with s 76 of the 1984 Act, which obliges the court to exclude evidence of a disputed confession on which the CPS seeks to rely if the defendant alleges that such evidence was obtained through oppression, or in circumstances rendering it unreliable, unless the prosecution can prove beyond a reasonable doubt that the evidence was not so obtained (see **20.4**).

Common examples of prosecution evidence which a defendant may seek to persuade a court to exclude under s 78 are:

(a)   evidence obtained following an illegal search;

(b)   identification evidence;

(c)   confession evidence (including confessions made on arrest, as well as in interview at the police station);

(d)   no comment interviews given at the police station;

(e)   evidenced obtained from the use of covert listening and surveillance devices; and

(f)   evidence obtained in 'undercover' police operations.

21.3   Illegal searches

The pre-PACE position, as set out in *Jeffrey v Black* (see **21.2** above), remains unchanged. In *R v Stewart* [1995] Crim LR 500, the CPS was allowed to rely on evidence obtained following an illegal search where there had been a number of breaches of Code B (the Code of Practice concerned with searching premises and the seizure of property found on premises – see **Chapter 2**). The court reiterated that if items found following an illegal search are relevant to the charge the defendant faces, the fact that such items were found only as a result of an illegal search does not affect the fairness of the trial because such evidence is relevant to the defendant's guilt. There was also nothing in the case to suggest that there were any doubts as to the reliability of the items found as genuine pieces of evidence.

The only occasion on which evidence obtained following an illegal search should be excluded is if a court considers there to be a real risk that the way in which the evidence has been obtained has affected the reliability of such evidence and, in consequence, the fairness of the trial. An example of such a situation is where police officers conducting a search have ignored Code B completely, and the defendant alleges that the officers in fact planted the evidence which they claimed to have found. In this case, although the items recovered following a search may be relevant to the charge faced by the defendant, doubts as to the authenticity of the items found may lead a court to exercise its discretion under s 78 in favour of the defendant, and to exclude the evidence.

21.4 Identification evidence

21.4.1 Identification procedures

The court may exclude identification evidence on which the CPS wishes to rely if the defendant can establish a significant breach of Code D (the Code of Practice concerned with the identification of persons by police officers – see **Chapter 3**). A breach of Code D will not automatically render such evidence inadmissible, but the court will exclude this evidence under s 78 if the defendant can show that it would be unfair to admit it. To do this, the defendant will need to satisfy the court that the breach of Code D cast doubts upon the reliability of the identification evidence on which the CPS seeks to rely.

The court may exclude identification evidence obtained in breach of Code D if either:

(a) *the police have not used the appropriate identification procedure.* For example, if:

    (i) the police arrange a group identification after making an insufficient effort to arrange an identification parade or video identification, or

    (ii) the police arrange a confrontation after the defendant has requested an identification parade and it is practicable to hold such a parade; or

(b) *there is a defect in the conduct of the identification procedure chosen.* This is most likely to arise in the case of an identification parade or video identification. Arguments casting doubt on the reliability of identification evidence obtained at an identification parade or video identification may be raised if, for example:

    (i) the other participants in the identification parade or video identification did not resemble the defendant (in age, general appearance and position in life), with the resulting possibility that the witness identified the defendant only because there were insufficient volunteers who resembled him,

    (ii) there is a breach of the rule that the investigating officer should take no part in an identification procedure (since there would then be a suspicion that the officer may have 'contaminated' the procedure by indicating to a witness, inadvertently or otherwise, the person whom the witness should pick out),

    (iii) the police had not properly segregated witnesses before and/or after the procedure, so that the witnesses had either been brought into contact with each other or, in the case of an identification parade, had seen the defendant separately from the other volunteers taking part in the parade. In particular, if there is more than one witness and the witnesses are kept together in the same room, there would be a possibility that the first witness attending the identification procedure might, on returning to the room, tell the other witnesses the number of the person he picked out.

The court will exercise its discretion to exclude identification evidence under s 78 only if it considers that evidence to be unreliable as a result of breaches of Code D.

Example 1

Sebastian is arrested on suspicion of theft. He agrees to take part in a video identification. Sebastian has a slim build, is clean shaven and has short blond hair. The other volunteers whose images are taken for use in the video identification are of medium or large build, and none of them has short blond hair. Some of them have a moustache. Sebastian is picked out by the witness. At trial, Sebastian's solicitor will ask the court to exclude the identification evidence under s 78. The basis of the application will be that the video identification has been carried out in breach of Code D (see **3.5.3.2**), and it would be unfair to allow the CPS to rely on such evidence because the reason for Sebastian having been picked out by the witness might have been not that the witness actually recognised Sebastian, but that Sebastian was the only participant in the video identification who in any way resembled the person the witness saw carrying out the theft.

(Had this been an identification parade instead of a video identification, and the volunteers who attended the parade did not resemble Sebastian, the same type of application would be made to the court to exclude the identification evidence under s 78.)

Example 2

Ronald is arrested on suspicion of causing criminal damage and agrees to take part in identification parade. When the parade takes place, the investigating officer (PC Roberts) is present and is given the responsibility of escorting the witness from a waiting room to the room where the parade is to take place. Ronald is picked out at the parade. At his trial, Ronald's solicitor will ask the court to exclude this identification evidence under s 78. The basis of the application will be that the identification parade has been carried out in breach of Code D (see **3.5.3.3**), and it would be unfair to allow the CPS to rely on the identification evidence because PC Roberts might have contaminated the parade by indicating to the witness the person on the parade whom the witness should pick out.

Example 3

Jessica is arrested on suspicion of assault and agrees to take part in an identification parade which is to be attended by two witnesses. Prior to the parade taking place, the witnesses are asked to wait together in the same room. After the first witness has attended the parade, she returns to the room where the second witness is still waiting. Jessica is picked out at the identification parade by the second witness. At her trial, Jessica's solicitor will ask the court to exclude the identification evidence under s 78. The basis of the application will be that the identification parade has been carried out in breach of Code D (see **3.5.3.3**), and it would be unfair to allow the CPS to rely on such evidence because the witnesses were not properly segregated either prior to or, in the case of the first witness, after attending the parade. As a result, the parade may have been contaminated if the witnesses spoke to each other about their respective recollections of the incident and the person they saw, and also if the first witness spoke to the second witness after the first witness had attended the parade. The consequence of this might have been that the second witness picked Jessica out not as a result of her own recollection, but as a result of something said to her by the other witness.

The court may also exclude disputed identification evidence if, whilst the defendant was detained at the police station, the police failed to hold an identification procedure when such a procedure should have been held pursuant to para 3.12 of Code D (see **3.5.3.7**). The purpose of holding an identification procedure at the police station is to test the ability of the witness to identify the person he saw on a previous occasion and to provide a safeguard against mistaken identification. If the police fail to carry out an identification procedure, the defendant has lost the benefit of these safeguards.

Example

Tariq is arrested on suspicion of theft. A witness who saw the theft take place identifies Tariq as the thief . The witness claims to know Tariq, because he and Tariq had worked together at the same factory for six months several years beforehand. Tariq raises the defence of alibi. Tariq vaguely recalls the witness, but he says that he never worked in the same department as the witness and that he is not well known to the witness. The police decide not to hold an identification procedure. This is a breach of Code D, para 3.12. Tariq disputes the identification made by the witness, and he disputes that he is well known to the witness. In these circumstances an identification procedure should have been held at the police station, both to test the ability of the witness to identify the person he saw committing the theft and to provide a safeguard against mistaken identification. Tariq has lost the benefit of this, and his solicitor should therefore ask the court to exclude the disputed identification evidence under s 78.

21.4.2 Samples

If the police obtain a sample from a suspect in breach of PACE 1984 and the Codes of Practice, such evidence is unlikely to be excluded by the courts if it is relevant to the charge which the defendant faces. In *R v Cooke* [1995] 1 Cr App R 318, a sample of hair was obtained from a suspect at the police station in breach of the 1984 Act. This sample was then used to prepare a DNA profile which implicated the suspect in the crime. The court refused to exclude such evidence under s 78. It said that the method used to obtain the sample, whilst illegal, did not cast any doubt on the relevance or reliability of the evidence subsequently obtained.

21.5 Confessions and police interviews

The ability of the court to exclude confession evidence under s 78 is explained in **Chapter 20**, which deals with the admissibility of confession evidence.

Even if a defendant does not make an admission or a confession in an interview at the police station, it may still be in his interests to have the record of his interview at the police station ruled inadmissible by the court. Examples of when a defendant may not wish to have his interview record used as part of the prosecution case are:

(a) if the defendant failed to mention in the interview a fact which he now wants to raise as part of his defence (because the court may draw an inference under s 34 of the CJPOA 1994 if the interview record is used as part of the prosecution case – see **18.2**);

(b) if, after being given a 'special caution', the defendant failed in the interview to account for the presence of an object, substance or mark, or failed to account for his presence at a particular place (because the court may draw an inference under ss 36 or 37 of the CJPOA 1994 if the interview record is used as part of the prosecution case – see **18.3** and **18.4**); or

(c) if the defendant gave the facts of his defence during the interview (and so avoided the risk of adverse inferences being drawn), but the answers he gave were muddled or confusing, and might lead the jury or magistrates to doubt the credibility of his evidence at trial.

To persuade the court that the record of his interview at the police station should be ruled inadmissible, the defendant will need to show why it would be unfair for the CPS to be allowed to use this record in evidence. An application to exclude an interview record is likely to succeed only if the police carried out the interview in an inappropriate manner (for example, by breaching PACE 1984 or the Codes of

Practice), or if there are factors personal to the defendant (whilst he was detained at the police station) which would make it unfair to allow the interview record to be admitted in evidence.

Examples of inappropriate behaviour by the police in the conduct of an interview would include asking a suspect several questions at the same time (with the result that the suspect does not know which question to answer so that his answers are unclear), or interrupting a suspect when he is replying to questions (so that he is unable to answer properly the questions that have been put to him).

Example of factors personal to a suspect which may lead to the exclusion of the interview record are the suspect being unduly tired or emotional when being interviewed, or suffering from the effects of an illness or medication, such that he was unable to answer properly the questions which were being put to him, or was unable to appreciate the evidential significance of such questions. Paragraph 11.8 of Code C (the Code of Practice for the Detention, Treatment and Questioning of Persons by Police Officers) provides that unless exceptional circumstances exist, a suspect should not be interviewed if he would be unable to understand what was happening because of the effects of drink or drugs, or any illness, ailment or condition (see **3.5.2.2**).

21.6 Covert listening and surveillance devices

The police often attempt to obtain evidence by secretly audio-recording the words of a suspect. Following the case of *R v Khan* [1997] AC 558, the courts are unlikely to exclude such evidence under s 78. Khan was charged with the importation of heroin. The only evidence against him was from a recording the police had made (using a covert listening device) of a conversation Khan had with another person concerning the importation of heroin. Khan's application to have this evidence excluded under s 78 was rejected on the basis that such a recording did not affect the fairness of the proceedings against Khan. The court said that such evidence should not be excluded because it was relevant to the charge Khan faced, and there was nothing in the way in which the evidence had been obtained which cast any doubt on its reliability or credibility as a piece of evidence.

This case subsequently went to the European Court of Human Rights (*Khan v United Kingdom* [2000] Crim LR 684). Khan alleged that the obtaining of the evidence against him using a covert listening device was in breach of his rights under Article 6 (the right to a fair trial) and Article 8 (the right to respect for private and family life) of the ECHR (see **1.8.3**).

The European Court of Human Rights held that there had been a violation of Article 8 because, at the time of Khan's conviction, domestic law in the United Kingdom did not regulate the use of covert listening devices. However, the Court did not find there to have been a breach of Article 6. The Court said that the recording of Khan's conversation, whilst in breach of Article 8, had not been unlawful in the sense of being contrary to domestic criminal law. It went on to say that had the trial judge thought that the admission of the conversation would have given rise to unfairness, he would have exercised his discretion under s 78 to exclude it. The Court was satisfied that the ability of the trial judge to exclude evidence under s 78 was sufficient to guarantee Khan's right to a fair trial, and thus there had been no breach of Article 6. (For more on the right to a fair trial and s 78, see **21.8** below.)

In *R v Bailey* [1993] 3 All ER 513, two co-accused who had refused to answer questions in police interview were charged and then placed together in a cell which the police had bugged. Whilst in the cell the co-accused had an incriminating conversation, which the trial judge subsequently refused to declare inadmissible under s 78. Although the conversation had taken place only as a result of some deception on the part of the police, it was held that there was nothing in either PACE 1984 or the Codes of Practice to prevent a cell from being bugged. The conversation was therefore admissible in evidence.

In *R v Rosenberg* [2006] EWCA Crim 6, the prosecution were permitted to use in evidence video-recordings made by the defendant's neighbours showing the defendant engaged in drug-dealing activities. The defendant argued that this evidence should have been excluded by the trial judge under s 78 as the recordings breached both domestic law (the Regulation of Investigatory Powers Act 2000) and also Article 8 of the ECHR. The Court of Appeal dismissed this argument because the surveillance was not covert and the defendant had been fully aware of it. In addition, the surveillance had not been carried out by the police and neither had they encouraged its use. The Court held that although the police had in fact warned the neighbours that the surveillance might breach Article 8, the prosecution were still entitled to use evidence obtained by means of that surveillance.

21.7 Police undercover operations

Sometimes the police will employ 'entrapment' techniques in order to induce the committing of a criminal offence. Evidence obtained as a result of such entrapment may be excluded by the court under s 78. The test which the courts employ is to decide whether the police did nothing more than give the defendant an opportunity to commit a crime. For example, in *Williams v DPP* [1993] 3 All ER 365, the police were investigating a spate of thefts from vehicles. Plain-clothed police officers parked an insecure van, containing a substantial quantity of cigarettes, in a busy area. The defendant was subsequently observed by the officers taking the cigarettes from the van. It was held on appeal that the trial court had been correct in refusing to exercise its discretion under s 78 to rule that the evidence from the police officers should be inadmissible. The Court said that the officers had done nothing more than give the defendant an opportunity to commit a crime. The defendant had not been actively encouraged by police officers to commit the crime.

In *R v Harmes & Another* [2006] EWCA Crim 928, the defendants were convicted of conspiracy to commit various customs offences. During a police undercover operation, an officer supplied the first defendant with soft drinks in exchange for a small amount of drugs worth half the value of the drinks. The first defendant subsequently revealed to another officer a system whereby large amounts of drugs could be imported into Heathrow airport with the assistance of the second defendant (an airport employee). On appeal, the defendants argued that it was only the conduct of the officers in agreeing to supply soft drinks in exchange for drugs that led to the first defendant's revelation of a system for the importation of drugs. The Court of Appeal held that although the police had acted improperly, the officers' suggestion that they should be supplied with drugs in exchange for the soft drinks did not trap the defendants into agreeing to import substantial quantities of drugs. It was not the supply of drinks that persuaded the defendants to become involved in the supposed importation, but rather their hope of substantial financial gain for themselves.

In *R v Loosely* [2001] 1 WLR 2060, the House of Lords said that the courts should be more willing to exercise their discretion to exclude evidence under s 78 if it could be shown that the police have caused the commission of the offence, as opposed to simply providing the defendant with the chance to commit an offence.

Thus, in *R v Moon* [2004] EWCA Crim 2872, the Court of Appeal held that proceedings against a drug addict for supplying an undercover police officer with a small quantity of drugs should have been stayed as an abuse of process (see **21.9** below) where:

(a)   the addict was approached by the officer;

(b)   the officer had persistently asked the addict for drugs;

(c)   the officer pretended that she was an addict suffering from withdrawal symptoms; and

(d)   the addict told the officer never to approach her again for drugs.

The Court considered that the undercover officer had caused crime and had lured the defendant into committing crime.

21.8   Section 78 and the right to a fair trial

Article 6 of the ECHR (see **1.8.3**) provides that anyone charged with a criminal offence is entitled to a 'fair' hearing. The appellate courts have held, on several occasions, that the discretion given to a trial judge to exclude evidence under s 78 where the admission of that evidence would otherwise lead to unfairness, ensures that a defendant will receive a fair trial. Similarly, in cases such as *Khan* (see **21.6** above), the European Court of Human Rights has stated repeatedly that the key question to be answered when determining whether the defendant's rights under Article 6 have been breached is whether the proceedings as a whole were fair. The width of the discretion given to the trial judge by s 78 should ensure that proceedings are conducted in a manner which is fair to the defendant.

21.9   Abuse of process

In cases where misconduct by the police or the prosecuting authorities is so grave as to threaten the rule of law, the court will not simply exclude evidence obtained as a result of that misconduct but rather will stay the proceedings against the defendant as an abuse of process. This means that the proceedings against the defendant will not be permitted to go any further.

An example of this is *R v Grant* [2005] EWCA Crim 1089. The defendant was arrested on suspicion of conspiracy to murder. The police deliberately eavesdropped upon and tape-recorded privileged conversations between the defendant and his solicitor in the exercise yard at the police station. The trial judge refused to stay the proceedings as an abuse of process. On appeal, the Court of Appeal said that the proceedings should have been stayed. Although the defendant suffered no prejudice as a result of the eavesdropping (because no information gained as a result of the eavesdropping was used against him at trial), the Court said that such unlawful acts were an affront to the integrity of the justice system and consequently the rule of law. The duty of a court in such a situation was to stop the case from proceeding any further.

In *A v Secretary of State for the Home Department* [2005] UKHL 71, the House of Lords held that evidence obtained by torture carried out by officials of a foreign state was not admissible under UK law. Needless to say, if evidence against a defendant was obtained as a result of torture carried out by the police, the court would stay any proceedings against the defendant as an abuse of process.

21.10 Procedure for excluding prosecution evidence

21.10.1 Crown Court

In the Crown Court, the admissibility of the evidence which the defendant seeks to persuade the trial judge to exclude under s 78 will usually be determined at a voire dire in the absence of the jury (see **10.10.1**). The judge will ask the jury to retire and he will then hear evidence from witnesses about the disputed piece of evidence and legal submissions from prosecuting and defence counsel. If the judge rules the item of evidence to be inadmissible, the jury will hear no evidence about it. If the judge rules that the evidence is admissible, it may then be raised during the trial. The defendant will still be able to attempt to undermine the reliability or cogency of that evidence, however, either when cross-examining the prosecution witnesses or when giving evidence in chief. It will then be a matter for the jury as to the weight to be attached to the evidence when considering their verdict.

As an alternative to holding a voire dire during the course of the trial, the judge may determine the admissiblity of a piece of prosecution evidence which the defendant seeks to persuade him to exclude under s 78 at a pre-trial hearing (see **10.9**).

21.10.2 Magistrates' court

In the magistrates' court, a voire dire may be held to decide upon the admissibility of the piece of evidence. Alternatively, the defendant's solicitor may make a submission to the magistrates that the item of evidence should be excluded either as part of a submission of no case to answer made at the conclusion of the prosecution case, or in his closing speech before the magistrates retire to consider their verdict. If the magistrates rule that the item of evidence is inadmissible, they will disregard it when considering their verdict. If the magistrates decide not to exclude the evidence under s 78, the defendant may still challenge the reliability or cogency of that evidence either when cross-examining the prosecution witnesses, or when giving evidence in chief. It will then be a matter for the magistrates as to the weight to be attached to the evidence when considering their verdict.

As an alternative to the above, the magistrates may determine the admissibility of a piece of prosecution evidence which the defendant seeks to exclude under s 78 at a pre-trial review (see **8.2.2**).

21.11   Flowchart – the operation of s 78

Although the court may exercise its discretion to exclude prosecution evidence in situations where the police have not acted inappropriately but there are factors personal to the defendant which would make it unfair for the evidence to be admitted at trial (see **21.5** above), most occasions when the court excludes evidence under s 78 will involve the police having breached either PACE 1984 or the Codes of Practice. The flowchart below sets out how the court will approach an application by the defendant to exclude evidence in such circumstances.

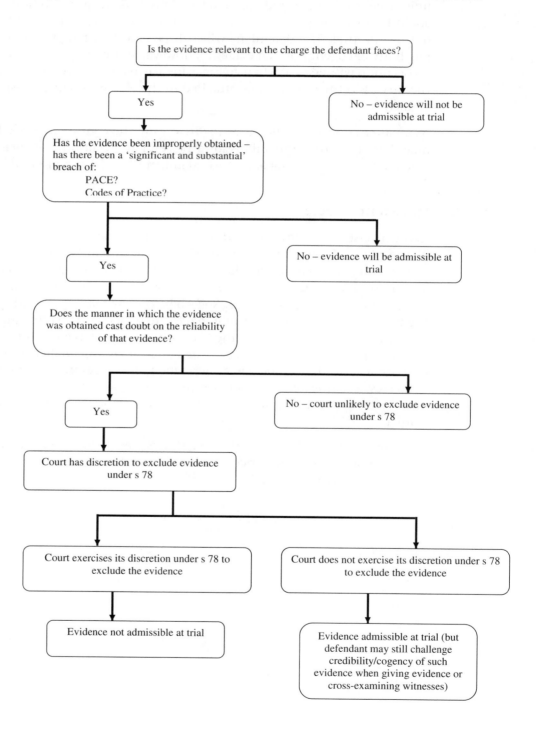

Is the evidence relevant to the charge the defendant faces?

Yes → Has the evidence been improperly obtained – has there been a 'significant and substantial' breach of:
PACE?
Codes of Practice?

No – evidence will not be admissible at trial

Yes → Does the manner in which the evidence was obtained cast doubt on the reliability of that evidence?

No – evidence will be admissible at trial

Yes → Court has discretion to exclude evidence under s 78

No – court unlikely to exclude evidence under s 78

Court exercises its discretion under s 78 to exclude the evidence

Court does not exercise its discretion under s 78 to exclude the evidence

Evidence not admissible at trial

Evidence admissible at trial (but defendant may still challenge credibility/cogency of such evidence when giving evidence or cross-examining witnesses)

21.12 Checklist

At the end of this chapter you should be able to explain:

- the meaning of PACE 1984, s 78;
- the circumstances in which s 78 may be used by the defendant to persuade the court to exclude evidence on which the CPS seeks to rely at trial;
- the relationship between s 78 and the following types of prosecution evidence:
  — evidence obtained following an illegal search,
  — visual identification evidence or samples obtained in breach of PACE 1984 or the Codes of Practice,
  — evidence obtained in an interview at the police station (including confession evidence),
  — evidence obtained using covert listening devices,
  — evidence obtained in undercover operations by the police;
- the relationship between s 78 and the right to a fair trial in Article 6 of the ECHR;
- what is meant by the term 'abuse of process';
- the procedure by which a defendant may challenge the admissibility of prosecution evidence under s 78 either in the Crown Court, or in the magistrates' court.

Chapter 22

Character Evidence

22.1 Introduction

Defendants in a criminal case will often have previous convictions for offences they have committed in the past. Similarly, persons other than the defendant who are involved in the case (such as witnesses for the prosecution or the defence) may have such convictions. This chapter will examine the circumstances in which such previous convictions may be admitted in evidence at trial and the evidential significance of such convictions. It will begin by explaining the law regarding the admissibility of previous convictions prior to the enactment of the Criminal Justice Act (CJA) 2003. The 2003 Act made significant changes to the law in this area, but it is important to understand the pre-CJA position in order to place these changes in context. The chapter will then examine the law as it now stands in relation to the admissibility of a defendant's previous convictions, before looking at when the previous convictions of persons other than the defendant may be raised at trial. It will conclude by examining the evidential significance of a defendant having no previous convictions and so being of good character.

22.2 Admissibility of previous convictions pre-Criminal Justice Act 2003

22.2.1 Previous convictions of the defendant

Prior to the CJA 2003 coming into effect, an *exclusionary* approach was adopted in relation to a defendant's previous convictions. In other words, evidence that a defendant had previous convictions was not admissible at trial except in very limited circumstances. The rationale behind this was that if the magistrates or the jury heard about a defendant's previous convictions, they would decide upon his guilt or innocence of the offence with which he was currently charged not on the basis of the evidence they heard about that offence, but on the basis of his previous convictions. Evidence of the defendan's bad character was considered to be more prejudicial than probative.

The CPS could raise as part of the its case evidence that a defendant had previous convictions only if those convictions amounted to 'similar fact' evidence. Similar fact evidence was evidence that the defendant had previously committed offences that were so strikingly similar to the current offence in the manner in which they were carried out as to be positively probative of the defendant's guilt, rather than just showing that the defendant had a tendency to commit the offence charged.

Example

In *R v Straffen* [1952] 2 QB 911, the defendant, who had escaped from Broadmoor psychiatric hospital, was accused of strangling a girl a short distance away from the hospital. Evidence was admitted of the fact that the defendant had previous convictions for strangling two other girls, and that the features of the two previous crimes were strikingly similar to the offence charged. This similar fact evidence was admitted not to show that the defendant had a disposition to commit murder, but because the features of the case provided a strong indication that the defendant was guilty of the offence charged.

The only other way in which a defendant's previous convictions could be raised in evidence prior to the CJA 2003 taking effect was if the defendant entered the witness box to give evidence as part of his defence case. The general rule was that if the defendant entered the witness box, he had a shield against being cross-examined by the prosecution (or by a co-accused) as to his previous convictions. This shield could be lost, however, if:

(a)   the defendant had previous convictions which amounted to similar fact evidence (see above);

(b)   the defendant gave evidence to suggest that he was of good character;

(c)   the defendant attacked the character of a prosecution witness; or

(d)   the defendant gave evidence implicating a co-accused.

Even if the defendant lost his shield against cross-examination as to his previous convictions, any cross-examination on such convictions was relevant only to the defendant's credibility as a witness (ie, whether the defendant's account of events should be believed) rather than to his propensity to commit the crime with which he had been charged. This meant that a jury or bench of magistrates were not permitted to infer that the fact a defendant had previous convictions for a similar offence made it more likely that the defendant had committed the offence with which he was currently charged.

22.2.2   Previous convictions of other witnesses

Prior to the CJA 2003 being enacted, an *inclusionary* approach was adopted towards evidence that any witness in the case other than the defendant (whether giving evidence for the prosecution or defence) had previous convictions. Such a witness could always be cross-examined as to his previous convictions. This cross-examination was relevant to the credibility of the evidence given by the witness (ie, whether the evidence given by the witness should be believed).

22.3   Criminal Justice Act 2003 – what is meant by bad character?

Under s 98 of the CJA 2003, evidence of a person's bad character is defined as 'evidence of, or a disposition towards, misconduct on his part', other than evidence connected with the offence for which the defendant has been charged or evidence of misconduct in connection with the investigation or prosecution of that offence (see the **Example** below). 'Misconduct' is defined in s 112 as 'the commission of an offence or other reprehensible behaviour'.

This is potentially an extremely wide definition. It is likely that, in time, the appellate courts will define what is meant by the term 'other reprehensible behaviour'. At present, however, it is likely that this definition of 'misconduct' will include not only previous convictions, but also evidence that a person:

(a)   was charged for an offence that was not subsequently prosecuted;

(b)   was prosecuted for an offence but was acquitted at trial – if, for example, the acquittal was in any way tainted or was on a legal technicality (it has also been argued that any acquittal should be admissible on the basis that an acquittal does not mean that a defendant is innocent of the offence charged, merely that a court or jury have not found him guilty beyond a reasonable doubt);

(c)   has received a warning, caution or a conditional caution in respect of a previous matter, or, in the case of a juvenile, a reprimand or final warning;

(d)   has behaved in a blameworthy manner which was not the subject of criminal proceedings (for example, if a person is alleged to have used violence, or told lies on a previous occasion);

(e)   is the subject of an anti-social behaviour order or has been made the subject of an injunction in civil or family law proceedings;

(f)   was dismissed from a previous job for misconduct;

(g)   has been involved in a sexual, financial or other type of scandal; or

(h)   is, or was, a member of an organisation that most people find objectionable.

If the alleged misconduct by the defendant is connected to the offence with which he has been charged, this will not fall within the definition of bad character and will therefore be admissible in evidence *without* needing to consider whether one of the seven 'gateways' applies (*R v Edwards & Rowlands* [2005] EWCA Crim 3244; see **22.4** below). This is particularly relevant when the CPS seeks to suggest that the defendant had a motive for committing the offence.

Example

Adrian is charged with the murder of Frank, his father. The CPS alleges that Adrian fabricated a will in Frank's name, leaving all Frank's assets to Adrian, and that Adrian then murdered Frank so that he could take these assets. The allegation that Adrian fabricated Frank's will is an allegation of misconduct on the part of Adrian. It will not fall within s 98 of the CJA 2003, however, because it is connected to the subsequent murder of Frank. Evidence of the fabrication of the will is therefore admissible without needing to consider whether it satisfies the test for admissibility of bad character evidence set out in the CJA 2003.

This distinction between evidence of bad character within the meaning of s 98 and evidence concerning the facts of the alleged offence also applies to witnesses other than the defendant. In *R v Machado* [2006] All ER (D) 28 (Mar), the Court of Appeal held that the trial judge had been wrong to exclude evidence that the victim of an alleged robbery was under the influence of an ecstasy tablet at the time of the alleged offence. The judge had excluded this evidence on the basis that this was evidence of the victim's bad character and did not satisfy any of the potential grounds for admissibility under s 100 (see **22.6** below). The Court held that the judge did not need to consider the provisions of the CJA 2003 concerning the admissibility of evidence of the character of persons other than the defendant because evidence that the victim may have been taking drugs at the time of the offence was evidence in connection with the 'very circumstances in which the offence had allegedly occurred', rather than being evidence of bad character.

22.4 Bad character of the defendant – the seven 'gateways'

22.4.1 Introduction

Evidence of a defendant's bad character may be raised at trial through one or more of seven 'gateways' which are set out in s 101(1) of the CJA 2003. Section 101(1) provides that:

> (1)   In criminal proceedings evidence of a defendant's bad character is admissible if, but only if:
>
> (a)   all parties to the proceedings agree to the evidence being admissible,
>
> (b)   the evidence is adduced by the defendant himself or is given in answer to a question asked by him in cross-examination and intended to elicit it,
>
> (c)   it is important explanatory evidence,
>
> (d)   it is relevant to an important matter in issue between the defendant and the prosecution,
>
> (e)   it has substantial probative value in relation to an important matter in issue between the defendant and a co-defendant,
>
> (f)   it is evidence to correct a false impression given by the defendant, or
>
> (g)   the defendant has made an attack on another person's character.

If the defendant is aged 21 or over, evidence of his conviction for an offence when under the age of 14 will not be admissible unless *both* offences (ie, the offence for which the defendant was convicted previously and the offence with which the defendant is currently charged) are triable only on indictment, and the court is satisfied that it is in the interests of justice for the evidence to be admissible (s 108(2)).

Each of these seven gateways will now be examined in more detail. A flowchart summarising the operation of s 101(1)(a)–(g) is set out at **22.9.1** below.

22.4.2 Gateway (a) – all parties to the proceedings agree to the evidence being admissible

This gateway is self-explanatory. If the CPS and the defendant are in agreement that the evidence is admissible, it may be admitted under this gateway.

22.4.3 Gateway (b) – the evidence is adduced by the defendant himself or is given in answer to a question asked by him in cross-examination and intended to elicit it

This gateway allows a defendant to introduce evidence of his own bad character either by telling the court about this when he gives evidence-in-chief, or by asking a prosecution witness (such as a police officer) to confirm that he has previous convictions. A defendant may seek to do this if he has only very minor previous convictions and does not want the jury or magistrates to think that, because he is not adducing evidence of his own good character, he may have extensive previous convictions.

Example

Chris is on trial in the Crown Court for unlawful wounding. The only previous conviction Chris has is for a minor public order offence committed three years previously. The fact that Chris has a previous conviction means that he cannot place before the court evidence that he is of good character. Chris is concerned that if the jury notice that he has not put forward evidence of his good character, they may think that he has extensive previous convictions which may prejudice them against him. Therefore, when he is giving evidence in chief, Chris confirms to the court that he has one previous conviction for a minor public order offence.

22.4.4 Gateway (c) – it is important explanatory evidence

This gateway may be used by the CPS to introduce evidence of a defendant's bad character, although it is likely to arise only in limited circumstances. Evidence is important explanatory evidence if:

(a) without it, the magistrates or jury would find it impossible or difficult properly to understand the case; and

(b) the value of the evidence for understanding the case as a whole is substantial (CJA 2003, s102) ('substantial' in this context is likely to mean more than merely trivial or marginal – see **22.4.5.1** below).

Evidence of a defendant's previous convictions will be admissible under this gateway only if, without such evidence being admitted, the case would not make sense to the court.

Example 1

Victoria is on trial in the magistrates' court for driving while disqualified. Victoria was disqualified one year previously for the offence of driving whilst over the prescribed alcohol limit. The disqualification was for 18 months. The magistrates will need to be told about this earlier offence in order to understand why Victoria was disqualified from driving. Unless they hear about the earlier offence, the magistrates will find it impossible to understand details of the current offence.

Example 2

Oliver is on trial for the offence of unlawful wounding. The CPS alleges that Oliver launched a completely unprovoked attack against James while James was having drink in his local pub. Three years previously, Oliver was convicted of possession of Class A drugs with intent to supply, for which he received a custodial sentence from which he has only just been released. James was the key witness for the prosecution who gave evidence against Oliver at his trial for the drugs offence. The CPS may seek to raise in evidence at Oliver's trial his conviction for the drugs offence, on the basis that this is important evidence to explain why Oliver may have carried out an unprovoked attack on James.

Example 3

In *R v Edwards* [2005] EWCA Crim 1813, the defendant was charged with robbery. The prosecution relied on identification evidence from an eye-witness who claimed to have recognised the defendant as he was running away from the scene. The defendant raised the defence of alibi, claiming that he was elsewhere at the time the robbery occurred. The trial judge permitted the eye-witness to give evidence that she recognised the defendant because she had regularly bought drugs from him in the past. The Court of Appeal held that the trial judge had correctly allowed this evidence to be admitted under gateway (c), since it was necessary to explain the basis on which she had recognised the defendant.

The court will not allow the CPS to adduce evidence of a defendant's previous bad character, however, if such evidence is not necessary for a proper understanding of the case. In *R v Dolan* [2003] 1 Cr App R 281, the defendant was charged with murder, the allegation being that he shook his baby son to death. The trial judge allowed the CPS to raise evidence of the defendant's violence during the course of a previous relationship towards inanimate objects, on the basis that this was important explanatory evidence. The Court of Appeal subsequently held that this evidence should not have been admitted since the jury's understanding of the case would not have been incomplete without the admission of the evidence.

This decision may be contrasted with *R v s* [2006] EWCA Crim 756. The defendant was convicted in April 2005 of various sexual offences committed against his sisters during the 1970s. The allegations which formed the basis of these charges were made by his sisters only in 2004, after the sisters heard that the defendant had recently received a caution for indecent assault on a child. The Court of Appeal held that the trial judge had correctly allowed the CPS to raise the caution for the indecent assault at the defendant's trial as important explanatory evidence under gateway (c). Evidence of the caution was held to be important explanatory evidence without which the jury would not have been able properly to understand the case because it was hearing about the caution which had triggered the sisters' recollection of the sexual assaults the defendant had committed against them. Evidence of the caution would thus help the jury to understand why the sisters had not made their complaints at an earlier time and why the defendant came to be prosecuted some three decades after the crimes were committed.

The trial judge has *no* discretion to prevent the admission of bad character evidence under s 101(1)(c) if the CPS can establish that the above test for this gateway has been satisfied.

22.4.5   Gateway (d) – it is relevant to an important matter in issue between the defendant and the prosecution

22.4.5.1   Introduction

This gateway is the most contentious of all the gateways created by the CJA 2003, because it expands hugely the scope for the CPS to raise evidence of the defendant's bad character at trial.

'An important matter' is defined as 'a matter of substantial importance in the context of the case as a whole' (CJA 2003, s 112(1)). Although the word 'substantial' is not defined in the Act, the 'Explanatory Notes' accompanying it suggest that 'substantial' should be taken to mean something that is more than merely trivial or marginal.

Important matters in issue between the defendant and prosecution are defined in s 103(1) of the CJA 2003 as including:

(a)   the question whether the defendant has a *propensity to commit offences of the kind with which he is charged* (except where his having such propensity makes it no more likely that he is guilty of the offence); and

(b)   the question whether the defendant has a *propensity to be untruthful* (except where it is not suggested that the defendant's case is untruthful in any respect).

22.4.5.2   Propensity to commit offences of the kind with which he is charged

Introduction

The CPS is now permitted to place before the court evidence that a defendant has previous convictions in order to suggest that the defendant has a propensity to commit offences of the type with which he is currently charged. To place such evidence before the court, the CPS must first satisfy the court that establishing such propensity makes it more likely that the defendant committed the offence.

Section 103(2) of the CJA 2003 states that

> a defendant's propensity to commit offences of the kind with which he is charged may (without prejudice to any other way of doing so) be established by evidence that he has been convicted of:
>
> (a)   an offence of the same *description* as the one with which he is charged, or
>
> (b)   an offence of the same *category* as the one with which he is charged. (emphasis added)

This subsection does not apply in the case of a particular defendant if the court is satisfied that, as a result of the time which has passed since the conviction (or for any other reason), it would be unjust for it to be applied (CJA 2003, s 103(3)). This is most likely to arise in situations where a defendant's previous convictions are 'spent' (see **22.4.5.4** below).

Example

Peter is on trial for common assault. Peter has a previous conviction for common assault. This conviction occurred 10 years ago. Peter's solicitor will argue that this previous conviction should not be admitted in evidence at Peter's trial to show that Peter has a propensity to commit this type of offence. Given the amount of time that has elapsed since Peter's previous conviction, he will argue under s 103(3) that it would be unjust for this conviction to be used in the present case.

Similarly, the CPS may not raise a defendant's previous convictions to show propensity to commit offences of the kind with which he is charged if such a propensity makes it no more likely that he is guilty of the offence (s 103(1)(a)). This covers situations where there is no dispute about the facts of a case and the question is whether those facts constitute an offence.

Example

Jeremy is charged with the possession of a controlled drug under the Misuse of Drugs Act 1971. Jeremy has several previous convictions for such offences. Jeremy's defence to the current charge is that whilst he admits to having possession of the drug, he denies that it is a controlled drug as defined in s 2 of the Act. The question for the court to decide is not whether Jeremy had the drugs, but whether the drugs he had satisfied the legal definition of a controlled drug. Jeremy's previous convictions for the same offence will not be admissible, since they do not make it more likely that he is guilty of the offence.

Offences of the same description

Two offences will be of the same *description* as each other if the statement of the offence in a written charge or an indictment would, in each case, be in the same terms (CJA 2003, s103(4)(a)).

Example

Stephen is charged with assault occasioning actual bodily harm. He pleads not guilty on the basis that he was acting in reasonable self-defence. He has two previous convictions for the same offence. These will be offences of the same description because they would be described in the same way in a written charge or an indictment. The CPS may therefore attempt to raise these convictions at trial to show that Stephen has a propensity to commit offences of this type.

It is not necessary for the earlier conviction to be described in identical terms. What matters is whether the facts of the earlier conviction would be sufficient to support an offence charged in the same terms. For example, on a charge of burglary, a previous conviction for theft committed on premises whilst the defendant was a trespasser, would be in the same terms as the burglary.

Offences of the same category

Two offences will be of the same *category* as each other if they belong to the same category of offences prescribed by the Secretary of State (CJA 2003, s 103(4)(b)). The Secretary of State has so far prescribed two categories of offences which are in the same category:

(a)   the *sexual offences category*, which specifies a number of sexual offences committed against children under 16 years of age; and

(b)   the *theft category*, which includes the following offences:

    (i)   theft;

    (ii)   robbery;

    (iii)   burglary;

    (iv)   aggravated burglary;

    (v)   taking a motor vehicle or conveyance without authority;

    (vi)   aggravated vehicle taking;

    (vii)   handling stolen goods;

    (viii) going equipped for stealing;

    (ix)   making off without payment;

    (x)   any attempt to commit any of the above substantive offences;

    (xi)   aiding, abetting, counselling, procuring or inciting the commission of any of the above offences.

Example

Felicity pleads not guilty to a charge of theft. She has two previous convictions for the offence of burglary and one previous conviction for the offence of handling stolen goods. These will be offences of the same category because they fall within the 'theft category' prescribed by the Secretary of State. The CPS may therefore seek to raise these convictions in evidence to show that Felicity has a propensity to commit offences of this type.

May other offences be used to demonstrate a propensity to commit offences of the same kind?

Even if an earlier offence is not of the same description or in the same category as the offence charged, evidence of the defendant's conviction for the earlier offence may still be admissible under this gateway if there are significant factual similarities between the offences, since this would fall within the definition of having a propensity to commit offences of the kind with which the defendant is charged. This is much wider than the old 'similar fact' evidence provisions referred to at **22.2.1** above.

Example 1

In *R v Brima* [2006] EWCA Crim 408, the defendant was convicted of murder by stabbing his victim. The Court of Appeal held that the trial judge had correctly allowed the prosecution to adduce evidence of the defendant's previous convictions for two much less serious offences, each involving the use of a knife.

The first conviction in November 2002 was for assault occasioning actual bodily harm. After an altercation with the victim earlier the same day, the defendant stabbed him in the leg with a knife. This case had certain other similarities with the murder charge, in which the stabbing followed an earlier altercation between the deceased and a friend of the defendant. The second conviction in April 2003 was for robbery. The facts were that the defendant had held a knife to the throat of the victim, and demanded his training shoes and top which the victim handed over.

Although the previous convictions were not in the same category or of the same description as the murder charge, the prosecution contended that the defendant had a propensity to commit offences of violence using knives, either by inflicting or by threatening injury.

Example 2

Arthur is charged with common assault. The allegation is that, whilst under the influence of drink, Arthur punched a fellow customer at a pub after that customer had barged past Arthur, spilling his drink. Arthur pleads not guilty, alleging that the fellow customer attacked him first and he was acting in reasonable self-defence. Arthur has previous convictions for offences of affray and causing fear or provocation of violence (Public Order Act 1986, s 4). Both convictions arose out of incidents at a pub when Arthur became drunk and started arguing with fellow customers. Although these previous convictions are not in the same category or of the same description as the current offence, they may still be admissible to show Arthur's propensity to act in a violent manner when under the influence of drink.

May a propensity to commit offences of the kind charged be demonstrated other than through evidence of a defendant's previous convictions?

Although in most cases, propensity under s 101(1)(d) will be established by the CPS adducing evidence of the defendant's previous convictions, s 103(2) provides that this is 'without prejudice' to any other way of proving propensity to commit offences of the kind with which the defendant has been charged. This means that the CPS may attempt to show propensity other than through a defendant's previous convictions.

Example 1

Clive pleads not guilty to a charge of unlawful wounding. Shortly before the events giving rise to this charge, Clive was acquitted at trial on another charge of unlawful wounding. Clive was acquitted only after the victim of the assault failed to attend the trial to give evidence against him. The CPS may attempt to adduce in evidence the fact that Clive was previously tried for the same offence (and acquitted only after his victim failed to attend court) to show a propensity to commit this type of offence.

Example 2

Martin is charged with common assault following an allegation that he punched his next-door neighbour over a dispute about a right of way. Martin pleads not guilty, alleging that he was acting only in reasonable self-defence. Two years previously a similar incident had occurred and Martin was charged with the same offence, although the charge was dropped when the neighbour said that he did not want the matter to go to court. The CPS may attempt to adduce in evidence the fact that Martin was previously charged with the same offence to show a propensity to commit this type of offence.

Example 3

Wayne is charged with criminal damage. It is alleged that he was part of a gang that sprayed graffiti on a wall. Wayne pleads not guilty, claiming that although he was present at the time, he had nothing to do with the graffiti. Twelve months earlier Wayne received a caution from the police for spraying graffiti on another wall. The CPS may attempt to adduce evidence of the fact that Wayne has previously received a caution for the same offence to show a propensity to commit this type of offence.

R v Hanson, Gilmore & Pickstone

In *R v Hanson, Gilmore & Pickstone* [2005] Crim LR 787, the Court of Appeal set out guidelines for judges or magistrates to consider when the CPS seeks to adduce evidence of a defendant's previous convictions in order to demonstrate his propensity to commit offences of the kind with which he is charged. The Court stated as follows:

(a)   Three questions need to be considered should the CPS seek to adduce evidence of the defendant's bad character under this part of gateway (d):

   (i)   Does the defendant's history of offending show a propensity to commit offences?

   (ii)   If so, does that propensity make it more likely that the defendant committed the current offence?

   (iii) If so, is it just to rely on convictions of the same description or category, having in mind the overriding principle that proceedings must be fair?

   Only if the answer to each of these questions is in the affirmative should the convictions be allowed in evidence.

(b)   Offences which can be relied upon by the CPS to show this propensity may go beyond offences of the same description or of the same category.

(c)   The fewer the number of previous convictions the defendant has, the less likely it is that propensity will be established. If the defendant has only one previous conviction of the same description or category, this is unlikely to show propensity unless there are distinguishing circumstances or a tendency towards unusual behaviour. The Court gave examples of unusual behaviour as including fire starting and the sexual abuse of children.

(d)   The manner in which the previous and current offences were carried out may be highly relevant to propensity and the probative value of a defendant's previous convictions. The Court said that it was the factual circumstances of previous convictions that were important, rather than the simple fact that the defendant had been convicted.

Example 1

Norma is on trial for unlawful wounding involving the use of a knife. She is alleged to have stabbed her husband after she found out he had been having an affair. She has previous convictions for assaulting a police officer in the execution of his duty and common assault. These convictions arose after Norma got drunk in a pub and refused the landlord's request that she leave the pub premises. Norma punched the landlord and then punched a policeman who tried to arrest her. It is likely that these convictions would not be admissible through this gateway. They are not offences of the same description, neither are they offences of the same category (as they do not fall within the two categories prescribed by the Secretary of State). Nor are they admissible generally to show 'propensity'. They would be admissible only if there were significant factual similarities between them and the current offence with which Norma is charged. Such similarities do not exist here because there is a marked difference between punching a stranger when drunk and attacking a spouse with a knife.

Example 2

Sharon, a juvenile, is on trial for the theft of a mobile phone from the school locker of a fellow pupil. Sharon is pleading not guilty. Sharon has three previous convictions for offences of theft. On each occasion Sharon entered shop premises and stole cosmetic items. The prosecution will seek to adduce evidence of these convictions under gateway (d) to show that Sharon has a propensity to commit offences of the same description as the offence she is currently charged with. Sharon's solicitor may, however, argue that her previous convictions do not show a propensity to commit this type of offence because of the significant factual differences between the circumstances of these offences (thefts from a shop) and the facts of the current offence (theft from the locker of another pupil). It would then be for the court to determine whether the factual differences were such that the previous convictions could not be said to demonstrate a propensity to commit offences of theft.

Example 3

Mick is on trial for burglary. The CPS alleges that, after an argument over the ownership of some gardening equipment, Mick broke into a neighbour's garden shed and removed a quantity of tools. Mick has two previous convictions for theft. Both convictions arose after Mick stole groceries from a supermarket. At the time, Mick was unemployed and stole the groceries in order to provide food for his family. Mick has committed offences of the same category as the offence he is currently charged with, and the prosecution will therefore seek to adduce evidence of such convictions at trial under gateway (d). Mick's solicitor may, however, argue that Mick's previous convictions do not show a propensity to commit this type of offence because of the significant factual differences between the circumstances of these offences and the facts of the current offence. It would then be for the court to determine whether the factual differences were such that the previous convictions could not be said to demonstrate a propensity to commit offences of theft.

Example 4

Max is on trial for threatening behaviour (Public Order Act 1986, s 4) after he threatened some children who had thrown stones at his front door. Max has two previous convictions for the same offence. These convictions arose out of incidents at a local nightclub where Max works as a bouncer. On both occasions Max used threatening behaviour towards people in a drunken state who were attempting to gain entry to the nightclub. Max has committed offences of the same description as the offence he is currently charged with, and at his trial the prosecution will seek to adduce evidence of these convictions under gateway (d). Max's solicitor may, however, argue that Max's previous convictions do not show a propensity to commit this type of offence because of the significant factual differences between the circumstances of these offences and the facts of the current offence. It would then be for the court to determine whether the factual differences were such that the previous convictions could not be said to demonstrate a propensity to commit the offence of threatening behaviour.

Example 5

In *R v Tully* [2006] All ER (D) 249 (Mar), the defendant was convicted of robbery (involving the use of a knife). At his trial, the defendant's numerous previous convictions for offences of dishonesty were adduced under gateway (d) to show a propensity to commit offences of the kind charged. Although some of these convictions were for robbery, most of them were for more general dishonesty offences (such as theft), being offences of the same category (ie, the theft category). On appeal, the Court of Appeal held that whilst the robbery convictions were clearly admissible under gateway (d), the convictions for the other offences of dishonesty merely showed a propensity to acquire other people's property and were not therefore admissible under this gateway. Such convictions could not be said to show that the defendant had a propensity to commit the offence of robbery.

22.4.5.3 Propensity to be untruthful

When may the CPS suggest that the defendant has a propensity to be untruthful?

The CPS may now place before the court evidence of a defendant's previous convictions to show that the defendant has a propensity to be untruthful (and therefore that evidence given by the defendant at trial may lack credibility). The CPS will be permitted to do this only if it is suggested that the defendant's case is in any way untruthful (s 103(1)(b)).

Example 1

John is on trial for assaulting Martin. John has two previous convictions for perjury. John denies the charge, claiming that he was elsewhere at the time of the assault and that this is a case of mistaken identity. To obtain a conviction, the CPS will need to prove that John's defence is untruthful, and it may therefore seek to use evidence of John's previous convictions to show that John has a propensity to be untruthful.

Example 2

John is on trial for assaulting Martin. John has two previous convictions for perjury. John denies the charge, claiming that he acted only in self-defence. The CPS accepts that Martin attacked John first, but claims that the degree of force used by John went beyond what constitutes reasonable self-defence. There is no dispute between the parties as to the actual level of force used by John, merely a legal argument as to whether this level of force constitutes reasonable self-defence. The CPS is not seeking to prove that John's version of events is untruthful, and will therefore be unable to use evidence of John's previous convictions to show that John has a propensity to be untruthful.

Which offences will demonstrate a propensity to be untruthful?

In *R v Hanson, Gilmore & Pickstone* (see **22.4.5.2** above), the Court of Appeal said that previous convictions will not be admissible under this part of gateway (d) unless:

(a)   the offence itself demonstrates that the defendant has been untruthful; or

(b)   the defendant has pleaded not guilty in previous proceedings and has been disbelieved by a jury.

Specific offences which demonstrate a propensity to be untruthful

The Court drew a distinction between a propensity to be dishonest and a propensity to be untruthful. Only if a defendant's previous convictions demonstrated a propensity to be *untruthful* will they become admissible under this gateway. The Court stressed that the only specific types of offence that would demonstrate a propensity to be untruthful were offences where the defendant had actively sought to deceive or mislead another person. This includes previous convictions for perjury and offences involving an active deception of another (such as obtaining property by deception), but not other offences where dishonesty forms part of the mental element of the offence but where the defendant has not actually been untruthful and has not actively deceived anyone. For example, a previous conviction for theft is unlikely to demonstrate a propensity to be untruthful because, unless the defendant had actually sought to mislead or had lied to another person as part of the commission of the theft, although the defendant had acted dishonestly, he had not been untruthful. In practical terms this means that if the CPS seeks to rely on offences such as theft to demonstrate the defendant's propensity to be untruthful, it will need to investigate the actual circumstances of the offence to find out if the defendant was in any way untruthful during its commission.

Example 1

Duleep is charged with common assault. The CPS alleges that he punched his victim in the face for no reason. Duleep denies the charge, claiming that he was initially attacked by his victim and that he was acting only in self-defence. Duleep's alleged victim refutes this. Duleep has previous convictions for perjury and obtaining property by deception. These are offences which the CPS may attempt to raise in evidence to demonstrate that Duleep has a propensity to be untruthful.

Example 2

Miranda is charged with burglary. She denies the charge, raising the defence of alibi. Miranda has two previous convictions for obtaining services by deception and a previous conviction for theft from a shop. The CPS may seek to use the convictions for the deception to demonstrate that Miranda has a propensity to be untruthful, because such offences involve actively misleading another person. The CPS will not be allowed to use the conviction for theft for the same purpose. Although this conviction shows that Miranda acted dishonestly, it does not show that she was untruthful.

(The only exception to this would be if Miranda had actively misled or lied to someone during the commission of the theft. If, for example, Miranda had told the shop owner that there was a fire in another part of the shop in order to distract him and to give her the opportunity to steal items from the shop without being seen, this would demonstrate a propensity to be untruthful because she has told a lie as part of the commission of the offence.)

Although a previous conviction for theft will not in itself demonstrate a propensity to be untruthful, it is likely that the prosecution will seek to adduce evidence of a conviction for theft in breach of trust (in particular, theft from an employer) to demonstrate that the defendant has a propensity to be untruthful, since the commission of such an offence is likely to have involved the defendant having been untruthful to another person.

Example

Jordan is on trial for common assault. She denies the charge and enters a not guilty plea, claiming that the case against her has been fabricated by her alleged victim. Jordan has two previous convictions for theft in breach of trust. These convictions occurred when Jordan was employed as a check-out assistant at a supermarket. At the end of her shift, Jordan was required to calculate that day's takings at her till and to prepare a written slip recording the takings. On the occasions when she committed the thefts, Jordan filled in the slip to show that the day's takings were £20 less than they actually were. Jordan did this to cover up for the fact that on each occasion she had removed a £20 note from the till and put this in her pocket. These convictions are likely to be admissible to show that Jordan has a propensity to be untruthful, because Jordan told a lie when completing the slip in order to conceal her theft of the money from the till.

In his commentary on the *Hanson* case, Professor J R Spencer QC stated:

> ... s 103(1)(b) does not make potentially admissible evidence of previous convictions generally, or even previous offences of dishonesty. It does, however, make admissible evidence for convictions of offences that involve telling lies – and also previous convictions in fought cases where the defendant gave evidence, and his word was plainly disbelieved. (*New Law Journal*, 28 April 2005)

Convictions following a not guilty plea

Offences of *any* description may also fall within this part of gateway (d) if the defendant pleaded not guilty but was convicted following a trial at which the magistrates or jury disbelieved his version of events, since this will demonstrate that the defendant has been found by a court to have been untruthful on a previous occasion. This will be particularly significant when, on a prior occasion, the defendant employed the same defence as he is raising in the current proceedings, and was disbelieved by the jury or magistrates.

Example 1

Kathy is charged with common assault. She is pleading not guilty and will raise the defence of alibi at trial. Kathy has several previous convictions for various offences. On each occasion she pleaded not guilty and raised the defence of alibi, but was convicted following a trial in which her alibi was disbelieved. The CPS may attempt to raise these previous convictions in evidence to show that Kathy has a propensity to be untruthful.

Example 2

Barry is stopped by the police in the early hours of the morning driving a car that has been reported stolen. Barry is charged with taking the vehicle without consent (TWOC) and pleads not guilty. His defence is that he had the authority of the owner to be driving the vehicle. Barry has two previous convictions for theft. On both occasions he pleaded not guilty on the basis that he had the authority of the owner to be in possession of the stolen items, but was convicted following a trial at which his defence was disbelieved. The CPS may attempt to raise these previous convictions to show that Barry has a propensity to be untruthful.

Example 3

Indira is charged with theft of goods from a shop. She pleads not guilty on the basis that she forgot to pay for the items. Indira has two previous convictions for theft from a shop. On both occasions she raised as her defence the fact that she had merely forgotten to pay for the items, but was convicted following a trial at which her version of events was disbelieved. The prosecution will attempt to raise these previous convictions to show that Indira has a propensity to be untruthful.

Example 4

Tim is charged with affray after a fight between two groups of men which was caught on a CCTV camera. Tim denies the charge and raises an alibi defence. He claims that the image caught on the camera is that of someone else and that he was at home at the time of the alleged affray. Tim has two previous convictions for assault occasioning actual bodily harm. On both occasions Tim pleaded not guilty on the basis that he was acting in reasonable self-defence. He was convicted, however, following a trial before the magistrates. Although Tim's defence to the charge of affray is not the same defence which he raised when accused of assault (and which was disbelieved by the magistrates), the CPS may nevertheless attempt to use the convictions for assault to show that Tim has a propensity to be untruthful.

Although it is not necessary for the CPS to show that when he was convicted of the previous offence(s), the defendant raised the same defence as he is raising in the current proceedings, it will be of huge evidential significance for the CPS to demonstrate that a defendant has a 'stock' defence which a previous jury or bench of magistrates have disbelieved.

May a propensity to be untruthful be shown other than through previous convictions?

The CPS may attempt to show that a defendant has a propensity to be untruthful other than by reference to his previous convictions (*R v Somanathan & Others* [2005] EWCA Crim 2866). In this case the defendant was a priest, who was alleged to have raped his victim on two occasions following a prolonged period of sexual 'grooming' at a time when the victim was emotionally vulnerable. The defendant denied the rapes, and also denied that he had behaved improperly at any time either in relation to his alleged victim or in relation to any other women. The Court of Appeal held that the trial judge had acted correctly in permitting the prosecution to call evidence from three other women who, at a time when they had been emotionally vulnerable, had been subjected to sexually-charged approaches from the defendant (but who had not then been raped). The Court said that this evidence was admissible to demonstrate that the defendant had a propensity to be untruthful, because it cast doubt on the credibility of his assertion that he has not previously acted improperly towards women.

Other evidence which the court may be prepared to admit to show that the defendant has a propensity to be untruthful includes:

(a)   evidence that a defendant told lies about himself on a job application form; or

(b)   evidence that a defendant has told lies about himself in order to gain some position of public trust or responsibility within the community.

22.4.5.4   Excluding evidence admitted under gateway (d)

Only the prosecution may adduce evidence of a defendant's previous convictions under gateway (d). Under s 101(3) of the CJA 2003, the court *must* not admit this evidence if:

> ... on an application by the defendant to exclude it, it appears to the court that the admission of the evidence would have such an adverse effect on the fairness of the proceedings that the court ought not to admit it.

This is the same test that that the court must apply when deciding whether to exclude unfairly obtained evidence under s 78 of PACE 1984 (see **21.21** above), save that under s 78 the court has a *discretion* to exclude the evidence if the test is satisfied, whereas under s 101(3) the court *must* exclude the evidence if the test is satisfied. The courts are most likely to use their powers under s 101(3) in three situations:

(a)   When the nature of a defendant's previous convictions is such that the jury are likely to convict a defendant on the basis of these convictions alone, rather than examining the other evidence placed before them, or where the evidence of the previous convictions is more prejudicial than probative.

Example 1

Gareth is charged with the theft of a bottle of whisky from a supermarket, to which he enters a not guilty plea. Gareth elects trial in the Crown Court. Gareth has a previous conviction for rape. Gareth raised the defence of consent in relation to this charge, but was convicted following a trial at which his defence was disbelieved. Although the prosecution may attempt to use this conviction to show that Gareth has a propensity to be untruthful, it is likely that the judge would exclude evidence of this previous conviction under s 101(3). The offence Gareth is currently charged with is relatively minor and, in the circumstances, allowing the jury to hear that Gareth has a previous conviction for a very serious sexual offence is likely to be more prejudicial to his case than probative of his propensity to be untruthful. There is a danger that a jury hearing about the conviction for rape would be prejudiced against Gareth and may convict him on this basis alone, rather than considering the other evidence in the case.

Example 2

Seamus is charged with shoplifting. Seamus has 15 previous convictions for the same offence. The prosecution will seek to adduce evidence of these convictions at trial to show that Seamus has a propensity to commit this kind of offence. Although these convictions clearly show that Seamus does have such a propensity, the sheer number of such convictions may result in the jury assuming that Seamus is guilty of the current offence solely on the basis of these convictions, rather than examining the evidence placed before them (ie the convictions may be more prejudicial than probative). In such a case, the judge may use his power under s 101(3) to limit the number of Seamus's previous convictions, evidence of which the prosecution may place before the jury. For example, the judge may allow the prosecution to adduce evidence of Seamus's three most recent convictions for this offence.

(b)   When the CPS seeks to adduce previous convictions to support a case which is otherwise weak (*R v Hanson, Gilmore & Pickstone* [2005] Crim LR 787 – see **22.4.10** below).

(c)   When the defendant's previous convictions are 'spent'. The Rehabilitation of Offenders Act 1974 provides that after a prescribed period of time, certain convictions are spent. This means that, for most purposes (such as completing an application form for a job), the convicted person is to be treated as never having been convicted of the spent offence. The rehabilitation period varies with the sentence, as follows:

absolute discharge	6 months
conditional discharge	1 year or period of order
fine/community sentence	5 years
custodial sentence up to 6 months	7 years
custodial sentence between 6 and 30 months	10 years

A conviction for an offence which was punished by a custodial sentence exceeding 30 months cannot become spent.

Although the Act specifically does not prevent 'spent' convictions from being admissible in evidence in subsequent criminal proceedings, it is likely that the court will consider exercising its discretion under s101(3) in such cases. In particular, s 101(4) provides that when an application to exclude evidence is made under s 101(3), the court must have regard to the length of time between the matters to which that evidence relates and the matters which form the subject of the offence charged.

In *R v Somanathan & Others* (see **22.4.5.3** above), the Court of Appeal held that, bearing in mind the defendant's right to a fair trial under Article 6 of the ECHR (see **1.8.3**), the trial judge should if necessary encourage a defendant to make an application to exclude evidence of his bad character under s 101(3).

(In addition to the court's discretionary power to exclude evidence of a defendant's previous convictions under s 101(3), the court must not allow the prosecution to adduce evidence of a previous conviction of a defendant in order to show that the defendant has a propensity to commit offences of the kind charged if the court is satisfied that, as a result of the time which has passed since the conviction, it would be unjust for it to be applied (CJA 2003, s 103(3)) – see **22.4.5.2** above. As with its discretionary power under s 101(3), the court is likely to consider it unjust to rely on a previous conviction to demonstrate a propensity to commit offences of the kind charged when that previous conviction is spent.)

22.4.5.5   Gateway (d) – summary

The prosecution will seek to adduce evidence of a defendant's previous convictions under gateway (d) to demonstrate that:

(a)   the defendant has a propensity to commit offences of the kind charged; or

(b)   the defendant has a propensity to be untruthful.

Previous convictions showing a propensity to commit offences of the kind charged will be convictions for offences of the same description or category, or convictions for offences where there is a significant factual similarity between the previous conviction and the current offence.

Previous convictions showing a propensity to be untruthful will be convictions for specific offences where a lie has been told (eg, obtaining property by deception or perjury), or offences where the defendant pleaded not guilty but was convicted following a trial. Offences of dishonesty (such as theft) will not generally show a propensity to be untruthful, unless the defendant has told a lie as part of the commission of the offence.

The defendant's solicitor may seek to challenge the admissibility of previous convictions which the prosecution seek to admit under gateway (d) in two ways:

(a)   He may argue that the previous convictions do not actually demonstrate the relevant propensity and so do not satisfy gateway (d). For example:

   (i)   How many convictions does the defendant have? One conviction is unlikely to show a propensity.

   (ii)   If the previous convictions are being adduced to show a propensity to commit offences of the same kind:

     —   do the factual circumstances of the previous convictions differ from the facts of the current offence;

     —   would it be unjust to rely on them given the time which has elapsed since they occurred (s 103(3)); or

     —   does the propensity make it no more likely that the defendant is guilty of the offence?

   (iii)   If the previous convictions are being adduced to show a propensity to be untruthful, is it not suggested that the defendant's case is in any way untruthful?

(b)   If the previous convictions do show the relevant propensity, can the court be persuaded to exercise its discretionary power under s 101(3) to exclude the convictions? Arguments that may be raised include:

   (i)   Would the convictions be more prejudicial than probative? Is there a danger that the defendant would be convicted on the basis of his previous convictions alone, due either to the extent or to the nature of such convictions?

   (ii)   Are the convictions being used to support a prosecution case that is otherwise weak?

   (iii)   Are the previous convictions spent?

A flowchart to illustrate the operation of gateway (d) is set out at **22.9.3** below.

22.4.6   Gateway (e) – it has substantial probative value in relation to an important matter in issue between the defendant and a co-defendant

22.4.6.1   Introduction

This gateway may be used only by a defendant to admit evidence of a co-defendant's bad character, not by the CPS. The Explanatory Notes to the CJA 2003 (see **22.4.5.1** above) suggest that the term 'substantial probative value' is to be widely construed, and that a court should exclude evidence only where its value is no more than 'marginal or trivial'. 'An important matter' is defined as 'a matter of substantial importance in the context of the case as a whole' (CJA 2003, s 112(1)). A defendant is likely to want to admit evidence of a co-defendant's bad character to show either that the co-defendant has a propensity to be untruthful (and thus to undermine the credibility of the evidence that defendant gives), or to show that the co-defendant has a propensity to commit the kind of offence with which they have both been charged (thereby suggesting that it is the co-defendant, rather than the defendant, who is guilty of having committed the offence).

22.4.6.2   Propensity to be untruthful

Section 104(1) of the CJA 2003 states:

> (1)   Evidence which is relevant to the question whether the defendant has a propensity to be untruthful is admissible on that basis under section 101(1)(e) only if the nature or conduct of his defence is such as to undermine the co-defendant's defence.

This gateway preserves the pre-CJA 2003 position in relation to what are commonly known as 'cut-throat' defence situations. Such situations will arise where there are two (or more) defendants jointly charged with an offence, with each defendant pleading not guilty and accusing the other defendant(s) of having committed the offence. It will be advantageous to a defendant in such a situation to be allowed to cross-examine his fellow defendant about his previous convictions so as to undermine the credibility of that co-defendant's evidence, and to demonstrate that the co-defendant has a propensity to be untruthful.

As with gateway (d) (see **22.4.5**), the previous convictions of a co-defendant which a defendant will be able to adduce in evidence in order to show that the co-defendant has a propensity to be untruthful will be specific offences involving the making of a false statement or representation (for example, obtaining property by deception or perjury), or any offence where the co-defendant was convicted at trial after entering a not guilty plea but having his defence disbelieved by the court. More general offences of dishonesty (such as theft) will be admissible only if the defendant can show that the co-defendant told a lie as part of the commission of the offence.

Example

Albert and Harold are jointly charged with the burglary of a warehouse. Each pleads not guilty, alleging that the other was solely responsible for the crime. Albert has a previous conviction for obtaining services by deception. He also has two previous convictions for offences of theft, both convictions following a trial at which his alibi defence was disbelieved. As Albert's defence (that Harold was solely responsible for the burglary) will undermine Harold's defence, Harold will raise Albert's previous convictions at trial in order to show that Albert has a propensity to be untruthful.

Although the use of this gateway to show that a co-defendant has a propensity to be untruthful will most commonly be used in a 'cut-throat' defence situation, the gateway may also apply if the co-defendant's defence is merely inconsistent with that of the defendant, as opposed to contradicting it completely.

Example

Albert and Harold are jointly charged with the burglary of a warehouse. The CPS alleges that they forced open a window and stole the contents of the warehouse. Each pleads not guilty. Albert raises an alibi defence and claims that he does not know Harold. Harold raises a separate alibi defence. He does, however, admit to knowing Albert and to selling Albert a crowbar shortly before the burglary occurred. Harold has previous convictions for perjury and attempting to pervert the course of justice. Although Harold is not raising a cut-throat defence, his defence is inconsistent with Albert's defence because Harold says that he knows Albert and sold him a crowbar, both of which allegations Albert will deny. Albert will therefore seek to raise Harold's previous convictions at trial to show that Harold has a propensity to be untruthful.

This gateway cannot be used by a defendant against his co-defendant if the co-defendant merely denies participating in the offence and does not say anything to undermine the defence put forward by the defendant (*R v Edwards & Rowlands* [2005] EWCA Crim 3244 – see **22.3** above).

Example

Graham and Arthur are jointly charged with assaulting Brian. Both enter not guilty pleas. Graham has several previous convictions for offences of deception. Graham raises the defence of alibi, claiming that he was elsewhere at the time of the assault and that he has been mistakenly identified as one of the assailants. Arthur claims that he was acting in self-defence after he had been attacked by Brian. Arthur says that a third person pulled Brian off him, but the incident happened so quickly that he cannot recall what that person looked like. If Graham raises the defence of alibi at trial, Arthur will not be able to raise Graham's previous convictions under s 101(1)(e) to demonstrate that Graham has a propensity to be untruthful. Graham's defence does not contradict the defence put forward by Arthur: Graham is not saying that Arthur carried out the assault; neither is Arthur saying that Graham was the other person involved in the assault.

22.4.6.3   Propensity to commit offences of the same kind

A defendant may also want to raise in evidence the fact that a co-defendant has previous convictions for offences of the kind with which they have both been charged, in order to demonstrate that the co-defendant has a propensity to commit such offences and is therefore the more likely of the two to have committed the current offence.

A defendant who seeks to use a co-defendant's previous convictions for this purpose does *not* need to show that the nature or conduct of the co-defendant's defence undermines his own defence (*R v Edwards & Rowlands* – see **22.3** above). He will, however, need to demonstrate that such convictions are relevant to an important matter in issue between himself and the co-defendant, and that the relevance of such convictions is more than merely marginal or trivial (see **22.4.6.1** above). This will be the case when the defendant denies having committed the offence and seeks to blame his co-defendant.

Example

Helen and Andrei are jointly charged with wounding with intent. The CPS alleges that they stabbed their victim with a knife. Both are pleading not guilty. Helen claims to have been an innocent bystander and that the attack was committed by Andrei alone. Helen has no previous convictions. Andrei has two previous convictions for wounding with intent. On both occasions Andrei used a weapon. Helen will seek to use Andrei's previous convictions in order to show that Andrei has a propensity to commit offences of violence using a weapon, and that he rather than Helen is more likely to have committed the current offence.

The previous convictions of a co-defendant which a defendant is likely to be able to adduce in evidence in order to show that the co-defendant has a propensity to commit offences of the kind with which they have both been charged will be convictions for any offence where the factual circumstances are similar to the facts of the current offence.

The trial judge has *no* discretion to prevent the admission of evidence of the bad character of a co-defendant under s 101(1)(e) if the defendant can establish that the above test for admitting evidence under this gateway is satisfied.

22.4.7   Gateway (f) – it is evidence to correct a false impression given by the defendant

A defendant will give a false impression 'if he is responsible for the making of an express or implied assertion which is apt to give the court or jury a false or misleading impression about the defendant' (CJA 2003, s 105(1)(a)).

A defendant will be treated as being responsible for making such an assertion if the assertion is:

(a)   made by the defendant in the proceedings (for example, when giving evidence in the witness box, or in a defence statement served on the CPS);

(b)   made by the defendant when being questioned under caution by the police before charge, or on being charged;

(c)   made by a witness called by the defendant;

(d)   made by any witness in cross-examination in response to a question asked by the defendant that is intended to elicit it; or

(e)   made by any person out of court, and the defendant adduces evidence of it in the proceedings (CJA 2003, s 105(2)).

Example 1

Alan is on trial for theft. He has several previous convictions for various offences. When giving evidence-in-chief, Alan says that he is of previous good character and has no previous convictions. The CPS will be permitted to correct the false impression given by Alan by by adducing evidence of his previous convictions.

Example 2

Malik is charged with indecently assaulting Sarah. He has convictions for various offences against the person. Malik gives evidence at trial about specific occasions when he has behaved well towards women, and says that he would never use violence against a woman. The CPS will be permitted to correct the false impression Malik has given about his character by adducing evidence of his previous convictions. Although the previous convictions do not relate to Malik's behaviour towards women, he has given a false impression about his character which the CPS is entitled to correct.

Example 3

Phillip is on trial for common assault. Phillip has several previous convictions for offences involving violence. When the allegation of assault was put to Phillip in interview at the police station, Phillip said: 'I would never do such a thing. I'm a good Christian and I go to church every Sunday.' The CPS will be permitted to correct the false impression given by Phillip in the police interview by adducing evidence of his previous convictions.

Example 4

Frances is on trial for theft. She has two previous convictions for theft. Frances calls her mother Doreen as an alibi witness. When giving evidence Doreen says: 'My daughter would never steal anything. I've brought her up better than that.' The CPS will be permitted to correct the false impression Doreen has given about her daughter by adducing evidence of Frances' previous convictions.

Example 5

Jeremy is on trial for theft from his employer, a large building company. Jeremy has a number of previous convictions for property-related offences (about which Jeremy's employer knew nothing). In cross-examination of the foreman under whom Jeremy worked, Jeremy's solicitor says: 'Jeremy isn't the kind of person to steal anything, is he?' The foreman replies: 'I agree. He always struck me as an honest sort of lad.' The CPS will be permitted to correct the false impression which this gives by adducing evidence of Jeremy's previous convictions.

Section 105(4) of the CJA 2003 widens the manner in which a defendant may create a false impression by providing that:

> (4)   Where it appears to the Court that a defendant, by means of his conduct (other than the giving of evidence) in the proceedings, is seeking to give the Court or jury an impression about himself that is false or misleading, the Court may if it appears just to do so treat the defendant as being responsible for the making of an assertion which is apt to give that impression.

'Conduct' here includes appearance or dress. This subsection is designed to cover situations where a defendant changes his appearance, or dresses in a manner which is intended to create a false or misleading impression about him.

Example

William is on trial for armed robbery. He appears before the jury wearing an army uniform and several medals for gallantry. William has never served in the army. He does, however, have previous convictions for offences of violence. The CPS will be permitted to correct the false impression given by William by adducing evidence of his previous convictions.

Only prosecution evidence is admissible under gateway (f). Evidence may be admitted under this gateway 'only if it goes no further than is necessary to correct the false impression' (CJA 2003, s 105(6)). Further, the defendant's bad character cannot be admitted under this gateway if, having made a false impression, the defendant 'withdraws or disassociates himself from it'. This provision is intended to cover the situation where the defendant says or does something to create a false impression, but subsequently (and prior to trial) makes some form of retraction.

The trial judge has *no* discretion to prevent the admission of bad character evidence under s 101(1)(f) if the prosecution can establish that the above test for this gateway has been satisfied.

22.4.8   Gateway (g) – the defendant has made an attack on another person's character

22.4.8.1   What constitutes an attack on another person's character?

Under the law prior to the CJA 2003 coming into force, a defendant was given some latitude in what he was permitted to say about prosecution witnesses before he lost his shield against cross-examination as to his bad character (see **22.2.1** above). In particular, a defendant was permitted to make an emphatic denial of guilt (which often by implication meant an accusation that a prosecution witness was lying) without losing his shield. The defendant's shield would be lost only if he:

(a)   alleged that a prosecution witness had committed the offence with which he (the defendant) was charged;

(b)   alleged that a witness for the prosecution had a specific reason for telling lies (such as an allegation that the witness was biased or had a grudge against him);

(c)   alleged that the police had acted improperly either by purposely breaching PACE 1984 or the Codes of Practice, or by fabricating evidence; or

(d)   cross-examined a witness for the prosecution about that witness's previous convictions.

Simply accusing a witness of lying was not in itself sufficient to lose his shield unless the defendant said that the witness had a particular reason for lying.

Gateway (g) widens considerably the way in which a defendant may now have his bad character raised at trial. Under this gateway, a defendant's bad character will become admissible against him (even if he does not himself give evidence at trial) if he makes an attack on *any* person's character. The attack does not necessarily need to be on the character of a witness for the prosecution who is attending court to give evidence. It may be an attack on the character of a person who is dead, or a person whom the CPS does not intend to call to give evidence. Furthermore, the attack on the character of the other person does not necessarily need to take place at trial. The attack may be made when the defendant is being questioned at the police station, or in a defence statement which is served on the CPS.

Section 106(1) of the CJA 2003 provides that:

(1)   For the purposes of section 101(1)(g) a defendant makes an attack on another person's character if—

(a)   he adduces evidence attacking the other person's character,

(b)   he [or his legal representative] asks questions in cross-examination that are intended to elicit such evidence, or are likely to do so, or

(c)   evidence is given of an imputation about the other person made by the defendant—

(i)   on being questioned under caution, before charge, about the offence for which he is charged, or

(ii)   on being charged with the offence or officially informed that he might be prosecuted for it.

Evidence attacking another person's character is evidence to the effect that the other person has:

(a)   committed an offence (whether a different offence from the one with which the defendant is charged or the same one); or

(b)   behaved, or is disposed to behave, in a reprehensible way (CJA 2003, s 106(2)).

In *R v Hanson, Gilmore & Pickstone* [2005] Crim LR 787 (see **22.4.5.2** above), the Court of Appeal said that when considering this gateway, authorities preceding the CJA 2003 will remain relevant. This will be particularly important if there is a dispute as to whether comments made by the defendant (or questions asked of a witness for the prosecution in cross-examination) constitute an attack on the character of that witness. Although the courts are still likely to find that a defendant who makes an emphatic denial of guilt has not attacked the character of another (even if this denial suggests that a prosecution witness is lying), it is likely that the courts will give a very wide interpretation to s 106(2). For example, in *R v Ball* [2005] EWCA Crim 2826, the defendant was charged with rape and raised the defence of consent. When interviewed at the police station, the defendant emphatically denied the complainant's version of what had taken place, but then went further and made a disparaging remark about the complainant's sexual promiscuity, referring to her as a 'slag'. This imputation was held to be sufficient to enable the CPS to raise at trial evidence of the defendant's previous convictions. The Court of Appeal did say, however, that the defendant's statement that the complainant had fabricated the allegation of rape would not have been sufficient in itself to invoke s 101(1)(g). This section came into play only because the defendant had gone further and made a sweeping attack on the complainant's character.

Evidence of a defendant's bad character which is adduced under gateway (g) may be used to suggest that the defendant:

(a) is not a credible witness (if the defendant has convictions for offences where he has been untruthful, or has been convicted of any offence following a trial at which his version of the facts was disbelieved);

(b) has a propensity to commit a particular type of offence (if the defendant's previous convictions are for offences of the same kind as the offence with which the defendant is currently charged); or

(c) is generally predisposed to act in a criminal way (if the defendant has previous convictions for any other type of offence).

Example 1

John is on trial for murder. John has previous convictions for perjury and attempting to pervert the course of justice. Part of the evidence relied upon by the CPS is an alleged confession that John made to PC Smith when he was initially arrested for the offence. When John gives evidence at trial he tells the jury: 'The confession is a pack of lies. I never said anything and PC Smith is as bent as they come.' Accusing PC Smith of being a liar and being corrupt is an attack on PC Smith's character. At trial the CPS will seek to adduce evidence of John's previous convictions because John has attacked the character of PC Smith.

(It is very common for defendants to allege that police officers are lying. To suggest to a police officer who is giving evidence that he is lying or has fabricated evidence will always constitute an attack on that officer's character. It would not, however, be an attack on a police officer's character to suggest that the officer was merely 'mistaken' as to what he saw or heard.)

Example 2

Jim is on trial for the burglary of factory premises where he had worked until recently. Jim has a number of previous convictions for similar offences. One of the witnesses for the prosecution is PC Gray, who claims to have found the items stolen in the burglary at Jim's flat. In cross-examination, Jim's solicitor puts to PC Gray the allegation that he (PC Gray) planted the stolen items in Jim's flat in order to frame him for the crime. Suggesting that PC Gray planted evidence in this way is an attack on the character of PC Gray. At trial the CPS will seek to adduce evidence of Jim's previous convictions because Jim has attacked the character of PC Gray.

Example 3

Trudy is on trial for common assault. She has several previous convictions for offences involving the use of violence, and also convictions for various offences of deception. Her defence is one of mistaken identity. She claims the assault was in fact carried out by Carrie, a witness for the prosecution. When giving evidence, Trudy tells the magistrates: 'It wasn't me that did it, it was Carrie. It wouldn't be the first time she's smacked someone. She's got a real temper on her.' This is an attack on the character of Carrie. At trial the CPS will seek to adduce evidence of Trudy's previous convictions because she has made an attack on the character of Carrie.

Example 4

Veronica is on trial for theft of items from a jewellery shop. Veronica has several previous convictions for offences of theft and deception. When she was questioned under caution at the police station, Veronica told the police: 'I had nothing to do with the theft. The owner of the shop is just trying to swindle his insurance company.' This is an attack on the character of the owner of the shop. At trial, the CPS will seek to adduce evidence of Veronica's previous convictions because Veronica has attacked the character of the owner of the shop.

Example 5

Henry is on trial for rape. He has previous convictions for various sexual offences. In his defence statement, Henry raises the defence of alibi and accuses Vincent of having committed the rape. This is an attack on Vincent's character. Vincent has not been charged with any offence and will not be giving evidence at Henry's trial. Even though Vincent will not be attending court to give evidence, at trial the CPS will seek to adduce evidence of Henry's previous convictions because Henry has attacked the character of Vincent.

Example 6

Margaret is on trial for assault occasioning actual bodily harm. She alleges that the complainant, Jennifer, attacked her and that she was merely acting in self-defence. Both Margaret and Jennifer have several previous convictions for offences of violence. Margaret makes an application to the court for leave to raise Jennifer's previous convictions in evidence at trial under s 100(1)(b) (see **22.5.3** below). This is an attack on Jennifer's character. At trial the CPS will seek to adduce evidence of Margaret's previous convictions because Margaret has sought to attack the character of Jennifer.

(In such a case the court is likely either to give leave for the previous convictions of both Margaret and Jennifer to be admissible at trial, or to rule that neither person's previous convictions are admissible.)

22.4.8.2 Excluding evidence admitted under gateway (g)

Only the prosecution may adduce evidence of a defendant's previous convictions under gateway (g). As with gateway (d), the court must exclude evidence that would otherwise be admitted under this gateway if, on an application by the defendant, the admission of the evidence would have such an adverse effect on the fairness of the proceedings that the court ought not to admit it (CJA 2003, s 101(3)) (see **22.4.5.4** above).

The court is likely to exercise its discretion here when the effect of allowing the CPS to bring forward evidence of the defendant's previous convictions would be out of proportion to the significance of the defendant's attack on the character of another person (ie, where the evidence would be more prejudicial than probative). In such a situation, admitting evidence of previous convictions would have an adverse effect on the fairness of the trial because there would be a danger that the jury would convict the defendant on the basis of his previous convictions alone, rather than considering all the evidence in the case.

Example

Fergus is charged with assault occasioning actual bodily harm following a fight in a pub when he is alleged to have pushed a fellow customer (John) to the ground, causing a gash to John's cheek. Fergus pleads not guilty and elects trial at the Crown Court. In his interview at the police station, Fergus said to the police: 'John's had it in for me ever since I complained about his dog running across my garden. He's nothing but a troublemaker.'

This is an attack on John's character which would then permit the prosecution to adduce evidence of Fergus's previous convictions at his trial. Fergus has previous convictions for a number of sexual offences, including sexual assault and gross indecency with children. Although these convictions would be admissible under gateway (g), the trial judge may exercise his discretion under s 101(3) to prevent the prosecution adducing evidence of these convictions at trial. It is likely that the prejudicial effect of the jury finding out about such convictions would outweigh the probative value of such convictions in determining Fergus's guilt.

The court may also exercise its discretion to exclude a defendant's previous convictions which the CPS seeks to adduce under s 101(1)(g) if those convictions are 'spent' (see **22.4.5.4** above), or if the CPS is attempting to raise such convictions to support a case which is otherwise weak.

If the defendant has attacked the character of another person during the course of an interview at the police station, the court may exercise its discretion under s 101(3) to prevent the prosecution from adducing evidence at trial of the defendant's previous convictions if the defendant can argue that he made an attack on the character of that other person only because of the nature of the questioning techniques employed by the police (if, for example, the defendant was goaded into attacking the character of a prosecution witness, or the interviewing officer specifically asked the defendant what his opinion of a particular person was).

If the court rules that because of the manner in which the police conducted the interview, the entire interview record is inadmissible, any attack which the defendant made on the character of another person during the course of the interview will not entitle the prosecution to adduce evidence of the defendant's bad character under gateway (g), since details of the defendant's attack on the character of that other person will not be adduced in evidence. The court will not need to exercise its discretion under s 101(3) in such a situation, since the prosecution will be unable to argue that the test for admitting evidence of the defendant's bad character under gateway (g) is satisfied.

22.4.8.3 Gateway (g) – summary

The prosecution will seek to adduce evidence of a defendant's previous convictions under gateway (g) if the defendant has attacked the character of a prosecution witness. The defendant may do this by:

(a) attacking the character of the witness when he is interviewed at the police station;

(b) attacking the character of the witness in his defence statement;

(c) asking the witness about his previous convictions in cross-examination; or

(d) adducing evidence of the witness's previous convictions.

If this gateway is satisfied, the prosecution will be entitled to adduce evidence of *all* the previous convictions which the defendant has.

The defendant's solicitor may seek to challenge the admissibility of previous convictions which the prosecution seek to admit under gateway (g) in two ways:

(a)   He may argue that the test for admitting evidence of the defendant's bad character under gateway (g) has not been satisfied. For example:

    (i)   If the defendant has merely accused a witness of lying, this is unlikely to satisfy gateway (g) (unless the witness is a police officer). An attack on the witness's character generally needs to go beyond this and to suggest a reason for the lie.

    (ii)   If the attack on the character of the witness was made during an interview at the police station, can the interview record be excluded because of breaches of PACE 1984 or the Codes of Conduct by the police?

(b)   If (a) is unsuccessful, can the court be persuaded to exercise its discretionary power under s 101(3) to exclude the convictions? Arguments that may be raised include:

    (i)   Would the convictions be more prejudicial than probative? Is there a danger that the defendant would be convicted on the basis of his previous convictions alone, due to the extent or the nature of such convictions?

    (ii)   Are the convictions being used to support a prosecution case that is otherwise weak?

    (iii)   Are the previous convictions spent?

    (iv)   If the attack on the character of the witness was made during an interview at the police station, did the defendant make the attack only because of the questioning techniques adopted by the police? Was he goaded into making the attack?

A flowchart summarising the operation of s 101(1)(a)–(g) is set out at **22.9.1** below.

22.4.9   Does the court have any other power to exclude bad character evidence?

The court has no power under the provisions of the CJA 2003 to exclude bad character evidence admitted under any gateway other than (d) and (g). Bad character evidence under gateways (a), (b), (c), (e) and (f) is automatically admissible if the requirements for each of these gateways are satisfied.

The court does, however, retain a discretionary power under s 78 of PACE 1984 to exclude evidence on which the prosecution propose to rely if the admission of the evidence would have such an adverse effect on the fairness of the proceedings that it ought not to be admitted (see **Chapter 21**). In *R v Highton & Others* [2005] EWCA Crim 1985, the Court of Appeal held that judges should apply the provisions of s 78 when making rulings as to the use of evidence of bad character, and exclude evidence where it would be appropriate to do so under s 78. The Court went on to say that adopting such a policy would also ensure that the court complied with the defendant's right to a fair trial under Article 6 of the ECHR (see **1.8.3**).

22.4.10 General guidance about the bad character provisions of the Criminal Justice Act 2003

22.4.10.1 General principles

In *R v Hanson, Gilmore & Pickstone* [2005] Crim LR 787 (see **22.4.5.2** above), the Court of Appeal took the opportunity to lay down general guidelines for dealing with evidence of a defendant's bad character under the CJA 2003:

(a) Prosecution applications to adduce evidence of the defendant's bad character should *not* be made as a matter of routine. Such applications should be carefully balanced, depending on the facts of the case. Anecdotal evidence from around the country suggests that, in certain regions, the CPS is making applications to adduce evidence of a defendant's bad character as a matter of course. This should not happen.

(b) Where the evidence against the defendant is otherwise weak, it may be unfair to admit evidence of the defendant's previous convictions to bolster this evidence. Courts should also have regard to the amount of time which has elapsed between the earlier conviction(s) and the commission of the offence for which the defendant is charged. Old convictions may affect the fairness of current proceedings.

(c) Each individual previous conviction needs to be examined separately, rather than the court simply applying a broad-brush approach and deciding that all previous convictions should be admissible.

(d) Details of the sentence passed in relation to the earlier offence are unlikely to be probative or admissible, even if the offence itself is admissible.

(e) The Court of Appeal will be slow to interfere with a trial judge's discretion to admit evidence of a defendant's bad character, and will interfere only if such discretion has been exercised in an irrational manner.

(f) When the CPS makes an application to adduce evidence of the defendant's bad character, it should decide at that point whether it seeks to rely on the fact of the conviction alone or on the factual circumstances of the offence as well.

22.4.10.2 Role of the trial judge

In addition to providing general guidelines about the new rules, the Court of Appeal also said in *Hanson* that a judge, when directing a jury in a case where the jury had been told about the defendant's previous convictions, should tell the jury that:

(a) they should not conclude that a defendant is guilty or untruthful merely because he has previous convictions;

(b) although previous convictions may show a propensity either to commit offences or to be untruthful, this does not mean that the defendant has committed the current offence or has been untruthful in the current case;

(c) whether the previous convictions do show a propensity is for them to decide;

(d) they must take into account what (if anything) a defendant has said about his previous convictions; and

(e) although they are entitled, if they find propensity is shown, to take this into account when determining guilt, propensity is only one relevant factor and they must assess its significance in the light of all the other evidence in the case.

The Court of Appeal stressed that the judge should warn the jury against placing undue reliance on previous convictions and should direct the jury that evidence of bad character cannot be used to bolster a weak case or to prejudice the minds of the jury against a defendant.

In the subsequent case of *R v Chohan* [2005] EWCA Crim 1813, the Court of Appeal held that a trial judge, when allowing evidence of a defendant's bad character to be placed before the jury, had to give a clear warning that reliance on previous convictions could not by itself prove guilt. Subject to this, the question of what weight is to be attached to a defendant's previous convictions is matter for the jury rather than the judge.

In *R v Renda & Others* [2005] EWCA Crim 2826, which involved several conjoined appeals concerning the practical application by trial judges of the bad character provisions in the 2003 Act, the Court of Appeal held that, having provided general guidance in the *Hanson* case as to how these provisions were to be interpreted, the detailed application of these principles was a matter for the judge at trial rather than an appellate court. The Court said that the trial judge's 'feel' for the case (and whether it would be unfair to admit evidence of the defendant's bad character) was important. This was confirmed in *R v Edwards & Rowlands* (see **22.3** above), when the Court of Appeal said that it would interfere with the decision of a trial judge only if it considered a conviction to be unsafe.

22.4.11   May bad character evidence admitted under one gateway be used for another purpose?

The CJA 2003 does not expressly identify the purpose for which bad character evidence may be used if it passes through one of the seven gateways created by s 101(1). However, in *R v Highton & Others* [2005] EWCA Crim 1985 (see **22.4.9** above), the Court of Appeal held that evidence of a defendant's bad character which is adduced under one gateway may then be used for any purpose for which bad character evidence was relevant in the particular case. Thus, for example, evidence of a defendant's previous convictions adduced as important explanatory evidence under gateway (c) may, once admitted in evidence, be used to show that the defendant has a propensity to commit the type of offence charged (under gateway (d)).

In the *Highton* case, the Court of Appeal held that a distinction had to be drawn between the admissibility of evidence of bad character (which depended on that evidence getting through one of the seven gateways) and the use to which that evidence could be put when admitted. Once bad character became admissible through one of gateways, it could then be used for any purpose for which bad character evidence was relevant in the particular case. The Court considered that the width of the definition as to what amounted to bad character in s 98 suggested that, wherever such evidence was admitted, it could be admitted for any purpose for which it was relevant in the case in which it was being admitted.

The Court went on to say that this would not result in unfairness to the defendant, because the trial judge retained the discretionary power to exclude evidence under s 101(3) if the CPS sought to adduce bad character evidence under s 101(1)(d) or (g) and the judge considered that the admission of this evidence would cause unfairness to the defendant.

In *R v M* [2006] All ER (D) 472 (Mar), the Court of Appeal emphasised that evidence of a defendant's previous convictions introduced under one gateway could then be used for another purpose only if the convictions were relevant for that purpose. In this case, the defendant had convictions for offences of violence, similar to that with which he was currently charged, but he had pleaded guilty on those previous occasions. He had entered a plea of not guilty to the current offence. The Court of Appeal held that the trial judge had erred when suggesting to the jury that the previous convictions could be taken to impact adversely on the defendant's credibility as a witness in his own defence.

22.5 Stopping contaminated cases

Section 107 of the CJA 2003 permits a judge in a Crown Court trial either to direct the jury to acquit the defendant, or to order a retrial in circumstances when evidence of the defendant's previous convictions has been adduced under s 101(c)–(g) above but *other* evidence called in support of the prosecution case has been contaminated. Contamination may occur where there has been an agreement between witnesses as to the evidence they are to give, or if the evidence given by one witness is affected by what that witness has heard someone else say. The purpose behind s 107 is to cover the potential danger in situations where the prosecution evidence is contaminated, and the evidence of bad character that the prosecution call in support of this contaminated evidence is then given too much emphasis by the jury.

Example

In *R v Card* [2006] EWCA Crim 1079, following a Crown Court trial, the defendant was convicted of the sexual assault of a 10-year-old boy. As part of its case, the prosecution adduced under s 101(1)(d) evidence of the defendant's previous convictions for offences of rape, buggery, indecent assault and taking indecent photographs of children. When giving evidence, the boy agreed that he had made some things up about the defendant and that his mother had told him what to say. The Court of Appeal held that the boy's evidence was contaminated and that, in those circumstances, there was a risk that the jury had convicted the defendant only because they had given a disproportionate emphasis to his previous convictions. The Court held that the trial judge should have stopped the trial at the end of the prosecution case and directed that the jury acquit the defendant.

In the *Card* case, the Court of Appeal directed that, in future cases, if the defendant alleges that evidence called in support of the prosecution case is contaminated, the trial judge should postpone any decision to admit evidence of the defendant's bad character until *after* the complainant and any other prosecution witnesses have given evidence. The judge can then determine whether s 107 applies and, if necessary, direct the jury to acquit the defendant (or to order a retrial) because the prosecution evidence has been contaminated.

Section 107 does not apply to trials before the magistrates' court.

22.6 Bad character of persons other than the defendant

22.6.1 Introduction

In contrast to the numerous ways in which a defendant's bad character may now be admissible in evidence at trial, the bad character of *persons other than the defendant* (ie, not just other witnesses in the case) is now admissible only on very limited grounds. These grounds are set out in s 100(1) of the CJA 2003:

(1)   ... evidence of the bad character of a person other than the defendant is admissible if and only if—

(a)   it is important explanatory evidence,

    (b)   it has substantial probative value in relation to a matter which—

        (i)   is a matter in issue in the proceedings, and

        (ii)   is of substantial importance in the context of the case as a whole, or

    (c)   all parties agree to the evidence being admissible.

22.6.2 Section 100(1)(a) – it is important explanatory evidence

This is very similar to gateway (c) for evidence of a defendant's previous convictions (see **22.4.4** above). The evidence will be important explanatory evidence only if:

(a)   without it, the court or jury would find it impossible or difficult properly to understand other evidence in the case; and

(b)   its value for understanding the case as a whole is substantial (s 100(2)).

'Substantial' in this context is likely to mean more than merely trivial or marginal (see **22.4.5.1** above).

Example 1

Michael is the former manager of a care home for children. He is on trial for sexually abusing the children in his care. The offences are alleged to have taken place over a number of years and the CPS needs to explain why the victims of the abuse did not seek help from another person. The only other person to whom the victims could have spoken was Laura, the matron at the home. The reason why the victims did not report the abuse to Laura was because she also participated in the abuse. Laura has already been prosecuted (and convicted) for her role in the abuse. The CPS will be able to raise Laura's convictions for abuse to explain why Michael's victims did not go to her for help.

Example 2

Kabir is charged with dangerous driving after a vehicle he is alleged to have been driving is caught on a CCTV camera going through a red traffic light and colliding with a pedestrian. Kabir pleads not guilty. His defence is that he was a passenger in the vehicle which was in fact being driven by Anil, who is the owner and registered keeper of the vehicle. The CPS accepts that Anil is the owner and registered keeper of the vehicle but alleges that Anil was merely the passenger on this occasion. To explain why Anil was not driving the vehicle (when ordinarily he would have been expected to be the driver given that he is the owner), the CPS may seek to adduce evidence of Anil's conviction six months previously for driving whilst over the prescribed alcohol limit, for which Anil was banned from driving for 18 months.

Example 3

Derrick is charged with assaulting Tracey, his partner. The CPS alleges that Derrick grabbed Tracey by the hair as she was attempting to put Matthew, their baby son, to bed. Tracey has a previous conviction for assaulting Matthew after she punched him when he wouldn't stop crying. Derrick's defence is that he grabbed Tracey by the hair because he thought she was going to assault Matthew. As Tracey went to put Matthew to bed, he heard her say: 'For God's sake, will he never shut up!' On hearing this, Derrick thought that Tracey might assault Matthew again. To explain why he grabbed Tracey by the hair, Derrick may seek to adduce evidence of Tracey's previous conviction for assaulting Matthew.

Example 4

Ben is charged with murder and raises the defence of alibi, claiming that at the time of the murder he was in a pub some miles away from where the murder took place, and that the landlord of the pub will confirm this. The police approach the landlord, who says that Ben was not in the pub at the time he claims. Shortly before Ben's trial, the landlord retracts his previous statement and tells Ben's solicitor that he can confirm Ben's alibi. The landlord tells Ben's solicitor that he initially refused to confirm Ben's alibi because he had been threatened by David, who actually committed the murder. David told the landlord that if he confirmed Ben's alibi, he would be killed. David, however, has since been sent to prison for several years for a separate offence of robbery. To explain why the landlord took David's threat seriously and initially failed to confirm the alibi, Ben may seek to raise in evidence David's previous convictions for wounding with intent and attempting to pervert the course of justice, both of which arose out of a previous attempt made by David to prevent a witness from giving evidence in criminal proceedings. Ben may also seek to adduce evidence of David's recent conviction for robbery (and David's subsequent imprisonment) to explain why the landlord has only now felt able to come forward to confirm Ben's alibi.

Under s 100(4), leave of the court will be required if a party wishes to adduce evidence of the bad character of a person other than the defendant under s 100(1)(a). The court is likely to grant leave only if the case cannot properly be understood in the absence of such convictions being adduced in evidence.

22.6.3 Section 100 (1)(b) – it has substantial probative value in relation to a matter in issue in the proceedings

22.6.3.1 Introduction

Although this ground may apply to any person other than the defendant (and so may apply to a witness for the defence as well as to a witness for the prosecution), it is most likely to arise when the defendant seeks to adduce evidence of the previous convictions of a witness for the prosecution in order to support an allegation that the witness is either:

(a) lying or has fabricated evidence against the defendant; or

(b) is himself either guilty of the offence with which the defendant has been charged, or has engaged in misconduct in connection with the alleged offence.

In assessing the probative value of the evidence of another person's previous convictions, the court must have regard to:

(a) the nature and number of the events, or other things, to which the evidence relates; and

(b) when those events or things are alleged to have happened or to have existed (s 100(3)).

The term 'substantial' is likely to be construed by the courts as meaning more than merely marginal or trivial (see **22.4.5.1** above).

22.6.3.2 Credibility as a witness

Evidence which is adduced under s 100(1)(b) may be used to suggest either that the person other than the defendant may have engaged in misconduct in connection with the current offence (see **22.6.3.3** below), or that the person is not a credible witness because he has a propensity to be untruthful (*R v Weir & Others* [2005] EWCA Crim 2866).

Previous convictions of a witness for the prosecution which may be used to suggest that the evidence given by the witness lacks credibility may be either:

(a)   convictions for specific offences where the witness has made a false statement or representation (such as perjury, obtaining property by deception, or theft where the witness has lied to or deceived another person as part of the commission of the theft). As is the position with defendants, any previous convictions which another person may have for more general offences of dishonesty will not usually be admissible to demonstrate a propensity to be untruthful (*R v S* – see **22.6.3.3** below); or

(b)   convictions when the witness has been found guilty of an offence to which he pleaded not guilty but was convicted following a trial at which his version of events was disbelieved (when the CPS discloses to the defendant's solicitor details of the previous convictions of any witnesses it intends to call, the defendant's solicitor will need to ask the CPS to confirm whether the witness pleaded guilty or not guilty to these offences); or

(c)   other convictions which may cast doubt on the credibility of the evidence given by the witness.

Example 1

George is on trial for theft of a gold watch from a jewellery shop. Peter, the owner of the shop, is a witness for the prosecution, and will say that he saw George place the watch in his pocket and walk out of the shop without paying for it. George denies this and claims that Peter has made up the allegation as part of an insurance swindle. Peter has two previous convictions for obtaining property by deception. George will seek to use Peter's previous convictions to undermine Peter's credibility as a witness when he gives evidence at George's trial by showing that twice previously Peter has been convicted of an offence involving untruthfulness.

Example 2

Kathryn is on trial for assault occasioning actual bodily harm, following an incident outside a pizza shop when she is alleged to have punched Michelle. The CPS alleges that Kathryn punched Michelle after Michelle accidentally knocked Kathryn's pizza to the floor. Kathryn accepts that Michelle knocked her pizza to the floor, but denies punching her. She claims that Michelle has made up the allegation because she (Kathryn) has just started going out with Michelle's ex-boyfriend. Michelle has previous convictions for offences of theft and criminal damage. Michelle pleaded not guilty to both of these offences, but on both occasions was convicted following a trial. Kathryn will seek to use Michelle's previous convictions to undermine Michelle's credibility as a witness when she gives evidence at Kathryn's trial, by showing that Michelle has twice previously given evidence in criminal proceedings which has been disbelieved.

Example 3

Tracy is charged with the theft of a mobile phone belonging to Diane. The key witness for the prosecution is Kate. Kate claims to have heard Tracy boasting to a friend about having stolen the phone. Tracy alleges that Kate has fabricated this evidence because Tracy is seeing Kate's ex-boyfriend. Kate did not come forward to tell the police about overhearing Tracy's admission until two weeks after the theft took place. Kate claims this was because she was frightened that Tracy would attack her if she came forward. Kate has several previous convictions for common assault and threatening behaviour. Although Kate pleaded guilty to these offences and they are not offences which in themselves demonstrate a propensity to be untruthful, Tracy may still seek to use these convictions to undermine the credibility of Kate's evidence. Tracy will argue that Kate's convictions for offences of violence show that Kate's claim that she was frightened of Tracy is untrue, and that this is not a credible reason for Kate not coming forward to give her story until two weeks had elapsed.

Tracy will argue that Kate failed to come forward immediately because Kate's evidence is fabricated.

22.6.3.3 Misconduct in connection with the current offence or guilty of that offence

The other reason for a defendant wanting to raise the bad character of a person other than himself is to use such evidence to suggest either that:

(a)   the other person has committed some form of misconduct in connection with the current offence (for example, a defendant charged with assault may claim that he was acting merely in self-defence, and that he was in fact attacked by his alleged victim); or

(b)   the other person is in fact guilty of the offence with which the defendant has been charged.

Although this ground applies equally to witnesses called either by the defence or by the prosecution, it is likely to be used most regularly by a defendant to suggest that a witness for the prosecution either committed the offence with which the defendant is charged, or is guilty of some other form of misconduct in connection with that offence.

Misconduct in connection with the current offence

If it is alleged that evidence of another person's misconduct has probative value because there is a similarity between that misconduct and alleged misconduct in connection with the current offence, the court will have regard to the nature and extent of the similarities and dissimilarities between each of the alleged instances of misconduct (s 100(3)(c)). In order to establish such similarity in a case where the defendant alleges that a prosecution witness has engaged in misconduct in connection with the offence with which the defendant has been charged, the defendant's solicitor will need to ask the CPS to disclose details of the factual circumstances of that witness's previous convictions.

> **Example**
>
> Michael is on trial for assaulting Brian at a pub. The CPS alleges that Michael punched Brian in the face. Michael denies the offence, claiming that he was in fact attacked by Brian (who was in a drunken state) after Michael had made a provocative remark about Brian's girlfriend. Brian has previous convictions for offences of common assault and threatening behaviour. Michael will seek to use evidence of Brian's previous convictions to show that Brian is more likely to have been the aggressor on this occasion.
>
> In deciding whether evidence of Brian's previous convictions is admissible, the court will have regard to the nature and extent of the similarities and dissimilarities between his previous convictions and the facts of the current offence. The court will want to know if Brian's previous convictions arose in similar circumstances, and in particular if Brian committed these offences after any provocation and/or whilst in a drunken state. If so, this would be evidence to support Michael's argument that Brian becomes aggressive when either drunk or provoked, and that Brian attacked Michael first. If, however, Brian's previous convictions arose in circumstances different from the facts of the current matter (if, for example, they arose in the context of a dispute with a neighbour that got out of hand but where there was no provocation and drink was not involved), the court is unlikely to allow Michael to rely on them in evidence.

In *R v Bovell* [2005] EWCA Crim 1091, the Court of Appeal held that a judge could admit evidence of previous convictions relied upon to show the propensity of a prosecution witness to commit a particular type of offence, if the defendant could show sufficient factual similarities between the earlier offence and the current incident. The complainant had been stabbed three times following an altercation. The defence was self-defence, the defendant suggesting that the knife used was originally in the possession of the complainant. The complainant had a conviction for handling stolen goods 11 years previously. He also had a conviction for robbery 10 years previously, for which he had received a four-year sentence following a guilty plea. At trial, the defendant claimed that s 100(1)(b) applied and that the complainant's previous convictions could be used both to show that the complainant had a propensity to use violence and to undermine his credibility as a witness. The trial judge refused to admit these convictions on the basis that the defendant could not show any factual similarities between these offences and the incident involving the defendant.

On appeal, it was discovered that the complainant had actually once been accused of wounding (using a knife), although the allegation was withdrawn. It was also found that there was some factual similarity between the earlier robbery and the current altercation, because evidence came to light that the complainant had used a knife in the commission of the robbery. The Court of Appeal felt, however, that the mere making of an allegation was not evidence of bad character, and so the allegation of wounding was not admissible. The Court also declined to overturn the trial judge's ruling that the previous convictions of the complainant were inadmissible, despite the new evidence that had come to light. The Court went on to say that had the defendant been allowed at trial to raise evidence of the complainant's previous convictions, this would have constituted an attack on the character of another which would have enabled the prosecution to adduce evidence of the defendant's extensive criminal record under s 101(1)(g) (see **22.4.8** above).

In *R v S* [2006] All ER (D) 273, however, the Court of Appeal appeared to widen the scope of the types of previous conviction which may be used to support an allegation of misconduct on the part of the complainant in connection with the offence with which the defendant is charged. The defendant was convicted of indecent assault following a complaint made by a prostitute. The defendant accepted that he had approached the complainant for sexual services but claimed that, after such services had been provided, the complainant demanded more money from him, tried to grab him and threatened to accuse him of rape. The defendant denied that he had committed any form of assault. The complainant had previous convictions for offences of theft, burglary and going equipped to steal. The defendant applied for leave to cross-examine the complainant about these convictions, on the basis that such convictions went to her credibility (ie, that they demonstrated a propensity to be untruthful). The trial judge refused this application.

The Court of Appeal held that the trial judge had correctly refused the defendant's application because the complainant's previous convictions were for offences of dishonesty, and did not in themselves show a propensity to be untruthful (this is analogous to the ruling of the Court of Appeal in the *Hanson* case that a defendant's previous convictions for offences of dishonesty do not demonstrate a propensity to be untruthful – see **22.4.5.3** above). The Court did, however, go on to say that evidence of the complainant's previous convictions *would* have been admissible had the defendant sought leave to raise them on the basis that they supported an allegation that the complainant was guilty of misconduct in connection with the offence with which the defendant was charged. The allegation of misconduct that the defendant was making was that the complainant had acted in a dishonest manner towards him, by initially agreeing to accept payment for sexual services but subsequently demanding further payment and threatening to accuse him of rape (essentially demanding money with menace). The Court said that the offences for which the complainant had previous convictions (theft, burglary and going equipped to steal) were all offences of dishonesty. The complainant's previous convictions therefore had substantial probative value in relation to a matter in issue, namely to support the argument that the complainant was liable to behave, or had a propensity to act, dishonestly.

This case widens considerably the admissibility of the previous convictions of a complainant. An allegation of misconduct made by the defendant in connection with the current offence may now include an allegation that the complainant has acted in a dishonest manner. If the defendant makes such an allegation, he may then be granted leave to cross-examine the complainant about any previous convictions the complainant has which demonstrate a propensity to act or behave in a dishonest manner. This will include *any* offence where dishonesty forms part of the *mens rea* of the offence.

(If the defendant is charged with having committed an offence involving dishonesty (for example, theft or burglary), any previous convictions which the defendant has for other offences involving dishonesty will be admissible under s 101(1)(d) to show that the defendant has a propensity to commit offences of the kind with which he is charged. Such previous convictions will usually be admissible either if they are for offences of the same description as the offence with which the defendant is charged, or if they are offences falling within the same category (ie, the theft category) as the offence charged (see **22.4.5.2** above).)

Guilty of committing the current offence

If it is alleged that evidence of another person's misconduct has probative value because it is suggested that the person is responsible for having committed the offence with which the defendant has been charged, the court will have regard to the extent to which the evidence shows or tends to show that the same person was responsible each time (s 100(3)(d)). To establish a similarity between these offences and the current offence, the defendant's solicitor will need to obtain from the CPS details of the factual circumstances of the previous convictions of a witness for the prosecution whom the defendant alleges committed the offence with which the defendant has been charged.

Example

Terry is on trial for the theft of items from a warehouse. One of the witnesses for the prosecution is Gordon, the night watchman at the warehouse. Gordon claims to have seen Terry committing the theft. Terry denies the offence and alleges that Gordon has fabricated evidence against him because he (Gordon) was in fact responsible for the theft. Gordon has two previous convictions for offences of theft. Terry will seek to use evidence of Gordon's previous convictions to show Gordon to have been the more likely of the two to have been responsible for the theft. In deciding whether the evidence of Gordon's previous convictions is admissible, the court will have regard to the nature and extent of the similarities and dissimilarities between Gordon's previous convictions and the facts of the current offence. For example, if Gordon's previous convictions were for theft from an employer or theft from commercial premises, such convictions could have substantial probative value. Alternatively, if the factual circumstances of Gordon's previous convictions were very different from the facts of the current offence (for example, if the thefts arose out of a dispute with a family member over the ownership of family heirlooms), it is unlikely that they would have such value.

If the facts of the previous conviction are markedly different, it is highly unlikely that the court will permit the defendant to raise this conviction at trial. In *R v Gadsby* [2005] EWCA Crim 3206, the defendant was charged with the attempted murder of his wife by placing an explosive device containing petrol beneath her bed. He denied having done this and informed the police that other people had had access to his wife's bedroom during the period of time when the device was planted. One of these people was the defendant's sister, who had a previous conviction for arson committed over 20 years previously. The defendant sought leave of the trial judge to admit this evidence at trial to show that his sister had a propensity to commit offences of this type. The trial judge refused leave and the defendant was convicted. The Court of Appeal held that the trial judge had correctly excluded evidence of the sister's previous conviction. The Court found that the factual circumstances of the sister's previous conviction did not demonstrate a propensity to commit the crime with which the defendant was charged. The offence of arson had been committed over 20 years earlier, whilst the sister was a teenager, and involved setting fire to a box of toys in her bedroom after an argument with her mother. The Court did say, however, that the sister's previous conviction for arson would have been admissible had it been capable of increasing or diminishing the probability of facts indicating that the sister had committed the crime (ie, if it had substantial probative value in determining who had actually placed the explosive device under the bed).

22.6.3.4   Witnesses who are not giving evidence

Although the defendant will usually rely upon s 100(1)(b) in respect of a witness for the prosecution who has previous convictions, it may also be used in relation to persons who are not giving evidence in the case.

Example

Oscar is on trial for the murder of Claude. It is alleged that Oscar stabbed Claude with a knife. Oscar raises the defence of self-defence. He alleges that Claude attacked him with a knife and that Claude was stabbed after he (Oscar) managed to turn the knife against him. Claude had a previous conviction for carrying a knife as an offensive weapon. Oscar will want to use this previous conviction to support his defence of self-defence. In deciding whether the evidence of Claude's previous conviction is admissible, the court will have regard to the nature and extent of the similarities and dissimilarities between the facts of Claude's previous conviction and the facts of the current case.

22.6.3.5   Leave of the court

Under s 100(4), leave of the court will be required if a party wishes to adduce evidence of the bad character of a person other than the defendant under s 100(1)(b). It will be rare for a court to allow the bad character of a person other than the defendant to be admissible at trial under s 100(1)(b). When the CJA 2003 was in its parliamentary stages, it was stressed repeatedly by the Government that this part of the legislation was intended to prevent witnesses in criminal trials being made to feel that it was they, rather than the defendant, who were on trial by having their previous convictions brought up in cross-examination and their character attacked.

The court will grant leave for the bad character of a non-defendant to be used in evidence at trial only if this is both of great importance in determining a fact in issue in the case and is significant to the case as a whole. The court will not allow the bad character of a non-defendant to be used simply as a means of attacking that person's credibility or suggesting that the person is himself guilty of misconduct, unless either that person's credibility as a witness goes to the heart of the case, or the defendant's defence rests on the allegation that the other person actually committed the offence with which the defendant is charged or was otherwise guilty of misconduct in connection with that alleged offence.

22.6.4 Section 100(1)(c) – all parties to the proceedings agree to the evidence being admissible

This ground is self-explanatory. If all parties to the case are in agreement, evidence of the bad character of a person other than the defendant will always be admissible.

If s 100(1)(c) applies, leave of the court is not required to admit evidence of the bad character of a person other than the defendant.

A flowchart summarising the operation of s 100(1) is set out at **22.9.2** below.

22.7 Procedure for admitting bad character evidence

22.7.1 Introduction

If the CPS wishes to adduce evidence of the defendant's bad character at trial, notice of this intention must be given both to the court and to the other parties in the case (CrimPR, r 35.4(1)). If either the CPS or the defendant wishes to adduce evidence of the bad character of a non-defendant at trial, an application must be made to the court, with the application also being served on the other parties to the case (CrimPR, r 35.2). In either case, a prescribed set of forms must be used. These forms are reproduced at **22.11** below.

As part of the standard directions that will be given in both the magistrates' court (see **8.2.3**) and the Crown Court (see **10.5.1**), the court will impose time limits for the parties to serve any notice or make any application to adduce bad character evidence at trial. The relevant time limits are set out in r 35.4 (for the CPS to give notice of its intention to introduce evidence of the defendant's bad character) and r 35.2 (for either the CPS or the defendant to apply to introduce evidence of the bad character of a non-defendant). If a party opposes the introduction of bad character evidence, it must serve a counter-notice. The time limits for serving a counter notice are set out in r 35.6 (when the defendant applies to exclude evidence of his own bad character) and r 35.3 (when either the CPS or the defendant opposes the introduction of evidence of a non-defendant's bad character).

22.7.2 Magistrates' court

If the defendant wishes to introduce evidence of the bad character of a prosecution witness at trial, r 35.2(a) provides that he must serve an application for permission to do this within *14 days* of the date on which the prosecution disclose details of those convictions (details of such convictions will normally be part of the disclosure obligations on the CPS in respect of their unused material, since such convictions will be capable of undermining the prosecution case – see **8.4.6.2**). If the CPS wishes to oppose this application, it must serve a notice opposing the application within *14 days* of receiving the application (CrimPR, r 35.3). The notice must be served on the court and on the other parties in the case.

If the CPS wishes to adduce evidence of the bad character of a witness (other than the defendant) who is to give evidence for the defence, r 35.2(b) provides that it must serve an application to do this 'as soon as reasonably practicable'. If the defendant wishes to oppose this application, he must serve a notice opposing the application within *14 days* of receiving the application (CrimPR, r 35.3). The notice must be served both on the court and on the other parties in the case.

If the CPS wishes to adduce evidence of the defendant's bad character at trial, it must serve a notice of intention to do this at the same time as it complies with its initial duty to disclose to the defendant any unused material it has (CrimPR, r 35.4(2)(a). The defendant must serve any application he wishes to make to exclude evidence of his bad character at trial within *14 days* of receiving the prosecution notice (CrimPR, r 35.6).

22.7.3 Crown Court

The defendant will have *14 days* from the date on which the CPS discloses details of the previous convictions of any prosecution witnesses to make an application to introduce the bad character of any such witness at trial (CrimPR, r 35.2(a)). As with the magistrates' court, details of such convictions should form part of the unused material which the CPS will disclose to the defence (see **Chapter 10**). The CPS will have *14 days* from receipt of the defendant's application to serve a notice opposing this (CrimPR, r 35.3). The notice must be served on the court and the other parties in the case.

If the CPS wishes to adduce evidence of the bad character of a defence witness at trial, it must make an application to do so 'as soon as reasonably practicable' (CrimPR, r 35.2(b)). If this application is opposed by the defendant, a counter-notice must be served on the court and the other parties within *14 days* of the defendant receiving the application made by the CPS (CrimPR, r 35.3).

If the CPS wishes to adduce evidence of the defendant's bad character at trial, it must serve notice of its intention to do so within *14 days* of the service of the prosecution case papers on the defendant (CrimPR, r 35.4(2)(b)). The defendant will have *14 days* from receipt of this notice to serve an application to exclude evidence of his bad character at trial (CrimPR, r 35.6).

22.7.4 Co-defendants

In either the magistrates' court or the Crown Court, a defendant who wants to introduce at trial evidence of a co-defendant's bad character, or who wants to cross-examine a witness to elicit such evidence, must give notice of this both to the court and to the other parties in the case within *14 days* of the CPS complying with its initial duty to disclose any unused material in its possession (CrimPR, r 35.5). If the co-defendant wishes to oppose this notice, he must serve an application to exclude evidence of his own bad character at trial within *14 days* of receiving the defendant's application (CrimPR, r 35.6).

22.7.5 Must the parties comply with the above time limits?

The court may allow oral notice to be given at trial and extend or shorten any time limit for the giving of any notice under Part 35 if it is in the interests of justice to do so (CrimPR, r 35.8). This would, for example, allow the CPS to apply to adduce evidence of a defendant's bad character when at trial the defendant gives a false impression about himself when giving evidence.

In *R (Robinson) v Sutton Coldfield Magistrates' Court* [2006] EWHC (Admin) 307, the CPS served a notice to adduce evidence of the defendant's bad character at trial three days prior to the date of the trial. The Court of Appeal held that it was the duty of all parties to comply with the Criminal Procedure Rules 2005 and that all necessary time limits should be adhered to. The Court went on to say, however, that there was a discretionary power under r 35.8 to extend the time limit for service of the notice, and that it was unnecessary for the court to find 'exceptional' reasons before allowing an extension. What the court should take into account in such a situation was the overriding objective under r 1.1 of the Criminal Procedure Rules (see **1.4.2**), the reasons for the failure to comply with the Rules, and whether the position of the defendant has been prejudiced by the late service of the notice. In the *Robinson* case, the Court of Appeal held that the defendant had not been prejudiced by the late service of the notice because he clearly knew he had these convictions, the CPS had previously given an indication that the previous convictions would be relied upon at trial, and the defendant had not sought an adjournment on the day of the trial.

22.7.6   Procedure for adducing bad character evidence at trial

Where either the CPS or the defendant has made an application to adduce bad character evidence at trial, and this application is opposed by the other party, the court will usually determine the admissibility of such evidence at a pre-trial hearing. In the magistrates' court, this is likely to be at the case management hearing/pre-trial review, or at a specific pre-trial hearing to resolve disputes about the admissibility of evidence. In the Crown Court, this is likely to be at the plea and case management hearing, or at a specific pre-trial hearing as in the magistrates' court.

The method by which the previous convictions either of the defendant or any other witness are proved at trial is by the party seeking to adduce this evidence producing a certificate of conviction to the court (PACE 1984, s 73(1); *DPP v Parker* [2006] EWHC 1270). If the CPS is seeking to adduce the previous convictions of the defendant, the certificate will usually be produced by the police officer in the case when he gives evidence in chief. If either the CPS or the defence are seeking to adduce the previous convictions of a witness (or a defendant is seeking to adduce the previous convictions of a co-defendant), such convictions will usually be put to the witness (or co-defendant) in cross-examination. A certificate of conviction will be required only if the defendant or witness denies having the previous conviction(s). In practice, if the court has ruled that a previous conviction of a defendant or other person is admissible, the party against whom the evidence is to be adduced will often make a formal admission as to the existence of the conviction under s 10 of the CJA 1967 (see **16.3.3**).

If, in order to demonstrate a defendant's propensity to commit a particular type of offence, the CPS wants to adduce evidence of the *details* of what the defendant was alleged to have done when committing previous offences (rather than just the fact that the defendant was convicted of a particular offence), it must call witnesses at trial who can give first-hand evidence of what happened, such as the victims of the previous offences (*R v Humphries* (2005) *The Times*, 19 September). Merely having a police officer repeat details of what is alleged to have happened when the previous offences were committed is not sufficient.

22.8   Evidence of good character

22.8.1   Good character of the defendant

A defendant who is of good character (in other words, a defendant who has no previous convictions and who has not otherwise engaged in any 'reprehensible behaviour') is entitled to have this taken into account by the magistrates or jury at his trial. The accepted method of confirming the defendant's good character at trial is for the defendant's solicitor or counsel to ask the police officer who gives evidence verifying the record of the interview in the police station, to confirm that the defendant is of good character. The defendant may also be allowed to give brief details of his good character when he starts to give evidence in the witness box (for example, details of any charitable works he has done). He may also call witnesses as to his good character. Such witnesses are likely to be either persons in a position of respect or trust within the community (for example, a teacher or doctor), or the defendant's current or former employer.

If a defendant is of good character, this will be relevant both to his credibility as a witness (provided he has put his defence 'on record') and to show the absence of a propensity to commit the offence with which he has been charged (*R v Vye, Wise & Stephenson* (1993) 97 Cr App R 134). In the Crown Court, if a defendant of previous good character gives evidence in his own defence at his trial, the judge will give a direction to the jury that this is relevant both to matters of credibility and propensity (a '*Vye*' direction'). If the defendant does not give evidence at his trial, the judge will give a direction as to propensity only, unless the defendant has put his defence on record elsewhere (if, for example, the defendant does not give evidence at trial, but did give details of his defence when interviewed at the police station). In the magistrates' court, the defendant's solicitor will remind the magistrates of the significance of the defendant's good character as to matters of propensity and credibility when giving his closing speech to the court.

Example

Charles in on trial for possession of Class A drugs with intent to supply. Charles has no previous convictions. When being cross-examined by Charles's counsel, the officer in the case confirms that Charles is of good character. Charles subsequently gives evidence in his own defence. When he is summing up the case to the jury before they retire to consider their verdict, the judge will give the jury a '*Vye*' direction. He will direct the jury that they should take Charles's good character into account when deciding whether the prosecution have satisfied them as to Charles's guilt. The jury are entitled to conclude that Charles's good character enhances the credibility of the evidence he has given, *and* that his good character means that he is less likely to have committed the offence for which he is on trial.

In *R v Barrington Payton* [2006] EWCA Crim 1226, the Court of Appeal held that a trial judge's failure to give a '*Vye*' direction where appropriate was a misdirection which would render any subsequent conviction unsafe.

If two co-defendants are tried together, with one being of good character and the other having previous convictions, the defendant who is of previous good character is entitled to have the judge give a '*Vye* direction'. If the bad character of the co-defendant has not come out during the course of the trial, the trial judge may either say nothing about his character when summing up to the jury, or may tell the jury that they have heard nothing about his character but should not speculate as to the reason for this (*R v Aziz* [1995] 3 All ER 149).

22.8.2 Good character of other witnesses

Evidence of the good character of a witness other than the defendant is inadmissible at common law and should not be raised at trial. Such evidence is said to be 'oath helping' (ie, adduced to bolster the credibility of the evidence given by the witness) and is not permitted. In *R v Beard* [1998] Crim LR 585, the defendant was charged with robbery. It was alleged that his victim was vulnerable as he had learning difficulties. When giving evidence, the victim stated that he had been threatened with a 'kicking' by the defendant if he did not give him money. In his defence, the defendant claimed that the victim was a compulsive liar. The prosecution were granted leave to call a social worker to rebut this assertion, saying that the victim was an honest and truthful person. The defendant's subsequent conviction was quashed by the Court of Appeal. The Court held that the trial judge had been wrong to allow the prosecution to adduce such evidence since it amounted to 'oath helping' and served no useful purpose.

In cases involving sexual conduct, however, differences between questions that go to the credibility of a complainant and questions going to an issue in the case (eg, consent in a rape case) are sometimes impossible to separate, and the court may allow some evidence to be given as to the character of the complainant (*R v Tobin* [2003] Crim LR 408).

22.9 Procedural flowcharts

22.9.1 Bad character of the defendant

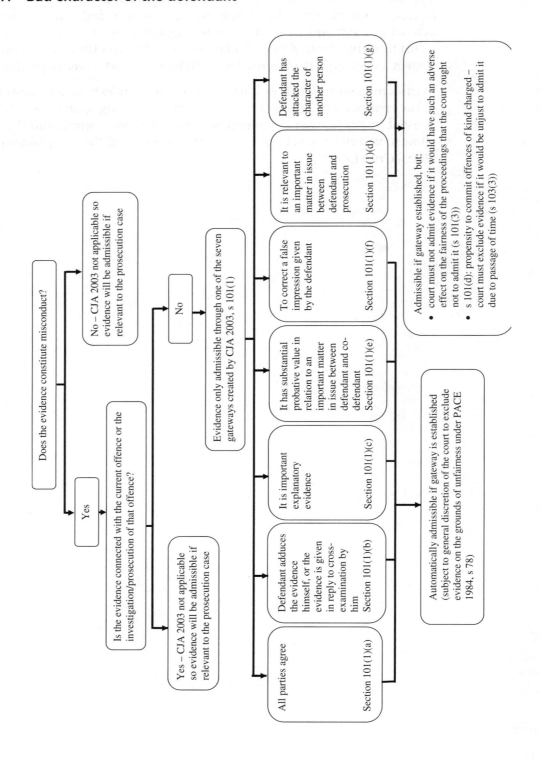

22.9.2 Bad character of persons other than the defendant

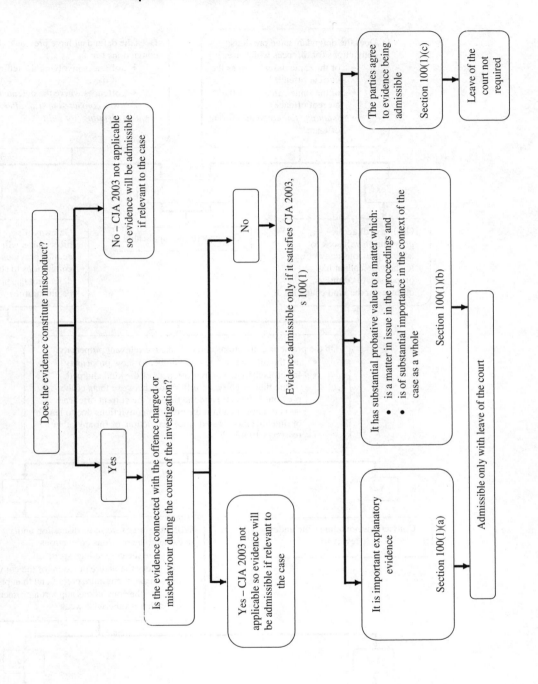

22.9.3 The operation of gateway (d)

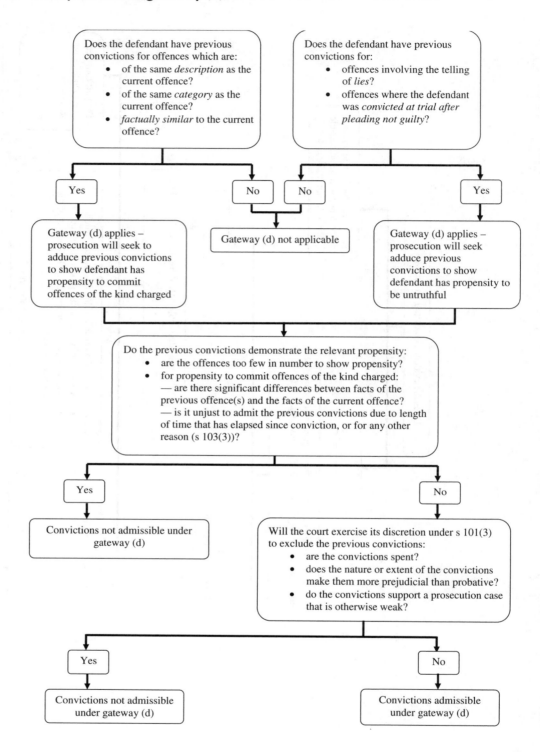

22.10 Checklist

At the end of this chapter you should be able to explain:

- the statutory definition of 'bad character' in the CJA 2003;
- the seven 'gateways' through which a defendant's bad character may become admissible in evidence at trial:
  - all the parties agree to the evidence being admissible (s 101(1)(a)),
  - evidence that is adduced by the defendant himself (s 101(1)(b)),
  - important explanatory evidence (s 101(1)(c)),
  - evidence that is relevant to an important matter in issue between the defendant and the prosecution (s 101(1)(d)),
  - evidence that has substantial probative value in relation to an important matter in issue between the defendant and a co-defendant (s 101(1)(e)),
  - evidence to correct a false impression given by the defendant (s 101(1)(f)),
  - defendant has made an attack on another person's character (s 101(1)(g));
- the discretion which the court has to exclude evidence of the defendant's bad character that would otherwise be admissible under gateways (d) and (g) (s 101(3));
- the significance of the guidelines in *R v Hanson, Gilmore & Pickstone*;
- the circumstances in which the bad character of a person other than the defendant may become admissible in evidence at trial (s 100(1)(a)–(c));
- the procedure to be followed if a party wishes to rely upon bad character evidence at trial, or to challenge bad character evidence upon which another party seeks to rely (CrimPR, Part 35);
- how the good character of the defendant may be established at trial, and the evidential significance of the defendant being of good character.

22.11 Key forms

22.11.1 Introduction

Three forms are set out below:

(a) notice of intention to adduce evidence of the defendant's bad character (see **22.11.2**);

(b) application to exclude evidence of the defendant's bad character (see **22.11.3**); and

(c) application for leave to adduce non-defendant's bad character (see **22.1.4**).

Each form has been completed to illustrate how this should be done and the level of detail required.

22.11.2 Notice of intention to adduce evidence of the defendant's bad character

<table>
<tr>
<td colspan="2"> Notice of intention to adduce bad character evidence
under s 101 Criminal Justice Act 2003
(Criminal Procedure Rules, IT 35.4(1), 68.21) </td>
</tr>
<tr>
<td>Details Required</td>
<td>Notes</td>
</tr>
<tr>
<td>1. Details of applicant

Name: Crown Prosecution Service
Address: 2 The Avenue, Bishoptown, Guildshire GU1 5RQ
Name of prosecuting agency (if relevant)</td>
<td></td>
</tr>
<tr>
<td>2. Case details

Case reference numbers: GL/0231/07
Date of trial or proceedings is due to start/or started: 21/02/07
Name of defendant(s): Paul Grayson
Charges:
Assault occasioning actual bodily harm on Graham Hull on 13th August 2006 in The Sick Parrot Public House, Bishoptown</td>
<td>Give brief details of those charges to which this application applies.</td>
</tr>
<tr>
<td>3. Details of this Notice

To the named defendant:
You are hereby given notice that bad character evidence, particulars of which are detailed below, is to be adduced or elicited in these proceedings.
The particulars of that bad character evidence are as follows:
(a) Evidence of the accused's record of previous convictions (record attached). The officer in charge of the case, PC 1042 Asquith, will be called to give this evidence.
(b) Grounds:
<u>s 101(1)(d) CJA 2003</u> – relevant to an important matter in issue between the prosecution and defence as to propensity to commit offences of the type charged [convictions for common assault on 3rd March 2000 and threatening behaviour on 5th June 2004] and to truthfulness [conviction for theft on 18th May 2003]
<u>s 101(1)(g)</u> – defendant made an attack on another person's character when interviewed at the police station [interview record attached]. All convictions on attached list are relevant.</td>
<td>In this section include:
(a) a description of the bad character evidence and how it is to be adduced or elicited in the proceedings (including the names of any relevant witnesses); and
(b) the grounds for the admission of evidence of the defendant's bad character under section 101 of the Criminal Justice Act 2003. Please attach any relevant documentation.</td>
</tr>
<tr>
<td>4. Extension of time

Are you applying for an extension of time for service? (~~yes~~/no)

If yes, state your reasons.</td>
<td></td>
</tr>
<tr>
<td>Signed: J. Boothroyd

Dated: 8th October 2006</td>
<td></td>
</tr>
</table>

[Note: Formerly set out in the Schedule to the Magistrates' Courts (Amendment) Rules 2004 (SI 2004/2993) relating to rule 72A of the Magistrates' Court Rules 1981 and form BC2 of the Crown Court (Amendment No 3) Rules 2004 (SI 2004/2991) relating to rule 23D of the Crown Court Rules 1982 and form 22 of the Criminal Appeal (Amendment No 2) Rules 2004 (SI 2004/2992) relating to rule 9D of the Criminal Appeal Rules 1968.]

22.11.3 Application to exclude evidence of the defendant's bad character

Application to exclude evidence of the defendant's bad character under ss 101, 108(2) Criminal Justice Act 2003 (Criminal Procedure Rules, IT 35.6, 68.21)	
Details Required	*Notes*
1. Details of applicant Name: *Paul Grayson* Address: *4 The Limes, Bishoptown, Guildshire* Date of Birth: *21/09/78* If you are in custody, please give your Prison Index No and address where detained:	
2. Case details Case reference numbers: *GL/0231/07* Date of trial or proceedings is due to start/or started: *21/02/07* Charges: *Assault occasioning actual bodily harm on Graham Hull on 13th August 2006 in The Sick Parrot Public House, Bishoptown* Date that you were served with the notice of the intention to adduce bad character evidence in these proceedings: *8th October 2006*	
3. Details of this Notice This section must include the following information: (a) why the admission of the bad character evidence would have such an adverse effect on the fairness of the proceedings that the court should not admit it. *Convictions for common assault on 3rd March 2000 and threatening behaviour on 5th June 2004 not for same kind of offence as offence currently charged and occurred in the context of a domestic dispute (whereas the current offence is alleged to have occurred following an incident in a pub when the defendant was in drink). Such offences do not demonstrate a propensity to commit offences of the kind charged, and would be more prejudicial than probative in the eyes of the jury.* *Conviction for common assault on 3rd March 2000 occurred too long ago to be relevant to demonstrate propensity.* *Conviction for theft on 18th May 2003 not relevant to issue of truthfulness since not committed in a way that would reflect on propensity to be untruthful [R v Hanson], and defendant pleaded guilty to this charge. Evidential value of offence would be more prejudicial than probative.* *Admissibility of interview record will be challenged at trial. Alternatively attack on character of prosecution witness made only as a result of the officer's style of questioning and it would be unfair to admit evidence of the defendant's previous convictions in such circumstances.*	*Note that an application to exclude this evidence under section 101(3) of the Criminal Justice Act 2003 can only be made if you have been notified of a party's intentions to adduce this evidence under subsection 101(1)(d) (it is relevant to an important matter in issue between the defendant and the prosecution) or subsection 101(1)(g) (that the defendant has made an attack on another person's character)* *Section 101(4) of the 2003 Act.*

(b)   details as to the length of time between the matters to which the bad character evidence relates and the matters which form the subject of the offence charged.

Conviction for common assault on 3rd March 2000 is spent and is too long ago to be of any evidential value.

(c)   if you are applying for the exclusion of this evidence on grounds other than section 101(3) of CJA 2003, please set out such objections.

Section 103(3) – in relation to propensity to commit offences of the type charged, by reason of the length of time which has elapsed since the conviction for common assault on 3rd March 2000, it would be unjust for it to apply in this case.

Defendant's previous convictions do not satisfy the test for admissibility in s 101(1)(d) – see (a) above:
– offences alleged to show propensity to commit this kind of offence arose in entirely different factual circumstances;
– Hanson judgment makes it clear that conviction for offence of theft may demonstrate dishonesty, but does not demonstrate propensity to be untruthful.

4. Extension of time

Are you applying for an extension of time for service? (~~yes~~/no)

If yes, state your reasons.

Signed: *P Grayson*

Dated*: 19th October 2006*

[Note: Formerly set out in the Schedule to the Magistrates' Courts (Amendment) Rules 2004 (SI 2004/2993) relating to rule 72A of the Magistrates' Court Rules 1981 and form BC3 of the Crown Court (Amendment No 3) Rules 2004 (SI 2004/2991) relating to rule 23D of the Crown Court Rules 1982 and form 23 of the Criminal Appeal (Amendment No 2) Rules 2004 (SI 2004/2992) relating to rule 9D of the Criminal Appeal Rules 1968.]

22.11.4 Application for leave to adduce non-defendant's bad character

EVIDENCE OF BAD CHARACTER
(CRIMINAL PROCEDURE RULES, PART 35)

<table>
<tr>
<td colspan="2"> Application for leave to adduce non-defendant's bad character
under s 100 Criminal Justice Act 2003
(Criminal Procedure Rules, IT 35.2, 68.21) </td>
</tr>
<tr>
<td>Details Required</td>
<td>Notes</td>
</tr>
<tr>
<td>1. Details of applicant

Name: Paul Grayson
Address: 4 The Limes, Bishoptown, Guildshire GU8 5JP
Name of prosecuting agency (if relevant)</td>
<td></td>
</tr>
<tr>
<td>2. Case details

Case reference numbers: GL/0231/07
Date of trial or proceedings is due to start/or started: 21/02/07
Name of defendant(s): Paul Grayson
Charges:
Assault occasioning actual bodily harm on Graham Hull on 13th August 2006 in The Sick Parrot Public House, Bishoptown</td>
<td>Give brief details of those charges to which this application applies.</td>
</tr>
<tr>
<td>3. Details of this application

Please provide the following details
(a) the particulars of the bad character evidence including how it is to be adduced or elicited in the proceedings (including the name of the relevant non-defendant and all other relevant witnesses)

Previous convictions of the complainant Graham Hull for common assault (9th July 2004), assault occasioning actual bodily harm (2nd September 2005) and affray (30th January 2006).

(b) the grounds for the admission of evidence of a non-defendant's bad character under section 100 of CJA 2003.

Section 100(1)(b) – convictions have substantial probative value in relation to a matter in issue in the proceedings. The matter in issue is whether the defendant was responsible for causing the fight at the Sick Parrot. The defendant alleges that he was acting in self-defence. The previous convictions of the complainant are relevant to the allegation that the complainant was the aggressor.</td>
<td>s 100 Criminal Justice Act 2003

Please attach any relevant documentation.</td>
</tr>
<tr>
<td>4. Extension of time

Are you applying for an extension of time for service? (<s>yes</s>/no)

If so provide details.</td>
<td></td>
</tr>
<tr>
<td>Signed: Paul Grayson

Dated: 19th October 2006</td>
<td></td>
</tr>
</table>

[Note: Formerly set out in the Schedule to the Magistrates' Courts (Amendment) Rules 2004 (SI 2004/2993) relating to rule 72A of the Magistrates' Court Rules 1981 and form BC1 of the Crown Court (Amendment No 3) Rules 2004 (SI 2004/2991) relating to rule 23D of the Crown Court Rules 1982 and form 21 of the Criminal Appeal (Amendment No 2) Rules 2004 (SI 2004/2992) relating to rule 9D of the Criminal Appeal Rules 1968.]

Appendix 1
PACE Codes of Practice

Police and Criminal Evidence Act 1984 (PACE) Code C

Code of practice for the detention, treatment and questioning of persons by police officers

Commencement — Transitional Arrangements

This Code applies to people in police detention after midnight on 31 December 2005, notwithstanding that their period of detention may have commenced before that time.

1 General

1.1 All persons in custody must be dealt with expeditiously, and released as soon as the need for detention no longer applies.

1.1A A custody officer must perform the functions in this Code as soon as practicable. A custody officer will not be in breach of this Code if delay is justifiable and reasonable steps are taken to prevent unnecessary delay. The custody record shall show when a delay has occurred and the reason. See Note 1H

1.2 This Code of Practice must be readily available at all police stations for consultation by:
- police officers
- police staff
- detained persons
- members of the public.

1.3 The provisions of this Code:
- include the Annexes
- do not include the Notes for Guidance.

1.4 If an officer has any suspicion, or is told in good faith, that a person of any age may be mentally disordered or otherwise mentally vulnerable, in the absence of clear evidence to dispel that suspicion, the person shall be treated as such for the purposes of this Code. See Note 1G

1.5 If anyone appears to be under 17, they shall be treated as a juvenile for the purposes of this Code in the absence of clear evidence that they are older.

1.6 If a person appears to be blind, seriously visually impaired, deaf, unable to read or speak or has difficulty orally because of a speech impediment, they shall be treated as such for the purposes of this Code in the absence of clear evidence to the contrary.

1.7 'The appropriate adult' means, in the case of a:

(a) juvenile:
   (i) the parent, guardian or, if the juvenile is in local authority or voluntary organisation care, or is otherwise being looked after under the Children Act 1989, a person representing that authority or organisation;
   (ii) a social worker of a local authority social services department;
   (iii) failing these, some other responsible adult aged 18 or over who is not a police officer or employed by the police.

(b) person who is mentally disordered or mentally vulnerable: See Note 1D
   (i) a relative, guardian or other person responsible for their care or custody;
   (ii) someone experienced in dealing with mentally disordered or mentally vulnerable people but who is not a police officer or employed by the police;

(iii)   failing these, some other responsible adult aged 18 or over who is not a police officer or employed by the police.

1.8   If this Code requires a person be given certain information, they do not have to be given it if at the time they are incapable of understanding what is said, are violent or may become violent or in urgent need of medical attention, but they must be given it as soon as practicable.

1.9   References to a custody officer include any:—
    •   police officer; or
    •   designated staff custody officer acting in the exercise or performance of the powers and duties conferred or imposed on them by their designation,
performing the functions of a custody officer. See Note 1J.

1.9A   When this Code requires the prior authority or agreement of an officer of at least inspector or superintendent rank, that authority may be given by a sergeant or chief inspector authorised to perform the functions of the higher rank under the Police and Criminal Evidence Act 1984 (PACE), section 107.

1.10   Subject to paragraph 1.12, this Code applies to people in custody at police stations in England and Wales, whether or not they have been arrested, and to those removed to a police station as a place of safety under the Mental Health Act 1983, sections 135 and 136. Section 15 applies solely to people in police detention, e.g. those brought to a police station under arrest or arrested at a police station for an offence after going there voluntarily.

1.11   People in police custody include anyone detained under the Terrorism Act 2000, Schedule 8 and section 41, having been taken to a police station after being arrested under the Terrorism Act 2000, section 41. In these cases, reference to an offence in this Code includes the commission, preparation and instigation of acts of terrorism.

1.12   This Code's provisions do not apply to people in custody:
    (i)   arrested on warrants issued in Scotland by officers under the Criminal Justice and Public Order Act 1994, section 136(2), or arrested or detained without warrant by officers from a police force in Scotland under section 137(2). In these cases, police powers and duties and the person's rights and entitlements whilst at a police station in England or Wales are the same as those in Scotland;
    (ii)   arrested under the Immigration and Asylum Act 1999, section 142(3) in order to have their fingerprints taken;
    (iii) whose detention is authorised by an immigration officer under the Immigration Act 1971;
    (iv)   who are convicted or remanded prisoners held in police cells on behalf of the Prison Service under the Imprisonment (Temporary Provisions) Act 1980;
    (v)   detained for examination under the Terrorism Act 2000, Schedule 7 and to whom the Code of Practice issued under that Act, Schedule 14, paragraph 6 applies;
    (vi)   detained for searches under stop and search powers except as required by Code A.

The provisions on conditions of detention and treatment in sections 8 and 9 must be considered as the minimum standards of treatment for such detainees.

1.13   In this Code:
    (a)   'designated person' means a person other than a police officer, designated under the Police Reform Act 2002, Part 4 who has specified powers and duties of police officers conferred or imposed on them;
    (b)   reference to a police officer includes a designated person acting in the exercise or performance of the powers and duties conferred or imposed on them by their designation.

1.14   Designated persons are entitled to use reasonable force as follows:—
    (a)   when exercising a power conferred on them which allows a police officer exercising that power to use reasonable force, a designated person has the same entitlement to use force; and

(b)   at other times when carrying out duties conferred or imposed on them that also entitle them to use reasonable force, for example:

- when at a police station carrying out the duty to keep detainees for whom they are responsible under control and to assist any other police officer or designated person to keep any detainee under control and to prevent their escape.
- when securing, or assisting any other police officer or designated person in securing, the detention of a person at a police station.
- when escorting, or assisting any other police officer or designated person in escorting, a detainee within a police station.
- for the purpose of saving life or limb; or
- preventing serious damage to property.

1.15   Nothing in this Code prevents the custody officer, or other officer given custody of the detainee from allowing police staff who are not designated persons to carry out individual procedures or tasks at the police station if the law allows. However, the officer remains responsible for making sure the procedures and tasks are carried out correctly in accordance with the Codes of Practice. Any such person must be:

(a)   a person employed by a police authority maintaining a police force and under the control and direction of the Chief Officer of that force;

(b)   employed by a person with whom a police authority has a contract for the provision of services relating to persons arrested or otherwise in custody.

1.16   Designated persons and other police staff must have regard to any relevant provisions of the Codes of Practice.

1.17   References to pocket books include any official report book issued to police officers or other police staff.

Notes for guidance

1A   Although certain sections of this Code apply specifically to people in custody at police stations, those there voluntarily to assist with an investigation should be treated with no less consideration, e.g. offered refreshments at appropriate times, and enjoy an absolute right to obtain legal advice or communicate with anyone outside the police station.

1B   A person, including a parent or guardian, should not be an appropriate adult if they:

- are
  — suspected of involvement in the offence
  — the victim
  — a witness
  — involved in the investigation
- received admissions prior to attending to act as the appropriate adult.

Note: If a juvenile's parent is estranged from the juvenile, they should not be asked to act as the appropriate adult if the juvenile expressly and specifically objects to their presence.

1C   If a juvenile admits an offence to, or in the presence of, a social worker or member of a youth offending team other than during the time that person is acting as the juvenile's appropriate adult, another appropriate adult should be appointed in the interest of fairness.

1D   In the case of people who are mentally disordered or otherwise mentally vulnerable, it may be more satisfactory if the appropriate adult is someone experienced or trained in their care rather than a relative lacking such qualifications. But if the detainee prefers a relative to a better qualified stranger or objects to a particular person their wishes should, if practicable, be respected.

1E   A detainee should always be given an opportunity, when an appropriate adult is called to the police station, to consult privately with a solicitor in the appropriate adult's absence if they want. An appropriate adult is not subject to legal privilege.

1F   A solicitor or independent custody visitor (formerly a lay visitor) present at the police station in that capacity may not be the appropriate adult.

1G   'Mentally vulnerable' applies to any detainee who, because of their mental state or capacity, may not understand the significance of what is said, of questions or of their replies. 'Mental disorder' is defined in the Mental Health Act 1983, section 1(2) as 'mental illness, arrested or incomplete development of mind, psychopathic disorder and any other disorder or disability of mind'. When the custody officer has any doubt about the mental state or capacity of a detainee, that detainee should be treated as mentally vulnerable and an appropriate adult called.

1H   Paragraph 1.1A is intended to cover delays which may occur in processing detainees e.g. if:

- a large number of suspects are brought into the station simultaneously to be placed in custody;
- interview rooms are all being used;
- there are difficulties contacting an appropriate adult, solicitor or interpreter.

1I   The custody officer must remind the appropriate adult and detainee about the right to legal advice and record any reasons for waiving it in accordance with section 6.

1J   The designation of police staff custody officers applies only in police areas where an order commencing the provisions of the Police Reform Act 2002, section 38 and Schedule 4A, for designating police staff custody officers is in effect.

1K   This Code does not affect the principle that all citizens have a duty to help police officers to prevent crime and discover offenders. This is a civic rather than a legal duty; but when a police officer is trying to discover whether, or by whom, an offence has been committed he is entitled to question any person from whom he thinks useful information can be obtained, subject to the restrictions imposed by this Code. A person's declaration that he is unwilling to reply does not alter this entitlement

2 Custody records

2.1A When a person is brought to a police station:

- under arrest;
- is arrested at the police station having attended there voluntarily; or
- attends a police station to answer bail

they should be brought before the custody officer as soon as practicable after their arrival at the station or, if appropriate, following arrest after attending the police station voluntarily. This applies to designated and non-designated police stations. A person is deemed to be 'at a police station' for these purposes if they are within the boundary of any building or enclosed yard which forms part of that police station.

2.1   A separate custody record must be opened as soon as practicable for each person brought to a police station under arrest or arrested at the station having gone there voluntarily or attending a police station in answer to street bail. All information recorded under this Code must be recorded as soon as practicable in the custody record unless otherwise specified. Any audio or video recording made in the custody area is not part of the custody record.

2.2   If any action requires the authority of an officer of a specified rank, subject to paragraph 2.6A, their name and rank must be noted in the custody record.

2.3   The custody officer is responsible for the custody record's accuracy and completeness and for making sure the record or copy of the record accompanies a detainee if they are transferred to another police station. The record shall show the:

- time and reason for transfer;
- time a person is released from detention.

2.4   A solicitor or appropriate adult must be permitted to consult a detainee's custody record as soon as practicable after their arrival at the station and at any other time whilst the person is detained. Arrangements for this access must be agreed with the custody officer and may not unreasonably interfere with the custody officer's duties.

2.4A   When a detainee leaves police detention or is taken before a court they, their legal representative or appropriate adult shall be given, on request, a copy of the custody record as soon as practicable. This entitlement lasts for 12 months after release.

2.5   The detainee, appropriate adult or legal representative shall be permitted to inspect the original custody record after the detainee has left police detention provided they give reasonable notice of their request. Any such inspection shall be noted in the custody record.

2.6   Subject to paragraph 2.6A, all entries in custody records must be timed and signed by the maker. Records entered on computer shall be timed and contain the operator's identification.

2.6A   Nothing in this Code requires the identity of officers or other police staff to be recorded or disclosed:

(a)   in the case of enquiries linked to the investigation of terrorism; or

(b)   if the officer or police staff reasonably believe recording or disclosing their name might put them in danger.

In these cases, they shall use their warrant or other identification numbers and the name of their police station. See Note 2A

2.7   The fact and time of any detainee's refusal to sign a custody record, when asked in accordance with this Code, must be recorded.

Note for guidance

2A   The purpose of paragraph 2.6A(b) is to protect those involved in serious organised crime investigations or arrests of particularly violent suspects when there is reliable information that those arrested or their associates may threaten or cause harm to those involved. In cases of doubt, an officer of inspector rank or above should be consulted.

3   Initial action

(a)   Detained persons — normal procedure

3.1   When a person is brought to a police station under arrest or arrested at the station having gone there voluntarily, the custody officer must make sure the person is told clearly about the following continuing rights which may be exercised at any stage during the period in custody:

(i)   the right to have someone informed of their arrest as in section 5;

(ii)   the right to consult privately with a solicitor and that free independent legal advice is available;

(iii)   the right to consult these Codes of Practice. See Note 3D

3.2   The detainee must also be given:

•   a written notice setting out:

—   the above three rights;

—   the arrangements for obtaining legal advice;

—   the right to a copy of the custody record as in paragraph 2.4A;

—   the caution in the terms prescribed in section 10.

•   an additional written notice briefly setting out their entitlements while in custody, see Notes 3A and 3B.

Note: The detainee shall be asked to sign the custody record to acknowledge receipt of these notices. Any refusal must be recorded on the custody record.

3.3   A citizen of an independent Commonwealth country or a national of a foreign country, including the Republic of Ireland, must be informed as soon as practicable about their rights of communication with their High Commission, Embassy or Consulate. See section 7

3.4   The custody officer shall:

•   record the offence(s) that the detainee has been arrested for and the reason(s) for the arrest on the custody record. See paragraph 10.3 and Code G paragraphs 2.2 and 4.3.

- note on the custody record any comment the detainee makes in relation to the arresting officer's account but shall not invite comment. If the arresting officer is not physically present when the detainee is brought to a police station, the arresting officer's account must be made available to the custody officer remotely or by a third party on the arresting officer's behalf. If the custody officer authorises a person's detention the detainee must be informed of the grounds as soon as practicable and before they are questioned about any offence;

- note any comment the detainee makes in respect of the decision to detain them but shall not invite comment;

- not put specific questions to the detainee regarding their involvement in any offence, nor in respect of any comments they may make in response to the arresting officer's account or the decision to place them in detention. Such an exchange is likely to constitute an interview as in paragraph 11.1A and require the associated safeguards in section 11.

See paragraph 11.13 in respect of unsolicited comments.

3.5   The custody officer shall:

(a)   ask the detainee, whether at this time, they:

(i)   would like legal advice, see paragraph 6.5;

(ii)   want someone informed of their detention, see section 5;

(b)   ask the detainee to sign the custody record to confirm their decisions in respect of (a);

(c)   determine whether the detainee:

(i)   is, or might be, in need of medical treatment or attention, see section 9;

(ii)   requires:

- an appropriate adult;

- help to check documentation;

- an interpreter;

(d)   record the decision in respect of (c).

3.6   When determining these needs the custody officer is responsible for initiating an assessment to consider whether the detainee is likely to present specific risks to custody staff or themselves. Such assessments should always include a check on the Police National Computer, to be carried out as soon as practicable, to identify any risks highlighted in relation to the detainee. Although such assessments are primarily the custody officer's responsibility, it may be necessary for them to consult and involve others, e.g. the arresting officer or an appropriate health care professional, see paragraph 9.13. Reasons for delaying the initiation or completion of the assessment must be recorded.

3.7   Chief Officers should ensure that arrangements for proper and effective risk assessments required by paragraph 3.6 are implemented in respect of all detainees at police stations in their area.

3.8   Risk assessments must follow a structured process which clearly defines the categories of risk to be considered and the results must be incorporated in the detainee's custody record. The custody officer is responsible for making sure those responsible for the detainee's custody are appropriately briefed about the risks. If no specific risks are identified by the assessment, that should be noted in the custody record. See Note 3E and paragraph 9.14

3.9   The custody officer is responsible for implementing the response to any specific risk assessment, e.g.:

- reducing opportunities for self harm;

- calling a health care professional;

- increasing levels of monitoring or observation.

3.10 Risk assessment is an ongoing process and assessments must always be subject to review if circumstances change.

3.11   If video cameras are installed in the custody area, notices shall be prominently displayed showing cameras are in use. Any request to have video cameras switched off shall be refused.

(b)   *Detained persons — special groups*

3.12   If the detainee appears deaf or there is doubt about their hearing or speaking ability or ability to understand English, and the custody officer cannot establish effective communication, the custody officer must, as soon as practicable, call an interpreter for assistance in the action under paragraphs 3.1–3.5. See section 13

3.13   If the detainee is a juvenile, the custody officer must, if it is practicable, ascertain the identity of a person responsible for their welfare. That person:

- may be:
  — the parent or guardian;
  — if the juvenile is in local authority or voluntary organisation care, or is otherwise being looked after under the Children Act 1989, a person appointed by that authority or organisation to have responsibility for the juvenile's welfare;
  — any other person who has, for the time being, assumed responsibility for the juvenile's welfare.
- must be informed as soon as practicable that the juvenile has been arrested, why they have been arrested and where they are detained. This right is in addition to the juvenile's right in section 5 not to be held incommunicado. See Note 3C

3.14   If a juvenile is known to be subject to a court order under which a person or organisation is given any degree of statutory responsibility to supervise or otherwise monitor them, reasonable steps must also be taken to notify that person or organisation (the 'responsible officer'). The responsible officer will normally be a member of a Youth Offending Team, except for a curfew order which involves electronic monitoring when the contractor providing the monitoring will normally be the responsible officer.

3.15   If the detainee is a juvenile, mentally disordered or otherwise mentally vulnerable, the custody officer must, as soon as practicable:

- inform the appropriate adult, who in the case of a juvenile may or may not be a person responsible for their welfare, as in paragraph 3.13, of:
  — the grounds for their detention;
  — their whereabouts.
- ask the adult to come to the police station to see the detainee.

3.16   It is imperative that a mentally disordered or otherwise mentally vulnerable person, detained under the Mental Health Act 1983, section 136, be assessed as soon as possible. If that assessment is to take place at the police station, an approved social worker and a registered medical practitioner shall be called to the station as soon as possible in order to interview and examine the detainee. Once the detainee has been interviewed, examined and suitable arrangements made for their treatment or care, they can no longer be detained under section 136. A detainee must be immediately discharged from detention under section 136 if a registered medical practitioner, having examined them, concludes they are not mentally disordered within the meaning of the Act.

3.17   If the appropriate adult is:

- already at the police station, the provisions of paragraphs 3.1 to 3.5 must be complied with in the appropriate adult's presence;
- not at the station when these provisions are complied with, they must be complied with again in the presence of the appropriate adult when they arrive.

3.18   The detainee shall be advised that:

- the duties of the appropriate adult include giving advice and assistance;
- they can consult privately with the appropriate adult at any time.

3.19   If the detainee, or appropriate adult on the detainee's behalf, asks for a solicitor to be called to give legal advice, the provisions of section 6 apply.

3.20 If the detainee is blind, seriously visually impaired or unable to read, the custody officer shall make sure their solicitor, relative, appropriate adult or some other person likely to take an interest in them and not involved in the investigation is available to help check any documentation. When this Code requires written consent or signing the person assisting may be asked to sign instead, if the detainee prefers. This paragraph does not require an appropriate adult to be called solely to assist in checking and signing documentation for a person who is not a juvenile, or mentally disordered or otherwise mentally vulnerable (see paragraph 3.15).

(c)   Persons attending a police station voluntarily

3.21 Anybody attending a police station voluntarily to assist with an investigation may leave at will unless arrested. See Note 1K. If it is decided they shall not be allowed to leave, they must be informed at once that they are under arrest and brought before the custody officer, who is responsible for making sure they are notified of their rights in the same way as other detainees. If they are not arrested but are cautioned as in section 10, the person who gives the caution must, at the same time, inform them they are not under arrest, they are not obliged to remain at the station but if they remain at the station they may obtain free and independent legal advice if they want. They shall be told the right to legal advice includes the right to speak with a solicitor on the telephone and be asked if they want to do so.

3.22 If a person attending the police station voluntarily asks about their entitlement to legal advice, they shall be given a copy of the notice explaining the arrangements for obtaining legal advice. See paragraph 3.2

(d)   Documentation

3.23 The grounds for a person's detention shall be recorded, in the person's presence if practicable.

3.24 Action taken under paragraphs 3.12 to 3.20 shall be recorded.

(e)   Persons answering street bail

3.25 When a person is answering street bail, the custody officer should link any documentation held in relation to arrest with the custody record. Any further action shall be recorded on the custody record in accordance with paragraphs 3.23 and 3.24 above.

Notes for guidance

3A   The notice of entitlements should:
- list the entitlements in this Code, including:
  — visits and contact with outside parties, including special provisions for Commonwealth citizens and foreign nationals;
  — reasonable standards of physical comfort; -adequate food and drink;
  — access to toilets and washing facilities, clothing, medical attention, and exercise when practicable.
- mention the:
  — provisions relating to the conduct of interviews;
  — circumstances in which an appropriate adult should be available to assist the detainee and their statutory rights to make representation whenever the period of their detention is reviewed.

3B   In addition to notices in English, translations should be available in Welsh, the main minority ethnic languages and the principal European languages, whenever they are likely to be helpful. Audio versions of the notice should also be made available.

3C   If the juvenile is in local authority or voluntary organisation care but living with their parents or other adults responsible for their welfare, although there is no legal obligation to inform them, they should normally be contacted, as well as the authority or organisation unless suspected of involvement in the offence concerned. Even if the juvenile is not living with their parents, consideration should be given to informing them.

3D   The right to consult the Codes of Practice does not entitle the person concerned to delay unreasonably any necessary investigative or administrative action whilst they do so. Examples of action which need not be delayed unreasonably include:

- procedures requiring the provision of breath, blood or urine specimens under the Road Traffic Act 1988 or the Transport and Works Act 1992
- searching detainees at the police station
- taking fingerprints, footwear impressions or non-intimate samples without consent for evidential purposes

3E   Home Office Circular 32/2000 provides more detailed guidance on risk assessments and identifies key risk areas which should always be considered.

4 Detainee's property

(a)   Action

4.1   The custody officer is responsible for:

(a)   ascertaining what property a detainee:

(i)   has with them when they come to the police station, whether on:

- arrest or re-detention on answering to bail;
- commitment to prison custody on the order or sentence of a court;
- lodgement at the police station with a view to their production in court from prison custody;
- transfer from detention at another station or hospital;
- detention under the Mental Health Act 1983, section 135 or 136;
- remand into police custody on the authority of a court

(ii)   might have acquired for an unlawful or harmful purpose while in custody;

(b)   the safekeeping of any property taken from a detainee which remains at the police station.

The custody officer may search the detainee or authorise their being searched to the extent they consider necessary, provided a search of intimate parts of the body or involving the removal of more than outer clothing is only made as in Annex A.A search may only be carried out by an officer of the same sex as the detainee. See Note 4A

4.2   Detainees may retain clothing and personal effects at their own risk unless the custody officer considers they may use them to cause harm to themselves or others, interfere with evidence, damage property, effect an escape or they are needed as evidence. In this event the custody officer may withhold such articles as they consider necessary and must tell the detainee why.

4.3   Personal effects are those items a detainee may lawfully need, use or refer to while in detention but do not include cash and other items of value.

(b)   Documentation

4.4   It is a matter for the custody officer to determine whether a record should be made of the property a detained person has with him or had taken from him on arrest. Any record made is not required to be kept as part of the custody record but the custody record should be noted as to where such a record exists. Whenever a record is made the detainee shall be allowed to check and sign the record of property as correct. Any refusal to sign shall be recorded.

4.5   If a detainee is not allowed to keep any article of clothing or personal effects, the reason must be recorded.

Notes for guidance

4A   PACE, Section 54(1) and paragraph 4.1 require a detainee to be searched when it is clear the custody officer will have continuing duties in relation to that detainee or when that detainee's behaviour or offence makes an inventory appropriate. They do not require every detainee to be searched, e.g. if it is clear a person will only be detained for a short period and is not to be placed in a cell, the custody officer may decide not to search them. In such a case the custody record will be endorsed 'not searched', paragraph 4.4 will not apply, and the detainee will be invited to sign the entry. If the detainee refuses, the custody officer will be obliged to ascertain what property they have in accordance with paragraph 4.1.

4B   Paragraph 4.4 does not require the custody officer to record on the custody record property in the detainee's possession on arrest if, by virtue of its nature, quantity or size, it is not practicable to remove it to the police station.

4C   Paragraph 4.4 does not require items of clothing worn by the person be recorded unless withheld by the custody officer as in paragraph 4.2.

5   Right not to be held incommunicado

(a)   Action

5.1   Any person arrested and held in custody at a police station or other premises may, on request, have one person known to them or likely to take an interest in their welfare informed at public expense of their whereabouts as soon as practicable. If the person cannot be contacted the detainee may choose up to two alternatives. If they cannot be contacted, the person in charge of detention or the investigation has discretion to allow further attempts until the information has been conveyed. See Notes 5C and 5D

5.2   The exercise of the above right in respect of each person nominated may be delayed only in accordance with Annex B.

5.3   The above right may be exercised each time a detainee is taken to another police station.

5.4   The detainee may receive visits at the custody officer's discretion. See Note 5B

5.5   If a friend, relative or person with an interest in the detainee's welfare enquires about their whereabouts, this information shall be given if the suspect agrees and Annex B does not apply. See Note 5D

5.6   The detainee shall be given writing materials, on request, and allowed to telephone one person for a reasonable time, see Notes 5A and 5E. Either or both these privileges may be denied or delayed if an officer of inspector rank or above considers sending a letter or making a telephone call may result in any of the consequences in:

(a)   Annex B paragraphs 1 and 2 and the person is detained in connection with an indictable offence; or

(b)   Annex B paragraphs 8 and 9 and the person is detained under the Terrorism Act 2000, Schedule 7 or section 41

Nothing in this paragraph permits the restriction or denial of the rights in paragraphs 5.1 and 6.1.

5.7   Before any letter or message is sent, or telephone call made, the detainee shall be informed that what they say in any letter, call or message (other than in a communication to a solicitor) may be read or listened to and may be given in evidence. A telephone call may be terminated if it is being abused. The costs can be at public expense at the custody officer's discretion.

5.7A   Any delay or denial of the rights in this section should be proportionate and should last no longer than necessary.

(b)   Documentation

5.8   A record must be kept of any:

(a)   request made under this section and the action taken;

(b)   letters, messages or telephone calls made or received or visit received;

(c)   refusal by the detainee to have information about them given to an outside enquirer. The detainee must be asked to countersign the record accordingly and any refusal recorded.

Notes for guidance

5A   A person may request an interpreter to interpret a telephone call or translate a letter.

5B   At the custody officer's discretion, visits should be allowed when possible, subject to having sufficient personnel to supervise a visit and any possible hindrance to the investigation.

5C   If the detainee does not know anyone to contact for advice or support or cannot contact a friend or relative, the custody officer should bear in mind any local voluntary bodies or other organisations who might be able to help. Paragraph 6.1 applies if legal advice is required.

5D   In some circumstances it may not be appropriate to use the telephone to disclose information under paragraphs 5.1 and 5.5.

5E   The telephone call at paragraph 5.6 is in addition to any communication under paragraphs 5.1 and 6.1.

6   Right to legal advice

(a)   Action

6.1   Unless Annex B applies, all detainees must be informed that they may at any time consult and communicate privately with a solicitor, whether in person, in writing or by telephone, and that free independent legal advice is available from the duty solicitor. See paragraph 3.1, Note 6B and Note 6J

6.2   Not Used

6.3   A poster advertising the right to legal advice must be prominently displayed in the charging area of every police station. See Note 6H

6.4   No police officer should, at any time, do or say anything with the intention of dissuading a detainee from obtaining legal advice.

6.5   The exercise of the right of access to legal advice may be delayed only as in Annex B. Whenever legal advice is requested, and unless Annex B applies, the custody officer must act without delay to secure the provision of such advice. If, on being informed or reminded of this right, the detainee declines to speak to a solicitor in person, the officer should point out that the right includes the right to speak with a solicitor on the telephone. If the detainee continues to waive this right the officer should ask them why and any reasons should be recorded on the custody record or the interview record as appropriate. Reminders of the right to legal advice must be given as in paragraphs 3.5, 11.2, 15.4, 16.4, 2B of Annex A, 3 of Annex K and 16.5 and Code D, paragraphs 3.17(ii) and 6.3. Once it is clear a detainee does not want to speak to a solicitor in person or by telephone they should cease to be asked their reasons. See Note 6K

6.5A   In the case of a juvenile, an appropriate adult should consider whether legal advice from a solicitor is required. If the juvenile indicates that they do not want legal advice, the appropriate adult has the right to ask for a solicitor to attend if this would be in the best interests of the person. However, the detained person cannot be forced to see the solicitor if he is adamant that he does not wish to do so.

6.6   A detainee who wants legal advice may not be interviewed or continue to be interviewed until they have received such advice unless:

(a)   Annex B applies, when the restriction on drawing adverse inferences from silence in Annex C will apply because the detainee is not allowed an opportunity to consult a solicitor; or

(b)   an officer of superintendent rank or above has reasonable grounds for believing that:

(i)   the consequent delay might:
- lead to interference with, or harm to, evidence connected with an offence;
- lead to interference with, or physical harm to, other people;
- lead to serious loss of, or damage to, property;
- lead to alerting other people suspected of having committed an offence but not yet arrested for it;
- hinder the recovery of property obtained in consequence of the commission of an offence.

(ii)   when a solicitor, including a duty solicitor, has been contacted and has agreed to attend, awaiting their arrival would cause unreasonable delay to the process of investigation.

Note: In these cases the restriction on drawing adverse inferences from silence in Annex C will apply because the detainee is not allowed an opportunity to consult a solicitor;

(c)   the solicitor the detainee has nominated or selected from a list:

(i)   cannot be contacted;

(ii)   has previously indicated they do not wish to be contacted; or

(iii)   having been contacted, has declined to attend; and

the detainee has been advised of the Duty Solicitor Scheme but has declined to ask for the duty solicitor.

In these circumstances the interview may be started or continued without further delay provided an officer of inspector rank or above has agreed to the interview proceeding.

Note: The restriction on drawing adverse inferences from silence in Annex C will not apply because the detainee is allowed an opportunity to consult the duty solicitor;

(d)   *the detainee changes their mind, about wanting legal advice.*

In these circumstances the interview may be started or continued without delay provided that:

(i)   the detainee agrees to do so, in writing or on the interview record made in accordance with Code E or F; and

(ii)   an officer of inspector rank or above has inquired about the detainee's reasons for their change of mind and gives authority for the interview to proceed.

Confirmation of the detainee's agreement, their change of mind, the reasons for it if given and, subject to paragraph 2.6A, the name of the authorising officer shall be recorded in the written interview record or the interview record made in accordance with Code E or F. See Note 6I.

Note: In these circumstances the restriction on drawing adverse inferences from silence in Annex C will not apply because the detainee is allowed an opportunity to consult a solicitor if they wish.

6.7   If paragraph 6.6(b)(i) applies, once sufficient information has been obtained to avert the risk, questioning must cease until the detainee has received legal advice unless paragraph 6.6(a), (b)(ii), (c) or (d) applies.

6.8   A detainee who has been permitted to consult a solicitor shall be entitled on request to have the solicitor present when they are interviewed unless one of the exceptions in paragraph 6.6 applies.

6.9   The solicitor may only be required to leave the interview if their conduct is such that the interviewer is unable properly to put questions to the suspect. See Notes 6D and 6E

6.10   If the interviewer considers a solicitor is acting in such a way, they will stop the interview and consult an officer not below superintendent rank, if one is readily available, and otherwise an officer not below inspector rank not connected with the investigation. After speaking to the solicitor, the officer consulted will decide if the interview should continue in the presence of that solicitor. If they decide it should not, the suspect will be given the opportunity to consult another solicitor before the interview continues and that solicitor given an opportunity to be present at the interview. See Note 6E

6.11   The removal of a solicitor from an interview is a serious step and, if it occurs, the officer of superintendent rank or above who took the decision will consider if the incident should be reported to the Law Society. If the decision to remove the solicitor has been taken by an officer below superintendent rank, the facts must be reported to an officer of superintendent rank or above who will similarly consider whether a report to the Law Society would be appropriate. When the solicitor concerned is a duty solicitor, the report should be both to the Law Society and to the Legal Services Commission.

6.12   'Solicitor' in this Code means:
- a solicitor who holds a current practising certificate
- an accredited or probationary representative included on the register of representatives maintained by the Legal Services Commission.

6.12A An accredited or probationary representative sent to provide advice by, and on behalf of, a solicitor shall be admitted to the police station for this purpose unless an officer of inspector rank or above considers such a visit will hinder the investigation and directs otherwise. Hindering the investigation does not include giving proper legal advice to a detainee as in Note 6D. Once admitted to the police station, paragraphs 6.6 to 6.10 apply.

6.13   In exercising their discretion under paragraph 6.12A, the officer should take into account in particular:
- whether:
  - the identity and status of an accredited or probationary representative have been satisfactorily established;
  - they are of suitable character to provide legal advice, e.g. a person with a criminal record is unlikely to be suitable unless the conviction was for a minor offence and not recent.
- any other matters in any written letter of authorisation provided by the solicitor on whose behalf the person is attending the police station. See Note 6F

6.14   If the inspector refuses access to an accredited or probationary representative or a decision is taken that such a person should not be permitted to remain at an interview, the inspector must notify the solicitor on whose behalf the representative was acting and give them an opportunity to make alternative arrangements. The detainee must be informed and the custody record noted.

6.15   If a solicitor arrives at the station to see a particular person, that person must, unless Annex B applies, be so informed whether or not they are being interviewed and asked if they would like to see the solicitor. This applies even if the detainee has declined legal advice or, having requested it, subsequently agreed to be interviewed without receiving advice. The solicitor's attendance and the detainee's decision must be noted in the custody record.

(b)   Documentation

6.16   Any request for legal advice and the action taken shall be recorded.

6.17   A record shall be made in the interview record if a detainee asks for legal advice and an interview is begun either in the absence of a solicitor or their representative, or they have been required to leave an interview.

Notes for guidance

6A   In considering if paragraph 6.6(b) applies, the officer should, if practicable, ask the solicitor for an estimate of how long it will take to come to the station and relate this to the time detention is permitted, the time of day (i.e. whether the rest period under paragraph 12.2 is imminent) and the requirements of other investigations. If the solicitor is on their way or is to set off immediately, it will not normally be appropriate to begin an interview before they arrive. If it appears necessary to begin an interview before the solicitor's arrival, they should be given an indication of how long the police would be able to wait before 6.6(b) applies so there is an opportunity to make arrangements for someone else to provide legal advice.

6B   A detainee who asks for legal advice should be given an opportunity to consult a specific solicitor or another solicitor from that solicitor's firm or the duty solicitor. If advice is not available by these means, or they do not want to consult the duty solicitor, the detainee should be given an opportunity to choose a solicitor from a list of those willing to provide legal advice. If this solicitor is unavailable, they may choose up to two alternatives. If these attempts are unsuccessful, the custody officer has discretion to allow further attempts until a solicitor has been contacted and agrees to provide legal advice. Apart from carrying out these duties, an officer must not advise the suspect about any particular firm of solicitors.

6C   Not Used

6D   A detainee has a right to free legal advice and to be represented by a solicitor. The solicitor's only role in the police station is to protect and advance the legal rights of their client. On occasions this may require the solicitor to give advice which has the effect of the client avoiding giving evidence which strengthens a prosecution case. The solicitor may intervene in order to seek clarification, challenge an improper question to their client or the manner in which it is put, advise their client not to reply to particular questions, or if they wish to give their client further legal advice. Paragraph 6.9 only applies if the solicitor's approach or conduct prevents or unreasonably obstructs proper questions being put to the suspect or the suspect's response being recorded. Examples of unacceptable conduct include answering questions on a suspect's behalf or providing written replies for the suspect to quote.

6E   An officer who takes the decision to exclude a solicitor must be in a position to satisfy the court the decision was properly made. In order to do this they may need to witness what is happening.

6F   If an officer of at least inspector rank considers a particular solicitor or firm of solicitors is persistently sending probationary representatives who are unsuited to provide legal advice, they should inform an officer of at least superintendent rank, who may wish to take the matter up with the Law Society.

6G   Subject to the constraints of Annex B, a solicitor may advise more than one client in an investigation if they wish. Any question of a conflict of interest is for the solicitor under their professional code of conduct. If, however, waiting for a solicitor to give advice to one client may lead to unreasonable delay to the interview with another, the provisions of paragraph 6.6(b) may apply.

6H   In addition to a poster in English, a poster or posters containing translations into Welsh, the main minority ethnic languages and the principal European languages should be displayed wherever they are likely to be helpful and it is practicable to do so.

6I   Paragraph 6.6(d) requires the authorisation of an officer of inspector rank or above to the continuation of an interview when a detainee who wanted legal advice changes their mind. It is permissible for such authorisation to be given over the telephone, if the authorising officer is able to satisfy themselves about the reason for the detainee's change of mind and is satisfied it is proper to continue the interview in those circumstances.

6J   Whenever a detainee exercises their right to legal advice by consulting or communicating with a solicitor, they must be allowed to do so in private. This right to consult or communicate in private is fundamental. Except as allowed by the Terrorism Act 2000, Schedule 8, paragraph 9, if the requirement for privacy is compromised because what is said or written by the detainee or solicitor for the purpose of giving and receiving legal advice is overheard, listened to, or read by others without the informed consent of the detainee, the right will effectively have been denied. When a detainee chooses to speak to a solicitor on the telephone, they should be allowed to do so in private unless this is impractical because of the design and layout of the custody area or the location of telephones. However, the normal expectation should be that facilities will be available, unless they are being used, at all police stations to enable detainees to speak in private to a solicitor either face to face or over the telephone.

6K   A detainee is not obliged to give reasons for declining legal advice and should not be pressed to do so.

8   Conditions of detention

(a)   Action

8.1   So far as it is practicable, not more than one detainee should be detained in each cell.

8.2   Cells in use must be adequately heated, cleaned and ventilated. They must be adequately lit, subject to such dimming as is compatible with safety and security to allow people detained overnight to sleep. No additional restraints shall be used within a locked cell unless absolutely necessary and then only restraint equipment, approved for use in that force by the Chief Officer, which is reasonable and necessary in the circumstances having regard to the detainee's demeanour and with a view to ensuring their safety and the safety of others. If a detainee is deaf, mentally disordered or otherwise mentally vulnerable, particular care must be taken when deciding whether to use any form of approved restraints.

8.3 Blankets, mattresses, pillows and other bedding supplied shall be of a reasonable standard and in a clean and sanitary condition. See Note 8A

8.4 Access to toilet and washing facilities must be provided.

8.5 If it is necessary to remove a detainee's clothes for the purposes of investigation, for hygiene, health reasons or cleaning, replacement clothing of a reasonable standard of comfort and cleanliness shall be provided. A detainee may not be interviewed unless adequate clothing has been offered.

8.6 At least two light meals and one main meal should be offered in any 24 hour period. See Note 8B. Drinks should be provided at meal times and upon reasonable request between meals. Whenever necessary, advice shall be sought from the appropriate health care professional, see Note 9A, on medical and dietary matters. As far as practicable, meals provided shall offer a varied diet and meet any specific dietary needs or religious beliefs the detainee may have. The detainee may, at the custody officer's discretion, have meals supplied by their family or friends at their expense. See Note 8A

8.7 Brief outdoor exercise shall be offered daily if practicable.

8.8 A juvenile shall not be placed in a police cell unless no other secure accommodation is available and the custody officer considers it is not practicable to supervise them if they are not placed in a cell or that a cell provides more comfortable accommodation than other secure accommodation in the station. A juvenile may not be placed in a cell with a detained adult.

(b) *Documentation*

8.9 A record must be kept of replacement clothing and meals offered.

8.10 If a juvenile is placed in a cell, the reason must be recorded.

8.11 The use of any restraints on a detainee whilst in a cell, the reasons for it and, if appropriate, the arrangements for enhanced supervision of the detainee whilst so restrained, shall be recorded. See paragraph 3.9

Notes for guidance

8A The provisions in paragraph 8.3 and 8.6 respectively are of particular importance in the case of a person detained under the Terrorism Act 2000, immigration detainees and others likely to be detained for an extended period. In deciding whether to allow meals to be supplied by family or friends, the custody officer is entitled to take account of the risk of items being concealed in any food or package and the officer's duties and responsibilities under food handling legislation.

8B Meals should, so far as practicable, be offered at recognised meal times, or at other times that take account of when the detainee last had a meal.

9   Care and treatment of detained persons

(a) *General*

9.1 Nothing in this section prevents the police from calling the police surgeon or, if appropriate, some other health care professional, to examine a detainee for the purposes of obtaining evidence relating to any offence in which the detainee is suspected of being involved. See Note 9A

9.2 If a complaint is made by, or on behalf of, a detainee about their treatment since their arrest, or it comes to notice that a detainee may have been treated improperly, a report must be made as soon as practicable to an officer of inspector rank or above not connected with the investigation. If the matter concerns a possible assault or the possibility of the unnecessary or unreasonable use of force, an appropriate health care professional must also be called as soon as practicable.

9.3   Detainees should be visited at least every hour. If no reasonably foreseeable risk was identified in a risk assessment, see paragraphs 3.6 — 3.10, there is no need to wake a sleeping detainee. Those suspected of being intoxicated through drink or drugs or having swallowed drugs, see Note 9CA, or whose level of consciousness causes concern must, subject to any clinical directions given by the appropriate health care professional, see paragraph 9.13:

- be visited and roused at least every half hour
- have their condition assessed as in Annex H
- and clinical treatment arranged if appropriate

See Notes 9B, 9C and 9H

9.4   When arrangements are made to secure clinical attention for a detainee, the custody officer must make sure all relevant information which might assist in the treatment of the detainee's condition is made available to the responsible health care professional. This applies whether or not the health care professional asks for such information. Any officer or police staff with relevant information must inform the custody officer as soon as practicable.

(b)   Clinical treatment and attention

9.5   The custody officer must make sure a detainee receives appropriate clinical attention as soon as reasonably practicable if the person:

(a)   appears to be suffering from physical illness; or

(b)   is injured; or

(c)   appears to be suffering from a mental disorder;

(d)   appears to need clinical attention.

9.5A   This applies even if the detainee makes no request for clinical attention and whether or not they have already received clinical attention elsewhere. If the need for attention appears urgent, e.g. when indicated as in Annex H, the nearest available health care professional or an ambulance must be called immediately.

9.5B   The custody officer must also consider the need for clinical attention as set out in Note for Guidance 9C in relation to those suffering the effects of alcohol or drugs.

9.6   Paragraph 9.5 is not meant to prevent or delay the transfer to a hospital if necessary of a person detained under the Mental Health Act 1983, section 136. See Note 9D. When an assessment under that Act takes place at a police station, see paragraph 3.16, the custody officer must consider whether an appropriate health care professional should be called to conduct an initial clinical check on the detainee. This applies particularly when there is likely to be any significant delay in the arrival of a suitably qualified medical practitioner.

9.7   If it appears to the custody officer, or they are told, that a person brought to a station under arrest may be suffering from an infectious disease or condition, the custody officer must take reasonable steps to safeguard the health of the detainee and others at the station. In deciding what action to take, advice must be sought from an appropriate health care professional. See Note 9E. The custody officer has discretion to isolate the person and their property until clinical directions have been obtained.

9.8   If a detainee requests a clinical examination, an appropriate health care professional must be called as soon as practicable to assess the detainee's clinical needs. If a safe and appropriate care plan cannot be provided, the police surgeon's advice must be sought. The detainee may also be examined by a medical practitioner of their choice at their expense.

9.9   If a detainee is required to take or apply any medication in compliance with clinical directions prescribed before their detention, the custody officer must consult the appropriate health care professional before the use of the medication. Subject to the restrictions in paragraph 9.10, the custody officer is responsible for the safekeeping of any medication and for making sure the detainee is given the opportunity to take or apply prescribed or approved medication. Any such consultation and its outcome shall be noted in the custody record.

9.10   No police officer may administer or supervise the self-administration of medically prescribed controlled drugs of the types and forms listed in the Misuse of Drugs

Regulations 2001, Schedule 2 or 3. A detainee may only self-administer such drugs under the personal supervision of the registered medical practitioner authorising their use. Drugs listed in Schedule 4 or 5 may be distributed by the custody officer for self-administration if they have consulted the registered medical practitioner authorising their use, this may be done by telephone, and both parties are satisfied self-administration will not expose the detainee, police officers or anyone else to the risk of harm or injury.

9.11   When appropriate health care professionals administer drugs or other medications, or supervise their self-administration, it must be within current medicines legislation and the scope of practice as determined by their relevant professional body.

9.12   If a detainee has in their possession, or claims to need, medication relating to a heart condition, diabetes, epilepsy or a condition of comparable potential seriousness then, even though paragraph 9.5 may not apply, the advice of the appropriate health care professional must be obtained.

9.13   Whenever the appropriate health care professional is called in accordance with this section to examine or treat a detainee, the custody officer shall ask for their opinion about:

- any risks or problems which police need to take into account when making decisions about the detainee's continued detention;
- when to carry out an interview if applicable; and
- the need for safeguards.

9.14   When clinical directions are given by the appropriate health care professional, whether orally or in writing, and the custody officer has any doubts or is in any way uncertain about any aspect of the directions, the custody officer shall ask for clarification. It is particularly important that directions concerning the frequency of visits are clear, precise and capable of being implemented. See Note 9F.

(c)   Documentation

9.15   A record must be made in the custody record of:

(a)   the arrangements made for an examination by an appropriate health care professional under paragraph 9.2 and of any complaint reported under that paragraph together with any relevant remarks by the custody officer;

(b)   any arrangements made in accordance with paragraph 9.5;

(c)   any request for a clinical examination under paragraph 9.8 and any arrangements made in response;

(d)   the injury, ailment, condition or other reason which made it necessary to make the arrangements in (a) to (c), see Note 9G;

(e)   any clinical directions and advice, including any further clarifications, given to police by a health care professional concerning the care and treatment of the detainee in connection with any of the arrangements made in (a) to (c), see Note 9F;

(f)   if applicable, the responses received when attempting to rouse a person using the procedure in Annex H, see Note 9H.

9.16   If a health care professional does not record their clinical findings in the custody record, the record must show where they are recorded. See Note 9G. However, information which is necessary to custody staff to ensure the effective ongoing care and well being of the detainee must be recorded openly in the custody record, see paragraph 3.8 and Annex G, paragraph 7.

9.17   Subject to the requirements of Section 4, the custody record shall include:

- a record of all medication a detainee has in their possession on arrival at the police station;
- a note of any such medication they claim to need but do not have with them.

Notes for guidance

9A   A 'health care professional' means a clinically qualified person working within the scope of practice as determined by their relevant professional body. Whether a health care professional is 'appropriate' depends on the circumstances of the duties they carry out at the time.

9B   Whenever possible juveniles and mentally vulnerable detainees should be visited more frequently.

9C   A detainee who appears drunk or behaves abnormally may be suffering from illness, the effects of drugs or may have sustained injury, particularly a head injury which is not apparent. A detainee needing or dependent on certain drugs, including alcohol, may experience harmful effects within a short time of being deprived of their supply. In these circumstances, when there is any doubt, police should always act urgently to call an appropriate health care professional or an ambulance. Paragraph 9.5 does not apply to minor ailments or injuries which do not need attention. However, all such ailments or injuries must be recorded in the custody record and any doubt must be resolved in favour of calling the appropriate health care professional.

9CA   Paragraph 9.3 would apply to a person in police custody by order of a magistrates' court under the Criminal Justice Act 1988, section 152 (as amended by the Drugs Act 2005, section 8) to facilitate the recovery of evidence after being charged with drug possession or drug trafficking and suspected of having swallowed drugs. In the case of the healthcare needs of a person who has swallowed drugs, the custody officer subject to any clinical directions, should consider the necessity for rousing every half hour. This does not negate the need for regular visiting of the suspect in the cell.

9D   Whenever practicable, arrangements should be made for persons detained for assessment under the Mental Health Act 1983, section 136 to be taken to a hospital. There is no power under that Act to transfer a person detained under section 136 from one place of safety to another place of safety for assessment.

9E   It is important to respect a person's right to privacy and information about their health must be kept confidential and only disclosed with their consent or in accordance with clinical advice when it is necessary to protect the detainee's health or that of others who come into contact with them.

9F   The custody officer should always seek to clarify directions that the detainee requires constant observation or supervision and should ask the appropriate health care professional to explain precisely what action needs to be taken to implement such directions.

9G   Paragraphs 9.15 and 9.16 do not require any information about the cause of any injury, ailment or condition to be recorded on the custody record if it appears capable of providing evidence of an offence.

9H   The purpose of recording a person's responses when attempting to rouse them using the procedure in Annex H is to enable any change in the individual's consciousness level to be noted and clinical treatment arranged if appropriate.

10   Cautions

(a)   When a caution must be given

10.1 A person whom there are grounds to suspect of an offence, see Note 10A, must be cautioned before any questions about an offence, or further questions if the answers provide the grounds for suspicion, are put to them if either the suspect's answers or silence, (i.e. failure or refusal to answer or answer satisfactorily) may be given in evidence to a court in a prosecution. A person need not be cautioned if questions are for other necessary purposes, e.g.:

(a)   solely to establish their identity or ownership of any vehicle;

(b)   to obtain information in accordance with any relevant statutory requirement, see paragraph 10.9;

(c)   in furtherance of the proper and effective conduct of a search, e.g. to determine the need to search in the exercise of powers of stop and search or to seek cooperation while carrying out a search;

(d)   to seek verification of a written record as in paragraph 11.13;

(e)   when examining a person in accordance with the Terrorism Act 2000, Schedule 7 and the Code of Practice for Examining Officers issued under that Act, Schedule 14, paragraph 6.

10.2   Whenever a person not under arrest is initially cautioned, or reminded they are under caution, that person must at the same time be told they are not under arrest and are free to leave if they want to. See Note 10C

10.3   A person who is arrested, or further arrested, must be informed at the time, or as soon as practicable thereafter, that they are under arrest and the grounds for their arrest, see paragraph 3.4, Note 10B and Code G, paragraphs 2.2 and 4.3.

10.4   As per Code G, section 3, a person who is arrested, or further arrested, must also be cautioned unless:

(a)   it is impracticable to do so by reason of their condition or behaviour at the time;

(b)   they have already been cautioned immediately prior to arrest as in paragraph 10.1.

(b)   *Terms of the cautions*

10.5   The caution which must be given on:

(a)   arrest;

(b)   all other occasions before a person is charged or informed they may be prosecuted, see section 16,

should, unless the restriction on drawing adverse inferences from silence applies, see Annex C, be in the following terms:

"You do not have to say anything. But it may harm your defence if you do not mention when questioned something which you later rely on in Court. Anything you do say may be given in evidence."

See Note 10G

10.6   Annex C, paragraph 2 sets out the alternative terms of the caution to be used when the restriction on drawing adverse inferences from silence applies.

10.7   Minor deviations from the words of any caution given in accordance with this Code do not constitute a breach of this Code, provided the sense of the relevant caution is preserved. See Note 10D

10.8   After any break in questioning under caution, the person being questioned must be made aware they remain under caution. If there is any doubt the relevant caution should be given again in full when the interview resumes. See Note 10E

10.9   When, despite being cautioned, a person fails to co-operate or to answer particular questions which may affect their immediate treatment, the person should be informed of any relevant consequences and that those consequences are not affected by the caution. Examples are when a person's refusal to provide:

•   their name and address when charged may make them liable to detention;

•   particulars and information in accordance with a statutory requirement, e.g. under the Road Traffic Act 1988, may amount to an offence or may make the person liable to a further arrest.

(c)   *Special warnings under the Criminal Justice and Public Order Act 1994, sections 36 and 37*

10.10   When a suspect interviewed at a police station or authorised place of detention after arrest fails or refuses to answer certain questions, or to answer satisfactorily, after due warning, see Note 10F, a court or jury may draw such inferences as appear proper under the Criminal Justice and Public Order Act 1994, sections 36 and 37. Such inferences may only be drawn when:

(a)   the restriction on drawing adverse inferences from silence, see Annex C, does not apply; and

(b)   the suspect is arrested by a constable and fails or refuses to account for any objects, marks or substances, or marks on such objects found:

•   in or on their clothing or footwear;

•   otherwise in their possession; or

•   in the place they were arrested;

(c)   the arrested suspect was found by a constable at a place at or about the time the offence for which that officer has arrested them is alleged to have been committed, and the suspect fails or refuses to account for their presence there.

•   on their person;

When the restriction on drawing adverse inferences from silence applies, the suspect may still be asked to account for any of the matters in (b) or (c) but the special warning described in paragraph 10.11 will not apply and must not be given.

10.11 For an inference to be drawn when a suspect fails or refuses to answer a question about one of these matters or to answer it satisfactorily, the suspect must first be told in ordinary language:

(a)   what offence is being investigated;

(b)   what fact they are being asked to account for;

(c)   this fact may be due to them taking part in the commission of the offence;

(d)   a court may draw a proper inference if they fail or refuse to account for this fact;

(e)   a record is being made of the interview and it may be given in evidence if they are brought to trial.

(d)   Juveniles and persons who are mentally disordered or otherwise mentally vulnerable

10.12 If a juvenile or a person who is mentally disordered or otherwise mentally vulnerable is cautioned in the absence of the appropriate adult, the caution must be repeated in the adult's presence.

(e)   Documentation

10.13 A record shall be made when a caution is given under this section, either in the interviewer's pocket book or in the interview record.

Notes for guidance

10A   There must be some reasonable, objective grounds for the suspicion, based on known facts or information which are relevant to the likelihood the offence has been committed and the person to be questioned committed it.

10B   An arrested person must be given sufficient information to enable them to understand that they have been deprived of their liberty and the reason they have been arrested, e.g. when a person is arrested on suspicion of committing an offence they must be informed of the suspected offence's nature, when and where it was committed. The suspect must also be informed of the reason or reasons why the arrest is considered necessary. Vague or technical language should be avoided.

10C   The restriction on drawing inferences from silence, see Annex C, paragraph 1, does not apply to a person who has not been detained and who therefore cannot be prevented from seeking legal advice if they want, see paragraph 3.21.

10D   If it appears a person does not understand the caution, the person giving it should explain it in their own words.

10E   It may be necessary to show to the court that nothing occurred during an interview break or between interviews which influenced the suspect's recorded evidence. After a break in an interview or at the beginning of a subsequent interview, the interviewing officer should summarise the reason for the break and confirm this with the suspect.

10F   The Criminal Justice and Public Order Act 1994, sections 36 and 37 apply only to suspects who have been arrested by a constable or Customs and Excise officer and are given the relevant warning by the police or customs officer who made the arrest or who is investigating the offence. They do not apply to any interviews with suspects who have not been arrested.

10G   Nothing in this Code requires a caution to be given or repeated when informing a person not under arrest they may be prosecuted for an offence. However, a court will not be able to draw any inferences under the Criminal Justice and Public Order Act 1994, section 34, if the person was not cautioned.

11   Interviews — general

(a)   Action

11.1A An interview is the questioning of a person regarding their involvement or suspected involvement in a criminal offence or offences which, under paragraph 10.1, must be carried out under caution. Whenever a person is interviewed they must be informed of the nature of the offence, or further offence. Procedures under the Road Traffic Act 1988, section 7 or the Transport and Works Act 1992, section 31 do not constitute interviewing for the purpose of this Code.

11.1   Following a decision to arrest a suspect, they must not be interviewed about the relevant offence except at a police station or other authorised place of detention, unless the consequent delay would be likely to:

(a)   lead to:
- interference with, or harm to, evidence connected with an offence;
- interference with, or physical harm to, other people; or
- serious loss of, or damage to, property;

(b)   lead to alerting other people suspected of committing an offence but not yet arrested for it; or

(c)   hinder the recovery of property obtained in consequence of the commission of an offence.

Interviewing in any of these circumstances shall cease once the relevant risk has been averted or the necessary questions have been put in order to attempt to avert that risk.

11.2   Immediately prior to the commencement or re-commencement of any interview at a police station or other authorised place of detention, the interviewer should remind the suspect of their entitlement to free legal advice and that the interview can be delayed for legal advice to be obtained, unless one of the exceptions in paragraph 6.6 applies. It is the interviewer's responsibility to make sure all reminders are recorded in the interview record.

11.3   Not Used

11.4   At the beginning of an interview the interviewer, after cautioning the suspect, see section 10, shall put to them any significant statement or silence which occurred in the presence and hearing of a police officer or other police staff before the start of the interview and which have not been put to the suspect in the course of a previous interview. See Note 11A. The interviewer shall ask the suspect whether they confirm or deny that earlier statement or silence and if they want to add anything.

11.4A A significant statement is one which appears capable of being used in evidence against the suspect, in particular a direct admission of guilt. A significant silence is a failure or refusal to answer a question or answer satisfactorily when under caution, which might, allowing for the restriction on drawing adverse inferences from silence, see Annex C, give rise to an inference under the Criminal Justice and Public Order Act 1994, Part III.

11.5   No interviewer may try to obtain answers or elicit a statement by the use of oppression. Except as in paragraph 10.9, no interviewer shall indicate, except to answer a direct question, what action will be taken by the police if the person being questioned answers questions, makes a statement or refuses to do either. If the person asks directly what action will be taken if they answer questions, make a statement or refuse to do either, the interviewer may inform them what action the police propose to take provided that action is itself proper and warranted.

11.6   The interview or further interview of a person about an offence with which that person has not been charged or for which they have not been informed they may be prosecuted, must cease when:

(a)   the officer in charge of the investigation is satisfied all the questions they consider relevant to obtaining accurate and reliable information about the offence have been put to the suspect, this includes allowing the suspect an opportunity to give an innocent explanation and asking questions to test if the explanation is accurate and reliable, e.g. to clear up ambiguities or clarify what the suspect said;

(b) the officer in charge of the investigation has taken account of any other available evidence; and

(c) the officer in charge of the investigation, or in the case of a detained suspect, the custody officer, see paragraph 16.1, reasonably believes there is sufficient evidence to provide a realistic prospect of conviction for that offence. See Note 11B

This paragraph does not prevent officers in revenue cases or acting under the confiscation provisions of the Criminal Justice Act 1988 or the Drug Trafficking Act 1994 from inviting suspects to complete a formal question and answer record after the interview is concluded.

(b) *Interview records*

11.7 (a) An accurate record must be made of each interview, whether or not the interview takes place at a police station

(b) The record must state the place of interview, the time it begins and ends, any interview breaks and, subject to paragraph 2.6A, the names of all those present; and must be made on the forms provided for this purpose or in the interviewer's pocket book or in accordance with the Codes of Practice E or F;

(c) Any written record must be made and completed during the interview, unless this would not be practicable or would interfere with the conduct of the interview, and must constitute either a verbatim record of what has been said or, failing this, an account of the interview which adequately and accurately summarises it.

11.8 If a written record is not made during the interview it must be made as soon as practicable after its completion.

11.9 Written interview records must be timed and signed by the maker.

11.10 If a written record is not completed during the interview the reason must be recorded in the interview record.

11.11 Unless it is impracticable, the person interviewed shall be given the opportunity to read the interview record and to sign it as correct or to indicate how they consider it inaccurate. If the person interviewed cannot read or refuses to read the record or sign it, the senior interviewer present shall read it to them and ask whether they would like to sign it as correct or make their mark or to indicate how they consider it inaccurate. The interviewer shall certify on the interview record itself what has occurred. See Note 11E

11.12 If the appropriate adult or the person's solicitor is present during the interview, they should also be given an opportunity to read and sign the interview record or any written statement taken down during the interview.

11.13 A written record shall be made of any comments made by a suspect, including unsolicited comments, which are outside the context of an interview but which might be relevant to the offence. Any such record must be timed and signed by the maker. When practicable the suspect shall be given the opportunity to read that record and to sign it as correct or to indicate how they consider it inaccurate. See Note 11E

11.14 Any refusal by a person to sign an interview record when asked in accordance with this Code must itself be recorded.

(c) *Juveniles and mentally disordered or otherwise mentally vulnerable people*

11.15 A juvenile or person who is mentally disordered or otherwise mentally vulnerable must not be interviewed regarding their involvement or suspected involvement in a criminal offence or offences, or asked to provide or sign a written statement under caution or record of interview, in the absence of the appropriate adult unless paragraphs 11.1, 11.18 to 11.20 apply. See Note 11C

11.16 Juveniles may only be interviewed at their place of education in exceptional circumstances and only when the principal or their nominee agrees. Every effort should be made to notify the parent(s) or other person responsible for the juvenile's welfare and the appropriate adult, if this is a different person, that the police want to interview the juvenile and reasonable time should be allowed to enable the appropriate adult to be present at the interview. If awaiting the appropriate adult would cause unreasonable delay, and unless the juvenile is suspected of an offence against the educational establishment, the principal or their nominee can act as the appropriate adult for the purposes of the interview.

11.17 If an appropriate adult is present at an interview, they shall be informed:
- they are not expected to act simply as an observer; and
- the purpose of their presence is to:
  — advise the person being interviewed;
  — observe whether the interview is being conducted properly and fairly;
  — facilitate communication with the person being interviewed.

(d)   Vulnerable suspects — urgent interviews at police stations

11.18 The following persons may not be interviewed unless an officer of superintendent rank or above considers delay will lead to the consequences in paragraph 11.1(a) to (c), and is satisfied the interview would not significantly harm the person's physical or mental state (see Annex G):

(a)   a juvenile or person who is mentally disordered or otherwise mentally vulnerable if at the time of the interview the appropriate adult is not present;

(b)   anyone other than in (a) who at the time of the interview appears unable to:
- appreciate the significance of questions and their answers; or
- understand what is happening because of the effects of drink, drugs or any illness, ailment or condition;

(c)   a person who has difficulty understanding English or has a hearing disability, if at the time of the interview an interpreter is not present.

11.19 These interviews may not continue once sufficient information has been obtained to avert the consequences in paragraph 11.1(a) to (c).

11.20 A record shall be made of the grounds for any decision to interview a person under paragraph 11.18.

Notes for guidance

11A   Paragraph 11.4 does not prevent the interviewer from putting significant statements and silences to a suspect again at a later stage or a further interview.

11B   The Criminal Procedure and Investigations Act 1996 Code of Practice, paragraph 3.4 states 'In conducting an investigation, the investigator should pursue all reasonable lines of enquiry, whether these point towards or away from the suspect. What is reasonable will depend on the particular circumstances.' Interviewers should keep this in mind when deciding what questions to ask in an interview.

11C   Although juveniles or people who are mentally disordered or otherwise mentally vulnerable are often capable of providing reliable evidence, they may, without knowing or wishing to do so, be particularly prone in certain circumstances to provide information that may be unreliable, misleading or self-incriminating. Special care should always be taken when questioning such a person, and the appropriate adult should be involved if there is any doubt about a person's age, mental state or capacity. Because of the risk of unreliable evidence it is also important to obtain corroboration of any facts admitted whenever possible.

11D   Juveniles should not be arrested at their place of education unless this is unavoidable. When a juvenile is arrested at their place of education, the principal or their nominee must be informed.

11E   Significant statements described in paragraph 11.4 will always be relevant to the offence and must be recorded. When a suspect agrees to read records of interviews and other comments and sign them as correct, they should be asked to endorse the record with, e.g. 'I agree that this is a correct record of what was said' and add their signature. If the suspect does not agree with the record, the interviewer should record the details of any disagreement and ask the suspect to read these details and sign them to the effect that they accurately reflect their disagreement. Any refusal to sign should be recorded.

12   Interviews in police stations

(a)   Action

12.1   If a police officer wants to interview or conduct enquiries which require the presence of a detainee, the custody officer is responsible for deciding whether to deliver the detainee into the officer's custody.

12.2   Except as below, in any period of 24 hours a detainee must be allowed a continuous period of at least 8 hours for rest, free from questioning, travel or any interruption in connection with the investigation concerned. This period should normally be at night or other appropriate time which takes account of when the detainee last slept or rested. If a detainee is arrested at a police station after going there voluntarily, the period of 24 hours runs from the time of their arrest and not the time of arrival at the police station. The period may not be interrupted or delayed, except:

(a)   when there are reasonable grounds for believing not delaying or interrupting the period would:

(i)   involve a risk of harm to people or serious loss of, or damage to, property;

(ii)   delay unnecessarily the person's release from custody;

(iii)   otherwise prejudice the outcome of the investigation;

(b)   at the request of the detainee, their appropriate adult or legal representative;

(c)   when a delay or interruption is necessary in order to:

(i)   comply with the legal obligations and duties arising under section 15;

(ii)   to take action required under section 9 or in accordance with medical advice.

If the period is interrupted in accordance with (a), a fresh period must be allowed. Interruptions under (b) and (c), do not require a fresh period to be allowed.

12.3   Before a detainee is interviewed the custody officer, in consultation with the officer in charge of the investigation and appropriate health care professionals as necessary, shall assess whether the detainee is fit enough to be interviewed. This means determining and considering the risks to the detainee's physical and mental state if the interview took place and determining what safeguards are needed to allow the interview to take place. See Annex G. The custody officer shall not allow a detainee to be interviewed if the custody officer considers it would cause significant harm to the detainee's physical or mental state. Vulnerable suspects listed at paragraph 11.18 shall be treated as always being at some risk during an interview and these persons may not be interviewed except in accordance with paragraphs 11.18 to 11.20.

12.4   As far as practicable interviews shall take place in interview rooms which are adequately heated, lit and ventilated.

12.5   A suspect whose detention without charge has been authorised under PACE, because the detention is necessary for an interview to obtain evidence of the offence for which they have been arrested, may choose not to answer questions but police do not require the suspect's consent or agreement to interview them for this purpose. If a suspect takes steps to prevent themselves being questioned or further questioned, e.g. by refusing to leave their cell to go to a suitable interview room or by trying to leave the interview room, they shall be advised their consent or agreement to interview is not required. The suspect shall be cautioned as in section 10, and informed if they fail or refuse to co-operate, the interview may take place in the cell and that their failure or refusal to co-operate may be given in evidence. The suspect shall then be invited to co-operate and go into the interview room.

12.6   People being questioned or making statements shall not be required to stand.

12.7   Before the interview commences each interviewer shall, subject to paragraph 2.6A, identify themselves and any other persons present to the interviewee.

12.8   Breaks from interviewing should be made at recognised meal times or at other times that take account of when an interviewee last had a meal. Short refreshment breaks shall be provided at approximately two hour intervals, subject to the interviewer's discretion to delay a break if there are reasonable grounds for believing it would:

(i)   involve a:

- risk of harm to people;
- serious loss of, or damage to, property;

(ii)   unnecessarily delay the detainee's release;

(iii)   otherwise prejudice the outcome of the investigation.

See Note 12B

12.9   If during the interview a complaint is made by or on behalf of the interviewee concerning the provisions of this Code, the interviewer should:

(i)   record it in the interview record;

(ii)   inform the custody officer, who is then responsible for dealing with it as in section 9.

(b)   Documentation

12.10 A record must be made of the:

- time a detainee is not in the custody of the custody officer, and why
- reason for any refusal to deliver the detainee out of that custody

12.11 A record shall be made of:

(a)   the reasons it was not practicable to use an interview room; and

(b)   any action taken as in paragraph 12.5.

The record shall be made on the custody record or in the interview record for action taken whilst an interview record is being kept, with a brief reference to this effect in the custody record.

12.12 Any decision to delay a break in an interview must be recorded, with reasons, in the interview record.

12.13 All written statements made at police stations under caution shall be written on forms provided for the purpose.

12.14 All written statements made under caution shall be taken in accordance with Annex D. Before a person makes a written statement under caution at a police station they shall be reminded about the right to legal advice. See Note 12A

Notes for guidance

12A   It is not normally necessary to ask for a written statement if the interview was recorded in writing and the record signed in accordance with paragraph 11.11 or audibly or visually recorded in accordance with Code E or F. Statements under caution should normally be taken in these circumstances only at the person's express wish. A person may however be asked if they want to make such a statement.

12B   Meal breaks should normally last at least 45 minutes and shorter breaks after two hours should last at least 15 minutes. If the interviewer delays a break in accordance with paragraph 12.8 and prolongs the interview, a longer break should be provided. If there is a short interview, and another short interview is contemplated, the length of the break may be reduced if there are reasonable grounds to believe this is necessary to avoid any of the consequences in paragraph 12.8(i) to (iii).

13   Interpreters

(a)   General

13.1   Chief officers are responsible for making sure appropriate arrangements are in place for provision of suitably qualified interpreters for people who:

- are deaf;
- do not understand English.

Whenever possible, interpreters should be drawn from the National Register of Public Service Interpreters (NRPSI) or the Council for the Advancement of Communication with Deaf People (CADCP) Directory of British Sign Language/English Interpreters.

(b)   Foreign languages

13.2   Unless paragraphs 11.1, 11.18 to 11.20 apply, a person must not be interviewed in the absence of a person capable of interpreting if:

(a)   they have difficulty understanding English;

(b)   the interviewer cannot speak the person's own language;

(c)   the person wants an interpreter present.

13.3   The interviewer shall make sure the interpreter makes a note of the interview at the time in the person's language for use in the event of the interpreter being called to give evidence, and certifies its accuracy. The interviewer should allow sufficient time for the interpreter to note each question and answer after each is put, given and interpreted. The person should be allowed to read the record or have it read to them and sign it as correct or indicate the respects in which they consider it inaccurate. If the interview is audibly recorded or visually recorded, the arrangements in Code E or F apply.

13.4   In the case of a person making a statement to a police officer or other police staff other than in English:

(a)   the interpreter shall record the statement in the language it is made;

(b)   the person shall be invited to sign it;

(c)   an official English translation shall be made in due course.

(c)   Deaf people and people with speech difficulties

13.5   If a person appears to be deaf or there is doubt about their hearing or speaking ability, they must not be interviewed in the absence of an interpreter unless they agree in writing to being interviewed without one or paragraphs 11.1, 11.18 to 11.20 apply.

13.6   An interpreter should also be called if a juvenile is interviewed and the parent or guardian present as the appropriate adult appears to be deaf or there is doubt about their hearing or speaking ability, unless they agree in writing to the interview proceeding without one or paragraphs 11.1, 11.18 to 11.20 apply.

13.7   The interviewer shall make sure the interpreter is allowed to read the interview record and certify its accuracy in the event of the interpreter being called to give evidence. If the interview is audibly recorded or visually recorded, the arrangements in Code E or F apply.

(d)   Additional rules for detained persons

13.8   All reasonable attempts should be made to make the detainee understand that interpreters will be provided at public expense.

13.9   If paragraph 6.1 applies and the detainee cannot communicate with the solicitor because of language, hearing or speech difficulties, an interpreter must be called. The interpreter may not be a police officer or any other police staff when interpretation is needed for the purposes of obtaining legal advice. In all other cases a police officer or other police staff may only interpret if the detainee and the appropriate adult, if applicable, give their agreement in writing or if the interview is audibly recorded or visually recorded as in Code E or F.

13.10   When the custody officer cannot establish effective communication with a person charged with an offence who appears deaf or there is doubt about their ability to hear, speak or to understand English, arrangements must be made as soon as practicable for an interpreter to explain the offence and any other information given by the custody officer.

(e)   Documentation

13.11   Action taken to call an interpreter under this section and any agreement to be interviewed in the absence of an interpreter must be recorded.

14   Questioning — special restrictions

14.1   If a person is arrested by one police force on behalf of another and the lawful period of detention in respect of that offence has not yet commenced in accordance with PACE, section 41 no questions may be put to them about the offence while they are in transit between the forces except to clarify any voluntary statement they make.

14.2   If a person is in police detention at a hospital they may not be questioned without the agreement of a responsible doctor. See Note 14A

Note for guidance

14A   If questioning takes place at a hospital under paragraph 14.2, or on the way to or from a hospital, the period of questioning concerned counts towards the total period of detention permitted.

15   Reviews and extensions of detention

(a)   Persons detained under PACE

15.1   The review officer is responsible under PACE, section 40 for periodically determining if a person's detention, before or after charge, continues to be necessary. This requirement continues throughout the detention period and except as in paragraph 15.10, the review officer must be present at the police station holding the detainee. See Notes 15A and 15B

15.2   Under PACE, section 42, an officer of superintendent rank or above who is responsible for the station holding the detainee may give authority any time after the second review to extend the maximum period the person may be detained without charge by up to 12 hours. Further detention without charge may be authorised only by a magistrates' court in accordance with PACE, sections 43 and 44. See Notes 15C, 15D and 15E

15.2A Section 42(1) of PACE as amended extends the maximum period of detention for indictable offences from 24 hours to 36 hours. Detaining a juvenile or mentally vulnerable person for longer than 24 hours will be dependent on the circumstances of the case and with regard to the person's:

   (a)   special vulnerability;

   (b)   the legal obligation to provide an opportunity for representations to be made prior to a decision about extending detention;

   (c)   the need to consult and consider the views of any appropriate adult; and

   (d)   any alternatives to police custody.

15.3   Before deciding whether to authorise continued detention the officer responsible under paragraphs 15.1 or 15.2 shall give an opportunity to make representations about the detention to:

   (a)   the detainee, unless in the case of a review as in paragraph 15.1, the detainee is asleep;

   (b)   the detainee's solicitor if available at the time; and

   (c)   the appropriate adult if available at the time.

15.3A Other people having an interest in the detainee's welfare may also make representations at the authorising officer's discretion.

15.3B Subject to paragraph 15.10, the representations may be made orally in person or by telephone or in writing. The authorising officer may, however, refuse to hear oral representations from the detainee if the officer considers them unfit to make representations because of their condition or behaviour. See Note 15C

15.3C The decision on whether the review takes place in person or by telephone or by video conferencing (see Note 15G) is a matter for the review officer. In determining the form the review may take, the review officer must always take full account of the needs of the person in custody. The benefits of carrying out a review in person should always be considered, based on the individual circumstances of each case with specific additional consideration if the person is:

   (a)   a juvenile (and the age of the juvenile); or

   (b)   mentally vulnerable; or

   (c)   has been subject to medical attention for other than routine minor ailments; or

   (d)   there are presentational or community issues around the person's detention.

15.4   Before conducting a review or determining whether to extend the maximum period of detention without charge, the officer responsible must make sure the detainee is reminded of their entitlement to free legal advice, see paragraph 6.5, unless in the case of a review the person is asleep.

15.5   If, after considering any representations, the officer decides to keep the detainee in detention or extend the maximum period they may be detained without charge, any comment made by the detainee shall be recorded. If applicable, the officer responsible under paragraph 15.1 or 15.2 shall be informed of the comment as soon as practicable. See also paragraphs 11.4 and 11.13

15.6   No officer shall put specific questions to the detainee:
- regarding their involvement in any offence; or
- in respect of any comments they may make:
    — when given the opportunity to make representations; or
    — in response to a decision to keep them in detention or extend the maximum period of detention.

Such an exchange could constitute an interview as in paragraph 11.1A and would be subject to the associated safeguards in section 11 and, in respect of a person who has been charged, paragraph 16.5. See also paragraph 11.13

15.7   A detainee who is asleep at a review, see paragraph 15.1, and whose continued detention is authorised must be informed about the decision and reason as soon as practicable after waking.

(b)   Persons detained under the Terrorism Act 2000

15.8   In terrorism cases:
    (a)   the powers and duties of the review officer are in the Terrorism Act 2000, Schedule 8, Part II;
    (b)   a police officer of at least superintendent rank may apply to a judicial authority for a warrant of further detention under the Terrorism Act 2000, Schedule 8, Part III.
    (c)   Telephone review of detention

15.9   PACE, section 40A provides that the officer responsible under section 40 for reviewing the detention of a person who has not been charged, need not attend the police station holding the detainee and may carry out the review by telephone.

15.9A PACE, section 45A(2) provides that the officer responsible under section 40 for reviewing the detention of a person who has not been charged, need not attend the police station holding the detainee and may carry out the review by video conferencing facilities (See Note 15G).

15.9B A telephone review is not permitted where facilities for review by video conferencing exist and it is practicable to use them.

15.9C The review officer can decide at any stage that a telephone review or review by video conferencing should be terminated and that the review will be conducted in person. The reasons for doing so should be noted in the custody record.
See Note 15F

15.10 When a telephone review is carried out, an officer at the station holding the detainee shall be required by the review officer to fulfil that officer's obligations under PACE section 40 or this Code by:
    (a)   making any record connected with the review in the detainee's custody record;
    (b)   if applicable, making a record in (a) in the presence of the detainee; and
    (c)   giving the detainee information about the review.

15.11 When a telephone review is carried out, the requirement in paragraph 15.3 will be satisfied:
    (a)   if facilities exist for the immediate transmission of written representations to the review officer, e.g. fax or email message, by giving the detainee an opportunity to make representations:
        (i)   orally by telephone; or
        (ii)   in writing using those facilities; and
    (b)   in all other cases, by giving the detainee an opportunity to make their representations orally by telephone.

(d)   Documentation

15.12 It is the officer's responsibility to make sure all reminders given under paragraph 15.4 are noted in the custody record.

15.13 The grounds for, and extent of, any delay in conducting a review shall be recorded.

15.14 When a telephone review is carried out, a record shall be made of:

    (a)   the reason the review officer did not attend the station holding the detainee;

    (b)   the place the review officer was;

    (c)   the method representations, oral or written, were made to the review officer, see paragraph 15.11.

15.15 Any written representations shall be retained.

15.16 A record shall be made as soon as practicable about the outcome of each review or determination whether to extend the maximum detention period without charge or an application for a warrant of further detention or its extension. If paragraph 15.7 applies, a record shall also be made of when the person was informed and by whom. If an authorisation is given under PACE, section 42, the record shall state the number of hours and minutes by which the detention period is extended or further extended. If a warrant for further detention, or extension, is granted under section 43 or 44, the record shall state the detention period authorised by the warrant and the date and time it was granted.

Notes for guidance

15A   Review officer for the purposes of:

- PACE, sections 40 and 40A means, in the case of a person arrested but not charged, an officer of at least inspector rank not directly involved in the investigation and, if a person has been arrested and charged, the custody officer;

- the Terrorism Act 2000, means an officer not directly involved in the investigation connected with the detention and of at least inspector rank, for reviews within 24 hours of the detainee's arrest or superintendent for all other reviews.

15B   The detention of persons in police custody not subject to the statutory review requirement in paragraph 15.1 should still be reviewed periodically as a matter of good practice. Such reviews can be carried out by an officer of the rank of sergeant or above. The purpose of such reviews is to check the particular power under which a detainee is held continues to apply, any associated conditions are complied with and to make sure appropriate action is taken to deal with any changes. This includes the detainee's prompt release when the power no longer applies, or their transfer if the power requires the detainee be taken elsewhere as soon as the necessary arrangements are made. Examples include persons:

    (a)   arrested on warrant because they failed to answer bail to appear at court;

    (b)   arrested under the Bail Act 1976, section 7(3) for breaching a condition of bail granted after charge;

    (c)   in police custody for specific purposes and periods under the Crime (Sentences) Act 1997, Schedule 1;

    (d)   convicted, or remand prisoners, held in police stations on behalf of the Prison Service under the Imprisonment (Temporary Provisions) Act 1980, section 6;

    (e)   being detained to prevent them causing a breach of the peace;

    (f)   detained at police stations on behalf of the Immigration Service.

    (g)   detained by order of a magistrates' court under the Criminal Justice Act 1988, section 152 (as amended by the Drugs Act 2005, section 8) to facilitate the recovery of evidence after being charged with drug possession or drug trafficking and suspected of having swallowed drugs.

The detention of persons remanded into police detention by order of a court under the Magistrates' Courts Act 1980, section 128 is subject to a statutory requirement to review that detention. This is to make sure the detainee is taken back to court no later than the end of the period authorised by the court or when the need for their detention by police ceases, whichever is the sooner.

The detention of persons remanded into police detention by order of a court under the Magistrates' Courts Act 1980, section 128 is subject to a statutory requirement to review that detention. This is to make sure the detainee is taken back to court no later than the end of the period authorised by the court or when the need for their detention by police ceases, whichever is the sooner.

15C   In the case of a review of detention, but not an extension, the detainee need not be woken for the review. However, if the detainee is likely to be asleep, e.g. during a period of rest allowed as in paragraph 12.2, at the latest time a review or authorisation to extend detention may take place, the officer should, if the legal obligations and time constraints permit, bring forward the procedure to allow the detainee to make representations. A detainee not asleep during the review must be present when the grounds for their continued detention are recorded and must at the same time be informed of those grounds unless the review officer considers the person is incapable of understanding what is said, violent or likely to become violent or in urgent need of medical attention.

15D   An application to a Magistrates' Court under PACE, sections 43 or 44 for a warrant of further detention or its extension should be made between 10am and 9pm, and if possible during normal court hours. It will not usually be practicable to arrange for a court to sit specially outside the hours of 10am to 9pm. If it appears a special sitting may be needed outside normal court hours but between 10am and 9pm, the clerk to the justices should be given notice and informed of this possibility, while the court is sitting if possible.

15E   In paragraph 15.2, the officer responsible for the station holding the detainee includes a superintendent or above who, in accordance with their force operational policy or police regulations, is given that responsibility on a temporary basis whilst the appointed long-term holder is off duty or otherwise unavailable.

15F   The provisions of PACE, section 40A allowing telephone reviews do not apply to reviews of detention after charge by the custody officer or to reviews under the Terrorism Act 2000, Schedule 8, Part II in terrorism cases. When video conferencing is not required, they allow the use of a telephone to carry out a review of detention before charge. The procedure under PACE, section 42 must be done in person.

15G   The use of video conferencing facilities for decisions about detention under section 45A of PACE is subject to the introduction of regulations by the Secretary of State.

16   Charging detained persons

(a)   Action

16.1   When the officer in charge of the investigation reasonably believes there is sufficient evidence to provide a realistic prospect of conviction for the offence (see paragraph 11.6), they shall without delay, and subject to the following qualification, inform the custody officer who will be responsible for considering whether the detainee should be charged. See Notes 11B and 16A. When a person is detained in respect of more than one offence it is permissible to delay informing the custody officer until the above conditions are satisfied in respect of all the offences, but see paragraph 11.6. If the detainee is a juvenile, mentally disordered or otherwise mentally vulnerable, any resulting action shall be taken in the presence of the appropriate adult if they are present at the time. See Notes 16B and 16C.

16.1A   Where guidance issued by the Director of Public Prosecutions under section 37A is in force the custody officer must comply with that Guidance in deciding how to act in dealing with the detainee. See Notes 16AA and 16AB.

16.1B   Where in compliance with the DPP's Guidance the custody officer decides that the case should be immediately referred to the CPS to make the charging decision, consultation should take place with a Crown Prosecutor as soon as is reasonably practicable. Where the Crown Prosecutor is unable to make the charging decision on the information available at that time, the detainee may be released without charge and on bail (with conditions if necessary) under section 37(7)(a). In such circumstances, the detainee should be informed that they are being released to enable the Director of Public Prosecutions to make a decision under section 37B.

16.2   When a detainee is charged with or informed they may be prosecuted for an offence, see Note 16B, they shall, unless the restriction on drawing adverse inferences from silence applies, see Annex C, be cautioned as follows:

> 'You do not have to say anything. But it may harm your defence if you do not mention now something which you later rely on in court. Anything you do say may be given in evidence.'

Annex C, paragraph 2 sets out the alternative terms of the caution to be used when the restriction on drawing adverse inferences from silence applies.

16.3   When a detainee is charged they shall be given a written notice showing particulars of the offence and, subject to paragraph 2.6A, the officer's name and the case reference number. As far as possible the particulars of the charge shall be stated in simple terms, but they shall also show the precise offence in law with which the detainee is charged. The notice shall begin:

> 'You are charged with the offence(s) shown below.' Followed by the caution.

If the detainee is a juvenile, mentally disordered or otherwise mentally vulnerable, the notice should be given to the appropriate adult.

16.4   If, after a detainee has been charged with or informed they may be prosecuted for an offence, an officer wants to tell them about any written statement or interview with another person relating to such an offence, the detainee shall either be handed a true copy of the written statement or the content of the interview record brought to their attention. Nothing shall be done to invite any reply or comment except to:

(a)   caution the detainee, 'You do not have to say anything, but anything you do say may be given in evidence.'; and

(b)   remind the detainee about their right to legal advice.

16.4A If the detainee:

- cannot read, the document may be read to them
- is a juvenile, mentally disordered or otherwise mentally vulnerable, the appropriate adult shall also be given a copy, or the interview record shall be brought to their attention

16.5   A detainee may not be interviewed about an offence after they have been charged with, or informed they may be prosecuted for it, unless the interview is necessary:

- to prevent or minimise harm or loss to some other person, or the public
- to clear up an ambiguity in a previous answer or statement
- in the interests of justice for the detainee to have put to them, and have an opportunity to comment on, information concerning the offence which has come to light since they were charged or informed they might be prosecuted

Before any such interview, the interviewer shall:

(a)   caution the detainee, 'You do not have to say anything, but anything you do say may be given in evidence.';

(b)   remind the detainee about their right to legal advice.

See Note 16B

16.6   The provisions of paragraphs 16.2 to 16.5 must be complied with in the appropriate adult's presence if they are already at the police station. If they are not at the police station then these provisions must be complied with again in their presence when they arrive unless the detainee has been released.

See Note 16C

16.7   When a juvenile is charged with an offence and the custody officer authorises their continued detention after charge, the custody officer must try to make arrangements for the juvenile to be taken into the care of a local authority to be detained pending appearance in court unless the custody officer certifies it is impracticable to do so or, in the case of a juvenile of at least 12 years old, no secure accommodation is available and there is a risk to the public of serious harm from that juvenile, in accordance with PACE, section 38(6). See Note 16D

(b)   Documentation

16.8   A record shall be made of anything a detainee says when charged.

16.9   Any questions put in an interview after charge and answers given relating to the offence shall be recorded in full during the interview on forms for that purpose and the record signed by the detainee or, if they refuse, by the interviewer and any third parties present. If the questions are audibly recorded or visually recorded the arrangements in Code E or F apply.

16.10   If it is not practicable to make arrangements for a juvenile's transfer into local authority care as in paragraph 16.7, the custody officer must record the reasons and complete a certificate to be produced before the court with the juvenile. See Note 16D

Notes for guidance

16A   The custody officer must take into account alternatives to prosecution under the Crime and Disorder Act 1998, reprimands and warning applicable to persons under 18, and in national guidance on the cautioning of offenders, for persons aged 18 and over.

16AA   When a person is arrested under the provisions of the Criminal Justice Act 2003 which allow a person to be re-tried after being acquitted of a serious offence which is a qualifying offence specified in Schedule 5 to that Act and not precluded from further prosecution by virtue of section 75(3) of that Act the detention provisions of PACE are modified and make an officer of the rank of superintendent or above who has not been directly involved in the investigation responsible for determining whether the evidence is sufficient to charge.

16AB   Where Guidance issued by the Director of Public Prosecutions under section 37B is in force, a custody officer who determines in accordance with that Guidance that there is sufficient evidence to charge the detainee, may detain that person for no longer than is reasonably necessary to decide how that person is to be dealt with under PACE, section 37(7)(a) to (d), including, where appropriate, consultation with the Duty Prosecutor. The period is subject to the maximum period of detention before charge determined by PACE, sections 41 to 44. Where in accordance with the Guidance the case is referred to the CPS for decision, the custody officer should ensure that an officer involved in the investigation sends to the CPS such information as is specified in the Guidance.

16B   The giving of a warning or the service of the Notice of Intended Prosecution required by the Road Traffic Offenders Act 1988, section 1 does not amount to informing a detainee they may be prosecuted for an offence and so does not preclude further questioning in relation to that offence.

16C   There is no power under PACE to detain a person and delay action under paragraphs 16.2 to 16.5 solely to await the arrival of the appropriate adult. After charge, bail cannot be refused, or release on bail delayed, simply because an appropriate adult is not available, unless the absence of that adult provides the custody officer with the necessary grounds to authorise detention after charge under PACE, section 38.

16D   Except as in paragraph 16.7, neither a juvenile's behaviour nor the nature of the offence provides grounds for the custody officer to decide it is impracticable to arrange the juvenile's transfer to local authority care. Similarly, the lack of secure local authority accommodation does not make it impracticable to transfer the juvenile. The availability of secure accommodation is only a factor in relation to a juvenile aged 12 or over when the local authority accommodation would not be adequate to protect the public from serious harm from them. The obligation to transfer a juvenile to local authority accommodation applies as much to a juvenile charged during the daytime as to a juvenile to be held overnight, subject to a requirement to bring the juvenile before a court under PACE, section 46.

ANNEX B — DELAY IN NOTIFYING ARREST OR ALLOWING ACCESS TO LEGAL ADVICE

A   *Persons detained under PACE*

1.   The exercise of the rights in Section 5 or Section 6, or both, may be delayed if the person is in police detention, as in PACE, section 118(2), in connection with an indictable offence, has not yet been charged with an offence and an officer of superintendent rank or above, or inspector rank or above only for the rights in Section 5, has reasonable grounds for believing their exercise will:

(i)   lead to:

- interference with, or harm to, evidence connected with an indictable offence; or
- interference with, or physical harm to, other people; or

(ii)   lead to alerting other people suspected of having committed an indictable offence but not yet arrested for it; or

(iii)   hinder the recovery of property obtained in consequence of the commission of such an offence.

2.   These rights may also be delayed if the officer has reasonable grounds to believe that:

(i)   the person detained for an indictable offence has benefited from their criminal conduct (decided in accordance with Part 2 of the Proceeds of Crime Act 2002); and

(ii)   the recovery of the value of the property constituting that benefit will be hindered by the exercise of either right.

3.   Authority to delay a detainee's right to consult privately with a solicitor may be given only if the authorising officer has reasonable grounds to believe the solicitor the detainee wants to consult will, inadvertently or otherwise, pass on a message from the detainee or act in some other way which will have any of the consequences specified under paragraphs 1 or 2. In these circumstances the detainee must be allowed to choose another solicitor. See Note B3

4.   If the detainee wishes to see a solicitor, access to that solicitor may not be delayed on the grounds they might advise the detainee not to answer questions or the solicitor was initially asked to attend the police station by someone else. In the latter case the detainee must be told the solicitor has come to the police station at another person's request, and must be asked to sign the custody record to signify whether they want to see the solicitor.

5.   The fact the grounds for delaying notification of arrest may be satisfied does not automatically mean the grounds for delaying access to legal advice will also be satisfied.

6.   These rights may be delayed only for as long as grounds exist and in no case beyond 36 hours after the relevant time as in PACE, section 41. If the grounds cease to apply within this time, the detainee must, as soon as practicable, be asked if they want to exercise either right, the custody record must be noted accordingly, and action taken in accordance with the relevant section of the Code.

7.   A detained person must be permitted to consult a solicitor for a reasonable time before any court hearing.

B   *Persons detained under the Terrorism Act 2000*

8.   The rights as in sections 5 or 6, may be delayed if the person is detained under the Terrorism Act 2000, section 41 or Schedule 7, has not yet been charged with an offence and an officer of superintendent rank or above has reasonable grounds for believing the exercise of either right will:

(i)   lead to:

- interference with, or harm to, evidence connected with an indictable offence;
- interference with, or physical harm to, other people; or

(ii)   lead to the alerting of other people suspected of having committed an indictable offence but not yet arrested for it; or

      (iii)   hinder the recovery of property:
- obtained in consequence of the commission of such an offence; or
- in respect of which a forfeiture order could be made under that Act, section 23;

      (iv)   lead to interference with the gathering of information about the commission, preparation or instigation of acts of terrorism; or

      (v)   by alerting any person, make it more difficult to prevent an act of terrorism or secure the apprehension, prosecution or conviction of any person in connection with the commission, preparation or instigation of an act of terrorism.

9. These rights may also be delayed if the officer has reasonable grounds for believing that:

      (i)   the person detained has benefited from their criminal conduct (decided in accordance with Part 2 of the Proceeds of Crime Act 2002), and

      (ii)   the recovery of the value of the property constituting that benefit will be hindered by the exercise of either right.

10. In these cases paragraphs 3 (with regards to the consequences specified at paragraphs 8 and 9), 4 and 5 apply.

11. These rights may be delayed only for as long as is necessary but not beyond 48 hours from the time of arrest if arrested under section 41, or if detained under the Terrorism Act 2000, Schedule 7 when arrested under section 41, from the beginning of their examination. If the above grounds cease to apply within this time the detainee must as soon as practicable be asked if they wish to exercise either right, the custody record noted accordingly, and action taken in accordance with the relevant section of this Code.

12. In this case paragraph 7 applies.

C   *Documentation*

13. The grounds for action under this Annex shall be recorded and the detainee informed of them as soon as practicable.

14. Any reply given by a detainee under paragraphs 6 or 11 must be recorded and the detainee asked to endorse the record in relation to whether they want to receive legal advice at this point.

D   *Cautions and special warnings*

When a suspect detained at a police station is interviewed during any period for which access to legal advice has been delayed under this Annex, the court or jury may not draw adverse inferences from their silence.

Notes for guidance

B1   Even if Annex B applies in the case of a juvenile, or a person who is mentally disordered or otherwise mentally vulnerable, action to inform the appropriate adult and the person responsible for a juvenile's welfare if that is a different person, must nevertheless be taken as in paragraph 3.13 and 3.15.

B2   In the case of Commonwealth citizens and foreign nationals, see Note 7A.

B3   A decision to delay access to a specific solicitor is likely to be a rare occurrence and only when it can be shown the suspect is capable of misleading that particular solicitor and there is more than a substantial risk that the suspect will succeed in causing information to be conveyed which will lead to one or more of the specified consequences.

ANNEX C — RESTRICTION ON DRAWING ADVERSE INFERENCES FROM SILENCE AND TERMS OF THE CAUTION WHEN THE RESTRICTION APPLIES

(a)   *The restriction on drawing adverse inferences from silence*

1. The Criminal Justice and Public Order Act 1994, sections 34, 36 and 37 as amended by the Youth Justice and Criminal Evidence Act 1999, section 58 describe the conditions under which adverse inferences may be drawn from a person's failure or refusal to say anything about their involvement in the offence when interviewed, after being

charged or informed they may be prosecuted. These provisions are subject to an overriding restriction on the ability of a court or jury to draw adverse inferences from a person's silence. This restriction applies:

(a)   to any detainee at a police station, see Note 10C who, before being interviewed, see section 11 or being charged or informed they may be prosecuted, see section 16, has:

    (i)   asked for legal advice, see section 6, paragraph 6.1;

    (ii)   not been allowed an opportunity to consult a solicitor, including the duty solicitor, as in this Code; and

    (iii)   not changed their mind about wanting legal advice, see section 6, paragraph 6.6(d)

    Note the condition in (ii) will

    —   apply when a detainee who has asked for legal advice is interviewed before speaking to a solicitor as in section 6, paragraph 6.6(a) or (b).

    —   not apply if the detained person declines to ask for the duty solicitor, see section 6, paragraphs 6.6(c) and (d).

(b)   to any person charged with, or informed they may be prosecuted for, an offence who:

    (i)   has had brought to their notice a written statement made by another person or the content of an interview with another person which relates to that offence, see section 16, paragraph 16.4;

    (ii)   is interviewed about that offence, see section 16, paragraph 16.5; or

    (iii)   makes a written statement about that offence, see Annex D paragraphs 4 and 9.

(b)   *Terms of the caution when the restriction applies*

2.   When a requirement to caution arises at a time when the restriction on drawing adverse inferences from silence applies, the caution shall be:

    'You do not have to say anything, but anything you do say may be given in evidence.'

3.   Whenever the restriction either begins to apply or ceases to apply after a caution has already been given, the person shall be re-cautioned in the appropriate terms. The changed position on drawing inferences and that the previous caution no longer applies shall also be explained to the detainee in ordinary language. See Note C2

Notes for guidance

C1   The restriction on drawing inferences from silence does not apply to a person who has not been detained and who therefore cannot be prevented from seeking legal advice if they want to, see paragraphs 10.2 and 3.15.

C2   The following is suggested as a framework to help explain changes in the position on drawing adverse inferences if the restriction on drawing adverse inferences from silence:

(a)   begins to apply:

    'The caution you were previously given no longer applies. This is because after that caution:

    (i)   you asked to speak to a solicitor but have not yet been allowed an opportunity to speak to a solicitor. See paragraph 1(a); or

    (ii)   you have been charged with/informed you may be prosecuted.' See paragraph 1(b).

    'This means that from now on, adverse inferences cannot be drawn at court and your defence will not be harmed just because you choose to say nothing. Please listen carefully to the caution I am about to give you because it will apply from now on. You will see that it does not say anything about your defence being harmed.'

(b)   ceases to apply before or at the time the person is charged or informed they may be prosecuted, see paragraph 1(a);

'The caution you were previously given no longer applies. This is because after that caution you have been allowed an opportunity to speak to a solicitor. Please listen carefully to the caution I am about to give you because it will apply from now on. It explains how your defence at court may be affected if you choose to say nothing.'

ANNEX D – WRITTEN STATEMENTS UNDER CAUTION

(a)   Written by a person under caution

1.   A person shall always be invited to write down what they want to say.

2.   A person who has not been charged with, or informed they may be prosecuted for, any offence to which the statement they want to write relates, shall:

  (a)   unless the statement is made at a time when the restriction on drawing adverse inferences from silence applies, see Annex C, be asked to write out and sign the following before writing what they want to say:

  'I make this statement of my own free will. I understand that I do not have to say anything but that it may harm my defence if I do not mention when questioned something which I later rely on in court. This statement may be given in evidence.';

  (b)   if the statement is made at a time when the restriction on drawing adverse inferences from silence applies, be asked to write out and sign the following before writing what they want to say;

  'I make this statement of my own free will. I understand that I do not have to say anything. This statement may be given in evidence.'

3.   When a person, on the occasion of being charged with or informed they may be prosecuted for any offence, asks to make a statement which relates to any such offence and wants to write it they shall:

  (a)   unless the restriction on drawing adverse inferences from silence, see Annex C, applied when they were so charged or informed they may be prosecuted, be asked to write out and sign the following before writing what they want to say:

  'I make this statement of my own free will. I understand that I do not have to say anything but that it may harm my defence if I do not mention when questioned something which I later rely on in court. This statement may be given in evidence.';

  (b)   if the restriction on drawing adverse inferences from silence applied when they were so charged or informed they may be prosecuted, be asked to write out and sign the following before writing what they want to say:

  'I make this statement of my own free will. I understand that I do not have to say anything. This statement may be given in evidence.'

4.   When a person, who has already been charged with or informed they may be prosecuted for any offence, asks to make a statement which relates to any such offence and wants to write it they shall be asked to write out and sign the following before writing what they want to say:

  'I make this statement of my own free will. I understand that I do not have to say anything. This statement may be given in evidence.';

5.   Any person writing their own statement shall be allowed to do so without any prompting except a police officer or other police staff may indicate to them which matters are material or question any ambiguity in the statement.

(b)   Written by a police officer or other police staff

6.   If a person says they would like someone to write the statement for them, a police officer, or other police staff shall write the statement.

7.   If the person has not been charged with, or informed they may be prosecuted for, any offence to which the statement they want to make relates they shall, before starting, be asked to sign, or make their mark, to the following:

  (a)   unless the statement is made at a time when the restriction on drawing adverse inferences from silence applies, see Annex C:

'I, ..., wish to make a statement. I want someone to write down what I say. I understand that I do not have to say anything but that it may harm my defence if I do not mention when questioned something which I later rely on in court. This statement may be given in evidence.';

(b)   if the statement is made at a time when the restriction on drawing adverse inferences from silence applies:

'I, ..., wish to make a statement. I want someone to write down what I say. I understand that I do not have to say anything. This statement may be given in evidence.'

8.   If, on the occasion of being charged with or informed they may be prosecuted for any offence, the person asks to make a statement which relates to any such offence they shall before starting be asked to sign, or make their mark to, the following:

(a)   unless the restriction on drawing adverse inferences from silence applied, see Annex C, when they were so charged or informed they may be prosecuted:

'I, ..., wish to make a statement. I want someone to write down what I say. I understand that I do not have to say anything but that it may harm my defence if I do not mention when questioned something which I later rely on in court. This statement may be given in evidence.';

(b)   if the restriction on drawing adverse inferences from silence applied when they were so charged or informed they may be prosecuted:

'I, ..., wish to make a statement. I want someone to write down what I say. I understand that I do not have to say anything. This statement may be given in evidence.'

9.   If, having already been charged with or informed they may be prosecuted for any offence, a person asks to make a statement which relates to any such offence they shall before starting, be asked to sign, or make their mark to:

'I, ..., wish to make a statement. I want someone to write down what I say. I understand that I do not have to say anything. This statement may be given in evidence.'

10.   The person writing the statement must take down the exact words spoken by the person making it and must not edit or paraphrase it. Any questions that are necessary, e.g. to make it more intelligible, and the answers given must be recorded at the same time on the statement form.

11.   When the writing of a statement is finished the person making it shall be asked to read it and to make any corrections, alterations or additions they want. When they have finished reading they shall be asked to write and sign or make their mark on the following certificate at the end of the statement:

'I have read the above statement, and I have been able to correct, alter or add anything I wish. This statement is true. I have made it of my own free will.'

12.   If the person making the statement cannot read, or refuses to read it, or to write the above mentioned certificate at the end of it or to sign it, the person taking the statement shall read it to them and ask them if they would like to correct, alter or add anything and to put their signature or make their mark at the end. The person taking the statement shall certify on the statement itself what has occurred.

ANNEX E — SUMMARY OF PROVISIONS RELATING TO MENTALLY DISORDERED AND OTHERWISE MENTALLY VULNERABLE PEOPLE

1.   If an officer has any suspicion, or is told in good faith, that a person of any age may be mentally disordered or otherwise mentally vulnerable, or mentally incapable of understanding the significance of questions or their replies that person shall be treated as mentally disordered or otherwise mentally vulnerable for the purposes of this Code. See paragraph 1.4

2.   In the case of a person who is mentally disordered or otherwise mentally vulnerable, 'the appropriate adult' means:

(a)   a relative, guardian or other person responsible for their care or custody;

(b)   someone experienced in dealing with mentally disordered or mentally vulnerable people but who is not a police officer or employed by the police;

(c)   failing these, some other responsible adult aged 18 or over who is not a police officer or employed by the police.

See paragraph 1.7(b) and Note 1D

3.   If the custody officer authorises the detention of a person who is mentally vulnerable or appears to be suffering from a mental disorder, the custody officer must as soon as practicable inform the appropriate adult of the grounds for detention and the person's whereabouts, and ask the adult to come to the police station to see them. If the appropriate adult:

- is already at the station when information is given as in paragraphs 3.1 to 3.5 the information must be given in their presence

- is not at the station when the provisions of paragraph 3.1 to 3.5 are complied with these provisions must be complied with again in their presence once they arrive.

See paragraphs 3.15 to 3.17

4.   If the appropriate adult, having been informed of the right to legal advice, considers legal advice should be taken, the provisions of section 6 apply as if the mentally disordered or otherwise mentally vulnerable person had requested access to legal advice. See paragraph 3.19 and Note E1

5.   The custody officer must make sure a person receives appropriate clinical attention as soon as reasonably practicable if the person appears to be suffering from a mental disorder or in urgent cases immediately call the nearest health care professional or an ambulance. It is not intended these provisions delay the transfer of a detainee to a place of safety under the Mental Health Act 1983, section 136 if that is applicable. If an assessment under that Act is to take place at a police station, the custody officer must consider whether an appropriate health care professional should be called to conduct an initial clinical check on the detainee. See paragraph 9.5 and 9.6

6.   It is imperative a mentally disordered or otherwise mentally vulnerable person detained under the Mental Health Act 1983, section 136 be assessed as soon as possible. If that assessment is to take place at the police station, an approved social worker and registered medical practitioner shall be called to the station as soon as possible in order to interview and examine the detainee. Once the detainee has been interviewed, examined and suitable arrangements been made for their treatment or care, they can no longer be detained under section 136. A detainee should be immediately discharged from detention if a registered medical practitioner having examined them, concludes they are not mentally disordered within the meaning of the Act. See paragraph 3.16

7.   If a mentally disordered or otherwise mentally vulnerable person is cautioned in the absence of the appropriate adult, the caution must be repeated in the appropriate adult's presence. See paragraph 10.12

8.   A mentally disordered or otherwise mentally vulnerable person must not be interviewed or asked to provide or sign a written statement in the absence of the appropriate adult unless the provisions of paragraphs 11.1 or 11.18 to 11.20 apply. Questioning in these circumstances may not continue in the absence of the appropriate adult once sufficient information to avert the risk has been obtained. A record shall be made of the grounds for any decision to begin an interview in these circumstances. See paragraphs 11.1, 11.15 and 11.18 to 11.20

9.   If the appropriate adult is present at an interview, they shall be informed they are not expected to act simply as an observer and the purposes of their presence are to:

- advise the interviewee

- facilitate communication with the interviewee

- observe whether or not the interview is being conducted properly and fairly

See paragraph 11.17

10.   If the detention of a mentally disordered or otherwise mentally vulnerable person is reviewed by a review officer or a superintendent, the appropriate adult must, if

available at the time, be given an opportunity to make representations to the officer about the need for continuing detention. See paragraph 15.3

11.   If the custody officer charges a mentally disordered or otherwise mentally vulnerable person with an offence or takes such other action as is appropriate when there is sufficient evidence for a prosecution this must be done in the presence of the appropriate adult. The written notice embodying any charge must be given to the appropriate adult. See paragraphs 16.1 to 16.4A

12.   An intimate or strip search of a mentally disordered or otherwise mentally vulnerable person may take place only in the presence of the appropriate adult of the same sex, unless the detainee specifically requests the presence of a particular adult of the opposite sex. A strip search may take place in the absence of an appropriate adult only in cases of urgency when there is a risk of serious harm to the detainee or others. See Annex A, paragraphs 5 and 11(c)

13.   Particular care must be taken when deciding whether to use any form of approved restraints on a mentally disordered or otherwise mentally vulnerable person in a locked cell. See paragraph 8.2

Notes for guidance

E1   The purpose of the provision at paragraph 3.19 is to protect the rights of a mentally disordered or otherwise mentally vulnerable detained person who does not understand the significance of what is said to them. If the detained person wants to exercise the right to legal advice, the appropriate action should be taken and not delayed until the appropriate adult arrives. A mentally disordered or otherwise mentally vulnerable detained person should always be given an opportunity, when an appropriate adult is called to the police station, to consult privately with a solicitor in the absence of the appropriate adult if they want.

E2   Although people who are mentally disordered or otherwise mentally vulnerable are often capable of providing reliable evidence, they may, without knowing or wanting to do so, be particularly prone in certain circumstances to provide information that may be unreliable, misleading or self-incriminating. Special care should always be taken when questioning such a person, and the appropriate adult should be involved if there is any doubt about a person's mental state or capacity. Because of the risk of unreliable evidence, it is important to obtain corroboration of any facts admitted whenever possible.

E3   Because of the risks referred to in Note E2, which the presence of the appropriate adult is intended to minimise, officers of superintendent rank or above should exercise their discretion to authorise the commencement of an interview in the appropriate adult's absence only in exceptional cases, if it is necessary to avert an immediate risk of serious harm. See paragraphs 11.1, 11.18 to 11.20

ANNEX G – FITNESS TO BE INTERVIEWED

1.   This Annex contains general guidance to help police officers and health care professionals assess whether a detainee might be at risk in an interview.

2.   A detainee may be at risk in an interview if it is considered that:

   (a)   conducting the interview could significantly harm the detainee's physical or mental state;

   (b)   anything the detainee says in the interview about their involvement or suspected involvement in the offence about which they are being interviewed might be considered unreliable in subsequent court proceedings because of their physical or mental state.

3.   In assessing whether the detainee should be interviewed, the following must be considered:

   (a)   how the detainee's physical or mental state might affect their ability to understand the nature and purpose of the interview, to comprehend what is being asked and to appreciate the significance of any answers given and make rational decisions about whether they want to say anything;

(b)   the extent to which the detainee's replies may be affected by their physical or mental condition rather than representing a rational and accurate explanation of their involvement in the offence;

(c)   how the nature of the interview, which could include particularly probing questions, might affect the detainee.

4.   It is essential health care professionals who are consulted consider the functional ability of the detainee rather than simply relying on a medical diagnosis, e.g. it is possible for a person with severe mental illness to be fit for interview.

5.   Health care professionals should advise on the need for an appropriate adult to be present, whether reassessment of the person's fitness for interview may be necessary if the interview lasts beyond a specified time, and whether a further specialist opinion may be required.

6.   When health care professionals identify risks they should be asked to quantify the risks. They should inform the custody officer:
   •   whether the person's condition:
      —   is likely to improve
      —   will require or be amenable to treatment; and
   •   indicate how long it may take for such improvement to take effect

7.   The role of the health care professional is to consider the risks and advise the custody officer of the outcome of that consideration. The health care professional's determination and any advice or recommendations should be made in writing and form part of the custody record.

8.   Once the health care professional has provided that information, it is a matter for the custody officer to decide whether or not to allow the interview to go ahead and if the interview is to proceed, to determine what safeguards are needed. Nothing prevents safeguards being provided in addition to those required under the Code. An example might be to have an appropriate health care professional present during the interview, in addition to an appropriate adult, in order constantly to monitor the person's condition and how it is being affected by the interview.

ANNEX H — DETAINED PERSON: OBSERVATION LIST

1.   If any detainee fails to meet any of the following criteria, an appropriate health care professional or an ambulance must be called.

2.   When assessing the level of rousability, consider:
Rousability – can they be woken?
   •   go into the cell
   •   call their name
   •   shake gently
Response to questions – can they give appropriate answers to questions such as:
   •   What's your name?
   •   Where do you live?
   •   Where do you think you are?
Response to commands – can they respond appropriately to commands such as:
   •   Open your eyes!
   •   Lift one arm, now the other arm!

3.   Remember to take into account the possibility or presence of other illnesses, injury, or mental condition, a person who is drowsy and smells of alcohol may also have the following:
   •   Diabetes
   •   Epilepsy
   •   Head injury
   •   Drug intoxication or overdose
   •   Stroke

Police and Criminal Evidence Act 1984 (PACE) Code D

Code of practice for the identification of persons by police officers

Commencement — Transitional Arrangements

This Code applies to people in police detention after midnight on 31 December 2005, notwithstanding that their period of detention may have commenced before that time.

This code has effect in relation to any identification procedure carried out after midnight on 31 December 2005

1   Introduction

1.1   This Code of Practice concerns the principal methods used by police to identify people in connection with the investigation of offences and the keeping of accurate and reliable criminal records.

1.2   Identification by witnesses arises, e.g., if the offender is seen committing the crime and a witness is given an opportunity to identify the suspect in a video identification, identification parade or similar procedure. The procedures are designed to:

- test the witness' ability to identify the person they saw on a previous occasion
- provide safeguards against mistaken identification.

While this Code concentrates on visual identification procedures, it does not preclude the police making use of aural identification procedures such as a 'voice identification parade', where they judge that appropriate.

1.3   Identification by fingerprints applies when a person's fingerprints are taken to:

- compare with fingerprints found at the scene of a crime
- check and prove convictions
- help to ascertain a person's identity.

1.3A   Identification using footwear impressions applies when a person's footwear impressions are taken to compare with impressions found at the scene of a crime.

1.4   Identification by body samples and impressions includes taking samples such as blood or hair to generate a DNA profile for comparison with material obtained from the scene of a crime, or a victim.

1.5   Taking photographs of arrested people applies to recording and checking identity and locating and tracing persons who:

- are wanted for offences
- fail to answer their bail.

1.6   Another method of identification involves searching and examining detained suspects to find, e.g., marks such as tattoos or scars which may help establish their identity or whether they have been involved in committing an offence.

The provisions of the Police and Criminal Evidence Act 1984 (PACE) and this Code are designed to make sure fingerprints, samples, impressions and photographs are taken, used and retained, and identification procedures carried out, only when justified and necessary for preventing, detecting or investigating crime. If these provisions are not observed, the application of the relevant procedures in particular cases may be open to question.

2   General

2.1   This Code must be readily available at all police stations for consultation by:

- police officers and police staff
- detained persons
- members of the public

2.2   The provisions of this Code:

- include the Annexes
- do not include the Notes for guidance.

2.3   Code C, paragraph 1.4, regarding a person who may be mentally disordered or otherwise mentally vulnerable and the Notes for guidance applicable to those provisions apply to this Code.

2.4   Code C, paragraph 1.5, regarding a person who appears to be under the age of 17 applies to this Code.

2.5   Code C, paragraph 1.6, regarding a person who appears blind, seriously visually impaired, deaf, unable to read or speak or has difficulty orally because of a speech impediment applies to this Code.

2.6   In this Code:

•   'appropriate adult' means the same as in Code C, paragraph 1.7,

•   'solicitor' means the same as in Code C, paragraph 6.12 and the Notes for guidance applicable to those provisions apply to this Code.

2.7   References to custody officers include those performing the functions of custody officer, see paragraph 1.9 of Code C.

2.8   When a record of any action requiring the authority of an officer of a specified rank is made under this Code, subject to paragraph 2.18, the officer's name and rank must be recorded.

2.9   When this Code requires the prior authority or agreement of an officer of at least inspector or superintendent rank, that authority may be given by a sergeant or chief inspector who has been authorised to perform the functions of the higher rank under PACE, section 107.

2.10   Subject to paragraph 2.18, all records must be timed and signed by the maker.

2.11   Records must be made in the custody record, unless otherwise specified. References to 'pocket book' include any official report book issued to police officers or police staff.

2.12   If any procedure in this Code requires a person's consent, the consent of a:

•   mentally disordered or otherwise mentally vulnerable person is only valid if given in the presence of the appropriate adult

•   juvenile, is only valid if their parent's or guardian's consent is also obtained unless the juvenile is under 14, when their parent's or guardian's consent is sufficient in its own right. If the only obstacle to an identification procedure in section 3 is that a juvenile's parent or guardian refuses consent or reasonable efforts to obtain it have failed, the identification officer may apply the provisions of paragraph 3.21. See Note 2A.

2.13   If a person is blind, seriously visually impaired or unable to read, the custody officer or identification officer shall make sure their solicitor, relative, appropriate adult or some other person likely to take an interest in them and not involved in the investigation is available to help check any documentation. When this Code requires written consent or signing, the person assisting may be asked to sign instead, if the detainee prefers. This paragraph does not require an appropriate adult to be called solely to assist in checking and signing documentation for a person who is not a juvenile, or mentally disordered or otherwise mentally vulnerable (see Note 2B and Code C paragraph 3.15).

2.14   If any procedure in this Code requires information to be given to or sought from a suspect, it must be given or sought in the appropriate adult's presence if the suspect is mentally disordered, otherwise mentally vulnerable or a juvenile. If the appropriate adult is not present when the information is first given or sought, the procedure must be repeated in the presence of the appropriate adult when they arrive. If the suspect appears deaf or there is doubt about their hearing or speaking ability or ability to understand English, and effective communication cannot be established, the information must be given or sought through an interpreter.

2.15   Any procedure in this Code involving the participation of a suspect who is mentally disordered, otherwise mentally vulnerable or a juvenile must take place in the presence of the appropriate adult. See Code C paragraph 1.4.

2.15A   Any procedure in this Code involving the participation of a witness who is or appears to be mentally disordered, otherwise mentally vulnerable or a juvenile should take place in the presence of a pre-trial support person. However, the support-person must not be allowed to prompt any identification of a suspect by a witness. See Note 2AB.

2.16 References to:

- 'taking a photograph', include the use of any process to produce a single, still or moving, visual image
- 'photographing a person', should be construed accordingly
- 'photographs', 'films', 'negatives' and 'copies' include relevant visual images recorded, stored, or reproduced through any medium
- 'destruction' includes the deletion of computer data relating to such images or making access to that data impossible.

2.17 Except as described, nothing in this Code affects the powers and procedures:

(i) for requiring and taking samples of breath, blood and urine in relation to driving offences, etc, when under the influence of drink, drugs or excess alcohol under the:

- Road Traffic Act 1988, sections 4 to 11
- Road Traffic Offenders Act 1988, sections 15 and 16
- Transport and Works Act 1992, sections 26 to 38;

(ii) under the Immigration Act 1971, Schedule 2, paragraph 18, for taking photographs and fingerprints from persons detained under that Act, Schedule 2, paragraph 16 (Administrative Controls as to Control on Entry etc.); for taking fingerprints in accordance with the Immigration and Asylum Act 1999; sections 141 and 142(3), or other methods for collecting information about a person's external physical characteristics provided for by regulations made under that Act, section 144;

(iii) under the Terrorism Act 2000, Schedule 8, for taking photographs, fingerprints, skin impressions, body samples or impressions from people:

- arrested under that Act, section 41,
- detained for the purposes of examination under that Act, Schedule 7, and to whom the Code of Practice issued under that Act, Schedule 14, paragraph 6, applies ('the terrorism provisions')

See Note 2C;

(iv) for taking photographs, fingerprints, skin impressions, body samples or impressions from people who have been:

- arrested on warrants issued in Scotland, by officers exercising powers under the Criminal Justice and Public Order Act 1994, section 136(2)
- arrested or detained without warrant by officers from a police force in Scotland exercising their powers of arrest or detention under the Criminal Justice and Public Order Act 1994, section 137(2), (Cross Border powers of arrest etc.).

Note: In these cases, police powers and duties and the person's rights and entitlements whilst at a police station in England and Wales are the same as if the person had been arrested in Scotland by a Scottish police officer.

2.18 Nothing in this Code requires the identity of officers or police staff to be recorded or disclosed:

(a) in the case of enquiries linked to the investigation of terrorism;

(b) if the officers or police staff reasonably believe recording or disclosing their names might put them in danger.

In these cases, they shall use warrant or other identification numbers and the name of their police station. See Note 2D

2.19 In this Code:

(a) 'designated person' means a person other than a police officer, designated under the Police Reform Act 2002, Part 4, who has specified powers and duties of police officers conferred or imposed on them;

(b) any reference to a police officer includes a designated person acting in the exercise or performance of the powers and duties conferred or imposed on them by their designation.

2.20   If a power conferred on a designated person:

    (a)   allows reasonable force to be used when exercised by a police officer, a designated person exercising that power has the same entitlement to use force;

    (b)   includes power to use force to enter any premises, that power is not exercisable by that designated person except:

        (i)   in the company, and under the supervision, of a police officer; or

        (ii)   for the purpose of:

        •   saving life or limb; or

        •   preventing serious damage to property.

2.21   Nothing in this Code prevents the custody officer, or other officer given custody of the detainee, from allowing police staff who are not designated persons to carry out individual procedures or tasks at the police station if the law allows. However, the officer remains responsible for making sure the procedures and tasks are carried out correctly in accordance with the Codes of Practice. Any such person must be:

    (a)   a person employed by a police authority maintaining a police force and under the control and direction of the Chief Officer of that force;

    (b)   employed by a person with whom a police authority has a contract for the provision of services relating to persons arrested or otherwise in custody.

2.22   Designated persons and other police staff must have regard to any relevant provisions of the Codes of Practice.

Notes for guidance

2A   For the purposes of paragraph 2.12, the consent required from a parent or guardian may, for a juvenile in the care of a local authority or voluntary organisation, be given by that authority or organisation. In the case of a juvenile, nothing in paragraph 2.12 requires the parent, guardian or representative of a local authority or voluntary organisation to be present to give their consent, unless they are acting as the appropriate adult under paragraphs 2.14 or 2.15. However, it is important that a parent or guardian not present is fully informed before being asked to consent. They must be given the same information about the procedure and the juvenile's suspected involvement in the offence as the juvenile and appropriate adult. The parent or guardian must also be allowed to speak to the juvenile and the appropriate adult if they wish. Provided the consent is fully informed and is not withdrawn, it may be obtained at any time before the procedure takes place.

2AB   The Youth Justice and Criminal Evidence Act 1999 guidance "Achieving Best Evidence in Criminal Proceedings" indicates that a pre-trial support person should accompany a vulnerable witness during any identification procedure. It states that this support person should not be (or not be likely to be) a witness in the investigation.

2B   People who are seriously visually impaired or unable to read may be unwilling to sign police documents. The alternative, i.e. their representative signing on their behalf, seeks to protect the interests of both police and suspects.

2C   Photographs, fingerprints, samples and impressions may be taken from a person detained under the terrorism provisions to help determine whether they are, or have been, involved in terrorism, as well as when there are reasonable grounds for suspecting their involvement in a particular offence.

2D   The purpose of paragraph 2.18(b) is to protect those involved in serious organised crime investigations or arrests of particularly violent suspects when there is reliable information that those arrested or their associates may threaten or cause harm to the officers. In cases of doubt, an officer of inspector rank or above should be consulted.

3   Identification by witnesses

3.1   A record shall be made of the suspect's description as first given by a potential witness. This record must:

(a)   be made and kept in a form which enables details of that description to be accurately produced from it, in a visible and legible form, which can be given to the suspect or the suspect's solicitor in accordance with this Code; and

(b)   unless otherwise specified, be made before the witness takes part in any identification procedures under paragraphs 3.5 to 3.10, 3.21 or 3.23.

A copy of the record shall where practicable, be given to the suspect or their solicitor before any procedures under paragraphs 3.5 to 3.10, 3.21 or 3.23 are carried out. See Note 3E

(a)   Cases when the suspect's identity is not known

3.2   In cases when the suspect's identity is not known, a witness may be taken to a particular neighbourhood or place to see whether they can identify the person they saw. Although the number, age, sex, race, general description and style of clothing of other people present at the location and the way in which any identification is made cannot be controlled, the principles applicable to the formal procedures under paragraphs 3.5 to 3.10 shall be followed as far as practicable. For example:

(a)   where it is practicable to do so, a record should be made of the witness' description of the suspect, as in paragraph 3.1(a), before asking the witness to make an identification;

(b)   care must be taken not to direct the witness' attention to any individual unless, taking into account all the circumstances, this cannot be avoided. However, this does not prevent a witness being asked to look carefully at the people around at the time or to look towards a group or in a particular direction, if this appears necessary to make sure that the witness does not overlook a possible suspect simply because the witness is looking in the opposite direction and also to enable the witness to make comparisons between any suspect and others who are in the area; See Note 3F

(c)   where there is more than one witness, every effort should be made to keep them separate and witnesses should be taken to see whether they can identify a person independently;

(d)   once there is sufficient information to justify the arrest of a particular individual for suspected involvement in the offence, e.g., after a witness makes a positive identification, the provisions set out from paragraph 3.4 onwards shall apply for any other witnesses in relation to that individual. Subject to paragraphs 3.12 and 3.13, it is not necessary for the witness who makes such a positive identification to take part in a further procedure;

(e)   the officer or police staff accompanying the witness must record, in their pocket book, the action taken as soon as, and in as much detail, as possible. The record should include: the date, time and place of the relevant occasion the witness claims to have previously seen the suspect; where any identification was made; how it was made and the conditions at the time (e.g., the distance the witness was from the suspect, the weather and light); if the witness's attention was drawn to the suspect; the reason for this; and anything said by the witness or the suspect about the identification or the conduct of the procedure.

3.3   A witness must not be shown photographs, computerised or artist's composite likenesses or similar likenesses or pictures (including 'E-fit' images) if the identity of the suspect is known to the police and the suspect is available to take part in a video identification, an identification parade or a group identification. If the suspect's identity is not known, the showing of such images to a witness to obtain identification evidence must be done in accordance with Annex E.

(b)   Cases when the suspect is known and available

3.4   If the suspect's identity is known to the police and they are available, the identification procedures set out in paragraphs 3.5 to 3.10 may be used. References in this section to a suspect being 'known' mean there is sufficient information known to the police to justify the arrest of a particular person for suspected involvement in the offence. A suspect being 'available' means they are immediately available or will be within a reasonably short time and willing to take an effective part in at least one of the following which it is practicable to arrange:

- video identification;
- identification parade; or
- group identification.

Video identification

3.5   Change to: 'A 'video identification' is when the witness is shown moving images of a known suspect, together with similar images of others who resemble the suspect. Moving images must be used unless:

- the suspect is known but not available (see paragraph 3.21 of this Code); or
- in accordance with paragraph 2A of Annex A of this Code, the identification officer does not consider that replication of a physical feature can be achieved or that it is not possible to conceal the location of the feature on the image of the suspect.

The identification officer may then decide to make use of video identification but using still images.

3.6   Video identifications must be carried out in accordance with Annex A.

Identification parade

3.7   An 'identification parade' is when the witness sees the suspect in a line of others who resemble the suspect.

3.8   Identification parades must be carried out in accordance with Annex B.

Group identification

3.9   A 'group identification' is when the witness sees the suspect in an informal group of people.

3.10   Group identifications must be carried out in accordance with Annex C.

Arranging identification procedures

3.11   Except for the provisions in paragraph 3.19, the arrangements for, and conduct of, the identification procedures in paragraphs 3.5 to 3.10 and circumstances in which an identification procedure must be held shall be the responsibility of an officer not below inspector rank who is not involved with the investigation, 'the identification officer'. Unless otherwise specified, the identification officer may allow another officer or police staff, see paragraph 2.21, to make arrangements for, and conduct, any of these identification procedures. In delegating these procedures, the identification officer must be able to supervise effectively and either intervene or be contacted for advice. No officer or any other person involved with the investigation of the case against the suspect, beyond the extent required by these procedures, may take any part in these procedures or act as the identification officer. This does not prevent the identification officer from consulting the officer in charge of the investigation to determine which procedure to use. When an identification procedure is required, in the interest of fairness to suspects and witnesses, it must be held as soon as practicable.

Circumstances in which an identification procedure must be held

3.12   Whenever:

(i)   a witness has identified a suspect or purported to have identified them prior to any identification procedure set out in paragraphs 3.5 to 3.10 having been held; or

(ii)   there is a witness available, who expresses an ability to identify the suspect, or where there is a reasonable chance of the witness being able to do so, and they have not been given an opportunity to identify the suspect in any of the procedures set out in paragraphs 3.5 to 3.10,

and the suspect disputes being the person the witness claims to have seen, an identification procedure shall be held unless it is not practicable or it would serve no useful purpose in proving or disproving whether the suspect was involved in committing the offence. For example, when it is not disputed that the suspect is already well known to the witness who claims to have seen them commit the crime.

3.13 Such a procedure may also be held if the officer in charge of the investigation considers it would be useful.

Selecting an identification procedure

3.14 If, because of paragraph 3.12, an identification procedure is to be held, the suspect shall initially be offered a video identification unless:

(a) a video identification is not practicable; or

(b) an identification parade is both practicable and more suitable than a video identification; or

(c) paragraph 3.16 applies.

The identification officer and the officer in charge of the investigation shall consult each other to determine which option is to be offered. An identification parade may not be practicable because of factors relating to the witnesses, such as their number, state of health, availability and travelling requirements. A video identification would normally be more suitable if it could be arranged and completed sooner than an identification parade.

3.15 A suspect who refuses the identification procedure first offered shall be asked to state their reason for refusing and may get advice from their solicitor and/or if present, their appropriate adult. The suspect, solicitor and/or appropriate adult shall be allowed to make representations about why another procedure should be used. A record should be made of the reasons for refusal and any representations made. After considering any reasons given, and representations made, the identification officer shall, if appropriate, arrange for the suspect to be offered an alternative which the officer considers suitable and practicable. If the officer decides it is not suitable and practicable to offer an alternative identification procedure, the reasons for that decision shall be recorded.

3.16 A group identification may initially be offered if the officer in charge of the investigation considers it is more suitable than a video identification or an identification parade and the identification officer considers it practicable to arrange.

Notice to suspect

3.17 Unless paragraph 3.20 applies, before a video identification, an identification parade or group identification is arranged, the following shall be explained to the suspect:

(i) the purposes of the video identification, identification parade or group identification;

(ii) their entitlement to free legal advice; see Code C, paragraph 6.5;

(iii) the procedures for holding it, including their right to have a solicitor or friend present;

(iv) that they do not have to consent to or co-operate in a video identification, identification parade or group identification;

(v) that if they do not consent to, and co-operate in, a video identification, identification parade or group identification, their refusal may be given in evidence in any subsequent trial and police may proceed covertly without their consent or make other arrangements to test whether a witness can identify them, see paragraph 3.21;

(vi) whether, for the purposes of the video identification procedure, images of them have previously been obtained, see paragraph 3.20, and if so, that they may co-operate in providing further, suitable images to be used instead;

(vii) if appropriate, the special arrangements for juveniles;

(viii) if appropriate, the special arrangements for mentally disordered or otherwise mentally vulnerable people;

(ix) that if they significantly alter their appearance between being offered an identification procedure and any attempt to hold an identification procedure, this may be given in evidence if the case comes to trial, and the identification officer may then consider other forms of identification, see paragraph 3.21 and Note 3C;

(x) that a moving image or photograph may be taken of them when they attend for any identification procedure;

(xi) whether, before their identity became known, the witness was shown photographs, a computerised or artist's composite likeness or similar likeness or image by the police, see Note 3B;

(xii) that if they change their appearance before an identification parade, it may not be practicable to arrange one on the day or subsequently and, because of the appearance change, the identification officer may consider alternative methods of identification, see Note 3C;

(xiii) that they or their solicitor will be provided with details of the description of the suspect as first given by any witnesses who are to attend the video identification, identification parade, group identification or confrontation, see paragraph 3.1.

3.18 This information must also be recorded in a written notice handed to the suspect. The suspect must be given a reasonable opportunity to read the notice, after which, they should be asked to sign a second copy to indicate if they are willing to co-operate with the making of a video or take part in the identification parade or group identification. The signed copy shall be retained by the identification officer.

3.19 The duties of the identification officer under paragraphs 3.17 and 3.18 may be performed by the custody officer or other officer not involved in the investigation if:

(a) it is proposed to release the suspect in order that an identification procedure can be arranged and carried out and an inspector is not available to act as the identification officer, see paragraph 3.11, before the suspect leaves the station; or

(b) it is proposed to keep the suspect in police detention whilst the procedure is arranged and carried out and waiting for an inspector to act as the identification officer, see paragraph 3.11, would cause unreasonable delay to the investigation.

The officer concerned shall inform the identification officer of the action taken and give them the signed copy of the notice. See Note 3C

3.20 If the identification officer and officer in charge of the investigation suspect, on reasonable grounds that if the suspect was given the information and notice as in paragraphs 3.17 and 3.18, they would then take steps to avoid being seen by a witness in any identification procedure, the identification officer may arrange for images of the suspect suitable for use in a video identification procedure to be obtained before giving the information and notice. If suspect's images are obtained in these circumstances, the suspect may, for the purposes of a video identification procedure, co-operate in providing new images which if suitable, would be used instead, see paragraph 3.17(vi).

(c) Cases when the suspect is known but not available

3.21 When a known suspect is not available or has ceased to be available, see paragraph 3.4, the identification officer may make arrangements for a video identification (see Annex A). If necessary, the identification officer may follow the video identification procedures but using still images. Any suitable moving or still images may be used and these may be obtained covertly if necessary. Alternatively, the identification officer may make arrangements for a group identification. See Note 3D. These provisions may also be applied to juveniles where the consent of their parent or guardian is either refused or reasonable efforts to obtain that consent have failed (see paragraph 2.12).

3.22 Any covert activity should be strictly limited to that necessary to test the ability of the witness to identify the suspect.

3.23 The identification officer may arrange for the suspect to be confronted by the witness if none of the options referred to in paragraphs 3.5 to 3.10 or 3.21 are practicable. A 'confrontation' is when the suspect is directly confronted by the witness. A confrontation does not require the suspect's consent. Confrontations must be carried out in accordance with Annex D.

3.24 Requirements for information to be given to, or sought from, a suspect or for the suspect to be given an opportunity to view images before they are shown to a witness, do not apply if the suspect's lack of co-operation prevents the necessary action.

(d)   *Documentation*

3.25   A record shall be made of the video identification, identification parade, group identification or confrontation on forms provided for the purpose.

3.26   If the identification officer considers it is not practicable to hold a video identification or identification parade requested by the suspect, the reasons shall be recorded and explained to the suspect.

3.27   A record shall be made of a person's failure or refusal to co-operate in a video identification, identification parade or group identification and, if applicable, of the grounds for obtaining images in accordance with paragraph 3.20.

(e)   *Showing films and photographs of incidents and information released to the media*

3.28   Nothing in this Code inhibits showing films or photographs to the public through the national or local media, or to police officers for the purposes of recognition and tracing suspects. However, when such material is shown to potential witnesses, including police officers, see Note 3A, to obtain identification evidence, it shall be shown on an individual basis to avoid any possibility of collusion, and, as far as possible, the showing shall follow the principles for video identification if the suspect is known, see Annex A, or identification by photographs if the suspect is not known, see Annex E.

3.29   When a broadcast or publication is made, see paragraph 3.28, a copy of the relevant material released to the media for the purposes of recognising or tracing the suspect, shall be kept. The suspect or their solicitor shall be allowed to view such material before any procedures under paragraphs 3.5 to 3.10, 3.21 or 3.23 are carried out, provided it is practicable and would not unreasonably delay the investigation. Each witness involved in the procedure shall be asked, after they have taken part, whether they have seen any broadcast or published films or photographs relating to the offence or any description of the suspect and their replies shall be recorded. This paragraph does not affect any separate requirement under the Criminal Procedure and Investigations Act 1996 to retain material in connection with criminal investigations.

(f)   *Destruction and retention of photographs taken or used in identification procedures*

3.30   PACE, section 64A, see paragraph 5.12, provides powers to take photographs of suspects and allows these photographs to be used or disclosed only for purposes related to the prevention or detection of crime, the investigation of offences or the conduct of prosecutions by, or on behalf of, police or other law enforcement and prosecuting authorities inside and outside the United Kingdom or the enforcement of a sentence. After being so used or disclosed, they may be retained but can only be used or disclosed for the same purposes.

3.31   Subject to paragraph 3.33, the photographs (and all negatives and copies), of suspects not taken in accordance with the provisions in paragraph 5.12 which are taken for the purposes of, or in connection with, the identification procedures in paragraphs 3.5 to 3.10, 3.21 or 3.23 must be destroyed unless the suspect:

(a)   is charged with, or informed they may be prosecuted for, a recordable offence;

(b)   is prosecuted for a recordable offence;

(c)   is cautioned for a recordable offence or given a warning or reprimand in accordance with the Crime and Disorder Act 1998 for a recordable offence; or

(d)   gives informed consent, in writing, for the photograph or images to be retained for purposes described in paragraph 3.30.

3.32   When paragraph 3.31 requires the destruction of any photograph, the person must be given an opportunity to witness the destruction or to have a certificate confirming the destruction if they request one within five days of being informed that the destruction is required.

3.33   Nothing in paragraph 3.31 affects any separate requirement under the Criminal Procedure and Investigations Act 1996 to retain material in connection with criminal investigations.

Notes for guidance

3A   Except for the provisions of Annex E, paragraph 1, a police officer who is a witness for the purposes of this part of the Code is subject to the same principles and procedures as a civilian witness.

3B   When a witness attending an identification procedure has previously been shown photographs, or been shown or provided with computerised or artist's composite likenesses, or similar likenesses or pictures, it is the officer in charge of the investigation's responsibility to make the identification officer aware of this.

3C   The purpose of paragraph 3.19 is to avoid or reduce delay in arranging identification procedures by enabling the required information and warnings, see sub-paragraphs 3.17(ix) and 3.17(xii), to be given at the earliest opportunity.

3D   Paragraph 3.21 would apply when a known suspect deliberately makes themself 'unavailable' in order to delay or frustrate arrangements for obtaining identification evidence. It also applies when a suspect refuses or fails to take part in a video identification, an identification parade or a group identification, or refuses or fails to take part in the only practicable options from that list. It enables any suitable images of the suspect, moving or still, which are available or can be obtained, to be used in an identification procedure. Examples include images from custody and other CCTV systems and from visually recorded interview records, see Code F Note for Guidance 2D.

3E   When it is proposed to show photographs to a witness in accordance with Annex E, it is the responsibility of the officer in charge of the investigation to confirm to the officer responsible for supervising and directing the showing, that the first description of the suspect given by that witness has been recorded. If this description has not been recorded, the procedure under Annex E must be postponed. See Annex E paragraph 2

3F   The admissibility and value of identification evidence obtained when carrying out the procedure under paragraph 3.2 may be compromised if:

     (a)   before a person is identified, the witness' attention is specifically drawn to that person; or

     (b)   the suspect's identity becomes known before the procedure.

4   Identification by fingerprints and footwear impressions

(A)   Taking fingerprints in connection with a criminal investigation

(a)   General

4.1   References to 'fingerprints' means any record, produced by any method, of the skin pattern and other physical characteristics or features of a person's:

     (i)   fingers; or

     (ii)   palms.

(b)   Action

4.2   A person's fingerprints may be taken in connection with the investigation of an offence only with their consent or if paragraph 4.3 applies. If the person is at a police station consent must be in writing.

4.3   PACE, section 61, provides powers to take fingerprints without consent from any person over the age of ten years:

     (a)   under section 61(3), from a person detained at a police station in consequence of being arrested for a recordable offence, see Note 4A, if they have not had their fingerprints taken in the course of the investigation of the offence unless those previously taken fingerprints are not a complete set or some or all of those fingerprints are not of sufficient quality to allow satisfactory analysis, comparison or matching.

     (b)   under section 61(4), from a person detained at a police station who has been charged with a recordable offence, see Note 4A, or informed they will be reported for such an offence if they have not had their fingerprints taken in the course of the investigation of the offence unless those previously taken fingerprints are not a complete set or some or all of those fingerprints are not of sufficient quality to allow satisfactory analysis, comparison or matching.

(c) under section 61(4A), from a person who has been bailed to appear at a court or police station if the person:

(i) has answered to bail for a person whose fingerprints were taken previously and there are reasonable grounds for believing they are not the same person; or

(ii) who has answered to bail claims to be a different person from a person whose fingerprints were previously taken;

and in either case, the court or an officer of inspector rank or above, authorises the fingerprints to be taken at the court or police station;

(d) under section 61(6), from a person who has been:

(i) convicted of a recordable offence;

(ii) given a caution in respect of a recordable offence which, at the time of the caution, the person admitted; or

(iii) warned or reprimanded under the Crime and Disorder Act 1998, section 65, for a recordable offence.

4.4 PACE, section 27, provides power to:

(a) require the person as in paragraph 4.3(d) to attend a police station to have their fingerprints taken if the:

(i) person has not been in police detention for the offence and has not had their fingerprints taken in the course of the investigation of that offence; or

(ii) fingerprints that were taken from the person in the course of the investigation of that offence, do not constitute a complete set or some, or all, of the fingerprints are not of sufficient quality to allow satisfactory analysis, comparison or matching; and

(b) arrest, without warrant, a person who fails to comply with the requirement.

Note: The requirement must be made within one month of the date the person is convicted, cautioned, warned or reprimanded and the person must be given a period of at least 7 days within which to attend. This 7 day period need not fall during the month allowed for making the requirement.

4.5 A person's fingerprints may be taken, as above, electronically.

4.6 Reasonable force may be used, if necessary, to take a person's fingerprints without their consent under the powers as in paragraphs 4.3 and 4.4.

4.7 Before any fingerprints are taken with, or without, consent as above, the person must be informed:

(a) of the reason their fingerprints are to be taken;

(b) of the grounds on which the relevant authority has been given if the power mentioned in paragraph 4.3 (c) applies;

(c) that their fingerprints may be retained and may be subject of a speculative search against other fingerprints, see Note 4B, unless destruction of the fingerprints is required in accordance with Annex F, Part (a); and

(d) that if their fingerprints are required to be destroyed, they may witness their destruction as provided for in Annex F, Part (a).

(c) Documentation

4.8 A record must be made as soon as possible, of the reason for taking a person's fingerprints without consent. If force is used, a record shall be made of the circumstances and those present.

4.9 A record shall be made when a person has been informed under the terms of paragraph 4.7(c), of the possibility that their fingerprints may be subject of a speculative search.

(B)   Taking fingerprints in connection with immigration enquiries

Action

4.10   A person's fingerprints may be taken for the purposes of Immigration Service enquiries in accordance with powers and procedures other than under PACE and for which the Immigration Service (not the police) are responsible, only with the person's consent in writing or if paragraph 4.11 applies.

4.11   Powers to take fingerprints for these purposes without consent are given to police and immigration officers under the:

(a)   Immigration Act 1971, Schedule 2, paragraph 18(2), when it is reasonably necessary for the purposes of identifying a person detained under the Immigration Act 1971, Schedule 2, paragraph 16 (Detention of person liable to examination or removal);

(b)   Immigration and Asylum Act 1999, section 141(7)(a), from a person who fails to produce, on arrival, a valid passport with a photograph or some other document satisfactorily establishing their identity and nationality if an immigration officer does not consider the person has a reasonable excuse for the failure;

(c)   Immigration and Asylum Act 1999, section 141(7)(b), from a person who has been refused entry to the UK but has been temporarily admitted if

an immigration officer reasonably suspects the person might break a condition imposed on them relating to residence or reporting to a police or immigration officer, and their decision is confirmed by a chief immigration officer;

(d)   Immigration and Asylum Act 1999, section 141(7)(c), when directions are given to remove a person:

•   as an illegal entrant,

•   liable to removal under the Immigration and Asylum Act 1999, section 10,

•   who is the subject of a deportation order from the UK;

(e)   Immigration and Asylum Act 1999, section 141(7)(d), from a person arrested under UK immigration laws under the Immigration Act 1971, Schedule 2, paragraph 17;

(f)   Immigration and Asylum Act 1999, section 141(7)(e), from a person who has made a claim:

•   for asylum

•   under Article 3 of the European Convention on Human Rights; or

(g)   Immigration and Asylum Act 1999, section 141(7)(f), from a person who is a dependant of someone who falls into (b) to (f) above.

4.12   The Immigration and Asylum Act 1999, section 142(3), gives a police and immigration officer power to arrest, without warrant, a person who fails to comply with a requirement imposed by the Secretary of State to attend a specified place for fingerprinting.

4.13   Before any fingerprints are taken, with or without consent, the person must be informed:

(a)   of the reason their fingerprints are to be taken;

(b)   the fingerprints, and all copies of them, will be destroyed in accordance with Annex F, Part B.

4.14   Reasonable force may be used, if necessary, to take a person's fingerprints without their consent under powers as in paragraph 4.11.

4.15   Paragraphs 4.1 and 4.8 apply.

(C)   Taking footwear impressions in connection with a criminal investigation

(a)   Action

4.16   Impressions of a person's footwear may be taken in connection with the investigation of an offence only with their consent or if paragraph 4.17 applies. If the person is at a police station consent must be in writing.

4.17 PACE, section 61A, provides power for a police officer to take footwear impressions without consent from any person over the age of ten years who is detained at a police station:

(a) in consequence of being arrested for a recordable offence, see Note 4A; or if the detainee has been charged with a recordable offence, or informed they will be reported for such an offence; and

(b) the detainee has not had an impression of their footwear taken in the course of the investigation of the offence unless the previously taken impression is not complete or is not of sufficient quality to allow satisfactory analysis, comparison or matching (whether in the case in question or generally).

4.18 Reasonable force may be used, if necessary, to take a footwear impression from a detainee without consent under the power in paragraph 4.17.

4.19 Before any footwear impression is taken with, or without, consent as above, the person must be informed:

(a) of the reason the impression is to be taken;

(b) that the impression may be retained and may be subject of a speculative search against other impressions, see Note 4B, unless destruction of the impression is required in accordance with Annex F, Part (a); and

(c) that if their footwear impressions are required to be destroyed, they may witness their destruction as provided for in Annex F, Part (a).

(b)   Documentation

4.20 A record must be made as soon as possible, of the reason for taking a person's footwear impressions without consent. If force is used, a record shall be made of the circumstances and those present.

4.21 A record shall be made when a person has been informed under the terms of paragraph 4.19(b), of the possibility that their footwear impressions may be subject of a speculative search.

Notes for guidance

4A   References to 'recordable offences' in this Code relate to those offences for which convictions, cautions, reprimands and warnings may be recorded in national police records. See PACE, section 27(4). The recordable offences current at the time when this Code was prepared, are any offences which carry a sentence of imprisonment on conviction (irrespective of the period, or the age of the offender or actual sentence passed) as well as the non-imprisonable offences under the Vagrancy Act 1824 sections 3 and 4 (begging and persistent begging), the Street Offences Act 1959, section 1 (loitering or soliciting for purposes of prostitution), the Road Traffic Act 1988, section 25 (tampering with motor vehicles), the Criminal Justice and Public Order Act 1994, section 167 (touting for hire car services) and others listed in the National Police Records (Recordable Offences) Regulations 2000 as amended.

4B   Fingerprints, footwear impressions or a DNA sample (and the information derived from it) taken from a person arrested on suspicion of being involved in a recordable offence, or charged with such an offence, or informed they will be reported for such an offence, may be subject of a speculative search. This means the fingerprints, footwear impressions or DNA sample may be checked against other fingerprints, footwear impressions and DNA records held by, or on behalf of, the police and other law enforcement authorities in, or outside, the UK, or held in connection with, or as a result of, an investigation of an offence inside or outside the UK. Fingerprints, footwear impressions and samples taken from a person suspected of committing a recordable offence but not arrested, charged or informed they will be reported for it, may be subject to a speculative search only if the person consents in writing. The following is an example of a basic form of words:

"I consent to my fingerprints, footwear impressions and DNA sample and information derived from it being retained and used only for purposes related to the prevention and detection of a crime, the investigation of an offence or the conduct of a prosecution either nationally or internationally.

I understand that my fingerprints, footwear impressions or DNA sample may be checked against other fingerprint, footwear impressions and DNA records held by or on behalf of relevant law enforcement authorities, either nationally or internationally.

I understand that once I have given my consent for my fingerprints, footwear impressions or DNA sample to be retained and used I cannot withdraw this consent."

See Annex F regarding the retention and use of fingerprints and footwear impressions taken with consent for elimination purposes.

5 Examinations to establish identity and the taking of photographs

(A)   Detainees at police stations

(a)   Searching or examination of detainees at police stations

5.1   PACE, section 54A (1), allows a detainee at a police station to be searched or examined or both, to establish:

(a)   whether they have any marks, features or injuries that would tend to identify them as a person involved in the commission of an offence and to photograph any identifying marks, see paragraph 5.5;or

(b)   their identity, see Note 5A.

A person detained at a police station to be searched under a stop and search power, see Code A, is not a detainee for the purposes of these powers.

5.2   A search and/or examination to find marks under section 54A (1) (a) may be carried out without the detainee's consent, see paragraph 2.12, only if authorised by an officer of at least inspector rank when consent has been withheld or it is not practicable to obtain consent, see Note 5D.

5.3   A search or examination to establish a suspect's identity under section 54A (1) (b) may be carried out without the detainee's consent, see paragraph 2.12, only if authorised by an officer of at least inspector rank when the detainee has refused to identify themselves or the authorising officer has reasonable grounds for suspecting the person is not who they claim to be.

5.4   Any marks that assist in establishing the detainee's identity, or their identification as a person involved in the commission of an offence, are identifying marks. Such marks may be photographed with the detainee's consent, see paragraph 2.12; or without their consent if it is withheld or it is not practicable to obtain it, see Note 5D.

5.5   A detainee may only be searched, examined and photographed under section 54A, by a police officer of the same sex.

5.6   Any photographs of identifying marks, taken under section 54A, may be used or disclosed only for purposes related to the prevention or detection of crime, the investigation of offences or the conduct of prosecutions by, or on behalf of, police or other law enforcement and prosecuting authorities inside, and outside, the UK. After being so used or disclosed, the photograph may be retained but must not be used or disclosed except for these purposes, see Note 5B.

5.7   The powers, as in paragraph 5.1, do not affect any separate requirement under the Criminal Procedure and Investigations Act 1996 to retain material in connection with criminal investigations.

5.8   Authority for the search and/or examination for the purposes of paragraphs 5.2 and 5.3 may be given orally or in writing. If given orally, the authorising officer must confirm it in writing as soon as practicable. A separate authority is required for each purpose which applies.

5.9   If it is established a person is unwilling to co-operate sufficiently to enable a search and/or examination to take place or a suitable photograph to be taken, an officer may use reasonable force to:

(a)   search and/or examine a detainee without their consent; and

(b)   photograph any identifying marks without their consent.

5.10   The thoroughness and extent of any search or examination carried out in accordance with the powers in section 54A must be no more than the officer considers necessary to achieve the required purpose. Any search or examination which involves the removal of more than the person's outer clothing shall be conducted in accordance with Code C, Annex A, paragraph 11.

5.11   An intimate search may not be carried out under the powers in section 54A.

(b)   Photographing detainees at police stations and other persons elsewhere than at a police station

5.12   Under PACE, section 64A, an officer may photograph :

(a)   any person whilst they are detained at a police station; and

(b)   any person who is elsewhere than at a police station and who has been:—

(i)   arrested by a constable for an offence;

(ii)   taken into custody by a constable after being arrested for an offence by a person other than a constable;

(iii)   made subject to a requirement to wait with a community support officer under paragraph 2(3) or (3B) of Schedule 4 to the Police Reform Act 2002;

(iv)   given a penalty notice by a constable in uniform under Chapter 1 of Part 1 of the Criminal Justice and Police Act 2001, a penalty notice by a constable under section 444A of the Education Act 1996, or a fixed penalty notice by a constable in uniform under section 54 of the Road Traffic Offenders Act 1988;

(v)   given a notice in relation to a relevant fixed penalty offence (within the meaning of paragraph 1 of Schedule 4 to the Police Reform Act 2002) by a community support officer by virtue of a designation applying that paragraph to him; or

(vi)   given a notice in relation to a relevant fixed penalty offence (within the meaning of paragraph 1 of Schedule 5 to the Police Reform Act 2002) by an accredited person by virtue of accreditation specifying that that paragraph applies to him.

5.12A   Photographs taken under PACE, section 64A:

(a)   may be taken with the person's consent, or without their consent if consent is withheld or it is not practicable to obtain their consent, see Note 5E; and

(b)   may be used or disclosed only for purposes related to the prevention or detection of crime, the investigation of offences or the conduct of prosecutions by, or on behalf of, police or other law enforcement and prosecuting authorities inside and outside the United Kingdom or the enforcement of any sentence or order made by a court when dealing with an offence. After being so used or disclosed, they may be retained but can only be used or disclosed for the same purposes. see Note 5B.

5.13   The officer proposing to take a detainee's photograph may, for this purpose, require the person to remove any item or substance worn on, or over, all, or any part of, their head or face. If they do not comply with such a requirement, the officer may remove the item or substance.

5.14   If it is established the detainee is unwilling to co-operate sufficiently to enable a suitable photograph to be taken and it is not reasonably practicable to take the photograph covertly, an officer may use reasonable force, see Note 5F.

(a)   to take their photograph without their consent; and

(b)   for the purpose of taking the photograph, remove any item or substance worn on, or over, all, or any part of, the person's head or face which they have failed to remove when asked.

5.15   For the purposes of this Code, a photograph may be obtained without the person's consent by making a copy of an image of them taken at any time on a camera system installed anywhere in the police station.

(c)   Information to be given

5.16   When a person is searched, examined or photographed under the provisions as in paragraph 5.1 and 5.12, or their photograph obtained as in paragraph 5.15, they must be informed of the:

(a)   purpose of the search, examination or photograph;

(b)   grounds on which the relevant authority, if applicable, has been given; and

(c)   purposes for which the photograph may be used, disclosed or retained.

This information must be given before the search or examination commences or the photograph is taken, except if the photograph is:

(i)   to be taken covertly;

(ii)   obtained as in paragraph 5.15, in which case the person must be informed as soon as practicable after the photograph is taken or obtained.

(d)   Documentation

5.17 A record must be made when a detainee is searched, examined, or a photograph of the person, or any identifying marks found on them, are taken. The record must include the:

(a)   identity, subject to paragraph 2.18, of the officer carrying out the search, examination or taking the photograph;

(b)   purpose of the search, examination or photograph and the outcome;

(c)   detainee's consent to the search, examination or photograph, or the reason the person was searched, examined or photographed without consent;

(d)   giving of any authority as in paragraphs 5.2 and 5.3, the grounds for giving it and the authorising officer.

5.18 If force is used when searching, examining or taking a photograph in accordance with this section, a record shall be made of the circumstances and those present.

(B)   Persons at police stations not detained

5.19 When there are reasonable grounds for suspecting the involvement of a person in a criminal offence, but that person is at a police station voluntarily and not detained, the provisions of paragraphs 5.1 to 5.18 should apply, subject to the modifications in the following paragraphs.

5.20 References to the 'person being detained' and to the powers mentioned in paragraph 5.1 which apply only to detainees at police stations shall be omitted.

5.21 Force may not be used to:

(a)   search and/or examine the person to:

(i)   discover whether they have any marks that would tend to identify them as a person involved in the commission of an offence; or

(ii)   establish their identity, see Note 5A;

(b)   take photographs of any identifying marks, see paragraph 5.4;or

(c)   take a photograph of the person.

5.22 Subject to paragraph 5.24, the photographs of persons or of their identifying marks which are not taken in accordance with the provisions mentioned in paragraphs 5.1 or 5.12, must be destroyed (together with any negatives and copies) unless the person:

(a)   is charged with, or informed they may be prosecuted for, a recordable offence;

(b)   is prosecuted for a recordable offence;

(c)   is cautioned for a recordable offence or given a warning or reprimand in accordance with the Crime and Disorder Act 1998 for a recordable offence; or

(d)   gives informed consent, in writing, for the photograph or image to be retained as in paragraph 5.6.

5.23 When paragraph 5.22 requires the destruction of any photograph, the person must be given an opportunity to witness the destruction or to have a certificate confirming the destruction provided they so request the certificate within five days of being informed the destruction is required.

5.24 Nothing in paragraph 5.22 affects any separate requirement under the Criminal Procedure and Investigations Act 1996 to retain material in connection with criminal investigations.

Notes for guidance

5A   The conditions under which fingerprints may be taken to assist in establishing a person's identity, are described in Section 4.

5B   Examples of purposes related to the prevention or detection of crime, the investigation of offences or the conduct of prosecutions include:

    (a)   checking the photograph against other photographs held in records or in connection with, or as a result of, an investigation of an offence to establish whether the person is liable to arrest for other offences;

    (b)   when the person is arrested at the same time as other people, or at a time when it is likely that other people will be arrested, using the photograph to help establish who was arrested, at what time and where;

    (c)   when the real identity of the person is not known and cannot be readily ascertained or there are reasonable grounds for doubting a name and other personal details given by the person, are their real name and personal details. In these circumstances, using or disclosing the photograph to help to establish or verify their real identity or determine whether they are liable to arrest for some other offence, e.g. by checking it against other photographs held in records or in connection with, or as a result of, an investigation of an offence;

    (d)   when it appears any identification procedure in section 3 may need to be arranged for which the person's photograph would assist;

    (e)   when the person's release without charge may be required, and if the release is:

        (i)   on bail to appear at a police station, using the photograph to help verify the person's identity when they answer their bail and if the person does not answer their bail, to assist in arresting them; or

        (ii)   without bail, using the photograph to help verify their identity or assist in locating them for the purposes of serving them with a summons to appear at court in criminal proceedings;

    (f)   when the person has answered to bail at a police station and there are reasonable grounds for doubting they are the person who was previously granted bail, using the photograph to help establish or verify their identity;

    (g)   when the person arrested on a warrant claims to be a different person from the person named on the warrant and a photograph would help to confirm or disprove their claim;

    (h)   when the person has been charged with, reported for, or convicted of, a recordable offence and their photograph is not already on record as a result of (a) to (f) or their photograph is on record but their appearance has changed since it was taken and the person has not yet been released or brought before a court.

5C   There is no power to arrest a person convicted of a recordable offence solely to take their photograph. The power to take photographs in this section applies only where the person is in custody as a result of the exercise of another power, e.g. arrest for fingerprinting under PACE, section 27.

5D   Examples of when it would not be practicable to obtain a detainee's consent, see paragraph 2.12, to a search, examination or the taking of a photograph of an identifying mark include:

    (a)   when the person is drunk or otherwise unfit to give consent;

    (b)   when there are reasonable grounds to suspect that if the person became aware a search or examination was to take place or an identifying mark was to be photographed, they would take steps to prevent this happening, e.g. by violently resisting, covering or concealing the mark etc and it would not otherwise be possible to carry out the search or examination or to photograph any identifying mark;

    (c)   in the case of a juvenile, if the parent or guardian cannot be contacted in sufficient time to allow the search or examination to be carried out or the photograph to be taken.

5E   Examples of when it would not be practicable to obtain the person's consent, see paragraph 2.12, to a photograph being taken include:

    (a)   when the person is drunk or otherwise unfit to give consent;

(b)   when there are reasonable grounds to suspect that if the person became aware a photograph, suitable to be used or disclosed for the use and disclosure described in paragraph 5.6, was to be taken, they would take steps to prevent it being taken, e.g. by violently resisting, covering or distorting their face etc, and it would not otherwise be possible to take a suitable photograph;

(c)   when, in order to obtain a suitable photograph, it is necessary to take it covertly; and

(d)   in the case of a juvenile, if the parent or guardian cannot be contacted in sufficient time to allow the photograph to be taken.

5F   The use of reasonable force to take the photograph of a suspect elsewhere than at a police station must be carefully considered. In order to obtain a suspect's consent and co-operation to remove an item of religious headwear to take their photograph, a constable should consider whether in the circumstances of the situation the removal of the headwear and the taking of the photograph should be by an officer of the same sex as the person. It would be appropriate for these actions to be conducted out of public view.

6   Identification by body samples and impressions

(A)   General

6.1   References to:

(a)   an 'intimate sample' mean a dental impression or sample of blood, semen or any other tissue fluid, urine, or pubic hair, or a swab taken from any part of a person's genitals or from a person's body orifice other than the mouth;

(b)   a 'non-intimate sample' means:

(i)   a sample of hair, other than pubic hair, which includes hair plucked with the root, see Note 6A;

(ii)   a sample taken from a nail or from under a nail;

(iii)   a swab taken from any part of a person's body other than a part from which a swab taken would be an intimate sample;

(iv)   saliva;

(v)   a skin impression which means any record, other than a fingerprint, which is a record, in any form and produced by any method, of the skin pattern and other physical characteristics or features of the whole, or any part of, a person's foot or of any other part of their body.

(B)   Action

(a)   Intimate samples

6.2   PACE, section 62, provides that intimate samples may be taken under:

(a)   section 62(1), from a person in police detention only:

(i)   if a police officer of inspector rank or above has reasonable grounds to believe such an impression or sample will tend to confirm or disprove the suspect's involvement in a recordable offence, see Note 4A, and gives authorisation for a sample to be taken; and

(ii)   with the suspect's written consent;

(b)   section 62(1A), from a person not in police detention but from whom two or more non-intimate samples have been taken in the course of an investigation of an offence and the samples, though suitable, have proved insufficient if:

(i)   a police officer of inspector rank or above authorises it to be taken; and

(ii)   the person concerned gives their written consent. See Notes 6B and 6C

6.3   Before a suspect is asked to provide an intimate sample, they must be warned that if they refuse without good cause, their refusal may harm their case if it comes to trial, see Note 6D. If the suspect is in police detention and not legally represented, they must also be reminded of their entitlement to have free legal advice, see Code C, paragraph 6.5, and the reminder noted in the custody record. If paragraph 6.2(b) applies and the person is attending a station voluntarily, their entitlement to free legal advice as in Code C, paragraph 3.21 shall be explained to them.

6.4   Dental impressions may only be taken by a registered dentist. Other intimate samples, except for samples of urine, may only be taken by a registered medical practitioner or registered nurse or registered paramedic.

(b)   Non-intimate samples

6.5   A non-intimate sample may be taken from a detainee only with their written consent or if paragraph 6.6 applies.

6.6   (a)   under section 63, a non-intimate sample may not be taken from a person without consent and the consent must be in writing

   (aa)   A non-intimate sample may be taken from a person without the appropriate consent in the following circumstances:

      (i)   under section 63(2A) where the person is in police detention as a consequence of his arrest for a recordable offence and he has not had a non-intimate sample of the same type and from the same part of the body taken in the course of the investigation of the offence by the police or he has had such a sample taken but it proved insufficient.

      (ii)   Under section 63(3) (a) where he is being held in custody by the police on the authority of a court and an officer of at least the rank of inspector authorises it to be taken.

   (b)   under section 63(3A), from a person charged with a recordable offence or informed they will be reported for such an offence: and

      (i)   that person has not had a non-intimate sample taken from them in the course of the investigation; or

      (ii)   if they have had a sample taken, it proved unsuitable or insufficient for the same form of analysis, see Note 6B;or

   (c)   under section 63(3B), from a person convicted of a recordable offence after the date on which that provision came into effect. PACE, section 63A, describes the circumstances in which a police officer may require a person convicted of a recordable offence to attend a police station for a non-intimate sample to be taken.

6.7   Reasonable force may be used, if necessary, to take a non-intimate sample from a person without their consent under the powers mentioned in paragraph 6.6.

6.8   Before any intimate sample is taken with consent or non-intimate sample is taken with, or without, consent, the person must be informed:

   (a)   of the reason for taking the sample;

   (b)   of the grounds on which the relevant authority has been given;

   (c)   that the sample or information derived from the sample may be retained and subject of a speculative search, see Note 6E, unless their destruction is required as in Annex F, Part A.

6.9   When clothing needs to be removed in circumstances likely to cause embarrassment to the person, no person of the opposite sex who is not a registered medical practitioner or registered health care professional shall be present, (unless in the case of a juvenile, mentally disordered or mentally vulnerable person, that person specifically requests the presence of an appropriate adult of the opposite sex who is readily available) nor shall anyone whose presence is unnecessary. However, in the case of a juvenile, this is subject to the overriding proviso that such a removal of clothing may take place in the absence of the appropriate adult only if the juvenile signifies, in their presence, that they prefer the adult's absence and they agree.

(c)   Documentation

6.10   A record of the reasons for taking a sample or impression and, if applicable, of its destruction must be made as soon as practicable. If force is used, a record shall be made of the circumstances and those present. If written consent is given to the taking of a sample or impression, the fact must be recorded in writing.

6.11   A record must be made of a warning given as required by paragraph 6.3.

6.12   A record shall be made of the fact that a person has been informed as in paragraph 6.8(c) that samples may be subject of a speculative search.

Notes for guidance

6A   When hair samples are taken for the purpose of DNA analysis (rather than for other purposes such as making a visual match), the suspect should be permitted a reasonable choice as to what part of the body the hairs are taken from. When hairs are plucked, they should be plucked individually, unless the suspect prefers otherwise and no more should be plucked than the person taking them reasonably considers necessary for a sufficient sample.

6B   (a)   An insufficient sample is one which is not sufficient either in quantity or quality to provide information for a particular form of analysis, such as DNA analysis. A sample may also be insufficient if enough information cannot be obtained from it by analysis because of loss, destruction, damage or contamination of the sample or as a result of an earlier, unsuccessful attempt at analysis.

        (b)   An unsuitable sample is one which, by its nature, is not suitable for a particular form of analysis.

6C   Nothing in paragraph 6.2 prevents intimate samples being taken for elimination purposes with the consent of the person concerned but the provisions of paragraph 2.12 relating to the role of the appropriate adult, should be applied. Paragraph 6.2(b) does not, however, apply where the non-intimate samples were previously taken under the Terrorism Act 2000, Schedule 8, paragraph 10.

6D   In warning a person who is asked to provide an intimate sample as in paragraph 6.3, the following form of words may be used:

        'You do not have to provide this sample/allow this swab or impression to be taken, but I must warn you that if you refuse without good cause, your refusal may harm your case if it comes to trial.'

6E   Fingerprints or a DNA sample and the information derived from it taken from a person arrested on suspicion of being involved in a recordable offence, or charged with such an offence, or informed they will be reported for such an offence, may be subject of a speculative search. This means they may be checked against other fingerprints and DNA records held by, or on behalf of, the police and other law enforcement authorities in or outside the UK or held in connection with, or as a result of, an investigation of an offence inside or outside the UK. Fingerprints and samples taken from any other person, e.g. a person suspected of committing a recordable offence but who has not been arrested, charged or informed they will be reported for it, may be subject to a speculative search only if the person consents in writing to their fingerprints being subject of such a search. The following is an example of a basic form of words:

        'I consent to my fingerprints/DNA sample and information derived from it being retained and used only for purposes related to the prevention and detection of a crime, the investigation of an offence or the conduct of a prosecution either nationally or internationally.

        I understand that this sample may be checked against other fingerprint/DNA records held by or on behalf of relevant law enforcement authorities, either nationally or internationally.

        I understand that once I have given my consent for the sample to be retained and used I cannot withdraw this consent.'

    See Annex F regarding the retention and use of fingerprints and samples taken with consent for elimination purposes.

6F   Samples of urine and non-intimate samples taken in accordance with sections 63B and 63C of PACE may not be used for identification purposes in accordance with this Code. See Code C note for guidance 17D.

ANNEX A — VIDEO IDENTIFICATION

(a)   *General*

1.   The arrangements for obtaining and ensuring the availability of a suitable set of images to be used in a video identification must be the responsibility of an identification officer, who has no direct involvement with the case.

2.   The set of images must include the suspect and at least eight other people who, so far as possible, resemble the suspect in age, general appearance and position in life. Only one suspect shall appear in any set unless there are two suspects of roughly similar appearance, in which case they may be shown together with at least twelve other people.

2A   If the suspect has an unusual physical feature, e.g., a facial scar, tattoo or distinctive hairstyle or hair colour which does not appear on the images of the other people that are available to be used, steps may be taken to:

(a)   conceal the location of the feature on the images of the suspect and the other people; or

(b)   replicate that feature on the images of the other people.

For these purposes, the feature may be concealed or replicated electronically or by any other method which it is practicable to use to ensure that the images of the suspect and other people resemble each other. The identification officer has discretion to choose whether to conceal or replicate the feature and the method to be used. If an unusual physical feature has been described by the witness, the identification officer should, if practicable, have that feature replicated. If it has not been described, concealment may be more appropriate.

2B   If the identification officer decides that a feature should be concealed or replicated, the reason for the decision and whether the feature was concealed or replicated in the images shown to any witness shall be recorded.

2C   If the witness requests to view an image where an unusual physical feature has been concealed or replicated without the feature being concealed or replicated, the witness may be allowed to do so.

3.   The images used to conduct a video identification shall, as far as possible, show the suspect and other people in the same positions or carrying out the same sequence of movements. They shall also show the suspect and other people under identical conditions unless the identification officer reasonably believes:

(a)   because of the suspect's failure or refusal to co-operate or other reasons, it is not practicable for the conditions to be identical; and

(b)   any difference in the conditions would not direct a witness' attention to any individual image.

4.   The reasons identical conditions are not practicable shall be recorded on forms provided for the purpose.

5.   Provision must be made for each person shown to be identified by number.

6.   If police officers are shown, any numerals or other identifying badges must be concealed. If a prison inmate is shown, either as a suspect or not, then either all, or none of, the people shown should be in prison clothing.

7.   The suspect or their solicitor, friend, or appropriate adult must be given a reasonable opportunity to see the complete set of images before it is shown to any witness. If the suspect has a reasonable objection to the set of images or any of the participants, the suspect shall be asked to state the reasons for the objection. Steps shall, if practicable, be taken to remove the grounds for objection. If this is not practicable, the suspect and/or their representative shall be told why their objections cannot be met and the objection, the reason given for it and why it cannot be met shall be recorded on forms provided for the purpose.

8.   Before the images are shown in accordance with paragraph 7, the suspect or their solicitor shall be provided with details of the first description of the suspect by any witnesses who are to attend the video identification. When a broadcast or publication is made, as in paragraph 3.28, the suspect or their solicitor must also be allowed to view any material released to the media by the police for the purpose of

recognising or tracing the suspect, provided it is practicable and would not unreasonably delay the investigation.

9.   The suspect's solicitor, if practicable, shall be given reasonable notification of the time and place the video identification is to be conducted so a representative may attend on behalf of the suspect. If a solicitor has not been instructed, this information shall be given to the suspect. The suspect may not be present when the images are shown to the witness(es). In the absence of the suspect's representative, the viewing itself shall be recorded on video. No unauthorised people may be present.

(b)   Conducting the video identification

10.   The identification officer is responsible for making the appropriate arrangements to make sure, before they see the set of images, witnesses are not able to communicate with each other about the case, see any of the images which are to be shown, see, or be reminded of, any photograph or description of the suspect or be given any other indication as to the suspect's identity, or overhear a witness who has already seen the material. There must be no discussion with the witness about the composition of the set of images and they must not be told whether a previous witness has made any identification.

11.   Only one witness may see the set of images at a time. Immediately before the images are shown, the witness shall be told that the person they saw on a specified earlier occasion may, or may not, appear in the images they are shown and that if they cannot make a positive identification, they should say so. The witness shall be advised that at any point, they may ask to see a particular part of the set of images or to have a particular image frozen for them to study. Furthermore, it should be pointed out to the witness that there is no limit on how many times they can view the whole set of images or any part of them. However, they should be asked not to make any decision as to whether the person they saw is on the set of images until they have seen the whole set at least twice.

12.   Once the witness has seen the whole set of images at least twice and has indicated that they do not want to view the images, or any part of them, again, the witness shall be asked to say whether the individual they saw in person on a specified earlier occasion has been shown and, if so, to identify them by number of the image. The witness will then be shown that image to confirm the identification, see paragraph 17.

13.   Care must be taken not to direct the witness' attention to any one individual image or give any indication of the suspect's identity. Where a witness has previously made an identification by photographs, or a computerised or artist's composite or similar likeness, the witness must not be reminded of such a photograph or composite likeness once a suspect is available for identification by other means in accordance with this Code. Nor must the witness be reminded of any description of the suspect.

14.   After the procedure, each witness shall be asked whether they have seen any broadcast or published films or photographs, or any descriptions of suspects relating to the offence and their reply shall be recorded.

(c)   Image security and destruction

15.   Arrangements shall be made for all relevant material containing sets of images used for specific identification procedures to be kept securely and their movements accounted for. In particular, no-one involved in the investigation shall be permitted to view the material prior to it being shown to any witness.

16.   As appropriate, paragraph 3.30 or 3.31 applies to the destruction or retention of relevant sets of images.

(d)   Documentation

17.   A record must be made of all those participating in, or seeing, the set of images whose names are known to the police.

18.   A record of the conduct of the video identification must be made on forms provided for the purpose. This shall include anything said by the witness about any identifications or the conduct of the procedure and any reasons it was not practicable

to comply with any of the provisions of this Code governing the conduct of video identifications.

ANNEX B — IDENTIFICATION PARADES

(a)   General

1.   A suspect must be given a reasonable opportunity to have a solicitor or friend present, and the suspect shall be asked to indicate on a second copy of the notice whether or not they wish to do so.

2.   An identification parade may take place either in a normal room or one equipped with a screen permitting witnesses to see members of the identification parade without being seen. The procedures for the composition and conduct of the identification parade are the same in both cases, subject to paragraph 8 (except that an identification parade involving a screen may take place only when the suspect's solicitor, friend or appropriate adult is present or the identification parade is recorded on video).

3.   Before the identification parade takes place, the suspect or their solicitor shall be provided with details of the first description of the suspect by any witnesses who are attending the identification parade. When a broadcast or publication is made as in paragraph 3.28, the suspect or their solicitor should also be allowed to view any material released to the media by the police for the purpose of recognising or tracing the suspect, provided it is practicable to do so and would not unreasonably delay the investigation.

(b)   Identification parades involving prison inmates

4.   If a prison inmate is required for identification, and there are no security problems about the person leaving the establishment, they may be asked to participate in an identification parade or video identification.

5.   An identification parade may be held in a Prison Department establishment but shall be conducted, as far as practicable under normal identification parade rules. Members of the public shall make up the identification parade unless there are serious security, or control, objections to their admission to the establishment. In such cases, or if a group or video identification is arranged within the establishment, other inmates may participate. If an inmate is the suspect, they are not required to wear prison clothing for the identification parade unless the other people taking part are other inmates in similar clothing, or are members of the public who are prepared to wear prison clothing for the occasion.

(c)   Conduct of the identification parade

6.   Immediately before the identification parade, the suspect must be reminded of the procedures governing its conduct and cautioned in the terms of Code C, paragraphs 10.5 or 10.6, as appropriate.

7.   All unauthorised people must be excluded from the place where the identification parade is held.

8.   Once the identification parade has been formed, everything afterwards, in respect of it, shall take place in the presence and hearing of the suspect and any interpreter, solicitor, friend or appropriate adult who is present (unless the identification parade involves a screen, in which case everything said to, or by, any witness at the place where the identification parade is held, must be said in the hearing and presence of the suspect's solicitor, friend or appropriate adult or be recorded on video).

9.   The identification parade shall consist of at least eight people (in addition to the suspect) who, so far as possible, resemble the suspect in age, height, general appearance and position in life. Only one suspect shall be included in an identification parade unless there are two suspects of roughly similar appearance, in which case they may be paraded together with at least twelve other people. In no circumstances shall more than two suspects be included in one identification parade and where there are separate identification parades, they shall be made up of different people.

10. If the suspect has an unusual physical feature, e.g., a facial scar, tattoo or distinctive hairstyle or hair colour which cannot be replicated on other members of the

identification parade, steps may be taken to conceal the location of that feature on the suspect and the other members of the identification parade if the suspect and their solicitor, or appropriate adult, agree. For example, by use of a plaster or a hat, so that all members of the identification parade resemble each other in general appearance.

11. When all members of a similar group are possible suspects, separate identification parades shall be held for each unless there are two suspects of similar appearance when they may appear on the same identification parade with at least twelve other members of the group who are not suspects. When police officers in uniform form an identification parade any numerals or other identifying badges shall be concealed.

12. When the suspect is brought to the place where the identification parade is to be held, they shall be asked if they have any objection to the arrangements for the identification parade or to any of the other participants in it and to state the reasons for the objection. The suspect may obtain advice from their solicitor or friend, if present, before the identification parade proceeds. If the suspect has a reasonable objection to the arrangements or any of the participants, steps shall, if practicable, be taken to remove the grounds for objection. When it is not practicable to do so, the suspect shall be told why their objections cannot be met and the objection, the reason given for it and why it cannot be met, shall be recorded on forms provided for the purpose.

13. The suspect may select their own position in the line, but may not otherwise interfere with the order of the people forming the line. When there is more than one witness, the suspect must be told, after each witness has left the room, that they can, if they wish, change position in the line. Each position in the line must be clearly numbered, whether by means of a number laid on the floor in front of each identification parade member or by other means.

14. Appropriate arrangements must be made to make sure, before witnesses attend the identification parade, they are not able to:
    (i)   communicate with each other about the case or overhear a witness who has already seen the identification parade;
    (ii)   see any member of the identification parade;
    (iii) see, or be reminded of, any photograph or description of the suspect or be given any other indication as to the suspect's identity; or
    (iv)   see the suspect before or after the identification parade.

15. The person conducting a witness to an identification parade must not discuss with them the composition of the identification parade and, in particular, must not disclose whether a previous witness has made any identification.

16. Witnesses shall be brought in one at a time. Immediately before the witness inspects the identification parade, they shall be told the person they saw on a specified earlier occasion may, or may not, be present and if they cannot make a positive identification, they should say so. The witness must also be told they should not make any decision about whether the person they saw is on the identification parade until they have looked at each member at least twice.

17. When the officer or police staff (see paragraph 3.11) conducting the identification procedure is satisfied the witness has properly looked at each member of the identification parade, they shall ask the witness whether the person they saw on a specified earlier occasion is on the identification parade and, if so, to indicate the number of the person concerned, see paragraph 28.

18. If the witness wishes to hear any identification parade member speak, adopt any specified posture or move, they shall first be asked whether they can identify any person(s) on the identification parade on the basis of appearance only. When the request is to hear members of the identification parade speak, the witness shall be reminded that the participants in the identification parade have been chosen on the basis of physical appearance only. Members of the identification parade may then be asked to comply with the witness' request to hear them speak, see them move or adopt any specified posture.

19. If the witness requests that the person they have indicated remove anything used for the purposes of paragraph 10 to conceal the location of an unusual physical feature, that person may be asked to remove it.

20. If the witness makes an identification after the identification parade has ended, the suspect and, if present, their solicitor, interpreter or friend shall be informed. When this occurs, consideration should be given to allowing the witness a second opportunity to identify the suspect.

21   After the procedure, each witness shall be asked whether they have seen any broadcast or published films or photographs or any descriptions of suspects relating to the offence and their reply shall be recorded.

22. When the last witness has left, the suspect shall be asked whether they wish to make any comments on the conduct of the identification parade.

(d)   Documentation

23. A video recording must normally be taken of the identification parade. If that is impracticable, a colour photograph must be taken. A copy of the video recording or photograph shall be supplied, on request, to the suspect or their solicitor within a reasonable time.

24. As appropriate, paragraph 3.30 or 3.31, should apply to any photograph or video taken as in paragraph 23.

25. If any person is asked to leave an identification parade because they are interfering with its conduct, the circumstances shall be recorded.

26. A record must be made of all those present at an identification parade whose names are known to the police.

27. If prison inmates make up an identification parade, the circumstances must be recorded.

28. A record of the conduct of any identification parade must be made on forms provided for the purpose. This shall include anything said by the witness or the suspect about any identifications or the conduct of the procedure, and any reasons it was not practicable to comply with any of this Code's provisions.

ANNEX C — GROUP IDENTIFICATION

(a)   General

1. The purpose of this Annex is to make sure, as far as possible, group identifications follow the principles and procedures for identification parades so the conditions are fair to the suspect in the way they test the witness' ability to make an identification.

2. Group identifications may take place either with the suspect's consent and cooperation or covertly without their consent.

3. The location of the group identification is a matter for the identification officer, although the officer may take into account any representations made by the suspect, appropriate adult, their solicitor or friend.

4. The place where the group identification is held should be one where other people are either passing by or waiting around informally, in groups such that the suspect is able to join and be capable of being seen by the witness at the same time as others in the group. For example people leaving an escalator, pedestrians walking through a shopping centre, passengers on railway and bus stations, waiting in queues or groups or where people are standing or sitting in groups in other public places.

5. If the group identification is to be held covertly, the choice of locations will be limited by the places where the suspect can be found and the number of other people present at that time. In these cases, suitable locations might be along regular routes travelled by the suspect, including buses or trains or public places frequented by the suspect.

6. Although the number, age, sex, race and general description and style of clothing of other people present at the location cannot be controlled by the identification officer, in selecting the location the officer must consider the general appearance and numbers of people likely to be present. In particular, the officer must reasonably expect that over the period the witness observes the group, they will be able to see,

from time to time, a number of others whose appearance is broadly similar to that of the suspect.

7. A group identification need not be held if the identification officer believes, because of the unusual appearance of the suspect, none of the locations it would be practicable to use satisfy the requirements of paragraph 6 necessary to make the identification fair.

8. Immediately after a group identification procedure has taken place (with or without the suspect's consent), a colour photograph or video should be taken of the general scene, if practicable, to give a general impression of the scene and the number of people present. Alternatively, if it is practicable, the group identification may be video recorded.

9. If it is not practicable to take the photograph or video in accordance with paragraph 8, a photograph or film of the scene should be taken later at a time determined by the identification officer if the officer considers it practicable to do so.

10. An identification carried out in accordance with this Code remains a group identification even though, at the time of being seen by the witness, the suspect was on their own rather than in a group.

11. Before the group identification takes place, the suspect or their solicitor shall be provided with details of the first description of the suspect by any witnesses who are to attend the identification. When a broadcast or publication is made, as in paragraph 3.28, the suspect or their solicitor should also be allowed to view any material released by the police to the media for the purposes of recognising or tracing the suspect, provided that it is practicable and would not unreasonably delay the investigation.

12. After the procedure, each witness shall be asked whether they have seen any broadcast or published films or photographs or any descriptions of suspects relating to the offence and their reply recorded.

(b)   Identification with the consent of the suspect

13. A suspect must be given a reasonable opportunity to have a solicitor or friend present. They shall be asked to indicate on a second copy of the notice whether or not they wish to do so.

14. The witness, the person carrying out the procedure and the suspect's solicitor, appropriate adult, friend or any interpreter for the witness, may be concealed from the sight of the individuals in the group they are observing, if the person carrying out the procedure considers this assists the conduct of the identification.

15. The person conducting a witness to a group identification must not discuss with them the forthcoming group identification and, in particular, must not disclose whether a previous witness has made any identification.

16. Anything said to, or by, the witness during the procedure about the identification should be said in the presence and hearing of those present at the procedure.

17. Appropriate arrangements must be made to make sure, before witnesses attend the group identification, they are not able to:

(i)   communicate with each other about the case or overhear a witness who has already been given an opportunity to see the suspect in the group;

(ii)   see the suspect; or

(iii)   see, or be reminded of, any photographs or description of the suspect or be given any other indication of the suspect's identity.

18. Witnesses shall be brought one at a time to the place where they are to observe the group. Immediately before the witness is asked to look at the group, the person conducting the procedure shall tell them that the person they saw may, or may not, be in the group and that if they cannot make a positive identification, they should say so. The witness shall be asked to observe the group in which the suspect is to appear. The way in which the witness should do this will depend on whether the group is moving or stationary.

Moving group

19. When the group in which the suspect is to appear is moving, e.g. leaving an escalator, the provisions of paragraphs 20 to 24 should be followed.

20. If two or more suspects consent to a group identification, each should be the subject of separate identification procedures. These may be conducted consecutively on the same occasion.

21. The person conducting the procedure shall tell the witness to observe the group and ask them to point out any person they think they saw on the specified earlier occasion.

22. Once the witness has been informed as in paragraph 21 the suspect should be allowed to take whatever position in the group they wish.

23. When the witness points out a person as in paragraph 21 they shall, if practicable, be asked to take a closer look at the person to confirm the identification. If this is not practicable, or they cannot confirm the identification, they shall be asked how sure they are that the person they have indicated is the relevant person.

24. The witness should continue to observe the group for the period which the person conducting the procedure reasonably believes is necessary in the circumstances for them to be able to make comparisons between the suspect and other individuals of broadly similar appearance to the suspect as in paragraph 6.

Stationary groups

25. When the group in which the suspect is to appear is stationary, e.g. people waiting in a queue, the provisions of paragraphs 26 to 29 should be followed.

26. If two or more suspects consent to a group identification, each should be subject to separate identification procedures unless they are of broadly similar appearance when they may appear in the same group. When separate group identifications are held, the groups must be made up of different people.

27. The suspect may take whatever position in the group they wish. If there is more than one witness, the suspect must be told, out of the sight and hearing of any witness, that they can, if they wish, change their position in the group.

28. The witness shall be asked to pass along, or amongst, the group and to look at each person in the group at least twice, taking as much care and time as possible according to the circumstances, before making an identification. Once the witness has done this, they shall be asked whether the person they saw on the specified earlier occasion is in the group and to indicate any such person by whatever means the person conducting the procedure considers appropriate in the circumstances. If this is not practicable, the witness shall be asked to point out any person they think they saw on the earlier occasion.

29. When the witness makes an indication as in paragraph 28, arrangements shall be made, if practicable, for the witness to take a closer look at the person to confirm the identification. If this is not practicable, or the witness is unable to confirm the identification, they shall be asked how sure they are that the person they have indicated is the relevant person.

All cases

30. If the suspect unreasonably delays joining the group, or having joined the group, deliberately conceals themselves from the sight of the witness, this may be treated as a refusal to co-operate in a group identification.

31. If the witness identifies a person other than the suspect, that person should be informed what has happened and asked if they are prepared to give their name and address. There is no obligation upon any member of the public to give these details. There shall be no duty to record any details of any other member of the public present in the group or at the place where the procedure is conducted.

32. When the group identification has been completed, the suspect shall be asked whether they wish to make any comments on the conduct of the procedure.

33. If the suspect has not been previously informed, they shall be told of any identifications made by the witnesses.

(c)   Identification without the suspect's consent

34.   Group identifications held covertly without the suspect's consent should, as far as practicable, follow the rules for conduct of group identification by consent.

35.   A suspect has no right to have a solicitor, appropriate adult or friend present as the identification will take place without the knowledge of the suspect.

36.   Any number of suspects may be identified at the same time.

(d)   Identifications in police stations

37.   Group identifications should only take place in police stations for reasons of safety, security or because it is not practicable to hold them elsewhere.

38.   The group identification may take place either in a room equipped with a screen permitting witnesses to see members of the group without being seen, or anywhere else in the police station that the identification officer considers appropriate.

39.   Any of the additional safeguards applicable to identification parades should be followed if the identification officer considers it is practicable to do so in the circumstances.

(e)   Identifications involving prison inmates

40.   A group identification involving a prison inmate may only be arranged in the prison or at a police station.

41.   When a group identification takes place involving a prison inmate, whether in a prison or in a police station, the arrangements should follow those in paragraphs 37 to 39.If a group identification takes place within a prison, other inmates may participate. If an inmate is the suspect, they do not have to wear prison clothing for the group identification unless the other participants are wearing the same clothing.

(f)   Documentation

42.   When a photograph or video is taken as in paragraph 8 or 9, a copy of the photograph or video shall be supplied on request to the suspect or their solicitor within a reasonable time.

43.   Paragraph 3.30 or 3.31, as appropriate, shall apply when the photograph or film taken in accordance with paragraph 8 or 9 includes the suspect.

44.   A record of the conduct of any group identification must be made on forms provided for the purpose. This shall include anything said by the witness or suspect about any identifications or the conduct of the procedure and any reasons why it was not practicable to comply with any of the provisions of this Code governing the conduct of group identifications.

ANNEX D — CONFRONTATION BY A WITNESS

1.   Before the confrontation takes place, the witness must be told that the person they saw may, or may not, be the person they are to confront and that if they are not that person, then the witness should say so.

2.   Before the confrontation takes place the suspect or their solicitor shall be provided with details of the first description of the suspect given by any witness who is to attend. When a broadcast or publication is made, as in paragraph 3.28, the suspect or their solicitor should also be allowed to view any material released to the media for the purposes of recognising or tracing the suspect, provided it is practicable to do so and would not unreasonably delay the investigation.

3.   Force may not be used to make the suspect's face visible to the witness.

4.   Confrontation must take place in the presence of the suspect's solicitor, interpreter or friend unless this would cause unreasonable delay.

5.   The suspect shall be confronted independently by each witness, who shall be asked 'Is this the person?'. If the witness identifies the person but is unable to confirm the identification, they shall be asked how sure they are that the person is the one they saw on the earlier occasion.

6.   The confrontation should normally take place in the police station, either in a normal room or one equipped with a screen permitting a witness to see the suspect without being seen. In both cases, the procedures are the same except that a room

equipped with a screen may be used only when the suspect's solicitor, friend or appropriate adult is present or the confrontation is recorded on video.

7. After the procedure, each witness shall be asked whether they have seen any broadcast or published films or photographs or any descriptions of suspects relating to the offence and their reply shall be recorded.

ANNEX E — SHOWING PHOTOGRAPHS

(a)   Action

1. An officer of sergeant rank or above shall be responsible for supervising and directing the showing of photographs. The actual showing may be done by another officer or police staff, see paragraph 3.11.

2. The supervising officer must confirm the first description of the suspect given by the witness has been recorded before they are shown the photographs. If the supervising officer is unable to confirm the description has been recorded they shall postpone showing the photographs.

3. Only one witness shall be shown photographs at any one time. Each witness shall be given as much privacy as practicable and shall not be allowed to communicate with any other witness in the case.

4. The witness shall be shown not less than twelve photographs at a time, which shall, as far as possible, all be of a similar type.

5. When the witness is shown the photographs, they shall be told the photograph of the person they saw may, or may not, be amongst them and if they cannot make a positive identification, they should say so. The witness shall also be told they should not make a decision until they have viewed at least twelve photographs. The witness shall not be prompted or guided in any way but shall be left to make any selection without help.

6. If a witness makes a positive identification from photographs, unless the person identified is otherwise eliminated from enquiries or is not available, other witnesses shall not be shown photographs. But both they, and the witness who has made the identification, shall be asked to attend a video identification, an identification parade or group identification unless there is no dispute about the suspect's identification.

7. If the witness makes a selection but is unable to confirm the identification, the person showing the photographs shall ask them how sure they are that the photograph they have indicated is the person they saw on the specified earlier occasion.

8. When the use of a computerised or artist's composite or similar likeness has led to there being a known suspect who can be asked to participate in a video identification, appear on an identification parade or participate in a group identification, that likeness shall not be shown to other potential witnesses.

9. When a witness attending a video identification, an identification parade or group identification has previously been shown photographs or computerised or artist's composite or similar likeness (and it is the responsibility of the officer in charge of the investigation to make the identification officer aware that this is the case), the suspect and their solicitor must be informed of this fact before the identification procedure takes place.

10. None of the photographs shown shall be destroyed, whether or not an identification is made, since they may be required for production in court. The photographs shall be numbered and a separate photograph taken of the frame or part of the album from which the witness made an identification as an aid to reconstituting it.

(b)   Documentation

11. Whether or not an identification is made, a record shall be kept of the showing of photographs on forms provided for the purpose. This shall include anything said by the witness about any identification or the conduct of the procedure, any reasons it was not practicable to comply with any of the provisions of this Code governing the showing of photographs and the name and rank of the supervising officer.

12. The supervising officer shall inspect and sign the record as soon as practicable.

ANNEX F — FINGERPRINTS, FOOTWEAR IMPRESSIONS AND SAMPLES — DESTRUCTION AND SPECULATIVE SEARCHES

(a)   *Fingerprints, footwear impressions and samples taken in connection with a criminal investigation*

1.   When fingerprints, footwear impressions or DNA samples are taken from a person in connection with an investigation and the person is not suspected of having committed the offence, see Note F1, they must be destroyed as soon as they have fulfilled the purpose for which they were taken unless:

    (a)   they were taken for the purposes of an investigation of an offence for which a person has been convicted; and

    (b)   fingerprints, footwear impressions or samples were also taken from the convicted person for the purposes of that investigation.

However, subject to paragraph 2, the fingerprints, footwear impressions and samples, and the information derived from samples, may not be used in the investigation of any offence or in evidence against the person who is, or would be, entitled to the destruction of the fingerprints, footwear impressions and samples, see Note F2.

2.   The requirement to destroy fingerprints, footwear impressions and DNA samples, and information derived from samples, and restrictions on their retention and use in paragraph 1 do not apply if the person gives their written consent for their fingerprints, footwear impressions or sample to be retained and used after they have fulfilled the purpose for which they were taken, see Note F1.

When a person's fingerprints, footwear impressions or sample are to be destroyed:

    (a)   any copies of the fingerprints and footwear impressions must also be destroyed;

    (b)   the person may witness the destruction of their fingerprints, footwear impressions or copies if they ask to do so within five days of being informed destruction is required;

    (c)   access to relevant computer fingerprint data shall be made impossible as soon as it is practicable to do so and the person shall be given a certificate to this effect within three months of asking; and

    (d)   neither the fingerprints, footwear impressions, the sample, or any information derived from the sample, may be used in the investigation of any offence or in evidence against the person who is, or would be, entitled to its destruction.

4.   Fingerprints, footwear impressions or samples, and the information derived from samples, taken in connection with the investigation of an offence which are not required to be destroyed, may be retained after they have fulfilled the purposes for which they were taken but may be used only for purposes related to the prevention or detection of crime, the investigation of an offence or the conduct of a prosecution in, as well as outside, the UK and may also be subject to a speculative search. This includes checking them against other fingerprints, footwear impressions and DNA records held by, or on behalf of, the police and other law enforcement authorities in, as well as outside, the UK.

(b)   *Fingerprints taken in connection with Immigration Service enquiries*

5.   Fingerprints taken for Immigration Service enquiries in accordance with powers and procedures other than under PACE and for which the Immigration Service, not the police, are responsible, must be destroyed as follows:

    (a)   fingerprints and all copies must be destroyed as soon as practicable if the person from whom they were taken proves they are a British or Commonwealth citizen who has the right of abode in the UK under the Immigration Act 1971, section 2(1)(b);

    (b)   fingerprints taken under the power as in paragraph 4.11(g) from a dependant of a person in 4.11 (b) to (f) must be destroyed when that person's fingerprints are to be destroyed;

    (c)   fingerprints taken from a person under any power as in paragraph 4.11 or with the person's consent which have not already been destroyed as above, must be destroyed within ten years of being taken or within such period specified by the Secretary of State under the Immigration and Asylum Act 1999, section 143(5).

Notes for guidance

F1   Fingerprints, footwear impressions and samples given voluntarily for the purposes of elimination play an important part in many police investigations. It is, therefore, important to make sure innocent volunteers are not deterred from participating and their consent to their fingerprints, footwear impressions and DNA being used for the purposes of a specific investigation is fully informed and voluntary. If the police or volunteer seek to have the fingerprints, footwear impressions or samples retained for use after the specific investigation ends, it is important the volunteer's consent to this is also fully informed and voluntary.

Examples of consent for:

- DNA/fingerprints/footwear impressions — to be used only for the purposes of a specific investigation;
- DNA/fingerprints/footwear impressions — to be used in the specific investigation and retained by the police for future use.

To minimise the risk of confusion, each consent should be physically separate and the volunteer should be asked to sign each consent.

(a)   DNA:

    (i)   DNA sample taken for the purposes of elimination or as part of an intelligence-led screening and to be used only for the purposes of that investigation and destroyed afterwards:

> 'I consent to my DNA/mouth swab being taken for forensic analysis. I understand that the sample will be destroyed at the end of the case and that my profile will only be compared to the crime stain profile from this enquiry. I have been advised that the person taking the sample may be required to give evidence and/or provide a written statement to the police in relation to the taking of it'.

    (ii)   DNA sample to be retained on the National DNA database and used in the future:

> 'I consent to my DNA sample and information derived from it being retained and used only for purposes related to the prevention and detection of a crime, the investigation of an offence or the conduct of a prosecution either nationally or internationally.'
>
> 'I understand that this sample may be checked against other DNA records held by, or on behalf of, relevant law enforcement authorities, either nationally or internationally'.
>
> 'I understand that once I have given my consent for the sample to be retained and used I cannot withdraw this consent.'

(b)   Fingerprints:

    (i)   Fingerprints taken for the purposes of elimination or as part of an intelligence-led screening and to be used only for the purposes of that investigation and destroyed afterwards:

> 'I consent to my fingerprints being taken for elimination purposes. I understand that the fingerprints will be destroyed at the end of the caseand that my fingerprints will only be compared to the fingerprints from this enquiry. I have been advised that the person taking the fingerprints may be required to give evidence and/or provide a written statement to the police in relation to the taking of it.'

    (ii)   Fingerprints to be retained for future use:

> 'I consent to my fingerprints being retained and used only for purposes related to the prevention and detection of a crime, the

investigation of an offence or the conduct of a prosecution either nationally or internationally'.

'I understand that my fingerprints may be checked against other records held by, or on behalf of, relevant law enforcement authorities, either nationally or internationally.'

'I understand that once I have given my consent for my fingerprints to be retained and used I cannot withdraw this consent.'

(c)   Footwear impressions:

(i)   Footwear impressions taken for the purposes of elimination or as part of an intelligence-led screening and to be used only for the purposes of that investigation and destroyed afterwards:

'I consent to my footwear impressions being taken for elimination purposes. I understand that the footwear impressions will be destroyed at the end of the case and that my footwear impressions will only be compared to the footwear impressions from this enquiry. I have been advised that the person taking the footwear impressions may be required to give evidence and/or provide a written statement to the police in relation to the taking of it.'

(ii)   Footwear impressions to be retained for future use:

'I consent to my footwear impressions being retained and used only for purposes related to the prevention and detection of a crime, the investigation of an offence or the conduct of a prosecution, either nationally or internationally'.

'I understand that my footwear impressions may be checked against other records held by, or on behalf of, relevant law enforcement authorities, either nationally or internationally.'

'I understand that once I have given my consent for my footwear impressions to be retained and used I cannot withdraw this consent.'

F2   The provisions for the retention of fingerprints, footwear impressions and samples in paragraph 1 allow for all fingerprints, footwear impressions and samples in a case to be available for any subsequent miscarriage of justice investigation.

Appendix 2
Magistrates' Court Sentencing Guidelines

Introduction

These Sentencing Guidelines cover offences with which magistrates deal regularly and frequently in the adult criminal courts. They provide a sentencing structure which sets out how to:

- establish the seriousness of each case
- determine the most appropriate way of dealing with it.

The Sentencing Guidelines provide a method for considering individual cases and a guideline from which discussion should properly flow; but they are not a tariff and should never be used as such. **The guideline sentences are based on a first-time offender pleading not guilty.**

Using the sentencing structure

The sentencing structure used for these Guidelines was established by the Criminal Justice Act 1991. This reaffirms the principle of 'just deserts' so that any penalty must reflect the seriousness of the offence for which it is imposed and the personal circumstances of the offender. Magistrates must always start the sentencing process by taking full account of all the circumstances of the offence and making a judicial assessment of the seriousness category into which it falls. It is important that the court makes clear the factual basis on which the sentence is based.

In every case, the Criminal Justice Act 1991 requires sentencers to consider:

- Is discharge or a fine appropriate?
- Is the offence serious enough for a community penalty?
- Is it so serious that only custody is appropriate?

If the last, in either way cases, justices will also need to consider if magistrates' courts' powers are sufficient.

The format of the Sentencing Guidelines

1.	**CONSIDER THE SERIOUSNESS OF THE OFFENCE**

Magistrates must always make an assessment of seriousness following the structure of the Criminal Justice Act 1991. **The guideline sentences are based on a first-time offender pleading not guilty.**

Where this guideline is discharge or fine, a suggested starting point guideline fine is also given. Refer to the guidance on pages 85–87 and 101–102.

Where the starting point guideline is a community penalty, refer to the guidance on pages 91 and 92.

Where the starting point guideline is custody, think in terms of weeks and credit as appropriate for a timely guilty plea.

For some either way offences the guideline is 'are your sentencing powers sufficient?'. This indicates that magistrates should be considering whether the seriousness of the offence is such that six months (or 12 months in the case of two or more offences) is insufficient, so that the case must be committed to the Crown Court (consult the legal adviser with regard to Crown Court sentencing and guideline cases). If the case is retained in the magistrates' court a substantial custodial sentence is likely to be necessary.

It should be noted that if magistrates consider (say) nine months to be the appropriate sentence, to be reduced for a timely guilty plea to six months, then the case falls within their powers and must be retained. Subject to offender mitigation, six months would appear to be the appropriate sentence. However, if sentence is passed on this basis the court should specifically say so in its reasons.

2.	**CONSIDER AGGRAVATING AND MITIGATING FACTORS**

Make sure that all aggravating and mitigating factors are considered. The lists in the Sentencing Guidelines are neither exhaustive nor a substitute for the personal judgment of magistrates. **Factors which do not appear in the Guidelines may be important in individual cases.**

If the offence was racially or religiously aggravated, the court must treat that fact as an aggravating factor under statute (s.153 of the Powers of Criminal Courts (Sentencing) Act 2000). Refer to page 98 for further guidance.

If the offence was committed while the offender was on bail, the court must treat that as an aggravating factor under statute (s.151 Powers of Criminal Courts (Sentencing) Act 2000).

Consider previous convictions, or any failure to respond to previous sentences, in assessing seriousness. Courts should identify any convictions relevant for this purpose and then consider to what extent they affect the seriousness of the present offence.

3.

TAKE A PRELIMINARY VIEW OF SERIOUSNESS, THEN CONSIDER OFFENDER MITIGATION

When an initial assessment of the seriousness of the offence has been formed, consider the offender.

The Guidelines set out some examples of offender mitigation but there are frequently others to be considered in individual cases. Any offender mitigation that the court accepts must lead to some downward revision of the provisional assessment of seriousness, although this revision may be minor. **Remember, however, that the guideline sentences are based on a first-time offender pleading not guilty.**

A previous criminal record may deprive the defendant of being able to say that he is a person of good character.

4.

CONSIDER YOUR SENTENCE

The law requires the court to consider reducing the sentence for a timely guilty plea. Credit for a timely guilty plea may result in a sentencing reduction of up to one-third but the precise amount of credit will depend upon the facts of each case and a last minute plea of guilty may attract only a minimal reduction.

Credit may be given in respect of the amount of a fine or periods of community service or custody. Periods of mandatory disqualification or mandatory penalty points cannot be reduced for a guilty plea.

5.

DECIDE YOUR SENTENCE

Remember that magistrates have a duty to consider the award of compensation in all appropriate cases, and to give reasons if compensation is not awarded. See pages 89–90, Section Three.

Agree the form of words that the Chairman will use when announcing sentence.

Assault – actual bodily harm	Offences Against the Person Act 1861 s.47 Triable either way – see Mode of Trial Guidelines Penalty: Level 5 and/or 6 months

CONSIDER THE SERIOUSNESS OF THE OFFENCE
(INCLUDING THE IMPACT ON THE VICTIM)

IS DISCHARGE OR FINE APPROPRIATE?

IS IT SERIOUS ENOUGH FOR A COMMUNITY PENALTY?

GUIDELINE: → IS IT SO SERIOUS THAT ONLY CUSTODY IS APPROPRIATE?

ARE YOUR SENTENCING POWERS SUFFICIENT?

THIS IS A GUIDELINE FOR A FIRST-TIME OFFENDER PLEADING NOT GUILTY

 ## CONSIDER AGGRAVATING AND MITIGATING FACTORS AND THE WEIGHT TO ATTACH TO EACH

for example	for example
Abuse of trust (domestic setting) Deliberate kicking or biting Extensive injuries (may be psychological) Headbutting Group action Offender in position of authority On hospital/medical or school premises Premeditated Victim particularly vulnerable Victim serving the public Weapon *This list is not exhaustive*	Minor injury Provocation Single blow *This list is not exhaustive*

If offender is on bail, this offence is more serious

If offender has previous convictions, their relevance and any failure to respond to previous sentences should be considered – they may increase the seriousness. The court should make it clear, when passing sentence, that this was the approach adopted.

TAKE A PRELIMINARY VIEW OF SERIOUSNESS, THEN CONSIDER OFFENDER MITIGATION

for example
    Age, health (physical or mental)
    Co-operation with police
    Evidence of genuine remorse
    Voluntary compensation

CONSIDER YOUR SENTENCE

Compare it with the suggested guideline level of sentence and reconsider your reasons carefully if you have chosen a sentence at a different level. Consider a reduction for a timely guilty plea.

DECIDE YOUR SENTENCE
NB. COMPENSATION – Give reasons if not awarding compensation

Burglary (dwelling)	Theft Act 1968 s.9 Triable either way – see Mode of Trial Guidelines Penalty: Level 5 and/or 6 months

CONSIDER THE SERIOUSNESS OF THE OFFENCE
(INCLUDING THE IMPACT ON THE VICTIM)

IS DISCHARGE OR FINE APPROPRIATE?

IS IT SERIOUS ENOUGH FOR A COMMUNITY PENALTY?

IS IT SO SERIOUS THAT ONLY CUSTODY IS APPROPRIATE?

GUIDELINE: →   *ARE YOUR SENTENCING POWERS SUFFICIENT?*

THIS IS A GUIDELINE FOR A FIRST-TIME OFFENDER PLEADING NOT GUILTY

 ## CONSIDER AGGRAVATING AND MITIGATING FACTORS AND THE WEIGHT TO ATTACH TO EACH

for example
- Force used or threatened
- Group enterprise
- High value (in economic or sentimental terms) property stolen
- More than minor trauma caused
- Professional planning/organisation/ execution
- Significant damage or vandalism
- Victim injured
- Victim present at the time
- Vulnerable victim

IF ANY of the above factors are present you should commit for sentence.

for example
- First offence of its type AND low value property stolen AND no significant damage or disturbance AND no injury or violence
- Minor part played
- Theft from attached garage
- Vacant property

ONLY if one or more of the above factors are present AND none of the aggravating factors listed are present should you consider NOT committing for sentence.

If racially or religiously aggravated, or offender is on bail, this offence is more serious
If offender has previous convictions, their relevance and any failure to respond to previous sentences should be considered – they may increase the seriousness. The court should make it clear, when passing sentence, that this was the approach adopted.

TAKE A PRELIMINARY VIEW OF SERIOUSNESS, THEN CONSIDER WHETHER THE CASE SHOULD BE COMMITTED FOR SENTENCE, THEN CONSIDER OFFENDER MITIGATION

for example
- Age, health (physical or mental)
- Co-operation with police
- Evidence of genuine remorse
- Voluntary compensation

CONSIDER COMMITTAL OR YOUR SENTENCE

Compare it with the suggested guideline level of sentence and reconsider your reasons carefully if you have chosen a sentence at a different level. Consider a reduction for a timely guilty plea.

DECIDE YOUR SENTENCE
NB. COMPENSATION – Give reasons if not awarding compensation

Theft Act 1968 s.9 Triable either way – see Mode of Trial Guidelines Penalty: Level 5 and/or 6 months	**Burglary (non-dwelling)**

CONSIDER THE SERIOUSNESS OF THE OFFENCE
(INCLUDING THE IMPACT ON THE VICTIM)

IS DISCHARGE OR FINE APPROPRIATE?

GUIDELINE: →   *IS IT SERIOUS ENOUGH FOR A COMMUNITY PENALTY?*

IS IT SO SERIOUS THAT ONLY CUSTODY IS APPROPRIATE?

ARE YOUR SENTENCING POWERS SUFFICIENT?

THIS IS A GUIDELINE FOR A FIRST-TIME OFFENDER PLEADING NOT GUILTY

 ## CONSIDER AGGRAVATING AND MITIGATING FACTORS AND THE WEIGHT TO ATTACH TO EACH

for example	**for example**
Forcible entry Group offence Harm to business Occupants frightened Professional operation Repeat victimisation School or medical premises Soiling, ransacking, damage *This list is not exhaustive*	Low value Nobody frightened No damage or disturbance *This list is not exhaustive*

If racially or religiously aggravated, or offender is on bail, this offence is more serious
If offender has previous convictions, their relevance and any failure to respond to previous sentences should be considered – they may increase the seriousness. The court should make it clear, when passing sentence, that this was the approach adopted.

TAKE A PRELIMINARY VIEW OF SERIOUSNESS, THEN CONSIDER OFFENDER MITIGATION

for example
Age, health (physical or mental)
Co-operation with police
Evidence of genuine remorse
Voluntary compensation

CONSIDER YOUR SENTENCE

Compare it with the suggested guideline level of sentence and reconsider your reasons carefully if you have chosen a sentence at a different level. Consider a reduction for a timely guilty plea.

DECIDE YOUR SENTENCE
NB. COMPENSATION – Give reasons if not awarding compensation

Common assault	Criminal Justice Act 1988 s.39 Triable only summarily Penalty: Level 5 and/or 6 months

CONSIDER THE SERIOUSNESS OF THE OFFENCE
(INCLUDING THE IMPACT ON THE VICTIM)

IS DISCHARGE OR FINE APPROPRIATE?

GUIDELINE: →   *IS IT SERIOUS ENOUGH FOR A COMMUNITY PENALTY?*

IS IT SO SERIOUS THAT ONLY CUSTODY IS APPROPRIATE?

THIS IS A GUIDELINE FOR A FIRST-TIME OFFENDER PLEADING NOT GUILTY

 ## CONSIDER AGGRAVATING AND MITIGATING FACTORS
AND THE WEIGHT TO ATTACH TO EACH

for example
Abuse of trust (domestic setting)
Group action
Injury
Offender in position of authority
On hospital/medical or school premises
Premeditated
Spitting
Victim particularly vulnerable
Victim serving the public
Weapon
This list is not exhaustive

for example
Impulsive
Minor injury
Provocation
Single blow
This list is not exhaustive

If offender is on bail, this offence is more serious
If offender has previous convictions, their relevance and any failure to respond to previous sentences should be considered – they may increase the seriousness. The court should make it clear, when passing sentence, that this was the approach adopted.

TAKE A PRELIMINARY VIEW OF SERIOUSNESS, THEN
CONSIDER OFFENDER MITIGATION

for example
Age, health (physical or mental)
Co-operation with police
Evidence of genuine remorse
Voluntary compensation

CONSIDER YOUR SENTENCE

Compare it with the suggested guideline level of sentence and reconsider
your reasons carefully if you have chosen a sentence at a different level.
Consider a reduction for a timely guilty plea.

DECIDE YOUR SENTENCE
NB. COMPENSATION – Give reasons if not awarding compensation

Bail Act 1976 s.6 Triable only summarily Penalty: Level 5 and/or 3 months	**Failure to surrender to bail**

CONSIDER THE SERIOUSNESS OF THE OFFENCE

IS DISCHARGE OR FINE APPROPRIATE?
GUIDELINE: → *IS IT SERIOUS ENOUGH FOR A COMMUNITY PENALTY?*
IS IT SO SERIOUS THAT ONLY CUSTODY IS APPROPRIATE?

THIS IS A GUIDELINE FOR A FIRST-TIME OFFENDER PLEADING NOT GUILTY

 ## CONSIDER AGGRAVATING AND MITIGATING FACTORS AND THE WEIGHT TO ATTACH TO EACH

for example	**for example**
Leaves jurisdiction	Appears late on day of hearing
Long term evasion	Genuine misunderstanding
Results in ineffective trial date	Voluntary surrender
Wilful evasion	*This list is not exhaustive*
This list is not exhaustive	

A curfew order may be particularly suitable

Previous convictions for this offence increase the seriousness – consider custody

TAKE A PRELIMINARY VIEW OF SERIOUSNESS, THEN CONSIDER OFFENDER MITIGATION

for example
Age, health (physical or mental)
Co-operation with police
Evidence of genuine remorse

CONSIDER YOUR SENTENCE

Compare it with the suggested guideline level of sentence and reconsider your reasons carefully if you have chosen a sentence at a different level. Consider a reduction for a timely guilty plea.

DECIDE YOUR SENTENCE

Handling stolen goods	Theft Act 1968 s.22 Triable either way – see Mode of Trial Guidelines Penalty: Level 5 and/or 6 months

CONSIDER THE SERIOUSNESS OF THE OFFENCE
(INCLUDING THE IMPACT ON THE VICTIM)

IS DISCHARGE OR FINE APPROPRIATE?
GUIDELINE: →   *IS IT SERIOUS ENOUGH FOR A COMMUNITY PENALTY?*
IS IT SO SERIOUS THAT ONLY CUSTODY IS APPROPRIATE?
ARE YOUR SENTENCING POWERS SUFFICIENT?

THIS IS A GUIDELINE FOR A FIRST-TIME OFFENDER PLEADING NOT GUILTY

 CONSIDER AGGRAVATING AND MITIGATING FACTORS AND THE WEIGHT TO ATTACH TO EACH

for example	for example
High level of profit accruing to handler High value (including sentimental) of goods Provision by handler of regular outlet for stolen goods Proximity of the handler to the primary offence Seriousness of the primary offence Sophistication The particular facts, eg the goods handled were the proceeds of a domestic burglary Threats of violence or abuse of power by handler in order to obtain goods *This list is not exhaustive*	Isolated offence Little or no benefit accruing to handler Low monetary value of goods *This list is not exhaustive*

If offender is on bail, this offence is more serious
If offender has previous convictions, their relevance and any failure to respond to previous sentences should be considered – they may increase the seriousness. The court should make it clear, when passing sentence, that this was the approach adopted.

TAKE A PRELIMINARY VIEW OF SERIOUSNESS, THEN CONSIDER OFFENDER MITIGATION

for example
   Age, health (physical or mental)
   Co-operation with police
   Evidence of genuine remorse
   Voluntary compensation

CONSIDER YOUR SENTENCE

Compare it with the suggested guideline level of sentence and reconsider your reasons carefully if you have chosen a sentence at a different level. Consider a reduction for a timely guilty plea.

DECIDE YOUR SENTENCE
NB. COMPENSATION – Give reasons if not awarding compensation

Theft Act 1968 s.15 Triable either way – see Mode of Trial Guidelines Penalty: Level 5 and/or 6 months	**Obtaining by deception**

CONSIDER THE SERIOUSNESS OF THE OFFENCE
(INCLUDING THE IMPACT ON THE VICTIM)

IS DISCHARGE OR FINE APPROPRIATE?

GUIDELINE: →   *IS IT SERIOUS ENOUGH FOR A COMMUNITY PENALTY?*

IS IT SO SERIOUS THAT ONLY CUSTODY IS APPROPRIATE?

ARE YOUR SENTENCING POWERS SUFFICIENT?

THIS IS A GUIDELINE FOR A FIRST-TIME OFFENDER PLEADING NOT GUILTY

 ## CONSIDER AGGRAVATING AND MITIGATING FACTORS AND THE WEIGHT TO ATTACH TO EACH

for example	for example
Committed over lengthy period Large sums or valuable goods Two or more involved Use of stolen credit/debit card, cheque books, or giros Victim particularly vulnerable *This list is not exhaustive*	Impulsive action Short period Small sum *This list is not exhaustive*

If offender is on bail, this offence is more serious
If offender has previous convictions, their relevance and any failure to respond to previous sentences should be considered – they may increase the seriousness. The court should make it clear, when passing sentence, that this was the approach adopted.

TAKE A PRELIMINARY VIEW OF SERIOUSNESS, THEN CONSIDER OFFENDER MITIGATION

for example
Age, health (physical or mental)
Co-operation with police
Evidence of genuine remorse
Voluntary compensation

CONSIDER YOUR SENTENCE

Compare it with the suggested guideline level of sentence and reconsider your reasons carefully if you have chosen a sentence at a different level.
Consider a reduction for a timely guilty plea.

DECIDE YOUR SENTENCE
NB. COMPENSATION – Give reasons if not awarding compensation

Theft	Theft Act 1968 s.1 Triable either way – see Mode of Trial Guidelines Penalty: Level 5 and/or 6 months May disqualify where committed with reference to the theft or taking of a vehicle

CONSIDER THE SERIOUSNESS OF THE OFFENCE
(INCLUDING THE IMPACT ON THE VICTIM)

IS DISCHARGE OR FINE APPROPRIATE?

GUIDELINE: → *IS IT SERIOUS ENOUGH FOR A COMMUNITY PENALTY?*

IS IT SO SERIOUS THAT ONLY CUSTODY IS APPROPRIATE?

ARE YOUR SENTENCING POWERS SUFFICIENT?

THIS IS A GUIDELINE FOR A FIRST-TIME OFFENDER PLEADING NOT GUILTY

 CONSIDER AGGRAVATING AND MITIGATING FACTORS AND THE WEIGHT TO ATTACH TO EACH

for example	for example
High value	Impulsive action
Planned	Low value
Sophisticated	*This list is not exhaustive*
Adult involving children	
Organised team	
Related damage	
Vulnerable victim	
This list is not exhaustive	

If racially or religiously aggravated, or offender is on bail, this offence is more serious
If offender has previous convictions, their relevance and any failure to respond to previous
sentences should be considered – they may increase the seriousness. The court should make
it clear, when passing sentence, that this was the approach adopted.

TAKE A PRELIMINARY VIEW OF SERIOUSNESS, THEN CONSIDER OFFENDER MITIGATION

for example
　　Age, health (physical or mental)
　　Co-operation with police
　　Evidence of genuine remorse
　　Voluntary compensation

CONSIDER YOUR SENTENCE

Compare it with the suggested guideline level of sentence and reconsider
your reasons carefully if you have chosen a sentence at a different level.
Consider a reduction for a timely guilty plea.

DECIDE YOUR SENTENCE
NB. COMPENSATION – Give reasons if not awarding compensation

Theft Act 1968 s.1 Triable either way – see Mode of Trial Guidelines Penalty: Level 5 and/or 6 months	Theft in breach of trust

CONSIDER THE SERIOUSNESS OF THE OFFENCE
(INCLUDING THE IMPACT ON THE VICTIM)

IS DISCHARGE OR FINE APPROPRIATE?

IS IT SERIOUS ENOUGH FOR A COMMUNITY PENALTY?

GUIDELINE: → IS IT SO SERIOUS THAT ONLY CUSTODY IS APPROPRIATE?

ARE YOUR SENTENCING POWERS SUFFICIENT?

THIS IS A GUIDELINE FOR A FIRST-TIME OFFENDER PLEADING NOT GUILTY

 ## CONSIDER AGGRAVATING AND MITIGATING FACTORS AND THE WEIGHT TO ATTACH TO EACH

for example	**for example**
Casting suspicion on others Committed over a period High value Organised team Planned Senior employee Sophisticated Vulnerable victim *This list is not exhaustive*	Impulsive action Low value Previous inconsistent attitude by employer Single item Unsupported junior *This list is not exhaustive*

If racially or religiously aggravated, or offender is on bail, this offence is more serious
If offender has previous convictions, their relevance and any failure to respond to previous sentences should be considered – they may increase the seriousness. The court should make it clear, when passing sentence, that this was the approach adopted.

TAKE A PRELIMINARY VIEW OF SERIOUSNESS, THEN CONSIDER OFFENDER MITIGATION

for example
 Age, health (physical or mental)
 Co-operation with police
 Evidence of genuine remorse
 Voluntary compensation

CONSIDER YOUR SENTENCE

Compare it with the suggested guideline level of sentence and reconsider your reasons carefully if you have chosen a sentence at a different level. Consider a reduction for a timely guilty plea.

DECIDE YOUR SENTENCE
NB. COMPENSATION – Give reasons if not awarding compensation

Wounding – grievous bodily harm	Offences Against the Person Act 1861 s.20 Triable either way – see Mode of Trial Guidelines Penalty: Level 5 and/or 6 months

CONSIDER THE SERIOUSNESS OF THE OFFENCE
(INCLUDING THE IMPACT ON THE VICTIM)

IS DISCHARGE OR FINE APPROPRIATE?

IS IT SERIOUS ENOUGH FOR A COMMUNITY PENALTY?

IS IT SO SERIOUS THAT ONLY CUSTODY IS APPROPRIATE?

GUIDELINE: →   *ARE YOUR SENTENCING POWERS SUFFICIENT?*

THIS IS A GUIDELINE FOR A FIRST-TIME OFFENDER PLEADING NOT GUILTY

 ## CONSIDER AGGRAVATING AND MITIGATING FACTORS AND THE WEIGHT TO ATTACH TO EACH

for example	for example
Abuse of trust (domestic setting) Deliberate kicking/biting Extensive injuries Group action Offender in position of authority On hospital/medical or school premises Premeditated Prolonged assault Victim particularly vulnerable Victim serving the public Weapon *This list is not exhaustive*	Minor wound Provocation *This list is not exhaustive*

If offender is on bail, this offence is more serious

If offender has previous convictions, their relevance and any failure to respond to previous sentences should be considered – they may increase the seriousness. The court should make it clear, when passing sentence, that this was the approach adopted.

TAKE A PRELIMINARY VIEW OF SERIOUSNESS, THEN CONSIDER WHETHER THE CASE SHOULD BE COMMITTED FOR SENTENCE, THEN CONSIDER OFFENDER MITIGATION

for example
- Age, health (physical or mental)
- Co-operation with police
- Evidence of genuine remorse
- Voluntary compensation

CONSIDER COMMITTAL OR YOUR SENTENCE

Compare it with the suggested guideline level of sentence and reconsider your reasons carefully if you have chosen a sentence at a different level. Consider a reduction for a timely guilty plea.

DECIDE YOUR SENTENCE
NB. COMPENSATION – Give reasons if not awarding compensation

Road Traffic Act 1988 s.3 Triable only summarily Penalty: Level 4 Must endorse (3-9 points OR may disqualify)	**Careless driving**

CONSIDER THE SERIOUSNESS OF THE OFFENCE

GUIDELINE: →   *IS DISCHARGE OR FINE APPROPRIATE?*

IS IT SERIOUS ENOUGH FOR A COMMUNITY PENALTY?

*(COMMUNITY REHABILITATION AND CURFEW ORDERS ARE THE ONLY
AVAILABLE COMMUNITY PENALTIES FOR THIS OFFENCE)*

THIS IS A GUIDELINE FOR A FIRST-TIME OFFENDER PLEADING NOT GUILTY

GUIDELINE FINE – STARTING POINT B

 ## CONSIDER AGGRAVATING AND MITIGATING FACTORS
AND THE WEIGHT TO ATTACH TO EACH

for example	**for example**
Excessive speed	Minor risk
High degree of carelessness	Momentary lapse
Serious risk	Negligible/parking damage
Using a hand-held mobile telephone	Sudden change in weather conditions
This list is not exhaustive	*This list is not exhaustive*

Death, serious injury or damage is capable of being aggravation

---

If offender is on bail, this offence is more serious
*If offender has previous convictions, their relevance and any failure to respond to previous
sentences should be considered – they may increase the seriousness. The court should make
it clear, when passing sentence, that this was the approach adopted.*

TAKE A PRELIMINARY VIEW OF SERIOUSNESS, THEN
CONSIDER OFFENDER MITIGATION

for example
    Co-operation with police
    Evidence of genuine remorse
    Voluntary compensation

CONSIDER YOUR SENTENCE

Endorse (3-9 points OR period of disqualification)
*Consider other measures (including disqualification until test passed if appropriate –
for example, age, infirmity or medical condition)*
*Compare it with the suggested guideline level of sentence and reconsider
your reasons carefully if you have chosen a sentence at a different level.*
Consider a reduction for a timely guilty plea.

DECIDE YOUR SENTENCE

Dangerous driving	Road Traffic Act 1988 s.2 Triable either way – see Mode of Trial Guidelines Penalty: Level 5 and/or 6 months Must endorse and disqualify at least 12 months Must endorse (3-11 points) if not disqualified **MUST ORDER EXTENDED RE-TEST**

CONSIDER THE SERIOUSNESS OF THE OFFENCE
(INCLUDING THE IMPACT ON THE VICTIM)

IS DISCHARGE OR FINE APPROPRIATE?
IS IT SERIOUS ENOUGH FOR A COMMUNITY PENALTY?
GUIDELINE: → *IS IT SO SERIOUS THAT ONLY CUSTODY IS APPROPRIATE?*
ARE YOUR SENTENCING POWERS SUFFICIENT?

THIS IS A GUIDELINE FOR A FIRST-TIME OFFENDER PLEADING NOT GUILTY

 ## CONSIDER AGGRAVATING AND MITIGATING FACTORS
AND THE WEIGHT TO ATTACH TO EACH

for example
    Avoiding detection or apprehension
    Competitive driving, racing, showing off
    Disregard of warnings, eg from passengers
       or others in vicinity
    Evidence of alcohol or drugs
    Excessive speed
    Police pursuit
    Prolonged, persistent, deliberate bad driving
    Serious risk
    Using a mobile telephone
    This list is not exhaustive

for example
    Emergency
    Speed not excessive
    This list is not exhaustive

Serious injury or damage is capable of being aggravation

If offender is on bail, this offence is more serious
If offender has previous convictions, their relevance and any failure to respond to previous sentences should be considered – they may increase the seriousness. The court should make it clear, when passing sentence, that this was the approach adopted.

TAKE A PRELIMINARY VIEW OF SERIOUSNESS,
THEN CONSIDER OFFENDER MITIGATION

for example
    Co-operation with police
    Evidence of genuine remorse
    Voluntary compensation

CONSIDER YOUR SENTENCE

Endorse licence and disqualify at least 12 months unless special reasons apply.
MUST ORDER EXTENDED RE-TEST.
Compare it with the suggested guideline level of sentence and reconsider your reasons carefully if you have chosen a sentence at a different level.
Consider a reduction for a timely guilty plea.

DECIDE YOUR SENTENCE

Excess alcohol (drive or attempt to drive)

Road Traffic Act 1988 s.5(1)(a)
Penalty: Level 5 and/or 6 months
Triable only summarily
Must endorse and disqualify *at least* 12 months:
disqualify at least 36 months for a further
offence within 10 years

CONSIDER THE SERIOUSNESS OF THE OFFENCE
THE LEVEL OF SERIOUSNESS AND GUIDELINE SENTENCE ARE RELATED TO THE BREATH/BLOOD/URINE LEVEL

 CONSIDER AGGRAVATING AND MITIGATING FACTORS AND THE WEIGHT TO ATTACH TO EACH

for example
- Ability to drive seriously impaired
- Caused injury/fear/damage
- Police pursuit
- Evidence of nature of the driving
- Type of vehicle, eg carrying passengers for reward/large goods vehicle
- High reading (and in combination with above)

This list is not exhaustive

for example
- Emergency
- Moving a vehicle a very short distance
- Spiked drinks

This list is not exhaustive

If offender is on bail, this offence is more serious
If offender has previous convictions, their relevance and any failure to respond to previous sentences should be considered – they may increase the seriousness. The court should make it clear, when passing sentence, that this was the approach adopted.

TAKE A PRELIMINARY VIEW OF SERIOUSNESS, THEN CONSIDER OFFENDER MITIGATION

for example
- Co-operation with police

CONSIDER YOUR SENTENCE

Offer a rehabilitation course.
Compare your decision with the suggested guideline level of sentence and reconsider your reasons carefully if you have chosen a sentence at a different level.
Consider a reduction for a timely guilty plea.

DECIDE YOUR SENTENCE

BREATH	BLOOD	URINE	DISQUALIFY NOT LESS THAN	GUIDELINE
36-55	80-125	107-170	12 months	B
56-70	126-160	171-214	16 months	C
71-85	161-195	215-260	20 months	C
86-100	196-229	261-308	24 months	CONSIDER COMMUNITY PENALTY
101-115	230-264	309-354	28 months	
116-130	265-300	355-400	32 months	CONSIDER CUSTODY
131+	301+	401+	36 months	

© The Magistrates' Association   70   *Issued October 2003 for implementation 1 January 2004*

Road Traffic Act 1984 s.89(10) Triable only summarily Penalty: Level 3 (Level 4 if motorway) Must endorse (3-6 points OR may disqualify)	Speeding

CONSIDER THE SERIOUSNESS OF THE OFFENCE

GUIDELINE: → ***IS DISCHARGE OR FINE APPROPRIATE?***

(COMMUNITY REHABILITATION AND CURFEW ORDERS ARE THE ONLY

AVAILABLE COMMUNITY PENALTIES FOR THIS OFFENCE)

THIS IS A GUIDELINE FOR A FIRST-TIME OFFENDER PLEADING NOT GUILTY

 ## CONSIDER AGGRAVATING AND MITIGATING FACTORS AND THE WEIGHT TO ATTACH TO EACH

for example LGV, HGV, PCV or taxi or private-hire vehicles Location/time of day/visibility Serious risk Towing caravan/trailer *This list is not exhaustive*	**for example** Emergency established *This list is not exhaustive*

If offender is on bail, this offence is more serious
If offender has previous convictions, their relevance and any failure to respond to previous sentences should be considered – they may increase the seriousness. The court should make it clear, when passing sentence, that this was the approach adopted.

GUIDELINE PENALTY POINTS	LEGAL SPEED LIMITS	EXCESS SPEED – MPH	FINE
3	20-30 mph 40-50 mph 60-70 mph	Up to 10 mph Up to 15 mph Up to 20 mph	A
4 or 5 OR disqualify up to 42 days	20-30 mph 40-50 mph 60-70 mph	From 11-20 mph From 16-25 mph From 21-30 mph	B
6 OR disqualify up to 56 days	20-30 mph 40-50 mph 60-70 mph	From 21-30 mph From 26-35 mph From 31-40 mph	B

TAKE A PRELIMINARY VIEW OF SERIOUSNESS, THEN CONSIDER OFFENDER MITIGATION

for example
Co-operation with police
Fixed penalty not taken up for valid reason

CONSIDER YOUR SENTENCE

Endorse (3-6 points OR period of disqualification. If a new driver accumulates 6 points this will result in automatic revocation of the licence by the DVLA, see note on page 100.)
Consider other measures (including disqualification until test passed if appropriate).
Compare it with the suggested guideline level of sentence and reconsider your reasons carefully if you have chosen a sentence at a different level.
Consider a reduction for a timely guilty plea.

DECIDE YOUR SENTENCE

Road traffic offences

Disqualification

Some offences carry mandatory disqualification. This mandatory disqualification period may be automatically lengthened by the existence of certain previous convictions and disqualifications.

Sentencers should not disqualify defendants in their absence although there is provision in statute to do so provided that an offender is given adequate notice of the hearing at which the court will consider disqualification. This discretionary power should only be exercised in out of the ordinary circumstances. As with all decisions of this type, account should be taken of human rights legislation. The court must give cogent and explicit reasons for any decision to disqualify in absence.

Penalty points and disqualification

All endorsable offences carry also as an alternative discretionary power to disqualify instead of imposing penalty points.

Dangerous driving carries an obligatory minimum disqualification of one year and a mandatory extended re-test.

For any offence which carries penalty points the courts have a discretion to order a re-test provided there is evidence of inexperience, incompetence or infirmity. It would be an ordinary test except where disqualification is obligatory when an extended test would be required.

The number of variable penalty points or the period of disqualification is targeted strictly at the seriousness of the offence and in either case must not be reduced below the statutory minimum, where applicable.

Offences committed on different occasions may carry points, even where they are dealt with on the same occasion.

Disqualification until a test is passed

A magistrates' court **must** disqualify an offender until he passes an *extended driving test* where he is convicted of an offence of dangerous driving.

The court has a **discretion** to disqualify until a test is passed where the offender has been convicted of an offence involving obligatory disqualification. In this case it is the ordinary driving test that must be undertaken.

An offender disqualified as a 'totter' under the penalty points provisions **may** also be ordered to re-take a driving test, in which case it will be the *extended test*.

The discretion is likely to be exercised where there is evidence of inexperience, incompetence or infirmity; or the disqualification period imposed is lengthy (ie the offender is going to be 'off the road' for a considerable time).

Disqualifications for less than 56 days

A disqualification for less than 56 days is also more lenient in that it does not revoke the licence and cannot increase subsequent mandatory periods even if it is imposed under the points provisions.

Reduction for guilty plea

The precise amount of credit for a timely guilty plea will depend on the facts of each case. It should be given in respect of the fine or periods of community sentence or custody. An early guilty plea may also affect the length of a disqualification or the number of penalty points but cannot apply so as to reduce minimum mandatory periods of disqualification.

The multiple offender

Where an offender is convicted of several offences committed on one occasion, it is suggested that the court should concentrate on the most serious offence, carrying the greatest number of penalty points or period of disqualification.

The application of the totality principle may then result in the court deciding to impose no separate penalty for the lesser offences, or to reduce fines for these offences below the level which might normally be imposed.

Totting

Repeat offenders who reach 12 points or more within a period of three years become liable to a minimum disqualification for 6 months, and in some instances 12 months or 2 years – but must be given an opportunity to address the court and/or bring evidence to show why such disqualification should not be ordered or should be reduced. Totting disqualifications, unlike other disqualifications, erase all penalty points.

Totting disqualifications can be reduced or avoided for exceptional hardship or other circumstances. No account is to be taken of non-exceptional hardship or circumstances alleged to make the offence(s) not serious. No such ground can be used again to mitigate totting, if previously taken into account in totting mitigation within the three years preceding the conviction.

New drivers

Newly qualified drivers who incur 6 points or more during a two-year probationary period from the date of passing the driving test will automatically have their licence revoked by the Secretary of State and will have to apply for a provisional licence until they pass a repeat test. This total must include any points imposed prior to passing the test provided they are within three years.

Fixed penalties

If a fixed penalty was offered, the court should consider any reasons for not taking it up and, if valid, fine the amount of the appropriate fixed penalty (provided the amount is within the means of the offender), endorse if required, waive costs and allow a maximum of 28 days to pay. If a fixed penalty was refused or not offered, the court should consider whether there are aggravating factors which merit increasing the fine or there should be any credit for a guilty plea.

Appendix 3
The Criminal Procedure Rules 2005

PART 1 – THE OVERRIDING OBJECTIVE

1.1 The overriding objective

(1) The overriding objective of this new code is that criminal cases be dealt with justly.

(2) Dealing with a criminal case justly includes—

    (a) acquitting the innocent and convicting the guilty;

    (b) dealing with the prosecution and the defence fairly;

    (c) recognising the rights of a defendant, particularly those under Article 6 of the European Convention on Human Rights;

    (d) respecting the interests of witnesses, victims and jurors and keeping them informed of the progress of the case;

    (e) dealing with the case efficiently and expeditiously;

    (f) ensuring that appropriate information is available to the court when bail and sentence are considered; and

    (g) dealing with the case in ways that take into account—

        (i) the gravity of the offence alleged,

        (ii) the complexity of what is in issue,

        (iii) the severity of the consequences for the defendant and others affected, and

        (iv) the needs of other cases.

1.2 The duty of the participants in a criminal case

(1) Each participant, in the conduct of each case, must—

    (a) prepare and conduct the case in accordance with the overriding objective;

    (b) comply with these Rules, practice directions and directions made by the court; and

    (c) at once inform the court and all parties of any significant failure (whether or not that participant is responsible for that failure) to take any procedural step required by these Rules, any practice direction or any direction of the court. A failure is significant if it might hinder the court in furthering the overriding objective.

(2) Anyone involved in any way with a criminal case is a participant in its conduct for the purposes of this rule.

1.3 The application by the court of the overriding objective

The court must further the overriding objective in particular when—

(a) exercising any power given to it by legislation (including these Rules);

(b) applying any practice direction; or

(c) interpreting any rule or practice direction.

PART 3 — CASE MANAGEMENT

3.1 The scope of this Part

This Part applies to the management of each case in a magistrates' court and in the Crown Court (including an appeal to the Crown Court) until the conclusion of that case.

3.2 The duty of the court

(1) The court must further the overriding objective by actively managing the case.

(2)   Active case management includes—

    (a)   the early identification of the real issues;

    (b)   the early identification of the needs of witnesses;

    (c)   achieving certainty as to what must be done, by whom, and when, in particular by the early setting of a timetable for the progress of the case;

    (d)   monitoring the progress of the case and compliance with directions;

    (e)   ensuring that evidence, whether disputed or not, is presented in the shortest and clearest way;

    (f)   discouraging delay, dealing with as many aspects of the case as possible on the same occasion, and avoiding unnecessary hearings;

    (g)   encouraging the participants to co-operate in the progression of the case; and

    (h)   making use of technology.

(3)   The court must actively manage the case by giving any direction appropriate to the needs of that case as early as possible.

3.3   The duty of the parties

Each party must—

(a)   actively assist the court in fulfilling its duty under rule 3.2, without or if necessary with a direction; and

(b)   apply for a direction if needed to further the overriding objective.

3.4   Case progression officers and their duties

(1)   At the beginning of the case each party must, unless the court otherwise directs—

    (a)   nominate an individual responsible for progressing that case; and

    (b)   tell other parties and the court who he is and how to contact him.

(2)   In fulfilling its duty under rule 3.2, the court must where appropriate—

    (a)   nominate a court officer responsible for progressing the case; and

    (b)   make sure the parties know who he is and how to contact him.

(3)   In this Part a person nominated under this rule is called a case progression officer.

(4)   A case progression officer must—

    (a)   monitor compliance with directions;

    (b)   make sure that the court is kept informed of events that may affect the progress of that case;

    (c)   make sure that he can be contacted promptly about the case during ordinary business hours;

    (d)   act promptly and reasonably in response to communications about the case; and

    (e)   if he will be unavailable, appoint a substitute to fulfil his duties and inform the other case progression officers.

3.5   The court's case management powers

(1)   In fulfilling its duty under rule 3.2 the court may give any direction and take any step actively to manage a case unless that direction or step would be inconsistent with legislation, including these Rules.

(2)   In particular, the court may—

    (a)   nominate a judge, magistrate, justices' clerk or assistant to a justices' clerk to manage the case;

    (b)   give a direction on its own initiative or on application by a party;

    (c)   ask or allow a party to propose a direction;

    (d)   for the purpose of giving directions, receive applications and representations by letter, by telephone or by any other means of electronic communication, and conduct a hearing by such means;

    (e)   give a direction without a hearing;

    (f)   fix, postpone, bring forward, extend or cancel a hearing;

(g)   shorten or extend (even after it has expired) a time limit fixed by a direction;

(h)   require that issues in the case should be determined separately, and decide in what order they will be determined; and

(i)   specify the consequences of failing to comply with a direction.

(3)   A magistrates' court may give a direction that will apply in the Crown Court if the case is to continue there.

(4)   The Crown Court may give a direction that will apply in a magistrates' court if the case is to continue there.

(5)   Any power to give a direction under this Part includes a power to vary or revoke that direction.

3.6   Application to vary a direction

(1)   A party may apply to vary a direction if—

(a)   the court gave it without a hearing;

(b)   the court gave it at a hearing in his absence; or

(c)   circumstances have changed.

(2)   A party who applies to vary a direction must—

(a)   apply as soon as practicable after he becomes aware of the grounds for doing so; and

(b)   give as much notice to the other parties as the nature and urgency of his application permits.

3.7   Agreement to vary a time limit fixed by a direction

(1)   The parties may agree to vary a time limit fixed by a direction, but only if—

(a)   the variation will not—

(i)   affect the date of any hearing that has been fixed, or

(ii)   significantly affect the progress of the case in any other way;

(b)   the court has not prohibited variation by agreement; and

(c)   the court's case progression officer is promptly informed.

(2)   The court's case progression officer must refer the agreement to the court if he doubts the condition in paragraph (1)(a) is satisfied.

3.8   Case preparation and progression

(1)   At every hearing, if a case cannot be concluded there and then the court must give directions so that it can be concluded at the next hearing or as soon as possible after that.

(2)   At every hearing the court must, where relevant—

(a)   if the defendant is absent, decide whether to proceed nonetheless;

(b)   take the defendant's plea (unless already done) or if no plea can be taken then find out whether the defendant is likely to plead guilty or not guilty;

(c)   set, follow or revise a timetable for the progress of the case, which may include a timetable for any hearing including the trial or (in the Crown Court) the appeal;

(d)   in giving directions, ensure continuity in relation to the court and to the parties' representatives where that is appropriate and practicable; and

(e)   where a direction has not been complied with, find out why, identify who was responsible, and take appropriate action.

3.9   Readiness for trial or appeal

(1)   This rule applies to a party's preparation for trial or (in the Crown Court) appeal, and in this rule and rule 3.10 trial includes any hearing at which evidence will be introduced.

(2)   In fulfilling his duty under rule 3.3, each party must—

(a)   comply with directions given by the court;

(b)   take every reasonable step to make sure his witnesses will attend when they are needed;

(c)   make appropriate arrangements to present any written or other material; and

(d)   promptly inform the court and the other parties of anything that may—

(i)   affect the date or duration of the trial or appeal, or

(ii)   significantly affect the progress of the case in any other way.

(3)   The court may require a party to give a certificate of readiness.

3.10   Conduct of a trial or an appeal

In order to manage the trial or (in the Crown Court) appeal, the court may require a party to identify—

(a)   which witnesses he intends to give oral evidence;

(b)   the order in which he intends those witnesses to give their evidence;

(c)   whether he requires an order compelling the attendance of a witness;

(d)   what arrangements, if any, he proposes to facilitate the giving of evidence by a witness;

(e)   what arrangements, if any, he proposes to facilitate the participation of any other person, including the defendant;

(f)   what written evidence he intends to introduce;

(g)   what other material, if any, he intends to make available to the court in the presentation of the case;

(h)   whether he intends to raise any point of law that could affect the conduct of the trial or appeal; and

(i)   what timetable he proposes and expects to follow.

3.11   Case management forms and records

(1)   The case management forms set out in the Practice Direction must be used, and where there is no form then no specific formality is required.

(2)   The court must make available to the parties a record of directions given.

PART 12 — SENDING FOR TRIAL

12.1   Documents to be sent to the Crown Court

(1)   As soon as practicable after any person is sent for trial (pursuant to section 51 of the Crime and Disorder Act 1998), and in any event within 4 days from the date on which he is sent (not counting Saturdays, Sundays, Good Friday, Christmas Day or Bank Holidays), the magistrates' court officer shall, subject to section 7 of the Prosecution of Offences Act 1985 (which relates to the sending of documents and things to the Director of Public Prosecutions), send to the Crown Court officer—

(a)   the information, if it is in writing;

(b)   the notice required by section 51(7) of the 1998 Act;

(c)   a copy of the record made in pursuance of section 5 of the Bail Act 1976 relating to the granting or withholding of bail in respect of the accused on the occasion of the sending;

(d)   any recognizance entered into by any person as surety for the accused together with any enlargement thereof under section 129(4) of the Magistrates' Courts Act 1980;

(e)   the names and addresses of any interpreters engaged for the defendant for the purposes of the appearance in the magistrates' court, together with any telephone numbers at which they can be readily contacted, and details of the languages or dialects in connection with which they have been so engaged;

(f)   if any person under the age of 18 is concerned in the proceedings, a statement whether the magistrates' court has given a direction under section 39 of the Children and Young Persons Act 1933 (prohibition of publication of certain matter in newspapers);

(g) a copy of any representation order previously made in the case;

(h) a copy of any application for a representation order previously made in the case which has been refused; and

(i) any documents relating to an appeal by the prosecution against the granting of bail.

(2) The period of 4 days specified in paragraph (1) may be extended in relation to any sending for trial for so long as the Crown Court officer directs, having regard to any relevant circumstances.

12.2 Time for first appearance of accused sent for trial

A Crown Court officer to whom notice has been given under section 51(7) of the Crime and Disorder Act 1998, shall list the first Crown Court appearance of the person to whom the notice relates in accordance with any directions given by the magistrates' court.

PART 13 — DISMISSAL OF CHARGES TRANSFERRED OR SENT TO THE CROWN COURT

13.1 Interpretation of this Part

In this Part:

'notice of transfer' means a notice referred to in section 4(1) of the Criminal Justice Act 1987 or section 53(1) of the Criminal Justice Act 1991; and

'the prosecution' means the authority by or on behalf of whom notice of transfer was given under the 1987 or 1991 Acts, or the authority by or on behalf of whom documents were served under paragraph 1 of Schedule 3 to the Crime and Disorder Act 1998.

13.2 Written notice of oral application for dismissal

(1) Where notice of transfer has been given under the Criminal Justice Act 1987 or the Criminal Justice Act 1991, or a person has been sent for trial under the Crime and Disorder Act 1998, and the person concerned proposes to apply orally—

(a) under section 6(1) of the 1987 Act;

(b) under paragraph 5(1) of Schedule 6 to the 1991 Act; or

(c) under paragraph 2(1) of Schedule 3 to the 1998 Act

for any charge in the case to be dismissed, he shall give notice of his intention in writing to the Crown Court officer at the place specified by the notice of transfer under the 1987 or 1991 Acts or the notice given under section 51(7) of the 1998 Act as the proposed place of trial. Notice of intention to make an application under the 1987 or 1991 Acts shall be in the form set out in the Practice Direction.

(2) Notice of intention to make an application shall be given—

(a) in the case of an application to dismiss charges transferred under the 1987 Act, not later than 28 days after the day on which notice of transfer was given;

(b) in the case of an application to dismiss charges transferred under the 1991 Act, not later than 14 days after the day on which notice of transfer was given; and

(c) in the case of an application to dismiss charges sent under the 1998 Act, not later than 14 days after the day on which the documents were served under paragraph 1 of Schedule 3 to that Act,

and a copy of the notice shall be given at the same time to the prosecution and to any person to whom the notice of transfer relates or with whom the applicant for dismissal is jointly charged.

(3) The time for giving notice may be extended, either before or after it expires, by the Crown Court, on an application made in accordance with paragraph (4).

(4) An application for an extension of time for giving notice shall be made in writing to the Crown Court officer, and a copy thereof shall be given at the same time to the prosecution and to any other person to whom the notice of transfer relates or with whom the applicant for dismissal is jointly charged. Such an application made in

proceedings under the 1987 or 1991 Acts shall be in the form set out in the Practice Direction.

(5)   The Crown Court officer shall give notice in the form set out in the Practice Direction of the judge's decision on an application under paragraph (3)—

(a)   to the applicant for dismissal;

(b)   to the prosecution; and

(c)   to any other person to whom the notice of transfer relates or with whom the applicant for dismissal is jointly charged.

(6)   A notice of intention to make an application under section 6(1) of the 1987 Act, paragraph 5(1) of Schedule 6 to the 1991 Act or paragraph 2(1) of Schedule 3 to the 1998 Act shall be accompanied by a copy of any material on which the applicant relies and shall—

(a)   specify the charge or charges to which it relates;

(b)   state whether the leave of the judge is sought under section 6(3) of the 1987 Act, paragraph 5(4) of Schedule 6 to the 1991 Act or paragraph 2(4) of Schedule 3 to the 1998 Act to adduce oral evidence on the application, indicating what witnesses it is proposed to call at the hearing; and

(c)   in the case of a transfer under the 1991 Act, confirm in relation to each such witness that he is not a child to whom paragraph 5(5) of Schedule 6 to that Act applies.

(7)   Where leave is sought from the judge for oral evidence to be given on an application, notice of his decision, indicating what witnesses are to be called if leave is granted, shall be given in writing by the Crown Court officer to the applicant for dismissal, the prosecution and to any other person to whom the notice of transfer relates or with whom the applicant for dismissal is jointly charged. Notice of a decision in proceedings under the 1987 or 1991 Acts shall be in the form set out in the Practice Direction.

(8)   Where an application for dismissal under section 6(1) of the 1987 Act, paragraph 5(1) of Schedule 6 to the 1991 Act or paragraph 2(1) of Schedule 3 to the 1998 Act is to be made orally, the Crown Court officer shall list the application for hearing before a judge of the Crown Court and the prosecution shall be given the opportunity to be represented at the hearing.

13.3 Written application for dismissal

(1)   Application may be made for dismissal under section 6(1) of the Criminal Justice Act 1987, paragraph 5(1) of Schedule 6 to the Criminal Justice Act 1991 or paragraph 2(1) of Schedule 3 to the Crime and Disorder Act 1998 without an oral hearing. Such an application shall be in writing, and in proceedings under the 1987 or 1991 Acts shall be in the form set out in the Practice Direction.

(2)   The application shall be sent to the Crown Court officer and shall be accompanied by a copy of any statement or other document, and identify any article, on which the applicant for dismissal relies.

(3)   A copy of the application and of any accompanying documents shall be given at the same time to the prosecution and to any other person to whom the notice of transfer relates or with whom the applicant for dismissal is jointly charged.

(4)   A written application for dismissal shall be made—

(a)   not later than 28 days after the day on which notice of transfer was given under the 1987 Act;

(b)   not later than 14 days after the day on which notice of transfer was given under the 1991 Act; or

(c)   not later than 14 days after the day on which documents required by paragraph 1 of Schedule 3 to the 1998 Act were served

unless the time for making the application is extended, either before or after it expires, by the Crown Court; and rule 13.2(4) and (5) shall apply for the purposes of this paragraph as if references therein to giving notice of intention to make an oral application were references to making a written application under this rule.

13.4 Prosecution reply

(1) Not later than seven days from the date of service of notice of intention to apply orally for the dismissal of any charge contained in a notice of transfer or based on documents served under paragraph 1 of Schedule 3 to the Crime and Disorder Act 1998, the prosecution may apply to the Crown Court under section 6(3) of the Criminal Justice Act 1987, paragraph 5(4) of Schedule 6 to the Criminal Justice Act 1991 or paragraph 2(4) of Schedule 3 to the 1998 Act for leave to adduce oral evidence at the hearing of the application, indicating what witnesses it is proposed to call.

(2) Not later than seven days from the date of receiving a copy of an application for dismissal under rule 13.3, the prosecution may apply to the Crown Court for an oral hearing of the application.

(3) An application under paragraph (1) or (2) shall be served on the Crown Court officer in writing and, in the case of an application under paragraph (2), shall state whether the leave of the judge is sought to adduce oral evidence and, if so, shall indicate what witnesses it is proposed to call. Where leave is sought to adduce oral evidence under paragraph 5(4) of Schedule 6 to the 1991 Act, the application should confirm in relation to each such witness that he is not a child to whom paragraph 5(5) of that Schedule applies. Such an application in proceedings under the 1987 or 1991 Acts shall be in the form set out in the Practice Direction.

(4) Notice of the judge's determination upon an application under paragraph (1) or (2), indicating what witnesses (if any) are to be called shall be served in writing by the Crown Court officer on the prosecution, on the applicant for dismissal and on any other party to whom the notice of transfer relates or with whom the applicant for dismissal is jointly charged. Such a notice in proceedings under the 1987 or 1991 Acts shall be in the form set out in the Practice Direction.

(5) Where, having received the material specified in rule 13.2 or, as the case may be, rule 13.3, the prosecution proposes to adduce in reply thereto any written comments or any further evidence, the prosecution shall serve any such comments, copies of the statements or other documents outlining the evidence of any proposed witnesses, copies of any further documents and, in the case of an application to dismiss charges transferred under the 1991 Act, copies of any video recordings which it is proposed to tender in evidence, on the Crown Court officer not later than 14 days from the date of receiving the said material, and shall at the same time serve copies thereof on the applicant for dismissal and any other person to whom the notice of transfer relates or with whom the applicant is jointly charged. In the case of a defendant acting in person, copies of video recordings need not be served but shall be made available for viewing by him.

(6) The time for—

    (a) making an application under paragraph (1) or (2) above; or

    (b) serving any material on the Crown Court officer under paragraph (5) above

    may be extended, either before or after it expires, by the Crown Court, on an application made in accordance with paragraph (7) below.

(7) An application for an extension of time under paragraph (6) above shall be made in writing and shall be served on the Crown Court officer, and a copy thereof shall be served at the same time on to the applicant for dismissal and on any other person to whom the notice of transfer relates or with whom the applicant for dismissal is jointly charged. Such an application in proceedings under the 1987 or 1991 Acts shall be in the form set out in the Practice Direction.

13.5 Determination of applications for dismissal—procedural matters

(1) A judge may grant leave for a witness to give oral evidence on an application for dismissal notwithstanding that notice of intention to call the witness has not been given in accordance with the foregoing provisions of this Part.

(2) Where an application for dismissal is determined otherwise than at an oral hearing, the Crown Court officer shall as soon as practicable, send to all the parties to the case

written notice of the outcome of the application. Such a notice in proceedings under the 1987 and 1991 Acts shall be in the form set out in the Practice Direction.

13.6   Service of documents

(1)   Any notice or other document which is required by this Part to be given to any person may be served personally on that person or sent to him by post at his usual or last known residence or place of business in England and Wales or, in the case of a company, at the company's registered office in England or Wales.

(2)   If the person to be served is acting by a solicitor, the notice or other document may be served by delivering it, or sending it by post, to the solicitor's address for service.

PART 14 — THE INDICTMENT

14.1   Method of preferring an indictment

Subject as hereinafter provided, a bill of indictment shall be preferred before the Crown Court by delivering the bill to the Crown Court officer:

Provided that where with the assent of the prosecutor the bill is prepared by, or under the supervision of, the court officer it shall not be necessary for the bill to be delivered to the court officer, but as soon as it has been settled to his satisfaction it shall be deemed to have been duly preferred.

14.2   Time for preferring an indictment

(1)   Subject to the provisions of this Part, a bill of indictment shall be preferred—

(a)   where a defendant has been committed for trial, within a period of 28 days commencing with the date of committal;

(b)   where a notice of transfer has been given under section 4 of the Criminal Justice Act 1987 (serious fraud), within a period of 28 days commencing with the date on which notice is given;

(c)   where a notice of transfer has been served under section 53 of the Criminal Justice Act 1991 (certain cases involving children), within a period of 28 days commencing with the date on which notice is served; and

(d)   where a person is sent for trial under section 51 of the Crime and Disorder Act 1998, within a period of 28 days commencing with the date on which copies of the documents containing the evidence on which the charge or charges are based are served under paragraph 1 of Schedule 3 to that Act .

(2)   The period referred to in paragraph (1) may, on the application of the person preferring the bill of indictment or otherwise, be extended by a judge of the Crown Court before or after it has expired; and any period so extended may be further extended in like manner.

(3)   Notwithstanding paragraph (2), the first extension of the period may be granted by the Crown Court officer provided that the period of the extension does not exceed 28 days; but if the court officer is of the opinion that the first extension of the period should not be granted, he shall refer the application to a judge of the Crown Court who shall determine the application himself.

(4)   An application under paragraph (2) above shall—

(a)   be in writing unless a judge of the Crown Court otherwise directs; and

(b)   include a statement of the reasons why an extension of the period referred to in paragraph (1) is necessary.

(5)   Where an application under paragraph (2) is made after the expiry of the period referred to in paragraph (1) or, as the case may be, the expiry of that period as extended under paragraph (2), the application shall in addition include a statement of the reasons why the application was not made before the expiry of the period or, as the case may be, the extended period.

14.3 Committal documents to be made available to person wishing to prefer an indictment

It shall be the duty of any person in charge of any committal documents to give to any person desiring to make an application for leave to prefer a bill of indictment against a person in respect of whom committal proceedings have taken place, a reasonable opportunity to inspect the committal documents and, if so required by him, to supply him with copies of the documents or any part thereof.

PART 15 — PREPARATORY HEARINGS IN CASES OF SERIOUS FRAUD AND OTHER COMPLEX, SERIOUS OR LENGTHY CASES IN THE CROWN COURT

15.1 Application for a preparatory hearing

(1) A party who wants the court to order a preparatory hearing under section 7(2) of the Criminal Justice Act 1987 or under section 29(4) of the Criminal Procedure and Investigations Act 1996 must –

   (a) apply in the form set out in the Practice Direction;

   (b) include a short explanation of the reasons for applying; and

   (c) serve the application on the court officer and all other parties.

(2) A prosecutor who wants the court to order that the trial will be conducted without a jury under section 43 or section 44 of the Criminal Justice Act 2003 must apply under this rule for a preparatory hearing, whether or not the defendant has applied for one.

15.2 Time for applying for a preparatory hearing

(1) A party who applies under rule 15.1 must do so not more than 28 days after—

   (a) the committal of the defendant;

   (b) the consent to the preferment of a bill of indictment in relation to the case;

   (c) the service of a notice of transfer; or

   (d) where a person is sent for trial, the service of copies of the documents containing the evidence on which the charge or charges are based.

(2) A prosecutor who applies under rule 15.1 because he wants the court to order a trial without a jury under section 44 of the Criminal Justice Act 2003 (jury tampering) must do so as soon as reasonably practicable where the reasons do not arise until after that time limit has expired.

(3) The court may extend the time limit, even after it has expired.

15.3 Representations concerning an application

(1) A party who wants to make written representations concerning an application made under rule 15.1 must –

   (a) do so within 7 days of receiving a copy of that application; and

   (b) serve those representations on the court officer and all other parties.

(2) A defendant who wants to oppose an application for an order that the trial will be conducted without a jury under section 43 or section 44 of the Criminal Justice Act 2003 must serve written representations under this rule, including a short explanation of the reasons for opposing that application.

15.4 Determination of an application

(1) Where an application has been made under rule 15.1(2), the court must hold a preparatory hearing for the purpose of determining whether to make an order that the trial will be conducted without a jury under section 43 or section 44 of the Criminal Justice Act 2003.

(2) Other applications made under rule 15.1 should normally be determined without a hearing.

(3) The court officer must serve on the parties in the case, in the form set out in the Practice Direction –

   (a) notice of the determination of an application made under rule 15.1; and

(b)   an order for a preparatory hearing made by the court of its own initiative, including one that the court is required to make.

15.5   Orders for disclosure by prosecution or defence

(1)   Any disclosure order under section 9 of the Criminal Justice Act 1987, or section 31 of the Criminal Procedure and Investigations Act 1996, must identify any documents that are required to be prepared and served by the prosecutor under that order.

(2)   A disclosure order under either of those sections does not require a defendant to disclose who will give evidence, except to the extent that disclosure is required –

(a)   by section 6A(2) of the 1996 Act (disclosure of alibi); or

(b)   by Part 24 of these Rules (disclosure of expert evidence).

(3)   The court officer must serve notice of the order, in the relevant form set out in the Practice Direction, on the parties.

15.6   Service

(1)   For the purposes of this Part, a notice or document may be served on any person by any of the following methods—

(a)   personally on that person or their solicitor;

(b)   by first class post to, or by leaving it at—

(i)   that person's usual or last known residence or place of business in England and Wales,

(ii)   in the case of a company, that company's registered address in England and Wales, or

(iii)   the business address of that person's solicitor;

(c)   by fax or other electronic means, but only if the person has agreed to accept service by that method;

(d)   where the person or their solicitor has given a number of a box at a document exchange and has not indicated that they are unwilling to accept service through a document exchange, by leaving it at the document exchange addressed to the box number.

(2)   Where a document or notice is served under this Part by any method other than personal service it is deemed to be served—

(a)   if left at an address, on the next business day after the day on which it was left;

(b)   if sent by first class post, on the second business day after the day on which it was posted;

(c)   if transmitted by fax or other electronic means—

(i)   on a business day before 5 p.m., on that day, and

(ii)   at any other time, on the next business day after the day on which it is transmitted; and

(d)   if left at a document exchange, on the second business day after the day on which it was left.

(3)   In this rule, 'business day' means any day other than a Saturday, Sunday, Christmas Day, Good Friday or a bank holiday.

PART 19 — BAIL IN MAGISTRATES' COURTS AND THE CROWN COURT

19.1   Application to a magistrates' court to vary conditions of police bail

(1)   An application under section 43B(1) of the Magistrates' Courts Act of 1980 shall—

(a)   be made in writing;

(b)   contain a statement of the grounds upon which it is made;

(c)   specify the offence with which the applicant was charged before his release on bail;

(d)   specify, or be accompanied by a copy of the note of, the reasons given by the custody officer for imposing or varying the conditions of bail; and

(e)   specify the name and address of any surety provided by the applicant before his release on bail to secure his surrender to custody.

(2)   Any such application shall be sent to the court officer for—

(a)   the magistrates' court (if any) appointed by the custody officer as the court before which the applicant has a duty to appear; or

(b)   if no such court has been appointed, a magistrates' court acting for the local justice area in which the police station at which the applicant was granted bail or at which the conditions of his bail were varied, as the case may be, is situated,

and, in either case, a copy shall be sent to a custody officer appointed for that police station.

(3)   The court officer to whom an application is sent under paragraph (2) above shall send a notice in writing of the date, time and place fixed for the hearing of the application to—

(a)   the applicant;

(b)   the prosecutor; and

(c)   any surety in connection with bail in criminal proceedings granted to, or the conditions of which were varied by a custody officer in relation to, the applicant.

(4)   The time fixed for the hearing shall be not later than 72 hours after receipt of the application. In reckoning for the purposes of this paragraph any period of 72 hours, no account shall be taken of Christmas Day, Good Friday, any bank holiday, or any Saturday or Sunday.

(5)   Any notice required by this rule to be sent to any person shall either be delivered to him or be sent by post in a letter and, if sent by post to the applicant or a surety of his, shall be addressed to him at his last known or usual place of abode.

(6)   If the magistrates' court hearing an application under section 43B(1) of the 1980 Act discharges or enlarges any recognizance entered into by any surety or increases or reduces the amount in which that person is bound, the court officer shall forthwith give notice thereof to the applicant and to any such surety.

(7)   In this rule, 'the applicant' means the person making an application under section 43B(1) of the 1980 Act.

19.2   Application to a magistrates' court to reconsider grant of police bail

(1)   The appropriate court for the purposes of section 5B of the Bail Act 1976 in relation to the decision of a constable to grant bail shall be—

(a)   the magistrates' court (if any) appointed by the custody officer as the court before which the person to whom bail was granted has a duty to appear; or

(b)   if no such court has been appointed, a magistrates' court acting for the local justice area in which the police station at which bail was granted is situated.

(2)   An application under section 5B(1) of the 1976 Act shall—

(a)   be made in writing;

(b)   contain a statement of the grounds on which it is made;

(c)   specify the offence which the proceedings in which bail was granted were connected with, or for;

(d)   specify the decision to be reconsidered (including any conditions of bail which have been imposed and why they have been imposed); and

(e)   specify the name and address of any surety provided by the person to whom the application relates to secure his surrender to custody.

(3)   Where an application has been made to a magistrates' court under section 5B of the 1976 Act,

(a)   the clerk of that magistrates' court shall fix a date, time and place for the hearing of the application; and

(b)   the court officer shall—

(i)   give notice of the application and of the date, time and place so fixed to the person affected, and

(ii)   send a copy of the notice to the prosecutor who made the application and to any surety specified in the application.

(4)   The time fixed for the hearing shall be not later than 72 hours after receipt of the application. In reckoning for the purpose of this paragraph any period of 72 hours, no account shall be taken of Christmas Day, Good Friday, any bank holiday or any Sunday.

(5)   Service of a notice to be given under paragraph (3) to the person affected may be effected by delivering it to him.

(6)   At the hearing of an application under section 5B of the 1976 Act the court shall consider any representations made by the person affected (whether in writing or orally) before taking any decision under that section with respect to him; and, where the person affected does not appear before the court, the court shall not take such a decision unless it is proved to the satisfaction of the court, on oath or in the manner set out by rule 4.2(1), that the notice required to be given under paragraph (3) of this rule was served on him before the hearing.

(7)   Where the court proceeds in the absence of the person affected in accordance with paragraph (6)—

(a)   if the decision of the court is to vary the conditions of bail or impose conditions in respect of bail which has been granted unconditionally, the court officer shall notify the person affected;

(b)   if the decision of the court is to withhold bail, the order of the court under section 5B(5)(b) of the 1976 Act (surrender to custody) shall be signed by the justice issuing it or state his name and be authenticated by the signature of the clerk of the court.

(8)   Service of any of the documents referred to in paragraph (7) may be effected by delivering it to the person to whom it is directed or by leaving it for him with some person at his last known or usual place of abode.

19.3   Notice of change of time for appearance before magistrates' court

Where—

(a)   a person has been granted bail under the Police and Criminal Evidence Act 1984 (4) subject to a duty to appear before a magistrates' court and the court before which he is to appear appoints a later time at which he is to appear; or

(b)   a magistrates' court further remands a person on bail under section 129 of the Magistrates' Courts Act 1980 in his absence,

it shall give him and his sureties, if any, notice thereof.

19.4   Directions by a magistrates' court as to security, etc

Where a magistrates' court, under section 3(5) or (6) of the Bail Act 1976, imposes any requirement to be complied with before a person's release on bail, the court may give directions as to the manner in which and the person or persons before whom the requirement may be complied with.

19.5   Requirements to be complied with before release on bail granted by a magistrates' court

(1)   Where a magistrates' court has fixed the amount in which a person (including any surety) is to be bound by a recognizance, the recognizance may be entered into—

(a)   in the case of a surety where the accused is in a prison or other place of detention, before the governor or keeper of the prison or place as well as before the persons mentioned in section 8(4)(a) of the Bail Act 1976;

(b)   in any other case, before a justice of the peace, a justices' clerk, a magistrates' court officer, a police officer who either is of the rank of inspector or above or is in charge of a police station or, if the person to be bound is in a prison or other place of detention, before the governor or keeper of the prison or place; or

(c) where a person other than a police officer is authorised under section 125A or 125B of the Magistrates' Courts Act 1980 to execute a warrant of arrest providing for a recognizance to be entered into by the person arrested (but not by any other person), before the person executing the warrant.

(2) The court officer for a magistrates' court which has fixed the amount in which a person (including any surety) is to be bound by a recognizance or, under section 3(5), (6) or (6A) of the 1976 Act (8) imposed any requirement to be complied with before a person's release on bail or any condition of bail shall issue a certificate showing the amount and conditions, if any, of the recognizance, or as the case may be, containing a statement of the requirement or condition of bail; and a person authorised to take the recognizance or do anything in relation to the compliance with such requirement or condition of bail shall not be required to take or do it without production of such a certificate as aforesaid.

(3) If any person proposed as a surety for a person committed to custody by a magistrates' court produces to the governor or keeper of the prison or other place of detention in which the person so committed is detained a certificate to the effect that he is acceptable as a surety, signed by any of the justices composing the court or the clerk of the court and signed in the margin by the person proposed as surety, the governor or keeper shall take the recognizance of the person so proposed.

(4) Where the recognizance of any person committed to custody by a magistrates' court or of any surety of such a person is taken by any person other than the court which committed the first-mentioned person to custody, the person taking the recognizance shall send it to the court officer for that court:

Provided that, in the case of a surety, if the person committed has been committed to the Crown Court for trial or under any of the enactments mentioned in rule 43.1(1), the person taking the recognizance shall send it to the Crown Court officer.

19.6 Notice to governor of prison, etc, where release from custody is ordered by a magistrates' court

Where a magistrates' court has, with a view to the release on bail of a person in custody, fixed the amount in which he or any surety of such a person shall be bound or, under section 3(5), (6) or (6A) of the Bail Act 1976, imposed any requirement to be complied with before his release or any condition of bail—

(a) the magistrates' court officer shall give notice thereof to the governor or keeper of the prison or place where that person is detained by sending him such a certificate as is mentioned in rule 19.5(2); and

(b) any person authorised to take the recognizance of a surety or do anything in relation to the compliance with such requirement shall, on taking or doing it, send notice thereof by post to the said governor or keeper and, in the case of a recognizance of a surety, shall give a copy of the notice to the surety.

19.7 Release when notice received by governor of prison that recognizances have been taken or requirements complied with

Where a magistrates' court has, with a view to the release on bail of a person in custody, fixed the amount in which he or any surety of such a person shall be bound or, under section 3(5) or (6) of the Bail Act 1976, imposed any requirement to be complied with before his release and given notice thereof in accordance with this Part to the governor or keeper of the prison or place where that person is detained, the governor or keeper shall, when satisfied that the recognizances of all sureties required have been taken and that all such requirements have been complied with, and unless he is in custody for some other cause, release him.

19.8 Notice from a magistrates' court of enlargement of recognizances

(1) If a magistrates' court before which any person is bound by a recognizance to appear enlarges the recognizance to a later time under section 129 of the Magistrates' Courts Act 1980 in his absence, it shall give him and his sureties, if any, notice thereof.

(2)   If a magistrates' court, under section 129(4) of the 1980 Act, enlarges the recognizance of a surety for a person committed for trial on bail, it shall give the surety notice thereof.

19.9   Further remand of minors by a youth court

Where a child or young person has been remanded, and the period of remand is extended in his absence in accordance with section 48 of the Children and Young Persons Act 1933, notice shall be given to him and his sureties (if any) of the date at which he will be required to appear before the court.

19.10   Notes of argument in magistrates' court bail hearings

Where a magistrates' court hears full argument as to bail, the clerk of the court shall take a note of that argument.

19.11   Bail records to be entered in register of magistrates' court

Any record required by section 5 of the Bail Act 1976 to be made by a magistrates' court (together with any note of reasons required by section 5(4) to be included and the particulars set out in any certificate granted under section 5(6A)) shall be made by way of an entry in the register.

19.12   Notification of bail decision by magistrate after arrest while on bail

Where a person who has been released on bail and is under a duty to surrender into the custody of a court is brought under section 7(4)(a) of the Bail Act 1976 before a justice of the peace, the justice shall cause a copy of the record made in pursuance of section 5 of that Act relating to his decision under section 7(5) of that Act in respect of that person to be sent to the court officer for that court:

Provided that this rule shall not apply where the court is a magistrates' court acting for the same local justice area as that for which the justice acts.

19.13   Transfer of remand hearings

(1)   Where a magistrates' court, under section 130(1) of the Magistrates' Courts Act 1980, orders that an accused who has been remanded in custody be brought up for any subsequent remands before an alternate magistrates' court, the court officer for the first-mentioned court shall, as soon as practicable after the making of the order and in any case within 2 days thereafter (not counting Sundays, Good Friday, Christmas Day or bank holidays), send to the court officer for the alternate court—

(a)   a statement indicating the offence or offences charged;

(b)   a copy of the record made by the first-mentioned court in pursuance of section 5 of the Bail Act 1976 relating to the withholding of bail in respect of the accused when he was last remanded in custody;

(c)   a copy of any representation order previously made in the same case;

(d)   a copy of any application for a representation order;

(e)   if the first-mentioned court has made an order under section 8(2) of the 1980 Act (removal of restrictions on reports of committal proceedings), a statement to that effect.

(f)   a statement indicating whether or not the accused has a solicitor acting for him in the case and has consented to the hearing and determination in his absence of any application for his remand on an adjournment of the case under sections 5, 10(1) and 18(4) of the 1980 Act together with a statement indicating whether or not that consent has been withdrawn;

(g)   a statement indicating the occasions, if any, on which the accused has been remanded under section 128(3A) of the 1980 Act without being brought before the first-mentioned court; and

(h)   if the first-mentioned court remands the accused under section 128A of the 1980 Act on the occasion upon which it makes the order under section 130(1) of that Act, a statement indicating the date set under section 128A(2) of that Act.

(2) Where the first-mentioned court is satisfied as mentioned in section 128(3A) of the 1980 Act, paragraph (1) shall have effect as if for the words 'an accused who has been remanded in custody be brought up for any subsequent remands before' there were substituted the words 'applications for any subsequent remands of the accused be made to'.

(3) The court officer for an alternate magistrates' court before which an accused who has been remanded in custody is brought up for any subsequent remands in pursuance of an order made as aforesaid shall, as soon as practicable after the order ceases to be in force and in any case within 2 days thereafter (not counting Sundays, Good Friday, Christmas Day or bank holidays), send to the court officer for the magistrates' court which made the order—

(a) a copy of the record made by the alternate court in pursuance of section 5 of the 1976 Act relating to the grant or withholding of bail in respect of the accused when he was last remanded in custody or on bail;

(b) a copy of any representation order made by the alternate court;

(c) a copy of any application for a representation order made to the alternate court;

(d) if the alternate court has made an order under section 8(2) of the 1980 Act (removal of restrictions on reports of committal proceedings), a statement to that effect;

(e) a statement indicating whether or not the accused has a solicitor acting for him in the case and has consented to the hearing and determination in his absence of any application for his remand on an adjournment of the case under sections 5, 10(1) and 18(4) of the 1980 Act together with a statement indicating whether or not that consent has been withdrawn; and

(f) a statement indicating the occasions, if any, on which the accused has been remanded by the alternate court under section 128(3A) of the 1980 Act without being brought before that court.

(4) Where the alternate court is satisfied as mentioned in section 128(3A) of the 1980 Act paragraph (2) above shall have effect as if for the words 'an accused who has been remanded in custody is brought up for any subsequent remands' there shall be substituted the words 'applications for the further remand of the accused are to be made'.

19.14 Notice of further remand in certain cases

Where a transfer direction has been given by the Secretary of State under section 47 of the Mental Health Act 1983 in respect of a person remanded in custody by a magistrates' court and the direction has not ceased to have effect, the court officer shall give notice in writing to the managers of the hospital where he is detained of any further remand under section 128 of the Magistrates' Courts Act 1980.

19.15 Cessation of transfer direction

Where a magistrates' court directs, under section 52(5) of the Mental Health Act 1983, that a transfer direction given by the Secretary of State under section 48 of that Act in respect of a person remanded in custody by a magistrates' court shall cease to have effect, the court officer shall give notice in writing of the court's direction to the managers of the hospital specified in the Secretary of State's direction and, where the period of remand has not expired or the person has been committed to the Crown Court for trial or to be otherwise dealt with, to the Governor of the prison to which persons of the sex of that person are committed by the court if remanded in custody or committed in custody for trial.

19.16 Lodging an appeal against a grant of bail by a magistrates' court

(1) Where the prosecution wishes to exercise the right of appeal, under section 1 of the Bail (Amendment) Act 1993, to a judge of the Crown Court against a decision to grant

bail, the oral notice of appeal must be given to the justices' clerk and to the person concerned, at the conclusion of the proceedings in which such bail was granted and before the release of the person concerned.

(2)   When oral notice of appeal is given, the justices' clerk shall announce in open court the time at which such notice was given.

(3)   A record of the prosecution's decision to appeal and the time the oral notice of appeal was given shall be made in the register and shall contain the particulars set out.

(4)   Where an oral notice of appeal has been given the court shall remand the person concerned in custody by a warrant of commitment.

(5)   On receipt of the written notice of appeal required by section 1(5) of the 1993 Act, the court shall remand the person concerned in custody by a warrant of commitment, until the appeal is determined or otherwise disposed of.

(6)   A record of the receipt of the written notice of appeal shall be made in the same manner as that of the oral notice of appeal under paragraph (3).

(7)   If, having given oral notice of appeal, the prosecution fails to serve a written notice of appeal within the two hour period referred to in section 1(5) of the 1993 Act the justices' clerk shall, as soon as practicable, by way of written notice (served by a court officer) to the persons in whose custody the person concerned is, direct the release of the person concerned on bail as granted by the magistrates' court and subject to any conditions which it imposed.

(8)   If the prosecution serves notice of abandonment of appeal on a court officer, the justices' clerk shall, forthwith, by way of written notice (served by the court officer) to the governor of the prison where the person concerned is being held, or the person responsible for any other establishment where such a person is being held, direct his release on bail as granted by the magistrates' court and subject to any conditions which it imposed.

(9)   A court officer shall record the prosecution's failure to serve a written notice of appeal, or its service of a notice of abandonment.

(10)   Where a written notice of appeal has been served on a magistrates' court officer, he shall provide as soon as practicable to a Crown Court officer a copy of that written notice, together with—

(a)   the notes of argument made by the court officer for the court under rule 19.10; and

(b)   a note of the date, or dates, when the person concerned is next due to appear in the magistrates' court, whether he is released on bail or remanded in custody by the Crown Court.

(11)   References in this rule to 'the person concerned' are references to such a person within the meaning of section 1 of the 1993 Act.

19.17   Crown Court procedure on appeal against grant of bail by a magistrates' court

(1)   This rule shall apply where the prosecution appeals under section 1 of the Bail (Amendment) Act 1993 against a decision of a magistrates' court granting bail and in this rule, 'the person concerned' has the same meaning as in that Act.

(2)   The written notice of appeal required by section 1(5) of the 1993 Act shall be in the form set out in the Practice Direction and shall be served on—

(a)   the magistrates' court officer; and

(b)   the person concerned.

(3)   The Crown Court officer shall enter the appeal and give notice of the time and place of the hearing to—

(a)   the prosecution;

(b)   the person concerned or his legal representative; and

(c)   the magistrates' court officer.

(4)   The person concerned shall not be entitled to be present at the hearing of the appeal unless he is acting in person or, in any other case of an exceptional nature, a judge of the Crown Court is of the opinion that the interests of justice require him to be present and gives him leave to be so.

(5)   Where a person concerned has not been able to instruct a solicitor to represent him at the appeal, he may give notice to the Crown Court requesting that the Official Solicitor shall represent him at the appeal, and the court may, if it thinks fit, assign the Official Solicitor to act for the person concerned accordingly.

(6)   At any time after the service of written notice of appeal under paragraph (2), the prosecution may abandon the appeal by giving notice in writing in the form set out in the Practice Direction.

(7)   The notice of abandonment required by the preceding paragraph shall be served on—

(a)   the person concerned or his legal representative;

(b)   the magistrates' court officer; and

(c)   the Crown Court officer.

(8)   Any record required by section 5 of the Bail Act 1976 (together with any note of reasons required by subsection (4) of that section to be included) shall be made by way of an entry in the file relating to the case in question and the record shall include the following particulars, namely—

(a)   the effect of the decision;

(b)   a statement of any condition imposed in respect of bail, indicating whether it is to be complied with before or after release on bail; and

(c)   where bail is withheld, a statement of the relevant exception to the right to bail (as provided in Schedule 1 to the 1976 Act) on which the decision is based.

(9)   The Crown Court officer shall, as soon as practicable after the hearing of the appeal, give notice of the decision and of the matters required by the preceding paragraph to be recorded to—

(a)   the person concerned or his legal representative;

(b)   the prosecution;

(c)   the police;

(d)   the magistrates' court officer; and

(e)   the governor of the prison or person responsible for the establishment where the person concerned is being held.

(10)   Where the judge hearing the appeal grants bail to the person concerned, the provisions of rule 19.18(9) (informing the Court of any earlier application for bail) and rule 19.22 (conditions attached to bail granted by the Crown Court) shall apply as if that person had applied to the Crown Court for bail.

(11)   In addition to the methods of service permitted by rule 4.3 (service of documents in Crown Court proceedings), the notices required by paragraphs (3), (5), (7) and (9) of this rule may be sent by way of facsimile transmission and the notice required by paragraph (3) may be given by telephone.

19.18   Applications to Crown Court relating to bail

(1)   This rule applies where an application to the Crown Court relating to bail is made otherwise than during the hearing of proceedings in the Crown Court.

(2)   Subject to paragraph (7) below, notice in writing of intention to make such an application to the Crown Court shall, at least 24 hours before it is made, be given to the prosecutor and if the prosecution is being carried on by the Crown Prosecution Service, to the appropriate Crown Prosecutor or, if the application is to be made by the prosecutor or a constable under section 3(8) of the Bail Act 1976, to the person to whom bail was granted.

(3)   On receiving notice under paragraph (2), the prosecutor or appropriate Crown Public Prosecutor or, as the case may be, the person to whom bail was granted shall—

(a)   notify the Crown Court officer and the applicant that he wishes to be represented at the hearing of the application;

(b)   notify the Crown Court officer and the applicant that he does not oppose the application; or

(c)   give to the Crown Court officer, for the consideration of the Crown Court, a written statement of his reasons for opposing the application, at the same time sending a copy of the statement to the applicant.

(4)   A notice under paragraph (2) shall be in the form set out in the Practice Direction or a form to the like effect, and the applicant shall give a copy of the notice to the Crown Court officer.

(5)   Except in the case of an application made by the prosecutor or a constable under section 3(8) of the 1976 Act, the applicant shall not be entitled to be present on the hearing of his application unless the Crown Court gives him leave to be present.

(6)   Where a person who is in custody or has been released on bail desires to make an application relating to bail and has not been able to instruct a solicitor to apply on his behalf under the preceding paragraphs of this rule, he may give notice in writing to the Crown Court of his desire to make an application relating to bail, requesting that the Official Solicitor shall act for him in the application, and the Court may, if it thinks fit, assign the Official Solicitor to act for the applicant accordingly.

(7)   Where the Official Solicitor has been so assigned the Crown Court may, if it thinks fit, dispense with the requirements of paragraph (2) and deal with the application in a summary manner.

(8)   Any record required by section 5 of the 1976 Act (together with any note of reasons required by section 5(4) to be included) shall be made by way of an entry in the file relating to the case in question and the record shall include the following particulars, namely—

(a)   the effect of the decision;

(b)   a statement of any condition imposed in respect of bail, indicating whether it is to be complied with before or after release on bail;

(c)   where conditions of bail are varied, a statement of the conditions as varied; and

(d)   where bail is withheld, a statement of the relevant exception to the right to bail (as provided in Schedule 1 to the 1976 Act) on which the decision is based.

(9)   Every person who makes an application to the Crown Court relating to bail shall inform the Court of any earlier application to the High Court or the Crown Court relating to bail in the course of the same proceedings.

19.19   Notice to governor of prison of committal on bail

(1)   Where the accused is committed or sent for trial on bail, a magistrates' court officer shall give notice thereof in writing to the governor of the prison to which persons of the sex of the person committed or sent are committed or sent by that court if committed or sent in custody for trial and also, if the person committed or sent is under 21, to the governor of the remand centre to which he would have been committed or sent if the court had refused him bail.

(2)   Where a corporation is committed or sent for trial, a magistrates' court officer shall give notice thereof to the governor of the prison to which would be committed or sent a man committed or sent by that court in custody for trial.

19.20   Notices on committal of person subject to transfer direction

Where a transfer direction has been given by the Secretary of State under section 48 of the Mental Health Act 1983 in respect of a person remanded in custody by a magistrates' court and, before the direction ceases to have effect, that person is committed or sent for trial, a magistrates' court officer shall give notice—

(a)   to the governor of the prison to which persons of the sex of that person are committed or sent by that court if committed or sent in custody for trial; and

(b)   to the managers of the hospital where he is detained.

19.21   Variation of arrangements for bail on committal to Crown Court

Where a magistrates' court has committed or sent a person on bail to the Crown Court for trial or under any of the enactments mentioned in rule 43.1(1) and subsequently varies any conditions of the bail or imposes any conditions in respect of the bail, the magistrates' court officer shall send to the Crown Court officer a copy of the record made in pursuance of section 5 of the Bail Act 1976 relating to such variation or imposition of conditions.

19.22　Conditions attached to bail granted by the Crown Court

(1)　Where the Crown Court grants bail, the recognizance of any surety required as a condition of bail may be entered into before an officer of the Crown Court or, where the person who has been granted bail is in a prison or other place of detention, before the governor or keeper of the prison or place as well as before the persons specified in section 8(4) of the Bail Act 1976.

(2)　Where the Crown Court under section 3(5) or (6) of the 1976 Act imposes a requirement to be complied with before a person's release on bail, the Court may give directions as to the manner in which and the person or persons before whom the requirement may be complied with.

(4)　A person who, in pursuance of an order made by the Crown Court for the grant of bail, proposes to enter into a recognizance or give security must, unless the Crown Court otherwise directs, give notice to the prosecutor at least 24 hours before he enters into the recognizance or gives security as aforesaid.

(5)　Where, in pursuance of an order of the Crown Court, a recognizance is entered into or any requirement imposed under section 3(5) or (6) of the 1976 Act is complied with (being a requirement to be complied with before a person's release on bail) before any person, it shall be his duty to cause the recognizance or, as the case may be, a statement of the requirement to be transmitted forthwith to the court officer; and a copy of the recognizance or statement shall at the same time be sent to the governor or keeper of the prison or other place of detention in which the person named in the order is detained, unless the recognizance was entered into or the requirement was complied with before such governor or keeper.

(6)　Where, in pursuance of section 3(5) of the 1976 Act, security has been given in respect of a person granted bail with a duty to surrender to the custody of the Crown Court and either—

(a)　that person surrenders to the custody of the Court; or

(b)　that person having failed to surrender to the custody of the Court, the Court decides not to order the forfeiture of the security,

the court officer shall as soon as practicable give notice of the surrender to custody or, as the case may be, of the decision not to forfeit the security to the person before whom the security was given.

19.23　Estreat of recognizances in respect of person bailed to appear before the Crown Court

(1)　Where a recognizance has been entered into in respect of a person granted bail to appear before the Crown Court and it appears to the Court that a default has been made in performing the conditions of the recognizance, other than by failing to appear before the Court in accordance with any such condition, the Court may order the recognizance to be estreated.

(2)　Where the Crown Court is to consider making an order under paragraph (1) for a recognizance to be estreated, the court officer shall give notice to that effect to the person by whom the recognizance was entered into indicating the time and place at which the matter will be considered; and no such order shall be made before the expiry of 7 days after the notice required by this paragraph has been given.

19.24　Forfeiture of recognizances in respect of person bailed to appear before the Crown Court

(1)　Where a recognizance is conditioned for the appearance of an accused before the Crown Court and the accused fails to appear in accordance with the condition, the Court shall declare the recognizance to be forfeited.

(2)　Where the Crown Court declares a recognizance to be forfeited under paragraph (1), the court officer shall issue a summons to the person by whom the recognizance was entered into requiring him to appear before the Court at a time and place specified in the summons to show cause why the Court should not order the recognizance to be estreated.

(3)   At the time specified in the summons the Court may proceed in the absence of the person by whom the recognizance was entered into if it is satisfied that he has been served with the summons.

PART 20 — CUSTODY TIME LIMITS

20.1   Appeal to the Crown Court against a decision of a magistrates' court in respect of a custody time limit

(1)   This rule applies—

(a)   to any appeal brought by an accused, under section 22(7) of the Prosecution of Offences Act 1985, against a decision of a magistrates' court to extend, or further extend, a custody time limit imposed by regulations made under section 22(1) of the 1985 Act; and

(b)   to any appeal brought by the prosecution, under section 22(8) of the 1985 Act, against a decision of a magistrates' court to refuse to extend, or further extend, such a time limit.

(2)   An appeal to which this rule applies shall be commenced by the appellant's giving notice in writing of appeal—

(a)   to the court officer for the magistrates' court which took the decision;

(b)   if the appeal is brought by the accused, to the prosecutor and, if the prosecution is to be carried on by the Crown Prosecution Service, to the appropriate Crown Prosecutor;

(c)   if the appeal is brought by the prosecution, to the accused; and

(d)   to the Crown Court officer.

(3)   The notice of an appeal to which this rule applies shall state the date on which the custody time limit applicable to the case is due to expire and, if the appeal is brought by the accused under section 22(7) of the 1985 Act, the date on which the custody time limit would have expired had the court decided not to extend or further extend that time limit.

(4)   On receiving notice of an appeal to which this rule applies, the Crown Court officer shall enter the appeal and give notice of the time and place of the hearing to—

(a)   the appellant;

(b)   the other party to the appeal; and

(c)   the court officer for the magistrates' court which took the decision.

(5)   Without prejudice to the power of the Crown Court to give leave for an appeal to be abandoned, an appellant may abandon an appeal to which this rule applies by giving notice in writing to any person to whom notice of the appeal was required to be given by paragraph (2) of this rule not later than the third day preceding the day fixed for the hearing of the appeal:

Provided that, for the purpose of determining whether notice was properly given in accordance with this paragraph, there shall be disregarded any Saturday and Sunday and any day which is specified to be a bank holiday in England and Wales under section 1(1) of the Banking and Financial Dealings Act 1971.

PART 21 — ADVANCE INFORMATION

21.1   Scope of procedure for furnishing advance information

This Part applies in respect of proceedings against any person ('the accused') for an offence triable either way.

21.2   Notice to accused regarding advance information

As soon as practicable after a person has been charged with an offence in proceedings in respect of which this Part applies or a summons has been served on a person in connection with such an offence, the prosecutor shall provide him with a notice in writing explaining the effect of rule 21.3 and setting out the address at which a request under that section may be made.

21.3 Request for advance information

(1) If, in any proceedings in respect of which this Part applies, either before the magistrates' court considers whether the offence appears to be more suitable for summary trial or trial on indictment or, where the accused has not attained the age of 18 years when he appears or is brought before a magistrates' court, before he is asked whether he pleads guilty or not guilty, the accused or a person representing the accused requests the prosecutor to furnish him with advance information, the prosecutor shall, subject to rule 21.4, furnish him as soon as practicable with either—

    (a) a copy of those parts of every written statement which contain information as to the facts and matters of which the prosecutor proposes to adduce evidence in the proceedings; or

    (b) a summary of the facts and matters of which the prosecutor proposes to adduce evidence in the proceedings.

(2) In paragraph (1) above, 'written statement' means a statement made by a person on whose evidence the prosecutor proposes to rely in the proceedings and, where such a person has made more than one written statement one of which contains information as to all the facts and matters in relation to which the prosecutor proposes to rely on the evidence of that person, only that statement is a written statement for purposes of paragraph (1) above.

(3) Where in any part of a written statement or in a summary furnished under paragraph (1) above reference is made to a document on which the prosecutor proposes to rely, the prosecutor shall, subject to rule 21.4, when furnishing the part of the written statement or the summary, also furnish either a copy of the document or such information as may be necessary to enable the person making the request under paragraph (1) above to inspect the document or a copy thereof.

21.4 Refusal of request for advance information

(1) If the prosecutor is of the opinion that the disclosure of any particular fact or matter in compliance with the requirements imposed by rule 21.3 might lead to any person on whose evidence he proposes to rely in the proceedings being intimidated, to an attempt to intimidate him being made or otherwise to the course of justice being interfered with, he shall not be obliged to comply with those requirements in relation to that fact or matter.

(2) Where, in accordance with paragraph (1) above, the prosecutor considers that he is not obliged to comply with the requirements imposed by rule 21.3 in relation to any particular fact or matter, he shall give notice in writing to the person who made the request under that section to the effect that certain advance information is being withheld by virtue of that paragraph.

21.5 Duty of court regarding advance information

(1) Subject to paragraph (2), where an accused appears or is brought before a magistrates' court in proceedings in respect of which this Part applies, the court shall, before it considers whether the offence appears to be more suitable for summary trial or trial on indictment, satisfy itself that the accused is aware of the requirements which may be imposed on the prosecutor under rule 21.3.

(2) Where the accused has not attained the age of 18 years when he appears or is brought before a magistrates' court in proceedings in respect of which this rule applies, the court shall, before the accused is asked whether he pleads guilty or not guilty, satisfy itself that the accused is aware of the requirements which may be imposed on the prosecutor under rule 21.3.

21.6   Adjournment pending furnishing of advance information

(1)   If, in any proceedings in respect of which this Part applies, the court is satisfied that, a request under rule 21.3 having been made to the prosecutor by or on behalf of the accused, a requirement imposed on the prosecutor by that section has not been complied with, the court shall adjourn the proceedings pending compliance with the requirement unless the court is satisfied that the conduct of the case for the accused will not be substantially prejudiced by non-compliance with the requirement.

(2)   Where, in the circumstances set out in paragraph (1) above, the court decides not to adjourn the proceedings, a record of that decision and of the reasons why the court was satisfied that the conduct of the case for the accused would not be substantially prejudiced by non-compliance with the requirement shall be entered in the register kept under rule 6.1.

PART 24 — DISCLOSURE OF EXPERT EVIDENCE

24.1   Requirement to disclose expert evidence

(1)   Following—

(a)   A plea of not guilty by any person to an alleged offence in respect of which a magistrates' court proceeds to summary trial;

(b)   the committal for trial of any person;

(c)   the transfer to the Crown Court of any proceedings for the trial of a person by virtue of a notice of transfer given under section 4 of the Criminal Justice Act 1987;

(d)   the transfer to the Crown Court of any proceedings for the trial of a person by virtue of a notice of transfer served on a magistrates' court under section 53 of the Criminal Justice Act 1991;

(e)   the sending of any person for trial under section 51 of the Crime and Disorder Act 1998;

(f)   the preferring of a bill of indictment charging a person with an offence under the authority of section 2(2)(b) of the Administration of Justice (Miscellaneous Provisions) Act 1933; or

(g)   the making of an order for the retrial of any person,

if any party to the proceedings proposes to adduce expert evidence (whether of fact or opinion) in the proceedings (otherwise than in relation to sentence) he shall as soon as practicable, unless in relation to the evidence in question he has already done so or the evidence is the subject of an application for leave to adduce such evidence in accordance with section 41 of the Youth Justice and Criminal Evidence Act 1999—

(i)   furnish the other party or parties with a statement in writing of any finding or opinion which he proposes to adduce by way of such evidence, and

(ii)   where a request in writing is made to him in that behalf by any other party, provide that party also with a copy of (or if it appears to the party proposing to adduce the evidence to be more practicable, a reasonable opportunity to examine) the record of any observation, test, calculation or other procedure on which such finding or opinion is based and any document or other thing or substance in respect of which any such procedure has been carried out.

(2)   A party may by notice in writing waive his right to be furnished with any of the matters mentioned in paragraph (1) and, in particular, may agree that the statement mentioned in paragraph (1)(a) may be furnished to him orally and not in writing.

(3)   In paragraph (1), 'document' means anything in which information of any description is recorded.

24.2 Withholding evidence

(1) If a party has reasonable grounds for believing that the disclosure of any evidence in compliance with the requirements imposed by rule 24.1 might lead to the intimidation, or attempted intimidation, of any person on whose evidence he intends to rely in the proceedings, or otherwise to the course of justice being interfered with, he shall not be obliged to comply with those requirements in relation to that evidence.

(2) Where, in accordance with paragraph (1), a party considers that he is not obliged to comply with the requirements imposed by rule 24.1 with regard to any evidence in relation to any other party, he shall give notice in writing to that party to the effect that the evidence is being withheld and the grounds for doing so.

24.3 Effect of failure to disclose

A party who seeks to adduce expert evidence in any proceedings and who fails to comply with rule 24.1 shall not adduce that evidence in those proceedings without the leave of the court.

PART 28 — WITNESS SUMMONSES AND ORDERS

28.1 Application to a magistrates' court for summons to witness or warrant for his arrest

(1) An application for the issue of a summons or warrant under section 97 or 97A of the Magistrates' Courts Act 1980 or paragraph 4 of Schedule 3 to the Crime and Disorder Act 1998 may be made by the applicant in person or by his counsel or solicitor.

(2) An application for the issue of such a summons may be made by delivering or sending the application in writing to the magistrates' court officer.

28.2 Taking a deposition in a magistrates' court

(1) Where a person attends before a justice of the peace in pursuance of section 97A of the Magistrates' Courts Act 1980 or paragraph 4 of Schedule 3 to the Crime and Disorder Act 1998 the justice shall—

(a) where that person attends for the purpose of giving evidence, cause his evidence to be put in writing;

(b) where that person attends for the purpose of producing a document or other exhibit, cause the document or exhibit to be handed over for examination and any evidence given by that person in respect of it to be put in writing;

(c) where that person refuses to have his evidence taken or to produce the document or other exhibit, as the case may be, explain to him the consequences of so refusing without just excuse, and ask him to explain why he has so refused; and

(d) cause a record of any such refusal to be made in writing.

(2) As soon as practicable after the examination by the prosecutor of a witness whose evidence is put in writing the justice shall cause his deposition to be read to him, and shall require the witness to sign the deposition.

(3) Any such deposition shall be authenticated by a certificate signed by the justice.

(4) Subject to rule 10.5 (material to be sent to Crown Court following committal) the court officer, on sending a copy of any deposition or documentary exhibit to the prosecutor under section 97A(9) or (10) of the 1980 Act, as the case may be—

(a) shall retain the original deposition or documentary exhibit; and

(b) may retain any other exhibit produced in pursuance of that section.

28.3 Application to the Crown Court for witness summons

(1) This rule applies to an application under section 2 of the Criminal Procedure (Attendance of Witnesses) Act 1965 for the issue of a witness summons and in this rule references to 'the application' and 'the applicant' shall be construed accordingly.

(2)   Subject to paragraphs (8) to (10), the application shall be made in writing to the Crown Court officer and shall—

(a)   contain a brief description of the stipulated evidence, document or thing;

(b)   set out the reasons why the applicant considers that the stipulated evidence, document or thing is likely to be material evidence;

(c)   set out the reason why the applicant considers that the directed person will not voluntarily attend as a witness or produce the document or thing; and

(d)   if the witness summons is proposed to require the directed person to produce a document or thing—

(i)   inform the directed person of his right to make representations in writing and at a hearing, under paragraph (5), and

(ii)   state whether the applicant seeks a requirement also to be imposed under section 2A of the 1965 Act (advance production) and, if such a requirement is sought, specify the place and time at which the applicant wishes the document or thing to be produced.

(3)   The application shall be supported by an affidavit—

(a)   setting out any charge on which the proceedings concerned are based;

(b)   specifying the stipulated evidence, document or thing in such a way as to enable the directed person to identify it;

(c)   specifying grounds for believing that the directed person is likely to be able to give the stipulated evidence or to produce the stipulated evidence or thing; and

(d)   specifying grounds for believing that the stipulated evidence is likely to be material evidence or, as the case may be, that the stipulated document or thing is likely to be material evidence.

(4)   A copy of the application and the supporting affidavit shall be served on the directed person at the same time as it is served on the court officer.

(5)   The directed person may, within 7 days of receiving a copy of the application under paragraph (4) above, inform the court officer whether or not he wishes to make representations, concerning the issue of the witness summons proposed to be directed to him, at a hearing and may also make written representations to the court officer.

(6)   The court officer shall—

(a)   if the directed person indicates that he wishes to have the application considered at a hearing, fix a time, date and place for the hearing;

(b)   if the directed person does not indicate in accordance with paragraph (5) that he wishes to make representations at a hearing, refer the application to a judge of the Crown Court for determination with or without a hearing; and

(c)   notify the applicant and, where paragraph (6)(a) above applies, the directed person of the time, date and place fixed for any hearing of the application.

(7)   Any hearing under this rule shall, unless the judge directs otherwise, take place in private and the proceedings at the hearing shall be recorded.

(8)   In the case of an application for a witness summons which it is proposed shall require the directed person to give evidence but not to produce any document or thing, that application may be made orally to a judge or in writing and, in such a case—

(a)   paragraphs (3) to (7) shall not have effect; and

(b)   the application shall, in addition to the matters set out in paragraph (2)(a) to (c), specify—

(i)   any charge on which the proceedings concerned are based, and

(ii)   the grounds for believing that the directed person is likely to be able to give the stipulated evidence.

(9)   Subject to paragraph (10), in the case of an application for a witness summons which it is proposed shall require the directed person to produce any document or thing and which is made within 7 days of the date fixed for trial, the court officer shall refer the notice of application to the trial judge, or such other judge as may be available, to determine the application or to give such directions as the judge to whom the notice

is referred considers appropriate, and paragraphs (2)(d)(i) and (4) to (6) shall not have effect.

(10)   In the case of an application for a witness summons which it is proposed shall require the directed person to produce any document or thing and which is made during the trial, such application shall be made orally to the trial judge, to determine the application or to give such directions as he considers appropriate, and in such a case—

(a)   paragraphs (3) to (7) shall not have effect; and

(b)   the application shall, in addition to the matters set out in paragraph (2)(a) to (c), specify the grounds for believing that the directed person is likely to be able to produce the document or thing.

(11)   In this rule references to 'the directed person' and 'the stipulated evidence, document or thing' shall be construed in accordance with section 2(10) of the 1965 Act.

28.4 Application to set aside Crown Court witness summons where no longer needed

(1)   This rule applies to an application under section 2B of the Criminal Procedure (Attendance of Witnesses) Act 1965 and references in this rule to 'the applicant' and 'the application' shall be construed accordingly.

(2)   The application shall be made in writing to the Crown Court officer as soon as reasonably practicable after the document or thing has been produced for inspection in pursuance of a requirement imposed by the witness summons under section 2A of the 1965 Act.

(3)   The application shall state that the applicant concludes that the requirement imposed by the witness summons under section 2(2) of the 1965 Act is no longer needed.

(4)   If a direction is given under section 2B of the 1965 Act following the application, the court officer shall notify the person to whom the witness summons is directed as to the effect of the direction.

28.5 Application to set aside witness summons issued on application to the Crown Court

(1)   This rule applies to an application under section 2C of the Criminal Procedure (Attendance of Witnesses) Act 1965 and in this rule references to 'the application' and 'the applicant' shall, unless the contrary intention appears, be construed accordingly.

(2)   The application shall be made in writing to the Crown Court officer and shall—

(a)   state that the applicant was not served with notice of the application to issue the summons and that he was neither present nor represented at any hearing of that application; and

(b)   set out the reasons why the applicant considers that he cannot give any evidence likely to be material evidence or, as the case may be, produce any document or thing likely to be material evidence.

(3)   On receiving the application, the court officer shall serve notice of the application on the person on whose application the witness summons was issued.

(4)   The court shall not grant or, as the case may be, refuse the application unless the applicant and the person on whose application the witness summons has been issued have been given an opportunity of making representations, whether at a hearing or (where they agree to do so) in writing without a hearing.

(5)   In a case where the witness summons to which the application relates imposed a requirement to produce any document or thing, then if—

(a)   the applicant can produce that document or thing; but

(b)   he seeks to satisfy the court that the document or thing is not likely to be material evidence, the applicant must, unless the judge directs otherwise, arrange for the document or thing to be available at the hearing of the application.

(6)   Any hearing under this rule shall, unless the judge directs otherwise, take place in private and the proceedings at the hearing shall be recorded.

(7)   The court officer shall notify the applicant and the person on whose application the witness summons was issued of the decision of the court in relation to the application.

28.6 Application to set aside witness summons issued of Crown Court's own motion

(1)   Rule 28.5 shall apply to an application under section 2E of the Criminal Procedure (Attendance of Witnesses) Act 1965 as it applies to an application under section 2C, subject to the following modifications.

(2)   Paragraphs (2)(a) and (3) shall be omitted.

(3)   In paragraphs (4) and (7), the words 'and the person on whose application the witness summons was issued' shall be omitted.

(4)   In paragraph (4), for the words '(where they agree to do so)', there shall be substituted the words '(where he agrees to do so)'.

PART 29 — SPECIAL MEASURES DIRECTIONS

29.1 Application for special measures directions

(1)   An application by a party in criminal proceedings for a magistrates' court or the Crown Court to give a special measures direction under section 19 of the Youth Justice and Criminal Evidence Act 1999 must be made in writing in the form set out in the Practice Direction.

(2)   If the application is for a special measures direction—

(a)   enabling a witness to give evidence by means of a live link, the information sought in Part B of that form must be provided;

(b)   providing for any examination of a witness to be conducted through an intermediary, the information sought in Part C of that form must be provided; or

(c)   enabling a video recording of an interview of a witness to be admitted as evidence in chief of the witness, the information sought in Part D of that form must be provided.

(3)   The application under paragraph (1) above must be sent to the court officer and at the same time a copy thereof must be sent by the applicant to every other party to the proceedings.

(4)   The court officer must receive the application—

(a)   in the case of an application to a youth court, within 28 days of the date on which the defendant first appears or is brought before the court in connection with the offence;

(b)   in the case of an application to a magistrates' court, within 14 days of the defendant indicating his intention to plead not guilty to any charge brought against him and in relation to which a special measures direction may be sought; and

(c)   in the case of an application to the Crown Court, within 28 days of

(i)   the committal of the defendant, or

(ii)   the consent to the preferment of a bill of indictment in relation to the case, or

(iii)   the service of a notice of transfer under section 53 of the Criminal Justice Act 1991, or

(iv)   where a person is sent for trial under section 51 of the Crime and Disorder Act 1998, the service of copies of the documents containing the evidence on which the charge or charges are based under paragraph 1 of Schedule 3 to that Act, or

(v)   the service of a Notice of Appeal from a decision of a youth court or a magistrates' court.

(5)   A party to whom an application is sent in accordance with paragraph (3) may oppose the application for a special measures direction in respect of any, or any particular, measure available in relation to the witness, whether or not the question whether the witness is eligible for assistance by virtue of section 16 or 17 of the 1999 Act is in issue.

(6)   A party who wishes to oppose the application must, within 14 days of the date the application was served on him, notify the applicant and the court officer, as the case may be, in writing of his opposition and give reasons for it.

(7)   Paragraphs (5) and (6) do not apply in respect of an application for a special measures direction enabling a child witness in need of special protection to give evidence by means of a live link if the opposition is that the special measures direction is not likely to maximise the quality of the witness's evidence.

(8)   In order to comply with paragraph (6)—

(a)   a party must in the written notification state whether he—

(i)   disputes that the witness is eligible for assistance by virtue of section 16 or 17 of the 1999 Act,

(ii)   disputes that any of the special measures available would be likely to improve the quality of evidence given by the witness or that such measures (or a combination of them) would be likely to maximise the quality of that evidence, and

(iii)   opposes the granting of a special measures direction; and

(b)   where the application relates to the admission of a video recording, a party who receives a recording must provide the information required by rule 29.7(7) below.

(9)   Except where notice is received in accordance with paragraph (6), the court (including, in the case of an application to a magistrates' court, a single justice of the peace) may—

(a)   determine the application in favour of the applicant without a hearing; or

(b)   direct a hearing.

(10)   Where a party to the proceedings notifies the court in accordance with paragraph (6) of his opposition to the application, the justices' clerk or the Crown Court must direct a hearing of the application.

(11)   Where a hearing of the application is to take place in accordance with paragraph (9) or (10) above, the court officer shall notify each party to the proceedings of the time and place of the hearing.

(12)   A party notified in accordance with paragraph (11) may be present at the hearing and be heard.

(13)   The court officer must, within 3 days of the decision of the court in relation to an application under paragraph (1) being made, notify all the parties of the decision, and if the application was made for a direction enabling a video recording of an interview of a witness to be admitted as evidence in chief of that witness, the notification must state whether the whole or specified parts only of the video recording or recordings disclosed are to be admitted in evidence.

(14)   In this Part:

'an intermediary' has the same meaning as in section 29 of the 1999 Act; and

'child witness in need of protection' shall be construed in accordance with section 21(1) of the 1999 Act.

29.2 Application for an extension of time

(1)   An application may be made in writing for the period of 14 days or, as the case may be, 28 days specified in rule 29.1(4) to be extended.

(2)   The application may be made either before or after that period has expired.

(3)   The application must be accompanied by a statement setting out the reasons why the applicant is or was unable to make the application within that period and a copy of

the application and the statement must be sent to every other party to the proceedings.

(4)   An application for an extension of time under this rule shall be determined by a single justice of the peace or a judge of the Crown Court without a hearing unless the justice or the judge otherwise directs.

(5)   The court officer shall notify all the parties of the court's decision.

29.3   Late applications

(1)   Notwithstanding the requirements of rule 29.1—
 (a)   an application may be made for a special measures direction orally at the trial; or
 (b)   a magistrates' court or the Crown Court may of its own motion raise the issue whether a special measures direction should be given.

(2)   Where an application is made in accordance with paragraph (1)(a)—
 (a)   the applicant must state the reasons for the late application; and
 (b)   the court must be satisfied that the applicant was unable to make the application in accordance with rule 29.1.

(3)   The court shall determine before making a special measures direction—
 (a)   whether to allow other parties to the proceedings to make representations on the question;
 (b)   the time allowed for making such representations (if any); and
 (c)   whether the question should be determined following a hearing at which the parties to the proceedings may be heard.

(4)   Paragraphs (2) and (3) do not apply in respect of an application made orally at the trial for a special measures direction—
 (a)   enabling a child witness in need of special protection to give evidence by means of a live link; or
 (b)   enabling a video recording of such a child to be admitted as evidence in chief of the witness,
 if the opposition is that the special measures direction will not maximise the quality of the witness's evidence.

PART 30 — USE OF LIVE TELEVISION LINK OTHER THAN FOR VULNERABLE WITNESSES

30.1   Evidence by live television link in the Crown Court where witness is outside the United Kingdom

(1)   Any party may apply for leave under section 32(1) of the Criminal Justice Act 1988 for evidence to be given through a live television link by a witness who is outside the United Kingdom.

(2)   An application under paragraph (1), and any matter relating thereto which, by virtue of the following provisions of this rule, falls to be determined by the Crown Court, may be dealt with in chambers by any judge of the Crown Court.

(3)   An application under paragraph (1) shall be made by giving notice in writing, which shall be in the form set out in the Practice Direction.

(4)   An application under paragraph (1) shall be made within 28 days after the date of the committal of the defendant or, as the case may be, of the giving of a notice of transfer under section 4(1)(c) of the Criminal Justice Act 1987, or of the service of copies of the documents containing the evidence on which the charge or charges are based under paragraph 1 of Schedule 3 to the Crime and Disorder Act 1998, or of the preferring of a bill of indictment in relation to the case.

(5)   The period of 28 days in paragraph (4) may be extended by the Crown Court, either before or after it expires, on an application made in writing, specifying the grounds of the application. The court officer shall notify all the parties of the decision of the Crown Court.

(6)   The notice under paragraph (3) or any application under paragraph (5) shall be sent to the court officer and at the same time a copy thereof shall be sent by the applicant to every other party to the proceedings.

(7)   A party who receives a copy of a notice under paragraph (3) shall, within 28 days of the date of the notice, notify the applicant and the court officer, in writing—

(a)   whether or not he opposes the application, giving his reasons for any such opposition; and

(b)   whether or not he wishes to be represented at any hearing of the application.

(8)   After the expiry of the period referred to in paragraph (7), the Crown Court shall determine whether an application under paragraph (1) is to be dealt with—

(a)   without a hearing; or

(b)   at a hearing at which the applicant and such other party or parties as the court may direct may be represented;

(c)   and the court officer shall notify the applicant and, where necessary, the other party or parties, of the time and place of any such hearing.

(9)   The court officer shall notify all the parties of the decision of the Crown Court in relation to an application under paragraph (1) and, where leave is granted, the notification shall state—

(a)   the country in which the witness will give evidence;

(b)   if known, the place where the witness will give evidence;

(c)   where the witness is to give evidence on behalf of the prosecutor, or where disclosure is required by section 5(7) of the Criminal Procedure and Investigations Act 1996 (alibi) or by rules under section 81 of the Police and Criminal Evidence Act 1984 (expert evidence), the name of the witness;

(d)   the location of the Crown Court at which the trial should take place; and

(e)   any conditions specified by the Crown Court in accordance with paragraph (10).

(10)   The Crown Court dealing with an application under paragraph (1) may specify that as a condition of the grant of leave the witness should give the evidence in the presence of a specified person who is able and willing to answer under oath or affirmation any questions the trial judge may put as to the circumstances in which the evidence is given, including questions about any persons who are present when the evidence is given and any matters which may affect the giving of the evidence.

PART 31 — RESTRICTION ON CROSS-EXAMINATION BY A DEFENDANT ACTING IN PERSON IN THE CROWN COURT

31.1   Restrictions on cross-examination of witness in the Crown Court

(1)   This rule and rules 31.2 and 31.3 apply where an accused is prevented from cross-examining a witness in person by virtue of section 34, 35 or 36 of the Youth Justice and Criminal Evidence Act 1999.

(2)   The court shall explain to the accused as early in the proceedings as is reasonably practicable that he—

(a)   is prevented from cross-examining a witness in person; and

(b)   should arrange for a legal representative to act for him for the purpose of cross-examining the witness.

(3)   The accused shall notify the court officer within 7 days of the court giving its explanation, or within such other period as the court may in any particular case allow, of the action, if any, he has taken.

(4)   Where he has arranged for a legal representative to act for him, the notification shall include details of the name and address of the representative.

(5)   The notification shall be in writing.

(6)   The court officer shall notify all other parties to the proceedings of the name and address of the person, if any, appointed to act for the accused.

(7)   Where the court gives its explanation under paragraph (2) to the accused either within 7 days of the day set for the commencement of any hearing at which a witness

in respect of whom a prohibition under section 34, 35 or 36 of the 1999 Act applies may be cross-examined or after such a hearing has commenced, the period of 7 days shall be reduced in accordance with any directions issued by the court.

(8)   Where at the end of the period of 7 days or such other period as the court has allowed, the court has received no notification from the accused it may grant the accused an extension of time, whether on its own motion or on the application of the accused.

(9)   Before granting an extension of time, the court may hold a hearing at which all parties to the proceedings may attend and be heard.

(10)   Any extension of time shall be of such period as the court considers appropriate in the circumstances of the case.

(11)   The decision of the court as to whether to grant the accused an extension of time shall be notified to all parties to the proceedings by the court officer.

31.2   Appointment of legal representative by the Crown Court

(1)   Where the court decides, in accordance with section 38(4) of the Youth Justice and Criminal Evidence Act 1999, to appoint a qualified legal representative, the court officer shall notify all parties to the proceedings of the name and address of the representative.

(2)   An appointment made by the court under section 38(4) of the 1999 Act shall, except to such extent as the court may in any particular case determine, terminate at the conclusion of the cross-examination of the witness or witnesses in respect of whom a prohibition under section 34, 35 or 36 of the 1999 Act applies.

31.3   Appointment arranged by the accused in the Crown Court

(1)   The accused may arrange for the qualified legal representative, appointed by the court under section 38(4) of the Youth Justice and Criminal Evidence Act 1999, to be appointed to act for him for the purpose of cross-examining any witness in respect of whom a prohibition under section 34, 35 or 36 of the 1999 Act applies.

(2)   Where such an appointment is made—
   (a)   both the accused and the qualified legal representative appointed shall notify the court of the appointment; and
   (b)   the qualified legal representative shall, from the time of his appointment, act for the accused as though the arrangement had been made under section 38(2)(a) of the 1999 Act and shall cease to be the representative of the court under section 38(4).

(3)   Where the court receives notification of the appointment either from the qualified legal representative or from the accused but not from both, the court shall investigate whether the appointment has been made, and if it concludes that the appointment has not been made, paragraph (2)(b) shall not apply.

(4)   An accused may, notwithstanding an appointment by the court under section 38(4) of the 1999 Act, arrange for a legal representative to act for him for the purpose of cross-examining any witness in respect of whom a prohibition under section 34, 35 or 36 of the 1999 Act applies.

(5)   Where the accused arranges for, or informs the court of his intention to arrange for, a legal representative to act for him, he shall notify the court, within such period as the court may allow, of the name and address of any person appointed to act for him.

(6)   Where the court is notified within the time allowed that such an appointment has been made, any qualified legal representative appointed by the court in accordance with section 38(4) of the 1999 Act shall be discharged.

(7)   The court officer shall, as soon as reasonably practicable after the court receives notification of an appointment under this rule or, where paragraph (3) applies, after the court is satisfied that the appointment has been made, notify all the parties to the proceedings—
   (a)   that the appointment has been made;

(b)   were paragraph (4) applies, of the name and address of the person appointed; and

(c)   that the person appointed by the Crown Court under section 38(4) of the 1999 Act has been discharged or has ceased to act for the court.

31.4 Prohibition on cross-examination of particular witness in the Crown Court

(1)   An application by the prosecutor for the court to give a direction under section 36 of the Youth Justice and Criminal Evidence Act 1999 in relation to any witness must be sent to the court officer and at the same time a copy thereof must be sent by the applicant to every other party to the proceedings.

(2)   In his application the prosecutor must state why, in his opinion—

(a)   the evidence given by the witness is likely to be diminished if cross-examination is undertaken by the accused in person;

(b)   the evidence would be improved if a direction were given under section 36(2) of the 1999 Act; and

(c)   it would not be contrary to the interests of justice to give such a direction.

(3)   On receipt of the application the court officer must refer it—

(a)   if the trial has started, to the trial judge; or

(b)   if the trial has not started when the application is received—

(i)   to the judge who has been designated to conduct the trial, or

(ii)   if no judge has been designated for that purpose, to such judge who may be designated for the purposes of hearing that application.

(4)   Where a copy of the application is received by a party to the proceedings more than 14 days before the date set for the trial to begin, that party may make observations in writing on the application to the court officer, but any such observations must be made within 14 days of the receipt of the application and be copied to the other parties to the proceedings.

(5)   A party to whom an application is sent in accordance with paragraph (1) who wishes to oppose the application must give his reasons for doing so to the court officer and the other parties to the proceedings.

(6)   Those reasons must be notified—

(a)   within 14 days of the date the application was served on him, if that date is more than 14 days before the date set for the trial to begin;

(b)   if the trial has begun, in accordance with any directions issued by the trial judge; or

(c)   if neither paragraph (6)(a) nor (b) applies, before the date set for the trial to begin.

(7)   Where the application made in accordance with paragraph (1) is made before the date set for the trial to begin and—

(a)   is not contested by any party to the proceedings, the court may determine the application without a hearing;

(b)   is contested by a party to the proceedings, the court must direct a hearing of the application.

(8)   Where the application is made after the trial has begun—

(a)   the application may be made orally; and

(b)   the trial judge may give such directions as he considers appropriate to deal with the application.

(9)   Where a hearing of the application is to take place, the court officer shall notify each party to the proceedings of the time and place of the hearing.

(10)   A party notified in accordance with paragraph (9) may be present at the hearing and be heard.

(11)   The court officer must, as soon as possible after the determination of an application made in accordance with paragraph (1), give notice of the decision and the reasons for it to all the parties to the proceedings.

(12)   A person making an oral application under paragraph (8)(a) must—

(a)   give reasons why the application was not made before the trial commenced; and

(b)   provide the court with the information set out in paragraph (2).

PART 34 — HEARSAY EVIDENCE

34.1   When this applies

This Part applies in a magistrates' court and in the Crown Court where a party wants to introduce evidence on one or more of the grounds set out in section 114(1)(d), section 116, section 117 and section 121 of the Criminal Justice Act 2003, and in this Part that evidence is called 'hearsay evidence'.

34.2   Notice of hearsay evidence

The party who wants to introduce hearsay evidence must give notice in the form set out in the Practice Direction to the court officer and all other parties.

34.3   When the prosecutor must give notice of hearsay evidence

The prosecutor must give notice of hearsay evidence—

(a)   in a magistrates' court, at the same time as he complies or purports to comply with section 3 of the Criminal Procedure and Investigations Act 1996 (disclosure by prosecutor); or

(b)   in the Crown Court, not more than 14 days after—

    (i)   the committal of the defendant, or

    (ii)   the consent to the preferment of a bill of indictment in relation to the case, or

    (iii) the service of a notice of transfer under section 4 of the Criminal Justice Act 1987 (serious fraud cases) or under section 53 of the Criminal Justice Act 1991 (certain cases involving children), or

    (iv) where a person is sent for trial under section 51 of the Crime and Disorder Act 1998 (indictable-only offences sent for trial), the service of copies of the documents containing the evidence on which the charge or charges are based under paragraph 1 of Schedule 3 to the 1998 Act.

34.4   When a defendant must give notice of hearsay evidence

A defendant must give notice of hearsay evidence not more than 14 days after the prosecutor has complied with or purported to comply with section 3 of the Criminal Procedure and Investigations Act 1996 (disclosure by prosecutor).

34.5   Opposing the introduction of hearsay evidence

A party who receives a notice of hearsay evidence may oppose it by giving notice within 14 days in the form set out in the Practice Direction to the court officer and all other parties.

34.6   Methods of giving notice

Where this Part requires a notice to be given it may, with the consent of the addressee, be sent by fax or other means of electronic communication.

34.7   Court's power to vary requirements under this Part

The court may —

(a)   dispense with the requirement to give notice of hearsay evidence;

(b)   allow notice to be given in a different form, or orally; or

(c)   shorten a time limit or extend it (even after it has expired).

34.8   Waiving the requirement to give a notice of hearsay evidence

A party entitled to receive a notice of hearsay evidence may waive his entitlement by so informing the court and the party who would have given the notice.

PART 35 — EVIDENCE OF BAD CHARACTER

35.1 When this applies

This Part applies in a magistrates' court and in the Crown Court when a party wants to introduce evidence of bad character as defined in section 98 of the Criminal Justice Act 2003.

35.2 Introducing evidence of non-defendant's bad character

A party who wants to introduce evidence of a non-defendant's bad character or who wants to cross-examine a witness with a view to eliciting that evidence, under section 100 of the Criminal Justice Act 2003 must apply in the form set out in the Practice Direction and the application must be received by the court officer and all other parties to the proceedings–

(a)   not more than 14 days after the prosecutor has –

    (i)   complied or purported to comply with section 3 of the Criminal Procedure and Investigations Act 1996 (initial disclosure by the prosecutor), or

    (ii)   disclosed the previous convictions of that non-defendant; or

(b)   as soon as reasonably practicable, where the application concerns a non-defendant who is to be invited to give (or has given) evidence for a defendant.

35.3 Opposing introduction of evidence of non-defendant's bad character

A party who receives a copy of an application under rule 35.2 may oppose that application by giving notice in writing to the court officer and all other parties to the proceedings not more than 14 days after receiving that application.

35.4 Prosecutor introducing evidence of defendant's bad character

(1)   A prosecutor who wants to introduce evidence of a defendant's bad character or who wants to cross-examine a witness with a view to eliciting that evidence, under section 101 of the Criminal Justice Act 2003 must give notice in the form set out in the Practice Direction to the court officer and all other parties to the proceedings.

(2)   Notice under paragraph (1) must be given–

    (a)   in a case to be tried in a magistrates' court, at the same time as the prosecutor complies or purports to comply with section 3 of the Criminal Procedure and Investigations Act 1996; and

    (b)   in a case to be tried in the Crown Court, not more than 14 days after—

        (i)   the committal of the defendant, or

        (ii)   the consent to the preferment of a bill of indictment in relation to the case, or

        (iii)   the service of notice of transfer under section 4(1) of the Criminal Justice Act 1987 (notices of transfer) or under section 53(1) of the Criminal Justice Act 1991 (notices of transfer in certain cases involving children), or

        (iv)   where a person is sent for trial under section 51 of the Crime and Disorder Act 1998 (sending cases to the Crown Court) the service of copies of the documents containing the evidence on which the charge or charges are based under paragraph 1 of Schedule 3 to that Act.

35.5 Co-defendant introducing evidence of defendant's bad character

A co-defendant who wants to introduce evidence of a defendant's bad character or who wants to cross-examine a witness with a view to eliciting that evidence under section 101 of the Criminal Justice Act 2003 must give notice in the form set out in the Practice Direction to the court officer and all other parties to the proceedings not more than 14 days after the prosecutor has complied or purported to comply with section 3 of the Criminal Procedure and Investigations Act 1996.

35.6   A defendant's application to exclude bad character evidence must be in the form set out in the Practice Direction and received by the court officer and all other parties to the proceedings not more than 14 days after receiving a notice given under rules 35.4 or 35.5.

35.7   Methods of giving notice

Where this rule requires a notice or application to be given or sent it may, with the consent of the addressee, be sent by fax or other means of electronic communication.

35.8   Court's power to vary requirements under this Part

The court may—

(a)   allow a notice or application required under this rule to be given in a different form, or orally; or

(b)   shorten a time-limit under this rule or extend it even after it has expired.

35.9   Defendant waiving right to receive notice

A defendant entitled to receive a notice under this Part may waive his entitlement by so informing the court and the party who would have given the notice.

PART 36 — EVIDENCE OF A COMPLAINANT'S PREVIOUS SEXUAL BEHAVIOUR

36.1   Evidence in the Crown Court of a complainant's previous sexual behaviour

(1)   An application for leave under section 41(2) of the Youth Justice and Criminal Evidence Act 1999 must be made in writing to the Crown Court officer and must either—

(a)   be received by the court officer within 28 days of—

(i)   the committal of the defendant, or

(ii)   the consent to the preferment of a bill of indictment in relation to the case, or

(iii)   the service of notice of transfer under section 53 of the Criminal Justice Act 1991, or

(iv)   where a person is sent for trial under section 51 of the Crime and Disorder Act 1998, the service of copies of the documents containing the evidence on which the charge or charges are based under paragraph 1 of Schedule 3 to the 1998 Act,

(v)   or within such period as the court may in any particular case determine; or

(b)   be accompanied by a full written explanation specifying the reasons why the application could not have been made within the 28 days mentioned above.

(2)   Such an application must contain the following—

(a)   a summary of the evidence it is proposed to adduce and of the questions it is proposed to put to any witness;

(b)   a full explanation of the reasons why it is considered that the evidence and questions fall within section 41(3) or (5) of the 1999 Act;

(c)   a summary of any document or other evidence to be submitted in support of such evidence and questions; and

(d)   where it is proposed that a witness at the trial give evidence as to the complainant's sexual behaviour, the name and date of birth of any such witness.

(3)   A copy of the application must be sent to all the parties to the proceedings at the same time as it is sent to the court officer.

(4)   Where a copy of the application is received by the prosecutor more than 14 days before the date set for the trial to begin, the prosecutor must, within 14 days of the receipt of the application, notify the other parties to the proceedings and the court officer in writing whether or not—

(a)   he opposes the application, giving reasons for any such opposition; and

(b)   he wishes to be represented at any hearing of the application.

(5)   Where a copy of the application is received by a party to the proceedings other than the prosecutor more than 14 days before the date set for the trial to begin, that party may make observations in writing on the application to the court officer, but any such observations must be made within 14 days of the receipt of the application and be copied to the other parties to the proceedings.

(6)   In considering any application under this rule, the court may request a party to the proceedings to provide the court with such information as it may specify and which the court considers would assist it in determining the application.

(7)   Where the court makes such a request, the person required to provide the information must do so within 14 days of the court making the request or by such time as the court considers appropriate in the circumstances of the case.

(8)   An application under paragraph (1) must be determined by a judge of the Crown Court following a hearing if—

(a)   the prosecutor has notified the court officer that he opposes the application; or

(b)   the copy of the application was received by any of the parties to the proceedings less than 14 days before the date set for the trial to begin.

(9)   An application under paragraph (1) must be determined by a judge of the Crown Court following a hearing in any case where he considers such a hearing is appropriate in the circumstances of the particular case.

(10)   The date and time of the hearing must be—

(a)   determined by the court or the court officer after taking into consideration—

(i)   any time which a party to the proceedings has been given to respond to a request for information, and

(ii)   the date fixed for any other hearing relevant to the proceedings; and

(b)   notified by the court officer to all the parties to the proceedings.

(11)   Except where paragraph (8) or (9) above applies, an application under paragraph (1) must be determined by a judge of the Crown Court without a hearing.

(12)   The court officer must, as soon as possible after the determination of an application made in accordance with paragraph (1), give notice of the decision and the reasons for it to all the parties to the proceedings.

(13)   An application under section 41(2) of the 1999 Act may be made orally where the application is made after the trial has begun.

(14)   The person making the application under paragraph (13) must—

(a)   give reasons why the applicant failed to make the application in writing in accordance with paragraph (1); and

(b)   provide the court with the information set out in paragraph (2)(a) to (d).

PART 37 — SUMMARY TRIAL

37.1   Order of evidence and speeches: information

(1)   On the summary trial of an information, where the accused does not plead guilty, the prosecutor shall call the evidence for the prosecution, and before doing so may address the court.

(2)   At the conclusion of the evidence for the prosecution, the accused may address the court, whether or not he afterwards calls evidence.

(3)   At the conclusion of the evidence, if any, for the defence, the prosecutor may call evidence to rebut that evidence.

(4)   At the conclusion of the evidence for the defence and the evidence, if any, in rebuttal, the accused may address the court if he has not already done so.

(5)   Either party may, with the leave of the court, address the court a second time, but where the court grants leave to one party it shall not refuse leave to the other.

(6)   Where both parties address the court twice the prosecutor shall address the court for the second time before the accused does so.

37.2   Procedure on information where accused is not legally represented

(1)   The court shall explain to an accused who is not legally represented the substance of the charge in simple language.

(2)   If an accused who is not legally represented, instead of asking a witness in support of the charge questions by way of cross-examination, makes assertions, the court shall then put to the witness such questions as it thinks necessary on behalf of the accused and may for this purpose question the accused in order to bring out or clear up any point arising out of such assertions.

37.3   Adjournment of trial of information

(1)   Where in the absence of the accused a magistrates' court adjourns the trial of an information, the court officer shall give to the accused notice in writing of the time and place at which the trial is to be resumed.

(2)   Service of the notice required to be given by paragraph (1) may be effected in any manner in which service of a summons may be effected under rule 4.1(1) or (3).

37.4   Formal admissions

Where under section 10 of the Criminal Justice Act 1967 a fact is admitted orally in court by or on behalf of the prosecutor or defendant for the purposes of the summary trial of an offence the court shall cause the admission to be written down and signed by or on behalf of the party making the admission.

37.5   Notice of intention to cite previous convictions

Service on any person of a notice of intention to cite previous convictions under section 104 of the Magistrates' Courts Act 1980 or section 13 of the Road Traffic Offenders Act 1988 may be effected by delivering it to him or by sending it by post in a registered letter or by recorded delivery service, or by first class post addressed to him at his last known or usual place of abode.

37.6   Preservation of depositions where offence triable either way is dealt with summarily

The magistrates' court officer for the magistrates' court by which any person charged with an offence triable either way has been tried summarily shall preserve for a period of three years such depositions as have been taken.

37.7   Order of evidence and speeches: complaint

(1)   On the hearing of a complaint, except where the court determines under section 53(3) of the Magistrates' Courts Act 1980 to make the order with the consent of the defendant without hearing evidence, the complainant shall call his evidence, and before doing so may address the court.

(2)   At the conclusion of the evidence for the complainant the defendant may address the court, whether or not he afterwards calls evidence.

(3)   At the conclusion of the evidence, if any, for the defence, the complainant may call evidence to rebut that evidence.

(4)   At the conclusion of the evidence for the defence and the evidence, if any, in rebuttal, the defendant may address the court if he has not already done so.

(5)   Either party may, with the leave of the court, address the court a second time, but where the court grants leave to one party it shall not refuse leave to the other.

(6)   Where the defendant obtains leave to address the court for a second time his second address shall be made before the second address, if any, of the complainant.

PART 38 — TRIAL OF CHILDREN AND YOUNG PERSONS

38.1 Application of this Part

(1) This Part applies, subject to paragraph (3) of this rule, where proceedings to which paragraph (2) applies are brought in a magistrates' court in respect of a child or young person ('the relevant minor').

(2) This paragraph applies to proceedings in which the relevant minor is charged with an offence, and, where he appears or is brought before the court, to proceedings under—

(a) Paragraphs 1, 2, 5 and 6 of Schedule 7 to the Powers of Criminal Courts (Sentencing) Act 2000 (breach, revocation and amendment of supervision orders);

(b) Part II, III or IV of Schedule 3 to the 2000 Act (breach, revocation and amendment of certain community orders);

(c) Paragraphs 4, 5, 6 and 7 of Schedule 5 to the 2000 Act (breach, revocation and amendment of attendance centre orders); and

(d) Schedule 8 to the 2000 Act (breach, revocation and amendment of action plan orders and reparation orders).

(3) Where the court is inquiring into an offence as examining justices, only rules 38.2, 38.3 and 38.5(3) apply, and where the proceedings are of a kind mentioned in paragraph (2)(a), (b) or (c) rule 38.4 does not apply.

38.2 Assistance in conducting case

(1) Except where the relevant minor is legally represented, the magistrates' court shall allow his parent or guardian to assist him in conducting his case.

(2) Where the parent or guardian cannot be found or cannot in the opinion of the court reasonably be required to attend, the court may allow any relative or other responsible person to take the place of the parent or guardian for the purposes of this Part.

38.3 Duty of court to explain nature of proceedings etc

(1) The magistrates' court shall explain to the relevant minor the nature of the proceedings and, where he is charged with an offence, the substance of the charge.

(2) The explanation shall be given in simple language suitable to his age and understanding.

38.4 Duty of court to take plea to charge

Where the relevant minor is charged with an offence the magistrates' court shall, after giving the explanation required by rule 38.3, ask him whether he pleads guilty or not guilty to the charge.

38.5 Evidence in support of charge

(1) Where—

(a) the relevant minor is charged with an offence and does not plead guilty, or

(b) the proceedings are of a kind mentioned in rule 38.1(2)(a), (b) or (c),

the magistrates' court shall hear the witnesses in support of the charge or, as the case may be, the application.

(2) Except where—

(a) the proceedings are of a kind mentioned in rule 38.1(2)(a), (b) or (c), and

(b) the relevant minor is the applicant,

each witness may at the close of his evidence-in-chief be cross-examined by or on behalf of the relevant minor.

(3) If in any case where the relevant minor is not legally represented or assisted as provided by rule 38.2, the relevant minor, instead of asking questions by way of cross-examination, makes assertions, the court shall then put to the witness such

questions as it thinks necessary on behalf of the relevant minor and may for this purpose question the relevant minor in order to bring out or clear up any point arising out of any such assertions.

38.6 Evidence in reply

If it appears to the magistrates' court after hearing the evidence in support of the charge or application that a prima facie case is made out, the relevant minor shall, if he is not the applicant and is not legally represented, be told that he may give evidence or address the court, and the evidence of any witnesses shall be heard.

PART 39 — TRIAL ON INDICTMENT

39.1 Time limits for beginning of trials

The periods set out for the purposes of section 77(2)(a) and (b) of the Supreme Court Act 1981 shall be 14 days and 8 weeks respectively and accordingly the trial of a person committed by a magistrates' court—

(a)   shall not begin until the expiration of 14 days beginning with the date of his committal, except with his consent and the consent of the prosecution; and

(b)   shall, unless the Crown Court has otherwise ordered, begin not later than the expiration of 8 weeks beginning with the date of his committal.

PART 44 — SENTENCING CHILDREN AND YOUNG PERSONS

44.1 Procedure after finding against minor in a magistrates' court

(1)   This rule applies where—

    (a)   the relevant minor (as defined in rule 38.1) is found guilty by a magistrates' court of an offence, whether after a plea of guilty or otherwise; or

    (b)   in proceedings of a kind mentioned in rule 38.1(2)(a), (b) or (c) the court is satisfied that the case for the applicant—

        (i)   if the relevant minor is not the applicant, has been made out, or

        (ii)   if he is the applicant, has not been made out.

(2)   Where this rule applies—

    (a)   the relevant minor and his parent or guardian, if present, shall be given an opportunity of making a statement;

    (b)   the court shall take into consideration all available information as to the general conduct, home surroundings, school record and medical history of the relevant minor and, in particular, shall take into consideration such information as aforesaid which is provided in pursuance of section 9 of the Children and Young Persons Act 1969;

    (c)   if such information as aforesaid is not fully available, the court shall consider the desirability of adjourning the proceedings for such inquiry as may be necessary;

    (d)   any written report of a probation officer, local authority, local education authority, educational establishment or registered medical practitioner may be received and considered by the court without being read aloud; and

    (e)   if the court considers it necessary in the interests of the relevant minor, it may require him or his parent or guardian, if present, to withdraw from the court.

(3)   The court shall arrange for copies of any written report before the court to be made available to—

    (a)   the legal representative, if any, of the relevant minor;

    (b)   any parent or guardian of the relevant minor who is present at the hearing; and

    (c)   the relevant minor, except where the court otherwise directs on the ground that it appears to it impracticable to disclose the report having regard to his age and understanding or undesirable to do so having regard to potential serious harm which might thereby be suffered by him.

(4)   In any case in which the relevant minor is not legally represented and where a report which has not been made available to him in accordance with a direction under paragraph (3)(c) has been considered without being read aloud in pursuance of paragraph (2)(d) or where he or his parent or guardian has been required to withdraw from the court in pursuance of paragraph (2)(e), then—

(a)   the relevant minor shall be told the substance of any part of the information given to the court bearing on his character or conduct which the court considers to be material to the manner in which the case should be dealt with unless it appears to it impracticable so to do having regard to his age and understanding; and

(b)   the parent or guardian of the relevant minor, if present, shall be told the substance of any part of such information which the court considers to be material as aforesaid and which has reference to his character or conduct or to the character, conduct, home surroundings or health of the relevant minors, and if such a person, having been told the substance of any part of such information, desires to produce further evidence with reference thereto, the court, if it thinks the further evidence would be material, shall adjourn the proceedings for the production thereof and shall, if necessary in the case of a report, require the attendance at the adjourned hearing of the person who made the report.

44.2   Duty of magistrates' court to explain manner in which it proposes to deal with case and effect of order

(1)   Before finally disposing of the case or before remitting the case to another court in pursuance of section 8 of the Powers of Criminal Courts (Sentencing) Act 2000, the magistrates' court shall inform the relevant minor and his parent or guardian, if present, or any person assisting him in his case, of the manner in which it proposes to deal with the case and allow any of those persons so informed to make representations; but the relevant minor shall not be informed as aforesaid if the court considers it undesirable so to do.

(2)   On making any order, the court shall explain to the relevant minor the general nature and effect of the order unless, in the case of an order requiring his parent or guardian to enter into a recognizance, it appears to it undesirable so to do.

PART 50 — SUPPLEMENTARY ORDERS MADE ON CONVICTION

50.1   Sexual offences prevention orders made by a magistrates' court on conviction

(1)   A sexual offences prevention order made by a magistrates' court under section 104 of the Sexual Offences Act 2003 shall be in the form set out in the Practice Direction.

(2)   An interim sexual offences prevention order made by a magistrates' court under section 109 of the 2003 Act shall be in the form set out in the Practice Direction.

(3)   As soon as reasonably practicable after a sexual offences prevention order or an interim sexual offences prevention order has been made, the court officer shall serve a copy of that order on the defendant. Any copy of an order required to be sent under this rule to the defendant shall be either given to him in person or sent by post to his last known address and, if so given or sent, shall be deemed to have been received by him, unless the defendant proves that it was not received by him.

50.2   Parenting orders made by a magistrates' court on conviction

(1)   A parenting order made by a magistrates' court under section 8 of the Crime and Disorder Act 1998 shall be in the form set out in the Practice Direction.

(2)   A parenting order made by a magistrates' court under paragraph 9D of Schedule 1 to the Powers of Criminal Courts (Sentencing) Act 2000 shall be in the form set out in the Practice Direction.

50.3   Variation of certain orders by a magistrates' court

(1)   An application to a magistrates' court for variation or discharge of any of the following orders shall be by complaint:

(a)   a parenting order made under section 9(5) of the Crime and Disorder Act 1998;

(b)   a parenting order made under paragraph 9D of Schedule 1 to the Powers of Criminal Courts (Sentencing) Act 2000;

(c)   a reparation order, under paragraph 5 of Schedule 8 to the Powers of Criminal Courts (Sentencing) Act 2000; or

(d)   an action plan order, under that paragraph.

(2)   An application under paragraph (1)(b) above shall be made to the magistrates' court which made the order, and shall specify the reason why the applicant for variation or discharge believes the court should vary or discharge the order, as the case may be.

50.4   Anti-social behaviour orders made by the Crown Court on conviction

An order made by the Crown Court under section 1C of the Crime and Disorder Act 1998 on conviction in criminal proceedings shall be in the form set out in the Practice Direction.

PART 55 — ROAD TRAFFIC PENALTIES

55.1   Endorsement of driving licence by magistrates' court

(1)   Where a magistrates' court convicts a person of an offence and, under section 44 of the Road Traffic Offenders Act 1988 orders that particulars of the conviction, and, if the court orders him to be disqualified, particulars of the disqualification, shall be endorsed on any licence held by him, the particulars to be endorsed shall include—

(a)   the name of the local justice area for which the court is acting;

(b)   the date of the conviction and the date on which sentence was passed (if different);

(c)   particulars of the offence including the date on which it was committed; and

(d)   particulars of the sentence of the court (including the period of disqualification, if any).

(2)   Where a magistrates' court orders that the licence of an offender be endorsed as mentioned in paragraph (1) or imposes an interim disqualification as mentioned in rule 43.1(1)(f) and the court officer knows or is informed of the date of birth and sex of the offender, the court officer shall send the information to the licensing authority which granted the licence.

55.2   Application to magistrates' court for removal of disqualification

(1)   An application under section 42 of the Road Traffic Offenders Act 1988 or paragraph 7 of Schedule 4 to the Road Traffic (Consequential Provisions) Act 1988 for an order removing a disqualification or disqualifications for holding or obtaining a licence shall be by complaint.

(2)   The justice to whom the complaint is made shall issue a summons directed to the chief officer of police requiring him to appear before a magistrates' court to show cause why an order should not be made on the complaint.

(3)   Where a magistrates' court makes an order under either of the provisions mentioned in paragraph (1) the court shall cause notice of the making of the order and a copy of the particulars of the order endorsed on the licence, if any, previously held by the applicant for the order to be sent to the licensing authority to which notice of the applicant's disqualification was sent.

55.3   Application to magistrates' court for review of course organiser's refusal to issue certificate of satisfactory completion of driving course

(1)   An application to the supervising court under section 34B(6) or (7) of the Road Traffic Offenders Act 1988 shall be served on the court officer within 28 days after the date

specified in an order under section 34A(2) of the1988 Act, where that date falls on or after 24th May 1993.

(2)   An application under section 34B(6) of the 1988 Act shall be accompanied by the notice under section 34B(5) of the 1988 Act.

(3)   Where such an application is served on the court officer—

    (a)   he shall fix a date and time for the hearing of the application; and

    (b)   he shall—

        (i)   serve a copy of the application on the course organiser, and

        (ii)   serve notice of the hearing on the applicant and course organiser.

(4)   If the course organiser fails to appear or be represented at the hearing of the application without reasonable excuse, the court may proceed to decide the application in his absence.

(5)   In this rule, 'course organiser' and 'supervising court' have the meanings assigned to them in England and Wales by section 34C of the 1988 Act.

55.4   Notice of registration to defaulter under section 71(6) of the Road Traffic Offenders Act 1988

Where a magistrates' court officer gives notice of registration to a defaulter under section 71(6) of the Road Traffic Offenders Act 1988 (registration of sums payable in default for enforcement as a fine) the court officer shall send the notice by delivering it at, or by sending it by post to, the defaulter's address as given in the certificate of registration issued under section 70(4) of that Act.

PART 63 — APPEAL TO THE CROWN COURT AGAINST CONVICTION OR SENTENCE

63.1   Application of this Part

This Part shall apply to any appeal under section 108(1) of the Magistrates' Courts Act 1980 (conviction and sentence), section 45(1) of the Mental Health Act 1983 (hospital or guardianship order in the absence of conviction) and paragraph 11 of Schedule 3 to the Powers of Criminal Courts (Sentencing) Act 2000 (re-sentencing on failure to comply with supervision order).

63.2   Notice of appeal

(1)   An appeal shall be commenced by the appellant's giving notice of appeal in accordance with the following provisions of this rule.

(2)   The notice required by the preceding paragraph shall be in writing and shall be given to a court officer for the magistrates' court and to any other party to the appeal.

(3)   Notice of appeal shall be given not later than 21 days after the day on which the decision appealed against is given and, for this purpose, where the court has adjourned the trial of an information after conviction, that day shall be the day on which the court sentences or otherwise deals with the offender:

Provided that, where a court exercises its power to defer sentence under section 1(1) of the Powers of Criminal Courts (Sentencing) Act 2000, that day shall, for the purposes of an appeal against conviction, be the day on which the court exercises that power.

(4)   A notice of appeal shall state the grounds of appeal.

(5)   The time for giving notice of appeal may be extended, either before or after it expires, by the Crown Court, on an application made in accordance with paragraph (6).

(6)   An application for an extension of time shall be made in writing, specifying the grounds of the application and sent to a Crown Court officer.

(7)   Where the Crown Court extends the time for giving notice of appeal, the Crown Court officer shall give notice of the extension to—

    (a)   the appellant; and

    (b)   the magistrates' court officer,

and the appellant shall give notice of the extension to any other party to the appeal.

63.3 Documents to be sent to Crown Court

(1)   The magistrates' court officer shall as soon as practicable send to the Crown Court officer any notice of appeal to the Crown Court given to the magistrates' court officer.

(2)   the magistrates' court officer shall send to the Crown Court officer, with the notice of appeal, a copy of the extract of the magistrates' court register relating to that decision and of the last known or usual place of abode of the parties to the appeal.

(3)   Where any person, having given notice of appeal to the Crown Court, has been granted bail for the purposes of the appeal the magistrates' court officer for the court from whose decision the appeal is brought shall before the day fixed for the hearing of the appeal send to the Crown Court officer a copy of the record made in pursuance of section 5 of the Bail Act 1976.

(4)   Where a notice of appeal is given in respect of a hospital order or guardianship order made under section 37 of the Mental Health Act 1983 (powers of courts to order hospital admission or guardianship), a magistrates' court officer for the court from which the appeal is brought shall send with the notice to the Crown Court officer any written evidence considered by the court under section 37(2) of the 1983 Act.

(5)   Where a notice of appeal is given in respect of an appeal against conviction by a magistrates' court the magistrates' court officer shall send with the notice to the Crown Court officer any admission of facts made for the purposes of the summary trial under section 10 of the Criminal Justice Act 1967 (proof by formal admission).

(6)   Where a notice of appeal is given in respect of an appeal against sentence by a magistrates' court, and where that sentence was a custodial sentence, the magistrates' court officer shall send with the notice to the Crown Court officer a statement of whether the magistrates' court obtained and considered a pre-sentence report before passing such sentence.

63.4 Entry of appeal and notice of hearing

On receiving notice of appeal, the Crown Court officer shall enter the appeal and give notice of the time and place of the hearing to—

(a)   the appellant;

(b)   any other party to the appeal; and

(c)   the magistrates' court officer.

63.5 Abandonment of appeal — notice

(1)   Without prejudice to the power of the Crown Court to give leave for an appeal to be abandoned, an appellant may abandon an appeal by giving notice in writing, in accordance with the following provisions of this rule, not later than the third day before the day fixed for hearing the appeal.

(2)   The notice required by the preceding paragraph shall be given—

(a)   to the magistrates' court officer;

(b)   to the Crown Court officer; and

(c)   to any other party to the appeal.

(3)   For the purposes of determining whether notice of abandonment was given in time there shall be disregarded any Saturday, Sunday and any day which is specified to be a bank holiday in England and Wales under section 1(1) of the Banking and Financial Dealings Act 1971.

63.6 Abandonment of appeal — bail

Where notice to abandon an appeal has been given by the appellant, any recognizance conditioned for the appearance of the appellant at the hearing of the appeal shall have effect as if conditioned for the appearance of the appellant before the court from whose decision the appeal was brought at a time and place to be notified to the appellant by the court officer for that court.

63.7 Number and qualification of justices — appeals from youth courts

Subject to the provisions of rule 63.8 and to any directions under section 74(4) of the Supreme Court Act 1981 (directions disapplying the set out number and qualifications of justices), on the hearing of an appeal from a youth court the Crown Court shall consist of a judge sitting with two justices each of whom is a member of a youth court panel and who are chosen so that the Court shall include a man and a woman.

63.8 Number and qualification of justices — dispensation for special circumstances

(1)   The Crown Court may enter on any appeal notwithstanding that the Court is not constituted as required by section 74(1) of the Supreme Court Act 1981 or rule 63.7 if it appears to the judge that the Court could not be constituted without unreasonable delay and the Court includes one justice who is a member of a youth court panel.

(2)   The Crown Court may at any stage continue with any proceedings with a Court from which any one or more of the justices initially comprising the Court has withdrawn, or is absent for any reason.

63.9 Disqualifications

A justice of the peace shall not sit in the Crown Court on the hearing of an appeal in a matter on which he adjudicated.

PART 64 — APPEAL TO THE HIGH COURT BY WAY OF CASE STATED

64.1 Application to a magistrates' court to state a case

(1)   An application under section 111(1) of the Magistrates' Courts Act 1980 shall be made in writing and signed by or on behalf of the applicant and shall identify the question or questions of law or jurisdiction on which the opinion of the High Court is sought.

(2)   Where one of the questions on which the opinion of the High Court is sought is whether there was evidence on which the magistrates' court could come to its decision, the particular finding of fact made by the magistrates' court which it is claimed cannot be supported by the evidence before the magistrates' court shall be specified in such application.

(3)   Any such application shall be sent to a court officer for the magistrates' court whose decision is questioned.

64.2 Consideration of a draft case by a magistrates' court

(1)   Within 21 days after receipt of an application made in accordance with rule 64.1, a court officer for the magistrates' court whose decision is questioned shall, unless the justices refuse to state a case under section 111(5) of the Magistrates' Courts Act 1980, send a draft case in which are stated the matters required under rule 64.6 (content of case stated) to the applicant or his legal representative and shall send a copy thereof to the respondent or his legal representative.

(2)   Within 21 days after receipt of the draft case under paragraph (1), each party may make representations thereon. Any such representations shall be in writing and signed by or on behalf of the party making them and shall be sent to the magistrates' court officer.

(3)   Where the justices refuse to state a case under section 111(5) of the 1980 Act and they are required by a mandatory order of the High Court under section 111(6) to do so, this rule shall apply as if in paragraph (1)—

    (a)   for the words 'receipt of an application made in accordance with rule 64.1' there were substituted the words 'the date on which a mandatory order under section 111(6) of the 1980 Act is made'; and

    (b)   the words 'unless the justices refuse to state a case under section 111(5) of the 1980 Act' were omitted.

64.3   Preparation and submission of final case to a magistrates' court

(1)   Within 21 days after the latest day on which representations may be made under rule 64.2, the justices whose decision is questioned shall make such adjustments, if any, to the draft case prepared for the purposes of that rule as they think fit, after considering any such representations, and shall state and sign the case.

(2)   A case may be stated on behalf of the justices whose decision is questioned by any 2 or more of them and may, if the justices so direct, be signed on their behalf by the justices' clerk.

(3)   Forthwith after the case has been stated and signed a court officer for the court shall send it to the applicant or his legal representative, together with any statement required by rule 64.4.

64.4   Extension of time limits by a magistrates' court

(1)   If a magistrates' court officer is unable to send to the applicant a draft case under rule 64.2(1) within the time required by that paragraph, he shall do so as soon as practicable thereafter and the provisions of that rule shall apply accordingly; but in that event a court officer shall attach to the draft case, and to the final case when it is sent to the applicant or his legal representative under rule 64.3(3), a statement of the delay and the reasons for it.

(2)   If a magistrates' court officer receives an application in writing from or on behalf of the applicant or the respondent for an extension of the time within which representations on the draft case may be made under rule 64.2(2), together with reasons in writing for it, the justices' clerk may, by notice in writing sent to the applicant, or respondent as the case may be, by the magistrates' court officer, extend the time and the provisions of that paragraph and of rule 64.3 shall apply accordingly; but in that event the court officer shall attach to the final case, when it is sent to the applicant or his legal representative under rule 64.3(3), a statement of the extension and the reasons for it.

(3)   If the justices are unable to state a case within the time required by rule 64.3(1), they shall do so as soon as practicable thereafter and the provisions of that rule shall apply accordingly; but in that event a court officer shall attach to the final case, when it is sent to the applicant or his legal representative under rule 64.3(3), a statement of the delay and the reasons for it.

64.5   Service of documents where application made to a magistrates' court

Any document required by rules 64.1 to 64.4 to be sent to any person shall either be delivered to him or be sent by post in a registered letter or by recorded delivery service and, if sent by post to an applicant or respondent, shall be addressed to him at his last known or usual place of abode.

64.6   Content of case stated by a magistrates' courts

(1)   A case stated by the magistrates' court shall state the facts found by the court and the question or questions of law or jurisdiction on which the opinion of the High Court is sought.

(2)   Where one of the questions on which the opinion of the High Court is sought is whether there was evidence on which the magistrates' court could come to its decision, the particular finding of fact which it is claimed cannot be supported by the evidence before the magistrates' court shall be specified in the case.

(3)   Unless one of the questions on which the opinion of the High Court is sought is whether there was evidence on which the magistrates' court could come to its decision, the case shall not contain a statement of evidence.

64.7   Application to the Crown Court to state a case

(1)   An application under section 28 of the Supreme Court Act 1981 to the Crown Court to state a case for the opinion of the High Court shall be made in writing to a court

officer within 21 days after the date of the decision in respect of which the application is made.

(2) The application shall state the ground on which the decision of the Crown Court is questioned.

(3) After making the application, the applicant shall forthwith send a copy of it to the parties to the proceedings in the Crown Court.

(4) On receipt of the application, the Crown Court officer shall forthwith send it to the judge who presided at the proceedings in which the decision was made.

(5) On receipt of the application, the judge shall inform the Crown Court officer as to whether or not he has decided to state a case and that officer shall give notice in writing to the applicant of the judge's decision.

(6) If the judge considers that the application is frivolous, he may refuse to state a case and shall in that case, if the applicant so requires, cause a certificate stating the reasons for the refusal to be given to him.

(7) If the judge decides to state a case, the procedure to be followed shall, unless the judge in a particular case otherwise directs, be the procedure set out in paragraphs (8) to (12) of this rule.

(8) The applicant shall, within 21 days of receiving the notice referred to in paragraph (5), draft a case and send a copy of it to the Crown Court officer and to the parties to the proceedings in the Crown Court.

(9) Each party to the proceedings in the Crown Court shall, within 21 days of receiving a copy of the draft case under paragraph (8), either—

    (a) give notice in writing to the applicant and the Crown Court officer that he does not intend to take part in the proceedings before the High Court;

    (b) indicate in writing on the copy of the draft case that he agrees with it and send the copy to a court officer; or

    (c) draft an alternative case and send it, together with the copy of the applicant's case, to the Crown Court officer.

(10) The judge shall consider the applicant's draft case and any alternative draft case sent to the Crown Court officer under paragraph (9)(c).

(11) If the Crown Court so orders, the applicant shall, before the case is stated and delivered to him, enter before the Crown Court officer into a recognizance, with or without sureties and in such sum as the Crown Court considers proper, having regard to the means of the applicant, conditioned to prosecute the appeal without delay.

(12) The judge shall state and sign a case within 14 days after either—

    (a) the receipt of all the documents required to be sent to a court officer under paragraph (9); or

    (b) the expiration of the period of 21 days referred to in that paragraph,

    whichever is the sooner.

(13) A case stated by the Crown Court shall state the facts found by the Crown Court, the submissions of the parties (including any authorities relied on by the parties during the course of those submissions), the decision of the Crown Court in respect of which the application is made and the question on which the opinion of the High Court is sought.

(14) Any time limit referred to in this rule may be extended either before or after it expires by the Crown Court.

(15) If the judge decides not to state a case but the stating of a case is subsequently required by a mandatory order of the High Court, paragraphs (7) to (14) shall apply to the stating of the case save that—

    (a) in paragraph (7) the words 'If the judge decides to state a case' shall be omitted; and

    (b) in paragraph (8) for the words 'receiving the notice referred to in paragraph (5)' there shall be substituted the words 'the day on which the mandatory order was made'.

PART 68 — APPEAL TO THE COURT OF APPEAL AGAINST CONVICTION OR SENTENCE

68.1 Service of documents

(1)   Except where any other rule contains provision to the contrary, service of a document in proceedings in the Court of Appeal may be effected—

(a)   in the case of a document to be served on the Registrar—

(i)   in the case of an appellant who is in custody, by delivering it to the person having custody of him,

(ii)   by delivering it to the Registrar,

(iii)   by addressing it to him and leaving it at his office in the Royal Courts of Justice, London, W.C.2, or

(iv)   by sending it by post addressed to him at the said office;

(b)   in the case of a document to be served on a Crown Court officer—

(i)   in the case of an appellant who is in custody, by delivering it to the person having custody of him,

(ii)   by delivering it to, or sending it by post addressed to, a court officer at the Crown Court centre at which the conviction, verdict, finding or sentence appealed against was given or passed;

(c)   in the case of a document to be served on a body corporate by delivering it to the secretary or clerk of the body at its registered or principal office or sending it by post addressed to the secretary or clerk of the body at that office; or

(d)   in the case of a document to be served on any other person—

(i)   by delivering it to the person to whom it is directed,

(ii)   by leaving it for him with some person at his last known or usual place of abode, or

(iii)   by sending it by post addressed to him at his last known or usual place of abode.

(2)   A person having custody of an appellant to whom a document is delivered in pursuance of paragraph (1)(a)(i) or (1)(b)(i) of this rule shall endorse on it the date of delivery and cause it to be forwarded forthwith to the Registrar or to a Crown Court officer, as the case may be.

(3)   In this rule, a reference to an appellant includes an appellant—

(a)   an appellant under section 13 of the Administration of Justice Act 1960 (appeal in cases of contempt of court);

(b)   a defendant in proceedings in the Crown Court in respect of which an application is made for leave to appeal under section 159 of the Criminal Justice Act 1988 (Crown Court proceedings – orders restricting or preventing reports or restricting public access);

(c)   an appellant under paragraph 14 of Schedule 22 to the Criminal Justice Act 2003 (mandatory life sentences: appeals in transitional cases); and

(d)   in the case of an application under section 8(1) or 8(1A) of the Criminal Appeal Act 1968, a person who has been ordered to be retried.

68.2 Certificate of trial judge

(1)   The certificate of the judge of the court of trial under section 1(2), 12 or 15(2) of the Criminal Appeal Act 1968 that a case is a fit case for appeal shall be in the form set out in the Practice Direction.

(2)   The certificate shall be forwarded forthwith to the Registrar, whether or not the person to whom the certificate relates has applied for a certificate.

(3)   A copy of the certificate shall be forwarded forthwith to the person to whom the certificate relates or to his legal representative.

68.3 Notice of appeal and application for extension of time

(1) Notice of appeal or of an application for leave to appeal under Part I of the Criminal Appeal Act 1968 or notice of appeal under section 13 (appeal in cases of contempt of court) of the Administration of Justice Act 1960 (as required by section 18A of the 1968 Act) against an order or decision of the Crown Court shall be given by completing the form set out in the Practice Direction and serving it on a Crown Court officer.

(1A) Notice of an application for leave to appeal under paragraph 14 of Schedule 22 to the Criminal Justice Act 2003 shall be given by completing the form set out in the Practice Direction and serving it on the Registrar.

(2) A notice of appeal or of an application for leave to appeal shall be accompanied by a notice in the form set out in the Practice Direction containing the grounds of the appeal or application.

(3) A notice of the grounds of appeal or application in the form set out in the Practice Direction shall include notice—

    (a) of any application to be made to the court for a declaration of incompatibility under section 4 of the Human Rights Act 1998; or

    (b) of any issue for the court to decide which may lead to the court making such a declaration.

(4) Where the grounds of appeal or application include notice in accordance with paragraph (3)(b) above, a copy of the notice shall be served on the prosecutor by the appellant.

(5) If the appellant has been convicted of more than one offence, the notice of appeal or of an application for leave, referred to in paragraph (2), shall specify the convictions or sentences against which the appellant is appealing or applying for leave to appeal.

(6) The grounds of an appeal or application, referred to in paragraph (2), may, with the consent of the court, be varied or amplified within such time as the court may allow.

(7) Notice of an application to extend the time within which notice of appeal or of an application for leave to appeal may be given under—

    (a) Part I of the 1968 Act; or

    (b) article 3 of the Criminal Justice Act 2003 (Mandatory Life Sentences: Appeals in Transitional Cases) Order 2005;

by completing so much of the form, referred to in paragraph (2), as relates to the application and by giving notice of appeal or of an application for leave to appeal in accordance with the foregoing provisions of this rule.

(8) Notice of an application to extend the time within which notice of appeal or of an application for leave to appeal may be given under—

    (a) Part I of the 1968 Act; or

    (b) article 3 of the 2005 Order;

shall specify the grounds of the application.

(9) An appellant who is appealing or applying for leave to appeal against conviction shall specify in the form, referred to in paragraph (2), any exhibit produced at the trial which he wishes to be kept in custody for the purposes of his appeal.

(10) The forms to which this rule relates, shall be signed by, or on behalf of, the appellant.

(11) If a form is not signed by the appellant and the appellant is in custody, the Registrar shall, as soon as practicable after receiving the form from the Crown Court, send a copy of it to the appellant.

(12) Where an appellant does not require leave to appeal, a notice of application for leave to appeal shall be treated as a notice of appeal; and where an appellant requires leave to appeal but serves only a notice of appeal, the notice of appeal shall be treated as an application for leave to appeal.

68.4 Appeal following reference by Criminal Cases Review Commission

(1) In this rule:

'the Commission' means the Criminal Cases Review Commission, and 'reference' means the reference of a conviction, verdict, finding or sentence to the Court of Appeal by the Commission under section 9 of the Criminal Appeal Act 1995.

(2)   The Registrar must serve on the appellant written notice of receipt of a reference.

(3)   The appellant must give notice of appeal under rule 68.3 by serving it on the Registrar within—

  (a)   28 days of the date of the notice served under paragraph (2), in the case of an appeal against sentence; or

  (b)   56 days of the date of that notice, in the case of an appeal against conviction, verdict of not guilty by reason of insanity, finding that the appellant was under a disability, or finding that the appellant did the act or made the omission charged.

(4)   The court may extend the time for giving notice of appeal, either before or after it expires.

(5)   The grounds of appeal accompanying a notice of appeal must include—

  (a)   where a ground of appeal is said to relate to a reason given by the Commission for making the reference, an explanation of how it is related; and

  (b)   where a ground of appeal is said not to be so related, notice of application for leave to appeal on that ground.

(6)   If a notice of appeal is not received within the time specified in paragraph (3), or within such longer period as the court allows under paragraph (4), the reasons given by the Commission for making the reference shall stand as the grounds of appeal.

(7)   On receiving a notice of appeal the Registrar must serve a copy on the prosecutor and on any other party to the appeal.

68.5   Exercise of court's powers to give leave to appeal, etc: general rules

(1)   This rule and rule 68.6 apply when the Registrar or a single judge exercises a power conferred by one of the following provisions—

  (a)   section 31 of the Criminal Appeal Act 1968 or article 8 of the Criminal Justice Act 2003 (Mandatory Life Sentences: Appeals in Transitional Cases) Order 2005 (powers exercisable by a single judge);

  (b)   section 31A of the 1968 Act or article 9 of the 2005 Order (powers exercisable by the Registrar);

  (c)   section 31B of the 1968 Act or article 10 of the 2005 Order (procedural directions by a single judge or the Registrar); or

  (d)   section 31C of the 1968 Act or article 11 of the 2005 Order (appeals against procedural directions).

(2)   An application to the Registrar, a single judge or the court for the exercise of any of the powers referred to in paragraph (1) should be in the relevant form set out in the Practice Direction or in the form required by the Registrar.

(3)   An application by an appellant must be signed by him or on his behalf. If it is not signed by him and he is in custody, the Registrar must send him a copy as soon as practicable after receiving it.

(4)   If an appellant makes an application for the exercise of any of the powers under the 1968 Act and he makes it when he gives notice of appeal or notice of an application for leave to appeal, the application must be served on the Crown Court officer . In all other cases, the application must be served on the Registrar.

(5)   Neither a single judge nor the Registrar need sit in court to exercise any of the powers referred to in paragraph (1) of this rule.

68.6   Further applications to a judge or to the court: additional rules

(1)   Where—

  (a)   an appellant renews an application for the exercise of a power conferred by section 31 of the Criminal Appeal Act 1968 or article 8 of the Criminal Justice Act 2003 (Mandatory Life Sentences: Appeals in Transitional Cases) Order 2005 (powers exercisable by a single judge); or

(b)   an appellant renews an application for the exercise of a power conferred by section 31A of the 1968 Act or by article 9 of the 2005 Order (powers exercisable by the Registrar); or

(c)   an appellant or a respondent applies for procedural directions under section 31C of the 1968 Act or article 11 of the 2005 Order (appeals against procedural directions),

then he must do so within 14 days. That period begins when the Registrar serves on him notice of the decision that prompts his further application. That period may be extended before or after it expires by the Registrar, by a single judge or by the court. The general rule is that an application for an extension of that period will be considered at the same time as the further application itself.

(2)   Where—

(a)   an appellant may renew to the court an application for the exercise of a power conferred by section 31 of the 1968 Act or article 8 of the 2005 Order ; but

(b)   he does not do so within the period fixed by this rule or extended under it,

then his application shall be treated as having been refused by the court.

68.7   Application for bail pending appeal

(1)   Notice of an application by the appellant to be granted bail pending the determination of his appeal or pending his retrial shall be in the form set out in the Practice Direction and, unless notice of appeal or of an application for leave to appeal has previously been given, shall be accompanied by such a notice and shall be served on the Registrar; save that where notice of such an application is given together with a notice of appeal or notice of application for leave to appeal, it shall be served on the Crown Court officer.

(2)   An application as aforesaid may be made to the court orally.

(3)   Notice in writing of intention to make an application relating to bail to the court shall, unless the court or a judge thereof otherwise directs, at least 24 hours before it is made be served on the prosecutor and on the Director of Public Prosecutions, if the prosecution was carried on by him or, if the application is to be made by the prosecutor or a constable under section 3(8) of the Bail Act 1976, on the appellant.

68.8   Bail with condition of surety

(1)   Where the court grants bail to the appellant, the recognizance of any surety required as a condition of bail may be entered into before the Registrar or, where the person who has been granted bail is in a prison or other place of detention, before the governor or keeper of the prison or place as well as before the persons specified in section 8(4) of the Bail Act 1976.

(2)   The recognizance of a surety shall be in the form set out in the Practice Direction, there being an alternative form for use in relation to an appellant granted bail pending his retrial or on the issue of a writ of venire de novo.

(3)   Where, under section 3(5) or (6) of the 1976 Act, the court imposes a requirement to be complied with before a person's release on bail, the court may give directions as to the manner in which and the person or persons before whom the requirement may be complied with.

(4)   A person who, in pursuance of an order for the grant of bail made by the court, proposes to enter into a recognizance as a surety or give security shall, unless the court or a judge thereof otherwise directs, give notice to the prosecutor at least 24 hours before he enters into the recognizance or gives security as aforesaid.

(5)   Where the court has fixed the amount in which a surety is to be bound by a recognizance or, under section 3(5) or (6) of the 1976 Act, has imposed any requirement to be complied with before the appellant's release on bail, the Registrar shall issue a certificate in the form set out in the Practice Direction showing the amount and conditions, if any, of the recognizance or, as the case may be, containing a statement of the requirement; and a person authorised to take the recognizance or

do anything in relation to the compliance with such requirement shall not be required to take or do it without production of such a certificate as aforesaid.

(6)   Where, in pursuance of an order for the grant of bail made by the court, a recognizance is entered into or requirement complied with before any person, it shall be the duty of that person to cause the recognizance or, as the case may be, a statement that the requirement has been complied with, to be transmitted forthwith to the Registrar; and a copy of such recognizance or statement shall at the same time be sent to the governor or keeper of the prison or other place of detention in which the appellant is detained, unless the recognizance was entered into or the requirement complied with before such governor or keeper.

(7)   A person taking a recognizance in pursuance of such an order shall give a copy thereof to the person entering into the recognizance.

(8)   Where the court has fixed the amount in which a surety is to be bound by a recognizance or, under section 3(5) or (6) of the 1976 Act, has imposed any requirement to be complied with before the appellant's release on bail, the governor or keeper of the prison or other place of detention in which the appellant is detained shall, on receipt of a certificate in the appropriate form stating that the recognizances of all sureties required have been taken and that all such requirements have been complied with or on being otherwise so satisfied, release the appellant.

(9)   Where the court has granted bail pending retrial or on ordering the issue of a writ of venire de novo, the Registrar shall forward to the Crown Court officer a copy of any record made in pursuance of section 5 of the 1976 Act relating to such bail and also all recognizances and statements sent to the Registrar under paragraph (6) of this rule.

(10)   Any record required by section 5 of the 1976 Act shall be made by including in the file relating to the case in question—

(a)   where bail is granted, a copy of the form issued under paragraph (5) of this rule and a statement of the day on which, and the time and place at which, the appellant is notified to surrender to custody; and

(b)   in any other case, a copy of the notice served under rule 68.29(1) (notice of determination of court).

69.9 Forfeiture of recognizance in respect of person bailed to appear

(1)   Where a recognizance has been entered into in respect of an appellant and it appears to the court that a default has been made in performing the conditions of the recognizance, the court may order the recognizance to be forfeited and such an order may—

(a)   allow time for the payment of the amount due under the recognizance;

(b)   direct payment of that amount by instalments of such amounts and on such dates respectively as may be specified in the order; or

(c)   discharge the recognizance or reduce the amount due thereunder.

(2)   Where the court is to consider making an order under paragraph (1) for a recognizance to be forfeited, the Registrar shall give notice to that effect to the person by whom the recognizance was entered into indicating the time and place at which the matter will be considered; and no such order shall be made before the expiry of seven days after the notice required by this paragraph has been given.

68.10 Custody of exhibits

(1)   On a conviction on indictment or on a coroner's inquisition a court officer of the court of trial shall, subject to any directions of the judge of the court of trial, make arrangements for any exhibit at the trial which in his opinion may be required for the purposes of an appeal against conviction to be kept in the custody of the court, or given into the custody of the person producing it at the trial or any other person for retention, until the expiration of 35 days from the date of conviction.

(2)   Where an appellant has given notice of appeal, or of an application for leave to appeal, against conviction, the Registrar shall inform a court officer of the notice and

give directions concerning the continued retention in custody of any exhibit which appears necessary for the proper determination of the appeal or application.

(3)   Where the court orders an appellant to be retired, it shall make arrangements pending his retrial for the continued retention in custody of exhibits.

(4)   Any arrangements under this rule may include arrangements for the inspection of an exhibit by an interested party.

68.11 Supply of documentary and other exhibits

(1)   The Registrar shall, on request, supply to the appellant or respondent copies of documents or other things required for the appeal and in such case may make charges in accordance with scales and rates fixed for the time being by the Treasury.

(2)   The Registrar shall, on request, make arrangements for the appellant or respondent to inspect any document or other thing required for the appeal.

(3)   This rule shall not apply to the supply of the transcripts of any proceedings or part thereof.

68.12 Record of proceedings

(1)   Except as provided by this rule, the whole of any proceedings in respect of which an appeal lies (with or without leave) to the court shall be recorded by means of shorthand notes or, with the permission of the Lord Chancellor, by mechanical means.

(2)   Where such proceedings are recorded by means of shorthand notes, it shall not be necessary to record—

(a)   the opening or closing addresses to the jury on behalf of the prosecution or an accused person unless the judge of the court of trial otherwise directs; or

(b)   any other part of such proceedings which the judge of the court of trial directs need not be recorded.

(3)   Where it is not practicable for such proceedings to be recorded by means of shorthand notes or by mechanical means, the judge of the court of trial shall direct how and to what extent the proceedings shall be recorded.

(4)   The permission of the Lord Chancellor may contain conditions concerning the custody, and supply of transcripts, of a recording made by mechanical means.

68.13 Transcripts

(1)   A transcript of the record of any proceedings or part thereof in respect of which an appeal lies, with or without leave, to the court and which are recorded in accordance with the provisions of rule 68.12—

(a)   shall, on request be supplied to the Registrar or any interested party; and

(b)   may, on request, be supplied to any other person on payment of such charge as may be fixed for the time being by the Treasury.

(2)   Without prejudice to the provisions of paragraph (1) of this rule, the Registrar may, on request, supply to any interested party a transcript of the record of any proceedings or part thereof which is in his possession for the purposes of the appeal or application in question and in such case may make charges in accordance with scales and rates fixed for the time being by the Treasury:

Provided that in the case of an interested party who has been granted a right to representation by the Criminal Defence Service under Schedule 3 to the Access to Justice Act 1999 for the purpose of the appeal or any proceedings preliminary or incidental thereto such a transcript shall be supplied free.

68.14 Verification of record of proceedings

(1)   An official shorthand writer who takes shorthand notes of any proceedings or part thereof in respect of which an appeal lies (with or without leave) to the court shall—

(a)   at the beginning of the notes state the name of the parties to the proceedings;

(b)   in the case of shorthand notes of part of any proceedings, state the part concerned;

(c)   record his name in the notes; and

(d)   retain the shorthand notes for not less than five years.

(2)   Verification of a transcript of the shorthand notes taken by an official shorthand writer of any proceedings or part thereof in respect of which an appeal lies (with or without leave) to the court shall be by a certificate by the person making the transcript that—

(a)   he has made a correct and complete transcript of the notes to the best of his skill and ability; and

(b)   the notes were either taken by him and were to the best of his skill and ability a complete and correct account of those proceedings or part thereof or were taken by another official shorthand writer.

(3)   Verification of a transcript of the record of the proceedings or part thereof if recorded by mechanical means shall be by—

(a)   a certificate by the person making the transcript that he has made a correct and complete transcript of the recording to the best of his skill and ability; and

(b)   a certificate by a person responsible for the recording or a successor that the recording records so much of the proceedings as is specified in the certificate.

(4)   Verification of a transcript of the record of the proceedings or part thereof if recorded in any other way shall be by—

(a)   a certificate by the person who made the record that he recorded the proceedings or part thereof to the best of his ability; and

(b)   a certificate by the person making the transcript that he has made a correct and complete transcript of the record to the best of his skill and ability.

68.15   Application for a witness order and for evidence to be received

(1)   Notice of an application by the appellant—

(a)   that a witness who would have been a compellable witness at the trial be ordered to attend for examination by the court; or

(b)   that the evidence of a witness be received by the court;

shall be in the form set out in the Practice Direction and shall be served on the Registrar; save that where a notice of an application under sub-paragraph (a) or (b) is given together with a notice of appeal or notice of application for leave to appeal, it shall be served on the Crown Court officer.

(2)   An application as aforesaid may be made to the court orally.

68.16   Examination of witnesses by the court

(1)   An order of the court to a person to attend for examination as a witness shall be in the form set out in the Practice Direction and shall specify the time and place of attendance.

(2)   The examination of a witness shall be conducted by the taking of a deposition and, unless the court directs otherwise, shall take place in public.

68.17   Vulnerable witness giving video recorded testimony

(1)   A party to an appeal who applies for leave to call a witness may also apply for leave under section 32A of the Criminal Justice Act 1988 to tender in evidence a video recording of testimony from a witness where—

(a)   the offence charged is one to which section 32(2) of the 1988 Act applies;

(b)   in the case of an offence falling within section 32(2)(a) or (b) of the 1988 Act, the proposed witness is under the age of 14 or, if he was under 14 when the video recording was made, is under the age of 15;

(c)   in the case of an offence falling within section 32(2)(c) of the 1988 Act, the proposed witness is under the age of 17 or, if he was under 17 when the video recording was made, is under the age of 18; and

     (d)   the video recording is of an interview conducted between an adult and a person coming within sub-paragraph (b) or (c) above (not being the accused or one of the accused) which relates to any matter in issue in the proceedings;

and references in this rule to an offence include references to attempting or conspiring to commit, or aiding, abetting, counselling, procuring or inciting the commission of, that offence.

(2)   An application under paragraph (1) shall be made by serving a notice in writing on the Registrar. The application shall be accompanied by the video recording which it is proposed to tender in evidence and shall include the following, namely—

    (a)   the name of the appellant and the offence or offences charged;

    (b)   the name and date of birth of the witness in respect of whom the application is made;

    (c)   the date on which the video recording was made;

    (d)   a statement that in the opinion of the applicant the witness is willing and able to attend the appeal for cross-examination; and

    (e)   a statement of the circumstances in which the video recording was made which complies with paragraph (4).

(3)   Where it is proposed to tender part only of a video recording of an interview with the witness, an application under paragraph (1) must specify that part and be accompanied by a video recording of the entire interview, including those parts which it is not proposed to tender in evidence, and by a statement of the circumstances in which the video recording of the entire interview was made which complies with paragraph (4).

(4)   The statement of the circumstances in which the video recording was made referred to in paragraphs (2)(e) and (3) shall include the following information, except in so far as it is contained in the recording itself, namely—

    (a)   the times at which the recording commenced and finished, including details of any interruptions;

    (b)   the location at which the recording was made and the usual function of the premises;

    (c)   the name, age and occupation of any person present at any point during the recording, the time for which he was present, his relationship (if any) to the witness and to the appellant;

    (d)   a description of the equipment used including the number of cameras used and whether they were fixed or mobile, the number and location of microphones, the video format used and whether there were single or multiple recording facilities; and

    (e)   the location of the mastertape if the video recording is a copy and details of when and by whom the copy was made.

(5)   An application under paragraph (1) shall be made at the same time as the application for leave to call the witness or at any time thereafter, but no less than 14 days before the date fixed for the hearing of the appeal except with the leave of the court.

(6)   The Registrar shall, as soon as practicable after receiving an application under paragraph (1), send a copy of the notice to the other parties to the appeal. Copies of any video recording required by paragraph (2) or (3) to accompany the notice shall be provided by the applicant and sent by the Registrar to any party to the appeal not already served with a copy. In the case of an appellant acting in person, a copy shall be made available for viewing by him.

(7)   An application under paragraph (1) shall be determined without a hearing, unless the Court otherwise directs, and the Registrar shall notify the applicant and the other parties of the time and place of any hearing.

(8)   Without prejudice to rule 68.29, the Registrar shall notify all the parties of the decision of the Court in relation to an application under paragraph (1) and, where leave is granted, the notification shall state whether the whole or specified parts only of the video recording or recordings disclosed are to be admitted in evidence.

68.18   Vulnerable witness giving evidence by live television link

(1)   A party to an appeal who applies for leave to call a witness may also apply for leave under section 32(1)(b) of the Criminal Justice Act 1988 for the evidence of that witness to be given through a live television link where—

    (a)   the offence charged is one to which section 32(2) of the 1988 Act applies; and

    (b)   the evidence is to be given by a witness who is either–

        (i)   in the case of an offence falling within section 32(2)(a) or (b) of the 1988 Act, under the age of 14,

        (ii)   in the case of an offence falling within section 32(2)(c) of the 1988 Act, under the age of 17, or

        (iii)   a person who is to be cross-examined following the admission under section 32A of the 1988 Act of a video recording of testimony from him,

    and references in this rule to an offence include references to attempting or conspiring to commit, or aiding, abetting, counselling, procuring or inciting the commission of, that offence.

(2)   An application under paragraph (1) shall be made by serving a notice in writing on the Registrar which shall state—

    (a)   the grounds of the application;

    (b)   the date of birth of the witness;

    (c)   the name of the witness; and

    (d)   the name, occupation and relationship (if any) to the witness of any person proposed to accompany the witness and the grounds for believing that person should accompany the witness.

(3)   An application under paragraph (1) shall be made at the same time as the application for leave to call the witness or at any time thereafter, but no less than 14 days before the date fixed for the hearing of the appeal except with the leave of the court.

(4)   The Registrar shall, as soon as practicable after receiving an application under paragraph (1), send a copy of the notice to the other parties to the appeal.

(5)   An application under paragraph (1) shall be determined without a hearing, unless the Court otherwise directs, and the Registrar shall notify the applicant and the other parties of the time and place of any hearing.

(6)   Without prejudice to rule 68.29, the Registrar shall notify all the parties and the person who is to accompany the witness (if known) of the decision of the court in relation to an application under paragraph (1). Where leave is granted, the notification shall state the name of the witness, and, if known, the name, occupation and relationship (if any) to the witness of the person who is to accompany the witness.

(7)   A witness giving evidence through a television link pursuant to leave granted in accordance with this rule shall be accompanied by a person acceptable to the Court and, unless the Court otherwise directs, by no other person.

68.19   Evidence through live television link where witness is outside the United Kingdom

(1)   A party to an appeal who applies for leave to call a witness may also apply for leave under section 32(1) of the Criminal Justice Act 1988 for the evidence of that witness to be given through a live television link where the witness is outside the United Kingdom.

(2)   An application under paragraph (1) shall be made by serving a notice in writing on the Registrar which shall state—

    (a)   the grounds of the application;

    (b)   the name of the witness;

    (c)   the country and place where it is proposed the witness will be when giving evidence; and

    (d)   the name and occupation of any person who it is proposed should be available for the purpose specified in paragraph (3).

(3)   The purpose referred to in paragraph (2)(d) is that of answering any questions the court may put, before or after the evidence of the witness is given, as to the circumstances in which the evidence is given, including questions about any persons who are present when the evidence is given and any matters which may affect the giving of the evidence.

(4)   An application under paragraph (1) shall be made at the same time as the application for leave to call the witness or at any time thereafter, but no less than 14 days before the date fixed for the hearing of the appeal except with the leave of the court.

(5)   The Registrar shall, as soon as practicable after receiving an application under paragraph (1), send a copy of the notice to the other parties to the appeal.

(6)   An application under paragraph (1) shall be determined without a hearing, unless the court otherwise directs, and the Registrar shall notify the applicant and the other parties of the time and place of any such hearing.

(7)   Without prejudice to rule 68.29, the Registrar shall notify all the parties of the decision of the court in relation to an application under paragraph (1), and, where leave is granted, the notification shall state the name of the witness and, where applicable, the name and occupation of any person specified by the court for the purpose set out in paragraph (3).

68.20   Procedure for the admission of hearsay evidence

(1)   Part 34 applies where a party wants to introduce hearsay evidence in an appeal or application for leave to appeal, except for rules 34.2, 34.3 and 34.4 (relating to the notice of hearsay evidence).

(2)   An appellant who wants to introduce hearsay evidence to support a ground of appeal contained in his notice under rule 68.3(2)—

    (a)   must give notice in the form set out in the Practice Direction to the Crown Court officer with his notice of application for leave to appeal under rule 68.3(1); but

    (b)   need not give a separate notice of application under rule 68.15(1) for that same evidence to be received by the court.

(3)   A party who wants to introduce hearsay evidence in any other circumstances must give notice in the form set out in the Practice Direction to the Registrar and all other parties not more than 28 days after—

    (a)   leave to appeal is given; or

    (b)   notice of appeal is given, if leave is not required.

68.21   Procedure for the admission of evidence of bad character

Part 35 applies to the introduction of evidence of bad character in proceedings before the Court of Appeal, except for rule 35.1 and with the following modifications—

(a)   a reference to a defendant should be read as a reference to an appellant, and 'non-defendant' and 'co-defendant' read accordingly;

(b)   a reference to a court officer should be read as a reference to the Registrar; and

(c)   an application under rule 35.2 (non-defendant's bad character) must be received, and a notice under rule 35.4 or 35.5 (defendant's bad character) must be given, not more than 28 days after—

    (i)   leave to appeal is given, or

    (ii)   notice of appeal is given, if leave is not required.

68.22   Abandonment of proceedings

(1)   An appeal or an application for leave to appeal under Part I of the Criminal Appeal Act 1968 or under paragraph 14 of Schedule 22 to the Criminal Justice Act 2003 may be abandoned before the hearing of the appeal or application by serving on the Registrar notice thereof in the form set out in the Practice Direction.

(2)   The notice shall be signed by, or on behalf of, the appellant.

(3)   The Registrar shall, as soon as practicable after receiving a notice under this rule, send a copy of it, endorsed with the date of receipt, to the appellant, to the Secretary of State and to a court officer of the court of trial.

(4)   Where an appeal or an application for leave to appeal is abandoned, the appeal or application shall be treated as having been dismissed or refused by the court.

68.23   The Registrar

(1)   The Registrar may require the court of trial to furnish the court with any assistance or information which it may require for the purpose of exercising its jurisdiction.

(2)   The Registrar shall give as long notice in advance as reasonably possible of the date on which the court will hear any appeal or application by an appellant to—

(a)   the appellant;

(b)   any person having custody of the appellant; and

(c)   any other interested party whom the court requires to be represented at the hearing.

(3)   This paragraph shall not apply to proceedings before a single judge of the court under section 31 of the Criminal Appeal Act 1968.

68.24   Sittings in vacation

The Lord Chief Justice shall determine the days on which the court shall, if necessary, sit during vacations; and the court shall sit on such days in accordance with arrangements made by the Lord Chief Justice after consultation with the Master of the Rolls.

68.25   Opinion of court on point referred by Criminal Cases Review Commission

Where the Criminal Cases Review Commission refers a point to the court under section 14(3) of the Criminal Appeal Act 1995 the court may consider the point in private if appropriate.

68.26   Application to the Court of Appeal for leave to be present

(1)   Notice of an application by the appellant to be given leave by the court to be present at proceedings for which such leave is required shall be in the form set out in the Practice Direction and shall be served on the Registrar; save that where a notice of such an application is given together with a notice of appeal or notice of application for leave to appeal, it shall be served on a Crown Court officer.

(2)   An application as aforesaid may be made to the court orally.

68.27   Declaration of incompatibility

(1)   The court shall not consider making a declaration of incompatibility under section 4 of the Human Rights Act 1998 unless it has given written notice to the Crown.

(2)   Where notice has been given to the Crown, a Minister, or other person entitled under the 1998 Act to be joined as a party, shall be so joined on giving written notice to the court.

(3)   A notice given under paragraph (1) above shall be given to—

(a)   the person named in the list published under section 17(1) of the Crown Proceedings Act 1947 (22); or

(b)   in the case of doubt as to whether any and if so which of those departments is appropriate, the Treasury Solicitor.

(4)   A notice given under paragraph (1) above, shall provide an outline of the issues in the case and specify—

(a)   the prosecutor and appellant;

(b)   the date, judge and court of the trial in the proceedings from which the appeal lies; and

(c)   the provision of primary legislation and the Convention right under question.

(5)   Any consideration of whether a declaration of incompatibility should be made, shall be adjourned for—

(a)   21 days from the date of the notice given under paragraph (1) above; or

(b)   such other period (specified in the notice), as the court shall allow in order that the relevant Minister or other person, may seek to be joined and prepare his case.

(6)   Unless the court otherwise directs, the Minister or other person entitled under the 1998 Act to be joined as a party shall, if he is to be joined, give written notice to the court and every other party.

(7)   Where a Minister of the Crown has nominated a person to be joined as a party by virtue of section 5(2)(a) of the 1998 Act, a notice under paragraph (6) above shall be accompanied by a written nomination signed by or on behalf of the Minister.

68.28   Dismissal of appeal against hospital order

If the court dismisses an appeal or an application for leave to appeal by an appellant who is subject to a hospital order under the Mental Health Act 1983 or an order under section 5(1) of the Criminal Procedure (Insanity) Act 1964 (power to deal with persons not guilty by reason of insanity or unfit to plead etc.) or the court affirms the order and the appellant has been released on bail pending his appeal, the court shall give such directions as it thinks fit for his conveyance to the hospital from which he was released on bail and for his detention, if necessary, in a place of safety as defined in section 55 of the 1983 Act pending his admission to the said hospital.

68.29   Notice of determination of court

(1)   The Registrar shall, as soon as practicable, serve notice of any determination by the court or by any judge of the court under section 31 of the Criminal Appeal Act 1968 or under article 8 of the Criminal Justice Act 2003 (Mandatory Life Sentences: Appeals in Transitional Cases) Order 2005 (powers exercisable by a single judge) on any appeal or application by an appellant on—

(a)   the appellant;

(b)   the Secretary of State;

(c)   any person having custody of the appellant;

(d)   in the case of an appellant detained under the Mental Health Act 1983 the responsible authority; and

(e)   in the case of a declaration of incompatibility under section 4 of the Human Rights Act 1998, the declaration shall be served on—

(i)   all of the parties to the proceedings, and

(ii)   where a Minister of the Crown has not been joined as a party, the Crown (in accordance with rule 68.27(3) above).

(2)   The Registrar shall, as soon as practicable, serve notice on a court officer of the court of trial of the order of the court disposing of an appeal or application for leave to appeal.

(3)   In this rule the expression 'responsible authority' means—

(a)   in relation to a patient liable to be detained under the 1983 Act in a hospital or mental nursing home, the managers of the hospital or home as defined in section 145(1) of that Act; and

(b)   in relation to a patient subject to guardianship, the responsible local health authority as defined in section 34(3) of the 1983 Act.

68.30   Enforcement of fines

(1)   Where the court imposes a fine on an appellant, the court shall make an order fixing a term of imprisonment, not exceeding 12 months, which the appellant is to undergo if the fine is not duly paid or recovered.

(2)   Such an order may—

(a)   allow time for the payment of the fine; or

(b)   direct payment of the fine by instalments of such amounts and on such dates respectively as may be specified in the order.

68.31   Notice of application after order for retrial

Notice of an application under section 8(1) of the Criminal Appeal Act 1968 for leave to arraign, and notice of an application under section 8(1A) of that Act to set aside an order for retrial shall be in the form set out in the Practice Direction and shall be served on the prosecutor or the person ordered to be retried as the case may be, and on the Registrar.

PART 69 — REFERENCE TO THE COURT OF APPEAL OF POINT OF LAW

69.1   References

(1)   Every reference under section 36 of the Criminal Justice Act 1972 shall be in writing and shall—

    (a)   specify the point of law referred and, where appropriate, such facts of the case as are necessary for the proper consideration of the point of law;

    (b)   summarise the arguments intended to be put to the court; and

    (c)   specify the authorities intended to be cited:

Provided that no mention shall be made in the reference of the proper name of any person or place which is likely to lead to the identification of the respondent.

(2)   A reference shall be entitled 'Reference under section 36 of the Criminal Justice Act 1972' together with the year and number of the reference.

69.2   Registrar's notice to respondent

(1)   The Registrar shall cause to be served on the respondent notice of the reference which shall also—

    (a)   inform the respondent that the reference will not affect the trial in relation to which it is made or any acquittal in that trial; and

    (b)   invite the respondent, within such period as may be specified in the notice (being not less than 28 days from the date of service of the notice), to inform the Registrar if he wishes to present any argument to the court and, if so, whether he wishes to present such argument in person or by counsel on his behalf.

(2)   The court shall not hear argument by or on behalf of the Attorney General until the period specified in the notice has expired unless the respondent agrees or has indicated that he does not wish to present any argument to the court.

69.3   Withdrawal or amendment of reference

The Attorney General may withdraw or amend the reference at any time before the court have begun the hearing, or, after that, and until the court have given their opinion, may withdraw or amend the reference by leave of the court, and notice of such withdrawal or amendment shall be served on the respondent on behalf of the Attorney General.

69.4   Anonymity of respondent

The court shall ensure that the identity of the respondent is not disclosed during the proceedings on a reference except where the respondent has given his consent to the use of his name in the proceedings.

69.5   Reference to House of Lords

An application under section 36(3) of the Criminal Justice Act 1972 (reference to the House of Lords) may be made orally immediately after the court give their opinion or by notice served on the Registrar within the 14 days next following.

69.6   Service of documents

(1)   For the purpose of this Part service of a document on the respondent may be effected—

(a) in the case of a document to be served on a body corporate by delivering it to the secretary or clerk of the body at its registered or principal office or sending it by post addressed to the secretary or clerk of that body at that office; and

(b) in the case of a document to be served on any other person by—

(i) delivering it to the person to whom it is directed,

(ii) leaving it for him with some person at his last known or usual place of abode, or

(iii) sending it by post addressed to him at his last known or usual place of abode.

(2) For the purpose of this Part, service of a document on the Registrar may be effected by—

(a) delivering it to the Registrar;

(b) addressing it to him and leaving it at his office in the Royal Courts of Justice, London, WC2; or

(c) sending it by post addressed to him at the said office.

PART 70 — REFERENCE TO THE COURT OF APPEAL OF UNDULY LENIENT SENTENCE

70.1 Applications

(1) Every application for a reference under section 36 of the Criminal Justice Act 1988 shall be in writing and shall—

(a) specify—

(i) the name of the offender,

(ii) the date on which, and the offence of which, he was convicted,

(iii) the sentence passed on him in respect of that offence,

(iv) the date on which the sentence was passed (if later than the date under sub-paragraph (ii)), and

(v) the judge by whom, and the location of the Crown Court at which, the sentence was passed; and

(b) state the reason why it appears to the Attorney General that the sentencing of the offender was unduly lenient.

(2) An application shall be entitled 'Reference under section 36 of the Criminal Justice Act 1988' together with the year and number of the application and the name of the offender.

70.2 Notice of application

The sending of the application to the Registrar shall constitute the giving of notice of the application for the purpose of paragraph 1 of Schedule 3 to the Criminal Justice Act 1988 (notice to be given within 28 days of passing of sentence).

70.3 Registrar's notice to offender

(1) The Registrar shall, as soon as practicable after receiving the application, cause to be served on the offender a copy of it together with a notice which—

(a) informs him that the result of any reference could be that the court would quash the sentence passed on him in the proceeding and in place of it pass such sentence as they thought appropriate for the case and as the court below had power to pass when dealing with him (including a greater punishment);

(b) informs him of the effect of paragraph 6 (entitlement of offender to be present at hearing of reference, although he may be in custody), 7 (offender in custody requires leave of court to be present at hearing of application), 8 (power of court to pass sentence on offender who is not present) and 11 (entitlement of offender to reasonable costs out of central funds) of Schedule 3 to the Criminal Justice Act 1988;

(c)   invites him, within such period as the Registrar may specify (being not less than 14 days from the date of service on him of the notice), to serve notice on the Registrar if he wishes—

(i)   to apply to the court for leave to be present under paragraph 7 of Schedule 3 to the 1988 Act, and

(ii)   to present any argument to the court on the hearing of the application or, if leave is given, of the reference, and whether to present it in person or by counsel on his behalf;

(d)   draws to his attention the effect of rule 70.7 (supply of documentary and other exhibits); and

(e)   advises him to consult a solicitor as to his position as soon as possible.

(2)   The court shall not hear argument by or on behalf of the Attorney General until the period specified by the Registrar has expired unless the offender agrees or has indicated that he does not wish to present any argument to the Court.

70.4   References

(1)   Every reference shall be in writing and shall—

(a)   contain the information required by rule 70.1(1)(a) to be specified in an application;

(b)   summarise the arguments intended to be put to the court; and

(c)   specify the authorities intended to be cited.

(2)   The reference shall bear the same title as the application.

(3)   Subject to paragraph (4), the reference shall be sent on behalf of the Attorney General to the Registrar, who shall, as soon as practicable after receiving it, cause to be served a copy of it on the offender.

(4)   Where the court gives leave for a case to be referred to it and is satisfied that the document comprising the application also contains the material required by paragraph (1) to be contained in a reference, the court may order that the document be treated for the purpose of this Part as the reference; and in that case paragraph (3) shall not apply.

70.5   Withdrawal or amendment of application or reference

The Attorney General may withdraw or amend an application or reference at any time before the court have begun the hearing of the application or reference as the case may be, or, after that, and until the court have given their decision, may withdraw or amend the application or reference by leave of the court, and notice of such withdrawal or amendment shall be served on the Registrar and on the offender on behalf of the Attorney General.

70.6   Registrar's power to require information from court of trial

The Registrar may require the court of trial to furnish the Court with any assistance or information which they may require for the purpose of exercising their jurisdiction.

70.7   Supply of documentary and other exhibits

(1)   The Registrar shall, on request, supply to the offender copies or reproductions of documents or other things required for the application or reference and in such case may make charges in accordance with scales and rates fixed from time to time by the Treasury.

(2)   The Registrar shall, on request, make arrangements for the offender to inspect any document or other thing required for the application or reference.

(3)   This rule shall not apply to the supply of transcripts of any proceedings or part of proceedings.

70.8   Service of documents

(1)   For the purposes of this Part service of a document on the offender may be effected—

(a) in the case of a document to be served on a body corporate by delivering it to the secretary or clerk of the body at its registered or principal office or sending it by post addressed to the secretary or clerk of the body at that office; and

(b) in the case of a document to be served on any other person—

   (i) by delivering it to the person to whom it is directed,

   (ii) by leaving it for him with some person at his last known or usual place of abode, or

   (iii) by sending it by post addressed to him at his last known or usual place of abode.

(2) For the purpose of this Part service of a document on the Registrar may be effected—

   (a) in the case of an offender who is in custody, by delivering it to the person having custody of him;

   (b) by delivering it to the Registrar;

   (c) by addressing it to him and leaving it at his office in the Royal Courts of Justice, London, WC2; or

   (d) by sending it by post addressed to him at the said office.

(3) A person having custody of an offender and to whom a document is delivered in pursuance of paragraph (2)(a) shall endorse on it the date of delivery and cause it to be forwarded to the Registrar.

PART 74 — APPEAL TO THE HOUSE OF LORDS

74.1 Application for leave to appeal from the Criminal Division of the Court of Appeal to the House of Lords

(1) An application to the criminal division of the Court of Appeal—

   (a) for leave to appeal to the House of Lords under Part II of the Criminal Appeal Act 1968 or section 13 of the Administration of Justice Act 1960 or Part 3 of the Criminal Justice Act 2003 (Mandatory Life Sentences: Appeals in Transitional Cases) Order 2005;

   (b) to extend the time within which an application may be made by the defendant to the House of Lords or the court under section 34(1) of the 1968 Act or that subsection as applied by section 13(4) of the 1960 Act or article 13(2) of the 2005 Order;

   (c) by the defendant to be given leave to be present on the hearing of the appeal or of any proceedings preliminary or incidental thereto; or

   (d) by the defendant to be granted bail pending the appeal,

   shall either be made orally immediately after the decision of the court from which an appeal lies to the House of Lords or notice thereof shall be in the form set out in the Practice Direction and shall be served on the Registrar.

(2) The recognizance of a surety shall be in the form set out in the Practice Direction.

(3) Rules 68.8 (bail with condition of surety) and 68.9 (forfeiture of recognizances) shall apply with respect to a defendant pending his appeal to the House of Lords as they apply with respect to an appellant with the necessary modifications.

(4) An application to the court for leave to appeal to the House of Lords under Part II of the 1968 Act or section 13 of the 1960 Act, or Part 3 of the 2005 Order may be abandoned before the hearing of the application by serving on the Registrar notice to that effect.

(5) For the purpose of having an application determined by the court in pursuance of section 44 of the 1968 Act, rules 68.5 (exercise of court's power to give leave) and 68.6 (further application to the court) shall apply with the necessary modifications.

(6) Rule 68.29 (notice if determination of court) shall apply to a determination under Part II of the 1968 Act or section 13 of the 1960 Act with the necessary modifications.

(7) Rules 68.11 (supply of documentary and other exhibits), 68.13(2) (transcripts) and 68.23 (the Registrar) shall apply in relation to an appeal under Part II of the 1968 Act or section 13 of the 1960 Act as they apply in relation to an appeal under Part I of the

1968 Act, except that any reference to section 31 of the 1968 Act shall be construed as a reference to section 44 of the 1968 Act.

(8)   In this rule any reference to a defendant includes an appellant under section 13 of the 1960 Act or under the 2005 Order.

Index